Beginnings
Discovering Your World
New Horizons
Our World Today
American Voices
The Literary Heritage

The aim of The Living Literature Series is to make the study of imaginative literature more meaningful and more productive for today's students. The series offers materials designed to help students become capable and appreciative readers.

# CONTRIBUTORS AND CONSULTANTS

**Adolescent Literature**

*Gabriele L. Rico, Ph.D.*
*San Jose State University, California*

**Regional Literature**

*Patricia Strandness Shnider*
*Minneapolis, Minnesota*

**Cultural Minorities**

*Pearl Thomas, Ph.D.*
*New York, New York*

**Humanities**

*Sondra Melzer*
*Stamford, Connecticut*

**American Literature**

*Mary Pauline McElroy, Ph.D.*
*Houston, Texas*

**Teaching Helps**

*Barbara Johnston*
*San Jose, California*

*Barbara Laswell*
*Pittsburgh, Pennsylvania*

Series Editor: *Karen Madsen*
Volume Editor: *Barbara St. Laurent*
Copyeditor: *Mary Alice Richardson*
Designer: *Designworks, Inc.*
Art Director: *Deborah A. Flynn*
Picture Research: *Pembroke Herbert*

# American Voices

**Hans P. Guth**

General Editor and Senior Author

**D. C. Heath and Company**

Lexington, Massachusetts / Toronto, Ontario

# SERIES CONSULTANTS

Francis J. Adams, Ph.D
*Scituate High School*
*Scituate, Massachusetts*

Karen K. Albeck
*McKinley Junior High School*
*Racine, Wisconsin*

Patricia S. Alford
*Belmont Junior High School*
*Belmont, North Carolina*

Barbara Anderson
*Nelsen Middle School*
*Renton, Washington*

Sister Marie Therese Artis, IHM
*St. Joachim School*
*Philadelphia, Pennsylvania*

Ann Arnold
*Edward White Middle School*
*San Antonio, Texas*

Hazel Clemons
*Happy Valley High School*
*Elizabethton, Tennessee*

Helen L. Fowler
*South Caldwell High School*
*Hudson, North Carolina*

Jane Gilliam
*Westwood Junior High School*
*Manchester, Tennessee*

Dorothy A. Hwopek, Ph.D.
*New Castle County*
*School District*
*Wilmington, Delaware*

Vivian L. Johnston
*North High School*
*Denver, Colorado*

Grace Louise McCall
*Smiley Junior High School*
*Denver, Colorado*

Irwin Maimen
*Clara Barton High School*
*Brooklyn, New York*

Lynn W. Miller
*Boise High School*
*Boise, Idaho*

Henry F. Mooney
*Danvers Public Schools*
*Danvers, Massachusetts*

Ann Nelson
*Johnston Junior High School*
*Houston, Texas*

Patricia A. Newell
*Padua Franciscan High School*
*Parma, Ohio*

James C. Olsen
*Niles North High School*
*Skokie, Illinois*

James J. Pfander
*Padua Franciscan High School*
*Parma, Ohio*

Lorraine A. Plasse
*Springfield Public Schools*
*Springfield, Massachusetts*

Helen A. Pounds
*Kashmere Senior High School*
*Houston, Texas*

Delores M. Pringle
*Pendleton Middle School*
*Pendleton, South Carolina*

Connie Reinhardt
*Hot Springs High School*
*Hot Springs, Arkansas*

Susan F. Robinson
*Trinity High School*
*Euless, Texas*

Louis J. Sessinger, Jr.
*North Penn High School*
*Lansdale, Pennsylvania*

Genevieve Setton
*Jerstad-Agerholm Junior*
*High School*
*Racine, Wisconsin*

Judy Smith
*South West Junior High School*
*Gastonia, North Carolina*

Astrid L. Sinclair
*Sonoma High School*
*Sonoma, California*

Imogene Springer
*Denver Public Schools*
*Denver, Colorado*

Mary Starnes
*East Ridge High School*
*Chattanooga, Tennessee*

Mary A. Swafford
*Central Middle School*
*Murfreesboro, Tennessee*

Dorothy Threlkeld
*Central Junior High School*
*Hot Springs, Arkansas*

Jane B. Turner
*Hickory High School*
*Hickory, North Carolina*

Vestina Young
*Orangeburg-Wilkinson*
*High School*
*Orangeburg, South Carolina*

Copyright © 1981 by D. C. Heath and Company

Acknowledgments for copyrighted material begin on page 744 and constitute an extension of this page.

Printed in the United States of America

International Standard Book Number: 0-669-93914-5

# Teacher's Preface

The purpose of this book is to give students a mature understanding of the American literary heritage. A special effort has been made to make high-quality literature accessible to the students in today's classrooms. The following points help explain the organization of the volume:

1. *This book presents major themes in American literary history in a meaningful historical order.* Literary history goes beyond the accidents of surface chronology to reveal the patterns that give shape and meaning to our shared literary tradition. It makes literature come to life by focusing on the challenges and vital purposes that shaped our literary heritage.

2. *This book pays special attention to authors and books that have become true classics.* It starts with "A Historical Overview" of authors and books that had a lasting influence and that are remembered and loved when the work of many contemporaries has been forgotten. This preview is followed by "A Gallery of American Authors" that pays tribute to the personalities and special influence of selected major authors.

3. *This book helps students see living literature in its larger cultural context.* PART ONE, "New World: American Beginnings," relates American literature to major themes in American history. It stresses the rootedness of literature, helping students see imaginative literature not as an esoteric or academic pursuit but as part of the shared experience of a people.

4. *This book stresses major themes that give our literature its unmistakable American quality.* PART TWO, "American Voices: American Classics Today," pays special attention to authors who give voice to the major recurrent concerns of American literature: The Belief in Innocence (Whitman, Twain); The Wilderness and Our Relation to Nature (Cooper, Melville, Crane); The Gothic Imagination (Poe, Hawthorne, Faulkner); American Individualism (Dickinson, Emerson, Thoreau).

5. *This book tries to do justice to the true diversity and pluralism of American life and literature.* Women included among major authors range from Ellen Glasgow, Willa Cather, and Katherine Anne Porter to Tillie Olsen and Lorraine Hansberry. Major authors from minority backgrounds include N. Scott Momaday, Richard Wright, Ralph Ellison, and others. PART THREE, "On Native Soil: A Manifold Heritage," pays special attention to the contributions of cultural minorities to our common heritage.

*H. Guth*

# Contents

PART ONE    **New World:**
**American Beginnings**     12

*Unit One*    **Growing Up in America**     15

*poems*    *Looking in the Album*   16

JOHN UPDIKE **Home Movies**   16
EVELYN TOOLEY HUNT **Taught Me Purple**   17
RICHARD WILBUR **Running**   18
COUNTEE CULLEN **Saturday's Child**   19
C. K. WILLIAMS **Hood**   20

*short story*    EUDORA WELTY **A Visit of Charity**   21
*short story*    JOHN KNOWLES **A Turn With the Sun**   27
*autobiography*    M. CARL HOLMAN **The Afternoon of a Young Poet**   42

*Unit Two*    **O Pioneers**     54

*poems*    *There Is Wealth in the Earth*   56

STEPHEN VINCENT BENÉT **Western Star**   56
ARCHIBALD MAC LEISH **To Thomas Jefferson, Esquire**   59
DUNCAN CAMPBELL SCOTT **On the Way to the Mission**   61
MARY OLIVER **Stark Boughs on the Family Tree**   63
ELISABETH PECK **Walthena**   64

*novel excerpt*    ELLEN GLASGOW **Only Yesterday** from *Vein of Iron*   66
*essay*    IRVING STONE **Death Valley Earns Its Name**   70
*novel excerpt*    WILLA CATHER **The New Country** from *My Ántonia*   77
*short story*    JOHN STEINBECK **The Leader of the People**   87

| *Unit Three* | **The Immigrants' America** | *100* |

*poems*   Origins   *103*

HENRY WADSWORTH LONGFELLOW **The Jewish Cemetery**   *103*
EDWARD FIELD **My Polish Grandma**   *104*
DAVID IGNATOW **Europe and America**   *107*
LINDA PASTAN **My Grandmother**   *108*
KATHERINE EDELMAN **Irish Grandmother**   *109*

*short story* BERNARD MALAMUD **The Magic Barrel**   *111*
*autobiography* JADE SNOW WONG from **Fifth Chinese Daughter**   *125*
*novel excerpt* JOE VERGARA **A Letter From Home** from *Love and Pasta*   *137*


| *Unit Four* | **The American Tradition** | *141* |

*poems*   *Home Thoughts*   *142*
ROBERT FROST **Mending Wall**   *142*
WILLIAM STAFFORD **One Home**   *144*
EDGAR LEE MASTERS **Lucinda Matlock**   *145*
ROBERT HAYDEN **Those Winter Sundays**   *146*
EVE MERRIAM
**Robin Hood**   *147*
**Landscape**   *147*

*poems*   *The Puritan Heritage*   *148*
EDWARD TAYLOR
**The Golden Key**   *148*
**The Spiderweb**   *149*
**The Creation**   *149*
ANNE BRADSTREET
**The Poet's Art**   *150*
**Human Vanity**   *150*
*sermon* JONATHAN EDWARDS
**Sinners in the Hands of an Angry God**   *152*
*autobiography* BENJAMIN FRANKLIN from **Autobiography**   *157*
*short story* SHERWOOD ANDERSON **The Egg**   *166*
*short story* TILLIE OLSEN **I Stand Here Ironing**   *175*

PART TWO  **American Voices:**
**American Classics Today**                                                    184

Unit Five  **Innocence and Experience**                                        187

poems  *Poet of Democracy: Walt Whitman*  188

WALT WHITMAN
**I Am One of the Nation** from *Song of Myself*  189
**A March in the Ranks Hard-Pressed**  193
from **When Lilacs Last in the Dooryard Bloomed**  195

novel excerpt  JAMES FENIMORE COOPER
**Deerslayer Escapes** from *The Deerslayer*  199

novel excerpt  MARK TWAIN **Huck Runs Away**
from *The Adventures of Huckleberry Finn*  207

short story  BRET HARTE **The Outcasts of Poker Flat**  237

short story  KATHERINE ANNE PORTER **The Grave**  246

Unit Six  **The Faces of Nature**                                              252

poems  *The Changing Seasons*  254

HENRY WADSWORTH LONGFELLOW **Afternoon in February**  254
E. E. CUMMINGS **in Just-spring**  255
ROBERT FROST
**The Tuft of Flowers**  256
**Once by the Pacific**  258
SYLVIA PLATH **Frog Autumn**  259
KAY BOYLE **October 1954**  260

poems  *Nature Poet: William Cullen Bryant*  261
WILLIAM CULLEN BRYANT
**The Love of Nature** from *Thanatopsis*  261
**The Groves Were God's First Temples**  264

novel excerpt  HERMAN MELVILLE from **Moby Dick**  266
short story  STEPHEN CRANE **The Open Boat**  287
short story  ERNEST HEMINGWAY **Big Two-Hearted River (Part One)**  307

*Unit Seven*  **The Gothic Imagination**  *316*

*poems*  *The Owl Shall Stoop*  *318*

SYLVIA PLATH **The Water Rat**  *318*
ROBINSON JEFFERS **Vulture**  *319*
DENISE LEVERTOV **The Sharks**  *320*
RUTH HERSCHBERGER **Displays of Skill: The Bat**  *321*
DANIELA GIOSEFFI **Some Slippery Afternoon**  *322*

*poems*  *Master of the Macabre: Edgar Allan Poe*  *324*
EDGAR ALLAN POE
**Annabel Lee**  *324*
from **Ulalume**  *326*
*short story*  **The Black Cat**  *328*
*short story*  NATHANIEL HAWTHORNE **Young Goodman Brown**  *338*
*short story*  WILLIAM FAULKNER **The Tall Men**  *351*
*short story*  CYNTHIA RICH **My Sister's Marriage**  *364*


*Unit Eight*  **A Different Drummer**  *375*

*poems*  *Moths and Angels: Emily Dickinson*  *376*

EMILY DICKINSON
**Presentiment**  *376*
**A Bird Came Down the Walk**  *377*
**A Narrow Fellow in the Grass**  *378*
**I Stepped From Plank to Plank**  *379*
**Because I Could Not Stop for Death**  *380*
**The Bustle in a House**  *381*
**Hope Is the Thing With Feathers**  *381*
*essay*  THOMAS PAINE **The American Crisis**  *382*
*essay*  RALPH WALDO EMERSON **On Self-Reliance**  *388*
*autobiography*  HENRY DAVID THOREAU
**An Experiment in Simple Living** from *Walden*  *392*
*novel excerpt*  RICHARD WRIGHT **A Separate Road** from *Black Boy*  *401*

| | | |
|---|---|---|
| *Unit Nine* | **The Secret Heart** | *413* |

*poems*   *Where Is Happiness?*   *414*

      STEPHEN CRANE **Four Poems**   *414*
      COUNTEE CULLEN **Any Human to Another**   *416*
      GWENDOLYN BROOKS **The Sonnet-Ballad**   *417*
      ELINOR WYLIE **Sanctuary**   *418*
      MARGE PIERCY **Simple Song**   *419*

*poems*   *Love Is Not All: Edna St. Vincent Millay*   *420*
      EDNA ST. VINCENT MILLAY
        **Pity Me Not Because the Light of Day**   *420*
        **I Shall Go Back Again to the Bleak Shore**   *421*
        **Love Is Not All**   *422*
        **Dirge Without Music**   *423*
        **Apostrophe to Man**   *424*
*play*   THORNTON WILDER **Our Town**   *425*


| | | |
|---|---|---|
| *PART THREE* | **On Native Soil:**<br>**A Manifold Heritage** | *476* |


| | | |
|---|---|---|
| *Unit Ten* | **A Proud Nation** | *478* |

*poems*   *The Land Shall Remain*   *480*

      INDIAN CHANTS AND PRAYERS
        **Calling for Rain (Zuñi)**   *480*
        **The War God's Horse Song (Navajo)**   *482*
        **A Prayer to the Dead (Assiniboine)**   *483*
        **Song of the Sky Loom (Tewa)**   *484*
        **Song of Defeat (Sioux)**   *485*
      VACHEL LINDSAY **The Flower-Fed Buffaloes**   *486*
      MARY AUSTIN **The Grass on the Mountain**   *487*
      W. D. SNODGRASS **Powwow**   *488*
      N. SCOTT MOMADAY **Earth and I Gave You Turquoise**   *490*
*essay*   N. SCOTT MOMADAY from **The Way to Rainy Mountain**   *491*
*oral history*   BLACK ELK
      **The Earth Is All That Lasts** from *Black Elk Speaks*   *497*
*short story*   DANIEL DE PAOLA **The Returning**   *517*

Unit Eleven **Let My People Go** 526

poems *Free at Last* 528

SPIRITUALS
**Go Down, Moses** *528*
**I Thank God I'm Free at Last** *529*
LANGSTON HUGHES **Uncle Tom** *530*
**Porter** *530*
**Graduation** *531*
ARNA BONTEMPS **A Black Man Talks of Reaping** *532*
ROBERT HAYDEN **Runagate, Runagate** *534*
**Frederick Douglass** *537*
choral reading JAMES WELDON JOHNSON
**Noah Built the Ark** from *God's Trombones* *538*
autobiography MAYA ANGELOU **Lift Every Voice and Sing**
from *I Know Why the Caged Bird Sings* *543*
short story RALPH ELLISON **Mister Toussan** *554*
play LORRAINE HANSBERRY **A Raisin in the Sun** *562*

Unit Twelve **Between Two Worlds** 628

poems *If Sun Comes* 630

STEPHEN BERG **Five Aztec Poems** *630*
NIKKI GIOVANNI **Legacies** *632*
GWENDOLYN BROOKS **Truth** *634*
IMAMU AMIRI BARAKA (LE ROI JONES)
**Preface to a Twenty-Volume Suicide Note** *636*
JAMES A. EMANUEL **Get Up, Blues** *637*
short story AMADO MURO **Cecilia Rosas** *638*
autobiography EDNA FERBER
**An Iowa Childhood** from *A Peculiar Treasure* *649*
short story SIMON J. ORTIZ **Kaiser and the War** *656*
short story JOHN STEINBECK **Flight** *664*

*Index of Literary Terms* 682
*Handbook of Literary Terms* 683
*Author Biographies* 702
*Glossary* 722

*Acknowledgments* 744
*Art Credits* 749
*Index of Authors and Titles* 752

# Language/Composition Activities

**Words**

A 2    RELATED TERMS: The Vocabulary of Status   *41*
A 4    LANGUAGE AND LIFE: The Language of Worship   *69*
A 5    WORDS IN CONTEXT: Conquering the Desert   *76*
A 8    WORDS IN ACTION: What Adjectives Tell Us   *124*
A 10   LANGUAGE HISTORY: Old Country Memories   *140*
A 13   WORDS IN CONTEXT: A Trip to the Eighteenth Century   *164*
B 4    WORDS IN CONTEXT: A Far-Off Day   *251*
B 8    WORD CLUSTERS: The Cruel Sea   *306*
B 10   THE READER'S VOCABULARY: The Monster Within the Tomb   *336*
B 12   THE RANGE OF VOCABULARY: Country People   *363*
B 13   ACCURATE DISTINCTIONS: Weighty Words   *374*
C 1    FOR VOCABULARY BUILDING: Reading About Our History   *496*
C 2    FOR DICTIONARY WORK: Language and History   *516*
C 3    WORKING WITH ETYMOLOGY: Going to the Roots   *553*
C 6    STUDYING COHERENCE: Charting Related Terms   *648*

**Sentences**

A 1    WRITING AND OBSERVATION: The Unusual Touch   *26*
A 3    FOR SENTENCE PRACTICE: The One-Sentence Portrait   *53*
A 11   IMAGINATIVE COMPARISON: Stretching Your Imagination   *151*
B 2    FOR SENTENCE PRACTICE: Thoughts and Afterthoughts
           by Mark Twain   *236*
B 15   THE BALANCED SENTENCE: Simplicity, Simplicity, Simplicity!   *400*
C 4    FOR SENTENCE PRACTICE: The Added Touch   *561*
C 8    FOR SENTENCE PRACTICE: Writing the Close-Up Sentence   *678*

**Composition**

A 6    FOR WRITING PRACTICE: An Exercise in Point of View   *99*
A 7    OBSERVING A GROUP: Rediscovering the Ethnic American   *110*
A 9    COMPARISON AND CONTRAST: Writing the Point-by-Point
           Comparison   *135*
A 12   STUDYING PARALLELISM: The Uses of Repetition   *156*
B 3    WRITING ABOUT LITERATURE: A Touch of Melodrama   *245*
B 9    WRITING AND OBSERVATION: A Stickler for Detail   *315*
B 16   FOLLOWING THROUGH: You Are on Your Own   *412*
B 18   THE TWO-PARAGRAPH THEME: The Important Thing Is
           to Be Happy   *459*
B 19   THE BIOGRAPHICAL REPORT: A Memorable Person   *473*
C 7    IMAGINATIVE DESCRIPTION: A Scene I Would Like to See   *655*

**Usage**

B 1    FORMAL AND INFORMAL: A Nineteenth-Century Style   *206*
B 5    A FORMAL STYLE: In Small Boats on the Omnipotent Sea   *275*
B 6    A FORMAL STYLE: The Mighty Whale   *280*
B 7    A FORMAL STYLE: Heart of Steel   *286*
B 11   OUR CHANGING LANGUAGE: The Heart of the Wilderness   *349*
B 14   OUR READING VOCABULARY: The Times That Try Men's Souls   *387*
B 17   INFORMAL ENGLISH: Small-Town Talk   *444*
C 5    WORKING WITH USAGE: Down-Home Talk   *590*

# American Voices

# American Literature
## *A Historical Overview*

A great poem is for ages and ages in common and for all degrees
and complexions and all departments and sects and for a woman
as much as a man and a man as much as a woman. . . . The proof of a
poet is that his country absorbs him as affectionately as he has
absorbed it.

—Walt Whitman

What makes a classic? What causes writers to be remembered
long after their contemporaries have been forgotten? Some writers
become successful for a time because they know how to cater to
their public. Entertainment literature helps people keep their
minds off their troubles. Much popular reading matter helps readers see the silver lining in the dark clouds of the day. It helps them
build up their self-esteem, or it helps them find words for their
anger or indignation. But as times and fashions change, the readers find new objects for their hopes and their anger. As a result,
much day-to-day literature soon disappears from view.

As we look back over the history of our literature, which are the
books that have stood the test of time? To which authors do readers return in spite of changing fashions? Often the books that last
have a strength that has its roots in a basic honesty. Their authors
wrote about life as they saw it, from their own personal point of
view. They recorded their own view of the world, whether it was
popular at the time or not. They used their own eyes and ears, and
they took in things that others had been too busy or too prejudiced
to notice. They spoke up and made themselves heard.

### Early Beginnings

The history of American literature takes us from the records and
diaries of colonial times to the full flowering of a national literature rich in writers with a powerful individuality. The story
begins with the arrival of the first colonists in the New World.
The first books written in America were histories of the early
explorations and settlements. They were stories of Indian wars
and of battles against disease and near-starvation. In the best
known of these, the *History of the Plymouth Plantation*, William
Bradford told his eyewitness story of the crossing of the *Mayflower* in 1620 and the fortunes of the first settlers in the "wild
and savage" country they had reached. Much of the literature of
the early colonial times was written by Puritan ministers like

The crossing of the Mayflower in
1620.

Cotton Mather and Jonathan Edwards, preaching their zealous Protestantism to their New England audience. Later, the struggle for independence from the English mother country brought fame to writers who helped shape the political ideals of the new nation. They included Benjamin Franklin, Thomas Jefferson, and Thomas Paine.

## The Nineteenth Century

During the nineteenth century, American writers at first wrote poems and stories similar to those that were admired at the time in England and other European countries. But more and more, they dealt with new materials from American history and American life. They developed new styles and new forms that pointed toward a homegrown, independent national literature. Edgar Allan Poe (1809–1849) wrote tales of mystery and horror that carried on traditions already popular in Europe, and that were later in turn widely read and appreciated by European readers. Nathaniel Hawthorne wrote tales in the leisurely style of British nineteenth-century storytellers. But many of his stories dealt with a sense of guilt and a suspicion of secret sin that were rooted in the traditions of his native New England. For many readers around the world, his novel *The Scarlet Letter* (1850) painted an unforgettable picture of the Puritan past. Herman Melville first became known for his stories of a sailor's life and of South Seas adventure. His *Moby Dick* (1851) started out as a collection of whaling lore and whaling adventures. It became one of the great American classics, the story of the pursuit of the Great White Whale by the obsessed Captain Ahab and his strange crew.

In the second half of the nineteenth century, several great writers took up a theme that for a long time remained part of the image Americans had of themselves. From the beginning, the growth of a new nation on the North American continent had brought to many the hope of a new dawn for humanity. In the Old World, many people had always been taught to accept the place in which Providence had placed them. They had learned to be resigned to poverty, oppression, and war. In the New World, people had to believe from the beginning that it was possible to make a new start. It became part of the American creed that the open spaces and the challenges of the new continent required a new breed of people. This new kind of person would be unhampered by age-old prejudices and the dead weight of custom. The first major American novelist, James Fenimore Cooper, in his Leatherstocking Tales helped create the myth of the sturdy, self-reliant hero of the American frontier. These books included titles like *The Pioneers* (1823), *The Last of the Mohicans* (1826), and *The Deerslayer* (1841). Over the years, these books brought to millions of readers

*The link between the East and the West created by the Erie Canal in 1825.*

*The Westward Movement of the mid-nineteenth century.*

*The outbreak of Civil War in 1861.*

*The first transcontinental railroad, completed in 1869.*

*The rise of American industry during the closing decades of the nineteenth century.*

*The trend toward mechanization at the turn of the twentieth century.*

everywhere the idealized picture of an unspoiled, adventurous life close to nature, without the frills of city civilization.

After Cooper, several of the most widely heard voices in American literature preached the gospel of independence and sturdy self-reliance. The business of America was with the present and with the future. In the forties and fifties, Ralph Waldo Emerson published many essays and lectures, including his famous essay "Self-Reliance," that told Americans to discover their own native genius and to trust their own spiritual resources. His friend and admirer Henry David Thoreau published *Walden* (1854), the story of Thoreau's attempt to live close to nature and without the unnecessary baggage of tradition and custom. Walt Whitman, in his *Leaves of Grass* (first published in 1855), included long, sprawling poems unlike any poetry of the past. He chanted the glories of a democratic America. He painted a picture of a country brawny, tough, and full of untrammeled energy, dedicated to liberty, brotherhood, and common sense.

The literature of self-reliance had its counterpart in the boisterous, irreverent tradition of American humor. Mark Twain wrote many books whose deadpan humor appealed hugely to a people suspicious of sham and pomp. His masterpiece, *Huckleberry Finn* (1885), took millions of readers on an unforgettable journey down the Mississippi with the youthful hero who keeps his unspoiled sense of right and wrong in a corrupt and violent world.

## The Twentieth Century

Many of the great names of twentieth-century American literature are known far beyond America's borders. American poets were pioneers in the search for modern forms to express modern themes. Twentieth-century readers rediscovered the poetry of Emily Dickinson, whose poems, mostly unpublished in her own time, were strangely different from the harmonious, mellow verses of her more popular contemporaries. Among the great innovators in modern poetry were American poets like Ezra Pound, T. S. Eliot, and E. E. Cummings. The modern American novel became the most widely read and translated around the world. Ernest Hemingway wrote novels that became classics of world literature: *The Sun Also Rises* (1926), *A Farewell to Arms* (1929), *For Whom the Bell Tolls* (1940), and *The Old Man and the Sea* (1953). His characters are often lonely modern individuals who have lost faith in big words and in institutions and who try to live by a personal code of honesty and courage. John Steinbeck, best known for his *Grapes of Wrath* (1939), wrote immensely popular stories about ordinary people coping with their troubles. William Faulkner wrote difficult, rich tales of conflict and violence. *The Sound and the Fury* (1929) and *Absalom, Absalom* (1936) are two of his best-known novels. He chronicled the history of successive generations of the American South in transition, with old standards threatened by the ruthlessness of individuals and by new ways of life.

The modern American short story was developed by many gifted storytellers, including Willa Cather, Sherwood Anderson, Katherine Anne Porter, Bernard Malamud, Shirley Jackson, Eudora Welty, and Flannery O'Connor. Short story classics like Willa Cather's "Paul's Case" or Shirley Jackson's "The Lottery" were read by many thousands of readers.

Modern American dramatists wrote plays that have become familiar to audiences everywhere. Thornton Wilder wrote the nostalgic *Our Town* (1938) and a number of other plays that were successes with audiences here and abroad. Arthur Miller used the stage for a gripping kind of truth-telling in plays like *Death of a Salesman* (1949) and *The Crucible* (1953). Tennessee Williams became famous with plays like *The Glass Menagerie* (1944) and *A Streetcar Named Desire* (1947), stories of lonely people searching for happiness in a callous or brutal world.

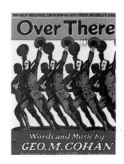

*U.S. entrance into World War I in 1917.*

## Today and Tomorrow

In recent years, America's literary tradition has been challenged as a too one-sided mirror of its people and their history. There has been increasing recognition for writers who have written from the experience of America's minorities and questioned the sincerity of the nation's promise of liberty and justice for all. Readers have rediscovered Frederick Douglass, an escaped former slave who in his speeches and writings fought for the abolition of slavery. Readers have gone back to the novels of Richard Wright, who in his bitter, powerful autobiographical *Black Boy* (1945) attacked the image white Americans had of black people and the image black people had of themselves. Black poets like Langston Hughes and Gwendolyn Brooks have become more widely known. Writers like N. Scott Momaday have helped readers rediscover America's Indian heritage. Piri Thomas, José Antonio Villareal, and others wrote about the lives of Spanish-speaking Americans.

*The Great Depression of the 1930's.*

What is the future of books and readers in America? For a time, the prophets of an electronic tomorrow predicted that radio, television, and movies would take the place of magazines and books. But today Americans read as much as ever for entertainment, for information, for encouragement and advice. As many people as ever rely on the printed word to share in the grievances and daydreams and aspirations of their fellows. And every so often a writer with something important to say reaches millions of readers and makes them think about what it is like to be alive at this time, on this planet.

*New frontiers of the twentieth century.*

# A Gallery of American Authors

*Song of Himself*
## Walt Whitman

Whitman is one of those passionate geniuses who appear once every one hundred years or so and are so far ahead of their contemporaries that they are misunderstood during their lifetime.

Other nations have such men—artists, musicians, poets, writers—whose memory they honor and whose works they cherish. Walt Whitman is one of *our* geniuses—a particularly American one—whose praises should be sung along with those of Lincoln, Washington, and Jefferson in every schoolhouse in the land.

His output was small, but his magnificent *Leaves of Grass* left an imprint on the world of poetry that is incalculable and still being felt. That lovely line hidden deep within "Song of Myself" still gives me a feeling of joy whenever I think of it:

> A leaf of grass is no less than the journeywork of the stars . . .

Whitman hoped to be a poet of the people and dreamed that his exuberance for the hearty, unpolished heart of America would stir even the roughest of his young countrymen. Needless to say, he stirred Emerson, Thoreau, Stevenson, and every poet in the world ever since— including his imitators today.

—Terrence O'Flaherty

*Legacy of the Heart*
*From a Shy Recluse*
## Emily Dickinson

Even in prose her words were poetry. She possessed no portrait of herself, Emily Dickinson wrote in 1862 to a friend who had requested one; "but," she continued in a style clear as engraved glass, "am small, like the Wren, and my Hair is bold, like the Chestnut Bur—and my eyes, like the Sherry in the Glass, that the Guest leaves." She was the daughter of a domineering Yankee lawyer-congressman who bade her stay close to home, and she acquiesced. The world thus discovered her verse only after she died. In her lifetime just seven of her poems saw print. There were hundreds more in her room, and they have earned her acclaim, from students of literature, as one of the greatest poets in the history of the English language.

*Life Special Report: Remarkable American Women*

*America's*
*Greatest Humorist*

# Mark Twain

Mark Twain is one of the most widely read authors around the world. He took in and preserved for future generations much of nineteenth-century America: the bustling life of the Mississippi River, with its wharves, rafts, and riverboats; the open spaces of the West; the beckoning freedom and random violence of a rapidly changing and growing society. Critics have called his *Huckleberry Finn* "a joy forever" and "unquestionably one of the masterpieces of American and world literature." Millions of readers have loved him for his horse sense, his endless supply of extravagant yarns, his friendliness toward the underdog and instinctive hostility toward bullies. He wrote many books and lectured to countless audiences. His white clothes became famous, and his birthdays became national events. He made millions laugh, but he never completely let them forget that life has a darker side, like the moon.

*A Modest Author*
*Whose Epic Moved the Nation*

# Harriet Beecher Stowe

"I am a little bit of a woman," Harriet Beecher Stowe wrote of herself in 1853, "somewhat more than 40, about as thin and dry as a piece of snuff." The daughter of one preacher and the sister of seven more, she found a focus for her own Christian idealism in the antislavery cause. Her book *Uncle Tom's Cabin* sharpened moral issues that led to civil war. "The soul of eloquence is feeling," her father had written, and Stowe's book limned the human anguish of slavery, so arousing Americans that 10,000 copies were sold in a week, over 300,000 in a year. In 1862 she was in Washington urging Abraham Lincoln to sign the Emancipation Proclamation. The legend is that Lincoln shook her hand and said, "So this is the little lady who made this big war."

*Life Special Report: Remarkable American Women*

*Clear Eye and Kindly Heart*
# William Saroyan

There are very few things which have captured the spirit of San Francisco of the 1930's in such an affectionately flamboyant manner as William Saroyan's "The Time of Your Life" and yet managed to make it seem universal. It was produced on Broadway in 1939 and won a Pulitzer Prize.

"In the time of your life, live—so that in that good time there shall be no ugliness or death for yourself or for any life your life touches. Seek goodness everywhere, and when it is found, bring it out of its hiding place and let it be free and unashamed. Place in matter and in flesh the least of values, for these are the things that hold death and must pass away," says Saroyan.

"Discover in all things that which shines and is beyond corruption. Encourage virtue in whatever heart it may have been driven into secrecy and sorrow by the shame and terror of the world.

"Ignore the obvious, for it is unworthy of the clear eye and the kindly heart. Be the inferior of no man, nor of any man be the superior. Remember that every man is a variation of yourself. No man's guilt is not yours, nor is any man's innocence a thing apart.

"Despise evil and ungodliness, but not men of ungodliness or evil. These, understand. . . In the time of your life, live—so that in that wondrous time you shall not add to the misery and sorrow of the world, but shall smile to the infinite delight and mystery of it."

That is the credo which has inspired the play, and it still has a lovely ring to it.

—Terrence O'Flaherty

*I Am What I Am*
# Ralph Ellison

Ralph Ellison was born in 1914 in Oklahoma City. He says, "I heard stories of searching for buried treasure and of headless horsemen . . . of Jesse James, of Negro outlaws and black United States marshals, of slaves who became chiefs of Indian tribes, and of the exploits of Negro cowboys." Ellison studied to be a musician and played in school orchestras and jazz bands. But after he went to New York in search of work, he was encouraged to become a writer by Richard Wright, then the best-known black novelist. Ralph Ellison published his *Invisible Man* in 1952. It is the story of a young black struggling to find independence and self-respect. *Invisible Man* has been called "one of the classic American novels written since World War II."

# Joyce Carol Oates

Joyce Carol Oates grew up near a small town in upstate New York. In the sixties and seventies, she published many prize-winning stories. Many of these stories take place in an everyday urban or suburban setting that is immediately recognized by many of her readers. Her characters, as one critic said, "are typically immersed in a middle-class culture full of TV and radio announcers' clichés." Many readers have been fascinated and at times made angry by the mirror her stories hold up to our everyday lives.

*Indians and the Land*

# N. Scott Momaday

N. Scott Momaday, a full-blooded Kiowa from a Southwest reservation and professor of English and comparative literature, saw the anniversary of the nation as a timely occasion to renew "an attitude of reverence for the American landscape" that was traditional with the country's first settlers, the Indians.

"A feeling for our land, which would help strengthen the national spirit, is characteristic of Indian ceremonies and oral literature," he said. The poet-novelist, who won the Pulitzer Prize in 1969 for his novel *House Made of Dawn,* put the feeling and the occasion in an eloquent way:

"Once in his life a man ought to concentrate his mind upon the remembered earth, I believe. He ought to give himself up to a particular landscape in his experience, to look at it from as many angles as he can, to wonder upon it, to dwell upon it.

"He ought to imagine that he touches it with his hands at every season and listens to the sounds that are made upon it. He ought to imagine the creatures there and all the faintest motions of the wind. He ought to recollect the glare of moon and the colors of the dawn and dusk."

# New World

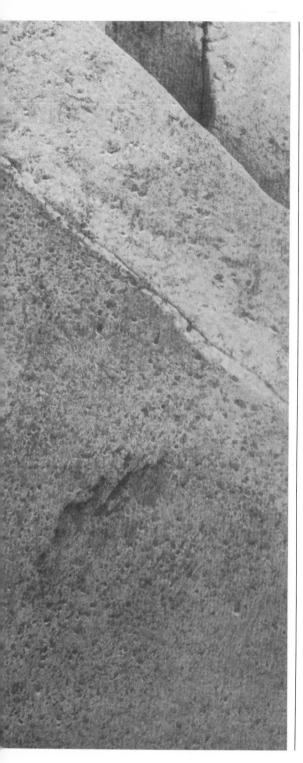

Part One of this book is a collection of readings about beginnings. It includes many selections that make the reader think about origins, about roots. The collection as a whole asks where Americans come from—in body, and in spirit. When we ask "Who am I?" part of the answer is that we exist at a given point in a common history. Both what we accept and what we reject is shaped to a great extent by "where we came in."

In recent years, the search for roots has become an urgent preoccupation of people concerned about the spiritual condition of our times. For decades, a central theme of modern art and literature has been alienation. Many modern writers document their struggles to escape the nets thrown by the family, by the church, by the belligerent patriotism of their elders. Some of the great modern stories are stories of rejection—of the father by the son, of the state by the citizen, of the citizen by the state. A familiar modern hero is the outsider— Holden Caulfield in *The Catcher in the Rye,* Sylvia Plath's heroine in *The Bell Jar,* Ralph Ellison's *Invisible Man.*

On the positive side, some of the literature of alienation makes us experience a sense of liberation, a pride in a hard-won, uncompromising personal integrity. But much of it also makes us experience a profound sense of homelessness, of loneliness, of being adrift in a world without meaning. Where do we turn in our modern world to experience a sense of solidarity? When do we feel a sense of belonging? This collection makes us look in our common spiritual history for clues to our identity. It reminds us of ties we may have forgotten.

# Growing Up in America

It took me a long time and much painful
boomeranging of my expectations to achieve a
realization everyone else seems to have been
born with: That I am nobody but myself.

—Ralph Ellison

What is it like to grow up in America?

Though Columbus discovered America centuries
ago, each young person has to rediscover it, and chart
and measure it for personal use. There is a time for
each of us when we see the familiar landmarks for the
first time. There is a first time for our discovery of
some of the detours and dead ends along the road. What
are some of the road signs and roadblocks encountered
by the young person growing up in this country yesterday or today? What map or compass do young people
follow who are making their way into the future? The
section that follows contains a brief sampling of poems
and stories about "Young America." Many readers find
that some of the most fascinating or absorbing literature they encounter is literature about childhood and
adolescence. When we are young, our own experiences
often seem to us unique: We feel that no one really
understands; we are given advice that does not really
fit our problems. But in reading about the experiences
of other people, we may find that others have traveled a
similar route. Or, dealing with problems different from
ours, they may have had thoughts and feelings similar
to our own.

## POEMS: **Looking in the Album**

> Even snapshots meant to gather afternoons
> with casual ease are rigid . . .
> > Tinny laughter
> echoes from the staged scene on an artificial
> beach.
>
> —Vern Rutsala, "Looking in the Album"

When we are asked to look at an album of childhood memories, we know that the pictures cannot tell the whole or the real story. Too many of them are posed or staged especially for the occasion, with the people in them making special Sunday faces. Too much of real life is left out since we do not always have a camera ready when something important is happening to us. How real are the following poetic snapshots of childhood scenes? What kind of pictures came to these poets' minds when they turned to the past for childhood memories?

---

### John Updike
# Home Movies

How the children have changed! Rapt we stare
    At flickering lost Edens where
    Pale infants, squinting, seem to hark
To their older selves laughing in the dark.

And then, by the trellis in some old Spring—
    The seasons are unaltering—
    We gather, smoother and less bald,
Innocently clowning, have been called

By the cruelly invisible cameraman.
    How silently time ran!
    We cannot climb back, nor can our friends,
To that calm light. The brief film ends.

---

### YOU AND THE POEM

(1) Many older people look back on childhood as a "lost Eden." What was lost in the original Eden? Some of the details in the poem, such as the "pale" and "squinting" children, do not seem to tie in with the idea of "Eden" very well. But other words and details *do*. Which ones? How?

(2) Imagine you are watching a home movie of a typical scene from your own childhood. Describe what you see.

## Evelyn Tooley Hunt
# Taught Me Purple

My mother taught me purple
Although she never wore it.
Wash-gray was her circle,
The tenement her orbit.

My mother taught me golden
And held me up to see it,
Above the broken molding,
Beyond the filthy street.

My mother reached for beauty
And for its lack she died,
Who knew so much of duty
She could not teach me pride.

---

### YOU AND THE POEM

(1) A **symbol** carries with it a larger meaning over and above its practical or everyday significance. For instance, green is a familiar everyday color, used for all kinds of things. But it is also the color of plants. It therefore reminds us of growing, "greening" things. It can easily become a symbol for natural and healthy life. What are some of the possible symbolic meanings of the colors used in this poem: purple, gray, gold? What is their symbolic meaning as they are used in this poem?

(2) This and the preceding poem use **rhyme**. Two lines rhyme when the final accented vowels and the sounds that follow them are identical: *stare/where; hark/dark.* In both poems, rhyme helps group each set of four lines together as a unit, or **stanza**. In "Taught Me Purple," several of the rhymes are only half-rhymes: *purple/circle.* They illustrate **assonance**. Assonance is a "sounding together," a resemblance of sounds, that is not complete enough for a full rhyme. Find the full rhymes in this poem. Also, explain what makes the other ones examples of half-rhyme or assonance.

Richard Wilbur

# Running

What were we playing? Was it prisoner's base?
I ran with whacking keds
Down the cart-road past Rickard's place,
And where it dropped beside the tractor-sheds

Lept out into the air above a blurred
Terrain, through jolted light,
Took two hard lopes, and at the third
Spanked off a hummock-side exactly right,

And made the turn, and with delighted strain
Sprinted across the flat
By the bullpen, and up the lane.
Thinking of happiness, I think of that.

## YOU AND THE POEM

(1) What do all the following words have in common? What keynote do they strike for the poem as a whole? Try to read the poem in such a way that whatever common charge the following words carry comes through clearly to the listener: *whack, leap, blur, jolt, lope, spank, strain, sprint.* The word *delight* often makes us think of a relaxed, happy feeling. Can you explain how someone could have a feeling of "delighted *strain*"?

(2) In this poem, the poet first takes us through the actual run. (Can you visualize his actual route?) Then he lets us know how it made him feel. We get the point of the experience at the very end. Can you think of some experience that made you feel exceptionally happy, or angry, or sad? Write a paragraph about it that takes us through the experience first—lead up to how you felt.

## Countee Cullen
### (1903–1946)

# Saturday's Child

Some are teethed on a silver spoon,
With the stars strung for a rattle;
I cut my teeth as the black raccoon—
For implements of battle.

Some are swaddled in silk and down,
And heralded by a star;
They swathed my limbs in a sackcloth gown
On a night that was black as tar.

For some, godfather and goddame
The opulent fairies be;
Dame Poverty gave me my name,
And Pain godfathered me.

For I was born on Saturday—
"Bad time for planting a seed,"
Was all my father had to say,
And, "One mouth more to feed."

Death cut the strings that gave me life,
And handed me to Sorrow,
The only kind of middle wife
My folks could beg or borrow.

### YOU AND THE POEM

(1) We call a very clear-cut confrontation of opposites an **antithesis**. Spell out as fully as you can the extreme opposite meanings summed up in the following pairs from the poem:
rattle—battle; silk—sackcloth; star—tar; opulent—poverty.

(2) Countee Cullen, one of America's best-known black poets, was raised by foster parents. Is there any hint in this poem of this biographical fact?

(3) People react to poverty and sorrow in different ways. How could you describe this poet's attitude toward his childhood experiences? What is the *spirit* of this poem? With what **tone** of voice should it be read? Would you say this poet is "feeling sorry for himself"? Why or why not?

C. K. Williams

# Hood

Remember me? I was the one
in high school you were always afraid of.
I kept cigarettes in my sleeve, wore
engineer's boots, long hair, my collar
up in back and there were always
girls with me in the hallways.

You were nothing. I had it in for you—
when I peeled rubber at the lights
you cringed like a teacher.
And when I crashed and broke both lungs
on the wheel, you were so relieved
that you stroked the hard Ford paint
And your hands shook.

## YOU AND THE POEM

(1) One of the facts of life of youth is our encounter with people bigger and meaner than we are. What is your first natural reaction to the person who is talking in this poem? Do you recognize the type?

(2) How do you feel about the *other* person—the one the speaker in the poem is talking to? Do you think the poet himself was more like the first person when he was in high school, or like the second?

(3) Would you have material for a story called "An Encounter With a Bully"? (Or, do you have a vivid memory of bullying someone else?)

● Part of growing up is getting into situations that make us say: "I'm not ready to handle this!" A familiar definition of adolescence is growing up into a world we did not create. It presents us with situations we did not ask for. Eudora Welty is a short-story writer from Mississippi who is well-known for her sharp eye and ear. She does not believe in glossing over things, or in making people seem kind when they are not. She here takes a sharp look at a young girl in the kind of unsettling situation that is part of growing up.

## Eudora Welty

# A Visit of Charity

It was mid-morning—a very cold, bright day. Holding a potted plant before her, a girl of fourteen jumped off the bus in front of the Old Ladies' Home, on the outskirts of town. She wore a red coat, and her straight yellow hair was hanging down loose from the pointed white cap all the little girls were wearing that year. She stopped for a moment beside one of the prickly dark shrubs with which the city had beautified the Home, and then proceeded slowly toward the building, which was of whitewashed brick and reflected the winter sunlight like a block of ice. As she walked vaguely up the steps she shifted the small pot from hand to hand; then she had to set it down and remove her mittens before she could open the heavy door.

"I'm a Campfire Girl. . . . I have to pay a visit to some old lady," she told the nurse at the desk. This was a woman in a white uniform who looked as if she were cold; she had close-cut hair which stood up on the very top of her head exactly like a sea wave. Marian, the little girl, did not tell her that this visit would give her a minimum of only three points in her score.

"Acquainted with any of our residents?" asked the nurse. She lifted one eyebrow and spoke like a man.

"With any old ladies? No—but—that is, any of them will do," Marian stammered. With her free hand she pushed her hair behind her ears, as she did when it was time to study Science.

The nurse shrugged and rose. "You have a nice *multiflora cineraria* there," she remarked as she walked ahead down the hall of closed doors to pick out an old lady.

There was loose, bulging linoleum on the floor. Marian felt as if she were walking on the waves, but the nurse paid no attention to it. There was a smell in the hall like the interior of a clock. Everything was silent until, behind one of the doors, an old lady of some kind cleared her throat like a sheep bleating. This decided the nurse. Stopping in her tracks, she first extended her arm, bent her elbow, and leaned forward from the hips—all for the purpose of examining the watch strapped to her wrist; then she gave a loud double-rap on the door.

"There are two in each room," the nurse remarked over her shoulder.

"Two what?" asked Marian without thinking. The sound like a sheep's bleating almost made her turn around and run back.

One old woman was pulling the door open in short, gradual jerks, and when she saw the nurse a strange smile forced her old face dangerously awry. Marian, suddenly propelled by the strong, impatient arm of the nurse, saw next the side-face of another old woman, even older, who was lying flat in bed with a cap on and a counterpane drawn up to her chin.

"Visitor," said the nurse, and after one more shove she was off up the hall.

Marian stood tongue-tied; both hands held the potted plant. The old woman, still with that terrible, square smile (which was a smile of welcome) stamped on her bony face, was waiting. . . . Perhaps she said something. The old woman in bed said nothing at all, and she did not look around.

Suddenly Marian saw a hand, quick as a bird claw, reach up in the air and pluck the white cap off her head. At the same time, another claw to match drew her all the way into the room, and the next moment the door closed behind her.

"My, my, my," said the old lady at her side.

Marian stood enclosed by a bed, a washstand, and a chair; the tiny room had altogether too much furniture. Everything smelled wet—even the bare floor. She held onto the back of the chair, which was wicker and felt soft and damp. Her heart beat more and more slowly, her hands got colder and colder, and she could not hear whether the old women were saying anything or not. She could not see them very

clearly. How dark it was! The window shade was down, and the only door was shut. Marian looked at the ceiling. . . . It was like being caught in a robber's cave, just before one was murdered.

"Did you come to be our little girl for awhile?" the first robber asked.

Then something was snatched from Marian's hand—the little potted plant.

"Flowers!" screamed the old woman. She stood holding the pot in an undecided way. "Pretty flowers," she added.

Then the old woman in bed cleared her throat and spoke. "They are not pretty," she said, still without looking around, but very distinctly.

Marian suddenly pitched against the chair and sat down in it.

"Pretty flowers," the first old woman insisted. "Pretty—pretty. . . ."

Marian wished she had the little pot back for just a moment—she had forgotten to look at the plant herself before giving it away. What did it look like?

"Stinkweeds," said the other old woman sharply. She had a bunchy white forehead and red eyes like a sheep. Now she turned them toward Marian. The fogginess seemed to rise in her throat again, and she bleated, "Who—are—you?"

To her surprise, Marian could not remember her name. "I'm a Campfire Girl," she said finally.

"Watch out for the germs," said the old woman like a sheep, not addressing anyone.

"One came out last month to see us," said the first old woman.

A sheep or a germ? wondered Marian dreamily, holding onto the chair.

"Did not!" cried the other old woman.

"Did so! Read to us out of the Bible, and we enjoyed it!" screamed the first.

"Who enjoyed it!" said the woman in bed. Her mouth was unexpectedly small and sorrowful, like a pet's.

"We enjoyed it," insisted the other. "You enjoyed it—I enjoyed it."

"We all enjoyed it," said Marian, without realizing that she had said a word.

The first old woman had just finished putting the potted plant high, high on the top of the wardrobe, where it could hardly be seen from below. Marian wondered how she had ever succeeded in placing it there, how she could ever have reached so high.

"You mustn't pay any attention to old Addie," she now said to the little girl. "She's ailing today."

"Will you shut your mouth?" said the woman in bed. "I am not."

"You're a story."

"I can't stay but a minute—really, I can't," said Marian suddenly. She looked down at the wet floor and thought that if she were sick in here they would have to let her go.

With much to-do the first old woman sat down in a rocking chair—still another piece of furniture!—and began to rock. With the fingers of one hand she touched a very dirty cameo pin on her chest. "What do you do at school?" she asked.

"I don't know . . ." said Marian. She tried to think but she could not.

"Oh, but the flowers are beautiful," the old woman whispered. She seemed to rock faster and faster; Marian did not see how anyone could rock so fast.

"Ugly," said the woman in bed.

"If we bring flowers—" Marian began, and then fell silent. She had almost said that if Campfire Girls brought flowers to the Old Ladies' Home, the visit would count one extra point, and if they took a Bible with them on the bus and read it to the old ladies, it counted double. But the old woman had not listened, anyway; she was rocking and watching the other one, who watched back from the bed.

"Poor Addie is ailing. She has to take medicine—see?" she said, pointing a horny finger at a row of bottles on the table, and rocking so high that her black comfort shoes lifted off the floor like a little child's.

"I am no more sick than you are," said the woman in bed.

"Oh yes you are!"

"I just got more sense than you have, that's all," said the other old woman, nodding her head.

"That's only the contrary way she talks when *you all* come," said the first old lady with sudden intimacy. She stopped the rocker with a neat pat of her feet and leaned toward Marian. Her hand reached over—it felt like a petunia leaf, clinging and just a little sticky.

"Will you hush! Will you hush!" cried the other one.

Marian leaned back rigidly in her chair.

"When I was a little girl like you, I went to school and all," said the old woman in the same intimate, menacing voice. "Not here—another town. . . ."

"Hush!" said the sick woman. "You never went to school. You never came and you never went. You never were anywhere—only here. You never were born! You don't know anything. Your head is empty, your heart and hands and your old black purse are all empty, even that little old box that you brought with you you brought empty—you showed it to me. And yet you talk, talk, talk, talk, talk all the time until I think I'm losing my mind. Who are you? You're a stranger—a perfect stranger! Don't you know you're a stranger? Is it possible that they have actually done a thing like this to anyone—sent them in a stranger to talk, and rock, and tell away her whole long rigmarole? Do you seriously suppose that I'll be able to keep it up, day in, day out, night in, night out, living in the same room with a terrible old woman—forever?"

Marian saw the old woman's eyes grow bright and turn toward her. This old woman was looking at her with despair and calculation in her face. Her small lips suddenly dropped apart, and exposed a half circle of false teeth with tan gums.

"Come here, I want to tell you something," she whispered. "Come here!"

Marian was trembling, and her heart nearly stopped beating altogether for a moment.

"Now, now, Addie," said the first old woman. "That's not polite. Do you know what's really the matter with old Addie today?" She, too, looked at Marian; one of her eyelids drooped low.

"The matter?" the child repeated stupidly. "What's the matter with her?"

"Why, she's mad because today is her birthday!" said the first old woman, beginning to rock again and giving a little crow as though she had answered her own riddle.

"It is not, it is not!" screamed the old woman in bed. "It is not my birthday, no one knows when that is but myself, and will you please be quiet and say nothing more, or I'll go straight out of my mind!" She turned her eyes toward Marian again, and presently she said in the soft, foggy voice, "When the worst comes to the worst, I ring this bell, and the nurse comes." One of her hands was drawn out from under the patched counterpane—a thin little hand with enormous black freckles. With a finger which would not hold still she pointed to a little bell on the table among the bottles.

"How old are you?" Marian breathed. Now she could see the old woman in bed very closely and plainly, and very abruptly, from all sides, as in dreams. She wondered about her—she wondered for a moment as though there was nothing else in the world to wonder about. It was the first time such a thing had happened to Marian.

"I won't tell!"

The old face on the pillow, where Marian was bending over it, slowly gathered and collapsed. Soft whimpers came out of the small open mouth. It was a sheep that she sounded like—a little lamb. Marian's face drew very close, the yellow hair hung forward.

"She's crying!" She turned a bright, burning face up to the first old woman.

"That's Addie for you," the old woman said spitefully.

Marian jumped up and moved toward the door. For the second time, the claw almost touched her hair, but it was not quick enough. The little girl put her cap on.

"Well, it was a real visit," said the old woman, following Marian through the doorway and all the way out into the hall. Then from behind she suddenly clutched the child with her sharp little fingers. In an affected, high-pitched whine she cried, "Oh, little girl, have you a penny to spare for a poor old woman that's not got anything of her own? We don't have a thing in the world—not a penny for candy—not a thing! Little girl, just a nickel—a penny—"

Marian pulled violently against the old hands for a moment before she was free.

Then she ran down the hall, without looking behind her and without looking at the nurse, who was reading *Field & Stream* at her desk. The nurse, after another triple motion to consult her wrist watch, asked automatically the question put to visitors in all institutions: "Won't you stay and have dinner with *us*?"

Marian never replied. She pushed the heavy door open into the cold air and ran down the steps.

Under the prickly shrub she stooped and quickly, without being seen, retrieved a red apple she had hidden there.

Her yellow hair under the white cap, her scarlet coat, her bare knees all flashed in the sunlight as she ran to meet the big bus rocketing through the street.

"Wait for me!" she shouted. As though at an imperial command, the bus ground to a stop.

She jumped on and took a big bite out of the apple.

## YOU AND THE STORY

What do you think of the way the young girl acted in this story? Describe why she came to the home, how she felt, and what she did. Do you think you would have acted differently in her place? Was her behavior immature? Why or why not? Would there have been a more adult way for her to act? How?

## A Closer Look

(1) In much fiction, the **setting** is not just a location where the action takes place. It helps shape the way we feel—cozy or uncomfortable, crowded or alone. It's a particular place that leads us to expect certain kinds of things to happen. To what kind of place does the author take us in this story, and how does it make us feel? Look at how the author introduces us to the Old Ladies' Home in the opening paragraphs of her story. Point out several details that help us see and feel what the place is like. Describe the nurse. What picture of her does the author give us?

(2) Eudora Welty is an author with a quick eye and ear for how people act and talk with each other. Here she shows us people who experience strong feelings in a situation that might look ordinary on the surface. The following are some of the words she uses to describe the feelings and attitudes of her characters. Explain several of these. (Choose some of them to act out to show what kinds of gestures and facial expressions would go with them.)

impatient   tongue-tied   sorrowful
contrary   rigid   menacing
calculating   spiteful   affected   imperial

(3) In recent years, much has been written about what it means to be old in our society. What picture of old people does the author give us in this story? Describe the two old people. Point out striking or unusual details. How does the author expect us to feel about them? Are we supposed to dislike them? Can we feel sympathy for them? Defend your answer.

(4) What is the significance of the apple that appears at the end of the story? Does it show something about the girl—or about life in general? Did the author intend it as a **symbol** of some kind? What would it stand for—what would it symbolize?

### Your Turn

Compare the old people in this story with an old person you know or knew well. Or, compare Eudora Welty's old people with another fictitious older person you have read about or seen on the screen.

---

Language/Composition Activity A1

WRITING AND OBSERVATION

# The Unusual Touch

Eudora Welty is a writer who has a quick eye for the unusual. Look at the italicized parts of each of the following sentences. Why would each get the reader's attention? Choose three of these as model sentences. For each model, fill in a very similar sentence frame with material of your own. Use a separate sheet of paper. Aim at finished sentences of your own that also have an unusual touch.

1. *Holding a potted plant before her*, a girl of fourteen jumped off the bus in front of the Old Ladies' Home, on the outskirts of town.

SENTENCE FRAME: _____ing a _____, a _____
(stepped off a bus) (boarded a subway) (climbed out of a car) _____.

2. She proceeded slowly toward the building, which was of whitewashed brick and reflected the winter sunlight *like a block of ice*.

3. Marian, *suddenly propelled by the strong, impatient arm of the nurse*, saw next the side-face of another old woman, even older.

4. Suddenly Marian saw a hand, *quick as a bird claw*, reach up in the air and pluck the white cap off her head.

5. Stopping in her tracks, she first *extended her arm, bent her elbow, and leaned forward* from the hips—all to examine the watch strapped to her wrist.

● Some young people seem to make friends easily and naturally. They blend easily into a group; they are part of the "crowd." But for others, becoming accepted by a group is not an easy or a simple task. They may want very badly to be made welcome or be respected or be admired, but they are unsure of how they should act. They may try very hard to impress others, to attract their attention. Or they may "retreat into a shell," afraid of ridicule, afraid that others will laugh at them. John Knowles, in the following story, writes about an exclusive private school where the "competition for importance" and the whole question of "who fitted where" becomes a deadly serious matter. The outsider struggles to become part of the "in" group. He is obsessed by the fear of being left out, of being rejected by the group. In your own experience, have you encountered anything that reminds you of the struggle for acceptance and position in this story? Or does the world of this private boys' school seem like a distant planet?

## John Knowles

# A Turn With the Sun

It was dusk; the warm air of the early spring afternoon was edged with an exhilarating chill, and in the half-light the dark green turf of the playing field acquired the smooth perfection of a thick rug, spreading up to the thin woods lightly brushed with color along one sideline and down to the river, with the stolid little bridge arching over it, along the other. Across the stream more playing fields, appearing smoother still in the distance, sloped gently up to the square gray shape of the gymnasium; and behind it the towers and turrets of the boys' school were etched against the darkening blue sky.

The lacrosse game was over, and the Red team, pleased by a three-to-two victory, but only mildly pleased since it was just an intramural game, formed a loose circle and cheered for themselves and their opponents: "Reds, Reds, Reds, Reds, Rah, Rah, Rah, Blues!" A few players tarried for some extra shots at the cage, which the second-string Blue goalie made halfhearted attempts to defend; but most of them straggled off toward the bridge, swinging their lacrosse sticks carelessly along beside them. Three boys played catch as they went; one of them missed a pass near the bridge and the ball plopped into the stream.

"Nuts!" he said. "I'm not going in after it."

"No, too cold," the others agreed.

As Lawrence stepped onto the gravel road which led over the bridge he experienced that thrill of feeling himself strong and athletic which the sound of his cleats on a hard surface always excited. His stride became more free swinging, more authoritative.

"I scored," he said simply. "D'you see that, Bead? I scored my first goal."

"Yeah." Bead's scratchy voice had an overtone of cordiality. "Good going, boy. The winning point too."

They crunched along in silence up to the bridge, and then Lawrence was emboldened to issue an invitation. "You going to the flick tonight? I mean I guess it's Shelley Winters or someone. . . ."

Bead balanced his companion's possible new status for an indecisive instant and then elected to hedge. "Yeah, well I'll see you after dinner in the Butt Room for a smoke. I'm prob'ly going. Bruce," he added with careful casualness, "said something about it."

Bruce! Lawrence sensed once again that he was helplessly sliding back, into the foggy social bottomland where unacceptable first-year boys dwell. He had risen out of it just now: the goal he had scored, the sweaty ease of his body, the grump-grump of his shoes on the gravel had suggested something better. But here was Bead, like himself only seven months at the school, and yet going to the movies with Bruce. Lawrence marveled at the speed with which Bead was settling into the school, and he marveled again at his own failure, after seven months, to win a single close friend.

Not that Lawrence Stuart was a pariah; the hockey captain had never invaded his room, as he had Fruitcake Putsby's next door, and festooned his clothes through the hall; he had never found a mixture of sour cream and cereal in his bed at night; no one had ever poured ink into the tub while he was bathing. The victims of such violations were genuine outcasts. But the very fact of their persecutions had, Lawrence reflected, some kind of negative value. They were at least notable in their way. "There goes Fruitcake Putsby!" someone would shout, "Hi ya, Fruitie." They had a status all their own; and a few of them, by senior year, could succeed by some miraculous alchemy in becoming accepted and even respected by the whole school.

Lawrence Stuart was neither grotesque enough nor courageous enough for that. He merely inhabited the nether world of the unregarded, where no one bothered him or bothered about him. He had entered in fourth form year, when the class was already clearly stratified, knowing only one person in the school; he came from a small Virginia town which no one had ever heard of, his clothes were wrong, his vocabulary was wrong, and when he talked at all it was about the wrong things.

He had been assigned to an out-of-the-way house (instead of to one of the exuberant dormitories) with six other nebulous flotsam, and there on the edge of the school he had been waiting all year for something to happen to him, living alone in a little room tucked up under the eaves.

His failure to strike out in some, in any, direction puzzled him in October, when he had been at Devon six weeks, angered him in December, made him contemptuous in February, and on this burgeoning April day when everything else around him stirred with life, took on the coloration of tragedy.

He crossed over the bridge with Bead, and his heart stopped for an instant as it always did on this bridge; in his imagination he again stood on the railing, with his image white and mysterious in the green-black water twenty-five feet below, and he leaped out and over, as he had done last September on his fourth day there, somersaulting twice while most of the school looked on in admiration at the new boy, and knifed cleanly into the icy water.

Last September, his fourth day at school. He hadn't been thinking of anything in particular there on the bridge; everyone was diving from it so he did too. When he plunged from the railing he had been just another of the unknown new boys, but when he broke the surface of the water in that remarkable dive, one that he

had never attempted before and was never to repeat, he became for his schoolmates a boy to be considered. That is why Ging Powers, a senior from his own town who had seemed these first days to be decisively avoiding him, came over in the shower room afterward and dropped an invitation to dinner like a negligible piece of soap. "Come over to the Inn for dinner tonight. Got a couple of friends I want you to meet."

There is a trophy room in the Devon School gymnasium much visited by returning alumni; during June reunions they wander whispering past its softly lighted cases, in which gleam the cups and medals of athletic greatness. Proud banners hang from its paneled walls, inscribed with the records of triumphant, forgotten afternoons. The room is like a small, peculiarly sacred chapel in a great cathedral.

At the far end, standing long and bright in the focal niche, the alumni would admire the James Harvey Fullerton Cup, Awarded Each Year to That Member of the Sixth Form Who, in the Opinion of His Fellows and Masters, Most Closely Exemplifies the Highest Traditions of Devon. There is no mention of athletics on the inscription, but it has come to rest in the gymnasium, in the place of honor, because the highest tradition of Devon is the thinking athlete. Thirty-four names have been engraved on its burnished surface since Mr. Fullerton, feeling disturbed by the activities of German submarines,* decided to confirm the reality of his untroubled childhood by donating it, with a small endowment, to his old school, like some symbol of royalty.

Lawrence had approached it that afternoon, his fourth day at the school, and

*activities of German submarines: a reference to World War I.

was struck by the beauty and sacredness of the place. This surely was the heart of Devon: the chapel was like an assembly hall, the library was a clearing house, the houses were dormitories, the classrooms, classrooms; only here did he sense that behind the visible were deeper meanings, that these trophies and banners were clues to the hidden core of the school. He left the gymnasium lost in thought.

He had felt he was still in the air as he walked from the gym back to his room that afternoon, still spinning down upon his own bright image in the murky water. He dressed hurriedly for the dinner at the Inn, for this was surely the beginning of his career at Devon. He explained how wonderfully everything was going in an ardent letter to Janine, and then walked, holding himself back from running by an intoxicating exercise of will power, and arrived at last at the Inn. Everything within him was released; it was as though his dive into the river had washed away his boyhood, and he stood clean and happy, wondering dreamily what he would be like now.

The hushed dining room was pervaded by the atmosphere of middle-aged gentility characteristic of Inns at boys' schools: the dull walnut woodwork, the pink and green wallpaper depicting Colonial scenes, the virginal fireplace. At the far end of the room Lawrence saw his dinner partners huddled conspiratorily at a corner table. He wheeled past other, empty tables, bright with white cloths and silver, realized dimly that there were murmuring groups dining here and there in the room; and then Ging, his thin frame unfolding from a chair, was muttering introductions. "This is Vinnie Ump," he seemed to say, and Lawrence recognized Vinnie James, vice-chairman of the senior council, a calm, blond Bostonian who was allowed to be as articulate as he chose because he was so unassertively sure of himself. "And this," said Ging, in a somewhat more stately cadence, "is Charles Morrell." Lawrence recognized him too, of course; this was Morrell, the fabled "Captain Marvel" of the football field, the baseball field, and the hockey rink. Lawrence had never seen him at close quarters before; he seemed more formidable than ever.

Vinnie James was talking, and after pausing for a neutral, birdlike nod to Lawrence, he continued. "So if you want to put up with being patronized by a lot of crashing bores, then you can go to Harvard, and be Punched all sophomore year."

Captain Marvel leaned his heavily handsome face out over the table, "I don't get you, Vinnie, what's this Punching?"

"That's how you get into the clubs at Harvard, Dim One," Vinnie's eyes flickered humorously at him for an instant. "They invite you to Punch parties all sophomore year, and when they stop inviting you then you know you're not going to be asked to join the club."

"Well," Ging looked with masked apprehension from one to the other, "they've got to take *some* guys, don't they? And Devon isn't such a terrible background."

"It's not Groton," said Vinnie mercilessly, "of course."

"Groton!" Ging clutched his tastefully striped tie savagely. "I wouldn't be caught dead at that snobatorium. I could 'ev', if I'd wanted to I could 'ev' gone to Groton. But mother said wild horses couldn't drag a son of hers to that snobatorium."

Lawrence felt dizzy at the barefacedness of this lie. He knew that Mrs. Powers would cheerfully have violated most of the customs of civilization to get a son of hers into Groton. Devon had been a hasty compromise after Groton had proved out of the question.

"In any case," Vinnie remarked drily,

"Marvel here won't have any trouble. Personable athletes are kidnaped by the most desirable clubs the moment they appear." Vinnie made no comment on Ging's chances.

Lawrence disliked and felt superior to Ging at once. The climber! He had never realized before what a fool Ging was, it made him feel older to realize it now. It was so clear when you could see him beside Captain Marvel, cool, unconcerned Marvel, who would easily rise to the top of every group he entered, leaving Ging clawing and snarling below.

Lawrence looked away irritably, regretting that it was Ging who had introduced him to the others. At the same time he felt himself more thoroughly aware than he had ever been of how the world went, of who fitted where, of what was grand and genuine and what was shoddy and fake. Devon had posed a question to him and demanded that he do something. This afternoon he had done a single, beautiful dive, it was just right and he knew it the moment he hit the water. And now he had come to understand Captain Marvel. The answer was athletics; not just winning a major D, but the personality of the athlete itself, the unconscious authority which his strength, his skill, his acclaim gave him. Lawrence stirred his tomato soup reflectively, and felt his diffuse ambitions coming into focus, experienced a vision of himself as the Majestic Athlete; he decided instinctively and immediately to accept it, there at dinner among the walnut and silver and the polite murmurings of the other diners. He gathered about himself the mantle of the Olympiad, and lost in its folds, he burst into speech.

"I have some cousins, two cousins, you know, Ging—George and Carter—they're in clubs at Harvard, I mean a club at Harvard, one club, both of 'em are in the same club. It's the . . . the . . ." Lawrence was suddenly stricken with the thought that George and Carter might very easily not be in the best Harvard club, or even the second best; but everyone, even Marvel, was listening with interest, "It's called," he felt his color rising at the inelegance of the name, "The Gas—or something."

"Oh yes," said Vinnie crisply, "that's a very good club, for New Yorkers mostly, they have some very good men."

"Oh," Lawrence breathed with fake innocence and real relief. This success swept him spinning on. "George and Carter, they go there for dinners, but they always have lunch in the—is it the Houses?" his wide, brightened blue eyes searched his listeners' faces avidly; Vinnie nodded a brief assent. "They said those clubs make you so ingrown, you just know all these fancy socialites and everything they wanted to know, you know, everybody, they didn't want to be exclusive or anything like that. It isn't like up here, I mean there isn't, aren't all these clubs and things. They said that I'd get raided but nothing like that seems to happen up here; but they *did* say that when I went on to Harvard, if I do go there, that after being here it'll be easier and I'll know people and not have to study, but I don't really study so hard here, 'course it's only been four days, but after what everybody said about prep school I thought I'd be studying all the time, but, well, take this afternoon"— that was good, *take this afternoon* smacked of maturity; he paused an instant for the two important seniors (Ging was a bystander now) to catch the overtone of authority in it—"we went swimming off the bridge, and that flip, I thought a two-and-a-half flip might be tough, but . . ." he paused again, hoping Ging might make himself useful as a witness to this feat; nothing happened so he finished a little out of breath, "it wasn't."

"Yeah," Captain Marvel said, "I saw you do it."

This swept down Lawrence's last controls. His best moment had been seen, and doubtless admired, by the most important athlete in school. He rushed ahead now, eager to impress him even more; no, by golly, he was through impressing people. Now he was ready to leap, in one magnificent bound, to the very peak of his ambitions, to become Captain Marvel's protégé, to learn what it meant to be unconcerned, powerful, and a man. So he stuttered gaily on, snatching at everything inside him that seemed presentable— home, his family, Janine, the play he had seen in New York; he assumed every grown-up attitude he could find. All of it he brought forth, as an offering of fealty.

The seniors followed this unwinding of a new boy carefully, looked where he pointed, gauging all his information and attitudes according to their own more precisely graded yardsticks, and took his measure.

"Devon is like some kind of country-club penitentiary, where the inmates don't take walks around the courtyard, they go to the private penitentiary golf course for eighteen holes. And the dean, is that who he is? that queer, stuttery old bird, you know, the one in chapel the first day, the one who looks like Hoover with an Oxford accent. . . ."

"Yes, that's the dean," said Vinnie, fingering his water glass, "Dean Eleazer Markham Bings-Smith."

"No!" exploded Lawrence, "is that his name! His honest name?" He regretted the *honest*, it should have been *actual*.

"Why does he talk that way, and *look* that way! Like my beagle, that's the way he looks, like the beagle I've got at home, my beagle looks just like that right after he's had a bath."

There was something like consternation passing around the table. Lawrence felt it and looked wonderingly from one to the other. Ging was watching an elderly couple making their way toward the door. The others examined their desserts.

"Was that the dean?" Lawrence asked in a shocked whisper. "Did he hear me?"

No one really answered, but Lawrence, alive in every nerve now, responded symbolically. He slipped like a boneless organism from his chair and sank beneath the table; there he performed the appropriate expiation; he banged his head, not too hard, against the table's underside.

There was a scraping of chairs, Lawrence saw napkins flutter onto the seats, and suddenly he realized the impossibility of his position: under a table in the Anthony Wayne Dining Room of the Devon Inn, making a fool of himself.

He could not recall afterward how he got to his feet, but he remembered very clearly what was said.

"I have an appointment," Vinnie was informing Ging, and then to Lawrence: "That was not the dean, that was Dr. Farnham, the registrar. I doubt whether he heard you. And if he did, I doubt whether he knows or cares *who* you are."

"Are you British?" demanded Captain Marvel with heavy distaste. "Is that why you talk so queer?"

Lawrence felt the exuberance within him turn over, leaving a sob pressing against his chest. He could not speak and would not cry, but drew a deep, shuddering breath.

Marvel and Vinnie strode out through the door, Ging followed, and Lawrence roamed out a few paces behind, out into the damp September night, down the deserted street to the quadrangle, where the dormitory lights streamed hospitably from cozy windows. Ging said "G'night" there as though he were saying "pass" during a dull bridge game, and Lawrence was left to wander down the lane to the cluttered old house, to the little room stuck up under the eaves where he lived.

In the next weeks, after the first storms had subsided, Lawrence tried again and again to analyze his failure. Whom had he offended, how, why? Why was everything he had ever wanted sparkling like a trophy in his hands one minute, and smashed to bits at his feet the next?

Defeat seemed to follow upon defeat after that. Having missed the peak of his ambition, he assumed that lesser heights could be attained automatically; he felt like a veteran of violent foreign wars whose scars entitled him to homage and precedence. Instead he was battered on every occasion: one day he offered to move into the empty half of a double room down the hall and the boy living there had simply ignored him, had pretended not to hear. Then he turned wildly delinquent; he threw his small steamer trunk, filled with shoes and books, down the long flight of stairs under which the housemaster lived. It slammed against Mr. Kuzak's door at the bottom, and the resultant methodical investigation and punishment made him briefly notable to his housemates, until they concluded that he was strange.

This was the final, the unbearable affront; they thought him strange, undisciplined, an inferior boy given to pettish tantrums. He would show them. If there was one thing he was sure he possessed, it was a capacity for self-discipline. If there was one thing he would not be, it was a clown, a butt. He knew there was a certain dignity in his bearing, even though it shaded into pomposity, and he would not violate that, he would not become a Fruitcake Putsby, even if people would like him better that way.

He decided, in the season when the last leaves were drifting down from the trees bordering the playing fields, and the sunlight cut obliquely across the town, that there remained this one quality on which he could rely: his capacity for self-discipline. He would turn his back upon the school, he would no longer be embroiled in Devon's cheap competition for importance. He would be intelligent; yes, he told himself, he would be *exceedingly* intelligent; and by God, if he only could, he would be the greatest athlete ever to electrify a crowd on the playing fields of Devon. The greatest, and the most inaccessible.

The earth was turning wintery; the season of Steam Heat arrived. It filled every inhabited room in the school, the steam hissed and clanged with power, and could not be shut off. Slowly the heat drained the spirit from them, dried their healthy faces, seared the freshest skin. The usual number of colds appeared, the usual amount of force faded from lectures and application from homework, the usual apathy slipped into the school through the radiators. Winter was here.

Lawrence moved from one steaming box to another, crossing the sharp, drily cold outdoors in between, and felt his own inner strength grow as it waned in those about him. He had learned to study very systematically, and as his responses in class were apt and laconic, several of his teachers became noticeably interested in winning his good opinion; would make remarks about Kafka or Turgenev* and then glance at him. He would smile knowingly back, and resolve to find out who these people might be.

His free time he spent watching athletes, religiously following the major sports, football games and football drill, enjoying every moment except when

*Kafka or Turgenev: great European writers of the twentieth and nineteenth centuries respectively.

Captain Marvel made a really brilliant play, which made him feel uneasy and guilty. He watched soccer and track and tennis and squash, and as winter sports replaced them, he watched basketball, wrestling, hockey, and even fencing.

In the fall he had played a little intramural football at which he was generally inept and abstracted, but once in a while he would startle everyone, including himself, with a brilliantly skillful play. But there was too much freedom on a football field, too much room to maneuver, too many possibilities; so in the winter he turned to swimming, in which the lanes were rigidly predetermined, and he had only to swim up and down, up and down. Into this he poured all the intensity he possessed, and as a result made the junior varsity squad. He was uniformly cooperative with his teammates, and the coach thought him a promising boy.

His housemates now felt disposed to revise their opinion of him; yes, Stuart was strange, but if he was going to turn out to be not only bright but also something of an athlete, they thought they had better accept him.

The proctor and the others made a few fumbling, gruff overtures. Lawrence sensed this at once and became more thoroughly disturbed than at any time since the dinner at the inn. He loathed them all, of course, and he felt cheated; now that his defenses were invulnerable they were calling off the assault, inviting him to talk terms, asking for a conference out in the open. The cold wind tore around the angles of the old house, and Lawrence camped in his steamy room, speaking politely to those who came to his door, doing his homework, and feeling confusedly vindicated. He had proved the strongest of all, for what was strength if not the capacity for self-denial? He had divorced himself from them so successfully that now he didn't care; *they* cared, so it seemed, now; they were seeking his friendship, therefore they were weak. Strength, Lawrence was sure, was the capacity for self-denial; life was conquered by the strong-willed, success was demonstrated by austerity; it was the bleak who would inherit the earth. Yes, that was right and he would not allow them to change the rules now that he had won; he decided to continue his triumphant game, even though he was playing it alone.

Only in his anger did he draw close to them; one dismal afternoon in February Billy Baldwin, the boy down the hall who had refused to room with him in September, came to his door:

"Hi, Varsity." This was the nickname Lawrence had been given by the other boys, who understood him better than he thought. "You going to Bermuda for spring vacation?" Since he was excluded from the gay round of parties which the boys from Boston and New York described as typical of their holidays, Lawrence had intimated that he was going to Bermuda with his family. This afternoon he was too depressed to lie.

"No," he parroted, "I'm not going to Bermuda for spring vacation."

Billy was a little put off, but continued with determined good humor. "Well then how about coming down, I mean if you aren't going home. . . ." Billy had no champagne vacation in the offing either, but he had grown up a little during the winter and forgiven his parents for making their home in Bridgeport, Connecticut. He had also changed his mind about Lawrence, whom he now thought pleasantly temperamental and handsome. "Why don't you, if you want, you could always. . . ."

"What?" interrupted Lawrence irritably. "Why don't I what?"

"All I was going to say," Billy continued on a stronger note, "what I was going to say if you didn't interrupt all the time. . . ." but then he couldn't say it.

"You were going to say nothing," Lawrence said disgustedly, turning back to his book, "as usual."

"Just one thing," Billy exclaimed sharply. "All I was going to say was why *don't* you go to Bermuda? If you're so rich."

"Rich enough," Lawrence's voice thickening with controlled anger, "richer than some people who live in little dump towns on the New Haven Railroad."

"Yeah!" Billy shouted. "Yeah, so rich your pop couldn't pay the last bursar's bill on time!"

"What!" screamed Lawrence, tearing the book from his lap and jumping up, "what'd you say?" His blood was pounding because it wasn't the truth, but it was close to it. He was standing now in the middle of his little garret, his shoulders slightly forward. His voice turned coarse, "Get out." Neither of them knew his voice had a savage depth like that. "Just get out of my room." Then in a single motion, he snatched the book from the floor and hurled it at Billy's head. Billy sprang back from the doorway, deeply frightened, not so much *of* him as *with* him. Both of them stood panting on either side of the doorway, and then Billy went back to his own room.

Lawrence pretended to be totally unconcerned about such flare-ups, which occurred several times in the late winter. He eventually allowed Billy to reestablish a civil relationship with him; *After all,* Lawrence reasoned, *he should be the one to make up, after the way he insulted me right in my own room. I never did like him,* he reflected with strengthening satisfaction, *no I never did.* Billy didn't matter to him; in September when he was so alone, Billy could have helped. But now; what good was Billy? He was no athlete, no star, he did not possess that unconcerned majesty, he was a person of no importance. And Billy, who was just finding out about kindness, looked regretfully elsewhere for friends.

Except for these explosions, Lawrence maintained his admirable outer imperviousness throughout the winter. He spent spring vacation in Virginia with his family. It was an uneventful two weeks except for a bitter little fight with Janine. "You're changed and I hate you," she cried at the end of it, and then indignantly, "who do you think you are, anyhow? I hate you!"

He returned in the middle of April to find Devon transformed. He had forgotten that the bleak lanes and roads were beautiful when the earth turned once again toward the sun. Tiny leaves of callow green sprouted from the gray branches of the skeletal trees, and the living scents of the earth hung in the air. Windows which had been stuck closed with winter were opened to allow the promising air to circulate; the steamy dryness of his little room drifted away; when he opened the single window and the door, a tantalizing breeze whipped across his papers and notebooks, fluttered the college pennants on his wall, and danced on to the other rooms where his housemates stirred restlessly.

Then, unexpectedly, he began to slip in his studies. For two successive French classes he appeared unprepared, and when called on to discuss the lesson, he fumbled. The others snickered behind their notebooks. But the boy sitting next to him, with whom he had had a relationship consisting only of "Excuse me," and "Hard assignment, wasn't it?", nudged him in the ribs as they were going out after the second class and exclaimed robustly, "Boy, did *you* stink today!" Lawrence was about to coin some cutting rejoinder when the boy grinned broadly. "You were really lousy," he added, as he punched him again. Lawrence tried and failed to keep from grinning back, and then muttered that Well, after all, it was spring wasn't it.

That afternoon he went as usual to watch the varsity lacrosse team practice. His own intramural team was having a game that day and could have used even his unsteady stick, but he had wrangled a medical excuse. Varsity lacrosse was almost as meaningful for him as varsity baseball, and he didn't have to watch Captain Marvel there. So he sat alone on the empty bleachers and followed the practice shots intently, watching the careless skill of the players, marveling at the grand unawareness with which they played. *This is the best part of the day*, he thought, *this is wonderful*. He pondered the assumptions on which these athletes operated, that they would not miss the ball, that if they did they would catch it next time, that their teammates accepted them regardless, that there was a basic peace among them taken for granted. Lawrence could take nothing for granted; *yes, this is the best part of the day*, he told himself, and as he watched the skillful, confident boys warming to the game he saw only himself, he watched the others but he was seeing himself, doing all the skillful, impossible things. He looked very pleased, *This is the best*, he thought, and despair flamed up in him.

He decided not to stay for the whole practice, and wandering back to the gym he met his own team coming out; Hey, Lawrence, get dressed, There's a game, Lawrence, C'mon, Stuart, Whathaheckeryadoin? The one thing he had wanted to avoid that day was his own team. Lately he always seemed to be stumbling into the very situations he wanted fervently to avoid.

"Yeah," he called lamely to them, "but I got a . . ." *medical excuse*? An Olympian unable to take the field because he had

sniffles? It wouldn't do. "Yeah, okay, I was just . . . the varsity . . . I thought maybe if I watched them . . ." Shouting out complicated explanations was impossible. "You know," he yelled even though they were moving away, not listening, "I thought I might learn something."

"Forget the varsity, Varsity," someone called over his shoulder. "The second-string Red midfield wants you."

. . . This then was the afternoon when Lawrence scored his first goal. He felt an odd looseness playing that day, the hot rays of the sun seemed to draw the rigidity out of his body, leaving his muscles and sinews free to function as they would. Something about the way he held his stick was different, he found himself in

the right place at the right time; his team-mates sensed the change and passed the ball to him, and in the last minutes of the game he made a fast instinctive turn around a burly Blue defenseman and scored the winning goal with a quick, sure shot.

It was a minor triumph which calmed his spirit for approximately seven minutes, until the invitation to the movies was issued and turned aside, until he crossed over the little arching bridge, observed the water where his heroic reflection had shone, and stepped onto the turf on the other side, the varsity field. By the time they reached the gym it was Lawrence the unrecognized Olympian all over again, Lawrence the unknown and unloved.

After his shower he dressed and went, as he so often did, into the trophy room for a pacifying moment of dreaming. He knew the inscription and most of the names on the Fullerton Cup by heart, and in the space below 1951—Robert Graves Hartshorne, he would visualize 1952—Charles Taylor Morrell, for unquestionably the cup would be Marvel's this year. And the list should go on and on, with one celebrated name after another (even perhaps 1954—Lawrence Bates Stuart); but here reality always intervened. The fact, the shocking fact was that the front plate of the cup was almost filled, after Marvel's name had been inscribed the list would reach the little silver relief statues around the base—the old-fashioned football player looking slim and inadequate, the pompous baseball player with his squarely planted little cap, and for the others—there would be no more room. Nor was there any space to start a second list, since all the remaining circumference of the cup was devoted to an etched allegorical representation of the flame of knowledge passing from hand to hand through the ages, until it found its way into a device at the top, a coat-of-arms of birds and Latin and moons which was the seal of Devon.

Always a little amazed at this finiteness of the cup, Lawrence backed thoughtfully away from it. Wasn't this the core of everything, didn't it sum up, absorb, glorify everything at Devon? And still, the cup would be full this year. One of these days it would be moved to a case along the walls with the other old trophies which had once reigned in the niche, it would be honorably, obscurely retired. In his imagination the heroic list stretched back over cup after cup, into the past, and forward, upon cups not yet conceived, into the future. It was odd, he thought, all these great names fading into the past, getting less important every year, until finally they must just go out, like the last burned-out ember in a fire. It was sad of course, but well, there was something almost *monotonous* about it.

Lawrence squirmed. He had never thought about time's passage before. It made him feel better to realize it now, to understand that the circle of the years changed things; it wasn't all up to him personally.

Puzzled, he gazed around this chilly and damp chamber which had seemed so cool and serene in February, untouched by the bone-chilling winds outside or the rasping steam in the other rooms of the school.

But now it was April, and Lawrence felt and saw April everywhere. This room isn't a chapel at all, he thought with a passing wave of indignation, it's a crypt.

Then, right there in the trophy room, he yawned, comfortably. And stretching his legs, to get a feeling of cramp out of them, he strode contentedly toward the door, through which the sunlight poured, and as he stepped into it he felt its warmth on his shoulders. It was going to be a good summer.

He never knew that he was right in this, because Lawrence drowned that night, by the purest accident, in the river which winds between the playing fields. Bead and Bruce tried to save him; the water was very cold and black and the night moonless. They eventually found him, doubled over among some rushes. He had not cried out when the cramp convulsed him, so they did not know where to begin searching and after they found him, it was a hard, clumsy job getting him to shore. They tried artificial respiration at first, and then becoming very frightened, started for help. But then Bruce thought again and came back to try to revive him while Bead ran to the gym, completely disrupting the movie in his frantic search for a master.

There was a conference two days later,

attended by the headmaster, the dean, Mr. Kuzak from Lawrence's house, Bruce, and Bead. The boys explained that it had been just a little dark; students always swam in the river in the spring, and although they usually waited until it was warmer, they had decided in the Butt Room Saturday night to have the first swim of the season while the rest of the school was at the movie. Bruce and Bead had planned it alone, but Lawrence had been there, very enthusiastic to go to the movie. Then when he heard they were going swimming, that had become the one thing he wanted to do.

"You know, sir," Bruce explained earnestly, "he was a good swimmer, and he wanted to go so much."

"Yeah," Bead confirmed this eagerly, "we didn't ask him to go, did we, Bruce?"

"No, he just asked if he could and we said yes."

Bead set his face maturely, "He wasn't a very good friend of ours, but he just wanted to go. So we said okay, but it wasn't like we planned it together. I didn't know him very well, did you, Bruce?"

Mr. Kuzak studied the backs of his hands, and the headmaster asked, "Who were his close friends?"

"I don't know," Bead answered.

"The fellows in his house, I guess," said Bruce. Everyone looked at Mr. Kuzak, who thought of several perfunctory ways of confirming this, but knowing it was not true, he was unable to say anything. It is easy to write, "Lawrence Stuart is beginning to find himself" on a report to the dean, when Stuart was alive and could be heard trudging up the stairs every day; undoubtedly he *would* have found himself. But now the boy was dead, Mr. Kuzak had seen his body, had telephoned his parents; he said nothing.

Irritated, the headmaster leaned out of his thronelike chair. "He *had* close

friends?" he persisted.

Still Mr. Kuzak could not speak.

"Well," the dean broke the uneasy silence, his kind, mournful eyes studying the two boys, "Well how did he, was he—" his fingers searched the lines in his forehead, "he enjoyed it, did he?" The dean's face reddened, he indulged in his chronic cough for several seconds. "He seemed lively? I mean did he act . . . happy, before, before this cramp seized him?"

"Oh sure!" Bead exclaimed. "Yes, yes he did," Bruce said at the same time.

"When we first got there," Bruce continued, "he got up on the bridge. Bead and I just slipped into the water from the bank, it was awfully cold."

"I never was in such cold water," Bead agreed.

"But Stuart got up on the bridge and stood there a minute."

"Then he dove," said Bead.

"Dived," someone corrected him abstractly.

"It was a real dive," Bruce added thoughtfully. "He did a beautiful dive."

It had been like the free curve of powerful wings. Lawrence had cut the water almost soundlessly, and then burst up again a moment later, breaking a foaming silver circle on the black surface. Then he twisted over on his back and sank out of sight.

"I believe he enjoyed the water," said Mr. Kuzak quietly.

"Yeah," Bead agreed, "he liked it a lot, I think. That was the one thing he did like. He was good in the water."

"I don't think he cared," Bruce remarked suddenly.

The headmaster straightened sharply. "What do you mean?" Bruce's thoughts doubled over this instinctive statement to censor it or deny it, but then because this was death and the first he had ever really encountered, he persisted. "I mean in the dive, he just seemed to trust everything, all of a sudden. He looked different, standing up there on the bridge."

"Happy?" asked the dean in a very low voice.

"Something like that. He wasn't scared, I know that."

The conference ended afterward, with everyone agreed that it had been a wholly accidental death. A photograph of Lawrence in his swimming suit, taken when he made the junior varsity team, was enlarged, framed, and hung on the wall of the gym among pictures of athletic teams. He stood very straight in the picture and his young eyes looked directly at the camera.

But the season moved on; that summer was the most beautiful and fruitful anyone could remember at Devon. Blossoms scented the air and hung over the river winding through the playing fields. And the earth, turned full toward the sun, brought forth its annual harvest.

## YOU AND THE STORY

What is a "snob"? (What does the boy in the story mean when he calls another school a "snobatorium"?) Are the people in this story all snobs? Or is the struggle for status and acceptance a natural part of everybody's life? Do you think Lawrence was too sensitive, too "touchy," about what happened to him at school?

## A Closer Look

Some authors create one-dimensional, **flat characters** that are easy to recognize and to understand. Such characters may have one powerful motive, like greed; they may have one dominant trait, like anger. Every time we see the character act greedy, or angry, we can say: "There he (or she) goes again!" John Knowles in this story gives us a more **rounded character**— more complicated, like real people. When we watch Lawrence, we know there are confused thoughts and contradictory feelings going through his mind. We see him do strange things on the spur of the moment, and we suspect that he will regret them later. Do you always understand what he is thinking, and why he acts the way he does? Discuss the following questions with your classmates to see how well you can come to understand the central character.

(1) Often the physical appearance of a school tells us much about how it feels to be there. How do you picture the grounds, the buildings? What kind of colors and textures do you expect to see? How would they make you feel?

(2) What kind of "school spirit" is strong at this school? By visiting places like the trophy room, what would a visitor learn about the traditions of the school? What does it take to impress or please teachers at this school? In short, what kind of a school is it?

(3) Look at the "high points" in Lawrence's experience at the school. What were the things that helped him impress the others, that helped him in his struggle to become accepted? (What advice could you give to someone trying to "do things right" in this setting?)

(4) Look at the "low points" in Lawrence's experience. We are told "he tried again and again to analyze his failure." What exactly did he do wrong? How did he "offend"? What did he do that alienated everyone further after the first "looking over"? Why?

(5) People in Lawrence's situation often try to "get back" at the others. What was his strategy for "showing them"? When they

were ready to make friendly overtures, what was his reaction? Can you understand what went on in his mind?

(6) Were you surprised at the way the quarrel with Billy came about? What had been Billy's intention in coming to Lawrence's room? Can you retrace how " one thing led to another"? Does this quarrel seem "true to life" to you? Why or why not?

(7) Look at the passage where Lawrence watches the spring practice of the varsity lacrosse team. He says admiringly again and again, "This is the best." What did these boys have that he did not have?

(8) At the end, the dean is trying to find out what really happened. How do *you* explain the accident at the end of the story?

---

### Your Turn

---

What opportunities have you had to observe people seeking status or maneuvering for prestige? Do a study of the role of status in your own school. Is there any kind of "pecking order"? Are there any groups that enjoy special status or prestige? Can you set up three of four major *categories* or *ranks* of people that would help guide the newcomer?

---

Language/Composition Activity A2

RELATED TERMS

# The Vocabulary of Status

Lawrence Stuart lives in a world where everything has its place. He and the other boys are very status-conscious; they worry about their standing in the school and in the larger world. Many of the terms used in the story have something to do with how we judge and rank other people. Look at the related terms in each of the following sets. What does each word mean? Where or in what connection would you expect to find the word? What ideas or associations does it bring to mind?

1. Here are some of the basic words connected with the idea of status. How are they related? *stratified exclusive precedence*

2. Here are some words that apply to things or people associated with the "in" group. What do they mean? *gentility socialites protégé*

3. Here are some words that apply to people who are left out. What ideas or associations does each word bring to mind? *unacceptable pariah outcast grotesque undesirable*

4. Here are some labels for the personal manner someone might adopt to impress or please other people. Do you know all of the words? *authoritative articulate unassertive inaccessible laconic impervious cooperative civil avid*

5. Here are some words for attitudes or reactions that people in the story show toward one another. Which words are favorable or positive? Which words are unfavorable or negative? *cordiality consternation distaste homage fealty*

6. All of the following words are used in the story to express a favorable judgment or admiration. How would you rank these words in order from "just barely favorable" to "most favorable of all"? *formidable notable personable grand presentable promising*

● Much has been written about what it means to grow up. But most people agree that to grow up means in some way or other declaring our independence. Childhood is often in many ways sheltered and protected. We are mothered or fussed over or led by the hand. To become grown up, we finally have to venture forth on our own. We have to discover the world outside and try to make our own kind of sense of the way it operates. In the autobiographical account that follows, a high school boy ventures forth from his own neighborhood to discover the world outside. He reports in faithful detail his contradictory feelings, his mixed emotions: shyness and ambition, surprise and recognition, hope and disappointment. Would you have experienced similar feelings if you had been in his place?

## M. Carl Holman

# The Afternoon of a Young Poet

In the late winter of my senior year in high school I entered a poem in an annual literary competition sponsored by the Arts Club of St. Louis. Because I was almost pathologically shy, and because I was not sure I actually intended to go through with it until I was picking my way back up the icy street from the corner mailbox, I told no one what I had done. Until that night I had submitted poems to Negro newspapers and magazines and had won one or two small prizes, but I had never before ventured to enter a "white" contest.

I had found the announcement of the Arts Club competition in the section of one of the white dailies where I read avidly about plays, concerts, and ballets which might just as well have been taking place on the moon. During that period of my life I was strongly influenced by three or four university-trained teachers on our

high school faculty who were still caught up in the afterglow of the Negro Renaissance.[1] Mr. Watts, Miss Armstrong, Mr. Blanton, and Miss Lewis taught us from the "lily-white" textbooks prescribed by the St. Louis school system, but they also mounted on their bulletin boards the works and pictures of Langston Hughes, James Weldon Johnson, Claude McKay, Sterling Brown, Countee Cullen, and Jean Toomer.[2]

Entering the contest, however secretly, represented unusual daring for me, though it would have been as easy as breathing for Miss Armstrong, a vibrant

[1]**Negro Renaissance:** also known as the "Harlem Renaissance," the term refers to the great outburst of literary accomplishment by blacks in the 1920's.

[2]**Langston Hughes . . . Jean Toomer:** writers who were part of the Negro Renaissance.

and energetic mahogany-skinned woman whose voice flayed our budding manhood with comtempt when she read McKay's poem "If We Must Die." (Her voice accused and disturbed me, conjuring up two confusing memories from my childhood downtown on Carroll Street—the first, that day in the depths of the Depression when half the fathers on the block straggled back from their protest march on City Hall, their heads broken and bleeding. Some of them weeping, but only one of them laughing. The potbellied little man next door who came stumbling up the alley apart from the others, tittering like a drunken woman, one eye puffed shut, his bloody rag of a shirt dragging in the dust. Giggling and whispering. *"Don't hit me no mo, Cap'n. You the boss. You sho is the boss. . . ."* And less than five years later, Big Crew, standing in the middle of the yard, his lips drawn back from his blue gums in a wolfish grin, smashing his black fist like a hammer into the rent man's face, picking the man up like a sack of flour and knocking him down again. All the time talking to him as quietly as one friend to another: *"Git up and fight, you peckerwood. Git up and fight for you country."*)

I yearned during those high school years to write something as defiantly bitter as McKay's "If We Must Die" or Sterling Brown's "Strong Men." My temper was capable of flaring up and consuming me so utterly that during a period of a few months I found myself in wildly hopeless fights with the older boys. Deep in hostile north St. Louis I had placed my life and those of two boys with me in jeopardy when, without thinking, I spat in the face of a young white boy seated on the stoop surrounded by at least seven members of his beefy family, because he called me a "skinny black nigger" as my friends and I were passing. My mother's long campaign to curb my temper had only taught me at last to swallow my feelings, hiding them so deep that I could not have dredged up my rages and despairs and found words for them even if I had wanted to. The long poem I finally mailed to the Arts Club was called "Nocturne on a Hill." Though it was probably honest enough in its way, it echoed more of the white writers I had been reading and told more about my reactions to the shapes and sound of the city than it did about the people I loved and hated, or the things which delighted, hurt, or confused me most.

We had moved from Carroll Street downtown three years earlier and we were living that year on Driscoll Avenue in midtown, halfway between the river on the east and that section of West End the whites had ceded to the Negro doctors, schoolteachers, and postal workers. For a long time after the move to Driscoll Avenue I had continued to go back to the old neighborhood. In part this was because the customers to whom I sold Negro weekly newspapers lived there (ranging from an ancient self-ordained bishop, whose wife was never permitted to expose anything more than a slender wax-yellow hand and a black-clad sleeve as I handed the paper through the double-chained door, to the heavily powdered ladies in the big house on Seymour Street who had bought a dozen papers from me every Friday for a month before I learned how they made their living). But even on days when I had no papers to sell, Carroll Street for a long time continued to have the same love-fear magnetism for me it had exercised when I lived there; racked by sweaty nightmares on nights when the patrol wagons and ambulances pounded past our house, listening by the hour to the Italians singing from the backyards where they had strung light bulbs for the parties that left the alley littered with snail shells and the discarded bottles the winos fought over the next morning. On

Carroll Street we had lived closely, though not intimately, with whites: the Italians on Bouie Avenue to the rear, the Jewish storekeepers, the Germans who worked in the bakery and the bank, the Irish truck drivers and policemen. . . .

Driscoll Avenue was a less impoverished and more self-contained world than Carroll Street. Except for the merchants and bill collectors, it was possible to walk through midtown for blocks without seeing a white face. We lived on the first floor of a three-story brick house set on a concrete terrace from which three stone steps led down to the street. My chores during the long winter included keeping the steps salted down and making sure the heavy hall door was kept tightly shut.

My mother was ill for a long time that winter, and the grown-ups came to visit her, stamped into the house wrapped like mummies with only their eyes showing, bringing pots of stew, pickled preserves, and the latest tale of some drunk who had been found frozen stiff in an alley or a neighbor who had been taken to "Old Number Two" with double pneumonia. Number Two was the nearest city hospital, and the neighborhood saying was that they did more killing there than Mr. Swift did over at his packing house. Old people in the neighborhood sometimes clung stubbornly to their beds at home, hiding the seriousness of their ailments, for fear they would be sent to Number Two to die. My mother was not old, but I lay awake many nights that winter, listening to her rasping breathing and praying that she would not have to be taken to Number Two. Sometimes, after her breathing had smoothed out and she had fallen asleep, I would get out of bed and go over to the window, raising the shade enough to let in the white winter moonlight. Fumbling for a pencil and piece of paper, I would write lines and fragments which I could not see, then fold the paper and stuff it into my hiding place back of the piano which nobody in the house played.

My mother's conviction that both her children were going to finish high school and college and "amount to something" had persisted in the face of the bleakest realities her native Mississippi and a half-flat near the tracks in south St. Louis could marshal against her. Even in her illness, hollow-eyed and feverish, she wanted to know what we had done in school daily, what the teachers had said, whether our homework was done. A gifted seamstress and a careful manager of small change for most of her life, she never doubted she would one day find the proper use for the patterns, scraps of cloth, Eagle stamps, buttons, and pins she scrupulously put aside, each in its proper place. She cooked huge pots of soup, with opulent aromas suggesting magnitudes of power and promise out of all proportion to the amount of meat in the pot. She felt she had ample reason to sing "He Leadeth Me," and when we had amazed ourselves and our teachers by prodigies of nerve-straining effort she only said mildly, "Didn't He promise He would make a way out of no way for those who believed in Him?"

Lacking in faith, I was so beset with premonitions and terrors during those months of her illness that I lost all recollection of the poem I had mailed to the Arts Club. The cousin I loved most had died in childbirth just two years before, at the age of nineteen, and I had been tormented ever since by the fragility of the web separating life and death. Though she met the slightest ache or pain visited on her children as if it were an outrider of the Devil's legions fully armed, my mother regarded her own illnesses as nuisances to be gotten through with as little fuss as possible. By the time the snow had melted in the gutters she was on her feet again, halfway through her spring cleaning, and

fretting to have the last frost gone so that she could start planting the narrow rectangle of earth out front she called her garden.

I came home from school one afternoon in early May to find a letter from the Arts Club in our mailbox. I was afraid to open it until I had first made sure it was not bulky enough to contain the rejected poem. There was only a single sheet inside, a note typed on the most elegant stationery I had ever seen, congratulating me on the selection of my poem as one of the five best works submitted in that year's contest and inviting me to meet the other winners at the club two weeks later.

The first surge of surprise and pleasure was followed almost at once by a seizure of blind panic. How could I go out there to Westmoreland Place, a street I had never seen, to meet a group of strangers, most if not all of them white—when I stammered or fell silent whenever I had to talk to one of my teachers without the supporting presence of the rest of the class? Reading the note again I saw that the meeting had been scheduled for mid-afternoon of a school day. For most of that next week I debated whether I should accept the club's invitation or prepare to be sick on that day. Finally, just forty-eight hours before the date set in the letter, I went down to the principal and secured permission to be excused from my afternoon classes to attend the Arts Club meeting.

That same afternoon I showed my mother the letter. She knew me well enough to play down the pride she felt, complaining instead about people who would miss Heaven one day because they always waited until the last minute. She consulted with a friend who worked in the section where the club was located and wrote down the directions for me, dryly reminding me to have the conductor give me a transfer when I boarded the trolley near the school. I had once had to walk home a distance of some six miles away because I forgot to ask for a transfer.

Actually, I was less concerned about the transfer than about the possibility that on the way out to the club I might develop motion sickness. This often happened when I rode the trolleys. Usually I got off the car as soon as the first queasy stirrings began in the pit of my stomach, and walked the rest of the way. But this time I would be in a part of town that I did not know at all. I resolved to ride standing up all the way, trusting that my mother's God would not let me be sick.

I left school on a hazily bright afternoon alive with the tarry tang of smoke and the green smell of growing things which I associate still with spring in St. Louis. It was good to be a privileged truant with the whole block in front of the school to myself, the typewriters clicking behind me in the principal's office and the unheeded voices of the teachers floating out of the classroom windows overhead. The first trolley was a long time coming. When I got on I remembered to ask for the transfer, and though over half the seats were empty on both trolleys, I stood up all the way. But when I got off the second car I found that I had managed to lose the directions my mother had given me. I could not remember whether I was to go north or south from the trolley stop. My palms promptly began sweating and I took out the letter from the Arts Club, reading the address again as if that would give me a clue. In my neighborhood most of the houses were row houses, or were separated from each other by nothing more than a narrow passageway. Even houses like the one we lived in, though not flush with the pavement, were close enough so that the addresses could be easily read from the sidewalk. But out here the houses were set back from wide lawns under shade trees and there was no way of making out the addresses without going up a long walk to the front door. No small children were playing outside, there were

no stores into which a stranger might go and ask directions, and the whole neighborhood was wrapped in a fragrant but forbidding stillness. Remembering that my mother had said the club was only two blocks away from the trolley stop, I started walking south, deciding that if it turned out I was going the wrong way I could always come back and go two blocks in the other direction. I walked three blocks for good measure without finding Westmoreland Place, then turned and started back.

A red-faced old man with bushy military whiskers that reminded me of pictures I had seen of the Kaiser[3] came down one of the walks with a bulldog on a leash. I braced myself to ask him where Westmoreland Place was, but before I could speak, his china blue eyes suddenly glared at me with such venomous hatred that I had the feeling he was about to set the dog on me. I averted my eyes and walked on, trembling suddenly with an answering hatred as senseless as his. Not noticing where I was going, I was about to cross into the next block when I looked up at the street sign and found that I was on Westmoreland Place. It was a street of thick hedges and houses which, if anything, were more inaccessible than those I had already passed. I walked up the street in one direction, then crossed and reversed my course. By now the letter was wilting in my hand. The trolley ride had taken longer than I had estimated and I was sure I was already late. One of the last things my mother had said to me that morning was, "Now try to be sure not to get out there on Colored People's Time." My mind groped for a plausible lie that would let me give up the whole business and go home. I thought of saying that the meeting had been called off, that the place

[3]**Kaiser:** Kaiser William II, German emperor during World War I.

was closed when I got there, that I had caught the wrong car and gone too far out of the way to get back in time. At one point, I almost convinced myself that I should go back to the trolley stop and catch a car that would take me downtown to my old refuge, the main public library. I could stay there reading for an hour or two, then claim I had actually attended the tea. But my spirit quailed at the prospect of inventing answers to all the questions that would follow. And what if in the meantime someone from the club had already called my home or the school? I hated myself for entering the competition and felt sick with envy when I thought of my schoolmates who by now were idling down the halls on free period or dreaming their way through the last classes before the liberating bell.

I was plodding down the same block for the second time when around the corner of a big stone house across the street came an unmistakably colored man in work clothes, uncoiling a garden hose. We might have been the only two living souls on a desert island. Almost faint with relief I angled across the street toward him. But the handyman, his high shiny forehead furrowed in elaborate concentration, adjusted the nozzle and began playing rainbow jets of spray across the grass. I halted at the edge of the lawn and waited for him to take note of my presence. In due time he worked himself close enough so that I was able to ask him if he knew where the Arts Club was. I held out the letter as I asked him, but he merely turned his rusty deepset eyes on me with a look that said plainly *I hope you ain't come out here to make trouble for the rest of us.* In later years I have seen that look in the eyes of Negro businessmen, schoolteachers, college presidents, reverend ministers—and a trio of cooks and dishwashers peering through the swinging doors of a restaurant kitchen at the dark-skinned students

sitting at counters where no one of their color ever presumed to sit before.

But I was of another generation, another temperament and state of mind from those students. So when the handyman flicked one hand in the direction from which I had just come and said, "There 'tis, over there," I thanked him—rather thanked his back, which was already turned to me.

I would never have taken the two-story brick building at the end of the flagstone walk to be anything other than the residence of a comfortably well-off family. Just before I pushed the button beside the broad door it occurred to me that the handyman might be playing his notion of a joke on me. Then I looked down at the thick mat on which I was standing and saw the letters "A-C." I pressed the button, waited, and was about to press it again when the door swung open. The rake-thin white maid standing there had composed for her plain freckled face a smile of deferential welcome. The smile faded and her body stiffened in the neat gray uniform. For an instant I thought she would close the door in my face, but she braked it so that it was barely ajar and said, "Yes?" I mumbled something and held out the letter. She squinted at the envelope and said, "You wait here." The door closed and I stood there with my face burning, wanting to turn and go away but unwilling to confront the expression of sour satisfaction I expected to see on the face of the handyman across the street. After what seemed fifteen full minutes a gray-haired woman in a blue uniform with starched cuffs came to the door. "All right, what is it now?" she said, sounding like a very busy woman. I held out the letter and she took it, measured me up and down with her shrewd eyes, and said to the younger woman hovering behind her, "I'll be right back." The freckle-faced thin one looked miles above my head toward the street but we shared the unspoken understanding that I was not to move from where I stood and that she was to watch me.

I stood rooted there, calling myself every kind of black fool for coming in the first place, my undershirt cleaving to my damp skin. It had become clear to me that I had received the invitation by mistake. And now that I had surrendered the letter, the only proof that I had been invited, my sole excuse for being there at all was gone. I pictured them huddled inside, talking in whispers, waiting for me to have the good sense to leave. Then I heard voices coming toward the door. My keeper faded back into the gloom of the hallway and an attractive woman in her forties held the door open and smiled at me. Everything about her, her fine-textured skin, the soft-colored dress and the necklace she was wearing, her candid gaze, defined an order of relationships which did away with any need for me to deal further with the other two women. "Hello," she said. "So you're the boy who came over to tell us Mr. Holman couldn't come?"

I stared dumbly at her, wondering how I could have been fooled into thinking she was one of those white women my mother would have described approvingly as "a real lady, as nice as they come."

"Please tell him we hope he'll be feeling better soon," the woman said. "We had so hoped to meet him."

"I'm—I got the letter saying to come out here," I blurted. We stood here for a minute staring at one another and then her pink skin flushed red. "Oh, you mean you—oh, I *am* so sorry," she said. "Please do come in. I didn't know." She glanced back at the maids. "I mean, we thought—"

It was finally clear to all of us what she had thought. That the white boy who wrote the poem had been unable to come so his family had thoughtfully sent their colored boy to tender his regrets.

"You come right on in," the woman said. "I'm your hostess. All the others are already here and we've been waiting for you." She drew me inside the cool, dim hallway and guided me up the stairs like an invalid. I could not remember ever walking on such thick carpets. I had a hazy impression of cut flowers in vases, and paintings hanging along the walls like those I had seen in the Art Museum in the park. As she went up she kept on talking, but I made very little of what she was saying because now I could hear the murmur of other voices and laughter coming from the floor above us. I had the feeling that an intimate and very pleasant family party was in progress which we were about to ruin and I wanted to ask my hostess if I might not be excused after all. Instead I let myself be piloted into a sunny high-ceilinged room which at one and the same time seemed as spacious as a playing field and so intimate that no one could move without touching the person beside him. A blur of white faces turned toward us, some of them young, some middle-aged, some older, but all of them clearly belonging to a different world from that of the uniformed women downstairs. A different world from mine. For a flickering moment there was a drop in energy like that sudden dimming of lights during a summer storm and then I was being introduced in a flurry of smiles, bobbing heads, and a refrain seeming to consist of variations on "Delightful . . . delighted . . . so good you could come . . . a pleasure."

Whenever I have tried to recollect that afternoon since, the faces in that upstairs room elude me like objects seen through sunlit water. I remember that one of the girls was blond and turned eagerly from one speaker to another as if anxious not to miss one word, that there was a boy there from a school out in the country who talked and moved with the casual, almost insulting assurance which for a long time afterward I automatically associated with private schools. All of the other students there who had won prizes or honorable mentions in the area-wide competition were either from private schools or from white high schools whose very names were new to me. One of the girls was from a Catholic school and one of the sisters from the faculty had come along with her. I discovered that other winners were accompanied by their teacher and I mentally kicked myself for not realizing that I might have been buttressed by the presence of Miss Armstrong or Mr. Blanton. Certainly they would have been much more at home in this company than I was. Gradually, as cookies, tea, and punch were passed and the talk again swirled back and forth, I began to relax somewhat, content to be on the periphery of that closed circle. I kept stealing glances around the room, taking in the wide fireplace and the portrait above the mantel of some famous man whose identity kept eluding me, the rows of books in the recessed shelves along the wall, and the magazines scattered tantalizingly just out of reach on the long oaken table in the center of the room.

In school, except to recite, I had rarely ever talked even to my English teachers about poems, books, and writers. But this group, comfortably seated or standing about the pleasant room with the haze of spring sunlight sifting through the windows, shared a community of language and interests which enabled them largely to ignore differences of age and individual preference and to move from one idea or work to another as effortlessly as fish in a pond. They talked of Shakespeare and Keats, Milton and Shelley, but there were other writers whose lines I had spoken aloud, sometimes in puzzlement, when I was alone. Now they were being argued over, attacked, defended, ridiculed: Eliot, Frost, Sandburg, Millay, Vachel Lindsay, Amy Lowell, Yeats. There were moments when someone touched on something I had read and I was tempted to speak out in agreement or disagreement. At other times I was overcome by the gloomy conviction that I could never in the years there were left to me read all the works some of them seemed to know by heart. I felt particularly lost as the talk shifted to novels only recently written, to concerts they had attended and plays seen at the American Theatre downtown or "on our last trip to New York." (I had been drunk for days on the free concert given for Negro high school students by the St. Louis Symphony the year before, shutting myself off in my room with an umbrella spoke for a baton, trying to be all the voices of the orchestra and graceful Mr. Golschmann conducting the *New World Symphony*.) Later I was to go to the American as often as I could to see the road companies in performance and, during intermissions, to devour the posters advertising the plays I would not be able to see. Often my companion and I were among less than a dozen Negroes present. (Years afterward, on a trip back to St. Louis I was triumphantly informed that Negroes were no longer segregated in the second-balcony seats at the American. Second-balcony seats being all we could afford, my friend and I had never asked for anything else, a neat dovetailing of covert discrimination and economic necessity.)

Toward the end of the long afternoon, it was proposed that the young writers read their poems. Once again I was plunged into sweaty-palmed agony. My torment only increased as the first two readers read their poems like seasoned professionals, or so it seemed to me. When my turn came I tried to beg off, but the additional attention this focused upon me only increased my discomfort and I plunged in, at first reading too fast and almost inaudibly but finally recollecting some of the admonitions my teachers had dinned into my head in preparation for "recitations" before Negro school and church audiences as far back as the second grade. I had not realized how long a poem it was when I was writing it and I was squirmingly conscious of certain flaws and failures which had never before loomed so large. The applause and praise that followed when I finished, if anything, exceeded that given the others; a situation which, even then, aroused the fleeting suspicion that the dancing bear was being given higher marks than a man might get for the same performance. One of the older women murmured something about Paul Laurence Dunbar. Someone else asked me if I liked Pushkin. I could only look blank, since at that time I knew almost nothing about the great Russian's poetry and even less about his Negro lineage. Inevitably, there was a flattering and irrelevant comparison to Langston Hughes. A wavy-haired gentleman took his pipe out of his mouth to ask if I didn't think "The Negro Speaks of Rivers" was a marvelous poem. I said I certainly did. . . .

Gradually, as the light faded outside the window, people began looking at their watches and saying good-bye. One of the club members thanked all of us for coming and said she could not remember when the Arts Club had had such a fine and talented group. The blonde girl clapped her hands for attention, her eyes shining with the enthusiasm of the born organizer. Why, she wanted to know, did this year's group really have to scatter? It seemed to her that we should not let our companionship, our new friendships, die. Some of us were going away for the summer, but there were still several weeks left yet before school would be out. Some might be going off to college in the fall, but others would not, and probably some of those who would be entering college would be going no farther away than the University of Missouri at Columbia, or St. Louis, Washington, or one of the other schools in the St. Louis area. I was silent as the others chimed in, suggesting that we meet at the various high schools or rotate meetings from one home to another before and after summer vacations. Such a point was made of including me, and I felt already so much the witch at the wedding party that I was not inclined to remind them that I would have a much harder time getting into a meeting at the schools they attended or the colleges in the area than I had had getting into the Arts Club that afternoon. To say nothing of what their parents and friends and mine would make of those meetings in the homes. I tried to picture those well-dressed, self-assured young white poets strolling past the cleaning and pressing shop to a meeting at my house. Nevertheless, my Driscoll Avenue cynicism began crumbling under the effervescent pressures of their youth and mine. We made our way down thick-carpeted stairs, true poets and comrades, a verbal skyscraper of plans and projects rising as we descended. We would do a volume of poems together and a famous novelist who was a good friend of our hostess would get the book published for us. The Arts Club would serve as secretariat and haven, keeping track of addresses and phone numbers and providing a place where we could meet, read, and write.

Good will, mutual admiration, flowering ambition united us as we parted in the gathering spring dusk. The air was scented with the watermelony smell of freshly cut grass. The lights were on in the stone house across the street, but the handyman was gone.

I did not hear from the young men and women I met that afternoon at the Arts Club the next week, the next month, or

ever. But I had a great many more serious disappointments than that, along with a decent amount of good fortune, in the two remaining years I spent in my home town. Like many other young men similarly situated I was involved during those pre-war years in a quiet but no less desperate scramble simply to hold on to life and not go under. By the end of that period of twenty-odd months I had run an elevator, worked as a machine operator, delivered parcels, patrolled a lake stocked with fish nobody ever tried to steal, and stood in half a hundred job lines with white and black men who showed up every morning less out of hope than the need to put off as long as possible that time of day when they must once again face their families. For me and a good many others my age it was not a question really of having something to eat and a place to sleep. Rather, the battle was to find ways of withstanding the daily erosion, through tedium, through humiliation, through various short-term pleasures, of the sense of your own possibilities. Necessary, too, was some sensitivity to possibilities outside yourself. Here I do not exclude chance, the lucky break. For me it came with the opportunity to become a part-time student at a college I might have attended full time two years earlier.

On the night before I left for college my mother gave a party for me, inviting a dozen of my friends. Some of them brought gifts. As I was walking past the Catholic church on Garth Avenue, shortly after midnight, going home to the flat I shared with my father, a squad car pulled up and two officers jumped out. Night sticks at the ready, they flashed a light in my face and wanted to know where I was coming from and where I had picked up all that stuff. They pawed through the presents I was carrying until they came across an anthology of poetry autographed for me that night by my friends. The first officer grunted and snapped off his light. The second seemed tempted to take a swipe at me anyhow for wasting their time. They got back in the car and drove off, leaving me to walk the two blocks remaining between the church and home.

The next morning, on a cold, sooty, old-style St. Louis day, I left home. I got on a bus and headed for Jefferson City, Missouri. That trip away from home has been a much longer journey than I had anticipated and a very much different one. On certain occasions, as when my poetry was published or while lecturing at Atlanta University, I have remembered that afternoon. And I have thought that perhaps when I next visited St. Louis, I would try once again to find my way to the Arts Club. I never have and it is probably just as well. It may be that I got as much as could reasonably be expected on that first visit.

## YOU AND THE STORY

When people approach something that spells trouble to them, they often react with ready-made attitudes, or in set ways. (This is what several people in this story do when they encounter what to them is a "problem.") The value of first-rate autobiography is that it keeps us from any "kneejerk" response. In honest autobiographical writing, someone who really cares tries to give a faithful accounting of something that happened in his or her own life. It is as if the writer were turning to us to say: "Here, let me replay this incident for you. Let us keep out our preconceived notions and ready-made ideas. Remember these are real people. Remember they are looking at things from their own point of view." Can you read this autobiographical story as a faithful account of "the way it actually was"? Can you leave some of your own ready-made ideas aside? How would you answer questions like the following?

(1) Several of the people in the story react to the boy's appearance in set, ready-made ways: the red-faced man walking his dog, the handyman, the maid. In your own words, how would you describe and explain the reactions of each?

(2) Were you surprised by the reception the boy received at the actual meeting, after he had made his way past the door? How would you describe and explain the reactions and attitudes of the people there? Do they seem familiar or strange to you?

(3) The author talks about the "Driscoll Avenue cynicism" that he had brought to the meeting. He says it began crumbling in the atmosphere of "good will." How do you think the incident as a whole would have looked to a person of determined good will? How do you think it would have looked to a determined cynic? (You may want to volunteer for one of these roles in a debate between cynicism and good will.)

(4) The author gives us some brief glimpses of the boy's life both before and after the memorable afternoon. How does this *framework* for the main part of the story affect your reactions to the major incident?

**Your Turn**

Do you remember an incident that was an "eye-opener" to you about the adult world or the "world outside"? Give a faithful accounting of what happened.

Language/Composition Activity A3

FOR SENTENCE PRACTICE

# The One-Sentence Portrait

Carl Holman is the kind of writer who can take a look at people and tell us much about them in one single sentence. Each of the following sentences sizes up one of the people in his story. Can you spell out in your own words everything the sentence tells us about the person? Can you write some similar "one-sentence portraits" about people that you have had a chance to observe?

A gifted seamstress and a careful manager of small change for most of her life, she never doubted she would one day find the proper use for the patterns, scraps of cloth, Eagle stamps, buttons, and pins she scrupulously put aside, each in its proper place.

A red-faced old man with bushy military whiskers that reminded me of pictures I had seen of the Kaiser came down one of the walks with a bulldog on a leash.

The handyman, his high shiny forehead furrowed in elaborate concentration, adjusted the nozzle and began playing rainbow jets of spray across the grass.

The rake-thin white maid standing there had composed for her plain freckled face a smile of deferential welcome.

A wavy-haired gentleman took his pipe out of his mouth to ask if I didn't think "The Negro Speaks of Rivers" was a marvelous poem.

Write a set of similar one-sentence portraits about a group like one of the following:

—the people around the dinner table at your house

—a group of teachers in the faculty lounge at your school

—a group of passengers on a bus or on the subway

—the members of a team in the gym or out on the field

—the members of a band, orchestra, or other similar group

# O Pioneers

Come, my tan-faced children,
Follow well in order, get your weapons ready;
Have you your pistols? have you your sharp-edged axes?
Pioneers! O Pioneers!

—Walt Whitman

Oh, paint your wagons with "Pike's Peak or Bust!"
Pack up the fiddle, rosin up the bow,
Vamoose, skedaddle, mosey, hit the grit! . . .
We're off for Californ-iay,
We're off down the wild O-hi-o!

—Stephen Vincent Benét

When Americans look into the mirror of their literature, what image of themselves do they expect to see? How do they think of themselves, and how do they want others to think of them? What kind of people are their true heroes? One of the most popular and most lasting of idealized American images has been that of the pioneer. The pioneer has become a kind of American "archetype"—summing up traits that many people consider fundamental in their national character. For many people, the image of the pioneer continues to sum up what they really want to be—not a number in a computer, not a cog in a machine, but a free spirit, taming the wilderness, opening up new territories, crossing the mountains and plains in search of a new life.

The central symbol of the pioneering spirit has been the westward journey, first across the ocean and then across the new continent, opening up new frontiers. "Americans are always moving on," said Stephen Vincent Benét. The inheritance of the "westering spirit" has helped Americans think of themselves as people

hard to hem in and fence in, willing to pull up stakes if need be. They like the feel of open spaces and the open road.

The image of the pioneer has helped keep alive a basic part of the American creed: the belief in individual initiative, in self-reliance. The pioneer is a guiding light to people who believe that basically "you have to make it on your own." The lone rider, the small band of settlers, the isolated family on the homestead—these are the true popular heroes in much American folklore and entertainment.

These are different heroes from the aristocrats and conquerors and generals of much traditional history. Americans like to think of their history as having been made by unknown, unsung heroes—ordinary people. They have their great leaders and patriotic monuments, but their true hero is the common man or woman. How true to life is the image we have of the American pioneer? Is it possible to turn back the clock and relive some of the experiences of pioneering days?

## POEMS: **There Is Wealth in the Earth**

When we study history, we are often looking at memorials and mementos.
We look at an inscription on a rock, a yellowed document under glass,
names engraved on a plaque. We often have to use our imagination to bring
back the human side of history. We wonder what the *people* were like—how
they looked, how they talked, what they thought. One age-old function of
poets has been to preserve the living memory of the past. They have used
their imagination to help keep alive the memory of history as a human
experience. The following poems make us look at some pages from the early
history of our country. See how successful these poets are in making you
say: "This is the way it was. This is how it felt to be there."

## Stephen Vincent Benét
### (1898–1943)

# Western Star

She was a sturdy ship, with her double-decks,
High-sterned, slow-sailing, chunky, hard to wear out,
Long in the wine-trade, smelling of it still,
And known for that as a "sweet" ship, meaning a healthy one.
They steered her hundred and eighty tons with a whipstaff.
And she'd trudged the seas for years,
Slow, roomy, durable, smelling of salt and wine,
—A housewife of a ship, not a gallant lady,
Who would groan at storms but get through them and get home,
Like a housewife plodding, market basket in hand—
The *Mayflower*—a common name for ships—

With Christopher Jones of Harwich for her master.
—And what he thought of the voyage, heaven knows,
His business being to sail the ship across,
Land his queer passengers somewhere and return home,
But that was his last voyage, though he knew it not,
For he died ten months after getting back to England,
Neither Puritan nor rogue, but the mere seaman
Who had done his seaman's task and gotten his death
And brought his ship home to sail under other captains.
For that is the chance of the sea.
                                        And the trudging housewife
Went on with her work, and plodded from port to port
Till she met the end of every laboring ship,
Though we do not know what it was.
                                        We only know
They appraised her, later—at least we think it was she—
And valued her at a hundred and sixty pounds,
Including fifteen pounds for a suit of worn sails.

Now she meets Atlantic, and labors in the gray seas.
And, for those aboard,
We think of them all of one stamp, which they were not.
There were a hundred and one of them all told
But only thirty-five from the Leyden church.
The rest were drawn from London and Southampton
And drawn sometimes, as needs must, from the sort of folk
Willing to stake their lives and seven years
Against a possible future and free land.
They did their best at the choosing, no doubt of that.
They chose Miles Standish, the little chimney soon fired,
Who was to be their buckler in the wilderness;
They picked up young John Alden at the last moment,
For he was a cooper and a hopeful youth;
But there were a number, neither saints nor Puritans,
Who grumbled even while they were still on board
At being ruled by the small band of Zion's men
And swore they would have their liberties, once ashore, . . .
And, hearing them, Zion's leaders thought it well
To draw a compact, binding their own together
In a lawful government for the town to be.
—And that was to be a cornerstone, in time,
Of something they never visioned from first to last.
But they did not know it then. How could they know it?
They were taking emergency measures in an emergency;
They were founding Zion, not the United States.
—And the seed is sown, and it grows in the deep earth,
And from it comes what the sower never dreamed.

. . . think of them through the sixty-five long days
Of tempest and fair weather, of calm and storm,
They were not yet Pilgrim Fathers in steeple-hats,
Each with an iron jaw and a musketoon,
They were not Pilgrim Mothers, sure of their fame.
They were men and women and children, cramped in a ship,
Bound for an unknown land and wondering.
The godly prayed, the ungodly spat overside,
The sailors jeered now and then at the pious speeches,
The Billington boys behaved like limbs of Satan,
And the three pregnant women walked the decks
Or lay in their cabins, wondering at night
What hour their pains would strike and what would be born.

## YOU AND THE POEM

(1) Poets often make more *resourceful* use of words than do ordinary people. They often use words that add "something extra." In each of the following pairs, the second word is the one actually used in this poem. What does it add?

a. What is the difference between *travel* and *trudge*?
b. What is the difference between saying "a brave woman" and "a gallant lady"?
c. What is the difference between a journey and a voyage?
d. What is the difference between an ordinary dishonest person and a rogue?
e. Is there a difference between a contract and a compact?
f. What is the difference between being crowded and being cramped?

(2) Everyone knows that the *Mayflower* brought Pilgrims in search of a new Zion, a heavenly city they were going to build in the wilderness. But the poet who wrote this poem said, "There were human beings aboard the *Mayflower*, not merely ancestors." When we hear about "ancestors," we may think of pictures in a museum, with people in strange clothes posed stiffly for a historic portrait. Benét was a writer whose goal was to make history come back to life, to make us *relive* moments in history. What facts or details did he include in this poem to help us see that what is now history was once part of real people's lives? What details in this poem help you think of the people involved as human beings? What details about the ship or the voyage are the kind of thing people sometimes do *not* find in a history book?

## Archibald MacLeish
# To Thomas Jefferson, Esquire

"To Thos. Jefferson Esq. his obd't serv't
M. Lewis: captain: detached:
Sir:

Having in mind your repeated commands in this matter,
And the worst half of it done and the streams mapped,

And we here on the back of this beach beholding the
Other ocean—two years gone and the cold

Breaking with rain for the third spring since St. Louis,
The crows at the fishbones on the frozen dunes,

The first cranes going over from south north,
And the river down by a mark of the pole since the morning,

And time near to return, and a ship (Spanish)
Lying in for the salmon: and fearing chance or the

Drought or the Sioux should deprive you of these discoveries—
Therefore we send by sea in this writing.

Above the
Platte there were long plains and a clay country:
Rim of the sky far off, grass under it,

Dung for the cook fires by the sulphur licks.
After that there were low hills and the sycamores,

And we poled up by the Great Bend in the skiffs:
The honey bees left us after the Osage River.

The wind was west in the evenings, and no dew and the
Morning Star larger and whiter than usual—

The winter rattling in the brittle haws.
The second year there was sage and the quail calling.

All that valley is good land by the river:
Three thousand miles and the clay cliffs and
Rue and beargrass by the water banks
And many birds and the brant going over and tracks of

Bear, elk, wolves, marten: the buffalo
Numberless so that the cloud of their dust covers them:

The antelope fording the fall creeks, and the mountains and
Grazing lands and the meadow lands and the ground

Sweet and open and well-drained.
                        We advise you to
Settle troops at the forks and to issue licenses:

Many men will have living on these lands.
There is wealth in the earth for them all and the wood standing

And wild birds on the water where they sleep.
There is stone in the hills for the towns of a great people . . ."

## YOU AND THE POEM

(1) Can you imagine yourself living in the nation's capital when Lewis and Clark first left on their mission to explore the Western wilderness? What kind of report would you have *expected* to get back from them? Improvise a description of the "wilderness" as you would have imagined it.

(2) When we receive a lengthy letter or report, we often say: "What is the gist of it? What is the word?" What *overall impression* do you get from the "letter" reconstructed here by the poet? What are some of the most striking details? (How is the letter different from what you might have expected it to be?)

(3) What do you think the members of the expedition felt when after two years of travel they first reached the "other ocean"? Pretend you were a member of the original expedition. Reconstruct this historic moment, and tell us what you saw and thought and felt.

Duncan Campbell Scott

# On the Way to the Mission

They dogged him all one afternoon,
Through the bright snow,
Two whitemen servants of greed;
He knew that they were there,
But he turned not his head;
He was an Indian trapper;
He planted his snowshoes firmly,
He dragged the long toboggan
Without rest.

The three figures drifted
Like shadows in the mind of a seer;
The snowshoes were whisperers
On the threshold of awe;
The toboggan made the sound of wings,
A wood pigeon sloping to her nest.

The Indian's face was calm.
He strode with the sorrow
  of foreknowledge,

But his eyes were jewels of content
Set in circles of peace.

They would have shot him;
But momently in the deep forest,
They saw something flit by his side;
Their hearts stopped with fear.
Then the moon rose.
They would have left him to the spirit,
But they saw the long toboggan
Rounded well with furs,
With many a silver foxskin,
With the pelts of mink and of otter.

They were the servants of greed;
When the moon grew brighter
And the spruces were dark with sleep,
They shot him.
When he fell on a shield of moonlight,

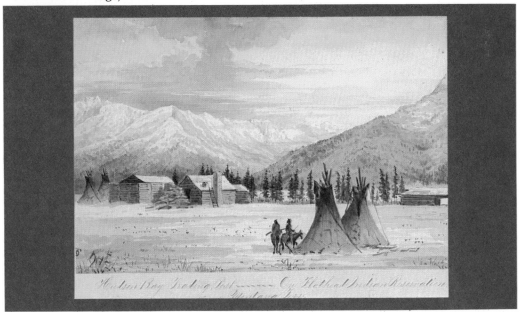

One of his arms clung to his burden;
The snow was not melted:
The spirit passed away.

Then the servants of greed
Tore off the cover to count their gains;
They shuddered away into the shadows,
Hearing each the loud heart of the other.
Silence was born.

There in the tender moonlight,
    As sweet as they were in life,
Glimmered the ivory features,
    Of the Indian's wife.

In the manner of Montagnais women
    Her hair was rolled with braid;
Under her waxen fingers
    A crucifix was laid.

He was drawing her down to the Mission,
    To bury her there in spring,
When the bloodroot comes and the windflower
    To silver everything.

But as a gift of plunder
    Side by side were they laid,
The moon went on to her setting
    And covered them with shade.

---

## YOU AND THE POEM

(1) The picture we get of the Indian in this poem is quite different from the familiar one of the "bloodthirsty savage." How many different details can you point out that go counter to the familiar stereotype?

(2) The events described in this poem are treated **ballad-style**. What are some of the features that make this poem read like the ballads that street singers used to recite, or that were passed on orally from one generation to the next?

## Your Turn

For contrast, could you retell the events of the poem in a style *different* from the ballad style it employs? Retell the story as it might be told by one of the following:

—a modern small-town or backcountry newspaper

—a sensational big-city newspaper

—an old-style preacher using the story in a sermon

—the script for an old movie melodrama

Mary Oliver

# Stark Boughs on the Family Tree

Up in the attic on row on row,
In dusty frames, with stubborn eyes,
My thin ancestors slowly fade
Under the flat Ohio skies.

And so, I think, they always were:
Like their own portrait, years ago,
They paced the blue and windy fields,
Aged in the polished rooms below.

For name by name I find no sign
Of hero in this distant life,
But only men as calm as snow
Who took some faithful girl as wife,

Who labored while the drought, the flood
Crisscrossed the fickle summer air,
Who built great barns and propped
    their lives
Upon a slow heart-breaking care.

Why do I love them as I do,
Who dared no glory, won no fame?
In a harsh land that lies subdued,
They are the good boughs of my name.

If music sailed their dreams at all,
They were not heroes, and slept on;
As one by one they left the small
Accomplished, till the great was done.

---

## YOU AND THE POEM

(1) Can you explain the *contradictory* signals that a reader might get from this poem? What are familiar negative associations of words like the following: *stark, dusty, stubborn, thin, flat*? What are some of the more positive things and feelings that come into the poem? How do the negative and the positive balance out.

(2) The people discussed in the poem were not "heroes"; they did not win "fame" or "glory." Yet they helped bring about something "great." What? How?

### Your Turn

If there were an attic with portraits of some of your own ancestors, what kind of people would be shown in them? Describe one or two of the imaginary portraits.

Elisabeth Peck

# Walthena
*Kentucky, c. 1785*

I turned my back when in the pot they tossed
My pewter spoons, to mold as shot for guns.
My mother owned a shelf of shining spoons and plates;—
Can we have none but homemade wooden ones,
    Just handmade wooden ones?

I asked your father once if we might have
Crock plates to set our table. He said, "No,"
They dulled men's knives. So we must eat from plates
        of wood,
To keep knife-blades well sharped against the foe,
    The ever-lurking foe.

Back home each Saturday my mother made
White candles, clean and straight. But out west here
Your father, laughing, scorns to make a candle mold,
When we have fatty pine-knots always near,
    Pine-knots and greasy bear-dips always near.

If I could hope some day to own a gown
Of smooth, fine store-cloth, little would I care
That I have only homespun linsey-woolsey now,
And shapeless shoepacks stiffed with moss to wear,
    Coarse, shapeless clothes to wear.

But though I could not own a pewter spoon nor store-
        cloth dress,
I snatched at least some beauty for my brood.
When pappy gave the boys their names, and I the girls,
He gave man-names that seemed like puncheons rude,
    Ax-hewn puncheons rude.

But I chose names for loveliness alone.
Fair-Anna is a spoon of silver bright,
Lizelle a silken gown, Morene a china bowl,
And you, Walthena, are a candle white,
    A tall, smooth candle white,
        Walthena.

## YOU AND THE POEM

When we talk about the **form** of a poem or of a work of art, we talk about what makes it a finished whole. This poem is exceptionally well unified. Look at some of the things that make it seem all of one piece:

(1) The parts of this poem go together in their external shape. In all six **stanzas,** the poet uses the same pattern of **rhyme** and **repetition.** How is this pattern repeated in each stanza?

(2) The first four stanzas follow a very similar pattern in their content: Each gives us a different example of the contrast between the speaker's earlier life "back home" and her present life "out west." What are the three examples? What do they have in common?

(3) The fifth stanza further rounds out our picture of what the present is like for the speaker. But at the same time, it looks at the present from a different perspective, or point of view. How or in what way?

(4) Names often mean something special to the people who choose them. The boys' names chosen by the father were like "ax-hewn puncheons"—like rough pieces of timber. What did the names of her daughters mean to the speaker in the poem? How does the last stanza help tie all the parts of this poem together?

### Your Turn

What's in a name? Do you remember any names that meant something special to someone? Do you remember names that seemed exceptionally fitting—or exceptionally out of place? What names do you especially like, and why? If you were asked to name a child, a ship, or a street, what name would you choose?

● What were the people like who first settled in the eastern part of the continent? Where did they come from? What did they believe and think and feel? In her novel *Vein of Iron,* Ellen Glasgow takes us to Appalachian Virginia. She takes us to the Blue Ridge and the Alleghenies, to a country with many rivers and creeks, to valleys with scattered farmhouses with roofs of red-painted tin or gray weatherbeaten shingles. The people in her novel are descended from Scotch-Irish pioneers who had first moved from Scotland into Ulster (in Northern Ireland) and from there to the New World in the early eighteenth century. A great-great-grandfather had been John Fincastle, a Presbyterian minister who had brought his flock with him from Ireland, all the elders and deacons of his church and some other members of his congregation. They had sailed from Ulster in the ship *Martha and Mary,* and it had taken them one hundred and eighteen days to cross the Atlantic Ocean to Philadelphia. At first they had settled and practiced their religion in Pennsylvania, but after a few years the more restless spirits among them had pushed southward over the old Indian Road into Virginia. After many years in Virginia, there were still memories and reminders of the Indian past:

Lower down on Thunder Mountain you could still see signs of the Shawnee warpath. Indian trail, they called it; and Ralph McBride had followed it with some deer-hunters last fall. Over that trail the Shawnees had come for the massacre of Smiling Creek. Ralph had found arrowheads and part of a tomahawk down under the rocks in the deepest bottom of the creek. When the Indians went back they had taken Great-great-grandmother Tod away into captivity. A little girl she had been, ten years old. She had lived for seven long years a captive in a Shawnee village. When she was sixteen, they had married her to a young chief, and she had gone into his wigwam. Then peace with the red men had come soon afterwards, and when she was seventeen she was returned under the treaty, Father said, that ended Pontiac's War [1766]. After all she had endured, she lived to be over a hundred.

Ellen Glasgow's novel deals with the descendants of the early Fincastles and Tods. A tower of strength to the other members of her family is Grandmother Fincastle. Like other people her age she lives partly in the present and partly in the past. In the following excerpt, the grandmother thinks about some of the people and places she has known and heard about during her life.

---

Ellen Glasgow

# Only Yesterday

Her youth had suffered from hardships; she had spent her childhood in a log cabin, yet she had not been ashamed. When she was five years old her father was called to a mission on Wildcat Mountain, and from that time she had not seen a railway train until she was grown. Mr. Fincastle met her when he came to preach at the mission, and he had felt from the first minute, he told her afterwards, that this also was appointed. That was the Sabbath she was admitted to sealing ordinances.* But even before she had reached the years of discretion, her faith had been strong. When she was no bigger than a slip of a girl she had felt that she was ready to do or die, or even to be damned, if it would redound to the greater glory of God.

Though she knew that bricks are no more than straws in the sight of the Lord, she would always remember how wonderful the manse had appeared to her, as a bride, when she had first seen it on a spring morning. Everything had seemed to her to be provided; the grove of oaks to cast shade; the vegetable garden at the back of the house; the well so close to the kitchen porch; the springhouse at the bottom of the yard under the big willow; and the house inside, with the solid furniture, the rows of books that had always been there, and the shining pewter plates, so bright you could see your face in them, on the sideboard. She could imagine nothing more luxurious than eating in a dining room, with a cloth on the table, and

*admitted to sealing ordinances: admitted to full membership in the Church and, therefore, to the sacraments of Baptism and Communion.

having hot water to wash in. As a bride she used to say that she praised the Lord whenever she took up that big kettle from the trivet in front of the fire. . . .

How in the world, Grandmother still asked herself, had those early settlers been able to enjoy living without such simple comforts as featherbeds and kettles of hot water? In fear, too, whenever they had taken time to stop and think, of the savages. Yet they also had loved life. They had loved it the more because it was fugitive; they had loved it for the sake of the surprise, the danger, the brittleness of the moment. Her husband, she knew, had felt this, though what he had said sounded so different. Life will yield up its hidden sweetness, she had heard him preach from the pulpit, only when it is being sacrificed to something more precious than life.

They had believed this in the old days. Time and again, they had risen from the ruins of happiness. Yet they had gone on; they had rebuilt the ruins; they had scattered life more abundantly over the ashes. There was a near neighbor of her grandfather who had held his cabin twice when others fled to the stockade. For the sake of his crop, he had held his ground. All within the space of ten years, he had seen two wives and two families of children scalped and killed by the savages. He himself had once been left to die, and a second time he had escaped from an Indian village and made his way home through the wilderness. For the rest of his life he had worn a handkerchief tied over his head, and one Sunday morning, while the congregation sang the Doxology,* he had fallen down in a fit. In his later years he had married a third wife and had brought up a new family, after the manner of Job, to inherit the land. Though he had seen men burned at the stake, he had never lost his trust in Divine goodness.

*Doxology: a hymn of praise.

And nearer still, there was her own grandmother, Martha Tod. She had liked the young chief too well, people had whispered. He was a noble figure; he had many virtues; she had wept when they came to redeem her. One story ran that her Indian husband had come to the settlement in search of her, and that her two brothers had killed him in the woods, from ambush, and had hidden his body. This may have been true, and again it may not have been. The age was a wild one. Many of the men who had come to the wilderness to practice religion appeared to have forgotten its true nature. Whatever happened, Martha Tod's lips were sealed tight. No one, not even her mother, had ever won her confidence again, or heard her speak of her life with the Shawnees. But as long as she lived, after her marriage to an elder in the church, she had suffered from spells of listening, a sort of wildness, which would steal upon her in the fall of the year, especially in the blue haze of weather they called Indian summer. Then she would leap up at the hoot of an owl or the bark of a fox and disappear into the forest. When she returned from these flights, her husband would notice a strange stillness in her eyes, as if she were listening to silence. But gradually, as her children grew up, ten of them in all, fine, sturdy, professing Christians, her affliction became lighter. To the end of her days, even after her reason had tottered, she could still card, spin, weave, dye, or knit as well as the best of them. Grandmother had heard that when she was dying, her youth, with the old listening look, had flashed back into her face, and she had tried to turn toward the forest. But that was too much to credit. It couldn't have happened. Not when her mind was addled, not when she was well over a hundred. Grandmother remembered her well . . .

A closed memory unfolded as a fan in her thoughts. She saw the pale red loop of the road round the manse on a spring morning, the narrow valley, deep as a river, and the lofty Endless Mountains thronging beneath the April blue of the sky. It was more than fifty years ago, but it seemed only yesterday!

---

## YOU AND THE READING

In the early chapters of her novel, Ellen Glasgow gradually fills in much of the Fincastle family history. On the basis of the excerpts you have read, could you put together a brief "family chronicle" of a typical pioneer family? (How "typical" do you think the Fincastles were? Why?) Prepare a *report* that includes the highlights from the material you have read. Include the details that you considered most important.

---

### A Closer Look

(1) In many accounts of pioneer life, we get only short glimpses of the Indians into whose lands the early settlers were moving. What picture of the Indians can you piece together from this?

(2) In recent years, there has been much discussion of the role women play in modern society. What kind of women do we encounter in these excerpts? What role do they seem to have played in pioneer society? (How is their role like what you would expect? How is it different?)

---

### Your Turn

In a dramatic **monologue,** one single character speaks to the audience. What would you include in a brief script for dramatic monologues in which the following characters tell the audience their story: John Fincastle, Martha Tod, the young chief, Grandmother Fincastle? Your class may want to split up into groups to prepare the scripts, and to prepare the presentation of each monologue to the class.

---

Language/Composition Activity A4

LANGUAGE AND LIFE

# The Language of Worship

Religion played a large role in the lives of the early settlers. The following words all appear in the early pages of Ellen Glasgow's novel. Could you explain all or most of them?

ELDERS    DEACON    CATECHISM    SABBATH    CONGREGATION

COVENANT    KIRK    THEOLOGY

To the Presbyterians of Ellen Glasgow's novel, the following words had a special meaning, different from the most common everyday use of each word. What is the special meaning in each case?

VOCATION    ELECTION    REDEEM

- What was it like on the westward trail?

Soon, notice was formally circulated among the emigrants that a certain man, whose name I forget, professing to be an experienced traveler, and explorer of the Great Basin, would lead a company to California by a route far south of the one followed by emigrants thus far. . . .

So begins the diary of a traveler who survived to tell the story of how these people "conquered the desert." Sarah Royce, who wrote these lines, was part of the great westward trek of 1849. She joined thousands of others who were crossing the mountains and the "Great American Desert" in search of land or gold. They encountered legendary hardships: unmapped territory, hostile Indians, thirst, and exhaustion. Some perished in accidents along the way. Some lost their cattle and abandoned their wagons to escape with their bare lives. Some, like the ill-fated Donner Party, were surprised by winter and left stranded as deep snow blocked the mountain passes. In the following selection, a well-known modern writer retells the story of one party of travelers on the westward trail. He calls the story of their trek through Death Valley "one of the West's great sagas of man's will against the implacable elements." His writing is an example of the kind of documentary literature that attracts thousands of readers to stories of endurance and survival.

## Irving Stone

# Death Valley Earns Its Name

In October of 1849 there assembled at Provo on Utah Lake, some sixty miles south of Salt Lake, a number of traveling groups, families and young men on horseback, unknown to each other prior to this meeting, which would make up the Death Valley Party. The majority of the party had come south to Provo instead of north around Salt Lake to join the California Trail because they had heard the grisly details of the Donner Party. Judging that it was too late to risk the winter snows of the Sierra Nevada, they decided to take the longer but safer route into southern California, then north to the mines. Word had been spread that there would be a rendezvous at Provo for all wishing to travel the Old Spanish Trail.

In the party when it started for Los Angeles on October 9 there were eighty wagons, two hundred fifty people, and one thousand head of horses and cattle. For their guide they hired Captain Jefferson Hunt, a member of the Mormon Battalion who was being sent to California to buy cattle and seed for the community in Salt Lake. Hunt imposed Mormon military discipline on the train: it moved like an army, divided into seven divisions, each under its captain. The train named itself the Sand Walking Company.

No crueler nor more accurate title could be divined.

Captain Hunt made an early error: he took a wrong turning. Though he was soon back on the main trail this undermined confidence in him, and when a Captain Smith with a party of nine Mormons heading for the California mines rode up with a map or waybill which claimed that there was a cutoff, what James Reed of the Donner Party had called "a nigher way," over Walker's Pass from which they could descend into the Tulare Valley close to the mines, and save themselves four hundred wearisome miles, the Sand Walking Company went into a Committee of the Whole around a campfire to debate the desirability of taking Smith's cutoff. When Captain Hunt was asked his opinion, he said he doubted if any white man had ever traveled it; that young men alone might make it but families with wagons would have serious trouble:

"If you all wish to go and follow Smith I will go also. But if even one wagon decides to go the original route, I shall feel bound by my promise to go with that lone wagon."

The Reverend John W. Brier, described in the journal of one of the listeners as a "man who always liked to give his opinion on every subject," declared forcibly for the cutoff, despite the fact he was traveling with a wife and three young sons. So did a number of others.

The next morning, as the wagons and men came to the fork in the road, Smith and the Reverend Mr. Brier prevailed, even as Lansford Hastings and James Reed had helped make the decision for the Donners over the advice of experienced mountain men. Only seven wagons continued on the known trail with Captain Hunt. A hundred wagons seceded,

including the Briers, Bennetts, and Arcanes, the Wade and Dale families, all of whom had children, and the entire Jayhawker* party of single men.

For two days Smith's party crossed green valleys with plenty of water. But that was as far as the anonymous mapmaker had traveled. Caught in an impassable canyon, with evidence of worse terrain ahead, seventy-two wagons turned back to the Old Spanish Trail. Though they never caught up with Hunt, they followed him into southern California, and arrived in Los Angeles before the seceders had even reached the heart of their inferno.

Smith had also thought better of his decision; he cut back with his mounted

*Jayhawker: antislavery guerrillas in Kansas and Missouri before and during the Civil War.

Mormons to the Old Spanish Trail and safety without informing the remaining eighty-five emigrants that he had changed his mind. Meeting about their campfire at Misery Mountain, guideless, they too seemed to have little choice but to turn back, when scouts rode into the camp with the message that they had seen a good pass which would carry them into California.

They decided to plunge ahead, but not as a unified train with a leader; instead they split into three separate groups. The Jayhawkers, young, unencumbered, started out first and fast; the Reverend Mr. Brier's party came next with his three children and two young men who were part of their mess; third, and bringing up the rear, the Bennett, Arcane, and Wade families, the two Earhart brothers with two sons, several unattached men, and twenty-one-year-old William Manly, who was to be their guide. It was Manly's first trip west.

Juliet Brier was born in Bennington, Vermont, September 26, 1813, and educated at a seminary. She was a wisp of a woman, nervous by nature, the mother of three sons, aged eight, seven, and four. The first white woman to enter Death Valley, the sight that greeted her eyes from the ridge of the eastern range was one to strike terror into the stoutest heart: utter, hopeless, unalleviated desolation: eight to fourteen miles wide, one hundred thirty miles long, with the lower-lying, aptly named Funeral Range in the center. There was nothing living as far as the eye could sweep, only windblown and rippled Sahara wastes of sunbaked sand and crusted salt-mud flats, with mountains surrounding on all sides and bearing not a tree, bush, or blade of grass; what H. H. Bancroft, historian of the West, calls:

"The region of mirage, accursed to all living things, its atmosphere destructive even to the passing bird."

When the Reverend Mr. Brier went ahead looking for water, says Mrs. Brier, "I was left with our three little boys to help bring up the cattle. Poor little Kirke gave out and I carried him on my back, barely seeing where I was going."

She stumbled on, hour after hour, in the hot choking dust, the cattle bellowing for water. When darkness fell she lost the two men of the group and had to get on her knees to search out the ox tracks in the starlight. Not until three in the morning did she reach camp, where the men had found hot and cold springs.

It was Christmas morning. At the springs, which they named Furnace Creek, one of the men asked, "Don't you think you and the children better remain here?"

"I have never kept the company waiting," replied Mrs. Brier. "Neither have my children. *Every step I take will be towards California.*"

The next morning when they reached the Jayhawker camp the Briers found the young men burning their wagons in order to travel faster: for it needed only one surveying look about them to know that they all faced imminent death.

The Briers also abandoned their wagons, packing their rapidly vanishing foodstuffs on the failing oxen. The Reverend Mr. Brier asked the Jayhawkers for permission to travel with them; the Jayhawkers did not want to be encumbered by a woman and small children, and objected. Then they looked at Mrs. Brier, all skin and bones, and relented. William Manly, leading the Bennett Party, also arrived at the springs. He reports:

"She was the one who put the packs on the oxen in the morning. She it was who took them off at night, built the fires, cooked the food, helped the children, and did all sorts of work when the father of the family was too tired, which was almost all of the time."

The combined train struggled through mile after mile of salt marsh, sinking in sand to their shoe tops. One of the Brier boys remembers:

"Twenty miles across naked dunes, the wind driving the sand like shot into the faces and eyes."

Their tongues grew swollen, their lips cracked, the oxen lay down in the sand never to rise again. That night the men climbed up the rock-strewn mountain to the snow line, bringing back snow in their shirts, some eating it hard, others melting it for the cattle.

They went for the next forty-eight hours without water, unable to eat the meat of their slaughtered oxen because they could get nothing down their parched throats. A Dr. Carr suggested that they return to Furnace Creek where there was water; he broke down and cried when Mrs. Brier repeated, "Every step we take will be towards California."

By New Year's Day they camped at the head of the Panamint Valley, totally lost. The stronger of the Jayhawkers pushed ahead, leaving in Mrs. Brier's care the older and weaker men.

The first to die of thirst was the fifty-year-old Reverend Mr. Fish, who was traveling to California in hopes of finding the money to pay off his church's debt in Indiana.

On January 6 the two single men who had been in the Brier mess, and who had the only flour in the party, decided they would strike out alone in the hopes of saving themselves. They baked up all their dough except for a small piece they gave to Mrs. Brier, then shook hands good-bye. Mrs. Brier baked her dough into twenty-two crackers, all they would have for twenty-two days of nightmare and terror.

Next to die was middle-aged William Isham, who crawled four miles on his hands and knees searching for water, then dropped on his face.

"Give up?" cried Juliet Brier. "Oh! I knew what that meant—a shallow grave in the sand."

Their tongues became black and hung out of their mouths. Ahead there was the cruel mirage of the desert: water, an oasis, trees, greenery. When water came it was a muddy pool at what is now Borax Lake; the few remaining cattle stamped into it first, then the humans scooped up the mud-laden water, forcing it down their parched throats.

The next waterless stretch lasted nearly five days. In camp the men, with burnt faces and skeletal frames, lay down and waited for death. Mrs. Brier went behind a rock, prayed to God for strength, then gave them a combined sermon and tongue-lashing that shocked them back onto their feet. At that moment the Reverend Mr. Richards came running into camp, crying:

"Water! Water! I have found water!"

Four miles away he had come upon a group of Indians, had made friendly signs, then gestures of thirst. The Indians guided him to a brook at the base of the mountains, hidden by shrubs, which ran clear and cold before disappearing into the sands of the desert.

When the party finally struggled to the top of the range and looked back at the valley behind them, they named it Death Valley. But the Mojave Desert into which they descended in the middle of January 1850 was little better: a desert of alkali, with no known trails or springs. Emaciated from dysentery and exhaustion, they faced days of heat, dust, thirst, rocks that cut their feet. One man said, "I will just take a little nap," and never woke up. Another said, "I have a presentiment I shall never reach California," fell off his pony and died. At a spring, one drank too copiously; he was the seventh to perish.

The Reverend Mr. Brier, who had been hobbling along with the aid of crutches, lay down in camp, bade his wife farewell, and closed his eyes. Juliet Brier pleaded with her husband to hold on, gathered some acorns, ground and cooked them and fed them to him from a spoon. He survived.

The Bennett-Manly Party had equally bad luck in trying a southerly trail: they got trapped in the hopeless waste bordered by a black range of mountains through which there could be no conceivable pass. Finding a spring at Tule, near the southern end of the valley, they decided not to dissipate their failing strength, but to remain encamped. Bennett asked young Manly and Rogers, a burly butcher, if they would push on alone, find civilization, and bring back relief. There was neither map nor food the men could take with them, nor knowledge of what lay ahead except days of purgatory.

But they went . . . passing the dead bodies of Jayhawkers who had given out. Their trek, as told by Manly in *Death Valley in '49*, is one of the West's great sagas of man's will against the implacable elements:

"Black and desolate ranges and buttes to the south, great dry plains, salt lakes and slippery alkali water to which we walked, only to turn away again in bitter disappointment, little sheets of ice that saved our lives, hawk and crow diet, lameness . . . "

They got out in fourteen days, sustaining life by sucking on rocks or single blades of grass, breaking trail over trailless mountains, deserts, and valleys until, more dead than alive, they cleared one more range and saw below them the green cattle ranch of San Francisquito.

Settling in for a long wait, the Bennetts took off their wagon covers to make protecting tents for themselves and for the cattle against the heat and sandstorms, rationed their food, watched it vanish. Mrs. Arcane, knowing she must abandon her clothing but not wanting it to be too good for the Indians who would inherit it, dressed herself in her finest garments every day. Captain Richard Culverwell, who had gone exploring, died trying to get back to camp. After three weeks the men agreed:

"If those boys ever get out of this hole they are fools if they ever come back to help anybody."

Manly and Rogers waited only four days to regain their strength, then borrowed horses to load with oranges and other foodstuffs, and spent the next week retracing their steps, exploring for better passes and water holes. When they got their first view of the camp not a soul was in sight; they concluded they had made the journey for nothing.

Manly fired a shot. From under a wagon a man emerged. He threw his arms high over his head and shouted:

"The boys have come! The boys have come!"

They were saved.

The Brier party also emerged, as images of death, onto the opulent hospitality of the Californios who owned San Francisquito ranch. Mrs. Brier came down out of the San Gabriel Mountains, leading her three sons, in rags, the last of the moccasins she had made of the hides of dead oxen worn through; seventy pounds of bone, grit, and indestructibility.

Thirteen men had lost their lives in the Sand Walking Company. The women were tougher; they endured. Juliet Brier's inner strength saved not only her own family but several of the Jayhawkers as well.

---

## YOU AND THE STORY

The **sagas** of old often centered on a great leader whose reputation was known far and wide. This saga of struggle and survival on the Western trail deals with the heroism of ordinary people. Strong individuals come to stand out as hardships put people to the test. As the story proceeds, Juliet Brier stands out as someone whose leadership inspired and saved others. Describe her and her role in this account. Who was she? What did she do? How did she act? What did she accomplish?

### A Closer Look

(1) During the westward trek, much depended on the people serving as guides and leaders. Describe Captain Hunt and his role in the events of the story.

(2) In this account, people alone or in a group make fateful decisions. They show good judgment or bad. Discuss several examples.

(3) When hardship puts people to the test, we are sometimes disappointed in them. At other times, we are impressed. How did the people traveling with Juliet Brier measure up? Discuss examples of travelers proving selfish or dedicated, courageous or afraid, and the like.

(4) How much of what happened to these people depended on accident? Discuss examples of good or bad luck that play a role in this account.

### Your Turn

Does your school library or public library have firsthand accounts of the westward trek or of pioneer life, such as Sarah Royce's *A Frontier Lady*? Read a chapter or a section from an account by an eyewitness. Report on the experiences and the spirit of the people.

WORDS IN CONTEXT

# Conquering the Desert

Which of the italicized words in the following phrases make sense to you in the context of the story? Which do you have to check in a dictionary? From each set of three choices, select the one that is closest to the meaning of the italicized word.

1. the *grisly* details of the Donner Party
   a. petty     b. horrible     c. encouraging

2. there would be a *rendezvous* at Provo
   a. meeting     b. celebration     c. fair

3. no more accurate title could be *divined*
   a. reported     b. imagined
   c. forgotten

4. a hundred wagons *seceded*
   a. turned back     b. joined     c. split off

5. the *anonymous* mapmaker
   a. skillful     b. helpful     c. unknown

6. caught in an *impassable* canyon
   a. scenic     b. without a way through
   c. sloping

7. worse *terrain* ahead
   a. ground     b. weather
   c. exhaustion

8. the heart of their *inferno*
   a. religion     b. hell     c. effort

9. young, *unencumbered* single men
   a. not burdened     b. not experienced
   c. not strong

10. educated at a *seminary*
    a. orphanage     b. girls' school
    c. school for Indians

11. hopeless, *unalleviated* desolation
    a. unexpected     b. unknown
    c. unlightened

12. they all faced *imminent* death
    a. unexpected     b. painful
    c. coming very soon

13. the cruel *mirage* of the desert
    a. trick picture     b. tracks
    c. pitfall

14. *emaciated* from dysentery
    a. angry     b. spared     c. bone-thin

15. have a *presentiment*
    a. vague fear     b. strong conviction
    c. mistaken notion

16. drank too *copiously*
    a. often     b. little     c. much

17. no *conceivable* pass
    a. avoidable     b. scalable
    c. imaginable

18. *dissipate* their strength
    a. waste     b. save     c. build up

19. the *implacable* elements
    a. hospitable     b. wild     c. merciless

20. the *opulent* hospitality of the Californios
    a. grudging     b. very rich     c. too late

● Willa Cather (1873–1947) loved the land and the people of the Midwest where she grew up. In her youth in the grasslands of Nebraska, the plows of European immigrants from countries like Sweden, Norway, and what is now Czechoslovakia were turning the wild plains into the wheat country of today. In books like *O Pioneers!* (1913) and *My Ántonia* (1918), she told the story of people who wanted life and happiness and went after them in spite of the obstacles put in their path by the rough farm life in a raw, unmade new world. In the following selection from *My Ántonia,* she takes us among the last pioneers—immigrants who farmed the uncharted plains of the Midwest. They often spoke no English, and they had to make their way in an environment where all the familiar landmarks were missing. What would it have been like to be one of them? If you could, would you be willing to turn back the clock?

Willa Cather

# The New Country

On Sunday morning Otto Fuchs was to drive us over to make the acquaintance of our new Bohemian neighbors. We were taking them some provisions, as they had come to live on a wild place where there was no garden or chicken house, and very little broken land. Fuchs brought up a sack of potatoes and a piece of cured pork from the cellar, and grandmother packed some loaves of Saturday's bread, a jar of butter, and several pumpkin pies in the straw of the wagon box. We clambered up to the front seat and jolted off past the little pond and along the road that climbed to the big cornfield.

I could hardly wait to see what lay beyond that cornfield; but there was only red grass like ours, and nothing else, though from the high wagon seat one could look off a long way. The road ran about like a wild thing, avoiding the deep draws, crossing them where they were wide and shallow. And all along the road, wherever it looped or ran, the sunflowers grew; some of them were as big as little trees, with great rough leaves and many branches which bore dozens of blossoms. They made a gold ribbon across the prairie. Occasionally one of the horses would tear off with his teeth a plant full of blossoms and walk along munching it, the flowers nodding in time to his bites as he ate down toward them.

The Bohemian family, grandmother told me as we drove along, had bought the homestead of a fellow countryman, Peter Krajiek, and had paid him more than it was worth. Their agreement with him was made before they left the old country, through a cousin of his, who was also a relative of Mrs. Shimerda. The Shimerdas were the first Bohemian family to come to this part of the county. Krajiek was their only interpreter, and could tell them anything he chose. They could not speak enough English to ask for advice, or even to make their most pressing wants known. One son, Fuchs said, was well-grown, and strong enough to work the land; but the father was old and frail and knew nothing about farming. He was a weaver by trade and had been a skilled workman on tapestries and upholstery materials. He had brought his fiddle with him, which wouldn't be of much use here, though he used to pick up money by it at home.

"If they're nice people, I hate to think of them spending the winter in that cave of Krajiek's," said grandmother. "It's no better than a badger hole; no proper dugout at all. And I hear he's made them pay twenty dollars for his old cookstove that ain't worth ten."

"Yes'm," said Otto; "and he's sold them his oxen and his two bony old horses for the price of good work teams. I'd have interfered about the horses—the old man can understand some German—if I'd have thought it would do any good. But Bohemians has a natural distrust of Austrians."

Grandmother looked interested. "Now, why is that, Otto?"

Fuchs wrinkled his brow and nose. "Well, ma'm, it's politics. It would take me a long while to explain."

The land was growing rougher. I was told that we were approaching Squaw Creek, which cut up the west half of the Shimerdas' place and made the land of little value for farming. Soon we could see the broken, grassy clay cliffs which indicated the windings of the stream, and the glittering tops of the cottonwoods and ash trees that grew down in the ravine. Some of the cottonwoods had already turned, and the yellow leaves and shining white bark made them look like the gold and silver trees in fairy tales.

As we approached the Shimerdas' dwelling, I could still see nothing but rough red hillocks, and draws with shelving banks and long roots hanging out where the earth had crumbled away. Presently, against one of those banks, I saw a sort of shed, thatched with the same wine-colored grass that grew everywhere. Near it tilted a shattered windmill frame that had no wheel. We drove up to this skeleton to tie our horses, and then I saw a door and window sunk deep in the draw-bank. The door stood open, and a woman and a girl of fourteen ran out and looked up at us hopefully. A little girl trailed along behind them. The woman had on her head the same embroidered shawl with silk fringes that she wore when she had alighted from the train at Black Hawk. She was not old, but she was certainly not young. Her face was alert and lively, with a sharp chin and shrewd little eyes. She shook grandmother's hand energetically.

"Very glad, very glad!" she ejaculated. Immediately she pointed to the bank out of which she had emerged and said, "House no good, house no good!"

Grandmother nodded consolingly. "You'll get fixed up comfortable after while, Mrs. Shimerda; make good house."

My grandmother always spoke in a very loud tone to foreigners, as if they were deaf. She made Mrs. Shimerda understand the friendly intention of our visit, and the Bohemian woman handled the loaves of bread and even smelled them, and examined the pies with lively curiosity, exclaiming, "Much good, much thank!"—and again she wrung grandmother's hand.

The oldest son, Ambrož—they called it Ambrosch—came out of the cave and stood beside his mother. He was nineteen years old, short and broad-backed, with a close-cropped, flat head, and a wide, flat face. His hazel eyes were little and shrewd, like his mother's, but more sly and suspicious; they fairly snapped at the food. The family had been living on corncakes and sorghum molasses for three days.

The little girl was quite pretty, but Án-tonia—they accented the name thus, strongly, when they spoke to her—was still prettier. I remembered what the conductor had said about her eyes. They were big and warm and full of light, like the sun shining on brown pools in the wood. Her skin was brown, too, and in her cheeks she had a glow of rich, dark color. Her brown hair was curly and wild-looking. The little sister, whom they called Yulka (Julka), was fair, and seemed mild and obedient. While I stood awkwardly confronting the two girls, Krajiek came up from the barn to see what was going on. With him was another Shimerda son. Even from a distance one could see that there was something strange about this boy. As he approached us, he began to make uncouth noises and held up his hands to show us his fingers, which were webbed to the first knuckle, like a duck's foot. When he saw me draw back, he began to crow delightedly, "Hoo, hoo-hoo, hoo-hoo!" like a rooster. His mother scowled and then she said sternly, "Marek!" then spoke rapidly to Krajiek in Bohemian.

"She wants me to tell you he won't hurt nobody, Mrs. Burden. He was born like that. The others are smart. Ambrosch, he make good farmer." Then he slapped Ambrosch on the back, and the boy smiled knowingly.

At that moment the father came out of the hole in the bank. He wore no hat, and his thick, iron-gray hair was brushed straight back from his forehead. It was so long that it bushed out behind his ears, and made him look like the old portraits I remembered in Virginia. He was tall and slender, and his thin shoulders stooped.

He looked at us understandingly, then took grandmother's hand and bent over it. I noticed how white and well-shaped his own hands were. They looked calm, somehow, and skilled. His eyes were melancholy, and were set back deep under his brow. His face was ruggedly formed, but it looked like ashes—like something from which all the warmth and light had died out. Everything about this old man was in keeping with his dignified manner. He was neatly dressed. Under his coat he wore a knitted gray vest, and, instead of a collar, a silk scarf of a dark bronze-green, carefully crossed and held together by a red coral pin. While Krajiek was translating for Mr. Shimerda, Ántonia came up to me and held out her hand coaxingly. In a moment we were running up the steep drawside together, Yulka trotting along after us.

When we reached the level and could see the gold treetops, I pointed toward them, and Ántonia laughed and squeezed my hand as if to tell me how glad she was I had come. We raced off toward Squaw Creek and did not stop until the ground itself stopped—fell away before us so abruptly that the next step would have been out into the treetops. We stood panting on the edge of the ravine, looking down at the trees and bushes that grew below us. The wind was so strong that I had to hold my hat on, and the girls' skirts were blown out before them. Ántonia seemed to like it; she held her little sister by the hand and chattered away in that language which seemed to me spoken so much more rapidly than mine. She looked at me, her eyes fairly blazing with things she could not say.

"Name? What name?" she asked, touching me on the shoulder. I told her my name, and she repeated it after me and made Yulka say it. She pointed into the gold cottonwood tree behind whose top we stood and said again, "What name?"

We sat down and made a nest in the long red grass. Yulka curled up like a baby rabbit and played with a grasshopper. Ántonia pointed up to the sky and questioned me with her glance. I gave her the word, but she was not satisfied and pointed to my eyes. I told her, and she repeated the word, making it sound like "ice." She pointed up to the sky, then to my eyes, then back to the sky, with movements so quick and impulsive that she distracted me, and I had no idea what she wanted. She got up on her knees and wrung her hands. She pointed to her own eyes and shook her head, then to mine and to the sky, nodding violently.

"Oh," I exclaimed, "blue; blue sky."

She clapped her hands and murmured, "Blue sky, blue eyes," as if it amused her. While we snuggled down there out of the wind, she learned a score of words. She was quick, and very eager. We were so deep in the grass that we could see nothing but the blue sky over us and the gold tree in front of us. It was wonderfully pleasant. After Ántonia had said the new words over and over, she wanted to give me a little chased silver ring she wore on her middle finger. When she coaxed and insisted, I repulsed her quite sternly. I didn't want her ring, and I felt there was something reckless and extravagant about her wishing to give it away to a boy she had never seen before. No wonder Krajiek got the better of these people, if this was how they behaved.

While we were disputing about the ring, I heard a mournful voice calling, "Ántonia, Án-tonia!" She sprang up like a hare. *"Tatinek! Tatinek!"* she shouted, and we ran to meet the old man who was coming toward us. Ántonia reached him first, took his hand and kissed it. When I came up, he touched my shoulder and looked searchingly down into my face for several seconds. I became somewhat embarrassed, for I was used to being taken for granted by my elders.

We went with Mr. Shimerda back to the dugout, where grandmother was waiting for me. Before I got into the wagon, he took a book out of his pocket, opened it, and showed me a page with two alphabets, one English and the other Bohemian. He then placed this book in my grandmother's hands, looked entreatingly at her, and said, with an earnestness which I shall never forget, "Te-e-ach, te-e-ach my Ántonia!"

On the afternoon of that same Sunday I took my first long ride on my pony, under Otto's direction. After that, Dude and I went twice a week to the post office, six miles east of us, and I saved the men a good deal of time by riding on errands to our neighbors. When we had to borrow anything, or to send about word that there would be preaching at the sod schoolhouse, I was always the messenger. Formerly Fuchs attended to such things after working hours.

All the years that have passed have not dimmed my memory of that first glorious autumn. The new country lay open before me: there were no fences in those days, and I could choose my own way over the grass uplands, trusting the pony to get me home again. Sometimes I followed the sunflower-bordered roads. Fuchs told me that the sunflowers were introduced into that country by the Mormons; that at the time of the persecution, when they left Missouri and struck out into the wilderness to find a place where they could worship God in their own way, the members of the first exploring party, crossing the plains to Utah, scattered sunflower seed as they went. The next summer, when the long trains of wagons came through with all the women and children, they had the sunflower trail to follow. I believe botanists do not confirm this story, but insist that the sunflower was

native to those plains. Nevertheless, that legend has stuck in my mind, and sunflower-bordered roads always seem to me the roads to freedom.

I used to love to drift along the pale-yellow cornfields, looking for the damp spots one sometimes found at their edges, where the smartweed soon turned a rich copper color and the narrow brown leaves hung curled like cocoons about the swollen joints of the stem. Sometimes I went south to visit our German neighbors and to admire their catalpa grove, or to see the big elm tree that grew up out of a deep crack in the earth and had a hawk's nest in its branches. Trees were so rare in that country, and they had to make such a hard fight to grow, that we used to feel anxious about them, and visit them as if they were persons. It must have been the scarcity of detail in that tawny landscape that made detail so precious.

Sometimes I rode north to prairie-dog town to watch the brown earth owls fly home in the late afternoon and go down to their nests underground with the dogs. Ántonia Shimerda liked to go with me, and we used to wonder a great deal about these birds of subterranean habit. We had to be on our guard there, for rattlesnakes were always lurking about. They came to pick up an easy living among the dogs and owls, which were quite defenseless against them; took possession of their comfortable houses and ate the eggs and puppies. We felt sorry for the owls. It was always mournful to see them come flying home at sunset and disappear under the earth. But, after all, we felt, winged things who would live like that must be rather degraded creatures. The dog town was a long way from any pond or creek. Otto Fuchs said he had seen populous dog towns in the desert where there was no surface water for fifty miles; he insisted that some of the holes must go down to water—nearly two hundred feet, hereabouts. Ántonia said she didn't believe it; that the dogs probably lapped up the dew in the early morning, like the rabbits.

Ántonia had opinions about everything, and she was soon able to make them known. Almost every day she came running across the prairie to have her reading lesson with me. Mrs. Shimerda grumbled, but realized it was important that one member of the family should learn English. When the lesson was over, we used to go up to the watermelon patch behind the garden. I split the melons with an old cornknife, and we lifted out the hearts and ate them with the juice trickling through our fingers. The white Christmas melons we did not touch, but we watched them with curiosity. They were to be picked late, when the hard frosts had set in, and put away for winter use. After weeks on the ocean, the Shimerdas were famished for fruit. The two girls would wander for miles along the edge of the cornfields, hunting for ground-cherries.

Ántonia loved to help grandmother in the kitchen and to learn about cooking and housekeeping. She would stand beside her, watching her every movement. We were willing to believe that Mrs. Shimerda was a good housewife in her own country, but she managed poorly under new conditions: the conditions were bad enough, certainly!

I remember how horrified we were at the sour, ashy-gray bread she gave her family to eat. She mixed her dough, we discovered, in an old tin peck-measure that Krajiek had used about the barn. When she took the paste out to bake it, she left smears of dough sticking to the sides of the measure, put the measure on the shelf behind the stove, and let this residue ferment. The next time she made bread, she scraped this sour stuff down into the fresh dough to serve as yeast.

In those first months the Shimerdas never went to town. Krajiek encouraged them in the belief that in Black Hawk they would somehow be mysteriously separated from their money. They hated Krajiek, but they clung to him because he was the only human being with whom they could talk or from whom they could get information. He slept with the old man and the two boys in the dugout barn, along with the oxen. They kept him in their hole and fed him for the same reason that the prairie dogs and the brown owls house the rattlesnakes—because they did not know how to rid themselves of him.

We knew that things were hard for our Bohemian neighbors, but the two girls were lighthearted and never complained. They were always ready to forget their troubles at home and to run away with me over the prairie, scaring rabbits or starting up flocks of quail.

I remember Ántonia's excitement when she came into our kitchen one afternoon and announced: "My papa find friends up north, with Russian mans. Last night he take me for see, and I can understand very much talk. Nice mans, Mrs. Burden. One is fat and all the time laugh. Everybody laugh. The first time I see my papa laugh in this kawn-tree. Oh, very nice!"

I asked her if she meant the two Russians who lived up by the big dog town. I had often been tempted to go to see them when I was riding in that direction, but one of them was a wild-looking fellow and I was a little afraid of him. Russia seemed to me more remote than any other country—farther away than China, almost as far as the North Pole. Of all the strange, uprooted people among the first settlers, those two men were the strangest and the most aloof. Their last names were unpronounceable, so they were called Pavel and Peter. They went about making signs to people, and until the Shimerdas came they had no friends. Krajiek could understand them a little, but he had cheated them in a trade, so they avoided him. Pavel, the tall one, was said to be an anarchist; since he had no means of imparting his opinions, probably his wild gesticulations and his generally excited and rebellious manner gave rise to this supposition. He must once have been a very strong man, but now his great frame, with big, knotty joints, had a wasted look, and the skin was drawn tight over his high cheekbones. His breathing was hoarse, and he always had a cough.

Peter, his companion, was a very different sort of fellow: short, bow-legged, and as fat as butter. He always seemed pleased when he met people on the road, smiled and took off his cap to everyone, men as well as women. At a distance, on his wagon, he looked like an old man; his hair and beard were of such a pale flaxen color that they seemed white in the sun. They were as thick and curly as carded wool. His rosy face, with its snub nose, set in this fleece, was like a melon among its leaves. He was usually called "Curly Peter," or "Rooshian Peter."

The two Russians made good farmhands, and in summer they worked out together. I had heard our neighbors laughing when they told how Peter always had to go home at night to milk his cow. Most bachelor homesteaders just used canned milk, to save trouble. Sometimes Peter came to church at the sod schoolhouse. It was there I first saw him, sitting on a low bench by the door, his plush cap in his hands, his bare feet tucked apologetically under the seat.

After Mr. Shimerda discovered the Russians, he went to see them almost every evening, and sometimes took Ántonia with him. She said they came from a part of Russia where the language was not very different from Bohemian, and if I wanted to go to their place, she could talk to them for me. One afternoon, before the heavy frosts began, we rode up there together on my pony.

The Russians had a neat log house built on a grassy slope, with a windlass well beside the door. As we rode up the draw, we skirted a big melon patch, and a garden where squashes and yellow cucumbers lay about on the sod. We found Peter out behind his kitchen, bending over a washtub. He was working so hard that he did not hear us coming. His whole body moved up and down as he rubbed, and he was a funny sight from the rear, with his shaggy head and bandy legs. When he straightened himself up to greet us, drops of perspiration were rolling from his thick nose down onto his curly beard. Peter dried his hands and seemed glad to leave his washing. He took us down to see his chickens, and his cow that was grazing on the hillside. He told Ántonia that in his country only rich people had cows, but here any man could have one who would take care of her. The milk was good for Pavel, who was often sick, and he could make butter by beating sour cream with a wooden spoon. Peter was very fond of his cow. He patted her flanks and talked to her in Russian while he pulled up her lariat pin and set it in a new place.

After he had shown us his garden, Peter trundled a load of watermelons up the hill in his wheelbarrow. Pavel was not at home. He was off somewhere helping to dig a well. The house I thought very comfortable for two men who were "batching." Besides the kitchen, there was a living room, with a wide double bed built against the wall, properly made up with blue gingham sheets and pillows. There was a little storeroom, too, with a window, where they kept guns and saddles and tools, and old coats and boots. That day the floor was covered with garden things, drying for winter; corn and beans and fat yellow cucumbers. There were no screens or window blinds in the house, and all the doors and windows stood wide open, letting in flies and sunshine alike.

Peter put the melons in a row on the oilcloth-covered table and stood over them, brandishing a butcher knife. Before the blade got fairly into them, they split of their own ripeness, with a delicious sound. He gave us knives, but no plates, and the top of the table was soon swimming with juice and seeds. I had never seen anyone eat so many melons as Peter ate. He assured us that they were good for one—better than medicine; in his country people lived on them at this time of year. He was very hospitable and jolly. Once, while he was looking at Ántonia, he sighed and told us that if he had stayed at home in Russia perhaps by this time he would have had a pretty daughter of his own to cook and keep house for him. He said he had left his country because of a "great trouble."

When we got up to go, Peter looked about in perplexity for something that would entertain us. He ran into the storeroom and brought out a gaudily painted harmonica, sat down on a bench, and spreading his fat legs apart began to play like a whole band. The tunes were either very lively or very doleful.

Before we left, Peter put ripe cucumbers into a sack for Mrs. Shimerda and gave us a lardpail full of milk to cook them in. I had never heard of cooking cucumbers, but Ántonia assured me they were very good. We had to walk the pony all the way home to keep from spilling the milk.

One afternoon we were having our reading lesson on the warm, grassy bank where the badger lived. It was a day of amber sunlight, but there was a shiver of coming winter in the air. I had seen ice on the little horsepond that morning, and as we went through the garden we found the tall asparagus, with its red berries, lying on the ground, a mass of slimy green.

Tony was barefooted, and she shivered in her cotton dress and was comfortable only when we were tucked down on the baked earth, in the full blaze of the sun. She could talk to me about almost anything by this time. That afternoon she was telling me how highly esteemed our friend the badger was in her part of the world, and how men kept a special kind of dog, with very short legs, to hunt him. Those dogs, she said, went down into the hole after the badger and killed him there in a terrific struggle underground; you could hear the barks and yelps outside. Then the dog dragged himself back, covered with bites and scratches, to be rewarded and petted by his master. She knew a dog who had a star on his collar for every badger he had killed.

The rabbits were unusually spry that afternoon. They kept starting up all about us, and dashing off down the draw as if they were playing a game of some kind. But the little buzzing things that lived in the grass were all dead—all but one. While we were lying there against the warm bank, a little insect of the palest, frailest green hopped painfully out of the buffalo grass and tried to leap into a bunch of bluestem. He missed it, fell back, and sat with his head sunk between his long legs, his antennae quivering, as if he were waiting for something to come and finish him. Tony made a warm nest for him in her hands; talked to him gaily and indulgently in Bohemian. Presently he began to sing for us—a thin, rusty little chirp. She held him close to her ear and laughed, but a moment afterward I saw there were tears in her eyes. She told me that in her village at home there was an old beggar woman who went about selling herbs and roots she had dug up in the forest. If you took her in and gave her a warm place by the fire, she sang old songs to the children in a cracked voice, like this. Old Hata, she was called, and the children loved to see her coming and saved their cakes and sweets for her.

When the bank on the other side of the draw began to throw a narrow shelf of shadow, we knew we ought to be starting homeward; the chill came on quickly when the sun got low, and Ántonia's dress was thin. What were we to do with the frail little creature we had lured back to life by false pretences? I offered my pockets, but Tony shook her head and carefully put the green insect in her hair, tying her big handkerchief down loosely over her curls. I said I would walk with her until we could see Squaw Creek, and then turn and run home. We drifted along lazily, very happy, through the magical light of the late afternoon.

All those fall afternoons were the same, but I never got used to them. As far as we could see, the miles of copper-red grass were drenched in sunlight that was stronger and fiercer than at any other time of the day. The blond cornfields were red gold, the haystacks turned rosy and threw long shadows. The whole prairie was like the bush that burned with fire and was not consumed. That hour always had the exultation of victory, of triumphant ending, like a hero's death—heroes who died young and gloriously. It was a sudden transfiguration, a lifting-up of day.

How many an afternoon Ántonia and I have trailed along the prairie under that magnificence! And always two long black shadows flitted before us or followed after, dark spots on the ruddy grass.

We had been silent a long time, and the edge of the sun sank nearer and nearer the prairie floor, when we saw a figure moving on the edge of the upland, a gun over his shoulder. He was walking slowly, dragging his feet along as if he had no purpose. We broke into a run to overtake him.

"My papa sick all the time," Tony panted as we flew. "He not look good, Jim."

As we neared Mr. Shimerda she shouted, and he lifted his head and peered about. Tony ran up to him, caught his hand and pressed it against her cheek. She was the only one of his family who could rouse the old man from the torpor in which he seemed to live. He took the bag from his belt and showed us three rabbits he had shot, looked at Ántonia with a wintry flicker of a smile and began to tell her something. She turned to me.

"My *tatinek* make me little hat with the skins, little hat for win-ter!" she exclaimed joyfully. "Meat for eat, skin for hat"—she told off these benefits on her fingers.

Her father put his hand on her hair, but she caught his wrist and lifted it carefully away, talking to him rapidly. I heard the name of old Hata. He untied the handkerchief, separated her hair with his fingers, and stood looking down at the green insect. When it began to chirp faintly, he listened as if it were a beautiful sound.

I picked up the gun he had dropped; a queer piece from the old country, short and heavy, with a stag's head on the cock. When he saw me examining it, he turned to me with his faraway look that always made me feel as if I were down at the bottom of a well. He spoke kindly and gravely, and Ántonia translated:

"My *tatinek* say when you are big boy, he give you his gun. Very fine, from Bohemia. It was belong to a great man, very rich, like what you not got here; many fields, many forests, many big house. My papa play for his wedding, and he give my papa fine gun, and my papa give you."

I was glad that this project was one of futurity. There never were such people as the Shimerdas for wanting to give away everything they had. Even the mother was always offering me things, though I knew she expected substantial presents in return. We stood there in friendly silence, while the feeble minstrel sheltered in Ántonia's hair went on with its scratchy chirp. The old man's smile, as he listened, was so full of sadness, of pity for things, that I never afterward forgot it. As the sun sank there came a sudden coolness and the strong smell of earth and drying grass. Ántonia and her father went off hand in hand, and I buttoned up my jacket and raced my shadow home.

---

## YOU AND THE READING

(1) Willa Cather writes in loving detail about the **setting** of her story. She dwells on the sights, the sounds, the smells of the land. Look at the story she tells about the sunflowers on the prairie. Look at what she says about the attitude that the people living on the prairies have toward trees. Pretend you are Ántonia, the girl in the story. You are writing a letter home to friends or relatives who stayed behind in Czechoslovakia. Tell them about the new land to which you have come. Tell them about the land, the plant life, the animal life in your new setting.

(2) Many people pent up in crowded cities have always yearned for a life closer to the land—self-sustained, drawing on what is locally available. What was it like when people were less cut off than they are today from their natural environment? Suppose you were writing to people in the big cities of the East about the early farm life in Nebraska. Drawing your description from this selection, how would you describe the *way of life* of these people? How do they live? How do they manage for basic necessities? Look at what we learn about the boy's family, about Ántonia's family, and about the two Russians. What picture emerges of a pioneer economy, of an earlier life-style?

(3) How do you expect people to react to "foreigners"? What pictures or ideas does the word bring to mind? What is the attitude toward the foreigners in this selection? What kind of people are they? What kind of picture do you get of the father, the mother, Ántonia, the two Russians? (Your teacher may ask you to do a *capsule portrait* of one or more of them.) What label best describes the attitude of the people in the story toward their "foreign" neighbors?

---

### Your Turn

In this selection, people go out of their way to make their neighbors welcome. How much survives today of the traditional ideal of being a good neighbor? What is people's attitude today toward the newcomer, the new arrival? Can you tell a story about the arrival of a new neighbor, or the arrival of a new student at your school? Can you generalize after thinking over some relevant incidents from your own experience or observation?

● "Let bygones be bygones!" say people who want to live in the here and now. "The spirit of the old days is dead," say people who mourn the passing of what they believed in and worked for. In the following story, set in the Salinas Valley of California, John Steinbeck (1902–1968), one of the best-known storytellers of the American West, writes about the spirit of the old pioneering days. But he writes about a time when the old days lived on mainly in the memory of older people who spent much of their time reliving the past. They would tell one more time the old familiar story about the hardships of more heroic days. What did the stories about the wagon trains and the trek west mean to the young boy in the story?

John Steinbeck

# The Leader of the People

On Saturday afternoon Billy Buck, the ranch hand, raked together the last of the old year's haystack and pitched small forkfuls over the wire fence to a few mildly interested cattle. High in the air small clouds like puffs of cannon smoke were driven eastward by the March wind. The wind could be heard whishing in the brush on the ridge crests, but no breath of it penetrated down into the ranch-cup.

The little boy, Jody, emerged from the house eating a thick piece of buttered bread. He saw Billy working on the last of the haystack. Jody tramped down scuffling his shoes in a way he had been told was destructive to good shoe leather. A flock of white pigeons flew out of the black cypress tree as Jody passed, and circled the tree and landed again. A half-grown tortoise-shell cat leaped from the bunkhouse porch, galloped on stiff legs across the road, whirled, and galloped back again. Jody picked up a stone to help the game along, but he was too late, for the cat was under the porch before the stone could be discharged. He threw the stone into the cypress tree and started the white pigeons on another whirling flight.

Arriving at the used-up haystack, the boy leaned against the barbed wire fence. "Will that be all of it, do you think?" he asked.

The middle-aged ranch hand stopped his careful raking and stuck his fork into the ground. He took off his black hat and smoothed down his hair. "Nothing left of it that isn't soggy from ground moisture," he said. He replaced his hat and rubbed his dry leathery hands together.

"Ought to be plenty of mice," Jody suggested.

"Lousy with them," said Billy, "Just crawling with mice."

"Well, maybe, when you get all through, I could call the dogs and hunt the mice."

"Sure, I guess you could," said Billy Buck. He lifted a forkful of the damp ground-hay and threw it into the air. Instantly three mice leaped out and burrowed frantically under the hay again.

Jody sighed with satisfaction. Those plump, sleek, arrogant mice were doomed. For eight months they had lived and multiplied in the haystack. They had been immune from cats, from traps, from poison, and from Jody. They had grown smug in their security, overbearing and fat. Now the time of disaster had come; they would not survive another day.

Billy looked up at the top of the hills that surrounded the ranch. "Maybe you better ask your father before you do it," he suggested.

"Well, where is he? I'll ask him now."

"He rode up to the ridge ranch after dinner. He'll be back pretty soon."

Jody slumped against the fence post. "I don't think he'd care."

As Billy went back to his work he said ominously, "You'd better ask him anyway. You know how he is."

Jody did know. His father, Carl Tiflin, insisted upon giving permission for anything that was done on the ranch, whether it was important or not. Jody sagged farther against the post until he was sitting on the ground. He looked up at the little puffs of wind-driven cloud. "Is it like to rain, Billy?"

"It might. The wind's good for it, but not strong enough."

"Well, I hope it don't rain until after I kill those mice." Billy worked on without comment.

Jody turned back and looked at the side-hill where the road from the outside world came down. The hill was washed with lean March sunshine. Silver thistles, blue lupins, and a few poppies bloomed among the sage bushes. Halfway up the hill Jody could see Doubletree Mutt, the black dog, digging in a squirrel hole. He paddled for a while and then paused to kick bursts of dirt out between his hind legs, and he dug with an earnestness which belied the knowledge he must have possessed that no dog had ever caught a squirrel simply by digging in a hole.

Suddenly, while Jody watched, the black dog stiffened, and backed out of the hole and looked up the hill toward the cleft in the ridge where the road came through. Jody looked up too. For a moment Carl Tiflin on horseback stood out against the pale sky and then he moved down the road toward the house. He carried something white in his hand.

The boy started to his feet. "He's got a letter," Jody cried. He trotted away toward the ranch house, for the letter would probably be read aloud and he wanted to be there. He reached the house before his father did, and ran in. He heard Carl dismount from his creaking saddle and slap the horse on the side to send it to the barn where Billy would unsaddle it, and turn it out.

Jody ran into the kitchen. "We got a letter!" he cried.

His mother looked up from a pan of beans. "Who has?"

"Father has. I saw it in his hand."

Carl strode into the kitchen then, and Jody's mother asked, "Who's the letter from, Carl?"

He frowned quickly. "How did you know there was a letter?"

She nodded her head in the boy's direction. "Big-Britches Jody told me."

Jody was embarrassed.

His father looked down at him contemptuously. "He *is* getting to be a Big-Britches," Carl said. "He's minding everybody's business but his own. Got his big nose into everything."

Mrs. Tiflin relented a little. "Well, he hasn't enough to keep him busy. Who's the letter from?"

Carl still frowned on Jody. "I'll keep him busy if he isn't careful." He held out a sealed letter. "I guess it's from your father."

Mrs. Tiflin took a hairpin from her head and slit open the flap. Her lips pursed judiciously. Jody saw her eyes snap back and forth over the lines. "He says," she translated, "he says he's going to drive out Saturday to stay for a little while. Why, this is Saturday. The letter must have been delayed." She looked at the postmark. "This was mailed day before yesterday. It should have been here yesterday." She looked up questioningly at her husband, and then her face darkened angrily. "Now what have you got that look on you for? He doesn't come often."

Carl turned his eyes away from her anger. He could be stern with her most of the time, but when occasionally her temper arose, he could not combat it.

"What's the matter with you?" she demanded again.

In his explanation there was a tone of apology Jody himself might have used. "It's just that he talks," Carl said lamely. "Just talks."

"Well, what of it? You talk yourself."

"Sure I do. But your father only talks about one thing."

"Indians!" Jody broke in excitedly. "Indians and crossing the plains!"

Carl turned fiercely on him. "You get out, Mr. Big-Britches! Go on, now! Get out!"

Jody went miserably out the back door and closed the screen with elaborate quietness. Under the kitchen window his shamed, downcast eyes fell upon a curiously shaped stone, a stone of such fascination that he squatted down and picked it up and turned it over in his hands.

The voices came clearly to him through the open kitchen window. "Jody's right," he heard his father say. "Just Indians and crossing the plains. I've heard that story about how the horses got driven off about a thousand times. He just goes on and on, and he never changes a word in the things he tells."

When Mrs. Tiflin answered her tone was so changed that Jody, outside the window, looked up from his study of the stone. Her voice had become soft and explanatory. Jody knew how her face would have changed to match the tone. She said quietly, "Look at it this way, Carl. That was the big thing in my father's life. He led a wagon train clear across the plains to the coast, and when it was finished, his life was done. It was a big thing to do, but it didn't last long enough. Look!" she continued, "it's as though he was born to do that, and after he finished it, there wasn't anything more for him to do but think about it and talk about it. If there'd been any farther west to go, he'd have gone. He's told me so himself. But at last there was the ocean. He lives right by the ocean where he had to stop."

She had caught Carl, caught him and entangled him in her soft tone.

"I've seen him," he agreed quietly. "He goes down and stares off west over the ocean." His voice sharpened a little. "And then he goes up to the Horseshoe Club in Pacific Grove, and he tells people how the Indians drove off the horses."

She tried to catch him again. "Well, it's everything to him. You might be patient with him and pretend to listen."

Carl turned impatiently away. "Well, if it gets too bad, I can always go down to the bunkhouse and sit with Billy," he said irritably. He walked through the house and slammed the front door after him.

Jody ran to his chores. He dumped the grain to the chickens without chasing any of them. He gathered the eggs from the nests. He trotted into the house with the wood and interlaced it so carefully in the woodbox that two armloads seemed to fill it to overflowing.

His mother had finished the beans by now. She stirred up the fire and brushed off the stove top with a turkey wing. Jody peered cautiously at her to see whether any rancor toward him remained. "Is he coming today?" Jody asked.

"That's what his letter said."

"Maybe I better walk up the road to meet him."

Mrs. Tiflin clanged the stove lid shut. "That would be nice," she said. "He'd probably like to be met."

"I guess I'll just do it then."

Outside, Jody whistled shrilly to the dogs. "Come on up the hill," he commanded. The two dogs waved their tails and ran ahead. Along the roadside the sage had tender new tips. Jody tore off some pieces and rubbed them on his hands until the air was filled with the sharp wild smell. With a rush the dogs leaped from the road and yapped into the brush after a rabbit. That was the last Jody saw of them, for when they failed to catch the rabbit, they went back home.

Jody plodded on up the hill toward the

ridge top. When he reached the little cleft where the road came through, the afternoon wind struck him and blew up his hair and ruffled his shirt. He looked down on the little hills and ridges below and then out at the huge green Salinas Valley. He could see the white town of Salinas far out in the flat and the flash of its windows under the waning sun. Directly below him, in an oak tree, a crow congress had convened. The tree was black with crows all cawing at once.

Then Jody's eyes followed the wagon road down from the ridge where he stood, and lost it behind a hill, and picked it up again on the other side. On that distant stretch he saw a cart slowly pulled by a bay horse. It disappeared behind the hill. Jody sat down on the ground and watched the place where the cart would reappear again. The wind sang on the hilltops and the puff-ball clouds hurried eastward.

Then the cart came into sight and stopped. A man dressed in black dismounted from the seat and walked to the horse's head. Although it was so far away, Jody knew he had unhooked the checkrein, for the horse's head dropped forward. The horse moved on, and the man walked slowly up the hill beside it. Jody gave a glad cry and ran down the road toward them. The squirrels bumped along off the road, and a roadrunner flirted its tail and raced over the edge of the hill and sailed out like a glider.

Jody tried to leap into the middle of his shadow at every step. A stone rolled under his foot and he went down. Around a little bend he raced, and there, a short distance ahead, were his grandfather and the cart. The boy dropped from his unseemly running and approached at a dignified walk.

The horse plodded stumble-footedly up the hill and the old man walked beside it. In the lowering sun their giant shadows flickered darkly behind them. The grandfather was dressed in a black broadcloth suit and he wore kid congress gaiters and a black tie on a short, hard collar. He carried his black slouch hat in his hand. His white beard was cropped close and his white eyebrows overhung his eyes like moustaches. The blue eyes were sternly merry. About the whole face and figure there was a granite dignity, so that every motion seemed an impossible thing. Once at rest, it seemed the old man would be stone, would never move again. His steps were slow and certain. Once made, no step could ever be retraced; once headed in a direction, the path would never bend nor the pace increase nor slow.

When Jody appeared around the bend, Grandfather waved his hat slowly in welcome, and he called, "Why, Jody! Come down to meet me, have you?"

Jody sidled near and turned and matched his step to the old man's step and stiffened his body and dragged his heels a little. "Yes, sir," he said. "We got your letter only today."

"Should have been here yesterday," said Grandfather. "It certainly should. How are all the folks?"

"They're fine, sir." He hesitated and then suggested shyly, "Would you like to come on a mouse hunt tomorrow, sir?"

"Mouse hunt, Jody?" Grandfather chuckled. "Have the people of this generation come down to hunting mice? They aren't very strong, the new people, but I hardly thought mice would be game for them."

"No, sir. It's just play. The haystack's gone. I'm going to drive out the mice to the dogs. And you can watch, or even beat the hay a little."

The stern, merry eyes turned down on them. "I see. You don't eat them, then. You haven't come to that yet."

Jody explained, "The dogs eat them, sir. It wouldn't be much like hunting Indians, I guess."

"No, not much—but then later, when

the troops were hunting Indians and shooting children and burning tepees, it wasn't much different from your mouse hunt."

They topped the rise and started down into the ranch-cup, and they lost the sun from their shoulders. "You've grown," Grandfather said. "Nearly an inch, I should say."

"More," Jody boasted. "Where they mark me on the door, I'm up more than an inch since Thanksgiving even."

Grandfather's rich throaty voice said, "Maybe you're getting too much water and turning to pith and stalk. Wait until you head out, and then we'll see."

Jody looked quickly into the old man's face to see whether his feelings should be hurt, but there was no will to injure, no punishing nor putting-in-your-place light in the keen blue eyes. "We might kill a pig," Jody suggested.

"Oh, no! I couldn't let you do that. You're just humoring me. It isn't the time and you know it."

"You know Riley, the big boar, sir?"

"Yes. I remember Riley well."

"Well, Riley ate a hole into that same haystack, and it fell down on him and smothered him."

"Pigs do that when they can," said Grandfather.

"Riley was a nice pig, for a boar, sir. I rode him sometimes, and he didn't mind."

A door slammed at the house below them, and they saw Jody's mother standing on the porch waving her apron in welcome. And they saw Carl Tiflin walking up from the barn to be at the house for the arrival.

The sun had disappeared from the hills by now. The blue smoke from the house chimney hung in flat layers in the purpling ranch-cup. Numerous puff-ball clouds, dropped by the falling wind, hung listlessly in the sky.

Billy Buck came out of the bunkhouse and flung a wash basin of soapy water on the ground. He had been shaving in midweek, for Billy held Grandfather in reverence, and Grandfather said that Billy was one of the few men of the new generation who had not gone soft. Although Billy was in middle age, Grandfather considered him a boy. Now Billy was hurrying toward the house too.

When Jody and Grandfather arrived, the three were waiting for them in front of the yard gate.

Carl said, "Hello, sir. We've been looking for you."

Mrs. Tiflin kissed Grandfather on the side of his beard, and stood still while his big hand patted her shoulder. Billy shook hands solemnly, grinning under his straw moustache. "I'll put up your horse," said Billy, and he led the rig away.

Grandfather watched him go, and then, turning back to the group, he said as he had said a hundred times before, "There's a good boy. I knew his father, old Muletail Buck. I never knew why they called him Mule-tail except he packed mules."

Mrs. Tiflin turned and led the way into the house. "How long are you going to stay, Father? Your letter didn't say."

"Well, I don't know. I thought I'd stay about two weeks. But I never stay as long as I think I'm going to."

In a short while they were sitting at the white oilcloth table eating their supper. The lamp with the tin reflector hung over the table. Outside the dining-room windows the big moths battered softly against the glass.

Grandfather cut his steak into tiny pieces and chewed slowly. "I'm hungry," he said. "Driving out here got my appetite up. It's like when we were crossing. We all got so hungry every night we could hardly wait to let the meat get done. I could eat about five pounds of buffalo meat every night."

"It's moving around does it," said Billy. "My father was a government packer. I helped him when I was a kid. Just the two of us could about clean up a deer's ham."

"I knew your father, Billy," said Grandfather. "A fine man he was. They called him Mule-tail Buck. I don't know why except he packed mules."

"That was it," Billy agreed. "He packed mules."

Grandfather put down his knife and fork and looked around the table. "I can remember one time we ran out of meat—" His voice dropped to a curious low sing-song, dropped into a tonal groove the story had worn for itself. "There was no buffalo, no antelope, not even rabbits. The hunters couldn't even shoot a coyote. That was the time for the leader to be on the watch. I was the leader, and I kept my eyes open. Know why? Well, just the minute the people began to get hungry they'd start slaughtering the team oxen. Do you believe that? I've heard of parties that just ate up their draft cattle. Started from the middle and worked toward the ends. Finally they'd eat the lead pair, and then the wheelers. The leader of a party had to keep them from doing that."

In some manner a big moth got into the room and circled the hanging kerosene lamp. Billy got up and tried to clap it between his hands. Carl struck with a cupped palm and caught the moth and broke it. He walked to the window and dropped it out.

"As I was saying," Grandfather began again, but Carl interrupted him. "You'd better eat some more meat. All the rest of us are ready for our pudding."

Jody saw a flash of anger in his mother's eyes. Grandfather picked up his knife and fork. "I'm pretty hungry, all right," he said. "I'll tell you about that later."

When supper was over, when the family and Billy Buck sat in front of the fireplace in the other room, Jody anxiously watched Grandfather. He saw the signs he knew. The bearded head leaned forward; the eyes lost their sternness and looked wonderingly into the fire; the big lean fingers laced themselves on the black knees. "I wonder," he began, "I just wonder whether I ever told you how those thieving Piutes drove off thirty-five of our horses."

"I think you did," Carl interrupted. "Wasn't it just before you went up into the Tahoe country?"

Grandfather turned quickly toward his son-in-law. "That's right. I guess I must have told you that story."

"Lots of times," Carl said cruelly, and he avoided his wife's eyes. But he felt the angry eyes on him, and he said, " 'Course I'd like to hear it again."

Grandfather looked back at the fire. His fingers unlaced and laced again. Jody knew how he felt, how his insides were collapsed and empty. Hadn't Jody been called a Big-Britches that very afternoon? He arose to heroism and opened himself to the term Big-Britches again. "Tell about Indians," he said softly.

Grandfather's eyes grew stern again. "Boys always want to hear about Indians. It was a job for men, but boys want to hear about it. Well, let's see. Did I ever tell you how I wanted each wagon to carry a long iron plate?"

Everyone but Jody remained silent. Jody said, "No. You didn't."

"Well, when the Indians attacked, we always put the wagons in a circle and fought from between the wheels. I thought that if every wagon carried a long plate with rifle holes, the men could stand the plates on the outside of the wheels when the wagons were in the circle and they would be protected. It would save lives and that would make up for the extra weight of the iron. But of course the party wouldn't do it. No party had done it before and they couldn't see why they should go to the expense. They lived to regret it, too.''

Jody looked at his mother, and knew from her expression that she was not listening at all. Carl picked at a callus on his thumb and Billy Buck watched a spider crawling up the wall.

Grandfather's tone dropped into its narrative groove again. Jody knew in advance exactly what words would fall. The story droned on, speeded up for the attack, grew sad over the wounds, struck a dirge at the burials on the great plains. Jody quietly sat watching Grandfather. The stern blue eyes were detached. He looked as though he were not very interested in the story himself.

When it was finished, when the pause had been politely respected as the frontier of the story, Billy Buck stood up and stretched and hitched his trousers. ''I guess I'll turn in,'' he said. Then he faced Grandfather. ''I've got an old powder horn and a cap and ball pistol down to the bunkhouse. Did I ever show them to you?''

Grandfather nodded slowly. ''Yes, I think you did, Billy. Reminds me of a pistol I had when I was leading the people across.'' Billy stood politely until the little story was done, and then he said, ''Good night,'' and went out of the house.

Carl Tiflin tried to turn the conversation then. ''How's the country between here and Monterey? I've heard it's pretty dry.''

''It is dry,'' said Grandfather. ''There's not a drop of water in the Laguna Seca. But it's a long pull from '87. The whole country was powder then, and in '61 I believe all the coyotes starved to death. We had fifteen inches of rain this year.''

''Yes, but it all came too early. We could do with some now.'' Carl's eyes fell on Jody. ''Hadn't you better be getting to bed?''

Jody stood up obediently. ''Can I kill the mice in the old haystack, sir?''

''Mice? Oh! Sure, kill them all off. Billy said there isn't any good hay left.''

Jody exchanged a secret and satisfying look with Grandfather. ''I'll kill every one tomorrow,'' he promised.

Jody lay in his bed and thought of the impossible world of Indians and buffaloes, a world that had ceased to be forever. He wished he could have been living in the heroic time, but he knew he was not of heroic timber. No one living now, save possibly Billy Buck, was worthy to do the things that had been done. A race of giants had lived then, fearless men, men of a staunchness unknown in this day. Jody thought of the wide plains and of the wagons moving across like centipedes. He thought of Grandfather on a huge white horse, marshaling the people. Across his mind marched the great phantoms, and they marched off the earth and they were gone.

He came back to the ranch for a moment, then. He heard the dull rushing sound that space and silence make. He heard one of the dogs, out in the doghouse, scratching a flea and bumping his elbow against the floor with every stroke. Then the wind arose again and the black cypress groaned and Jody went to sleep.

He was up half an hour before the triangle sounded for breakfast. His mother was rattling the stove to make the flames roar when Jody went through the kitchen. ''You're up early,'' she said. ''Where are you going?''

''Out to get a good stick. We're going to kill the mice today.''

''Who is 'we'?''

''Why, Grandfather and I.''

''So you've got him in it. You always like to have someone in with you in case there's blame to share.''

''I'll be right back,'' said Jody. ''I just want to have a good stick ready for after

breakfast, for the mice."

He closed the screen door after him and went out into the cool blue morning. The birds were noisy in the dawn and the ranch cats came down from the hill like blunt snakes. They had been hunting gophers in the dark, and although the four cats were full of gopher meat, they sat in a semi-circle at the back door and mewed piteously for milk. Doubletree Mutt and Smasher moved sniffing along the edge of the brush, performing the duty with rigid ceremony, but when Jody whistled, their heads jerked up and their tails waved. They plunged down to him, wriggling their skins and yawning. Jody patted their heads seriously, and moved on to the weathered scrap pile. He selected an old broom handle and a short piece of inch-square scrap wood. From his pocket he took a shoelace and tied the ends of the sticks loosely together to make a flail. He whistled his new weapon through the air and struck the ground experimentally, while the dogs leaped aside and whined with apprehension.

Jody turned and started down past the house toward the old haystack to look over the field of slaughter, but Billy Buck, sitting patiently on the back steps, called to him, "You better come back. It's only a couple of minutes till breakfast."

Jody changed his course and moved toward the house. He leaned his flail against the steps. "That's to drive the mice out," he said. "I'll bet they're fat. I'll bet they don't know what's going to happen to them today."

"No, nor you either," Billy remarked philosophically, "nor me, nor anyone."

Jody was staggered by this thought. He knew it was true. His imagination twitched away from the mouse hunt. Then his mother came out on the back porch and struck the triangle, and all thoughts fell in a heap.

Grandfather hadn't appeared at the table when they sat down. Billy nodded at his empty chair. "He's all right? He isn't sick?"

"He takes a long time to dress," said Mrs. Tiflin. "He combs his whiskers and rubs up his shoes and brushes his clothes."

Carl scattered sugar on his mush. "A man that's led a wagon train across the plains has got to be pretty careful how he dresses."

Mrs. Tiflin turned on him. "Don't do that, Carl! Please don't!" There was more of threat than of request in her tone. And the threat irritated Carl.

"Well, how many times do I have to listen to the story of the iron plates, and the thirty-five horses? That time's done. Why can't he forget it, now it's done? He grew angrier while he talked, and his voice rose. "Why does he have to tell them over and over? He came across the plains. All right! Now it's finished. Nobody wants to hear about it over and over."

The door into the kitchen closed softly. The four at the table sat frozen. Carl laid his mush spoon on the table and touched his chin with his fingers.

Then the kitchen door opened and Grandfather walked in. His mouth smiled tightly and his eyes were squinted. "Good morning," he said, and he sat down and looked at his mush dish.

Carl could not leave it there. "Did—did you hear what I said?"

Grandfather jerked a little nod.

"I don't know what got into me, sir. I didn't mean it. I was just being funny."

Jody glanced in shame at his mother, and he saw that she was looking at Carl, and that she wasn't breathing. It was an awful thing that he was doing. He was tearing himself to pieces to talk like that. It was a terrible thing to him to retract a word, but to retract it in shame was infinitely worse.

Grandfather looked sidewise. "I'm trying to get right side up," he said gently. "I'm not being mad. I don't mind what you said, but it might be true, and I would mind that."

"It isn't true," said Carl. "I'm not feeling well this morning. I'm sorry I said it."

"Don't be sorry, Carl. An old man doesn't see things sometimes. Maybe you're right. The crossing is finished. Maybe it should be forgotten, now it's done."

Carl got up from the table. "I've had enough to eat. I'm going to work. Take your time, Billy!" He walked quickly out of the dining room. Billy gulped the rest of his food and followed soon after. But Jody could not leave his chair.

"Won't you tell any more stories?" Jody asked.

"Why, sure I'll tell them, but only when—I'm sure people want to hear them."

"I like to hear them, sir."

"Oh! Of course you do, but you're a little boy. It was a job for men, but only little boys like to hear about it."

Jody got up from his place. "I'll wait outside for you, sir. I've got a good stick for those mice."

He waited by the gate until the old man came out on the porch. "Let's go down and kill the mice now," Jody called.

"I think I'll just sit in the sun, Jody. You go kill the mice."

"You can use my stick if you like."

"No, I'll just sit here a while."

Jody turned disconsolately away, and walked down toward the old haystack. He tried to whip up his enthusiasm with thoughts of the fat juicy mice. He beat the ground with his flail. The dogs coaxed and whined about him, but he could not go. Back at the house he could see Grandfather sitting on the porch, looking small and thin and black.

Jody gave up and went to sit on the steps at the old man's feet.

"Back already? Did you kill the mice?"

"No, sir. I'll kill them some other day."

The morning flies buzzed close to the ground and the ants dashed about in front of the steps. The heavy smell of sage slipped down the hill. The porch boards grew warm in the sunshine.

Jody hardly knew when Grandfather started to talk. "I shouldn't stay here, feeling the way I do." He examined his strong old hands. "I feel as though the crossing wasn't worth doing." His eyes moved up the sidehill and stopped on a motionless hawk perched on a dead limb. "I tell those old stories, but they're not what I want to tell. I only know how I want people to feel when I tell them.

"It wasn't Indians that were important, nor adventures, nor even getting out here. It was a whole bunch of people made into one big crawling beast. And I was the head. It was westering and westering. Every man wanted something for himself, but the big beast that was all of them wanted only westering. I was the leader, but if I hadn't been there, someone else would have been the head. The thing had to have a head.

"Under the little bushes the shadows were black at white noonday. When we saw the mountains at last, we cried—all of us. But it wasn't getting here that mattered; what mattered was movement and westering.

"We carried life out here and set it down the way those ants carry eggs. And I was the leader. The westering was as big as God, and the slow steps that made the movement piled up and piled up until the continent was crossed.

"Then we came down to the sea, and it was done." He stopped and wiped his eyes until the rims were red. "That's what I should be telling instead of stories."

When Jody spoke, Grandfather started and looked down at him. "Maybe I could lead the people some day," Jody said.

The old man smiled. "There's no place to go. There's the ocean to stop you. There's a line of old men along the shore hating the ocean because it stopped them."

"In boats I might, sir."

"No place to go, Jody. Every place is taken. But that's not the worst—no, not the worst. Westering has died out of the people. Westering isn't a hunger any more. It's all done. Your father is right. It is finished." He laced his fingers on his knee and looked at them.

Jody felt very sad. "If you'd like a glass of lemonade I could make it for you."

Grandfather was about to refuse, and then he saw Jody's face. "That would be nice," he said. "Yes, it would be nice to drink a lemonade."

Jody ran into the kitchen where his mother was wiping the last of the breakfast dishes. "Can I have a lemon to make a lemonade for Grandfather?"

His mother mimicked—"And another lemon to make a lemonade for you."

"No, ma'am. I don't want one."

"Jody! You're sick!" Then she stopped suddenly. "Go take a lemon out of the cooler," she said softly. "Here, I'll reach the squeezer down to you."

---

## YOU AND THE STORY

What are some of the features or qualities that keep us interested while we are reading a good story? Often there is some basic **conflict**—some opposition or contest that produces tension. It keeps the outcome in doubt and thus creates suspense. Often there is a high point in the story when we see the opposites in some kind of direct confrontation that helps decide the outcome. We can call the high point the **climax** of the story. In this story by John Steinbeck, the real outdoor action seems to be in the remembered "heroic" past. What actually happens in the story itself? What would you include in a *plot summary* or a *plot outline* of this story? Does this story have some basic conflict—some contest or opposition? How would you describe it? Does the story have a high point or climax? If so, where would you place it in the story?

### A Closer Look

(1) In "The Leader of the People" by John Steinbeck, how much opportunity does the grandfather actually have to reminisce and tell his stories to the family? Pretend that you are the grandfather, and you have just miraculously found a new audience that has never heard the old stories. How would you relate the story of "westering" as you knew it? What significance do the events and achievements have for you?

(2) What are the **character traits** that set apart the characters in this story? Look at the following sets of words. Each set collects words that the author uses in talking about one of the characters in the story. Which set is the set of words that fits Jody, or the father, or the mother, or Billy, or the grandfather? Taken together, what kind of story do the words in a set tell about the character? Do a *character portrait* of one or more of the people in the story. Try to use all the words in that character's list of words.

| | |
|---|---|
| frown | careful |
| contemptuous | solemn |
| impatient | polite |
| stern | patient |
| irritable | philosophical |
| cruel | reverence |

| | | |
|---|---|---|
| dignity | judicious | excited |
| stern | questioning | miserable |
| merry | temper | fascination |
| sad | relent | cautious |
| staunch | soft | glad |
| wonder | flash | disconsolate |
| keen | mimic | obedient |

(3) Sometimes the **characters** in a story simply stay true to their nature. They act "in character"; they act the way we expect them to act. But sometimes—often in a novel, and less frequently in a short story— we see a character *develop*. We have to revise our estimate of who and what the character was. Do you have to revise your estimate of Jody's father when the father apologizes to the mother, when he apologizes to the grandfather and "retracts" what he has said? (Why is it hard for someone like the father to apologize?) In turn, are you surprised by the grandfather's reactions during this crucial scene? How would you have expected him to act?

(4) The characters in this story seem to agree that the westward movement is over, that now "there is no place to go." So the realistic father wants to be done with it, but the son seems much more receptive to the tales of the old times. Do you think he will "grow out" of his interest in these stories? Should he? In this conflict between father and son, on which side do you see the author?

### Your Turn

At the end of the story, the grandfather says, "Westering has died out of the people." Do you see any area in our society, or in modern life, where something like the pioneering spirit is still alive?

---

Language/Composition Activity A6

FOR WRITING PRACTICE
# An Exercise in Point of View

We want people to take us as we are. We want them to do justice to whatever we have to offer. But at the same time we realize that people see us from their own perspective. They see us in terms of their own lives. They judge us in part according to how we help or hinder them in their affairs. What we remind them of, or what they judge us by, is part of their own personal history. When a story or a play is well-made, the characters in it look at each other from their own perspective, as we do in real life. Each has his or her personal **point of view**. In this story, the grandfather means something different in the lives of each of the four other characters. The father, the mother, Jody, Billy—they each think of him differently; they greet him differently; and they treat him differently. What material would you use in a paper that shows how each character looks at the grandfather from a different point of view? Collect the details that you would need in each paragraph of a *three-paragraph* paper:

    I. the grandfather as seen from the point of view of Jody's father
    II. the grandfather as seen from Jody's own point of view
    III. the grandfather as seen from either the mother's or Billy's point of view

# The Immigrants' America

Even the most incorrigible maverick has
to be born somewhere. He may leave the
group that produced him—he may be
forced to—but nothing will efface his
origins, the marks of which he carries with
him everywhere. I think it is important
to know this and even find it a matter
for rejoicing, as the strongest people do,
regardless of their station.

—James Baldwin,
*Nobody Knows My Name*

For many years, a steady stream of immigrants came into this country from the Old World. No one can know what made this country without understanding "the hunger of people to come to America." For millions and millions of people in Europe and other parts of the world, America was a magic word that stood for the distant golden shore. Millions came to this country as a refuge from persecution and oppression. To them America was a sanctuary: English Puritans persecuted as dissenters; Irish immigrants fleeing from oppression and famine; Jews in Poland and Russia persecuted under the government of the Czars; Armenians and Greeks fleeing from massacres under the Turks. Millions of poor people in the countryside and factory towns of Europe dreamed of a second chance in the land where "the streets were paved with gold." People defeated by century-old barriers in traditional status societies came here to learn the meaning of what one immigrant called "the most American of all idioms: 'to start all over again.' "

But though millions of people came to America to make a new start, they did not leave behind everything that had been. When we see pictures of immigrants

arriving with no baggage other than a battered suitcase or a bundle of clothes, we realize that they carried with them other things that the eye does not see. While learning to talk and live like Americans, they preserved Old Country memories and some of their Old Country ways. They kept their native language for use with friends and relatives. They kept alive familiar ways of thinking and feeling: familiar dos and don'ts, ways of showing affection, ways of being polite, ways to know your friends and your enemies. They kept alive the stories and anecdotes and humor of their native land. For many in the first generation and second generation of immigrants, being American meant sharing in two cultures: one new and at first in many ways unsettling and strange; the other old and familiar but slowly fading into the past.

Behind the tired anonymous faces and the strange peasantlike costumes that we see on old pictures of immigrant ships, there were real people. What was coming to a strange country like for them? Do you know any people, within your own family or outside, who remember what this country was like for the immigrant, or for the children of immigrants?

## Terrence O'Flaherty

# Through the Golden Door

We Americans are often reminded of our great diversity, but there is one common condition which all of us share: we are immigrants from foreign shores, or their descendants, with the exceptions of the Indians who were already here and African slaves who were transported forcibly, the remaining 89 percent of our present population and their relatives came voluntarily and with great hope for a new life in a welcome land.

That poem at the base of the Statue of Liberty written by Emma Lazarus in 1883 was more than a promise; it was a reminder of our beginnings as Americans:

**"Keep, ancient lands, your storied pomp**
. . . . . . . . .
**Give me your tired, your poor,**
**Your huddled masses yearning to breathe**
  **free,**
**The wretched refuse of your teeming shore.**
**Send these, the homeless, tempest-tost to**
  **me.**
**I lift my lamp beside the golden door!''**

Even in the present day of inflated figures, the actual numbers involved in the emigration to America are astonishing. It is not known exactly how many people came to the colonies before 1776 but the so-called Puritan migration to Massachusetts between 1628 and 1640 totalled only 20,000 people. For 30 years after independence the arrivals didn't increase much. Then, from the close of the Napoleonic Wars until the restrictive laws were enacted in the 1920s, a total of 35 million people entered the U.S., eventually at the rate of a million a year.

*San Francisco Chronicle*
(Wednesday, June 9, 1976)

We are often told that for people comfortable in their own homes it is hard to imagine themselves sharing the experience of the exile or the refugee. How distant, or how close, does the experience treated in the following poems seem to you?

Henry Wadsworth Longfellow
(1807–1882)

# The Jewish Cemetery

The very names recorded here are strange,
    Of foreign accent, and of different climes;
Alvares and Rivera interchange
    With Abraham and Jacob of old times.

How came they here? What burst of Christian hate,
    What persecution, merciless and blind,
Drove over the sea—that desert desolate—
    These Ishmaels and Hagars of mankind?

All their lives long, with the unleavened bread
    And bitter herbs of exile and its fears,
The wasting famine of the heart they fed,
    And slaked its thirst with marah of their tears.

Pride and humiliation hand in hand
    Walked with them through the world where'er they went;
Trampled and beaten were they as the sand,
    And yet unshaken as the continent.

For in the background figures vague and vast
    Of patriarchs and of prophets rose sublime,
And all the great traditions of the Past
    They saw reflected in the coming time.

## YOU AND THE POEM

(1) In the Old Testament, Hagar and Ishmael are the names of a mother and her son who are driven into exile. In Jewish history and literature, the theme of exile plays a central, dominant role. But the same theme—of people driven from their homes or compelled to flee their native country—occurs in much other history. What historical associations do the following words, all related to the idea of exile, carry: *exodus,*

diaspora, expatriate, proscription, deport, transport, excommunicate, ostracism, DP, émigré.

(2) In the Old Testament, Marah is the name of a spring of bitter, undrinkable water found in the wilderness. Longfellow uses figurative expressions that are obvious or self-explanatory. Can you show how well and how clearly expressions like the following convey the intended meaning? Discuss several: a "burst of hate"; "blind persecution"; the "desert" of the sea; the "unleavened bread" of exile; the "famine of the heart."

(3) What does the word *sublime* mean? Where have you encountered it? In the poem, what words that precede it help prepare us for something "sublime"?

Edward Field

# My Polish Grandma

Grandma and the children left at night.
It was forbidden to go. In those days
the Czar and his cossacks rode through the town at whim
killing Jews and setting fire to straw roofs
while just down the road the local Poles
sat laughing as they drank liquor.

Grandpa had gone to America first
and earned the money for the rest of the family to come over.
So they left finally, the whole brood of them
with the hired agent running the show,
an impatient man, and there were so many kids
and the bundles kept falling apart
and poor grandma was frightened of him.

She gave the man all the money
but she couldn't round up the kids fast enough for him.
They were children after all and didn't understand
and she was so stupid and clumsy herself,
carrying food for all of them and their clothes
and could she leave behind her pots?
Her legs hurt already; they were always swollen
from the hard work, the childbearing, and the cold.

They caught the train and there was a terrible moment
when the conductor came by for the tickets:
The children mustn't speak or he would know they were Jewish,
they had no permits to travel—Jews weren't allowed.
But the agent knew how to handle it,
everybody got *shmeared*, that means money got you
    everywhere.

The border was the worst. They had to sneak across at night.
The children mustn't make a sound, not even the babies.
Momma was six and she didn't want to do anything wrong
but she wasn't sure what to do.
The man led them through the woods
and beyond they could hear dogs barking from the sentry hut,
and then they had to run all of them down the ravine to the
    other side,
grandma broken down from childbearing with her bundles
and bad legs and a baby in her arms,
they ran all the children across the border
or the guards might shoot them
and if the little ones cried, the agent said he would smother
    them.

They got to a port finally.
Grandpa had arranged for cabin passage, not steerage,
but the agent cheated and put them in the hold
so they were on the low deck looking up at the rich people.
My momma told me how grandma took care of all her children,
how Jake didn't move anymore he was so seasick, maybe even
    dead,
and if people thought he was dead
they would throw him overboard like garbage, so she hid him.
The rich tossed down oranges to the poor children—
my momma had never had one before.

They came to New York, to the tenements,
a fearful new place, a city, country people in the city.
My momma, who had been roly-poly in slow Poland,
got skinny and pimply in zippy New York.
Everybody grew up in a new way.
And now my grandma is dead and my momma is old
and we her children are all scattered over the earth
speaking a different language and forgetting
why it was so important
to go to a new country.

---

### YOU AND THE POEM

One of the most basic and lasting plot patterns in literature is the flight, the escape, the breaking away. In this poem about the flight to the "fearful new place," what are elements that must have been part of the *common experience* of many immigrants? How does the poet remind us that these were real people? Did any parts of this poem make you feel as if you could have been one of the refugees?

David Ignatow

# Europe and America

My father brought the emigrant bundle
of desperation and worn threads,
that in anxiety as he stumbles
tumble out distractedly;
while I am bedded upon soft green money
that grows like grass. Thus,
between my father who lives on a bed of anguish
for his daily bread, and I who tear money
at leisure by the roots,
where I lie in sun or shade,
a vast continent of breezes, storms to him,
shadows, darkness to him, small lakes,
difficult channels to him, and hills,
mountains to him, lie between us.

My father comes of a hell
where bread and man have been kneaded
and baked together. You have heard the scream
as the knife fell; while I have slept
as guns pounded on the shore.

---

### YOU AND THE POEM

(1) Poets who write short poems know how to say much in a small space. They often select *one single detail* in order to bring a whole larger picture to the reader's mind. What makes "the emigrant bundle" and the "worn threads" the kind of telling details that bring a larger picture to mind? What ideas do they convey to you?

(2) When David Ignatow wrote this poem, the danger and suffering of the father's European past were foremost in the poet's mind. Point out half a dozen words and details that echo this central theme.

(3) The poet is struck by the *contrast* between his own more protected life and the father's experience. Choose the three examples that for you show this contrast most strongly or strikingly.

(4) How much "darkness" and "anguish" in the father's present life is real? Do you think some of it might exist in his imagination? Why?

# Linda Pastan
# My Grandmother

My grandmother
of the bitter mouth
and the capable hands
taught us how long you can live
without love
and be forgiven
and never forgive.
She married knowingly,
at her father's bidding,
the wrong man.
And though she called
each granddaughter "shaneh madeleh,"
which means "lovely girl,"
when my cousin married
a gentile boy for love
she covered her mirrors
as for death:
for seven days
she didn't see
her once beautiful face
wasted in the glass.

## YOU AND THE POEM

(1) Many modern writers have written on the theme of waste—wasted opportunities, wasted capacity for love. Where and in what ways are we made to feel a sense of waste in this poem? What causes it? Are there several different causes? Often people feel about the losses or sufferings of the past that they "could not be helped." Do you feel that way about the causes of waste in this poem?

(2) People who object to the waste of opportunities often encourage us to believe in our potential—what might be, what we might be able to do. Are there any hints in this poem of the grandmother's gifts or potential as a person?

## Katherine Edelman
# Irish Grandmother

Great-grandmother talks by the hour to me
Of a little cottage in Ballybree,
Of whitewashed walls and a roof of thatch
And a gay green ribbon that raised the latch.

Great-grandmother tells of a wee boreen,
With fern and shamrock, moisty-green,
Of a thrush that sang in a hawthorn bough,
Of an old furze patch, and a Kerry cow.

Great-grandmother speaks of the little folk,
Of blazing peat, with its tangy smoke,
Of quaint tall cups they used for tea,
When she was a child in Ballybree.

---

**YOU AND THE POEM**

(1) Irish folkways and Irish folklore are familiar to many Americans. How much do you know about Ireland and Irish history? Give the meaning of each of the following terms, and indicate their connection with Ireland: *bard, colleen, banshee, jig, St. Patrick, boreen, peat, leprechaun, shamrock.*

(2) In much autobiographical writing, the most vivid passages deal with childhood memories—children's games, childhood friends, older relatives, family gatherings, holidays. Imagine yourself talking to a future grandchild about the world of your own childhood. What memories would you pass on? What people, events, and traditions stand out most in your mind?

OBSERVING A GROUP

# Rediscovering the Ethnic American

In the following magazine article, a descendant of the New York Irish describes the kind of gathering where the traditional food and entertainment remind ethnic Americans of their Old Country ties. The occasion makes the author think about the American Irish in general and about early memories of his childhood among them. What in this article is new to you, what familiar? Can you do a short introduction to a similar group with which you yourself have had an experience either as an observer or as a member? Do a brief piece called "Notes on the _____." Try to include the kind of authentic touches that will be familiar to the insider.

## Pete Hamill
## Notes on the Irish

We were standing in a far corner of the McFadden Brothers Post of the American Legion, crushed against a wall beside the midday feast of boiled ham, pickles, cheese, olives and scalding coffee, and all around us were the Brooklyn Irish. Busdrivers, cops, ironworkers, firemen, carpenters: all in Sunday clothes, their faces raw from the bitter cold outside, talking to each other in muted tones, while a visiting group of Irish folk dancers moved in ancient elegant steps to the hard skirl of pipes, and children ran between the long tables, and the wooden folding chairs filled up with some of those extraordinary white-haired women who sat in the front parlor during every wake of every Irish kid's New York childhood.

They were the American Irish and that meant 40 years of work, a certain cargo of resentment, and some glittering small triumphs, displayed like heirlooms: the son who made it through college, the daughter who married a solid man, the grandson who hit .376 at the Parade Grounds. But the world had changed around them. Once, the Irish ran New York; they were the bone and muscle of political power in every

borough. They had Tammany and the Brooklyn organization, Jimmy Walker and the Fire Department and always the cops, in good times and bad. The saloons and restaurants were Irish, and they ran the crime for a while, too, and they had a great brawling sense of themselves. . . .

They called the place Wanderer's Oval and it was located at the base of Greenwood Cemetery, on Fifth Avenue and 35th Street in Brooklyn. It was really only a large dusty lot, with wooden slat fences, where men in heavy greatcoats drank from cups, and a few scattered women stood beside them, and all of them watched the soccer teams play across the cold Sunday afternoons. They were always full

of mass, Sunday breakfasts of sausage, eggs, and fresh white mountain rolls, and the *Daily News*. The men all wore hats then, gray fedoras or brown blocked lids that I see now only in pictures, and the few women were silent with the men and soft with the children. There were no benches on the playing field. This was a hard Depression field; mud caked your shoes for days afterwards, that thick gooey paste of the yellow Brooklyn clay turning mortar-hard in the cold. Across the street, there was a small cellar clubhouse where the players changed clothes at halftime; a tightly packed cave without furniture, smelling of honest workingmen's sweat. And then they would be out on the field again:

cleats pounding the frozen earth into mud, roars from the sidelines, shoving and sometimes punches. And then, the game finished, they would go back to dress and then walk along Fifth Avenue to a place called Keating's on 39th Street, where brown pictures of old soccer teams covered the walls, and as the winter afternoon turned dark, someone would begin to sing. They would always sing about a place called Ireland.

I mention all of this at length because it was in places like Keating's or at soccer games at Wanderer's Oval that a lot of us learned for the first time that we were something called Irish. There were never major pronouncements, no manifestoes issued, no statements of purpose. You were born in America, but you were Irish. You were Irish because your parents were Irish and all their friends were Irish. And it was all mixed up with songs and drinking, of course, but there was something else there too: it had to do with the Depression. Like the Jews, the Irish are a people to whom things were done. And while many were mauled by the Depression, few were surprised that it happened. In the places where they lived, they managed to overcome the Depression. . . . No matter how long the lines of unemployment would last, they would retain some pride and some love of each other. And so in Keating's and in Farrell's and in Rattigan's, in all those saloons that served as the private social clubs for the Irish of my neighborhood, there was some sense of shared disaster and shared courage that got them through.

*New York* magazine (March 13, 1972)

● Several of America's most widely read modern novelists draw on the rich cultural heritage of the American Jewish community. In their books we encounter echoes of a common past: memories of persecution, the folkways of the ghetto, the customs of Jewish religion, the tradition of Jewish humor. Bernard Malamud is one of these writers, and, like many of them, he is a great storyteller who knows how to make his readers laugh and cry. He was born and grew up in Brooklyn and finished his education at Columbia University. In his novel *The Assistant* (1956), he told the story of a poor Jewish neighborhood grocer and the down-and-out young man he tries to help. In his story "The Magic Barrel," Malamud recreates ways of talking and ways of living that many Americans of Jewish descent remember.

# Bernard Malamud

# The Magic Barrel

Not long ago there lived in uptown New York, in a small, almost meager room, though crowded with books, Leo Finkle, a rabbinical student in the Yeshivah University. Finkle, after six years of study, was to be ordained in June and had been advised by an acquaintance that he might find it easier to win a congregation if he were married. Since he had no present prospects of marriage, after two tormented days of turning it over in his mind, he called in Pinye Salzman, a marriage broker, whose two-line advertisement he had read in the *Forward*.[1]

[1] the *Forward:* a New York newspaper written in Yiddish.

The matchmaker appeared one night out of the dark fourth-floor hallway of the graystone rooming house, grasping a black, strapped portfolio that had been worn thin with use. Salzman, who had been long in the business, was of slight but dignified build, wearing an old hat and an overcoat too short and tight for him. He smelled frankly of fish, which he loved to eat, and although he was missing a few teeth, his presence was not displeasing, because of an amiable manner curiously contrasted by mournful eyes. His voice, his lips, his wisp of beard, his bony fingers were animated, but give him a moment of repose, and his mild blue eyes soon revealed a depth of sadness, a characteristic that put Leo a little at ease although the situation, for him, was inherently tense.

He at once informed Salzman why he had asked him to come, explaining that his home was in Cleveland, and that but for his parents, who had married comparatively late in life, he was alone in the world. He had for six years devoted himself entirely to his studies, as a result of which, quite understandably, he had found himself without time for a social life and the company of young women. Therefore he thought it the better part of trial and error—of embarrassing fumbling—to call in an experienced person to advise him in these matters. He remarked in passing that the function of the marriage broker was ancient and honorable, highly approved in the Jewish community, because it made practical the necessary without hindering joy. Moreover, his own parents had been brought together by a matchmaker. They had made, if not a financially profitable marriage—since neither had possessed any worldly goods to speak of—at least a successful one in the sense of their everlasting devotion to one another. Salzman listened in embarrassed surprise, sensing a sort of apology. Later, however, he experienced a glow of pride in his work, an emotion that had left him years ago, and he heartily approved of Finkle.

The two men went to their business. Leo had led Salzman to the only clear place in the room, a table near a window that overlooked the lamplit city. He seated himself at the matchmaker's side but facing him, attempting by an act of will to suppress the unpleasant tickle in his throat. Salzman eagerly unstrapped his portfolio and removed a loose rubber band from a thin packet of much-handled cards. As he flipped through them, a gesture and sound that physically hurt Leo, the student pretended not to see and gazed steadfastly out the window. Although it was still February, winter was on its last legs, signs of which he had for the first time in years begun to notice. He now observed the round white moon, moving high in the sky through a cloud-menagerie, and watched with half-open mouth as it penetrated a huge hen and dropped out of her like an egg laying itself. Salzman, though pretending through eyeglasses he had just slipped on to be engaged in scanning the writing on the cards, stole occasional glances at the young man's distinguished face, noting with pleasure the long, severe scholar's nose, brown eyes heavy with learning, sensitive yet ascetic lips, and a certain almost hollow quality of the dark cheeks. He gazed around at shelves upon shelves of books and let out a soft but happy sigh.

When Leo's eyes fell upon the cards, he counted six spread out in Salzman's hand.

"So few?" he said in disappointment.

"You wouldn't believe me how much cards I got in my office," Salzman replied. "The drawers are already filled to the top, so I keep them now in a barrel, but is every girl good for a new rabbi?"

Leo blushed at this, regretting all he had

revealed of himself in a curriculum vitae[2] he had sent to Salzman. He had thought it best to acquaint him with his strict standards and specifications, but in having done so now felt he had told the marriage broker more than was absolutely necessary to reveal.

He hesitantly inquired, "Do you keep photographs of your clients on file?"

"First comes family, amount of dowry, and also what kind promises," Salzman replied, unbuttoning his tight coat and settling himself in the chair. "After comes pictures, rabbi."

"Call me Mr. Finkle. I'm not a rabbi yet."

Salzman adjusted his horn-rimmed spectacles, gently cleared his throat, and read in an eager voice the contents of the top card:

"Sophie P. Twenty-four years. Widow for one year. No children. Educated high school and two years college. Father promises eight thousand dollars. Has a wonderful wholesale business. Also real estate. On mother's side comes teachers, also one actor. Well known on Second Avenue."

Leo gazed up in surprise. "Did you say a widow?"

"A widow don't mean spoiled, rabbi. She lived with her husband maybe four months. He was a sick boy; she made a mistake to marry him."

"Marrying a widow has never entered my mind."

"This is because you have no experience. A widow, specially if she is young and healthy like this girl, is a wonderful person to marry. She will be thankful to you the rest of her life. Believe me, if I was looking now for a bride, I would marry a widow."

Leo reflected, then shook his head.

[2]**curriculum vitae:** a short account of one's career and qualifications.

Salzman hunched his shoulders in an almost imperceptible gesture of disappointment. He placed the card down on the wooden table and proceeded to read another:

"Lily H. High-school teacher. Regular. Not a substitute. Has savings and new Dodge car. Lived in Paris one year. Father is successful dentist thirty-five years. Interested in professional man. Well Americanized family. Wonderful opportunity.

"I know her personally," said Salzman. "I wish you could see this girl. She is a doll. Also very intelligent. All day you could talk to her about books and theater and what not. She also knows current events."

"I don't believe you mentioned her age?"

"Her age?" Salzman said, raising his brows in surprise. "Her age is thirty-two years."

Leo said after a while, "I'm afraid that seems a little too old."

Salzman let out a laugh. "So how old are you, rabbi?"

"Twenty-seven."

"So what is the difference, tell me, between twenty-seven and thirty-two? My own wife is seven years older than me. So what did I suffer?—Nothing. If Rothschild's daughter wants to marry you, would you say on account of her age, no?"

"Yes," Leo said dryly.

Salzman shook off the no in the yes. "Five years don't mean a thing. I give you my word that when you will live with her for one week, you will forget her age. What does it mean five years—that she lived more and knows more than somebody who is younger? On this girl, God bless her, years are not wasted. Each one that it comes makes better the bargain."

"What subject does she teach in high school?"

"Languages. If you heard the way she

reads French, you will think it is music. I am in the business twenty-five years, and I recommend her with my whole heart. Believe me, I know what I'm talking, rabbi."

"What's on the next card?" Leo said abruptly.

Salzman reluctantly turned up the third card:

"Ruth K. Nineteen years old. Honor student. Father offers thirteen thousand dollars cash to the right bridegroom. He is a medical doctor. Stomach specialist with marvelous practice. Brother-in-law owns own garment business. Particular people."

Salzman looked up as if he had read his trump card.

"Did you say nineteen?" Leo asked with interest.

"On the dot."

"And is she attractive?" He blushed. "Pretty?"

Salzman kissed his fingertips. "A little doll. On this I give you my word. Let me call the father tonight and you will see what means pretty."

But Leo was troubled. "You're sure she's that young?"

"This I am positive. The father will show you the birth certificate."

"Are you positive there isn't something wrong with her?" Leo insisted.

"Who says there is wrong?"

"I don't understand why an American girl her age should go to a marriage broker."

A smile spread over Salzman's face.

"So for the same reason you went, she comes."

Leo flushed. "I am pressed for time."

Salzman, realizing he had been tactless, quickly explained. "The father came, not her. He wants she should have the best, so he looks around himself. When we will locate the right boy, he will introduce him and encourage. This makes a much better

marriage than if a young girl without experience takes for herself. I don't have to tell you this."

"But don't you think this young girl believes in love?" Leo spoke uneasily.

Salzman was about to guffaw, but caught himself and said soberly, "Love comes with the right person, never before."

Leo parted dry lips but did not speak. Noticing that Salzman had snatched a quick glance at the next card, he cleverly asked, "How is her health?"

"Perfect," Salzman said, breathing with difficulty. "Of course, she is a little lame on her right foot from an auto accident that it happened to her when she was twelve years old, but nobody notices on account she is so brilliant and also beautiful."

Leo got up heavily and went to the window. He felt curiously bitter and upbraided himself for having called in the marriage broker. Finally, he shook his head.

"Why not?" Salzman persisted, the pitch of his voice rising.

"Because I hate stomach specialists."

"So what do you care what is his business? After you marry her, do you need him? Who says he must come every Friday night to your house?"

Ashamed of the way the talk was going, Leo dismissed Salzman, who went home with melancholy eyes.

Though he had felt only relief at the marriage broker's departure, Leo was in low spirits the next day. He explained it as arising from Salzman's failure to produce a suitable bride for him. He did not care for his type of clientele. But when Leo found himself hesitating over whether to seek out another matchmaker, one more polished than Pinye, he wondered if it could be—his protestations to the contrary, and although he honored his father and mother—that he did not, in essence,

care for the matchmaking institution? This thought he quickly put out of his mind yet found himself still upset. All day he ran around in a fog—missed an important appointment, forgot to give out his laundry, walked out of a Broadway cafeteria without paying and had to run back with the ticket in his hand; had even not recognized his landlady in the street when she passed with a friend and courteously called out, "A good evening to you, Doctor Finkle." By nightfall, however, he had regained sufficient calm to sink his nose into a book and there found peace from his thoughts.

Almost at once there came a knock on the door. Before Leo could say enter, Salzman, commercial cupid, was standing in the room. His face was gray and meager, his expression hungry, and he looked as if he would expire on his feet. Yet the marriage broker managed, by some trick of the muscles, to display a broad smile.

"So good evening. I am invited?"

Leo nodded, disturbed to see him again, yet unwilling to ask him to leave.

Beaming still, Salzman laid his portfolio on the table. "Rabbi, I got for you tonight good news."

"I've asked you not to call me rabbi. I'm still a student."

"Your worries are finished. I have for you a first-class bride."

"Leave me in peace concerning this subject." Leo pretended lack of interest.

"At your wedding the world will dance."

"Please, Mr. Salzman, no more."

"But first must come back my strength," Salzman said weakly. He fumbled with the portfolio straps and took out of the leather case an oily paper bag, from which he extracted a hard seeded roll and a small smoked whitefish. With one motion of his hand he stripped the fish out of its skin and began ravenously to chew. "All day in a rush," he muttered.

Leo watched him eat.

"A sliced tomato you have maybe?" Salzman hesitantly inquired.

"No."

The marriage broker shut his eyes and ate. When he had finished, he carefully cleaned up the crumbs and rolled up the remains of the fish in the paper bag. His spectacled eyes roamed the room until he discovered, amid some piles of books, a one-burner gas stove. Lifting his hat, he humbly asked, "A glass of tea you got, rabbi?"

Conscience-stricken, Leo rose and brewed the tea. He served it with a chunk of lemon and two cubes of lump sugar, delighting Salzman.

After he had drunk his tea, Salzman's strength and good spirits were restored.

"So tell me, rabbi," he said amiably, "you considered any more the three clients I mentioned yesterday?"

"There was no need to consider."

"Why not?"

"None of them suits me."

"What, then, suits you?"

Leo let it pass because he could give only a confused answer.

Without waiting for a reply, Salzman asked, "You remember this girl I talked to you—the high-school teacher?"

"Age thirty-two?"

But surprisingly, Salzman's face lit in a smile. "Age twenty-nine."

Leo shot him a look. "Reduced from thirty-two?"

"A mistake," Salzman avowed. "I talked today with the dentist. He took me to his safety deposit box and showed me the birth certificate. She was twenty-nine last August. They made her a party in the mountains where she went for her vacation. When her father spoke to me the first time, I forgot to write the age and I told you thirty-two, but now I remember this was a different client, a widow."

"The same one you told me about? I thought she was twenty-four?"

"A different. Am I responsible that the world is filled with widows?"

"No, but I'm not interested in them, nor for that matter, in schoolteachers."

Salzman passionately pulled his clasped hands to his breast. Looking at the ceiling he exclaimed, "Jewish children, what can I say to somebody that he is not interested in high-school teachers? So what then you are interested?"

Leo flushed but controlled himself.

"In who else you will be interested," Salzman went on, "if you not interested in this fine girl that she speaks four languages and has personally in the bank ten thousand dollars? Also her father guarantees further twelve thousand. Also she has a new car, wonderful clothes, talks on all subjects, and she will give you a first-class home and children. How near do we come in our life to paradise?"

"If she's so wonderful, why wasn't she married ten years ago?"

"Why," said Salzman with a heavy laugh. "—Why? Because she is *partikler*. This is why. She wants only the *best*."

Leo was silent, amused at how he had trapped himself. But Salzman had aroused his interest in Lily H., and he began seriously to consider calling on her. When the marriage broker observed how intently Leo's mind was at work on the facts he had supplied, he felt positive they would soon come to an agreement.

Late Saturday afternoon, conscious of Salzman, Leo Finkle walked with Lily Hirschorn along Riverside Drive. He walked briskly and erectly, wearing with distinction the black fedora he had that morning taken with trepidation out of the dusty hatbox on his closet shelf, and the heavy black Saturday coat he had thoroughly whisked clean. Leo also owned a walking stick, a present from a distant relative, but had decided not to use it. Lily, petite and not unpretty, had on something signifying the approach of spring. She was *au courant*,[3] animatedly, with all subjects, and he weighed her words and found her surprisingly sound— score another for Salzman, whom he uneasily sensed to be somewhere around, hiding perhaps high in a tree along the street, flashing the lady signals; or perhaps a cloven-hoofed Pan,[4] piping nuptial ditties as he danced his invisible way before them, strewing wild buds on the walk and purple summer grapes in their path, symbolizing fruit of a union, of which there was yet none.

[3]*au courant:* French, up-to-date.

[4]**Pan:** Greek god of hunters and shepherds who was half-man and half-goat and is usually pictured playing the flute.

Lily startled Leo by remarking, "I was thinking of Mr. Salzman, a curious figure, wouldn't you say?"

Not certain what to answer, he just nodded.

She bravely went on, blushing, "I for one am grateful for his introducing us. Aren't you?"

He courteously replied, "I am."

"I mean," she said with a little laugh— and it was all in good taste, or at least gave the effect of being not in bad—"do you mind that we came together so?"

He was not afraid of her honesty, recognizing that she meant to set the relationship aright, and understanding that it took a certain amount of experience in life, and courage, to want to do it quite that way. One had to have some sort of past to make that kind of beginning.

He said that he did not mind. Salzman's function was traditional and honorable— valuable for what it might achieve, which, he pointed out, was frequently nothing.

Lily agreed with a sigh. They walked on for a while, and she said after a long silence, again with a nervous laugh, "Would you mind if I asked you something a little bit personal? Frankly, I find the subject fascinating." Although Leo shrugged, she went on half embarrassedly, "How was it that you came to your calling? I mean, was it a sudden passionate inspiration?"

Leo, after a time, slowly replied, "I was always interested in the Law."

"You saw revealed in it the presence of the Highest?"

He nodded and changed the subject. "I understand you spent a little time in Paris, Miss Hirschorn?"

"Oh, did Mr. Salzman tell you, Rabbi Finkle?" Leo winced, but she went on, "It was ages and ages ago and almost forgotten. I remember I had to return for my sister's wedding."

But Lily would not be put off. "When," she asked in a trembly voice, "did you become enamored of God?"

He stared at her. Then it came to him that she was talking not about Leo Finkle, but a total stranger, some mystical figure, perhaps even passionate prophet that Salzman had conjured up for her—no relation to the living or dead. Leo trembled with rage and weakness. The trickster had obviously sold her a bill of goods, just as he had him, who'd expected to become acquainted with a young lady of twenty-nine, only to behold, the moment he laid eyes upon her strained and anxious face, a woman past thirty-five and aging very rapidly. Only his self-control, he thought, had kept him this long in her presence.

"I am not," he said gravely, "a talented religious person," and in seeking words to go on, found himself possessed by fear and shame. "I think," he said in a strained manner, "that I came to God not because I love Him, but because I did not."

This confession he spoke harshly because its unexpectedness shook him.

Lily wilted. Leo saw a profusion of loaves of bread sailing like ducks high over his head, not unlike the loaves by which he had counted himself to sleep last night. Mercifully, then, it snowed, which he would not put past Salzman's machinations.

He was infuriated with the marriage broker and swore he would throw him out of the room the moment he reappeared. But Salzman did not come that night, and when Leo's anger had subsided, an unaccountable despair grew in its place. At first he thought this was caused by his disappointment in Lily, but before long it became evident that he had involved himself with Salzman without a true knowledge of his own intent. He gradually realized—with an emptiness that seized him with six hands—that he had called in the broker to find him a bride because he was incapable of doing it himself. This terrifying insight he had derived as a result of his meeting and conversation with Lily Hirschorn. Her probing questions had somehow irritated him into revealing—to himself more than her—the true nature of his relationship with God, and from that it had come upon him, with shocking force, that apart from his parents, he had never loved anyone. Or perhaps it went the other way, that he did not love God so well as he might, because he had not loved man. It seemed to Leo that his whole life stood starkly revealed and he saw himself, for the first time, as he truly was—unloved and loveless. This bitter but somehow not fully unexpected revelation brought him to a point of panic controlled only by extraordinary effort. He covered his face with his hands and wept.

The week that followed was the worst of his life. He did not eat, and lost weight. His beard darkened and grew ragged. He stopped attending lectures and seminars and almost never opened a book. He seriously considered leaving the Yeshivah, although he was deeply troubled at the thought of the loss of all his years of study—saw them like pages from a book strewn over the city—and at the devastating effect of this decision upon his parents. But he had lived without knowledge of himself, and never in the Five Books and all the Commentaries[5] had the truth been revealed to him. He did not know where to turn, and in all this desolating loneliness there was no *to whom*, although he often thought of Lily but not once could bring himself to go downstairs and make the call. He became touchy and irritable, especially with his landlady,

[5]**Five Books . . . .Commentaries:** the books of Moses, the first five books of the Old Testament, believed to contain all knowledge. The commentaries, written by Jewish scholars in the Middle Ages, explain the books' meaning—plain and hidden—line by line.

who asked him all manner of questions; on the other hand, sensing his own disagreeableness, he waylaid her on the stairs and apologized abjectly, until mortified, she ran from him. Out of this, however, he drew the consolation that he was yet a Jew and that a Jew suffered. But gradually, as the long and terrible week drew to a close, he regained his composure and some idea of purpose in life: to go on as planned. Although he was imperfect, the ideal was not. As for his quest of a bride, the thought of continuing afflicted him with anxiety and heartburn, yet perhaps with this new knowledge of himself he would be more successful than in the past. Perhaps love would now come to him and a bride to that love. And for this sanctified seeking who needed a Salzman?

The marriage broker, a skeleton with haunted eyes, returned that very night. He looked, withal, the picture of frustrated expectancy—as if he had steadfastly waited the week at Miss Lily Hirschorn's side for a telephone call that never came.

Casually coughing, Salzman came immediately to the point: "So how did you like her?"

Leo's anger rose and he could not refrain from chiding the matchmaker: "Why did you lie to me, Salzman?"

Salzman's pale face went dead white, as if the world had snowed on him.

"Did you not state that she was twenty-nine?" Leo insisted.

"I give you my word—"

"She was thirty-five. At *least* thirty-five."

"Of this I would not be too sure. Her father told me—"

"Never mind. The worst of it was that you lied to her."

"How did I lie to her, tell me?"

"You told her things about me that weren't true. You made me out to be more, consequently less, than I am. She

had in mind a totally different person, a sort of semimystical Wonder Rabbi."

"All I said, you was a religious man."

"I can imagine."

Salzman sighed. "This is my weakness that I have," he confessed. "My wife says to me I shouldn't be a salesman, but when I have two fine people that they would be wonderful to be married, I am so happy that I talk too much." He smiled wanly. "This is why Salzman is a poor man."

Leo's anger went. "Well, Salzman, I'm afraid that's all."

The marriage broker fastened hungry eyes on him.

"You don't want any more a bride?"

"I do," said Leo, "but I have decided to seek her in a different way. I am no longer interested in an arranged marriage. To be frank, I now admit the necessity of premarital love. That is, I want to be in love with the one I marry."

"Love?" said Salzman, astounded. After a moment he said, "For us, our love is our life, not for the ladies. In the ghetto they—"

"I know, I know," said Leo. "I've thought of it often. Love, I have said to myself, should be a by-product of living and worship rather than its own end. Yet for myself I find it necessary to establish the level of my need and to fulfill it."

Salzman shrugged but answered, "Listen, rabbi, if you want love, this I can find for you also. I have such beautiful clients that you will love them the minute your eyes will see them."

Leo smiled unhappily. "I'm afraid you don't understand."

But Salzman hastily unstrapped his portfolio and withdrew a manila packet from it.

"Pictures," he said, quickly laying the envelope on the table.

Leo called after him to take the pictures away, but as if on the wings of the wind, Salzman had disappeared.

March came. Leo had returned to his

regular routine. Although he felt not quite himself yet—lacked energy—he was making plans for a more active social life. Of course it would cost something, but he was an expert in cutting corners; and when there were no corners left he could make circles rounder. All the while Salzman's pictures had lain on the table, gathering dust. Occasionally as Leo sat studying, or enjoying a cup of tea, his eyes fell on the manila envelope, but he never opened it.

The days went by, and no social life to speak of developed with a member of the opposite sex—it was difficult, given the circumstances of his situation. One morning Leo toiled up the stairs to his room and stared out the window at the city. Although the day was bright, his view of it was dark. For some time he watched the people in the street below hurrying along and then turned with a heavy heart to his little room. On the table was the packet. With a sudden relentless gesture he tore it open. For a half-hour he stood there, in a state of excitement, examining the photographs of the ladies Salzman had included. Finally, with a deep sigh he put them down. There were six, of varying degrees of attractiveness, but look at them long enough and they all became Lily Hirschorn: all past their prime, all starved behind bright smiles, not a true personality in the lot. Life, despite their anguished struggles and frantic yoohooings, had passed them by; they were photographs in a briefcase that stank of fish. After a while, however, as Leo attempted to return the pictures into the envelope, he found another in it, a small snapshot of the type taken by a machine for a quarter. He gazed at it a moment and let out a cry.

Her face deeply moved him. Why, he could at first not say. It gave him the impression of youth—all spring flowers—yet age—a sense of having been used to the bone, wasted; this all came from the eyes, which were hauntingly familiar, yet absolutely strange. He had a strong impression that he had met her before, but try as he might he could not place her, although he could almost recall her name, as if he had read it written in her own handwriting. No, this couldn't be; he would have remembered her. It was not, he affirmed, that she had an extraordinary beauty—no, although her face was attractive enough; it was that *something* about her moved him. Feature for feature, even some of the ladies of the photographs could do better; but she leaped forth to the heart—had lived, or wanted to—more than just wanted, perhaps regretted it— had somehow deeply suffered: it could be seen in the depths of those reluctant eyes, and from the way the light enclosed and shone from her, and within her, opening whole realms of possibility: this was her own. Her he desired. His head ached and eyes narrowed with the intensity of his gazing, then, as if a black fog had blown up in the mind, he experienced fear of her. He shuddered, saying softly, it is thus with us all. Leo brewed some tea in a small pot and sat sipping it, without sugar, to calm himself. But before he had finished drinking, again with excitement he examined the face and found it good: good for him. Only such a one could truly understand Leo Finkle and help him to seek whatever he was seeking. How she had come to be among the discards in Salzman's barrel he could never guess, but he knew he must urgently go find her.

Leo rushed downstairs, grabbed up the Bronx telephone book, and searched for Salzman's home address. He was not listed, nor was his office. Neither was he in the Manhattan book. But Leo remembered having written down the address on a slip of paper after he had read Salzman's advertisement in the "personals" column of the *Forward*. He ran up to his room and tore through his papers, without luck. It was exasperating. Just when he needed the matchmaker he was nowhere to be found. Fortunately Leo remembered to look in his wallet. There on a card he found his name written and a Bronx address. No phone number was listed, which, Leo now recalled, was the reason he had originally communicated with Salzman by letter. He got on his coat, put a hat on over his skull cap and hurried to the subway station. All the way to the far end of the Bronx he sat on the edge of his seat. He was more than once tempted to take out the picture and see if the girl's face was as he remembered it, but he refrained, allowing the snapshot to remain in his inside coat pocket, content to have her so close. When the train pulled into the station, he was waiting at the door and bolted out. He quickly located the street Salzman had advertised.

The building he sought was less than a block from the subway, but it was not an office building, nor even a loft, nor a store in which one could rent office space. It was an old and grimy tenement. Leo found Salzman's name in pencil on a soiled tag under the bell and climbed three dark flights to his apartment. When he knocked, the door was opened by a thin, asthmatic, gray-haired woman, in felt slippers.

"Yes?" she said, expecting nothing. She listened without listening. He could have sworn he had seen her somewhere before but knew it was illusion.

"Salzman—does he live here? Pinye Salzman," he said, "the matchmaker?"

She stared at him a long time. "Of course."

He felt embarrassed. "Is he in?"

"No." Her mouth was open, but she offered nothing more.

"This is urgent. Can you tell me where his office is?"

"In the air." She pointed upward.

"You mean he has no office?" Leo said.

"In his socks."

He peered into the apartment. It was sunless and dingy, one large room divided by a half-open curtain, beyond which he could see a sagging metal bed. The nearer side of the room was crowded with rickety chairs, old bureaus, a three-legged table, racks of cooking utensils, and all the apparatus of a kitchen. But there was no sign of Salzman or his magic barrel, probably also a figment of his imagination. An odor of frying fish made Leo weak to the knees.

"Where is he?" he insisted. "I've got to see your husband."

At length she answered, "So who knows where he is? Every time he thinks a new thought he runs to a different place. Go home, he will find you."

"Tell him Leo Finkle."

She gave no sign that she had heard.

He went downstairs, deeply depressed.

But Salzman, breathless, stood waiting at his door.

Leo was overjoyed and astounded. "How did you get here before me?"

"I rushed."

"Come inside."

They entered. Leo fixed tea and a sardine sandwich for Salzman.

As they were drinking, he reached behind him for the packet of pictures and handed them to the marriage broker.

Salzman put down his glass and said expectantly, "You found maybe somebody you like?"

"Not among these."

The marriage broker turned sad eyes away.

"Here's the one I like." Leo held forth the snapshot.

Salzman slipped on his glasses and took the picture into his trembling hand. He turned ghastly and let out a miserable groan.

"What's the matter?" cried Leo.

"Excuse me. Was an accident this picture. She is not for you."

Salzman frantically shoved the manila packet into his portfolio. He thrust the snapshot into his pocket and fled down the stairs.

Leo, after momentary paralysis, gave chase and cornered the marriage broker in the vestibule of the rooming house. The landlady made hysterical outcries, but neither of them listened.

"Give me back the picture, Salzman."

"No." The pain evident in his eyes was terrible.

"Tell me where she is then."

"This I can't tell you. Excuse me."

He made to depart, but Leo, forgetting himself, seized the matchmaker by his tight coat and shook him frenziedly.

"Please," sighed Salzman. *"Please."*

Leo ashamedly let him go. "Tell me who she is," he begged. "It's very important for me to know."

"She is not for you. She is a wild one— wild, without shame. This is not a bride for a rabbi."

"What do you mean wild?"

"Like an animal. Like a dog. For her to be poor was a sin. This is why she is dead now."

"In God's name, what do you mean?"

"Her I can't introduce to you," Salzman cried.

"Why are you so excited?"

"Why he asks," Salzman said, bursting into tears. "This is my baby, my Stella, she should burn in hell."

Leo hurried up to bed and hid under the covers. Under the covers he thought his whole life through. Although he soon fell asleep he could not sleep her out of his mind. He woke, beating his breast. Though he prayed to be rid of her, his prayers went unanswered. Through days of torment he struggled endlessly not to love her; fearing success, he escaped it. He then concluded to convert her to goodness, himself to God. The idea alternately nauseated and exalted him.

He perhaps did not know that he had come to a final decision until he encountered Salzman in a Broadway cafeteria. He was sitting alone at a rear table sucking the bony remains of a fish. The marriage broker appeared haggard, and transparent to the point of vanishing.

Salzman looked up at first without recognizing him. Leo had grown a pointed beard, and his eyes were weighted with wisdom.

"Salzman," he said, "love has at last come to my heart."

"Who can love from a picture?" mocked the marriage broker.

"It is not impossible."

"If you can love her, then you can love anybody. Let me show you some new clients that they just sent me their photographs. One is a little doll."

"Just her I want," Leo murmured.

"Don't be a fool, doctor. Don't bother with her."

"Put me in touch with her, Salzman," Leo said humbly. "Perhaps I can do her a service."

Salzman had stopped chewing, and Leo understood with emotion that it was now arranged.

Leaving the cafeteria, he was, however, afflicted by a tormenting suspicion that Salzman had planned it all to happen this way.

Leo was informed by letter that she would meet him on a certain corner, and she was there one spring night, waiting under a street lamp. He appeared, carrying a small bouquet of violets and rosebuds. Stella stood by the lamppost, smoking. She wore white with red shoes, which fitted his expectations, although in a troubled moment he had imagined the dress red, and only the shoes white. She waited uneasily and shyly. From afar he saw that her eyes—clearly her father's—were filled with desperate innocence. He pictured, in hers, his own redemption. Violins and lit candles revolved in the sky. Leo ran forward with the flowers outthrust.

Around the corner, Salzman, leaning against a wall, chanted prayers for the dead.

## YOU AND THE STORY

(1) What kind of story do you expect when someone starts by saying, "Not long ago there lived . . ."? *Retell* what happens in this story as if it were a simple folktale. Is there anything about this story that reminds you of a fairy tale?

(2) Toward the end of the story, the matchmaker asks his client: "Who can love from a picture?" What would *you* answer? Do you think that what Leo feels for the girl in the picture is really "love"?

### A Closer Look

(1) Leo first repeats the *traditional* view of the function of the matchmaker but then changes his mind later in the story. Describe the institution of the marriage broker—first as it looks to someone who wants to keep up the tradition of the ghettos, and second as it would look to someone who is fully "Americanized."

(2) Have you ever encountered the kind of person that Salzman represents? He is in some ways a *sad* person, a kind of hard-luck character. He knows a lot about suffering. (As Leo says to himself about being a Jew, "a Jew suffered.") But on the other hand, Salzman can also "bounce back" surprisingly, and be full of joy or vitality. Do a "portrait in words" of Salzman. Use examples from the story that show *both* his sad and his more joyful side.

(3) Imagine yourself as a more modern or up-to-date version of a matchmaker. Make out a description of Leo Finkle, rabbinical student, for use with prospective clients. What would you include?

(4) While going through his experience with the matchmaker, Leo learns quite a bit about what he really wants and does not want in a future bride. Suppose he had known ahead of time what he learns the hard way in the story. Draw up the kind of specifications he might have given the matchmaker, telling him what was desirable and undesirable, what was important and what unimportant. Do you think Leo's expectations or requirements are reasonable, or unreasonable? What would a girl think of his ideas about marriage?

---

### Your Turn

(1) Pretend you are preparing a detailed description of *yourself* as a person for a modern matchmaking service. What are you going to include? What kind of picture of yourself are you going to give?

(2) Pretend that at some future time you are turning to a modern matchmaking service to help you find the ideal person you are looking for. Describe that imaginary ideal person as fully as you can to help them in their search.

---

Language/Composition Activity A8

WORDS IN ACTION

# What Adjectives Tell Us

If you were in the business of a matchmaker or a marriage broker, you would often be asked: "*What kind* of person? What is the person like?" All the words in the left-hand column below are *adjectives*—words we can use to answer the question "what kind?" All of these adjectives are used in Malamud's story—some of them several times. Match the number of each adjective in the left-hand column with the letter of the word or phrase that gives its meaning.

| | |
|---|---|
| 1. amiable | a. not ordinary |
| 2. animated | b. friendly |
| 3. distinguished | c. has lively feelings |
| 4. sensitive | d. knows how to do without |
| 5. ascetic | e. always sad |
| 6. tactless | f. intensely religious or otherworldly |
| 7. ravenous | g. very humble |
| 8. petite | h. has a lively manner |
| 9. mystical | i. overexcited |
| 10. enamored | j. ashamed |
| 11. irritable | k. of small build |
| 12. mortified | l. very hungry |
| 13. hysterical | m. embarrassing others |
| 14. melancholy | n. in love |
| 15. abject | o. easily made angry |

● In 1950, Jade Snow Wong published a book called *Fifth Chinese Daughter* about growing up in Chinatown. Thousands of Chinese immigrants had come to the land of the "Golden Mountains" to work as laborers building the railroads across the West or as laundry workers, waiters, and cooks in the towns. Where they settled, they often maintained many of the ways of their homeland. The family was a strong traditional unit. People looked for protection and justice to the clan that included many of their close relatives. Parents and more distant ancestors were revered; the upkeep of the graves of ancestors in the distant homeland was an important responsibility. Children were taught obedience and filial respect—the respect of a child for its parents. Originally, many of the Chinese workers who came to this country hoped to save money, to return to China, and to marry or buy property there. But many stayed, and gradually adopted the ways and the language of their new environment. Jade Snow Wong's father, who had come to San Francisco as a young man, became a naturalized citizen when he was over seventy years old. Like many other young Americans, Jade Snow Wong had to chart her way between two cultures. In the following excerpt from an autobiographical essay, she tells us about the Oriental and the Western influences in her growing up.

Jade Snow Wong

*from*

# Fifth Chinese Daughter

From infancy to my sixteenth year, I was reared according to nineteenth century ideals of Chinese womanhood. I was never left alone, though it was not unusual for me to feel lonely, while surrounded by a family of seven others, and often by ten (including bachelor cousins) at meals.

My father (who enjoyed our calling him Daddy in English) was the unquestioned head of our household. He was not talkative, being preoccupied with his business affairs and with reading constantly otherwise. My mother was mistress of domestic affairs. Seldom did these two converse before their children, but we knew them to be a united front, and suspected that privately she both informed and influenced him about each child.

In order to support the family in America, Daddy tried various occupations—candy making, the ministry to which he was later ordained—but finally settled on manufacturing men's and children's denim garments. He leased sewing equipment, installed machines in a basement where rent was cheapest, and there he and his family lived and worked. There was no thought that dim, airless quarters were terrible conditions for living and working, or that child labor was unhealthful. The only goal was for all in the family to work, to save, and to become educated. It was possible, so it would be done.

My father, a meticulous bookkeeper,

used only an abacus, a brush, ink, and Chinese ledgers. Because of his newly learned ideals, he pioneered for the right of women to work. Concerned that they have economic independence, but not with the long hours of industrial home work, he went to shy housewives' apartments and taught them sewing.

My earliest memories of companionship with my father were as his passenger in his red wheelbarrow, sharing space with the piles of blue-jean materials he was delivering to a worker's home. He must have been forty. He was lean, tall, inevitably wearing blue overalls, rolled shirt sleeves, and high black kid shoes. In his pockets were numerous keys, tools, and pens. On such deliveries, I noticed that he always managed time to show a mother how to sew a difficult seam, or to help her repair a machine, or just to chat.

I observed from birth that living and working were inseparable. My mother was short, sturdy, young looking, and took pride in her appearance. She was at her machine the minute housework was done, and she was the hardest-working seamstress, seldom pausing, working after I went to bed. The hum of sewing machines continued day and night, seven days a week. She knew that to have more than the four necessities, she must work and save. We knew that to overcome poverty, there were only two methods: working and education.

Having provided the setup for family industry, my father turned his attention to our education. Ninety-five percent of the population in China had been illiterate. He knew that American public schools would take care of our English, but he had to be the watchdog to nurture our Chinese knowledge. Only the Cantonese tongue was ever spoken by him or my mother. When the two oldest girls arrived from China, the schools of Chinatown received only boys. My father tutored his daughters each morning before breakfast. In the midst of a foreign environment, he clung to a combination of the familiar old standards and what was permissible in the newly learned Christian ideals.

My eldest brother was born in America, the only boy for fourteen years, and after him three daughters—another older sister, myself, and my younger sister. Then my younger brother, Paul, was born. That older brother, Lincoln, was cherished in the best Chinese tradition. He had his own room; he kept a German shepherd as his pet; he was tutored by a Chinese scholar; he was sent to private school for American classes. As a male Wong, he would be responsible some day for the preservation of and pilgrimages to ancestral graves—his privileges were his birthright. We girls were content with the unusual opportunities of working and attending two schools.

For by the time I was six, times in Chinatown were changing. The Hip Wo Chinese Christian Academy (in the same building as the Methodist Mission) had been founded on a coeducational basis, with nominal tuition. Financial support came from three Protestant church boards: the Congregational, Presbyterian, and Methodist churches contributed equal shares. My father was on the Hip Wo School Board for many years. By day, I attended American public school near our home. From 5:00 P.M. to 8:00 P.M. on five weekdays and from 9:00 A.M. to 12 noon on Saturdays, I attended the Chinese school. Classes numbered twenty to thirty students, and were taught by educated Chinese from China. We studied poetry, calligraphy, philosophy, literature, history, correspondence, religion, all by exacting memorization. The Saturday morning chapel services carried out the purposes of the supporting churches.

Daddy emphasized memory development; he could still recite fluently many lengthy lessons of his youth. Every evening after both schools, I'd sit by my father, often as he worked at his sewing machine, sing-songing my lessons above its hum. Sometimes I would stop to hold a light for him as he threaded the difficult holes of a specialty machine, such as one for bias bindings. After my Chinese lessons passed his approval, I was allowed to attend to American homework. I was made to feel luckier than other Chinese girls who didn't study Chinese, and also luckier than Western girls without a dual heritage.

We lived on both levels of our factory, which had moved out of the basement to street level. The kitchen, bathroom, and sitting-dining room were at the rear of the street floor. Kitchen privileges were granted employee seamstresses, who might wish to heat lunch or wash hands; our family practically never had privacy. Floorboards ran the length of the factory; we were never permitted to play on them because of the danger of splinters. My mother carried each child on her back with a traditional Chinese support until he was able to walk firmly, to eliminate the necessity of crawling and the danger of injury by machine pulleys and motor belts. Only the living quarters were laid with what was known as "battleship linoleum," which was an uninspired brown, but unquestionably durable. There was little time for play, and toys were unknown to me. In any spare time, I was supplied with embroidery and sewing for my mother. The Chinese New Year, which by the old lunar calendar would fall sometime in late January or early February of the Western Christian calendar, was the most special time of the year, for then the machines stopped for three days. Mother would clean our living quarters very thoroughly, decorate the sitting room with flowering branches and fresh oranges, and arrange candied fruits or salty melon seeds for callers. All of us would be dressed in bright new clothes, and relatives or close friends, who came to call, would give each of us a red paper packet containing a good luck coin—usually a quarter. I remember how my classmates would gleefully talk of *their* receipts. But my mother made us give our money to her, for she said that she needed it to reciprocate to others.

Yet there was little reason for unhappiness. I was never hungry. Though we had no milk, there was all the rice we wanted. We had hot and cold running water—a rarity in Chinatown—as well as our own bathtub. Our sheets were pieced from dishtowels, but we had sheets. I was never neglected, for my mother and father were always at home. During school vacation periods, I was taught to operate many types of machines—tacking (for pockets), overlocking (for the raw edges of seams), buttonhole, double seaming; and I learned all the stages in producing a pair of jeans to its final inspection, folding, and tying in bundles of a dozen pairs by size, ready for pickup. Denim jeans are heavy—my shoulders ached often. My father set up a modest nickel-and-dime piecework reward for me, which he recorded in my own notebook, and paid me regularly.

My mother dutifully followed my father's leadership. She was extremely thrifty, but the thrifty need pennies to manage, and the old world had denied her those. Upon arrival in the new world of San Francisco, she accepted the elements her mate had selected to shape her new life: domestic duties, seamstress work in the factory-home, mothering each child in turn, church once a week, and occasional movies. Daddy frowned upon the community Chinese operas because of their very late hours (they did not finish till past midnight) and their mixed audiences.

Very early in my life, the manners of a Chinese lady were taught to me. How to hold a pair of chopsticks (palm up, not down); how to hold a bowl of rice (one thumb on top, not resting in an open palm); how to pass something to elders (with both hands, never one); how to pour tea into the tiny, handleless porcelain cups (seven-eighths full so that the top edge would be cool enough to hold); how to eat from a center serving dish (only the piece in front of your place; never pick around); not to talk at table, not to show up outside of one's room without being fully dressed; not to be late, ever; not to be too playful—in a hundred and one ways, we were molded to be trouble-free, unobtrusive, cooperative.

We were disciplined by first being told, and then by punishment if we didn't remember. Punishment was instant and unceremonious. At the table, it came as a sudden whack from Daddy's chopsticks. Away from the table, punishment could be the elimination of a privilege or the blow on our legs from a bundle of cane switches. My father used the switch, but mother favored a wooden clotheshanger. Now that I have four children myself, I can see that my parents' methods insured "domestic tranquillity." Once, when I screamed from the sting of his switch, my father reminded me of my good fortune. In China, he had been hung by his thumbs before being whipped by an uncle or other older family member, called to do the job dispassionately.

Only Daddy and Oldest Brother were allowed individual idiosyncrasies. Daughters were all expected to be of one standard. To allow each one of many daughters to be different would have posed enormous problems of cost, energy, and attention. No one was shown physical affection. Such familiarity would have weakened my parents and endangered the one-answer authoritative system. One

standard from past to present, whether in China or in San Francisco, was simpler to enforce.

Thirty-five years later, I have four children, two sons and two daughters. In principle we remain true to my father's and mother's tradition, I believe. Our children respect my husband and me, but it is not a blind obedience enforced by punishment. It is a respect won from observing us and rounded by friendship. My parents never said "please" and "thank you" for any service or gift. In Chinese, both "please" and "thank you" can be literally translated as "I am not worthy" and naturally, no parent is going to say that about a service which should be their just due. Now I say "thank you," "please," and "sorry" to my children, in English, and I do not think it lessens my dignity. The ultimate praise I ever remember from my parents was a single word, "good." We do not abhor a show of affection. Each child looks forward to his goodnight kiss and tuck-in. Sometimes one or more of them will throw his arms around one of us and cry out, "I love you so."

Traditional Chinese parents pit their children against a standard of perfection without regard to personality, individual ambitions, tolerance for human error, or exposure to the changing social scene. It never occurred to that kind of parent to be friends with their children on common ground. Unlike our parents, we think we tolerate human error and human change. Our children are being encouraged to develop their individual abilities. They all draw and can use their hands in crafts, are all familiar with our office and love to experiment with the potter's wheel or enameling supplies at our studio. Sometimes I have been asked, "What would you like your children to be?" Let each choose his or her career. The education of our girls will be provided by us as well as that of our boys. My father used to say, "If

no one educated girls, how can we have educated mothers for our sons?"

During the Depression, my mother and father needed even more hours to work. Daddy had been shopping daily for groceries (we had no icebox) and my mother cooked. Now I was told to assume both those duties. The management of money, time, and cookery had to be mastered. My mother would give me fifty cents to buy enough fresh food for dinner and breakfast. In those years, twenty-five cents could buy a small chicken or three sanddabs, ten cents bought three bunches of green vegetables, and fifteen cents bought some meat to cook with these. After American school I rushed to the stores only a block or so away, returned and cleaned the foods, and cooked in a hurry in order to eat an early dinner and get to Chinese school on time. When I came home at 8:00 P.M., I took care of the dinner dishes before starting to do my homework. Saturdays and Sundays were for housecleaning and the family laundry, which I scrubbed on a board, using big galvanized buckets in our bathtub.

I had no sympathetic guidance as an eleven-year-old in my own reign in the kitchen, which lasted for four years. I finished junior high school, started high school, and continued studying Chinese. With the small earnings from summer work in my father's basement factory (we moved back to the basement during the Depression), I bought materials to sew my own clothes. But the routine of keeping house only to be dutiful, to avoid tongue or physical lashings, became exasperating. The tiny space which was the room for three sisters was confining. After I graduated from Chinese evening school, I began to look for part-time paying jobs as a mother's helper. Those jobs varied from cleaning house to baking a cake, amusing a naughty child to ironing shirts, but wearying, exhausting as they were, they meant money earned for myself.

As I advanced in American high school and worked at those jobs, I was gradually introduced to customs not of the Chinese world. American teachers were mostly kind. I remember my third-grade teacher's skipping me half a year. I remember my fourth-grade teacher—with whom I am still friendly. She was the first person to hold me to her physically and affectionately—because a baseball bat had been accidentally flung against my hand. I also remember that I was confused by being held, since physical comfort had not been offered by my parents. I remember my junior high school principal, who skipped me half a grade and commended me before the school assembly, to my great embarrassment.

In contrast, Chinese schoolteachers acted as extensions of Chinese parental discipline. There was a formal "disciplinarian dean" to apply the cane to wayward boys, and girls were not exempt either. A whisper during chapel was sufficient provocation to be called to the dean's office. No humor was exchanged; no praise or affection expressed by the teachers. They presented the lessons, and we had to learn to memorize all the words, orally, before the class. Then followed the written test, word for word. Without an alphabet, the Chinese language requires exact memorization. No originality or deviation was permitted and grading was severe. One word wrong during an examination could reduce a grade by 10 percent. It was the principle of learning by punishment.

Interest and praise, physical or oral, were rewards peculiar to the American world. Even employers who were paying me thanked me for a service or complimented me on a meal well cooked, and sometimes helped me with extra dishes. Chinese often said that "foreigners" talked too much about too many personal things. My father used to tell me to think three times before saying anything, and if I said nothing, no one would say I was stupid. I perceived a difference between two worlds.

The difference was not always lovely. One day after junior high school classes (I was one of only two Chinese faces there), a tormentor chased me, taunting me with "Chinky, chinky, Chinaman . . ." and tacked on some insults. Suddenly, I wondered if by my difference, I was inferior. This question had to be resolved again and again later: when I looked for my first job, when I looked for an apartment, when I met with unexplained rejection. It was a problem I felt that I could not discuss with my parents . . .

By the time I was graduating from high school, my parents had done their best to produce an intelligent, obedient daughter, who would know more than the average Chinatown girl and should do better than average at a conventional job, her earnings brought home to them in repayment for their years of child support. Then, they hoped, she would marry a nice Chinese boy and make him a good wife, as well as an above-average mother for his children. Chinese custom used to decree that families should "introduce" chosen partners to each other's children—a custom which has some merits and which has not been abandoned. The groom's family should pay handsomely to the bride's family for rearing a well-bred daughter. They should also pay all bills for a glorious wedding banquet for several hundred guests. Then the bride's family could consider their job done. Their daughter belonged to the groom's family and must henceforth seek permission from all persons in his home before returning to her parents for a visit.

But having been set upon a new path, I did not oblige my parents with the expected conventional ending. At fifteen, I had moved away from home to work for room and board and a salary of twenty dollars per month. Having found that I could subsist independently, I thought it regretful to terminate my education. Upon graduating from high school at the age of sixteen, I asked my parents to assist me in college expenses. I pleaded with my father, for his years of encouraging me to be above mediocrity in both Chinese and American studies had made me wish for some undefined but brighter future.

My father was briefly adamant. He must conserve his resources for my oldest brother's medical training. Though I desired to continue on an above-average course, his material means were insufficient to support that ambition. He added that if I had the talent, I could provide for my own college education. When he had spoken, no discussion was expected. After his edict, no daughter questioned.

But this matter involved my whole future—it was not simply asking for permission to go to a night church meeting (forbidden also). Though for years I had accepted the authority of the one I honored most, his decision that night embittered me as nothing ever had. My oldest brother had so many privileges, had incurred unusual expenses for luxuries which were taken for granted as his birthright, yet these were part of a system I had accepted. Now I suddenly wondered at my father's interpretation of the Christian code: was it intended to discriminate against a girl after all, or was it simply convenient for my father's economics and cultural prejudice? Did a daughter have any right to expect more than a fate of obedience, according to the old Chinese standard? As long as I could remember, I had been told that a female followed three men during her lifetime: as a girl, her father; as a wife, her husband; as an old woman, her son.

My indignation mounted against that tradition and I decided then that my past could not determine my future. I knew

that more education would prepare me for a different expectation than my other female schoolmates, few of whom were to complete a college degree. I, too, had my father's unshakable faith in the justice of God, and I shared his unconcern with popular opinion.

So I decided to enter junior college, now San Francisco's City College, because the fees were lowest. I lived at home and supported myself with an after-school job which required long hours of housework and cooking but paid me twenty dollars per month, of which I saved as much as possible. The thrills derived from reading and learning, in ways ranging from chemistry experiments to English compositions, from considering new ideas of sociology to the logic of Latin, convinced me that I had made a correct choice. I was kept in a state of perpetual mental excitement by new Western subjects and concepts and did not mind long hours of work and study. I also made new friends, which led to another painful incident with my parents, who had heretofore discouraged even girlhood friendships.

The college subject which had most jolted me was sociology. The instructor fired my mind with his interpretation of family relationships. As he explained to our class, it used to be an economic asset for American farming families to be large, since children were useful to perform agricultural chores. But this situation no longer applied and children should be regarded as individuals with their own rights. Unquestioning obedience should be replaced with parental understanding. So at sixteen, discontented as I was with my parents' apparent indifference to me, those words of my sociology professor gave voice to my sentiments. How old-fashioned was the dead-end attitude of my parents! How ignorant they were of modern thought and progress! The family unit had been China's strength for centuries,

but it had also been her weakness, for corruption, nepotism, and greed were all justified in the name of the family's welfare. My new ideas festered; I longed to release them.

One afternoon on a Saturday, which was normally occupied with my housework job, I was unexpectedly released by my employer, who was departing for a country weekend. It was a rare joy to have free time and I wanted to enjoy myself for a change. There had been a Chinese-American boy who shared some classes with me. Sometimes we had found each other walking to the same 8:00 A.M. class. He was not a special boyfriend, but I had enjoyed talking to him and had confided in him some of my problems. Impulsively, I telephoned him. I knew I must be breaking rules, and I felt shy and scared. At the same time, I was excited at this newly found forwardness, with nothing more purposeful than to suggest another walk together.

He understood my awkwardness and shared my anticipation. He asked me to "dress up" for my first movie date. My clothes were limited but I changed to look more graceful in silk stockings and found a bright ribbon for my long black hair. Daddy watched, catching my mood, observing the dashing preparations. He asked me where I was going without his permission and with whom.

I refused to answer him. I thought of my rights! I thought he surely would not try to understand. Thereupon Daddy thundered his displeasure and forbade my departure.

I found a new courage as I heard my voice announce calmly that I was no longer a child, and if I could work my way through college, I would choose my own friends. It was my right as a person.

My mother heard the commotion and joined my father to face me; both appeared shocked and incredulous. Daddy at once demanded the source of this unfilial, non-Chinese theory. And when I quoted my college professor, reminding him that he had always felt teachers should be revered, my father denounced that professor as a foreigner who was disregarding the superiority of our Chinese culture, with its sound family strength. My father did not spare me; I was condemned as an ingrate for echoing dishonorable opinions which should only be temporary whims, yet nonetheless inexcusable.

The scene was not yet over. I completed my proclamation to my father, who had never allowed me to learn how to dance, by adding that I was attending a movie, unchaperoned, with a boy I had met at college.

My startled father was sure that my reputation would be subject to whispered innuendos. I must be bent on disgracing the family name; I was ruining my future, for surely I would yield to temptation. My mother underscored him by saying that I hadn't any notion of the problems endured by parents of a young girl.

I would not give in. I reminded them that they and I were not in China, that I wasn't going out with just anybody but someone I trusted! Daddy gave a roar that no man could be trusted, but I devastated them in declaring that I wished the freedom to find my own answers.

Both parents were thoroughly angered, scolded me for being shameless, and predicted that I would some day tell them I was wrong. But I dimly perceived that they were conceding defeat and were perplexed at this breakdown of their training. I was too old to beat and too bold to intimidate.

## YOU AND THE ESSAY

(1) Pretend you are one of the elders giving the younger people instructions concerning their role in life. Prepare "Advice to a Chinese Daughter." What would be the traditional advice concerning behavior, manners, duties, responsibilities? How much of what you are going to say deals with general attitudes? How much deals with specific details of etiquette?

(2) Pretend you are the American daughter who is beginning to question the traditional ways. State and defend your major objections to the traditional Chinese ways. (Which part of this assignment can you do with special conviction? What are you going to emphasize? Why?)

(3) Do you think a "bicultural" background like that of the author is a liability or an asset? What do you think the author especially valued about her dual heritage? What do you think were major handicaps?

## A Closer Look

(1) What words in this essay might be unfamiliar to the ordinary reader? One way a dictionary helps us with new or unfamiliar words is to "go to the roots." Very often a dictionary provides the Latin or Greek *word roots* from which words that at one time were new to the English language were derived. Show how the following word roots would help a reader with the italicized words in each sentence.

a. We studied poetry, *calligraphy*, history, correspondence and religion. (*kalli*: beauty; *graphy*: writing)

b. Only Daddy and Oldest Brother were allowed individual *idiosyncrasies*. (*idio*: one's own; *syncrasy*: temperament)

c. The routine of keeping house only to be dutiful became *exasperating*. (*ex*: thoroughly; *asper*: bitter)

d. No originality or *deviation* was ever permitted. (*de*: away from; *via*: the way)

e. My father was *adamant*; he must conserve his resources. (*adamant*: very hard metal)

f. Corruption, *nepotism*, and greed were all justified in the name of the family's welfare. (*nepot*: nephew, grandson)

(2) Many of the words in this essay deal with the relationships in the family during the author's growing up. Many of the words deal with the feelings and emotional reactions of parents and children. With each of the italicized words, how much help do you get from the context—from how they "fit in"?

a. Such familiarity would have weakened the one-answer *authoritative* system.

b. The tiny space was *confining*.

c. After the father's *edict*, no daughter questioned.

d. My *indignation* mounted against the tradition.

e. Both parents appeared shocked and *incredulous*.

f. My father did not spare me; I was

condemned as an *ingrate.*

g. My father was convinced that my reputation would be subject to whispered *innuendos.*

h. I dimly sensed that my parents were *conceding* defeat.

i. They were *perplexed* at this breakdown of their training.

j. I was too bold to *intimidate.*

Turn to your own experience or observation: Where have you seen two different ways of looking at things, or two different ways of doing things, come into conflict? Describe an incident or an episode where this conflict played a major role. What did you learn from the experience?

---

Language/Composition Activity A9

COMPARISON AND CONTRAST
# Writing the Point-by-Point Comparison

Jade Snow Wong was one of the millions of young Americans whose own upbringing showed them the contrast between two different cultures, two different ways of life. In her essay, we see some of the major differences between a traditional Chinese and an American or "Western" way of life. How would you line up some of the material from the essay to help a reader see what these differences are? Working alone or in a group, sort out some of what the author tells us for a point-by-point comparison. A point-by-point comparison takes up "one thing at a time." It asks one limited question at a time, and then answers it for *both* of the subjects that are being compared. Then it goes on to the next question, and again looks at both of the subjects to answer it. Follow this outline for your comparison of the Chinese and the American way as we see it in Jade Snow Wong's description:

## Chinese Tradition and the American Way

   I. The authority of parents
      A. The traditional Chinese way
      B. The American way

   II. The methods of education
      A. The traditional Chinese way
      B. The American way

   III. The different roles of men and women
      A. The traditional Chinese way
      B. The American way

(You may want to prepare this point-by-point comparison as a group project, with one or more people assigned to prepare the material for each separate point.)

Arshile Gorky, *The Artist and His Mother*, 1926–29. Oil on canvas. 60 × 50 inches. Collection of the Whitney Museum of American Art. Gift of Julien Levy for Maro and Natasha Gorky in memory of their father.

*A haunting portrait*

While many artist-immigrants looked around them, others continued to look back. Armenian Vosdanig Manoog Adoian, better known as Arshile Gorky, was such an artist, and one of the most dramatic figures in modern American art history. To avoid conscription into the Turkish army, his father had emigrated to the United States in 1908. Four years later, when Gorky was eight, he and his mother posed for a photograph to send to the father in Providence, Rhode Island. In 1915, the Turks began a massacre of all Armenians within their borders. Gorky, his mother, and sisters were forced to make a 150-mile march into what is now Soviet Armenia. In 1919 his 39-year-old mother died of starvation in his arms. After he finally arrived in America in 1920, Gorky painted a haunting double portrait based on the old photograph of him with his mother taken when Gorky was eight years old.

● In recent years, many Americans have rediscovered their varied ethnic history. Actors no longer automatically change their names to more Anglo-Saxon sounding names like Curtis or Monroe. Children read books in which the characters are no longer always called Jack and Jill but perhaps Stanislaw and Magda or Maria and Gustavo. But at the same time, for most children and grandchildren of immigrants, the old-country ways and the old-country language are slowly receding into the past. It used to be a common experience of young Americans to grow up with immigrant parents. What was it like to grow up with parents whose language and memories were tied to a country that the younger generation knew only from hearsay?

## Joe Vergara

# A Letter From Home

One evening, shortly after Pop came home, Mom told him that a letter had come from Calabria.

"Why you don't tell me before? Read-a to me right away."

We knew how important these letters were to Pop, so while Mom went to get the letter and Pop stretched out on the couch, Al, Wheezer, and I left the piano and other preoccupations and sat around on the floor. We had heard enough of these letters from Pop's hometown to know what to expect. The first page would tell how welcome our last letter had been, how eagerly they had waited for it, what good use Pop's last check had been put to, how often they thought of us and prayed for us and longed to see us. Then there would be a page or two of news—lists of who had died, who had left the town, reports on the health and well-being of various members of the family. The last page would be filled with gracious and flowery wishes that Mom and Pop and each of us, in turn, would enjoy health and success and that God would grant us long life and happiness. Reading the first and last pages, Mom usually raced along. So when Mom opened the letter, we were not expecting to learn any startling news.

But this letter was different, we saw at once. Mom didn't start reading the first page aloud quickly as usual. She didn't read aloud at all. As her eyes ran over the page, her lips began to tremble uncontrollably. Her left hand went to her forehead. Her whole body seemed suddenly to sag.

"What's wrong? What happen'?" Pop jumped up from the couch and reached for the letter in Mom's hand. He could barely read. Only with slow, painful effort could he puzzle out the words. Mom held the letter away from him, and all at once she began to cry. The tears told Pop the truth. "My mother—is it my mother?" he said in Italian, his voice strained, demanding. "What's happened to my mother? An accident? Is she dead?"

Mom nodded her head, looking tearfully into his eyes. Pop took a few unsteady steps backward and let himself down heavily on the couch. His head rocked slowly back and forth, his eyes glassy and unseeing. So quick to react in little things, he appeared drained of all emotion by the enormity of his loss. Mom went to the couch, sat down close to Pop, and took one of his hands in both of hers.

Al and Wheezer moved over to the couch and stood behind it, as though to shield Pop from further blows.

"Tell-a me, Lena. How it happen," Pop said, at length.

Mom read the letter slowly, trying to control the quiver in her voice: "We are distressed, more than we can describe," I translated to myself as Mom read, "by the sad news we must give you. God, for reasons unknown to ordinary men, has called your beloved mother to Him. Last night, while she slept peacefully, He took her from this poor world to join Him in eternal bliss. . . ."

Pop listened numbly. I suffered along with him. Never again would he see her. Never. The fine words could not change that. No need now to send monthly checks to Italy. When he went back to his home town, she would not be there to welcome him. If only he hadn't left her. If only he'd gone back to see her. If only . . .

Pop, please say something, I thought. Scream, curse, cry—anything. But Pop seemed unable to react. Finally, when Mom finished reading the letter, all he could say was "Addio, Mamma mia, addio," over and over—Good-bye, mother, good-bye.

He took the letter from Mom's hand, folded it carefully, and put it in his pocket. Then, with an effort, he lifted himself up from the couch and walked out the kitchen door to the backyard, where he began digging up the soil with a shovel—furiously—as though he hoped to drown the pain in physical exhaustion. Wheezer went out after him, picked up a smaller shovel, and began digging alongside him.

"Don't worry, your father be all right," Mom said to Al and me. "Best thing now is for him to work—to work hard. Joe, go upstairs and get your father's jacket and look for his black tie. Al, you get the big box from closet and find me a piece of black silk." Then she sat at the telephone and was shortly telling Coma' Angelina* the sad news.

I ran upstairs and got Pop's jacket and tie out of his closet. And then, not knowing how I got there, I was on the bed sobbing, "Please, dear God," I heard myself saying, "don't take Mom and Pop. Let me die first." How could I live in a world without them? Let Pop make me a shoemaker. Let Mom call me Little Swede. I didn't care. Just so long as they stayed alive. Maybe I was being selfish. For if I died first they would suffer rather than me. I couldn't help it. I didn't want them to die. . . .

Mom called me to hurry with the jacket. I got up from the bed, went into the bathroom, and soaked my face with cold water. Then I took the jacket and tie to Mom. While I watched, she sewed a black band, about three inches wide, around one upper sleeve. This done, she folded the jacket neatly and placed it, along with the black tie, on the arm of a chair.

Al and I, unable to sit still, got out our bikes and rode aimlessly about, pedaling considerably faster than usual. We had never seen our grandmother, not even a picture of her. But Pop had spoken of her so often and so fondly that we could almost feel her presence. And now . . .

Back at the house, we found Mom in the kitchen baking. She had changed into a black dress. Pop and Wheezer were still digging in the yard. We were glad when the bell rang and Coma' Angelina appeared at the front door. She was dressed all in black and carried a huge covered pot. Al took the pot from her, and she and Mom embraced affectionately.

"Here, Coma' Lena, I bring you some nice hot soup, how Compa' Charley* likes it, with pasta and little meatballs."

*Coma', Compa': abbreviated forms of *comare* and *compare*, feminine and masculine forms of the Italian for *close friend*.

"Thank you, Coma'. I'm so glad you come," said Mom, and she and Coma' Angelina went into the kitchen with the soup.

A few minutes later, Pop, carrying Wheezer in his arms, came back into the house followed by Compa' Alfonso. The sleeve of Compa' Alfonso's jacket bore a black mourning band. Pop picked up his jacket and tie and put them on. He looked very tired, his eyes puffy, but some of the strain was gone. The hard work, plus Compa' Alfonso's presence, had helped.

Later, Compa' Francesco came, bearing a box of Italian pastries. Then The Gink and Il Lungo. Seated around the big kitchen table, the old friends talked of the old country while Coma' Angelina and Mom served soup, sandwiches, and coffee. Compa' Francesco saw to it that the wine-glasses were always filled, especially Pop's. As they talked, ate, and drank, the atmosphere became livelier, less restrained. Compa' Alfonso told of once ordering a yard of sand for some small cement job around the house. A yard seemed a decent quantity. When it was delivered, he found himself inundated with the stuff. It completely covered his driveway so he couldn't get his car out. He shoveled it away for days. Compa' Francesco pulled three odd-shaped pieces of metal from his pocket. Left over from the stitching machine in his shoe-repair shop, he maintained. He had taken it apart to fix it. When he put it back together again, he could find no place for the "extra" pieces. The machine worked fine, so he carried the leftovers with him as a good-luck charm. The men, including Pop, laughed at these stories.

But beneath the laughter lay an under-current of tense uneasiness. Pop's loss was not his alone. It was shared by all of them. With the death of Pop's mother, each of the men lost a bit of himself—one more tie with the old country had been broken.

## YOU AND THE STORY

People in different societies have different ways of showing their feelings. They have different ways of reacting to serious loss, of showing—or not showing—their grief. How do the people in this selection show their grief? How do they try to overcome it?

### A Closer Look

(1) The parents of the person telling the story were from Calabria, in southern Italy. To him, the letters from there sound "gracious and flowery," full of "fine words." Point out several examples of what he means.

(2) Do the children in this story share in the emotions of their parents? When or how?

(3) Toward the end of the story, we see people eating and drinking. We hear the sound of laughter. Is the author trying to show that these people are unfeeling, or that their feelings of sorrow are not sincere? (Support your answer.)

### Your Turn

Does your family have any ties with a place that they or their ancestors at one time left behind? Write an imaginary letter from old-country or down-home relatives that stayed behind when other members of the family left for their present location.

---

Language/Composition Activity A10

LANGUAGE HISTORY

# Old Country Memories

Each ethnic group among the immigrants handed on to the next generation words and expressions related to their own history and experience. Choose one of the following groups. What was the common history and experience of people who knew and used these words? Which of the words do you know? Which of them would you have to check in a dictionary? If necessary, where else would you turn for help?

1. *Verein, Yiddish, samovar, Sabbath, menorah, medina, ghetto, anti-Semite, Czarist, mishmash, pogrom, kibitzer.*

2. *Lasagna, bocce, espresso, pasta, bambino, padre, padrone, madonna, bravo, primadonna.*

3. *Fjord, skoal, smorgasbord, lutefisk, yule, lag, skijoring, slalom.*

4. *Samurai, kimono, sake, banzai, Bushido, haiku, karate.*

BONUS: How often do we encounter ethnic names in areas like American science, American art and music, American entertainment? Study biographical dictionaries or other sources of biographical information for one such area. What is the ethnic background of some of the prominent people? What kinds of names do you encounter?

# The American Tradition

Americans have long been proud of having no set ideology. No set of beliefs or ideas is compulsory for everyone. From Thomas Jefferson's and Tom Paine's time down to our own, Americans have assumed that the citizens are free to make up their own minds, and that they are entitled to their own opinions. But at the same time, there are familiar ways of thinking and talking that have long been part of the American tradition. There are traditional values that have shaped the outlook of many generations of Americans. For instance, historians have stressed the influence of the Puritan attitude toward life. We may no longer believe in some of the doctrines the Puritans preached. We have different ways of looking at authority and organizing our communities. But we have inherited from the Puritans some of their ways of looking at other people and at the tasks of everyday life: They believed in thrift and hard work, and they did not believe in spoiling themselves or others. They helped make Americans serious, reliable, businesslike people who appreciate the satisfaction of a job well done. At the same time, they often had a tendency to mind other people's business as well as their own. To them, morality often meant a concern for the morals of other people as well as theirs. What are some of the other influences that have shaped the way Americans traditionally look at life? What are traditional American ways of looking at ambition and success? What are traditional American attitudes toward misfortune or the unfortunate? The selections in the following unit will give you a chance to think about influences and traditions that help shape our way of life.

To live in this country means to become influenced by familiar attitudes, by widely shared ways of looking at life. As John Steinbeck once said, "No one can define the American way of life or point to any person or group who lives it, but it is real nevertheless. . . . We have amassed a set of feelings which grew out of our background, but which are just as strongly held when we do not know that background." Which of the following poems express feelings that you recognize? How do they reflect traditional American ways of looking at life?

Robert Frost

# Mending Wall

Something there is that doesn't love a wall,
That sends the frozen ground swell under it,
And spills the upper boulders in the sun;
And makes gaps even two can pass abreast.
The work of hunters is another thing:
I have come after them and made repair
Where they have left not one stone on a stone,
But they would have the rabbit out of hiding,
To please the yelping dogs. The gaps I mean,
No one has seen them made or heard them made,
But at spring mending time we find them there.
I let my neighbor know beyond the hill;
And on a day we meet to walk the line
And set the wall between us once again.
We keep the wall between us as we go.
To each the boulders that have fallen to each.
And some are loaves and some so nearly balls
We have to use a spell to make them balance:
"Stay where you are till our backs are turned!"
We wear our fingers rough with handling them.
Oh, just another kind of outdoor game,
One on a side. It comes to little more:
There where it is we do not need the wall:
He is all pine and I am apple orchard.
My apple trees will never get across
And eat the cones under his pines, I tell him.
He only says, "Good fences make good neighbors."
Spring is the mischief in me, and I wonder

If I could put a notion in his head:
"*Why* do they make good neighbors? Isn't it
Where there are cows? But here there are no cows.
Before I built a wall I'd ask to know
What I was walling in or walling out,
And to whom I was like to give offense.
Something there is that doesn't love a wall,
That wants it down." I could say "Elves" to him,
But it's not elves exactly, and I'd rather
He said it for himself. I see him there
Bringing a stone grasped firmly by the top
In each hand, like an old stone savage armed.
He moves in darkness as it seems to me,
Not of woods only and the shade of trees.
He will not go behind his father's saying,
And he likes having thought of it so well
He says again, "Good fences make good neighbors."

---

## YOU AND THE POEM

(1) How do *you* feel about fences? What is the attitude of the poet's neighbor? What can be said in its favor? What is the attitude of the poet? What are the arguments on his side? Which of the two positions do you think is in tune with traditional American ideas about being "a good neighbor"?

(2) When you read this poem, what kind of voice do you seem to be hearing? What kind of person is the poet as he presents himself in this poem? Would you call him argumentative? emotional? persistent? overly serious? inclined to quarrel? What label would *you* use?

## William Stafford
# One Home

Mine was a Midwest home—you can keep your world.
Plain black hats rode the thoughts that made our code.
We sang hymns in the house; the roof was near God.

The light bulb that hung in the pantry made a wan light,
but we could read by it the names of preserves—
outside, the buffalo grass, and the wind in the night.

A wildcat sprang at Grandpa on the Fourth of July
when he was cutting plum bushes for fuel,
before Indians pulled the West over the edge of the sky.

To anyone who looked at us we said, "My friend";
liking the cut of a thought, we could say, "Hello."
(But plain black hats rode the thoughts that made our code.)

The sun was over our town; it was like a blade.
Kicking cottonwood leaves we ran toward storms.
Wherever we looked the land would hold us up.

---

### YOU AND THE POEM

(1) Americans have often liked to think of themselves as "plain folks." They are often suspicious of what is too frilly or too fancy. What kind of mentality or spirit do you think goes with the "plain black hats" in this poem? What other "plain" touches are there in the poem? What else seems to be part of the same attitude toward life?

(2) The first thing the poet says is "Mine was a Midwest home." What does that have to do with what he goes on to say? Is it an accident that the poet's home was in the Midwest?

### Your Turn

If you were asked to take sides in a debate between "plain" and "fancy," what side would you choose? (You may want to write your own poem or short passage in defense of plain or fancy.)

## Edgar Lee Masters
# Lucinda Matlock

I went to dances at Chandlerville,
And played snap-out at Winchester.
One time we changed partners,
Driving home in the moonlight of middle June,
And then I found Davis.
We were married and lived together for seventy years,
Enjoying, working, raising the twelve children,
Eight of whom we lost
Ere I had reached the age of sixty.
I spun, I wove, I kept the house, I nursed the sick,
I made the garden, and for holiday
Rambled over the fields where sang the larks,
And by Spoon River gathering many a shell,
And many a flower and medicinal weed—
Shouting to the wooded hills, singing to the green valleys.
At ninety-six I had lived enough, that is all,
And passed to a sweet repose.
What is this I hear of sorrow and weariness,
Anger, discontent, and drooping hopes?
Degenerate sons and daughters,
Life is too strong for you—
It takes life to love Life.

### YOU AND THE POEM

(1) Americans have long had a reputation around the world as *optimists.* Critics of American popular preachers and philosophers have often criticized them for their "Pollyanna" spirit. Writers and artists in America are often admonished to take an affirmative attitude toward life. What do these different terms mean? How well would any or all of them fit the person speaking from the grave in this imaginary epitaph?

(2) An **epitaph** can be literally an inscription on a tombstone or a statement commemorating someone who has departed. What would you like to see in your own imaginary epitaph? What thoughts would you like to convey to the reader? Write it as you would like to see it.

## Robert Hayden
# Those Winter Sundays

Sundays too my father got up early,
and put his clothes on in the blueblack cold,
then with cracked hands that ached
from labor in the weekday weather made
banked fires blaze. No one ever thanked him.

I'd wake and hear the cold splintering, breaking.
When the rooms were warm, he'd call,
and slowly I would rise and dress,
fearing the chronic angers of that house,

Speaking indifferently to him,
who had driven out the cold
and polished my good shoes as well.
What did I know, what did I know
of love's austere and lonely offices?

---

### YOU AND THE POEM

(1) What word would you naturally use to fit in before *anger* in phrases like "a _____ anger" or "a _____ kind of anger"? What would *chronic* angers be? How would they be different from what we might normally expect? What kinds of words would naturally fit in before the word *love*? What is strange about using the word *austere* in connection with love?

(2) It is part of our national customs to "express appreciation" for the efforts of ordinary little-noticed individuals. We try to give recognition not just to great leaders and important persons but to the unsung heroes among the common people. How does this poem by a well-known black American poet fit into this familiar American tradition? (How is this poem *different* from what you might expect?)

### Your Turn

Write your own poem or brief prose piece about a person who to you is an "unsung hero."

Eve Merriam

# Robin Hood

has returned
to Sherwood Forest
as
Secretary of the Interior

and the greenery
is to be preserved
for the public good

directly alongside
the parts reserved
for Hood enterprises

for Sherwood Homesites
Shop-and-Sher Parking Plaza
and
Sherburger Franchises.

# Landscape

Some of
the more expensive lobbies
now have
mixed in with the artificial
so cunningly
you can scarcely tell they are
real plantings

only when
brown spots appear
can you be sure
they are real
because then you know they are
dying

---

**YOU AND THE POEMS**

The author of these two poems is aiming her satire at features of modern American life that are often criticized. What are her targets? **Satire** combines criticism with telling use of humor or slashing ridicule. What's funny in these poems?

## POEMS: **The Puritan Heritage**

When the Puritans first came to New England, they brought with them a religious spirit that played a large role in the early history of the American colonies. Puritans were people who took their religion seriously. In England, "Puritans" was the name for zealous Protestant reformers bent on purifying the Christian faith that in their judgment had become too worldly and insincere. They rejected the pomp and circumstance of the established churches. They criticized the wealth and power of bishops and popes. They insisted on strict observance of God's word as they studied it in the Bible. They preached a strict religious morality, designed to wean people away from their sinful ways. In England for a short interval, and to some extent in the New England colonies, the Puritans came close to establishing a Puritan *theocracy*—a Christian commonwealth in which the will of God, and not the will of Man, would be supreme. But England returned to its "Church of England ways," and the descendants of Puritans of the New World learned to live side by side with Quakers, Mormons, and Catholics, in a society that separated church and state. But Puritanism as a frame of mind, as a set of attitudes, played a major role in shaping the ways and the character of the new nation.

America's earliest poets were Puritans who had come to New England in search of the "New Jerusalem." Edward Taylor (1645–1729) was one of many seventeenth-century Puritans who came to this country from England, leaving behind discrimination and persecution. Anne Bradstreet (1612–1672) had been on the ship that brought the first Puritan settlers from England to Massachusetts Bay. These poets thought of their Lord as an ever-present God whose workings could be seen everywhere in the world. Their poems expressed their strong religious feelings: guilt for their sins, fear of eternal damnation, and hope in God's mercy. Like other religious poets of their time, they expressed their ideas about God and His creation in striking, vivid images. In what spirit do you think the following poems should be read? What should they sound like?

---

## Edward Taylor
# The Golden Key

Earth once was Paradise of Heaven below,
Till ink-faced sin had it with poison stocked
And chased this Paradise away into
Heaven's upmost loft, and it in Glory locked.
But thou, sweet Lord, hast with thy golden key
unlocked the door, and made a golden day.

# The Spiderweb

Hell's spider gets
His entrails spun to whipcords thus
And woven to nets
and sets.

To tangle Adam's race
In his stratagems
To their destruction, spoiled, made base
By venom things—
Damned sins.

But, mighty, gracious Lord,
Communicate
Thy grace to break the cord, afford
Us Glory's gate
and state.

# The Creation

Who blew the bellows of His furnace vast?
Or held the mold wherein the world was cast?
Who laid its cornerstone? Or whose command?
Where stand the pillars upon which it stands?
Who spread its canopy, or curtains spun?
Who in this bowling alley bowled the sun?

## YOU AND THE POEMS

(1) The religious poets of the seventeenth century were fond of striking **metaphors**. A metaphor compares one thing to another, but it is worded as if the one thing actually *were* the other. In "The Golden Key," Edward Taylor talks as if sin actually had an inky face, and as if it actually brought physical "poison" into Paradise. We ask about metaphors: How *apt* are they—how well do they fit? Think about each of the metaphors in the first poem: What does each mean? How well does each fit? Explain the ink and poison; the loft; the door, the lock, and the key; the gold.

(2) What is your reaction when you see a spider? The Puritans *hated* sin, and they used every means to make people detest it and shrink away from it. How many words can you find in the spider poem that produce a negative reaction? How many words refer to something that we would want to avoid, escape, shrink away from?

(3) Religious poets talk about things that concern the soul and the conscience. But they try to make these things as real as the material things of our everyday world. Many of the metaphors the earlier poets used necessarily compared spiritual ideas to the material things of the world of *yesterday*. Explain the comparisons that underlie the different metaphors in the creation poem. How many of them still fit well today? How many of them take us into the world of yesteryear?

## Anne Bradstreet
# The Poet's Art

I heard the merry grasshopper then sing;
The black clad cricket bear a second part.
They kept one tune and played on the
    same string,
Seeming to glory in their little art.
Shall creatures abject thus their voices
    raise,
And in their kind resound their Maker's
    praise,
While I, as mute, can warble forth no
    higher lays?*

*lays: poems.

# Human Vanity

Man's at the best a creature frail and vain,
In knowledge ignorant, in strength but weak,
Subject to sorrows, losses, sickness, pain.
Each storm his state, his mind, his body break.
From some of these he never finds cessation,
But day or night, within, without, vexation—
Troubles from foes, from friends, from dearest, nearest relation.

And yet this sinful creature, frail and vain,
This lump of wretchedness, of sin and sorrow,
This weather-beaten vessel wracked with pain,
Joys not in hope of an eternal morrow;
Nor all his losses, crosses, and vexation,
In weight, in frequency and long duration,
Can make him deeply groan for that divine translation.

When we translate something, we transfer it from one language to another. What kind of transfer is the poet talking about in the last line of "Human Vanity"? In traditional religious thinking, the greatest human sin was *pride*—the human tendency to glory in our own human wisdom and strength. The Puritans preached *humility*. In the poem "Human Vanity," what words can you find that in one way or another remind us of the shortcomings, the disadvantages, of our human state?

---

Language/Composition Activity A11

IMAGINATIVE COMPARISON
# Stretching Your Imagination

The religious poets of the seventeenth century were not afraid to use their imagination. They were not afraid to make the reader say: "I never thought of it that way before!" They used bold, unusual imaginative comparisons to make sure their readers would vividly imagine the things they were writing about. Try your hand at some comparisons of your own that would stretch your readers' imagination. Use the kind of comparison that will make them see and feel something more vividly than usual. On a separate sheet of paper, write imaginative comparisons that would complete the following frames:

1. On a hot summer day, the sun is like _____.
2. A modern river is like _____.
3. To the city dweller, the prairies are like _____.
4. To someone who grew up away from it, the ocean is like _____.
5. After the first storm of winter, the snow is like _____.
6. On a clear night, the stars are like _____.
7. On a hot summer night, my neighborhood is like _____.
8. A typical highway in my part of the state is like _____.
9. Where I grew up, the vegetation is like _____.
10. For me, a farm is like _____.

● Puritan preachers were famous for the brimstone-and-hellfire sermons they used to arouse the religious fervor of their congregations. The most famous of them all was Jonathan Edwards (1703–1758). Born in Connecticut, he studied at Yale and became a minister in Massachusetts. He tried to promote a "Great Awakening" and helped bring about a wave of evangelism that spread through the colonies. Like other Puritan preachers, Edwards painted in vivid colors the great drama of humanity's sins and salvation. He drove home the Puritan doctrine that human actions are worthless in the sight of God, that "in the course of justice, none of us should see salvation." Our only course is to throw ourselves upon God's mercy and be saved through *grace*—at God's "pleasure"; of His own arbitrary, "sovereign" will. Edwards insisted that the outward form of religion was not enough. The outward appearance of a moral and religious life was not enough. The *spirit* had to be there. The spirit of Edwards' ministry survives in his famous sermon, "Sinners in the Hands of an Angry God." The following is a much shortened version.

## Jonathan Edwards

# Sinners in the Hands of an Angry God

Almost every natural man that hears of Hell flatters himself that he shall escape it. He depends upon himself for his own security. He flatters himself in what he has done, in what he is now doing, or what he intends to do. Everyone lays out matters in his own mind how he shall avoid damnation, and flatters himself that he contrives well for himself, and that his schemes won't fail. They hear indeed that there are but few saved, and that the bigger part of men that have died are gone to Hell. But each one imagines that he lays out matters better for his own escape than others have done. He doesn't intend to come to that place of torment. He says within himself that he intends to take care and order matters so for himself as not to fail.

But the foolish children of men do miserably delude themselves in their own schemes, and in their confidence in their own strength and wisdom. They trust to nothing but a shadow. The bigger part of those that have lived under the same means of grace and are now dead are undoubtedly gone to Hell; and it was not because they were not as wise as those that are now alive. It was not because they did not lay out matters as well for themselves to secure their own escape. If we could speak with them, could inquire of them, one by one, whether they expected when alive ever to be the subjects of that misery, we doubtless should hear one and another reply, "No, I never intended to come here. I had laid out matters otherwise in my mind. I thought I should

contrive well for myself. I thought my scheme good. I intended to take care, but it came upon me unexpected. I did not look for it at that time, and in that manner. It came as a thief. Death outwitted me. God's wrath was too quick for me. O my cursed foolishness! I was flattering myself, and pleasing myself with vain dreams of what I would do hereafter, and when I was saying peace and safety, then sudden destruction came upon me."

Natural men are held in the hand of God over the pit of Hell. They have deserved the fiery pit, and are already sentenced to it; and God is dreadfully provoked, his anger is as great towards them as to those that are actually suffering the executions of the fierceness of his wrath in Hell, and they have done nothing in the least to appease or abate that anger, neither is God in the least bound by any promise to hold them up one moment. The Devil is waiting for them. Hell is gaping for them. The flames gather and flash about them, and would fain lay hold on them, and swallow them up. The fire pent up in their own hearts is struggling to break out; and there are no means within reach that can be any security to them.

Your wickedness makes you heavy as lead, and to tend downwards with great weight and pressure towards Hell. If God should let you go, you would immediately sink and swiftly descend and plunge into the bottomless gulf, and your healthy constitution, and your own care and prudence, and all your righteousness, would have no more influence to uphold you and keep you out of Hell than a spider's web would have to stop a falling rock. Were it not the sovereign pleasure of God, the earth would not bear you one moment, for you are a burden to it. The creation groans with you. The creature is made subject to the bondage of your corruption, not willingly. The sun doesn't willingly shine upon you to give you light to serve sin and Satan. The earth doesn't willingly yield her increase to satisfy your lusts, nor is it willingly a stage for your wickedness to be acted upon. The air doesn't willingly serve you for breath to maintain the flame of life in your vitals, while you spend your life in the service of God's enemies.

There are the black clouds of God's wrath now hanging directly over your heads, full of the dreadful storm, and big with thunder. Were it not for the restraining hand of God, it would immediately burst forth upon you. The sovereign pleasure of God for the present stays his rough wind; otherwise it would come with fury, and your destruction would come like a whirlwind, and you would be like the chaff of the summer threshing floor.

The wrath of God is like great waters that are dammed for the present. They increase more and more, and rise higher and higher, till an outlet is given, and the longer the stream is stopped, the more rapid and mighty is its course, when once it is let loose. It is true that judgment against your evil works has not been executed hitherto. The floods of God's vengeance have been withheld, but your guilt in the meantime is constantly increasing, and you are every day treasuring up more wrath. The waters are continually rising and waxing more and more mighty; and there is nothing but the mere pleasure of God that holds the waters back that are unwilling to be stopped, and press hard to go forward. If God should only withdraw his hand from the floodgate, it would immediately fly open, and the fiery floods of the fierceness and wrath of God would rush forth with inconceivable fury, and would come upon you with omnipotent power; and if your strength were ten thousand times greater than it is, yea ten thousand times greater than the strength of the stoutest, sturdiest devil in Hell, it would be nothing to withstand or endure it.

The bow of God's wrath is bent, and the arrow made ready on the string, and justice bends the arrow at your heart, and strains the bow, and it is nothing but the mere pleasure of God, and that of an angry God, without any promise or obligation at all, that keeps the arrow one moment from being made drunk with your blood.

Thus are all you that never passed under a great change of heart, by the mighty power of the spirit of God upon your souls—all that were never born again, and made new creatures, and raised from being dead in sin, to a state of new light and life—you are thus in the hands of an angry God. It is nothing but his mere pleasure that keeps you from being this moment swallowed up in everlasting destruction.

The God that holds you over the pit of Hell, much as one holds a spider, or some loathsome insect, over the fire, abhors you and is dreadfully provoked. His wrath towards you burns like fire. He looks upon you as worthy of nothing else but to be cast into the fire. He is of purer eyes than to bear to have you in his sight. You are ten thousand times so abominable in his eyes as the most hateful venomous serpent is in ours. You have offended him infinitely more than ever a stubborn rebel did his prince: and yet 'tis nothing but his hand that holds you from falling into the fire every moment. It is to be ascribed to nothing else, that you did not go to Hell the last night, after you closed your eyes to sleep.

O sinner! Consider the fearful danger

you are in: It is a great furnace of wrath, a wide and bottomless pit, that you are held over in the hand of that God, whose wrath is provoked and incensed as much against you as against many of the damned in Hell. You hang by a slender thread, with the flames of divine wrath flashing about it, and ready every moment to singe it, and burn it asunder. You have nothing to lay hold of to save yourself, nothing to keep off the flames of wrath, nothing of your own, nothing that you ever have done, nothing that you can do, to induce God to spare you one moment.

And now you have an extraordinary opportunity, a day wherein Christ has flung the door of mercy wide open, and stands in the door calling and crying with a loud voice to poor sinners—a day wherein many are flocking to him, and pressing into the kingdom of God. Many are daily coming from the east, west, north and south. Many that were very lately in the same miserable condition that you are in are in now a happy state, with their hearts filled with love to Him that has loved them and washed them from their sins in his own blood, and rejoicing in hope of the glory of God. How awful is it to be left behind at such a day! To see so many others feasting, while you are pining and perishing! To see so many rejoicing and singing for joy of heart, while you have cause to mourn for sorrow of heart and howl for vexation of spirit! How can you rest one moment in such a condition?

And you that are *young men*, and *young women*, will you neglect this precious season that you now enjoy, when so many others of your age are renouncing all youthful vanities, and flocking to Christ? You especially have now an extraordinary opportunity; but if you neglect it, it will soon be with you as it is with those persons that spent all the precious days of youth in sin, and are now come to such a dreadful pass in blindness and hardness.

Therefore let every one that is out of Christ now awake and fly from the wrath to come. The wrath of Almighty God is now undoubtedly hanging over a great part of this congregation: let every one fly out of Sodom.* *Haste and escape for your lives. Look not behind you. Escape to the mountain, lest you be consumed.*

*Sodom:* a city of ancient Palestine, notorious in the Bible for wickedness.

## YOU AND THE SERMON

People used to travel from afar to hear a truly eloquent preacher, someone who knew how to make sure that his voice and message reached the audience. Select a short passage from this sermon. Practice reading it aloud with the right feeling. (Your class may want to stage a reenactment of this famous sermon, with different speakers spelling each other as the preacher.)

## A Closer Look

(1) In a **sustained metaphor,** we trace the parallel between two things in detail. The reader or the listener comes to see the *several different* ways in which the things being compared are alike. For instance, when we compare a human being to a ship at sea, sunshine could be prosperity. A storm could be sickness or disaster. The distant harbor could be God's love. Trace in detail the imaginative comparison that Edwards develops in some of the following sustained metaphors:

—the rock and the abyss
—the storm
—the water and the dam
—the bow and the arrow
—the insect and the fire
—the open door

*Sinners in the Hands of an Angry God* **155**

(2) Part of the secret of eloquence is copiousness—having a copious, rich supply of words. The speaker always seems to have *more than enough* words to choose from. Edwards is the kind of eloquent speaker who often seems to be able to draw on a whole range of *synonyms,* words with roughly the same meaning. In your own words, how would you sum up the common meanings of the synonyms or closely related terms in each of the following sets? What differences, if any, set the words in each set apart?

a. schemes—prudence—contrive
b. delude—outwit
c. provoked—wrath—fury—incensed
d. wickedness—corruption—evil—sin
e. appease—abate
f. loathsome—abhor—abominable

---

**Your Turn**

The Puritans painted a vivid picture of God's anger and human wickedness. Many religious people today take a more liberal stand on these two topics. *Interview* someone with a strong background or interest in religion. Question the person about the "modern" view on these two topics. Report your findings and conclusions. Compare them with those of your classmates.

---

Language/Composition Activity A12

STUDYING PARALLELISM

# The Uses of Repetition

Edwards is a speaker who knows how to drive a point home. He follows through—he piles up related examples or similar images that all reinforce the same basic idea. Often he presents such related ideas in sentences that follow the same ground plan. When several sentences are laid out in a similar way, their *parallel structure* is a signal that helps us keep going in the same direction. When a speaker or writer uses such parallelism well, the repetition of a similar pattern helps channel our attention. But at the same time there is enough *variety* to keep the repetition from becoming monotonous. Can you see the parallel structure in passages like the following?

The sun doesn't willingly shine. . . . The earth doesn't willingly yield. . . . The air doesn't willingly serve. . . .

The devil is waiting. . . . Hell is gaping. . . . The flames gather. . . . The fire pent up in their hearts is struggling to break out. . . .

On a separate sheet of paper, write a paragraph that starts with one of the following phrases. Use parallel structure to help tie the various related ideas in your paragraph together. Choose one of the following opening phrases:

"A true leader . . ."
"A true friend . . ."
"A real woman . . ."
"A real man . . ."
"A real _____ (fill in a word of your choice) . . ."

● Benjamin Franklin (1706–1790) early became a kind of national institution. Among early Americans whose names have become household words, he stands out as someone we can easily come to know as a human being. To many readers of his *Autobiography*, he has always seemed not a historical monument but a live person who was in many ways a typical American. Benjamin Franklin was successful in business as a printer and publisher. In his adopted city of Philadelphia, he promoted public service projects of various kinds. He became known for his scientific experiments and inventions. He played an active role in local self-government in the early colonies. He later served as one of the first American diplomats in Europe after independence. What kind of person speaks to you in the following selections from his autobiography? How familiar are some of his ideas and attitudes to present-day Americans?

# Benjamin Franklin
## *from*
# Autobiography

I disliked the trade of tallow-chandler[1] and had a strong inclination for the sea, but my father declared against it; however, living near the water, I was much in and about it, learned early to swim well, and to manage boats; and when in a boat or canoe with other boys, I was commonly allowed to govern, especially in any case of difficulty; and upon other occasions I was generally a leader among the boys, and sometimes led them into scrapes, of which I will mention one instance, as it shows an early projecting public spirit, tho' not then justly conducted.

There was a salt-marsh that bounded part of the millpond, on the edge of which, at high water, we used to stand to fish for minnows. By much tramping, we had made it a mere quagmire. My proposal was to build a wharf there fit for us to stand upon, and I showed my comrades a large heap of stones, which were intended for a new house near the marsh, and which would very well suit our purpose. Accordingly, in the evening, when the workmen were gone, I assembled a number of my playfellows, and working with them diligently like so many emmets, sometimes two or three to a stone, we brought them all away and built our little wharf. The next morning the workmen

[1]**tallow-chandler:** maker of soap and candles.

were surprised at missing the stones, which were found in our wharf. Inquiry was made after the removers; we were discovered and complained of; several of us were corrected by our fathers; and, though I pleaded the usefulness of the work, mine convinced me that nothing was useful which was not honest.

I think you may like to know something of his person and character. He had an excellent constitution of body, was of middle stature, but well set, and very strong; he was ingenious, could draw prettily, was skilled a little in music, and had a clear pleasing voice, so that when he played psalm tunes on his violin and sung withal, as he sometimes did in an evening after the business of the day was over, it was extremely agreeable to hear. He had a mechanical genius too, and, on occasion, was very handy in the use of other tradesmen's tools; but his great excellence lay in a sound understanding and solid judgment in prudential matters, both in private and public affairs. In the latter, indeed, he was never employed, the numerous family he had to educate and the straitness of his circumstances keeping him close to his trade; but I remember well his being frequently visited by leading people, who consulted him for his opinion in affairs of the town or of the church he belonged to, and showed a good deal of respect for his judgment and advice: he was also much consulted by private persons about their affairs when any difficulty occurred, and frequently chosen an arbitrator between contending parties. At his table he liked to have, as often as he could, some sensible friend or neighbor to converse with, and always took care to start some ingenious or useful topic for discourse, which might tend to improve the minds of his children. By this means he turned our attention to what was good, just, and prudent in the conduct of life; and little or no notice was ever taken of what related to the victuals on the table, whether it was well or ill dressed, in or out of season, of good or bad flavor, preferable or inferior to this or that other thing of the kind, so that I was brought up in such a perfect inattention to those matters as to be quite indifferent what kind of food was set before me, and so unobservant of it that to this day if I am asked I can scarce tell a few hours after dinner what I dined upon. This has been a convenience to me in traveling, where my companions have been sometimes very unhappy for want of a suitable gratification of their more delicate, because better instructed, tastes and appetites.

My mother had likewise an excellent constitution: she suckled all her ten children. I never knew either my father or mother to have any sickness but that of which they died, he at 89, and she at 85. They lie buried together at Boston, where I some years since placed a marble over their grave, with this inscription:

JOSIAH FRANKLIN,
and
ABIAH his wife,
lie here interred.
They lived lovingly together in wedlock
fifty-five years,
Without an estate, or any gainful employment,
By constant labor and industry,
with God's blessing,
They maintained a large family
comfortably,
and brought up thirteen children
and seven grandchildren
reputably.
From this instance, reader,
Be encouraged to diligence in thy calling,
And distrust not Providence.
He was a pious and prudent man;
She, a discreet and virtuous woman.
Their youngest son,
In filial regard to their memory,
Places this stone.
J. F. born 1655, died 1744, Ætat 89.
A. F. born 1667, died 1752,——85.

By my rambling digressions I perceive myself to be grown old. I used to write more methodically. But one does not dress for private company as for a public ball. 'Tis perhaps only negligence.

To return: I continued thus employed in my father's business for two years, that is, till I was twelve years old; and my brother John, who was bred to that business, having left my father, married, and set up for himself at Rhode Island, there was all appearance that I was destined to supply his place, and become a tallow-chandler. But my dislike to the trade continuing, my father was under apprehensions that if he did not find one for me more agreeable, I should break away and get to sea, as his son Josiah had done, to his great vexation. He therefore sometimes took me to walk with him, and see joiners, bricklayers, turners, braziers,[2] etc., at their work, that he might observe my inclination, and endeavor to fix it on some trade or other on land. It has ever since been a pleasure to me to see good workmen handle their tools; and it has been useful to me, having learned so much by it as to be able to do little jobs myself in my house when a workman could not readily be got, and to construct little machines for my experiments, while the intention of making the experiment was fresh and warm in my mind. My father at last fixed upon the cutler's trade, and my uncle Benjamin's son Samuel, who was bred to that business in London, being about that time established in Boston, I was sent to be with him some time on liking. But his expectations of a fee with me displeasing my father, I was taken home again.

From a child I was fond of reading, and all the little money that came into my hands was ever laid out in books. Pleased with the *Pilgrim's Progress*, my first collection was of John Bunyan's works in separate little volumes. I afterward sold them to enable me to buy R. Burton's Historical Collections; they were small chapmen's books, and cheap, 40 or 50 in all. . . .

This bookish inclination at length determined my father to make me a printer, though he had already one son (James) of that profession. In 1717 my brother James returned from England with a press and letters to set up his business in Boston. I liked it much better than that of my father, but still had a hankering for the sea. To prevent the apprehended effect of such an inclination, my father was impatient to have me bound to my brother. I stood out some time, but at last was persuaded, and signed the indentures[3] when I was yet but twelve years old. I was to serve as an apprentice till I was twenty-one years of age, only I was to be allowed journeyman's wages during the last year. In a little time I made great proficiency in the business, and became a useful hand to my brother. I now had access to better books. An acquaintance with the apprentices of booksellers enabled me sometimes to borrow a small one, which I was careful to return soon and clean. Often I sat up in my room reading the greatest part of the night, when the book was borrowed in the evening and to be returned early in the morning, lest it should be missed or wanted.

And after some time an ingenious tradesman, Mr. Matthew Adams, who had a pretty collection of books, and who frequented our printing house, took notice of me, invited me to his library, and very kindly lent me such books as I chose to read. I now took a fancy to poetry, and

---

[2]**joiners; turners; braziers:** makers of furniture; persons who work wood and metal on a lathe; persons who work with brass.

[3]**indentures:** a contract that binds one person to work for another for a stated period of time.

Bookbinder

Letter Press Printer

Typefounder

made some little pieces; my brother, thinking it might turn to account, encouraged me, and put me on composing occasional ballads. One was called *The Lighthouse Tragedy*, and contained an account of the drowning of Captain Worthilake, with his two daughters: the other was a sailor's song, on the taking of *Teach* (or Blackbeard) the pirate. They were wretched stuff, in the Grub Street ballad style; and when they were printed he sent me about the town to sell them. The first sold wonderfully, the event being recent, having made a great noise. This flattered my vanity; but my father discouraged me by ridiculing my performances, and telling me verse-makers were generally beggars. So I escaped being a poet, most probably a very bad one; but as prose writing has been of great use to me in the course of my life, and was a principal means of my advancement, I shall tell you how, in such a situation, I acquired what little ability I have in that way.

There was another bookish lad in the town, John Collins by name, with whom I was intimately acquainted. We sometimes disputed, and very fond we were of argument, and very desirous of confuting one another, which disputatious turn, by the way, is apt to become a very bad habit, making people often extremely disagreeable in company by the contradiction that is necessary to bring it into practice; and thence, besides souring and spoiling the conversation, is productive of disgusts and, perhaps, enmities where you may have occasion for friendship. I had caught it by reading my father's books of dispute about religion. Persons of good sense, I have since observed, seldom fall into it . . . .

A question was once, somehow or other, started between Collins and me, of the propriety of educating the female sex in learning, and their abilities for study. He was of opinion that it was improper, and that they were naturally unequal to it. I took the contrary side, perhaps a little for dispute's sake. He was naturally more eloquent, had a ready plenty of words; and sometimes, as I thought, bore me down more by his fluency than by the strength of his reasons. As we parted without settling the point, and were not to see one another again for some time, I sat down to put my arguments in writing, which I copied fair and sent to him. He answered, and I replied. Three or four letters of a side had passed, when my father happened to find my papers and read them. Without entering into the discussion, he took occasion to talk to me about the manner of my writing; observed that, though I had the advantage of my antagonist in correct spelling and pointing[4] (which I owed to the printing house), I fell far short in elegance of expression, in method and in perspicuity, of which he convinced me by several instances. I saw the justice of his remarks, and thence grew more attentive to the manner in writing, and determined to endeavor at improvement.

When about 16 years of age I happened to meet with a book, written by one Tryon, recommending a vegetable diet. I determined to go into it. My brother, being yet unmarried, did not keep house, but boarded himself and his apprentices in another family. My refusing to eat flesh occasioned an inconveniency, and I was frequently chid for my singularity. I made myself acquainted with Tryon's manner of preparing some of his dishes, such as boiling potatoes or rice, making hasty pudding, and a few others, and then proposed to my brother, that if he would give me, weekly, half the money he paid for my board, I would board myself. He instantly agreed to it, and I presently found that I could save half what he paid me. This was an additional fund for buying books. But I had another advantage in it.

[4] **pointing:** punctuation.

My brother and the rest going from the printing house to their meals, I remained there alone, and, dispatching presently my light repast, which often was no more than a biscuit or a slice of bread, a handful of raisins or a tart from the pastry-cook's, and a glass of water, had the rest of the time till their return for study, in which I made the greater progress, from that greater clearness of head and quicker apprehension which usually attend temperance in eating and drinking.

And now it was that, being on some occasion made ashamed of my ignorance in figures, which I had twice failed in learning when at school, I took Cocker's book of Arithmetic, and went through the whole by myself with great ease. I also read Seller's and Shermy's books of Navigation, and became acquainted with the little geometry they contain; but never proceeded far in that science . . . .

My brother had, in 1720 or 1721, begun to print a newspaper. It was the second that appeared in America, and was called the New England Courant. The only one before it was the Boston News-Letter. I remember his being dissuaded by some of his friends from the undertaking, as not likely to succeed, one newspaper being, in their judgment, enough for America. At this time (1771) there are not less than five-and-twenty. He went on, however, with the undertaking, and after having worked in composing the types and printing off the sheets, I was employed to carry the papers through the streets to the customers.

He had some ingenious men among his friends, who amused themselves by writing little pieces for this paper, which gained it credit and made it more in demand, and these gentlemen often visited us. Hearing their conversations, and their accounts of the approbation their papers were received with, I was excited to try my hand among them; but, being still a boy, and suspecting that my brother would object to printing anything of mine in his paper if he knew it to be mine, I contrived to disguise my hand, and, writing an anonymous paper, I put it in at night under the door of the printing house. It was found in the morning, and communicated to his writing friends when they called in as usual. They read it, commented on it in my hearing, and I had the exquisite pleasure of finding it met with their approbation, and that, in their different guesses at the author, none were named but men of some character among us for learning and ingenuity. I suppose now that I was rather lucky in my judges, and that perhaps they were not really so very good ones as I then esteemed them.

Encouraged, however, by this, I wrote and conveyed in the same way to the press several more papers which were equally approved; and I kept my secret till my small fund of sense for such performances was pretty well exhausted, and then I discovered it, when I began to be considered a little more by my brother's acquaintance, and in a manner that did not quite please him, as he thought, probably with reason, that it tended to make me too vain. And, perhaps, this might be one occasion of the differences that we began to have about this time. Though a brother, he considered himself as my master, and me as his apprentice, and, accordingly, expected the same services from me as he would from another, while I thought he demeaned me too much in some he required of me, who from a brother expected more indulgence. Our disputes were often brought before our father, and I fancy I was either generally in the right, or else a better pleader, because the judgment was generally in my favor. But my brother was passionate, and had often beaten me, which I took extremely amiss; and, thinking my apprenticeship very tedious, I was continually wishing for some opportunity of shortening it, which at length offered in a manner unexpected.

One of the pieces in our newspaper on some political point, which I have now forgotten, gave offense to the Assembly. He was taken up, censured, and imprisoned for a month, by the speaker's warrant, I suppose, because he would not discover his author. I too was taken up and examined before the council; but, though I did not give them any satisfaction, they contented themselves with admonishing me, and dismissed me, considering me, perhaps, as an apprentice, who was bound to keep his master's secrets.

During my brother's confinement, which I resented a good deal, notwithstanding our private differences, I had the management of the paper; and I made bold to give our rulers some rubs in it, which my brother took very kindly, while others began to consider me in an unfavorable light, as a young genius that had a turn for libelling and satire. My brother's discharge was accompanied with an order of the House (a very odd one), that "James Franklin should no longer print the paper called the New England Courant."

There was a consultation held in our printing house among his friends, what he should do in this case. Some proposed to evade the order by changing the name of the paper; but my brother seeing inconveniences in that, it was finally concluded on as a better way, to let it be printed for the future under the name of BENJAMIN FRANKLIN; and to avoid the censure of the Assembly, that might fall on him as still printing it by his apprentice, the contrivance was that my old indenture should be returned to me, with a full discharge on the back of it, to be shown on occasion, but to secure to him the benefit of my service, I was to sign new indentures for the remainder of the term, which were to be kept private. A very flimsy scheme it was; however, it was immediately executed, and the paper went on accordingly, under my name, for several months.

At length, a fresh difference arising between my brother and me, I took upon me to assert my freedom, presuming that he would not venture to produce the new indentures. It was not fair in me to take this advantage, and this I therefore reckon one of the first errata of my life; but the unfairness of it weighed little with me, when under the impressions of resentment for the blows his passion too often urged him to bestow upon me, though he was otherwise not an ill-natured man: perhaps I was too saucy and provoking.

When he found I would leave him, he took care to prevent my getting employment in any other printing house of the town, by going round and speaking to every master, who accordingly refused to give me work. I then thought of going to New York, as the nearest place where there was a printer; and I was rather inclined to leave Boston when I reflected that I had already made myself a little obnoxious to the governing party, and, from the arbitrary proceedings of the Assembly in my brother's case, it was likely I might, if I stayed, soon bring myself into scrapes. . . . I determined on the point, but my father now siding with my brother, I was sensible that, if I attempted to go openly, means would be used to prevent me. My friend Collins, therefore, undertook to manage a little for me. He agreed with the captain of a New York sloop for my passage, under the notion of my being a young acquaintance of his, that had got a naughty girl with child, whose friends would compel me to marry her, and therefore I could not appear or come away publicly. So I sold some of my books to raise a little money, was taken on board privately, and as we had a fair wind, in three days I found myself in New York, near 300 miles from home, a boy of but 17, without the least recommendation to, or knowledge of any person in the place, and with very little money in my pocket.

My inclinations for the sea were by this time worn out, or I might now have gratified them. But, having a trade, and supposing myself a pretty good workman, I offered my service to the printer in the place, old Mr. William Bradford, who had been the first printer in Pennsylvania, but removed from thence upon the quarrel of George Keith. He could give me no employment, having little to do, and help enough already; but says he, "My son at Philadelphia has lately lost his principal hand, Aquila Rose, by death; if you go thither, I believe he may employ you." Philadelphia was a hundred miles further; I set out, however, in a boat for Amboy, leaving my chest and things to follow me round by sea.

---

## YOU AND THE READING

Many readers have always considered Benjamin Franklin "as American as apple pie." When we know and understand some of his attitudes toward life, we understand some of the values that helped shaped the way of life of many generations of Americans. Could you pull together from this account what helps us know and understand one or more of the following?

—his attitude toward *work*
—his attitude toward *education*
—his attitude toward *authority*

How familiar are the views and attitudes that you find here?

---

### A Closer Look

(1) How much do you learn about the life of the early tradesmen here? What does the word "trade" mean usually in this account?

What are "indentures"?

(2) Franklin uses many everyday expressions along with words that suit a fairly formal, dignified eighteenth-century style. For each of the following, what would be a more familiar everyday word?

arbitrator    proficiency    converse

disputatious    victuals

perspicuity    gratification

approbation    vexation    errata

(3) Franklin says that he "was generally a leader among the boys." Do you think he had qualities that would make him a "natural leader"? Does he have qualities that you would look for in a leader?

(4) What was Franklin's attitude toward his father? What was his attitude toward his brother? How typical or familiar would his attitudes be today?

(5) Franklin was a great "moralizer." He was always telling people what he considered the right thing. Pretend you are Benjamin Franklin. Prepare to give a brief moral lecture on one of the following:

diligence    honesty    prudence

public spirit    temperance

---

Language/Composition Activity A13

WORDS IN CONTEXT

# A Trip to the Eighteenth Century

Some of Benjamin Franklin's language has become strange to our ears. Some of the words he uses we seldom hear anymore. Some of the words he uses *sound* familiar, but he uses them with slightly different meaning from what we are used to. Often we can find out what such a word means by looking at how it is used and what *goes with it* in Franklin's account. We look at the word *in context*—in a sentence, or in a whole paragraph. Look at each of the italicized words in the following sentences. What did Franklin mean when he used the word? What helps you decide?

1. We were found out, and several of us were *corrected* by our fathers.
2. He had a mechanical *genius* and was handy in the use of tools.
3. The youngest son placed the tombstone in *filial* regard of their memory.
4. My father was a chandler and my brother was *bred to* that business.
5. The apprentice was *bound* to his master.
6. Writing was of great use to me and a *principal* cause of my advancement.
7. We were fond of debating and tried to *confute* one another.
8. Contradiction produces *enmity* instead of friendship.
9. We had a debate on the *propriety* of educating the female sex.
10. He was naturally more *eloquent* and had a ready plenty of words.
11. When I refused to eat meat, I was criticized for my *singularity.*
12. I dispatched my light *repast,* which was often only a biscuit and some raisins.
13. His friends *dissuaded* him from the undertaking as not likely to succeed.
14. He *demeaned* me too much in some of the services he required of me.
15. During my brother's *confinement,* I managed the paper.

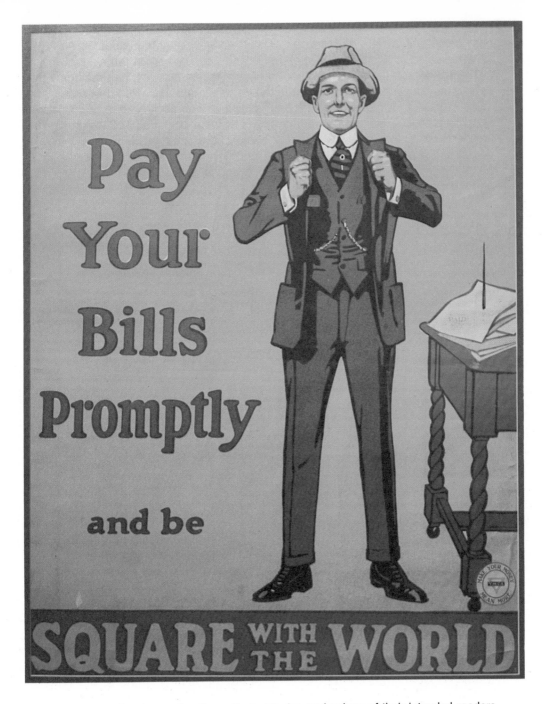

Old-time advertisements often reflect attitudes and values of their intended readers. Look at these favorite American words: *square, straight, fair, clean-cut, common sense, sincere.* Select one or more of these. What do these words bring to mind? What do they show about how Americans like to think of themselves?

● Sherwood Anderson grew up in Clyde, Ohio. He became one of the best-known chroniclers of American small-town life. Many of his best stories were collected in *Winesburg, Ohio* (1919) and *The Triumph of the Egg* (1921). Anderson tried to write about ordinary people the way they really are, behind the respectable or glib facade they present in public. He knew that there is often a lot more to people than shows in their social status or official accomplishments. He wrote about people who were confused and looking for answers. His stories often try to get at some of the basic problems that defeat and frustrate people. He had the kind of humor that makes us smile at people rather than laugh at them. The following is his sad and funny story about his parents, who had "the American passion for getting up in the world."

## Sherwood Anderson

# The Egg

My father was, I am sure, intended by nature to be a cheerful, kindly man. Until he was thirty-four years old he worked as a farmhand for a man named Thomas Butterworth whose place lay near the town of Bidwell, Ohio. He had then a horse of his own, and on Saturday evenings drove into town to spend a few hours in social intercourse with other farmhands. In town he drank several glasses of beer and stood about in Ben Head's saloon—crowded on Saturday evenings with visiting farmhands. Songs were sung and glasses thumped on the bar. At ten o'clock father drove home along a lonely country road, made his horse comfortable for the night, and himself went to bed, quite happy in his position in life. He had at that time no notion of trying to rise in the world.

It was in the spring of his thirty-fifth year that father married my mother, then a country schoolteacher, and in the following spring I came wriggling and crying into the world. Something happened to the two people. They became ambitious. The American passion for getting up in the world took possession of them.

It may have been that mother was responsible. Being a schoolteacher she had no doubt read books and magazines. She had, I presume, read of how Garfield, Lincoln, and other Americans rose from poverty to fame and greatness, and as I lay beside her—in the days of her lying-in—she may have dreamed that I would some day rule men and cities. At any rate she induced father to give up his place as a farmhand, sell his horse, and embark on an independent enterprise of his own. She was a tall silent woman with a long nose and troubled gray eyes. For herself she wanted nothing. For father and myself she was incurably ambitious.

The first venture into which the two people went turned out badly. They rented ten acres of poor stony land on Grigg's Road, eight miles from Bidwell, and launched into chicken-raising. I grew into boyhood on the place and got my first impressions of life there. From the beginning they were impressions of disaster, and if, in my turn, I am a gloomy man inclined to see the darker side of life, I attribute it to the fact that what should have been for me the happy joyous days of childhood were spent on a chicken farm.

One unversed in such matters can have no notion of the many and tragic things that can happen to a chicken. It is born out of an egg, lives for a few weeks as a tiny fluffy thing such as you will see pictured on Easter cards, then becomes hideously naked, eats quantities of corn and meal bought by the sweat of your father's brow, gets diseases called pip, cholera, and other names, stands looking with stupid eyes at the sun, becomes sick and dies. A few hens and now and then a rooster, intended to serve God's mysterious ends, struggle through to maturity. The hens lay eggs out of which come other chickens and the dreadful cycle is thus made complete. It is all unbelievably complex. Most philosophers must have been raised on chicken farms. One hopes for so much from a chicken and is so dreadfully disillusioned. Small chickens, just setting out on the journey of life, look so bright and alert and they are in fact so dreadfully stupid. They are so much like people they mix one up in one's judgments of life. If disease does not kill them, they wait until your expectations are thoroughly aroused and then walk under the wheels of a wagon—to go squashed and dead back to their maker. Vermin infest their youth, and fortunes must be spent for curative powders. In later life I have seen how a literature has been built up on the subject of fortunes to be made out of the raising of chickens. It is intended to be read by the gods who have just eaten of the tree of the knowledge of good and evil. It is a hopeful literature and declares that much may be done by simple ambitious people who own a few hens. Do not be led astray by it. It was not written for you. Go hunt for gold on the frozen hills of Alaska, put your faith in the honesty of a politician, believe if you will that the world is daily growing better and that good will triumph over evil, but do not read and believe the literature that is written concerning the hen. It was not written for you.

I, however, digress. My tale does not primarily concern itself with the hen. If correctly told it will center on the egg. For ten years my father and mother struggled to make our chicken farm pay and then they gave up that struggle and began another. They moved into the town of Bidwell, Ohio, and embarked in the restaurant business. After ten years of worry with incubators that did not hatch, and with tiny—and in their own way lovely—balls of fluff that passed on into semi-naked pullethood and from that into dead henhood, we threw all aside and, packing our belongings on a wagon, drove down Grigg's Road toward Bidwell, a tiny caravan of hope looking for a new place from which to start on our upward journey through life.

We must have been a sad-looking lot, not, I fancy, unlike refugees fleeing from a battlefield. Mother and I walked in the road. The wagon that contained our goods had been borrowed for the day from Mr. Albert Griggs, a neighbor. Out of its sides stuck the legs of cheap chairs, and at the back of the pile of beds, tables, and boxes filled with kitchen utensils was a crate of live chickens, and on top of that the baby carriage in which I had been wheeled about in my infancy. Why we stuck to the baby carriage I don't know. It was unlikely other children would be born and the wheels were broken. People who have few possessions cling tightly to those they have. That is one of the facts that make life so discouraging.

Father rode on top of the wagon. He was then a bald-headed man of forty-five, a little fat, and from long association with mother and the chickens he had become habitually silent and discouraged. All during our ten years on the chicken farm he had worked as a laborer on neighboring farms and most of the money he had earned had been spent for remedies to cure chicken diseases, on Wilmer's White Wonder Cholera Cure or Professor Bidlow's Egg Producer or some other preparations that mother found advertised in the poultry papers. There were two little patches of hair on father's head just above his ears. I remember that as a child I used to sit looking at him when he had gone to sleep in a chair before the stove on Sunday afternoons in the winter. I had at that time already begun to read books and have notions of my own, and the bald path that led over the top of his head was, I fancied, something like a broad road, such a road as Caesar might have made on which to lead his legions out of Rome and into the wonders of an unknown world. The tufts of hair that grew above father's ears were, I thought, like forests. I fell into a half-sleeping, half-waking state and dreamed I was a tiny thing going along the road into a far beautiful place where there were no chicken farms and where life was a happy eggless affair.

One might write a book concerning our flight from the chicken farm into town. Mother and I walked the entire eight miles—she to be sure that nothing fell from the wagon and I to see the wonders of the world. On the seat of the wagon beside father was his greatest treasure. I will tell you of that.

On a chicken farm, where hundreds and even thousands of chickens come out of eggs, surprising things sometimes happen. Grotesques are born out of eggs as out of people. The accident does not often occur—perhaps once in a thousand births. A chicken is, you see, born that has four legs, two pairs of wings, two heads, or what not. The things do not live. They go quickly back to the hand of their maker that has for a moment trembled. The fact that the poor little things could not live was one of the tragedies of life to father. He had some sort of notion that if he could but bring into henhood or roosterhood a five-legged hen or a two-headed rooster his fortune would be made. He dreamed of taking the wonder about the county fairs and of growing rich by exhibiting it to other farmhands.

At any rate, he saved all the little monstrous things that had been born on our chicken farm. They were preserved in alcohol and put each in its own glass bottle. These he had carefully put into a box, and on our journey into town it was carried on the wagon seat beside him. He drove the horses with one hand and with the other clung to the box. When we got to our destination, the box was taken down at once and the bottles removed. All during our days as keepers of a restaurant in the town of Bidwell, Ohio, the grotesques in their little glass bottles sat on a shelf back of the counter. Mother sometimes protested, but father was a rock on the subject of his treasure. The grotesques were, he declared, valuable. People, he said, liked to look at strange and wonderful things.

Did I say that we embarked in the restaurant business in the town of Bidwell, Ohio? I exaggerated a little. The town itself lay at the foot of a low hill and

on the shore of a small river. The railroad did not run through the town and the station was a mile away to the north at a place called Pickleville. There had been a cider mill and pickle factory at the station, but before the time of our coming they had both gone out of business. In the morning and in the evening busses came down to the station along a road called Turner's Pike from the hotel on the main street of Bidwell. Our going to that out-of-the-way place to embark in the restaurant business was mother's idea. She talked of it for a year and then one day went off and rented an empty store building opposite the railroad station. It was her idea that the restaurant would be profitable. Traveling men, she said, would be always waiting around to take trains out of town and town people would come to the station to await incoming trains. They would come to the restaurant to buy pieces of pie and drink coffee. Now that I am older I know that she had another motive in going. She was ambitious for me. She wanted me to rise in the world, to get into a town school and become a man of the towns.

At Pickleville father and mother worked hard, as they always had done. At first there was the necessity of putting our place into shape to be a restaurant. That took a month. Father built a shelf on which he put tins of vegetables. He painted a sign on which he put his name in large red letters. Below his name was the sharp command—"EAT HERE"— that was so seldom obeyed. A showcase was bought and filled with cigars and tobacco. Mother scrubbed the floor and the walls of the room. I went to school in the town and was glad to be away from the farm and from the presence of the discouraged, sad-looking chickens. Still I was not very joyous. In the evening I walked home from school along Turner's Pike and re-membered the children I had seen playing in the town school yard. A troop of little girls had gone hopping about and singing. I tried that. Down along the frozen road I went hopping solemnly on one leg. "Hip-pity Hop To The Barber Shop," I sang shrilly. Then I stopped and looked doubt-fully about. I was afraid of being seen in my gay mood. It must have seemed to me that I was doing a thing that should not be done by one who, like myself, had been raised on a chicken farm where death was a daily visitor.

Mother decided that our restaurant should remain open at night. At ten in the evening a passenger train went north past our door followed by a local freight. The freight crew had switching to do in Pick-leville, and when the work was done they came to our restaurant for hot coffee and food. Sometimes one of them ordered a fried egg. In the morning at four they returned northbound and again visited us. A little trade began to grow up. Mother slept at night and during the day tended the restaurant and fed our boarders while father slept. He slept in the same bed mother had occupied during the night and I went off to the town of Bidwell and to school. During the long nights, while mother and I slept, father cooked meats that were to go into sandwiches for the lunch baskets of our boarders. Then an idea in regard to getting up in the world came into his head. The American spirit took hold of him. Father also became ambitious.

In the long nights when there was little to do, father had time to think. That was his undoing. He decided that he had in the past been an unsuccessful man because he had not been cheerful enough and that in the future he would adopt a cheerful outlook on life. In the early morning he came upstairs and got into bed with mother. She woke and the two talked. From my bed in the corner I listened.

It was father's idea that both he and

mother should try to entertain the people who came to eat at our restaurant. I cannot now remember his words, but he gave the impression of one about to become in some obscure way a kind of public entertainer. When people, particularly young people from the town of Bidwell, came into our place, as on very rare occasions they did, bright entertaining conversation was to be initiated. From father's words I gathered that something of the jolly innkeeper effect was to be sought. Mother must have been doubtful from the first, but she said nothing discouraging. It was father's notion that a passion for the company of himself and mother would spring up in the breasts of the younger people of the town of Bidwell. In the evening bright happy groups would come singing down Turner's Pike. They would troop shouting with joy and laughter into our place. There would be song and festivity. I do not mean to give the impression that father spoke so elaborately of the matter. He was, as I have said, an uncommunicative man. "They want some place to go. I tell you they want some place to go," he said over and over. That was as far as he got. My own imagination has filled in the blanks.

For two or three weeks this notion of father's invaded our house. We did not talk much, but in our daily lives tried earnestly to make smiles take the place of glum looks. Mother smiled at the boarders and I, catching the infection, smiled at our cat. Father became a little feverish in his anxiety to please. There was, no doubt, lurking somewhere in him, a touch of the spirit of the showman. He did not waste much of his ammunition on the railroad men he served at night, but seemed to be waiting for a young man or woman from Bidwell to come in to show what he could do. On the counter in the restaurant there was a wire basket kept always filled with eggs, and it must have

been before his eyes when the idea of being entertaining was born in his brain. There was something pre-natal about the way eggs kept themselves connected with the development of his idea. At any rate, an egg ruined his new impulse in life. Late one night I was awakened by a roar of anger coming from father's throat. Both mother and I sat upright in our beds. With trembling hands she lighted a lamp that stood on a table by her head. Downstairs the front door of our restaurant went shut with a bang and in a few minutes father tramped up the stairs. He held an egg in his hand and his hand trembled as though he were having a chill. There was a half-insane light in his eyes. As he stood glaring at us I was sure he intended throwing the egg at either mother or me. Then he laid it gently on the table beside the lamp and dropped on his knees beside mother's bed. He began to cry like a boy, and I, carried away by his grief, cried with him. The two of us filled the little upstairs room with our wailing voices. It is ridiculous, but of the picture we made I can remember only the fact that mother's hand continually stroked the bald path that ran across the top of his head. I have forgotten what mother said to him and how she induced him to tell her of what had happened downstairs. His explanation also has gone out of my mind. I remember only my own grief and fright and the shiny path over father's head glowing in the lamplight as he knelt by the bed.

As to what happened downstairs: For some unexplainable reason I know the story as well as though I had been a witness to my father's discomfiture. One in time gets to know many unexplainable things. On that evening young Joe Kane, son of a merchant of Bidwell, came to Pickleville to meet his father, who was expected on the ten-o'clock evening train from the South. The train was three hours late and Joe came into our place to loaf about and to wait for its arrival. The local freight train came in and the freight crew were fed. Joe was left alone in the restaurant with father.

From the moment he came into our place the Bidwell young man must have been puzzled by my father's actions. It was his notion that father was angry at him for hanging around. He noticed that the restaurant-keeper was apparently disturbed by his presence and he thought of going out. However, it began to rain and he did not fancy the long walk to town and back. He bought a five-cent cigar and ordered a cup of coffee. He had a newspaper in his pocket and took it out and began to read. "I'm waiting for the evening train. It's late," he said apologetically.

For a long time father, whom Joe Kane had never seen before, remained silently gazing at his visitor. He was no doubt suffering from an attack of stage fright. As so often happens in life he had thought so much and so often of the situation that now confronted him that he was somewhat nervous in its presence.

For one thing, he did not know what to do with his hands. He thrust one of them nervously over the counter and shook hands with Joe Kane. "How-de-do," he said. Joe Kane put his newspaper down and stared at him. Father's eyes lighted on the basket of eggs that sat on the counter and he began to talk. "Well," he began hesitatingly, "well, you have heard of Christopher Columbus, eh?" He seemed to be angry. "That Christopher Columbus was a cheat," he declared emphatically. "He talked of making an egg stand on its end. He talked, he did, and then he went and broke the end of the egg."

My father seemed to his visitor to be beside himself at the duplicity of Christopher Columbus. He muttered and swore. He declared it was wrong to teach children that Christopher Columbus was a great man when, after all, he cheated at the critical moment. He had declared he would make an egg stand on end and then, when his bluff had been called, he had done a trick. Still grumbling at Columbus, father took an egg from the basket on the counter and began to walk up and down. He rolled the egg between the palms of his hands. He smiled genially. He began to mumble words regarding the effect to be produced on an egg by the electricity that comes out of the human body. He declared that, without breaking its shell and by virtue of rolling it back and forth in his hands, he could stand the egg on its end. He explained that the warmth of his hands and the gentle rolling movement he gave the egg created a new center of gravity, and Joe Kane was mildly interested. "I have handled thousands of eggs," father said. "No one knows more about eggs than I do."

He stood the egg on the counter and it fell on its side. He tried the trick again and again, each time rolling the egg between the palms of his hands and saying the words regarding the wonders of electricity and the laws of gravity. When after a half-hour's effort he did succeed in making the egg stand for a moment, he looked up to find that his visitor was no longer watching. By the time he had succeeded in calling Joe Kane's attention to the success of his effort, the egg had again rolled over and lay on its side.

Afire with the showman's passion and at the same time a good deal disconcerted by the failure of his first effort, father now took the bottles containing the poultry monstrosities down from their place on the shelf and began to show them to his visitor. "How would you like to have seven legs and two heads like this fellow?" he asked, exhibiting the most remarkable of his treasures. A cheerful smile played over his face. He reached over the counter and tried to slap Joe Kane

on the shoulder as he had seen men do in Ben Head's saloon when he was a young farmhand and drove to town on Saturday evenings. His visitor was made a little ill by the sight of the body of the terribly deformed bird floating in the alcohol in the bottle and got up to go. Coming from behind the counter, father took hold of the young man's arm and led him back to his seat. He grew a little angry and for a moment had to turn his face away and force himself to smile. Then he put the bottles back on the shelf. In an outburst of generosity he fairly compelled Joe Kane to have a fresh cup of coffee and another cigar at his expense. Then he took a pan and filling it with vinegar, taken from a jug that sat beneath the counter, he declared himself about to do a new trick. "I will heat this egg in this pan of vinegar," he said. "Then I will put it through the neck of a bottle without breaking the shell. When the egg is inside the bottle it will resume its normal shape and the shell will become hard again. Then I will give the bottle with the egg in it to you. You

can take it with you wherever you go. People will want to know how you got the egg in the bottle. Don't tell them. Keep them guessing. That is the way to have fun with this trick."

Father grinned and winked at his visitor. Joe Kane decided that the man who confronted him was mildly insane but harmless. He drank the cup of coffee that had been given him and began to read his paper again. When the egg had been heated in vinegar, father carried it on a spoon to the counter and going into a back room got an empty bottle. He was angry because his visitor did not watch him as he began to do his trick, but nevertheless went cheerfully to work. For a long time he struggled, trying to get the egg to go through the neck of the bottle. He put the pan of vinegar back on the stove, intending to reheat the egg, then picked it up and burned his fingers. After a second bath in the hot vinegar, the shell of the egg had been softened a little, but not enough for his purpose. He worked and worked and a spirit of desperate determination took possession of him. When he thought that at last the trick was about to be consummated, the delayed train came in at the station and Joe Kane started to go nonchalantly out at the door. Father made a last desperate effort to conquer the egg and make it do the thing that would establish his reputation as one who knew how to entertain guests who came into his restaurant. He worried the egg. He attempted to be somewhat rough with it. He swore and the sweat stood out on his forehead. The egg broke under his hand. When the contents spurted over his clothes, Joe Kane, who had stopped at the door, turned and laughed.

A roar of anger rose from my father's throat. He danced and shouted a string of inarticulate words. Grabbing another egg from the basket, he threw it, just missing the head of the young man as he dodged through the door and escaped.

Father came upstairs to mother and me with an egg in his hand. I do not know what he intended to do. I imagine he had some idea of destroying it, of destroying all eggs, and that he intended to let mother and me see him begin. When, however, he got into the presence of mother, something happened to him. He laid the egg gently on the table and dropped on his knees by the bed as I have already explained. He later decided to close the restaurant for the night and to come upstairs and get into bed. When he did so, he blew out the light and after much muttered conversation both he and mother went to sleep. I suppose I went to sleep also, but my sleep was troubled. I awoke at dawn and for a long time looked at the egg that lay on the table. I wondered why eggs had to be and why from the egg came the hen who again laid the egg. The question got into my blood. It has stayed there, I imagine, because I am the son of my father. At any rate, the problem remains unsolved in my mind. And that, I conclude, is but another evidence of the complete and final triumph of the egg—at least as far as my family is concerned.

## YOU AND THE STORY

Both the father and the mother in the story seem to be fully attuned to the "American Dream." They seem to share similar ideas about success and ambition, about getting on in the world. Describe traditional American ideas about success. Use the father and mother in this story as examples.

## A Closer Look

(1) What seems to be the father's problem? Why do things go wrong or badly? Is it something in his character? If you were his best friend trying to give him comfort or advice, what would you say? (Do any of your classmates agree with you?)

(2) What are some of the major influences that shape a child's character? We are sometimes told that a child's character is often formed at least in part by a reaction *against* what the parents do and stand for and expect. Do you see this kind of influence or reaction in this story? How does it seem to work?

(3) What accounts for the *humor* in this story? What kind of humor is it? (Could you retell some of the humorous highlights of the story?) How serious, or how funny, is the story overall?

## Your Turn

Much popular humor is found in things that go wrong. Tell a humorous story, or a sad-and-funny story, about things that went wrong in your own experience.

# Tillie Olsen

# I Stand Here Ironing

I stand here ironing, and what you asked me moves tormented back and forth with the iron.

"I wish you would manage the time to come in and talk with me about your daughter. I'm sure you can help me understand her. She's a youngster who needs help and whom I'm deeply interested in helping."

"Who needs help." Even if I came, what good would it do? You think because I am her mother I have a key, or that in some way you could use me as a key? She has lived for nineteen years. There is all that life that has happened outside of me, beyond me.

And when is there time to remember, to sift, to weigh, to estimate, to total? I will start and there will be an interruption and I will have to gather it all together again. Or I will become engulfed with all I did or did not do, with what should have been and what cannot be helped.

She was a beautiful baby. The first and only one of our five that was beautiful at birth. You do not guess how new and uneasy her tenancy in her now-loveliness. You did not know her all those years she was thought homely, or see her poring over her baby pictures, making me tell her over and over how beautiful she had been—and would be, I would tell her—and was now, to the seeing eye. But the seeing eyes were few or nonexistent. Including mine.

I nursed her. They feel that's important nowadays. I nursed all the children, but with her, with all the fierce rigidity of first motherhood, I did like the books then said. Though her cries battered me to trembling, I waited until the clock decreed.

Why do I put that first? I do not even know if it matters at all, or if it explains anything.

She was a beautiful baby. She blew shining bubbles of sound. She loved motion, loved light, loved color and music and textures. She would lie on the floor in her blue overalls patting the surface so hard in ecstasy her hands and feet would blur. She was a miracle to me, but when she was eight months old I had to leave her daytimes with the woman downstairs to whom she was no miracle at all, for I worked or looked for work and for Emily's father, who "could no longer endure" (he wrote in his good-bye note) "sharing want with us."

I was nineteen. It was the pre-relief, pre-WPA* world of the depression. I would start running as soon as I got off the streetcar, running up the stairs, the place smelling sour, and awake or asleep to startle awake, when she saw me she would break into a clogged weeping that could not be comforted, a weeping I can hear yet.

After a while I found a job hashing at night so I could be with her days, and it was better. But it came to where I had to bring her to his family and leave her.

It took a long time to raise the money for her fare back. Then she got chicken pox and I had to wait longer. When she finally came, I hardly knew her, walking quick and nervous like her father, looking like her father, thin, and dressed in a shoddy red that yellowed her skin and glared at the pockmarks. All the baby loveliness gone.

*WPA: Works Progress Administration, a program of the federal government, begun in 1935, that provided useful public jobs for needy unemployed people.

She was two. Old enough for nursery school they said, and I did not know then what I know now—the fatigue of the long day, and the lacerations of group life in the kinds of nurseries that are only parking places for children.

Except that it would have made no difference if I had known. It was the only place there was. It was the only way we could be together, the only way I could hold a job.

And even without knowing, I knew. I knew the teacher that was evil because all these years it has curdled into my memory, the little boy hunched in the corner, her rasp, "why aren't you outside, because Alvin hits you? that's no reason, go out, scaredy." I knew Emily hated it even if she did not clutch and implore "don't go Mommy" like the other children, mornings.

She always had a reason why we should stay home. Momma, you look sick, Momma. I feel sick. Momma, the teachers aren't there today, they're sick. Momma, we can't go, there was a fire there last night. Momma, it's a holiday today, no school, they told me.

But never a direct protest, never rebellion. I think of our others in their three-, four-year-oldness—the explosions, the tempers, the denunciations, the demands—and I feel suddenly ill. I put the iron down. What in me demanded that goodness in her? And what was the cost, the cost to her of such goodness?

The old man living in the back once said in his gentle way: "You should smile at Emily more when you look at her." What *was* in my face when I looked at her? I loved her. There were all the acts of love.

It was only with the others I remembered what he said, and it was the face of joy, and not of care or tightness or worry I turned to them—too late for Emily. She does not smile easily, let alone almost always as her brothers and sisters do. Her face is closed and somber, but when she wants, how fluid. You must have seen it in her pantomimes, you spoke of her rare gift for comedy on the stage that rouses a laughter out of the audience so dear they applaud and applaud and do not want to let her go.

Where does it come from, that comedy? There was none of it in her when she came back to me that second time, after I had had to send her away again. She had a new daddy now to learn to love, and I think perhaps it was a better time.

Except when we left her alone nights, telling ourselves she was old enough.

"Can't you go some other time, Mommy, like tomorrow?" she would ask. "Will it be just a little while you'll be gone? Do you promise?"

The time we came back, the front door open, the clock on the floor in the hall. She rigid awake. "It wasn't just a little while. I didn't cry. Three times I called you, just three times, and then I ran downstairs to open the door so you could come faster. The clock talked loud. I threw it away, it scared me what it talked."

She said the clock talked loud again that night I went to the hospital to have Susan. She was delirious with the fever that comes before red measles, but she was fully conscious all the week I was gone and the week after we were home when she could not come near the new baby or me.

She did not get well. She stayed skeleton thin, not wanting to eat, and night after night she had nightmares. She would call for me, and I would rouse from exhaustion to sleepily call back: "You're all right, darling, go to sleep, it's just a dream," and if she still called, in a sterner voice, "now go to sleep, Emily, there's nothing to hurt you." Twice, only twice, when I had to get up for Susan anyhow, I went in to sit with her.

Now when it is too late (as if she would let me hold and comfort her like I do the others) I get up and go to her at once at her moan or restless stirring. "Are you awake, Emily? Can I get you something?" And the answer is always the same: "No, I'm all right, go back to sleep, Mother."

They persuaded me at the clinic to send her away to a convalescent home in the country where "she can have the kind of food and care you can't manage for her, and you'll be free to concentrate on the new baby." They still send children to that place. I see pictures on the society page of sleek young women planning affairs to raise money for it, or dancing at the affairs, or decorating Easter eggs or filling Christmas stockings for the children.

They never have a picture of the children so I do not know if the girls still wear those gigantic red bows and the ravaged looks on the every other Sunday when parents can come to visit "unless otherwise notified"—as we were notified the first six weeks.

Oh it is a handsome place, green lawns and tall trees and fluted flower beds. High up on the balconies of each cottage the children stand, the girls in their red bows and white dresses, the boys in white suits and giant red ties. The parents stand below shrieking up to be heard and the children shriek down to be heard, and between them the invisible wall "Not To Be Contaminated by Parental Germs or Physical Affection."

There was a tiny girl who always stood hand in hand with Emily. Her parents never came. One visit she was gone. "They moved her to Rose Cottage," Emily shouted in explanation. "They don't like you to love anybody here."

She wrote once a week, the labored writing of a seven-year-old. "I am fine. How is the baby. If I write my letter nicely I will have a star. Love." There never was

a star. We wrote every other day, letters she could never hold or keep but only hear read—once. "We simply do not have room for children to keep any personal possessions," they patiently explained when we pieced one Sunday's shrieking together to plead how much it would mean to Emily, who loved so to keep things, to be allowed to keep her letters and cards.

Each visit she looked frailer. "She isn't eating," they told us.

(They had runny eggs for breakfast or mush with lumps, Emily said later, I'd hold it in my mouth and not swallow. Nothing ever tasted good, just when they had chicken.)

It took us eight months to get her released home, and only the fact that she gained back so little of her seven lost pounds convinced the social worker.

I used to try to hold and love her after she came back, but her body would stay stiff, and after a while she'd push away. She ate little. Food sickened her, and I think much of life too. Oh she had physical lightness and brightness, twinkling by on skates, bouncing like a ball up and down up and down over the jump rope, skimming over the hill; but these were momentary.

She fretted about her appearance, thin and dark and foreign-looking at a time when every little girl was supposed to look or thought she should look a chubby blonde replica of Shirley Temple. The doorbell sometimes rang for her, but no one seemed to come and play in the house or be a best friend. Maybe because we moved so much.

There was a boy she loved painfully through two school semesters. Months later she told me how she had taken pennies from my purse to buy him candy. "Licorice was his favorite and I brought him some every day, but he still liked Jennifer better'n me. Why, Mommy?" The kind of question for which there is no answer.

School was a worry to her. She was not glib or quick in a world where glibness and quickness were easily confused with ability to learn. To her overworked and exasperated teachers she was an overconscientious "slow learner" who kept trying to catch up and was absent entirely too often.

I let her be absent, though sometimes the illness was imaginary. How different from my now-strictness about attendance with the others. I wasn't working. We had a new baby, I was home anyhow. Sometimes, after Susan grew old enough, I would keep her home from school, too, to have them all together.

Mostly Emily had asthma, and her breathing, harsh and labored, would fill the house with a curiously tranquil sound. I would bring the two old dresser mirrors and her boxes of collections to her bed. She would select beads and single earrings, bottle tops and shells, dried flowers and pebbles, old postcards and scraps, all sorts of oddments; then she and Susan would play Kingdom, setting up landscapes and furniture, peopling them with action.

Those were the only times of peaceful companionship between her and Susan. I have edged away from it, that poisonous feeling between them, that terrible

balancing of hurts and needs I had to do between the two, and did so badly, those earlier years.

Oh there are conflicts between the others too, each one human, needing, demanding, hurting, taking—but only between Emily and Susan, no, Emily toward Susan that corroding resentment. It seems so obvious on the surface, yet it is not obvious. Susan, the second child, Susan, golden- and curly-haired and chubby, quick and articulate and assured, everything in appearance and manner Emily was not; Susan, not able to resist Emily's precious things, losing or sometimes clumsily breaking them; Susan telling jokes and riddles to company for applause while Emily sat silent (to say to me later: that was *my* riddle, Mother, I told it to Susan); Susan, who for all the five years' difference in age was just a year behind Emily in developing physically.

I am glad for that slow physical development that widened the difference between her and her contemporaries, though she suffered over it. She was too vulnerable for that terrible world of youthful competition, of preening and parading, of constant measuring of yourself against every other, of envy, "If I had that copper hair," "If I had that skin. . . ." She tormented herself enough about not looking like the others, there was enough of the unsureness, the having to be conscious of words before you speak, the constant caring— what are they thinking of me? without having it all magnified by the merciless physical drives.

Ronnie is calling. He is wet and I change him. It is rare there is such a cry now. That time of motherhood is almost behind me when the ear is not one's own but must always be racked and listening for the child cry, the child call. We sit for a while and I hold him, looking out over the city spread in charcoal with its soft aisles of light. "*Shoogily,*" he breathes and curls closer. I carry him back to bed, asleep. *Shoogily.* A funny word, a family word, inherited from Emily, invented by her to say: *comfort.*

In this and other ways she leaves her seal, I say aloud. And startle at my saying it. What do I mean? What did I start to gather together, to try and make coherent? I was at the terrible, growing years. War years. I do not remember them well. I was working, there were four smaller ones now, there was not time for her. She had to help be a mother, and housekeeper, and shopper. She had to set her seal. Mornings of crisis and near hysteria trying to get lunches packed, hair combed, coats and shoes found, everyone to school or Child Care on time, the baby ready for transportation. And always the paper scribbled on by a smaller one, the book looked at by Susan then mislaid, the homework not done. Running out to that huge school where she was one, she was lost, she was a drop; suffering over the unpreparedness, stammering and unsure in her classes.

There was so little time left at night after the kids were bedded down. She would struggle over books, always eating (it was in those years she developed her enormous appetite that is legendary in our family) and I would be ironing, or preparing food for the next day, or writing V-mail to Bill, or tending the baby. Sometimes, to make me laugh, or out of her despair, she would imitate happenings or types at school.

I think I said once: "Why don't you do something like this in the school amateur show?" One morning she phoned me at work, hardly understandable through the weeping: "Mother, I did it. I won, I won; they gave me first prize; they clapped and clapped and wouldn't let me go."

Now suddenly she was Somebody, and as imprisoned in her difference as she had been in anonymity.

She began to be asked to perform at other high schools, even in colleges, then at city and statewide affairs. The first one we went to, I only recognized her that first moment when thin, shy, she almost drowned herself into the curtains. Then: Was this Emily? The control, the command, the convulsing and deadly clowning, the spell, then the roaring, stamping audience, unwilling to let this rare and precious laughter out of their lives.

Afterwards: You ought to do something about her with a gift like that—but without money or knowing how, what does one do? We have left it all to her, and the gift has as often eddied inside, clogged and clotted, as been used and growing.

She is coming. She runs up the stairs two at a time with her light graceful step, and I know she is happy tonight. Whatever it was that occasioned your call did not happen today.

"Aren't you ever going to finish the ironing, Mother? Whistler painted his mother in a rocker. I'd have to paint mine standing over an ironing board." This is one of her communicative nights and she tells me everything and nothing as she fixes herself a plate of food out of the icebox.

She is so lovely. Why did you want me to come in at all? Why were you concerned? She will find her way.

She starts up the stairs to bed. "Don't get me up with the rest in the morning." "But I thought you were having midterms." "Oh, those." she comes back in, kisses me, and says quite lightly, "in a couple of years when we'll all be atom-dead they won't matter a bit."

She has said it before. She *believes* it. But because I have been dredging the past, and all that compounds a human being is so heavy and meaningful in me, I cannot endure it tonight.

I will never total it all. I will never come in to say: She was a child seldom smiled at. Her father left me before she was a year old. I had to work her first six years when there was work, or I sent her home and to his relatives. There were years she had care she hated. She was dark and thin and foreign-looking in a world where the prestige went to blondness and curly hair and dimples, she was slow where glibness was prized. She was a child of anxious, not proud, love. We were poor and could not afford for her the soil of easy growth. I was a young mother, I was a distracted mother. There were the other children pushing up, demanding. Her younger sister seemed all that she was not. There were years she did not let me touch her. She kept too much in herself, her life was such she had to keep too much in herself. My wisdom came too late. She has much to her and probably little will come of it. She is a child of her age, of depression, of war, of fear.

Let her be. So all that is in her will not bloom—but in how many does it? There is still enough left to live by. Only help her to know—help make it so there is cause for her to know—that she is more than this dress on the ironing board, helpless before the iron.

## YOU AND THE STORY

We each look at the world and the people in it from our own personal **point of view**. Emily's whole story is here told from the mother's point of view. We see everything through the eyes of a person thinking about her responsibilities as Emily's mother. What was it like to be Emily? Can you imagine yourself in her place? Tell Emily's story from the girl's point of view.

### A Closer Look

(1) What pictures or ideas come to your mind when you hear about poor people? How does this story live up to your expectations of what poverty is like? How is this picture of what it means to be poor different from what you would expect?

(2) People who are well established in society expect to be served well or at least adequately by its institutions. Look at the mother's view of the institutions that played a major role in the child's life: the nursery school, the convalescent home, later schools. Describe each of these. What kind of picture of institutions emerges? (What is your own basic feeling about institutions?)

(3) We see everything in this selection from the subjective, personal point of view of the person telling the story. Things in the story are seen and judged as they relate to her worries, her hopes, her life. Is it possible to look at the mother from a more objective point of view? How would she look to a fair outside observer? What kind of mother is she? Try to give a full and fair description of her.

(4) The mother several times uses phrases like "now when it is too late" or "wisdom came too late." If she had known what she knows now, would it have made any difference? What could she have done differently?

### Your Turn

The old man in the story tells the mother: "You should smile at Emily more when you look at her." The mother says about her daughter, "She does not smile easily." Americans are famous around the world for the way they value the "big smile." The most famous American slogan around the world used to be "Keep Smiling!" In your own experience, do people smile enough? Do they smile too much? Do they smile easily? In your experience, how and when do Americans smile?

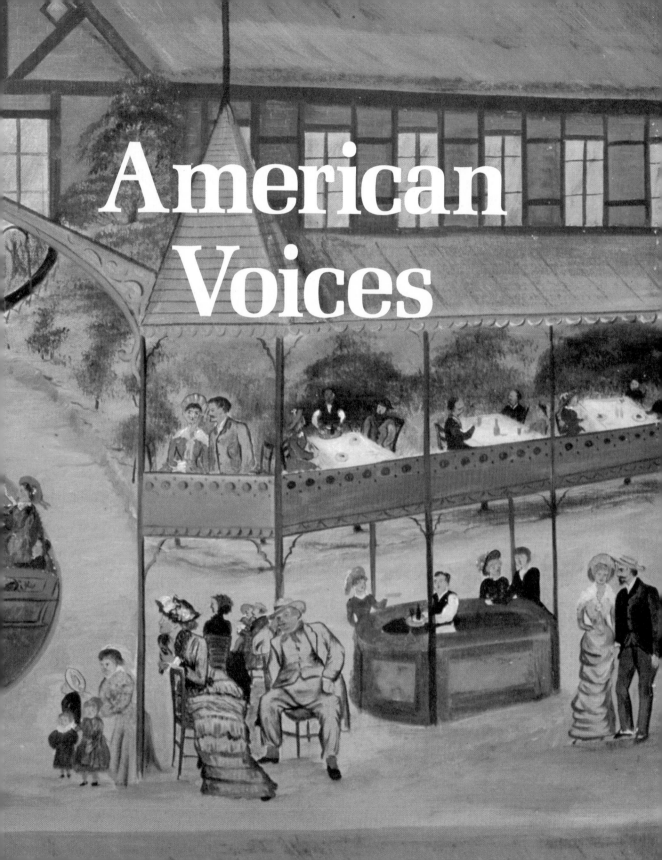

# PART TWO

# American
# Voices

# American Voices:
## American Classics Today

Whatever it is, it must have
A stomach that can digest
Rubber, coal, uranium, moons, poems.

Like the shark, it contains a shoe.
It must swim for miles through the desert
Uttering cries that are almost human.

—Louis Simpson, "American Poetry"

The literature of a nation tells us about the lives of its people. But it is not a dry factual record offered to us without comment. It is not like the reflection in the mirror, looking impartially at the good and bad. Literature is a living record, shaped by writers who select what they consider important. They try to make us see things as they appear to them. A book speaks to us strongly when the writer's point of view is in some basic way akin to the way we ourselves look at the world. A book becomes a classic when many readers everywhere recognize in it something that they themselves have felt. It puts something into words that they are ready to believe. It helps them make sense of their own experience.

Many of the classics of our national literature show the strong influence of traditions that are rooted in the American past. They were written by people attuned to the full range and sweep of American experience. Their authors responded to the elements in the American environment that are larger than life. They often used and adapted popular forms of storytelling, or they developed their own new literary forms to suit what they saw and felt.

Who are some of the best-known American authors, and what are their roots in the common experience of their people? Mark Twain, perhaps the best known and best loved of American authors, grew up with the tradition of the tall tale of the American frontier. He knew how to tell the most wildly exaggerated stories in a matter-of-fact, deadpan manner. He was a master of the most authentic kind of native American humor: the whopper that outdoes the wild stories told by everyone else. Mark Twain responded to what was rough and generous and unspoiled in the American people. When he

wrote about the bustling river traffic of the Mississippi, he could say:

In time this commerce . . . gave employment to hordes of rough and hardy men; rude, uneducated, brave, . . . heavy fighters, reckless fellows, . . . jolly, foul-witted, profane, prodigal of their money, bankrupt at the end of the trip, fond of barbaric finery, prodigious braggarts; yet, in the main, honest, trustworthy, faithful to promises and duty, and often picturesquely magnanimous.

Other American classics remind us of the tradition of popular *melodrama.* In much American popular entertainment, the good are very good and the bad very bad. This heightened contrast mirrors a traditional conflict in our view of the world: We want to believe in the native goodness of people, but we are also forever fascinated with their capacity for evil. The contrast between good and evil is strong in the writings of Nathaniel Hawthorne, who recreates for us the Puritan past. He shows us characters who want to believe in goodness. But they become obsessed with their suspicion of ever-present sin, or with their own feelings of guilt. Melodramatic evil plays a powerful role in the tradition of the Gothic tale of horror. Edgar Allan Poe was its great master.

Many of the best-known American authors threw off shackles that would have restrained less confident and less independent writers. Walt Whitman wrote with the sense of freedom and power of a poet speaking not to a small exclusive group but to a large mass of people. He celebrated American democracy in chanting *free verse* poems. When he wrote about the swirling masses of America, he could say, "The men and women I saw were all near to me":

I am with you, you men and women of a generation,
  or ever so many generations hence,
Just as you feel when you look on the river and sky,
  so I felt,
Just as any of you is one of a living crowd, I was one
  of a crowd,
Just as you are refreshed by the gladness of the river
  and the bright flow, I was refreshed, . . .
I consider'd long and seriously of you before you
  were born.
Who knows, for all the distance, but I am as good as
  looking at you now, for all you cannot see
  me?

In the following units, you will encounter some of the great names of American literature. You will encounter some of the great themes to which American writers have returned again and again. Some of the writers included, like Mark Twain or Edgar Allan Poe or Edna St. Vincent Millay, easily reached a large audience and built up a dedicated following. Others, like Herman Melville or Emily Dickinson or William Faulkner, are now remembered for works that seemed difficult and obscure to many of their early readers. You will be able to read some of the writers in this collection with ease. Others will be difficult for you. A few of the texts have been shortened and modernized somewhat to help today's reader. When a selection calls for special effort on your part, remember that many readers before you have found the effort worthwhile.

# Innocence and Experience

Every morning was a cheerful invitation
to make my life of equal simplicity, and I may
say innocence, with Nature herself.

—Henry David Thoreau, *Walden*

Great literature does not merely record life as it exists. It often mirrors the aspirations of a people. It shows what they want to believe about themselves and the future. Americans have long believed that the founding of their nation on this continent meant a new hope for humanity. Here people could leave behind the hatreds and oppression of the past. They could make a new start.

To make possible a new start and a better future, Americans had to believe that there was some native goodness in human beings. They had to believe that most people had good intentions. When confronted with challenges or problems, they had to be able to appeal to the better part of human nature. American folk heroes have often been people who basically believed in what was good and right. They have tended to be too trusting rather than too suspicious. Though they sometimes have encountered violence and treachery, they have kept their own innocence and good will.

Faith in human nature is the foundation of the American tradition of optimism—of looking at the more hopeful side of things, and of giving people the benefit of the doubt. The selections in the following unit are by writers who remind us of our traditional belief in innocence and good will, and who show how it is tested by experience.

## POET OF DEMOCRACY: **Walt Whitman**

Walt Whitman (1819–1892) considered himself the poet of American democracy. He grew up and worked as a young man on Long Island, in Brooklyn (then a small town), and in New York City. His father had been a farmer and a carpenter, and Whitman himself worked as a carpenter as well as a printer, teacher, and journalist. Walt Whitman marveled at the breadth and scope of America, and he admired the variety and the vigor of its people. He felt that an American poet should deal with

the enormous diversity of temperature and agriculture and mines—the tribes of red aborigines—the first settlements north or south . . . the perpetual coming of immigrants—the wharf-hemmed cities—the fisheries and whaling and golddigging. . . . the noble character of American workmen and workwomen . . . the general ardor and friendliness and enterprise . . . the factories and mercantile life and laborsaving machinery—the Yankee swap—the Southern plantation life—the character of the Northeast and of the Northwest and Southwest—slavery and the stern opposition to it which shall never cease.

Whitman recorded his vision of America in long, flowing **free verse** poems that read like catalogs of the inexhaustible sights and sounds of the New World. Much revised and expanded over the years, these poems became part of the collection called *Leaves of Grass,* first published in 1855 and

revised and reedited several times. Rather than showing us Utopia in a distant tomorrow, Whitman's poems described an America where the future had already begun. He painted a picture of a nation where every individual had as much dignity and importance as everyone else. No occupation was considered menial or inferior. He believed that in order to reach their full potential people had to break down the barriers that separated them from others and from parts of their own being. He encouraged everything that made people more outgoing and less embarrassed, inhibited, or superior in attitude to others. Whitman was the kind of creative genius who follows his own bent in spite of misunderstanding or ridicule. He had troubles with censors and with a reading public used to more genteel and traditional poetry. But he found supporters among the leading writers of his time, and he was gradually recognized here and abroad as one of the first great poets of a new age.

The Civil War was a serious challenge to Whitman's idealized vision of a nation of "comrades," dedicated to brotherhood and creative effort. He worked as a volunteer in army hospitals and wrote about his experiences, in poetry and prose. When President Lincoln was assassinated after the end of the war, Whitman wrote "When Lilacs Last in the Dooryard Bloomed," an elegy dedicated to a leader he had greatly admired. Two of the selections that follow are made up of passages chosen from longer poems.

Walt Whitman

# I Am One of the Nation

*from Song of Myself*

1

I am of old and young, of the foolish as much as the wise,
Stuffed with the stuff that is coarse and stuffed with the stuff that is fine,
One of the Nation of many nations, the smallest the same and the largest
    the same,
A Southerner soon as a Northerner, a planter nonchalant and hospitable
    down by the Oconee I live,
A Yankee bound my own way ready for trade, my joints the limberest
    joints on earth and the sternest joints on earth,
A Kentuckian walking the vale of the Elkhorn in my deerskin leggings,
    a Louisianian or Georgian,
A boatman over lakes or bays or along coasts, a Hoosier, Badger, Buckeye;*

*Hoosier, Badger, Buckeye: Indianan, Michigander, Ohioan.

At home on Canadian snowshoes or up in the bush, or with fishermen
off Newfoundland,
At home in the fleet of iceboats, sailing with the rest and tacking,
At home on the hills of Vermont or in the woods of Maine, or the
Texan ranch,
Comrade of Californians, comrade of free Northwesterners, (loving
their big proportions,)
Comrade of raftsmen and coal men, comrade of all who shake hands
and welcome to drink and meat,
A learner with the simplest, a teacher of the thoughtfullest,
A novice beginning yet experient of myriads of seasons,
Of every hue and caste am I, of every rank and religion,
A farmer, mechanic, artist, gentleman, sailor, quaker,
Prisoner, rowdy, lawyer, physician, priest.

## 2

Alone far in the wilds and mountains I hunt,
Wandering amazed at my own lightness and glee,
In the late afternoon choosing a safe spot to pass the night,
Kindling a fire and broiling the fresh-killed game,
Falling asleep on the gathered leaves with my dog and gun by my side.

## 3

I saw the marriage of the trapper in the open air in the far west, the
bride was a red girl,
Her father and his friends sat near cross-legged and dumbly smoking,
they had moccasins to their feet and large thick blankets
hanging from their shoulders;
On a bank lounged the trapper, he was dressed mostly in skins; his
luxuriant beard and curls protected his neck; he held his bride
by the hand;
She had long eyelashes, her head was bare, her coarse straight locks
descended upon her limbs and reached to her feet.

## 4

The runaway slave came to my house and stopped outside,
I heard his motions crackling the twigs of the woodpile,
Through the swung half-door of the kitchen I saw him limpsy
and weak.
And went where he sat on a log and led him in and assured him,
And brought water and filled a tub for his sweated body and bruised
feet,
And gave him a room that entered from my own, and gave him
some coarse clean clothes,
I had him sit next to me at table, my firelock leaned in the corner.

## 5

The big doors of the country barn stand open and ready,
The dried grass of the harvesttime loads the slow-drawn wagon,
The clear light plays on the brown gray and green intertinged,
The armfuls are packed to the sagging mow.
I am there, I help, I came stretched atop of the load,
I felt its soft jolts, one leg reclined on the other,
I jump from the crossbeams and seize the clover and timothy,
And roll head over heels and tangle my hair full of wisps.


## 6

I understand the large hearts of heroes,
The courage of present times and all times,
How the skipper saw the crowded and rudderless wreck of the
    steamship,* and Death chasing it up and down the storm,
How he knuckled tight and gave not back an inch, and was faithful
    of days and faithful of nights,
And chalked in large letters on a board, *Be of good cheer, we will
    not desert you;*
How he followed with them and tacked with them three days and
    would not give it up,
How he saved the drifting company at last,
How the lank loose-gowned women looked when boated from the
    side of their prepared graves,
How the silent old-faced infants and the lifted sick, and the sharp-
    lipped unshaved men;
All this I swallow; it tastes good. I like it well, it becomes mine,
I am the man, I suffered, I was there.


## 7

This is the city and I am one of the citizens,
Whatever interests the rest interests me: politics, wars, markets,
    newspapers, schools,
The mayor and councils, banks, tariffs, steamships, factories, stocks,
    stores, real estate and personal estate.


## 8

By the city's quadrangular houses—in log huts, camping with lumbermen,
Along the ruts of the turnpike, along the dry gulch and rivulet bed,
Weeding my onion patch or hoeing rows of carrots and parsnips,
    crossing savannas, trailing in forests.


*steamship: the *San Francisco*, which was shipwrecked and rescued three hundred miles outside of New York harbor in 1853.

Prospecting, gold digging, girdling the trees of a new purchase,
Scorched ankle-deep by the hot sand, hauling my boat down the
    shallow river.
Over the growing sugar, over the yellow-flowered cotton plant, over
    the rice in its low moist field,
Over the sharp-peaked farmhouse, with its scalloped scum and slender
    shoots from the gutters,
Where beehives range on a gray bench in the garden half hid by
    the high weeds,
Where cattle stand and shake away flies with the tremulous shuddering
    of their hides,
At the cidermill tasting the sweets of the brown mash, sucking the
    juice through a straw,
At apple-peelings wanting kisses for all the red fruit I find,
At musters, beach parties, friendly bees, huskings, house-raisings;
Where sundown shadows lengthen over the limitless and lonesome
    prairie,
Where the rattlesnake suns his flabby length on a rock, where the
    otter is feeding on fish,
Where the mockingbird sounds his delicious gurgles, cackles,
    screams, weeps,
Where the laughing gull scoots by the shore, where she laughs her
    near-human laugh,
Pleased with the native and pleased with the foreign, pleased with
    the new and old,
I tread day and night such roads.

## YOU AND THE POEM

With what part of the poem can you most easily identify? Where does the poet speak most directly for you or to you? Where does he touch on something that makes you say: "This is for me"? Explain what it is in your background or experience that makes you react as you do. What part (or parts) of the poem do you find it hardest to respond to? When or where do you feel left out? Why? (Compare your reactions with those of your classmates.)

## A Closer Look

(1) Although Whitman considered himself the poet of the common people, he liked big words that would give a solemn, elevated ring to his verse. Can you give a simpler word for each of the following?

nonchalant    vale    novice    myriad
    caste    quadrangular    rivulet
savanna    purchase    tremulous

(2) Whitman was always concerned about making his readers share in the whole range of the American experience. Show how fully this selection reflects the geographic range of the country, its range of occupations, and the variety of its lifestyles and opinions.

(3) Whitman often expressed his solidarity with the outcasts and the disinherited of society. He said, "I feel I am one of them. . . . How can I deny them?" Where

and how does he show this feeling of solidarity in this selection?

(4) What kind of "hero" does Whitman present to us in this poem, and where? What are the heroic qualities the passage illustrates?

---

**Your Turn**

---

Kenneth Rexroth, in *Classics Revisited*, says of Whitman: "His endless lists of the facts of life, which we expect to be tedious, are instead exhilarating, especially if read aloud." Arrange with your classmates for a *choral reading* of this poem. Help distribute the numbered sections among different voices. (You may further want to subdivide the first and last sections, as the poem moves from one person or one scene to another.) How should the poem be read so that the listener will share in the enthusiasm and "exhilaration" of the poet?

Walt Whitman
# A March in the Ranks Hard-Pressed

A march in the ranks hard-pressed, and the road unknown,
A route through the heavy wood with muffled steps in the darkness,
Our army foiled with loss severe, and the sullen remnant retreating,
Till after midnight glimmer upon us the lights of a dim-lighted building.
We come to an open space in the woods, and halt by the dim-lighted building,
'Tis a large old church at the crossing roads, now an impromptu hospital,
Entering but for a minute I see a sight beyond all the pictures and poems ever made,
Shadows of deepest, deepest black, just lit by moving candles and lamps,

And by one great pitchy torch stationary with wild red flame and clouds of
    smoke,
By these, crowds, groups of forms vaguely I see on the floor, some in the pews
    laid down,
At my feet more distinctly a soldier, a mere lad, in danger of bleeding to death
    (he is shot in the abdomen),
I stanch the blood temporarily (the youngster's face is white as a lily),
Then before I depart I sweep my eyes over the scene fain to absorb it all,
Faces, varieties, postures beyond description, most in obscurity, some of them
    dead,
Surgeons operating, attendants holding lights, the smell of ether, the odor of
    blood,
The crowd, O the crowd of the bloody forms, the yard outside also filled,
Some on the bare ground, some on planks or stretchers, some in the death spasm
    sweating,
An occasional scream or cry, the doctor's shouted orders or calls,
The glisten of the little steel instruments catching the glint of the torches,
These I resume as I chant, I see again the forms, I smell the odor,
Then hear outside the orders given, *Fall in, my men, fall in;*
But first I bend to the dying lad, his eyes open, a half-smile gives he me,
Then the eyes close, calmly close, and I speed forth to the darkness,
Resuming, marching, ever in darkness marching, on in the ranks,
The unknown road still marching.

## YOU AND THE POEM

Up to Whitman's time, poems about war had often been extremely partisan. They celebrated the just cause of the poet's own side and denounced the enemy. Are there any signs of partisan spirit in this poem? Point out some of the things in this poem that could have been experienced by people on either side.

## A Closer Look

(1) How was the army "foiled"? What is a "sullen remnant"? What is an "impromptu hospital"?

(2) In this poem, the poet takes us to a setting that is strange and unforgettable, like something seen in a dream. In the first ten lines, point out as many details as you can that help create a mood of gloom or foreboding.

(3) Inside the field hospital, the poet saw a "sight beyond all the pictures and poems ever made." His eyes swept over the scene "fain to absorb it all"—wanting to take everything in. Point out some of the most striking sights, sounds, and smells that the poet includes to make the scene seem real and come alive for us.

(4) Does it make a difference to the way we feel that the dying soldier is a "mere lad" and that he gives the poet a "half-smile"? How might our reaction to the poem be different if it ended when the soldier closed his eyes?

## Walt Whitman

*from*

# When Lilacs Last
# in the Dooryard Bloomed

### 1

When lilacs last in the dooryard bloomed,
And the great star early drooped in the western sky in the night,
I mourned, and yet shall mourn with ever-returning spring.
Ever-returning spring, trinity sure to me you bring,
Lilac blooming perennial and drooping star in the west,
And thought of him I love. . . .

### 2

In the dooryard fronting an old farmhouse near the whitewashed palings,
Stands the lilac bush tall-growing with heart-shaped leaves of rich green,
With many a pointed blossom rising delicate, with the perfume strong I love,
With every leaf a miracle— and from this bush in the dooryard,
With delicate-colored blossoms and heart-shaped leaves of rich green,
A sprig with its flower I break.

### 3

In the swamp in secluded recesses,
A shy and hidden bird is warbling a song.
Solitary the thrush,
The hermit withdrawn to himself, avoiding the settlements,
Sings by himself a song.
Song of the bleeding throat,
Death's outlet song of life (for well dear brother I know,
If thou wast not granted to sing thou would'st surely die).

### 4

Over the breast of the spring, the land, amid cities,
Amid lanes and through old woods, where lately the violets peeped from the
    ground spotting the gray debris,
Amid the grass in the fields each side of the lanes, passing the endless grass,
Passing the yellow-speared wheat, every grain from its shroud in the dark-
    brown fields uprisen,
Passing the apple-tree blows of white and pink in the orchards,
Carrying a corpse to where it shall rest in the grave,
Night and day journeys a coffin.

Coffin that passes through lanes and streets,
Through day and night with the great cloud darkening the land,
With the pomp of the inlooped flags with the cities draped in black,
With the show of the States themselves as of crepe-veiled women standing,
With processions long and winding and the flambeaus of the night,
With the countless torches lit, with the silent sea of faces and the bared
    heads,
With the waiting depot, the arriving coffin, and the somber faces,
With dirges through the night, with the thousand voices rising strong and
    solemn,
With all the mournful voices of the dirges poured around the coffin,
The dim-lit churches and the shuddering organs—where amid these you
    journey,
With the tolling, tolling bells' perpetual clang,
Here, coffin that slowly passes
I give you my sprig of lilac. . . .

THE FUNERAL OF PRESIDENT LINCOLN, NEW YORK, APRIL 25ᵗʰ 1865.

6

O what shall I hang on the chamber walls?
And what shall the pictures be that I hang on the walls,
To adorn the burial-house of him I love?

Pictures of growing spring and farms and homes,
With the Fourth-month eve at sundown, and the gray smoke lucid and bright,
With floods of the yellow gold of the gorgeous, indolent, sinking sun,
    burning, expanding the air,
With the fresh sweet herbage under foot, and the pale green leaves
    of the trees prolific,
In the distance the flowing glaze, the breast of the river, with a
    wind-dapple here and there,

With ranging hills on the banks, with many a line against the sky,
    and shadows,
And the city at hand with dwellings so dense, and stacks of chimneys,
And all the scenes of life and the workshops, and the workmen
    homeward returning.

## 7

Lo, body and soul—this land,
My own Manhattan with spires, and the sparkling and hurrying tides, and the
    ships,
The varied and ample land, the South and the North in the light, Ohio's
    shores and flashing Missouri,
And ever the far-spreading prairies covered with grass and corn.

Lo, the most excellent sun so calm and haughty,
The violet and purple morn with just-felt breezes,
The gentle soft-born measureless light,
The miracle spreading bathing all, the fulfilled noon,
The coming eve delicious, the welcome night and the stars,
Over my cities shining all, enveloping man and land.

## 8

Sing on, sing on you gray-brown bird,
Sing from the swamps, the recesses, pour your chant from the bushes,
Limitless out of the dusk, out of the cedars and pines.
Sing on dearest brother, warble your reedy song,
Loud human song, with voice of uttermost woe. . . .

Loud in the pines and cedars dim,
Clear in the freshness moist and the swamp-perfume,
And I with my comrades there in the night.
While my sight that was bound in my eyes unclosed,
As to long panoramas of visions.
And I saw the armies,
I saw as in noiseless dreams hundreds of battle-flags,
Borne through the smoke of the battles and pierced with missiles I saw them,
And carried hither and yon through the smoke, and torn and bloody,
And at last but a few shreds left on the staffs (and all in silence),
And the staffs all splintered and broken.

I saw battle-corpses, myriads of them,
And the white skeletons of young men, I saw them,
I saw the debris and debris of all the slain soldiers of the war,
But I saw they were not as was thought,
They themselves were fully at rest, they suffered not,
The living remained and suffered, the mother suffered,

And the wife and the child and the musing comrade suffered,
And the armies that remain'd suffer'd.

9

Passing the visions, passing the night,
Passing, unloosing the hold of my comrades' hands,
Passing the song of the hermit bird and the tallying song of my soul,
Victorious song, death's outlet song, yet varying ever-altering song,
As low and wailing, yet clear the notes, rising and falling, flooding the night,
Sadly sinking and fainting, as warning and warning, and yet again bursting
    with joy,
Covering the earth and filling the spread of the heaven,
As that powerful psalm in the night I heard from recesses,
Passing, I leave thee lilac with heart-shaped leaves,
I leave thee there in the dooryard, blooming, returning with spring.

---

### YOU AND THE POEM

Among the oldest known kinds of poetry are songs of praise and songs of mourning. Some of the oldest poems that survive are songs in which poets celebrated what was great and admirable in their world. Other ancient poems are **elegies**—poems that mourn the loss of what the poet had cherished. Walt Whitman wrote several elegies in memory of President Lincoln. One of these, "When Lilacs Last in the Dooryard Bloomed," is his greatest and best-known poem. Answer the following questions about these selections from the poem:

(1) Birdsong is often cheerful or joyful. Look at the poet's description of the bird early in the poem. What are some of the things here that help make the thrush an appropriate voice for a song of mourning?

(2) In the passage about the journey of the coffin, point out familiar sights and sounds associated with mourning. (*Flambeau* is the French word for "torch." What is a "dirge"?) This passage has a mournful, solemn rhythm like the slow muffled drum rolls of a funeral procession Listen to it read aloud.

(3) Lincoln had been the leader of one side in a conflict that had pitted brother against brother. In Section 8, the poet sees before his eyes a "panorama," a sweeping view, of the armies of the conflict recently concluded. Describe the vision he sees. (What does this vision add to the elegy? What is the connection between the death of the leader and what the poet sees in this vision?)

(4) Elegies have often followed a traditional pattern: from mourning the loss to finding hope or consolation. At the end of this poem, the song of the thrush is still sad, but it also at the same time has become "victorious" and "bursting with joy." What makes the lilac in this poem a good symbol for both sadness and joy? (Why does the poet tell us that the lilac bush is "perennial" and has leaves of "rich green"?) Where else in the poem do we see most strongly that in spite of the death of a loved leader the poet has kept his joyful belief in growth and life?

---

### Your Turn

You and your classmates may want to divide this poem for a choral reading.

• In the first half of the nineteenth century, James Fenimore Cooper (1789–1851) wrote a series of novels that turned into one of the great successes of popular literature in this country and in Europe. These were the Leatherstocking Tales, including *The Pioneers* (1823), *The Last of the Mohicans* (1826), *The Pathfinder* (1840), and *The Deerslayer* (1841). The hero of these tales is Natty Bumppo, the lone hunter and scout. At home in the wilderness, he does battle with hostile Indians and helps the forces of goodness. Natty became the ancestor of the folk hero of the American frontier found in countless dime novels, grade-B movies, and paleface-and-Indian games played by millions of children around the world. He was the prototype of the rugged hero of the American West: tall and lean, calm and unperturbed in the face of danger, gifted with uncanny marksmanship with a gun, stubbornly on the side of what is right. We find him in the forest with his faithful Indian comrade Chingachgook (the "friendly native"), far away from the luxuries and corruptions of city life, triumphing over treachery and greed. Cooper said in his preface to the complete edition of the Leatherstocking Tales that he had aimed at making his hero an ideal combination of the best in two worlds: what was best in white civilization and what was best in the Indian's life close to nature. The action of the tales takes place in the larger framework of the wars between England and France over their North American colonies. Indians were fighting the white man's battles on both sides: The Delawares were friendly to the British; they had trained young Natty Bumppo as a hunter and given him the name of Deerslayer. The Huron Indians, or "Mingos" as they are called in the excerpt that follows, were allies of the French. The following is a slightly shortened episode from *The Deerslayer*. Natty, who has killed one of the leading Huron warriors, is the prisoner of the hostile Hurons. He has been allowed to leave the Indian camp to settle important matters. Now, keeping his word, he has returned to meet his fate. What picture do we get here of Cooper's hero? What picture do we get of the hero's enemies?

## James Fenimore Cooper

# Deerslayer Escapes

It was an imposing scene into which Deerslayer now found himself advancing. All the older warriors were seated on the trunk of the fallen tree, waiting his approach with grave decorum. On the right stood the young men, armed, while the left was occupied by the women and children. In the center was an open space of considerable extent, always canopied by leaves, but from which the underbrush, dead wood, and other obstacles had been carefully removed. As was not unusual among the tribes, two chiefs shared, in nearly equal degrees, the authority that was wielded over these children of the forest. One was a senior, well known for eloquence in debate, wisdom in council, and prudence in measures. His great competitor, if not his rival, was a brave, distinguished in war, notorious for ferocity, and remarkable for the cunning and expedients of the warpath. The first was Rivenoak, who has already been introduced to the reader, while the last was called le Panthère, in the language of the Canadas; or the Panther, to resort to English. The appellation of the fighting chief was supposed to indicate the qualities of the warrior—ferocity, cunning, and treachery being perhaps the distinctive features of his character. The title had been received from the French, and was prized so much the more from that circumstance.

Rivenoak and the Panther sat side by side, awaiting the approach of their prisoner, as Deerslayer put his moccasined foot on the strand. Nor did either move or utter a syllable until the young man had advanced into the center of the area and proclaimed his presence with his voice. This was done firmly, though in the simple manner that marked the character of the individual.

"Here I am, Mingos," he said, in the dialect of the Delawares, a language that most present understood. "Here I am, and there is the sun. One is not more true to the laws of nature, than the other has proved true to his word. I am your prisoner; do with me what you please. My business with man and earth is settled. Nothing remains now but to meet the white man's God, according to a white man's duties and gifts."

A murmur of approbation escaped even the women at this address, and, for an instant there was a strong general desire to adopt into the tribe one who owned so brave a spirit. Still there were dissenters from this wish. Among the principal might be classed the Panther and his sister, le Sumach, so called from the number of her children, who was the widow of le Loup Cervier, now known to have fallen by the hand of the captive. Native ferocity held one in subjection, while the passion of revenge prevented the other from admitting any gentler feeling at the moment. Not so with Rivenoak. This chief arose, stretched his arm before him in a gesture of courtesy, and paid his compliments with an ease and dignity that a prince might have envied. As in that band his wisdom and eloquence were without rivals, he knew that on himself would properly fall the duty of first replying to the speech of the paleface.

"Paleface, you are honest," said the Huron orator. "My people are happy in having captured a man, and not a skulking fox. We now know you. We shall treat you like a brave. If you have slain one of our warriors, and helped to kill others, you have a life of your own ready to give away in return. Some of my young men thought that the blood of a paleface was too thin, that it would refuse to run under the Huron knife. You will show them it is not so. Your heart is stout as well as your body. It is a pleasure to make such a prisoner. My warriors say that the death of le Loup Cervier ought not to be forgotten, and that he cannot travel towards the land of spirits alone. His enemy must be sent to overtake him. They will remember that he fell by the hand of a brave, and send you after him with such signs of our friendship as shall not make him ashamed to keep your company. I have spoken. You know what I have said."

"True enough, Mingo, all true as the gospel," returned the simpleminded hunter. "You *have* spoken, and I *do* know not only what you have *said*, but, what is

still more important, what you *mean*. I dare to say your warrior the Lynx was a stouthearted brave, and worthy of your friendship and respect. But I do not feel unworthy to keep his company without any passport from your hands. Nevertheless, here I am, ready to receive judgment from your council, if indeed the matter was not determined among you before I got back."

"My old men would not sit in council over a paleface until they saw him among them," answered Rivenoak, looking around him a little ironically. "They said it would be like sitting in council over the winds. They go where they will, and come back as they see fit, and not otherwise. There was one voice that spoke in your favor, Deerslayer, but it was alone, like the song of the wren whose mate has been struck by the hawk."

"I thank that voice, whoever it may have been, Mingo, and will say it was as true a voice as the rest were lying voices. A furlough is as binding on a paleface, if he be honest, as it is on a redskin. And was it not so, I would never bring disgrace on the Delawares, among whom I may be said to have received my education. But words are useless and lead to bragging feelings. Here I am. Act your will on me."

Rivenoak made a sign of acquiescence, and then a short conference was privately held among the chiefs. As soon as the latter ended, three or four young men fell back from among the armed group and disappeared. Then it was signified to the prisoner that he was at liberty to go at large on the point, until a council was held concerning his fate. . . .

In the meantime the business of the camp appeared to proceed in its regular train. The chiefs consulted apart, admitting no one but the Sumach to their councils. She, the widow of the fallen warrior, had an exclusive right to be heard on such an occasion. The young men strolled about, awaiting the result with Indian patience, while the females prepared the feast that was to celebrate the termination of the affair, whether it proved fortunate or otherwise for our hero. No one betrayed feeling. An observer, beyond the extreme watchfulness of the sentinels, would have detected no extraordinary movement or sensation. Two or three old women put their heads together, and, it appeared, unfavorably to the Deerslayer, by their scowling looks and angry gesture. But a group of Indian girls were evidently animated by a different impulse, as was apparent by stolen glances that expressed pity and regret. In this condition of the camp, an hour soon glided away.

Suspense is perhaps the feeling, of all others, that is most difficult to be supported. When Deerslayer landed, he fully, in the course of a few minutes, expected to undergo the tortures of an Indian revenge, and he was prepared to meet his fate manfully. But the delay proved far more trying than the nearer approach of suffering. The intended victim began seriously to meditate some desperate effort at escape, when he was suddenly summoned to appear once more in front of his judges.

"Killer of the Deer!" commenced Rivenoak, as soon as his captive stood before him. "My aged men have listened to wise words. They are ready to speak. You are a man whose fathers came from beyond the rising sun. We are children of the setting sun. We turn our faces towards the Great Sweet Lakes when we look towards our villages. It may be a wise country and full of riches towards the morning, but it is very pleasant towards the evening. We love most to look in that direction. When we gaze at the east, we feel afraid, canoe after canoe bringing more and more of your people in the track of the sun, as if their land was so full as to run over. The redmen are few already. They have need of help. One of our best lodges has lately been emptied by the death of its master. It will be a long time before his son can grow big enough to sit in his place. There is his widow. She will want venison to feed her and her children, for her sons are yet like the young of the robin before they quit the nest. By your hand has this great calamity befallen her. She has two duties: one to le Loup Cervier, and one to his children. Scalp for scalp, life for life, blood for blood, is one law; to feed her young, another. We know you, Killer of the Deer. You are honest. When you say a thing, it is so. You have but one tongue, and that is not forked, like a snake's. Your head is never hid in the grass. All can see it. What you say, that will you do. You are just. When you have done wrong, it is your wish to do right again, as soon you can. Here is the Sumach: she is alone in her wigwam, with children crying around her for food. Yonder is a rifle: it is loaded and ready to be fired. Take the gun; go forth and shoot a deer. Bring the venison and lay it before the widow of le Loup Cervier. Feed her children; call yourself her husband. After which, your heart will no longer be Delaware, but Huron. Le Sumach's ears will not hear the cries of her children. My people will count the proper number of warriors."

"I feared this, Rivenoak," answered Deerslayer, when the other had ceased speaking. "Yes, I did dread that it would come to this. However, the truth is soon told, and that will put an end to all expectations on this head. Mingo, I'm Christian-born. It would ill become me to take a wife from among heathen. That which I wouldn't do in peaceable times, and under a bright sun, still less would I do behind clouds, in order to save my life. I may never marry. Most likely Providence, in putting me up here in the woods, has intended I should live single and without a lodge of my own. As for feeding the young of your dead warrior, I would do that cheerfully, could it be done without discredit. But it cannot, seeing that I can never live in a Huron village. Your own young men must find the Sumach venison, and the next time she marries, let her take a husband whose legs are not long enough to overrun territory that don't belong to him. We fought a fair battle, and he fell. In this there is nothing but what a brave expects and should be ready to meet. As for getting a Mingo heart, as well might you expect to see grey hairs on a boy, or the blackberry growing on the pine. No, no, Huron! My gifts are white so far as wives are concerned; it is Delaware in all things touching Indians."

These words were scarcely out of the mouth of Deerslayer before a common murmur betrayed the dissatisfaction with which they had been heard. The aged women, in particular, were loud in their expressions of disgust. The gentle Sumach herself, a woman quite old enough to be our hero's mother, was not the least pacific in her denunciations. But all the other manifestations of disappointment and discontent were thrown into the background by the fierce resentment of the Panther. This grim chief had thought it a degradation to permit his sister to become the wife of a paleface at all. . . . The animal from which he got his name does not glare on his intended prey with more frightful ferocity than his eyes gleamed on the captive.

"Dog of the palefaces!" he exclaimed, in Iroquois. "Go yell among the curs of your own evil hunting-grounds!"

The denunciation was accompanied by an appropriate action. Even while speaking, his arm was lifted, and the tomahawk hurled. Luckily the loud tones of the speaker had drawn the eye of Deerslayer towards him, else would that moment have probably closed his career. So great was the dexterity with which this dangerous weapon was thrown, and so deadly the intent, that it would have riven the skull of the prisoner, had he not stretched forth an arm and caught the handle in one of its turns, with a readiness quite as remarkable as the skill with which the missile had been hurled. The force was so great, notwithstanding, that when Deerslayer's arm was arrested, his hand was raised above and behind his own head, and in the very attitude necessary to return the attack. It is not certain whether the circumstance of finding himself unexpectedly in this menacing posture and armed tempted the young man to retaliate, or whether sudden resentment overcame his forbearance and prudence. His eye kindled, however, and a small red spot appeared on each cheek, while he cast all his energy in the effort of his arm and threw back the weapon at his assailant. The unexpectedness of this blow contributed to its success, the Panther neither raising an arm nor bending his head to avoid it. The keen little axe struck the victim in a perpendicular line with the nose, directly between the eyes. Sallying forward, as the serpent darts at his enemy even while receiving its own death wound, this man of powerful frame fell his length into the open area formed by the circle, quivering in death. A common rush to his relief left the captive for a single instant quite outside the crowd. Willing to make one desperate effort for life, he bounded off with the activity of a deer. There was but a breathless instant when the whole band, old and young, women and children, abandoning the lifeless body of the Panther where it lay, raised a yell of alarm and pursued him.

Sudden as had been the event which induced Deerslayer to make this desperate trial of speed, his mind was not wholly unprepared for the fearful emergency. In the course of the past hour, he had pondered well the chances of such an experiment and had shrewdly calculated all the details of success and failure. Several rifles were discharged as Deerslayer came out into the clear forest. But the direction of his line of flight, which partially crossed that of the fire, the haste with which the weapons had been aimed, and the general confusion that prevailed in the camp, prevented any harm from being done. Bullets whistled past him, and many cut twigs from the branches at his side, but not one touched even his dress. The delay caused by these fruitless attempts was of great service to the fugitive, who had gained more than a hundred yards on even the leading men of the Hurons. To think of following with rifle in hand was out of the question. After emptying their pieces in vague hopes of wounding their captive, the best runners of the Indians threw them aside, calling out to the women and boys to recover and load them again as soon as possible.

Deerslayer knew too well the desperate nature of the struggle in which he was engaged to lose one of the precious moments. He also knew that his only hope was to run in a straight line, for as soon as he began to turn or double the greater number of his pursuers would put escape out of the question. He held his way, therefore, in a diagonal direction up the mountain, which was sufficiently toilsome for one contending for life to render it painfully oppressive. There, however, he slackened his speed to recover breath, proceeding even at a quick walk or a slow trot, along the more difficult parts of the way. The Hurons were whooping and leaping behind him; but this he disregarded, well knowing they must overcome the difficulties he had surmounted before they could reach the elevation to which he had attained. The summit of the first hill was now quite near him, and he saw by the formation of the land that a deep glen intervened before the base of a second hill could be reached. Walking deliberately to the summit, he glanced eagerly about him in every direction in quest of a cover. A fallen tree lay near him, and desperate circumstances require desperate remedies. This tree lay in a line parallel to the glen, at the brow of the hill. To leap on it, and then to force his person as close as possible under its lower side, took but a moment. Previously to disappearing from his pursuers, however, Deerslayer stood on the height and gave a cry of triumph, as if exulting at the sight of the descent that lay before him. In the next instant he was stretched beneath the tree.

No sooner was this expedient adopted, than the young man ascertained how desperate had been his own efforts by the violence of the pulsations in his frame. He could hear his heart beat, and his breathing was like the action of a bellows in quick motion. Breath was gained, however, and the heart soon ceased to throb as if about to break through its confinement. The footsteps of those who toiled up the opposite side were now audible, and presently voices announced the arrival of the pursuers. The foremost shouted as they reached the height. Then, fearful that their enemy would escape, each leaped upon the fallen tree and plunged into the ravine, trusting to get a sight of the pursued before he reached the bottom. In this manner, Huron followed Huron, until Natty began to hope the whole had passed. Others succeeded, however, until quite forty had leaped over the tree; and then he counted them, as the surest mode of ascertaining how many could be behind. Presently all were in the bottom of the glen, quite a hundred feet below him, and some had even ascended part of the opposite hill. This was the critical moment. One of nerves less steady, or of a training that had been neglected, would have seized it to rise and fly. Not so with Deerslayer. He still lay quiet, watching with jealous vigilance every movement below, and fast regaining his breath.

The Hurons now resembled a pack of hounds at fault. Little was said, but each man ran about, examining the dead leaves, as the hound hunts for the lost scent. The great number of moccasins that had passed made the examination difficult. Believing that no more pursuers remained behind, and hoping to steal away unseen, Deerslayer suddenly threw himself over the tree, and fell on the upper side. This achievement appeared to be successful, and hope beat high in the bosom of the fugitive. Rising to his hands and feet, after a moment lost in listening to the sounds in the glen, the young man next scrambled to the top of the hill, a distance of only ten yards, in the expectation of getting its brow between him and his pursuers, and himself so far under cover. Even this was effected, as he rose to his feet, walking swiftly but steadily along the summit, in a direction opposite to that in which he had first fled.

## YOU AND THE STORY

(1) What made Cooper's Deerslayer one of the folk heroes of America? What are the two or three most essential or most striking qualities that he shows in this episode? How does he show them? What kind of person is he?

(2) Cooper sided with the missionaries and "humanitarians" who refused to see in the ways of the American Indian only superstition and "squalid misery." He was one of the minority among whites in his time who were "bent on the good of the red man" and respected in the Indian "the soul, reason, and characteristics of a fellow human being." What picture do we get of the Indians in this episode? What picture does Cooper show us of their customs, their standards, and their way of life? List several qualities that Cooper wants us to see in these Indians. Provide an example or illustration for each.

(3) Countless readers have allowed themselves to be carried away by the suspense and excitement of Cooper's tales. But from the beginning, some of his more skeptical readers have accused him

of a lack of **realism**. Look at the things that happen in this part of the story. Do you think something like them could have or might have happened in real life? Why or why not?

---

### A Closer Look

Each of the following sets of related words points to something that plays a role in this episode. What do the terms in each set have in common? How are they different? Which of these do you have to check in a dictionary?

1. decorum—courtesy—dignity
2. wisdom—prudence—vigilance
3. resentment—revenge
4. cunning—treachery—expedient
5. eloquence—orator
6. ferocity—fierceness
7. approbation—acquiescence

---

### Your Turn

Choose one of the speeches of Deerslayer or of the chief of the Mingos. Read it out loud. (Your class may want to stage the exchange of speeches between the two.)

---

Language/Composition Activity B1

FORMAL AND INFORMAL

# A Nineteenth-Century Style

To many nineteenth-century writers, writing was a serious and uplifting business. They often wrote in a solemn formal style. Just as the clothes that people in the nineteenth century wore on formal occasions have come to seem stiff and uncomfortable to us, so their writing style has come to seem stilted or artificial to many modern readers. Today, serious writing generally aims at a more natural effect. There is less of a gap between the language of informal everyday talk and the language of the printed page. Which of the following "book words" do you know? Which would slow you down in your reading? Match each very formal word in the column on the left with a less formal, more familiar word from the column on the right.

| | |
|---|---|
| 1. canopied | a. skill |
| 2. appellation | b. attacker |
| 3. approbation | c. prisoner |
| 4. acquiescence | d. name |
| 5. address | e. approval |
| 6. captive | f. caused |
| 7. dexterity | g. overcome |
| 8. assailant | h. speech |
| 9. perpendicular | i. beat |
| 10. induced | j. find out |
| 11. surmount | k. triumph |
| 12. attain | l. reach |
| 13. exult | m. vertical |
| 14. pulsation | n. shaded |
| 15. ascertain | o. consent |

# An Introduction to Mark Twain and Huck Finn

● Mark Twain (1835–1910) is at the same time the most American and the most universal of American writers. His books mirror the true range of American experience. He grew up in Missouri in a family whose loyalties were divided between the North and the South. He did newspaper work in the East, and he tried his fortunes in the West of frontier days. Mark Twain, whose real name was Samuel Clemens, grew up in Hannibal, a town on the banks of the Mississippi, in pre-Civil War times. He trained as a pilot for the steamboats that carried passengers, trade, news, and entertainment up and down the mighty river. He later told the story of his childhood and of the colorful life of the river pilot in his autobiographical *Life on the Mississippi* (1883). His pen name, "Mark Twain," echoes the report of water "two fathoms"—or twelve feet—deep, and safe for passage. After the war, he went west with his brothers, who had accepted government posts in the Nevada Territory. He described the rugged West of stagecoach days in *Roughing It*. Mark Twain first became famous as a writer of humorous sketches for newspapers and of travel stories and travel books. These included his *Innocents Abroad* (1869), his report on a trip to Europe and the Holy Land. Mark Twain always stayed close to the popular audience and to popular tradition. Millions of readers around the world loved him for his deadpan humor, his incredible yarns, his sharp eye for every kind of human foolishness, and his loyalty to what made people decent and human. Mark Twain was one of the great humorists of all time. But his observations of human callousness and trickery, and his own personal disappointments, made him increasingly bitter. This bitterness shows strongly in his last published stories: *The Man That Corrupted Hadleyburg* (1900) and *The Mysterious Stranger* (1916). He once said, "If you pick up a starving dog and make him prosperous, he will not bite you. This is the principal difference between a dog and a man."

Mark Twain's most widely read books are two books that recreate the world of his childhood days and that have been called "world classics of the remembrance of a lost and happy time." He had been extremely successful with his *Tom Sawyer* (1876), a story of boyhood tasks and adventures in a river town on the Mississippi. He took up the thread again in *The Adventures of Huckleberry Finn* (1885). In this book, Huck, Tom Sawyer's friend, tells the story of how he ran away from the Widow Douglas, who was trying to "civilize" him, and from his violent, drunken father, who was gone most of the time but would return sometimes to harass and abuse the boy. In Huck, the unspoiled country boy, Mark Twain created a true American folk hero. Huck does not have much book learning, and we often smile at his ignorance of the ways of the world. But we soon find that Huck has more shrewd common sense than many better-educated people, and his heart is in the right place. Huck and the runaway slave Jim journey down the river on a raft. They are two "innocents abroad" in a world in which they witness callousness, violence, and cunning. Their friendship, loyalty, and good will survive in a violent and corrupt world. In the book, Huck tells his own story,

(continued from previous page)

in the folksy, homey talk of ordinary people of his own time. At the beginning of the following selection, Huck is living with the Widow Douglas and going to school. Judge Thatcher is holding a large sum of money for him in trust—Huck's share of a treasure found by Tom Sawyer in the earlier book. In this selection from *Huckleberry Finn*, Chapters 4–11 appear in a slightly shortened form. Mark Twain's spelling has been modernized somewhat in some of the dialect passages. This selection omits racial labels that were used freely by both black and white people of Huck's time but that have become offensive to many modern readers.

## Mark Twain

# Huck Runs Away

### CHAPTER IV

Three or four months run along, and it was well into the winter now. I had been to school most all the time, and could spell, read, and write just a little, and could say the multiplication table up to six times seven is thirty-five, and I don't reckon I could ever get any further than that if I was to live forever. I don't take no stock in mathematics anyway.

At first I hated the school, and by and by I got so I could stand it. Whenever I got uncommon tired I played hookey, and the hiding I got next day done me good and cheered me up. So the longer I went to school the easier it got to be. I was getting sort of used to the widow's ways, too, and they warn't so raspy on me. Living in a house, and sleeping in a bed, pulled on me pretty tight, mostly, but before the cold weather I used to slide out and sleep in the woods, sometimes, and so that was a rest to me. I liked the old ways best, but I was getting so I liked the new ones, too, a little bit. The widow said I was coming along slow but sure, and doing very satisfactory. She said she warn't ashamed of me.

One morning I happened to turn over the salt cellar at breakfast. I reached for some of it as quick as I could, to throw over my left shoulder, and keep off the bad luck, but Miss Watson was in ahead of me, and crossed me off. She says, "Take your hands away, Huckleberry—what a mess you are always making." The widow put in a good word for me, but that warn't going to keep off the bad luck, I knowed that well enough. I started out, after breakfast, feeling worried and shaky, and wondering where it was going to fall on me, and what it was going to be. There is ways to keep off some kinds of bad luck, but this wasn't one of them kind; so I never tried to do anything, but just poked along low-spirited and on the watch-out.

I went down the front garden and clumb over the stile, where you go through the high board fence. There was an inch of new snow on the ground, and I seen somebody's tracks. They had come up from the quarry and stood around the stile a while,

and then went on around the garden fence. It was funny they hadn't come in, after standing around so. I couldn't make it out. It was very curious, somehow. I was going to follow around, but I stooped down to look at the tracks first. I didn't notice anything at first, but next I did. There was a cross in the left boot-heel made with big nails, to keep off the devil.

I was up in a second and shinning down the hill. I looked over my shoulder every now and then, but I didn't see nobody. I was at Judge Thatcher's as quick as I could get there. He said:

"Why, my boy, you are all out of breath. Did you come for your interest?"

"No sir," I says; "is there some for me?"

"Oh, yes, a half-yearly is in, last night. Over a hundred and fifty dollars. Quite a fortune for you. You better let me invest it along with your six thousand, because if you take it you'll spend it."

"No sir," I says, "I don't want to spend it. I don't want it at all—nor the six thousand, nuther. I want you to take it; I want to give it to you—the six thousand and all."

He looked surprised. He couldn't seem to make it out. He says:

"Why, what can you mean, my boy?"

I says, "Don't you ask me no questions about it, please. You'll take it—won't you?"

He says:

"Well I'm puzzled. Is something the matter?"

"Please take it," says I, "and don't ask me nothing—then I won't have to tell no lies."

He studied a while, and then he says:

"Oho-o. I think I see. You want to *sell* all your property to me—not give it. That's the correct idea."

Then he wrote something on a paper and read it over, and says:

"There—you see it says 'for a consideration.' That means I have bought it of you and paid you for it. Here's a dollar for you. Now, you sign it."

So I signed it, and left.

Miss Watson's slave, Jim, had a hair ball as big as your fist, which had been took out of the fourth stomach of an ox, and he used to do magic with it. He said there was a spirit inside of it, and it knowed everything. So I went to him that night and told him Pap was here again, for I found his tracks in the snow. What I wanted to know, was, what he was going to do, and was he going to stay? Jim got out his hair ball, and said something over it, and then he held it up and dropped it on the floor. It fell pretty solid, and only rolled about an inch. Jim tried it again, and then another time, and it acted just the same. Jim got down on his knees and put his ear against it and listened. But it warn't no use; he said it wouldn't talk. He said sometimes it wouldn't talk without money. I told him I had an old slick counterfeit quarter that warn't no good because the brass showed through the silver a little, and it wouldn't pass nohow, even if the brass didn't show, because it was so slick it felt greasy, and so that would tell on it every time. (I reckoned I wouldn't say nothing about the dollar I got from the judge.) I said it was pretty bad money, but maybe the hair ball would take it, because maybe it wouldn't know the difference. Jim smelt it, and bit it, and rubbed it, and said he would manage so the hair ball would think it was good. He said he would split open a raw Irish potato and stick the quarter in between and keep it there all night, and next morning you couldn't see no brass, and it wouldn't feel greasy no more, and so anybody in town would take it in a minute, let alone a hair ball. Well, I knowed a potato would do that, before, but I had forgot it.

Jim put the quarter under the hair ball and got down and listened again. This time he said the hair ball was all right. He said it would tell my whole fortune if I wanted it to. I says, go on. So the hair ball talked to Jim, and Jim told it to me. He says:

Your ole father don't know, yit, what he's goin' to do. Sometimes he expec' he'll go away, and then again he expec' he'll stay. The best way is to rest easy and let the ole man take his own way. They's two angels hoverin' round about him. One of 'em is good, and 'tother one is bad. The good one gets him to go right, a little while, then the bad one sail in and bust it all up. A body can't tell, yit, which one goin' to fetch him at the last. But you is all right. You goin' to have considable trouble in your life, and considable joy. Sometimes you goin' to git hurt, and sometimes you goin' to git sick; but every time you's goin' to git well agin. They's two gals flyin' about in your life. One of 'em is light and 'tother is dark. One is rich and 'tother is poor. You's goin' to marry the poor one first and the rich one by and by. You wants to keep away from the water as much as you kin, and don' run no risk, 'cause it's down in the bills that you's goin' to git hung.''

When I lit my candle and went up to my room that night, there set Pap, his own self!

CHAPTER V

I had shut the door to. Then I turned around, and there he was. I used to be scared of him all the time, he tanned me so much. I reckoned I was scared now, too; but in a minute I see I was mistaken. That is, after the first jolt, as you may say, when my breath sort of hitched—he being so unexpected; but right away after, I see I warn't scared of him worth bothering about.

He was most fifty, and he looked it. His hair was long and tangled and greasy, and hung down, and you could see his eyes shining through like he was behind vines. It was all black, no gray; so was his long, mixed-up whiskers. There warn't no color in his face, where his face showed; it was white; not like another man's white, but a white to make a body sick, a white to make a body's flesh crawl—a tree-toad white, a fish-belly white. As for his clothes—just rags, that was all. He had one ankle resting on 'tother knee; the boot on that foot was busted, and two of his toes stuck through, and he worked them now and then. His hat was laying on the floor; an old black slouch with the top caved in, like a lid.

I stood a-looking at him; he set there a-looking at me, with his chair tilted back a little. I set the candle down. I noticed the window was up; so he had clumb in by the shed. He kept a-looking me all over. By and by he says:

"Starchy clothes—very. You think you're a good deal of a big bug, *don't* you?"

"Maybe I am, maybe I ain't," I says.

"Don't you give me none o' your lip," says he. "You've put on considerble many frills since I been away. I'll take you down a peg before I get done with you. You're educated, too, they say; can read and write. You think you're better'n your father, now, don't you, because he can't? *I'll* take it out of you. Who told you you might meddle with such hifalut'n foolishness, hey?—who told you you could?"

"The widow. She told me."

"The widow, hey?—and who told the widow she could put in her shovel about a thing that ain't none of her business?"

"Nobody never told her."

"Well, I'll learn her how to meddle. And

looky here—you drop that school, you hear? I'll learn people to bring up a boy to put on airs over his own father and let on to be better'n what *he* is. You lemme catch you fooling around that school again, you hear? Your mother couldn't read, and she couldn't write, nuther, before she died. None of the family couldn't, before *they* died. *I* can't; and here you're a-swelling yourself up like this. I ain't the man to stand it—you hear? Say—lemme hear you read."

I took up a book and begun something about General Washington and the wars. When I'd read about a half a minute, he fetched the book a whack with his hand and knocked it across the house. He says:

"It's so. You can do it. I had my doubts when you told me. Now looky here; you stop that putting on frills. I won't have it. I'll lay for you, my smarty; and if I catch you about that school I'll tan you good. First you know you'll get religion, too. I never see such a son."

He took up a little blue and yaller picture of some cows and a boy, and says:

"What's this?"

"It's something they give me for learning my lessons good."

He tore it up, and says—

"I'll give you something better—I'll give you a cowhide."

He set there a minute a-mumbling and a-growling, and then he says—

"*Ain't* you a sweet-scented dandy, though? A bed; and bedclothes; and a look'n-glass; and a piece of carpet on the floor—and your own father got to sleep with the hogs in the tanyard. I never see such a son. I bet I'll take some o' these frills out o' you before I'm done with you. Why there ain't no end to your airs—they say you're rich. Hey?—how's that?"

"They lie—that's how."

"Looky here—mind how you talk to me; I'm a-standing about all I can stand, now—so don't gimme no sass. I've been in town two days, and I hain't heard nothing but about you bein' rich. I heard about it away down the river, too. That's why I come. You git me that money tomorrow—I want it."

"I hain't got no money."

"It's a lie. Judge Thatcher's got it. You git it. I want it."

"I hain't got no money, I tell you. You ask Judge Thatcher; he'll tell you the same."

"All right. I'll ask him; and I'll make him pay up, too, or I'll know the reason why. Say—how much you got in your pocket? I want it."

"I hain't got only a dollar, and I want that to—"

"It won't make no difference what you want it for—you just shell it out."

He took it and bit it to see if it was good, and then he said he was going downtown to get some whisky; said he hadn't had a drink all day. When he had got out on the shed, he put his head in again, and cussed me for putting on frills and trying to be better than him; and when I reckoned he was gone, he come back and put his head in again, and told me to mind about that school, because he was going to lay for me and lick me if I didn't drop that.

Next day he was drunk, and he went to Judge Thatcher's and bullyragged him and tried to make him give up the money, but he couldn't, and then he swore he'd make the law force him.

The judge and the widow went to law to get the court to take me away from him and let one of them be my guardian; but it was a new judge that had just come, and he didn't know the old man; so he said courts mustn't interfere and separate families if they can help it; said he'd druther not take a child away from its father. So

Judge Thatcher and the widow had to quit on the business.

That pleased the old man till he couldn't rest. He said he'd cowhide me till I was black and blue if I didn't raise some money for him. I borrowed three dollars from Judge Thatcher, and Pap took it and got drunk and went a-blowing around and cussing and whooping and carrying on; and he kept it up all over town, with a tin pan, till most midnight; then they jailed him, and next day they had him before court, and jailed him again for a week. But he said *he* was satisfied; said he was boss of his son, and he'd make it warm for *him*.

When he got out the new judge said he was agoing to make a man of him. So he took him to his own house, and dressed him up clean and nice, and had him to breakfast and dinner and supper with the family, and was just old pie to him, so to speak. And after supper he talked to him about temperance and such things till the old man cried, and said he'd been a fool, and fooled away his life; but now he was agoing to turn over a new leaf and be a man nobody wouldn't be ashamed of, and he hoped the judge would help him and not look down on him. The judge said he could hug him for them words; so *he* cried, and his wife she cried again; Pap said he's been a man that had always been misunderstood before, and the judge said he believed it. The old man said that what a man wanted that was down, was sympathy; and the judge said it was so; so they cried again. And when it was bedtime, the old man rose up and held out his hand, and says:

"Look at it gentlemen, and ladies all; take ahold of it; shake it. There's a hand that was the hand of a hog; but it ain't no more; it's the hand of a man that's started in on a new life, and 'll die before he'll go back. You mark them words—don't forget I said them. It's a clean hand now; shake it—don't be afeard."

So they shook it, one after the other, all around, and cried. The judge's wife she kissed it. Then the old man he signed a pledge—made his mark. The judge said it was the holiest time on record, or something like that. Then they tucked the old man into a beautiful room, which was the spare room, and in the night sometime he got powerful thirsty and clumb out onto the porch roof and slid down a stanchion and traded his new coat for a jug, and clumb back again and had a good old time; and towards daylight he crawled out again, drunk as a fiddler, and rolled off the porch and broke his left arm in two places and was most froze to death when somebody found him after sunup. And when they come to look at that spare room, they had to take soundings before they could navigate it.

The judge he felt kind of sore. He said he reckoned a body could reform the ole man with a shotgun, maybe, but he didn't know no other way.

CHAPTER VI

Well, pretty soon the old man was up and around again, and then he went for Judge Thatcher in the courts to make him give up that money, and he went for me, too, for not stopping school. He catched me a couple of times and thrashed me, but I went to school just the same, and dodged him or out-run him most of the time. I didn't want to go to school much, before, but I reckoned I'd go now to spite Pap. That law trial was a slow business; appeared like they warn't ever going to get started on it; so every now and then I'd borrow two or three dollars off the judge for him, to keep from getting a cowhiding. Every time he got money he got drunk; and every time he got drunk he raised Cain around town; and every time he raised Cain he got jailed. He was just suited—this kind of thing was right in his line.

He got to hanging around the widow's too much, and so she told him at last that if he didn't quit using around there she would make trouble for him. Well, *wasn't* he mad? He said he would show who was Huck Finn's boss. So he watched out for me one day in the spring, and catched me, and took me up the river about three mile in a skiff, and crossed over to the Illinois shore where it was woody and there warn't no houses but an old log hut in a place where timber was so thick you couldn't find it if you didn't know where it was.

He kept me with him all the time, and I never got a chance to run off. We lived in that old cabin, and he always locked the door and put the key under his head, nights. He had a gun which he had stole, I reckon, and we fished and hunted, and that was what we lived on. Every little while he locked me in and went down to the store, three miles, to the ferry, and traded fish and game for whisky and fetched it home and got drunk and had a good time, and licked me. The widow she found out where I was, by and by, and she sent a man over to try to get hold of me, but Pap drove him off with the gun, and it warn't long after that till I was used to being where I was, and liked it, all but the cowhide part.

It was kind of lazy and jolly, laying off comfortable all day, smoking and fishing, and no books nor study. Two months or more run along, and my clothes got to be all rags and dirt, and I didn't see how I'd ever got to like it so well at the widow's, where you had to wash, and eat on a plate, and comb up, and go to bed and get up regular, and be forever bothering over a book and have old Miss Watson pecking at you all the time. I didn't want to go back no more. I had stopped cussing, because the widow didn't like it; but now I took to it again because Pap hadn't no objections. It was pretty good times up in the woods there, take it all around.

But by and by Pap got too handy with his hick'ry, and I couldn't stand it. I was all over welts. He got to going away so much, too, and locking me in. Once he locked me in and was gone three days. It was dreadful lonesome. I judged he had got drowned and I wasn't ever going to get out any more. I was scared. I made up my mind I would fix up some way to leave there. I had tried to get out of that cabin many a time, but I couldn't find no way. There warn't a window to it big enought for a dog to get through. I couldn't get up the chimbly, it was too narrow. The door was thick solid oak slabs. Pap was pretty careful not to leave a knife or anything in the cabin when he was away; I reckon I had hunted the place over as much as a hundred times; well, I was 'most all the time at it, because it was about the only way to put in the time. But this time I found something at last; I found an old rusty wood saw without any handle; it was laid in between a rafter and the clap-boards of the roof. I greased it up and went to work. There was an old horse blanket nailed against the logs at the far end of the cabin behind the table, to keep the wind from blowing through the chinks and putting the candle out. I got under the table and raised the blanket and went to work to saw a section of the big bottom log out, big enough to let me through. Well, it was a good long job, but I was getting towards the end of it when I heard Pap's gun in the woods. I got rid of the signs of my work, and dropped the blanket and hid my saw, and pretty soon Pap come in.

Pap warn't in a good humor—so he was his natural self. He said he was down to town, and everything was going wrong. His lawyer said he reckoned he would win his lawsuit and get the money, if they ever got started on the trial; but then there was ways to put it off a long time, and Judge Thatcher knowed how to do it. And he said people allowed there'd be another trial to get me away from him and give me to the widow for my guardian, and they guessed it would win, this time. This shook me up considerable, because I didn't want to go back to the widow's any more and be so cramped up and sivilized, as they called it. Then the old man got to cussing, and cussed everything and everybody he could think of, and then cussed them all over again to make sure he hadn't skipped any, and after that he polished off with a kind of a general cuss all round, including a considerable parcel of people which he didn't know the names of, and so called them what's-his-name, when he got to them, and went right along with his cussing.

He said he would like to see the widow get me. He said he would watch out, and if they tried to come any such game on him he knowed of a place six or seven mile off, to stow me in, where they might hunt till they dropped and they couldn't find me. That made me pretty uneasy again, but only for a minute; I reckoned I wouldn't stay on hand till he got that chance.

The old man made me go to the skiff and fetch the things he had got. There was a fifty-pound sack of cornmeal, and a side of bacon, ammunition, and a four-gallon jug of whisky. I toted up a load, and went back and set down on the bow of the skiff to rest. I thought it all over, and I reckoned I would walk off with the gun and some lines, and take to the woods when I run away. I guessed I wouldn't stay in one place, but just tramp right across the country, mostly nighttimes, and hunt and fish to keep alive, and so get so far away

that the old man nor the widow couldn't ever find me any more. I judged I would saw out and leave that night if Pap got drunk enough, and I reckoned he would. I got so full of it that I didn't notice how long I was staying, till the old man hollered and asked me whether I was asleep or drownded.

I got the things all up to the cabin, and then it was about dark. While I was cooking supper the old man took a swig or two and got sort of warmed up, and went to ripping again. He had been drunk over in town, and laid in the gutter all night, and he was a sight to look at. A body would a thought he was Adam, he was just all mud. Whenever his liquor begun to work, he most always went for the govment. This time he says:

"Call this a govment! why, just look at it and see what it's like. Here's the law a-standing ready to take a man's son away from him—a man's own son, which he has had all the trouble and all the anxiety and all the expense of raising. Yes, just as that man has got that son raised at last, and ready to go to work and begin to do suthin' for *him* and give him a rest, the law up and goes for him. And they call *that* govment! That ain't all, nuther. The law backs that old Judge Thatcher up and helps him to keep me out o' my property. Here's what the law does. The law takes a man worth six thousand dollars and upards, and jams him into an old trap of a cabin like this, and lets him go round in clothes that ain't fitten for a hog. They call that govment! A man can't get his rights in a govment like this. Sometimes I've a mighty notion to just leave the country for good and all. Yes, and I *told* 'em so; I told old Thatcher so to his face. Lots of 'em heard me, and can tell what I said. Says I, for two cents I'd leave the blamed country and never come anear it agin. Them's the very words. I says, look at my hat—if you call it a hat—but the lid raises up and the rest of it goes down till it's below my chin, and then it ain't rightly a hat at all, but more like my head was shoved up through a jint o' stovepipe. Look at it, says I—such a hat for me to wear—one of the wealthiest men in this town, if I could git my rights. . . ."

Pap was agoing on so, he never noticed where his old limber legs was taking him to, so he went head over heels over the tub of salt pork, and barked both shins, and the rest of his speech was all the hottest kind of language—mostly hove at the govment, though he give the tub some, too, all along, here and there. He hopped around the cabin considerable, first on one leg, and then on the other, holding first one shin and then the other one, and at last he let out with his left foot all of a sudden and fetched the tub a rattling kick. But it warn't good judgment, because that was the boot that had a couple of his toes leaking out of the front end of it; so now he raised a howl that fairly made a body's hair raise, and down he went in the dirt, and rolled there, and held his toes; and the cussing he done then laid over anything he had ever done previous. He said so his own self, afterwards. He had heard old Sowberry Hagan in his best days, and he said it laid over him, too; but I reckon that was sort of piling it on, maybe.

After supper Pap took the jug, and said he had enough whisky there for two drunks and one delirium tremens. That was always his word. I judged he would be blind drunk in about an hour, and then I would steal the key, or saw myself out, one or 'tother. He drank, and drank, and tumbled down on his blankets, by and by; but luck didn't run my way. He didn't go sound asleep, but was uneasy. He groaned, and moaned, and thrashed around this way and that, for a long time. At last I got so sleepy I couldn't keep my eyes open, all I could do, and so before I knowed what I was about I was sound asleep, and the candle burning.

I don't know how long I was asleep, but all of a sudden there was an awful scream and I was up. There was Pap, looking wild and skipping around every which way and yelling about snakes. He said they was crawling up his legs; and then he would give a jump and a scream, and say one had bit him on the cheek—but I couldn't see no snakes. He started and run round and round the cabin, hollering "take him off! take him off! he's biting me on the neck!" I never see a man look so wild in the eyes. Pretty soon he was all fagged out, and fell down panting; then he rolled over and over, wonderful fast, kicking things every which way, and striking and grabbing at the air with his hands, and screaming, and saying there was devils ahold of him. He wore out, by and by, and laid still a while, moaning. Then he laid stiller, and didn't make a sound. I could hear the owls and the wolves, away off in the woods, and it seemed terrible still. He was laying over by the corner. By and by he raised up, partway, and listened, with his head to one side. He says very low:

"Tramp—tramp—tramp; that's the dead; tramp—tramp—tramp; they're coming after me; but I won't go—Oh, they're here! don't touch me—don't! hands off—they're cold; let go—Oh, let a poor devil alone!"

Then he went down on all fours and crawled off begging them to let him alone, and he rolled himself up in his blanket and wallowed in under the old pine table, still a-begging; and then he went to crying. I could hear him through the blanket.

By and by he rolled out and jumped up on his feet looking wild, and he see me and went for me. He chased me round and round the place, with a claspknife, calling me the Angel of Death and saying he would kill me and then I couldn't come for him no more. I begged, and told him I was only Huck, but he laughed *such* a screechy laugh, and roared and cussed, and kept on chasing me up. Once when I turned short and dodged under his arm he made a grab and got me by the jacket between my shoulders, and I thought I was gone; but I slid out of the jacket quick as lightning, and saved myself. Pretty soon he was all tired out, and dropped down with his back against the door, and said he would rest a minute and then kill me. He put his knife under him, and said he would sleep and get strong, and then he would see who was who.

So he dozed off, pretty soon. By and by I got the old split-bottom chair and clumb up, as easy I could, not to make any noise, and get down the gun. I slipped the ramrod down it to make sure it was loaded, and then I laid it across the turnip barrel, pointing towards Pap, and set down behind it to wait for him to stir. And how slow and still the time did drag along.

CHAPTER VII

"Git up! what you 'bout!"

I opened my eyes and looked around, trying to make out where I was. It was after sunup, and I had been sound asleep. Pap was standing over me, looking sour—and sick, too. He says—

"What you doin' with this gun?"

I judged he didn't know nothing about what he had been doing, so I says:

"Somebody tried to get in, so I was laying for him."

"Why didn't you roust me out?"

"Well, I tried to, but I couldn't; I couldn't budge you."

"Well, all right. Don't stand there palavering all day, but out with you and see if there's a fish on the lines for breakfast. I'll be along in a minute."

He unlocked the door and I cleared out, up the riverbank. I noticed some pieces of limbs and such things floating down, and a sprinkling of bark; so I knowed the river had begun to rise. I reckoned I would have great times now if I was over at the town. The June rise used to be always luck for me; because as soon as that rise begins, here comes cordwood floating down, and pieces of log rafts—sometimes a dozen logs together, so all you have to do is to catch them and sell them to the wood yards and the sawmill.

I went along up the bank with one eye out for Pap and 'tother one out for what the rise might fetch along. Well, all at once, here comes a canoe; just a beauty, too, about thirteen or fourteen foot long, riding high like a duck. I shot head first off the bank, like a frog, clothes and all on, and struck out for the canoe. I just expected there'd be somebody laying down in it, because people often done that to fool folks, and when a chap had pulled a skiff out most to it they'd raise up and laugh at him. But it warn't so this time. It was a drift canoe, sure enough, and I clumb in and paddled her ashore. Thinks I, the old man will be glad when he sees this—she's worth ten dollars. But when I got to shore Pap wasn't in sight yet, and as I was running her into a little creek like a gully, all hung over with vines and willows, I struck another idea; I judged I'd hide her good, and then, stead of taking to the woods when I run off, I'd go down the river about fifty mile and camp in one place for good, and not have such a rough time tramping on foot.

It was pretty close to the shanty, and I thought I heard the old man coming, all the time; but I got her hid; and then I out and looked around a bunch of willows, and there was the old man down the path apiece just drawing a bead on a bird with his gun. So he hadn't seen anything.

He abused me a little for being so slow, but I told him I fell in the river and that was what made me so long. I knowed he would see I was wet, and then he would be asking questions. We got five cat-fish off the lines and went home.

While we laid off, after breakfast, to sleep up, both of us being about wore out, I got to thinking that if I could fix up some way to keep Pap and the widow from trying to follow me, it would be a certainer thing than trusting to luck to get far enough off before they missed me; you see, all kinds of things might happen. Well, I didn't see no way for a while, but by and by Pap raised up a minute, to drink another barrel of water, and he says:

"Another time a man comes a-prowling round here, you roust me out, you hear? That man warn't here for no good. I'd a shot him. Next time, you roust me out, you hear?"

Then he dropped down and went to sleep again—but what he had been saying give me the very idea I wanted. I says to myself, I can fix it now so nobody won't think of following me.

About twelve o'clock we turned out and went along up the bank. The river was coming up pretty fast, and lots of driftwood going by on the rise. By and by, along comes part of a log raft—nine logs fast together. We went out with the skiff and towed it ashore. Then we had dinner. Anybody but Pap would a waited and seen the day through, so as to catch more stuff; but that warn't Pap's style. Nine logs was enough for one time; he must shove right over to town and sell. So he locked me in and took the skiff and started off towing the raft about half-past three. I judged he wouldn't come back that night. I waited till I reckoned he had got a good start, then I out with my saw and went to work on that log again. Before he was 'tother side of the river I was out of the hole; him and his raft was just a speck on the water away off yonder.

I took the sack of cornmeal and took it to where the canoe was hid, and shoved the vines and branches apart and put it in; then I done the same with the side of bacon; then the whisky jug; I took all the coffee and sugar there was, and all the ammunition; I took the bucket and gourd, I took a dipper and a tin cup, and my own saw and two blankets, and the skillet and the coffee pot. I took fishlines and matches and other things—everything that was worth a cent. I cleaned out the place. I wanted an ax, but there wasn't any, only the one out at the woodpile, and I knowed why I was going to leave that. I fetched out the gun, and now I was done.

I had wore the ground a good deal, crawling out of the hole and dragging out so many things. So I fixed that as good as I could from the outside by scattering dust on the place, which covered up the smoothness and the sawdust. Then I fixed the piece of log back into its place, and put two rocks under it and one against it to hold it there—for it was bent up at that place, and didn't quite touch ground. If you stood four or five foot away and didn't know it was sawed, you wouldn't ever notice it; and besides, this was the back of the cabin and it warn't likely anybody would go fooling around there.

It was all grass clear to the canoe; so I hadn't left a track. I followed around to see. I stood on the bank and looked out over the river. All safe. So I took the gun and went up a piece into the woods and was hunting around for some birds when I see a wild pig; hogs soon went wild in them bottoms after they had got away from the prairie farms. I shot this fellow and took him into camp.

I took the ax and smashed in the door— I beat it and hacked it considerable, a-doing it. I fetched the pig in and took him back nearly to the table and hacked into his throat with the ax, and laid him down on the ground to bleed—I say ground, because it *was* ground—hard packed, and no boards. Well, next I took an old sack and put a lot of big rocks in it,—all I could drag—and I started it from the pig and dragged it to the door and through the woods down to the river and dumped it in, and down it sunk, out of sight. You could easy see that something had been dragged over the ground. I did wish Tom Sawyer was there, I knowed he would take an interest in this kind of business and throw in the fancy touches. Nobody could spread himself like Tom Sawyer in such a thing as that.

Well, at last I pulled out some of my hair, and bloodied the ax good, and stuck it on the back side, and slung the ax in the corner. Then I took up the pig and held him to my breast with my jacket (so he couldn't drip) till I got a good piece below the house and then dumped him into the river. Now I thought of something else. So I went and got the bag of meal and my old saw out of the canoe and fetched them to the house. I took the bag to where it used to stand, and ripped a hole in the bottom of it with the saw, for there warn't no knives and forks on the place—Pap done everything with his claspknife, about the cooking. Then I carried the sack about a hundred yards across the grass and through the willows east of the house, to a shallow lake that was five miles wide and full of rushes—and ducks too, you might say, in the season. There was a slough or a creek leading out of it on the other side, that went miles away, I don't know where, but it didn't go to the river. The meal sifted out and made a little track all the way to the lake. I dropped Pap's whetstone there too, so as to look like it had been done by accident. Then I tied up the rip in the meal sack with a string, so it wouldn't leak no more, and took it and my saw to the canoe again.

It was about dark, now; so I dropped the canoe down the river under some willows that hung over the bank, and waited for the moon to rise. I made fast to a willow; then I took a bite to eat, and by and by laid down in the canoe to smoke a pipe and lay out a plan. I says to myself, they'll follow the track of that sackful of rocks to the shore and then drag the river for me. And they'll follow that meal track to the lake and go browsing down the creek that leads out of it to find the robbers that killed me and took the things. They won't ever hunt the river for anything but my dead carcass. They'll soon get tired of that, and won't bother no more about me. All right; I can stop anywhere I want to. Jackson's Island is good enough for me; I know that island pretty well, and nobody ever comes there. And then I can paddle over to town, nights, and slink around and pick up things I want. Jackson's Island's the place.

I was pretty tired, and the first thing I knowed I was asleep. When I woke up I didn't know where I was for a minute. I set up and looked around, a little scared. Then I remembered. The river looked miles and miles across. The moon was so bright I could a counted the drift logs that went a slipping along, black and still, hundred of yards out from shore. Everything was dead quiet, and it looked late, and *smelt* late. You know what I mean—I don't know the words to put it in.

I took a good gap and a stretch, and was just going to unhitch and start, when I heard a sound away over the water. I listened. Pretty soon I made it out. It was that dull kind of a regular sound that comes from oars working in rowlocks when it's a still night. I peeped through the willow branches, and there it was—a skiff, away across the water. I couldn't tell how many was in it. It kept a-coming, and when it was abreast of me I see there warn't but one man in it. Thinks I, maybe it's Pap, though I warn't expecting him. He dropped below me, with the current, and by and by he come a-swinging up shore in the easy water, and he went by so close I could a reached out the gun and touched him. Well, it *was* Pap, sure enough—and sober, too, by the way he laid to his oars.

I didn't lose no time. The next minute I was a-spinning downstream soft but quick in the shade of the bank. I made two mile and a half, and then struck out a quarter of a mile or more towards the middle of the river, because pretty soon I would be passing the ferry landing and people might see me and hail me. I got out amongst the driftwood and then laid down in the bottom of the canoe and let her float. I laid there and had a good rest and a smoke out of my pipe, looking away into the sky, not a cloud in it. The sky looks ever so deep when you lay down on your back in the moonshine; I never knowed it before. And how far a body can hear on the water such nights! I heard people talking at the ferry landing. I heard what they said, too, every word of it. One man said it was getting towards the long days and the short nights, now. 'Tother one said *this* warn't one of the short ones, he reckoned—and then they laughed, and he said it over again and they laughed again; then they waked up another fellow and told him, and laughed, but he didn't laugh; he ripped out something brisk and said let him alone. The first fellow said he 'lowed to tell it to his old woman—she would think it was pretty good; but he said that warn't nothing to some things he had said in his time. I heard one man say it was nearly three o'clock, and he hoped daylight wouldn't wait more than

about a week longer. After that, the talk got further and further away, and I couldn't make out the words any more, but I could hear the mumble, and now and then a laugh, too, but it seemed a long ways off.

I was away below the ferry now. I rose up and there was Jackson's Island, about two mile and a half downstream, heavy-timbered and standing up out of the middle of the river, big and dark and solid, like a steamboat without any lights. There warn't any signs of the bar at the head—it was all under water, now.

It didn't take me long to get there. I shot past the head at a ripping rate, the current was so swift, and then I got into the dead water and landed on the side towards the Illinois shore. I run the canoe into a deep dent in the bank that I knowed about; I had to part the willow branches to get in; and when I made fast nobody could a seen the canoe from the outside.

I went up and set down on a log at the head of the island and looked out on the big river and the black driftwood, and away over to the town, three miles away, where there was three or four lights twinkling. A monstrous big lumber raft was about a mile upstream, coming along down, and when it was most abreast of where I stood I heard a man say, "Stern oars, there! heave her head to stabboard!" I heard that just as plain as if the man was by my side.

There was a little gray in the sky now; so I stepped into the woods and laid down for a nap before breakfast.

### CHAPTER VIII

The sun was up so high when I waked that I judged it was after eight o'clock. I laid there in the grass and the cool shade; thinking about things and feeling rested and ruther comfortable and satisfied. I could see the sun out at one or two holes, but mostly it was big trees all about, and gloomy in there amongst them. There was freckled places on the ground where the light sifted down through the leaves, and the freckled places swapped about a little, showing there was a little breeze up there. A couple of squirrels set on a limb and jabbered at me very friendly.

I was powerful lazy and comfortable—didn't want to get up and cook breakfast. Well, I was dozing off again, when I thinks I hears a deep sound of "boom!" away up the river. I rouses up and rests on my elbow and listens, pretty soon I hears it again. I hopped up and went and looked out at a hole in the leaves, and I see a bunch of smoke laying on the water a long ways up—about abreast the ferry. And there was the ferryboat full of people, floating along down. I knowed what was the matter, now. "Boom!" I see the white smoke squirt out of the ferryboat's side. You see, they was firing cannon over the water, trying to make my carcass come to the top.

I was pretty hungry, but it warn't going to do for me to start a fire, because they might see the smoke. So I set there and watched the cannon smoke and listened to the boom. The river was a mile wide there, and it always looks pretty on a summer morning—so I was having a good enough time seeing them hunt for my remainders, if I only had a bite to eat. Well, then I happened to think how they always put quicksilver in loaves of bread and float them off because they always go right to the drownded carcass and stop there. So says I, I'll keep a lookout, and if any of them's floating around after me, I'll give them a show. I changed to the Illinois edge of the island to see what luck I could have, and I warn't disappointed. A big double loaf come along, and I most got it, with a long stick, but my foot slipped and she floated out further. Of course I was

where the current set in the closest to the shore—knowed enough for that. But by and by along comes another one, and this time I won. I took out the plug and shook out the little dab of quicksilver, and set my teeth in. It was "baker's bread"—what the quality eat—none of your low-down corn pone.

I got a good place amongst the leaves, and set there on a log, munching the bread and watching the ferryboat, and very well satisfied. And then something struck me. I says, now I reckon the widow or the parson or somebody prayed that this bread would find me, and here it has gone and done it. So there ain't no doubt but there is something in that thing. That is, there's something in it when a body like the widow or the parson prays, but it don't work for me, and I reckon it don't work for only just the right kind.

I lit a pipe and had a good long smoke and went on watching. The ferryboat was floating with the current, and I allowed I'd have a chance to see who was aboard when she come along, because she would come in close, where the bread did. When she'd got pretty well along down towards me, I put out my pipe and went to where I fished out the bread, and laid down behind a log on the bank in a little open place. Where the log forked I could peep through.

By and by she come along, and she drifted in so close that they could a run out a plank and walked ashore. Most everybody was on the boat. Pap, and Judge Thatcher, and Bessie Thatcher, and Jo Harper, and Tom Sawyer, and his old Aunt Polly, and Sid and Mary, and plenty more. Everybody was talking about the murder, but the captain broke in and says:

"Look sharp, now; the current sets in the closest here, and maybe he's washed ashore and got tangled amongst the brush

at the water's edge. I hope so, anyway."

I didn't hope so. They all crowded up and leaned over the rails, nearly in my face, and kept still, watching with all their might. I could see them first-rate, but they couldn't see me. Then the captain sung out:

"Stand away!" and the cannon let off such a blast right before me that it made me deef with the noise and pretty near blind with the smoke, and I judged I was gone. If they'd a had some bullets in, I reckon they'd a got the corpse they was after. Well, I see I wasn't hurt, thanks to goodness. The boat floated on and went out of sight around the shoulder of the island. I could hear the booming, now and then, further and further off, and by and by after an hour, I didn't hear it no more. The island was three miles long. I judged they had got to the foot, and was giving it up. But they didn't yet a while. They turned around the foot of the island and started up the channel on the Missouri side, under steam, and booming once in a while as they went. I crossed over to that side and watched them. When they got abreast the head of the island they quit shooting and dropped over to the Missouri shore and went home to the town.

I knowed I was all right now. Nobody else would come a-hunting after me. I got my traps out of the canoe and made me a nice camp in the thick woods. I made a kind of a tent out of my blankets to put my things under so the rain couldn't get at them. I catched a catfish and haggled him open with my saw, and towards sundown I started my campfire and had supper. Then I set out a line to catch some fish for breakfast.

When it was dark I set by my campfire smoking, and feeling pretty satisfied; but by and by it got sort of lonesome, and so I went and set on the bank and listened to the currents washing along, and counted the stars and driftlogs and rafts that come down, and then went to bed; there ain't no better way to put in time when you are lonesome; you can't stay so, you soon get over it.

And so for three days and nights. No difference—just the same thing. But the next day I went exploring around down through the island. I was boss of it; it all belonged to me, so to say, and I wanted to know all about it; but mainly I wanted to put in the time. I found plenty strawberries, ripe and prime; and green summer grapes, and green razberries; and the green blackberries was just beginning to show. They would all come handy by and by, I judged.

Well, I went fooling along in the deep woods till I judged I warn't far from the foot of the island. I had my gun along, but I hadn't shot nothing; it was for protection; thought I would kill some game nigh home. About this time I mighty near stepped on a good-sized snake, and it went sliding off through the grass and flowers, and I after it, trying to get a shot at it. I slipped along, and all of a sudden I bounded right onto the ashes of a campfire that was still smoking.

My heart jumped up amongst my lungs. I never waited for to look further, but uncocked my gun and went sneaking back on my tiptoes as fast as ever I could. Every now and then I stopped a second, amongst the thick leaves, and listened; but my breath come so hard I couldn't hear nothing else. I slunk along another piece further, then listened again; and so on, and so on; if I see a stump, I took it for a man; if I trod on a stick and broke it, it made me feel like a person had cut one of my breaths in two and I only got half, and the short half, too.

When I got to camp I warn't feeling very brash, there warn't much sand in my craw; but I says, this ain't no time to be fooling around. So I got all my traps into my canoe again so as to have them out of sight, and I put out the fire and scattered the ashes around to look like an old last year's camp, and then clumb a tree.

I reckon I was up in the tree two hours; but I didn't see nothing. I didn't hear nothing—I only *thought* I heard and seen as much as a thousand things. Well, I couldn't stay up there forever; so at last I got down, but I kept in the thick woods and on the lookout all the time. All I could get to eat was berries and what was left over from breakfast.

By the time it was night I was pretty hungry. So when it was good and dark, I slid out from shore before moonrise and paddled over to the Illinois bank—about a quarter of a mile. I went out in the woods and cooked a supper, and I had about made up my mind I would stay there all night when I hear a *plunkety-plunk, plunkety-plunk*, and says to myself, horses coming; and next I hear people's voices. I got everything into the canoe as quick as I could, and then went creeping through the woods to see what I could find out. I hadn't got far when I hear a man say:

"We better camp here, if we can find a good place; the horses is about beat out. Let's look around."

I didn't wait, but shoved out and paddled away easy. I tied up in the old place and reckoned I would sleep in the canoe.

I didn't sleep much. I couldn't, somehow, for thinking. And every time I waked up I thought somebody had me by the neck. So the sleep didn't do me no good. By and by I says to myself, I can't live this way; I'm agoing to find out who it is that's here on the island with me; I'll find it out or bust. Well, I felt better, right off.

So I took my paddle and slid out from shore just a step or two, and then let the canoe drop down amongst the shadows.

The moon was shining, and outside of the shadows it made it most as light as day. I poked along well onto an hour, everything still as rocks and sound asleep. A little ripply, cool breeze begun to blow, and that was as good as saying the night was about done. I give her a turn with the paddle and brung her nose to shore; then I got my gun and slipped out and into the edge of the woods. I set down there on a log and looked out through the leaves. I see the moon go off watch and the darkness begin to blanket the river. But in a little while I see a pale streak over the treetops, and knowed the day was coming. So I took my gun and slipped off towards where I had run across that campfire, stopping every minute or two to listen. But I hadn't no luck, somehow; I couldn't seem to find the place. But by and by, sure enough, I catched a glimpse of fire, away through the trees. I went for it, cautious and slow. By and by I was close enough to have a look, and there laid a man on the ground. It most give me the fantods.* He had a blanket around his head, and his head was just about in the fire. I set there behind a clump of bushes, in about six foot of him, and kept my eyes on him steady. It was getting gray daylight, now. Pretty soon he gapped, and stretched himself, and hove off the blanket, and it was Miss Watson's Jim! I bet I was glad to see him. I says:

"Hello, Jim!" and skipped out.

He bounced up and says:

"Don't hurt me! I ain't never done no harm to a ghost! You go and git in the river again, where you belongs!"

Well, I warn't long making him understand I warn't dead. I was ever so glad to see Jim. I warn't lonesome now. I told him I warn't afraid of *him* telling the people where I was. I talked along, but he only set

*fantods: the fidgets.

there and looked at me; never said nothing. Then I says:

"It's good daylight. Let's get breakfast. Make up your campfire good."

"What's the use of makin' up the campfire to cook strawberries and such truck? But you got a gun, ain't you? Then we kin git somethin' better than strawberries."

"Strawberries and such truck," I says. "Is that what you live on?"

"I couldn't get nothing else," he says.

"Why, how long you been on the island, Jim?"

"I come here the night after you's killed."

"What, all that time?"

"Yes-indeedy."

"And ain't you had nothing but that kind of rubbage to eat?"

"Nothin' else."

"Well, you must be most starved, ain't you?"

"I reckon I could eat a horse. I think I could. How long you ben on the islan'?"

"Since the night I got killed."

"No! Why, what has you lived on? But you got a gun. Oh, yes, you got a gun. That's good. Now you kill somethin' and I'll make up the fire."

So we went over to where the canoe was, and while he built a fire in a grassy open place amongst the trees, I fetched meal and bacon and coffee, and coffeepot and frying pan, and sugar and tin cups, and Jim was set back considerable, because he reckoned it was all done with witchcraft. I catched a good big catfish, too, and Jim cleaned him with his knife and fried him.

When breakfast was ready, we lolled on the grass and eat it smoking hot. Jim laid it in with all his might, for he was most about starved. Then when we had got pretty well stuffed, we laid off and just lazied.

By and by Jim says:

"But looky here, Huck, who was it that was killed in that shanty, if it warn't you?"

Then I told him the whole thing, and he said it was smart. He said Tom Sawyer couldn't get up no better plan than what I had. Then I says:

"How do you come to be here, Jim, and how'd you get here?"

He looked pretty uneasy, and didn't say nothing for a minute. Then he says:

"Maybe I better not tell."

"Why, Jim?"

"Well, they's reasons. But you wouldn't tell on me if I was to tell you, would you, Huck?"

"Blamed if I would, Jim."

"Well, I b'lieve you, Huck. I'll tell you. I—I *run off*."

"Jim!"

"But mind, you said you wouldn't tell—you know you said you wouldn't tell, Huck."

"Well, I did. I said I wouldn't, and I'll stick to it. Honest *injun* I will. People would call me a low-down Abolitionist and despise me for keeping mum—but that don't make no difference. I ain't agoing to tell, and I ain't agoing back there anyways. So now, le's know all about it."

"Well, you see, it was this way. Ole Missus—that's Miss Watson—she picks on me all the time, and treats me pretty rough, but she always said she wouldn' sell me down to Orleans. But I noticed they was a trader roun' the place considable lately, and I begin to git uneasy. Well, one night I creeps to the door, pretty late, and the door warn't quite shut, and I hear ole missus tell the widow she goin' to sell me down to Orleans, but she didn't want to, but she could git eight-hundred dollars for me, and it was such a big stack o' money she couldn' resist. The widow she try to git her to say she wouldn' do it, but I never waited to hear the rest. I lit out mighty quick, I tell you."

Some young birds come along, flying a yard or two at a time and lighting. Jim said it was a sign it was going to rain. He said it was a sign when young chickens flew that way, and so he reckoned it was the same way when young birds done it. I was going to catch some of them, but Jim wouldn't let me. He said it was death. He said his father laid mighty sick once, and some of them catched a bird, and his old granny said his father would die, and he did.

And Jim said you mustn't count the things you are going to cook for dinner, because that would bring bad luck. The same if you shook the tablecloth after sundown. And he said if a man owned a beehive, and that man died, the bees must be told about it before sunup next morning, or else the bees would all weaken down and quit work and die. Jim said bees wouldn't sting idiots; but I didn't believe that, because I had tried them lots of times myself, and they wouldn't sting me.

I had heard about some of these things before, but not all of them. Jim knowed all kinds of signs. He said he knowed most everything. I said it looked to me like all the signs was about bad luck, and so I asked him if there warn't any good-luck signs. He says:

"Mighty few—and they aint' no use to a body. What you want to know when good luck's a'comin' for? want to keep if off?" And he said: "If you's got hairy arms and a hairy breast, it's a sign that you's goin' to be rich. Well, they's some use in a sign like that, 'cause it's so far ahead. You see, maybe you's got to be poor a long time first, and so you might git discouraged and kill yourself if you didn't know by the sign that you goin' to be rich by and by."

"Have you got hairy arms and a hairy breast, Jim?"

"What's the use to ask that question? Don't you see I has?"

"Well, are you rich?"

"Yes—I's rich now, come to look at it. I owns myself, and I's worth eight hund'd dollars. I wisht I had the money, I wouldn't want no mo'."

## CHAPTER IX

I wanted to go and look at a place right about the middle of the island, that I'd found when I was exploring; so we started, and soon got to it, because the island was only three miles long and a quarter of a mile wide.

This place was a tolerable long steep hill or ridge, about forty foot high. We had a rough time getting to the top, the sides was so steep and the bushes so thick. We tramped and clumb around all over it, and by and by found a good big cavern in the rock, most up to the top on the side towards Illinois. The cavern was as big as two or three rooms bunched together, and Jim could stand up straight in it. It was cool in there. Jim was for putting our traps in there, right away, but I said we didn't want to be climbing up and down there all the time.

Jim said if we had the canoe hid in a good place, and had all the traps in the cavern, we could rush there if anybody was to come to the island, and they would never find us without dogs. And besides, he said them little birds had said it was going to rain, and did I want the things to get wet?

So we went back and got the canoe and paddled up abreast the cavern, and lugged all the traps up there. Then we hunted up a place close by to hide the canoe in, amongst the thick willows. We took some fish off of the lines and set them again, and begun to get ready for dinner.

The door of the cavern was big enough to roll a hogshead in, and on one side of the door the floor stuck out a little bit and was flat and a good place to build a fire on. So we built it there and cooked dinner.

We spread the blankets inside for a carpet, and eat our dinner in there. We put all the other things handy at the back of the cavern. Pretty soon it darkened up and begun to thunder and lighten; so the birds was right about it. Directly it begun to rain, and it rained like all fury, too, and I never see the wind blow so. It was one of these regular summer storms. It would get so dark that it looked all blue-black outside, and lovely; and the rain would thrash along by so thick that the trees off a little ways looked dim and spiderwebby; and here would come a blast of wind that would bend the trees down and turn up the pale underside of the leaves; and then a perfect ripper of a gust would follow along and set the branches to tossing their arms as if they was just wild; and next, when it was just about the bluest and blackest—*fst*! It was as bright as glory and you'd have a little glimpse of treetops a-plunging about, away off yonder in the storm, hundreds of yards further than you could see before; dark as sin again in a second, and now you'd hear the thunder let go with an awful crash and then go rumbling, grumbling, tumbling down the sky towards the underside of the world, like rolling empty barrels downstairs, where it's long stairs and they bounce a good deal, you know.

"Jim, this is nice," I says. "I wouldn't want to be nowhere else but here. Pass me along another hunk of fish and some hot cornbread."

"Well, you wouldn't have ben here, 'f it hadn't a ben for Jim. You'd have ben down in the woods widout any dinner, en gittn' mos' drownded, too, you would, honey. Chickens knows when its goin' to rain, and so do birds, chile."

The river went on raising and raising for

ten or twelve days, till at last it was over the banks. The water was three or four foot deep on the island in the low places and on the Illinois bottom. On that side it was a good many miles wide; but on the Missouri side it was the same old distance across—a half a mile—because the Missouri shore was just a wall of bluffs.

Daytimes we paddled all over the island in the canoe. It was mighty cool and shady in the deep woods even if the sun was blazing outside. We went winding in and out amongst the trees; and sometimes the vines hung so thick we had to back away and go some other way. Well, on every old broken-down tree, you could see rabbits, and snakes, and such things; and when the island had been overflowed a day or two, they got so tame, on account of being hungry, that you could paddle right up and put your hand on them if you wanted to; but not the snakes and turtles—they would slide off in the water. The ridge our cavern was in was full of them. We could a had pets enough if we'd wanted them.

One night we catched a little section of a lumber raft—nice pine planks. It was twelve foot wide and about fifteen or sixteen foot long, and the top stood above water six or seven inches, a solid level floor. We could see sawlogs go by in the daylight, sometimes, but we let them go; we didn't show ourselves in daylight.

Another night, when we was up at the head of the island, just before daylight, here comes a frame house down, on the west side. She was a two-story, and tilted over considerable. We paddled out and got aboard—clumb in at an upstairs window. But it was too dark to see yet, so we made the canoe fast and set in her to wait for daylight.

The light begun to come before we got to the foot of the island. Then we looked in at the window. We could make out a bed, and a table, and two old chairs, and lots of things around about on the floor; and there was clothes hanging against the wall. There was something laying on the floor in the far corner that looked like a man. So Jim says:

"Hello, you!"

But it didn't budge. So I hollered again, and then Jim says:

"The man ain't asleep—he's dead. You hold still—I'll go and see."

He went and bent down and looked, and says:

"It's a dead man. Yes, indeedy; naked, too. He's ben shot in the back. I reck'n he's ben dead two or three days. Come in, Huck, but don' look at his face—it's too ghastly."

I didn't look at him at all. Jim threw some old rags over him, but he needn't done it; I didn't want to see him. There was heaps of old greasy cards scattered around over the floor, and old whisky bottles, and a couple of masks made out of black cloth; and all over the walls was the ignorantest kind of words and pictures, made with charcoal. There was two old dirty calico dresses, and a sunbonnet, and some women's underclothes, hanging against the wall, and some men's clothing, too. We put the lot into the canoe; it might come good. There was a boy's old speckled straw hat on the floor; I took that too. And there was a bottle that had had milk in it; and it had a rag stopper for a baby to suck. We would a took the bottle, but it was broke. There was a seedy old chest, and an old hair trunk with the hinges broke. They stood open, but there warn't nothing left in them that was any account. The way things was scattered about, we reckoned the people left in a hurry and warn't fixed so as to carry off most of their stuff.

We got an old tin lantern, and a long butcherknife without any handle, and a bran-new Barlow knife worth two bits in any store, and a lot of tallow candles, and a tin candlestick, and a gourd, and a tin cup, and a ratty old bed quilt off the bed, and a reticule with needles and pins and beeswax and buttons and thread and all such truck in it, and a hatchet and some nails, and a fishline as thick as my little finger, with some monstrous hooks on it, and a roll of buckskin, and a leather dog collar, and a horseshoe, and some vials of medicine that didn't have no label on them; and just as we was leaving I found a tolerable good currycomb, and Jim he found a ratty old fiddle bow, and a wooden leg. The straps was broke off of it, but barring that, it was a good enough leg, though it was too long for me and not long enough for Jim, and we couldn't find the other one, though we hunted all around.

And so, take it all around, we made a good haul. When we was ready to shove off, we was a quarter of a mile below the island, and it was pretty broad day; so I made Jim lay down in the canoe and cover up with the quilt. I paddled over to the Illinois shore, and drifted down most a half a mile doing it. I crept up the dead water under the bank, and hadn't no accidents and didn't see nobody. We got home all safe.

CHAPTER X

After breakfast I wanted to talk about the dead man and guess out how he come to be killed, but Jim didn't want to. He said it would fetch bad luck; and besides, he said, he might come and ha'nt us; he said a man that warn't buried was more likely to go a-ha'nting around than one that was planted and comfortable. That sounded pretty reasonable, so I didn't say no more; but I couldn't keep from studying over it and wishing I knowed who shot the man, and what they done it for.

We rummaged the clothes we'd got, and found eight dollars in silver sewed up in the lining of an old blanket overcoat. Jim said he reckoned the people in that house stole the coat, because if they'd a knowed the money was there they wouldn't a left it. I said I reckoned they killed him, too; but Jim didn't want to talk about that. I says:

"Now you think it's bad luck; but what did you say when I fetched in the snakeskin that I found on the top of the ridge day before yesterday? You said it was the worst bad luck in the world to touch a snakeskin with my hands. Well, here's your bad luck! We've raked in all this truck and eight dollars besides. I wish we could have some bad luck like this every day, Jim."

"Never you mind, honey, don't never you mind. Don't you git too smart. It's a-comin'. Mind I tell you, it's a-comin'."

It did come, too. It was a Tuesday that we had that talk. Well, after dinner Friday, we was laying around in the grass at the upper end of the ridge, and got out of tobacco. I went to the cavern to get some, and found a rattlesnake in there. I killed him, and curled him up on the foot of Jim's blanket, ever so natural, thinking there'd be some fun when Jim found him there. Well, by night I forgot all about the snake, and when Jim flung himself down on the blanket while I struck a light, the snake's mate was there, and bit him.

He jumped up yelling, and the first thing the light showed was the varmint curled up and ready for another spring. I laid him out in a second with a stick, and Jim grabbed Pap's whisky jug and began to pour it down.

He was barefooted, and the snake bit him right on the heel. That all comes of my being such a fool as to not remember that wherever you leave a dead snake its mate always comes there and curls around it. Jim told me to chop off the snake's head and throw it away, and then skin the body and roast a piece of it. I done it, and he eat it and said it would help cure him. He made me take off the rattles and tie them around his wrist, too. He said that that would help. Then I slid out quiet and throwed the snakes clear away amongst the bushes; for I warn't going to let Jim find out it was all my fault, not if I could help it.

Jim sucked and sucked at the jug, and now and then he got out of his head and pitched around and yelled; but every time he come to himself he went to sucking at the jug again. His foot swelled up pretty big, and so did his leg; but by and by the drunk begun to come, and so I judged he was all right; but I'd druther been bit with a snake than Pap's whisky.

Jim was laid up for four days and nights. Then the swelling was all gone and he was around again. I made up my mind I wouldn't ever take aholt of a snakeskin again with my hands, now that I see what had come of it. Jim said he reckoned I would believe him next time. And he said that handling a snakeskin was such awful bad luck that maybe we hadn't got to the end of it yet. He said he druther see the new moon over his left shoulder as much as a thousand times than take up a snakeskin in his hand. Well, I was getting to feel that way myself, though I've always reckoned that looking at the new moon over your left shoulder is one of the carelessest and foolishest things a body can do. Old Hank Bunker done it once, and bragged about it; and in less than two years he got drunk and fell off of the shot tower and spread himself out so that he was just a kind of layer, as you may say; and they slid him edgeways between two barn doors for a coffin, and buried him so, so they say, but I didn't see it. Pap told me. But anyway, it all come of looking at the moon that way, like a fool.

Well, the days went along, and the river went down between its banks again; and about the first thing we done was to bait one of the big hooks with a skinned rabbit and set it and catch a catfish that was as big as a man, being six foot two inches long, and weighed over two hundred pounds. We couldn't handle him, of course; he would a flung us into Illinois. We just set there and watched him rip and tear around till he drowned. We found a brass button in his stomach, and a round ball, and lots of rubbage. We split the ball open with the hatchet, and there was a spool in it. Jim said he'd had it there a long time, to coat it over so and make a ball of it. It was as big a fish as was ever catched in the Mississippi, I reckon. Jim said he hadn't ever seen a bigger one. He would a been worth a good deal over at the village. They peddle out such a fish as that by the pound in the market house there; everybody buys some of him; his meat's as white as snow and makes a good fry.

Next morning I said it was getting slow and dull, and I wanted to get a stirring up, some way. I said I reckoned I would slip over the river and find out what was going on. Jim liked that notion; but he said I must go in the dark and look sharp. Then he studied it over and said, couldn't I put on some of them old things and dress up like a girl? That was a good notion, too. So we shortened up one of the calico gowns and I turned up my trouser legs to my knees and got into it. Jim hitched it behind with the hooks, and it was a fair fit. I put on the sunbonnet and tied it under my chin, and then for a body to look in and see my face was like looking down a joint of stovepipe. Jim said nobody would know me, even in the daytime, hardly. I practiced around all day to get the hang of the things, and by and by I could do pretty well in them, only Jim said I didn't walk like a girl; and he said I must quit pulling up my gown to get at

my britches pocket. I took notice, and done better.

I started up the Illinois shore in the canoe just after dark.

I started across to the town from a little below the ferry landing, and the drift of the current fetched me in at the bottom of the town. I tied up and started along the bank. There was a light burning in a little shanty that hadn't been lived in for a long time, and I wondered who had took up quarters there. I slipped up and peeped in at the window. There was a woman about forty year old in there, knitting by a candle that was on a pine table. I didn't know her face; she was a stranger, for you couldn't start a face in that town that I didn't know. Now this was lucky, because I was weakening; I was getting afraid I had come; people might know my voice and find me out. But if this woman had been in such a little town two days she could tell me all I wanted to know; so I knocked at the door, and made up my mind I wouldn't forget I was a girl.

### CHAPTER XI

"Come in," says the woman, and I did. She says:

"Take a cheer."

I done it. She looked me all over with her little shiny eyes, and says:

"What might your name be?"

"Sarah Williams."

"Where 'bouts do you live? In this neighborhood?"

"No'm. In Hookerville, seven mile below. I've walked all the way and I'm all tired out."

"Hungry, too, I reckon. I'll find you something."

"No'm, I ain't hungry. I was so hungry I

had to stop two mile below here at a farm; so I ain't hungry no more. It's what makes me so late. My mother's down sick, and out of money and everything, and I come to tell my Uncle Abner Moore. He lives at the upper end of the town, she says. I ain't ever been here before. Do you know him?"

"No; but I don't know everybody yet. I haven't lived here quite two weeks. It's a considerable ways to the upper end of the town. You better stay here all night. Take off your bonnet."

"No," I says, "I'll rest a while, I reckon, and go on. I ain't afeard of the dark."

She said she wouldn't let me go by myself, but her husband would be in by and by, maybe in a hour and a half, and she'd send him along with me. Then she got to talking about her husband, and about her relations up the river, and her relations down the river, and about how much better off they used to was, and how they didn't know but they'd made a mistake coming to our town, instead of letting well alone—and so on and so on, till I was afeard I had made a mistake coming to her to find out what was going on in the town; but by and by she dropped onto Pap and the murder, and then I was pretty willing to let her clatter right along. She told about me and Tom Sawyer ·finding the six thousand dollars (only she got it ten) and all about Pap and what a hard lot he was, and what a hard lot I was, and at last she got down to where I was murdered. I says:

"Who done it? We've heard considerable about these goings on, down in Hookerville, but we don't know who 'twas that killed Huck Finn."

"Well, I reckon there's a right smart chance of people *here* that'd like to know who killed him. Some thinks old Finn done it himself."

"No—is that so?"

"Most everybody thought it at first. He'll never know how nigh he come to getting lynched. But before night they changed around and judged it was done by a runaway named Jim."

"Why *he*—"

I stopped. I reckoned I better keep still. She run on, and never noticed I had put in at all.

"He run off the very night Huck Finn was killed. So there's a reward out for him—three hundred dollars. . . . Some folks thinks he ain't far from here. I'm one of them—but I ain't talked it around. A few days ago I was talking with an old couple that lives next door in the log shanty, and they happened to say hardly anybody ever goes to that island over yonder that they call Jackson's Island. Don't anybody live there? says I. No, nobody, says they. I didn't say any more, but I done some thinking. I was pretty near certain I'd seen smoke over there, about the head of the island, a day or two before that, so I says to myself, like as not that runaway is hiding over there; anyway, says I, it's worth the trouble to give the place a hunt. I ain't seen any smoke sence, so I reckon maybe he's gone, if it was him; but husband's going over to see—him and another man. He was gone up the river; but he got back today and I told him as soon as he got here two hours ago."

I had got so uneasy I couldn't set still. I had to do something with my hands; so I took up a needle off of the table and went to threading it. My hands shook, and I was making a bad job of it. When the woman stopped talking, I looked up, and she was looking at me pretty curious, and smiling a little. I put down the needle and thread and let on to be interested—and I was, too—and says:

"Three hundred dollars is a power of money. I wish my mother could get it. Is your husband going over there tonight?"

"Oh, yes. He went up town with the man I was telling you of, to get a boat and see if they could borrow another gun. They'll go over after midnight."

"Couldn't they see better if they was to wait till daytime?"

"Yes. And couldn't the runaway see better, too? After midnight he'll likely be asleep, and they can slip around through the woods and hunt up his campfire all the better for the dark, if he's got one."

"I didn't think of that."

The woman kept looking at me pretty curious, and I didn't feel a bit comfortable. Pretty soon she says:

"What did you say your name was, honey?"

"M—Mary Williams."

Somehow it didn't seem to me that I said it was Mary before, so I didn't look up; seemed to me I said it was Sarah; so I felt sort of cornered, and was afeard maybe I was looking it, too. I wished the woman would say something more; the longer she set still, the uneasier I was. But now she says:

"Honey, I though you said it was Sarah when you first come in?"

"Oh, yes'm, I did. Sarah Mary Williams. Sarah's my first name. Some calls me Sarah, some calls me Mary."

"Oh, that's the way of it?"

"Yes'm."

I was feeling better, then, but I wished I was out of there, anyway. I couldn't look up yet.

Well, the woman fell to talking about how hard times was, and how poor they had to live, and how the rats was as free as if they owned the place, and so forth, and so on, and then I got easy again. She was right about the rats. You'd see one stick his nose out of a hole in the corner every little while. She said she had to have things handy to throw at them when she was alone, or they wouldn't give her no peace. She showed me a bar of lead twisted up into a knot, and said she was a good shot with it generly, but she'd wrenched her arm a day or two ago, and didn't know whether she could throw true now. But she watched for a chance, and directly she banged away at a rat, but she missed him wide, and said "Ouch!" it hurt her arm so. Then she told me to try for the next one. I wanted to be getting away before the old man got back, but of course I didn't let on. I got the thing, and the first rat that showed his nose I let drive, and if he'd a stayed where he was he'd a been a tolerable sick rat. She said that that was first-rate, and she reckoned I would hive the next one. She went and got the lump of lead and fetched it back and brought along a hank of yarn, which she wanted me to help her with. I held up my two hands and she put the hank over them and went on talking about her and her husband's matters. But she broke off to say:

"Keep your eye on the rats. You better have the lead in your lap, handy."

So she dropped the lump into my lap, just at that moment, and I clapped my legs together on it and she went on talking. But only about a minute. Then she took off the hank and looked me straight in the face, but very pleasant, and says:

"Come, now—what's your real name?"

"Wh-what, mum?"

"What's your real name? Is it Bill, or Tom, or Bob?—or what is it?"

I reckon I shook like a leaf, and I didn't know hardly what to do. But I says:

"Please to don't poke fun at a poor girl like me, mum. If I'm in the way here, I'll—"

"No, you won't. Set down and stay where you are. I ain't going to hurt you, and I ain't going to tell on you nuther. You just tell me your secret, and trust me. I'll keep it; and what's more, I'll help you. So'll my old man, if you want him to. You see, you're a runaway 'prentice—that's all. It ain't anything. There ain't any harm in it. You've been treated bad, and you made up your mind to cut. Bless you, child, I wouldn't tell on you. Tell me all about it now—that's a good boy."

So I said it wouldn't be no use to try to play it any longer, and I would just make a clean breast and tell her everything, but she mustn't go back on her promise. Then I told her my father and mother was dead, and the law had bound me out to a mean old farmer in the country thirty mile back from the river, and he treated me so bad I couldn't stand it no longer; he went away to be gone a couple of days, and so I took my chance and stole some of his daughter's old clothes and cleared out, and I had been three nights coming the thirty miles; I traveled nights, and hid daytimes and slept, and the bag of bread and meat I carried from home lasted me all the way and I had a plenty. I said I believed my uncle Abner Moore would take care of me, and so that was why I struck out for this town of Goshen."

"Goshen, child? This ain't Goshen. This is St. Petersburg. Goshen's ten mile further up the river. Who told you this was Goshen?"

"Why, a man I met at daybreak this morning, just as I was going to turn into the woods for my regular sleep. He told me when the roads forked I must take the right hand, and five mile would fetch me to Goshen."

"He was drunk I reckon. He told you just exactly wrong."

"Well, he did act like he was drunk, but it ain't no matter now. I got to be moving along. I'll fetch Goshen before daylight."

"Hold on a minute. I'll put you up a snack to eat. You might want it."

So she put me up a snack, and says:

"Say—when a cow's laying down, which end of her gets up first? Answer up prompt, now—don't stop to study over it. Which end gets up first?"

"The hind end, mum."

"Well, then, a horse?"

"The for'rard end, mum."

"Which side of a tree does the most moss grow on?"

"North side."

"If fifteen cows is browsing on a hillside, how many of them eats with their heads pointed the same direction?"

"The whole fifteen, mum."

"Well, I reckon you *have* lived in the country. I thought maybe you was trying to hocus me again. What's your real name, now?"

"George Peters, mum."

"Well, try to remember it, George. Don't forget and tell me it's Elexander before you go, and then get out by saying it's George-Elexander when I catch you. And don't go about women in that old calico. You do a girl tolerable poor, but you might fool men maybe. Bless you, child, when you set out to thread a needle, don't hold the thread still and fetch the needle up to it; hold the needle still and poke the thread at it—that's the way a woman most always does; but a man always does 'tother way. And when you throw at a rat or anything, hitch yourself up a tiptoe, and fetch your hand up over your head as awkward as you can, and miss your rat about six or seven foot. Throw stiff-armed from the shoulder, like there was a pivot there for it to turn on— like a girl; not from the wrist and elbow, with your arm out to one side, like a boy. And mind you, when a girl tries to catch anything in her lap, she throws her knees apart; she don't clap them together, the way you did when you catched the lump of lead. Why, I spotted you for a boy when you was threading the needle; and I contrived the other things just to make certain. Now trot along to your uncle, Sarah Mary Williams George Elexander Peters, and if you get into trouble you send word to Mrs. Judith Loftus, which is me, and I'll do what I can to get you out of it. Keep the river road, all the way, and next time you tramp, take shoes and socks with you. The river road's a rocky one, and your feet'll be in a condition when you get to Goshen, I reckon."

I went up the bank about fifty yards, and then I doubled on my tracks and slipped back to where my canoe was, a good piece below the house. I jumped in and was off in a hurry. I went upstream far enough to make the head of the island, and then started across. I took off the sunbonnet, for I didn't want no blinders on then. When I was about the middle, I hear the clock begin to strike; so I stops and listens; the sound come faint over the water, but clear—eleven. When I struck the head of the island I never waited to blow, though I was most winded, but I shoved right into the timber where my old camp used to be, and started a good fire there on a high and dry spot.

Then I jumped in the canoe and dug out for our place a mile and a half below, as hard as I could go. I landed, and slopped through the timber and up the ridge and into the cavern. There Jim laid, sound asleep on the ground. I roused him out and says:

"Git up quick and hump yourself, Jim! There ain't a minute to lose. They're after us!"

Jim never asked no questions, he never said a word; but the way he worked for the next half an hour showed about how he was scared. By that time everything we had in the world was on our raft and she was ready to be shoved out from the willow cove where she was hid. We put out the campfire at the cavern the first thing, and didn't show a candle outside after that.

I took the canoe out from shore a little piece and took a look, but if there was a boat around I couldn't see it, for stars and shadows ain't good to see by. Then we got out the raft and slipped along down in the shade, past the foot of the island dead still, never saying a word.

## YOU AND MARK TWAIN

Mark Twain was a lifelong observer of human nature. His books are full of people that we remember as vividly as the people in our own lives. In *Huckleberry Finn*, the river journey becomes a journey through human experience, with Huck learning what human beings are like and what they are capable of. Answer the following questions about the picture of life and of people that we get in these selections from the book:

(1) Mark Twain greatly cared about people, but he had no illusions about them. He often tells us the unvarnished truth about a violent world.

—What kind of person is Huck's father? Describe his personality and his actions toward his son.

—The author's description of the house being carried along by the flood is a first example of some of the grim scenes that Huck witnesses during his river journey. Describe what Huck sees.

—What picture do we get of the slaveholding practices of Huck's time? What is an "abolitionist," and why does Huck think he will be called one?

(2) Mark Twain often shows us a world in which people are on their own. They have to

make their own decisions. They have to use their wits to survive.

—Huck encounters problems to which there are no simple solutions. At the beginning, Huck finds that life in town with the widow and life in the woods with his father both have advantages and disadvantages. Explain the pros and cons.

—Mark Twain shared the traditional American admiration for shrewdness and ingenuity. Where and how does ingenuity play a role in this selection?

(3) Mark Twain believed that when all was said and done people were capable of doing the decent thing. They were capable of offering understanding or support to their fellow human beings. How many examples of such actions can you find in this selection? How important are they?

## A Closer Look

Mark Twain was a great master of **satire:** He used humor to make us laugh—and to make us change our ways. He used humor as a weapon against conceitedness and callousness and greed. Like few other writers, Mark Twain knew the secrets of popular humor. Answer these questions about Mark Twain's humor in this selection:

(1) One of the oldest kinds of popular humor is the comedy of errors. We laugh at people's mistakes, at things done backwards, at things turned topsy-turvy or upside-down. What is funny about the father's attitude toward his son's education? What is funny about the first encounter between Huck and Jim on the island? What are some of the things that make us laugh during the episode when Huck is dressed as a girl?

(2) The most traditional American form of humor is the humor of the **tall tale**. It is the humor of the wildly exaggerated story told with a perfectly straight face. Show this kind of humor in Huck's account of his father's cussing, or in his account of Hank Bunker's fatal accident in Chapter 10.

(3) One of the oldest comic types is the simpleton—the naive or trusting person who knows less than we do. We smile at the person who is easily taken in, or who is less suspicious and less experienced than we are.

—When Huck consults Jim about the future, we see that Jim is in several ways more knowing than Huck. How?

—The new judge decides against the guardianship proposed by Judge Thatcher and the widow. How does he show how naive and trusting he is, and what happens as a result?

—Sometimes people who merely *seem* trusting or simple know more than we think. When Huck visits Mrs. Loftus in Chapter 11, we are not always sure who is fooling whom. Describe the battle of wits between the two.

(4) People who have a strong sense of humor sometimes cannot help noticing the funny side even of danger, or misfortune, or suffering. We call this shuddery kind of humor **macabre** or **grotesque**. It has often been a favorite with American readers. Can you find one or two gruesome comic touches or episodes in this selection?

## Your Turn

Mark Twain learned much of his art from traditional storytellers and jokesmiths who knew how to entertain a crowd. He lectured to audiences and knew the art of timing and of building up to a high point. In much of his writing, we are closer to the spoken language than we usually are when reading. We seem to hear the sound of a living voice. Select a passage from this selection for reading out loud. Practice making its drama or its humor come to life for an audience.

FOR SENTENCE PRACTICE

# Thoughts and Afterthoughts
# by Mark Twain

Sometimes when we state an opinion, we feel we are not really communicating. We are not getting any attention or any response. Mark Twain was the kind of writer who knew how to make a statement sink in. He knew how to provide a striking example or explanation that would drive the point home. He knew how to wake up an audience and make people think. Look at some of Mark Twain's sayings about human nature. The passages in each of the following sets show a pattern that Mark Twain used over and over again:

(1) Each of the following passages starts with a general statement and then drives it home by a striking example or other follow-up:

Training is everything. The peach was once a bitter almond; cauliflower is nothing but cabbage with a college education.

Noise proves nothing. Often a hen who has merely laid an egg cackles as if she had laid an asteroid.

We should be careful to get out of an experience only the wisdom that is in it—and stop there; lest we be like the cat that sits down on a hot stove lid. She will never sit down on a hot stove lid again, and that is well; but also she will never sit down on a cold one any more.

On a separate sheet of paper, write several passages of your own that follow a similar pattern of "statement-and-explanation":

1. _____ is everything. The _____.
2. _____ proves nothing. Often _____.
3. We should be careful to _____.

(2) Each of the following passages at first seems to lead us in a familiar direction. But it then takes a sudden turn that makes us notice and that makes us think:

The man with a new idea is a Crank—until the new idea succeeds.

Man is the only animal that blushes—or needs to.

The holy passion of Friendship is of so sweet and steady and loyal and enduring a nature that it will last through a whole lifetime—if not asked to lend money.

Write several statements of your own that follow a similar "thought-and-afterthought" pattern. Use a separate sheet of paper.

1. The person with _____—_____.
2. _____ are the only people who _____.
3. _____—if not _____.

● Bret Harte (1836–1902) had come to the American West from Albany, New York. He worked as a typesetter and journalist in the California of the mining towns of gold rush days. In his immensely popular stories, Bret Harte helped to create the folklore of the American West. He wrote about a rugged outdoor world in which people were on their own. They often were not choosy about their morals, often disregarding or skirting the law. At the same time, those trying to uphold the law tended to "take the law into their own hands," practicing rough and ready ways of dealing out justice. One of Bret Harte's best-known stories appears here in a slightly abridged form. (Though some passages have been shortened, the words are the author's own.)

Bret Harte

# The Outcasts of Poker Flat

As Mr. John Oakhurst, gambler, stepped into the main street of Poker Flat on the morning of the twenty-third of November, 1850, he was conscious of a change in its moral atmosphere since the preceding night. Two or three men, conversing earnestly together, ceased as he approached, and exchanged significant glances. There was a Sabbath lull in the air, which, in a settlement unused to Sabbath influences, looked ominous.

Mr. Oakhurst's calm, handsome face betrayed small concern. . . . "I reckon they're after somebody," he reflected. "Likely it's me." He returned to his pocket the handkerchief with which he had been whipping away the red dust of Poker Flat from his neat boots, and quietly discharged his mind of any further conjecture.

In point of fact, Poker Flat was "after somebody." It had lately suffered the loss of several thousand dollars, two valuable horses, and a prominent citizen. It was experiencing a spasm of virtuous reaction quite as lawless and ungovernable as any of the acts that had provoked it. A secret committee had determined to rid the town of all improper persons. This was done permanently in regard to two men who were then hanging from the boughs of a sycamore in the gulch, and temporarily in the banishment of certain other objectionable characters.

Mr. Oakhurst was right in supposing that he was included in this category. A few of the committee had urged hanging him as a possible example and a sure method of reimbursing themselves from his pockets of the sums he had won from them. "It's agin justice," said Jim Wheeler, "to let this yer young man from Roaring Camp—an entire stranger—carry away our money." But a crude sentiment of equity residing in the breasts of those who had been fortunate enough to win from Mr. Oakhurst overruled this narrower local prejudice.

Mr. Oakhurst received his sentence with calm, none the less coolly that he was aware of the hesitation of his judges. He was too much of a gambler not to accept fate. With him life was at best an uncertain game, and he recognized the usual percentage in favor of the dealer.

A body of armed men accompanied the deported wickedness of Poker Flat to the outskirts of the settlement. Besides Mr. Oakhurst, who was known to be a coolly desperate man, and for whose intimidation the armed escort was intended, the party consisted of a young woman familiarly known as "The Duchess"; another who had won the title of "Mother Shipton"; and "Uncle Billy," a suspected sluicerobber* and confirmed drunkard.

The cavalcade provoked no comments from the spectators, nor was any word uttered by the escort. Only when the gulch which marked the uttermost limit of Poker Flat was reached, the leader spoke briefly and to the point. The exiles were forbidden to return at the peril of their lives.

As the escort disappeared, their pent-up feelings found vent in a few tears from the Duchess, some bad language from Mother Shipton, and a volley of expletives from Uncle Billy. Oakhurst alone remained silent. He listened calmly to Mother Shipton's desire to cut somebody's heart out, to the repeated statements of the Duchess that she would die in the road, and to the alarming oaths that seemed to be bumped out of Uncle Billy as he rode forward.

With easy good humor, he insisted upon exchanging his own riding horse, "Five-Spot," for the sorry mule which the Duchess rode. But even this act did not draw the party into any closer sympathy. The young woman readjusted her somewhat draggled plumes; Mother Shipton eyed the possessor of "Five-Spot" with malevolence, and Uncle Billy included the whole party in one sweeping anathema.

*sluicerobber: a robber of troughs used to separate gold from gravel or sand.

The road to Sandy Bar—a camp that not having experienced the influence of Poker Flat seemed to offer some invitation to the emigrants—lay over a steep mountain range. It was distant a day's severe travel. In that advanced season the party soon passed out of the moist, temperate regions of the foothills into the dry, cold, bracing air of the Sierras. The trail was narrow and difficult. At noon the Duchess, rolling out of her saddle upon the ground, declared her intention of going no farther and the party halted.

The spot was wild and impressive. A wooded amphitheater, surrounded on three sides by cliffs of naked granite, sloped gently toward the crest of another precipice that overlooked the valley. It was, undoubtedly, the most suitable spot for a camp, had camping been advisable. But Mr. Oakhurst knew that scarcely half the journey to Sandy Bar was accomplished, and the party were not equipped or provisioned for delay. This fact he pointed out to his companions curtly, with a commentary on the folly of throwing up their hand before the game was played out.

But they were furnished with liquor, which in this emergency stood them in place of food, fuel, and rest. It was not long before they were more or less under its influence. Uncle Billy passed rapidly from a bellicose state into one of stupor, the Duchess became maudlin, and Mother Shipton snored. Mr. Oakhurst alone remained erect, leaning against a rock, calmly surveying them.

Mr. Oakhurst did not drink. It interfered with a profession which required coolness and presence of mind, and, in his own language, he "couldn't afford it." As he gazed at his fellow exiles, the loneliness begotten of his trade, his habits of life, his very vices, for the first time seriously oppressed him. He bestirred himself

in dusting his black clothes, washing his hands and face, and other acts characteristic of his neat habits, and for a moment forgot his annoyance.

The thought of deserting his weaker and more pitiable companions never perhaps occurred to him. . . . He looked at the gloomy walls that rose a thousand feet sheer above the circling pines around him, at the sky ominously clouded, at the valley below, already deepening into shadow. Doing so, suddenly he heard his own name called.

A horseman slowly ascended the trail. In the fresh, open face of the newcomer Mr. Oakhurst recognized Tom Simson, otherwise known as "The Innocent," of Sandy Bar. He had met him some months before over a "little game," and had won the entire fortune—amounting to some forty dollars—of that guileless youth. After the game was finished, Mr. Oakhurst drew the youthful speculator behind the door and thus addressed him: "Tommy, you're a good little man, but you can't gamble worth a cent. Don't try it over again." He then handed him his money back, pushed him gently from the room, and so made a devoted slave of Tom Simson.

There was a remembrance of this in his enthusiastic greeting of Mr. Oakhurst. He had started, he said, to go to Poker Flat to seek his fortune. "Alone?" No, not exactly alone; in fact (a giggle), he had run away with Piney Woods. Didn't Mr. Oakhurst remember Piney? She that used to wait on the table at the Temperance House? They had been engaged a long time, but old Jake Woods had objected, and so they had run away and were going to Poker Flat to be married, and here they were. And they were tired out, and how lucky it was they had found a place to camp, and company. All this the Innocent delivered rapidly,

while Piney, a stout damsel of fifteen, emerged from behind the pine tree and quickly rode to the side of her lover.

Mr. Oakhurst seldom troubled himself with sentiment, still less with propriety; but he had a vague idea that the situation was not fortunate. He retained, however, his presence of mind sufficiently to kick Uncle Billy, who was about to make his thoughts known, and Uncle Billy was sober enough to recognize in Mr. Oakhurst's kick a superior power that would not bear trifling.

He then endeavored to dissuade Tom Simson from delaying further, but in vain. He even pointed out the fact that there was no provision, nor means of making a camp. But, unluckily, the Innocent met this objection by assuring the party that he was provided with an extra mule loaded with provisions, and by the discovery of a rude attempt at a log house near the trail. "Piney can stay with Mrs. Oakhurst," said the Innocent, pointing to the Duchess, "and I can shift for myself."

Nothing but Mr. Oakhurst's admonishing foot saved Uncle Billy from bursting into a roar of laughter. As it was, he felt compelled to retire up the canyon. There he confided the joke to the tall pine trees, with many slaps of his leg, contortions of his face, and the usual profanity. But when he returned to the party, he found the group seated by a fire—for the air had grown strangely chill and the sky very overcast—in apparently amicable conversation.

Piney was actually talking in an impulsive girlish fashion to the Duchess, who was listening with an interest she had not shown for many days. The Innocent was also holding forth, apparently with equal effect, to Mr. Oakhurst and Mother Shipton, who was actually relaxing into amiability.

"Is this yer a picnic?" said Uncle Billy,

with inward scorn, as he surveyed the group, the glancing firelight, and the tethered animals in the foreground.

Suddenly an idea mingled with the alcoholic fumes that disturbed his brain. It was apparently of a jocular nature, for he felt impelled to slap his leg again and cram his fist into his mouth.

As the shadows crept slowly up the mountain, a slight breeze rocked the tops of the pine trees and moaned through their long and gloomy aisles. The ruined cabin, patched and covered with pine boughs, was set apart for the ladies. As the lovers parted, they exchanged a kiss, so honest and sincere that it might have been heard above the swaying pines. The Duchess and Mother Shipton were probably too stunned to remark upon this evidence of simplicity, and so turned without a word to the hut. The fire was replenished, the men lay down before the door, and in a few minutes were asleep.

Mr. Oakhurst was a light sleeper. Toward morning he awoke benumbed and cold. As he stirred the dying fire, the wind, which was now blowing strongly, brought to his cheek that which caused the blood to leave it—snow!

He started to his feet with the intention of awakening the sleepers, for there was no time to lose. But turning to where Uncle Billy had been lying, he found him gone. A suspicion leaped to his brain, and a curse to his lips. He ran to the spot where the mules had been tethered—they were no longer there. The tracks were already rapidly disappearing in the snow.

The momentary excitement brought Mr. Oakhurst back to the fire with his usual calm. He did not waken the sleepers. The Innocent slumbered peacefully, with a smile on his good-humored freckled face. Piney slept as sweetly as though attended by celestial guardians. Mr. Oakhurst, drawing his blanket over his shoulders, stroked his mustaches and waited for the dawn. It came slowly in a whirling mist of snowflakes that dazzled and confused the eye. What could be seen of the landscape appeared magically changed. He looked over the valley, and summed up the present and future in two words, "Snowed in!"

The provisions, fortunately for the party, had been stored within the hut, and so escaped the fingers of Uncle Billy. With care and prudence they might last ten days longer.

"That is," said Mr. Oakhurst to the Innocent, "if you're willing to board us. If you ain't—and perhaps you'd better not—you can wait till Uncle Billy gets back with provisions."

For some reason, Mr. Oakhurst could not bring himself to disclose Uncle Billy's rascality, and so offered the hypothesis that he had wandered from the camp and had accidentally stampeded the animals. He dropped a warning to the Duchess and Mother Shipton, who of course knew the facts.

"They'll find out the truth about us *all* when they find out anything," he added significantly, "and there's no good frightening them now."

Tom Simson not only put his entire worldly store at the disposal of Mr. Oakhurst, but seemed to enjoy their seclusion. "We'll have a camp for a week, and then the snow'll melt, and we'll all go back together."

The cheerful gaiety of the young man and Mr. Oakhurst's calm infected the others. The Innocent, with the aid of pine boughs, extemporized a thatch for the roofless cabin, and the Duchess directed Piney in the rearrangement of the interior with a taste and tact that opened the blue eyes of that provincial maiden to their fullest extent.

"I reckon now you're used to fine things

at Poker Flat," said Piney.

The Duchess turned away sharply to conceal something that reddened her cheeks, and Mother Shipton requested Piney not to "chatter." But when Mr. Oakhurst returned from a weary search for the trail, he heard the sound of happy laughter echoed from the rocks. He stopped in some alarm, and his thoughts first naturally reverted to the whiskey, which he had prudently cached. "And yet it don't somehow sound like whiskey," said the gambler. It was not until he caught sight of the blazing fire through the still blinding storm, and the group around it, that he settled to the conviction that it was "square fun."

Whether Mr. Oakhurst had cached his cards with the whiskey I cannot say. It was certain that, in Mother Shipton's words, he "didn't say 'cards' once" during that evening. Haply the time was beguiled by an accordion, produced somewhat ostentatiously by Tom Simson from his pack. Notwithstanding some difficulties, Piney Woods managed to pluck several reluctant melodies from its keys, to an accompaniment by the Innocent on a pair of bone castanets.

But the crowning festivity of the evening was reached in a rude camp-meeting hymn, which the lovers, joining hands, sang with great earnestness. I fear that a certain defiant tone to its chorus, rather than any devotional quality, caused it speedily to infect the others, who at last joined in the refrain:

I'm proud to live in the service of the Lord,
And I'm bound to die in His army.

The pines rocked, the storm eddied and whirled above the miserable group, and the flames of their altar leaped heavenward, as if in token of the vow.

At midnight the storm abated, the rolling clouds parted, and the stars glittered keenly above the sleeping camp. Mr. Oakhurst, whose professional habits had enabled him to live on the smallest possible amount of sleep, in dividing the watch with Tom Simson somehow managed to take upon himself the greatest part of that duty. He excused himself to the Innocent by saying that he had "often been a week without sleep."

"Doing what?" asked Tom.

"Poker!" replied Oakhurst. "When a man gets a streak of luck, he don't get tired. The luck gives in first. Luck," continued the gambler reflectively, "is a mighty queer thing. All you know about it for certain is that it's bound to change. And it's finding out when it's going to change that makes you. We've had a streak of bad luck since we left Poker Flat—you come along, and slap you get into it, too. If you can hold your cards right along you're all right. For," added the gambler,

I'm proud to live in the service of the Lord,
And I'm bound to die in His army.

The third day came, and the sun, looking through the white-curtained valley, saw the outcasts divide their slowly decreasing store of provisions for the morning meal. Its rays diffused a kindly warmth over the wintry landscape. But it revealed drift on drift of snow piled high around the hut—a hopeless, uncharted, trackless sea of white lying below the rocky shores to which the castaways still clung.

Through the marvelously clear air the smoke of the pastoral village of Poker Flat rose miles away. Mother Shipton saw it, and hurled in that direction a final malediction. It did her good, she privately informed the Duchess. "Just you go out there and cuss, and see."

She then set herself to the task of amusing "the child," as she and the Duchess were pleased to call Piney. Piney was no chicken, but it was a soothing and original theory of the pair thus to account for the fact that she didn't swear and wasn't improper.

When night crept up again through the gorges, the reedy notes of the accordion rose and fell in fitful spasms and long-drawn gasps by the flickering campfire. But music failed to fill entirely the aching void left by insufficient food. . . .

So, with small food and much of the accordion, a week passed over the heads of the outcasts. The sun again forsook them, and again from leaden skies the snow-flakes were sifted over the land. Day by day closer around them drew the snowy circle, until at last they looked from their prison over drifted walls of dazzling white that towered twenty feet above their heads. It became more and more difficult to replenish their fires, even from the fallen trees beside them, now half hidden in the drifts. And yet no one complained.

The lovers turned from the dreary prospect and looked into each other's eyes, and were happy. Mr. Oakhurst settled himself coolly to the losing game before him. The Duchess, more cheerful than she had been, assumed the care of Piney.

Only Mother Shipton—once the strongest of the party—seemed to sicken and fade. At midnight on the tenth day she called Oakhurst to her side. "I'm going," she said, in a voice of querulous weakness, "but don't say anything about it. Don't waken the kids. Take the bundle from under my head, and open it."

Mr. Oakhurst did so. It held Mother Shipton's rations for the last week, untouched. "Give 'em to the child," she said, pointing to the sleeping Piney.

"You've starved yourself," said the gambler.

"That's what they call it," said the woman querulously, as she lay down again, and, turning her face to the wall, passed quietly away.

The accordion and the bones were put aside that day. When the body of Mother Shipton had been committed to the snow, Mr. Oakhurst took the Innocent aside, and showed him a pair of snowshoes, which he had fashioned from the pack saddle.

"There's one chance in a hundred to save her yet," he said, pointing to Piney; "but it's there," he added, pointing toward Poker Flat. "If you can reach there in two days she's safe."

"And you?" asked Tom Simson.

"I'll stay here," was the curt reply.

The lovers parted with a long embrace. "You are not going, too?" said the Duchess, as she saw Mr. Oakhurst apparently waiting to accompany him.

"As far as the canyon," he replied. He turned suddenly and kissed the Duchess.

Night came, but not Mr. Oakhurst. It brought the storm again and the whirling snow. Then the Duchess, feeding the fire, found that someone had quietly piled beside the hut enough fuel to last a few days longer. The tears rose to her eyes, but she hid them from Piney.

The women slept but little. In the morning, looking into each other's faces, they read their fate. Neither spoke, but Piney, accepting the position of the stronger, drew near and placed her arm around the Duchess' waist. They kept this attitude for the rest of the day. That night the storm reached its greatest fury, and, rending asunder the protecting vines, invaded the very hut.

Toward morning they found themselves unable to feed the fire, which gradually died away. As the embers slowly blackened, the Duchess crept closer to Piney, and broke the silence of many hours: "Piney, can you pray?" "No, dear," said Piney simply. The Duchess, without knowing exactly why, felt relieved, and, putting her head upon Piney's shoulder, spoke no more. And so they fell asleep.

The wind lulled as if it feared to waken them. Feathery drifts of snow, shaken from the long pine boughs, flew like white-winged birds, and settled about them as they slept. The moon through the rifted clouds looked down upon what had been the camp. But all human stain, all trace of earthly travail, was hidden beneath the spotless mantle mercifully flung from above.

They slept all that day and the next, nor did they waken when voices and footsteps broke the silence of the camp. And when pitying fingers brushed the snow from their faces, equal peace dwelt upon them. Even the law of Poker Flat recognized this, and turned away, leaving them still locked in each other's arms.

But at the head of the gulch, on one of the largest pine trees, they found the deuce of clubs pinned to the bark with a bowie knife. It bore the following, written in pencil in a firm hand:

> BENEATH THIS TREE
> LIES THE BODY
> OF
> JOHN OAKHURST,
> WHO STRUCK A STREAK OF BAD LUCK
> ON THE 23D OF NOVEMBER, 1850,
> AND
> HANDED IN HIS CHECKS
> ON THE 7TH DECEMBER, 1850.

And pulseless and cold, with a Derringer by his side and a bullet in his heart, though still calm as in life, beneath the snow lay he who was at once the strongest and yet the weakest of the outcasts of Poker Flat.

## YOU AND THE STORY

The author's aim in this story was to make us feel sympathy for the underdog. We are asked to put ourselves in the place of the outcasts, those considered wicked by the community. How does the author enlist our sympathy for these "objectionable" characters? How successful is he? Answer the following questions about the way this story shapes the reader's reactions:

(1) From the beginning, the author lets us know how he feels about the citizens' methods of promoting virtue and justice. How does he describe those methods? Why does he object to them? Can you think of a label that would fit the kind of justice that is practiced in Poker Flat?

(2) What are the traits that are likely to make readers admire John Oakhurst, the gambler? When we first see him, what do we learn about his personal style and manners? What is striking about his behavior toward the other members of the party? What does his relationship with Tommy add to our picture of him? How does he meet his end?

(3) The outcasts in this story are a mixed lot. How do they act when they are put to the test? Show how some of them prove better than their reputation. Were you prepared for the actions of the one who proves truly bad?

## A Closer Look

In the following questions, various terms appear that play a role in this story. How many of them would you have to check in a dictionary?

(1) Early in the story, Oakhurst notices that the situation is turning serious and

threatening. How do the following words help establish this basic mood of the story?

> earnest    significant
> ominous    gloomy

(2) The events of the story are set in motion by the decision of the community to rid itself of undesirable characters. Explain how each of the words in the following set is related to this idea.

> banishment    deported
> exile    emigrant

(3) Poker Flat was experiencing a "virtuous reaction" against lawlessness, with a secret committee trying to establish law and order. Do all of the following terms used in connection with law and order mean the same?

> justice    equity    propriety

(4) Several of the characters in this story are given to rough language. How are the following words similar, and what sets each apart?

> oath    profanity    curse
> anathema    malediction

(5) The author reports to us in detail the changing moods of the different characters. What is the meaning of each of the following?

> bellicose    maudlin    guileless
> amicable    impulsive    jocular

---

### Your Turn

In this story, Oakhurst writes his own epitaph. What do you think a similar last word might be like for some of the other people in the story? Write an epitaph for one or two of the other characters in the story.

---

WRITING ABOUT LITERATURE

# A Touch of Melodrama

Like other successful nineteenth-century writers, Bret Harte used some of the techniques of **melodrama**. Melodrama was a kind of popular stage entertainment that stirred up strong emotions, and that made people feel very moral at the same time. Some of the characters were very good, and others very bad. The audience could love and admire the good people, and it could boo and hiss the sneering villains. Often the good people were very innocent and trusting, and they were persecuted or made to suffer by the bad. The audience felt warm sympathy for the victims and righteous anger toward the wicked. Often the spectators' emotions were aroused by sudden strokes of good luck or misfortune. Many of the things said or done on the stage were said and done with a flourish. Audiences liked especially an unexpected generous or unselfish gesture—especially one that came at a time when things looked hopeless for the hero or the heroine.

Can you see touches of melodrama in this story by Bret Harte? Which of the features mentioned above of melodrama can you see illustrated in this story? Where and how? Point out and describe the melodramatic elements in this story.

● Each generation tries to teach those who come after it what they should know about life. But what young people are told often does not become meaningful to them until it is tested by trial and error. The words slowly become real as the result of experiences big and small, some of them only half-understood at the time. Katherine Anne Porter (born 1890) wrote her best-known stories about characters who are trying to make sense of their experience. They are trying to understand what they have experienced, to explain it to themselves. Katherine Anne Porter was born in Texas and later lived in New York and Washington, D.C. She traveled in Europe and Mexico; and she made a living as a reporter, editor, and reviewer. She published her best-known stories in the thirties, and they have been reprinted in many collections of short stories since. Her novel *The Ship of Fools* was published in 1962. In many of her stories, she shows a special concern for characters who have been hurt in some way or who are in some way handicapped. Their spiritual resources are being tested by what they experience. As a person and as a writer, she has shown a special interest in what helps keep a warm and generous spirit alive in people and in what breeds callousness and hate. The following story is about an incident that played a role in someone's growing up.

## Katherine Anne Porter

# The Grave

The grandfather, dead for more than thirty years, had been twice disturbed in his long repose by the constancy and possessiveness of his widow. She removed his bones first to Louisiana and then to Texas as if she had set out to find her own burial place, knowing well she would never return to the places she had left. In Texas she set up a small cemetery in a corner of her first farm, and as the family connection grew, and oddments of relations came over from Kentucky to settle, it contained at last about twenty graves. After the grandmother's death, part of her land was to be sold for the benefit of certain of her children, and the cemetery happened to lie in the part set aside for sale. It was necessary to take up the bodies and bury them again in the family plot in the big new public cemetery, where the grandmother had been buried. At last her husband was to lie beside her for eternity, as she had planned.

The family cemetery had been a pleasant small neglected garden of tangled rose bushes and ragged cedar trees and cypress, the simple flat stones rising out of uncropped sweet-smelling wild grass. The graves were lying open and empty one burning day when Miranda and her brother Paul, who often went together to hunt rabbits and doves, propped their twenty-two Winchester rifles carefully against the rail fence, climbed over, and explored among the graves. She was nine years old and he was twelve.

They peered into the pits all shaped alike with such purposeful accuracy, and looking at each other with pleased adventurous eyes, they said in solemn tones: "These were graves!" trying by words to shape a special, suitable emotion in their minds, but they felt nothing except an agreeable thrill of wonder: they were seeing a new sight, doing something they had not done before. In them both there was also a small disappointment at the entire commonplaceness of the actual spectacle. Even if it had once contained a coffin for years upon years, when the coffin was gone a grave was just a hole in the ground. Miranda leaped into the pit that had held her grandfather's bones. Scratching around aimlessly and pleasurably as any young animal, she scooped up a lump of earth and weighed it in her palm. It had a pleasantly sweet, corrupt smell, being mixed with cedar needles and small leaves, and as the crumbs fell apart, she saw a silver dove no larger than a hazel nut, with spread wings and neat fan-shaped tail. The breast had a deep round hollow in it. Turning it up to the fierce sunlight, she saw that the inside of the hollow was cut in little whorls. She scrambled out, over the pile of loose earth that had fallen back into one end of the grave, calling to Paul that she had found something, he must guess what . . . His head appeared smiling over the rim of another grave. He waved a closed hand at her. "I've got something too!" They ran to compare treasures, making a game of it, so many guesses each, all wrong, and a final showdown with opened palms. Paul had found a thin wide gold ring carved with intricate flowers and leaves. Miranda was smitten at sight of the ring and wished to have it. Paul seemed more impressed by the dove. They made a trade, with some little bickering. After he had got the dove in his hand, Paul said, "Don't you know what this is? This is a screw head for a

coffin! . . . I'll bet nobody else in the world has one like this!"

Miranda glanced at it without covetousness. She had the gold ring on her thumb; it fitted perfectly. "Maybe we ought to go now," she said, "maybe somebody'll see us and tell." They knew the land had been sold, the cemetery was no longer theirs, and they felt like trespassers. They climbed back over the fence, slung their rifles loosely under their arms—they had been shooting at targets with various kinds of firearms since they were seven years old—and set out to look for the rabbits and doves or whatever small game might happen along. On these expeditions Miranda always followed at Paul's heels along the path, obeying instructions about handling her gun when going through fences; learning how to stand the gun up properly so it would not slip and fire unexpectedly; how to wait her time for a shot and not just bang away in the air without looking, spoiling shots for Paul, who really could hit things if given a chance. Now and then, in her excitement at seeing birds whizz up suddenly before her face, or a rabbit leap across her very toes, she lost her head, and almost without sighting she flung her rifle up and pulled the trigger. She hardly ever hit any sort of mark. She had no proper sense of hunting at all. Her brother would be often completely disgusted with her. "You don't care whether you get your bird or not," he said. "That's no way to hunt." Miranda could not understand his indignation. She had seen him smash his hat and yell with fury when he had missed his aim. "What I like about shooting," said Miranda, with exasperating inconsequence, "is pulling the trigger and hearing the noise."

"Then, by golly," said Paul, "whyn't you go back to the range and shoot at bull's-eyes?"

"I'd just as soon," said Miranda, "only like this, we walk around more."

"Well, you just stay behind and stop spoiling my shots," said Paul, who, when he made a kill, wanted to be certain he had made it. Miranda, who alone brought down a bird once in twenty rounds, always claimed as her own any game they got when they fired at the same moment. It was tiresome and unfair and her brother was sick of it.

"Now, the first dove we see, or the first rabbit, is mine," he told her. "And the next will be yours. Remember that and don't get smarty."

"What about snakes?" asked Miranda idly. "Can I have the first snake?"

Waving her thumb gently and watching her gold ring glitter, Miranda lost interest in shooting. She was wearing her summer roughing outfit: dark blue overalls, a light blue shirt, a hired-man's straw hat, and thick brown sandals. Her brother had on the same outfit except his was a sober hickory-nut color. Ordinarily Miranda preferred her overalls to any other dress, though it was making rather a scandal in the countryside, for the year was 1903, and in the back country the law of female decorum had teeth in it. Her father had been criticized for letting his girls dress like boys and go careering around astride barebacked horses. Big sister Maria, the really independent and fearless one, in spite of her rather affected ways, rode at a dead run with only a rope knotted around her horse's nose. It was said the motherless family was running down, with the Grandmother no longer there to hold it together. It was known that she had discriminated against her son Harry in her will, and that he was in straits about money. Some of his old neighbors reflected with vicious satisfaction that now he would probably not be so stiff-necked, nor have any more high-stepping horses either. Miranda knew this, though she could not say how. She had met along the road old women of the kind who smoked corncob pipes, who had treated her grandmother with most sincere respect. They slanted their gummy old eyes sideways at the granddaughter and said, "Ain't you ashamed of yoself, Missy? It's aginst the Scriptures to dress like that. Whut yo Pappy thinkin about?" Miranda, with her powerful social sense, which was like a fine set of antennae radiating from every pore of her skin, would feel ashamed because she knew it was rude and ill-bred to shock anybody, even bad-tempered old crones, though she had faith in her father's judgment and was perfectly comfortable in the clothes. Her father had said, "They're just what you need, and they'll save your dresses for school . . ." This sounded quite simple and natural to her. She had been brought up in rigorous economy. Wastefulness was vulgar. It was also a sin. These were truths; she had heard them repeated many times and never once disputed.

Now the ring, shining with the serene purity of fine gold on her rather grubby thumb, turned her feelings against her overalls and sockless feet, toes sticking through the thick brown leather straps. She wanted to go back to the farmhouse, take a good cold bath, dust herself with plenty of Maria's violet talcum powder—provided Maria was not present to object, of course—put on the thinnest, most becoming dress she owned, with a big sash, and sit in the wicker chair under the trees . . . These things were not all she wanted, of course; she had vague stirrings of desire for luxury and a grand way of living which could not take precise form in her imagination but were founded on family legend of past wealth and leisure. These immediate comforts were what she could have, and she wanted them at once. She lagged rather far behind Paul, and once she thought of just turning back without a word and going home. She stopped, thinking that Paul would never do that to her, and so she would have to tell him. When a rabbit leaped, she let Paul have it without dispute. He killed it with one shot.

When she came up with him, he was already kneeling, examining the wound, the rabbit trailing from his hands. "Right through the head," he said complacently, as if he had aimed for it. He took out his sharp, competent bowie knife and started to skin the body. He did it very cleanly and quickly. Uncle Jimbilly knew how to prepare the skins so that Miranda always had fur coats for her dolls, for though she never cared much for her dolls she liked seeing them in fur coats. The children knelt facing each other over the dead animal. Miranda watched admiringly while her brother stripped the skin away as if he were taking off a glove. The flayed flesh emerged dark scarlet, sleek, firm;

Miranda with thumb and finger felt the long fine muscles with the silvery flat strips binding them to the joints. Brother lifted the oddly bloated belly. "Look," he said, in a low amazed voice. "It was going to have young ones."

Very carefully he slit the thin flesh from the center ribs to the flanks, and a scarlet bag appeared. He slit again and pulled the bag open, and there lay a bundle of tiny rabbits, each wrapped in a thin scarlet veil. The brother pulled these off and there they were, dark gray, their sleek wet down lying in minute even ripples, like a baby's head just washed, their unbelievably small delicate ears folded close, their little blind faces almost featureless.

Miranda said, "Oh, I want to *see*," under her breath. She looked and looked—excited but not frightened, for she was accustomed to the sight of animals killed in hunting—filled with pity and astonishment and a kind of shocked delight in the wonderful little creatures for their own sakes, they were so pretty. She touched one of them so carefully, "Ah, there's blood running over them," she said and began to tremble without knowing why. Yet she wanted so deeply to see and to know. Having seen, she felt at once as if she had known all along. The very memory of her former ignorance faded, she had always known just this. No one had ever told her anything outright, she had been rather unobservant of the animal life around her because she was so accustomed to animals. They seemed simply disorderly and unaccountably rude in their habits, but altogether natural and not very interesting. Her brother had spoken as if he had known about everything all along. He may have seen all this before. He had never said a word to her, but she knew now a part at least of what he knew. She understood a little of the secret, formless intuitions in her own mind and body, which had been clearing up, taking form, so gradually and so steadily she had not realized that she was learning what she had to know. Paul said cautiously, as if he were talking about something forbidden: "They were just about ready to be born." His voice dropped on the last word. "I know," said Miranda, "like kittens. I know, like babies." She was quietly and terribly agitated, standing again with her rifle under her arm, looking down at the bloody heap. "I don't want the skin," she said, "I won't have it." Paul buried the young rabbits again in their mother's body, wrapped the skin around her, carried her to a clump of sage bushes, and hid her away. He came out again at once and said to Miranda, with an eager friendliness, a confidential tone quite unusual in him, as if he were taking her into an important secret on equal terms: "Listen now. Now you listen to me, and don't ever forget. Don't you ever tell a living soul that you saw this. Don't tell a soul. Don't tell Dad because I'll get into trouble. He'll say I'm leading you into things you ought not to do. He's always saying that. So now don't you go and forget and blab out something the way you're always doing . . . Now, that's a secret. Don't you tell."

Miranda never told, she did not even wish to tell anybody. She thought about the whole worrisome affair with confused unhappiness for a few days. Then it sank quietly into her mind and was heaped over by accumulated thousands of impressions, for nearly twenty years. One day she was picking her path among the puddles and crushed refuse of a market street in a strange city of a strange country, when without warning, plain and clear in its true colors as if she looked through a frame upon a scene that had not stirred nor changed since the moment it happened, the episode of that far-off day leaped from its burial place before her mind's eye. She was so reasonlessly horrified she halted suddenly staring, the scene before her eyes dimmed by the vision back of them. An Indian vendor had held up before her a tray of dyed sugar sweets, in the shapes of all kinds of small creatures: birds, baby chicks, baby rabbits, lambs, baby pigs. They were in gay colors and smelled of vanilla, maybe . . . It was a very hot day and the smell in the market, with its piles of raw flesh and wilting flowers, was like the mingled sweetness and corruption she had smelled that other day in the empty cemetery at home: the day she had remembered always until now vaguely as the time she and her brother had found treasure in the open graves. Instantly upon this thought the dreadful vision faded, and she saw clearly her brother, whose childhood face she had forgotten, standing again in the blazing sunshine, again twelve years old, a pleased sober smile in his eyes, turning the silver dove over and over in his hands.

## YOU AND THE STORY

If Miranda had been asked in later life what her relationship had been with her brother, what do you think she might have said? What kind of experiences did they share? How much difference did it make that he was older than she was? Do you think that their kind of sister-and-brother relationship is usual or unusual? Why?

## A Closer Look

Experiences like the one described in this story are often an important part of growing up. Katherine Anne Porter is a master at tracing impressions and feelings as they are taking shape in her characters' minds. Like other modern writers, she patiently explores the consciousness of her characters. The people in her stories seldom have simple, one-track thoughts. They often have mixed and half-formed feelings. They have confused hopes and fears—like real people. Answer the following questions about the influences that help shape Miranda's impressions and feelings, and about the thoughts and feelings that pass through her mind.

(1) What do we learn about Miranda's family and its history? What influence do you think the other members of the family had on the girl? What role did Miranda's father play? What was the role of her big sister?

(2) The way we dress at times seems an external or superficial thing. Yet what to wear, and how it will look to others, are often very serious questions in young people's minds. How and why does the question of how to dress first play a role in this story?

What role does it play in the thoughts brought to Miranda's mind by the gold ring?

(3) Part of growing up is learning about subjects that were once taboo for us. In examining the dead rabbit, the children have a glimpse of some of the basic mysteries of life that each generation discovers anew for itself. What do they learn? What are their feelings? Find several sentences in which the author tells us what Miranda and Paul think and feel.

### Your Turn

As people get older, they sometimes remember scenes from their childhood that they had long forgotten. Pretend you are much older than you are now. Describe a scene from your childhood that you think might come back to you in later years.

---

Language/Composition Activity B4

WORDS IN CONTEXT

# A Far-Off Day

What is the meaning of each italicized word in the following statements? How much does the context tell you about each word?

1. The long *repose* of the grandfather had been disturbed when his bones were moved to a new burial place.
2. The widow was *possessive* and moved his remains when she moved.
3. Miranda was not interested in the screw head from the coffin and looked at it without *covetousness*.
4. Dress that violated the law of female *decorum* caused a scandal.
5. The son had many problems because his mother had *discriminated* against him in her will.
6. Paul *complacently* examined the rabbit he had killed with one shot.
7. Animals were not very interesting to her, and she had been *unobservant* of the animal life around her.
8. She had not been told about birth but had secret, shapeless *intuitions* in her mind.
9. Her brother asked her in a *confidential* tone to keep their secret.
10. Many years later, Miranda remembered the *episode* of that far-off day.

# UNIT SIX

# The Faces of Nature

Go forth, under the open sky, and listen
To Nature's teachings.

—William Cullen Bryant

Civilization has often cut human beings off from their roots in the natural world. It has taught them how to shelter themselves from wind and cold and rain. It has taught them how to make themselves more independent of the cycles of growth that bring hunger or plenty. It has at times made them forget how much they are a part of nature, and how much they depend on it for their health and happiness. Part of the American experience has been the opportunity for people to rediscover their roots in nature. Pilgrims and pioneers were brought face to face with the wilderness. Early travelers discovered the virgin forest, the prairies, the Rocky Mountains, the mighty rivers, and the open sea.

From the beginning, the place that we as human beings occupy in nature has been a major theme of American writers. When American literature came into its own in the early nineteenth century, it strongly reflected the contemporary yearning to go back to nature, to find out what life had been like on God's earth before cities and roads and dams transformed the landscape. Romantic poets in Europe were telling restless, hemmed-in city dwellers to expose themselves to the healing influence of Nature's beauty. They attacked the artificial customs of civilized life and wrote about the spontaneous emotions of people in close touch with the unspoiled natural world.

Later in the nineteenth century, the Romantic tradition of celebrating Nature's beauty slowly gave way to a different view. Many people felt that the picture usually painted of nature had been too idealized and optimistic. Scientists wrote about the struggle for existence. They described untamed wild nature as ruled by the iron law of the jungle: eat or be eaten; kill or be killed. Poets discovered nature "red in tooth and claw." Around the turn of the century, naturalistic writers like Stephen Crane and Jack London were writing their grim sagas of human struggle against merciless natural forces.

In our day, we are again rethinking our relationship with nature. We are slowly becoming convinced that we have been too heedless in exploiting our apparently unlimited natural resources. Many writers are trying to teach human beings a new respect for the sources of life on this planet. They are trying to make us understand and respect the mutual dependence of living things on each other. They are trying to make us cherish our kinship with other forms of life. Slowly, we are gaining a better understanding of ecology, the great housekeeping system of life on this earth.

## POEMS: **The Changing Seasons**

Through the centuries, poets have written about the changing faces of nature. In the earliest days, the great yearly cycle of the seasons ruled everyone's life. There was a time to hunt or to move to new pastures. Or there was seedtime and harvest. Some of the oldest known poems express an age-old fear of cold and famine, or joy at the return of spring. In the following poems, some well-known American poets look at the changing seasons.

Henry Wadsworth Longfellow
# Afternoon in February

The day is ending,
The night is descending;
The marsh is frozen,
The river dead.

Through clouds like ashes
The red sun flashes
On village windows
That glimmer red.

The snow recommences;
The buried fences
Mark no longer
The road o'er the plain;

While through the meadows,
Like fearful shadows,
Slowly passes
A funeral train.

The bell is pealing,
And every feeling
Within me responds
To the dismal knell.

Shadows are trailing,
My heart is bewailing
And tolling within
Like a funeral bell.

### YOU AND THE POEM

(1) Henry Wadsworth Longfellow (1807–1882) wrote a very *regular* kind of poetry expected by most of his nineteenth-century readers. The **rhyme scheme** is very regular: The first two lines in each stanza rhyme. Where else is rhyme used in the poem? The **meter**, or length and rhythm of the lines, is also very regular. Usually, there are five syllables to a line. Each is a two-beat line, with two stresses or accents per line:

> The dáy is énding
> The béll is péaling
> On víllage wíndows

But even in this regular poem, variety keeps it from being monotonous. Find several lines in which the number of syllables differs. Find lines in which the location of the stresses, or accents, differs.

(2) Read this poem out loud. Try to make the listener hear the sad, mournful beat—like that of the drums in a funeral procession, or the ringing of a funeral bell. But try to vary your reading enough to keep it from becoming monotonous.

### Your Turn

Does a month like February have to be dreary or "dismal"? Write a short passage or poem "In Defense of February."

## E. E. Cummings
# in Just-spring

in Just-
spring   when the world is mud-
luscious the little
lame baloonman

whistles   far   and wee

and eddieandbill come
running from marbles and
piracies and it's
spring

when the world is puddle-wonderful

the queer
old baloonman whistles
far   and   wee
and bettyandisbel come dancing

from hop-scotch and jump-rope and

it's
spring
and
   the

       goat-footed

baloonMan   whistles
far
and
wee

---

### YOU AND THE POEM

(1) E. E. Cummings (1894–1962) became famous for his experimental and often humorous poems, and for his unconventional use of lower-case letters. This poem sets up the kind of *counter-rhythm* that many readers of modern poetry (and many listeners to modern music) prefer to the more regular patterns of the past. Often the sentence we are reading makes us want to go on—but the start of a new line, or a break in the line, makes us stop, at least briefly. Point out several such breaks—first those where a reader might have stopped naturally anyway. Then point out several such breaks where a reader probably would *not* have stopped. Several words or expressions appear after such a break several times, as if we were made to stop for them and notice them especially. Which are they? Practice reading this poem with the kind of skipping or jumpy rhythm that suits in a poem about childhood games and pursuits.

(2) How many sights and sounds and activities in this poem take us back into a child's world? Is spring especially a child's season?

(3) Pan, the Greek god of shepherds, had horns and goat feet. He wandered over the mountains and valleys, dancing and playing the shepherd's flute. The lame balloonman became linked in the poet's imagination with the ancient Greek god. Why is this **allusion** appropriate?

## Robert Frost
# The Tuft of Flowers

I went to turn the grass once after one
Who mowed it in the dew before the sun.

The dew was gone that made his blade so keen
Before I came to view the leveled scene.

I looked for him behind an isle of trees;
I listened for his whetstone on the breeze.

But he had gone his way, the grass all mown,
And I must be, as he had been,—alone.

"As all must be," I said within my heart,
"Whether they work together or apart."

But as I said it, swift there passed me by
On noiseless wing a bewildered butterfly,

Seeking with memories grown dim o'ernight
Some resting flower of yesterday's delight.

And once I marked his flight go round and round,
As where some flower lay withering on the ground.

And then he flew as far as eye could see,
And then on tremulous wing came back to me.

I thought of questions that have no reply,
And would have turned to toss the grass to dry;

But he turned first, and led my eye to look
At a tall tuft of flowers beside a brook,

A leaping tongue of bloom the scythe had spared
Beside a reedy brook the scythe had bared.

The mower in the dew had loved them thus,
By leaving them to flourish, not for us,

Nor yet to draw one thought of ours to him,
But from sheer morning gladness at the brim.

The butterfly and I had lit upon,
Nevertheless, a message from the dawn,

That made me hear the wakening birds around,
And hear his long scythe whispering to the ground,

And feel a spirit kindred to my own;
So that henceforth I worked no more alone;

But glad with him, I worked as with his aid,
And weary, sought at noon with him the shade;

And dreaming, as it were, held brotherly speech
With one whose thought I had not hoped to reach.

"Men work together," I told him from the heart,
"Whether they work together or apart."

## YOU AND THE POEM

(1) Robert Frost (1874–1963) wrote many poems about the ordinary sights and sounds of the New England countryside. Often these poems quietly describe some undramatic happening and then share with us the thoughts it brought to mind. The implements, the activities, the sights and smells of mowing were at one time familiar to everyone. What was it like? How much of it does the poem bring back?

(2) What happened in this poem that was unusual? What thoughts passed through the poet's mind at first, and why? How did he change his mind later, and why? Do you think what happened in this poem matters? Why or why not?

Robert Frost

# Once by the Pacific

The shattered water made a misty din.
Great waves looked over others coming in,
And thought of doing something to the shore
That water never did to land before.
The clouds were low and hairy in the skies,
Like locks blown forward in the gleam of eyes.
You could not tell, and yet it looked as if
The shore was lucky in being backed by cliff,
The cliff in being backed by continent;
It looked as if a night of dark intent
Was coming, and not only a night, an age.
Someone had better be prepared for rage.
There would be more than ocean-water broken
Before God's last *Put out the Light* was spoken.

## YOU AND THE POEM

(1) The poet talks about the ocean and the coast as though they both had human features, human thoughts, and human emotions. When a poet talks about things as if they were persons, we call the result **personification**. Pretend ocean and shore in this poem really *were* human beings. Describe as fully as you can the kind of person each would be.

(2) Can you find half a dozen words in the poem that in some way echo or reinforce the idea of threat, of fear? What's unexpected about the last line of the poem? Do you think readers would be ready for this kind of conclusion to the poem? (Does it depend on the reader? How?)

## Your Turn

Compare and contrast the two faces of nature that we see in these last two poems by the same poet.

## Sylvia Plath
# Frog Autumn

Summer grows old, cold-blooded mother.
The insects are scant, skinny.
In these palustral homes we only
Croak and wither.

Mornings dissipate in somnolence.
The sun brightens tardily
Among the pithless reeds. Flies fail us.
The fen sickens.

Frost drops even the spider. Clearly
The genius of plenitude
Houses himself elsewhere. Our folk thin
Lamentably.

---

### YOU AND THE POEM

(1) Sylvia Plath (1932–1963) was fascinated with the darker side of human nature. Many of her poems are about things that cast a shadow over people's lives. How should this poem be read—fast or slowly? loudly or softly? in a tone of sadness, or resignation, or despair?

(2) Poets use more of language than ordinary people do. Part of our pleasure in a poem is to look at or listen to *words:* Some may be words that we have not heard for some time. Some may be words that we do not know at all but that we come to know as we follow the poem. Some may be unusual words that fit better or add more to the poem than ordinary words would have done. Look at the following words from this poem. Show how the rest of the poem helps us understand each italicized word.

a. "In these *palustral* homes": The frogs live among reeds in fens or _____.

b. "Mornings dissipate [or come to nothing] in *somnolence*": The sun is coming up later, and the frogs, like people, may be awake but are still _____.

c. "The genius [or spirit] of *plenitude* houses himself elsewhere": When food is scarce and people are thin, they are experiencing the opposite of _____.

(3) Frogs are different from the cuddly pets that are most people's favorite animals. Why and how? Still, in this poem we are made to think of frogs as fellow creatures. Point out any words or expressions that we usually apply to fellow human beings. Point out any thoughts and feelings that human beings might experience. Explain why they might help create a fellow feeling.

Kay Boyle

# October 1954

Now the time of year has come for the leaves to be
    burning.
October, and the month fills me with grief
For the girl who used to run with the black dogs through
    them,
Singing, before they burned. Light as a leaf
Her heart, and her mouth red as the sumac turning.

Oh, girl, come back to tell them with your bell-like singing
That you are this figure who stands alone, watching the
    dead leaves burn.
(The wind is high in the trees, and the clang of bluejay
    voices ringing
Turns the air to metal. This is not a month for anyone who
    grieves.)
For they would say that a witch had passed in fury if I
    should turn,
Gray-haired and brooding, and run now as I once ran
    through the leaves.

## YOU AND THE POEM

(1) Kay Boyle (born 1903) in this poem records the rush of thoughts flowing through her mind at the thought of the burning leaves. She writes long, flowing sentences that may run through several lines but then come to a stop in the middle of a line. Give one or two examples of a strong break in the middle of a line. She uses an interlacing **rhyme scheme** that helps keep the poem flowing or gives it continuity. Which lines rhyme? Several words keep echoing through the poem. What are they?

(2) The yearly cycle of growth and decay in nature presents an obvious parallel to the human cycle of youth and age. Poets through the ages have used the falling leaf as a **symbol** for age and decay. What is the relationship between leaves and youth or age in this poem? What comparisons involving leaves are used in this poem? What other imaginative comparisons are used in the poem?

(3) Why is the month described in this poem "not a month for anyone who grieves"?

## Your Turn

To some people in the modern world, the changing seasons have come to mean very little. To others, they still matter a great deal. Write about the meaning for you of the changing seasons or of one of the four seasons.

Still came and lingered on my sight
Of flowers and streams the bloom and light,
And glory of the stars and sun;
And these and poetry are one.

William Cullen Bryant (1794–1878) was a lawyer and became a well-known newspaper editor. He was an active champion of political causes and one of the early organizers of the Republican party. He is best known, however, as a writer of the kind of Romantic nature poetry that was extremely popular in his youth. Romantic poetry had enjoyed a tremendous vogue in England, France, and Germany; and American readers were ready for a poet who would write poems about the natural scenes of their own country. The Romantic poets rebelled against the noise and dirt of crowded cities where dog-eat-dog competition made people callous and mean-spirited. They told the hectic, frustrated city dweller to find a remedy in the calm and purity of the natural world. For many readers to this day, poetry means the kind of poems that the Romantic nature poets wrote about trees, flowers, mountains, lakes, and the sea. To this day, many people consider it the first task of poets and painters to record the beauty of nature. What kind of beauty did poets like Bryant find in our natural environment?

William Cullen Bryant

# The Love of Nature

*from Thanatopsis*

(FIRST VOICE)     To him who in the love of Nature holds
Communion with her visible forms, she speaks
A various language. For her gayer hours,
She has a voice of gladness, and a smile
And eloquence of beauty, and she glides
Into his darker musings with a mild
And healing sympathy that steals away
Their sharpness ere he is aware. When thoughts      *before he is aware*
Of the last bitter hour come like a blight
Over thy spirit, and sad images
Of the stern agony, and shroud, and pall,
And breathless darkness, and the narrow house,
Make thee to shudder and grow sick at heart,
Go forth, under the open sky, and listen
To Nature's teachings, while from all around—
Earth and her waters, and the depths of air—
Comes a still voice:

(SECOND VOICE)                    Yet a few days, and thee
                The all-beholding sun shall see no more
                In all his course. Nor yet in the cold ground,
                Where thy pale form was laid with many tears,
                Nor in the embrace of ocean, shall exist
                Thy image. Earth, that nourished thee, shall claim
                Thy growth, to be resolved to earth again,
                And, lost each human trace, surrendering up     *And, with each trace of life lost*
                Thine individual being, shalt thou go
                To mix forever with the elements,
                To be a brother to the insensible rock
                And to the sluggish clod. . . .The oak
                Shall send his roots abroad, and pierce thy mould.


(THIRD VOICE)                  . . . The hills
                Rock-ribbed and ancient as the sun, the vales
                Stretching in pensive quietness between;
                The venerable woods—rivers that move
                In majesty, and the complaining brooks

That make the meadows green; and, poured round all,
Old Ocean's gray and melancholy waste—
Are but the solemn decorations all
Of the great tomb of man. The golden sun,
The planets, all the infinite host of heaven,
Are shining on the sad abodes of death,
Through the still lapse of ages.          *Through the quiet passing*

## YOU AND THE POEM

The Romantic poets wanted us to take time to look at nature and think about what we saw. At the beginning, the poet talks about how nature can change our "darker musings"—our sad or discouraged thoughts. Toward the end of the poem, the poet mentions "vales," or valleys, "stretching in pensive quietness." A *pensive* quietness" would be the kind of calm that allows us to think. Answer the following questions about the thoughts that nature brought to the poet's mind:

(1) "Communion" is a kind of communication that is not merely superficial but requires a deep mutual understanding, or a real kinship. How would a person hold communion with the "visible forms" of nature? Study the following series of related words from the poem: *love, communion, gladness, smile, mild, healing, still, nourished, brother.* How are these words related? Together, how do they make us think of nature? In your own words, describe the relationship between us and nature that these words paint for us.

(2) Of the changing faces of nature, the Romantic poets especially loved two or three that they returned to and wrote about again and again. Study the following series of related words from this poem: *rock-ribbed, ancient, venerable, majesty, old, solemn, infinite.* What central ideal holds all or most of these words together? What would be a good one-word label for the side

or aspect of nature that is hinted at in these words?

(3) What is the voice of Nature saying to the listener about death? What does it mean "to be resolved to earth again"? Is the thought of death meant to be frightening or depressing for us in this poem? Why or why not?

## A Closer Look

Like English nature poets, Bryant often used a flowing *un*rhymed line called **blank verse**. Blank verse fundamentally uses a five-beat line, with the stress usually on the *second* of each group of two syllables. (The basic pattern is "Detróit—Detróit—Detróit—Detróit—Detróit," not "Bóston—Bóston—Bóston—Bóston—Bóston.") Can you hear the basic beat in a passage like the following?

> She hás a vóice of gládness ànd a smíle
> And éloquènce of beáuty.

Notice that a new sentence often starts in the middle of a line, rather than at the beginning. It often runs on through two or more lines, coming to a stop again somewhere in the middle of a line, rather than at the end. The result is an *interlacing* effect and variety in rhythm from pauses occurring at different points in the line. You may want to arrange for a class reading of this poem with different voices. Aim at a reading that will do justice to the flowing rhythm of the lines, and to the strong emotional ties of the Romantic poet with Nature.

William Cullen Bryant

# The Groves Were God's First Temples

Father, thy hand
Hath reared these venerable columns, thou
Didst weave this verdant roof. Thou didst look down          *this roof of green*
Upon the naked earth, and forthwith rose
All these fair ranks of trees. They, in thy sun,
Budded and shook their green leaves in thy breeze,
And shot toward heaven. The century-living crow
Whose birth was in their tops, grew old and died
Among their branches, till at last they stood
As now they stand—massy, and tall, and dark,
Fit shrine for humble worshipper to hold
Communion with his Maker. These dim vaults,
These winding aisles, of human pomp or pride
Report not. No fantastic carvings show          *Tell no story of human pomp*
The boast of our vain race to change the form
Of thy fair works. But thou art here—
        in the soft winds
That run along the summit of these trees
In music. Thou art in the cooler breath
That from the inmost darkness of the place
Comes, scarcely felt. . . .
        Nature, here,
In the tranquillity that thou dost love,
Enjoys thy presence. Noiselessly around
From perch to perch, the solitary bird
Passes; and yon clear spring that, midst its herbs,          *among its green plant life*

Wells softly forth and wandering steeps the roots
Of half the mighty forest, tells no tale
Of all the good it does. Thou hast not left
Thyself without a witness, in the shades,
Of thy perfections. Grandeur, strength, and grace
Are here to speak of thee. This mighty oak—
By whose immovable stem I stand and seem
Almost annihilated—not a prince,                    *Almost turned to nothing*
In all that proud old world beyond the deep,
Ever wore his crown as loftily as he
Wears the green leaves with which
Thy hand had graced him. . . .
        O God!when thou
Dost scare the world with tempests, set on fire
The heavens with falling thunderbolts, or fill
With all the waters of the firmament
The swift dark whirlwind that uproots the woods
And drowns the villages; when at thy call
Uprises the great deep and throws himself                *Uprises the deep ocean*
Upon the continent, and overwhelms
Its cities—who forgets not, at the sight
Of these tremendous tokens of thy power,
His pride, and lays his strifes and follies by?
Oh, from these sterner aspects of thy face
Spare me and mine, nor let us need the wrath
Of the mad unchained elements to teach
Who rules them. Be it ours to meditate,
In these calm shades, thy milder majesty,
And to the beautiful order of thy works
Learn to conform the order of our lives.                *Learn to shape accordingly*

---

## YOU AND THE POEM

(1) Have you ever heard or seen a venerable forest compared to a temple or a cathedral? Find the many words and details that carry through the comparison between the forest and the building. What lines early in the poem show that the poet prefers the forest setting to places of worship built by human beings? Why does the poet prefer "nature's temples" to real ones?

(2) In the middle of the poem, what thoughts are brought to the poet's mind by the spring, or the oak?

(3) At the end, what picture do we get of the fierce or destructive side of nature? What idea or feeling seems to be uppermost in the poet's mind as he turns to this side of nature? Do these lines about the tempests and the thunderbolts make you change or revise your idea of the Romantic poet's view of the natural world? If so, why or how?

### Your Turn

Do you think people today still feel in some ways about nature the way Bryant did? How or where do they show it? Where do you have a chance to observe how people today feel about nature?

## An Introduction to Herman Melville and *Moby Dick*

● Herman Melville (1819–1891) had first gone to sea as a merchant sailor when he was nineteen. In 1841, he sailed from Massachusetts in a New England whaling ship bound for Cape Horn and the Pacific. After the first year and a half of the whaling voyage, he deserted the ship and during the next few years led a life of adventure. He lived for a time among the natives of the South Sea Islands. He worked on other whaling ships and finally signed on as a seaman in the U.S. Navy. He told the story of his adventures in the South Seas in two books that made him famous, *Typee* (1846) and *Omoo* (1847). *Moby Dick* (1851), his book about the hunt for the white whale, is one of the great masterpieces of American literature. He packed

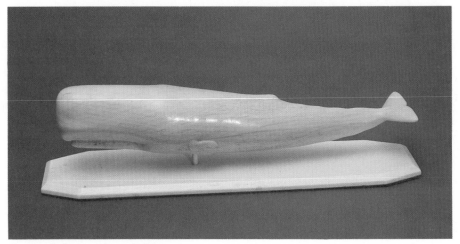

*Sperm whale carved in whalebone.*

the book with fascinating lore about the ways of whales and about the whaling ships he had known. He described the dangerous job of harpooning whales from small rowboats lowered from the mother ship. He described the equally dangerous task of cutting up the huge carcasses and boiling them down for oil. But above all, the book is the story of the moody Captain Ahab, who had lost a leg in an earlier encounter with a legendary white whale. He sets out to destroy the whale that has become his enemy. That whale is Moby Dick, an animal of huge size, with remarkable coloring, and with a mighty, deformed lower jaw: "It was not so much his uncommon bulk that so much distinguished him from other sperm whales but a peculiar snow-white wrinkled forehead, and a high white hump." These were the outstanding features by which "even in the limitless uncharted seas he revealed his identity at a long distance to those who knew him." The rest of his body was streaked and marbled with the same white hue, earning him the name of the White Whale—a name justified when he was seen "gliding at high noon through a dark blue sea, leaving a milky-way wake of creamy foam, all spangled with golden gleamings." Sailors who had tangled with the white whale claimed that he had given proof of conscious intelligence and deliberate, scheming malice. Swimming before his pursuers, apparently in panic, he had several times "been known to turn around suddenly, and bearing down upon them, either stave their boats to splinters or drive them back in consternation to their ship." More than once, his desperate and furious hunters had been left to swim for life among "the chips of chewed boats and the sinking limbs of torn comrades."

After the encounter that had cost him his leg, Captain Ahab had become obsessed with the need to revenge himself upon his enemy:

> All that most maddens and torments, . . . all truth with malice in it, . . . all evil, to crazy Ahab were visibly personified and made practically assailable in Moby Dick. He piled upon the whale's white hump the sum of all the general rage and hate felt by his whole race from Adam down.

Early in the book, we become acquainted with Ahab's ship, the *Pequod,* and its crew. The ship's chief mate is Starbuck, the calm second-in-command, who tries to restrain the bitter fury of the captain. Stubb and Flask are the two other officers of the ship. Among the strange crew, the three chief harpooners stand out: a tattooed, idol-worshipping South Sea islander called Queequeg; Tashtego, an Indian; and Daggoo, a tall black man. Later in the voyage, during the first hunt, we get our first glimpse of the crew that Ahab has hired secretly to serve under him in his own small boat: Fedallah and four other mysterious, Oriental-looking sailors. As the *Pequod* draws closer to the feeding grounds of the great whales of the Pacific, it encounters several ships whose crews had recently lost lives or limbs in ill-fated encounters with Moby Dick. Three of the chapters from the novel appear here in an abridged form. The first one tells the story of the first hunt of the voyage. The second chapter describes the first day of the final encounter with the great whale. The third chapter describes the third and last day of the battle. In this abridgement, paragraphs and sentences have been shortened, but the words are the author's own.

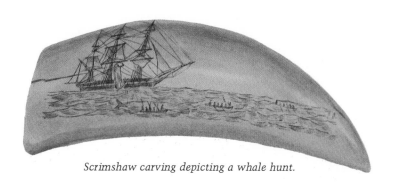

*Scrimshaw carving depicting a whale hunt.*

# Herman Melville

## *from*
# Moby Dick

"And God created great whales."

—*Genesis*

## 1. The First Hunt

It was a cloudy, sultry afternoon. The seamen were lazily lounging about the decks, or vacantly gazing over into the lead-colored waters. Queequeg and I were mildly employed weaving a mat for our boat. . . . We were weaving away when I started at a sound so strange, long drawn, and musically wild and unearthly, that I stood gazing up at the clouds whence that voice dropped like a wing. High aloft in the crosstrees[1] was Tashtego. His body was reaching eagerly forward, his hand stretched out, and at brief sudden intervals he continued his cries. To be sure, the same sound was that very moment perhaps being heard all over the seas, from hundreds of whalemen's lookouts perched as high in the air. But from few of those lungs could that accustomed old cry have derived such a marvellous cadence as from Tashtego, the Indian's.

As he stood hovering over you half suspended in air, so wildly and eagerly peering towards the horizon, you would have thought him some prophet beholding the shadows of Fate, and by those wild cries announcing their coming.

"There she blows! There! There! There! She blows! She blows!"

"Where-away?"

"On the leebeam, about two miles off! A school of them!"

Instantly all was commotion.

The Sperm Whale blows as a clock ticks, with the same reliable uniformity. And thereby whalemen distinguish this fish from other tribes.

"There go flukes!"[2] was now the cry from Tashtego, and the whales then disappeared.

"Quick, steward!" cried Ahab. "Time! Time!"

Dough-Boy hurried below, glanced at the watch, and reported the exact minute to Ahab.

The ship was now kept away from the wind, and she went gently rolling before it. Tashtego reporting that the whales had gone down heading to leeward, we confidently looked to see them again directly in advance of our bows. At times the Sperm Whale, sounding with his head in one direction, nevertheless, while concealed beneath the surface, mills round, and swiftly swims off in the opposite quarter. This deceitfulness of his could not now be in action, for there was no reason to suppose that the fish seen by Tashtego had been in any way alarmed, or indeed knew at all of our vicinity. One of the men selected for shipkeepers—that is, those not appointed to the boats—by this

[1]**crosstrees:** cross-pieces of timber on masthead.

[2]**flukes:** tail fins.

time relieved the Indian at the mainmast head. The sailors at the fore and mizzen had come down; the line tubs[3] were fixed in their places; the cranes were thrust out; and the three boats swung over the sea like baskets over high cliffs. Outside of the bulwarks[4] their eager crews with one hand clung to the rail, while one foot was expectantly poised on the gunwale. So look the long line of man-of-war's men about to throw themselves on board an enemy's ship.

But at this critical instant a sudden exclamation was heard that took every eye from the whale. With a start all glared at dark Ahab, who was surrounded by five dusky phantoms that seemed fresh formed out of air. The phantoms, for so they then seemed, were flitting on the other side of the deck and were casting loose the tackles[5] and bands of the boat which swung there. This boat had always been deemed one of the spare boats, though technically called the captain's, on account of its hanging from the starboard quarter. The figure that now stood by its bow was tall and swart, with one white tooth evilly protruding from its steel-like lips. A rumpled Chinese jacket of black cotton invested him, with wide black trousers of the same dark material. But strangely crowning this was a glistening white plaited turban, the living hair braided and coiled round and round upon his head. The companions of this figure were of that vivid complexion peculiar to some of the natives of the Manillas—a race by some honest mariners supposed to be the paid spies and secret confidential agents on the water of the devil, their lord,

whose counting room they suppose to be elsewhere.

All the while the wondering ship's company were gazing upon these strangers, Ahab cried out to the white-turbaned old man at their head, "All ready there, Fedallah?"

"Ready," was the half-hissed reply.

"Lower away then, d'ye hear?" shouting across the deck. "Lower away there, I say."

Such was the thunder of his voice, that inspite of their amazement the men sprang over the rail. The sheaves[6] whirled round in the blocks. The three boats dropped into the sea, while, with a dexterous, offhanded daring, unknown in any other vocation, the sailors, goatlike, leaped down the rolling ship's side into the tossed boats below.

Hardly had they pulled out from under the ship's lee when a fourth keel, coming from the windward side, pulled round under the stern and showed the five strangers rowing Ahab, who, standing erect in the stern, loudly hailed Starbuck, Stubb, and Flask, to spread themselves widely, so as to cover a large expanse of water. But with all their eyes again riveted upon the swart Fedallah and his crew, the inmates of the other boats obeyed not the command.

"Captain Ahab?" said Starbuck.

"Spread yourselves," cried Ahab, "give way, all four boats. Thou, Flask, pull out more to leeward!"

"Aye, aye, sir," cheerily cried Flask, sweeping round his great steering oar. "Lay back!" addressing his crew. "There! There! There again! There she blows right ahead, boys! Lay back!"

"Never heed yonder yellow boys, Archy."

"Oh, I don't mind 'em, sir," said Archy. "I knew it all before now. Didn't I hear

[3]**line tubs:** on a whale boat, barrels for storing rope to be attached to harpoons.

[4]**bulwarks:** the sides of a ship above the upper deck.

[5]**tackles** (TAY kel): pulleys.

[6]**sheaves:** pulleys.

'em in the hold? And didn't I tell Cabaco here of it? What say ye, Cabaco? They are stowaways, Mr. Flask."

"Pull, pull, my fine hearts-alive. Pull, my children. Pull, my little ones," drawlingly and soothingly sighed Stubb to his crew, some of whom still showed signs of uneasiness. "Why don't you break your backbones, my boys? What is it you stare at? Those chaps in yonder boat? They are only five more hands come to help us—never mind from where—the more the merrier. Pull, then, do pull; never mind the brimstone—devils are good fellows enough. So, so—there you are now. That's the stroke for a thousand pounds. That's the stroke to sweep the stakes! Three cheers, men—all hearts alive! Easy, easy; don't be in a hurry—don't be in a hurry. Why don't you snap your oars, you rascals? Bite something, you dogs! So, so, so, then—softly, softly! That's it—that's it! Long and strong. The devil fetch ye, ye ragamuffin rapscallions! Ye are all asleep. Stop snoring, ye sleepers, and pull. Pull, will ye? Pull, can't ye? Pull, won't ye? Why in the name of ginger cakes don't ye pull?

He would say the most terrific things to his crew, in a tone so strangely compounded of fun and fury, and the fury seemed so calculated merely as a spice to the fun, that no oarsman could hear such queer invocations without pulling for dear life, and yet pulling for the mere joke of the thing. Besides he all the time looked so easy and indolent himself, so loungingly managed his steering oar, and so broadly gaped—openmouthed at times—that the mere sight of such a yawning commander, by sheer force of contrast, acted like a charm upon the crew.

In obedience to a sign from Ahab, Starbuck was now pulling across Stubb's bow. When for a minute or so the two boats were pretty near to each other, Stubb hailed the mate.

"Mr. Starbuck! Larboard boat there, ahoy! A word with ye, sir, if ye please!"

"Halloa!" returned Starbuck, turning round not a single inch as he spoke, still earnestly but whisperingly urging his crew, his face set like a flint from Stubb's.

"What think ye of those yellow boys, sir!"

"Smuggled on board, somehow, before the ship sailed. (Strong, strong, boys!)" in a whisper to his crew, then speaking out loud again: "A sad business, Mr. Stubb! But never mind, Mr. Stubb, all for the best. Let all your crew pull strong, come what will. (Spring, my men, spring!)"

"Aye, ay, I thought as much," soliloquized Stubb, when the boats diverged, "as soon as I clapt eye on 'em, I thought

---

**THE WHALING SHIP AND *MOBY DICK*:** In reading this excerpt from the novel, we have to imagine ourselves on an old whaling ship. To find our way around the *Pequod* and the smaller whaling boats, we need to know some of the sailors' terms or *nautical* terms Melville uses. The *bow* is the foremost part of the boat and the *stern* is the rear. The *windward* is the side from which the wind is blowing, and the *leeward* (LOO werd) is the opposite side. The right side of a ship, as one faces the bow, is the *starboard*, while the left is the *port* or *larboard*. The *keel* is the bottom or spine of the ship, and the *gunwale* (GUN nel) is the upper edge of the side of a vessel. Melville mentions several *masts*—poles which rise from the deck and support the sails: the *mainmast*, usually located just behind the midpoint of the ship, is the principle mast; the *foremast* is the forwardmost mast, and the *mizzenmast* is the mast behind the mainmast.

so. Aye, and that's what he went into the after hold[7] for, so often, as Dough-Boy long suspected. They were hidden down there. The White Whale's at the bottom of it. Well, well, so be it! Can't be helped! All right! Give way, men! Give way!''

Now the advent of these outlandish strangers at such a critical instant as the lowering of the boats from the deck had awakened a sort of superstitious amazement in some of the ship's company. Meantime, Ahab, out of hearing of his officers, having sided the furthest to windward, was still ranging ahead of the other boats. Those tiger yellow creatures of his seemed all steel and whalebone. Like five trip-hammers they rose and fell with regular strokes of strength, which periodically started the boat along the water like a horizontal burst boiler out of a Mississippi steamer. As for Fedallah, who was seen pulling the harpooner oar, he had

[7]**after hold:** storage area, below decks, of a ship; in this case in the rear of the ship.

thrown aside his black jacket and displayed his naked chest with the whole part of his body above the gunwale clearly cut against the watery horizon. At the other end of the boat, Ahab—with one arm, like a fencer's, thrown half backward into the air, as if to counterbalance any tendency to trip—was seen steadily managing his steering oar as in a thousand boat lowerings ere the White Whale had torn him. All at once the outstretched arm gave a peculiar motion and then remained fixed, while the boat and crew sat motionless on the sea. Instantly the three spread boats in the rear paused on their way. The whales had irregularly settled bodily down into the blue.

"Every man look out along his oars!" cried Starbuck. "Thou Queequeg, stand up!"

Nimbly springing up on the triangular raised box in the bow, the savage stood erect there, and with intensely eager eyes gazed off towards the spot. Likewise upon the extreme stern of the boat where it was also triangularly platformed level with the gunwale, Starbuck himself was seen coolly balancing himself to the tossings of his chip of a craft and silently eyeing the vast blue eye of the sea.

Meanwhile Stubb, the third mate, betrayed no such solicitudes. The whales might have made one of their regular soundings, not a temporary dive from mere fright. If that were the case, Stubb, it seems, was resolved to solace the interval with his pipe. He withdrew it from his hatband, where he always wore it like a feather. He loaded it, and rammed home the loading with his thumb-end; but hardly had he ignited his match across the rough sandpaper of his hand, when Tashtego, his harpooner, whose eyes had been setting to windward like two fixed stars, suddenly dropped like light from his erect attitude to his seat, crying out, "Down, down all, and give way! There they are!"

To a landsman, no whale, nor any sign of a herring, would have been visible at that moment: nothing but a troubled bit of greenish white water, and thin scattered puffs of vapor hovering over it, and blowing off to leeward, like the confused scud from white rolling billows. The air around suddenly vibrated and tingled, as it were, like the air over heated plates of iron. Beneath this atmospheric waving and curling, and partially beneath a thin layer of water, also, the whales were swimming. Seen in advance of all the other indications, the puffs of vapor they spouted seemed their forerunning couriers and flying outriders.

All four boats were now in keen pursuit of that one spot of trouble water and air. But it flew on and on, as a mass of interblending bubbles borne down a rapid stream from the hills.

"Pull, pull, my good boys," said Starbuck, in the lowest possible but intensest concentrated whisper to his men, while the sharp fixed glance from his eyes darted straight ahead of the bow. He did not say much to his crew, though, nor did his crew say anything to him. Only the silence of the boat was at intervals startlingly pierced by one of his peculiar whispers, now harsh with command, now soft with entreaty.

But what it was that Ahab said to that crew of his—these were words best omitted here. Only the infidel sharks in the seas may give ear to such words, when, with tornado brow, and eyes of red murder, and foam-glued lips, Ahab leaped after his prey.

Meanwhile, all the boats tore on. It was a sight full of wonder and awe! The vast swells of the omnipotent sea; the surging, hollow roar they made, as they rolled along the eight gunwales; the brief suspended agony of the boat, as it would tip for an instant on the knifelike edge of the sharper waves, that almost seemed threatening to cut it in two; the sudden profound dip into the watery glens and hollows; the keen spurrings and goadings to gain the top of the opposite hill; the headlong, sledlike slide down its other side—all these, with the cries of the headsmen and harpooners, and the shuddering gasps of the oarsmen, with the sight of the ivory Pequod bearing down upon her boats with outstretched sails like a wild hen after her screaming brood—all this was thrilling. Not the raw recruit, marching from the bosom of his wife into the fever heat of his first battle; not the dead man's ghost encountering the first unknown phantom in the other world—neither of these can feel stranger and stronger emotions than that man does who for the first time finds himself pulling into the charmed, churned circle of a hunted sperm whale.

The dancing white water made by the chase was now becoming more and more visible, owing to the increasing darkness of the cloud-shadows flung upon the sea. The jets of vapor no longer blended, but tilted everywhere to right and left; the whales seemed separating their wakes. The boats were pulled more apart, Starbuck giving chase to three whales running to leeward. Our sail was now set, and, with the still rising wind, we rushed along—the boat going with such madness through the water that the oars could scarcely be worked rapidly enough to escape being torn from the rowlocks.[8]

Soon we were running through a wide veil of mist—neither ship nor boat to be seen.

"Give way, men," whispered Starbuck, drawing still further aft the sheet of his sail. "There is time to kill a fish yet before the squall comes. There's white water again!—close to! Spring!"

Soon after, two cries in quick succession on each side of us denoted that the other boats had got fast. Hardly were they overheard when with a lightninglike hurtling whisper Starbuck said "Stand up!" and Queequeg, harpoon in hand, sprang to his feet.

Though not one of the oarsmen was then facing the life and death peril so close to them ahead, yet with their eyes on the intense countenance of the mate in the stern of the boat, they knew that the instant had come. They heard, too, an enormous wallowing sound as of fifty elephants stirring in their litter. Meanwhile the boat was still booming through the mist, the waves curling and hissing around us like enraged serpents.

"That's his hump. *There, there,* give it to him!" whispered Starbuck.

A short rushing sound leaped out of the boat. It was the darted iron of Queequeg. Then all in one welded commotion came an invisible push from astern, while forward the boat seemed striking on a ledge. The sail collapsed and exploded; a gush of scalding vapor shot up nearby; something rolled and tumbled like an earthquake beneath us. The whole crew were half suffocated as they were tossed helter-skelter into the white curdling cream of the squall. Squall, whale, and harpoon had all blended together; and the whale, merely grazed by the iron, escaped.

Though completely swamped, the boat was nearly unharmed. Swimming round it we picked up the floating oars, and lashing them across the gunwale, tumbled back to our places. There we sat up to our knees in the sea, the water covering every rib and plank, so that the craft seemed a coral boat grown up to us from the bottom of the ocean.

[8] **rowlocks** (ROL locks): the resting place in the gunwale for the pulling oars.

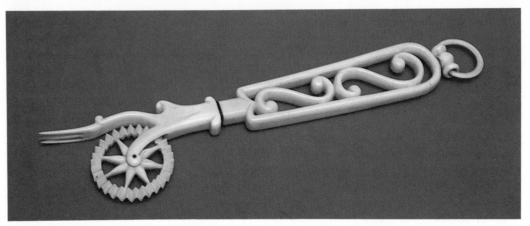

*Whalebone jagging wheel used for cutting cakes or pastry into ornamental figures.*

The wind increased to a howl. The waves dashed their bucklers together. The whole squall roared, forked, and crackled around us like a white fire upon the prairie in which, unconsumed, we were burning—immortal in these jaws of death! In vain we hailed the other boats. As well roar to the live coals down the chimney of a flaming furnace as hail those boats in that storm. Meanwhile the driving mist grew darker with the shadows of night. No sign of the ship could be seen. The rising sea forbade all attempts to bale out the boat. The oars were useless as propellers, performing now the office of life preservers. So, cutting the lashing of the waterproof match keg, after many failures Starbuck contrived to ignite the lamp in the lantern; then stretching it on a pole, handed it to Queequeg as the standard-bearer of this forlorn hope. There, then, he sat, holding up that candle in the heart of that almighty forlornness. There, then, he sat, the sign and symbol of a man without faith, hopelessly holding up hope in the midst of despair.

Wet, drenched through, and shivering cold, despairing of ship or boat, we lifted up our eyes as the dawn came on. The mist still spread over the sea, the empty lantern lay crushed in the bottom of the boat. Suddenly Queequeg started to his feet, hollowing his hand to his ear. We all heard a faint creaking, as of ropes and yards[9] hitherto muffled by the storm. The sound came nearer and nearer. The thick mists were dimly parted by a huge, vague form. Affrighted, we all sprang into the sea as the ship at last loomed into view, bearing right down upon us within a distance of not much more than its length.

Floating on the waves we saw the abandoned boat, as for one instant it tossed and gaped beneath the ship's bows like a chip at the base of a cataract. Then the vast hull[10] rolled over it, and it was seen no more till it came up weltering astern. Again we swam for it, were dashed against it by the seas, and were at last taken up and safely landed on board. The other boats had cut loose from their fish and returned to the ship in good time. The ship had given us up, but was still cruising, if haply it might light upon some token of our perishing—an oar or a lance pole.

[9]**yard:** a pole attached at right angles to the mast, used to attach the bottom of the sail.

[10]**hull:** the frame or body of a boat, not including the masts, yards, sails and rigging.

(1) Sailors have long had a reputation for their salty, colorful, resourceful use of language. We hear an example when Stubb urges on the crew of his boat. Listen to these orders and exhortations read aloud.

(2) All through the novel, Melville builds up our impression of Ahab as not the usual practical-minded, businesslike captain of a whaling voyage but as a brooding, mysterious, half-mad person. In this selection, what makes Ahab appear strange or unusual? What is the most striking example of Ahab's strange actions? What effect does it have on the rest of the crew?

(3) The story of the white whale is told to us by the sailor Ishmael, who serves as Melville's **narrator** in most of the novel. Ishmael is one of the crew of Starbuck's boat. In this selection, he recreates for us the thrill and the dangers of the first hunt. Retell the story of Ishmael's experience in Starbuck's boat.

Language/Composition Activity B5

A FORMAL STYLE

# In Small Boats on the Omnipotent Sea

Melville writes his story in a solemn, formal nineteenth-century style. Many of his words have come to sound old-fashioned for the modern reader. For each of the italicized words from the novel, find a more familiar and informal current expression in the list at the end.

1. With a *dexterous,* offhanded daring, the sailors leaped into the boats.
2. The boats spread wide so as to cover a vast *expanse* of water.
3. No oarsman could hear such strange *invocations* without pulling for dear life.
4. As the boats pulled apart, Stubb *soliloquized* about the stowaways.
5. The boats had been close together but then *diverged.*
6. The *advent* of the outlandish strangers had awakened a sort of superstitious amazement.
7. He was resolved to *solace* the interval with his pipe.
8. The vast swells of the *omnipotent* sea were a thrilling sight.
9. All their eyes were on the intense *countenance* of the mate in the stern of the boat.
10. *Affrighted,* we sprang into the sea.

Meanings:

a. all-powerful
b. afraid
c. the look on someone's face
d. solemn requests
e. while away in a cheering manner
f. stretch
g. arrival
h. very skillful
i. talked to himself
j. pulled apart

## 2. Sighting the White Whale

*[Captain Ahab had promised a gold coin—a doubloon—to the first man to sight the white whale. The book builds up to its high point as Ahab finally tracks down his old enemy.]*

"There she blows! There she blows! A hump like a snowhill! It is Moby Dick!"

Fired by the cry which seemed simultaneously taken up by the three lookouts, the men on deck rushed to the rigging to behold the famous whale they had so long been pursuing. Ahab had now gained his final perch, some feet above the other lookouts. Tashtego was standing just beneath him on the cap of the topgallant mast,[1] so that the Indian's head was almost on a level with Ahab's heel. From this height the whale was now seen some mile or so ahead, at every roll of the sea revealing his high sparkling hump and regularly jetting his silent spout into the air.

"And did none of ye see it before?" cried Ahab, hailing the perched men all around him.

"I saw him almost that same instant, sir, that Captain Ahab did, and I cried out," said Tashtego.

"Not the same instant! Not the same—no, the doubloon is mine! Fate reserved the doubloon for me. *I* only; none of ye could have raised the White Whale first. There she blows! There she blows! There she blows! There again! There again!" he cried, in long-drawn, lingering tones. "He's going to sound! Down topgallant sails![2] Stand by three boats. Mr. Starbuck, remember, stay on board, and keep the ship. All ready the boats there? Stand by, stand by! Lower me, Mr. Starbuck! Lower, lower—quick, quicker!" and he slid through the air to the deck.

"He is heading straight to leeward, sir," cried Stubb, "right away from us—cannot have seen the ship yet."

"Stand by the braces![3] Hard down the helm![4] . . . Boats, boats!"

Soon all the boats but Starbuck's were dropped, all the boatsails set—all the paddles plying, and Ahab heading the onset. A pale, death glimmer lit up Fedallah's sunken eyes. A hideous motion gnawed his mouth.

The light prows sped through the sea, but only slowly they neared the foe. As they neared him, the ocean grew still more smooth, seemed drawing a carpet over its waves. It seemed a noon meadow, so serenely it spread. At length the breathless hunter came so near his seemingly unsuspecting prey that his entire dazzling hump was distinctly visible, sliding along the sea as if an isolated thing, and continually set in a revolving ring of finest, fleecy, greenish foam. He saw the vast wrinkles of the slightly projecting head beyond. Before it, far out on the soft waters, went the glistening white shadow from his broad, milky forehead. Behind, the blue waters flowed over into the moving valley of his steady wake. On either hand, bright bubbles arose and danced by his side. But these were broken again by hundreds of fowl softly feathering the sea, alternate with their fitful flight. Like to some flagstaff rising from a painted hull, the tall but shattered pole of a recent lance projected from the white whale's back. At intervals, one of the cloud of soft-toed fowls hovering and skimming to and fro over the fish, silently perched and rocked on this pole.

---

[1]**topgallant mast:** the topmost part of the mast.

[2]**topgallant sails:** the topmost sails on the mast.

[3]**braces:** ropes used to change the position of the sails.

[4]**helm:** the steering device.

A gentle joy—a mighty mildness of repose in swiftness—invested the gliding whale. On each soft side—with the parted swell that but once leaving him then flowed so wide away—on each bright side, the whale shed off enticings. No wonder there had been some among the hunters who, allured by all this serenity, had ventured to assail it, but had fatally found that quiet but the vesture of tornadoes. Yet calm, enticing calm, oh, whale! thou glidest on, to all who for the first time eye thee, no matter how many in that same way thou may'st have bejuggled and destroyed before.

And thus, through the serene tranquillity of the tropical sea, Moby Dick moved on, still withholding from sight the full terrors of his submerged trunk, entirely hiding the wrenched hideousness of his jaw. But soon the fore part of him slowly rose from the water. For an instant his whole marble body formed a high arch, and warningly waving his bannered flukes in the air, the grand god revealed himself, sounded, and went out of sight. Hovering and dipping on the wing, the white sea fowls longingly lingered over the agitated pool that he left.

With oars apeak, and paddles down, the sheets of their sails adrift, the three boats now stilly floated, awaiting Moby Dick's reappearance.

"An hour," said Ahab, standing rooted in his boat's stern; and he gazed beyond the whale's place, towards the dim blue spaces to leeward. It was only an instant, for again his eyes seemed whirling round in his head as he swept the watery circle. The breeze now freshened. The sea began to swell.

"The birds! The birds!" was the cry from Tashtego.

In long Indian file, as when herons take wing, the white birds were now all flying towards Ahab's boat and began fluttering over the water there, wheeling round and round, with joyous, expectant cries. Their vision was keener than man's. Ahab could discover no sign in the sea. But suddenly as he peered down and down into its depths, he profoundly saw a white living spot no bigger than a white weasel, magnifying as it rose, till it turned, and then there were plainly revealed two long crooked rows of white, glistening teeth, floating up from the undiscoverable bottom. It was Moby Dick's open mouth and scrolled jaw, his vast, shadowed bulk still half blending with the blue of the sea. The glittering mouth yawned beneath the boat like an open-doored marble tomb; and giving one sidelong sweep with his steering oar, Ahab whirled the craft aside. Then, calling upon Fedallah to change places with him, he went forward to the bows, and seizing the harpoon, commanded his crew to grasp their oars.

Now, by reason of this timely spinning round the boat upon its axis, its bow was made to face the whale's head while yet underwater. But as if perceiving this stratagem, Moby Dick, with that malicious intelligence ascribed to him, transplanted himself, as it were, in an instant, shooting his pleated head lengthwise beneath the boat.

Through and through—through every plank and each rib, it thrilled for an instant, the whale lying on his back, in the manner of a biting shark, slowly taking its bows full within his mouth so that the long, narrow lower jaw curled high up into the open air, and one of the teeth caught in a rowlock. The bluish pearl-white of the inside of the jaw was within six inches of Ahab's head, and reached higher than that. In this attitude the White Whale now shook the slight cedar as a mildly cruel cat her mouse. With unastonished eyes Fedallah gazed and crossed his arms, but his crew were tumbling over each other's heads to gain the uttermost stern.

And now both elastic gunwales were springing in and out as the whale dallied with the doomed craft in this devilish way. His body being submerged beneath the boat, he could not be darted at from the bows, for the bows were almost inside of him, as it were. And while the other boats paused, as before a quick crisis impossible to withstand, then it was that Ahab, furious with this tantalizing vicinity of his foe, which placed him all alive and helpless in the very jaws he hated, seized the long bone with his naked hands and wildly strove to wrench it from its grip. As now he thus vainly strove, the jaw slipped from him. The frail gunwales bent in, collapsed, and snapped, as both jaws, like an enormous shears, bit the craft completely in two, and locked themselves fast again in the sea, midway between the two floating wrecks. These floated aside, the broken ends drooping, the crew at the stern-wreck clinging to the gunwales and striving to hold fast to the oars to lash them across.

Moby Dick swam swiftly round and round the wrecked crew; sideways churning the water in his vengeful wake, as if lashing himself up to still another and more deadly assault. The sight of the splintered boat seemed to madden him. Meanwhile Ahab was half smothered in the foam of the whale's tail. Too much of a cripple to swim, he could still keep afloat even in the heart of such a whirlpool as that. The clinging crew could not succor him. More than enough was it for them to look to themselves. For so appalling was the White Whale's aspect, and so swift the ever-contracting circles he made, that he seemed horizontally swooping upon them. The other boats, unharmed, still hovered hard by. Still they dared not pull into the eddy to strike, lest that should be the signal for the instant destruction of the jeopardized castaways,

Ahab and all. Nor in that case could they themselves hope to escape. With straining eyes, then, they remained on the outer edge of the zone, whose center had now become the old man's head.

Meantime, from the beginning all this had been described from the ship's mastheads. Squaring her yards, she had borne down upon the scene and was now so near that Ahab in the water hailed her: "Sail on the—" but that moment a breaking sea dashed on him from Moby Dick. Struggling out of it again, and rising on a towering crest, he shouted: "Sail on the whale! Drive him off!"

The Pequod's prows[5] were pointed, and breaking up the charmed circle, she effectually parted the white whale from his victim. As he sullenly swam off, the boats flew to the rescue.

Dragged into Stubb's boat with blood-shot, blinded eyes, Ahab's bodily strength did crack. For a time, he was lying crushed in the bottom of Stubb's boat, like one trodden underfoot of herds of elephants. Nameless wails came from him. . . .

"The harpoon," said Ahab, halfway rising and leaning on one bended arm. "Is it safe?"

"Aye, sir, for it was not darted. This is it," said Stubb, showing it.

"Lay it before me—any missing men?"

"One, two, three, four, five—there were five oars, sir, and here are five men."

[5]**prow:** the projecting front part of a ship; the bow.

"That's good. Help me, man; I wish to stand. So, so, I see him! there! there! Going to leeward still; what a leaping spout! Hands off from me! The eternal sap runs up in Ahab's bones again! Set the sail! Out oars!"

Often when a boat is stove, its crew, picked up by another boat, help to work that second boat. The chase is thus continued with what is called double-banked oars. It was thus now. But the added power of the boat did not equal the power of the whale, for he seemed to be swimming with a velocity which plainly showed that the chase would prove an indefinitely prolonged, if not a hopeless, one. Nor could any crew endure for so long a period such an intense straining at the oar. The ship itself, then, offered the most promising means of overtaking the chase. Accordingly, the boats now made for her and were soon swayed up to their cranes, the two parts of the wrecked boat having been previously secured by her. Then hoisting everything to her side, the Pequod bore down in the leeward wake of Moby Dick. At the well-known intervals, the whale's glittering spout was regularly announced from the manned mastheads. When he would be reported as just gone down, Ahab would take the time, and then pacing the deck, watch in hand, so soon as the last second of the allotted hour expired, his voice was heard: "Do you see him?" If the reply was, "No, sir!" straightway he commanded them to lift him to his perch. In this way the day wore on.

---

## YOU AND SECTION TWO

As Captain Ahab is no ordinary ship's captain, so Moby Dick is no ordinary whale. Many readers have long remembered the description of the white whale that the author gives in these pages. Be sure to listen to it read aloud. Then answer the following questions:

(1) Each of the following sets of synonyms describes one quality that is part of Melville's description of the whale. What do

the words in each set or cluster have in common? What is the common meaning, and what are the differences in meaning within the set? You may have to turn to a dictionary for help:

    a. dazzling—glistening
    b. gentle—serene—mildness
    c. repose—calm—tranquillity
    d. enticing—alluring—bejuggled
    e. mighty—terror—hideousness

(2) As the boat first approaches the legendary whale, "the ocean grew still more smooth" and seemed like a meadow at noon. Why is that strange? When a statement seems to claim two different and contradictory things at the same time, we call it a **paradox**. What is paradoxical about expressions like "mighty mildness" and "repose in swiftness"? What makes them contradictory?

(3) For Captain Ahab, Moby Dick summed up all the evil in the world. In his mind, the white whale had become a **symbol** for all the forces of destruction in the universe. To judge from the selections you have read, did the author want *us* to think of the whale as evil? Why or why not?

---

A FORMAL STYLE

# The Mighty Whale

What would be a simpler or more informal word or expression for each of the italicized words? In the list at the end, find the meaning that fits best into the context of each sentence.

1. The cry was *simultaneously* taken up by the three lookouts.
2. A gentle joy—a mighty mildness—*invested* the gliding whale.
3. The outward quiet of the whale was the *vesture* of tornadoes.
4. Sailors deceived by the quiet appearance of the whale had ventured to *assail* it.
5. The sailors *ascribed* a malicious intelligence to Moby Dick.
6. Ahab was helpless against the whale, furious at the *tantalizing* vicinity of his foe.
7. The crew of the wrecked boat could not *succor* their half-smothered captain.
8. Afraid to pull closer, the other boats watched the *jeopardized* castaways.
9. All this had been *descried* from the ship's mastheads.
10. The whale was swimming with a *velocity* the boat could not match.

Meanings:

| | | |
|---|---|---|
| a. help | d. attributed | g. a covering or garment |
| b. near and yet beyond reach | e. at exactly the same time | h. attack |
| c. seemed to fill | f. speed | i. in very serious danger |
| | | j. observed |

---

## 3. The Final Battle

*[During the second day of the chase, the white whale again turns on the pursuing boats. Two of the boats are destroyed. All the men in them are saved—except Fedallah, the harpooner in Ahab's own boat, who disappears in the waves. In the afternoon of the third day, the white whale is sighted one more time. Ahab leads his crew into the final contest with his hated enemy.]*

In due time the boats were lowered. But as Ahab just hovered upon the point of the descent, he waved to the mate—who held one of the tackleropes on deck—and bade him pause.

"Starbuck!"

"Sir?"

"For the third time my soul's ship starts upon this voyage, Starbuck."

"Aye, sir, thou wilt have it so."

"Some ships sail from their ports, and ever afterwards are missing, Starbuck!"

"Truth, sir: saddest truth."

"Some men die at ebb tide, some at the full of the flood—and I feel now like a billow that's all one crested comb, Starbuck. I am old—shake hands with me, man."

Their hands met; their eyes fastened.

"Oh, my captain, my captain!—Noble heart—go not—go not! See, it's a brave man that weeps!"

"Lower away!" cried Ahab, tossing the mate's arm from him. "Stand by the crew!"

In an instant the boat was pulling round close under the stern.

"The sharks! The sharks!" cried a voice from the low cabin window there. "O master, my master, come back!"

But Ahab heard nothing, for his own voice was high-lifted then, and the boat leaped on.

Yet the voice spoke true, for scarcely had he pushed from the ship, when large numbers of sharks, rising from the dark waters beneath the hull, maliciously snapped at the blades of the oars, every time they dipped in the water. It is a thing not uncommonly happening to the whale boats in those swarming seas. The sharks at times apparently follow them in the same way that vultures hover over the banners of marching regiments in the east.

"Heart of steel!" murmured Starbuck gazing over the side, and following with his eyes the receding boat, "canst thou yet ring boldly to that sight? Lowering thy keel among ravenous sharks, and followed by them, openmouthed to the chase—and this the critical third day? For when three days flow together in one continuous intense pursuit, be sure the first is the morning, the second the noon, and the third the evening and the end—be that end what it may!"

The boats had not gone very far, when by a signal from the mastheads, Ahab knew that the whale had sounded. Intending to be near him at the next rising, he held on his way a little sideways from the vessel, the crew maintaining the profoundest silence as the waves hammered and hammered against the opposing bow.

"Drive, drive in your nails, oh ye waves! To their uttermost heads drive them in! Ye but strike a thing without a lid!"

Suddenly the waters around them slowly swelled in broad circles; then quickly upheaved, as if sliding from a submerged iceberg swiftly rising to the surface. A low rumbling sound was heard, and then all held their breaths. Bedraggled with trailing ropes, and harpoons, and lances, a vast form shot from the sea. Shrouded in a thin drooping veil of mist, it hovered for a moment in the air and then fell back into the deep. Crushed thirty feet upwards, the waters flashed for an instant like heaps of fountains, then sank in a shower of flakes, leaving the circling surface creamed like new milk round the marble trunk of the whale.

"Give way!" cried Ahab to the oarsmen, and the boats darted forward to the attack, but maddened by yesterday's fresh irons that corroded in him, Moby Dick seemed possessed. The welded tendons overspreading his broad white forehead beneath the transparent skin looked knitted together as head on he came churning his tail among the boats and once more flailed them apart, spilling out the irons and lances from the two mates' boats, and dashing in one side of the upper part of their bows, but leaving Ahab's almost without a scar.

As the whale, swimming out from them, turned, and showed one entire flank as he shot by them again, a quick cry went up. Lashed round and round to the fish's back, pinioned in the turns upon turns in which, during the past night, the whale had reeled the lines around him, the half-torn body of Fedallah was seen— his eyes turned full upon old Ahab.

The harpoon dropped from his hand.

"Fooled. Fooled!"—drawing in a long breath—"Aye, I see thee again! Away, mates, to the ship! Those boats are useless now. Repair them if ye can in time, and return to me. If not, Ahab is enough to die. Down, men! the first thing that jumps from this boat I stand in, that thing I harpoon. Ye are not other men, but my arms and my legs. Obey me! Where's the whale? Gone down again?"

As if bent upon escaping with the corpse he bore, and as if the last encounter had been but a stage in his voyage, Moby Dick was now again steadily swimming forward and had almost passed the ship, which had been sailing in the contrary direction to him. He seemed now only intent upon pursuing his own straight path in the sea.

"Oh! Ahab," cried Starbuck, "not too late is it, even now, the third day, to desist. See! Moby Dick seeks thee not. It is thou, thou, that madly seekest him!"

Setting sail to the rising wind, the lonely boat was swiftly impelled to leeward by both oars and canvas. And at last when Ahab was sliding by the vessel, so near as plainly to distinguish Starbuck's face as he leaned over the rail, he hailed him to turn the vessel about and follow him.

Glancing upwards, he saw Tashtego, Queequeg, and Daggoo, eagerly mounting to the three mastheads. The oarsmen were rocking in the two staved boats which had but just been hoisted to the side and were busily at work in repairing them. One after the other, through the portholes,* as he sped, he also caught flying glimpses of Stubb and Flask, busying themselves on deck among bundles of new irons and lances. As he saw all this, as he heard the hammers in the broken boats, far other hammers seemed driving a nail into his heart.

Whether fagged by the three days' running chase or whether it was deceitfulness and malice in him—whichever was true, the White Whale's way now began to abate, as it seemed from the boat so rapidly nearing him once more. And still as Ahab glided over the waves the unpitying sharks accompanied him and stuck to the boat, and so continually bit at the plying oars that the blades became jagged and crunched and left small splinters in the sea at almost every dip.

"Heed them not! Pull on!"

"But at every bite, sir, the thin blades grow smaller and smaller!"

"They will last long enough! Pull on! But who can tell," he muttered, "whether these sharks swim to feast on the whale or on Ahab? But pull on! Aye, all alive,

*porthole: an opening in a ship's side, usually for a weapon or a window.

now—we near him. The helm! take the helm—let me pass!" Two of the oarsmen helped him forward to the bows of the still flying boat.

At length as the craft was cast to one side and ran ranging along with the White Whale's flank, he seemed strangely oblivious of its advance—as the whale sometimes will—and Ahab was fairly within the smoky mountain mist, which, thrown off from the whale's spout, curled round his great hump. He was thus close to him when, with body arched back and both arms lengthwise lifted, he darted his fierce iron and his far fiercer curse into the hated whale. As both steel and curse sank to the socket, as if sucked into a morass, Moby Dick sideways writhed. He rolled his flank against the bow, and, without staving a hole in it, so suddenly canted the boat over that had it not been for the elevated part of the gunwhale to which he then clung, Ahab would once more have been tossed into the sea. As it was, three of the oarsmen were flung out, but in an instant two of them clutched the gunwhale again and hurled themselves inboard, again. The third man was helplessly dropping astern, but still afloat and swimming.

Almost simultaneously, with a mighty swiftness, the White Whale darted through the weltering sea. Ahab cried out to the steersman to take new turns with the line and hold it so, and commanded the crew to turn round on their seats and tow the boat up to the mark. But the moment the treacherous line felt that double strain and tug, it snapped in the empty air!

"What breaks in me? Some sinew cracks!—'tis whole again. Oars! Oars! Burst in upon him!"

Hearing the tremendous rush of the sea-crashing boat, the whale wheeled round to present his blank forehead at bay. But the ship, seeing in it the source of all his persecutions, of a sudden he bore down upon its advancing prow, smiting his jaws amid fiery showers of foam.

Ahab staggered. His hand smote his forehead. "I grow blind. Hands, stretch out before me that I may yet grope my way. Is't night?"

"The whale! The ship!" cried the cringing oarsmen.

"Oars! Oars! Slope downwards to thy depths, O sea, that ere it be forever too late, Ahab may slide this last, last time upon his mark! I see: the ship! The ship! Dash on, my men! Will ye not save my ship?"

But as the oarsmen violently forced their boat through the sledge-hammering seas, two planks burst through, and in an instant almost the temporarily disabled boat lay nearly level with the waves, its half-wading, splashing crew trying hard to stop the gap and bale out the pouring water.

Meantime, Starbuck, standing upon the bowsprit, caught sight of the down-coming monster. "The whale, the whale! Up helm, up helm! Oh, all ye sweet powers of air, now hug me close! Let not Starbuck die, if die he must, in a fainting fit. Up helm, I say—ye fools. The jaw! The jaw! Is this the end of all my prayers? Oh, Ahab, Ahab, lo, thy work. Steady! helmsman, steady. Nay nay! Up helm again! He turns to meet us! Oh, his unappeasable brow drives on towards one whose duty tells him he cannot depart. My God, stand by me now!"

From the ship's bow nearly all the seamen now hung inactive—hammers, bits of plank, lances, and harpoons mechanically retained in their hands, just as they had darted from their various employments. All their eyes were upon the whale, which from side to side strangely vibrating his head, sent a broad band of spreading foam before him as he rushed. Retribution, swift vengeance, eternal malice were in his whole aspect, and in spite of all that mortal man could do, the solid white buttress of his forehead smote the ship's starboard bow, till men and timbers reeled. Some fell flat upon their faces. The heads of the harpooners aloft shook on their bull-like necks. Through the breach, they heard the waters pour, as mountain torrents down a flume.

Diving beneath the settling ship, the whale ran quivering along its keel, but turning under water, swiftly shot to the surface again, far off the other bow, but within a few yards of Ahab's boat, where, for a time, he lay. . . .

"Death-glorious ship! Must ye then perish, and without me? Am I cut off from the last pride of meanest shipwrecked captains? Oh, lonely death on lonely life! Towards thee I roll, thou all-destroying but unconquering whale. To the last I grapple with thee. From hell's heart I stab at thee. For hate's sake I spit my last breath at thee!"

The harpoon was darted. The stricken whale flew forward. The line ran through the groove—ran foul. Ahab stooped to clear it. He did clear it, but the flying turn caught him round the neck, and voicelessly he was shot out of the boat. Next instant, the heavy splice in the rope's final end flew out of the empty tub, knocked down an oarsman, and smiting the sea, disappeared in its depths.

For an instant, the boat's crew stood still, then turned. "The ship? Great God, where is the ship?" Soon they saw her sidelong fading phantom, only the uppermost masts out of water. Fixed by fidelity or fate to their once lofty perches, the pagan harpooners still maintained their sinking lookouts on the sea. And now, concentric circles seized the lone boat itself, and all its crew, and each floating oar, and spinning all round and round in one vortex, carried the smallest chip of the Pequod out of sight. . . .

Small fowls flew screaming over the yet yawning gulf. A sullen white surf beat against its steep sides. Then all collapsed, and the great shroud of the sea rolled on as it rolled five thousand years ago.

---

### YOU AND SECTION THREE

In this excerpt, the story of Ahab and the white whale reaches the **climax** for which all of Melville's novel has prepared the reader. In the end, only Ishmael of all the crew members of the *Pequod* is rescued and lives to tell the tale. Did you expect things to end as they finally did? Why or why not?

### A Closer Look

(1) At the beginning of this final excerpt, we witness the send-off of the boats to the final battle. In this section, Starbuck again several times plays the role that has become familiar to the readers of Melville's novel. Where and how? What does Ahab mean when he tells Starbuck: "I feel now like a billow that's all one crested comb"?

(2) What kind of feeling do the sharks help create? When the whale first surfaces, something else happens that on most people would have had an effect similar to the sight of the sharks. What is it?

(3) The final battle between Ahab and the whale is described as if it were a contest between two human opponents. Give several examples of feelings and reactions that

we might expect in a struggle between two human enemies.

(4) What is the story of the final battle? What are the actual events that take place? Describe what happens in your own words.

(5) Listen to Ahab's last words read out loud. At the end, Ahab calls the whale "all-destroying but unconquering." What do you think he means?

**Your Turn**

In Melville's *Moby Dick,* we see the struggle to the death between Captain Ahab and the great whale. In your own words, summarize how Captain Ahab felt about the whale. Do you think the captain was "mad"? If modern readers had to choose sides between the two enemies, which side do you think they would choose? Why? Which side would you choose?

---

Language/Composition Activity B7

A FORMAL STYLE

# Heart of Steel

What does each of the italicized words mean in the context of this selection? From the list at the end, select the meaning that fits best.

1. The boats were lowered among *ravenous* open-mouthed sharks.
2. Starbuck told Ahab that it was not too late to *desist.*
3. The missing harpooner's body was *pinioned* by the lines wrapped around the whale.
4. After three days of the chase, the speed of the white whale began to *abate.*
5. Though the boat approached the whale, he seemed *oblivious* of its advance.
6. To Starbuck, the front of the whale bearing down steadily upon the ship looked *unappeasable.*
7. After the harpoon was thrown, the *stricken* whale flew forward.
8. After *smiting* the sea, the heavy splice disappeared in its depth.
9. The harpooners were held by *fidelity* or fate in their once lofty perches.
10. The boat and each floating oar were spinning around in one *vortex.*

Meanings:

a. completely unaware
b. stop
c. lessen
d. cannot be made peaceful or harmless
e. held down

f. whirlpool
g. loyalty
h. wounded
i. striking
j. driven wild by hunger

● Stephen Crane (1871–1900) supported himself by various kinds of newspaper work. His most famous book is his Civil War classic *The Red Badge of Courage* (1895). In it, he painted the bloody realities of battle. Among his short story classics are "The Blue Hotel" and "The Bride Comes to Yellow Sky." Stephen Crane was one of the major representatives of a literary movement called *naturalism*. His aim was to look at the world, including its misery and suffering, without illusions. As a writer, he felt his duty was not to paint beautiful, unreal pictures but to look at nature and society and be honest about what he saw. The naturalistic writers liked to think of themselves as objective reporters, fearlessly facing the facts. In the twentieth century, writers like Sherwood Anderson and Ernest Hemingway continued the tradition of uncompromising truthtelling that writers like Crane had pioneered. "The Open Boat" is based on a real-life shipwreck that Stephen Crane experienced.

Stephen Crane

# The Open Boat

*A Tale Intended to be after the Fact: Being the Experience of Four Men from the Sunk Steamer* Commodore

## 1

None of them knew the color of the sky. Their eyes glanced level, and were fastened upon the waves that swept toward them. These waves were of the hue of slate, save for the tops, which were of foaming white, and all of the men knew the colors of the sea. The horizon narrowed and widened, and dipped and rose, and at all times its edge was jagged with waves that seemed thrust up in points like rocks.

Many a man ought to have a bathtub larger than the boat which here rode upon the sea. These waves were most wrongfully and barbarously abrupt and tall, and each froth-top was a problem in small-boat navigation.

The cook squatted in the bottom, and looked with both eyes at the six inches of gunwale[1] which separated him from the ocean. His sleeves were rolled over his fat forearms, and the two flaps of his unbuttoned vest dangled as he bent to bail out the boat. Often he said, "Lawd! that was a narrow clip." As he remarked it he invariably gazed eastward over the broken sea.

The oiler, steering with one of the two oars in the boat, sometimes raised himself suddenly to keep clear of water that swirled in over the stern. It was a thin little oar, and it seemed often ready to snap.

[1]**gunwale** (GUN nel): the upper edges of the sides of a boat.

The correspondent, pulling at the other oar, watched the waves and wondered why he was there.

The injured captain, lying in the bow, was at this time buried in that profound dejection and indifference which comes, temporarily at least, to even the bravest and most enduring when, willy-nilly, the firm fails, the army loses, the ship goes down. The mind of the master of a vessel is rooted deep in the timbers of her, though he command for a day or a decade; and this captain had on him the stern impression of a scene in the greys of dawn of seven turned faces, and later a stump of a topmast with a white ball on it, that slashed to and fro at the waves, went low and lower, and down. Thereafter there was something strange in his voice. Although steady, it was deep with mourning, and of a quality beyond oration or tears.

"Keep 'er a little more south, Billie," said he.

"A little more south, sir," said the oiler in the stern.

A seat in his boat was not unlike a seat upon a bucking broncho, and by the same token a broncho is not much smaller. The craft pranced and reared and plunged like an animal. As each wave came, and she rose for it, she seemed like a horse making at a fence outrageously high. The manner of her scramble over these walls of water is a mystic thing, and moreover, at the top of them were ordinarily these problems in white water, the foam racing down from the summit of each wave requiring a new leap, and a leap from the air. Then, after scornfully bumping a crest, she would slide and race and splash down a long incline, and arrive bobbing and nodding in front of the next menace.

A singular disadvantage of the sea lies in the fact that after successfully surmounting one wave you discover that there is another behind it just as important and just as nervously anxious to do something effective in the way of swamping boats. In a ten-foot dinghy[2] one can get an idea of the resources of the sea in the line of waves that is not probable to the average experience which is never at sea in a dinghy. As each salty wall of water approached, it shut all else from the view of the men in the boat, and it was not difficult to imagine that this particular wave was the final outburst of the ocean, the last effort of the grim water. There was a terrible grace in the move of the waves, and they came in silence, save for the snarling of the crests.

In the wan light the faces of the men must have been grey. Their eyes must have glinted in strange ways as they gazed steadily astern. Viewed from a balcony, the whole thing would doubtless have been weirdly picturesque. But the men in the boat had no time to see it, and if they had had leisure, there were other things to occupy their minds. The sun swung steadily up the sky, and they knew it was broad day because the color of the sea changed from slate to emerald green streaked with amber lights, and the foam was like tumbling snow. The process of the breaking day was unknown to them. They were aware only of this effect upon the color of the waves that rolled toward them.

In disjointed sentences the cook and the correspondent argued as to the difference between a lifesaving station and a house of refuge. The cook had said: "There's a house of refuge just north of the Mosquito Inlet Light, and as soon as they see us they'll come off in their boat and pick us up."

---

[2]**dinghy:** a small boat, usually propelled by oars or a sail, which is carried on a ship as a lifeboat.

"As soon as who see us?" challenged the correspondent.

"The crew," said the cook.

"Houses of refuge don't have crews," said the correspondent. "As I understand them, they are only places where clothes and grub are stored for the benefit of ship-wrecked people. They don't carry crews."

"Oh, yes, they do," said the cook.

"No, they don't," maintained the correspondent.

"Well, we're not there yet, anyhow," said the oiler, in the stern.

"Well," said the cook, "perhaps it's not a house of refuge that I'm thinking of as being near Mosquito Inlet Light; perhaps it's a lifesaving station."

"We're not there yet," said the oiler in the stern.

2

As the boat bounced from the top of each wave the wind tore through the hair of the hatless men, and as the craft plopped her stern down again the spray slashed past them. The crest of each of these waves was a hill, from the top of which the men surveyed for a moment a broad tumultuous expanse, shining and wind-riven. It was probably splendid, it was probably glorious, this play of the free sea, wild with lights of emerald and white and amber.

"Bully good thing it's an onshore wind," said the cook. "If not, where would we be? Wouldn't have a show."

"That's right," said the correspondent.

The busy oiler nodded his assent.

Then the captain, in the bow, chuckled in a way that expressed humor, contempt, tragedy, all in one. "Do you think we've got much of a show now, boys?" said he.

Whereupon the three were silent, save for a trifle of hemming and hawing. To express any particular optimism at this time they felt to be childish and stupid, but they all doubtless possessed this sense of the situation in their minds. A young man thinks doggedly at such times. On the other hand, the ethics of their condition was decidedly against any open suggestion of hopelessness. So they were silent.

"Oh, well," said the captain, soothing his children, "we'll get ashore all right."

But there was that in his tone which made them think; so the oiler quoth, "Yes! If this wind holds."

The cook was bailing. "Yes! if we don't get drowned in the surf."

Canton-flannel gulls flew near and far. Sometimes they sat down on the sea, near patches of brown seaweed that rolled over the waves with a movement like carpets on a line in a gale. The birds sat comfortably in groups, and they were envied by some in the dinghy, for the wrath of the sea was no more to them than it was to a covey of prairie chickens a thousand miles inland. Often they came very close and stared at the men with black beadlike eyes. At these times they were uncanny and sinister in their unblinking scrutiny, and the men hooted angrily at them, telling them to be gone. One came, and evidently decided to alight on the top of the captain's head. The bird flew parallel to the boat and did not circle, but made short sidelong jumps in the air in chicken-fashion. His black eyes were wistfully fixed upon the captain's head.

"Ugly brute," said the oiler to the bird. "You look as if you were made with a jackknife." The cook and the correspondent swore darkly at the creature. The captain naturally wished to knock it away with the end of the heavy painter, but he did not dare do it, because anything resembling an emphatic gesture would have capsized this freighted boat; and so, with his open hand, the captain gently and carefully waved the gull away. After it had been discouraged from the pursuit the captain breathed easier on account of his hair, and others breathed easier because the bird struck their minds at this time as being somehow gruesome and ominous.

In the meantime the oiler and the correspondent rowed. And also they rowed. They sat together in the same seat, and each rowed an oar. Then the oiler took both oars; then the correspondent took both oars; then the oiler; then the correspondent. They rowed and they rowed. The very ticklish part of the business was when the time came for the reclining one in the stern to take his turn at the oars. By the very last star of truth, it is easier to steal eggs from under a hen than it was to change seats in the dinghy. First the man in the stern slid his hand along the thwart[3] and moved with care. Then the man in the rowingseat slid his hand along the other thwart. It was all done with the most extraordinary care. As the two sidled past each other, the whole party kept watchful eyes on the coming wave, and the captain cried: "Look out, now! Steady, there!"

The brown mats of seaweed which appeared now and then were like islands, bits of earth. They were traveling, apparently, neither one way nor the other. They were, to all intents, stationary. They informed the men in the boat that it was making progress slowly toward the land.

The captain, rearing cautiously in the bow after the dinghy soared on a great swell, said that he had seen the lighthouse at Mosquito Inlet. Presently the cook remarked that he had seen it. The correspondent was at the oars then, and for some reason he too wished to look at the lighthouse; but his back was toward the

[3]**thwart:** a rower's seat in an open boat, which lies *athwart* or across the boat.

far shore, and the waves were important, and for some time he could not seize an opportunity to turn his head. But at last there came a wave more gentle than the others, and when at the crest of it he swiftly scoured the western horizon.

"See it?" said the captain.

"No," said the correspondent, slowly; "I didn't see anything."

"Look again," said the captain. He pointed. "It's exactly in that direction."

At the top of another wave the correspondent did as he was bid, and this time his eyes chanced on a small, still thing on the edge of the swaying horizon. It was precisely like the point of a pin. It took an anxious eye to find a lighthouse so tiny.

"Think we'll make it, Captain?"

"If this wind holds and the boat don't swamp, we can't do much else," said the captain.

The little boat, lifted by each towering sea and splashed viciously by the crests, made progress that in the absence of seaweed was not apparent to those in her. She seemed just a wee thing wallowing, miraculously top up, at the mercy of five oceans. Occasionally a great spread of water, like white flames, swarmed into her.

"Bail her, cook," uttered the captain, serenely.

"All right, Captain," said the cheerful cook.

3

It would be difficult to describe the subtle brotherhood of men that was here established on the seas. No one said that it was so. No one mentioned it. But it dwelt in the boat, and each man felt it warm him. They were a captain, an oiler, a cook, and a correspondent, and they were friends—friends in a more curiously ironbound degree than may be common. The hurt captain, lying against the water jar in

the bow, spoke always in a low voice and calmly; but he could never command a more ready and swiftly obedient crew than the motley three of the dinghy. It was more than a mere recognition of what was best for the common safety. There was surely in it a quality that was personal and heartfelt. And after this devotion to the commander of the boat, there was this comradeship, that the correspondent, for instance, who had been taught to be cynical of men, knew even at the time was the best experience of his life. But no one said that it was so. No one mentioned it.

"I wish we had a sail," remarked the captain. "We might try my overcoat on the end of an oar, and give you two boys a chance to rest." So the cook and the correspondent held the mast and spread wide the overcoat; the oiler steered; and the little boat made good way with her new rig. Sometimes the oiler had to scull sharply to keep a sea from breaking into the boat, but otherwise sailing was a success.

Meanwhile the lighthouse had been growing slowly larger. It had now almost assumed color and appeared like a little gray shadow on the sky. The man at the oars could not be prevented from turning his head rather often to try for a glimpse of this little gray shadow.

At last, from the top of each wave, the men in the tossing boat could see land. Even as the lighthouse was an upright shadow on the sky, this land seemed but a long black shadow on the sea. It certainly was thinner than paper. "We must be about opposite New Smyrna,"[4] said the cook, who had coasted this shore often in schooners. "Captain, by the way, I believe they abandoned that lifesaving station there about a year ago."

"Did they?" said the captain.

[4]**New Smyrna:** a city located on the Atlantic coast of Florida.

"The wind slowly died away. The cook and the correspondent were not now obliged to slave in order to hold high the oar. But the waves continued their old impetuous swooping at the dinghy, and the little craft, no longer under way, struggled woundily over them. The oiler or the correspondent took the oars again.

Shipwrecks are apropos of nothing. If men could only train for them and have them occur when the men had reached pink condition, there would be less drowning at sea. Of the four in the dinghy none had slept any time worth mentioning for two days and two nights previous to embarking in the dinghy, and in the excitement of clambering about the deck of a foundering ship they had also forgotten to eat heartily.

For these reasons, and for others, neither the oiler nor the correspondent was fond of rowing at this time. The correspondent wondered ingenuously how in the name of all that was sane could there be people who thought it amusing to row a boat. It was not an amusement; it was a diabolical punishment, and even a genius of mental aberrations could never conclude that it was anything but a horror to the muscles and a crime against the back. He mentioned to the boat in general how the amusement of rowing struck him, and the weary-faced oiler smiled in full sympathy. Previously to the foundering, by the way, the oiler had worked a double watch in the engine room of the ship.

"Take her easy now, boys," said the captain. "Don't spend yourselves. If we have to run a surf you'll need all your strength, because we'll sure have to swim for it. Take your time."

Slowly the land arose from the sea. From a black line it became a line of black and a line of white—trees and sand. Finally the captain said that he could make out a house on the shore. "That's the house of refuge, sure," said the cook. "They'll see us before long, and come out after us."

The distant lighthouse reared high. "The keeper ought to be able to make us out now, if he's looking through a glass," said the captain. "He'll notify the life-saving people."

"None of those other boats could have got ashore to give word of this wreck," said the oiler, in a low voice, "else the lifeboat would be out hunting us."

Slowly and beautifully the land loomed out of the sea. The wind came again. It had veered from the northeast to the southeast. Finally a new sound struck the ears of the men in the boat. It was the low thunder of the surf on the shore. "We'll never be able to make the lighthouse now," said the captain. "Swing her head a little more north, Billie."

"A little more north, sir," said the oiler.

Whereupon the little boat turned her nose once more down the wind, and all but the oarsman watched the shore grow. Under the influence of this expansion doubt and direful apprehension were leaving the minds of the men. The management of the boat was still most absorbing, but it could not prevent a quiet cheerfulness. In an hour, perhaps, they would be ashore.

Their backbones had become thoroughly used to balancing in the boat, and they now rode this wild colt of a dinghy like circus men. The correspondent thought that he had been drenched to the skin, but happening to feel in the top pocket of his coat, he found therein eight cigars. Four of them were soaked with seawater; four were perfectly scatheless. After a search, somebody produced three dry matches; and thereupon the four waifs rode impudently in their little boat and, with an assurance of an impending rescue shining in their eyes, puffed at the big cigars, and judged well and ill of all men. Everybody took a drink of water.

"Cook," remarked the captain, "there don't seem to be any signs of life about your house of refuge."

"No," replied the cook. "Funny they don't see us!"

A broad stretch of lowly coast lay before the eyes of the men. It was of low dunes topped with dark vegetation. The roar of the surf was plain, and sometimes they could see the white lip of a wave as it spun up the beach. A tiny house was blocked out black upon the sky. Southward, the slim lighthouse lifted its little gray length.

Tide, wind, and waves were swinging the dinghy northward. "Funny they don't see us," said the men.

The surf's roar was here dulled, but its tone was nevertheless thunderous and mighty. As the boat swam over the great rollers the men sat listening to this roar: "We'll swamp sure," said everybody.

It is fair to say here that there was not a lifesaving station within twenty miles in either direction; but the men did not know this fact, and in consequence they made dark and opprobious remarks concerning the eyesight of the nation's lifesavers. Four scowling men sat in the dinghy and surpassed records in the invention of epithets.

"Funny they don't see us."

The lightheartedness of a former time had completely faded. To their sharpened minds it was easy to conjure pictures of all kinds of incompetency and blindness and, indeed, cowardice. There was the shore of the populous land, and it was bitter and bitter to them that from it came no sign.

"Well," said the captain, ultimately, "I suppose we'll have to make a try for ourselves. If we stay out here too long, we'll none of us have strength left to swim after the boat swamps."

And so the oiler, who was at the oars, turned the boat straight for the shore. There was a sudden tightening of muscles. There was some thinking.

"If we don't all get ashore," said the captain—"if we don't all get ashore, I suppose you fellows know where to send news of my finish?"

They then briefly exchanged some addresses and admonitions. As for the reflections of the men, there was a great deal of rage in them. Perchance they might be formulated thus: "If I am going to be drowned—if I am going to be drowned—if I am going to be drowned, why, in the name of the seven mad gods who rule the sea, was I allowed to come thus far and contemplate sand and trees? Was I brought here merely to have my nose dragged away as I was about to nibble the sacred cheese of life? It is preposterous. If this old ninny-woman, Fate, cannot do better than this, she should be deprived of the management of men's fortunes. She is an old hen who knows not her intention. If she has decided to drown me, why did she not do it in the beginning, and save me all this trouble? The whole affair is absurd.—But no, she cannot mean to drown me. She dare not drown me. She cannot drown me. Not after all this work." Afterward the man might have had an impulse to shake his fist at the clouds. "Just you drown me, now, and then hear what I call you!"

The billows that came at this time were more formidable. They seemed always just about to break and roll over the little boat in a turmoil of foam. There was a preparatory and long growl in the speech of them. No mind unused to the sea would have concluded that the dinghy could ascend these sheer heights in time. The shore was still afar. The oiler was a wily surfman. "Boys," he said swiftly, "She won't live three minutes more, and we're too far out to swim. Shall I take her to sea again, Captain?"

"Yes, go ahead!" said the captain.

This oiler, by a series of quick miracles and fast and steady oarsmanship turned the boat in the middle of the surf and took her safely to sea again.

There was a considerable silence as the boat bumped over the furrowed sea to deeper water. Then somebody in gloom spoke: "Well, anyhow, they must have seen us from the shore by now."

The gulls went in slanting flight up the wind toward the gray, desolate east. A squall, marked by dingy clouds and clouds brick-red like smoke from a burning building, appeared from the southeast.

"What do you think of those lifesaving people? Ain't they peaches?"

"Funny they haven't seen us."

"Maybe they think we're out here for sport! Maybe they think we're fishin'. Maybe they think we're fools."

It was a long afternoon. A changed tide tried to force them southward, but wind and wave said northward. Far ahead, where coastline, sea, and sky formed their mighty angle, there were little dots which seemed to indicate a city on the shore.

"St. Augustine?"[5]

The captain shook his head. "Too near Mosquito Inlet."

And the oiler rowed, and then the correspondent rowed; then the oiler rowed. It was a weary business. The human back can become the seat of more aches and pains than are registered in books for the composite anatomy of a regiment. The back is a limited area, but it can become the theater of innumerable muscular conflicts, tangles, wrenches, knots, and other comforts.

"Did you ever like to row, Billie?" asked the correspondent.

"No," said the oiler, "hang it!"

When one exchanged the rowing seat for a place in the bottom of the boat, he suffered a bodily depression that caused him to be careless of everything save an obligation to wiggle one finger. There was cold seawater swashing to and fro in the boat, and he lay in it. His head, pillowed on a thwart, was within an inch of the swirl of a wave crest, and sometimes a particularly obstreperous sea came inboard and drenched him once more. But these matters did not annoy him. It is almost certain that if the boat had capsized he would have tumbled comfortably out upon the ocean as if he felt sure that it was a great soft mattress.

"Look! There's a man on the shore!"

"Where?"

"There! See 'im? See 'im?"

"Yes, sure! He's walking along."

"Now he's stopped. Look! He's facing us!"

"He's waving at us!"

"So he is! By thunder!"

"Ah, now we're all right! Now we're all right! There'll be a boat out here for us in half an hour."

"He's going on. He's running. He's going up to that house there."

The remote beach seemed lower than the sea, and it required a searching glance to discern the little black figure. The captain saw a floating stick, and they rowed to it. A bath towel was by some weird chance in the boat, and, tying this on the stick, the captain waved it. The oarsman did not dare turn his head, so he was obliged to ask questions.

"What's he doing now?"

"He's standing still again. He's looking, I think.—There he goes again—toward the house.—Now he's stopped again."

"Is he waving at us?"

"No, not now; he was, though."

"Look! There comes another man!"

"He's running."

"Look at him go, would you!"

[5]**St. Augustine:** a city on the Atlantic coast of Florida, sixty-five miles north of New Smyrna.

"Why, he's on a bicycle. Now he's met the other man. They're both waving at us. Look!"

"There comes something up the beach."

"What the devil is that thing?"

"Why, it looks like a boat."

"Why, certainly, it's a boat."

"No, it's on wheels."

"Yes, so it is. Well, that must be the lifeboat. They drag them along shore on a wagon."

"That's the lifeboat, sure."

"No, by God, it's—it's an omnibus."

"I tell you it's a lifeboat."

"It is not! It's an omnibus. I can see it plain. See? Look at it. One of these big hotel omnibuses."

"By thunder, you're right. It's an omnibus, sure as fate. What do you suppose they are doing with an omnibus? Maybe they are going around collecting the life-crew, hey?"

"That's it, likely. Look! There's a fellow waving a little black flag. He's standing on the steps of the omnibus. There come those other two fellows. Now they're all talking together. Look at the fellow with the flag. Maybe he ain't waving it!"

"That ain't a flag, is it? That's his coat. Why, certainly, that's his coat."

"So it is; it's his coat. He's taken it off and is waving it around his head. But would you look at him swing it!"

"Oh, say, there isn't any lifesaving station there. That's just a winter-resort hotel omnibus that has brought over some of the boarders to see us drown."

"What's that idiot with the coat mean? What's he signaling, anyhow?"

"It looks as if he were trying to tell us to go north. There must be a lifesaving station up there."

"No, he thinks we're only fishing. Just giving us a merry hand. See? Ah, there, Willie!"

"Well, I wish I could make something out of those signals. What do you suppose he means?"

"He don't mean anything; he's just playing."

"Well, if he'd just signal us to try the surf again, or to go to sea and wait, or go north, or go south, or go to hell, there would be some reason in it. But look at him! He just stands there and keeps his coat revolving like a wheel. The idiot!"

"There come more people."

"Now there's quite a mob. Look! Isn't that a boat?"

"Where? Oh, I see where you mean. No, that's no boat."

"That fellow is still waving his coat."

"He must think we like to see him do that. Why don't he quit it? It don't mean anything."

"I don't know. I think he is trying to make us go north. It must be that there's a lifesaving station there somewhere."

"Say, he ain't tired yet. Look at 'em wave!"

"Wonder how long he can keep that up. He's been revolving his coat ever since he caught sight of us. He's an idiot. Why aren't they getting men to bring a boat out? A fishing boat—one of those big yawls—could come out here all right. Why don't he do something?"

"Oh, it's all right now."

"They'll have a boat out here for us in less than no time, now that they've seen us."

A faint yellow tone came into the sky over the low land. The shadows on the sea slowly deepened. The wind bore coldness with it, and the men began to shiver.

"Holy smoke!" said one, allowing his voice to express his impious mood, "if we keep on monkeying out here! If we've got to flounder out here all night!"

"Oh, we'll never have to stay here all night! Don't you worry. They've seen us

now, and it won't be long before they'll
come chasing out after us."

The shore grew dusky. The man waving
a coat blended gradually into this gloom,
and it swallowed in the same manner the
omnibus and the group of people. The
spray, when it dashed uproariously over
the side, made the voyagers shrink and
swear like men who were being branded.

"I'd like to catch the chump who waved
the coat. I feel like socking him one, just
for luck."

"Why? What did he do?"

"Oh, nothing, but then he seemed so
cheerful."

In the meantime the oiler rowed, and

then the correspondent rowed, and then
the oiler rowed. Gray-faced and bowed
forward, they mechanically, turn by turn,
plied the leaden oars. The form of the
lighthouse had vanished from the southern horizon, but finally a pale star appeared, just lifting from the sea. The
streaked saffron in the west passed before
the all-merging darkness, and the sea to
the east was black. The land had vanished
and was expressed only by the low and
drear thunder of the surf.

"If I am going to be drowned—if I am
going to be drowned—if I am going to be
drowned, why, in the name of the seven
mad gods who rule the sea, was I allowed

to come thus far and contemplate sand and trees? Was I brought here merely to have my nose dragged away as I was about to nibble the sacred cheese of life?''

The patient captain, drooped over the water jar, was sometimes obliged to speak to the oarsman.

"Keep her head up! Keep her head up!''

"Keep her head up, sir.'' The voices were weary and low.

This was surely a quiet evening. All save the oarsman lay heavily and list-lessly in the boat's bottom. As for him, his eyes were just capable of noting the tall black waves that swept forward in a most sinister silence, save for an occasional subdued growl of a crest.

The cook's head was on a thwart, and he looked without interest at the water under his nose. He was deep in other scenes. Finally he spoke. "Billie,'' he mur-mured, dreamfully, "what kind of pie do you like best?''

### 5

"Pie!'' said the oiler and the correspon-dent, agitatedly. "Don't talk about those things, blast you!''

"Well,'' said the cook, "I was just think-ing about ham sandwiches and—''

A night on the sea in an open boat is a long night. As darkness settled finally, the shine of the light, lifting from the sea in the south, changed to full gold. On the northern horizon a new light appeared, a small bluish gleam on the edge of the waters. These two lights were the furni-ture of the world. Otherwise there was nothing but waves.

Two men huddled in the stern, and distances were so magnificent in the din-ghy that the rower was enabled to keep his feet partly warm by thrusting them under his companions. Their legs extended far under the rowing seat until they touched the feet of the captain forward.

Sometimes, despite the efforts of the tired oarsman, a wave came piling into the boat, an icy wave of the night, and the chilling water soaked them anew. They would twist their bodies for a mo-ment and groan, and sleep the dead sleep once more, while the water in the boat gurgled about them as the craft rocked.

The plan of the oiler and the correspon-dent was for one to row until he lost the ability, and then arouse the other from his seawater couch in the bottom of the boat.

The oiler plied the oars until his head drooped forward and the overpowering sleep blinded him; and he rowed yet after-ward. Then he touched a man in the bottom of the boat, and called his name. "Will you spell me for a little while?'' he said, meekly.

"Sure, Billie,'' said the correspondent, awaking and dragging himself to a sitting position. They exchanged places care-fully, and the oiler, cuddling down in the seawater at the cook's side, seemed to go to sleep instantly.

The particular violence of the sea had ceased. The waves came without snarling. The obligation of the man at the oars was to keep the boat headed so that the tilt of the rollers would not capsize her, and to preserve her from filling when the crests rushed past. The black waves were silent and hard to be seen in the darkness. Often one was almost upon the boat before the oarsman was aware.

In a low voice the correspondent ad-dressed the captain. He was not sure that the captain was awake, although this iron man seemed to be always awake. "Cap-tain, shall I keep her making for that light north, sir?''

The same steady voice answered him. "Yes. Keep it about two points off the port[6] bow.''

[6]**port:** the left side of a boat as one faces forward.

The cook had tied a life belt around himself in order to get even the warmth which this clumsy cork contrivance could donate, and he seemed almost stovelike when a rower, whose teeth invariably chattered wildly as soon as he ceased his labor, dropped down to sleep.

The correspondent, as he rowed, looked down at the two men sleeping underfoot. The cook's arm was around the oiler's shoulders, and, with their fragmentary clothing and haggard faces, they were the babes of the sea—a grotesque rendering of the old babes in the wood.

Later he must have grown stupid at his work, for suddenly there was a growling of water, and a crest came with a roar and a swash into the boat, and it was a wonder that it did not set the cook afloat in his life belt. The cook continued to sleep, but the oiler sat up, blinking his eyes and shaking with the new cold.

"Oh, I'm awful sorry, Billie," said the correspondent, contritely.

"That's all right, old boy," said the oiler, and lay down again and was asleep.

Presently it seemed that even the captain dozed, and the correspondent thought that he was the one man afloat on all the oceans. The wind had a voice as it came over the waves, and it was sadder than the end.

There was a long, loud swishing astern of the boat, and a gleaming trail of phosphorescence, like blue flame, was furrowed on the black waters. It might have been made by a monstrous knife.

Then there came a stillness, while the correspondent breathed with open mouth and looked at the sea.

Suddenly there was another swish and another long flash of bluish light, and this time it was alongside the boat and might almost have been reached with an oar. The correspondent saw an enormous fin speed like a shadow through the water, hurling the crystalline spray and leaving the long glowing trail.

The correspondent looked over his shoulder at the captain. His face was hidden, and he seemed to be asleep. He looked at the babes of the sea. They certainly were asleep. So, being bereft of sympathy, he leaned a little way to one side and swore softly into the sea.

But the thing did not then leave the vicinity of the boat. Ahead or astern, on one side or the other, at intervals long or short, fled the long sparkling streak, and there was to be heard the *whirroo* of the dark fin. The speed and power of the thing was greatly to be admired. It cut the water like a gigantic and keen projectile.

The presence of this thing did not affect the man with the same horror that it would if he had been a picnicker. He simply looked at the sea dully and swore in an undertone.

Nevertheless, it is true that he did not wish to be alone with the thing. He wished one of his companions to awake by chance and keep him company with it. But the captain hung motionless over the water jar, and the oiler and the cook in the bottom of the boat were plunged in slumber.

## 6

"If I am going to be drowned—if I am going to be drowned—if I am going to be drowned, why, in the name of the seven mad gods who rule the sea, was I allowed to come thus far and contemplate sand and trees?"

During this dismal night, it may be remarked that a man would conclude that it was really the intention of the seven mad gods to drown him, despite the abominable injustice of it. For it was certainly an abominable injustice to drown a man who had worked so hard, so hard. The man felt it would be a crime most unnatural. Other people had drowned at sea since galleys swarmed with painted sails, but still—

When it occurs to a man that nature does not regard him as important, and that she feels she would not maim the universe by disposing of him, he at first wishes to throw bricks at the temple, and he hates deeply the fact that there are no bricks and no temples. Any visible expression of nature would surely be pelleted with his jeers.

Then, if there be no tangible thing to hoot, he feels, perhaps, the desire to confront a personification and indulge in pleas, bowed to one knee, and with hands supplicant, saying, "Yes, but I love myself."

A high cold star on a winter's night is the word he feels that she says to him. Thereafter he knows the pathos of his situation.

The men in the dinghy had not discussed these matters, but each had, no doubt, reflected upon them in silence and according to his mind. There was seldom any expression upon their faces, save the general one of complete weariness. Speech was devoted to the business of the boat.

To chime the notes of his emotion, a verse mysteriously entered the correspondent's head. He had even forgotten that he had forgotten this verse, but it suddenly was in his mind.

A soldier of the Legion lay dying in Algiers;
There was lack of woman's nursing, there was dearth of woman's tears;
But a comrade stood beside him, and he took that comrade's hand,
And he said, "I never more shall see my own, my native land."

In his childhood the correspondent had been made acquainted with the fact that a soldier of the Legion lay dying in Algiers, but he had never regarded the fact as important. Myriads of his schoolfellows had informed him of the soldier's plight, but the dinning had naturally ended by making him perfectly indifferent. He had never considered it his affair that a soldier of the Legion lay dying in Algiers, nor had it appeared to him as a matter for sorrow. It was less to him than the breaking of a pencil's point.

Now, however, it quaintly came to him as a human, living thing. It was no longer merely a picture of a few throes in the breast of a poet, meanwhile drinking tea and warming his feet at the grate; it was an actuality—stern, mournful, and fine.

The correspondent plainly saw the soldier. He lay on the sand with his feet out straight and still. While his pale left hand was upon his chest in an attempt to thwart the going of his life, the blood came between his fingers. In the far Algerian distance, a city of low square forms was set against a sky that was faint with the last sunset hues. The correspondent, plying the oars and dreaming of the slow and slower movements of the lips of the soldier, was moved by a profound and perfectly impersonal comprehension. He was sorry for the soldier of the Legion who lay dying in Algiers.

The thing which had followed the boat and waited had evidently grown bored at the delay. There was no longer to be heard the slash of the cutwater, and there was no longer the flame of the long trail. The light in the north still glimmered, but it was apparently no nearer to the boat. Sometimes the boom of the surf rang in the correspondent's ears, and he turned the craft seaward then and rowed harder. Southward, someone had evidently built a watch fire on the beach. It was too low and too far to be seen, but it made a shimmering reflection upon the bluff in back of it, and this could be discerned from the boat. The wind came stronger, and sometimes a wave suddenly raged out like a mountain cat, and there was to be seen the sheen and sparkle of a broken crest.

The captain, in the bow, moved on his water jar and sat erect. "Pretty long night," he observed to the correspondent. He looked at the shore. "Those lifesaving people take their time."

"Did you see that shark playing around?"

"Yes, I saw him. He was a big fellow, all right."

"Wish I had known you were awake."

Later the correspondent spoke into the bottom of the boat. "Billie!" There was a slow and gradual disentanglement. "Billie, will you spell me?"

"Sure," said the oiler.

As soon as the correspondent touched the cold, comfortable seawater in the bottom of the boat and had huddled close to the cook's lifebelt he was deep in sleep, despite the fact that his teeth played all the popular airs. This sleep was so good to him that it was but a moment before he heard a voice call his name in a tone that demonstrated the last stages of exhaustion. "Will you spell me?"

"Sure, Billie."

The light in the north had mysteriously vanished, but the correspondent took his course from the wide-awake captain.

Later in the night they took the boat farther out to sea, and the captain directed the cook to take one oar at the stern and keep the boat facing the seas. He was to call out if he should hear the thunder of the surf. This plan enabled the oiler and the correspondent to get respite together. "We'll give those boys a chance to get into shape again," said the captain. They curled down and, after a few preliminary chatterings and trembles, slept once more the dead sleep. Neither knew they had bequeathed to the cook the company of another shark, or perhaps the same shark.

As the boat caroused on the waves, spray occasionally bumped over the side and gave them a fresh soaking, but this had no power to break their repose. The ominous slash of the wind and the water affected them as it would have affected mummies.

"Boys," said the cook, with the notes of every reluctance in his voice, "she's drifted in pretty close. I guess one of you had better take her to sea again." The correspondent, aroused, heard the crash of the toppled crests.

As he was rowing, the captain gave him some whiskey-and-water, and this steadied the chills out of him. "If I ever get ashore and anybody shows me even a photograph of an oar—"

At last there was a short conversation. "Billie!—Billie, will you spell me?"

"Sure," said the oiler.


### 7

When the correspondent again opened his eyes, the sea and the sky were each of the gray hue of the dawning. Later, carmine and gold was painted upon the waters. The morning appeared finally, in its splendor, with a sky of pure blue, and the sunlight flamed on the tips of the waves.

On the distant dunes were set many little black cottages, and a tall white windmill reared above them. No man, nor dog, nor bicycle appeared on the beach. The cottages might have formed a deserted village.

The voyagers scanned the shore. A conference was held in the boat. "Well," said the captain, "if no help is coming, we might better try a run through the surf right away. If we stay out here much longer we will be too weak to do anything for ourselves at all." The others silently acquiesced in this reasoning. The boat was headed for the beach. The correspondent wondered if none ever ascended the tall wind tower, and if then they never looked seaward. This tower was a giant, standing with its back to the plight of the ants. It represented in a degree, to the correspondent, the serenity of nature amid the struggles of the individual—nature in the wind, and nature in the vision of men. She did not seem cruel to him then, nor beneficent, nor treacherous, nor wise. But she was indifferent, flatly indifferent. It is, perhaps, plausible that a man in this situation, impressed with the unconcern of the universe, should see the innumerable flaws of his life, and have them taste wickedly in his mind, and wish for another chance. A distinction between right and wrong seems absurdly clear to him, then, in this new ignorance of the grave-edge, and he understands that if he were given another opportunity he would mend his conduct and his words, and be better and brighter during an introduction or at a tea.

"Now, boys," said the captain, "she is going to swamp sure. All we can do is to work her in as far as possible, and then when she swamps, pile out and scramble for the beach. Keep cool now, and don't jump until she swamps sure."

The oiler took the oars. Over his shoulder he scanned the surf. "Captain," he said, "I think I'd better bring her about and keep her head-on to the seas and back her in."

"All right, Billie," said the captain. "Back her in." The oiler swung the boat then, and, seated in the stern, the cook and the correspondent were obliged to look over their shoulders to contemplate the lonely and indifferent shore.

The monstrous inshore rollers heaved the boat high until the men were again enabled to see the white sheets of water scudding up the slanted beach. "We won't get in very close," said the captain. Each time a man could wrest his attention from the rollers, he turned his glance toward the shore, and in the expression of the eyes during this contemplation there was a singular quality. The correspondent, observing the others, knew that they were not afraid, but the full meaning of their glances was shrouded.

As for himself, he was too tired to grapple fundamentally with the fact. He tried to coerce his mind into thinking of it, but the mind was dominated at this time by the muscles, and the muscles said they did not care. It merely occurred to him that if he should drown it would be a shame.

There were no hurried words, no pallor, no plain agitation. The men simply looked at the shore. "Now, remember to get well clear of the boat when you jump," said the captain.

Seaward the crest of a roller suddenly fell with a thunderous crash, and the long white comber came roaring down upon the boat.

"Steady now," said the captain. The men were silent. They turned their eyes from the shore to the comber and waited. The boat slid up the incline, leaped at the furious top, bounced over it, and swung down the long back of the wave. Some water had been shipped, and the cook bailed it out.

But the next crest crashed also. The tumbling, boiling flood of white water caught the boat and whirled it almost perpendicular. Water swarmed in from all sides. The correspondent had his hands on the gunwhale at this time, and when the water entered at that place he swiftly withdrew his fingers, as if he objected to wetting them.

The little boat, drunken with this weight of water, reeled and snuggled deeper into the sea.

"Bail her out, cook! Bail her out!" said the capain.

"All right, Captain," said the cook.

"Now, boys, the next one will do for us

sure," said the oiler. "Mind to jump clear of the boat."

The third wave moved forward, huge, furious, implacable. It fairly swallowed the dinghy, and almost simultaneously the men tumbled into the sea. A piece of lifebelt had lain in the bottom of the boat, and as the correspondent went overboard he held this to his chest with his left hand.

The January water was icy, and he reflected immediately that it was colder than he had expected to find it off the coast of Florida. This appeared to his dazed mind as a fact important enough to be noted at the time. The coldness of the water was sad; it was tragic. This fact was somehow mixed and confused with his opinion of his own situation, so that it seemed almost a proper reason for tears. The water was cold.

When he came to the surface he was conscious of little but the noisy water.

Afterward he saw his companions in the sea. The oiler was ahead in the race. He was swimming strongly and rapidly. Off to the correspondent's left, the cook's great white and corked back bulged out of the water; and in the rear the captain was hanging with his one good hand to the keel of the overturned dinghy.

There is a certain immovable quality to a shore, and the correspondent wondered at it amid the confusion of the sea.

It seemed also very attractive; but the correspondent knew that it was a long journey, and he paddled leisurely. The piece of life preserver lay under him, and sometimes he whirled down the incline of a wave as it he were on a handsled.

But finally he arrived at a place in the sea where travel was beset with difficulty. He did not pause swimming to inquire what manner of current had caught him, but there his progress ceased. The shore was set before him like a bit of scenery on a stage, and he looked at it and understood with his eyes each detail of it.

As the cook passed, much farther to the left, the captain was calling to him. "Turn over on your back, cook! Turn over on your back and use the oar."

"All right, sir," The cook turned on his back, and, paddling with an oar, went ahead as if he were a canoe.

Presently the boat also passed to the left of the correspondent, with the captain clinging with one hand to the keel. He would have appeared like a man raising himself to look over a board fence if it were not for the extraordinary gymnastics of the boat. The correspondent marvelled that the captain could still hold to it.

They passed on nearer to shore—the oiler, the cook, the captain—and following them went the water jar, bouncing gaily over the seas.

The correspondent remained in the grip of this strange new enemy—a current. The shore, with its white slope of sand

and its green bluff topped with little silent cottages, was spread like a picture before him. It was very near to him then, but he was impressed as one who, in a gallery, looks at a scene from Brittany or Algiers.

He thought: "I am going to drown? Can it be possible? Can it be possible? Can it be possible?" Perhaps an individual must consider his own death to be the final phenomenon of nature.

But later a wave perhaps whirled him out of this small deadly current, for he found suddenly that he could again make progress toward the shore. Later still he was aware that the captain, clinging with one hand to the keel of the dinghy, had his face turned away from the shore and toward him, and was calling his name. "Come to the boat! Come to the boat!"

In his struggle to reach the captain and the boat, he reflected that when one gets properly wearied drowning must really be a comfortable arrangement—a cessation of hostilities accompanied by a large degree of relief; and he was glad of it, for the main thing in his mind for some moments had been horror of the temporary agony. He did not wish to be hurt.

Presently he saw a man running along the shore. He was undressing with most remarkable speed. Coat, trousers, shirt, everything flew magically off him.

"Come to the boat!" called out the captain.

"All right, Captain." As the correspondent paddled, he saw the captain let himself down to the bottom and leave the boat. Then the correspondent performed his one little marvel of the voyage. A large wave caught him and flung him with ease and supreme speed completely over the boat and far beyond it. It struck him even then as an event in gymnastics and a true miracle of the sea. An overturned boat in the surf is not a plaything to a swimming man.

The correspondent arrived in water that reached only to his waist, but his condition did not enable him to stand for more than a moment. Each wave knocked him into a heap, and the undertow pulled at him.

Then he saw the man who had been running and undressing, and undressing and running, come bounding into the water. He dragged ashore the cook, and then waded toward the captain; but the captain waved him away and sent him to the correspondent. He was naked—naked as a tree in winter; but a halo was about his head, and he shone like a saint. He gave a strong pull, and a long drag, and a bully heave at the correspondent's hand. The correspondent, schooled in the minor formulas, said "Thanks, old man." But suddenly the man cried, "What's that?" He pointed a swift finger. The correspondent said, "Go."

In the shallows, face downward, lay the oiler. His forehead touched sand that was periodically, between each wave, clear of the sea.

The correspondent did not know all that transpired afterward. When he achieved safe ground he fell, striking the sand with each particular part of his body. It was as if he had dropped from a roof, but the thud was grateful to him.

It seemed that instantly the beach was populated with men with blankets, clothes, and flasks, and women with coffeepots and all the remedies sacred to their minds. The welcome of the land to the men from the sea was warm and generous; but a still and dripping shape was carried slowly up the beach, and the land's welcome for it could only be the different sinister hospitality of the grave.

When it came night, the white waves paced to and fro in the moonlight, and the wind brought the sound of the great sea's voice to the men on the shore, and they felt that they could then be interpreters.

## YOU AND THE STORY

As we try to sum up the meaning of what has happened in a story or a play, we try to state its **theme**. At the end of this story, "the wind brought the sound of the great sea's voice to the men on the shore, and they felt that they could then be interpreters." As you look back over the experience of the people in this story, what do you think the voice of the sea would be saying to them? How do you think the author wants us to interpret what happened to them in the story? While we read the story, we are made to think long and hard about how nature treats us or deals with us as human beings. For you, what incident or what passage best sums up what Crane is trying to tell us about nature in this story? What to you is the major theme of his story?

## A Closer Look

Modern literature often appeals strongly to our sense of **irony**. Our sense of irony allows us to smile when things go counter to our hopes and expectations. Our sense of irony shows in our wry smile when we tell ourselves: "I should have known!" Though Stephen Crane wrote a hundred years ago, his poems and stories show the sense of irony that later becomes familiar in much twentieth-century literature. Answer the following questions about the role that irony plays in this story:

(1) Our sense of irony makes us notice the *contrast* between what we would like to see and what really exists. Find examples of such contrasts in this story: Show how Crane makes us aware of the contrast between the tasks facing people and their limited abilities. Show several examples of hopes being raised initially and then disappointed.

(2) When we use **verbal irony,** we say something that people might expect—but we show by the way we say it that we mean something different, and often the opposite. Crane's readers were used to reading praises of the beauty of nature. What is ironic about the following passages from his story?

—"Viewed from a balcony, the whole thing would doubtlessly have been wildly picturesque."
—"The crest of each of these waves was a hill, from the top of which the men surveyed for a moment a broad tumultuous expanse, shining and wind-riven. It was probably splendid, it was probably glorious, this play of the free sea, wild with lights of emerald and white and amber."
—"The correspondent saw an enormous fin speed like a shadow through the water. . . . The speed and power of the thing was greatly to be admired."

(3) Why were the men angry at the birds? Can you explain how they felt? Crane says later in the story that people in a bad situation need someone or something to blame or to jeer at. Find one or more other examples of this need to blame someone in this story.

(4) As the men jump from the boat in order to swim to shore, "the oiler was ahead in the race. He was swimming strongly and rapidly." Why would we expect him to do well compared with the other people? Why is this description of him ironic in the light of what happens later? Why is it ironic that the captain should be one of the survivors?

(5) When our hopes have often been disappointed, we hesitate to put positive or encouraging feelings into words. The people in the boat have strong positive feelings about each other—but no one mentions them or puts them into words. How and where in the story does Crane describe these feelings? Though the men do not talk about their feelings for each other, do they express or show them in other ways?

Compare and contrast the feelings and ideas about nature that we encounter in the selections from Melville's *Moby Dick* and in Stephen Crane's "The Open Boat":
—How do the authors shape our feelings toward our natural environment?
—How do the authors shape our feelings toward the creatures of the animal kingdom?
—How do the authors shape or influence our feelings toward our fellow human beings?

---

Language/Composition Activity B8

WORD CLUSTERS

# The Cruel Sea

Stephen Crane's program as a writer was to take a long honest look at things and let the truth about them sink in. He often uses related words, or word clusters, that help build and reinforce the same impression. What is the common meaning or common ground for the italicized words in each of the following excerpts? How do the words in each cluster differ? Which of these words do you have to check in a dictionary?

1. These waves were most wrongfully and *barbarously* abrupt and tall. . . . The *monstrous* inshore rollers heaved the boat high. . . . The third wave moved forward, huge, furious, *implacable*.

2. The captain was at this time buried in profound *dejection* and indifference. . . . The captain had on him the *stern* impression of a scene in the grays of dawn. . . . there was something strange in his voice. . . . It was deep with *mourning*.

3. The birds were *uncanny* and *sinister* in their unblinking scrutiny. . . . The birds struck their minds at this time as being somehow *gruesome* and *ominous*.

4. There was not a lifesaving station within twenty miles in either direction; but the men did not know this fact, and in consequence made *dark* and *opprobrious* remarks concerning the eyesight of the nation's lifesavers. Four *scowling* men sat in the dinghy and surpassed records in the invention of *epithets*.

5. If I am going to be drowned, why . . . was I allowed to come this far and contemplate sand and trees? . . . It is *preposterous*. . . . The whole affair is *absurd*.

6. Sometimes a particularly *obstreperous* sea came inboard and drenched him. . . . The spray, when it dashed *uproariously* over the side, made the voyagers shrink.

7. Any *visible* expression of nature would surely be pelleted with his jeers. Then, if there be no *tangible* thing to hoot, he feels, perhaps, the desire to confront a *personification* and indulge in pleas. . . .

8. It represented the *serenity* of nature amid the struggles of the individual. . . . She was *indifferent*, flatly indifferent. It is perhaps plausible that a man in this situation, impressed with the *unconcern* of the universe, should see . . . the flaws of his life.

• Ernest Hemingway (1898–1961) is among the half dozen American writers most famous around the world. Millions of readers in many countries have read his best-known books: *The Sun Also Rises* (1926), *A Farewell to Arms* (1929), *For Whom the Bell Tolls* (1940), and *The Old Man and the Sea* (1952). In many of his early stories, Hemingway wrote about war and its challenge to our values. He had served as a volunteer in World War I, first with an American ambulance unit in France and then with an Italian infantry unit on the Italian front. He later was a war correspondent in the Spanish civil war between the forces loyal to the Spanish Republic and the Fascist rebels led by Franco. Like other writers of his generation, Hemingway wrote about the realities of war behind the patriotic speeches. He wrote about the suffering of people in war and their conflicts of conscience. His characters are often survivors who are unable to forget and return to their old ways. They are often looking for a new code of values untainted by the dishonesties and hypocrisies of the past. They are suspicious of big words; they would rather keep silent than keep on "telling lies." Often they find a more honest way of life in close contact with nature and with the animal world. Like many other modern writers, Hemingway takes us back to nature in search for the answer to the doubts and frustrations of modern civilization. Some of his best-known stories show us the hunter, following a hunter's code; or the bullfighter, confronting the bull in the ring; or an old man alone in a boat, doing battle with the great fish.

Ernest Hemingway became a living legend in his own time. He was one of the many American writers and artists who left their country after World War I and lived abroad as expatriates. He lived for a time in Paris and later in Cuba. He pursued a rugged outdoor life. He loved bullfighting, deep-sea fishing, and hunting. The short stories he wrote about the challenges and adventures of the world he loved are ranked by many people among the best ever written. As a boy, Hemingway had gone camping and hunting in the Michigan woods. In the following selection, he takes us along on the first day of a camping trip. He describes with loving care the little things that make up the first day and evening of the trip.

## Ernest Hemingway

# Big Two-Hearted River

The train went on up the track out of sight, around one of the hills of burnt timber. Nick sat down on the bundle of canvas and bedding the baggage man had pitched out of the door of the baggage car. There was no town, nothing but the rails and the burned-over country. The thirteen saloons that had lined the one street of

Seney had not left a trace. The foundations of the Mansion House hotel stuck up above the ground. The stone was chipped and split by the fire. It was all that was left of the town of Seney. Even the surface had been burned off the ground.

Nick looked at the burned-over stretch of hillside, where he had expected to find the scattered houses of the town, and then walked down the railroad track to the bridge over the river. The river was there. It swirled against the log spiles of the bridge. Nick looked down into the clear, brown water, colored from the pebbly bottom, and watched the trout keeping themselves steady in the current with wavering fins. As he watched them they changed their positions by quick angles, only to hold steady in the fast water again. Nick watched them a long time.

He watched them holding themselves with their noses into the current, many trout in deep, fast moving water, slightly distorted as he watched far down through the glassy convex surface of the pool, its surface pushing and swelling smooth against the resistance of the log-driven piles of the bridge. At the bottom of the pool were the big trout. Nick did not see them at first. Then he saw them at the bottom of the pool, big trout looking to hold themselves on the gravel bottom in a varying mist of gravel and sand, raised in spurts by the current.

Nick looked down into the pool from the bridge. It was a hot day. A kingfisher flew up the stream. It was a long time since Nick had looked into a stream and seen trout. They were very satisfactory. As the shadow of the kingfisher moved up the stream, a big trout shot upstream in a long angle, only his shadow marking the angle, then lost his shadow as he came through the surface of the water, caught the sun, and then, as he went back into the stream under the surface, his shadow seemed to float down the stream with the current, unresisting, to his post under the bridge where he tightened facing up into the current.

Nick's heart tightened as the trout moved. He felt all the old feeling.

He turned and looked down the stream. It stretched away, pebbly-bottomed with shallows and big boulders and a deep pool as it curved away around the foot of a bluff.

Nick walked back up the ties to where his pack lay in the cinders beside the railway track. He was happy. He adjusted the pack harness around the bundle, pulling straps tight, slung the pack on his back, got his arms through the shoulder straps and took some of the pull off his shoulders by leaning his forehead against the wide band of the tumpline. Still, it was too heavy. It was much too heavy. He had his leather rod-case in his hand and leaning forward to keep the weight of the pack high on his shoulders he walked along the road that paralleled the railway track, leaving the burned town behind in the heat, and then turned off around a hill with a high, fire-scarred hill on either side onto a road that went back into the country. He walked along the road feeling the ache from the pull of the heavy pack. The road climbed steadily. It was hard work walking uphill. His muscles ached and the day was hot, but Nick felt happy. He felt he had left everything behind, the need for thinking, the need to write, other needs. It was all back of him.

From the time he had gotten down off the train and the baggage man had thrown his pack out of the open car door things had been different. Seney was burned, the country was burned over and changed, but it did not matter. It could not all be burned. He knew that. He hiked along the road, sweating in the sun, climbing to cross the range of hills that separated the railway from the pine plains.

The road ran on, dipping occasionally,

but always climbing. Nick went on up. Finally the road after going parallel to the burnt hillside reached the top. Nick leaned back against a stump and slipped out of the pack harness. Ahead of him, as far as he could see, was the pine plain. The burned country stopped off at the left with the range of hills. On ahead islands of dark pine trees rose out of the plain. Far off to the left was the line of the river. Nick followed it with his eye and caught glints of the water in the sun.

There was nothing but the pine plain ahead of him, until the far blue hills that marked the Lake Superior height of land. He could hardly see them, faint and far away in the heat-light over the plain. If he looked too steadily they were gone. But if he only half-looked they were there, the far-off hills of the height of land.

Nick sat down against the charred stump and smoked a cigarette. His pack balanced on the top of the stump, harness holding ready, a hollow molded in it from his pack. Nick sat smoking, looking out over the country. He did not need to get his map out. He knew where he was from the position of the river.

As he smoked, his legs stretched out in front of him, he noticed a grasshopper walk along the ground and up onto his woolen sock. The grasshopper was black. As he had walked along the road, climbing, he had started many grasshoppers from the dust. They were all black. They were not the big grasshoppers with yellow and black or red and black wings whirring out from their black wing sheathing as they fly up. These were just ordinary hoppers, but all a sooty black in color. Nick had wondered about them as he walked, without really thinking about them. Now, as he watched the black hopper that was nibbling at the wool of his sock with its fourway lip, he realized that they had all turned black from living in the burned-over land. He realized that the fire must have come the year before, but the grasshoppers were all black now. He wondered how long they would stay that way.

Carefully he reached his hand down and took hold of the hopper by the wings. He turned him up, all his legs walking in the air, and looked at his jointed belly. Yes, it was black too, iridescent where the back and head were dusty.

"Go on, hopper," Nick said, speaking out loud for the first time. "Fly away somewhere."

He tossed the grasshopper up into the air and watched him sail away to a charcoal stump across the road.

Nick stood up. He leaned his back against the weight of his pack where it rested upright on the stump and got his arms through the shoulder straps. He stood with the pack on his back on the brow of the hill looking out across the country, toward the distant river and then struck down the hillside away from the road. Underfoot the ground was good walking. Two hundred yards down the hillside the fire line stopped. Then it was sweet fern, growing ankle high, to walk through, and clumps of jack pines; a long undulating country with frequent rises and descents, sandy underfoot and the country alive again.

Nick kept his direction by the sun. He knew where he wanted to strike the river and he kept on through the pine plain, mounting small rises to see other rises ahead of him and sometimes from the top of a rise a great solid island of pines off to his right or his left. He broke off some sprigs of the heathery sweet fern, and put them under his pack straps. The chafing crushed it and he smelled it as he walked.

He was tired and very hot, walking across the uneven, shadeless pine plain. At any time he knew he could strike the river by turning off to his left. It could not be more than a mile away. But he kept on toward the north to hit the river as far upstream as he could go in one day's walking.

For some time as he walked Nick had been in sight of one of the big islands of pine standing out above the rolling high ground he was crossing. He dipped down and then as he came slowly up to the crest of the bridge he turned and made toward the pine trees.

There was no underbrush in the island of pine trees. The trunks of the trees went straight up or slanted toward each other. The trunks were straight and brown without branches. The branches were high above. Some interlocked to make a solid shadow on the brown forest floor. Around the grove of trees was a bare space. It was brown and soft underfoot as Nick walked on it. This was the overlapping of the pine needle floor, extending out beyond the width of the high branches. The trees had grown tall and the branches moved high, leaving in the sun this bare space they had once covered with shadow. Sharp at the edge of this extension of the forest floor commenced the sweet fern.

Nick slipped off his pack and lay down in the shade. He lay on his back and looked up into the pine trees. His neck and back and the small of his back rested as he stretched. The earth felt good against his back. He looked up at the sky, through the branches, and then shut his eyes. He opened them and looked up again. There was a wind high up in the branches. He shut his eyes again and went to sleep.

Nick woke stiff and cramped. The sun was nearly down. His pack was heavy and the straps painful as he lifted it on. He leaned over with the pack on and picked up the leather rod case and started out from the pine trees across the sweet fern swale, toward the river. He knew it could not be more than a mile.

He came down a hillside covered with stumps into a meadow. At the edge of the meadow flowed the river. Nick was glad to get to the river. He walked upstream through the meadow. His trousers were soaked with the dew as he walked. After the hot day, the dew had come quickly and heavily. The river made no sound. It was too fast and smooth. At the edge of the meadow, before he mounted to a piece of high ground to make camp, Nick looked down the river at the trout rising. They were rising to insects come from the swamp on the other side of the stream when the sun went down. The trout jumped out of water to take them. While Nick walked through the little stretch of meadow alongside the stream, trout had jumped high out of water. Now as he looked down the river, the insects must be settling on the surface, for the trout were feeding steadily all down the stream. As far down the long stretch as he could see, the trout were rising, making circles all down the surface of the water, as though it were starting to rain.

The ground rose, wooded and sandy, to overlook the meadow, the stretch of river and the swamp. Nick dropped his pack and rod case and looked for a level piece of ground. He was very hungry and he wanted to make his camp before he cooked. Between two jack pines, the ground was quite level. He took the ax out of the pack and chopped out two projecting roots. That leveled a piece of ground large enough to sleep on. He smoothed out the sandy soil with his hand and pulled the sweet fern bushes by their roots. His hands smelled good from the sweet fern. He smoothed the uprooted earth. He did not want anything making lumps under the blankets. When he had the ground smooth, he spread his three blankets. One he folded double, next to the ground. The other two he spread on top.

With the ax he slit off a bright slab of pine from one of the stumps and split it into pegs for the tent. He wanted them long and solid to hold in the ground. With the tent unpacked and spread on the ground, the pack, leaning against a jack pine, looked much smaller. Nick tied the rope that served the tent for a ridgepole to the trunk of one of the pine trees and pulled the tent up off the ground with the other end of the rope and tied it to the other pine. The tent hung on the rope like a canvas blanket on a clothesline. Nick poked a pole he had cut up under the back peak of the canvas and then made it a tent by pegging out the sides. He pegged the sides out taut and drove the pegs deep, hitting them down into the ground with the flat of the ax until the rope loops were buried and the canvas was drum tight.

Across the open mouth of the tent Nick fixed cheesecloth to keep out mosquitoes. He crawled inside under the mosquito bar with various things from the pack to put at the head of the bed under the slant of the canvas. Inside the tent the light came through the brown canvas. It smelled pleasantly of canvas. Already there was something mysterious and homelike. Nick was happy as he crawled inside the tent. He had not been unhappy all day. This was different though. Now things were done. There had been this to do. Now it was done. It had been a hard trip. He was very tired. That was done. He had made his camp. He was settled. Nothing could touch him. It was a good place to camp. He was there, in the good place. He was in his home where he had made it. Now he was hungry.

He came out, crawling under the cheesecloth. It was quite dark outside. It was lighter in the tent.

Nick went over to the pack and found, with his fingers, a long nail in a paper sack of nails, in the bottom of the pack. He drove it into the pine tree, holding it close and hitting it gently with the flat of the ax. He hung the pack up on the nail. All his supplies were in the pack. They were off the ground and sheltered now.

Nick was hungry. He did not believe he had ever been hungrier. He opened and emptied a can of pork and beans and a can of spaghetti into the frying pan.

"I've got a right to eat this kind of stuff, if I'm willing to carry it," Nick said. His voice sounded strange in the darkening woods. He did not speak again.

He started a fire with some chunks of pine he got with the ax from a stump. Over the fire he stuck a wire grill, pushing the four legs down into the ground with his boot. Nick put the frying pan on the grill over the flames. He was hungrier. The beans and spaghetti warmed. Nick stirred them and mixed them together. They began to bubble, making little bubbles that rose with difficulty to the surface. There was a good smell. Nick got out a bottle of tomato catsup and cut four slices of bread. The little bubbles were coming faster now. Nick sat down beside the fire and lifted the frying pan off. He poured about half the contents out into the tin plate. It spread slowly on the plate. Nick knew it was too hot. He poured on some tomato catsup. He knew the beans and spaghetti were still too hot. He looked at the fire, then at the tent; he was not going to spoil it all by burning his tongue. For years he had never enjoyed fried bananas because he had never been able to wait for them to cool. His tongue was very sensitive. He was very hungry. Across the river in the swamp, in the almost dark, he saw a mist rising. He looked at the tent once more. All right. He took a full spoonful from the plate.

He ate the whole plateful before he remembered the bread. Nick finished the second plateful with the bread, mopping the plate shiny. He had not eaten since a cup of coffee and a ham sandwich in the station restaurant at St. Ignace. It had been a very fine experience. He had been that hungry before, but had not been able to satisfy it. He could have made camp hours before if he had wanted to. There were plenty of good places to camp on the river. But this was good.

Nick tucked two big chips of pine under the grill. The fire flared up. He had forgotten to get water for the coffee. Out of the pack he got a folding canvas bucket and walked down the hill, across the edge of the meadow, to the stream. The other bank was in the white mist. The grass was wet and cold as he knelt on the bank and dipped the canvas bucket into the stream. It bellied and pulled hard in the current. The water was ice cold. Nick rinsed the bucket and carried it full up to the camp. Up away from the stream it was not so cold.

Nick drove another big nail and hung up the bucket full of water. He dipped the coffeepot half full, put some more chips under the grill onto the fire, and put the pot on. He could not remember which way he made coffee. He could remember an argument about it with Hopkins, but

not which side he had taken. He decided to bring it to a boil. He remembered now that was Hopkins's way. He had once argued about everything with Hopkins. While he waited for the coffee to boil, he opened a small can of apricots. He liked to open cans. He emptied the can of apricots out into a tin cup. While he watched the coffee on the fire, he drank the juice syrup of the apricots, carefully at first to keep from spilling, then meditatively, sucking the apricots down. They were better than fresh apricots.

The coffee boiled as he watched. The lid came up and coffee and grounds ran down the side of the pot. Nick took it off the grill. It was a triumph for Hopkins. He put sugar in the empty apricot cup and poured some of the coffee out to cool. It was too hot to pour and he used his hat to hold the handle of the coffeepot. . . .

Nick drank the steaming coffee, the

coffee according to Hopkins. The coffee was bitter. Nick laughed. . . . His mind was starting to work. He knew he could choke it because he was tired enough. He spilled the coffee out of the pot and shook the grounds loose into the fire. He lit a cigarette and went inside the tent. He took off his shoes and trousers, sitting on the blankets, rolled the shoes up inside the trousers for a pillow, and got in between the blankets.

Out through the front of the tent he watched the glow of the fire, when the night wind blew on it. It was a quiet night. The swamp was perfectly quiet. Nick stretched under the blanket comfortably. A mosquito hummed close to his ear. Nick sat up and lit a match. The mosquito was on the canvas, over his head. Nick moved the match quickly up to it. The mosquito made a satisfactory hiss in the flame. The match went out. Nick lay down again under the blanket. He turned on his side and shut his eyes. He was sleepy. He felt sleep coming. He curled up under the blanket and went to sleep.

## YOU AND THE STORY

Ernest Hemingway was a great lover of the outdoors. Many of his best stories show his patient attention to the natural life around us and his respect for the creatures of the animal kingdom. How are we asked to see, and react to, our natural environment in this story? Answer the following questions:

(1) Hemingway's aim as a writer was to record honest firsthand experience. Often the central character in his stories is someone like Nick—someone who does not look at things superficially, someone who takes things in. When the author first mentions the trout, for instance, he says that "Nick watched them for a long time." How real or how vivid do the sights and activities of the camping trip become for you? Describe one of the following: the countryside, the river, the trout. Use as many details from the story as you can.

(2) Hemingway wrote many of his stories about characters who believed that there was a right way to act, a right way to do their job. They are often perfectionists; they judge people by how they do things that at first might not seem important. Can you show that Nick in this story is one of Hemingway's perfectionists? Find several examples of how Nick tries to do things just right. Explain what it takes to do them the right or proper way—fill in a would-be camper on how to do some of the things Nick does.

(3) Hemingway was suspicious of big displays of emotion. His characters often seem tight-lipped and unemotional on the surface. Nevertheless, the most important part of a Hemingway story is what the experience *meant* to the people involved. To find out their thoughts and feelings, we sometimes have to read between the lines. Or we may have to wait for a gesture or a comment that gives us a clue to what a character feels. At other times, the author tells us outright what the feelings of a character are.

—How or where do we find out Nick's feelings about the burned-over countryside? Are they what you would have expected? What are Nick's thoughts and feelings about the grasshopper?
—In the author's description of the hike to the campsite, find half a dozen comments on what Nick is feeling and thinking. Find some similar comments later in the story.
—How would you sum up Nick's feelings

about the trip? Are they easy to summarize? Why or why not?

---

**Your Turn**

---

Hemingway had little use for big words, and for talk that was just talk. His search for honesty is reflected in his own use of language. In this story, some of the sentences are packed with authentic firsthand detail. Other sentences are the short, bare-fact sentences that became a trademark of the much-imitated Hemingway style:

It had been a hard trip. He was very tired. That was done. He had made his camp. He was settled. Nothing could touch him. It was a good place to camp.

Write a passage of your own in which you take your reader outdoors. Your topic could be a trip to a park; an afternoon at a playground; an exploration of a vacant lot; a hike into back country; or the like. Include as much exact and vivid detail as you can. Make at least some use of short, matter-of-fact Hemingway sentences.

---

Language/Composition Activity B9

WRITING AND OBSERVATION

# A Stickler for Detail

Hemingway was a stickler for detail. He tried to get the real thing down on paper—just as it was, with no faking. Look at the following sample passages. Compare the abbreviated "shortcut" passage with the original passage that Hemingway actually wrote. Point out all the details that someone in a hurry would not have noticed. Point out all the details that a writer-in-a-hurry would not have bothered to put in.

SHORTCUT: Nick pounded a nail into a tree and hung his pack up on the nail.

ORIGINAL: Nick went over to the pack and found, with his fingers, a long nail in a paper sack of nails, in the bottom of the pack. He drove it into the pine tree, holding it close and hitting it gently with the flat of the ax. He hung the pack up on the nail. All his supplies were in the pack. They were off the ground and sheltered now.

SHORTCUT: He went down to the stream and got water for his coffee.

ORIGINAL: He had forgotten to get water for the coffee. Out of the pack he got a folding canvas bucket and walked down the hill, across the edge of the meadow, to the stream. The other bank was in the white mist. The grass was wet and cold as he knelt on the bank and dipped the canvas bucket into the stream. It bellied and pulled hard in the current. The water was ice cold. Nick rinsed the bucket and carried it full up to the camp. Up away from the stream it was not so cold.

**Your Turn:** Do a similar passage of your own. Describe something you do every day. Be a stickler for detail.

# The Gothic Imagination

Everyone is a moon and has a darker side
which he never shows to anybody.

—Mark Twain

Americans are famous for their optimism. The early political leaders of our country shared the philosophy of the eighteenth-century Enlightenment, which looked forward to a more hopeful future for humanity. They believed in the dignity of every individual. They believed in the ability of human beings to live together in liberty and brotherhood. Americans are brought up to believe that there is some good in everyone, and that problems can be solved by the good will of all concerned.

At the same time, we can observe in American life and American literature an older and different way of looking at humankind. The New England Puritans were deeply religious people who took literally the traditional belief in our sinful nature. They reminded themselves to be ever watchful for the evil that lurks in the human heart. They believed that the path to virtue was narrow, and that temptation and corruption were ever present around us. Some of the best-known American literature reminds us of the Puritans' suspicion of secret sin and their fear of the unfathomed human capacity for evil.

Puritan or not, writers have long known that the vivid portrayal of evil has the power to fascinate and thrill readers. American writers early borrowed from Europe the Gothic tale of horror. Its setting often was the "Gothic" architecture of medieval castles or monasteries, with their gloomy vaults and hidden passageways. In a setting of gloom and decay, the Gothic tale makes us witness the results of ancient crimes or age-old feuds. Tales of treachery and revenge act out our

worst nightmare fears. Strange supernatural events bring back forgotten terrors of childhood days.

Although it often takes place in a modern and realistic setting, much twentieth-century American fiction continues some of the traditions of the Gothic tale. It explores the human capacity for crankiness and cruelty and spite. It may confront us with sudden unexplained horror. Much American literature since its beginning mirrors a basic paradox: We want to believe in the native goodness of human beings. But we are forever fascinated with and perplexed by their capacity for conflict and violence.

## POEMS: The Owl Shall Stoop

Many modern poets have felt that we are often too eager to escape to a fantasy world more cheerful than the real world we live in. When we feel too self-satisfied, they remind us of some of the more discouraging facts of life. In much modern poetry, we find a strong sense of irony that makes the poet quick to see the other and darker side. Modern poets are quick to see the difference between good intentions and unexpected results. They are quick to see the ironic difference between neat theories and messy facts. Study the role of irony in the following modern poems.

Sylvia Plath

# The Water Rat

Droll, vegetarian, the water rat
Saws down a reed and swims from his limber grove,
While the students stroll or sit,
Hands laced, in a moony indolence of love—
Black-gowned, but unaware
How in such mild air
The owl shall stoop from his turret, the rat cry out.

### YOU AND THE POEM

(1) **Irony** is the effect produced when things go counter to expectation. In this poem, the description of the rat is ironically different from what we are used to: We expect rats to be repulsive; we associate them with filth or disease. What are the things that help make this rat seem amusing and harmless? How at the end does the poet make us think of it as if it were almost a human being?

(2) The setting in this poem is *idyllic*—everything is restful and pleasant. Point out several of the things that help make it so. Show the ironic contrast between the setting and what happens at the end.

(3) Read this short poem out loud. Try to make your listeners smile at the droll rat and shudder at the grim ending.

# Robinson Jeffers
# **Vulture**

I had walked since dawn and lay down to rest on a
  bare hillside
Above the ocean. I saw through half-shut eyelids a
  vulture wheeling high up in heaven,
And presently it passed again, but lower and nearer,
  its orbit narrowing, I understood then
That I was under inspection. I lay death-still and
  heard the flight-feathers
Whistle above me and make their circle and come
  nearer.

I could see the naked red head between the great
  wings
Bear downward staring. I said, "My dear bird, we are
  wasting time here.
These old bones will still work; they are not for
  you." But how beautiful he looked, gliding down
On those great sails; how beautiful he looked, veer-
  ing away in the sea-light over the precipice. I tell
  you solemnly
That I was sorry to have disappointed him. To be
  eaten by that beak and become part of him, to
  share those wings and those eyes—
What a sublime end of one's body, what an enskyment; What a life after death.

## YOU AND THE POEM

Robinson Jeffers (1887–1962) became known in the twenties and thirties for his poems attacking a vulgar commercialized modern mass society. He looked for honesty and nobility in a life closer to unspoiled wild nature. Born in Pennsylvania, he traveled much before he went to live on the spectacular Big Sur coast south of San Francisco. Answer the following questions about the poem:

(1) The word *sublime* describes a kind of pure, majestic, and awe-inspiring beauty that Robinson Jeffers often celebrated in his poetry. Why is this a strange word to use in a poem about this bird? What words or details earlier in the poem help us see the beauty that the poet sees in this bird?

(2) What does the word *enskyment* mean in this poem? (Show that the prefix *en-* is used with a similar meaning or in a similar way in words like *entomb*, *entrap*, *encode*, *engirdle*, and *ensnare*.)

**(3)** The poet says he is speaking to us "solemnly." As in other poems, he uses exceptionally long lines. Even so, his sentences often spill over from one line into the next. Find several examples, and read them out loud. Why do this poet's long lines lend themselves easily to a "solemn" reading? Point to the kind of repetition of similar structures that a speaker might use to reinforce a point in a solemn speech. Are there any parts of this poem that are less solemn and more playful than the rest?

Denise Levertov
# The Sharks

Well, then, the last day the sharks appeared.
Dark fins appear, innocent
as if in fair warning. The sea becomes
sinister, are they everywhere?
I tell you, they break six feet of water.
Isn't it the same sea, and won't we
play in it any more?
I like it clear and not
too calm, enough waves
to fly in on. For the first time
I dared to swim out of my depth.
It was sundown when they came, the time
when a sheen of copper stills the sea,
not dark enough for moonlight, clear enough
to see them easily. Dark
the sharp lift of the fins.

## YOU AND THE POEM

**(1)** How could the fins at first have appeared "innocent"? The sharks cause the sea to become "sinister," and the poem as a whole gives us a good feeling for what the word *sinister* means. What feelings does the word sum up in this poem?

**(2)** Denise Levertov (born 1923) came to the United States from England. Her poems often explore what is strange and ironic about human life. What is **ironic** about the appearance of the sharks in this poem? What is ironic about the poet's description of the experience? Point out as many examples of irony in this poem as you can.

## Ruth Herschberger
# Displays of Skill: The Bat

Being a mammal, I have less care than birds,
Being a flight-borne creature, need no home,
So while the beaver builds its, robin its nest,
I hook my hind feet into a wall or ceiling
And hang there looking at the world made silly
By being turned around and upside-down.
Sleep, sleep is my nourishment, I sleep
All day, all winter, and my young's but one.
At first I fly with it at my breast, even hunting,
But if it bores me I hang it on a wall
And go alone, enjoying insects frankly.
Tons, tons, I devour tons of insects, half
Of my weight is insects eaten within one night,
Yet cleverer than the swift or swallow, I deploy
Twist, turn, dodge, catch mosquitoes one by one.
And if the human family finds me odd,
No odder they, locked in their crazy yards.

### YOU AND THE POEM

(1) Imaginative literature often mirrors our feelings about what is alien and what is akin to us in nature. In the world of the poet's imagination, birds are often part of our happier moments. Bats have in the past often been associated with gloomy thoughts. Bats are, however, contradictory or paradoxical animals: To the student of biology, bats are mammals and therefore closer to us than birds. Organize some of the features of birds and bats under the following headings:

—what makes birds a welcome or cheering part of human experience

—what makes bats seem frightening or strange
—what *should* make birds seem strange
—what *should* make bats seem closer to us

(2) What are some of the things the poet does to make bats seem *less* alien, and in some ways almost human? Point out several details and expressions that make the bat seem less alien than we might expect.

### Your Turn

Choose an animal that might seem "odd" or alien to most people. What might it say about itself if it could talk?

Daniela Gioseffi

# Some Slippery Afternoon

A silver watch you've worn for years
is suddenly gone
leaving a pale white stripe
blazing on your wrist.

A calendar in which you've marked all the appointments
you've kept
(or meant to keep)
disappears
leaving a faded spot on the wall
where it hung.
You search the house and yard and trash cans for weeks
and never find it.

One night the glass in your windows
vanishes
leaving you sitting in a gust of wind.

You think how a leg is suddenly lost
beneath a subway train
or a taxi wheel
some slippery afternoon.

The child you've raised for years
combing each lock,
tailoring each smile, each tear,
each valuable thought,
suddenly metamorphoses into a harlequin
and joins the circus passing in the street
never to be seen again.

One morning you wash your face,
look into the mirror,
and find the water has eroded your features,
worn them smooth as a rock in a brook.
A blank oval peers back at you
too mouthless to cry out.

## YOU AND THE POEM

(1) Describe some of the things that are happening in this poem. Which of them seem like things that really might happen? Which seem most strange? What if anything do they all have in common?

(2) A metamorphosis is a sudden miraculous change into a completely different kind of being. What is a "harlequin"? Is what happens to the child like anything that might happen in real life?

(3) This is a poem about people's fears. What do you think this poet was most afraid of? What part of the poem is most frightening to you?

### Your Turn

Write a brief report from a world from which one of the following has just mysteriously disappeared:

—all clocks and watches
—all calendars
—all glass windows
—all children

## MASTER OF THE MACABRE: **Edgar Allan Poe**

Edgar Allan Poe (1809–1849) is known around the world as the master of the Gothic tale of gloom and terror. Poe had little use for the "dull realities" of science. He said of himself that the spirit of romance "taught me my alphabet." His poems and stories take us to the world of dream and nightmare. It is a world of ancient vaults dimly lit by flickering torches, of heavy doors grating on their hinges, of phantoms and the walking dead. In this nightmare world, we see half-mad characters act out fiendish schemes of revenge. We see bereaved people crazed with grief, yearning for things that cannot be. Poe did not have a happy or settled life. Born in Boston, he early lost both parents, and he quarreled much with his wealthy foster father. After several false starts, he was for a time successful and influential as an editor, writer, and reviewer for magazines that published many of his famous stories. But he had a reputation for quarrelsomeness and eccentricity. He died in misery and poverty. His poem "The Raven" and stories like "The Tell-Tale Heart," "The Murders in the Rue Morgue," "The Fall of the House of Usher," and "The Pit and the Pendulum" have been read by millions of readers. Poe was a deliberate craftsman whose theories about the writer's art influenced fellow writers, both in America and abroad.

Edgar Allan Poe

# Annabel Lee

It was many and many a year ago,
　　In a kingdom by the sea,
That a maiden there lived whom you may know
　　By the name of Annabel Lee;
And this maiden she lived with no other thought
　　Than to love and be loved by me.

*She* was a child and *I* was a child,
　　In this kingdom by the sea,
But we loved with a love that was more than love—
　　I and my Annabel Lee—
With a love that the wingéd seraphs of Heaven
　　Coveted her and me.

And this was the reason that, long ago,
　　In this kingdom by the sea,
A wind blew out of a cloud by night
　　Chilling my Annabel Lee;

So that her highborn kinsmen came
    And bore her away from me,
To shut her up in a sepulchre
    In this kingdom by the sea.

The angels, not half so happy in Heaven,
    Went envying her and me:
Yes! that was the reason (as all men know,
    In this kingdom by the sea)
That the wind came out of the cloud, chilling
    And killing my Annabel Lee.

But our love it was stronger by far than the love
    Of those who were older than we—
    Of many far wiser than we—
And neither the angels in Heaven above
    Nor the demons down under the sea,
Can ever dissever my soul from the soul
    Of the beautiful Annabel Lee:

*Drawing of Poe's wife, Virginia Clemm Poe.*

For the moon never beams without bringing me dreams
    Of the beautiful Annabel Lee;
And the stars never rise but I see the bright eyes
    Of the beautiful Annabel Lee;
And so, all the nighttide, I lie down by the side
Of my darling, my darling, my life and my bride,
    In her sepulchre there by the sea—
    In her tomb by the side of the sea.

---

## YOU AND THE POEM

(1) Poe often achieves a heightened, solemn effect by preferring an unusual word to a more familiar one that means roughly the same thing. In this poem, what more *unusual* word does he use for each of the following words: *girl, angel, relatives, separate, tomb?*

(2) Several of Poe's best-known poems express the speaker's wild grief for a lost love. What has actually happened in this poem? What is the story behind the poem? What are some of the things in it that would remind a reader of ancient tales told and retold many times?

(3) Your class may want to divide the stanzas of this poem among different speakers for a *choral reading.* Poe often takes us away from our prosaic everyday surroundings to dim, faraway places where we watch mysterious events. How should this poem be read for the dim, faraway, mysterious effect?

## Edgar Allan Poe
*from*
# Ulalume

*[In this selection from a longer poem, the poet is imagining a conversation between himself and Psyche—his soul.]*

The skies they were ashen and sober;
    The leaves they were crispéd and sere—
    The leaves they were withering and sere:
It was night, in the lonesome October
    Of my most immemorial year:
It was hard by the dim lake of Auber,[1]
    In the misty mid region of Weir[2]—
It was down by the dank tarn of Auber,
    In the ghoul-haunted woodland of Weir.

. . . . . . . . . . . . . . . . . . . . . . . . . . . . . . . . . . .

Here Psyche, uplifting her finger,
    Said: "Sadly this star I mistrust—
    Her pallor I strangely mistrust:
Ah, hasten!—ah, let us not linger!
    Ah, fly!—let us fly!—for we must."
In terror she spoke, letting sink her
    Wings till they trailed in the dust—
In agony sobbed, letting sink her
    Plumes till they trailed in the dust—
    Till they sorrowfully trailed in the dust.

I replied: "This is nothing but dreaming:
    Let us on by this tremulous light!
    Let us bathe in this crystalline light!
Its Sibyllic[3] splendor is beaming
    With Hope and in Beauty tonight:—
    See!—it flickers up the sky through the night!
Ah, we safely may trust to its gleaming,

[1]**Auber:** (1782–1871) French composer of ballet music.

[2]**Weir:** (1803–1889) American painter of misty landscapes.

[3]**Sibyllic:** referring to the prophetesses, the Sibylls, of classic mythology.

And be sure it will lead us aright—
We surely may trust to a gleaming,
    That cannot but guide us aright,
    Since it flickers up to Heaven through the night."

Thus I pacified Psyche and kissed her,
    And tempted her out of her gloom—
    And conquered her scruples and gloom;
And we passed to the end of the vista,
    But were stopped by the door of a tomb—
    By the door of a legended tomb;
And I said: "What is written, sweet sister,
    On the door of this legended tomb?"
She replied: "Ulalume—Ulalume—
    'Tis the vault of thy lost Ulalume!"
Then my heart it grew ashen and sober
    As the leaves that were crispéd and sere—
    As the leaves that were withering and sere;
And I cried: "It was surely October
    On *this* very night of last year
    That I journeyed—I journeyed down here!—
    That I brought a dread burden down here—
    On this night of all nights in the year,
    Ah, what demon has tempted me here?
Well I know, now, this dim lake of Auber—
    This misty mid region of Weir—
Well I know, now, this dank tarn of Auber,
    This ghoul-haunted woodland of Weir."

## YOU AND THE POEM

(1) Our vocabulary of the occult is often drawn from the spirit lore of other countries. Look at the following names of imaginary creatures and of people in various ways in touch with the supernatural. Consult a dictionary about the origin and meaning of each word in the following sets:

    a. *ghoul, demon, phantom, specter, spirit*

    b. *sybil, prophet, augur, oracle, visionary*

(2) This poem illustrates the kind of hypnotic **repetition** that helps create the highly charged emotional atmosphere of Poe's most famous poems. Point out several different kinds of repetition in this poem. Practice reading one of the stanzas: Pay special attention to the strong rhythm and to the echoing words and phrases that create the lush sound effects of Poe's poetry.

(3) Like some of Poe's most famous stories, this poem builds up to a highly emotional **climax**. How?

# Edgar Allan Poe

# The Black Cat

For the most wild yet most homely narrative which I am about to pen, I neither expect nor solicit belief. Mad indeed would I be to expect it, in a case where my very senses reject their own evidence. Yet, mad am I not—and very surely do I not dream. But tomorrow I die, and today I would unburden my soul. My immediate purpose is to place before the world, plainly, succinctly, and without comment, a series of mere household events. In their consequences, these events have terrified—have tortured—have destroyed me. Yet I will not attempt to expound them. To me, they have presented little but horror. Hereafter, perhaps, some intellect may be found which will reduce my phantasm to the commonplace—some intellect more calm, more logical, and far less excitable than my own, which will perceive, in the circumstances I detail with awe, nothing more than an ordinary succession of natural causes and effects.

From my infancy I was noted for the docility and humanity of my disposition. My tenderness of heart was even so conspicuous as to make me the jest of my companions. I was especially fond of animals, and was indulged by my parents with a great variety of pets. With these I spent most of my time, and never was so happy as when feeding and caressing them. This peculiarity of character grew with my growth, and, in my manhood, I derived from it one of my principal sources of pleasure. To those who have cherished an affection for a faithful and sagacious dog, I need hardly be at the trouble of explaining the nature or the intensity of the gratification thus derivable.

There is something in the unselfish and self-sacrificing love of a brute which goes directly to the heart of him who has had frequent occasion to test the paltry friendship and gossamer fidelity of mere *Man*.

I married early, and was happy to find in my wife a disposition not uncongenial with my own. Observing my partiality for domestic pets, she lost no opportunity of procuring those of the most agreeable kind. We had birds, goldfish, a fine dog, rabbits, a small monkey, and a *cat*.

This latter was a remarkably large and beautiful animal, entirely black, and sagacious to an astonishing degree. In speaking of his intelligence, my wife, who at heart was not a little tinctured with superstition, made frequent allusion to the ancient popular notion, which regarded all black cats as witches in disguise. Not that she was ever *serious* upon this point—and I mention the matter at all for no better reason than that it happens, just now, to be remembered.

Pluto—this was the cat's name—was my favorite pet and playmate. I alone fed him, and he attended me wherever I went about the house. It was even with difficulty that I could prevent him from following me through the streets.

Our friendship lasted, in this manner, for several years, during which my general temperament and character—through the instrumentality of the Fiend Intemperance—had (I blush to confess it) experienced a radical alteration for the worse. I grew, day by day, more moody, more irritable, more regardless of the feelings of others. I suffered myself to use intemperate language to my wife. At length, I even offered her personal violence. My pets, of course, were made to feel the change in my disposition. I not only neglected, but ill-used them. For Pluto, however, I still retained sufficient regard to restrain me from maltreating him, as I made no scruple of maltreating the rabbits, the monkey, or even the dog, when, by accident, or through affection, they came in my way. But my disease grew upon me—for what disease is like Alcohol!—and at length even Pluto, who was now becoming old, and consequently somewhat peevish—even Pluto began to experience the effects of my ill temper.

One night, returning home, much intoxicated, from one of my haunts about town, I fancied that the cat avoided my presence. I seized him; when, in his fright at my violence, he inflicted a slight wound upon my hand with his teeth. The fury of a demon instantly possessed me. I knew myself no longer. My original soul seemed, at once, to take its flight from my body; and a more than fiendish malevolence, gin-nurtured, thrilled every fiber of my frame. I took from my waistcoat pocket a penknife, opened it, grasped the poor beast by the throat, and deliberately cut one of its eyes from the socket! I blush, I burn, I shudder, while I pen the damnable atrocity.

When reason returned with the morning—when I had slept off the fumes of the night's debauch—I experienced a sentiment half of horror, half of remorse, for the crime of which I had been guilty; but it was, at best, a feeble and equivocal feeling, and the soul remained untouched. I again plunged into excess, and soon drowned in wine all memory of it.

In the meantime the cat slowly recovered. The socket of the lost eye presented, it is true, a frightful appearance, but he no longer appeared to suffer any pain. He went about the house as usual, but, as might be expected, fled in extreme terror at my approach. I had so much of my old heart left as to be at first grieved by this evident dislike on the part of a creature which had once so loved me. But this feeling soon gave place to irritation. And then came, as if to my final and irrevocable overthrow, the spirit of PERVERSENESS. Of this spirit philosophy takes no account. Yet I am not more sure that my soul lives than I am that perverseness is one of the primitive impulses of the human heart—one of the faculties, or sentiments, which give direction to the character of Man. Who has not, a hundred times, found himself committing a vile or a stupid action for no other reason than because he knows he should *not*? Have we not a perpetual inclination, in the teeth of our best judgment, to violate that which is *Law*, merely because we understand it to be such? This spirit of perverseness, I say, came to my final overthrow. It was this unfathomable longing of the soul *to vex itself*—to offer violence to its own nature—to do wrong for the wrong's sake only—that urged me to continue and finally to consummate the injury I had inflicted upon the unoffending brute. One morning, in cold blood, I slipped a noose about its neck and hung it to the limb of a tree—hung it with the tears streaming from my eyes, and with the bitterest remorse at my heart—hung it *because* I knew that it had loved me, and *because* I felt it had given me no reason of offence—hung it *because* I knew that in so doing I was committing a sin—a deadly sin that would so jeopardize my immortal soul as to place it—if such a thing were possible—even beyond the reach of the infinite mercy of the Most Merciful and Most Terrible God.

On the night of the day on which this most cruel deed was done, I was aroused from sleep by the cry of fire. The curtains surrounding my bed were in flames. The whole house was blazing. It was with

"singular!" and other similar expressions, excited my curiosity. I approached and saw, as if graven upon the white surface, the figure of a gigantic *cat*. The impression was given with an accuracy truly marvellous. There was a rope about the animal's neck.

When I first beheld this apparition—for I could scarcely regard it as less—my wonder and my terror were extreme. But at length reflection came to my aid. The cat, I remembered, had been hung in a garden adjacent to the house. Upon the alarm of fire, this garden had been immediately filled by the crowd—by some one of whom the animal must have been cut from the tree and thrown, through an open window, into my chamber. This had probably been done with the view of arousing me from sleep. The falling of other walls had compressed the victim of my cruelty into the substance of the freshly spread plaster, the lime of which, with the flames and the *ammonia* from the carcass, had then accomplished the portraiture as I saw it.

Although I thus readily accounted to my reason, if not altogether to my conscience, for the startling fact just detailed, it did not the less fail to make a deep impression upon my fancy. For months I could not rid myself of the phantasm of the cat; and, during this period, there came back into my spirit a half-sentiment that seemed, but was not, remorse. I went so far as to regret the loss of the animal, and to look about me, among the vile haunts which I now habitually frequented, for another pet of the same species, and of somewhat similar appearance, with which to supply its place.

One night as I sat, half stupefied, in a den of more than infamy, my attention was suddenly drawn to some black object reposing upon the head of one of the immense hogsheads of gin, or of rum, which consituted the chief furniture of

great difficulty that my wife, a servant, and myself made our escape from the conflagration. The destruction was complete. My entire worldly wealth was swallowed up, and I resigned myself thenceforward to despair.

I am above the weakness of seeking to establish a sequence of cause and effect, between the disaster and the atrocity. But I am detailing a chain of facts—and wish not to leave even a possible link imperfect. On the day succeeding the fire, I visited the ruins. The walls, with one exception, had fallen in. This exception was found in a compartment wall, not very thick, which stood about the middle of the house and against which had rested the head of my bed. The plastering had here, in great measure, resisted the action of the fire—a fact which I attributed to its having been recently spread. About this wall a dense crowd were collected, and many persons seemed to be examining a particular portion of it with very minute and eager attention. The words "strange!"

the apartment. I had been looking steadily at the top of this hogshead for some minutes, and what now caused me surprise was the fact that I had not sooner perceived the object thereupon. I approached it and touched it with my hand. It was a black cat—a very large one—fully as large as Pluto, and closely resembling him in every respect but one. Pluto had not a white hair upon any portion of his body; but this cat had a large, although indefinite splotch of white, covering nearly the whole region of the breast.

Upon my touching him, he immediately arose, purred loudly, rubbed against my hand, and appeared delighted with my notice. This, then, was the very creature of which I was in search. I at once offered to purchase it of the landlord; but this person made no claim to it—knew nothing of it—had never seen it before.

I continued my caresses, and when I prepared to go home, the animal evinced a disposition to accompany me. I permitted it to do so; occasionally stooping and patting it as I proceeded. When it reached the house it domesticated itself at once, and became immediately a great favorite with my wife.

For my own part, I soon found a dislike to it arising within me. This was just the reverse of what I had anticipated; but—I know not how or why it was—its evident fondness for myself rather disgusted and annoyed me. By slow degrees these feelings of disgust and annoyance rose into the bitterness of hatred. I avoided the creature, a certain sense of shame, and the remembrance of my former deed of cruelty, preventing me from physically abusing it. I did not, for some weeks, strike or otherwise violently ill-use it; but gradually—very gradually—I came to look upon it with unutterable loathing and to flee silently from its odious presence, as from the breath of a pestilence.

What added, no doubt, to my hatred of the beast was the discovery, on the morning after I brought it home, that, like Pluto, it also had been deprived of one of its eyes. This circumstance, however, only endeared it to my wife, who, as I have already said, possessed, in a high degree, that humanity of feeling which had once been my distinguishing trait and the source of many of my simplest and purest pleasures.

With my aversion to this cat, however, its partiality for myself seemed to increase. It followed my footsteps with a pertinacity which it would be difficult to make the reader comprehend. Whenever I sat, it would crouch beneath my chair or spring upon my knees, covering me with its loathsome caresses. If I arose to walk, it would get between my feet and thus nearly throw me down, or, fastening its long and sharp claws in my dress, clamber, in this manner to my breast. At such times, although I longed to destroy it with a blow, I was yet withheld from so doing, partly by a memory of my former crime, but chiefly—let me confess it at once—by absolute *dread* of the beast.

This dread was not exactly a dread of physical evil—and yet I should be at a loss how otherwise to define it. I am almost ashamed to own—yes, even in this felon's cell, I am almost ashamed to own—that the terror and horror with which the animal inspired me had been heightened by one of the merest chimeras it would be possible to conceive. My wife had called my attention, more than once, to the character of the mark of white hair, of which I have spoken, and which constituted the sole visible difference between the strange beast and the one I had destroyed. The reader will remember that this mark, although large, had been originally very indefinite; but by slow degrees—degrees nearly imperceptible, and which for a long time my reason struggled to reject as fanciful—it had, at length, assumed a rigorous distinction of outline. It was now the representation of an object that I shudder to name—and for this, above all, I loathed, and dreaded, and would have rid myself of the monster *had I dared*—it was now, I say, the image of a hideous—of a ghastly thing—of the GALLOWS!—oh, mournful and terrible engine of Horror and of Crime—of Agony and of Death!

And now was I indeed wretched beyond the wretchedness of mere Humanity. And *a brute beast*—whose fellow I had contemptuously destroyed—*a brute beast* to work out for *me*—for me, a man fashioned in the image of the High God—so much of insufferable woe! Alas! neither by day nor by night knew I the blessing of rest any more! During the former the creature left me no moment alone, and in the latter I started hourly from dreams of unutterable fear to find the hot breath of *the thing* upon my face, and its vast weight—an incarnate nightmare that I had no power to shake off—eternally upon my *heart*!

Beneath the pressure of torments such as these the feeble remnant of the good within me succumbed. Evil thoughts became my sole intimates—the darkest and most evil of thoughts. The moodiness of my usual temper increased to hatred of all things and of all mankind; while from the sudden, frequent, and ungovernable outbursts of a fury to which I now blindly abandoned myself, my uncomplaining wife, alas, was the most usual and the most patient of sufferers.

One day she accompanied me, upon some household errand, into the cellar of the old building which our poverty compelled us to inhabit. The cat followed me down the steep stairs, and, nearly throwing me headlong, exasperated me to madness. Uplifting an axe, and forgetting in my wrath the childish dread which had hitherto stayed my hand, I aimed a blow at the animal, which, of course, would have proved instantly fatal had it descended as I wished. But this blow was arrested by the hand of my wife. Goaded by the interference into a rage more than demoniacal, I withdrew my arm from her grasp and buried the axe in her brain. She fell dead upon the spot without a groan.

This hideous murder accomplished, I set myself forthwith and with entire deliberation, to the task of concealing the body. I knew that I could not remove it from the house, either by day or by night, without the risk of being observed by the neighbors. Many projects entered my mind. At one period I thought of cutting the corpse into minute fragments and destroying them by fire. At another, I resolved to dig a grave for it in the floor of the cellar. Again, I deliberated about casting it in the well in the yard—about packing it in a box, as if merchandise, with the usual arrangements, and so getting a porter to take it from the house. Finally I hit upon what I considered a far better expedient than either of these. I determined to wall it up in the cellar, as the monks of the Middle Ages are recorded to have walled up their victims.

For a purpose such as this the cellar was well adapted. Its walls were loosely constructed and had lately been plastered throughout with a rough plaster, which the dampness of the atmosphere had prevented from hardening. Moreover, in one of the walls was a projection, caused by a false chimney, or fireplace, that had been filled up and made to resemble the rest of the cellar. I made no doubt that I could readily displace the bricks at this point, insert the corpse, and wall the whole up as before so that no eye could detect any thing suspicious.

And in this calculation I was not deceived. By means of a crowbar I easily dislodged the bricks, and, having carefully deposited the body against the inner wall,

I propped it in that position, while with little trouble I relaid the whole structure as it originally stood. Having procured mortar, sand, and hair, with every possible precaution, I prepared a plaster which could not be distinguished from the old, and with this I very carefully went over the new brickwork. When I had finished, I felt satisfied that all was right. The wall did not present the slightest appearance of having been disturbed. The rubbish on the floor was picked up with the minutest care. I looked around triumphantly and said to myself: "Here at least, then, my labor has not been in vain."

My next step was to look for the beast which had been the cause of so much wretchedness; for I had, at length, firmly resolved to put it to death. Had I been able to meet with it at the moment, there could have been no doubt of its fate; but it appeared that the crafty animal had been alarmed at the violence of my previous anger and forbore to present itself in my present mood. It is impossible to describe or to imagine the deep, the blissful sense of relief which the absence of the detested creature occasioned in my bosom. It did not make its appearance during the night; and thus for one night, at least, since its introduction into the house, I soundly and tranquilly slept—aye, *slept* even with the burden of murder upon my soul.

The second and the third day passed, and still my tormentor came not. Once again I breathed as a free man. The monster, in terror, had fled the premises forever! I should behold it no more! My happiness was supreme! The guilt of my dark deed disturbed me but little. Some few inquiries had been made, but these had been readily answered. Even a search had been instituted—but of course nothing was to be discovered. I looked upon my future felicity as secured.

Upon the fourth day of the assassination, a party of the police came into the house, very unexpectedly, and proceeded again to make rigorous investigation of the premises. Secure, however, in the inscrutability of my place of concealment, I felt no embarrassment whatever. The officers bade me accompany them in their search. They left no nook or corner unexplored. At length, for the third or fourth time, they descended into the cellar. I quivered not in a muscle. My heart beat calmly as that of one who slumbers in innocence. I walked the cellar from end to end. I folded my arms upon my bosom, and roamed easily to and fro. The police were thoroughly satisfied and prepared to depart. The glee at my heart was too strong to be restrained. I burned to say if but one word, by way of triumph, and to render doubly sure their assurance of my guiltlessness.

"Gentlemen," I said at last, as the party ascended the steps, "I delight to have allayed your suspicions. I wish you all health and a little more courtesy. By the bye, gentlemen, this—this is a very well-constructed house," (in the rabid desire to say something easily, I scarcely knew what I uttered at all)—"I may say an *excellently* well-constructed house. These walls—are you going, gentlemen?—these walls are solidly put together"; and here, through the mere frenzy of bravado, I rapped heavily with a cane which I held in my hand, upon that very portion of the brickwork behind which stood the corpse of the wife of my bosom.

But may God shield and deliver me from the fangs of the Arch-Fiend! No sooner had the reverberation of my blows sunk into silence than I was answered by a voice from within the tomb!—by a cry, at first muffled and broken, similar to the sobbing of a child, and then suddenly swelling into one long, loud, and continuous scream, utterly anomalous and inhuman—a howl—a wailing shriek, half of horror and half of triumph, such as might have arisen only out of hell, conjointly from the throats of the damned in their agony and of the demons that exult in the damnation.

Of my own thoughts it is folly to speak. Swooning, I staggered to the opposite wall. For one instant the party on the stairs remained motionless, through extremity of terror and awe. In the next a dozen stout arms were toiling at the wall. It fell bodily. The corpse, already greatly decayed and clotted with gore, stood erect before the eyes of the spectators. Upon its head, with red extended mouth and solitary eye of fire, sat the hideous beast whose craft had seduced me into murder, and whose informing voice had consigned me to the hangman. I had walled the monster up within the tomb.

## YOU AND THE STORY

Poe's classic tales of crime and terror have had an uncanny hold on the imagination of readers everywhere. He was a master at telling us horrible and frightening things that still do not come as a complete surprise: They bring out into the open our own buried fears. They remind us of violent feelings that people are taught to overcome through rational behavior and good manners. What view of the darker side of human nature do we get in this famous story? Answer the following questions:

(1) People who study dreams recognize common age-old fears that people have always relived in their nightmares: the fear of the dark, the fear of falling from high places, and the like. In some of Poe's other stories, we encounter the age-old fear of pestilence, or the fear of being buried alive. What common fears play a strong role in this story? What events in the story bring them out in the reader? Describe several events in the story that produce a strong feeling of fear in the reader.

(2) The characters in Poe's stories often act out violent or abnormal feelings that normal or well-adjusted people have been taught to control. What are some of the violent feelings that play a role in this story? Can you help explain how the central character felt in his violent or destructive moments? Can you understand how he felt, or do his thoughts, feelings and actions seem completely "irrational"?

(3) Poe knew how to make the fantastic seem real to us. He knew how to carry us along in a story and to break down our defenses. In this story, the narrator several times makes a special effort to tell his story calmly and rationally, as a "series of mere household events." Point out things in the story that helped make the setting and the events seem real or believable for you.

### A Closer Look

Edgar Allan Poe was a master at creating a **mood**—an emotional atmosphere that for a time colors everything we sense and feel. He knew how to draw us into a story and make us feel in turn anger and regret, fear and relief, triumph and despair. What is the range of moods in this story? Select one or more of the following passages from this story. Describe the mood of the passage in your own words. Practice reading the passage you have chosen in such a way that your listeners will share the mood set by the passage.

a. My immediate purpose is to place before the world, plainly, succinctly, and without comment, a series of mere household events. In their consequences, these events have terrified— have tortured—have destroyed me. Yet I will not attempt to expound them. To me, they have presented little but horror. Hereafter, perhaps, some intellect may be found which will reduce my phantasm to the commonplace—some intellect more calm, more logical, and far less excitable than my own, which will perceive, in the circumstances I detail with awe, nothing more than an ordinary succession of very natural causes and effects.

b.   From my infancy I was noted for the docility and humanity of my disposition. My tenderness of heart was even so conspicuous as to make me the jest of my companions. I was especially fond of animals, and was indulged by my parents with a great variety of pets. With these I spent most of my time, and never was so happy as when feeding and caressing them. This peculiarity of character grew with my growth, and, in my manhood, I derived from it one of my principal sources of pleasure. To those who have cherished an affection for a faithful and sagacious dog, I need hardly be at the trouble of explaining the nature or the intensity of the gratification thus derivable. There is something in the unselfish and self-sacrificing love of a brute which goes directly to the heart of him who has had frequent occasion to test the paltry friendship and gossamer fidelity of mere *Man*.

c.   "Gentlemen," I said at last, as the party ascended the steps, "I delight to have allayed your suspicions. I wish you all health and a little more courtesy. By the bye, gentlemen, this—this is a very well-constructed house," (in the rabid desire to say something easily, I scarcely knew what I uttered at all)—"I may say an *excellently* well-constructed house. These walls—are you going, gentlemen?—these walls are solidly put together"; and here, through the mere frenzy of bravado, I rapped heavily with a cane which I held in my hand, upon that very portion of the brickwork behind which stood the corpse of the wife of my bosom.

d.   But may God shield and deliver me from the fangs of the Arch-Fiend! No sooner had the reverberation of my blows sunk into silence than I was answered by a voice from within the tomb!—by a cry, at first muffled and broken, like the sobbing of a child, and then quickly swelling into one long, loud, and continuous scream, utterly anomalous and inhuman—a howl—a wailing shriek, half of horror and half of triumph, such as might have arisen only out of hell, conjointly from the throats of the damned in their agony and of the demons that exult in the damnation.

---

### Your Turn

Long before the invention of writing, people were fascinated by dreams and visions and illusions. The interpretation of dreams has often been a solemn art. Tell your listener or your reader something that you have learned about dreams in your own reading or from television or films.

---

Language/Composition Activity B10

THE READER'S VOCABULARY
# The Monster Within the Tomb

Poe loved solemn words and strange words that helped him create a mood of mystery and gloom. How different from a reader's ordinary speaking vocabulary is Poe's choice of words?

A. Give a simpler or more ordinary word for ten of the following:

| | | | |
|---|---|---|---|
| NARRATIVE | CONSPICUOUS | ALTERATION | COMPREHEND |
| SOLICIT | BRUTE | MALTREAT | LOATHING |
| PERCEIVE | PALTRY | ATROCITY | SUCCUMB |
| INFANCY | PROCURE | DEBAUCH | DISLODGE |
| DISPOSITION | INTEMPERANCE | CONFLAGRATION | CONCEAL |

B. What does each of the following sentences say? What is the meaning of each italicized word as it is used in its sentence? From the list at the end, choose the meaning that fits the context.

1. My purpose is to tell my story plainly, *succinctly,* and without comment.
2. I will not attempt to *expound* the events.
3. Some intellect may reduce my *phantasm* to the commonplace.
4. I was *indulged* by my parents with a great variety of pets.
5. To those who have cherished an affection for a dog, I need not explain the *gratification* thus derivable.
6. My wife observed my *partiality* for domestic pets.
7. The animal was *sagacious* to an astonishing degree, and my wife often spoke of its intelligence.
8. My wife was at heart not a little *tinctured* with superstition.
9. A more than fiendish *malevolence* thrilled every fiber of my frame.
10. When reason returned in the morning, I felt *remorse.*
11. I knew the sin would *jeopardize* my immortal soul.
12. It was a feeble and *equivocal* feeling.
13. The cat had been hung in a garden *adjacent* to the house.
14. The animal *evinced* a disposition to accompany me.
15. With my *aversion* to the cat, however, its liking for me increased.
16. It followed me wherever I went with a *pertinacity* hard to believe.
17. I would look upon it with loathing and flee from its *odious* presence.
18. My terror was heightened by one of the merest *chimeras* that it would be possible to conceive.
19. The mark became more definite by slow, almost *imperceptible* degrees.
20. The cat had become an *incarnate* nightmare.
21. Nothing was discovered, and I looked upon my future *felicity* as secured.
22. I felt secure because of the *inscrutability* of my place of concealment.
23. Through mere *bravado,* I knocked on the new brickwork that hid the corpse.
24. The *reverberation* of my blows sank into silence.
25. I was answered by a scream utterly *anomalous* and inhuman.

Meanings:

a. very strong, painful regret
b. explain
c. intense ill will
d. echo
e. half-hearted
f. wise
g. fondness
h. touched, influenced
i. pleasure
j. very briefly and clearly
k. fantastic experience
l. spoiled, pampered
m. hateful
n. showed
o. endanger
p. happiness
q. neighboring, adjoining
r. made flesh and blood
s. dislike
t. stubborn determination
u. completely out of the ordinary
v. protection against discovery
w. impossible, far-fetched idea
x. too small to notice
y. foolish showing-off

● For a long time, many readers formed their ideas about the Puritan past by reading the fiction of Nathaniel Hawthorne (1804–1864). Hawthorne grew up and lived most of his life in the part of New England where the Puritans had first built their communities. He was born and lived for a long time in Salem, Massachusetts; he later lived in Concord. He worked as a customs official in Boston and Salem. (For a period of four years, he was an American consul in Liverpool, England.) Among his friends and asssociates were such New England writers as Melville, Emerson, and Thoreau. *The Scarlet Letter* (1850), Hawthorne's most famous novel, takes us back to colonial Boston and the stern religious morality of Puritan times. We see offenders against the strict moral standards of the time pilloried and exposed to public shame, and we see a minister preaching God's word but tortured by secret guilt. We watch people whose hatred of sin has turned them into stern judges of others. The Puritan suspicion of sin and ever-present evil also plays a central role in Hawthorne's best-known short stories, such as "The Minister's Black Veil" and "Young Goodman Brown." In this last story, first published in 1835,

Hawthorne takes us back to the time of King William of England, who reigned from 1689 to 1702. We hear people talk about such events as the war fought by the Indians under "King Philip" against the white settlers in 1675–1676. We find ourselves in a world where people believed in spirits and witches and in the wiles of the ever-present devil. Some of the witches named in the story were among those sentenced in the witch trials of Salem in 1692. One of Hawthorne's own ancestors had been a member of the court that condemned the witches. Modern historians tell us that the Puritan world was not all harsh and gloomy. Many Puritans went about their business cheerfully; they enjoyed their holidays and the good things of life. But many readers of Hawthorne came to know the Puritan past as a world of mystery and terror. They remembered people living in fear of human malice, of evil spirits, and of divine punishment for their own secret sins. In this reprinting of Hawthorne's story, a few expressions and spellings that have gone out of use have been modernized.

## Nathaniel Hawthorne

# Young Goodman Brown

Young Goodman Brown came forth at sunset into the street at Salem Village, but put his head back, after crossing the threshold, to exchange a parting kiss with his young wife. And Faith, as the wife was aptly named, thrust her own pretty head into the street, letting the wind play with the pink ribbons of her cap while she called to Goodman Brown.

"Dearest heart," whispered she, softly and rather sadly, when her lips were close to his ear, "prithee put off your journey until sunrise and sleep in your own bed tonight. A lone woman is troubled with such dreams and such thoughts that she's afraid of herself sometimes. Pray tarry with me this night, dear husband, of all nights in the year."

"My love and my Faith," replied Goodman Brown, "of all nights in the year, this one night must I tarry away from thee. My journey, as thou callest it, forth and back again, must needs be done between now and sunrise. What, my sweet, pretty wife, dost thou doubt me already, and we but three months married?"

"Then God bless you!" said Faith with the pink ribbons, "and may you find all well when you come back."

"Amen!" cried Goodman Brown. "Say thy prayers, dear Faith, and go to bed at dusk, and no harm will come to thee."

So they parted; and the young man pursued his way until, being about to turn the corner by the meetinghouse, he looked back and saw the head of Faith still peeping after him with a melancholy air, in spite of her pink ribbons.

"Poor little Faith!" thought he, for his heart smote him. "What a wretch am I to leave her on such an errand! She talks of dreams, too. Methought as she spoke there was trouble in her face, as if a dream had warned her what work is to be done tonight. But no, no; 'twould kill her to think it. Well, she's a blessed angel on earth; and after this one night I'll cling to her skirts and follow her to heaven."

With this excellent resolve for the future, Goodman Brown felt himself justified in making more haste on his present evil purpose. He had taken a dreary road, darkened by all the gloomiest trees of the forest, which barely stood aside to let the narrow path creep through and closed immediately behind. It was all as lonely as could be; and there is this peculiarity in such a solitude, that the traveler knows not who may be concealed by the innumerable trunks and the thick boughs overhead; so that with lonely footsteps he may yet be passing through an unseen multitude.

"There may be a devilish Indian behind every tree," said Goodman Brown to himself; and he glanced fearfully behind him as he added, "What if the devil himself should be at my very elbow!"

His head being turned back, he passed a crook of the road, and, looking forward again, beheld the figure of a man, in grave and decent attire, seated at the foot of an old tree. He arose at Goodman Brown's approach and walked onward side by side with him.

"You are late, Goodman Brown," said he. "The clock of the Old South Church was striking as I came through Boston, and that is full fifteen minutes agone."

"Faith kept me back a while," replied the young man, with a slight tremor in his voice, caused by the sudden appearance of his companion, though not wholly unexpected.

It was now deep dusk in the forest, and deepest in that part of it where these two were journeying. As nearly as could be discerned, the second traveler was about fifty years old, apparently in the same rank of life as Goodman Brown, and bearing a considerable resemblance to him, though perhaps more in expression than features. Still they might have been taken for father and son. And yet, though the elder person was simply clad as the younger, and as simple in manner too, he had an indescribable air of one who knew the world, and who would not have felt abashed at the governor's dinner table or in King William's court, were it possible that his affairs should call him thither. But the only thing about him that could be fixed upon as remarkable was his staff, which bore the likeness of a great black snake, so curiously wrought that it might almost be seen to twist and wriggle itself like a living serpent. This, of course, must have been a deception, assisted by the uncertain light.

"Come, Goodman Brown," cried his fellow traveler, "this is a dull place for the beginning of a journey. Take my staff if you are so soon weary."

"Friend," said the other, exchanging his slow pace for a full stop, "having kept covenant by meeting thee here, it is my purpose now to return whence I came. I have scruples touching the matter thou knowest of."

"Sayest thou so?" replied he of the serpent, smiling apart. "Let us walk on, nevertheless, reasoning as we go; and if I convince thee not thou shalt turn back. We are but a little way in the forest yet."

"Too far! too far!" exclaimed the goodman, unconsciously resuming his walk. "My father never went into the woods on such an errand, nor his father before him. We have been a race of honest men and good Christians since the days of the martyrs; and shall I be the first of the name of Brown that ever took this path and kept—"

"Such company, thou wouldst say," observed the elder person, interpreting his pause. "Well said, Goodman Brown! I have been as well acquainted with your family as with ever a one among the Puritans; and that's no trifle to say. I helped your grandfather, the constable, when he lashed the Quaker woman so smartly through the streets of Salem; and it was I that brought your father a pitch-pine knot, kindled at my own hearth, to set fire to an Indian village, in King Philip's war. They were my good friends, both; and many a pleasant walk have we had along this path, and returned merrily after midnight. I would fain be friends with you for their sake."

"If it be as thou sayest," replied Goodman Brown, "I marvel they never spoke of these matters; or, verily, I marvel not at all, seeing that the least rumor of the sort would have driven them from New England. We are a people of prayer, and good works to boot, and abide no such wickedness."

"Wickedness or not," said the traveler with the twisted staff, "I have a very general acquaintance here in New England. The deacons of many a church have drunk the communion wine with me; the selectmen of divers towns make me their chairman; and a majority of the Great and General Court are firm supporters of my interest. The governor and I, too—But these are state secrets."

"Can this be so?" cried Goodman Brown, with a stare of amazement at his undisturbed companion. "Howbeit, I have nothing to do with the governor and council; they have their own ways and are no rule for a simple husbandman like me. But, were I to go on with thee, how should I meet the eye of that good old man, our minister, at Salem village? Oh, his voice would make me tremble both Sabbath day and lecture day."

Thus far the elder traveler had listened with due gravity; but now burst into a fit of irrepressible mirth, shaking himself so violently that his snakelike staff actually seemed to wriggle in sympathy.

"Ha! ha! ha!" shouted he again and again; then composing himself, "Well, go on, Goodman Brown, go on; but, prithee, don't kill me with laughing."

"Well, then, to end the matter at once," said Goodman Brown, considerably nettled, "there is my wife, Faith. It would break her dear little heart; and I'd rather break my own."

"Nay, if that be the case," answered the other, "go thy ways, Goodman Brown. I would not for twenty old women like the one hobbling before us that Faith should come to any harm."

As he spoke he pointed his staff at a female figure on the path, in whom Goodman Brown recognized a very pious and exemplary dame who had taught him his catechism in youth and was still his moral and spiritual adviser, jointly with the minister and Deacon Gookin.

"A marvel, truly, that Goody Cloyse should be so far in the wilderness at nightfall," said he. "But with your leave, friend, I shall take a cut through the woods until we have left this Christian woman behind. Being a stranger to you, she might ask whom I was consorting with and whither I was going."

"Be it so," said his fellow traveler. "Betake you to the woods, and let me keep the path."

Accordingly the young man turned aside, but took care to watch his companion, who advanced softly along the road until he had come within a staff's length of the old dame. She, meanwhile, was making the best of her way, with singular speed for so aged a woman, and mumbling some indistinct words—a prayer, doubtless—as she went. The traveler put forth his staff and touched her withered neck with what seemed the serpent's tail.

"The devil!" screamed the pious old lady.

"Then Goody Cloyse knows her old friend?" observed the traveler, confronting her and leaning on his writhing stick.

"Ah, forsooth, and is it your worship indeed?" cried the good dame. "Yea, truly it is, and in the very image of my old gossip, Goodman Brown, the grandfather of the silly fellow that now is. But—would your worship believe it?—my broomstick hath strangely disappeared, stolen, as I suspect, by that unhanged witch, Goody Cory, and that, too, when I was all anointed with the juice of small-age, and cinquefoil, and wolf's bane—"

"Mingled with fine wheat and the fat of a newborn babe," said the shape of old Goodman Brown.

"Ah, your worship knows the recipe," cried the old lady, cackling aloud. "So, as I was saying, being all ready for the meeting, and no horse to ride on, I made up my mind to foot it; for they tell me there is a nice young man to be taken into communion tonight. But now your good worship will lend me your arm, and we shall be there in a twinkling."

"That can hardly be," answered her friend. "I may not spare you my arm, Goody Cloyse; but here is my staff, if you will."

So saying, he threw it down at her feet, where, perhaps, it assumed life, being one of the rods which its owner had formerly lent to the Egyptian magi. Of this fact however, Goodman Brown could not take cognizance. He had cast up his eyes in astonishment, and, looking down again, beheld neither Goody Cloyse nor the serpentine staff, but his fellow traveler alone, who waited for him as calmly as if nothing had happened.

"That old woman taught me my catechism," said the young man, and there was a world of meaning in this simple comment.

They continued to walk onward, while the elder traveler exhorted his companion to make good speed and persevere in the path, discoursing so aptly that his arguments seemed rather to spring up in the bosom of his auditor than to be suggested by himself. As they went, he plucked a branch of maple to serve for a walking stick and began to strip it of the twigs and little boughs, which were wet with evening dew. The moment his fingers touched them they became strangely withered and dried up as with a week's sunshine. Thus the pair proceeded, at a good free pace, until suddenly, in a gloomy hollow of the road, Goodman Brown sat himself down on the stump of a tree and refused to go any farther.

"Friend," said he, stubbornly, "my mind is made up. Not another step will I budge on this errand. What if a wretched old woman do choose to go to the devil when I thought she was going to heaven: is that any reason why I should quit my dear Faith and go after her?"

"You will think better of this by and by," said his acquaintance, composedly. "Sit here and rest yourself a while; and when you feel like moving again, there is my staff to help you along."

Without more words, he threw his companion the maple stick, and was as speedily out of sight as if he had vanished into the deepening gloom. The young man sat a few moments by the roadside, applauding himself greatly, and thinking with how clear a conscience he should meet the minister in his morning walk, nor shrink from the eye of good old Deacon Gookin. And what calm sleep would be his that very night, which was to have been spent so wickedly, but so purely and sweetly now, in the arms of Faith! Amidst these pleasant and praiseworthy meditations, Goodman Brown heard the tramp of horses along the road and deemed it advisable to conceal himself within the verge of the forest, conscious of the guilty purpose that had brought him thither, though now so happily turned from it.

On came the hoof tramps and the voices of the riders, two grave old voices, conversing soberly as they drew near. These mingled sounds appeared to pass along the road, within a few yards of the young man's hiding place; but, owing doubtless to the depth of the gloom at that particular spot, neither the travelers nor their steeds were visible. Though their figures brushed the small boughs by the wayside, it could not be seen that they intercepted, even for a moment, the faint gleam from the strip of bright sky athwart which they must have passed. Goodman Brown alternately crouched and stood on tiptoe, pulling aside the branches and thrusting forth his head as far as he dared without discerning so much as a shadow. It vexed him the more, because he could have sworn, were such a thing possible, that he recognized the voices of the minister and Deacon Gookin, jogging along quietly, as they were wont to do when bound to some ordination or ecclesiastical council. While yet within hearing, one of the riders stopped to pluck a switch.

"Of the two, reverend sir," said the voice like the deacon's, "I had rather miss an ordination dinner than tonight's meeting. They tell me that some of our community are to be here from Falmouth and beyond, and others from Connecticut and Rhode Island, besides several of the Indian powwows, who, after their fashion, know almost as much deviltry as the best of us. Moreover, there is a goodly young woman to be taken into communion."

"Mighty well, Deacon Gookin!" replied the solemn old tones of the minister. "Spur up, or we shall be late. Nothing can be done, you know, until I get on the ground."

The hoofs clattered again; and the voices, talking so strangely in the empty air, passed on through the forest, where no church had ever been gathered or solitary Christian prayed. Whither, then, could these holy men be journeying so deep into the heathen wilderness? Young Goodman Brown caught hold of a tree for support, being ready to sink down on the ground, faint and overburdened with the heavy sickness of his heart. He looked up to the sky, doubting whether there really was a heaven above him. Yet there was the blue arch, and the stars brightening in it.

"With heaven above and Faith below, I will yet stand firm against the devil!" cried Goodman Brown.

While he still gazed upward into the deep arch of the firmament and had lifted his hands to pray, a cloud, though no wind was stirring, hurried across the zenith and hid the brightening stars. The blue sky was still visible, except directly overhead, where this black mass of cloud was sweeping swiftly northward. Aloft in the air, as if from the depths of the cloud, came a confused and doubtful sound of voices. Once the listener fancied that he could distinguish the accents of townspeople of his own, men and women, both pious and ungodly, many of whom he had met at the communion table, and had seen others rioting at the tavern. The next moment, so indistinct were the sounds, he doubted whether he had heard aught but the murmur of the old forest, whispering without a wind. Then came a stronger swell of those familiar tones, heard daily in the sunshine at Salem village, but never until now from a cloud of night. There was one voice, of a young woman, uttering lamentations, yet with an uncertain sorrow, and entreating for some favor, which, perhaps, it would grieve her to obtain; and all the unseen multitude, both saints and sinners, seemed to encourage her onward.

"Faith!" shouted Goodman Brown, his voice filled with agony and desperation; and the echoes of the forest mocked him, crying, "Faith! Faith!" as if bewildered wretches were seeking her all through the wilderness.

The cry of grief, rage, and terror was yet piercing the night when the unhappy husband held his breath for a response. There was a scream, drowned immediately in a louder murmur of voices, fading into far-off laughter, as the dark cloud swept away, leaving the clear and silent sky above Goodman Brown. But something fluttered lightly down through the air and caught on the branch of a tree. The young man seized it, and beheld a pink ribbon.

"My Faith is gone!" cried he, after one stupefied moment. "There is no good on earth, and sin is but a name. Come, devil, for to thee is this world given."

And, maddened with despair so that he laughed loud and long, did Goodman

Brown grasp his staff and set forth again at such a rate that he seemed to fly along the forest path rather than to walk or run. The road grew wilder and drearier and more faintly traced, and vanished at length, leaving him in the heart of the dark wilderness, still rushing onward with the instinct that guides mortal man to evil. The whole forest was peopled with frightful sounds—the creaking of the trees, the howling of wild beasts, and the yell of Indians; while sometimes the wind tolled like a distant church bell, and sometimes gave a broad roar around the traveler, as if all Nature were laughing him to scorn. But he was himself the chief horror of the terrible scene and shrank not from its other horrors.

"Ha! ha! ha!" roared Goodman Brown when the wind laughed at him. "Let us hear which will laugh loudest. Think not to frighten me with your deviltry. Come witch, come wizard, come Indian powwow, come devil himself, and here comes Goodman Brown. You may as well fear him as he fears you."

In truth, all through the haunted forest there could be nothing more frightful than the figure of Goodman Brown. On he flew along the black pines, brandishing his staff with frenzied gestures, now giving vent to an inspiration of horrid blasphemy, and now shouting forth such laughter as set all the echoes of the forest laughing like demons around him. The fiend in his own shape is less hideous than when he rages in the breast of man. Thus sped the demoniac on his course, until, quivering among the trees, he saw a red light before him, as when the felled trunks and branches of a clearing have been set on fire and throw up their lurid blaze against the sky at the hour of midnight. He paused, in a lull of the tempest that had driven him onward, and heard the swell of what seemed a hymn, rolling solemnly from a distance with the weight of many voices. He knew the tune; it was a familiar one in the choir of the village meetinghouse. The verse died heavily away and was lengthened by a chorus, not of human voices, but of all the sounds of the benighted wilderness pealing in awful harmony together. Goodman Brown cried out, and his cry was lost to his own ear by its unison with the cry of the desert.

In the interval of silence he stole forward until the light glared full upon his eyes. At one extremity of an open space, hemmed in by the dark wall of the forest, arose a rock bearing some rude, natural resemblance either to an altar or a pulpit and surrounded by four blazing pines, their tops aflame, their stems untouched, like candles at an evening meeting. The mass of foliage that had overgrown the summit of the rock was all on fire, blazing high into the night and fitfully illuminating the whole field. Each twig and leafy festoon was in a blaze. As the red light arose and fell, a numerous congregation alternately shone forth, then disappeared in shadow, and again grew, as it were, out of the darkness, peopling the heart of the solitary woods at once.

"A grave and dark-clad company," quoth Goodman Brown.

In truth they were such. Among them, quivering to and fro between gloom and splendor, appeared faces that would be seen next day at the council board of the province, and others which, Sabbath after Sabbath, looked devoutly heavenward and benignantly over the crowded pews from the holiest pulpits in the land. Some affirm that the lady of the governor was there. At least there were high dames well known to her, and wives of honored husbands, and widows, a great multitude, and ancient maidens, all of excellent repute, and fair young girls, who trembled lest their mothers should spy them. Either the sudden gleams of light flashing over the obscure field bedazzled Goodman Brown, or he recognized a score of the church members of Salem village famous for their especial sanctity. Good old Deacon Gookin had arrived and waited at the skirts of that venerable saint, his revered pastor. But, irreverently consorting with these grave, reputable, and pious people, these elders of the church, these chaste dames and dewy virgins, there were men of dissolute lives and women of spotted fame, wretches given over to all mean and filthy vice and suspected even of horrid crimes. It was strange to see that the good shrank not from the wicked, nor were the sinners abashed by the saints. Scattered also among their pale-faced enemies were the Indian priests, or powwows, who had often scared their native forest with more hideous incantations than any known to English witchcraft.

"But where is Faith?" thought Goodman Brown, and, as hope came into his heart, he trembled.

Another verse of the hymn arose, a slow and mournful strain such as the pious love, but joined to words which expressed all that our nature can conceive of sin, and darkly hinted at far more. Unfathomable to mere mortals is the lore of fiends. Verse after verse was sung; and still the chorus of the desert swelled between like the deepest tone of a mighty organ; and with the final peal of that dreadful anthem there came a sound, as if the roaring wind, the rushing streams, the howling beasts, and every other voice of the unconcerted wilderness were mingling and according with the voice of guilty man in homage to the prince of all. The four blazing pines threw up a loftier flame and obscurely discovered shapes and visages of horror on the smoke wreaths above the impious assembly. At the same moment the fire on the rock shot redly forth and formed a glowing arch above its base, where suddenly appeared a figure. With reverence be it spoken, the figure bore no slight similitude, both in garb and manner, to some grave divine of the New England churches.

"Bring forth the converts!" cried a voice echoed through the field and rolled into the forest.

At the word, Goodman Brown stepped forth from the shadow of the trees and approached the congregation, with whom he felt a loathful brotherhood by the sympathy of all that was wicked in his heart. He could have well-nigh sworn that the shape of his own dead father beckoned him to advance, looking downward from a smoke wreath, while a woman, with dim features of despair, threw out her hand to warn him back. Was it his mother? But he had no power to retreat one step, nor to resist, even in thought, when the minister and good old Deacon Gookin seized his arms and led him to the blazing rock. Thither came also the slender form of a veiled female, led between Goody Cloyse, that pious teacher of the catechism, and Martha Carrier, who had received the devil's promise to be queen of hell. A rampant hag was she. And there stood the proselytes beneath the canopy of fire.

"Welcome, my children," said the dark figure, "to the communion of your race. Ye have found thus young your nature and your destiny. My children look behind you!"

They turned, and flashing forth, as it were, in a sheet of flame, the fiend worshipers were seen; the smile of welcome gleamed darkly on every visage.

"There," resumed the sable form, "are all whom ye have reverenced from youth. Ye deemed them holier than yourselves and shrank from your own sin, contrasting it with their lives of righteousness and prayerful aspirations heavenward. Yet here are they all in my worshiping assembly. This night it shall be granted you to know their secret deeds: how hoary-bearded elders of the church have whispered wanton words to the young maids of their households; how many a woman, eager for widows' weeds, has given her husband a drink at bedtime and let him sleep his last sleep in her bosom; how beardless youths have made haste to inherit their fathers' wealth; and how fair damsels—blush not, sweet ones—have dug little graves in the garden, and bidden me, the sole guest, to an infant's funeral. By the sympathy of your human hearts for sin ye shall scent out all the places—whether in church, bedchamber, street, field, or forest—where crime has been committed, and shall exult to behold the whole earth one stain of guilt, one mighty blood spot. Far more than this. It shall be yours to penetrate, in every bosom, the deep mystery of sin, the fountain of all wicked arts, and which inexhaustibly supplies more evil impulses than human power—than my power at its utmost—can make manifest in deeds. And now, my children, look upon each other."

They did so; and, by the blaze of the hell-kindled torches, the wretched man beheld his Faith, and the wife her husband, trembling before that unhallowed altar.

"Lo, there ye stand, my children," said the figure, in a deep and solemn tone, almost sad with its despairing awfulness, as if his once angelic nature could yet mourn for our miserable race. "Depending upon one another's hearts, ye had still hoped that virtue were not all a dream. Now are ye undeceived. Evil is the nature of mankind. Evil must be your only happiness. Welcome again, my children, to the communion of your race."

"Welcome," repeated the fiend worshipers, in one cry of despair and triumph.

And there they stood, the only pair, as it seemed, who were yet hesitating on the verge of wickedness in this dark world. A basin was hollowed, naturally, in the rock. Did it contain water, reddened by the lurid light? or was it blood? or, perchance, a liquid flame? Herein did the shape of evil dip his hand and prepare to lay the mark of baptism upon their foreheads, that they might be partakers of the mystery of sin, more conscious of the secret guilt of others, both in deed and thought, than they could now be of their own. The husband cast one look at his pale wife, and Faith at him. What polluted wretches would the next glance show them to each other, shuddering alike at what they disclosed and what they saw!

"Faith! Faith!" cried the husband, "look up to heaven, and resist the wicked one."

Whether Faith obeyed he knew not. Hardly had he spoken when he found himself amid calm night and solitude, listening to a roar of the wind which died heavily away through the forest. He staggered against the rock and felt it chill and damp, while a hanging twig, that had been all on fire, besprinkled his cheek with the coldest dew.

The next morning young Goodman Brown came slowly into the street of Salem village, staring around him like a bewildered man. The good old minister was taking a walk along the graveyard to get an appetite for breakfast and meditate his sermon, and bestowed a blessing, as he passed, on Goodman Brown. He shrank from the venerable saint as if to avoid an anathema. Old Deacon Gookin was at domestic worship, and the holy words of his prayer were heard through the open window. "What God doth the wizard pray to?" quoth Goodman Brown. Goody Cloyse, that excellent old Christian, stood in the early sunshine at her own lattice, catechizing a little girl who had brought her a pint of morning's milk. Goodman Brown snatched away the child as from the grasp of the fiend himself. Turning the corner by the meetinghouse, he spied the head of Faith, with the pink ribbons, gazing anxiously forth, and bursting into such joy at the sight of him that she skipped along the street and almost kissed her husband before the whole village. But Goodman Brown looked sternly and sadly into her face and passed on without a greeting.

Had Goodman Brown fallen asleep in the forest and only dreamed a wild dream of a witch meeting?

Be it so if you will; but, alas! it was a dream of evil omen for young Goodman Brown. A stern, a sad, a darkly meditative, a distrustful, if not a desperate man did he become from the night of that fearful dream. On the Sabbath day, when the congregation were singing a holy psalm, he could not listen because an anthem of sin rushed loudly upon his ear and drowned all the blessed strain. When the minister spoke from the pulpit with power and fervid eloquence, and, with his hand on the open Bible, of the sacred truths of our religion, and of saintlike lives and triumphant deaths, and of future bliss or misery unutterable, then did Goodman Brown turn pale, dreading lest the roof should thunder down upon the gray blasphemer and his hearers. Often, waking suddenly at midnight, he shrank from the bosom of Faith; and at morning or eventide, when the family knelt down at prayer, he scowled and muttered to himself, and gazed sternly at his wife, and turned away. And when he lived long, and was borne to his grave a hoary corpse, followed by Faith, an aged woman, and children and grandchildren, a goodly procession, besides neighbors not a few, they carved no hopeful verse upon his tombstone, for his dying hour was gloom.

## YOU AND THE STORY

A story can help create a feeling of mystery by its **ambiguity**. It may raise questions in our minds that do not have one simple answer. It may show us events that could mean different things. Though this story starts in a tender and fairly cheerful mood, it gradually turns into a nightmare vision. Toward the end, the author asks, "Had Goodman Brown fallen asleep in the forest and only dreamed a wild dream of a witch meeting?" How would you answer this question? As you read the story, does it seem real or like a dream? The author tells us that Faith "was aptly named." Is she a real person or a symbol of the young man's faith? What evidence from the story can you present to support your answer?

### A Closer Look

(1) From the beginning Hawthorne creates a sense of foreboding. We are made to ponder things that may be ordinary—but that more likely are not. We suspect they have a serious or ominous meaning that will become clear to us later. When young Goodman Brown meets the second traveler at the beginning of the story, what is the meaning of the following hints?

—The sudden appearance of the other traveler caused a "tremor in his voice," but at the same time it was "not wholly unexpected."
—The traveler had a "considerable resemblance" to him, and they "might have been taken for father and son."
—The traveler seemed like someone "who knew the world" and would have been comfortable in the governor's mansion or the king's court.
—The traveler had a staff or cane similar to a great black snake, or serpent.
—The traveler says he assisted Goodman Brown's grandfather and father in certain activities. What kind? How and why?

(2) After watching the conversation between the second traveler and Goody Cloyse, the young man says, "That old woman taught me my catechism." And Hawthorne adds, "There was a world of meaning in this simple comment." What was that "world of meaning"? How does it fit in with other things we have heard or learned in the story so far?

(3) The Puritans stressed the need for a constant fight against temptation. They talked and wrote much about the struggle between good and evil that takes place in the human soul. Find several passages that show us Goodman Brown's *resistance* to evil—his reluctance or scruples. How or why are they overcome?

(4) People have often felt that the worst evil results from good things being corrupted and turned to evil uses. The story reminds us of the devil's own "once angelic nature": Satan had once been the brightest angel in heaven, before his sinful pride made him rebel against the Almighty. In this story, devil-worship is described as a **caricature** of traditional religious beliefs and practices—an imitation that holds them up to ridicule by turning them upside down. In the description of the witches' meeting, find half a dozen terms from the vocabulary of religion and worship. Show how they are used.

(5) At the end of the story, young Goodman Brown has become a sad and stern and perhaps even desperate man. But during the story, we witness various things that are strange in a way that makes us want to laugh or smile. Where in the story did you find evidence of the author's sense of humor?

---

## Your Turn

---

The Puritans lived far from traditional civilization, close to untamed nature. What role does nature play as a setting or as an influence in this story? What thoughts or associations does the natural setting bring to the author's or the reader's mind? Compare and contrast the role of nature in this story with its treatment by other writers in this volume.

---

Language/Composition Activity B11

OUR CHANGING LANGUAGE
# The Heart of the Wilderness

Hawthorne in this story takes us back to the end of the seventeenth century. He tries to make his characters sound the way their contemporaries might have spoken in those days. Dictionaries use the label *archaic* for words and expressions that have slowly gone out of use and that we encounter only rarely today: *whither* (where to?); *thither* (to that place, there); *methinks* or *methought* (I think or I thought); *prithee* (please); *thou, thee, thy* (you, your); *dost* (do); *quoth* (said); *must needs* (must). To modern readers, Hawthorne's own nineteenth-century language has come to sound old-fashioned. For

*(continued on page 350)*

(continued from previous page)

each of the italicized archaic or old-fashioned words, select the meaning that fits the context.

1. Faith asked him to put off his journey and *tarry* with her.
2. When Goodman Brown left his wife, his heart *smote* him, and he said, "What a wretch am I to leave her!"
3. As nearly as could be *discerned,* the second traveler was about fifty years old.
4. The traveler had the air of someone who knew the world and who would not have felt *abashed* at the governor's dinner table.
5. His staff was so curiously *wrought* that it seemed to wiggle like a serpent.
6. Young Brown had kept *covenant* by meeting the stranger in the forest.
7. I would *fain* be friends with you.
8. The traveler claimed to know well the public officials of *divers* towns.
9. The older man at first listened with due *gravity* but then burst into laughter.
10. Goodman Brown was considerably *nettled* when his companion laughed at him.
11. Goodman Brown was afraid Goody Cloyse would ask about the person he was *consorting* with.
12. The traveler asked his companion to *betake him* to the woods.
13. Goody Cloyse made her way with *singular* speed for so aged a woman.
14. The staff perhaps came to life, but Goodman Brown could not *take cognizance* of the fact.
15. The older traveler was *discoursing* so aptly that his arguments seemed to the listener like his own.
16. Goodman Brown was thinking of his pure and sweet wife, but his pleasant *meditations* were interrupted.
17. He did not see the speakers cross the faint beam of light from a strip of bright sky *athwart* which they must have passed.
18. The minister and the deacon were jogging along quietly, as they were *wont* to do.
19. The figure on the rock resembled some grave *divine* of the New England churches.
20. The smile of welcome gleamed darkly on every *visage.*

Meanings:

| | |
|---|---|
| a. bashful | k. talking |
| b. take in | l. thoughts |
| c. made out, observed | m. minister |
| d. across | n. seriousness |
| e. struck, hurt | o. gladly, willingly |
| f. made (by hand) | p. go |
| g. various | q. solemn agreement |
| h. keeping company | r. accustomed |
| i. exceptional | s. face |
| j. annoyed | t. stay |

● William Faulkner (1897–1962) was born in Mississippi. He served in the British Royal Air Force in World War I, and spent several years in New Orleans as a young writer. He spent most of his later years in Oxford, Mississippi. He became perhaps the most widely admired American novelist of the twentieth century and received the Nobel Prize for literature in 1950. His books include *The Sound and the Fury* (1929), *Light in August* (1932), and *Absalom, Absalom!* (1936). Many of his books and stories trace the history of several families living in his fictional Yoknapatawpha County: the Sartorises, the Compsons, the Sutpens, and others. In writing about these people, Faulkner brings back to life a story of pride, conflict, and defeat that had been part of his own family's past. His great-grandfather had made himself rich and famous in the Mississippi of the days before the Civil War. He became a colonel in the Confederate army and was killed years later in a duel. Faulkner's stories of the American South often show us families that were once wealthy but that are now impoverished after the War Between the States. They often show us people embittered by seeing their values threatened in an uprooted modern world. As a storyteller, Faulkner often did not report events in strict chronological order. Instead, he recorded the roundabout and contradictory thoughts and feelings of his characters. What goes on in their minds is as important as what happens in the world around them. Writers around the world have tried to imitate William Faulkner's difficult style. They have copied his flashbacks and hints and many-layered sentences. The following story illustrates some of the outstanding features of Faulkner's fiction.

William Faulkner

# The Tall Men

They passed the dark bulk of the cotton gin. Then they saw the lamplit house and the other car, the doctor's coupé, just stopping at the gate, and they could hear the hound baying.

"Here we are," the old deputy marshal said.

"What's that other car?" the younger man said, the stranger, the state draft investigator.

"Doctor Schofield's," the marshal said.

"Lee McCallum asked me to send him out when I telephoned we were coming."

"You mean you warned them?" the investigator said. "You telephoned ahead that I was coming out with a warrant for these two evaders? Is this the way you carry out the orders of the United States Government?"

The marshal was a lean, clean old man who chewed tobacco, who had been born and lived in the country all his life.

"I understood all you wanted was to arrest these two McCallum boys and bring them back to town," he said.

"It was!" the investigator said. "And now you have warned them, given them a chance to run. Possibly put the Government to the expense of hunting them down with troops. Have you forgotten that you are under a bond yourself?"

"I ain't forgot it," the marshal said. "And ever since we left Jefferson I been trying to tell you something for you not to forget. But I reckon it will take these McCallums to impress that on you. . . . Pull in behind the other car. We'll try to find out first just how sick whoever it is that is sick is."

The investigator drew up behind the other car and switched off and blacked out his lights. "These people," he said. Then he thought, *But this doddering, tobacco-chewing old man is one of them, too, despite the honor and pride of his office, which should have made him different.* So he didn't speak it aloud, removing the keys and getting out of the car, and then locking the car itself, rolling the windows up first, thinking, *These people who lie about and conceal the ownership of land and property in order to hold relief jobs which they have no intention of performing, standing on their constitutional rights against having to work, who jeopardize the very job itself through petty and transparent subterfuge to acquire a free mattress which they intend to attempt to sell; who would relinquish even the job, if by so doing they could receive free food and a place, any rathole, in town to sleep in; who, as farmers, make false statements to get seed loans which they will later misuse, and then react in loud vituperative outrage and astonishment when caught at it. And then, what at long last a suffering and threatened Government asks one thing of them in return, one thing simply, which is to put their names down on a selective-service list, they refuse to do it.*

The old marshal had gone on. The investigator followed, through a stout paintless gate in a picket fence, up a broad brick walk between two rows of old shabby cedars, toward the rambling and likewise paintless sprawl of the two-story house in the open hall of which the soft lamplight glowed and the lower story of which, as the investigator now perceived, was of logs.

He saw a hall full of soft lamplight beyond a stout paintless gallery running across the log front, from beneath which the same dog which they had heard, a big hound, came booming again, to stand four-square facing them in the walk, bellowing, until a man's voice spoke to it from the house. He followed the marshal up the steps onto the gallery. Then he saw the man standing in the door, waiting for them to approach—a man of about forty-five, not tall, but blocky, with a brown, still face and horseman's hands, who looked at him once, brief and hard, and then no more, speaking to the marshal, "Howdy, Mr. Gombault. Come in."

"Howdy, Rafe," the marshal said. "Who's sick?"

"Buddy," the other said. "Slipped and caught his leg in the hammer mill this afternoon."

"Is it bad?" the marshal said.

"It looks bad to me," the other said. "That's why we sent for the doctor instead of bringing him in to town. We couldn't get the bleeding stopped."

"I'm sorry to hear that," the marshal said. "This is Mr. Pearson." Once more the investigator found the other looking at him, the brown eyes still, courteous enough in the brown face, the hand he offered hard enough, but the clasp quite limp, quite cold. The marshal was still speaking. "From Jackson. From the draft board." Then he said, and the investigator

could discern no change whatever in his tone: "He's got a warrant for the boys."

The investigator could discern no change whatever anywhere. The limp hard hand merely withdrew from his, the still face now looking at the marshal. "You mean we have declared war?"

"No," the marshal said.

"That's not the question, Mr. McCallum," the investigator said. "All required of them was to register. Their numbers might not even be drawn this time; under the law of averages, they probably would not be. But they refused—failed, anyway—to register."

"I see," the other said. He was not looking at the investigator. The investigator couldn't tell certainly if he was even looking at the marshal, although he spoke to him, "You want to see Buddy? The doctor's with him now."

"Wait," the investigator said. "I'm sorry about your brother's accident, but I—" The marshal glanced back at him for a moment, his shaggy gray brows beetling, with something at once courteous yet a little impatient about the glance, so that during the instant the investigator sensed from the old marshal the same quality which had been in the other's brief look. The investigator was a man of better than average intelligence; he was already becoming aware of something a little different here from what he had expected. But he had been in relief work in the state several years, dealing almost exclusively with country people, so he still believed he knew them. So he looked at the old marshal, thinking, *Yes. The same sort of people, despite the office, the authority, and responsiblity which should have changed him.* Thinking again, *These people. These people.* "I intend to take the night train back to Jackson," he said. "My reservation is already made. Serve the warrant and we will—"

"Come along," the old marshal said. "We are going to have plenty of time."

So he followed—there was nothing else to do—fuming and seething, attempting in the short length of the hall to regain control of himself in order to control the situation, because he realized now that if the situation were controlled, it would devolve upon him to control it; that if their departure with their prisoners were expedited, it must be himself and not the old marshal who would expedite it. He had been right. The doddering old officer was not only at bottom one of these people, he had apparently been corrupted anew to his old, inherent, shiftless sloth and unreliability merely by entering the house. So he followed in turn, down the hall and into the bedroom; whereupon he looked about him not only with amazement but with something very like terror. The room was a big room, with a bare unpainted floor, and besides the bed, it contained only a chair or two and one other piece of old-fashioned furniture. Yet to the investigator it seemed so filled with tremendous men cast in the same mold as the man who had met them that the very walls themselves must bulge. Yet they were not big, not tall, and it was not vitality, exuberance, because they made no sound, merely looking quietly at him where he stood in the door, with faces bearing an almost identical stamp of kinship—a thin, almost frail old man of about seventy, slightly taller than the others; a second one, white-haired, too,

but otherwise identical with the man who had met them at the door; a third one about the same age as the man who had met them, but with something delicate in his face and something tragic and dark and wild in the same dark eyes; the two absolutely identical blue-eyed youths; and lastly the blue-eyed man on the bed over which the doctor, who might have been any city doctor, in his neat city suit, leaned—all of them turning to look quietly at him and the marshal as they entered. And he saw, past the doctor, the slit trousers of the man on the bed and the exposed, bloody, mangled leg, and he turned sick, stopping just inside the door under that quiet, steady regard while the marshal went up to the man who lay on the bed, smoking a cob pipe, a big, old-fashioned, wicker-covered demijohn, such as the investigator's grandfather had kept whisky in, on the table beside him.

"Well, Buddy," the marshal said, "this is bad."

"Ah, it was my own fault," the man on the bed said. "Stuart kept warning me about the frame I was using."

"That's correct," the second old one said.

Still the others said nothing. They just looked steadily and quietly at the investigator until the marshal turned slightly and said, "This is Mr. Pearson. From Jackson. He's got a warrant for the boys."

Then the man on the bed said, "What for?"

"That draft business, Buddy," the marshal said.

"We're not at war now," the man on the bed said.

"No," the marshal said, "It's that new law. They didn't register."

"What are you going to do with them?"

"It's a warrant, Buddy. Swore out."

"That means jail."

"It's a warrant," the old marshal said.

Then the investigator saw that the man on the bed was watching him, puffing steadily at the pipe.

"Pour me some whisky, Jackson," he said.

"No," the doctor said. "He's had too much already."

"Pour me some whisky, Jackson," the man on the bed said. He puffed steadily at the pipe, looking at the investigator. "You come from the Government?" he said.

"Yes," the investigator said. "They should have registered. That's all required of them yet. They did not—" His voice ceased, while the seven pairs of eyes contemplated him, and the man on the bed puffed steadily.

"We would have still been here," the man on the bed said. "We wasn't going to run." He turned his head. The two youths were standing side by side at the foot of the bed. "Anse, Lucius," he said.

To the investigator it sounded as if they answered as one, "Yes, father."

"This gentleman has come all the way from Jackson to say the Government is ready for you. I reckon the quickest place to enlist will be Memphis. Go upstairs and pack."

The investigator started, moved forward. "Wait!" he cried.

But Jackson, the eldest, had forestalled him. He said, "Wait," also, and now they were not looking at the investigator. They were looking at the doctor.

"What about his leg?" Jackson said.

"Look at it," the doctor said. "He almost amputated it himself. It won't wait. And he can't be moved now. I'll need my nurse to help me, and some ether, provided he hasn't had too much whiskey to stand the anesthetic too. One of you can drive to town in my car. I'll telephone—"

"Ether?" the man on the bed said. "What for? You just said yourself it's pretty near off now. I could whet up one of Jackson's butcher knives and finish it myself, with another drink or two. Go on. Finish it."

"You couldn't stand any more shock," the doctor said. "This is whisky talking now."

"Shucks," the other said. "One day in France we was running through a wheat field and I saw the machine gun, coming across the wheat, and I tried to jump it like you would jump a fence rail somebody was swinging at your middle, only I never made it. And I was on the ground then, and along toward dark that begun to hurt, only about that time something went whang on the back of my helmet, like when you hit a anvil, so I never knowed nothing else until I woke up. There was a heap of us racked up along a bank outside a field dressing station, only it took a long time for the doctor to get around to all of us, and by that time it was hurting bad. This here ain't hurt none to speak of since I got a-holt of this johnny-jug. You go on and finish it. If it's help you need, Stuart and Rafe will help you. . . . Pour me a drink, Jackson."

This time the doctor raised the demijohn and examined the level of the liquor. "There's a good quart gone," he said. "If you've drunk a quart of whisky since four o'clock, I doubt if you could stand the anesthetic. Do you think you could stand it if I finished it now?"

"Yes, finish it. I've ruined it; I want to get shut of it."

The doctor looked about at the others, at the still, identical faces watching him. "If I had him in town, in the hospital, with a nurse to watch him, I'd probably wait until he got over his first shock and got the whisky out of his system. But he can't be moved now, and I can't stop the bleeding like this, and even if I had ether or a local anesthetic—"

"Shucks," the man on the bed said. "God never made no better local nor general comfort or anesthetic neither than what's in this johnny-jug. And this ain't Jackson's leg nor Stuart's nor Rafe's nor Lee's. It's mine. I done started it; I reckon I can finish cutting it off any way I want to."

But the doctor was still looking at Jackson. "Well, Mr. McCallum?" he said. "You're the oldest."

But it was Stuart who answered. "Yes," he said. "Finish it. What do you want? Hot water, I reckon."

"Yes," the doctor said. "Some clean sheets. Have you got a big table you can move in here?"

"The kitchen table," the man who had met them at the door said. "Me and the boys—"

"Wait," the man on the bed said. "The boys won't have time to help you." He looked at them again. "Anse, Lucius," he said.

Again it seemed to the investigator that they answered as one. "Yes, father."

"This gentleman yonder is beginning to look impatient. You better start. Come to think of it, you won't need to pack. You will have uniforms in a day or two. Take the truck. There won't be nobody to drive you to Memphis and bring the truck back, so you can leave it at the Gayoso Feed Company until we can send for it. I'd like for you to enlist into the old Sixth Infantry, where I used to be. But I reckon that's too much to hope, and you'll just have to chance where they send you. But it likely won't matter, once you are in. The Government done right by me in my day, and it will do right by you. You just enlist wherever they want to send you, need you, and obey your sergeants and officers until you find out how to be soldiers. Obey them, but remember your name and don't take nothing from no man. You can go now."

"Wait!" the investigator cried again; again he started, moved forward into the center of the room. "I protest this! I'm sorry about Mr. McCallum's accident. I'm sorry about the whole business. But it's out of my hands and out of his hands now. This charge, failure to register according to law, has been made and the warrant issued. It cannot be evaded this way. The course of the action must be completed before any other step can be taken. They should have thought of this when these boys failed to register. If Mr. Gombault refuses to serve this warrant, I will serve it myself and take these men back to Jefferson with me to answer this charge as made. And I must warn Mr. Gombault that he will be cited for contempt!"

The old marshal turned, his shaggy eyebrows beetling again, speaking down to the investigator as if he were a child, "Ain't you found out yet that me or you neither ain't going nowhere for a while?"

"What?" the investigator cried. He looked about at the grave faces once more contemplating him with that remote speculative regard. "Am I being threatened?" he cried.

"Ain't anybody paying any attention to you at all," the marshal said. "Now you just be quiet for a while, and you will be all right, and after a while we can go back to town."

So he stopped again and stood while the grave, contemplative faces freed him once more of that impersonal and unbearable regard, and saw the two youths approach the bed and bend down in turn and kiss their father on the mouth, and then turn as one and leave the room, passing him without even looking at him. And sitting in the lamplit hall beside the old marshal, the bedroom door closed now, he heard the truck start up and back and turn and go down the road, the sound of it dying away, ceasing, leaving the silent hot night—the Mississippi Indian summer, which had already outlasted about half of

November—filled with the loud last shrilling of the summer's cicadas, as though they, too, were aware of the imminent season of cold weather and death.

"I remember old Anse," the marshal said pleasantly, chattily, in that tone in which an adult addresses a strange child. "He's been dead fifteen-sixteen years now. He was about sixteen when the old war* broke out, and he walked all the way to Virginia to get into it. He could have enlisted and fought right here at home, but his ma was a Carter, so wouldn't nothing do him but to go all the way back to Virginia to do his fighting, even though he hadn't never seen Virginia before himself; walked all the way back to a land he hadn't never even seen before and enlisted in Stonewall Jackson's army and stayed in it all through the Valley, and right up to Chancellorsville, where them Carolina boys shot Jackson by mistake, and right on up to that morning in 'Sixty-five when Sheridan's cavalry blocked the road from

---

*old war: the Civil War.

Appomattox to the Valley, where they might have got away again. And he walked back to Mississippi with just about what he had carried away with him when he left, and he got married and built the first story of this house—this here log story we're in right now—and started getting them boys—Jackson and Stuart and Raphael and Lee and Buddy.

"Buddy come along late, late enough to be in the other war, in France in it. You heard him in there. He brought back two medals, an American medal and a French one, and no man knows till yet how he got them, just what he done. I don't believe he even told Jackson and Stuart and them. He hadn't hardly got back home, with them numbers on his uniform and the wound stripes and them two medals, before he had found a girl, found her right off, and a year later them twin boys was born, the livin', spittin' image of old Anse McCallum. If old Anse had just been about seventy-five years younger, the three of them might have been thriblets. I remember them—two little critters exactly alike, and wild as spikehorn bucks, running around here day and night both with a pack of coon dogs until they got big enough to help Buddy and Stuart and Lee with the farm and the gin, and Rafe with the horses and mules, when he would breed and raise and train them and take them to Memphis to sell, right on up to three, four years back, when they went to the agricultural college for a year to learn more about whiteface cattle.

"That was after Buddy and them had quit raising cotton. I remember that too. It was when the Government first begun to interfere with how a man farmed his own land, raised his cotton. Stabilizing the price, using up the surplus, they called it, giving a man advice and help, whether he wanted it or not. You may have noticed them boys in yonder tonight; curious folks almost, you might call them. That first year, when county agents was trying to explain the new system to farmers, the agent come out here and tried to explain it to Buddy and Lee and Stuart, explaining how they would cut down the crop, but the Government would pay farmers the difference, and so they would actually be better off than attempting to farm by themselves.

"'Why, we're much obliged,' Buddy says. 'But we don't need no help. We'll just make the cotton like we always done; if we can't make a crop of it, that will just be our lookout and our loss, and we'll try again.

"So they wouldn't sign no papers nor no cards nor nothing. They just went on and made the cotton like old Anse had taught them to; it was like they just couldn't believe that the Government aimed to help a man whether he wanted help or not, aimed to interfere with how much of anything he could make by hard work on his own land, making the crop and ginning it right here in their own gin, like they had always done, and hauling it to town to sell, hauling it all the way into Jefferson before they found out they couldn't sell it because, in the first place, they had made too much of it and, in the second place, they never had no card to sell what they would have been allowed. So they hauled it back. The gin wouldn't hold all of it, so they put some of it under Rafe's mule shed and they put the rest of it right here in the hall where we are setting now, where they would have to walk around it all winter and keep themselves reminded to be sho and fill out that card next time.

"Only next year they didn't fill out no papers neither. It was like they still couldn't believe it, still believed in the freedom and liberty to make or break according to a man's fitness and will to work, guaranteed by the Government that old Anse had tried to tear in two once and failed, and admitted in good faith he had failed and taken the consequences, and that had give Buddy a medal and taken care of him when he was far away from home in a strange land and hurt.

"So they made their second crop. And they couldn't sell it to nobody neither because they never had no cards. This time they built a special shed to put it under, and I remember how in that second winter Buddy come to town one day to see Lawyer Gavin Stevens. Not for legal advice how to sue the Government or somebody into buying the cotton, even if they never had no card for it, but just to find out why. 'I was for going ahead and signing up for it,' Buddy says. 'If that's going to be the new rule. But we talked it over, and Jackson ain't no farmer, but he knowed father longer than the rest of us, and he said father would have said no, and I reckon now he would have been right.'

"So they didn't raise any more cotton; they had a plenty of it to last a while— twenty-two bales, I think it was. That was when they went into whiteface cattle, putting old Anse's cotton land into pasture, because that's what he would have wanted them to do if the only way they could raise cotton was by the Government telling them how much they could raise and how much they could sell it for, and where, and when, and then pay them for not doing the work they didn't do. Only even when they didn't raise cotton, every year the county agent's young fellow would come out to measure the pasture crops they planted so he could pay them for that, even if they never had no not-cotton to be paid for. Except that he never measured no crop on this place. 'You're welcome to look at what we are doing,' Buddy says. 'But don't draw it down on your map.'

" 'But you can get money for this,' the young fellow says. 'The Government wants to pay you for planting all this.'

" 'We are aiming to get money for it,' Buddy says. 'When we can't we will try something else. But not from the Government. Give that to them that want to take it. We can make out.'

"And that's about all. Them twenty-two bales of orphan cotton are down yonder in the gin right now, because there's room for it in the gin now because they ain't using the gin no more. And them boys grew up and went off a year to the agricultural college to learn right about whiteface cattle, and then come back to the rest of them—these here curious folks living off here to themselves, with the rest of the world all full of pretty neon lights burning night and day both, and easy, quick money scattering itself around everywhere for any man to grab a little, and every man with a shiny new automobile already wore out and throwed away and the new one delivered before the first one was even paid for and everywhere a fine loud grabble and snatch of AAA and WPA* and a dozen other three-letter reasons for a man not to work. Then this here draft comes along, and these curious folks ain't got around to signing that neither, and you come all the way from Jackson with your paper all signed and regular, and we come out here, and after a while we can go back to town. A man gets around, don't he?"

"Yes," the investigator said. "Do you suppose we can go back to town now?"

"No," the marshal told him in that same kindly tone, "not just yet. But we can leave after a while. Of course you will miss your train. But there will be another one tomorrow."

He rose, though the investigator had heard nothing. The investigator watched him walk down the hall and open the

*AAA, WPA: The Agricultural Adjustment Association and the Works Project Administration were agencies created during the Depression to provide assistance and jobs for farmers and laborers.

bedroom door, enter and close it behind him. The investigator sat quietly, listening to the night sounds and looking at the closed door until it opened presently and the marshal came back, carrying something wrapped in a bloody sheet, carrying it gingerly.

"Here," he said. "Hold it a minute."

"It's bloody," the investigator said.

"That's all right," the marshal said. "We can wash when we get through." So the investigator took the bundle and stood holding it while he watched the old marshal go back down the hall and on through it and vanish and return presently with a lighted lantern and a shovel. "Come along," he said. "We're pretty near through now."

The investigator followed him out of the house and across the yard, carrying gingerly the bloody, shattered, heavy bundle in which it still seemed to him he could feel some warmth of life, the marshal striding on ahead, the lantern swinging against his leg, the shadow of his striding scissoring and enormous along the earth, his voice still coming back over his shoulder, chatty and cheerful, "Yes, sir. A man gets around and sees a heap; a heap of folks in a heap of situations. The trouble is, we done got into the habit of confusing the situations with the folks. Take yourself, now," he said in that same kindly tone, chatty and easy; "you mean all right. You just went and got yourself all fogged up with rules and regulations. That's our trouble. We done invented ourselves so many alphabets and rules and recipes that we can't see anything else; if what we see can't be fitted to an alphabet or a rule, we are lost. We have come to be like critters doctor folks might have created in laboratories, that have learned how to slip off their bones and guts and still live, still be kept alive indefinite and forever maybe even without even knowing the bones and the guts are gone. We

have slipped our backbone; we have about decided a man don't need a backbone any more; to have one is old-fashioned. But the groove where the backbone used to be is still there, and the backbone has been kept alive, too, and someday we're going to slip back onto it. I don't know just when nor just how much of a wrench it will take to teach us, but someday."

They had left the yard now. They were mounting a slope; ahead of them the investigator could see another clump of cedars, a small clump, somehow shaggily formal against the starred sky. The marshal entered it and stopped and set the lantern down and, following with the bundle, the investigator saw a small rectangle of earth enclosed by a low brick coping. Then he saw the two graves, or the headstones—two plain granite slabs set upright in the earth.

"Old Anse and Mrs. Anse," the marshal said. "Buddy's wife wanted to be buried with her folks. I reckon she would have been right lonesome up here with just McCallums. Now, let's see." He stood for a moment, his chin in his hand; to the investigator he looked exactly like an old lady trying to decide where to set out a shrub. "They was to run from left to right, beginning with Jackson. But after the boys was born, Jackson and Stuart was to come up here by their pa and ma, so Buddy could move up some and make room. So he will be about here." He moved the lantern nearer and took up the shovel. Then he saw the investigator still holding the bundle. "Set it down," he said "I got to dig first."

"I'll hold it," the investigator said.

"Nonsense, put it down," the marshal said. "Buddy won't mind."

So the investigator put the bundle down on the brick coping and the marshal began to dig, skillfully and rapidly, still talking in that cheerful, interminable voice, "Yes, sir. We done forget about folks. Life has done got cheap, and life ain't cheap. Life's a pretty durn valuable thing. I don't mean just getting along from one WPA relief check to the next one, but honor and pride and discipline that make a man worth preserving, make him of any value. That's what we got to learn again. Maybe it takes trouble, bad trouble, to teach it back to us; maybe it was the walking to Virginia because that's where his ma come from, and losing a war and then walking back, that taught it to old Anse. Anyway, he seems to learned it, and to learned it good enough to bequeath it to his boys. Did you notice how all Buddy had to do was to tell them boys of his it was time to go, because the Government had sent them word? And how they told him good-bye? Growned men kissing one another without hiding and without shame. Maybe that's what I am trying to say. . . . There," he said. "That's big enough."

He moved quickly, easily; before the investigator could stir, he had lifted the bundle into the narrow trench and was covering it, covering it as rapidly as he had dug, smoothing the earth over it with the shovel. Then he stood up and raised the lantern—a tall, lean old man, breathing easily and lightly.

"I reckon we can go back to town now," he said.

## YOU AND THE STORY

William Faulkner was a storyteller who let a story build slowly, creating in the reader a sense of mystery or apprehension. He lingered over important parts, building up the mood and developing important details. The details in his stories work together. They help build up the central impression of the major theme that was his aim. What, in simple outline, is the story of "the tall men"? What happens in the story, taken as a whole? What are the things that to you seem most important in this story?

### A Closer Look

William Faulkner was one of the early modern experimenters with a limited **point of view**. Nineteenth-century authors had often written from the point of view of the all-knowing, or **omniscient,** storyteller. They moved freely from one place to the other, and they let us share in the thoughts and feelings of many different characters. Modern writers often limit their perspective to what *one actual observer* could really have taken in. In this story, we witness events, and we come to know things, the way the government investigator does. We try to make sense of things somewhat the way he observes and interprets them himself. Answer the following questions about what we learn in this story, and about how we learn the things we do:

(1) The opening conversation sets up for us the *initial situation* from which the plot of the story proceeds. A government investigator has come to the McCallum place to arrest two draft "evaders" who failed to register for "selective service" as required by law. For what does the investigator blame the local marshal, or law officer, who accompanies him?

(2) In his writing, Faulkner often uses the **stream-of-consciousness** technique that he helped pioneer in modern American fiction. We share in thoughts and feelings as they flow through a major character's mind. Often one idea blends into another without a clear break—just as our own thoughts actually flow and blend. The investigator has arrived with set notions about the kind of people he will have to deal with— "he believed he knew them." **a.** What

thoughts about these people in general flow through his mind at the beginning of the story? **b.** What does he think about the marshal? Why does he expect him to be different?

(3) The central characters in a Faulkner story are often *strong-willed* individuals. But they often in turn find themselves facing strong forces that will not bend easily to their will. As the story unfolds, the investigator faces a situation that he finds hard to take in hand. How is it different from what he might have expected? Why does it prove hard to control? Describe the situation and the events that challenge the ability of the investigator to control the course of the action.

(4) The central **conflict** in this story is between the *outsider*—the federal investigator—and the local people. **a.** Study the author's first description of the McCallum family. What was "tremendous" about them? Point out important words or details that the author uses to shape our impression of these people. **b.** How do the local people thwart the outsider's intentions? How do you react when they do?

(5) The author uses two **flashbacks** to help fill in the background and the family history of the McCallums. **a.** How does Buddy's talk about his service in France in World War I round out our impression of the kind of people the McCallums are? **b.** What do we learn from the story of old Anse as told by the marshal? What do we learn from the marshal's account of the family's dealings with the government?

(6) In this story, we first see the local people through the eyes of the outsider. But along with the outside observer, we slowly come to understand these people; we come to know their standards and values. Toward the end, the marshal sums up these standards or ideals for the investigator in a long *thematic passage*. Study it carefully and answer the questions that follow it:

"You mean all right. You just went and got yourself all fogged up with rules and regulations. That's our trouble. We done invented ourselves so many alphabets and rules and recipes that we can't see anything else; if what we see can't be fitted to an alphabet or a rule, we are lost. We have come to be like critters doctor folks might have created in laboratories, that have learned how to slip off their bones and guts and still live, still be kept alive indefinite and forever maybe even without even knowing the bones and the guts are gone. We have slipped our backbone; we have about decided a man don't need a backbone any more; to have one is old-fashioned. But the groove where the backbone used to be is still there, and the backbone has been kept alive, too, and someday we're going to slip back onto it. I don't know just when nor just how much of a wrench it will take to teach us, but someday."

**a.** This passage sums up the central **theme** of the story. It sums up the idea or message that we are likely to remember when we think about the story as a whole. In your own words, what is the marshal saying in this thematic passage? **b.** How do the events of the story act out or illustrate the theme summed up in this passage? **c.** At the very end, the marshal restates his theme in more general terms, saying that we have to learn again about "honor and pride and discipline." What do these terms mean to him? How are they related? How do they help sum up the theme of the story?

(7) This story does without some of the more external or superficial elements of the traditional Gothic story. There are no picturesque ruins, supernatural events, or age-old mysteries. But the story illustrates several major elements that American fiction has inherited from the Gothic tradition. Sum up in your own words how each of the following is illustrated in this story:

—*extraordinary characters* that seem somehow larger than life
—a *violent clash* of opposites, or violently conflicting points of view
—scenes and events that cause feelings of *terror* or horror on the part of the reader

Faulkner's sentences are rich in details and nuances. They often furnish us with several details that together create just the right impression or the right shade of meaning. Study the way details have been worked into the following three *model sentences* from the story. Each sentence describes a person. Write three sentences of your own in which you describe a person with the same amount of detail. Try to work your details into each sentence in such a way that its structure will be similar to that of the original.

1. Then he saw the man standing in the door, waiting for them to approach—a man of about forty-five, not tall, but blocky, with a brown, still face and horseman's hands.

2. The investigator found the other looking at him, the brown eyes still, courteous enough in the brown face, the hand he offered hard enough, but the clasp quite limp, quite cold.

3. The marshal glanced back at him for a moment, his shaggy gray brows beetling, with something at once courteous yet a little impatient about the glance.

---

Language Composition Activity B12

THE RANGE OF VOCABULARY

# Country People

Faulkner is known for the extreme richness and range of his vocabulary. How difficult is the vocabulary of this story for you? Do the following:

A. Look at the italicized words in the following sentences. For each, find the word or expression in the group below that is closest to it in meaning.

1. They *jeopardize* the very job itself through petty and transparent *subterfuge* to acquire a free mattress.
2. They would *relinquish* even the job if by doing so they could receive free food.
3. They react in loud *vituperative* outrage and astonishment when caught.
4. The investigator could *discern* no change whatever in his tone.
5. It would *devolve upon* him to control the situation.
6. He had to *expedite* their departure with the prisoners.
7. He had been corrupted anew to his old *inherent* shiftless *sloth.*
8. What made the men seem tremendous was not vitality or *exuberance,* for they made no sound.

| | | |
|---|---|---|
| LAZINESS | INHERITED, NATURAL | TAKE CARE OF EFFICIENTLY |
| ABUSIVE | ENDANGER | GIVE UP |
| DISCOVER | TRICK | |
| EXTREME LIVELINESS | BE UP TO | |

B. From Faulkner's story, select *ten* other words that are difficult for you. Find the right meaning in the glossary at the end of this book or in a dictionary. State the meaning in your own words.

● Many of the most successful writers of modern American short stories have been fascinated with the darker side of human nature. Many short story classics of the last thirty or forty years carry on a tradition of psychological probing, of bringing to light dark thoughts and hidden motives. Writers like Jean Stafford, Flannery O'Connor, and Shirley Jackson often explore the harrowing memories or the spiteful thoughts below a genteel outer surface. They often take us to an everyday setting, with people who could be next-door neighbors or ordinary passers-by. Often these authors tell us their story in a quiet, unpretentious way—as if to impress us with the *ordinariness* of what they describe. The following story, first published in 1955, carries on this tradition of a low-key exploring of the dark byways of the human heart.

## Cynthia Rich

# My Sister's Marriage

When my mother died she left just Olive and me to take care of Father. Yesterday when I burned the package of Olive's letters that left only me. I know that you'll side with my sister in all of this because you're only outsiders, and strangers can afford to sympathize with young love, and with whatever sounds daring and romantic, without thinking what it does to all the other people involved. I don't want you to hate my sister—I don't hate her—but I do want you to see that we're happier this way, Father and I, and as for Olive, she made her choice.

But if you weren't strangers, all of you, I wouldn't be able to tell you about this. "Keep yourself to yourself," my father has always said. "If you ever have worries, Sarah Ann, you come to me and don't go sharing your problems around town." And that's what I've always done. So if I knew you I certainly wouldn't ever tell you about Olive throwing the hairbrush, or about finding the letters buried in the back of the drawer.

I don't know what made Olive the way she is. We grew up together like twins—there were people who thought we were—and every morning before we went to school she plaited my hair and I plaited hers before the same mirror, in the same little twist of ribbons and braids behind our heads. We wore the same dresses and there was never a stain on the hem or a rip in our stockings to say to a stranger that we had lost our mother. And although we have never been well-to-do—my father is a doctor and his patients often can't pay—I know that there are people here in Conkling today who think we're rich, just because of little things like candlelight at dinner and my father's cigarette holder and the piano lessons that Olive and I had and the reproduction of *The Anatomy Lesson* that hangs above the mantelpiece instead of botanical prints. "You don't have to be rich to be a gentleman," my father says, "or to live like one."

My father is a gentleman and he raised Olive and myself as ladies. I can hear you

laughing, because people like to make fun of words like "gentleman" and "lady," but they are words with ideals and standards behind them, and I hope that I will always hold to those ideals as my father taught me to. If Olive has renounced them, at least we did all we could.

Perhaps the reason that I can't understand Olive is that I have never been in love. I know that if I had ever fallen in love it would not have been, like Olive, at first sight but only after a long acquaintance. My father knew my mother for seven years before he proposed—it is much the safest way. Nowadays people make fun of that too, and the magazines are full of stories about people meeting in the moonlight and marrying the next morning, but if you read those stories you know that they are not the sort of people you would want to be like.

Even today Olive couldn't deny that we had a happy childhood. She used to be very proud of being the lady of the house, of sitting across the candlelight from my father at dinner like a little wife. Sometimes my father would hold his carving knife poised above the roast to stand smiling at her and say: "Olive, every day you remind me more of your mother."

I think that although she liked the smile, she objected to the compliment, because she didn't like to hear about Mother. Once when my father spoke of her she said to him: "Papa, you're missing Mother again. I can't bear it when you miss Mother. Don't I take care of you all right? Don't I make everything happy for you?" It wasn't that she hadn't loved Mother but that she wanted my father to be completely happy.

To tell the truth, it was Olive Father loved best. There was a time when I couldn't have said that, it would have hurt me too much. Taking care of our father was like playing a long game of "let's pretend," and when little girls play

family nobody wants to be the children. I thought it wasn't fair, just because Olive was three years older, that she should always be the mother. I wanted to sit opposite my father at dinner and have him smile at me like that.

I was glad when Olive first began walking out with young men in the summer evenings. Then I would make lemonade for my father ("Is it as good as Olive's?") and we would sit out on the screened porch together watching the fireflies. I asked him about the patients he had seen that day, trying to think of questions as intelligent as Olive's. I knew that he was missing her and frowning into the long twilight for the swing of her white skirts. When she came up the steps he said, "I missed my housewife tonight," just as though I hadn't made the lemonade right after all. She knew, too, that it wasn't the same for him in the evenings without her and for a while, instead of going out, she brought the young men to the house. But soon she stopped even that ("I never realized how silly and shallow they were until I saw them with Papa," she said. "I was ashamed to have him talk to them"). I know that he was glad, and when my turn came I didn't want to go out because I hated leaving them alone together. It all seems a very long time ago. I used to hate it when Olive "mothered" me. Now I feel a little like Olive's mother, and she is like my rebellious child.

In spite of everything, I loved Olive. When we were children we used to play together. The other children disliked us because we talked like grown-ups and didn't like to get dirty, but we were happy playing by ourselves on the front lawn where my father, if he were home, could watch us from his study window. So it wasn't surprising that when we grew older we were still best friends. I loved Olive and I see now how she took advantage of that love. Sometimes I think she felt that if she was to betray my father she wanted me to betray him too.

I still believe that it all began, not really with Mr. Dixon, but with the foreign stamps. She didn't see many of them, those years after high school when she was working in the post office, because not very many people in Conkling have friends abroad, but the ones she saw—and even the postmarks from Chicago or California—made her dream. She told her dreams to Father, and of course he understood and said that perhaps some summer we could take a trip to New England as far as Boston. My father hasn't lived in Conkling all of his life. He went to Harvard, and that is one reason he is different from the other men here. He is a scholar and not bound to provincial ideas. People here respect him and come to him for advice.

Olive wasn't satisfied and she began to rebel. Even she admitted that there wasn't anything for her to rebel against. She told me about it, sitting on the windowsill in her long white nightgown, braiding and unbraiding the hair that she had never cut.

"It's not, don't you see, that I don't love Father. And it certainly isn't that I'm not happy here. But what I mean is, how can I ever know whether or not I'm really happy here unless I go somewhere else? When you graduate from school you'll feel the same way. You'll want—you'll want to know."

"I like it here," I said from the darkness of the room, but she didn't hear me.

"You know what I'm going to do, Sarah Ann? Do you know what I'm going to do? I'm going to save some money and go on a little trip—it wouldn't have to be expensive, I could go by bus—and I'll just see things, and then maybe I'll know."

"Father promised he'd take us to New England."

"No," said Olive, "no, you don't understand. Anyhow, I'll save the money."

And still she wasn't satisfied. She began to read. Olive and I always did well in school, and our names were called out for Special Recognition on Class Day. Miss Singleton wanted Olive to go to drama school after she played the part of Miranda in *The Tempest*, but my father talked to her, and when he told her what an actress's life is like she realized it wasn't what she wanted. Aside from books for school, though, we never read very much. We didn't need to because my father has read everything you've heard of, and people in town have said that talking to him about anything is better than reading three books.

Still, Olive decided to read. She would choose a book from my father's library and go into the kitchen, where the air was still heavy and hot from dinner, and sit on the very edge of the tall, hard three-legged stool. She had an idea that if she sat in a comfortable chair in the parlor she would not be attentive or would skip the difficult passages. So she would sit like that for hours, under the hard light of the unshaded bulb that hangs from the ceiling, until her arms ached from holding the book.

"What do you want to find out about?" my father would ask.

"Nothing," Olive said. "I'm just reading."

My father hates evasion.

"Now, Olive, nobody reads without a purpose. If you're interested in something, maybe I can help you. I might even know something about it myself."

When she came into our bedroom she threw the book on the quilt and said: "Why does he have to pry, Sarah Ann? It's so simple—just wanting to read a book. Why does he have to make a fuss about it as though I were trying to hide something from him?"

That was the first time that I felt a little like Olive's mother.

"But he's only taking an interest," I said. "He just wants us to share things with him. Lots of fathers wouldn't even care. You don't know how lucky we are."

"You don't understand, Sarah Ann. You're too young to understand."

"Of course I understand," I said shortly. "Only I've outgrown feeling like that."

It was true. When I was a little girl I wrote something on a piece of paper, something that didn't matter much, but it mattered to me because it was a private thought. My father came into my room and saw me shove the paper under the blotter, and he wanted me to show it to him. So I quickly said, "No, it's private. I wrote it to myself, I didn't write it to be seen," but he said he wanted to see it. And I said, "No, no, no, it was silly anyway," and he said, "Sarah Ann, nothing you have to say would seem silly to me, you never give me credit for understanding, I can understand a great deal," but I said it wasn't just him, really it wasn't, because I hadn't written it for anyone at all to see. Then he was all sad and hurt and said this wasn't a family where we keep things hidden and there I was hiding this from him. I heard his voice, and it went on and on, and he said I had no faith in him and that I shouldn't keep things from him— and I said it wasn't anything big or special, it was just some silly nonsense, but if it was nonsense, he said, why wouldn't I let him read it, since it would make him happy? And I cried and cried, because it was only a very little piece of paper and why did he have to see it anyway, but he was very solemn and said if you held back little things soon you would be holding back bigger things and the gap would grow wider and wider. So I gave him the paper. He read it and said nothing except that I was a good girl and he couldn't see what all the fuss had been about.

Of course now I know that he was only taking an interest and I shouldn't have minded that. But I was a little girl then and minded dreadfully, and that is why I understood how Olive felt, although she was grown-up then and should have known better.

She must have understood that she was being childish, because when my father came in a few minutes later and said, "Olive, you're our little mother. We mustn't quarrel. There should be only love between us," she rose and kissed him. She told him about the book she had been reading, and he said: "Well, as it happens, I do know something about that." They sat for a long time discussing the book, and I think he loved Olive better than ever. The next evening, instead of shutting herself in the bright, hot kitchen, Olive sat with us in the cool of the parlor until bedtime, hemming a slip. And it was just as always.

But I suppose that these things really had made a difference in Olive. For we had always been alike, and I cannot imagine allowing a perfect stranger to ask me personal questions before we had even been introduced. She told me about it afterward, how he had bought a book of three-cent stamps and stayed to chat through the half-open grilled window. Suddenly he said, quite seriously: "Why do you wear your hair like that?"

"Pardon me?" said Olive.

"Why do you wear your hair like that? You ought to shake it loose around your shoulders. It must be yards long."

That is when I would have remembered—if I had forgotten—that I was a lady. I would have closed the grill, not rudely but just firmly enough to show my displeasure, and gone back to my desk. Olive told me she thought of doing that but she looked at him and knew, she said, that he didn't mean to be impolite, that he really wanted to know.

And instead she said: "I only wear it down at night."

That afternoon he walked her home from the post office.

Olive told me everything long before my father knew anything. It was the beginning of an unwholesome deceit in her. And it was nearly a week later that she told even me. By that time he was meeting her every afternoon and they took long walks together, as far as Merton's Pond, before she came home to set the dinner table.

"Only don't tell Father," she said.

"Why not?"

"I think I'm afraid of him. I don't know why. I'm afraid of what he might say."

"He won't say anything," I said. "Unless there's something wrong. And if there's something wrong, wouldn't you want to know?"

Of course, I should have told Father myself right away. But that was how she played upon my love for her.

"I'm telling you," she said, "because I want so much to share it with you. I'm so happy, Sarah Ann, and I feel so free, don't you see. We've always been so close—I've been closer to you than to Father, I think—or at least differently." She had to qualify it, you see, because it wasn't true. But it still made me happy and I promised not to tell, and I was even glad for her because, as I've told you, I've always loved Olive.

I saw them together one day when I was coming home from school. They were walking together in the rain, holding hands like schoolchildren, and when Olive saw me from a distance she dropped his hand suddenly and then just as suddenly took it again.

"Hullo!" he said when she introduced us. "She does look like you!"

I want to be fair and honest with you— it is Olive's dishonesty that still shocks me—and so I will say that I liked Mr. Dixon that day. But I thought even then how different he was from my father, and that should have warned me. He was a big man with a square face and sun-bleached hair. I could see a glimpse of his bright, speckled tie under his tan raincoat, and his laugh sounded warm and easy in the rain. I liked him, I suppose, for the very things I should have distrusted in him. I liked his ease and the way that he accepted me immediately, spontaneously and freely, without waiting—waiting for whatever people wait for when they hold themselves back (as I should have done) to find out more about you. I could almost understand what had made Olive, after five minutes, tell him how she wore her hair at night.

I am glad, at least, that I begged Olive to tell my father about him. I couldn't understand why at first she refused. I think now that she was afraid of seeing them together, that she was afraid of seeing the difference. I have told you that my father is a gentleman. Even now you must be able to tell what sort of man Mr. Dixon was. My father knew at once, without even meeting him.

The weeks had passed and Olive told me that Mr. Dixon's business was completed but that his vacation was coming and he planned to spend it in Conkling. She said she would tell my father.

We were sitting on the porch after dinner. The evening had just begun to thicken and some children had wandered down the road, playing a game of pirates at the very edge of our lawn. One of them had a long paper sword and the others were waving tall sticks, and they were screaming. My father had to raise his voice to be heard.

"So this man whom you have been seeing behind my back is a traveling salesman for Miracle-wear soles."

*"Surrender in the name of the King."*

"I am more than surprised at you, Olive. That hardly sounds like the kind of man you would want to be associated with."

"Why not?" said Olive. "Why not?"

"It's notorious, my dear. Men like that have no respect for a girl. They'll flatter her with slick words but it doesn't mean anything. Just take my word for it, dear. It may seem hard, but I know the world."

*"Fight to the death! Fight to the death!"*

"I can't hear you, my dear. Sarah Ann, ask those children to play their games somewhere else."

I went down the steps and across the lawn.

"Doctor Landis is trying to rest after a long day," I explained. They nodded and vanished down the dusky road, brandishing their silent swords.

"I am saying nothing of the extraordinary manner of your meeting, not even of the deceitful way in which he has carried on this—friendship."

It was dark on the porch. I switched on the yellow overhead light, and the three of us blinked for a moment, rediscovering each other as the shadows leaped back.

"The cheapness of it is so apparent it amazes me that even in your innocence of the world—"

My father was fitting a cigarette into its black holder. He turned it slowly to and fro until it was firm before he struck a match and lit it. It is beautiful to watch him do even the most trivial things. He is always in control of himself and he never makes a useless gesture or thinks a useless thought. If you met him you might believe at first that he was totally relaxed, but because I have lived with him so long I know that there is at all times a tension controlling his body; you can feel it when you touch his hand. Tension is the wrong word. It is rather a self-awareness, as though not a muscle contracted without his conscious knowledge.

"You know it very well yourself, Olive. Could anything but shame have kept you from bringing this man to your home?"

His voice is like the way he moves. It is clear and considered and each word exists by itself. However common it may be, when he speaks it, it has become his, it has dignity because he has chosen it.

"Father, all I ask is that you'll have him here—that you will meet him. Surely that's not too much to ask before you—judge him."

Olive sat on the step at my father's feet. Her hands had been moving across her skirt, smoothing the folds over her knees, but when she spoke she clasped them tightly in her lap. She was trying to speak as he spoke, in that calm, certain voice, but it was a poor imitation.

"I'm afraid that it is too much to ask, Olive. I have seen too many of his kind to take interest in seeing another."

"I think you should see him, Father." She spoke very softly. "I think I am in love with him."

"Olive!" I said. I had known it all along, of course, but when she spoke it, in that voice trying so childishly to sound sure, I knew its absurdity. How could she say it after Father had made it so clear? As soon as he had repeated after her, "A salesman for Miracle-wear soles," even the inflections of his voice showed me that it was ludicrous; I realized what I had known all along, the cheapness of it all for Olive—for Olive with her ideals.

I looked across at my father but he had not stirred. The moths brushed their wings against the light bulb. He flicked a long gray ash.

"Don't use that word lightly, Olive," he said. "That is a sacred word. Love is the word for what I felt for your mother—what I hope you feel for me and for your sister. You must not confuse it with innocent infatuation."

"But I do love him—how can you know? How can you know anything about it? I do love him." Her voice was shrill and not pleasant.

"Olive," said my father. "I must ask you not to use that word."

She sat looking up at his face and from his chair he looked back at her. Then she rose and went into the house. He did not follow her, even with his eyes. We sat for a long time before I went over to him and took his hand. I think he had forgotten me. He started and said nothing and his hand did not acknowledge mine. I would rather he had slapped me. I left him and went into the house.

In our bedroom Olive was sitting before the dressing table in her nightgown, brushing her hair. You mustn't think I don't love her, that I didn't love her then. As I say, we were like twins, and when I saw her reflection in the tall, gilded mirror I might have been seeing my own eyes filled with tears. I tell you, I wanted to put my arms around her, but you must see that it was for her own sake that I didn't. She had done wrong, she had deceived my father and she had made me deceive him. It would have been wicked to give her sympathy then.

"It's hard, of course, Olive," I said gently. "But you know that Father's right."

She didn't answer. She brushed her hair in long strokes and it rose on the air. She did not turn even when the doorknob rattled and my father stood in the doorway and quietly spoke her name.

"Olive," he repeated. "Of course I must ask you not to see this—this man again."

Olive turned suddenly with her dark hair whirling about her head. She hurled the silver hairbrush at my father, and in that single moment when it leaped from her hand I felt an elation I have never

known before. Then I heard it clatter to the floor a few feet from where he stood, and I knew that he was unhurt and that it was I, not Olive, who had for that single moment meant it to strike him. I longed to throw my arms about him and beg his forgiveness.

He went over and picked up the brush and gave it to Olive. Then he left the room.

"How could you, Olive?" I whispered.

She sat with the brush in her hand. Her hair had fallen all about her face and her eyes were dark and bright. The next morning at breakfast she did not speak to my father and he did not speak to her, although he sat looking at her so intensely that if I had been Olive I would have blushed. I thought, He loves her more now, this morning, than when he used to smile and say she was like Mother. I remember thinking, Why couldn't he love me like that? I would never hurt him.

Just before she left for work he went over to her and brushed her arm slightly with his hand.

"We'll talk it all over tonight, Olive," he said. "I know you will understand that this is best."

She looked down at his hand as though it were a strange animal and shook her head and hurried down the porch steps.

That night she called from a little town outside of Richmond to say that she was married. I stood behind my father in the shadowy little hallway as he spoke to her. I could hear her voice, higher-pitched than usual over the static of the wires, and I heard her say that they would come, that very evening, if he would see them.

I almost thought he hadn't understood her, his voice was so calm.

"I suppose you want my blessings. I cannot give them to deceit and cowardice. You will have to find them elsewhere if you can, my dear. If you can."

After he had replaced the receiver he

still stood before the mouthpiece, talking into it.

"That she would give up all she has had—that she would stoop to a—for a—physical attraction—"

Then he turned to me. His eyes were dark.

"Why are you crying?" he said suddenly. "What are you crying for? She's made her choice. Am I crying? Do you think I would want to see her—now? If she—when she comes to see what she has done—but it's not a question of forgiveness. Even then it wouldn't be the same. She has made her choice."

He stood looking at me and I thought at first that what he saw was distasteful to him, but his voice was gentle when he spoke.

"Would you have done this to me, Sarah Ann? Would you have done it?"

"No," I said, and I was almost joyful, knowing it was true. "Oh, no."

That was a year ago. We never speak of Olive any more. At first letters used to come from her, long letters from New York and then from Chicago. Always she asked me about Father and whether he would read a letter if she wrote one. I wrote her long letters back and said that I would talk to him. But he wasn't well—even now he has to stay in bed for days at a time—and I knew that he didn't want to hear her name.

One morning he came into my room while I was writing to her. He saw me thrust the package of letters into a cubbyhole and I knew I had betrayed him again.

"Don't ally yourself with deception, Sarah Ann," he said quietly. "You did that once and you see what came of it."

"But if she writes to me—" I said. "What do you want me to do?"

He stood in the doorway in his long bathrobe. He had been in bed and his hair was slightly awry from the pillows and his face was a little pale. I have taken good care of him and he still looks young—not more than forty—but his cheekbones worry me. They are sharp and white.

"I want you to give me her letters," he said. "To burn."

"Won't you read them, Father? I know that what she did was wrong, but she sounds happy—"

I don't know what made me say that except that, you see, I did love Olive.

He stared at me and came into the room.

"And you believe her? Do you think that it's possible for happiness to come from deception?"

"But she's my sister," I said, and although I knew that he was right I began to cry. "And she's your daughter. And you love her so."

He came and stood beside my chair. This time he didn't ask me why I was crying.

He kneeled suddenly beside me and spoke very softly and quickly.

"We'll keep each other company, Sarah Ann, just the two of us. We can be happy that way, can't we? We'll always have each other, don't you know?" He put his hand on my hair.

I knew then that was the way it should be. I leaned my head on his shoulder, and when I had finished crying I smiled at him and gave him Olive's letters.

"You take them," I said. "I can't—"

He nodded and took them and then took my hand.

I know that when he took them he meant to burn them. I found them by chance yesterday in the back of his desk drawer, under a pile of old medical reports. They lay there like love letters from someone who had died or moved away. They were tied in a slim green hair ribbon—it was mine, but I suppose he had found it and thought it was Olive's.

I didn't wonder what to do. It wasn't fair, don't you see? He hadn't any right to keep those letters after he told me I was the only daughter he had left. He would always be secretly reading them and fingering them, and it wouldn't do him any good. I took them to the incinerator in the backyard and burned them carefully, one by one. His bed is by the window and I know that he was watching me, but of course he couldn't say anything.

Maybe you feel sorry for Father, maybe you think I was cruel. But I did it for his sake and I don't care what you think because you're all of you strangers, anyway, and you can't understand that there couldn't be two of us. As I said before, I don't hate Olive. But sometimes I think this is the way it was meant to be. First Mother died and left just the two of us to take care of Father. And yesterday when I burned Olive's letters I thought, Now there is only me.

## YOU AND THE STORY

This story takes up two classic **themes** familiar to readers of both traditional and modern literature. The first is the theme of the dominant parent: We see a strong-willed parent trying to mold the personalities of children and control their lives. The second theme is that of rivalry between sisters or brothers. We see sisters or brothers competing for love and attention at home, or for recognition in the world outside. Conflicts such as these take different shapes in the lives of different people. But many people know how it feels to grow up hemmed in or overshadowed by someone else. They know how it feels to have to struggle for their own place in the sun. Answer the following questions:

(1) At the beginning, the person telling the story says: "I know that you'll side with my sister in all this because you're only outsiders." As you read the story, do you find yourself siding with the sister? Why or why not? Do you think something can be said in defense of the woman telling the story?

(2) Do you think something can be said in defense of the father? At the end, the woman telling the story says: "Maybe you feel sorry for Father." Why would we? Why should we?

### A Closer Look

Many well-known contemporary authors are fascinated with *why* people do things that at first seem strange to us. They try to help us understand what is behind some of the strange things people do and say. Often they take us behind the scenes by having a central **character** take us into his or her confidence. We then look at what happens from the point of view of someone who is close to the scene—and who has a personal stake in what is going on. We thus have an exceptionally good chance to understand the **motivation** of the characters in a story—their reasons for doing what they do. Answer the following questions about the motives of the people in this story:

(1) Much of this story shows us the ideals and standards that the father has set up for his daughters. Is it true that people like to make fun of words like *gentleman* and *lady*? What were the "ideals and standards behind them"? The girls were taught to be

reserved rather than outgoing. They had been taught not to express their feelings freely or do things on the spur of the moment. Find evidence of this training and its effects in the story.

(2) The girls had lost their mother very early. How much difference did this loss make in their lives? How did this loss help shape their personalities? How did the girl telling the story become jealous of her sister Olive? Why? How did she show it?

(3) The central **conflict** of this story is the contest between the father and Olive, the older sister. What are some of the early signs of the conflict? What are the first hints of the girl's rebellion? How does the father try to impose his will? Describe the things he does and says in order to control the lives of his daughters. How and why does the father fail with Olive? What do you think made Dixon especially attractive to her?

(4) In the end, the girl telling the story in her own way asserts her independence from her father. And at the same time, she in her own way achieves a triumph over her sister. How?

## Your Turn

Do you remember reading a book in which rebellion against a strong-willed parent played a major part? Or, have you read a book in which rivalry among children in the same family was strong? Describe the conflict and its outcome.

---

Language/Composition Activity B13

ACCURATE DISTINCTIONS

# Weighty Words

In this story, people often use weighty words. They use words that are chosen with a purpose, words that make a difference. The father in the story, especially, knows how to speak in such a way that the words sink in. Help explain the weight the following words carry in the story:

1. When we "sympathize with young love," are we approving of it? Are we offering support?
2. The father had gone to Harvard and was not bound by "provincial" ideas. Is *provincial* the same as uneducated?
3. What is the difference between lies and "evasion"?
4. Is something that is "private" the same as something that is secret?
5. Is acting "spontaneously" the same thing as acting rashly? Is it the same thing as acting in an easygoing manner?
6. Is being "notorious" the same as being well-known?
7. Is "deceit" the same as deception? Which is the stronger word?
8. What is the difference between love and "infatuation"?
9. What is the difference between disobeying someone and "betraying" the person?
10. What is the difference between excitement and "elation"?

# A Different Drummer

If a man does not keep pace with his companions, perhaps it is because he hears a different drummer. Let him step to the music which he hears, however measured or far away.

—Henry David Thoreau

Americans have long believed that people have a right to their own opinions. They have a right to look at things for themselves and reach their own conclusions. To the leaders in the American War of Independence, liberty meant not only political independence from England but also freedom of thought and conscience. Thomas Jefferson said, "It behooves every man who values liberty of conscience for himself to resist invasions of it in the case of others." Thomas Paine said, "I have always strenuously supported the right of every man to his opinion, however different that opinion might be to mine."

When we respect the convictions and beliefs of others, we grant them the right to be different. We grant them the right to be individuals. Some of the strongest and most influential voices in American literature have been those of strong individualists. They distrusted established customs and ready-made opinions, and they set out to chart their own course.

The strong, independent individual often encounters opposition or ridicule from those who want everybody to be like everybody else. But in the long run, the American folk hero has often been someone who claimed his right to be a loner, someone who was not afraid to seem cranky or eccentric. The writers in the following unit include some of the best-known figures in the tradition of American individualism. What they said had the strength of honest personal conviction. They refused to follow the crowd, and they made themselves heard.

## MOTHS AND ANGELS: **Emily Dickinson**

In Amherst Emily lived on
though the world forgot
moving with calm coiled hair through tidy days.
Her face shrank to a locket. She explored
miniaturized worlds known only to moths and angels
walked to the far side of a raindrop—
trespassed
on Infinity.

—Olga Cabral

Emily Dickinson (1830–1886) spent most of her days living in Amherst, Massachusetts. Her father, a lawyer and later a Congressman, ruled over his family in a stern, old-fashioned manner. By today's standards, she lived a secluded life, spending much of her time alone. Only a few of her poems were published in her lifetime, but she continued writing, encouraged by a few close friends. Hundreds of her poems were collected and published after her death. They have strongly appealed to modern readers who have grown tired of poetry that seems too smooth, too sweet, and too predictable. Her strange, teasing, mysterious poems have become widely known in the twentieth century. She is today one of the best-known American writers of her time.

# Presentiment

Presentiment is that long shadow on the lawn
Indicative that suns go down;
The notice to the startled grass
That darkness is about to pass.

### YOU AND THE POEM

(1) When something is "indicative" of something else, it serves as an indicator—as a signal. A presentiment is a kind of signaling—it is the feeling we have when we know ahead of time that something is going to happen. To judge from this poem, does the feeling usually come slowly or suddenly? Is it usually of something pleasant or unpleasant?

(2) Emily Dickinson often talks about objects and animals as if they were capable of human actions and feelings. Find one or two examples of such **personification** in this short poem.

(3) Many people show that they are serious by adopting a very slow, solemn manner. In her poetry, Emily Dickinson often says serious things in a casual, almost light-hearted manner. How should this poem sound when it is read aloud?

# A Bird Came Down the Walk

A bird came down the walk:
He did not know I saw.
He bit an angleworm in halves
And ate the fellow, raw.

And then he drank a dew
From a convenient grass,
And then hopped sidewise to the wall
To let a beetle pass.

He glanced with rapid eyes
That hurried all around—
They looked like frightened beads, I thought.
He stirred his velvet head

Like one in danger. Cautious,
I offered him a crumb,
And he unrolled his feathers
And rowed him softer home

Than oars divide the ocean,
Too silver for a seam,
Or butterflies, off banks of noon,
Leap, plashless, as they swim.

---

## YOU AND THE POEM

(1) In this poem, how close do we come to a true bird's-eye view of a bird's world? Emily Dickinson often describes things in such a way that they seem familiar and strange at the same time. Early in the poem, point out several things that human beings would or could do—except for details that remind us that we are watching a bird.

(2) In the third stanza, the poet describes the eyes of the bird. What in her description fits especially well what she describes?

(3) In the last two stanzas, the poet uses two different imaginative comparisons for the flight of the bird. What are they? What do they have in common? (What might be the meaning of "too silver for a seam"? How does the phrase fit into the rest of the poem?)

(4) Photographs, paintings, and figurines of birds often appeal to people who like a pretty picture. Is this a pretty bird? Why or why not? Try to sum up what it is about this bird, or about birds in general, that fascinated the poet.

# A Narrow Fellow in the Grass

A narrow fellow in the grass
Occasionally rides.
You may have met him—did you not?
His notice sudden is.

The grass divides as with a comb—
A spotted shaft is seen,
And then it closes at your feet
And opens further on.

He likes a boggy acre,
A floor too cool for corn.
Yet when a child, and barefoot,
I more than once at noon

Have passed, I thought, a whiplash
Unbraiding in the sun—
When stooping to secure it
It wrinkled, and was gone.

Several of nature's people
I know, and they know me.
I feel for them a transport
Of cordiality,

But never met this fellow
Attended or alone
Without a tighter breathing,
And zero at the bone.

## YOU AND THE POEM

(1) When did you first realize this is a poem about a snake? Point out several details that fit in with what you know about snakes. How would the grass part when it is divided "as with a comb"? (How else could the grass be parted? What would be the difference?)

(2) As used here, the word *transport* means a sudden, strong, warm or happy feeling. Cordiality is a warm feeling of friendliness that comes "from the heart."

Who do you think might be "several of nature's people" for whom the poet has warm, friendly feelings? In this poem, what words or details do most to make the snake seem different? What kind of feeling does the snake make the poet experience? Is it familiar? How would you describe it in your own words?

(3) Even though the snake is more strange or alien to the poet than other animals, she still talks at times as if it were an almost human creature. Where and how?

# I Stepped From Plank to Plank

I stepped from plank to plank,
A slow and cautious way.
The stars about my head I felt,
About my feet the sea.

I knew not but the next
Would be my final inch—
This gave me that precarious gait
Some call experience.

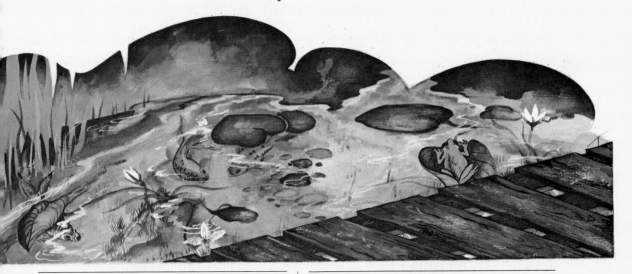

## YOU AND THE POEM

(1) Emily Dickinson had an uncanny ability to take familiar words and give us a lively feeling of what they really mean. The word *precarious* describes something that is insecure, unstable—balanced in such a way that it may tip over any minute. How does this poem act out the precariousness of human experience?

(2) "Gait" is the way we walk. How do you think that people who have developed this "precarious gait" would walk? How would they act?

## Your Turn

A very regular use of rhyme can make a poem sound pat. Emily Dickinson's use of rhyme is irregular and unpredictable—like other things about her poetry. She often uses **assonance,** or half-rhyme: Two words end in ways that make them sound *somewhat* alike. *Grass* and *pass* make a complete rhyme. But *lawn* and *down* make only a half-rhyme. Find examples of half-rhyme, or assonance, in this poem. Examine the poet's use of rhyme in some of the other poems.

# Because I Could Not Stop for Death

Because I could not stop for Death,
He kindly stopped for me.
The carriage held but just ourselves
And Immortality.

We slowly drove, he knew no haste,
And I had put away
My labor, and my leisure too,
For his civility.

We passed the school, where children strove
At recess, in the ring.
We passed the fields of gazing grain,
We passed the setting sun.

Or rather, he passed us.
The dews grew quivering and chill,
For only gossamer my gown,
My tippet only tulle.

We paused before a house that seemed
A swelling of the ground
The roof was scarcely visible,
The cornice in the ground.

Since then 'tis centuries, and yet
Feels shorter than the day
I first surmised the horses' heads
Were toward eternity.

## YOU AND THE POEM

(1) What is different or unexpected about the way the poet describes the arrival of Death in the first two stanzas? What does *civility* mean? Do you think readers of this poem would be ready to think of death as a journey?

(2) Is it a coincidence that the poet passes the school, the fields of grain, and then the setting sun, in that order? If they are intended as **symbols,** what is the symbolic meaning of each?

(3) *Gossamer* is a kind of cobweb floating in the late summer air. *Tulle* is a silky or lacy material used in veils. A *tippet* is a kind of scarf. Why are these materials appropriate to the kind of scene we are observing? How do they fit into the picture?

(4) What was the house that "seemed a swelling of the ground"? How do you know? (What is a "cornice"?)

(5) When we surmise, we guess, or reach a conclusion. Shouldn't the poet have known from the beginning that entering the carriage meant the end of her life and the beginning of "eternity"? Or is there anything about what happened that could have kept her from realizing it? What might have kept her from thinking about it for a time?

# The Bustle in a House

The bustle in a house
The morning after death
Is solemnest of industries
Enacted upon earth—

The sweeping up the heart,
And putting love away
We shall not want to use again
Until eternity.

# Hope Is the Thing With Feathers

Hope is the thing with feathers
That perches in the soul,
And sings the tune without the words,
And never stops at all,

And sweetest in the gale is heard;
And sore must be the storm
That could abash the little bird
That kept so many warm.

I've heard it in the chillest land,
And on the strangest sea;
Yet, never, in extremity,
It asked a crumb of me.

### YOU AND THE POEM

(1) Industry today means large organized factory production. It originally meant "keeping busy" on a more personal scale. What other words in this poem point toward familiar, homey activities—people keeping busy doing ordinary things?

(2) The activities described in this poem are **figurative**—they are imaginative comparisons that act out in front of us things that are really happening in our minds. What is really happening to the heart and to love?

(3) Do you think the poem would have been more sad or "solemn" if it had showed us a house of mourning as a very quiet place, where all activity had stopped?

### YOU AND THE POEM

(1) For you, is a bird a good **symbol** of hope? Point out as many hopeful things about this poem as you can.

(2) *Extremity* is a word for extreme danger or need. What does it mean that the bird never "asked a crumb" of the poet?

### Your Turn

Write about something that for you makes a good symbol of one of the following:

hope        despair
sadness     fear
happiness   danger

● Thomas Paine (1737–1809), an Englishman, came to America in 1774. He became a widely known and effective champion of American independence. His writing illustrates the kind of passionate appeal that in times of crisis can sway masses of people. The following selection is from a series of pamphlets published between 1776 and 1783. It appeared at a time when the American forces under Washington were threatened with defeat, and it helped restore their morale. Originally, the American colonists had objected to attempts of the British government to impose taxes that had not been approved by the colonial assemblies. As the conflict developed into the American War of Independence, American opinion was divided between the Revolutionists, or Whigs, and the loyalists, or Tories. The Tories were in favor of compromise with Britain, so that the colonies could remain united with the mother country. General Howe commanded one major part of the British forces. These were made up in large part of Hessians, who were mercenaries from Germany. The following passages are famous examples of Paine's ability to rally supporters to his cause.

## Thomas Paine

# The American Crisis

These are the times that try men's souls. The summer soldier and the sunshine patriot will, in this crisis, shrink from the service of his country, but he that stands it now deserves the love and thanks of man and woman. Tyranny, like hell, is not easily conquered. Yet we have this consolation with us that the harder the conflict, the more glorious the triumph. What we obtain too cheap, we esteem too lightly. It is dearness only that gives everything its value. Heaven knows how to put a proper price upon its good; and it would be strange indeed if so celestial an article as freedom should not be highly rated. Britain, with an army to enforce her tyranny, has declared that she has a right not only to tax but "to bind us in all cases whatsoever," and if being bound in that manner is not slavery, then is there not such a thing as slavery upon earth. Even the expression is impious, for so unlimited a power can belong only to God.

Whether the independence of the continent was declared too soon, or delayed too long, I will not now enter into as an argument. My own simple opinion is that had it been eight months earlier, it would have been much better. We did not make a proper use of last winter; neither could we, while we were in a dependent state. However, the fault, if it were one, was all our own. We have none to blame but ourselves. But no great deal is lost yet. All that Howe* has been doing for this month past is rather a ravage than a conquest, which the spirit of the Jerseys a year ago would have quickly repulsed, and which time and a little resolution will soon recover.

*Howe: Sir William, a British general in the American Revolution.

I have as little superstition in me as any man living, but my secret opinion has ever been, and still is, that God Almighty will not give up a people to military destruction, or leave them unsupportedly to perish, who have so earnestly and so repeatedly sought to avoid the calamities of war by every decent method which wisdom could invent. Neither have I so much of the infidel in me as to suppose that He has relinquished the government of the world and given us up to the care of devils. I cannot see on what grounds the king of Britain can look up to Heaven for help against us: a common murderer, a highwayman, or a housebreaker has as good a pretense as he.

It is surprising to see how rapidly a panic will sometimes run through a country. All nations and ages have been subject to them: Britain has trembled at the report of a French fleet of flat-bottomed boats. In the fourteenth century the whole English army, after ravaging the kingdom of France, was driven back like men petrified with fear; and this brave exploit was performed by a few broken forces collected and headed by a woman, Joan of Arc. Would that heaven might inspire some Jersey maid to spirit up her countrymen! Yet panics, in some cases, have their uses. They produce as much good as hurt. Their duration is always short. The mind soon grows through them and acquires a firmer habit than before. But their peculiar advantage is that they are the touchstones of sincerity and hypocrisy, and bring things and men to light which might otherwise have lain forever undiscovered. In fact, they have the same effect on secret traitors which an imaginary apparition would have upon a private murderer. They sift out the hidden thoughts of man and hold them up in public to the world. Many a disguised Tory has lately shown his head that shall curse the day on which Howe arrived upon the Delaware. . . .

Why is it that the enemy have left the New England provinces and made these middle ones the seat of war? The answer is easy: New England is not infested with Tories, and we are. I have been tender in raising the cry against these men, and used numberless arguments to show them their danger, but it will not do to sacrifice a world to either their folly or their baseness. The period is now arrived in which either they or we must change our sentiments, or one or both must fall. And what is a Tory? Good God! What is he? I should not be afraid to go with a hundred Whigs against a thousand Tories, were they to attempt to get into arms. Every Tory is a coward; for servile, slavish, self-interested fear is the foundation of Toryism; and a man under such influence, though he may be cruel, never can be brave.

But, before the line of irrecoverable separation be drawn between us, let us reason the matter together: Your conduct is an invitation to the enemy, yet not one in a thousand of you has heart enough to join him. Howe is as much deceived by you as the American cause is injured by you. He expects you will all take up arms and flock to his standard with muskets on your shoulders. Your opinions are of no use to him unless you support him personally, for it is soldiers and not Tories that he wants.

I once felt all that kind of anger which a man ought to feel against the mean principles that are held by the Tories. A noted one, who kept a tavern at Amboy, was standing at his door with as pretty a child in his hand, about eight or nine years old, as I ever saw, and, after speaking his mind as freely as he thought was prudent, finished with this unfatherly expression, "Well! give me peace in my day." Not a man lives on the continent but fully believes that a separation must sometime or other finally take place, and a generous parent should have said, "If there must be trouble, let it be in my day, that my child may have peace." This single reflection, well applied, is sufficient to awaken every man to duty. Not a place upon earth might be so happy as America. Her situation is remote from all the wrangling world, and she has nothing to do but to trade with them. A man can easily distinguish in himself between temper and principle, and I am as confident as I am that God governs the world that America will never be happy till she gets clear of foreign dominion. Wars without ceasing will break out till that period arrives, and the continent must in the end be conqueror. For though the flame of liberty may sometimes cease to shine, the coal can never expire. . . .

I call not upon a few, but upon all—not on this state or that state, but on every state: Up and help us! Lay your shoulders to the wheel! Better have too much force than too little, when so great an object is at stake. Let it be told to the future world that in the depth of winter, when nothing but hope and virtue could survive, the city and the country, alarmed at one common danger, came forth to meet it. Say not that thousands are gone, turn out your tens of thousands. Throw not the burden of the day upon Providence, but "show your faith by your works," that God may bless you. It matters not where you live, or what rank of life you hold, the evil or the blessing will reach you all. The far and the near, the home counties and the back, the rich and the poor, will suffer or rejoice alike. The heart that feels not now is dead. The blood of his children will curse his cowardice who shrinks back at a time when a little might have saved the whole and made *them* happy. I love the man that can smile in trouble, that can gather strength from distress, and grow brave by reflection. It is the business of little minds to shrink; but he whose heart is firm, and whose conscience approves his conduct, will pursue his principles unto death. My own line of reasoning is to myself as straight and clear as a ray of light. Not all the treasures of the world, so far as I believe, could have induced me to support an offensive war, for I think it murder. But if a thief breaks into my house, burns and destroys my property, and kills or threatens to kill me, or those that are in it, and to "bind me in all cases whatsoever" to his absolute will, am I to suffer it? What signifies it to me whether he who does it is a king or a common man, my countryman or not my countryman—whether it be done by an individual villain, or an army of them? If we reason to the root of things we shall find no difference. Neither can any just cause be assigned why we should punish in the one case and pardon in the other. Let them call me rebel, and welcome, I feel no concern from it; but I should suffer the misery of devils were I to swear allegiance to one whose character is that of a stupid, stubborn, worthless, brutish man. I conceive likewise a horrid idea in receiving mercy from a being who at the last day shall be shrieking to the rocks and mountains to cover him, and fleeing with terror from the orphan, the widow, and the slain America.

There are cases which cannot be overdone by language, and this is one. There are persons too who see not the full extent of the evil which threatens them. They solace themselves with hopes that the enemy, if they succeed, will be merciful. It is the madness of folly to expect mercy from those who have refused to do justice;

and even mercy, where conquest is the object, is only a trick of war. The cunning of the fox is as murderous as the violence of the wolf, and we ought to guard equally against both. . . .

I dwell not upon the powers of imagination. I bring reason to your ears: and in language as plain as ABC hold up truth to your eyes. I thank God that I fear not. I see no real cause for fear. I know our situation well and can see the way out of it. While our army was collected, Howe dared not risk a battle. It is no credit to him that he decamped from the White Plains and waited a mean opportunity to ravage the defenseless Jerseys; but it is great credit to us that, with a handful of men, we sustained an orderly retreat for near a hundred miles, brought off our ammunition, all our field pieces, the greatest part of our stores, and had four rivers to pass. None can say that our retreat was precipitate, for we were near three weeks in performing it, that the country might have time to come in. Twice we marched back to meet the enemy and remained out till dark. The sign of fear was not seen in our camp, and had not some of the cowardly and disaffected inhabitants spread false alarms through the country, the Jerseys had never been ravaged. Once more we are again collected and collecting. Our new army at both ends of the continent is recruiting fast, and we shall be able to open the next campaign with sixty thousand men, well armed and clothed. This is our situation, and who will may know it. By perseverance and fortitude we have the prospect of a glorious issue; by cowardice and submission, the sad choice of a variety of evils—a ravaged country, a depopulated city, habitations without safety, and slavery without hope. Look on this picture and weep over it! And if there yet remains one thoughtless wretch who believes it not, let him suffer it unlamented.

# YOU AND TOM PAINE

When Paine wrote, the tradition of political oratory was very much alive. Great political leaders knew how to inspire their followers. They knew how to best their opponents in debate. As we read Tom Paine's pamphlets, we can imagine hearing the voice of a rousing public speaker stirring up the enthusiasm of a crowd. How does Paine persuade readers who may have been bothered by doubt? How does he approach those who may have been wavering between the two sides? Answer the following questions:

(1) Like an effective public speaker, Paine alternates long, flowing sentences with short sentences that vigorously sum up a major point. These short sentences carry special emphasis: They stand out so that we can absorb and remember them. Read the following examples out loud. Try to make them ring with the right kind of emphasis:

> These are the times that try men's souls.
> Tyranny, like hell, is not easily conquered.
> We have none to blame but ourselves.
> The heart that feels not now is dead.

(2) An effective speaker sometimes uses *parallel* sentence structure to help line up ideas for our attention. Similar ideas appear in similar form, so that they can easily reinforce each other. Or, opposite ideas appear in similar form, so that the contrast stands out clearly. Study the clear lining-up of similar or opposite ideas in the following examples. Listen to them read out loud. Choose several as *model sentences*. For each, write a similar sentence of your own on a current topic. Imitate the parallel structure of the original.

a. We have this consolation with us that
    the harder the conflict,
    the more glorious the triumph.

b. What we obtain too cheap,
    we esteem too lightly.

c. The far and the near,
    the home counties and the back,
    the rich and the poor,
    will suffer or rejoice alike.

d. I love the man that can smile in trouble,
    that can gather strength from distress,
    and
    grow brave by reflection.

e. The cunning of the fox
    is as murderous as
    the violence of the wolf.

f. He whose heart is firm, and
    whose conscience approves his conduct,
    will pursue his principles unto death.

g. I bring reason to your ears:
    and in language as plain as ABC
    hold up truth to your eyes.

h. By perseverance and fortitude,
    we have the prospect of a glorious issue;
    by cowardice and submission,
    the sad choice of a variety of evils.

(3) The language of persuasion tends to polarize opposition: It makes the good seem very good, the bad extremely evil. Point out strong words of disapproval or denunciation. Which are some of Paine's most extreme or cutting attacks on the enemy and on backsliders? Point out words that do the opposite: Find words and expressions that help justify the American cause or inspire its supporters. Which words or expressions that Paine uses would still be "fighting words" today?

(4) Persuasive writers often make a claim to moderation: Their side has shown restraint, or is opposed to violence and aggression. They often know how to point out the good or encouraging side of apparent setbacks. Where and how does Paine employ these familiar strategies of persuasion in this selection?

| Your Turn | Abraham Lincoln, Susan B. Anthony, Eleanor Roosevelt, John F. Kennedy, Martin Luther King. Practice reading the passage out loud. |
|---|---|

Find a short passage from a speech by one of the following: Frederick Douglass,

Language/Composition Activity B14

OUR READING VOCABULARY

# The Times That Try Men's Souls

How much difficulty does a modern reader have with Paine's solemn, elevated style? Look at each italicized word. From the list of meanings at the end, choose the one that best fits the context. In your own words, what is each sentence as a whole saying?

1. It would be strange if so *celestial* an article as freedom should not be highly rated.
2. The expression is *impious,* for so unlimited a power can belong only to God.
3. All that Howe has been doing for this month is rather a *ravage* than a conquest.
4. The spirit of the Jerseys a year ago would have quickly *repulsed* the enemy.
5. We have earnestly sought to avoid the *calamities* of war.
6. Only an *infidel* could suppose that God has given up the government of the world.
7. All nations have been *subject to* panic.
8. The English army was driven back like men *petrified* with fear.
9. New England is not *infested* with Tories.
10. *Servile* fear is the foundation of Toryism.
11. Howe expects you to flock to his *standard.*
12. This single *reflection* is sufficient to awaken every man to his duty.
13. America will never be happy until she gets clear of foreign *dominion.*
14. Not all the treasures of the world could have *induced* me to support an offensive war.
15. If a thief breaks into my home, am I to *suffer* it?
16. They *solace* themselves with hopes that the enemy will be merciful.
17. No one can say that our retreat was *precipitate.*
18. Some of the cowardly and *disaffected* inhabitants spread false alarms.
19. We have the prospect of a glorious *issue.*
20. Let him suffer *unlamented.*

Meanings:

| | | |
|---|---|---|
| a. tolerate | h. persuaded | o. end result |
| b. thought | i. slavish | p. disasters |
| c. heavenly | j. rule | q. unbeliever |
| d. unmourned | k. turned to stone | r. console, cheer up |
| e. against religion | l. overhasty | s. no longer loyal |
| f. banner | m. plundering | t. victims of |
| g. thrown back | n. overrun | |

● Ralph Waldo Emerson (1803–1882) came from a family of New England clergymen. He started his own career as a Unitarian minister in Boston. But he left the church so that he could preach his own ideas in his own way. As an independent lecturer and writer, he spent a lifetime teaching people to trust their own moral sense and their own religious feelings. He became the leader of the American Transcendentalists, who looked beyond material reality to the divine force at work in human beings and in nature. (When we transcend surface appearances, we "go beyond" them to the real truth.) Emerson's essays and poems strengthened the traditional American belief in the importance of the individual. He called on people to trust their own powers and shape their own destiny. Most of the following selected passages are from his famous essay "Self-Reliance," first published in 1841.

## Ralph Waldo Emerson

# On Self-Reliance

Trust thyself: every heart vibrates to that iron string. Accept the place the divine providence has found for you, the society of your contemporaries, the connection of events. Great men have always done so, and confided themselves childlike to the genius of their age.

There is a time in every man's education when he arrives at the conviction that envy is ignorance; that imitation is suicide; that he must take himself for better for worse as his portion; that though the wide universe is full of good, no kernel of nourishing corn can come to him but through his toil bestowed on that plot of ground which is given to him to till.

Whoso would be a man, must be a nonconformist. He who would gather immortal palms must not be hindered by the name of goodness, but must explore if it be goodness. Nothing is at last sacred but the integrity of your own mind. Absolve you to yourself, and you shall have the suffrage of the world. I remember an answer which when quite young I was prompted to make to a valued adviser. On my saying, "What have I to do with the sacredness of traditions, if I live wholly from within?" my friend suggested, "But these impulses may be from below, not from above." I replied, "They do not seem to me to be such; but if I am the Devil's child, I will live then from the Devil." No law can be sacred to me but that of my nature. Good and bad are but names very readily transferable to that or this. The only right is what is after my constitution, the only wrong what is against it.

The popular fable of the drunk carried to the duke's house, washed and dressed and laid in the duke's bed, and, on his waking, treated like the duke, and assured that he had been insane, owes its popularity to the fact that it symbolizes so well the state of man, who now and then wakes up, exercises his reason, and finds himself a true prince.

Man is timid and apologetic. He is no longer upright. He dares not say "I think," "I am," but quotes some saint or sage. He is ashamed before the blade of grass or the blowing rose. These roses under my window make no reference to former roses or to better ones. They are for what they are. They exist with God today. There is no time to them. There is simply the rose. It is perfect in every moment of its existence. Before a leaf bud has burst, its whole life acts; in the full-blown flower there is no more; in the leafless root there is no less. Its nature is satisfied, and it satisfies nature, in all moments alike. But man postpones or remembers. He does not live in the present but laments the past, or, heedless of the riches that surround him, stands on tiptoe to foresee the future. He cannot be happy and strong until he too lives with nature in the present, above time.

I hope in these days we have heard the last of conformity and consistency. Let the words be ridiculous henceforward. Instead of the gong for dinner, let us hear a whistle from the Spartan fife. Let us never bow and apologize more. A great man is coming to eat at my house. I do not wish to please him; I wish that he should wish to please me. I will stand here for humanity, and though I would make it kind, I would make it true. Let us affront and reprimand the smooth mediocrity and squalid contentment of the times, and hurl in the face of custom, and trade, and office, the fact which is the upshot of all history, that there is a great responsible Thinker and Actor working wherever a man works. A true man belongs to no other time or place, but is the center of things. Where he is, there is nature.

We have become timorous, desponding whimperers. We are afraid of truth, afraid of fortune, afraid of death, and afraid of each other. Our age yields no great and perfect persons. We want men and women who shall renovate life and our social state, but we see that most natures cannot satisfy their own wants, have an ambition out of all proportion to their practical force, and do lean and beg day and night continually. If our young men miscarry in their first enterprises, they lose all heart. If the young merchant fails, men say he is ruined. If the finest genius studies at one of our colleges, and is not installed in an office within one year afterwards in the cities or suburbs of Boston or New York, it seems to his friends and to himself that he is right in being disheartened, and in complaining the rest of his life. A sturdy lad from New Hampshire or Vermont, who in turn tries all the professions, who teams it, farms it, peddles, keeps a school, preaches, edits a newspaper, goes to Congress, buys a township, and so forth, in successive years, and always, like a cat, falls on his feet, is worth a hundred of these city dolls. He walks abreast with his days, and feels no shame in not "studying a profession," for he does not postpone his life, but lives already.

The civilized man has built a coach, but has lost the use of his feet. He is supported on crutches, but lacks so much support of muscle. He has a fine watch, but he fails of the skill to tell the hour by the sun. The man in the street does not know a star in the sky. The solstice he does not observe, the equinox he knows as little, and the whole bright calendar of the year is without a dial in his mind. His notebooks impair his memory. His libraries overload his wit. It may be a question whether

machinery does not encumber, whether we have not lost by refinement some energy.

In this country we are very vain of our political institutions, which sprung, within the memory of living men, from the character and condition of the people, which they still express . . . But our institutions, though in coincidence with the spirit of the age, have not any exemption from the practical defects which have discredited other forms. Every actual state is corrupt. Good men must not obey the laws too well. What satire on government can equal the severity of censure conveyed in the word *politic*, which now for ages has signified *cunning*, intimating that the state is a trick?

Nature is loved by what is best in us. It is loved as the city of God, although, or rather because there is no citizen. The sunset is unlike anything that is underneath it. It lacks men. And the beauty of nature must always seem unreal and mocking, until the landscape has human figures that are as good as itself. If there were good men, there would never be this rapture in nature. If the king is in the palace, nobody looks at the walls. It is when he is gone, and the house is filled with grooms and gazers, that we turn from the people to find relief in the majestic men that are suggested by the pictures and the architecture. The critics who complain of the sickly separation of the beauty of nature from the thing to be done, must consider that our hunting of the picturesque is inseparable from our protest against false society. Nature serves as a thermometer, detecting the presence or absence of the divine sentiment in man.

## YOU AND EMERSON

The words *integrity* and *nonconformity* have long been inspiring words to people who believe in the dignity of an individual. The word *integrity* comes from the Latin word for being whole, "of one piece." The word *conform* originally meant to adjust to the shape of something else. How do you think a follower of Emerson would explain what integrity and nonconformity are, and why they are important?

## A Closer Look

(1) Why would someone with Emerson's outlook call envy "ignorance"? Why does he call imitation "suicide"?

(2) What is Emerson's attitude toward warnings that some of our impulses may be devilish or very evil?

(3) Emerson repeatedly gives symbolic meaning to things from the world of nature. What ideas does he communicate by his references to "immortal palms," and "nourishing corn," or the blooming rose?

(4) What is the point of the story about the drunk in the duke's palace?

(5) What does *mediocrity* mean? Why would Emerson object to it so strongly?

(6) How would machinery "encumber" people?

(7) What would be Emerson's advice to someone planning a career?

(8) What is Emerson's attitude toward our political institutions? How does it fit in with his general outlook?

(9) In the last passage, Emerson talks about the relationship between nature and human beings. According to Emerson, what do we see or look for in nature? What function does it serve for us?

## Your Turn

In Emerson's time, public speakers were trained to make themselves heard. They knew how to speak solemnly and firmly. Many of Emerson's essays were first delivered as lectures. Select one of these passages. Practice reading it aloud in a serious and formal manner.

• Henry David Thoreau (1817–1862) is one of the best-known voices of nineteenth-century American individualism. He lived in Concord, Massachusetts, and carried on the New England tradition of sturdy independence. He graduated from Harvard College and was strongly influenced by Emerson's gospel of self-reliance. Thoreau refused to tie himself to a definite career. He distrusted possessions and institutions as obstacles to true individual freedom. He taught off and on and traveled as a lecturer, but most of his life he supported himself by odd jobs. One of the most famous American books is his autobiographical *Walden* (1854). It describes Thoreau's experiment in living close to nature in a cabin by Walden Pond, trying to clear his life of everything artificial and unnecessary. *Walden* became the bible of countless readers everywhere who felt that life was meant to be less rushed and pressured than it often is in the modern world. Thoreau's famous essay "On Civil Disobedience" (1849) grew out of his opposition to the war with Mexico, a war that greatly expanded the territory of the United States in the West and Southwest. Asserting that "That government is best which governs least," Thoreau justified the citizen's refusal to cooperate with an oppressive government or to obey bad laws. Mahatma Gandhi in India and others around the world found in this essay the inspiration for twentieth-century movements of nonviolent resistance to immoral governments. Thoreau believed that finally the individual conscience was a higher authority than the will of a powerful majority. Thoreau's writings called upon Americans to rediscover basic, simple guidelines for a more meaningful life. The following excerpt is from the opening chapter, called "Economy," in *Walden.* It describes the building of Thoreau's cabin and records the thoughts that were passing through his mind.

Henry David Thoreau

# An Experiment in Simple Living

Every morning was a cheerful invitation to make my life of equal simplicity, and I may say innocence, with Nature herself.

—Henry David Thoreau,
*Walden*

Near the end of March, 1845, I borrowed an ax and went down to the woods by Walden Pond, nearest to where I intended to build my house, and began to cut down some tall arrowy white pines, still in their youth, for timber. It is difficult to begin without borrowing, but perhaps it is the most generous course thus to permit your fellowmen to have an interest in your enterprise. The owner of the ax, as he released his hold on it, said that it was the apple of his eye; but I returned it sharper than I received it. It was a pleasant hillside where I worked, covered with pine woods, through which I looked out on the pond, and a small open field in the woods where pines and hickories were springing up. The ice in the pond was not yet dissolved, though there were some open spaces, and it was all dark-colored and saturated with water. There were some slight flurries of snow during the days that I worked there. But for the most part when I came out on to the railroad, on my way home, its yellow sand heap stretched away gleaming in the hazy atmosphere, and the rails shone in the spring sun, and I heard the lark and pewee and other birds already come to commence another year with us. They were pleasant spring days, in which the winter of man's discontent was thawing as well as the earth, and the life that had lain torpid began to stretch itself. One day, when my ax had come off and I had cut a green hickory for a wedge, driving it with a stone, and had placed the whole to soak in a pond hole in order to swell the wood, I saw a striped snake run into the water. He lay on the bottom, apparently without inconvenience, as long as I stayed there, or more than a quarter of an hour—perhaps because he had not yet fairly come out of the torpid state. It appeared to me that for a like reason men remain in their present low and primitive condition. But if they should feel the influence of the spring of springs arousing them, they would of necessity rise to a higher life. I had previously seen the snakes in frosty mornings in my path with portions of their bodies still numb and inflexible, waiting for the sun to thaw them. On the 1st of April, it rained and melted the ice, and in the early part of the day, which was very foggy, I heard a stray goose groping about over the pond and cackling as if lost, or like the spirit of the fog.

So I went on for some days cutting and hewing timber, and also studs and rafters, all with my narrow ax, not having many communicable or scholar-like thoughts, singing to myself,—

> Men say they know many things;
> But lo! they have taken wings—
> The arts and sciences,
> And a thousand appliances;
> The wind that blows
> Is all that anybody knows.

I hewed the main timbers six inches square, most of the studs on two sides only, and the rafters and floor timbers on one side, leaving the rest of the bark on, so that they were just as straight and much stronger than sawed ones. Each stick was carefully mortised or tenoned by its stump, for I had borrowed other tools by this time. My days in the woods were not very long ones. Yet I usually carried my dinner of bread and butter, and read the newspaper in which it was wrapped, at noon, sitting amid the green pine boughs which I had cut off. To my bread was imparted some of their fragrance, for my hands were covered with a thick coat of pitch. Before I had done, I was more the friend than the foe of the pine tree, though I had cut down some of them, having become better acquainted with it. Sometimes a rambler in the wood was attracted by the sound of my ax, and we chatted pleasantly over the chips which I had made.

By the middle of April, for I made no haste in my work, but rather made the most of it, my house was framed and ready for the raising. I had already bought the shanty of James Collins, an Irishman who worked on the Fitchburg Railroad, for boards. James Collins' shanty was considered an uncommonly fine one. When I called to see it he was not at home. I walked about the outside, at first unobserved from within, the window was so deep and high. It was of small dimensions, with a peaked cottage roof, and not much else to be seen, the dirt being raised five

feet all around as if it were a compost heap. The roof was the soundest part, though a good deal warped and made brittle by the sun. Doorsill there was none, but a perennial passage for the hens under the door board. Mrs. C. came to the door and asked me to view it from the inside. The hens were driven in by my approach. It was dark, and had a dirt floor for the most part, dank and clammy, only here a board and there a board which would not bear removal. She lighted a lamp to show me the inside of the roof and the walls, and also that the board floor extended under the bed, warning me not to step into the cellar, a sort of dust hole two feet deep. In her own words, they were "good boards overhead, good boards all around, and a good window,"—of two whole squares originally, only the cat had passed out that way lately. There was a stove, a bed, and a place to sit, an infant in the house where it was born, a silk parasol, gilt-framed looking glass, and a patent new coffee mill nailed to an oak sapling, all told. The bargain was soon concluded, for James had in the meanwhile returned: I to pay four dollars and twenty-five cents tonight; he to vacate at five tomorrow morning, selling to nobody else meanwhile; I to take possession at six. It were well, he said, to be there early and anticipate certain wholly unjust claims on the score of ground rent and fuel. This he assured me was the only encumbrance. At six I passed him and his family on the road. One large bundle held their all—bed, coffee mill, looking glass, hens—all but the cat. She took to the woods and became a wild cat, and, as I learned afterward, trod in a trap set for woodchucks, and so became a dead cat at last.

I took down this dwelling the same morning, drawing the nails, and removed it to the pondside by small cartloads, spreading the boards on the grass there to bleach and warp back again in the sun. One early thrush gave me a note or two as I drove along the woodland path. I was informed treacherously by a young Patrick that neighbor Seeley, an Irishman, in the intervals of the carting, transferred the still tolerable, straight, and drivable nails, staples, and spikes to his pocket, and then stood when I came back to pass the time of day, and look freshly up, unconcerned, with spring thoughts, at the devastation; there being a dearth of work, as he said.

I dug my cellar in the side of a hill sloping to the south, where a woodchuck had formerly dug his burrow, down through sumach and blackberry roots, and the lowest stain of vegetation, six feet square by seven deep, to a fine sand where potatoes would not freeze in any winter. The sides were left shelving, and not stoned; but the sun having never shone on them, the sand still keeps its place. It was but two hours' work. I took particular pleasure in this breaking of ground, for in almost all latitudes men dig into the earth for an equable temperature. Under the most splendid house in the city is still to be found the cellar where they store their roots as of old, and long after the superstructure has disappeared, posterity remark its dent in the earth. The house is still but a sort of porch at the entrance of a burrow.

At length, in the beginning of May, with the help of some of my acquaintances, rather to improve so good an occasion for neighborliness than from any necessity, I set up the frame of my house. . . . I began to occupy my house on the 4th of July, as soon as it was boarded and roofed, for the boards were carefully feather-edged and lapped, so that it was perfectly impervious to rain. But before boarding I laid the foundation of a chimney at one end, bringing two cartloads of stones up the hill from the pond in my arms. I built the chimney after my hoeing in the fall, before a fire became necessary for warmth, doing my cooking in the meanwhile out-of-doors on the ground, early in the morning—which mode I still think is in some respects more convenient and agreeable than the usual one. When it stormed before my bread was baked, I fixed a few boards over the fire, and sat under them to watch my loaf, and passed some pleasant hours in that way. In those days, when my hands were much employed, I read but little, but the least scraps of paper which lay on the ground, my holder, or tablecloth, afforded me as much entertainment, in fact answered the same purpose as the Iliad.

It would be worthwhile to build still more deliberately than I did, considering, for instance, what foundation a door, a window, a cellar, a garret, have in the nature of man, and perhaps never raising any superstructure until we found a better reason for it than our temporal necessities even. There is some of the same fitness in a man's building his own house that there is in a bird's building its own nest. Who knows but if men constructed their dwellings with their own hands, and provided food for themselves and families simply and honestly enough, the poetic faculty would be universally developed, as birds universally sing when they are so engaged? But alas! we do like cowbirds and cuckoos, which lay their eggs in nests which other birds have built, and cheer no traveler with their chattering and unmusical notes. Shall we forever resign the pleasure of construction to the carpenter? What does architecture amount to in the experience of the mass of men? I never in all my walks came across a man engaged in so simple and natural an occupation as building his house. We belong to the community. It is not the tailor alone who is the ninth part of a man. It is as much the preacher, and the merchant, and the farmer. Where is this division of labor to end? And what object does it finally serve? No doubt another *may* also think for me, but it is not therefore desirable that he should do so to the exclusion of my thinking for myself. . . .

Before winter I built a chimney, and shingled the sides of my house, which were already impervious to rain, with imperfect and sappy shingles made of the first slice of the log, whose edges I was obliged to straighten with a plane.

I have thus a tight shingled and plastered house, ten feet wide by fifteen long, and eight-feet posts, with a garret and a closet, a large window on each side, two trapdoors, one door at the end, and a brick fireplace opposite. The exact cost of my house, paying the usual price for such materials as I used, but not counting the work, all of which was done by myself, was as follows. I give the details because very few are able to tell exactly what their houses cost, and fewer still, if any, the separate cost of the various materials which compose them:

| | |
|---|---|
| Boards, | $8.03½ |
| (*mostly shanty boards*) | |
| Refuse shingles for roof | |
| and sides, | 4.00 |
| Laths, | 4.00 |
| Two secondhand windows | |
| with glass, | 2.43 |
| One thousand old brick, | 4.00 |
| Two casks of lime, | 2.40 |
| (*That was high*) | |
| Hair, | 0.31 |
| (*More than I needed*) | |
| Mantle-tree iron, | 0.15 |
| Nails, | 3.90 |
| Hinges and screws, | 0.14 |
| Latch, | 0.10 |
| Chalk, | 0.01 |
| Transportation, | 1.40 |
| (*I carried a good part on* | |
| *my back*) | |
| In all, | $28.12½ |

These are all the materials except the timber, stones and sand, which I claimed by squatter's right. I have also a small woodshed adjoining, made chiefly of the stuff which was left after building the house.

I thus found that the student who wishes for a shelter can obtain one for a lifetime at an expense not greater than the rent which he now pays annually. . . . The student who secures his leisure and retirement by systematically shirking any labor obtains but an ignoble and unprofitable leisure, defrauding himself of the experience which alone can make leisure fruitful. "But," says one, "you do not mean that the students should go to work with their hands instead of their heads?" I do not mean that exactly, but I mean something which he might think a good deal like that. I mean that they should not *play* life, or *study* it merely, while the community supports them at this expensive game, but earnestly *live* it from beginning to end. How could youths better learn to live than by at once trying the experiment of living? This would exercise their minds as much as mathematics. If I wished a boy to know something about the arts and sciences, for instance, I would not pursue the common course, which is merely to send him into the neighborhood of some professor, where anything is practiced but the art of life: to survey the world through a telescope or a microscope, and never with his natural eye; to study chemistry, and not learn how his bread is made—or mechanics, and not learn how it is earned. . . . Which would have advanced the most at the end of a month—the boy who had made his own jackknife from the ore which he had dug and smelted, reading as much as would be necessary for this—or the boy who had attended the lectures on metallurgy at the Institute in the meanwhile, and had received a penknife from his father? Which would be most likely to cut his fingers?

One says to me, "I wonder that you do not lay up money. You love to travel. You might take the cars and go to Fitchburg today and see the country." But I am wiser than that. I have learned that the swiftest traveller is he that goes afoot. I say to my friend, "Suppose we try who will get there first. The distance is thirty miles, the fare ninety cents. That is almost a day's wages. I remember when wages were sixty cents a day for laborers on this very road. Well, I start now on foot and get there before night. I have travelled at that rate by the week together. You will in the meanwhile have earned your fare, and arrive there some time tomorrow, or possibly this evening, if you are lucky enough to get a job in season. Instead of going to Fitchburg, you will be working here the

greater part of the day. And so, if the railroad reached round the world, I think that I should keep ahead of you. As for seeing the country and getting experience of that kind, I should have to cut your acquaintance altogether."

Before I finished my house, wishing to earn ten or twelve dollars by some honest and agreeable method, in order to meet my unusual expenses, I planted about two acres and a half of light and sandy soil near it chiefly with beans, but also a small part with potatoes, corn, peas, and turnips. The lot contains eleven acres, mostly growing up to pines and hickories, and was sold the past season for eight dollars and eight cents an acre. One farmer said that it was "good for nothing but to raise cheeping squirrels on." I put no manure whatever on this land, not being the owner, but merely a squatter, and not expecting to cultivate so much again, and I did not quite hoe it all once. I got out several cords of stumps in plowing, which supplied me with fuel for a long time and left small circles of virgin mould, easily distinguishable through the summer by the greater luxuriance of the beans there. The dead and for the most part unmerchantable wood behind my house, and the driftwood from the pond, have supplied the remainder of my fuel. I was obliged to hire a team and a man for the plowing, though I held the plow myself. My farm outgoes for the first season were, for implements, seed, work, etc. $14.72½. The seed corn was given me. This never costs anything to speak of, unless you plant more than enough. I got twelve bushels of beans, and eighteen bushels of potatoes, besides some peas and sweet corn. The yellow corn and turnips were too late to come to anything. My whole income from the farm was

|  | $23.44. |
|---|---|
| Deducting the outgoes, | 14.72½ |
| There are left, | $8.71½, |

besides produce consumed and on hand at the time this estimate was made of the value of $4.50. . . . All things considered, I believe that that was doing better than any farmer in Concord did that year.

The next year I did better still, for I spaded up all the land which I required, about a third of an acre. I learned from the experience of both years that if one would live simply and eat only the crop which he raised, and raise no more than he ate, and not exchange it for an insufficient quantity of more luxurious and expensive things, he would need to cultivate only a few rods of ground. It would be cheaper to spade up than to use oxen to plow it, and to select a fresh spot from time to time than to manure the old, and he could do all his necessary farm work as it were with his left hand at odd hours in the summer. Thus he would not be tied to an ox, or horse, or cow, or pig, as at present. I desire to speak impartially on this point, and as one not interested in the success or failure of the present economical and social arrangements. I was more independent than any farmer in Concord, for I was not anchored to a house or farm, but could follow the bent of my genius, which is a very crooked one, every moment. Besides being better off than they already, if my house had been burned or my crops had failed, I should have been nearly as well off as before.

## YOU AND THOREAU

Henry David Thoreau set out to do things "deliberately" and "earnestly"—to do them only if they had purpose, a meaning. He makes us take a fresh look at many things that for other people might have seemed a familiar part of everyday routine. Answer the following questions about the things he did and thought about:

(1) Thoreau often makes us think about the simple events of a day and asks us to learn from them. Often the things he observes become **symbols** to him. They acquire a deeper meaning beyond themselves. Early in this selection, what was the symbolic meaning of the snake for him? Later, what for him was the symbolic meaning of cellars?

(2) Thoreau often puzzled or startled his contemporaries by his unconventional attitudes. What seems different about his attitude toward borrowing, or his attitude toward stealing?

(3) What is "division of labor"? How is the term usually used, and how is it usually justified? What would be some good examples? Why is Thoreau opposed to it? Describe Thoreau's thoughts about the advantages of people's building their own houses and raising their own food for themselves and for their families.

(4) What advice does Thoreau have for students? How does he make it persuasive? How much is it followed in the schools you have known?

(5) Like practical people that we can observe every day, Thoreau carefully totals up the cost of things. But the kind of reckoning he does leads him to unusual conclusions. What did he tell his friend about the cost of travel? What was his point?

(6) Thoreau's credo was "Simplicity, simplicity, simplicity!" How does his search for simplicity show in his experiments as a farmer? In what ways did he simplify the way farmers usually operate?

## A Closer Look

How well do you understand some of the old-fashioned expressions used by Thoreau? In each of the following statements, what is the meaning of the part quoted from Thoreau's essay? How much help do you get from the context of each unfamiliar expression? How does the modern meaning or use of some of the words help you?

1. The shanty had a dirt floor and only here and there a board "which would not bear removal."

2. By the middle of April, the house was "framed and ready for the raising."

3. The seller asked Thoreau to appear early in the morning to take over the property sold to him in order to "anticipate certain wholly unjust claims on the score of ground rent and fuel."

4. These possible claims against the property were "the only encumbrance."

5. Neighbor Seeley watched Thoreau, since there was "a dearth of work."

6. Because of the cellar, long after the superstructure of a house has disappeared, "posterity remark its dent in the earth."

7. According to Thoreau, we should have a better reason to start building "than our temporal necessities even."

8. Thoreau asked where the division of labor would end and "what object" it finally serves.

9. One of Thoreau's friends was surprised that he did not "lay up" money in order to travel.

10. Thoreau preferred not to be tied down by property, so that he "could follow the bent of my genius, which is a very crooked one."

### Your Turn

Writers with new or unusual ideas often make the reader want to say: "Yes, but . . ." Does Thoreau raise questions or doubts in your mind? Suppose you could raise your own personal doubts with the author. What would you say?

---

Language/Composition Activity B15

THE BALANCED SENTENCE
# Simplicity, Simplicity, Simplicity!

Many of Thoreau's sentences show us both what is desirable and its opposite. They describe the ideal and how we fall short. He often uses parallel sentence structure to balance off what we should do and what we should not do. Read several of the following sentences from other parts of *Walden* out loud. Select several of them as *model sentences*—for each, write a similarly balanced sentence of your own, on a current topic. Try to follow a very similar pattern, filling in ideas or opinions of your own. Use a separate sheet of paper.

1. MODEL: The morning wind forever blows, the poem of creation is uninterrupted; but few are the ears that hear it.

    SENTENCE FRAME: The _____, the _____; but _____.

2. MODEL: Let us spend one day as deliberately as Nature, and not be thrown off the track by every nutshell and mosquito's wing that falls on the rails.

    SENTENCE FRAME: Let us _____ and not _____.

3. MODEL: We should impart our courage, and not our despair, our health and ease, and not our disease, and take care that this does not spread by contagion.

    SENTENCE FRAME: We should _____ and not _____, _____ and not _____, and _____.

4. MODEL: There are a thousand hacking at the branches of evil to one who is striking at the root.

    SENTENCE FRAME: There are _____ to one who _____.

5. MODEL: As long as possible live free and uncommitted. It makes but little difference whether you are committed to a farm or the county jail.

    SENTENCE FRAME: As long as possible _____. It makes little difference whether _____.

**400**   *A Different Drummer*

• Richard Wright (1908–1960) was for many years the black American novelist best known in this country and abroad. Wright was born as the son of a sharecropper in Natchez, Mississippi. Though his mother moved from place to place in search of work, he graduated as valedictorian from grammar school. He read widely on his own. As a young man, he was strongly influenced by writers who stressed the influence of a person's environment, and by the radical ideologies of Depression times. He followed a path later traveled by other black American writers and artists who were searching for a place to breathe and to work: first from the small town to the city (Memphis); then north to Chicago; then overseas to Paris, France. His novel *Native Son* (1940) treated powerfully the anger and the pent-up violence that he saw as the heritage of a history of oppression. In later years, Wright became a leader in the search of black people for their roots in African history and culture. Richard Wright once said about himself that even as a young boy he knew about "the hunger of the human heart," the "thirst of the human spirit to conquer and transcend the implacable limitations of human life." *Black Boy* (1945) is the story of his own struggle against the limitations imposed on him as a young boy growing up in the American South. It is the story of a young black who refuses to behave in the traditional ways his society expects. His rebellious spirit alienated him from the older members of his own family. The following selections describe a time when the boy and his partially paralyzed mother are living with his aunt and grandmother. The boy is totally unable to get along with these two very strict and authoritarian relatives. As John Reilly said in an afterword to a recent edition of the book,

Richard Wright could not learn his role. Nor could he learn to be secure in the traditional consolation of the oppressed—the hope of a better world hereafter. *Black Boy* is the story of self-education achieved in rebellion against the conventions of Negro society.

## Richard Wright

# A Separate Road

I went to school, feeling that my life depended not so much upon my learning as upon getting into another world of people.

Until I entered Jim Hill public school, I had had but one year of unbroken study. With the exception of one year at the church school, each time I had begun a school term something happened to disrupt it. Already my personality was lopsided. My knowledge of feeling was far greater than my knowledge of fact.

Though I was not aware of it, the next four years were to be the only opportunity for formal study in my life.

The first school day presented the usual problem and I was emotionally prepared to meet it. Upon what terms would I be allowed to remain upon the school grounds? With pencil and tablet, I walked nonchalantly into the schoolyard, wearing a cheap, brand-new straw hat. I mingled with the boys, hoping to pass unnoticed, but knowing that sooner or later I would be spotted for a newcomer. And trouble came quickly. A black boy bounded past me, thumping my straw hat to the ground, and yelling:

"Straw katy!"

I picked up my hat and another boy ran past, slapping my hat even harder.

"Straw katy!"

Again I picked up my hat and waited. The cry spread. Boys gathered around, pointing, chanting:

"Straw katy! Straw katy!"

I did not feel that I had been really challenged so far. No particular boy had stood his ground and taunted me. I was hoping that the teasing would cease, and tomorrow I would leave my straw hat at home. But the boy who had begun the game came close.

"Mama bought me a straw hat," he sneered.

"Watch what you're saying," I warned him.

"Oh, look! He talks!" the boy said.

The crowd howled with laughter, waiting, hoping.

"Where you from?" the boy asked me.

"None of your business," I said.

"Now, look, don't you go and get sassy, or I'll cut you down," he said.

"I'll say what I please," I said.

The boy picked up a tiny rock and put it on his shoulder and walked close again.

"Knock it off," he invited me.

I hesitated for a moment, then acted. I

brushed the rock from his shoulder and ducked and grabbed him about the legs and dumped him to the ground. A volcano of screams erupted from the crowd. I jumped upon the fallen boy and started pounding him. Then I was jerked up. Another boy had begun to fight me. My straw hat had been totally crushed and forgotten.

"Don't you hit my brother!" the new boy yelled.

"Two fighting one ain't fair!" I yelled.

Both of them now closed in on me. A blow landed on the back of my head. I turned and saw a brick rolling away and I felt blood oozing down my back. I looked around and saw several brickbats scattered about. I scooped up a handful. The two boys backed away. I took aim as they circled me; I made a motion as if to throw and one of the boys turned and ran. I let go with the brick and caught him in the middle of his back. He screamed. I chased the other halfway around the schoolyard. The boys howled their delight; they crowded around me, telling me that I had fought with two bullies. Then suddenly the crowd quieted and parted. I saw a woman teacher bearing down upon me. I dabbed at the blood on my neck.

"Was it you who threw that brick?" she asked.

"Two boys were fighting me," I told her.

"Come," she said, taking my hand.

I entered school escorted by the teacher, under arrest. I was taken to a room and confronted with the two brothers.

"Are these the boys?" she asked.

"Both of 'em fought me," I said. "I had to fight back."

"He hit me first!" one brother yelled.

"You're lying!" I yelled back.

"Don't you use that language in here," the teacher said.

"But they're not telling the truth," I said. "I'm new here and they tore up my hat."

"He hit me first," the boy said again.

I reached around the teacher, who stood between us, and smacked the boy. He screamed and started at me. The teacher grabbed us.

"The very idea of you!" the teacher shouted at me. "You are trying to fight right in school! What's the matter with you?"

"He is not telling you the truth," I maintained.

She ordered me to sit down; I did, but kept my eyes on the two brothers. The teacher dragged them out of the room and I sat until she returned.

"I'm in a good mind not to let you off this time," she said.

"It wasn't my fault," I said.

"I know. But you hit one of those boys right in here," she said.

"I'm sorry."

She asked me my name and sent me to a room. For a reason I could not understand, I was assigned to the fifth grade. Would they detect that I did not belong there? I sat and waited. When I was asked my age I called it out and was accepted.

I studied night and day and within two weeks I was promoted to the sixth grade. Overjoyed, I ran home and babbled the news. The family had not thought it possible. How could a bad, bad boy do that? I told the family emphatically that I was going to study medicine, engage in research, make discoveries. Flushed with success, I had not given a second's thought to how I would pay my way through a medical school. But since I had leaped a grade in two weeks, anything seemed possible, simple, easy.

I was now with boys and girls who were studying, fighting, talking. It revitalized my being, whipped my senses to a high, keen pitch of receptivity. I knew that my life was revolving about a world that I had to encounter and fight when I grew up. Suddenly the future loomed tangibly for me, as tangible as a future can loom for a black boy in Mississippi.

Most of my schoolmates worked mornings, evenings, and Saturdays. They earned enough to buy their clothes and books, and they had money in their pockets at school. To see a boy go into a grocery store at noon recess and let his eyes roam over filled shelves and pick out what he wanted—even a dime's worth— was a hairbreadth short of a miracle to me. But when I broached the idea of my working to Granny, she would have none of it; she laid down the injunction that I could not work on Saturdays while I slept under her roof. I argued that Saturdays were the only days on which I could earn any worthwhile sum, and Granny looked me straight in the eyes and adamantly quoted Scripture:

*But the seventh day is the sabbath of the Lord thy God: in it thou shalt not do any work, thou, nor thy son, nor thy daughter, nor thy manservant, nor thy maidservant, nor thine ox, nor thine ass, nor any of thy cattle, nor thy stranger that is within thy gates; that thy manservant and thy maidservant may rest as well as thou . . .*

And that was the final word. Though we lived just on the borders of actual starvation, I could not bribe Granny with a promise of half or two-thirds of my salary. Her answer was no and never. Her refusal wrought me up to a high pitch of nervousness and I cursed myself for being made to live a different and crazy life. I told Granny that she was not responsible for my soul, and she replied that I was a minor, that my soul's fate rested in her hands, that I had no word to say in the matter.

To protect myself against pointed questions about my home and my life, to avoid being invited out when I knew that I could not accept, I was reserved with the boys and girls at school, seeking their company but never letting them guess how much I was being kept out of the world in which they lived, valuing their casual friendships but hiding it, acutely self-conscious but covering it with a quick smile and a ready phrase. Each day at noon I would follow the boys and girls into the corner store and stand against a wall and watch them buy sandwiches, and when they would ask me: "Why don't you eat a lunch?" I would answer with a shrug of my shoulders: "Aw, I'm not hungry at noon, ever." And I would swallow my saliva as I saw them split open loaves of bread and line them with juicy sardines. Again and again I vowed that someday I would end this hunger of mine, this apartness, this eternal difference; and I did not

suspect that I would never get intimately into their lives, that I was doomed to live with them but not of them, that I had my own strange and separate road, a road which in later years would make them wonder how I had come to tread it.

I now saw a world leap to life before my eyes because I could explore it, and that meant not going home when school was out, but wandering, watching, asking, talking. Had I gone home to eat my plate of greens, Granny would not have allowed me out again, so the penalty I paid for roaming was to forfeit my food for twelve hours. I would eat mush at eight in the morning and greens at seven or later at night. To starve in order to learn about my environment was irrational, but so were my hungers. With my books slung over my shoulder, I would tramp with a gang into the woods, to rivers, to creeks, into the business district, to the doors of poolrooms, into the movies when we could slip in without paying, to neighborhood ball games, to brick kilns, to lumberyards, to cottonseed mills to watch men work. There were hours when hunger would make me weak, would make me sway while walking, would make my heart give a sudden wild spurt of beating that would shake my body and make me breathless; but the happiness of being free would lift me beyond hunger, would enable me to discipline the sensations of my body to the extent that I could temporarily forget. . . .

As summer waned I obtained a strange job. Our next-door neighbor, a janitor, decided to change his profession and become an insurance agent. He was handicapped by illiteracy and he offered me the job of accompanying him on trips into the delta plantation area to write and figure for him, at wages of five dollars a week. I made several trips with Brother Mance, as he was called, to plantation shacks, sleeping on shuck mattresses, eating salt pork

and black-eyed peas for breakfast, dinner, and supper; and drinking, for once, all the milk I wanted.

I had all but forgotten that I had been born on a plantation and I was astonished at the ignorance of the children I met. I had been pitying myself for not having books to read, and now I saw children who had never read a book. Their chronic shyness made me seem bold and city-wise. A black mother would try to lure her brood into the room to shake hands with me and they would linger at the jamb of the door, peering at me with one eye, giggling hysterically. At night, seated at a crude table, with a kerosene lamp spluttering at my elbow, I would fill out insurance applications, and a share-cropper family, fresh from laboring in the fields, would stand and gape. Brother Mance would pace the floor, extolling my abilities with pen and paper. Many of the naïve black families bought their insurance from us because they felt that they were connecting themselves with something that would make their children "write 'n speak lak dat pretty boy from Jackson." . . .

I returned home with a pocketful of money that melted into the bottomless hunger of the household. My mother was proud; even Aunt Addie's hostility melted temporarily. To Granny, I had accomplished a miracle and some of my sinful qualities evaporated, for she felt that success spelled the reward of righteousness and that failure was the wages of sin. But God called Brother Mance to heaven that winter and, since the insurance company would not accept a minor as an agent, my status reverted to a worldly one. The holy household was still burdened with a wayward boy to whom, in spite of all, sin somehow insisted upon clinging.

School opened and I began the seventh grade. My old hunger was still with me and I lived on what I did not eat. Perhaps the sunshine, the fresh air, and the pot liquor from greens kept me going. Of an evening I would sit in my room reading, and suddenly I would become aware of smelling meat frying in a neighbor's kitchen and would wonder what it was like to eat as much meat as one wanted. My mind would drift into a fantasy and I would imagine myself a son in a family that had meat on the table at each meal; then I would become disgusted with my futile daydreams and would rise and shut the window to bar the torturing scent of meat.

When I came downstairs one morning and went into the dining room for my bowl of mush and lard gravy I felt at once that something serious was happening in the family. Grandpa, as usual, was not at the table; he always had his meals in his room. Granny nodded me to my seat; I sat and bowed my head. From under my brows I saw my mother's tight face. Aunt Addie's eyes were closed, her forehead furrowed, her lips trembling. Granny buried her face in her hands. I wanted to ask what had happened, but I knew that I would not get an answer.

Granny prayed and invoked the blessings of God for each of us, asking Him to guide us if it was His will, and then she told God that "my poor old husband lies sick this beautiful morning" and asked God, if it was His will, to heal him. That was how I learned of Grandpa's final illness. On many occasions I learned of some event, a death, a birth, or an impending visit, some happening in the neighborhood, at her church, or at some relative's home, first through Granny's informative prayers at the breakfast or dinner table.

Grandpa was a tall, black, lean man with a long face, snow-white teeth, and a head of woolly white hair. In anger he bared his teeth—a habit, Granny said, that he had formed while fighting in the trenches of the Civil War—and hissed, while his fists would clench until the veins swelled. In his rare laughs he bared his teeth in the same way, only now his teeth did not flash long and his body was relaxed. Grandpa owned a sharp pocketknife—which I had been forbidden to touch—and sat for long hours in the sun, whittling, whistling quietly, or maybe, if he was feeling well, humming some strange tune.

I had often tried to ask him about the Civil War, how he had fought, how he had felt, had he seen Lincoln, but he would never respond.

"You, git 'way frum me, you young'un," was all that he would ever say.

From Granny I learned—over a course of years—that he had been wounded in the Civil War and had never received his disability pension, a fact which he hugged close to his heart with bitterness. I never heard him speak of white people; I think he hated them too much to talk of them. In the process of being discharged from the Union Army, he had gone to a white officer to seek help in filling out his papers. In filling out the papers, the white officer misspelled Grandpa's name, making him Richard Vinson instead of Richard Wilson. It was possible that Grandpa's southern accent and his illiteracy made him mispronounce his own name. It was rumored that the white officer had been a Swede and had had a poor knowledge of English. Another rumor had it that the white officer had been a Southerner and had deliberately falsified Grandpa's papers. Anyway, Grandpa did not discover that he had been discharged in the name of Richard Vinson until years later; and when he applied to the War Department for a pension, no trace could be found of his ever having served in the Union Army under the name of Richard Wilson.

I asked endless questions about Grandpa's pension, but information was always denied me on the grounds that I was too young to know what was involved. For decades a long correspondence took place between Grandpa and the War Department; in letter after letter Grandpa would recount events and conversations (always dictating these long accounts to others); he would name persons long dead, citing their ages and descriptions, reconstructing battles in which he had fought, naming towns, rivers, creeks, roads, cities, villages, citing the names and numbers of regiments and companies with which he had fought, giving the exact day and the exact hour of the day of certain occurrences, and send it all to the War Department in Washington.

I used to get the mail early in the morning and whenever there was a long, businesslike envelope in the stack, I would know that Grandpa had got an answer from the War Department and I would run upstairs with it. Grandpa would lift his head from the pillow, take the letter from me and open it himself. He would stare at the black print for a long time, then reluctantly, distrustfully hand the letter to me.

"Well?" he would say.

And I would read him the letter—reading slowly and pronouncing each word with extreme care—telling him that his claims for a pension had not been substantiated and that his application had been rejected. Grandpa would not blink an eye, then he would curse softly under his breath.

"It's them rebels," he would hiss.

As though doubting what I had read, he would dress up and take the letter to at least a dozen of his friends in the neighborhood and ask them to read it to him; finally he would know it from memory. At last he would put the letter away carefully and begin his brooding again, trying to recall out of his past some telling fact that might help him get his pension. Like

"K" of Kafka's novel, *The Castle*, he tried desperately to persuade the authorities of his true identity right up to the day of his death, and failed.

Often, when there was no food in the house, I would dream of the Government's sending a letter that would read something like this:

Dear Sir:
Your claim for a pension has been verified. The matter of your name has been satisfactorily cleared up. In accordance with official regulations, we are hereby instructing the Secretary of the Treasury to compile and compute and send to you, as soon as it is convenient, the total amount of all moneys past due, together with interest, for the past ——years, the amount being $——.
We regret profoundly that you have been so long delayed in this matter. You may be assured that your sacrifice has been a boon and a solace to your country.

But no letter like that ever came, and Grandpa was so sullen most of the time that I stopped dreaming of him and his hopes. Whenever he walked into my presence I became silent, waiting for him to speak, wondering if he were going to upbraid me for something. I would relax when he left. My will to talk to him gradually died. . . .

I came in from school one afternoon and Aunt Addie met me in the hallway. Her face was trembling and her eyes were red.

"Go upstairs and say good-bye to your grandpa," she said.

"What's happened?"

She did not answer. I ran upstairs and was met by Uncle Clark, who had come from Greenwood. Granny caught my hand.

"Come and say good-bye to your grandpa," she said.

She led me to Grandpa's room; he was lying fully dressed upon the bed, looking as well as he ever looked. His eyes were open, but he was so still that I did not know if he was dead or alive.

"Papa, here's Richard," Granny said softly.

Grandpa looked at me, flashed his white teeth for a fraction of a second.

"Good-bye, grandpa," I whispered.

"Good-bye, son," he spoke hoarsely. "Rejoice, for God has picked out my s-s-e . . . in-in h-heaven . . ."

His voice died. I had not understood what he had said and I wondered if I should ask him to repeat it. But Granny took my hand and led me from the room. The house was quiet; there was no crying. My mother sat silent in her rocking chair, staring out the window; now and then she would lower her face to her hands. Granny and Aunt Addie moved silently about the house. I sat mute, waiting for Grandpa to die. I was still puzzled about what he had tried to say to me. It seemed important that I should understand his final words. I followed Granny into the kitchen.

"Granny, what did Grandpa say? I didn't quite hear him," I whispered.

She whirled and gave me one of her backhanded slaps across my mouth.

"Shut up! The angel of death's in the house!"

"I just wanted to know," I said, nursing my bruised lips.

She looked at me and relented.

"He said that God had picked out his seat in heaven," she said. "Now you know. So sit down and quit asking fool questions."

When I awakened the next morning my mother told me that Grandpa had "gone home."

"Get on your hat and coat," Granny said.

"What do you want me to do?" I asked.

"Quit asking questions and do what you are told," she said.

I dressed for the outdoors.

"Go to Tom and tell him that Papa's

gone home. Ask him to come here and take charge of things," Granny said.

Tom, her eldest son, had recently moved from Hazelhurst to Jackson and lived near the outskirts of town. Feeling that I was bearing an important message, I ran every inch of the two miles; I thought that news of a death should be told at once. I came in sight of my uncle's house with a heaving chest; I bounded up the steps and rapped on the door. My little cousin, Maggie, opened the door.

"Where's Uncle Tom?" I asked.

"He's sleeping," she said.

I ran into his room, went to his bed, and shook him.

"Uncle Tom, Granny says to come at once. Grandpa's dead," I panted.

He stared at me a long time.

"You certainly are a prize fool," he said quietly. "Don't you know that that's no way to tell a person that his father's dead?"

I stared at him, baffled, panting.

"I ran all the way out here," I gasped. "I'm out of breath. I'm sorry."

He rose slowly and began to dress, ignoring me; he did not utter a word for five minutes.

"What're you waiting for?" he asked me.

"Nothing," I said.

I walked home slowly, asking myself what on earth was the matter with me, why it was I never seemed to do things as people expected them to be done. Every word and gesture I made seemed to provoke hostility. I had never been able to talk to others, and I had to guess at their meanings and motives. I had not intentionally tried to shock Uncle Tom, and yet his anger at me seemed to outweigh his sorrow for his father. Finding no answer, I told myself that I was a fool to worry about it, that no matter what I did I would be wrong somehow as far as my family was concerned.

I was not allowed to go to Grandpa's funeral; I was ordered to stay home "and mind the house." I sat reading detective stories until the family returned from the graveyard. They told me nothing and I asked no questions. The routine of the house flowed on as usual. For me there was sleep, mush, greens, school, study, loneliness, yearning, and then sleep again.

My clothing became so shabby that I was ashamed to go to school. Many of the boys in my class were wearing their first long-pants suits. I grew so bitter that I decided to have it out with Granny; I would tell her that if she did not let me work on Saturdays I would leave home. But when I opened the subject, she would not listen. I followed her about the house, demanding the right to work on Saturday. Her answer was no and no and no.

"Then I'll quit school," I declared.

"Quit then. See how much I care," she said.

"I'll go away from here and you'll never hear from me!"

"No, you won't," she said tauntingly.

"How can I ever learn enough to get a job?" I asked her, switching my tactics. I showed her my ragged stockings, my patched pants. "Look, I won't go to school like this! I'm not asking you for money or to do anything. I only want to work!"

"I have nothing to do with whether you go to school or not," she said. "You left the church and you are on your own. You are with the world. You're dead to me, dead to Christ."

"That old church of yours is messing up my life," I said.

"Don't you say that in this house!"

"It's true and you know it!"

"God's punishing you," she said. "And you're too proud to ask Him for help."

"I'm going to get a job anyway."

"Then you can't live here," she said.

"Then I'll leave," I countered, trembling violently.

"You won't leave," she repeated.

"You think I'm joking, don't you?" I asked, determined to make her know how I felt. "I'll leave this minute!"

I ran to my room, got a battered suitcase, and began packing my ragged clothes. I did not have a penny, but I was going to leave. She came to the door.

"You little fool! Put that suitcase down!"

"I'm going where I can work!"

She snatched the suitcase out of my hands; she was trembling.

"All right," she said. "If you want to go to hell, then go. But God'll know that it was not my fault. He'll forgive me, but He won't forgive you."

Weeping, she rushed from the door. Her humanity had triumphed over her fear. I emptied the suitcase, feeling spent. I hated these emotional outbursts, these tempests of passion, because they always left me tense and weak. Now I was truly dead to Granny and Aunt Addie, but my mother smiled when I told her that I had defied them. She rose and hobbled to me on her paralytic legs and kissed me.

## YOU AND RICHARD WRIGHT

A book becomes a classic when in some way it has a universal appeal. It makes us relive things that many readers have themselves lived through, though in a different way. It reminds us of questions that we ourselves have asked. Richard Wright's *Black Boy* has had a powerful impact on readers who had found in their own lives that growing up means finding one's way in a world that often does not really care and that often is outright hostile or cruel. Do you feel at any point in reading this selection:

"This is like something I myself, or people I know well, have experienced"? Are any of the following like something you have experienced or thought about before?

(1) Among the things people remember most vividly in later years is their first real encounter with *injustice.* The boy in this selection feels unjustly treated during his first day at the new school. What happened? What made it unjust? What is there about this experience that many other people are likely to have encountered?

(2) We tend to remember vividly our first real experience of *denial:* We remember someone in authority who said no, or who blocked our way. The grandmother has this kind of authority in the boy's household. Describe how she uses it early in this selection. What did the boy want to do? Why was he denied permission? How would you have felt in his place?

(3) The first real job often opens a new world to people. What was the boy's first job of this kind? How did it broaden his outlook? What were its advantages and disadvantages? This job was important to the boy because it gave him an early taste of *achievement* or success. Did he have the opportunity to experience any similar feeling at school?

(4) Sometimes, a person's whole life and personality are influenced by a long-standing *grievance.* Something due was denied. Much time is taken up in retellings of what happened, in explanations and accusations, and in attempts to remedy the situation. Retell the story of the grandfather's grievance against the army. Does it remind you of any similar experiences of people you know?

(5) Many young people have experienced the feeling of being incurably *awkward.* They never seem to be able to "do things as people expected them to be done." The boy experiences this feeling very strongly during the events connected with his grandfather's death. How and why?

(6) We often vividly remember our first *defiance* of authority. We remember the first time we talked back. Tell the story of the boy's defiance of his grandmother at the end of this selection. What brought it about? How did it work out? What support, if any, did he get?

## A Closer Look

What is the meaning of each of the italicized words in its context? How does the rest of the passage help you narrow down the possible meaning of the word?

1. I had had only a year of unbroken study. Each time I had begun a school term something happened to *disrupt* it.

2. I walked *nonchalantly* into the schoolyard, hoping to pass unnoticed.

3. A volcano of screams *erupted* from the crowd.

4. I was escorted to the school by the teacher, under arrest, and *confronted* with the two brothers.

5. Being with boys and girls who were studying and talking *revitalized* my being and whipped my senses to a high, keen pitch.

6. The world I would have to encounter and fight was becoming more *tangible* for me.

7. When I *broached* the idea of my working to Granny, she would have none of it.

8. She laid down the *injunction* that I could not work on Saturdays while I slept under her roof.

9. Since the insurance company would not accept a minor as an agent, my status *reverted* to what it had been.

10. Granny prayed and *invoked* the blessings of God for each of us.

11. On many occasions I learned of some event first through Granny's *informative* prayers at the breakfast or dinner table.

12. Grandpa had been wounded in the

war but had never received his *disability* pension.

13. The officer had either misspelled or deliberately *falsified* his name.

14. His claim for a pension had not been *substantiated,* and his application had been rejected.

15. Your claim for a pension has been *verified;* the matter of your name has been satisfactorily cleared up.

**Your Turn**

The boy in this selection would often dream of a government letter that would announce that the grandfather's claim had been verified and that his pension would be paid. Can you imagine a letter that would solve a major problem, or make a real difference for you? Write an imaginary "Letter I Would Like to See."

Language/Composition Activity B16

FOLLOWING THROUGH

# You Are on Your Own

Richard Wright was an exceptionally serious writer. When he tells us things, he wants us to understand. He wants us to see his point of view. He often uses a basic pattern of *statement-and-explanation:* First, a shorter statement makes the point. Then, a longer statement (or a longer expanded part of the first statement) provides the follow-up or explanation. Study this pattern in the following model passages. Select three: For each, write a passage of your own that follows a very similar pattern of statement-and-explanation. Use a separate sheet of paper.

1. MODEL: *The routine of the house flowed on as usual.* For me there was sleep, mush, greens, school, study, loneliness, yearning, and then sleep again.

   YOUR TURN: The routine of the school flowed on as usual. ＿＿＿＿＿＿.

2. MODEL: *I did not feel that I had really been challenged so far.* No particular boy had stood his ground and taunted me.

   YOUR TURN: I do not feel that I have really been ＿＿＿＿＿＿＿＿.
   ＿＿＿＿＿＿＿.

3. MODEL: *Already my personality was lopsided.* My knowledge of feeling was far greater than my knowledge of fact.

   YOUR TURN: My personality is (was) ＿＿＿＿＿. ＿＿＿＿＿.

4. MODEL: *I was reserved with the boys and girls at school,* seeking their company but never letting them know how much I was being kept out of the world in which they lived, valuing their casual friendship but hiding it.

   YOUR TURN: I am ＿＿＿＿＿＿＿ with the boys and girls at school,
   ＿＿＿＿＿＿.

# The Secret Heart

In the deserts of the heart
Let the healing fountain start.

—W. H. Auden,
"In Memory of W. B. Yeats"

Much twentieth-century literature has dealt with people who felt walled off from others. People are naturally reluctant to tell strangers what they feel. But even when they are with someone very close to them, they often find it hard to put their real feelings into words. In much modern poetry and fiction, we see characters who want to reach out to others but do not succeed. They find themselves defeated in their attempts to communicate with others. Modern literature often takes us into a lonely world, where love and happiness are not easy to come by. At times, modern writers seem to leave us in a desert

where the sun beats,
And the dead tree gives no shelter, the cricket no relief,
And the dry stone no sound of water.

—T. S. Eliot, *The Waste Land*

Where can readers of our time turn when they feel starved for sincere feeling? Some of the best-loved American writers of our century have tried to counteract our modern sense of frustration and loneliness. They have probed into what makes us retreat into a shell, what teaches us to keep our feelings to ourselves. They have helped us read the strange or distorted ways in which others show their hidden thoughts and needs. The authors of the following selections include writers who were strongly aware of the barriers between people. They also include writers who led readers in search of their own buried selves, trying to restore their capacity for sincere, spontaneous feeling.

## POEMS: **Where Is Happiness?**

A short poem often expresses personal feelings. The traditional name for the kind of short poem that expresses personal feelings and attitudes is the **lyric**. The feelings we find expressed in lyrical poetry may be feelings of joy, but often also they are feelings of sadness and disappointment. The following poems are about people disappointed in their search for happiness. What do these poems tell us about the causes of unhappiness?

Stephen Crane

# Four Poems

### 1

I saw a man pursuing the horizon;
Round and round they sped.
I was disturbed at this;
I accosted the man.
"It is futile," I said,
"You can never—"

"You lie," he cried,
And ran on.

### 2

A man saw a ball of gold in the sky;
He climbed for it,
And eventually he achieved it—
It was clay.

Now this is the strange part:
When the man went to the earth
And looked again,
Lo, there was the ball of gold.
Now this is the strange part:
It was a ball of gold.
Ay, by the heavens, it was a ball of gold.

### 3

There was set before me a mighty hill,
And long days I climbed
Through regions of snow.
When I had before me the summit view,
It seemed that my labor
Had been to see gardens
Lying at impossible distances.

### 4

The wayfarer
Perceiving the pathway to truth,
Was struck with astonishment.
It was thickly grown with weeds.
"Ha," he said,
"I see that none has passed here
In a long time."
Later he saw that each weed
Was a singular knife.
"Well," he mumbled at last,
"Doubtless there are other roads."

## YOU AND THE POEMS

Stephen Crane (1871–1900), who is best known for his fiction, also wrote short poems that have appealed to the sense of irony of many modern readers. Answer the following questions:

(1) A **parable** acts out for us in simple, almost childlike form a general truth about life. Often, we have to spell out for ourselves what that truth is. Stephen Crane wrote short, parablelike poems that often seem to tell a very similar story. They show us yet one more time an ironic truth about human beings. What is Crane telling us about human beings in these poems? Is it the same or a similar story in each?

(2) **Dramatic irony** occurs when the spectators in the theater know more than a character they watch on the stage. For instance, the character on the stage may be very serious about something, but the audience may be smiling because they see the character's misunderstanding or mistake. Dramatic irony can also play a part in poetry. In which of these poems did you feel that you knew more, or knew something earlier, than the character in the poem?

### Your Turn

Choose one of these poems to read out loud. Read it with the right mock-solemn effect.

## Countee Cullen
# Any Human to Another

The ills I sorrow at
Not me alone
Like an arrow,
Pierce to the marrow,
Through the fat
And past the bone.

Your grief and mine
Must intertwine
Like sea and river,
Be fused and mingle,
Diverse yet single,
Forever and forever.

Let no man be so proud
And confident,
To think he is allowed
A little tent
Pitched in a meadow
Of sun and shadow
All his little own.

Joy may be shy, unique,
Friendly to a few,
Sorrow never scorned to speak
To any who
Were false or true.

Your every grief
Like a blade
Shining and unsheathed
Must strike me down.
Of bitter aloes wreathed,
My sorrow must be laid
On your head like a crown.

---

### YOU AND THE POEM

Countee Cullen (1903–1946) was one of the best-known black poets of the twenties and thirties. When this poem is read aloud, how should it sound—solemn? angry? bitter? sad? Answer the following questions:

(1) This poem about joy and sorrow uses several kinds of imaginative comparison. A **simile** is presented to us as a comparison, using words like *as* and *like*. The poet uses different similes to make us see what grief or sorrow is like. What are they? Which of them are similar, and in what way?

(2) A **metaphor** is a shorthand method for making a comparison—one thing is presented to us as if it really were another. The British poet John Donne said, "No man is an island." What metaphor in this poem expresses a very similar idea? How?

(3) **Personification** treats things or ideas as if they were human—making them do or say or feel things the way a person would. Find two examples of personification in this poem.

(4) How would you sum up in your own words what this poet is trying to tell us about joy and sorrow? What do you think makes the poet say what he does? Do you think many people would agree with him?

## Gwendolyn Brooks
# The Sonnet-Ballad

O mother, mother, where is happiness?
They took my lover's tallness off to war.
Left me lamenting. Now I cannot guess
What I can use an empty heart-cup for.
He won't be coming back here any more.
Some day the war will end, but, oh, I knew
When he went walking grandly out that door
That my sweet love would have to be untrue.
Would have to be untrue. Would have to court
Coquettish death, whose impudent and strange
Possessive arms and beauty (of a sort)
Can make a hard man hesitate—and change.
And he will be the one to stammer, "Yes."
Oh mother, mother, where is happiness?

---

### YOU AND THE POEM

Gwendolyn Brooks received the Pulitzer Prize in 1950 and became perhaps the best-known black American poet of the fifties and sixties. Using traditional forms, she wrote powerful poems on the topics of our time. Answer the following questions about this "sonnet-ballad":

(1) A **sonnet** is a traditional fourteen-line poem. Each line is basically a five-foot *iambic* line, with the stresses on the second syllable of each foot:

O móther, móther, whére is háppinéss?

Often a sonnet has an interlacing rhyme scheme, with more than two lines related by the same rhyme. Show how this poem illustrates these features.

(2) A **ballad** is a traditional folk poem in which we often seem to hear one or more people speaking—we seem to be listening to a conversation. Often a ballad has a songlike **refrain**—with all or part of a line repeated one or more times. Often the subject of a ballad is a sudden tragedy. Show how this poem is like a ballad.

(3) *Coquettish* means flirting or seductive. *Impudent* means shameless. How do people act when they act "possessive"? Not only these but also other words in this poem would fit into a story of love and jealousy—which ones? What is different about the way all these words are used here?

Elinor Wylie

# Sanctuary

This is the bricklayer; hear the thud
Of his heavy load dumped down on stone.
His lustrous bricks are brighter than blood,
His smoking mortar whiter than bone.

Set each sharp-edged, fire-bitten brick
Straight by the plumbline's shivering length;
Make my marvellous wall so thick
Dead nor living may shake its strength.

Full as a crystal cup with drink
Is my cell with dreams, and quiet, and cool. . . .
Stop, old man! You must leave a chink;
How can I breathe? *You can't, you fool!*

## YOU AND THE POEM

Elinor Wylie (1885–1928) liked things that were "sharp-edged," with clear outlines and nothing wasted. She liked "bare hills" and cold "thin blue" skies. This poem fits very neatly into a very definite form: **stanzas** of four lines each, with very regular **rhymes**. How "cold" or "bare" should this poem sound when it is read aloud? Should any emotion show through, and what kind?

## A Closer Look

(1) A wall offers protection. But a wall can also imprison us. What words or details help make the bricklayer's work seem beautiful or welcome? Are there any that make it sound frightening or ominous? Why does the poet change her mind about the wall?

(2) What is a sanctuary? What kind of sanctuary would you wish for if you wanted a quiet place where you could dream?

## Marge Piercy
# Simple Song

When we are going toward someone we say:
You are just like me
your thoughts are my brothers
word matches word
how easy to be together.

When we are leaving someone we say:
how strange you are
we cannot communicate
we can never agree
how hard, hard and weary to be together.

We are not different nor alike
but each strange in his leather body
sealed in skin and reaching out clumsy hands
and loving is an act
that cannot outlive
the open hand
the open eye
the door in the chest standing open.

## YOU AND THE POEM

When we find it hard to express our feelings, we often turn to something that can serve as a **symbol**. We choose an object or a gesture that has a meaning beyond itself. It expresses our feelings or attitudes for us. This is a poem by a contemporary poet about how hard it is to communicate. Look at the use she makes of symbolic gestures and other symbols. Answer the following questions:

(1) In this poem, going toward and leaving someone stand for the actual physical motions but they also have a symbolic meaning. How? When we talk about the way people communicate or relate to each other, we often refer to symbolic gestures of the hand, or symbolic movements of the eye. What is the symbolic meaning of the open hand, the open eye, the open door?

(2) Much twentieth-century poetry expresses a feeling of alienation, a feeling of being cut off from others or estranged from society. A famous modern poet talked about human beings "each in his prison," unable to reach out. How and where does this poem express a similar idea?

### Your Turn

The human hand can convey many different messages, and many of these are reflected in familiar expressions. Explore the possible meanings conveyed by or associated with one of the following: the hand, the eye, the door.

Edna St. Vincent Millay (1892–1950) was born in Maine. She became well-known as a poet in the years just before World War I and during the twenties. She wrote beautiful and sad poems on traditional themes, mourning lost happiness and the passing of young love. She also wrote passionate poems against injustice and oppression. Few twentieth-century poems have been as widely read and loved as hers. Choose one of the following poems to read out loud. How should it be read? How should it sound? Why?

# Pity Me Not Because the Light of Day

Pity me not because the light of day
At close of day no longer walks the sky;
Pity me not for beauties passed away
From field and thicket as the year goes by;
Pity me not the waning of the moon,
Nor that the ebbing tide goes out to sea,
Nor that a man's desire is hushed so soon,
And you no longer look with love on me.

This have I known always: Love is no more
Than the wide blossom which the wind assails,
Than the great tide that treads the shifting shore,
Strewing fresh wreckage gathered in the gales:
Pity me that the heart is slow to learn
What the swift mind beholds at every turn.

## YOU AND THE POEM

(1) This poem is the kind of traditional fourteen-line poem called a **sonnet**. In a sonnet, the first eight lines often go together as a closely knit group. Together they may sketch a scene, or set up a situation, or raise a question in our minds. Often the next six lines form a second group. This concluding part of the sonnet often interprets what has gone before, or draws a conclusion of some kind. In this sonnet, the first block of eight lines is further held together by the repetition of the poet's request: "Pity me not . . ." Each of these requests leads to something from the natural world that, for the poet, is similar to the way love passes or fades among human beings. What are these similarities or analogies? What do they all have in common?

(2) The concluding six lines again compare our human experience with love to things we see in nature. How are these similarities different from the earlier ones? What is the common element this time?

(3) A pair of rhymed lines that together state a complete thought is a **couplet**. In many sonnets, a final couplet sums up the main point. Sum up in your own words what the mind beholds and the heart learns. Why would the mind be swift about it but the heart slow?

# I Shall Go Back Again to the Bleak Shore

I shall go back again to the bleak shore
And build a little shanty on the sand,
In such a way that the extremest band
Of brittle seaweed will escape my door
But by a yard or two; and nevermore
Shall I return to take you by the hand;
I shall be gone to what I understand,
And happier than I ever was before.

The love that stood a moment in your eyes,
The words that lay a moment on your tongue,
Are one with all that in a moment dies,
A little undersaid and oversung.
But I shall find the sullen rocks and skies
Unchanged from what they were when I was young.

## YOU AND THE POEM

(1) How might love between two human beings be "undersaid" and "oversung"?

(2) The shore is bleak and sullen—but the poet will be "happier than I ever was before." Do you believe her? Explain this **paradox.**

## Your Turn

Suppose someone you cared for had bitterly disappointed you and you want to get away to forget or find happiness again. What kind of place do you think you would like to go to in order to forget or find happiness again?

# Love Is Not All

Love is not all: it is not meat nor drink
Nor slumber nor a roof against the rain;
Nor yet a floating spar to men that sink
And rise and sink and rise and sink again;
Love cannot fill the thickened lung with breath,
Nor clean the blood, nor set the fractured bone;
Yet many a man is making friends with death
Even as I speak, for lack of love alone.
It well may be that in a difficult hour,
Pinned down by pain and moaning for release,
Or nagged by want past resolution's power,
I might be driven to sell your love for peace,
Or trade the memory of this night for food.
It well may be. I do not think I would.

---

### YOU AND THE POEM

(1) Unlike many other modern poets, Millay is not reluctant to use **abstract** words like *love, peace, happiness,* and *pity.* Abstract words are the large umbrella terms that stand for general ideas and that often seem far removed from the specific sights and sounds of down-to-earth experience. But like other modern poets, Millay knows how to make abstract ideas **concrete** for us. She gives us a vivid picture, like the picture of people clinging to a floating spar, rising and sinking with the waves. Concrete words take us to the level of actual sense experience, giving us things to see, hear, smell, touch. What more general idea does this very concrete picture act out for us? Find other concrete details in this poem that stand for more general ideas.

(2) **Sonnets** first became a favorite form of poetry with English writers and their readers four hundred years ago. The early writers of sonnets often expressed similar feelings about love again and again. Are the feelings and ideas about love in this sonnet similar to those in the first two? Are they different? How?

# Dirge Without Music

I am not resigned to the shutting away of loving hearts in the
    hard ground.
So it is, and so it will be, for so it has been, time out of mind:
Into the darkness they go, the wise and the lovely.
Crowned with lilies and with laurel they go; but I am not
    resigned.

Lovers and thinkers, into the earth with you.
Be one with the dull, the indiscriminate dust.
A fragment of what you felt, of what you knew,
A formula, a phrase remains—but the best is lost.

The answers quick and keen, the honest look, the laughter,
    the love,—
They are gone. They are gone to feed the roses. Elegant and
    curled
Is the blossom. Fragrant is the blossom. I know. But I do
    not approve.
More precious was the light in your eyes than all the roses
    in the world.

Down, down, down into the darkness of the grave
Gently they go, the beautiful, the tender, the kind;
Quietly they go, the intelligent, the witty, the brave.
I know. But I do not approve. And I am not resigned.

---

### YOU AND THE POEM

(1) What is a dirge? How is this poem like a dirge? How do we act when we act resigned? When we discriminate, we tell people or things apart according to how we value them. Why or how can dust be "indiscriminate"?

(2) Would it make any difference if the poet had written "soft ground" in the first line instead of "hard ground"?

(3) Readers of poetry have long been familiar with the lily, laurel leaves, and the rose as symbols dear to poets. When familiar symbols appear with their usual meanings, we call them **conventional symbols**. Look at these three symbols as they are used in this poem. Which of them are used in a conventional way? Are any of them used unconventionally? How?

# Apostrophe to Man

(on reflecting that the world is ready to go to war again)

Detestable race, continue to expunge yourself, die out.
Breed faster, crowd, encroach, sing hymns, build bombing airplanes;
Make speeches, unveil statues, issue bonds, parade;
Convert again into explosives the bewildered ammonia and
    the distracted cellulose;
Convert again into putrescent matter drawing flies
The hopeful bodies of the young; exhort,
Pray, pull long faces, be earnest, be all but overcome,
    be photographed;
Confer, perfect your formulae, commercialize
Bacteria harmful to human tissue,
Put death on the market;
Breed, crowd, encroach, expand, expunge yourself, die out,
*Homo* called *sapiens.*

---

## YOU AND THE POEM

In times of conflict, poets and artists have often had to decide between staying apart from the struggle and choosing sides. Often they have felt it was their task to uphold the standard of beauty and truth and to stay clear of the partisan struggles of their time. Edna St. Vincent Millay felt there were times when the artist and writer could not stand aside. They had to make their voices heard in support of what they believed. Answer the following questions about this poem:

(1) An **apostrophe** is a solemn traditional speech or poem in which the speaker addresses or glorifies a godlike being. But in this modern apostrophe, the poet talks instead to the "detestable" human race. When people turn very bitter, they sometimes come to hate all humanity. Do you think the poet hated all human beings when she wrote this poem?

(2) Like other well-known writers of the period between the two World Wars, Edna St. Vincent Millay was passionately devoted to the cause of peace. In much of this poem, she mentions something we usually admire or at least accept. But she puts it next to something unflattering, or she makes us see its horrible results. In various ways, she tries to make us see the connection between some of our cherished familiar ways and the horrors of war. Point out and discuss several examples.

(3) What are the meanings of *encroach, exhort,* and *expunge* in this poem? What do ammonia and cellulose have to do with war? *Homo sapiens,* the scientific label for our species, calls us "knowing" or "reasoning" humans. The poet uses this label for a final bitter comment. How?

---

### Your Turn

In your reading, what has been the treatment of war that you remember best or that did most to shape your own ideas about war? Describe that treatment.

# An Introduction to *Our Town*

● In 1938, a playwright called Thornton Wilder wrote *Our Town,* a play that became a true classic of the American stage. It was a play filled with nostalgia for a simpler world. The author took the audience to a small town where "a dog could go to sleep all day in the middle of Main Street and nothing come along to disturb him." The events of the play were things "that repeat and repeat and repeat in the lives of millions." The people watching the play could feel that their own confusions and soul-searchings had been experienced in a very similar way by countless others before them—ordinary people like themselves.

Thornton Wilder (1897–1975) spent some of his childhood years in China when his father was serving as an American consul there. He spent part of his student years in Rome and got degrees from Yale and Princeton. In World War II, he served with the U.S. Air Force in North Africa and Italy. In later years, he traveled widely as a university teacher and lecturer. He wrote several novels whose setting was Rome, Peru, or Greece. He wrote several other plays that were very successful on the stage: *The Skin of Our Teeth* (1942) told the story of humanity from Cain and Abel to the rise of fascism and the start of World War II. *The Matchmaker* (1954) was later turned into a musical. But Wilder is best remembered for *Our Town,* his picture of American small-town life in the early years of the twentieth century.

When the play was first performed, two things made it different from plays that were familiar to audiences. Wilder had the play performed on a nearly empty stage, with hardly any scenery, and with very few props. His audiences saw a stage bare except for a table and a stool, or a folding chair. There was no curtain, and the audience could watch the stagehands who rearranged the few objects that were on the stage. Though this use of the stage seemed strange to many people, the playwright was actually going back to an old theater tradition. He wanted the audience to listen for lines that would help them create the setting and the scenery with their own imaginations. He wanted to exclude anything that would make the audience think of the play as taking place in one limited location. Wilder said about Shakespeare's *Romeo and Juliet:*

If Juliet is represented as a girl "very like Juliet" . . . moving about in a "real" house with marble staircases, rugs, lamps, and furniture, the impression is irresistibly conveyed that these events happened to this one girl, in one place, at one moment in time. When the play is staged as Shakespeare intended it, the bareness of the stage releases the events from the particular and the experience of Juliet partakes of that of all girls in love, in every time, place, and language.

Also strange or unusual for the audience of Wilder's play was the *stage manager* who tells much of the story. He wanders about the stage, helping to arrange the furniture, introducing each scene, commenting on the events, and occasionally playing a small part. According to Wilder, many playwrights have envied the novelist, who can explain the story while telling it, and who can point back to the past and forward to the future. In the ancient Greek plays, a **chorus** made up of elders of the community would come on stage

*(continued from previous page)*

between scenes to sum up what had happened. In later plays, an actor would sometimes speak a **prologue,** a kind of preview of the play. The stage manager in *Our Town* combines some of the functions of the chorus and the prologue. He serves as a guide to the audience, explaining and commenting as the play develops.

   *Our Town* covers a period from 1901 to 1913, the period Wilder lived through during his own youth. It shows us a place that could have been anywhere where there were small towns in America. It shows us people who were no different from many others like them. What about "our town" has changed? What has stayed the same?

## Thornton Wilder

# Our Town

*Characters (in the order of their appearance)*

| | |
|---|---|
| STAGE MANAGER | MR. WEBB |
| DR. GIBBS | WOMEN IN THE BALCONY |
| JOE CROWELL | MAN IN THE AUDITORIUM |
| HOWIE NEWSOME | LADY IN THE BOX |
| MRS. GIBBS | SIMON STIMSON |
| MRS. WEBB | MRS. SOAMES |
| GEORGE GIBBS | CONSTABLE WARREN |
| REBECCA GIBBS | SI CROWELL |
| WALLY WEBB | THREE BASEBALL PLAYERS |
| EMILY WEBB | SAM CRAIG |
| PROFESSOR WILLARD | JOE STODDARD |

The entire play takes place in Grover's Corners, New Hampshire.

*Costumes designed by Patricia Zipprodt for Off-Broadway production of* Our Town *at Circle in the Square, New York City.*

# Act One

*No curtain.*

*No scenery.*

*The audience, arriving, sees an empty stage in half-light.*

*Presently the Stage Manager, hat on and pipe in mouth, enters and begins placing a table and three chairs downstage left, and a table and three chairs downstage right. He also places a low bench at the corner of what will be the Webb house, left.*

*"Left" and "right" are from the point of view of the actor facing the audience. "Up" is toward the back wall.*

*As the house lights go down the Stage Manager has finished setting the stage and leaning against the right proscenium pillar watches the late arrivals in the audience.*

*When the auditorium is in complete darkness he speaks:*

STAGE MANAGER: This play is called "Our Town." It was written by Thornton Wilder; produced and directed by A . . . (or: produced by A . . .; directed by B . . .). In it you will see Miss C . . .; Miss D . . .; Miss E . . .; and Mr. F . . .; Mr. G . . .; Mr. H . . .; and many others. The name of the town is Grover's Corners, New Hampshire—just across the Massachusetts line: latitude 42 degrees 40 minutes; longitude 70 degrees 37 minutes. The First Act shows a day in our town. The day is May 7, 1901. The time is just before dawn.

[*A rooster crows.*]

The sky is beginning to show some streaks of light over in the East there, behind our mount'in. The morning star always gets wonderful bright the minute before it has to go,—doesn't it?

[*He stares at it for a moment, then goes upstage.*]

Well, I'd better show you how our town lies. Up here—[*that is: parallel with the back wall*] is Main Street. Way back there is the railway station; tracks go that way. Polish Town's across the tracks, and some Canuck families. [*toward the left*] Over there is the Congregational Church; across the street's the Presbyterian. Methodist and Unitarian are over there. Baptist is down in the holla' by the river. Catholic Church is over beyond the tracks. Here's the Town Hall and Post Office combined; jail's in the basement. Bryan once made a speech from these very steps here.

Along here's a row of stores. Hitching posts and horse blocks in front of them. First automobile's going to come along in about five years—belonged to Banker Cartwright, our richest citizen . . . lives in the big white house up on the hill. Here's the grocery store and here's Mr. Morgan's drugstore. Most everybody in town manages to look into those two stores once a day.

Public school's over yonder. High school's still farther over. Quarter of nine mornings, noontimes, and three o'clock afternoons, the hull town can hear the yelling and screaming from those schoolyards.

[*He approaches the table and chairs downstage right.*]

This is our doctor's house,—Doc Gibbs'. This is the back door.

[*Two arched trellises, covered with vines and flowers, are pushed out, one by each proscenium pillar.*]

There's some scenery for those who think they have to have scenery. This is Mrs. Gibbs' garden. Corn . . . peas . . . beans . . . hollyhocks . . . heliotrope . . . and a lot of burdock.

[*Crosses the stage.*]

In those days our newspaper come out twice a week—the Grover's Corners *Sentinel*—and this is Editor Webb's house. And this is Mrs. Webb's garden. Just like Mrs. Gibbs', only it's got a lot of sunflowers, too.

[*He looks upward, center stage.*]

Right here . . .'s a big butternut tree.

[*He returns to his place by the right proscenium pillar and looks at the audience for a minute.*]

Nice town, y'know what I mean? Nobody very remarkable ever come out of it, s'far as we know. The earliest tombstones in the cemetery up there on the mountain say 1670–1680—they're Grovers and Cartwrights and Gibbses and Herseys—same names as are around here now.

Well, as I said: it's about dawn. The only lights on in town are in a cottage over by the tracks where a Polish mother's just had twins. And in the Joe Crowell house, where Joe Junior's getting up so as to deliver the paper. And in the depot, where Shorty Hawkins is gettin' ready to flag the 5:45 for Boston.

[*A train whistle is heard. The Stage Manager takes out his watch and nods.*]

Naturally, out in the country—all around—there've been lights on for some time, what with milkin's and so on. But town people sleep late.

So—another day's begun. There's Doc Gibbs comin' down Main Street now, comin' back from that baby case.

And here's his wife comin' downstairs to get breakfast.

[*Mrs. Gibbs, a plump, pleasant woman in the middle thirties, comes "downstairs" right. She pulls up an imaginary window shade in her kitchen and starts to make a fire in her stove.*]

Doc Gibbs died in 1930. The new hospital's named after him. Mrs. Gibbs died first—long time ago, in fact. She went out to visit her daughter, Rebecca, who married an insurance man in Canton, Ohio, and died there—pneumonia—but her body was brought back here. She's up in the cemetery there now—in with a whole mess of Gibbses and Herseys—she was Julia Hersey 'fore she married Doc Gibbs in the Congregational Church over there. In our town we like to know the facts about everybody.

There's Mrs. Webb, coming downstairs to get her breakfast, too.—That's Doc Gibbs. Got that call at half past one this morning.

And there comes Joe Crowell, Jr., delivering Mr. Webb's *Sentinel*.

[*Dr. Gibbs has been coming along Main Street from the left. At the point where he would turn to approach his house, he stops, sets down his—imaginary—black bag, takes off his hat, and slowly rubs his face with fatigue, using an enormous handkerchief.*

*Mrs. Webb, a thin, serious woman, has entered her kitchen, left, tying on an apron. She goes through the motions of putting wood into a stove, lighting it, and preparing breakfast.*

*Suddenly, Joe Crowell, Jr., eleven, starts down Main Street from the right, hurling imaginary newspapers into each doorway.*]

JOE CROWELL, JR.: Morning, Doc Gibbs.

DR. GIBBS: Morning, Joe.

JOE CROWELL, JR.: Somebody been sick, Doc?

DR. GIBBS: No. Just some twins born over in Polish Town.

JOE CROWELL, JR.: Do you want your paper now?

DR. GIBBS: Yes, I'll take it. Anything serious goin' on in the world since Wednesday?

JOE CROWELL, JR.: Yessir, there is. My schoolteacher, Miss Foster, 's getting married to a fella over in Concord.

DR. GIBBS: I declare. How do you boys feel about that?

JOE CROWELL, JR.: Well, of course, it's none of my business—but I think if a person starts out to be a teacher, she ought to stay one.

DR. GIBBS: How's your knee, Joe?

JOE CROWELL, JR.: Fine, Doc, I never think

about it at all. Only like you said, it always tells me when it's going to rain.

DR. GIBBS: What's it telling you today? Goin' to rain?

JOE CROWELL, JR.: No, sir.

DR. GIBBS: Sure?

JOE CROWELL, JR.: Yessir.

DR. GIBBS: Knee ever make a mistake?

JOE CROWELL, JR.: No, sir.

[*Joe goes off. Dr. Gibbs stands reading his paper.*]

STAGE MANAGER: Want to tell you something about that boy Joe Crowell there. Joe was awful bright—graduated from high school here, head of his class. So he got a scholarship to Massachusetts Tech. Graduated head of his class there, too. It was all wrote up in the Boston paper at the time. Goin' to be a great engineer, Joe was. But the war broke out and he died in France.—All that education for nothing.

HOWIE NEWSOME: [*off left*] Giddap, Bessie! What's the matter with you today?

STAGE MANAGER: Here comes Howie Newsome, deliverin' the milk.

[*Howie Newsome, about thirty, in overalls, comes along Main Street from the left, walking beside an invisible horse and wagon and carrying an imaginary rack with milk bottles. The sound of clinking milk bottles is heard. He leaves some bottles at Mrs. Webb's trellis, then, crossing the stage to Mrs. Gibbs', he stops center to talk to Dr. Gibbs.*]

HOWIE NEWSOME: Morning, Doc.

DR. GIBBS: Morning, Howie.

HOWIE NEWSOME: Somebody sick?

DR. GIBBS: Pair of twins over to Mrs. Goruslawski's.

HOWIE NEWSOME: Twins, eh? This town's gettin' bigger every year.

DR. GIBBS: Goin' to rain, Howie?

HOWIE NEWSOME: No, no. Fine day— that'll burn through. Come on, Bessie.

DR. GIBBS: Hello Bessie.

[*He strokes the horse, which has remained up center.*]

How old is she, Howie?

HOWIE NEWSOME: Going on seventeen. Bessie's all mixed up about the route ever since the Lockharts stopped takin' their quart of milk every day. She wants to leave 'em a quart just the same— keeps scolding me the hull trip. [*He reaches Mrs. Gibbs' back door. She is waiting for him.*]

MRS. GIBBS: Good morning, Howie.

HOWIE NEWSOME: Morning, Mrs. Gibbs. Doc's just comin' down the street.

MRS. GIBBS: Is he? Seems like you're late today.

HOWIE NEWSOME: Yes. Somep'n went wrong with the separator. Don't know what 'twas.

[*He passes Dr. Gibbs up center.*]

Doc!

DR. GIBBS: Howie!

MRS. GIBBS: [*calling upstairs*] Children! Children! Time to get up.

HOWIE NEWSOME: Come on, Bessie! [*He goes off right.*]

MRS. GIBBS: George! Rebecca!

[*Dr. Gibbs arrives at his back door and passes through the trellis into his house.*]

MRS. GIBBS: Everything all right, Frank?

DR. GIBBS: Yes. I declare—was easy as kittens.

MRS. GIBBS: Bacon'll be ready in a minute. Set down and drink your coffee. You can catch a couple hours' sleep this morning, can't you?

DR. GIBBS: Hm! . . . Mrs. Wentworth's coming at eleven. Guess I know what it's about, too. Her stummick ain't what it ought to be.

MRS. GIBBS: All told, you won't get more'n three hours' sleep. Frank Gibbs, I don't know what's goin' to become of you. I do wish I could get you to go away someplace and take a rest. I think it would do you good.

MRS. WEBB: Emileeee! Time to get up! Wally! Seven o'clock!

MRS. GIBBS: I declare, you got to speak to George. Seems like something's come over him lately. He's no help to me at all. I can't even get him to cut me some wood.

DR. GIBBS:

[Washing and drying his hands at the sink. Mrs. Gibbs is busy at the stove.]

Is he sassy to you?

MRS. GIBBS: No. He just whines! All he thinks about is that baseball—George! Rebecca! You'll be late for school.

DR. GIBBS: M-m-m . . .

MRS. GIBBS: George!

DR. GIBBS: George, look sharp!

GEORGE'S VOICE: Yes, Pa!

DR. GIBBS: [as he goes off the stage] Don't you hear your mother calling you? I guess I'll go upstairs and get forty winks.

MRS. WEBB: Walleee! Emileee! You'll be late for school! Walleee! You wash yourself good or I'll come up and do it myself.

REBECCA GIBBS' VOICE: Ma! What dress shall I wear?

MRS. GIBBS: Don't make a noise. Your father's been out all night and needs his sleep. I washed and ironed the blue gingham for you special.

REBECCA: Ma, I hate that dress.

MRS. GIBBS: Oh, hush-up-with-you.

REBECCA: Every day I go to school dressed like a sick turkey.

MRS. GIBBS: Now, Rebecca, you always look *very* nice.

REBECCA: Mama, George's throwing soap at me.

MRS. GIBBS: I'll come and slap the both of you—that's what I'll do.

[A factory whistle sounds.

The children dash in and take their places at the tables. Right, George, about sixteen, and Rebecca, eleven. Left, Emily and Wally, same ages. All four carry strapped schoolbooks.]

STAGE MANAGER: We've got a factory in our town too—hear it? Makes blankets. Cartwrights own it and it brung 'em a fortune.

MRS. WEBB: Children! Now I won't have it. Breakfast is just as good as any other meal and I won't have you gobbling like wolves. It'll stunt your growth—that's a fact. Put away your book, Wally.

WALLY: Aw, Ma! By ten o'clock I got to know all about Canada.

MRS. WEBB: You know the rule's well as I do—no books at table. As for me, I'd rather have my children healthy than bright.

EMILY: I'm both, Mama: you know I am. I'm the brightest girl in school for my age. I have a wonderful memory.

MRS. WEBB: Eat your breakfast.

WALLY: I'm bright, too, when I'm looking at my stamp collection.

MRS. GIBBS: I'll talk to your father about it when he's rested. Seems to me twenty-five cents a week's enough for a boy your age. I declare I don't know how you spend it all.

GEORGE: Aw, Ma, I gotta lotta things to buy.

MRS. GIBBS: Strawberry phosphates—that's what you spend it on.

GEORGE: I don't see how Rebecca comes to have so much money. She has more'n a dollar.

REBECCA: [spoon in mouth, dreamily] I've been saving it up gradual.

MRS. GIBBS: Well, dear, I think it's a good thing to spend some every now and then.

REBECCA: Mama, do you know what I love most in the world—do you? Money.

MRS. GIBBS: Eat your breakfast.

THE CHILDREN: Mama, there's first bell— I gotta hurry—I don't want any more—I gotta hurry.

[*The children rise, seize their books and dash out through the trellises. They meet, down center, and chattering, walk to Main Street, then turn left.*

*The Stage Manager goes off, unobtrusively, right.*]

MRS. WEBB: Walk fast, but you don't have to run. Wally, pull up your pants at the knee. Stand up straight, Emily.

MRS. GIBBS: Tell Miss Foster I send her my best congratulations—can you remember that?

REBECCA: Yes, Ma.

MRS. GIBBS: You look real nice, Rebecca. Pick up your feet.

ALL: Good-bye.

[*Mrs. Gibbs fills her apron with food for the chickens and then comes down to the footlights.*]

MRS. GIBBS: Here, chick, chick, chick.
No, go away, you. Go away.
Here, chick, chick, chick.
What's the matter with *you*? Fight, fight, fight—that's all you do. Hm . . . *you* don't belong to me. Where'd you come from?

[*She shakes her apron.*]

Oh, don't be so scared. Nobody's going to hurt you.

[*Mrs. Webb is sitting on the bench by her trellis, stringing beans.*]

Good morning, Myrtle. How's your cold?

MRS. WEBB: Well, I still get that tickling feeling in my throat. I told Charles I didn't know as I'd go to choir practice tonight. Wouldn't be any use.

MRS. GIBBS: Have you tried singing over your voice?

MRS. WEBB: Yes, but somehow I can't do that and stay on the key. While I'm resting myself I thought I'd string some of these beans.

MRS. GIBBS: [*rolling up her sleeves as she crosses the stage for a chat*] Let me help you. Beans have been good this year.

MRS. WEBB: I've decided to put up forty quarts if it kills me. The children say they hate 'em, but I notice they're able to get 'em down all winter.

[*Pause. There is a brief sound of chickens cackling.*]

MRS. GIBBS: Now, Myrtle. I've got to tell you something, because if I don't tell somebody I'll burst.

MRS. WEBB: Why, Julia Gibbs!

MRS. GIBBS: Here, give me some more of those beans. Myrtle, did one of those secondhand-furniture men from Boston come to see you last Friday?

MRS. WEBB: No-o.

MRS. GIBBS: Well, he called on me. First I thought he was a patient wantin' to see Dr. Gibbs. 'N he wormed his way into my parlor, and, Myrtle Webb, he offered me three hundred and fifty dollars for Grandmother Wentworth's highboy, as I'm sitting here!

MRS. WEBB: Why, Julia Gibbs!

MRS. GIBBS: He did! That old thing! Why, it was so big I didn't know where to put it and I almost give it to Cousin Hester Wilcox.

MRS. WEBB: Well, you're going to take it, aren't you?

MRS. GIBBS: I don't know.

MRS. WEBB: You don't know—three hundred and fifty dollars! What's come over you?

MRS. GIBBS: Well, if I could get the Doctor to take the money and go away someplace on a real trip, I'd sell it like that. Y'know, Myrtle, it's been the dream of my life to see Paris, France.—Oh, I don't know. It sounds crazy, I suppose, but for years I've been promising myself that if we ever had the chance—

MRS. WEBB: How does the Doctor feel about it?

MRS. GIBBS: Well, I did beat about the bush a little and said that if I got a legacy—that's the way I put it—I'd make him take me somewhere.

MRS. WEBB: M-m-m . . . What did he say?

MRS. GIBBS: You know how he is. I haven't heard a serious word out of him since I've known him. No, he said, it might make him discontented with Grover's Corners to go traipsin' about Europe; better let well enough alone, he says. Every two years he makes a trip to the battlefields of the Civil War and that's enough treat for anybody, he says.

MRS. WEBB: Well, Mr. Webb just *admires* the way Dr. Gibbs knows everything about the Civil War. Mr. Webb's a good mind to give up Napoleon and move over to the Civil War, only Dr. Gibbs being one of the greatest experts in the country just makes him despair.

MRS. GIBBS: It's a fact! Dr. Gibbs is never so happy as when he's at Antietam or Gettysburg. The times I've walked over those hills, Myrtle, stopping at every bush and pacing it all out, like we were going to buy it.

MRS. WEBB: Well, if that secondhand man's really serious about buyin' it, Julia, you sell it. And then you'll get to see Paris, all right. Just keep droppin' hints from time to time—that's how I got to see the Atlantic Ocean, y'know.

MRS. GIBBS: Oh, I'm sorry I mentioned it. Only it seems to me that once in your life before you die you ought to see a country where they don't talk in English and don't even want to.

[The Stage Manager enters briskly from the right. He tips his hat to the ladies, who nod their heads.]

STAGE MANAGER: Thank you, ladies. Thank you very much.

[Mrs. Gibbs and Mrs. Webb gather up their things, return into their homes and disappear.]

Now we're going to skip a few hours. But first we want a little more information about the town, kind of a scientific account, you might say.

So I've asked Professor Willard of our State University to sketch in a few details of our past history here.

Is Professor Willard here?

[Professor Willard, a rural savant, pince-nez on a wide satin ribbon, enters from the right with some notes in his hand.]

May I introduce Professor Willard of our State University.

A few brief notes, if you please, Professor—unfortunately our time is limited.

PROFESSOR WILLARD: Grover's Corners . . . let me see . . . Grover's Corners lies on the old Pleistocene granite of the Appalachian range. I may say it's some of the oldest land in the world. We're very proud of that. A shelf of Devonian basalt crosses it with vestiges of Mesozoic shale, and some sandstone outcroppings; but that's all more recent: two hundred, three hundred million years old.

Some highly interesting fossils have been found . . . I may say: unique fossils . . . two miles out of town, in Silas Peckham's cow pasture. They can be seen at the museum in our University at any time—that is, at any reasonable time. Would you like me to read some of Professor Gruber's notes on the meteorological situation—mean precipitation, et cetera?

STAGE MANAGER: Afraid we won't have time for that, Professor. We might have a few words on the history of man here.

PROFESSOR WILLARD: Yes . . . anthropological data: Early Amerindian stock. Cotahatchee tribes . . . no evidence before the tenth century of this era . . . hm . . . now entirely disappeared . . . possible traces in three families. Migration toward the end of the seventeenth century of English brachiocephalic blue-eyed stock . . . for the most part. Since then some Slav and Mediterranean—

STAGE MANAGER: And the population, Professor Willard?

PROFESSOR WILLARD: Within the town limits: 2,640.

STAGE MANAGER: Just a moment, Professor. [He whispers into the professor's ear.]

PROFESSOR WILLARD: Oh, yes, indeed?— The population, *at the moment*, is 2,642. The Postal District brings in 507 more, making a total of 3,149. Mortality and birth rates: constant, 6.032 by MacPherson's gauge.

STAGE MANAGER: Thank you very much, Professor. We're all very much obliged to you, I'm sure.

PROFESSOR WILLARD: Not at all, sir; not at all.

STAGE MANAGER: This way, Professor, and thank you again.

[*Exit Professor Willard.*]

Now the political and social report: Editor Webb.—Oh, Mr. Webb?

[*Mrs. Webb appears at her back door.*]

MRS. WEBB: He'll be here in a minute. . . . He just cut his hand while he was eatin' an apple.

STAGE MANAGER: Thank you, Mrs. Webb.

MRS. WEBB: Charles! Everybody's waitin'.

[*Exit Mrs. Webb.*]

STAGE MANAGER: Mr. Webb is Publisher and Editor of the Grover's Corners *Sentinel*. That's our local paper, y'know.

[*Mr. Webb enters from his house, pulling on his coat as he walks. His finger is bound in a handkerchief.*]

MR. WEBB: Well . . . I don't have to tell you that we're run here by a Board of Selectmen.—All males vote at the age of twenty-one. Women vote indirect. We're lower middle class: sprinkling of professional men . . . ten per cent illiterate laborers. Politically, we're eighty-six per cent Republicans; six per cent Democrats; four per cent Socialists; rest, indifferent.

Religiously, we're eighty-five per cent Protestants; twelve per cent Catholics; rest, indifferent.

STAGE MANAGER: Have you any comments, Mr. Webb?

MR. WEBB: Very ordinary town, if you ask me. Little better behaved than most. Probably a lot duller. But our young people here seem to like it well enough. Ninety per cent of 'em graduating from high school settle down right here to live—even when they've been away to college.

STAGE MANAGER: Now, is there anyone in the audience who would like to ask Editor Webb anything about the town?

WOMAN IN THE BALCONY: Is there much drinking in Grover's Corners?

MR. WEBB: Well, ma'am, I wouldn't know what you'd call *much*. Satiddy nights the farmhands meet down in Ellery Greenough's stable and holler some. We've got one or two town drunks, but they're always having remorses every time an evangelist comes to town. No, ma'am, I'd say likker ain't a regular thing in the home here, except in the medicine chest. Right good for snake bite, y'know—always was.

BELLIGERENT MAN, BACK OF AUDITORIUM: Is there no one in town aware of—

STAGE MANAGER: Come forward, will you, where we can all hear you—What were you saying?

BELLIGERENT MAN: Is there no one in town aware of social injustice and industrial inequality?

MR. WEBB: Oh, yes, everybody is—somethin' terrible. Seems like they spend most of their time talking about who's rich and who's poor.

BELLIGERENT MAN: Then why don't they do something about it?

[*He withdraws without waiting for an answer.*]

MR. WEBB: Well, I dunno. . . . I guess we're all hunting like everybody else for a way the diligent and sensible can rise to the top and the lazy and quarrelsome can sink to the bottom. But it ain't easy to find. Meanwhile, we do all we can to help those that can't help themselves and those that can we leave alone.—Are there any other questions?

LADY IN A BOX: Oh, Mr. Webb? Mr. Webb, is there any culture or love of beauty in Grover's Corners?

MR. WEBB: Well, ma'am, there ain't much—not in the sense you mean. Come to think of it, there's some girls that play the piano at High School Commencement; but they ain't happy about it. No, ma'am, there isn't much culture; but maybe this is the place to tell you that we've got a lot of pleasures of a kind here: we like the sun comin' up over the mountain in the morning, and we all notice a good deal about the birds. We pay a lot of attention to them. And we watch the change of the seasons; yes, everybody knows about them. But those other things—you're right, ma'am—there ain't much. *Robinson Crusoe* and the Bible; and Handel's "Largo," we all know that; and Whistler's "Mother"—those are just about as far as we go.

LADY IN A BOX: So I thought. Thank you, Mr. Webb.

STAGE MANAGER: Thank you, Mr. Webb.

[*Mr. Webb retires.*]

Now, we'll go back to the town. It's early afternoon. All 2,642 have had their dinners and all the dishes have been washed.

[*Mr. Webb, having removed his coat, returns and starts pushing a lawn mower to and fro beside his house.*]

There's an early-afternoon calm in our town: a buzzin' and a hummin' from the school buildings; only a few buggies on Main Street—the horses dozing at the hitching posts; you all remember what it's like. Doc Gibbs is in his office, tapping people and making them say "ah." Mr. Webb's cuttin' his lawn over there; one man in ten thinks it is a privilege to push his own lawn mower. No, sir. It's later than I thought. There are the children coming home from school already.

[*Shrill girls' voices are heard, off left. Emily comes along Main Street, carrying some books. There are some signs that she is imagining herself to be a lady of startling elegance.*]

EMILY: I *can't*, Lois. I've got to go home and help my mother. I *promised*.

MR. WEBB: Emily, walk simply. Who do you think you are today?

EMILY: Papa, you're terrible. One minute you tell me to stand up straight and the next minute you call me names. I just don't listen to you.

[*She gives him an abrupt kiss.*]

MR. WEBB: Golly, I never got a kiss from such a great lady before.

[*He goes out of sight. Emily leans over and picks some flowers by the gate of her house.*

*George Gibbs comes careening down Main Street. He is throwing a ball up to dizzying heights, and waiting to catch it again. This sometimes requires his taking six steps backward. He bumps into an Old Lady invisible to us.*]

GEORGE: Excuse me, Mrs. Forrest.

STAGE MANAGER: [*as Mrs. Forrest*] Go out and play in the fields, young man. You got no business playing baseball on Main Street.

GEORGE: Awfully sorry, Mrs. Forrest.— Hello, Emily.

EMILY: H'lo.

GEORGE: You made a fine speech in class.

EMILY: Well . . . I was really ready to make a speech about the Monroe Doctrine, but at the last minute Miss Corcoran made me talk about the Louisiana Purchase instead. I worked an awful long time on both of them.

GEORGE: Gee, it's funny, Emily. From my window up there I can just see your head nights when you're doing your homework over in your room.

EMILY: Why, can you?

GEORGE: You certainly do stick to it, Emily. I don't see how you can sit still that long. I guess you like school.

EMILY: Well, I always feel it's something you have to go through.

GEORGE: Yeah.

EMILY: I don't mind it really. It passes the time.

GEORGE: Yeah—Emily, what do you think? We might work out a kinda telegraph from your window to mine; and once in a while you could give me a kinda hint or two about one of those algebra problems. I don't mean the answers, Emily, of course not . . . just some little hint . . .

EMILY: Oh, I think *hints* are allowed.—So—ah—if you get stuck, George, you whistle to me; and I'll give you some hints.

GEORGE: Emily, you're just naturally bright, I guess.

EMILY: I figure that it's just the way a person's born.

GEORGE: Yeah. But, you see, I want to be a farmer, and my Uncle Luke says whenever I'm ready I can come over and work on his farm and if I'm any good I can just gradually have it.

EMILY: You mean the house and the land and everything?

*[Enter Mrs. Webb with a large bowl and sits on the bench by her trellis.]*

GEORGE: Yeah. Well, thanks . . . I better be getting out to the baseball field. Thanks for the talk, Emily.—Good afternoon, Mrs. Webb.

MRS. WEBB: Good afternoon, George.

GEORGE: So long, Emily.

EMILY: So long, George.

MRS. WEBB: Emily, come and help me string these beans for the winter. George Gibbs let himself have a real conversation, didn't he? Why, he's growing up. How old would George be?

EMILY: I don't know.

MRS. WEBB: Let's see. He must be almost sixteen.

EMILY: Mama, I made a speech in class today and I was very good.

MRS. WEBB: You must recite it to your father at supper. What was it about?

EMILY: The Louisiana Purchase. It was like silk off a spool. I'm going to make speeches all my life.—Mama, are these big enough?

MRS. WEBB: Try and get them a little bigger if you can.

EMILY: Mama, will you answer me a question, serious?

MRS. WEBB: Seriously, dear—not serious.

EMILY: Seriously—will you?

MRS. WEBB: Of course, I will.

EMILY: Mama, am I good looking?

MRS. WEBB: Yes, of course you are. All my children have got good features; I'd be ashamed if they hadn't.

EMILY: Oh, Mama, that's not what I mean. What I mean is: am I *pretty*?

MRS. WEBB: I've already told you, yes. Now that's enough of that. You have a nice young pretty face. I never heard of such foolishness.

EMILY: Oh, Mama, you never tell us the truth about anything.

MRS. WEBB: I *am* telling you the truth.

EMILY: Mama, were *you* pretty?

MRS. WEBB: Yes, I was, if I do say it. I was the prettiest girl in town next to Mamie Cartwright.

EMILY: But, Mama, you've got to say *something* about me. Am I pretty enough . . . to get anybody . . . to get people interested in me?

MRS. WEBB: Emily, you make me tired. Now stop it. You're pretty enough for all normal purposes.—Come along now and bring that bowl with you.

EMILY: Oh, Mama, you're no help at all.

STAGE MANAGER: Thank you. Thank you! That'll do. We'll have to interrupt again here. Thank you, Mrs. Webb; thank you, Emily.

[*Mrs. Webb and Emily withdraw.*]

There are some more things we want to explore about this town.

[*He comes to the center of the stage. During the following speech the lights gradually dim to darkness, leaving only a spot on him.*]

I think this is a good time to tell you that the Cartwright interests have begun building a new bank in Grover's Corners—had to go to Vermont for the marble, sorry to say. And they've asked a friend of mine what they should put in the cornerstone for people to dig up . . . a thousand years from now. . . . Of course, they've put in a copy of the *New York Times* and a copy of Mr. Webb's *Sentinel*. . . . We're kind of interested in this because some scientific fellas have found a way of painting all that reading matter with a glue—a silicate glue—that'll make it keep a thousand—two thousand years.

We're putting in a Bible . . . and the Constitution of the United States—and a copy of William Shakespeare's plays. What do you say, folks? What do you think?

Y'know—Babylon once had two million people in it, and all we know about 'em is the names of the kings and some copies of wheat contracts . . . and contracts for the sale of slaves. Yet every night all those families sat down to supper, and the father came home from his work, and the smoke went up the chimney,—same as here. And even in Greece and Rome, all we know about the *real* life of the people is what we can piece together out of the joking poems and the comedies they wrote for the theater back then.

So I'm going to have a copy of this play put in the cornerstone and the people a thousand years from now'll know a few simple facts about us—more than the Treaty of Versailles and the Lindbergh flight. See what I mean?

So—people a thousand years from now—this is the way we were in the provinces north of New York at the beginning of the twentieth century. This is the way we were: in our growing up and in our marrying and in our living and in our dying.

[*A choir partially concealed in the orchestra pit has begun singing "Blessed Be the Tie That Binds."*

*Simon Stimson stands directing them. Two ladders have been pushed onto the stage; they serve as indication of the second story in the Gibbs and Webb houses. George and Emily mount them, and apply themselves to their schoolwork. Dr. Gibbs has entered and is seated in his kitchen reading.*]

Well!—good deal of time's gone by. It's evening. You can hear choir practice going on in the Congregational Church. The children are at home doing their schoolwork.

The day's running down like a tired clock.

SIMON STIMSON: Now look here, everybody. Music come into the world to give pleasure. Softer! Softer! Get it out of your heads that music's only good when it's loud. You leave loudness to the Methodists. You couldn't beat 'em, even if you wanted to. Now again. Tenors!

GEORGE: Hssst! Emily!

EMILY: Hello.

GEORGE: Hello!

EMILY: I can't work at all. The moonlight's so *terrible.*

GEORGE: Emily, did you get the third problem?

EMILY: Which?

GEORGE: The *third?*

EMILY: Why, yes, George—that one's the easiest of them all.

GEORGE: I don't see it. Emily, can you give me a hint?

EMILY: I'll tell you one thing: the answer's in yards.

GEORGE: ! ! ! In yards? How do you mean?

EMILY: In *square* yards.

GEORGE: Oh . . . in square yards.

EMILY: Yes, George, don't you see?

GEORGE: Yeah.

EMILY: In square yards of *wallpaper.*

GEORGE: Wallpaper—oh, I see. Thanks a lot, Emily.

EMILY: You're welcome. My, isn't the moonlight *terrible?* And choir practice going on.—I think if you hold your breath you can hear the train all the way to Contoocook. Hear it?

GEORGE: M-m-m—what do you know!

EMILY: Well, I guess I better go back and try to work.

GEORGE: Good night, Emily. And thanks.

EMILY: Good night, George.

SIMON STIMSON: Before I forget it: how many of you will be able to come in Tuesday afternoon and sing at Fred Hersey's wedding?—show your hands. That'll be fine; that'll be right nice. We'll do the same music we did for Jane Trowbridge's last month.

Now we'll do: "Art Thou Weary; Art Thou Languid?" It's a question, ladies and gentlemen, make it talk. Ready.

DR. GIBBS: Oh, George, can you come down a minute?

GEORGE: Yes, Pa.

[*He descends the ladder.*]

DR. GIBBS: Make yourself comfortable, George; I'll only keep you a minute. George, how old are you?

GEORGE: How old am I? I'm sixteen, almost seventeen.

DR. GIBBS: What do you want to do after school's over?

GEORGE: Why, you know, Pa. I want to be a farmer on Uncle Luke's farm.

DR. GIBBS: You'll be willing, will you, to get up early and milk and feed the stock . . . and you'll be able to hoe and hay all day?

GEORGE: Sure, I will. What are you . . . what do you mean, Pa?

DR. GIBBS: Well, George, while I was in my office today I heard a funny sound . . . and what do you think it was? It was your mother chopping wood. There you see your mother—getting up early; cooking meals all day long; washing and ironing;—and still she has to go out in the back yard and chop wood. I suppose she just got tired of asking you. She just gave up and decided it was easier to do it herself. And you eat her meals, and put on the clothes she keeps nice for you, and you run off and play baseball,—like she's some hired girl we keep around the house but that we don't like very much. Well, I knew all I had to do was call your attention to it. Here's a handkerchief, son. George, I've decided to raise your spending money twenty-five cents a week. Not, of course, for chopping wood for your mother, because that's a present you give her, but because you're getting older—and I imagine there are lots of things you must find to do with it.

GEORGE: Thanks, Pa.

DR. GIBBS: Let's see—tomorrow's your payday. You can count on it—hmm. Probably Rebecca'll feel she ought to have some more too. Wonder what could have happened to your mother. Choir practice never was as late as this before.

GEORGE: It's only half past eight, Pa.

DR. GIBBS: I don't know why she's in that old choir. She hasn't any more voice than an old crow. . . . Traipsin' around the streets at this hour of the night . . . Just about time you retired, don't you think?

GEORGE: Yes, Pa.

[George mounts to his place on the ladder.

Laughter and good nights can be heard on stage left and presently Mrs. Gibbs, Mrs. Soames, and Mrs. Webb come down Main Street. When they arrive at the corner of the stage they stop.]

MRS. SOAMES: Good night, Martha. Good night, Mr. Foster.

MRS. WEBB: I'll tell Mr. Webb; I know he'll want to put it in the paper.

MRS. GIBBS: My, it's late!

MRS. SOAMES: Good night, Irma.

MRS. GIBBS: Real nice choir practice, wa'n't it? Myrtle Webb! Look at that moon, will you! Tsk-tsk-tsk. Potato weather, for sure. [They are silent a moment, gazing up at the moon.]

MRS. SOAMES: Naturally I didn't want to say a word about it in front of those others, but now we're alone—really, it's the worst scandal that ever was in this town!

MRS. GIBBS: What?

MRS. SOAMES: Simon Stimson!

MRS. GIBBS: Now, Louella!

MRS. SOAMES: But, Julia! To have the organist of a church drink and drunk year after year. You know he was drunk tonight.

MRS. GIBBS: Now, Louella! We all know about Mr. Stimson, and we all know about the troubles he's been through, and Dr. Ferguson knows too, and if Dr. Ferguson keeps him on there in his job the only thing the rest of us can do is just not to notice it.

MRS. SOAMES: Not to notice it! But it's getting worse.

MRS. WEBB: That's not true, Louella. It's getting better. I've been in that choir longer than you have. It doesn't happen anywhere near so often. . . . My, I hate to go to bed on a night like this. . . . I better hurry. Those children'll be sitting up till all hours. Good night, Louella.

[They all exchange good nights. Mrs. Webb hurries downstage, enters her house, and disappears.]

MRS. GIBBS: Can you get home safe, Louella?

MRS. SOAMES: It's as bright as day. I can see Mr. Soames scowling at the window now. You'd think we'd been to a dance the way the menfolk carry on.

[*More good nights. Mrs. Gibbs arrives at her home and passes through the trellis into the kitchen.*]

MRS. GIBBS: Well, we had a real good time.

DR. GIBBS: You're late enough.

MRS. GIBBS: Why, Frank, it ain't any later 'n usual.

DR. GIBBS: And you stopping at the corner to gossip with a lot of hens.

MRS. GIBBS: Now, Frank, don't be grouchy.

Come out and smell the heliotrope in the moonlight.

[*They stroll out arm in arm along the footlights.*]

Isn't that wonderful? What did you do all the time I was away?

DR. GIBBS: Oh, I read—as usual. What were the girls gossiping about tonight?

MRS. GIBBS: Well, believe me, Frank—there is something to gossip about.

DR. GIBBS: Hmm! Simon Stimson far gone, was he?

MRS. GIBBS: Worst I've ever seen him. How'll that end, Frank? Dr. Ferguson can't forgive him forever.

DR. GIBBS: I guess I know more about Simon Stimson's affairs than anybody in this town. Some people ain't made for small-town life. I don't know how that'll end; but there's nothing we can do but just leave it alone. Come, get in.

MRS. GIBBS: No, not yet . . . Frank, I'm worried about you.

DR. GIBBS: What are you worried about?

MRS. GIBBS: I think it's my duty to make plans for you to get a real rest and change. And if I get that legacy, well, I'm going to insist on it.

DR. GIBBS: Now, Julia, there's no sense in going over that again.

MRS. GIBBS: Frank, you're just being *unreasonable!*

DR. GIBBS: [*starting into the house*] Come on, Julia, it's getting late. First thing you know you'll catch cold. I gave George a piece of my mind tonight. I reckon you'll have your wood chopped for a while anyway. No, no, start getting upstairs.

MRS. GIBBS: Oh, dear. There's always so many things to pick up, seems like. You know, Frank, Mrs. Fairchild always locks her front door every night. All those people up that part of town do.

DR. GIBBS: [*blowing out the lamp*] They're all getting citified, that's the trouble with them. They haven't got nothing fit to burgle and everybody knows it.

[*They disappear. Rebecca climbs up the ladder beside George.*]

GEORGE: Get out, Rebecca. There's only room for one at this window. You're always spoiling everything.

REBECCA: Well, let me look just a minute.

GEORGE: Use your own window.

REBECCA: I did, but there's no moon there. . . . George, do you know what I think, do you? I think maybe the moon's getting nearer and nearer and there'll be a big 'splosion.

GEORGE: Rebecca, you don't know anything. If the moon were getting nearer,

the guys that sit up all night looking through telescopes would see it first and they'd tell about it, and it'd be in all the newspapers.

REBECCA: George, is the moon shining on South America, Canada, and half the whole world?

GEORGE: Well—prob'ly is.

[*The Stage Manager strolls on. Pause. The sound of crickets is heard.*]

STAGE MANAGER: Nine thirty. Most of the lights are out. No, there's Constable Warren trying a few doors on Main Street. And here comes Editor Webb, after putting his newspaper to bed.

[*Mr. Warren, an elderly policeman, comes along Main Street from the right, Mr. Webb from the left.*]

MR. WEBB: Good evening, Bill.

CONSTABLE WARREN: Evenin', Mr. Webb.

MR. WEBB: Quite a moon!

CONSTABLE WARREN: Yepp.

MR. WEBB: All quiet tonight?

CONSTABLE WARREN: Simon Stimson is rollin' around a little. Just saw his wife movin' out to hunt for him so I looked the other way—there he is now.

[*Simon Stimson comes down Main Street from the left, only a trace of unsteadiness in his walk*]

MR. WEBB: Good evening, Simon . . . Town seems to have settled down for the night pretty well . . .

[*Simon Stimson comes up to him and pauses a moment and stares at him, swaying slightly.*]

MR. WEBB: Good evening . . . Yes, most of the town's settled down for the night, Simon. . . . I guess we better do the same. Can I walk along a ways with you?

[*Simon Stimson continues on his way*

*without a word and disappears at the right.*]

Good night.

CONSTABLE WARREN: I don't know how that's goin' to end, Mr. Webb.

MR. WEBB: Well, he's seen a peck of trouble, one thing after another. . . . Oh, Bill . . . if you see my boy smoking cigarettes, just give him a word, will you? He thinks a lot of you, Bill.

CONSTABLE WARREN: I don't think he smokes no cigarettes, Mr. Webb. Leastways, not more'n two or three a year.

MR. WEBB: Hm . . . I hope not. Well, good night, Bill.

CONSTABLE WARREN: Good night, Mr. Webb.

[*Exit.*]

MR. WEBB: Who's that up there? Is that you, Myrtle?

EMILY: No, it's me, Papa.

MR. WEBB: Why aren't you in bed?

EMILY: I don't know. I just can't sleep yet, Papa. The moonlight's so *won*-derful. And the smell of Mrs. Gibbs' heliotrope. Can you smell it?

MR. WEBB: Hm . . . Yes. Haven't any troubles on your mind, have you, Emily?

EMILY: *Troubles*, Papa? No.

MR. WEBB: Well, enjoy yourself, but don't let your mother catch you. Good night, Emily.

EMILY: Good night, Papa. [*Mr. Webb crosses into the house whistling "Blessed Be the Tie That Binds" and disappears.*]

REBECCA: I never told you about that letter Jane Crofut got from her minister when she was sick. He wrote Jane a letter and on the envelope the address was like this: It said: Jane Crofut; The Crofut Farm; Grover's Corners; Sutton County; New Hampshire; United States of America.

GEORGE: What's funny about that?

REBECCA: But listen, it's not finished: the United States of America; Continent of North America; Western Hemisphere; the Earth; the Solar System; the Universe; the Mind of God—that's what it said on the envelope.

GEORGE: What do you know!

REBECCA: And the postman brought it just the same.

GEORGE: What do you know!

STAGE MANAGER: That's the end of the First Act, friends. You can go and smoke now, those that smoke.

---

## YOU AND ACT ONE

*Our Town* is a play in which the **setting** plays a very important part. The author takes us to what he considers a typical small American town of its time. He shows us the kind of people that he feels we should expect to find there. Though they talk about going away for travel or education, their town with the people in it is what they really know. How much do we learn about "our town" in this first act? How much do we learn about the two families that receive most of our attention? What is an ordinary day like for them? Suppose you were the Stage Manager, and you had to sum up the things about these people and their lives that were most important to the author. What would you include?

---

### A Closer Look

(1) Do a brief portrait of the *teenagers* in Act One. What do they think about school? How are they treated by their parents—and how do they treat their parents in turn? How do they act toward each other? Do you think they were typical teenagers of their time?

(2) The Stage Manager at one point asks for questions from the *audience*. What questions is he asked? What attitudes do

they represent? What answers do they receive? How are the questioners different from the townspeople we have observed? Are they all "outsiders," and in what way?

(3) From the beginning, a major theme of Wilder's play is the *continuity* of human life. Life goes on. Some of the things that are a basic part of our human experience repeat themselves over and over—as they have in the past, and as they will in the future. Find passages in this first act that point back to the past and forward into the future. Describe several of them. Though the play takes place in one small town, we are constantly reminded that life at the same time goes on in other places everywhere. Find several examples.

---

### Your Turn

---

Suppose you were talking to an audience about everyday life in your own community, the way the Stage Manager does in this play. What would you say? Or, suppose that like the Stage Manager you wanted to put something in a cornerstone that would tell people many years from now about "the *real* life of the people." What would you include in your description of the real life of people in your community?

---

Language/Composition Activity B17

INFORMAL ENGLISH

# Small-Town Talk

The population of "our town" is mostly lower middle class, with some professional people. We come to know a doctor, a newspaper editor, and a college professor. They know educated English—office English and book English. But they talk it in a friendly small-town way, with a folksy touch. We call this kind of informal, conversational English *colloquial*—it is language we use in just "talking together." Each of the following sentences has a colloquial touch. With each sentence, find a more formal replacement for the italicized word or expression.

1. The morning star gets *wonderful* bright.
2. *Most* everybody in town manages to look into these two stores once a day.
3. The public school is over *yonder.*
4. In those days, our newspaper *come* out twice a week.
5. *Like* you said, the knee always tells me when it's going to rain.
6. It was all *wrote* up in the Boston paper at the time.
7. *Set* down and drink your coffee.
8. The Cartwrights own it, and it *brung* them a fortune.
9. I've been saving it *gradual.*
10. I've walked all over it, *like* we were going to buy it.
11. There *is* always many things to pick up.
12. He's seen *a peck of* trouble.
13. She told me to tell you *as how* we hope they'll be very happy.
14. Every now and then he says "I do," but it *don't* sound convincing.
15. *Ain't* been any burglars in town yet, but everybody's heard about them.

# Act Two

*The tables and chairs of the two kitchens are still on the stage. The ladders and the small bench have been withdrawn.*

*The Stage Manager has been at his accustomed place watching the audience return to its seats.*

STAGE MANAGER: Three years have gone by. Yes, the sun's come up over a thousand times. Summers and winters have cracked the mountains a little bit more and the rains have brought down some of the dirt. Some babies that weren't even born before have begun talking regular sentences already; and a number of people who thought they were right young and spry have noticed that they can't bound up a flight of stairs like they used to, without their heart fluttering a little. All that can happen in a thousand days.

Nature's been pushing and contriving in other ways, too: a number of young people fell in love and got married. Yes, the mountain got bit away a few fractions of an inch; millions of gallons of water went by the mill; and here and there a new home was set up under a roof. Almost everybody in the world gets married—you know what I mean? In our town there aren't hardly any exceptions at all. Most everybody in the world climbs into their graves married.

The First Act was called the Daily Life. This act is called Love and Marriage. There's another act coming after this: I reckon you can guess what that's about.

So: It's three years later. It's 1904. It's July 7th, just after High School Commencement. That's the time most of our young people jump up and get married. Soon as they've passed their last examinations in solid geometry and Cicero's Orations, looks like they suddenly feel themselves fit to be married.

It's early morning. Only this time it's been raining. It's been pouring and thundering. Mrs. Gibbs' garden, and Mrs. Webb's here: drenched. All those bean poles and pea vines: drenched. All yesterday over there on Main Street, the rain looked like curtains being blown along. Hm . . . it may begin again any minute.

There! You can hear the 5:45 for Boston.

*[Mrs. Gibbs and Mrs. Webb enter their kitchen and start the day as in the First Act.]*

And there's Mrs. Gibbs and Mrs. Webb come down to make breakfast, just as though it were an ordinary day. I don't have to point out to the women in my audience that those ladies they see before them, both of those ladies cooked three meals every day—one of 'em for twenty years, the other for forty—and no summer vacation. They brought up two children apiece, washed, cleaned the house—and *never had a nervous breakdown.*

It's like what one of those Middle West poets said: You've got to love life to have life, and you've got to have life to love life. . . . It's what they call a vicious circle.

HOWIE NEWSOME: *[off stage left]* Giddap, Bessie!

STAGE MANAGER: Here comes Howie Newsome delivering the milk. And there's Si Crowell delivering the papers like his brother before him.

*[Si Crowell has entered hurling imaginary newspapers into doorways; Howie*

*Newsome has come along Main Street with Bessie.*]

SI CROWELL: Morning, Howie.

HOWIE NEWSOME: Morning, Si.—Anything in the papers I ought to know?

SI CROWELL: Nothing much, except we're losing about the best baseball pitcher Grover's Corners ever had—George Gibbs.

HOWIE NEWSOME: Reckon he is.

SI CROWELL: He could hit and run bases, too.

HOWIE NEWSOME: Yep. Mighty fine ball player.—Whoa! Bessie! I guess I can stop and talk if I've a mind to!

SI CROWELL: I don't see how he could give up a thing like that just to get married. Would you, Howie?

HOWIE NEWSOME: Can't tell, Si. Never had no talent that way.

[*Constable Warren enters. They exchange good mornings.*]

You're up early, Bill.

CONSTABLE WARREN: Seein' if there's anything I can do to prevent a flood. River's been risin' all night.

HOWIE NEWSOME: Si Crowell's all worked up here about George Gibbs' retiring from baseball.

CONSTABLE WARREN: Yes, sir; that's the way it goes. Back in '84 we had a player, Si—even George Gibbs couldn't touch him. Name of Hank Todd. Went down to Maine and become a parson. Wonderful ball player.—Howie, how does the weather look to you?

HOWIE NEWSOME: Oh, 'tain't bad. Think maybe it'll clear up for good.

[*Constable Warren and Si Crowell continue on their way.*

*Howie Newsome brings the milk first to Mrs. Gibbs' house. She meets him by the trellis.*]

MRS. GIBBS: Good morning, Howie. Do you think it's going to rain again?

HOWIE NEWSOME: Morning, Mrs. Gibbs. It rained so heavy, I think maybe it'll clear up.

MRS. GIBBS: Certainly hope it will.

HOWIE NEWSOME: How much did you want today?

MRS. GIBBS: I'm going to have a houseful of relations, Howie. Looks to me like I'll need three-a-milk and two-a-cream.

HOWIE NEWSOME: My wife says to tell you we both hope they'll be very happy, Mrs. Gibbs. Know they *will*.

MRS. GIBBS: Thanks a lot, Howie. Tell your wife I hope she gits there to the wedding.

HOWIE NEWSOME: Yes, she'll be there; she'll be there if she kin.

[*Howie Newsome crosses to Mrs. Webb's house.*]

Morning, Mrs. Webb.

MRS. WEBB: Oh, good morning, Mr. Newsome. I told you four quarts of milk, but I hope you can spare me another.

HOWIE NEWSOME: Yes'm . . . and the two of cream.

MRS. WEBB: Will it start raining again, Mr. Newsome?

HOWIE NEWSOME: Well. Just sayin' to Mrs. Gibbs as how it may lighten up. Mrs. Newsome told me to tell you as how we hope they'll both be very happy, Mrs. Webb. Know they *will*.

MRS. WEBB: Thank you, and thank Mrs. Newsome and we're counting on seeing you at the wedding.

HOWIE NEWSOME: Yes, Mrs. Webb. We hope to git there. Couldn't miss that. Come on, Bessie.

[*Exit Howie Newsome.*

*Dr. Gibbs descends in shirt sleeves, and sits down at his breakfast table.*]

DR. GIBBS: Well, Ma, the day has come. You're losin' one of your chicks.

MRS. GIBBS: Frank Gibbs, don't you say

another word. I feel like crying every minute. Just sit down and drink your coffee.

DR. GIBBS: The groom's up shaving himself—only there ain't an awful lot to shave. Whistling and singing, like he's glad to leave us.—Every now and then he says "I do" to the mirror, but it don't sound convincing to me.

MRS. GIBBS: I declare, Frank, I don't know how he'll get along. I've arranged his clothes and seen to it he's put warm things on—Frank! they're too *young*. Emily won't think of such things. He'll catch his death of cold within a week.

DR. GIBBS: I was remembering my wedding morning, Julia.

MRS. GIBBS: Now don't start that, Frank Gibbs.

DR. GIBBS: I was the scaredest young fella in the State of New Hampshire. I thought I'd make a mistake for sure. And when I saw you comin' down that aisle I thought you were the prettiest girl I'd ever seen, but the only trouble was that I'd never seen you before. There I was in the Congregational Church marryin' a total stranger.

MRS. GIBBS: And how do you think I felt!—Frank, weddings are perfectly awful things. Farces—that's what they are!

[*She puts a plate before him.*]

Here, I've made something for you.

DR. GIBBS: Why, Julia Hersey—French toast!

MRS. GIBBS: 'Tain't hard to make and I had to do *something*.

[*Pause. Dr. Gibbs pours on the syrup.*]

DR. GIBBS: How'd you sleep last night, Julia?

MRS. GIBBS: Well, I heard a lot of the hours struck off.

DR. GIBBS: Ye-e-s! I get a shock every time I think of George setting out to be a family man—that great gangling thing!—I tell you Julia, there's nothing so terrifying in the world as a *son*. The relation of father and son is the darndest, awkwardest—

MRS. GIBBS: Well, mother and daughter's no picnic, let me tell you.

DR. GIBBS: They'll have a lot of troubles, I suppose, but that's none of our business. Everybody has a right to their own troubles.

MRS. GIBBS: [*at the table, drinking her coffee, meditatively*] Yes . . . people are meant to go through life two by two. 'Tain't natural to be lonesome.

[*Pause. Dr. Gibbs starts laughing.*]

DR. GIBBS: Julia, do you know one of the things I was scared of when I married you?

MRS. GIBBS: Oh, go along with you!

DR. GIBBS: I was afraid we wouldn't have material for conversation more'n'd last us a few weeks.

[*Both laugh.*]

I was afraid we'd run out and eat our meals in silence, that's a fact.—Well, you and I been conversing for twenty years now without any noticeable barren spells.

MRS. GIBBS: Well—good weather, bad weather—'tain't very choice, but I always find something to say.

[*She goes to the foot of the stairs.*]

Did you hear Rebecca stirring around upstairs?

DR. GIBBS: No. Only day of the year Rebecca hasn't been managing everybody's business up there. She's hiding up in her room.—I got the impression she's crying.

MRS. GIBBS: Lord's sakes!—This has got to stop.—Rebecca! Rebecca! Come and get your breakfast.

[*George comes rattling down the stairs, very brisk.*]

GEORGE: Good morning, everybody. Only five more hours to live.

[*Makes the gesture of cutting his throat, and a loud "k-k-k," and starts through the trellis.*]

MRS. GIBBS: George Gibbs, where are you going?

GEORGE: Just stepping across the grass to see my girl.

MRS. GIBBS: Now, George! You put on your overshoes. It's raining torrents. You don't go out of this house without you're prepared for it.

GEORGE: Aw, Ma. It's just a *step*!

MRS. GIBBS: George! You'll catch your death of cold and cough all through the service.

DR. GIBBS: George, do as your mother tells you!

[*Dr. Gibbs goes upstairs. George returns reluctantly to the kitchen and pantomimes putting on overshoes. Mrs. Gibbs oversees this operation.*]

MRS. GIBBS: From tomorrow on you can kill yourself in all weathers, but while you're in my house you'll live wisely, thank you.—Maybe Mrs. Webb isn't used to callers at seven in the morning.—Here, take a cup of coffee first.

GEORGE: Be back in a minute.

[*He crosses the stage, leaping over the puddles.*]

Good morning, Mother Webb.

MRS. WEBB: Goodness! You frightened me!—Now, George, you can come in a minute out of the wet, but you know I can't ask you in.

GEORGE: Why not—?

MRS. WEBB: George, you know's well as I do: the groom can't see his bride on his wedding day, not until he sees her in church.

GEORGE: Aw!—that's just a superstition.—Good morning, Mr. Webb.

[*Enter Mr. Webb.*]

MR. WEBB: Good morning, George.

GEORGE: Mr. Webb, you don't believe in that superstition, do you?

MR. WEBB: There's a lot of common sense in some superstitions, George.

[*He sits at the table, facing right.*]

MRS. WEBB: Millions have folla'd it, George, and you don't want to be the first to fly in the face of custom.

GEORGE: How is Emily?

MRS. WEBB: She hasn't waked up yet. I haven't heard a sound out of her.

GEORGE: Emily's *asleep*!!!

MRS. WEBB: No wonder! We were up 'til all ours, sewing and packing. Now I'll tell you what I'll do; you set down here a minute with Mr. Webb and drink this cup of coffee; and I'll go upstairs and see she doesn't come down and surprise you. There's some bacon, too; but don't be long about it.

[*Exit Mrs. Webb.
Embarrassed silence. Mr. Webb dunks doughnuts in his coffee.
More silence.*]

MR. WEBB: [*suddenly and loudly*] Well, George, how are you?

GEORGE: [*startled, choking over his coffee*] Oh, fine, I'm fine. [*Pause.*] Mr. Webb, what sense could there be in a superstition like that?

MR. WEBB: Well, you see—on her wedding morning a girl's head's apt to be full of . . . clothes and one thing and another. Don't you think that's probably it?

GEORGE: Ye-e-s. I never thought of that.

MR. WEBB: A girl's apt to be a mite nervous on her wedding day.

[*Pause.*]

GEORGE: I wish a fellow could get married without all that marching up and down.

MR. WEBB: Every man that's ever lived has felt that way about it, George; but it hasn't been any use. It's the womenfolk who've built up weddings, my boy. For a while now the women have it all their own. A man looks pretty small at a wedding, George. All those good women standing shoulder to shoulder making sure that the knot's tied in a mighty public way.

GEORGE: But . . . you *believe* in it, don't you, Mr. Webb?

MR. WEBB: [*with alacrity*] Oh, yes; oh, yes. Don't you misunderstand me, my boy. Marriage is a wonderful thing—wonderful thing. And don't you forget that, George.

GEORGE: No, sir.—Mr. Webb, how old were you when you got married?

MR. WEBB: Well, you see: I'd been to college and I'd taken a little time to get settled. But Mrs. Webb—she wasn't much older than what Emily is. Oh, age hasn't much to do with it, George—not compared with . . . uh . . . other things.

GEORGE: What were you going to say, Mr. Webb?

MR. WEBB: Oh, I don't know.—Was I going to say something?

[*Pause.*]

George, I was thinking the other night of some advice my father gave me when I got married. Charles, he said, Charles, start out early showing who's boss, he said. Best thing to do is to give an order, even if it don't make sense; just so she'll learn to obey. And he said: if anything about your wife irritates you—her conversation, or anything—just get up and leave the house. That'll make it clear to her, he said. And, oh, yes! he said never, *never* let your wife know how much money you have, never.

GEORGE: Well, Mr. Webb . . . I don't think I could . . .

MR. WEBB: So I took the opposite of my father's advice and I've been happy ever since. And let that be a lesson to you, George, never to ask advice on personal matters.—George, are you going to raise chickens on your farm?

GEORGE: What?

MR. WEBB: Are you going to raise chickens on your farm?

GEORGE: Uncle Luke's never been much interested, but I thought—

MR. WEBB: A book came into my office the other day, George, on the Philo System of raising chickens. I want you to read it. I'm thinking of beginning in a small way in the back yard, and I'm going to put an incubator in the cellar—

[*Enter Mrs. Webb.*]

MRS. WEBB: Charles, are you rambling on about that old incubator again? I thought you two would be talking about things worthwhile.

MR. WEBB: [*bitingly*] Well, Myrtle, if you want to give the boy some good advice, I'll go upstairs and leave you alone with him.

MRS. WEBB: [*pulling George up*] George, Emily's got to come downstairs and eat her breakfast. She sends you her love but she doesn't want to lay eyes on you. Good-bye.

GEORGE: Good-bye.

[*George crosses the stage to his own home, bewildered and crestfallen. He slowly dodges a puddle and disappears into his house.*]

MR. WEBB: Myrtle, I guess you don't know about that older superstition.

MRS. WEBB: What do you mean, Charles?

MR. WEBB: Ever since the cave men: no

bridegroom should see his father-in-law on the day of the wedding, or near it. Now remember that.

[*Both leave the stage.*]

STAGE MANAGER: Thank you very much, Mr. and Mrs. Webb.—Now I have to interrupt again here. You see, we want to know how all this began—this wedding, this plan to spend a lifetime together. I'm awfully interested in how big things like that begin.

You know how it is: you're twenty-one or twenty-two and you make some decisions; then whissh! you're seventy: you've been a lawyer for fifty years, and that white-haired lady at your side has eaten over fifty thousand meals with you.

How do such things begin? George and Emily are going to show you now the conversation they had when they first knew that . . . that . . . as the old saying goes . . . they were meant for one another.

But before they do it I want you to try and remember what it was like to have been very young. And particularly the days when you were first in love; when you were like a person sleepwalking, and you didn't quite see the street you were in, and didn't quite hear everything that was said to you. You're just a little bit crazy. Will you remember that, please?

Now they'll be coming out of high school at three o'clock. George has just been elected President of the Junior Class, and as it's June, that means he'll be President of the Senior Class all next year. And Emily's just been elected Secretary and Treasurer. I don't have to tell you how important that is.

[*He places a board across the backs of two chairs, which he takes from those at the Gibbs family's table. He brings two high stools from the wings and places them behind the board. Persons sitting on the stools will be facing the audience. This is the counter of Mr. Morgan's drugstore. The sounds of young people's voices are heard off left.*]

Yepp—there they are coming down Main Street now.

[*Emily, carrying an armful of—imaginary—schoolbooks, comes along Main Street from the left.*]

EMILY: I can't, Louise. I've got to go home. Good-bye. Oh, Ernestine! Ernestine! Can you come over tonight and do Latin? Isn't that Cicero the worst thing—! Tell your mother you *have* to. G'bye. G'bye, Helen. G'bye, Fred.

[*George, also carrying books, catches up with her.*]

GEORGE: Can I carry your books home for you, Emily?
EMILY: [*coolly*] Why . . . uh . . . Thank you. It isn't far.

[*She gives them to him.*]

GEORGE: Excuse me a minute, Emily.— Say, Bob, if I'm a little late, start practice anyway. And give Herb some long high ones.
EMILY: Good-bye, Lizzy.
GEORGE: Good-bye, Lizzy.—I'm awfully glad you were elected, too, Emily.
EMILY: Thank you.

[*They have been standing on Main Street, almost against the back wall. They take the first steps toward the audience when George stops and says:*]

GEORGE: Emily, why are you mad at me?
EMILY: I'm not mad at you.
GEORGE: You've been treating me funny lately.
EMILY: Well, since you ask me, I might as well say it right out, George—

[*She catches sight of a teacher passing.*]

Good-bye, Miss Corcoran.

GEORGE: Good-bye, Miss Corcoran.— Wha—what is it?

EMILY: [*not scoldingly, finding it difficult to say*] I don't like the whole change that's come over you in the last year. I'm sorry if that hurts your feelings, but I've got to—tell the truth and shame the devil.

GEORGE: A *change*?—Wha—what do you mean?

EMILY: Well, up to a year ago I used to like you a lot. And I used to watch you as you did everything . . . because we'd been friends so long . . . and then you began spending all your time at *base-ball* . . . and you never stopped to speak to anybody any more. Not even to your own family you didn't . . . and, George, it's a fact, you've got awful conceited and stuck-up, and all the girls say so. They may not say so to your face, but that's what they say about you behind your back, and it hurts me to hear them say it, but I've got to agree with them a little. I'm sorry if it hurts your feelings, but I can't be sorry I said it.

GEORGE: I . . . I'm glad you said it, Emily. I never thought that such a thing was happening to me. I guess it's hard for a fella not to have faults creep into his character.

[*They take a step or two in silence, then stand still in misery.*]

EMILY: I always expect a man to be perfect and I think he should be.

GEORGE: Oh . . . I don't think it's possible to be perfect, Emily.

EMILY: Well, my *father* is, and as far as I can see *your* father is. There's no reason on earth why you shouldn't be, too.

GEORGE: Well, I feel it's the other way round. That men aren't naturally good; but girls are.

EMILY: Well, you might as well know right now that I'm not perfect. It's not as easy for a girl to be as perfect as a man, because we girls are more— more—nervous.—Now I'm sorry I said all that about you. I don't know what made me say it.

GEORGE: Emily—

EMILY: Now I can see it's not the truth at all. And I suddenly feel that it isn't important, anyway.

GEORGE: Emily . . . would you like an ice-cream soda, or something, before you go home?

EMILY: Well, thank you. . . . I would.

[*They advance toward the audience and make an abrupt right turn, opening the door of Morgan's drugstore. Under strong emotion, Emily keeps her face down. George speaks to some passers-by.*]

GEORGE: Hello, Stew—how are you?— Good afternoon, Mrs. Slocum.

[*The Stage Manager, wearing spectacles and assuming the role of Mr. Morgan, enters abruptly from the right and stands between the audience and the counter of his soda fountain.*]

STAGE MANAGER: Hello, George. Hello, Emily.—What'll you have?—Why, Emily Webb—what you been crying about?

GEORGE:

[*He gropes for an explanation.*]

She . . . she just got an awful scare, Mr. Morgan. She almost got run over by that hardware-store wagon. Everybody says that Tom Huckins drives like a crazy man.

STAGE MANAGER: [*drawing a drink of water*] Well, now! You take a drink of water, Emily. You look all shook up. I tell you, you've got to look both ways before you cross Main Street these days. Gets worse every year.—What'll you have?

EMILY: I'll have a strawberry phosphate, thank you, Mr. Morgan.

GEORGE: No, no, Emily. Have an ice-cream soda with me. Two strawberry ice-cream sodas, Mr. Morgan.

STAGE MANAGER: [working the faucets] Two strawberry ice-cream sodas, yes sir. Yes, sir. There are a hundred and twenty-five horses in Grover's Corners this minute I'm talking to you. State Inspector was in here yesterday. And now they're bringing in these automobiles, the best thing to do is to just stay home. Why, I can remember when a dog could go to sleep all day in the middle of Main Street and nothing come along to disturb him.

[He sets the imaginary glasses before them.]

There they are. Enjoy 'em.

[He sees a customer, right.]

Yes, Mrs. Ellis. What can I do for you?

[He goes out right.]

EMILY: They're so expensive.

GEORGE: No, no—don't you think of that. We're celebrating our election. And then do you know what else I have to celebrate?

EMILY: No-no.

GEORGE: I'm celebrating because I've got a friend who tells me all the things that ought to be told me.

EMILY: George, please don't think of that. I don't know why I said it. It's not true. You're—

GEORGE: No, Emily, you stick to it. I'm glad you spoke to me like you did. But you'll see: I'm going to change so quick—you bet I'm going to change. And, Emily, I want to ask you a favor.

EMILY: What?

GEORGE: Emily, if I go away to State Agriculture College next year, will you write me a letter once in a while?

EMILY: I certainly will. I certainly will, George . . .

[Pause. They start sipping the sodas through the straws.]

It certainly seems like being away three years you'd get out of touch with things. Maybe letters from Grover's Corners wouldn't be so interesting after a while. Grover's Corners isn't a very important place when you think of all—New Hampshire; but I think it's a very nice town.

GEORGE: The day wouldn't come when I wouldn't want to know everything that's happening here. I know that's true, Emily.

EMILY: Well, I'll try to make my letters interesting.

[Pause.]

GEORGE: Y'know. Emily, whenever I meet a farmer I ask him if he thinks it's important to go to Agriculture School to be a good farmer.

EMILY: Why, George—

GEORGE: Yeah, and some of them say that it's even a waste of time. You can get all those things, anyway, out of the pamphlets the government sends out. And Uncle Luke's getting old—he's about ready for me to start in taking over his farm tomorrow, if I could.

EMILY: My!

GEORGE: And, like you say, being gone all that time . . . in other places and meeting other people . . . Gosh, if anything like that can happen I don't want to go away. I guess new people aren't any better than old ones. I'll bet they almost never are. Emily . . . I feel that you're as good a friend as I've got. I don't need to go and meet the people in other towns.

EMILY: But, George, maybe it's very important for you to go and learn all that about—cattle judging and soils and those things. . . . Of course, I don't know.

GEORGE: [after a pause, very seriously] Emily, I'm going to make up my mind right now. I won't go. I'll tell Pa about it tonight.

EMILY: Why, George, I don't see why you have to decide right now. It's a whole year away.

GEORGE: Emily, I'm glad you spoke to me about that . . . that fault in my character. What you said was right; but there was one thing wrong in it, and that was when you said that for a year I wasn't noticing people, and . . . you, for instance. Why, you say you were watching me when I did everything . . . I was doing the same about you all the time. Why, sure—I always thought about you as one of the chief people I thought about. I always made sure where you were sitting on the bleachers, and who you were with, and for three days now I've been trying to walk home with you; but something's always got in the way. Yesterday I was standing over against the wall waiting for you, and you walked home with *Miss Corcoran*.

EMILY: George! . . . Life's awful funny! How could I have known that? Why, I thought—

GEORGE: Listen, Emily, I'm going to tell you why I'm not going to Agriculture School. I think that once you've found a person that you're very fond of . . . I mean a person who's fond of you, too, and likes you enough to be interested in your character . . . Well, I think that's just as important as college is, and even more so. That's what I think.

EMILY: I think it's awfully important, too.

GEORGE: Emily.

EMILY: Y-yes, George.

GEORGE: Emily, if I *do* improve and make a big change . . . would you be . . . I mean: *could* you be . . .

EMILY: I . . . I am now; I always have been.

GEORGE: [*Pause.*] So I guess this is an important talk we've been having.

EMILY: Yes . . . yes.

GEORGE:

[*Takes a deep breath and straightens his back.*]

Wait just a minute and I'll walk you home.

[*With mounting alarm he digs into his pockets for the money. The Stage Manager enters, right. George, deeply embarrassed, but direct, says to him:*]

Mr. Morgan, I'll have to go home and get the money to pay you for this. It'll only take me a minute.

STAGE MANAGER: [*pretending to be affronted*] What's that? George Gibbs, do you mean to tell me—!

GEORGE: Yes, but I had reasons, Mr. Morgan.—Look, here's my gold watch to keep until I come back with the money.

STAGE MANAGER: That's all right. Keep your watch. I'll trust you.

GEORGE: I'll be back in five minutes.

STAGE MANAGER: I'll trust you ten years, George—not a day over.—Got all over your shock, Emily?

EMILY: Yes, thank you, Mr. Morgan. It was nothing.

GEORGE: [*taking up the books from the counter*] I'm ready.

[*They walk in grave silence across the stage and pass through the trellis at the Webbs' back door and disappear.*

*The Stage Manager watches them out, then turns to the audience, removing his spectacles.*]

STAGE MANAGER: Well—

[*He claps his hands as a signal.*]

Now we're all set to get on with the wedding.

[*He stands waiting while the set is prepared for the next scene.*

*Stagehands remove the chairs, tables, and trellises from the Gibbs and Webb houses. They arrange the pews for the church in the center of the stage. The congregation will sit facing the back wall. The aisle of the church starts at the center of the back wall and comes toward the audience. A small platform is placed against the back wall on which the Stage Manager will stand later, playing the minister. The image of a stained-glass window is cast from a lantern slide upon the back wall.*

*When all is ready the Stage Manager strolls to the center of the stage, down front, and, musingly, addresses the audience.*]

There are a lot of things to be said about a wedding; there are a lot of thoughts that go on during a wedding. We can't get them all into one wedding, naturally, and especially not into a wedding at Grover's Corners, where they're awfully plain and short. In this wedding I play the minister. That gives me the right to say a few more things about it. For a while now, the play gets pretty serious.

Y'see, some churches say that marriage is a sacrament. I don't quite know what that means, but I can guess. Like Mrs. Gibbs said a few minutes ago: People were made to live two-by-two. This is a good wedding, but people are so put together that even at a good wedding there's a lot of confusion way down deep in people's minds and we thought that that ought to be in our play, too.

The real hero of this scene isn't on the stage at all, and you know who that is. It's like what one of those European fellas said: every child born into the world is nature's attempt to make a perfect human being. Well, we've seen nature pushing and contriving for some time now. We all know that nature's interested in quantity; but I think she's interested in quality, too—that's why I'm in the ministry.

And don't forget all the other witnesses at this wedding—the ancestors. Millions of them. Most of them set out to live two by two, also. Millions of them.

Well, that's all my sermon. 'Twan't very long, anyway.

[*The organist starts playing Handel's "Largo." The congregation streams into the church and sits in silence. Church bells are heard.*

*Mrs. Gibbs sits in the front row, the first seat on the aisle, the right section; next to her are Rebecca and Dr. Gibbs. Across the aisle Mrs. Webb, Wally, and Mr. Webb. A small choir takes its place, facing the audience under the stained-glass window.*

*Mrs. Webb, on the way to her place, turns back and speaks to the audience.*]

MRS. WEBB: I don't know why on earth I should be crying. I suppose there's nothing to cry about. The sadness came over me at breakfast this morning; there was Emily eating her breakfast as she's done for seventeen years and now she's going off to eat it in someone else's house. I suppose that's it.

And Emily! She suddenly said: I can't eat another mouthful, and she put her head down on the table and *she* cried.

[*She starts toward her seat in the church, but turns back and adds:*]

Oh, I've got to say it: you know, there's something downright cruel about sending our girls out into marriage this way. I hope some of her girl friends have told her a thing or two. It's cruel, I know, but I couldn't bring myself to say anything. I went into it blind as a bat myself. [*in half-amused exasperation*] The whole world's wrong, that's what's the matter. There they come.

[*She hurries to her place in the pew. George starts to come down the right aisle of the theatre, through the audience. Suddenly Three Members of his baseball team appear by the right proscenium pillar and start whistling and catcalling to him. They are dressed for the ball field.*]

THE BASEBALL PLAYERS: [*tauntingly*] Eh, George, George! Hast—yaow! Look at him, fellas—he looks scared to death. Yaow! George, don't look so innocent, you old geezer. We know what you're thinking. Don't disgrace the team, big boy. Whoo-oo-oo.

STAGE MANAGER: All right! All right! That'll do. That's enough of that.

[*Smiling, he pushes them off the stage. They lean back to shout a few more catcalls.*]

There used to be an awful lot of that kind of thing at weddings in the old days—Rome, and later. We're more civilized now—so they say.

[*The choir starts singing "Love Divine, all Love Excelling—." George has reached the stage. He stares at the congregation a moment, then takes a few steps of withdrawal, toward the right proscenium pillar. His mother, from the front row, seems to have felt his confusion. She leaves her seat and comes down the aisle quickly to him.*]

MRS. GIBBS: George! George! What's the matter?

GEORGE: Ma, I don't want to grow old. Why's everybody pushing me so?

MRS. GIBBS: Why, George . . . you wanted it.

GEORGE: No, Ma, listen to me—

MRS. GIBBS: No, no, George—you're a man now.

GEORGE: Listen, Ma, for the last time I ask you . . . All I want to do is to be a fella—

MRS. GIBBS: George! If anyone should hear you! Now stop. Why, I'm ashamed of you!

GEORGE:

[*He comes to himself and looks over the scene.*]

What? Where's Emily?

MRS. GIBBS: [*relieved*] George! You gave me such a turn.

GEORGE: [*suddenly smiling*] Cheer up, Ma. I'm getting married.

MRS. GIBBS: Let me catch my breath a minute.

GEORGE: [*comforting her*] Now, Ma, you save Thursday nights. Emily and I are coming over to dinner every Thursday night . . . you'll see. Ma, what are you crying for? Come on; we've got to get ready for this.

[*Mrs. Gibbs, mastering her emotion, fixes his tie and whispers to him.*

*In the meantime, Emily, in white and wearing her wedding veil, has come through the audience and mounted onto the stage. She too draws back, frightened, when she sees the congregation in the church. The choir begins: "Blessed Be the Tie That Binds."*]

EMILY: I never felt so alone in my whole life. And George over there, looking so . . . ! I *hate* him. I wish I were dead. Papa! Papa!

MR. WEBB:

[*Leaves his seat in the pews and comes toward her anxiously.*]

Emily! Emily! Now don't get upset. . . .

EMILY: But, Papa—I don't want to get married. . . .

MR. WEBB: Sh—sh—Emily. Everything's all right.

EMILY: Why can't I stay for a while just as I am? Let's go away—

MR. WEBB: No, no, Emily. Now stop and think a minute.

EMILY: Don't you remember that you used to say—all the time you used to say—all the time: that I was *your* girl! There must be lots of places we can go to. I'll work for you. I could keep house.

MR. WEBB: Sh . . . You mustn't think of such things. You're just nervous, Emily.

[*He turns and calls:*]

George! George! Will you come here a minute?

[*He leads her toward George.*]

Why you're marrying the best young fellow in the world. George is a fine fellow.

EMILY: But Papa—

[*Mrs. Gibbs returns unobtrusively to her seat. Mr. Webb has one arm around his daughter. He places his hand on George's shoulder.*]

MR. WEBB: I'm giving away my daughter, George. Do you think you can take care of her?

GEORGE: Mr. Webb, I want to . . . I want to try. Emily, I'm going to do my best. I love you, Emily. I need you.

EMILY: Well, if you love me, help me. All I want is someone to love me.

GEORGE: I will, Emily. Emily, I'll try.

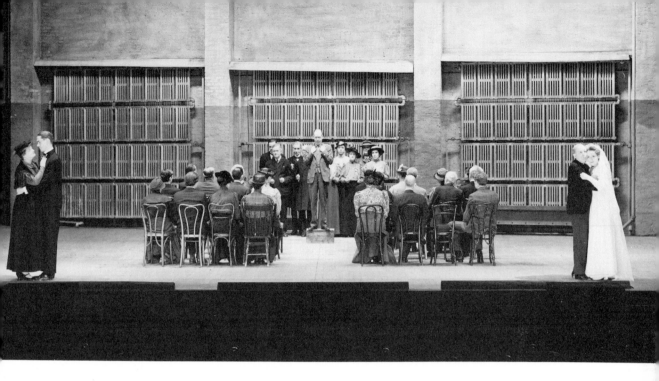

EMILY: And I mean for *ever*. Do you hear? For ever and ever.

[*They fall into each other's arms. The March from* Lohengrin *is heard. The Stage Manager, as Clergyman, stands on the box, up center.*]

MR. WEBB: Come, they're waiting for us. Now you know it'll be all right. Come, quick.

[*George slips away and takes his place beside the Stage Manager-Clergyman. Emily proceeds up the aisle on her father's arm.*]

STAGE MANAGER: Do you, George, take this woman, Emily, to be your wedded wife, to have . . .

[*Mrs. Soames has been sitting in the last row of the congregation. She now turns to her neighbors and speaks in a shrill voice. Her chatter drowns out the rest of the clergyman's words.*]

MRS. SOAMES: Perfectly lovely wedding! Loveliest wedding I ever saw. Oh, I do love a good wedding, don't you? Doesn't she make a lovely bride?

GEORGE: I do.

STAGE MANAGER: Do you, Emily, take this man, George, to be your wedded husband—

[*Again his further words are covered by those of Mrs. Soames.*]

MRS. SOAMES: Don't know *when* I've seen such a lovely wedding. But I always cry. Don't know why it is, but I always cry. I just like to see young people happy, don't you? Oh, I think it's lovely.

[*The ring. The kiss. The stage is suddenly arrested into silent tableau.*

*The Stage Manager, his eyes on the distance, as though to himself:*]

STAGE MANAGER: I've married over two hundred couples in my day. Do I believe in it? I don't know. M . . . marries N . . . millions of them. The small cottage, the go-cart, the Sunday-afternoon drives in the Ford, the first rheumatism, the grandchildren, the second rheumatism, the deathbed, the reading of the will—

[*He now looks at the audience for the first time, with a warm smile that removes any sense of cynicism from the next line.*]

Once in a thousand times it's interesting.—Well, let's have Mendelssohn's "Wedding March"!

[*The organ picks up the March.*
*The Bride and Groom come down the aisle, radiant, but trying to be very dignified.*]

MRS. SOAMES: Aren't they a lovely couple? Oh, I've never been to such a nice wedding. I'm sure they'll be happy. I always say: *happiness,* that's the great thing! The important thing is to be happy.

[*The Bride and Groom reach the steps leading into the audience. A bright light is thrown upon them. They descend into the auditorium and run up the aisle joyously.*]

STAGE MANAGER: That's all the Second Act, folks. Ten minutes' intermission.

---

## YOU AND ACT TWO

In most plays, the **plot** is a chain of events that make someone's life for a time more exciting or more dramatic. Something unusual happens to change the familiar patterns of ordinary lives. But Thornton Wilder wrote this play about events that he felt were part of everyone's everyday existence. In this act, the Stage Manager talks about what is happening as if it were as natural as the rain, or as the change from summer to winter. As you watch the people in the play, do you feel that many others have probably felt and acted in a very similar way? Answer the following questions:

(1) Traditionally, people in many different societies have treated *marriage* as a big occasion, as a very major milestone in a person's life. How does the author deal with marriage in this act? What feelings and thoughts go through the parents' minds? How does the groom act? How does the bride act? What are the first encounters with the new in-laws like? What is the minister telling the audience in his short sermon?

(2) Falling in love is treated in this play as something that happens sooner or later to just about everybody. Describe the author's picture of *young love.* How do Emily and George act toward each other? What do they talk about? Is this how you would expect lovers to act? Why or why not?

(3) Several times in this act people seem reluctant to do what they have decided to do. At other times, they say first one thing and then another. The Stage Manager says that "even at a good wedding there's a lot of confusion way down deep in people's minds." Find several examples of such reluctance and confusion in this act. Try to explain what the people involved feel. What makes them act the way they do?

---

## Your Turn

The play skips from the scene in the soda shop to the wedding of George and Emily, showing us nothing of what happened in between. Write a *script* for a short scene that could have occurred between these events. Use one of the following ideas, or an idea of your own.

—Emily talking with a friend about her marriage

—George talking with a friend—maybe one of the baseball players—about his marriage
—George and Emily discussing their plans
—George or Emily discussing their future with a parent
—a quarrel between George and Emily

Try to use the same language and style that Wilder does, so that your scene could become part of the play. Explain what furniture or props, if any, would be used. Describe any gestures or feelings an actor would need to know about. Feel free to include the Stage Manager in your scene, if he is needed.

---

Language/Composition Activity B18

THE TWO-PARAGRAPH THEME
# The Important Thing Is to Be Happy

In a well-organized piece of writing, the connection is clear between one paragraph and the next. The following kinds of two-paragraph papers give you a chance to practice writing paragraphs that are closely related.

A. *The Then-and-Now Paper.* A comparison often divides into two parts. We describe first the one thing to be compared, and then the other, pointing out things that are similar or different. As we watch the people in *Our Town,* we naturally compare how the people live with how the same people might live today. How would their daily lives or their roles in the family be different today? Write a two-paragraph theme on the role of a mother (father) (daughter) (son) then and now.

B. *The "Yes, but . . ." Paper.* The small-town characters in this play guide their lives by traditional folk wisdom. They often fall back on sayings that have a familiar ring:

> There's nothing we can do but just leave it alone.
> Everybody has a right to their own troubles.
> People are meant to go through life two by two.
> There's a lot of sense in some superstitions.
> You don't want to be the first to fly in the face of custom.
> Tell the truth and shame the devil.
> The important thing is to be happy.

Such traditional or proverbial sayings are very general—they may fit many situations but not all. When you listen to these, do you ever feel like saying: "That may be true up to a point, but there is something to be said on the other side"? Choose one of these sayings. Write a two-paragraph theme: In your first paragraph, show that the saying may be true up to a point. In the second, show what should be said on the other side.

● What is familiar in this report? What in it is new or especially interesting to you? Your teacher may ask you to collect material for a similar report on our country today: "The Way We Are."

# 1900: The Way We Were

In 1900 the total population of the United States was 76,094,000. The life expectancy was 46.3 for white males, 48.3 for white females and 33.0 for non-whites. The working force totalled 29,030,000 and the average work week 59 hours. Weekly wage was an average $12.74 but a pair of shoes could be had for $1.25, a shirt for 40 cents, and a root beer float for a nickel.

It was a time of abounding confidence. Anything was thought possible with good hard work. "Furnaces are glowing, spindles are singing their song. Happiness comes to us all with prosperity," declared Senator Mark Hanna of Ohio. His national euphoria was shared by most.

The first decade of this century with its overlying attitude of optimism presents a marked contrast to the present day. The new century provided a clean slate for new beginnings and every American seemed ready to take advantage of it. "The will to grow was everywhere written large," wrote Henry James, "and to grow at no matter what or at whose expense." Historians have tagged the era variously "the age of optimism", "the age of confidence," and "the age of innocence."

In many ways, it's easy to understand the optimism, the cocksureness. In the short period since the Civil War, the U.S. had been transformed from an agrarian nation to first

among the world's industrial nations. What had been a narrow fringe of population along the Eastern seaboard now extended across the continent. Columbus, Ohio, was now the geographical center of population—a move of about 475 miles west since 1800. Virtual "instant cities" were commonplace as the frontier was conquered and as emigrants swelled the urban population. "There is not a man here who does not feel 400 per cent bigger than he did in 1896— bigger intellectually, bigger patriotically!" exulted New York's Senator Depew. Senator Beveridge of Indiana was even more expansive. "God has marked the American people as his chosen nation to finally lead in the regeneration of the world . . . it holds for us all the profit, all the glory and all the happiness possible to man."

If Americans were intoxicated with geographical expansion, they were enraptured with the new technology. By 1900, 17.6 out of a 1000 had installed a telephone and typewriters, and sewing machines were increasingly in evidence in offices and homes. However, it was the automobile more than anything else, which symbolized progress and the good life. There were only 8000 cars and 150 miles of paved road but the mystique of an America on wheels had already taken hold. "Do not stare at another's car, nor, if at

a standstill, examine the mechanism. This is the height of rudeness," one read in *Everyday Etiquette* in 1905.

As yet unheard of, in 1900, was the concept of "women's rights". While four western states—Idaho, Utah, Colorado and Wyoming—allowed women to vote, her place was neither in the voting booth nor the office, but in the home as manager and purchasing agent. "The relative positions to be assumed by man and woman in the working out of our civilization were assigned long ago by a higher intelligence than ours," Grover Cleveland declared. Mark Twain, however, was a voice of dissent. "If women could vote they would vote on the side of morality . . . and set up some candidates fit for decent human beings to vote for."

While the working force was essentially all-male, women did predominate in the schoolhouses of America. 70% of the teachers were women, most of whom worked only until marriage for an average annual salary of $325. High value was placed on universal education, accounting for an illiteracy rate of only 10%. The average person attended school for six years—at a per pupil cost of $17 a year.

Good, hard work—in the classrooms, in the shops, and on the farms—was the key to that bountiful good life to which every American was entitled by birth.

# Act Three

*During the intermission the audience has seen the stagehands arranging the stage. On the right-hand side, a little right of the center, ten or twelve ordinary chairs have been placed in three openly spaced rows facing the audience. These are graves in the cemetery.*

*Toward the end of the intermission the actors enter and take their places. The front row contains: toward the center of the stage, an empty chair; then Mrs. Gibbs; Simon Stimson. The second row contains, among others, Mrs. Soames. The third row has Wally Webb.*

*The dead do not turn their heads or their eyes to right or left, but they sit in a quiet without stiffness. When they speak their tone is matter-of-fact, without sentimentality and, above all, without lugubriousness.*

*The Stage Manager takes his accustomed place and waits for the house lights to go down.*

STAGE MANAGER: This time nine years have gone by, friends—summer, 1913. Gradual changes in Grover's Corners. Horses are getting rarer. Farmers coming into town in Fords. Everybody locks their house doors now at night. Ain't been any burglars in town yet, but everybody's heard about 'em. You'd be surprised, though—on the whole, things don't change much around here.

This is certainly an important part of Grover's Corners. It's on a hilltop—a windy hilltop—lots of sky, lots of clouds, often lots of sun and moon and stars. You come up here on a fine afternoon and you can see range on range of hills—awful blue they are—up there by Lake Sunapee and Lake Winnipesaukee . . . and way up, if you've got a glass, you can see the White Mountains and Mt. Washington—where North Conway and Conway is. And, of course, our favorite mountain, Mt. Monadnock, 's right here—and all these towns that lie around it: Jaffrey, 'n East Jaffrey, 'n Peterborough, 'n Dublin; and [*then pointing down in the audience*] over there, quite a ways down is Grover's Corners.

Yes, beautiful spot up here. Mountain laurel and li-lacks. I often wonder why people like to be buried in Woodlawn and Brooklyn when they might pass the same time up here in New Hampshire. Over there—[*pointing to stage left*] are the old stones—1670, 1680. Strongminded people that come a long way to be independent. Summer people walk around there laughing at the funny words on the tombstones . . . it don't do any harm. And genealogists come up from Boston—get paid by city people for looking up their ancestors. They want to make sure they're Daughters of the American Revolution and of the *Mayflower*. . . . Well, I guess that don't do any harm, either. Wherever you come near the human race, there's layers and layers of nonsense. . . .

Over there are some Civil War veterans. Iron flags on their graves . . . New Hampshire boys . . . had a notion that the Union ought to be kept together, though they'd never seen more than fifty miles of it themselves. All they knew was the name, my friends—the United States of America. The United States of America. And they went and died about it.

This here is the new part of the cemetery. Here's your friend Mrs. Gibbs. 'N let me see—here's Mr. Stimson, organist at the Congregational Church. And

Mrs. Soames who enjoyed the wedding so—you remember? Oh, and a lot of others. And Editor Webb's boy, Wallace, whose appendix burst while he was on a Boy Scout trip to Crawford Notch.

Yes, an awful lot of sorrow has sort of quieted down up here. People just wild with grief have brought their relatives up to this hill. We all know how it is . . . and then time . . . and sunny days . . . and rainy days . . . 'n snow . . . We're all glad they're in a beautiful place and we're coming up here ourselves when our fit's over.

Now there are some things we all know, but we don't take'm out and look at'm very often. We all know that *something* is eternal. And it ain't houses and it ain't names, and it ain't earth, and it ain't even the stars . . . everybody knows in their bones that *something* is eternal, and that something has to do with human beings. All the greatest people ever lived have been telling us that for five thousand years and yet you'd be surprised how people are always losing hold of it. There's something way down deep that's eternal about every human being.

[*Pause.*]

You know as well as I do that the dead don't stay interested in us living people for very long. Gradually, gradually, they lose hold of the earth . . . and the ambitions they had . . . and the pleasures they had . . . and the things they suffered . . . and the people they loved. They get weaned away from earth—that's the way I put it—weaned away. And they stay here while the earth part of 'em burns away, burns out; and all that time they slowly get indifferent to what's goin' on in Grover's Corners.

They're waitin'. They're waitin' for something that they feel is comin'. Something important, and great. Aren't they waitin' for the eternal part in them to come out clear?

Some of the things they're going to say maybe'll hurt your feelings—but that's the way it is: mother'n daughter . . . husband 'n wife . . . enemy 'n enemy . . . money 'n miser . . . all those terribly important things kind of grow pale around here. And what's left when memory's gone, and your identity, Mrs. Smith?

[*He looks at the audience a minute, then turns to the stage.*]

Well! There are some *living* people. There's Joe Stoddard, our undertaker, supervising a new-made grave. And here comes a Grover's Corners boy, that left town to go out West.

[*Joe Stoddard has hovered about in the background. Sam Craig enters left, wiping his forehead from the exertion. He carries an umbrella and strolls front.*]

SAM CRAIG: Well, good afternoon, Joe Stoddard.

JOE STODDARD: Good afternoon to you, good afternoon. Let me see now: do I know you?

SAM CRAIG: I'm Sam Craig.

JOE STODDARD: Gracious sakes' alive! Of all people! I should'a knowed you'd be back for the funeral. You've been away a long time, Sam.

SAM CRAIG: Yes, I've been away over twelve years. I'm in business out in Buffalo now, Joe. But I was in the East when I got news of my cousin's death, so I thought I'd combine things a little and come and see the old home. You look well.

JOE STODDARD: Yes, yes, can't complain. Very sad, our journey today, Samuel.

SAM CRAIG: Yes.

JOE STODDARD: Yes, yes. I always say I hate to supervise when a young person is taken. They'll be here in a few minutes now. I had to come here early today—my son's supervisin' at the home.

SAM CRAIG: [*reading stones*] Old Farmer McCarty, I used to do chores for him—after school. He had the lumbago.

JOE STODDARD: Yes, we brought Farmer McCarty here a number of years ago now.

SAM CRAIG: [*staring at Mrs. Gibbs' knees*] Why, this is my Aunt Julia . . . I'd forgotten that she'd . . . of course, of course.

JOE STODDARD: Yes, Doc Gibbs lost his wife two-three years ago . . . about this time. And today's another pretty bad blow for him, too.

MRS. GIBBS: [*to Simon Stimson: in an even voice*] That's my sister Carey's boy, Sam . . . Sam Craig.

SIMON STIMSON: I'm always uncomfortable when *they're* around.

MRS. GIBBS: Simon.

SAM CRAIG: Do they choose their own verses much, Joe?

JOE STODDARD: No . . . not usual. Mostly the bereaved pick a verse.

SAM CRAIG: Doesn't sound like Aunt Julia. There aren't many of those Hersey sisters left now. Let me see: where are . . . I wanted to look at my father's and mother's . . .

JOE STODDARD: Over there with the Craigs . . . Avenue F.

SAM CRAIG: [*reading Simon Stimson's epitaph*] He was organist at church, wasn't he?—Hm, drank a lot, we used to say.

JOE STODDARD: Nobody was supposed to know about it. He'd seen a peck of trouble. [*behind his hand*] Took his own life, y' know?

SAM CRAIG: Oh, did he?

JOE STODDARD: Hung himself in the attic. They tried to hush it up, but of course it got around. He chose his own epy-taph. You can see it there. It ain't a verse exactly.

SAM CRAIG: Why, it's just some notes of music—what is it?

JOE STODDARD: Oh, I wouldn't know. It was wrote up in the Boston papers at the time.

SAM CRAIG: Joe, what did she die of?

JOE STODDARD: Who?

SAM CRAIG: My cousin.

JOE STODDARD: Oh, didn't you know? Had some trouble bringing a baby into the world. 'Twas her second, though. There's a little boy 'bout four years old.

SAM CRAIG: [*opening his umbrella*] The grave's going to be over there?

JOE STODDARD: Yes, there ain't much more room over here among the Gibbses, so they're opening up a whole new Gibbs section over by Avenue B. You'll excuse me now. I see they're comin'.

[*From left to center, at the back of the stage, comes a procession. Four men carry a casket, invisible to us. All the rest are under umbrellas. One can vaguely see: Dr. Gibbs, George, the Webbs, etc. They gather about a grave in the back center of the stage, a little to the left of center.*]

MRS. SOAMES: Who is it, Julia?

MRS. GIBBS: [*without raising her eyes*] My daughter-in-law, Emily Webb.

MRS. SOAMES: [*a little surprised, but no emotion*] Well, I declare! The road up here must have been awful muddy. What did she die of, Julia?

MRS. GIBBS: In childbirth.

MRS. SOAMES: Childbirth. [*almost with a laugh*] I'd forgotten all about that. My wasn't life awful—[*with a sigh*] and wonderful.

SIMON STIMSON: [*with a sideways glance*] Wonderful, was it?

MRS. GIBBS: Simon! Now, remember!

MRS. SOAMES: I remember Emily's wedding. Wasn't it a lovely wedding! And I remember her reading the class poem at

Graduation Exercises. Emily was one of the brightest girls ever graduated from High School. I've heard Principal Wilkins say so time after time. I called on them at their new farm, just before I died. Perfectly beautiful farm.

A WOMAN FROM AMONG THE DEAD: It's on the same road we lived on.

A MAN AMONG THE DEAD: Yepp, right smart farm.

[*They subside. The group by the grave starts singing "Blessed Be the Tie That Binds."*]

A WOMAN AMONG THE DEAD: I always liked that hymn. I was hopin' they'd sing a hymn.

[*Pause. Suddenly Emily appears from among the umbrellas. She is wearing a white dress. Her hair is down her back and tied by a white ribbon like a little girl. She comes slowly, gazing wonderingly at the dead, a little dazed. She stops halfway and smiles faintly. After looking at the mourners for a moment, she walks slowly to the vacant chair beside Mrs. Gibbs and sits down.*]

EMILY: [*to them all, quietly, smiling*] Hello.

MRS. SOAMES: Hello, Emily.

A MAN AMONG THE DEAD: Hello, M's Gibbs.

EMILY: [*warmly*] Hello, Mother Gibbs.

MRS. GIBBS: Emily.

EMILY: Hello. [*with surprise*] It's raining. [*Her eyes drift back to the funeral company.*]

MRS. GIBBS: Yes . . . They'll be gone soon, dear. Just rest yourself.

EMILY: It seems thousands and thousands of years since I . . . Papa remembered that that was my favorite hymn. Oh, I wish I'd been here a long time. I don't like being new here.—How do you do, Mr. Stimson?

SIMON STIMSON: How do you do, Emily.

[*Emily continues to look about her with a wondering smile; as though to shut out from her mind the thought of the funeral company she starts speaking to Mrs. Gibbs with a touch of nervousness.*]

EMILY: Mother Gibbs, George and I have made that farm into just the best place you ever saw. We thought of you all the time. We wanted to show you the new barn and a great long ce-ment drinking fountain for the stock. We bought that out of the money you left us.

MRS. GIBBS: I did?

EMILY: Don't you remember, Mother Gibbs—the legacy you left us? Why, it was over three hundred and fifty dollars.

MRS. GIBBS: Yes, yes, Emily.

EMILY: Well, there's a patent device on the drinking fountain so that it never overflows, Mother Gibbs, and it never sinks below a certain mark they have there. It's fine.

[*Her voice trails off and her eyes return to the funeral group.*]

It won't be the same to George without me, but it's a lovely farm.

[*Suddenly she looks directly at Mrs. Gibbs.*]

Live people don't understand, do they?

MRS. GIBBS: No, dear—not very much.

EMILY: They're sort of shut up in little boxes, aren't they? I feel as though I knew them last a thousand years ago . . . My boy is spending the day at Mrs. Carter's.

[*She sees Mr. Carter among the dead.*]

Oh, Mr. Carter, my little boy is spending the day at your house.

MR. CARTER: Is he?

EMILY: Yes, he loves it there.—Mother Gibbs, we have a Ford, too. Never gives any trouble. I don't drive, though. Mother Gibbs, when does this feeling go away?—Of being . . . one of *them*? How long does it . . . ?

MRS. GIBBS: Sh! dear. Just wait and be patient.

EMILY: [*with a sigh*] I know.—Look, they're finished. They're going.

MRS. GIBBS: Sh—.

[*The umbrellas leave the stage. Dr. Gibbs has come over to his wife's grave and stands before it a moment. Emily looks up at his face. Mrs. Gibbs does not raise her eyes.*]

EMILY: Look! Father Gibbs is bringing some of my flowers to you. He looks just like George, doesn't he? Oh, Mother Gibbs, I never realized before how troubled and how . . . how in the dark live persons are. Look at him. I loved him so. From morning till night, that's all they are—troubled.

[*Dr. Gibbs goes off.*]

THE DEAD: Little cooler than it was. Yes, that rain's cooled it off a little. Those northeast winds always do the same thing, don't they? If it isn't a rain, it's a three-day blow.

[*A patient calm falls on the stage. The Stage Manager appears at his proscenium pillar, smoking. Emily sits up abruptly with an idea.*]

EMILY: But, Mother Gibbs, one can go back; one can go back there again . . . into living. I feel it. I know it. Why just then for a moment I was thinking about . . . about the farm . . . and for a minute I *was* there, and my baby was on my lap as plain as day.

MRS. GIBBS: Yes, of course you can.

EMILY: I can go back there and live all those days over again . . . why not?

MRS. GIBBS: All I can say is, Emily, don't.

EMILY: [*She appeals urgently to the Stage Manager.*] But it's true, isn't it? I can go and live . . . back there . . . again.

STAGE MANAGER: Yes, some have tried—but they soon come back here.

MRS. GIBBS: Don't do it, Emily.

MRS. SOAMES: Emily, don't. It's not what you think it'd be.

EMILY: But I won't live over a sad day. I'll choose a happy one—I'll choose the day I first knew that I loved George. Why should that be painful?

[*They are silent. Her question turns to the Stage Manager.*]

STAGE MANAGER: You not only live it; but you watch yourself living it.

EMILY: Yes?

STAGE MANAGER: And as you watch it, you see the thing that they—down there—never know. You see the future and you know what's going to happen afterwards.

EMILY: But is that—painful? Why?

MRS. GIBBS: That's not the only reason why you shouldn't do it, Emily. When you've been here longer you'll see that our life here is to forget all that, and think only of what's ahead, and be ready for what's ahead. When you've been here longer you'll understand.

EMILY: [*softly*] But, Mother Gibbs, how can I *ever* forget that life? It's all I know. It's all I had.

MRS. SOAMES: Oh, Emily. It isn't wise. Really, it isn't.

EMILY: But it's a thing I must know for myself. I'll choose a happy day, at least.

MRS. GIBBS: *No!*—At least, choose an unimportant day. Choose the least important day in your life. It will be important enough.

EMILY: [*to herself*] Then it can't be since I was married; or since the baby was born. [*to the Stage Manager, eagerly*] I can choose a birthday at least, can't I?—I choose my twelfth birthday.

STAGE MANAGER: All right. February 11th, 1899. A Tuesday.—Do you want any special time of day?

EMILY: Oh, I want the whole day.

STAGE MANAGER: We'll begin at dawn. You remember it had been snowing for several days; but it had stopped the night before, and they had begun clearing the roads. The sun's coming up.

EMILY: [*with a cry; rising*] There's Main Street . . . why, that's Mr. Morgan's drugstore before he changed it! . . . And there's the livery stable.

[*The stage at no time in this act has been very dark; but now the left half of the stage gradually becomes very bright—the brightness of a crisp winter morning. Emily walks toward Main Street.*]

STAGE MANAGER: Yes, it's 1899. This is fourteen years ago.

EMILY: Oh, that's the town I knew as a little girl. And, *look*, there's the old white fence that used to be around our house. Oh, I'd forgotten that! Oh, I love it so! Are they inside?

STAGE MANAGER: Yes, your mother'll be coming downstairs in a minute to make breakfast.

EMILY: [softly] Will she?

STAGE MANAGER: And you remember: your father had been away for several days; he came back home on the early-morning train.

EMILY: No . . . ?

STAGE MANAGER: He'd been back to his college to make a speech—in western New York, at Clinton.

EMILY: Look! There's Howie Newsome. There's our policeman. But he's *dead*; he *died*.

[The voices of Howie Newsome, Constable Warren and Joe Crowell, Jr., are heard at the left of the stage. Emily listens in delight.]

HOWIE NEWSOME: Whoa, Bessie!—Bessie! 'Morning, Bill.

CONSTABLE WARREN: Morning, Howie.

HOWIE NEWSOME: You're up early.

CONSTABLE WARREN: Been rescuin' somebody; darn near froze to death, down by Polish Town thar. Got drunk and lay out in the snowdrifts. Thought he was in bed when I shook'm.

EMILY: Why, there's Joe Crowell. . . .

JOE CROWELL: Good morning, Mr. Warren. 'Morning, Howie.

[Mrs. Webb has appeared in her kitchen, but Emily does not see her until she calls.]

MRS. WEBB: Chil-*dren*! Wally! Emily! . . . Time to get up.

EMILY: Mama, I'm here! Oh! how young Mama looks! I didn't know Mama was ever that young.

MRS. WEBB: You can come and dress by the kitchen fire, if you like; but hurry.

[Howie Newsome has entered along Main Street and brings the milk to Mrs. Webb's door.]

Good morning, Mr. Newsome. Whhhh—it's cold.

HOWIE NEWSOME: Ten below by my barn, Mrs. Webb.

MRS. WEBB: Think of it! Keep yourself wrapped up.

[She takes her bottles in, shuddering.]

EMILY: [with an effort] Mama, I can't find my blue hair ribbon anywhere.

MRS. WEBB: Just open your eyes, dear, that's all. I laid it out for you special— on the dresser, there. If it were a snake it would bite you.

EMILY: Yes, yes . . .

[She puts her hand on her heart. Mr. Webb comes along Main Street, where he meets Constable Warren. Their movements and voices are increasingly lively in the sharp air.]

MR. WEBB: Good morning, Bill.

CONSTABLE WARREN: Good morning, Mr. Webb. You're up early.

MR. WEBB: Yes, just been back to my old college in New York State. Been any trouble here?

CONSTABLE WARREN: Well, I was called up this mornin' to rescue a Polish fella— darn near froze to death he was.

MR. WEBB: We must get it in the paper.

CONSTABLE WARREN: 'Twan't much.

EMILY: [Whispers.] Papa.

[Mr. Webb shakes the snow off his feet and enters his house. Constable Warren goes off, right.]

MR. WEBB: Good morning, Mother.

MRS. WEBB: How did it go, Charles?

MR. WEBB: Oh, fine, I guess. I told'm a few things.—Everything all right here?

MRS. WEBB: Yes—can't think of anything that's happened, special. Been right cold. Howie Newsome says it's ten below over to his barn.

MR. WEBB: Yes, well, it's colder than that at Hamilton College. Students' ears are falling off. It ain't Christian.—Paper have any mistakes in it?

MRS. WEBB: None that I noticed. Coffee's ready when you want it.

[*He starts upstairs.*]

Charles! Don't forget; it's Emily's birthday. Did you remember to get her something?

MR. WEBB: [*patting his pocket*] Yes, I've got something here. [*calling up the stairs*] Where's my girl? Where's my birthday girl?

[*He goes off left.*]

MRS. WEBB: Don't interrupt her now, Charles. You can see her at breakfast. She's slow enough as it is. Hurry up, children! It's seven o'clock. Now, I don't want to call you again.

EMILY: [*softly, more in wonder than in grief*] I can't bear it. They're so young and beautiful. Why did they ever have to get old? Mama, I'm here. I'm grown up. I love you all, everything.—I can't look at everything hard enough.

[*She looks questioningly at the Stage Manager, saying or suggesting: "Can I go in?" He nods briefly. She crosses to the inner door to the kitchen, left of her mother, and as though entering the room, says, suggesting the voice of a girl of twelve:*]

Good morning, Mama.

MRS. WEBB: [*crossing to embrace and kiss her; in her characteristic matter-of-fact manner*] Well, now, dear, a very happy birthday to my girl and many happy returns. There are some surprises waiting for you on the kitchen table.

EMILY: Oh, Mama, you *shouldn't* have.

[*She throws an anguished glance at the Stage Manager.*]

I can't—I can't.

MRS. WEBB: [*facing the audience, over her stove*] But birthday or no birthday, I want you to eat your breakfast good and slow. I want you to grow up and be a good strong girl.

That in the blue paper is from your Aunt Carrie; and I reckon you can guess who brought the postcard album. I found it on the doorstep when I brought in the milk—George Gibbs . . . must have come over in the cold pretty early . . . right nice of him.

EMILY: [*to herself*] Oh, George! I'd forgotten that. . . .

MRS. WEBB: Chew that bacon good and slow. It'll help keep you warm on a cold day.

EMILY: [*with mounting urgency*] Oh, Mama, just look at me one minute as though you really saw me. Mama, fourteen years have gone by. I'm dead. You're a grandmother, Mama. I married George Gibbs, Mama. Wally's dead, too. Mama, his apprendix burst on a camping trip to North Conway. We felt just terrible about it—don't you remember? But, just for a moment now we're all together. Mama, just for a moment we're happy. *Let's look at one another.*

MRS. WEBB: That in the yellow paper is something I found in the attic among your grandmother's things. You're old enough to wear it now, and I thought you'd like it.

EMILY: And this is from you. Why, Mama, it's just lovely and it's just what I wanted. It's beautiful!

[*She flings her arms around her mother's neck. Her mother goes on with her cooking, but is pleased.*]

MRS. WEBB: Well, I hoped you'd like it. Hunted all over. Your Aunt Norah couldn't find one in Concord, so I had to send all the way to Boston. [*laughing*] Wally has something for you, too. He made it at manual-training class and he's very proud of it. Be sure you make a big fuss about it.—Your father has a surprise for you, too; don't know what it is myself. Sh—here he comes.

MR. WEBB: [off stage] Where's my girl? Where's my birthday girl?

EMILY: [in a loud voice to the Stage Manager] I can't. I can't go on. It goes so fast. We don't have time to look at one another.

[She breaks down sobbing. The lights dim on the left half of the stage. Mrs. Webb disappears.]

I didn't realize. So all that was going on and we never noticed. Take me back—up the hill—to my grave. But first: Wait! One more look.

Good-bye, good-bye, world. Good-bye, Grover's Corners . . . Mama and Papa. Good-bye to clocks ticking . . . and Mama's sunflowers. And food and hot coffee. And new-ironed dresses and hot baths . . . and sleeping and waking up. Oh, earth, you're too wonderful for anybody to realize you.

[She looks toward the Stage Manager and asks abruptly, through her tears:]

Do any human beings ever realize life while they live it?—every, every minute?

STAGE MANAGER: No. [Pause.] The saints and poets, maybe—they do some.

EMILY: I'm ready to go back.

[She returns to her chair beside Mrs. Gibbs. Pause.]

MRS. GIBBS: Were you happy?

EMILY: No . . . I should have listened to you. That's all human beings are! Just blind people.

MRS. GIBBS: Look, it's clearing up. The stars are coming out.

EMILY: Oh, Mr. Stimson, I should have listened to them.

SIMON STIMSON: [with mounting violence, bitingly] Yes, now you know. Now you know! That's what it was to

be alive. To move about in a cloud of ignorance; to go up and down trampling on the feelings of those . . . of those about you. To spend and waste time as though you had a million years. To be always at the mercy of one self-centered passion, or another. Now you know—that's the happy existence that you wanted to go back to. Ignorance and blindness.

MRS. GIBBS: [spiritedly] Simon Stimson, that ain't the whole truth and you know it. Emily, look at that star. I forget its name.

A MAN AMONG THE DEAD: My boy Joel was a sailor—knew 'em all. He'd set on the porch evenings and tell 'em all by name. Yes, sir, wonderful!

ANOTHER MAN AMONG THE DEAD: A star's mighty good company.

A WOMAN AMONG THE DEAD: Yes. Yes, 'tis.

SIMON STIMSON: Here's one of them coming.

THE DEAD: That's funny. 'Tain't no time for one of them to be here—Goodness sakes.

EMILY: Mother Gibbs, it's George.

MRS. GIBBS: Sh, dear. Just rest yourself.

EMILY: It's George. [George enters from the left, and slowly comes toward them.]

A MAN FROM AMONG THE DEAD: And my boy, Joel, who knew the stars—he used to say it took millions of years for that speck o' light to git to the earth. Don't seem like a body could believe it, but that's what he used to say—millions of years.

[George sinks to his knees then falls full length at Emily's feet.]

A WOMAN AMONG THE DEAD: Goodness! That ain't no way to behave!

MRS. SOAMES: He ought to be home.

EMILY: Mother Gibbs?

MRS. GIBBS: Yes, Emily?

EMILY: They don't understand, do they?

MRS. GIBBS: No, Emily dear. They don't understand.

[*The Stage Manager appears at the right, one hand on a dark curtain which he slowly draws across the scene. In the distance a clock is heard striking the hour very faintly.*]

STAGE MANAGER: Well now, most everybody's asleep in Grover's Corners. There are a few lights on: Shorty Hawkins, down at the depot, has just watched the Albany train go by. And at the livery stable somebody's setting up late and talking.—Yes, it's clearing up. There are the stars—doing their old, old crisscross journeys in the sky. Scholars haven't settled the matter yet, but they seem to think there are no living beings up there. Just chalk . . . or fire. Only this one is straining away, straining away all the time to make something of itself. The strain's so bad that every sixteen hours everybody lies down and gets a rest.

[*He winds his watch.*]

Hm. . . . Eleven o'clock in Grover's Corners.—You get a good rest, too. Good night.

THE END

---

## YOU AND ACT THREE

In early parts of this play, the tone is often light and humorous. But as we approach the end, the tone becomes more solemn. The author wants us to think about the major **theme** of the play. What are our thoughts as we look back over the lives of the people we have met in this play? In this act, several people talk about our blindness as human beings. To what, according to the play, are we usually blind as we live from day to day? To what are Emily's eyes opened as she returns to the scene of her childhood? What if anything would be different if she had a chance to live her life over?

### A Closer Look

(1) The Stage Manager gets us ready for the more solemn tone of Act Three in his introductory remarks. We call a long passage in which an actor speaks alone to the audience (or with himself) a **monologue**— "words by a single speaker." Listen to the opening monologue of this act read out loud. Are there still some parts of it that should be read with a lighter touch? Where? Which parts do you think are the most solemn, and why?

(2) In the New England setting of this play, it is traditional not to "make a big fuss" over things. If someone does, others are likely to say: "That's no way to behave!" Find several examples in this play of people saying things or acting in ways that show they share this attitude. How does this attitude help shape the author's treatment of death in the last act? To judge from what we see in this play, are people who do not act very emotional therefore really unfeeling or cold-hearted? Point to specific evidence in the play to support your answer.

(3) Look closely at Simon Stimson's final description of life. How is his final judgment of life different from that of the others? What had we learned about him earlier in the play? What had been the attitude of others toward him? Mrs. Gibbs tells us that what Stimson says is only part of the truth. What is the other part? If you could add a few lines in which she explains that other part, what would you have her say?

## Your Turn

When you act out a part in a play, you do not just speak the words. You have to find the right tone of voice, the right gestures, and the right movements. Your appearance and your actions must help project the meaning of what you say. The author's **stage directions** tell actors how the author wanted different parts of the dialogue acted out. In the following selected stage directions from Acts Two and Three, some key words have been underlined. Explain what they tell the actors. Check in a dictionary those that are not clear from the context. Select several of these passages for acting out in accordance with the directions given by the author.

1. GEORGE: But . . . you *believe* in it, don't you, Mr. Webb?
   MR. WEBB: [*with alacrity*] Oh, yes; *oh, yes.* Don't you misunderstand me, my boy. Marriage is a wonderful thing—wonderful thing. And don't you forget that George.

2. MRS. WEBB: [*pulling George up*] George, Emily's got to come downstairs and eat her breakfast. She sends you her love but she doesn't want to lay eyes on you. Good-bye.
   GEORGE: Good-bye. [*George crosses the stage to his own home, bewildered and crestfallen. He slowly dodges a puddle and disappears into his house.*]

3. GEORGE: Mr. Morgan, I'll have to go home and get the money to pay you for this. It'll only take me a minute.
   STAGE MANAGER: [*pretending to be affronted*] What's that? George Gibbs, do you mean to tell me—?

4. STAGE MANAGER: [*When all is ready the Stage Manager strolls to the center of the stage, down front, and, musingly, addresses the audience.*] There are a lot of things to be said about a wedding; there are a lot of thoughts that go on during a wedding.

5. MRS. WEBB: Oh, I've got to say it: you know, there's something downright cruel about sending our girls out into marriage this way. I hope some of her girlfriends have told her a thing or two. It's cruel, I know, but I couldn't bring myself to say anything. I went into it as blind as a bat myself. [*in half-amused exasperation*] The whole world's wrong, that's what's the matter.

6. MR. WEBB: Why you're marrying the best young fellow in the world. George is a fine fellow.
   EMILY: But Papa—[*Mrs. Gibbs returns unobtrusively to her seat. Mr. Webb has one arm around his daughter. He places his hand on George's shoulder.*]

7. [*The dead do not turn their heads or their eyes to right or left, but they sit in a quiet without stiffness. When they speak their tone is matter-of-fact, without sentimentality and, above all, without lugubriousness.*]

8. [*Joe Stoddard has hovered about in the background. Sam Craig enters left, wiping his forehead from the exertion. He carries an umbrella and strolls front.*]

9. [*Emily sits up abruptly with an idea.*]
   EMILY: But, Mother Gibbs, one can go back; one can go back there again . . . into the living. I feel it. I know it.

10. MRS. WEBB: There are some surprises waiting for you on the kitchen table.
    EMILY: Oh, Mama, you shouldn't have. [*She throws an anguished glance at the Stage Manager.*] I can't—I can't.

THE BIOGRAPHICAL REPORT

# A Memorable Person

When Thornton Wilder died in 1975, a news magazine reported the event the way the Stage Manager might have in *Our Town*. Have you read about the career and writings of another well-known American author of the twentieth century? Research the author's life story. Write it in such a way that it could be printed as a memorial to the author.

# Exit the Stage Manager

*No curtain.*

*No scenery.*

*The Stage Manager enters, hat on and pipe in mouth, and arranges a table and chairs in the familiar setting for "Our Town." As the house lights go down, he turns to the audience and speaks:*

The name of the town is Grover's Corners—at least, that's what Thornton Wilder called it. Some folks up here in New Hampshire say that Our Town is really Peterborough, which is where Mr. Wilder was living when he wrote the play back in the 1930's. At the time, he was staying over to the MacDowell Colony where all those writers and artists come for a spell. Funny thing, for a fellow who wrote about a small town, Mr. Wilder never had any hometown that he grew up in. He was born out in Wisconsin but his father, old Amos Wilder, got to be a diplomat and took his family clear over to Hong Kong when Thorton was just a boy. Thornton come back to the States to go to college, and you might say he never got out of the habit. What a one he was for schoolin'! He went to Oberlin College in Ohio, and he went to Yale and Princeton and some schools over in Paris and Rome, and he learned pretty near all there is to know about stuff like history and philosophy and culture.

Fact is, Mr. Wilder stayed in school somewhere or other just about all his life, studying or teaching and lecturing. He was teaching French at Lawrenceville prep school down in New Jersey in the '20's when he wrote "The Bridge of San Luis Rey," about five people who got killed when a bridge collapsed in Peru 'way back when. They gave him the Pulitzer Prize for that novel, and Mr. Wilder won that same prize a couple more times for his plays—first for putting us Yankees on Broadway in "Our Town" and then for another hit, "The Skin of Our Teeth." Myself and folks I know, we thought Mr. Wilder's writing hit home, but some of those highfalutin critics started saying he didn't have a "social conscience," whatever that is. Mr. Wilder was a gentleman and he never let it bother him, but I've got an old clipping here that tells the way he felt. I'll read it to you: "I am not interested in the ephemeral. I am interested in those things that repeat and repeat and repeat in the lives of the millions."

That sounds like Mr. Wilder. He was interested in people and in what happened to them—all kinds of people in all kinds of places—and he was just full of enthusiasm all his life. He taught and he talked and he traveled, and he ate well and liked a drink or two—never too many—and he kept so doggoned busy that, as he always said, he just skipped getting married. He lived with his sister down in Connecticut, outside of New Haven, and he was getting up in years. Still, it was a jolt for us folks in Grover's Corners—and I'll bet for a whole lot of other people, too—when Thornton Wilder slipped away with a heart attack during his afternoon nap the other day. God rest him. H'm—11 o'clock in Grover's Corners. You get a good rest, too. Good night.

# On Native Soil

# PART THREE

# On Native Soil:
## A Manifold Heritage

Any day now I'll reach that land of freedom
  Yes, o yes
Any day now, know that promised land

At one time, American schools taught a fairly uniform view of what it meant to be an American. Teachers and schoolbooks seemed in agreement on what had happened in American history. They repeated familiar names in answer to questions about America's leaders and thinkers and artists. Literature books included familiar names in their list of American classics.

What was wrong with this accepted view of American culture and American literature was that large numbers of young people felt *left out.* They were from the wrong background, or the wrong part of the country, or the "wrong side of the tracks." As one of them said,

Nowhere in my schooling do I recall an attempt to put me in touch with my own history. The strategy was clearly to make an American of me. English literature, American literature, and even the history books, as I recall them, were peopled mainly by Anglo-Saxons from Boston (where most historians seemed to live). Not even my native Pennsylvania, let alone my Slovak forebears, counted for very many paragraphs. I don't remember feeling envy or regret: a feeling, perhaps, of unimportance, of remoteness, of not having heft enough to count.

—Michael Novak,
*The Rise of the Unmeltable Ethnics*

In recent decades, our views of American history and American literature have become more inclusive: Teachers and writers and artists have rediscovered the true richness and range of the American experience. They have developed a new respect for the pride of people in their region of the country, in their ethnic or racial identity, and in their religious traditions. Our attitude toward American culture has become

more responsive to the numerous elements that have fed into the mainstream of our national experience.

The selections in this collection of readings give you a chance to join representatives of ethnic, racial, or cultural minorities in the rediscovery of their history, in their search for identity. You will be able to follow them in their search for an answer to one of the oldest of all questions: "Who am I?"

# A Proud Nation

There were many, many of us, and we meant to ride right over them and rub them out. But our ponies were afraid of the ring of fire the guns of the Wasichus made, and would not go over. Our women were watching us from the hills and we could hear them singing and mourning whenever the shooting stopped. We tried hard, but we could not do it, and there were dead warriors and horses piled all around the boxes and scattered over the plain.

—Fire Thunder, in *Black Elk Speaks*

Around the middle of the nineteenth century, the Great Plains, stretching from Canada deep down into Texas, were the country of the Indian and the buffalo. As Mari Sandoz says in *Cheyenne Autumn*,

At that time the white men in the region were only a few little islands in a great sea of Indians and buffalos. Twenty-three years later, in 1877, the buffalo were about gone and the last of the Indians driven to the reservations—only a few little islands of Indians in a great sea of whites.

In the fantasy world of millions, the North American Indian lived on as a colorful romantic figure. He was a symbol of primitive freedom to people cooped up in modern cities. He symbolized a life close to nature. He was the "noble savage," whose courage inspired a mixture of fear and admiration. But in the real world of the rapidly expanding United States, there was no place for these native Americans. Millions of white settlers were coming into America from Europe. Like a stream out of control, these people swept over the territories

originally set aside for the remaining Indian tribes. The railroads, the cattlemen, the miners in search of silver and gold—for all these the Indian was an obstacle in their way, an obstacle in the path of "progress." One by one, the tribes were cut off from the lands they knew. The cycles of their hunting and wandering were broken up. The game was gone, and they had nowhere to turn. Their ceremonies and ancient ways were branded as heathen. War, starvation, and disease cut down the proud tribes of old and left small bands of humiliated, uprooted survivors. These, in the words of Mari Sandoz, were "shuffled off to land on which no white man could conceivably make a living."

In recent years, many American writers have retold the epic story of the Indians' last battles and their attempts to find a way of surviving in the modern world. Some of these writers are of Indian descent; others have been attracted to the Indian cause by the memory of old injustices. The following selections are from writings that have helped keep alive the American Indian heritage.

I shall vanish and be no more,
But the land over which I now roam
Shall remain
And change not.

—Omaha Warrior's Song

How do we come to know and understand the past? Facts and figures
can tell us much about what happened and how people lived. But we
need our imagination to help us see what things looked like, or to help us
share the feelings of people distant to us in place or in time. Do the following
poems help you to share imaginatively in the Indian past?

## Indian Chants and Prayers

# Calling for Rain
### *(Zuñi)*

When our earth mother is replete with living waters,
When spring comes,
The source of our flesh,
All the different kinds of corn,
We shall lay to rest in the ground.
With their earth mother's living waters,
They will be made into new beings.
Coming out standing into the daylight
Of their sun father,
Calling for rain,
To all sides they will stretch out their hands.
Then from wherever the rainmakers stay quietly
They will send forth their misty breath;
Their massed clouds filled with water will come out
    and sit with us,
Far from their homes,
With outstretched hands of water they will embrace
    the corn,
Stepping down to caress them with their fresh waters,
With their fine rain caressing the earth,

And yonder, wherever the roads of the rainmakers
    come forth,
Torrents will rush forth,
Silt will rush forth,
Mountains will be washed out,
Logs will be washed down,
Yonder all the mossy mountains will drip with water.
The clay-lined hollows of our earth mother
Will overflow with water,
Desiring that it should be thus,
I send forth my prayer.

A note from Margot Astrov, in *The Winged Serpent:*
Living in a semi-arid region, the minds of the Zuñi
dwell upon rain with greatest intensity, and their
hearts are made happy by the sight of wandering
clouds, the sound of clapping thunder, the flash of
lightning zigzagging across the parched fields. Their
prayers for life are prayers for rain. One would expect
in the vocabulary of a desert-dwelling people delicate nuances concerning climatological factors and
atmospheric changes. Thus all of the Pueblo people
discriminate between various forms of rain: fine and
heavy, female and male, misty and torrential.

# The War God's Horse Song
*(Navajo)*

I am the Turquoise Woman's son.
On top of Belted Mountain
Beautiful horses—slim like a weasel!
My horse has a hoof like striped agate;
His fetlock is like a fine eagle plume;
His legs are like quick lightning.
My horse's body is like an eagle-plumed arrow;
My horse has a tail like a trailing black cloud.
I put goods on my horse's back;
The Little Holy Wind blows through his hair.

His mane is made of short rainbows.
My horse's ears are made of round corn.
My horse's eyes are made of big stars.
My horse's head is made of mixed waters
(From the holy waters—he never knows thirst).
My horse's teeth are made of white shell.
The long rainbow is in his mouth for a bridle,
    And with it I guide him.
When my horse neighs, different-colored horses follow.
When my horse neighs, different-colored sheep follow.
    I am wealthy because of him.

*Magic pile erected by the Assiniboine Indians. Like many Plains people, the Assiniboine believed all nature's works possessed supernatural powers. A rock pile which resembled a buffalo was capped by a buffalo's skull to lure herds to the area.*

# A Prayer to the Dead
### *(Assiniboine)*

Spirits of our dead relatives, I make this feast for you to call you all around me. I smoke this tobacco which has been inclosed with your hair; be near us and hear.

My friends are around me, and you are called to the feast. Call on all the spirits of our dead friends to aid in giving us what we ask.

Make the buffalo come near and the clouds and wind fair to approach them, that we may always have meat in camp to feed us and you. Help us in every way; let our children live. Let us live. Call on all these spirits and ask them to assist you in helping us.

If we hunt, be with us. If we go to war, be with us. Enable us to revenge some of your deaths upon our enemies. They have killed you; they have brought our hearts low. Bring their hearts low also. Let us blacken our faces. Keep us from harm, rest quiet, we will not cease to cry for and remember you. You are remembered in this feast, eat some of it. This to you, my father. This for you, my grandfather, my uncle, my brother. The relatives of all present eat, rest in quiet, do not let disease trouble us.

We eat for you, we cry for you, we cut ourselves for you.

*Traditional Pueblo weaving. In addition to symbols of gods and spirits, the Pueblo Indians often wove representations of weather and geographical features bearing secret significance into their work. Thunder and lightning played a particularly important role in their religious beliefs.*

# Song of the Sky Loom
## *(Tewa)*

O our Mother the Earth, O our Father the Sky,
Your children are we, and with tired backs
We bring you the gifts you love.
Then weave for us a garment of brightness;
May the warp be the white light of morning,
May the weft be the red light of the evening,
May the fringes be the falling rain,
May the border be the standing rainbow.
Thus weave for us a garment of brightness,
That we may walk fittingly where birds sing,
That we may walk fittingly where grass is green,
O our Mother the Earth, O our Father the Sky.

A note from Herbert J. Spinden, in *Songs of the Tewa:* The Tewa Indians belong to a group of tribes inhabiting pueblos in New Mexico and northeastern Arizona. The sky loom refers to the small desert rain, characteristic of this part of the country: like wandering looms, rain-showers hang from the sky.

# Song of Defeat

*(Sioux)*

A wolf
I considered myself,
But the owls are hooting
And the night
I fear.

## YOU AND THE POEMS

Literature of the North American Indian was **oral literature**. Songs, prayers, and stories were handed on by word of mouth. Through the years, collectors have tried to translate and preserve what remains of the lore of the various tribes. How does this selection of chants and prayers fit in with what you have read or heard about Indian ways? If you had only these poems for evidence, what conclusions would you reach about Indian attitudes toward the land, toward nature, toward war, toward the dead? You and your classmates may want to present these poems orally.

## Vachel Lindsay
# The Flower-Fed Buffaloes

The flower-fed buffaloes of the spring
In the days of long ago,
Ranged where the locomotives sing
And the prairie flowers lie low:—
The tossing, blooming, perfumed grass
Is swept away by the wheat,
Wheels and wheels and wheels spin by
In the spring that still is sweet.

But the flower-fed buffaloes of the spring
Left us, long ago.
They gore no more, they bellow no more,
They trundle around the hills no more:—
With the Blackfeet, lying low,
With the Pawnees, lying low,
Lying low.

### YOU AND THE POEM

(1) Some people look back to the past with nostalgic yearning. Others tell us to live in the present. Is this a "nostalgia" poem? What is the poet's attitude toward the past? What is his attitude toward the present?

(2) Vachel Lindsay's poems have a strong rhythm caused by the very noticeable repetition of words and patterns. Point out several examples of the kind of repetition he uses in the poem. What do you think this poem should sound like when it is read aloud?

Mary Austin

# The Grass on the Mountain

Oh, long long
The snow has possessed the mountains.

The deer have come down and the bighorn,
They have followed the Sun to the South
To feed on the mesquite pods and the bunch grass.
Loud are the thunder drums
In the tents of the mountains.
Oh, long, long
Have we eaten chia seeds
And dried deer's flesh of the summer killing.
We are wearied of our huts
And the smoky smell of our garments.
We are sick with desire of the sun
And the grass on the mountains.

---

### YOU AND THE POEM

Writers sometimes tell us about the Indian past from the point of view of the outside observer. This poem asks us to use our imagination and share imaginatively in a vanished way of life. What do we learn about the people, their life, their feelings?

W. D. Snodgrass

# Powwow
*(Tama Reservation, Iowa, 1949)*

They all see the same movies.
    They shuffle on one leg,
       Scuffing the dust up,
    Shuffle on the other.
They are all the same:
    A Sioux dance to the spirits,
    A war dance by four Chippewa,
    A Dakota dance for rain.
       We wonder why we came.
Even tricked out in the various braveries—
    Black buffalo tassels, beadwork, or the brilliant
Feathers at the head, at the buttocks—
Even in long braids and the gaudy face paints,
       They all dance with their eyes turned
    Inward, like a woman nursing
A sick child she already knows
    Will die. For the time, she nurses it
       All the same. The loudspeakers shriek;
       We leave our bleacher seats to wander
    Among the wickiups and lean-tos
In a search for hot dogs. The Indians
       Are already packing; have
    Resumed green dungarees and khaki,
    Castoff combat issues of World War II.
       (Only the Iroquois do not come here;

They work in structural steel; they have a contract
    Building the United Nations
  And Air Force installations for our future wars.)
These, though, have dismantled their hot-dog stand
    And have to drive all night
To jobs in truck stops and all-night filling stations.
     We ask directions and
  They scuttle away from us like moths.
    Past the trailers,
  Beyond us, one tepee is still shining
Over all the rest. Inside, circled by a ring
    Of children, in the glare
  Of one bare bulb, a shrunken fierce-eyed man
Squats at his drum, all bones and parchment,
    While his dry hands move
  On the drumhead, always drumming, always
Raising his toothless, drawn jaw to the light
    Like a young bird drinking, like a chained dog,
Howling his tribe's song for the restless young
    Who wander in and out.
    Words of such great age,
Not even he remembers what they mean.
    We tramp back to our car,
  Then nearly miss the highway, squinting
Through red and yellow splatterings on the
  windshield,
    The garish and beautiful remains
    Of grasshoppers and dragonflies
That go with us, that do not live again.

---

## YOU AND THE POEM

(1) Look at the first few lines of this poem. What is the poet's attitude toward the exhibition he is watching? How can you tell? How much do we learn about his attitude before he leaves the bleacher seats?

(2) Contrast the everyday realities that become apparent later in the poem with the tourist-attraction image of the Indian presented earlier.

(3) The grasshoppers and dragonflies are in the poem not by accident. What is their *symbolic* meaning? How do they fit in with the rest of the poem?

(4) The old man beating the drum does not seem to fit into the overall pattern of the poem. What does he represent?

## N. Scott Momaday
# Earth and I Gave You Turquoise

Earth and I gave you turquoise
    when you walked singing
We lived laughing in my house
    and told old stories
You grew ill when the owl cried
We will meet on Black Mountain

I will bring corn for planting
    and we will make fire
Children will come to your breast
    You will heal my heart
I speak your name many times
The wild cane remembers you

My young brother's house is filled
    I go there to sing
We have not spoken of you
    but our songs are sad
When Moon Woman goes to you
I will follow her white way

Tonight they dance near Chinle
    by the seven elms
There your loom whispered beauty
    They will eat mutton
and drink coffee till morning
You and I will not be there

I saw a crow by Red Rock
    standing on one leg
It was the black of your hair
    The years are heavy
I will ride the swiftest horse
You will hear the drumming hooves

---

### YOU AND THE POEM

(1) In this poem, memories of the past and impressions of the present mingle with dreams of the future. What happened in the past, and what was the past like for the poet? What does he remember? What is the present like for the person speaking in the poem? What is his vision of the future?

(2) Some mourners express their grief in long flowing sentences, using rich, passionate words. This poet uses short *simple* statements that say much in little. Select the three short statements that for you are most effective in making you think, and making you share in the feelings of the poet.

- N. Scott Momaday is one of many Americans who did not find their own history in the history books they were asked to read in schools. He is one of the many American writers of recent years whose writings are a record of their search for roots. Like other writers, he went back to his home grounds to find the key to a half-forgotten past. He listened to the old-timers, searching their memories for clues to how his people once lived.

# N. Scott Momaday

*from*

# The Way to Rainy Mountain

A single knoll rises out of the plain in Oklahoma, north and west of the Wichita range. For my people, the Kiowas, it is an old landmark, and they gave it the name Rainy Mountain. The hardest weather in the world is there. Winter brings blizzards; hot tornadic winds arise in the spring; and in summer the prairie is an anvil's edge. The grass turns brittle and brown, and it cracks beneath your feet. There are green belts along the rivers and creeks, groves of hickory and pecan, willow and witch hazel. At a distance in July or August the steaming foliage seems almost to writhe in fire. Great green and yellow grasshoppers are everywhere in the tall grass, popping up like corn to sting the flesh, and tortoises crawl about on the red earth, going nowhere in the plenty of time. Loneliness is an aspect of the land. All things in the plain are isolated; there is no confusion of objects in the eyes, but *one* hill or *one* tree or *one* man. To look upon that landscape in the early morning, with the sun at your back, is to lose the sense of proportion. Your imagination comes to life, and this, you think, is where Creation was begun.

I returned to Rainy Mountain in July. My grandmother had died in the spring, and I wanted to be at her grave. She had lived to be very old and at last infirm. Her only living daughter was with her when she died, and I was told that in death her face was that of a child.

I like to think of her as a child. When she was born, the Kiowas were living the last great moment of their history. For more than a hundred years they had controlled the open range from the Smoky Hill River to the Red, from the headwaters of the Canadian to the fork of the Arkansas and Cimarron. In alliance with the Comanches, they had ruled the whole of the Southern Plains. War was their sacred business, and they were the finest horsemen the world has ever known. But warfare for the Kiowas was preeminently a matter of disposition rather than of survival, and they never understood the grim, unrelenting advance of the U.S. Cavalry. When at last, divided and ill provisioned, they were driven onto the Staked Plain* in the cold of autumn, they fell into panic. In Palo Duro Canyon they abandoned their crucial stores to pillage and had nothing then but their lives. In

*the Staked Plain: the great arid plateau of southeast New Mexico, northwest Oklahoma, and west Texas.

order to save themselves, they surrendered to the soldiers at Fort Sill and were imprisoned in the old stone corral that now stands as a military museum. My grandmother was spared the humiliation of those high gray walls by eight or ten years, but she must have known from birth the affliction of defeat, the dark brooding of old warriors.

Her name was Aho, and she belonged to the last culture to evolve in North America. Her forebears came down from the high country in western Montana nearly three centuries ago. They were a mountain people, a mysterious tribe of hunters whose language has never been classified in any major group. In the late seventeenth century they began a long migration to the south and east. It was a journey toward the dawn, and it led to a golden age. Along the way the Kiowas were befriended by the Crows, who gave them the culture and religion of the Plains. They acquired horses, and their ancient nomadic spirit was suddenly free of the ground. They acquired Tai-me, the sacred sun-dance doll, from that moment the object and symbol of their worship, and so shared in the divinity of the sun. Not least, they acquired the sense of destiny, therefore courage and pride. When they entered upon the Southern Plains they had been transformed. No longer were they slaves to the simple necessity of survival; they were a lordly and dangerous society of fighters and thieves, hunters and priests of the sun. According to their origin myth, they entered the world through a hollow log. From one point of view, their migration was the fruit of an old prophecy, for indeed they emerged from a sunless world.

Though my grandmother lived out her long life in the shadow of Rainy Mountain, the immense landscape of the continental interior lay like memory in her blood. She could tell of the Crows, whom she had never seen, and of the Black Hills, where she had never been. I wanted to see in reality what she had seen more perfectly in the mind's eye, and drove fifteen hundred miles to begin my pilgrimage.

A dark mist lay over the Black Hills, and the land was like iron. At the top of a ridge I caught sight of Devil's Tower upthrust against the gray sky as if in the birth of time the core of the earth had broken through its crust and the motion of the world was begun. There are things in nature that engender an awful quiet in the heart of man; Devil's Tower is one of them. Two centuries ago, because of their need to explain it, the Kiowas made a legend at the base of the rock. My grandmother said:

"Eight children were there at play, seven sisters and their brother. Suddenly the boy was struck dumb; he trembled and began to run upon his hands and feet. His fingers became claws, and his body was covered with fur. There was a bear where the boy had been. The sisters were terrified; they ran, and the bear after them. They came to the stump of a great tree, and the tree spoke to them. It bade them climb upon it, and as they did so, it began to rise into the air. The bear came to kill them, but they were just beyond its reach. It reared against the tree and scored the bark all around with its claws. The seven sisters were borne into the sky, and they became the stars of the Big Dipper." From that moment, and so long as the legend lives, the Kiowas have kinsmen in the night sky. Whatever they were in the mountains, they could be no more. However tenuous their well-being, however much they had suffered and would suffer again, they had discovered a way out of the wilderness.

My grandmother had a reverence for the sun, a holy regard that now is all but gone

*Devils Tower National Monument, northeastern Wyoming.*

out of mankind. There was a wariness in her, and an ancient awe. She was a Christian in her later years, but she had come a long way about, and she never forgot her birthright. As a child she had been to the sun dances; she had taken part in that annual rite, and by it she had learned the restoration of her people in the presence of Tai-me. She was about seven when the last Kiowa sun dance was held in 1887 on the Washita River above Rainy Mountain Creek. The buffalo were gone. In order to consummate the ancient sacrifice—to impale the head of a buffalo bull upon the Tai-me tree—a delegation of old men journeyed into Texas, there to beg and barter for an animal from the Goodnight herd. She was ten when the Kiowas came together for the last time as a living sundance culture. They could find no buffalo; they had to hang an old hide from the sacred tree. Before the dance could begin, a company of soldiers rode out from Fort Sill under orders to disperse the tribe. Forbidden without cause the essential act of their faith, having seen the wild herds slaughtered and left to rot upon the ground, the Kiowas backed away forever from the tree. That was July 20, 1890, at the great bend of the Washita. My grandmother was there.

Now that I can have her only in memory, I see my grandmother in the several postures that were peculiar to her: standing at the wood stove on a winter morning and turning meat in a great iron skillet; sitting at the south window, bent above her beadwork, and afterwards, when her vision failed, looking down for a long time into the fold of her hands; going out upon a cane, very slowly as she did when the weight of age came upon her; praying. I remember her most often at prayer. She made long, rambling prayers out of suffering and hope, having seen many things. I

was never sure that I had the right to hear, so exclusive were they of all mere custom and company. The last time I saw her she prayed standing by the side of her bed at night, naked to the waist, the light of a kerosene lamp moving upon her dark skin. Her long black hair, always drawn and braided in the day, lay upon her shoulders and against her breasts like a shawl. I do not speak Kiowa, and I never understood her prayers, but there was something sad in the sound, some merest hesitation upon the syllables of sorrow. She began in a high and descending pitch, exhausting her breath to silence; then again and again—and always the same intensity of effort, of something that is, and is not, like urgency in the human voice. Transported so in the dancing light among the shadows of her room, she seemed beyond the reach of time. But that was illusion; I think I knew then that I should not see her again.

Houses are like sentinels in the plain, old keepers of the weather watch. There, in a very little while, wood takes on the appearance of great age. All colors wear soon away in the wind and rain, and then the wood is burned gray and the grain appears and the nails turn red with rust. The windowpanes are black and opaque; you imagine there is nothing within, and indeed there are many ghosts, bones given up to the land. They stand here and there against the sky, and you approach them for a longer time than you expect. They belong in the distance; it is their domain.

Once there was a lot of sound in my grandmother's house, a lot of coming and going, feasting and talk. The summers there were full of excitement and reunion. The Kiowas are a summer people; they abide the cold and keep to themselves, but when the season turns and the land becomes warm and vital they cannot hold

still; an old love of going returns upon them. The aged visitors who came to my grandmother's house when I was a child were made of lean and leather, and they bore themselves upright. They wore great black hats and bright ample shirts that shook in the wind. They rubbed fat upon their hair and wound their braids with strips of colored cloth. Some of them painted their faces and carried the scars of old and cherished enmities. They were an old council of warlords, come to remind and be reminded of who they were. Their wives and daughters served them well. The women might indulge themselves; gossip was at once the mark and compensation of their servitude. They made loud and elaborate talk among themselves, full of jest and gesture, fright and false alarm. They went abroad in fringed and flowered shawls, bright beadwork and German silver. They were at home in the kitchen, and they prepared meals that were banquets.

There were frequent prayer meetings, and nocturnal feasts. When I was a child I played with my cousins outside, where the lamplight fell upon the ground and the singing of the old people rose up around us and carried away into the darkness. There were a lot of good things to eat, a lot of laughter and surprise. And afterwards, when the quiet returned, I lay down with my grandmother and could hear the frogs away by the river and feel the motion of the air.

Now there is a funeral silence in the rooms, the endless wake of some final word. The walls have closed in upon my grandmother's house. When I returned to it in mourning, I saw for the first time in my life how small it was. It was late at night, and there was a white moon, nearly full. I sat for a long time on the stone steps by the kitchen door. From there I could see out across the land; I could see the long row of trees by the creek, the low light upon the rolling plains, and the stars of the Big Dipper. Once I looked at the moon and caught sight of a strange thing. A cricket had perched upon the handrail, only a few inches away. My line of vision was such that the creature filled the moon like a fossil. It had gone there, I thought, to live and die, for there, of all places, was its small definition made whole and eternal. A warm wind rose up and purled like the longing within me.

The next morning, I awoke at dawn and went out on the dirt road to Rainy

Mountain. It was already hot, and the grasshoppers began to fill the air. Still, it was early in the morning, and birds sang out of the shadows. The long yellow grass on the mountain shone in the bright light, and a scissortail hied above the land. There, where it ought to be, at the end of a long and legendary way, was my grandmother's grave. She had at last succeeded to that holy ground. Here and there on the dark stones were ancestral names. Looking back once, I saw the mountain and came away.

## YOU AND THE READING

The job of a historian is to collect patiently many details and then fit them together in an overall picture. As you read about the old woman in N. Scott Momaday's account, many details about her ancient tribe emerge. Can you fit these together into an overall picture? Suppose you are the last tribal historian of the Kiowa tribe. Tell us about the tribe: their history, their legends, their habits and ways.

## A Closer Look

(1) The author's attitude toward the past is one of longing for something admirable and valuable that has passed away. Can you find a dozen words or expressions in this story that show that the author values or admires what he describes?

(2) Our memories of older people are often fragmentary—we often remember only certain parts of their appearance. We remember a few fragmentary incidents. If you had only one paragraph to describe the old woman in this account, what would you include?

(3) How much do we learn from the author about the Oklahoma setting? Describe the land where the people of his story lived.

---

Language/Composition Activity C1

FOR VOCABULARY BUILDING
# Reading About Our History

To understand N. Scott Momaday's account of the history of his people, the reader would have to know all or most of the words in the following list. Which of these words would be especially familiar to readers with a special interest in history? Which of the words have familiar uses in areas *other* than history, and should therefore be familiar to the "general reader"? Select *ten* of these words. Explain each word briefly to someone who does not know what it means or how it is used.

| | | | | |
|---|---|---|---|---|
| ALLIANCE | ILLPROVISIONED | PILLAGE | AFFLICTION | EVOLVE |
| FOREBEARS | MIGRATION | NOMADIC | DESTINY | MYTH | KINSMEN |
| RITE | SACRIFICE | DELEGATION | DISPERSE | SENTINELS |
| REUNION | ENMITY | COUNCIL | SERVITUDE | NOCTURNAL | LEGENDARY | ANCESTRAL |

## An Introduction to *The Earth Is All That Lasts*

• Black Elk was a holy man of the Sioux, or the Lakotas, as they called themselves. He was born and grew up at a time when his people were battling with white soldiers, the "Wasichus" of his story. Many years later, living as a lonely old man in a one-room log cabin among barren hills, he told his life story to John G. Neihardt, author of books and poems about the American Indian and the American West. When Black Elk was young, the talk among his people was that the white people were going to take the Indians' country, and that the Indians would all have to die fighting:

Once we were happy in our own country and we were seldom hungry, for then the two-leggeds and the four-leggeds lived together like relatives, and there was plenty for them and for us. But the Wasichus came, and they have made little islands for us and other little islands for the four-leggeds, and always these islands are becoming smaller, for around them surges the gnawing flood of the Wasichu; and it is dirty with lies and greed.

A long time ago my father told me what his father told him, that there was once a Lakota holy man, called Drinks Water, who dreamed what was to be; and this was long before the coming of the Wasichus. He dreamed that the four-leggeds were going back into the earth and that a strange race had woven a spider's web all around the Lakotas. And he said: "When this happens, you shall live in square gray houses, in a barren land, and beside those square gray houses you shall starve." They say he went back to Mother Earth soon after he saw this vision, and it was sorrow that killed him. You can look about you now and see that he meant these dirt-roofed houses we are living in, and that all the rest was true.

The following selection from *Black Elk Speaks* tells the story of General Custer's "Last Stand" from the Indians' point of view. It describes the fight at Little Big Horn in which Custer and many of his soldiers died. Custer had fought on the Union side in the American Civil War and assumed command of the U.S. Seventh Cavalry in 1866. A few years later, he had destroyed an Indian camp after the Indians there had been promised safety by a military agent. He had a son by an Indian girl that was taken as a captive there, along with other Cheyenne women and children. Black Elk and his friends were teenage boys when Custer or "Long Hair," attacked a large Indian encampment on the Little Big Horn in 1876.

The Old West—*The Indians.* Courtesy Time-Life Books Inc.

*Sioux standard. Carried in combat by a warrior who rode next to the war leader, the standard identified the leader in the confusion of battle so that he could be located quickly.*

# Black Elk

# The Earth Is All That Lasts

It was the next summer, when I was eleven years old (1874), that the first sign of a new trouble came to us. Our band had been camping on Split-Toe Creek in the Black Hills, and from there we moved to Spring Creek, then to Rapid Creek where it comes out into the prairie. That evening just before sunset, a big thundercloud came up from the west, and just before the wind struck, there were clouds of splittail swallows flying all around above us. . . . The boys tried to hit the swallows with stones and it hurt me to see them doing this, but I could not tell them. I got a stone and acted as though I were going to throw, but I did not. The swallows seemed holy. Nobody hit one, and when I thought about this I knew that of course they could not.

The next day some of the people were building a sweat tepee for a medicine man by the name of Chips, who was going to perform a ceremony and had to be purified first. They say he was the first man who made a sacred ornament for our great chief, Crazy Horse. While they were heating the stones for the sweat tepee, some boys asked me to go with them to shoot squirrels. We went out, and when I was about to shoot at one, I felt very uneasy all at once. So I sat down, feeling queer, and wondered about it. While I sat there I heard a voice that said: "Go at once! Go home!" I told the boys we must go home at once, and we all hurried. When we got back, everybody was excited, breaking camp, catching the ponies, and loading the drags; and I heard that while Chips was in the sweat tepee a voice had told him that the band must flee at once because something was going to happen there.

It was nearly sundown when we started, and we fled all that night on the back trail toward Spring Creek, then down that creek to the south fork of the Good River. I rode most of the night in a pony drag because I got too sleepy to stay on a horse. We camped at Good River in the morning, but we stayed only long enough to eat. Then we fled again, upstream, all day long until we reached the mouth of Horse Creek. We were going to stay there, but scouts came to us and said that many soldiers had come into the Black Hills; and that was what Chips saw while he was in the sweat tepee. So we hurried on in the night towards Smoky Earth River (the White), and when we got there, I woke up and it was daybreak. We camped a while to eat, and then went up the Smoky Earth, two camps, to Robinson, for we were afraid of the soldiers up there.

Afterward I learned that it was Pahuska (Long Hair, General Custer) who had led his soldiers into the Black Hills that summer to see what he could find. He had no right to go in there, because all that country was ours. Also the Wasichus had made a treaty with Red Cloud (1868) that said it would be ours as long as grass should grow and water flow. Later I learned too that Pahuska had found there much of the yellow metal that makes the Wasichus crazy; and that is what made the bad trouble, just as it did before, when the hundred were rubbed out.

Our people knew there was yellow

metal in little chunks up there; but they did not bother with it, because it was not good for anything.

We stayed all winter at the Soldiers' Town,* and all the while the bad trouble was coming fast; for in the fall we heard that some Wasichus had come from the Missouri River to dig in the Black Hills for the yellow metal, because Pahuska had told about it with a voice that went everywhere. Later he got rubbed out for doing that.

The people talked about this all winter. Crazy Horse was in the Powder River country and Sitting Bull was somewhere north of the Hills. Our people at the Soldiers' Town thought we ought to get together and do something. Red Cloud's people said that the soldiers had gone in

*Soldiers' Town: Fort Robinson, in western South Dakota.

there to keep the diggers out, but we, who were only visiting, did not believe it. We called Red Cloud's people "Hangs-Around-the-Fort," and our people said they were standing up for the Wasichus, and if we did not do something we should lose the Black Hills.

In the spring when I was twelve years old (1875), more soldiers with many wagons came up from the Soldiers' Town at the mouth of the Laramie River and went into the Hills.

There was much talk all summer, and in the Moon of Making Fat (June) there was a sun dance there at the Soldiers' Town to give the people strength, but not many took part; maybe because everybody was so excited talking about the Black Hills. I remember two men who danced together. One had lost a leg in the Battle of the Hundred Slain and one had lost an eye in the Attacking of the

Wagons, so they had only three eyes and three legs between them to dance with. We boys went down to the creek while they were sun dancing and got some elm leaves that we chewed up and threw on the dancers while they were all dressed up and trying to look their best. We even did this to some of the older people, and nobody got angry, because everybody was supposed to be in a good humor and to show their endurance in every kind of way; so they had to stand teasing too.

In the Moon When the Calves Grow Hair (September) there was a big council with the Wasichus on the Smoky Earth River at the mouth of White Clay Creek. I can remember the council, but I did not understand much of it then. Many of the Lakotas were there, also Shyelas and Blue Clouds (Cheyennes and Arapahoes); but Crazy Horse and Sitting Bull stayed away. In the middle of the circle there was a shade made of canvas. Under this the councilors sat and talked, and all around them there was a crowd of people on foot and horseback. They talked and talked for days, but it was just like wind blowing in the end. I asked my father what they were talking about in there, and he told me that the Grandfather at Washington wanted to lease the Black Hills so that the Wasichus could dig yellow metal, and that the chief of the soldiers had said if we did not do this, the Black Hills would be just like melting snow held in our hands, because the Wasichus would take that country anyway.

It made me sad to hear this. It was such a good place to play and the people were always happy in that country. . . .

After the council we heard that creeks of Wasichus were flowing into the Hills and becoming rivers, and that they were already making towns up there. It looked like bad trouble coming, so our band broke camp and started out to join Crazy Horse on Powder River. We camped on Horsehead Creek, then on the War Bonnet after we crossed the old Wasichu's road* that made the trouble that time when the hundred were rubbed out. Grass was growing on it. Then we camped at Sage Creek, then on the Beaver, then on Driftwood Creek, and came again to the Plain of Pine Trees at the edge of the Hills.

The nights were sharp now, but the days were clear and still; and while we were camping there I went up into the Hills alone and sat a long while under a tree. I tried to think how I could save that country for my people, but I could not see anything clear.

This made me sad, but something happened a few days later that made me feel good. We had gone over to Taking-the-Crow-Horses Creek, where we found many bison and made plenty of meat and tanned many hides for winter. In our band there was a man by the name of Fat, who was always talking about how fast his horse could run. One day while we were camping there I told Fat my pony could run faster than his could, and he laughed at me and said that only crows and coyotes would think my pony was any good. I asked him what he would give me if my pony could beat his, and he said he would give me some black medicine (coffee). So we ran, and I got the black medicine.

On Kills-Himself Creek we made more meat and hides and were ready to join Crazy Horse's camp on the Powder. There were some Hang-Around-the-Fort people with us, and when they saw that we were going to join Crazy Horse, they left us and started back to the Soldiers' Town. They were afraid there might be trouble, and they knew Crazy Horse would fight, so they wanted to be safe with the Wasichus. We did not like them very much.

*Wasichu's road: the Bozeman Trail, which began in Colorado and went to the mining town of Virginia City, in Montana.

After a while we came to the village on Powder River and went into camp at the downstream end. I was anxious to see my cousin, Crazy Horse, again, for now that it began to look like bad trouble coming, everybody talked about him more than ever and he seemed greater than before. Also I was getting older.

Of course I had seen him now and then ever since I could remember, and had heard stories of the brave things he did. I remember the story of how he and his brother were out alone on horseback, and a big band of Crows attacked them, so that they had to run. And while they were riding hard, with all those Crows after them, Crazy Horse heard his brother call out; when he looked back, his brother's horse was down and the Crows were almost on him. And they told how Crazy Horse charged back right into the Crows and fought them back with only a bow and arrows, then took his brother up behind him and got away. It was his sacred power that made the Crows afraid of him when he charged. And the people told stories of when he was a boy and used to be around with the older Hump all the time. Hump was not young any more at the time, and he was a very great warrior, maybe the greatest we ever had until then. They say people used to wonder at the boy and the old man always being together; but I think Hump knew Crazy Horse would be a great man and wanted to teach him everything.

Crazy Horse's father was my father's cousin, and there were no chiefs in our family before Crazy Horse; but there were holy men; and he became a chief because of the power he got in a vision when he was a boy. When I was a man, my father told me something about that vision. Of course he did not know all of it; but he said that Crazy Horse dreamed and went into the world where there is nothing but the spirits of all things. That is the real

world that is behind this one, and everything we see here is something like a shadow from that world. He was on his horse in that world, and the horse and himself on it and the trees and the grass and the stones and everything were made of spirit, and nothing was hard, and everything seemed to float. His horse was standing still there, and yet it danced around like a horse made only of shadow, and that is how he got his name, which does not mean that his horse was crazy or wild, but that in his vision it danced around in that queer way.

It was this vision that gave him his great power, for when he went into a fight, he had only to think of that world to be in it again, so that he could go through anything and not be hurt. Until he was murdered by the Wasichus at the Soldiers' Town on White River, he was wounded only twice, once by accident and both times by someone of his own people when he was not expecting trouble and was not thinking; never by an enemy. He was fifteen years old when he was wounded by accident; and the other time was when he was a young man and another man was jealous of him because the man's wife liked Crazy Horse.

They used to say too that he carried a sacred stone with him, like one he had seen in some vision, and that when he was in danger, the stone always got very heavy and protected him somehow. That, they used to say, was the reason no horse he ever rode lasted very long. I do not know about this; maybe people only thought it; but it is a fact that he never kept one horse long. They wore out. I think it was only the power of his great vision that made him great.

Now and then he would notice me and speak to me before this; and sometimes he would have the crier call me into his tepee to eat with him. Then he would say things to tease me, but I would not say

anything back, because I think I was a little afraid of him. I was not afraid that he would hurt me; I was just afraid. Everybody felt that way about him, for he was a queer man and would go about the village without noticing people or saying anything. In his own tepee he would joke, and when he was on the warpath with a small party, he would joke to make his warriors feel good. But around the village he hardly ever noticed anybody, except little children. All the Lakotas like to dance and sing; but he never joined a dance, and they say nobody ever heard him sing. But everybody liked him, and they would do anything he wanted or go anywhere he said. He was a small man among the Lakotas, and he was slender and had a thin face and his eyes looked through things, and he always seemed to be thinking hard about something. He never wanted to have many things for himself, and did not have many ponies like a chief. They say that when game was scarce and the people were hungry, he would not eat at all. . . .

Crazy Horse kept his village on Powder River with about a hundred tepees, and our band made camp on the Tongue. We built a corral of poles for the horses at night and herded them all day, because the Crows were great horsethieves and we had to be careful. The woman chopped and stripped cottonwood trees during the day and gave the bark to the horses at night. The horses liked it and it made them sleek and fat.

Beside the mouth of the corral there was a tepee for the horse guard, and one night Crow Nose was staying there and his wife was with him. He had a hole in the tepee so that he could look through.

Afterwhile he got very sleepy, so he woke his wife and told her to get up and watch while he had a little rest. By and by she saw something dark moving slowly on the snow out there, so she woke her husband and whispered, "Old man, you'd better get up, for I think I see something." So Crow Nose got up and peeped out and saw a man moving around the corral in the starlight looking for the best horse. Crow Nose told his wife to keep her eye at the hole and let him know when the man was coming out with a horse, and he lay down at the opening of the tepee with the muzzle of his gun sticking out of the flap. By and by they could hear the bar lifted at the mouth of the corral. When his wife touched him, Crow Nose thrust his head outside and saw the man just getting on a horse to ride away. He was black against the sky, so Crow Nose shot him, and the shot woke the whole camp so that many came running with guns and coup sticks. Yellow Shirt was the first to count coup* on the dead Crow, but many followed. A man who has killed an enemy must not touch him, for he has already had the honor of killing. He must let another count coup. When I got there to see, a pile of coup sticks was lying beside the Crow and the women had cut him up with axes and scattered him around. It was horrible. Then the people built a fire right there beside the Crow and we had a kill dance. Men, women, and children danced right in the middle of the night, and they sang songs about Crow Nose who had killed and Yellow Shirt who had counted the first coup.

Then it was daylight, and the crier told us we would move camp. Crow Nose dressed up for war, painted his face black and rode the horse the enemy had tried to steal. When the men paint their faces

---

*count coup: The act of striking an enemy, dead or alive, with a stick conferred distinction, the first coup naturally counting most.

black, the women all rejoice and make the tremolo, because it means their men are going to kill enemies.

When we camped again, one of Red Cloud's loafers who had started back for the Soldiers' Town because they were afraid there might be trouble, came in and said the Crows had killed all his party except himself, while they were sleeping, and he had escaped because he was out scouting.

During the winter, runners came from the Wasichus and told us we must come into the Soldiers' Town right away or there would be bad trouble. But it was foolish to say that, because it was very cold and many of our people and ponies would have died in the snow. Also, we were in our own country and were doing no harm.

Late in the Moon of the Dark Red Calves (February) there was a big thaw, and our little band started for the Soldiers' Town, but it was very cold again before we got there. Crazy Horse stayed with about a hundred tepees on Powder, and in the middle of the Moon of the Snowblind (March) something bad happened there. It was just daybreak. There was a blizzard and it was very cold. The people were sleeping. Suddenly there were many shots and horses galloping through the village. It was the cavalry of the Wasichus, and they were yelling and shooting and riding their horses against the tepees. All the people rushed out and ran, because they were not awake yet and they were frightened. The soldiers killed as many women and children and men as they could while the people were running toward a bluff. Then they set fire to some of the tepees and knocked the others down. But when the people were on the side of the bluff, Crazy Horse said something, and all the warriors began singing the death song and charged back upon the soldiers; and the soldiers ran, driving many of the people's ponies ahead of them. Crazy Horse followed them all that day with a band of warriors, and that night he took all the stolen ponies away from them, and some of their own horses, and brought them all back to the village.

These people were in their own country and were doing no harm. They only wanted to be let alone. We did not hear of this until quite a while afterward; but at the Soldiers' Town we heard enough to make us paint our faces black.

We stayed at the Soldiers' Town this time until the grass was good in the Moon When the Ponies Shed (May). Then my father told me we were going back to Crazy Horse and that we were going to have to fight from then on, because there was no other way to keep our country. He said that Red Cloud was a cheap man and wanted to sell the Black Hills to the Wasichus; that Spotted Tail and other chiefs were cheap men too, and that the Hang-Around-the-Fort people were all cheap and would stand up for the Wasichus. My aunt, who was living at the Soldiers' Town, must have felt the way we did, because when we were breaking camp she gave me a six-shooter like the soldiers had, and told me I was a man now. I was thirteen years old and not very big for my age, but I thought I should have to be a man anyway. We boys had practiced endurance, and we were all good riders, and I could shoot straight with either a bow or a gun.

We were a small band, and we started in the night and traveled fast. Before we got to War Bonnet Creek, some Shyelas joined us, because their hearts were bad like ours and they were going to the same place. Later I learned that many small bands were doing the same thing and coming together from everywhere.

Just after we camped on the War Bonnet, our scouts saw a wagon train of the Wasichus coming up the old road that caused the trouble before.* They had oxen hitched to their wagons and they were part of the river of Wasichus that was running into the Black Hills. They shot at our scouts, and we decided we would attack them. When the war party was getting ready, I made up my mind that, small as I was, I might as well die there, and if I did, maybe I'd be known. I told Jumping Horse, a boy about my age, that I was going along to die, and he said he would too. So we went, and so did Crab and some other boys.

When the Wasichus saw us coming, they put their wagons in a circle and got inside with their oxen. We rode around and around them in a wide circle that kept getting narrower. That is the best way to fight, because it is hard to hit ponies running fast in a circle. And sometimes there would be two circles, one inside the other, going fast in opposite directions, which made us still harder to hit. The cavalry of the Wasichus did not know how to fight. They kept together, and when they came on, you could hardly miss them. We kept apart in the circle. While we were riding around the wagons, we were hanging low on the outside of the ponies and shooting under their necks. This was not easy to do, even when your legs were long, and mine were not yet very long. But I stuck tight and shot with the six-shooter my aunt gave me. Before we started the attack I was afraid, but Big Man told us we were brave boys, and I soon got over being frightened. The Wasichus shot fast at us from behind the wagons, and I could hear bullets whizzing, but they did not hit any of us. I do not know whether we killed any Wasichus or not. We rode around several times, and once we got close, but there were not many of us and we could not get at the

*the old road: the Bozeman Trail. The Indians opposed the use of it by gold seekers.

Wasichus behind their wagons; so we went away. This was my first fight. When we were going back to camp, some Shyela warriors told us we were very brave boys, and that we were going to have plenty of fighting.

We were traveling very fast now, for we were in danger and wanted to get back to Crazy Horse. He had moved over west to the Rosebud River, and the people were gathering there. As we traveled, we met other little bands all going to the same place, until there were a good many of us all mixed up before we got there. Red Cloud's son was with us, but Red Cloud stayed at the Soldiers' Town.

When we came to the ridge on this side of the Rosebud River, we could see the valley full of tepees, and the ponies could not be counted. Many, many people were there—Oglalas, Hunkpapas, Minneconjous, Sans Arcs, Blackfeet, Brules, Santees, and Yanktonais; also many Shyelas and Blue Clouds had come to fight with us. The village was long, and you could not see all the camps with one look. The scouts came out to meet us and bring us in, and everybody rejoiced that we had come. Great men were there: Crazy Horse and Big Road of the Oglalas; Sitting Bull and Gall and Black Moon and Crow King of the Hunkpapas; Spotted Eagle of the Sans Arcs; the younger Hump and Fast Bull of the Minneconjous; Dull Knife and Ice Bear of the Shyelas; Inkpaduta with the Santees and Yanktonais. Great men were there with all those people and horses. Hetchetu aloh! [It is so indeed!]

About the middle of the Moon of Making Fat (June) the whole village moved a little way up the River to a good place for a sun dance. The valley was wide and flat there, and we camped in a great oval with the river flowing through it, and in the center they built the bower of branches in a circle for the dancers, with the opening of it to the east whence comes the light.

Scouts were sent out in all directions to guard the sacred place. Sitting Bull, who was the greatest medicine man of the nation at that time, had charge of this dance to purify the people and to give them power and endurance. It was held in the Moon of Fatness because that is the time when the sun is highest and the growing power of the world is strongest. I will tell you how it was done.

First a holy man was sent out all alone to find the *waga chun*, the holy tree that should stand in the middle of the dancing circle. Nobody dared follow to see what he did or hear the sacred words he would say there. And when he had found the right tree, he would tell the people, and they would come there singing, with flowers all over them. Then when they had gathered about the holy tree, some women who were bearing children would dance around it, because the Spirit of the Sun loves all fruitfulness. After that a warrior, who had done some very brave deed that summer, struck the tree, counting coup upon it; and when he had done this, he had to give gifts to those who had least of everything, and the braver he was, the more he gave away.

After this, a band of young maidens came singing, with sharp axes in their hands; and they had to be so good that nobody there could say anything against them, or that any man had ever known them; and it was the duty of anyone who knew anything bad about any of them to tell it right before all the people there and prove it. But if anybody lied, it was very bad for him.

The maidens chopped the tree down and trimmed its branches off. Then chiefs, who were the sons of chiefs, carried the sacred tree home, stopping four times on the way, once for each season, giving thanks for each.

Now when the holy tree had been brought home but was not yet set up in

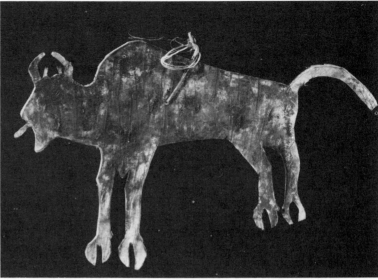

*Rawhide Indian and buffalo figures used by the Sioux in their ritual Sun Dance.*

the center of the dancing place, mounted warriors gathered around the circle of the village, and at a signal they all charged inward upon the center where the tree would stand, each trying to be the first to touch the sacred place; and whoever was the first could not be killed in war that year. When they all came together in the middle, it was like a battle, with the ponies rearing and screaming in a big cloud of dust and the men shouting and wrestling and trying to throw each other off the horses.

After that there was a big feast and plenty for everybody to eat, and a big dance just as though we had won a victory.

The next day the tree was planted in the center by holy men who sang sacred songs and made sacred vows to the Spirit. And the next morning nursing mothers brought their holy little ones to lay them at the bottom of the tree, so that the sons would be brave men and the daughters the mothers of brave men. The holy men pierced the ears of the little ones, and for each piercing the parents gave away a pony to someone who was in need.

The next day the dancing began, and those who were going to take part were ready, for they had been fasting and purifying themselves in the sweat lodges, and praying. First, their bodies were painted by the holy men. Then each would lie down beneath the tree as though he were dead, and the holy men would cut a place in his back or chest, so that a strip of rawhide, fastened to the top of the tree, could be pushed through the flesh and tied. Then the man would get up and dance to the drums, leaning on the rawhide strip as long as he could stand the pain or until the flesh tore loose.

We smaller boys had a good time during the two days of dancing, for we were allowed to do almost anything to tease the people, and they had to stand it. We would gather sharp spear grass, and when a man came along without a shirt, we would stick him to see if we could make him cry out, for everybody was supposed to endure everything. Also we made popguns out of young ash boughs and shot at the men and women to see if we could make them jump; and if they did, everybody laughed at them. The mothers carried water to their holy little ones in bladder bags, and we made little bows and arrows that we could hide under our robes so that we could steal up to the women and shoot holes in the bags. They were supposed to stand anything and not scold us when the water spurted out. We had a good time there.

Right after the sun dance was over, some of our scouts came in from the south, and the crier went around the circle and said: "The scouts have returned and they have reported that soldiers are camping up the river. So, young warriors, take courage and get ready to meet them."

While they were all getting ready, I was getting ready too, because Crazy Horse was going to lead the warriors and I wanted to go with him; but my uncle, who thought a great deal of me, said: "Young nephew, you must not go. Look at the helpless ones. Stay home, and maybe there will be plenty of fighting right here." So the war parties went on without me. Maybe my uncle thought I was too little to do much and might get killed.

Then the crier told us to break camp, and we moved over west towards the Greasy Grass (Little Big Horn) and camped at the head of Spring Creek while the war parties were gone. We learned later that it was Three Stars (General Crook) who fought with our people on the Rosebud that time. He had many walking soldiers and some cavalry, and there were many Crows and Shoshones with him. They were all coming to attack us where we had the sun dance, but Crazy Horse whipped them and they went back to Goose Creek where they had all their wagons. My friend, Iron Hawk, was there, and he can tell you how it was.

*Iron Hawk Speaks:*

I am a Hunkpapa. I was fourteen years old that summer, and I was a big boy. Two war parties went out, a very large one from the south end of the camp, and a small one from the north end. I went with the small one, and there were only about forty of us. The big party got there early in the morning, and when we came, they had been fighting a long while. There is a wide valley there at the bend of the river with some bluffs and hills around it, and it looked as though people were fighting all over that place. There were Crows with the soldiers, and we began fighting with some of them. It looked as though we were getting the best of them. Then the soldiers began to advance on the other side of us, and we had to retreat. We were heading for where the big party was, but the soldiers were after us, and the Crows got braver and fought harder because of the soldiers. When we got to the bend, the Crows were right among us, and it was all mixed up fighting there. I don't know whether I killed anybody or not, but I guess I did, for I was scared and fought hard, and the way it was you couldn't keep from killing somebody if you didn't get killed, and I am still alive. There was a Lakota with me by the name of Without-a-Tepee, and a big Crow pulled him right off his horse and he disappeared. Of course, me—I ran for my life, because we could not fight all those Crows and the soldiers too, and I was scared. But I was not running alone. We were all running, with the Crows after us. Then all at once we saw a band of cavalry coming right ahead of us—about thirty of them. I do not know how they got there. Maybe they were returning from a scouting trip. It looked bad for us. Then I heard voices crying in our language: "Take courage! This is a good day to die! Think of the children and the helpless at home!" So we all yelled "Hoka hey!" and charged on the cavalrymen and began shooting them off their horses, for they turned and ran. They were running toward their big party, and I could see many people were fighting over there, but everything was all mixed up, and you could not tell what was happening. It was a pitiful, long-stretched-out battle. They fought all day. Then the Crows were on us from behind, and we turned around and charged back on them. But many soldiers were behind them, coming. So we all had to run, crying "yea-hey" because there were not enough of us. By now I was very scared, and I ran for my life. I came to a rocky place, and my pony stepped between two stones and nearly tore his hoof off.

There was a very brave Shyela by the name of Sitting Eagle. He was a friend of mine and he had been with me in the fight. When I got off my pony to look at his hoof, a single Crow was coming after me. Then I saw my friend, the Shyela, going to meet the Crow. They fought hand-to-hand, and the Crow went down. I wish I had stayed with Sitting Eagle, because then I could have been the first to coup that Crow. But another man did it.

I ran on foot, leading my horse, who was hopping on three legs. Then I saw smoke coming out of a deep gully where there was a creek. I went over to the smoke, and there were three Lakotas who had killed a bison and were having a feast right there while all the fighting was going on over the hill. They invited me, so I sat there and ate, for I was about fourteen years old and I was always hungry. We had to watch out while we ate. One of the men took some clotted blood from the bison and put it in some raw bison hide and fastened it around my pony's hoof so that I could ride.

After we had been eating there a long time, a Lakota came up on his horse with blood and dirt all over his face, and he was angry. He said: "What are you doing here? We're fighting! All you think of is to eat! Why don't you think about the helpless ones at home? Come, make haste! We have got to stand our ground!"

I felt ashamed, so I got on my horse and we started. My horse could go better with his hoof tied up that way. We came to a ridge, and I could see all over the valley of the Rosebud where the fighting was going on. You could not tell who was getting whipped. It looked all mixed up. Some Crows attacked us there and I never got to the big party that was doing the hard fighting, but it was bad enough where I was, except when I was eating. I must have eaten a great deal, for it was evening now. Of course when we got there, they had been fighting a good while already.

We all came away when it was dark, to guard the women and children, and the enemy did not follow us. Of course I thought the Wasichus had whipped us; but I learned it was not so. It was not a finished battle because the night stopped it, but the Wasichus got whipped anyway, and did not attack our village. They went back to their wagons on Goose Creek and stayed there. . . .

*Black Elk Continues:*

Crazy Horse whipped Three Stars on the Rosebud that day, and I think he could have rubbed the soldiers out there. He could have called many more warriors from the villages and he could have rubbed the soldiers out at daybreak, for they camped there in the dark after the fight.

He whipped the cavalry of Three Stars when they attacked his village on the Powder that cold morning in the Moon of the Snowblind (March). Then he moved farther west to the Rosebud; and when the soldiers came to kill us there, he whipped them and made them go back. Then he moved farther west to the valley of the Greasy Grass. We were in our own country all the time and we only wanted to be let alone. The soldiers came there to kill us, and many got rubbed out. It was our country and we did not want to have any trouble.

We camped there in the valley along the south side of the Greasy Grass before the sun was straight above; and this was, I think, two days before the battle. It was a very big village and you could hardly count the tepees. Farthest up the stream toward the south were the Hunkpapas, and the Oglalas were next. Then came the Minneconjous, the Sans Arcs, the Black-feet, the Shyelas; and last, the farthest toward the north, were the Santees and Yanktonais. Along the side towards the east was the Greasy Grass, with some timber along it, and it was running full from the melting of the snow in the Big Horn Mountains. If you stood on a hill you could see the mountains off to the south and west. On the other side of the river, there were bluffs and hills beyond. Some gullies came down through the bluffs. On the westward side of us were lower hills, and there we grazed our ponies and guarded them. There were so many they could not be counted.

There was a man by the name of Rattling Hawk who was shot through the hip in the fight on the Rosebud, and people thought he could not get well. But there was a medicine man by the name of Hairy Chin who cured him.

The day before the battle I had greased myself and was going to swim with some boys, when Hairy Chin called me over to Rattling Hawk's tepee, and told me he wanted me to help him. There were five other boys there, and he needed us for bears in the curing ceremony, because he had his power from a dream of the bear. He painted my body yellow, and my face too, and put a black stripe on either side of my nose from the eyes down. Then he tied my hair up to look like bear's ears, and put some eagle feathers on my head.

Hairy Chin, who wore a real bear skin with the head on it, began to sing a song that went like this:

At the doorway, sacred herbs are rejoicing.

While he sang, two girls came in and stood one on either side of the wounded man; one had a cup of water and one some kind of an herb. They gave the cup and the herb to Rattling Hawk while Hairy Chin was singing. Then they gave him a red cane, and right away he stood up with it. The girls then started out of the tepee, and the wounded man followed, leaning on the sacred red stick; and we boys, who were the little bears, had to jump around him and make growling noises toward the man. When we did this, you could see something like feathers of all colors coming out of our mouths. Then Hairy Chin came out on all fours, and he looked just like a bear to me. Then Rattling Hawk began to walk better. He was not able to fight next day, but he got well in a little while.

After the ceremony, we boys went swimming to wash the paint off, and when we got back many of the people were dancing and having kill talks all over the village, remembering brave deeds done in the fight with Three Stars on the Rosebud.

When it was about sundown we boys had to bring the ponies in close, and when this was done it was dark and the people were still dancing around fires all over the village. We boys went around from one dance to another, until we got too sleepy to stay up any more.

My father woke me at daybreak and told me to go with him to take our horses out to graze, and when we were out there he said: "We must have a long rope on one of them, so that it will be easy to catch; then we can get the others. If anything happens, you must bring the horses back as fast as you can, and keep your eyes on the camp."

Several of us boys watched our horses together until the sun was straight above and it was getting very hot. Then we thought we would go swimming, and my cousin said he would stay with our horses till we got back. When I was greasing myself, I did not feel well; I felt queer. It seemed that something terrible was going to happen. But I went with the boys anyway. Many people were in the water now and many of the women were out west of the village digging turnips. We had been in the water quite a while when my cousin came down there with the horses to give them a drink, for it was very hot now.

Just then we heard the crier shouting in the Hunkpapa camp, which was not very far from us: "The Chargers are coming! They are charging! The chargers are coming!" Then the crier of the Oglalas shouted the same words; and we could hear the cry going from camp to camp northward clear to the Santees and the Yanktonais.

Everybody was running now to catch the horses. We were lucky to have ours right there just at that time. My older brother had a sorrel, and he rode away fast toward the Hunkpapas. I had a buckskin. My father came running and said: "Your brother has gone to the Hunkpapas without his gun. Catch him and give it to him. Then come right back to me." He had my six-shooter too—the one my aunt gave me. I took the guns, jumped on my pony and caught my brother. I could see a big dust rising just beyond the Hunkpapa camp and all the Hunkpapas were running around and yelling, and many were running wet from the river. Then out of the dust came the soldiers on their big horses.

They looked big and strong and tall and they were all shooting. My brother took his gun and yelled for me to go back. There was a brushy timber just on the other side of the Hunkpapas, and some warriors were gathering there. He made for that place, and I followed him. By now women and children were running in a crowd downstream. I looked back and saw them all running and scattering up a hillside down yonder.

When we got into the timber, a good many Hunkpapas were there already and the soldiers were shooting above us so that leaves were falling from the trees where the bullets struck. By now I could not see what was happening in the village below. It was all dust and cries and thunder; for the women and children were running there, and the warriors were coming on their ponies.

Among us there in the brush and out in the Hunkpapa camp a cry went up: "Take courage! Don't be a coward! The helpless are out of breath!" I think this was when Gall stopped the Hunkpapas, who had been running away, and turned them back.

Then another great cry went up out in the dust: "Crazy Horse is coming! Crazy Horse is coming!" Off toward the west and north they were yelling "Hoka hey!" like a big wind roaring, and making the tremolo; and you could hear eagle bone whistles screaming.

The valley went darker with dust and smoke, and there were only shadows and a big noise of many cries and hoofs and guns. On the left of where I was I could hear the shot hoofs of the soldiers' horses going back into the brush and there was shooting everywhere. Then the hoofs came out of the brush, and I came out and was in among men and horses weaving in and out and going upstream, and everybody was yelling, "Hurry! Hurry!" The soldiers were running upstream and we were all mixed there in the twilight and the great noise. I did not see much; but once I saw a Lakota charge at a soldier who stayed behind and fought and was a very brave man. The Lakota took the soldier's horse by the bridle, but the soldier killed him with a six-shooter. I was small and could not crowd in to where the soldiers were, so I did not kill anybody. There were so many ahead of me, and it was all dark and mixed up.

Soon the soldiers were all crowded into the river and many Lakotas too; and I was in the water awhile. Men and horses were all mixed up and fighting in the water, and it was like hail falling in the river. Then we were out of the river, and people were stripping dead soldiers and putting the clothes on themselves. There was a soldier on the ground and he was still kicking. A Lakota rode up and said to me: "Boy, get off and scalp him." I got off and started to do it. He had short hair and my knife was not very sharp. He ground his teeth. Then I shot him in the forehead and got his scalp.

Many of our warriors were following the soldiers up a hill on the other side of the river. Everybody else was turning back down stream, and on a hill away down yonder above the Santee camp there was a big dust, and our warriors whirling around in and out of it just like swallows, and many guns were going off.

I thought I would show my mother my scalp, so I rode over toward the hill where there was a crowd of women and children. On the way down there I saw a very pretty young woman among a band of warriors about to go up to the battle on the hill, and she was singing like this:

Brothers, now your friends have come!
Be brave! Be brave!
Would you see me taken captive?

When I rode through the Oglala camp I saw Rattling Hawk sitting up in his tepee with a gun in his hands, and he was all alone there singing a song of regret that went like this:

Brothers, what are you doing that I
can not do?

When I got to the women on the hill they were all singing and making the tremolo to cheer the men fighting across the river in the dust on the hill. My mother gave a big tremolo just for me when she saw my first scalp.

I stayed there awhile with my mother and watched the big dust whirling on the hill across the river, and horses were coming out of it with empty saddles.

*Standing Bear Speaks:*

I saw soldiers on horseback spreading out as they came down a slope to the river. They crossed and came on at a trot. I started down the butte, but I was barefoot and there was a big bed of cactus there. I had to go slow, picking my way. A dust cloud was rising up yonder; and then I could see that the Hunkpapas were running, and when I looked over onto the hills toward the south and east I saw other soldiers coming there on horseback. I did not go to the horses. I went down through the cactus as fast as I could and into the village. There were voices all over, and everybody was shouting something and running around. After awhile my older brother came driving our horses, and my uncle said: "Hurry up! We shall go forth!" I caught my gray horse and took my six-shooter and hung my bow and arrows over my shoulder. I had killed a red bird a few days before and I fastened this in my hair. I had made a vow that I would make an offering if this would keep me from getting hurt in the next fight; and it did.

We started and went downsteam to the mouth of Muskrat Creek beyond the

Santee camp. We were going to meet the second band of soldiers. By the time we got there, they must have been fighting on the hill already, because as we rode up east from the mouth of Muskrat Creek we met a Lakota with blood running out of his mouth and down over his horse's shoulders. His name was Long Elk. There were warriors ahead of us, the "fronters," who are the bravest and have had most practice in war. I was sixteen years old and I was in the rear with the less brave, and we had waited for our horses quite awhile.

Partway up we met another Lakota. He was on foot and he was bleeding and dizzy. He would get up and then he would fall down again. When we got farther up the hill, I could see the soldiers. They were off their horses, holding them by the bridles. They were ready for us and were shooting. Our people were all around the hill on every side by this time. I heard some of our men shouting: "They are gone!" And I saw that many of the soldiers' horses had broken loose and were running away. Everywhere our warriors began yelling: "Hoka hey! Hurry! Hurry!" Then we all went up, and it got dark with dust and smoke. I could see warriors flying all around me like shadows, and the noise of all those hoofs and guns and cries was so loud it seemed quiet in there and the voices seemed to be on top of the cloud. It was like a bad dream.

We could see the women coming over now in a swarm and they were all making the tremolo. We waited around there awhile, and then we saw soldiers coming on a hill toward the south and east. Everybody began yelling: "Hurry!" And we started for the soldiers. They ran back toward where they came from. One got killed, and many of us got off and couped him. Then we chased all the soldiers back to the hill where they were before. . . .

*Iron Hawk Speaks:*

When I got on my horse with the rope hitched around his nose, the soldiers were shooting up there and people were running and men and boys were catching their horses that were scared because of the shooting and yelling. I saw little children running up from the river where they had been swimming; and all the women and children were running quickly down the valley.

Our horses stampeded down toward the Minneconjous, but we rounded them up again and brought them back. By now warriors were running toward the soldiers, and getting on the ponies, and many of the Hunkpapas were gathering in the brush and timber near the place where the soldiers had stopped and got off their horses. I rode past a very old man who was shouting: "Boys, take courage! Would you see these little children taken away from me like dogs?"

I went into our tepee and got dressed for war as fast as I could; but I could hear bullets whizzing outside, and I was so shaky that it took me a long time to braid an eagle feather into my hair. Also, I had to hold my pony's rope all the time, and he kept jerking me and trying to get away. While I was doing this, crowds of warriors on horses were roaring by upstream, yelling: "Hoke hey!" Then I rubbed red paint all over my face and took my bow and arrows and got on my horse. I did not have a gun, only a bow and arrows.

When I was on my horse, the fight upstream seemed to be over, because everybody was starting back downstream and yelling: "It's a good day to die!" Soldiers were coming at the other end of the village, and nobody knew how many there were down there.

A man by the name of Little Bear rode up to me on a pinto horse, and he had a very pretty saddle blanket. He said: "Take courage, boy! The earth is all that lasts!" So I rode fast with him and the others downstream, and many of us Hunkpapas gathered on the east side of the river at the foot of a gulch that led back up the hill where the second soldier band was. . . .

I saw Little Bear's horse rear and race up hill toward the soldiers. When he got close, his horse was shot out from under him, and he got up limping because the bullet had gone through his leg; and he started hobbling back to us with the soldiers shooting at him. His brother-friend, Elk Nation, went up there on his horse and took Little Bear behind him and rode back safe with bullets striking all around him. It was his duty to go to his brother-friend even if he knew he would be killed.

*Black Elk Continues:*

After I showed my mother my first scalp, I stayed with the women awhile and they were all singing and making the tremolo. We could not see much of the battle for the big dust, but we knew there would be no soldiers left. There were many other boys about my age and younger up there with their mothers and sisters, and they asked me to go over to the battle with them. So we got on our ponies and started. While we were riding downhill toward the river we saw gray horses with empty saddles stampeding toward the water. We rode over across the Greasy Grass to the mouth of a gulch that led up through the bluff to where the fighting was.

Before we got there, the Wasichus were all down, and most of them were dead, but some of them were still alive and kicking. Many other little boys had come up by this time, and we rode around shooting arrows into the Wasichus. There was one who was squirming around with arrows sticking in him, and I started to take his coat, but a man pushed me away and took it for himself. Then I saw something bright hanging on this soldier's belt, and I pulled it out. It was round and bright and yellow and very beautiful and I put it on me for a necklace. At first it ticked inside, and then it did not anymore. I wore it around my neck a long time before I found out what it was and how to make it tick again.

Then the women all came over and we

*Sioux Pipe Bowl*

went to the top of the hill. Gray horses were lying dead there, and some of them were on top of dead Wasichus and dead Wasichus were on top of them. There were not many of our own dead there, because they had been picked up already; but many of our men were killed and wounded. . . .

I saw some Lakotas holding another Lakota up. I went over there, and it was Chase-in-the-Morning's brother, who was called Black Wasichu. He had been shot through the right shoulder downward, and the bullet stopped in his left hip, because he was hanging on the side of his horse when he was hit. They were trying to give him some medicine.

Everybody was up all night in the village. Next morning another war party went up to the hill where the other soldiers were, and the men who had been watching there all night came home. My mother and I went along. She rode a mare with a little colt tied beside her and it trotted along with its mother.

We could see the horses and pack mules up there, but the soldiers were dug in. Beneath the hill, right on the west side of the Greasy Grass, were some bullberry bushes, and there was a big boy by the name of Round Fool who was running around the bushes. We asked him what he was doing that for, and he said: "There is a Wasichu in that bush." And there was. He had hidden there when the other soldiers ran to the hilltop and he had been there all night. We boys began shooting at him with arrows, and it was like chasing a rabbit. He would crawl from one side to the other while we were running around the bush shooting at him with our bows. Once he yelled "Ow." After a while we set fire to the grass around the bushes, and he came out running. Some of our warriors killed him.

Once we went up the back of the hill, where some of our men were, and looked over. We could not see the Wasichus, who were lying in their dug-ins, but we saw the horses and pack mules, and many of them were dead. When we came down and crossed the river again, some soldiers shot at us and hit the water. Mother and I galloped back to the camp, and it was about sundown. By then our scouts had reported that more soldiers were coming upstream; so we all broke camp. Before dark we were ready and we started up the Greasy Grass, heading for Wood Louse Creek in the Big Horn Mountains. We fled all night, following the Greasy Grass. My two younger brothers and I rode in a pony drag, and my mother put some young pups in with us. They were always trying to crawl out and I was always putting them back in, so I didn't sleep much.

By morning we reached a little dry creek and made camp and had a big feast. The meat had spots of fat in it, and I wish I had some of it right now.

When it was full day, we started again and came to Wood Louse Creek at the foot of the mountains, and camped there. A badly wounded man by the name of Three Bears had fits there, and he would keep saying: "Jeneny, jeneny." I do not know what he meant. He died, and we used to call that place the camp where Jeneny died.

That evening everybody got excited and began shouting: "The soldiers are coming!" I looked, and there they were, riding abreast right toward us. But it was some of our own men dressed in the soldiers' clothes. They were doing this for fun.

The scouts reported that the soldiers had not followed us and that everything was safe now. All over the camp there were big fires and dances all night long.

I will sing you some of the songs that our people made up and sang that night. Some of them went like this:

> Long Hair has never returned,
> So his woman is crying, crying.
> Looking over here, she cries.
> . . . . . . . . .
> Long Hair, guns I had none.
> You brought me many. I thank you!
> You make me laugh!
> . . . . . . . . .
> Long Hair, horses I had none.
> You brought me many. I thank you!
> You make me laugh!
> . . . . . . . . .
> Long Hair, where he lies nobody knows.
> Crying, they seek him.
> He lies over here.
>
> Let go your holy irons (guns).
> You are not men enough to do any harm.
> Let go your holy irons!

After awhile I got so tired dancing that I went to sleep on the ground right where I was.

My cousin, Black Wasichu, died that night.

## YOU AND THE STORY

(1) The Sioux were famous as a *warrior nation*. From Black Elk's account, what do you learn about them as warriors? What were their reasons for fighting? What were their standards of courage, their attitudes toward their enemies? How did they put their people in a warlike spirit? What did they expect from young boys like Black Elk and his friends? What did they expect from the women?

(2) Throughout history, people have painted their enemies as savage and inhuman. What do you learn from Black Elk's story about the *human* side of his people? What parts of his story go counter to familiar stereotypes of the Indian?

(3) In recent times, there has been a tremendous revival of interest in the traditions, religion, and customs of "primitive" peoples. Bring together what you learn from Black Elk's account about the beliefs, legends, and ceremonies of his people.

### A Closer Look

(1) Crazy Horse, Black Elk's cousin, was a chief whose village was attacked by the U.S. Cavalry in March 1876. Study the account of Crazy Horse given in this narrative. He was admired by his people as a great leader. Which of the qualities or features they admired would be expected or easily understood in the white culture? Which would have been strange or unexpected for white people, and why? (If you were serving as an interpreter of Indian ways, how would you explain some of the

things that might seem different or strange?)

(**2**) To judge from this story, what were the relations between Indians of different tribes?

---

## Your Turn

You and your class may want to adapt Black Elk's story for a *dramatic presentation* on "Custer's Last Stand." Can you give your audience the Indian side of the events leading up to the battle and of the battle itself? You may want to prepare speaking parts for some of the following roles:

—a narrator who sets the scene and fills in essential facts

—Crazy Horse talking about his tribe and their dealings with the "Wasichus"

—one of the young maidens telling the story of the sun dance

—Black Elk, Iron Hawk, and Standing Bear as boys telling about their roles in the events of the story

—Black Elk's mother talking about the events as seen by the women in the story

—voices reciting the songs at the end of the story

---

Language/Composition Activity C2

FOR DICTIONARY WORK

# Language and History

History books give us more than just the "bare facts." What we say and write about history is seldom entirely neutral. The words we choose, like the facts we emphasize, show *where we stand*. They show how we want others to look at the people and events we describe. Often we do not have to ask a historian: "What side are you on?" We can tell from the *words* being used. Look at the following words that you might find in a book about early American history. How would they help show where the historian stands? How would they help show what the historian thinks and feels?

Select several of the following sets of words. About each set ask:

(1) What do the words in the set have *in common*? What "common denominator" do they have?

(2) How is each word or expression *different* from the other words in the set? Are they synonyms—"just about the same"—or does it make a difference which one we choose? What is different about the ideas, feelings, or pictures they bring to mind?

(3) Where does each of the words come from? Does its *origin* or history help us understand what the word means or how it is used?

1. natives, original inhabitants, aborigines
2. settlers, pioneers, immigrants
3. territory, habitat, homeland
4. savage, primitive, barbaric
5. migrants, nomads, hunters
6. civilization, culture, way of life
7. warrior, soldier, mercenary
8. alien, stranger, outsider
9. newcomer, arrival, invader
10. battle, skirmish, massacre
11. conquest, victory, triumph
12. scout, spy, informer
13. aggressive, warlike, belligerent
14. pacify, subdue, subjugate
15. mixing, blending, integration

● In the stories about the warriors of old, a hero had to meet hard but clear standards. A true hero had exceptional courage. He had great stamina or perseverance. He was capable of tremendous loyalty toward his people or his friends. But most modern writers write about a world where the old simple heroic virtues no longer seem self-evident. The battle lines no longer seem as simply or as clearly drawn. A modern hero or a modern heroine often has to make difficult *choices.* A modern character may be a hero to some readers and not to others. Look at the central character in the following story. Could you admire or respect him as a modern hero?

Daniel de Paola

# The Returning

It was the only house he had seen in three days; it nestled just at the base of the foothills which led to the Mexican border. For a long time, he sat in the brush and wondered whether he should chance it. His throat was so dry he couldn't swallow; his mouth and lips were sore from lack of water and he felt that if he didn't get some kind of food in his stomach soon, it wouldn't make any difference whether he made the border or not.

He moved closer; from fifty yards away, he could see only a few chickens inside the fence; there was no other sign of life, no sounds, no smoke coming from the chimney though it was nearing sundown. Whoever lived out here in such isolation must be independent and have a mind of his own, he thought. It didn't have to follow that they would suspect him just because he was an Indian. And perhaps they might even give him some food and water.

He went very slowly now; many of these outlying places had dogs to keep a watch. When he was satisfied there was none, he was no more than a score of

paces from the fence. At this point, he noted that the front door was ajar about a foot or so; this added to the strangeness of the place. The wind blew in gusts and he saw dust in small clouds swirl up on the porch and some of it enter the house. That and the quiet made him see there was something very odd about this place.

In a moment, he was up on the porch. After looking at the horizon, he squinted in beyond the door and saw a dust-covered living room, old furniture, and faded walls. There was no one about and he entered; then he heard the heavy breathing, like sighing from another room. The door on the left was half open, and when he reached it he heard the breathing more clearly. He pushed the door back silently and looked into a bedroom; and on the bed was a white woman and a small baby in her arms.

They were very sick, he saw close up; they seemed in a heavy, unnatural sleep, almost like a coma. The woman coughed several times, a harsh, wracking cough that left her breathing all the louder. Her face was a deathly white and her eyelids trembled but never opened. The baby was exhaling quickly in a hoarse tone; on closer look, he saw the reddish tinge of its throat and neck. Then he felt he knew what was wrong with them.

He looked all over the house quickly until he found a kerosene lamp in the kitchen; he took the top off, dipped a piece of cloth in it, and went back to the bedroom where he rubbed both their throats with it. With more kerosene-soaked cloths wrapped around their throats, he used one wad at the end of a spoon to coat the insides of their throats with more of the spirit, a procedure he had seen his own mother use many years ago when he and his sisters had had diphtheria.

After he had a sip of water and munched on a hard piece of bread he found, he began the second phase of his treatment. With a damp towel, he washed down both their bodies, then laid the baby out alongside the mother, who still wanted to hold it even in her condition. He then found two heavy blankets and threw them over the two patients. They slept on while he sat near and wondered what else he could do.

He recalled one old uncle saying that sufferers from the throat sickness seemed to get some relief from breathing fumes of gunpowder. Having only a knife, he began another search of the house. But though he could find no weapons or shells about, he did find a can out on the back porch which was half filled with kerosene; this he brought into the kitchen and placed under the table for use later.

Back in the bedroom, he redampened the cloths around their necks and felt their pulses and foreheads. They were still very hot and uneasy, but their breathing didn't sound quite so rough as it had earlier. He placed the chair near the window and gazed out. It was a lonely stretch—a few small trees beyond the small patch of prairie, and then the rocky slope leading up. A woman and baby here meant that there had to be a man about; and for a long time he thought of fleeing before the man returned. But then he saw a cow come into view around back and it made him see how thoughtless he had been.

He got a small fire going in the stove and put a pot of water on; he found some jelled soup in a larder and put that on the stove too to heat up. Then he took another small pan and went out to the cow which he milked for a long time before she would stand still long enough to give him a small amount. This too he put on the stove. He rechecked his patients and went outside to bring in more wood, to get the fire as hot as possible.

While he drank a small bit of the warm soup, he looked at the needlework in the dining room and scanned the living room which had small poems hanging up on the walls. One was entitled "Bless This Home," and another was a prayer to the Lord to give the occupants fortitude and patience. He stood before a third one a long time, reading "Everyman is me, I am his brother. No man is my enemy. I am Everyman and He is Myself."

Out on the porch, he looked back the way he had come. Ten days and one man's life back, he had left the reservation, vowing never to return to that shameful bondage. But no sooner had he set out on his way west than the chief notified the Indian agent, who sent several deputies to recapture him. He recalled how they had separated and the one had guessed his next move back in the Diablo mountains, surprising him in a narrow rocky pass. He had only wanted to get away; he hadn't wanted to stab the man who had been so careless and heavy-handed as to miss the knife in his pants and to cuss him out for a dumb injun who didn't know when he was well off.

He took the deputy's horse and rode south for three days before it fell to the ground, unable to move any farther or stand. He had gone about a hundred yards away when he turned and saw the buzzards circling in the sky above it. Throwing curses at them as a kind of relief and cover, he went back, drew his knife, and made a cut deep in the horse's neck. He sat near it, glaring up at the black birds while the life of the animal oozed out into the thick sandy stubble around them.

After he had been walking for a long while, he turned and looked back. He saw the birds beginning to glide lower and lower until they landed; and he tried to find some solace in the memory of the tribe elders explaining how buzzards and other ghouls helped keep the prairies clean. He tried to think of that but it didn't do much good. Just as it had never done any good to think of what the elders had said about their being brought into reservations. The whites *had* grown too numerous and powerful; his own people *had* grown weaker and fewer in number. It was a fact of life they had to accept in the long run. But even so, he did his best not to think about it. Things were bad enough without basking in their defeat.

So when the prospect of undergoing another summer of skimpy planting and harvesting on reservations faced him again, some weeks back, he began to drink all the more to bolster the decision he had made soon after they had been placed on the government land some two years before. And when the chief and several elders warned him two or three times in the past weeks, he knew the time had come. But before he could make a well-planned departure with supplies and a horse, he got into an argument with another man over a squaw and almost killed him in a fight; thus, before the elders could decide on his punishment, he slipped away one night with only the clothes he wore and his knife.

Knowing he had talked many times of heading west if and when he jumped the reservation, he decided to strike south instead, to throw off pursuers sent out by the chief and the agent. But they soon picked up his trail, and for a time he was desperate with the fear of being brought back to his people—not for the punishment they might set up for him, but for the shame he would have to bear, like an unruly hapless prisoner being brought back to his prison. He told himself many times that he would endure almost anything but that.

It was their passivity that he had found most unbearable back on the reservation. Not only had they become like orphans waiting for the charity of the whites, but the chief and his people seemed satisfied to get less and less of what they were originally promised. More than once, he and several other braves had told the chief it was shameful for them, a tribe once as strong as the Blackfeet, to accept each new insult without so much as a word of complaint. But the chief had always promised to talk to the agent and never did; he knew full well if he dared to complain another elder would soon be chief and receiving the little favors from the agent.

True, there had often been unrest and talk of deserting the reservation; but it had always occurred when men were drinking or bitter over the agent's shortcomings. Generally, the families accepted the few blankets and cows and horses and said that perhaps they were better off than other lone tribes who starved in bad weather. And when he had tried to argue that other tribes, even if some of them were starving, were still real people and not slaves to the whites, often he had been told that if he felt that way, why did he stay?

All through the night, he bathed and

rebathed the patients with hot cloths and painted their throats. Once or twice he tried to get some soup down them but it didn't work. So he kept them warm and continued to watch them when he wasn't out on the porch, watching the night. He wondered if he should continue south tomorrow or turn west as he had originally planned. He had heard tales of the opportunities in the Pacific Northwest or even up in the Yukon. Mexico was too close and offered only more land to flee through. He was weary and wanted to stop somewhere.

He dozed off in his chair and woke just before sunup; the woman was awake and saw him. She tried to sit up but was too weak; he moved to her and smiled down at her. "Are you feeling better?"

"Who are you?" Then before he could answer, she turned to her baby and held it close. "Is she going to be all right?"

"She is better," he nodded.

The woman scrutinized the baby for a moment and saw it was true. "Did you take care of her?"

He nodded again.

"Who are you?"

"I was passing and saw you were sick."

She looked over his dark, angular face, his stiff clothes and the way his odd appearance filled the room. "Are you a doctor?"

"No, but I have seen this sickness before."

She gazed at him. "It was very good of you to stop and help us."

"Is there no one else here? You have a husband?"

"He left a few days ago; he works for the sheriff of the county."

"Will he be back soon?"

"I don't know."

"You have no friends near, to help?"

"Only over in town," she said.

He nodded and told her, "You mustn't talk more. Rest, and I will stay until you are better."

When he had tucked her and the baby in and resumed his seat by the window, he found her eyes on him. "What is your name?" she asked.

"Nachobi," he said, giving the first name which came to him.

She smiled faintly and said, "Well, I'm very grateful to you."

When she slept again, he rose and went outside. Odd how the name of a dead kinsman had come to his lips, one who had been killed in battle and not been like those on the reservation. But then he realized it wasn't so odd after all; when he was a boy, his father had told him all the great names and he still remembered so many—Nachobi, Pionsomen, Long Face, Diniseau, and Laughing Cat after whom his father had wanted to name him. His mother had compromised on Darkcat, used as a white man's last name, and had given him the first name of Willis, after an agent she had admired.

He wondered if the woman's husband was on his trail, too. Perhaps not, since the reservation was up in Oklahoma; but he did know that he couldn't afford to remain here much longer. The deputy had to be coming home soon, and he wasn't going to like having Willis here, no matter what he had done for the woman and baby. He told himself that he would leave sometime this day, as soon as the woman was strong enough to get food for her baby. In the meanwhile, he could keep checking with her on the location of her husband.

He stood by the window of the bedroom and gazed in on the woman. He wondered if his several women friends in the tribe still spoke of him, although it was probably forbidden by the chief; and he wondered too if his old mother was being shunned by others because of this so-called shame. He pictured the small, bony woman with no teeth, who always watched him with those sad eyes when he grew from a wild boyhood into a bitter manhood; and he could still hear her saying, "You must see that we have to live thinner days now. Our ancestors, if they were alive with us, would be living just as we are." And he would never believe that; he told her more than once when drinking, that the ancestors would never accept such a trammeled life, they would erupt like a river over its banks.

He never got over feeling that he had been cursed in the time he was born; his life had spanned the whole decline and thus the memories he had as a boy led him into an empty maturity. Often when he had been a small boy, he had seen great chiefs and heard of victories over the whites. His father and his uncles had shown him bits of the glory; he had been like an observer of the epoch and didn't know until many years later that the epoch had been closing. If he had been born thirty years later, perhaps he would have listened to his mother's words and not felt quite so much dissatisfaction with himself and his people.

He had often envied the braves who had adapted themselves to the new life; they had taken their wives and plots of land and begun to work as any white would on his homestead. When Willis and other drunken braves gathered late at night, they talked of these "white braves" and scoffed at their methods and outlook. And he joined in with the most scornful tones and sarcastic laugh. But when he was alone, he now and then wondered if perhaps the white braves weren't the wisest of their tribe. Most of the time, however, he tried not to think of them and never had anything to do with them.

If he knew he could never be satisfied with the white braves' mode of life, he knew also that the existence of his cronies was as bad or worse. Night after night of drinking, gaming, and fighting was like letting out the pent-up emotion of his wasting years. Now and again he woke up with a hangover lying among a bunch of sprawled forms and felt he was a bigger fool than any of them. He too was becoming old and paunchy and idiotic. But when the others got up and did a little work to get money for more liquor, he sat around staring at the circle of the horizon. That was when his anger would reach its whitest pitch: their ancestors had roamed the continent from one coast to another and here they were confined to a three-hundred-square-mile plot like fishes in a lake.

He found a small bottle later and put some warm milk in it for the baby; the mother woke up and fed it while he watched. The mother seemed stronger now; her fever was down and she didn't cough too often. As the baby drank slowly, she gazed up at Willis.

"Do you have to be moving on?"

"Yes, I do. I was waiting to see if you were better. Does your throat hurt much?"

"A little, but I'm much better, thanks to you."

She gazed down at her baby drinking.

"She looks better too," he said.

"Yes, she does, I don't know what we would've done without you."

He asked her how it had all happened and she told him that she and the baby had been hit almost simultaneously with a sudden fever and sore throat; then coughing and dizziness set in so that she had to take to her bed. He told her he had had diphtheria as a boy and had remembered some of the symptoms and treatments used by his mother.

She smiled at him and said, "It was divine providence that you happened by."

He asked if her husband often stayed

away this long, and she replied he did when his job demanded it, knowing she could take care of herself and the baby. "Until this time," she smiled.

He asked if she could swallow some soup and she said she would try. He brought some in to her and sat at the window as she drank it. She was a fairly young woman, hardy looking, with a round face and long blond hair. Between sips, she asked where he came from and where he was bound. He made up a story of heading for a job in some Mexican gold fields. She said she wished he would stay long enough to receive the thanks of her husband who was probably on his way home by now. But that if he didn't he would understand.

For a moment, they were silent; he sat next to the window watching her and she, between turning to the baby and drinking her soup, was looking over at him. At another time and place, he wouldn't have wanted to linger in a room alone with a white woman. He had heard of more than one Indian in such an instance being accused of everything from attempted assault to terrorizing a helpless female. But here and now there was only friendliness between them; it was a kind of kinship he had never felt toward a white before. It made him think of the words he had read in the living room.

He saw that the woman was still weak; he took away the bottle and dish, and told her he would stay a while longer until she got a little more rest. She smiled tiredly and said it was very good of him, she didn't know how to thank him. He resumed his post at the window and took to scanning the northern prairie. He knew he was stretching his luck; if he was smart, he would wait until she dozed off and then leave. But somehow he just couldn't.

The longer he sat, however, the more restive he became. He began to think of the times his people had suffered at the hands of the whites, mainly for trusting the whites too much. One of his uncles had taught him early the saying that an Indian should trust the whites but keep his knife sharp. Perhaps the woman would never hurt him after what he had done for her, but the husband was something else again. He went outside and thought about what he should do.

While he tried to make a plan, he milked the cow, chopped more wood, fed the chickens, and cleaned the pots he had used. Then he brought several buckets of water in from the well out back; afterward, he went into the bedroom to see if she was awake. She was dozing and he took the chair to wait.

It was almost noon when she woke up. He smiled at her when she glanced over, and he said, "Feeling stronger?"

"Yes, very much so."

"I thought after I got you and the baby a lunch, I would leave."

"Of course we've kept you far too long already. In fact, I think I can get up now." She started to sit up and he moved to her.

"Not yet," he told her. "Have some more soup and take a few more hours of rest. You will feel much better by evening."

"Maybe you're right." She lay back. "You're the doctor here."

He returned to the kitchen and got the soup ready. While she fed the baby and had some herself, she said she had to pay him in some way for all this help. He tried to protest but she insisted. "Is your horse rested and fed?" she asked. When he told her he had no horse, she said, "There's the answer; you'll take our spare horse."

"I couldn't do that," he said.

"But you must."

"It's kind of you, generous, but I can't take your horse."

For the next few moments, she kept insisting and he kept refusing. He had a pretty good idea of what would happen if he was caught with a white man's horse. Back at the window, he noted a puff of dust in the distance. While he listened to her, he saw it grow until he could make out the form of a man on a horse. When she saw him gazing out, she asked, "Is someone coming?"

"Yes," he told her.

"It must be Jim, my husband." Perhaps she guessed his feelings, for she added, "I'm so glad he's come home before you left. I want to tell him all you've done for us."

He listened to her talk about moving closer to town and all the while he kept glancing at the approaching rider. Soon he could hear the hooves of the horse hitting the ground and presently the rider was coming through the fence up to the house.

"That's him, I can tell by the sound," she said. When they heard steps on the porch, she sat up and called out, "Jim? I'm in here." The man then came into the bedroom.

As he moved to his wife, he grew aware of Willis near the window. He stopped and stared at the Indian.

"This is Mr. Nachobi," the woman told him. "And if he hadn't come along yesterday, I don't know what you would've found here today." While the cowboy regarded the Indian searchingly, she gave him the whole story, laying a special stress on how Willis had worked like a doctor with only crude tools to save both her and the baby. The cowboy was around thirty, tall and lean, with the hard look of a man much in the saddle. He had fair skin and light eyes, which looked hard and soft at the same time. Now they seemed friendly as he said, "I'm much obliged to you; it was a fine thing you did here."

Willis nodded and waited.

"I told Mr. Nachobi that he had to take Daisy in payment," the woman went on. "He has no horse of his own and this is the least we can do. Don't you think so?"

"Of course," said the cowboy. "No buts about it, after all he did for us." He bent over his baby, eyed it closely, and then kissed it on the head. He then caressed the woman and looked back at Willis.

"He was just going to leave when you came," the woman told her husband.

"Sure glad you were here for me to thank you," he said to Willis.

"But I think he has to be on his way now," she went on.

The cowboy turned questioningly to Willis, who said this was true.

"Well then, I'll saddle up Daisy for you."

Willis said goodbye to the woman and followed the man out back. He watched the cowboy bring the mare out of the barn and throw a saddle over her. After he had tightened the cinches and patted the horse, he turned and studied the Indian. "You're Darkcat, aren't you?"

Now the blue eyes were cold and challenging. And Willis said it was so.

"I thought so as soon as I saw you." After a pause the cowboy went on, "For what you did, I can never repay you. It was as good as I've ever seen; not many white men would've done it." Another long pause. "We got the word on you last week." Their eyes met and locked. "You know I can't let you go, don't you?" said the cowboy.

"I know," nodded Willis.

"All right. But for saving my wife and baby, I can give you a day."

Willis stared, not understanding.

"I've been in the saddle for five days, so I'm taking a day's rest. By then my wife'll be up and I can leave again. And then I'm coming out after you. Understand?"

"I understand," said Willis.

"She's a good horse." He patted the mare. "She'll give you all she's got, you won't have to drive her much." He put a canteen of water up over the saddle horn and asked Willis if he wanted any food.

Willis refused, and they stood in silence. "Well," said Willis finally, "I'll leave now." He swung up into the saddle and gazed down at the man.

"I'll be starting out tomorrow about this time," said the cowboy.

Willis nodded.

"And make no mistake about it, I mean to get you."

"I understand," Willis repeated.

He moved the mare south toward the hills; he turned once and saw the cowboy still watching him. And he knew he was in for more and now perhaps even harder pursuit.

The farther he rode, the less did he feel the cowboy had been boyish or silly or downright crazy. He saw that even amid the whites, there was still a touch of the old, undying spirit. He felt he was closer to this blue-eyed white man than to any of his own people. When they finally did meet again over a gun or knife, it would be a more fitting finish for either than anything else that might come their way.

---

## YOU AND THE STORY

This is the kind of story that supports a major unifying idea, a central **theme**. In some stories, a major theme is hinted at but not spelled out. In this story, the central theme is spelled out in one of the poems on the living room wall: "Everyman is me, I am his brother." The author is trying to show us a common human bond stronger than the divisions created by a history of conflict. Our general human fellow feeling is stronger than resentment, prejudice, or distrust. Does this idea become believable or convincing in this story? Do you think the central character in this story would have done in real life what he did? Do you think the other people in the story would have reacted the way they did? How *real* is this story to you?

---

### A Closer Look

(1) Several **flashbacks** provided by the author fill in the background that the central character brings to the events in the story. Before he came to the house in the foothills, what kind of person was Darkcat? How would you describe him in a character sketch called something like "An Indian Born Too Late"? What is his attitude toward his tribe and its history? How much does he know about the past, and what does he think about it? What has been his experience with reservation life, and how does he feel about it? Why did he "jump" the reservation? What are his thoughts about his pursuers and about a possible capture? (Why does he kill the horse before he leaves it behind?)

(2) What is the role of the white people in the events of the actual story? How much is Darkcat aware of white people's attitudes toward Indians? (Where in the story does he show what he knows or thinks about their attitudes?) At the end, why does he feel "closer to this blue-eyed white man than to any of his own people"? Do you think that the way the white man acted at the end was "boyish or silly or downright crazy"?

---

### Your Turn

Who is your hero or your heroine? Tell your reader or your listener about a person you consider admirable. Choose a modern person that you can look up to, that comes close to your ideal standards.

# Let My People Go

Precious Lord, take my hand,
Lead me on, let me stand,
I am tired, I am weak, I am worn.
Through the storm, through the night
Lead me on to the light,
Take my hand, precious Lord,
Lead me home.

—Thomas A. Dorsey

In recent years, many black Americans have discovered their own heritage, their own history. They have begun to listen to leaders who taught pride in their own culture, faith in their own strength. As one young girl from Birmingham said: "I want to know what the old songs are. I want to know that my parents were working for fifteen cents a day. I want to know what made me." In poems, stories, and plays by black writers, this search for the black American's true identity is a powerful major theme. Many black writers and artists deal with what it means to be different in a society that is mostly white. They tell us what it is like to be taught the common American ideals, hopes, and ways and then find constant barriers, visible and invisible, in their path. Richard Wright, the author of *Black Boy* and *Native Son*, once talked about the kind of "double vision" that results when the ideas we are taught and our actual experience *contradict* each other:

> I have spent most of my adult life and most of my waking hours brooding upon the destiny of the race to which I belong by accident of birth and by accident of history. . . . Being a Negro living in a white Western Christian society, I've never been allowed to blend, in a natural and healthy manner, with the culture and civilization of the West. This contradiction of being both Western and a man of color creates a distance, so to speak, between me and my environment.

Black writers and artists show us how their people have coped with their history of persecution and discrimination. For many years, their people turned for strength and encouragement to their religion. In the emotional sermons of their preachers, in their powerful hymns and spirituals, and in the joyful rhythms of their gospel tunes, they found strength to bear the grim present and hope for a better future. Black music, "soul" music, has been a vital influence in the lives of black Americans. Richard Wright said about the blues that with all their "sense of defeat and downheartedness," they are deep down not really pessimistic:

> Their burden of woe and melancholy is redeemed . . . into an almost exultant affirmation of life, of love, . . . of movement, of hope. No matter how repressive was the American environment, the Negro never lost faith in or doubted his capacity to live.

In the old days, black leaders often counseled patience. They asked their followers to trust in the strength of the spirit and the justice of their cause. In the writings and the art of a younger generation, we often encounter a smouldering anger ready to burst into open flame. In a book like Ralph Ellison's *Invisible Man*, we see angry young blacks turn their backs upon leaders who preached humility, who asked them to "know their place." Many younger black writers admired leaders like Malcolm X, who openly expressed their feelings about white America. In the following selections, black Americans, of both the older and the younger generation, speak for themselves.

Because I had loved so deeply,
Because I had loved so long,
God in His great compassion
Gave me the gift of song.

—Paul Laurence Dunbar,
"Compensation"

Through the ages, people have expressed their deepest feelings through poetry and song. The poems and songs of black Americans eloquently express a whole range of powerful emotions, from anger, bitterness, and despair to pride and exuberant joy. As you listen to the voices speaking in the following selections, how often can you say: "I understand the way you feel. I would share in your feelings if I were in your shoes"?

Spirituals

# Go Down, Moses

Go down, Moses,
Way down in Egyptland
Tell old Pharaoh
To let my people go.

When Israel was in Egyptland
Let my people go
Oppressed so hard they could not stand
Let my people go.

Go down, Moses,
Way down in Egyptland
Tell old Pharaoh
"Let my people go."

"Thus saith the Lord," bold Moses said,
"Let my people go;
If not I'll smite your first-born dead
Let my people go.

"No more shall they in bondage toil,
Let my people go;
Let them come out with Egypt's spoil,
Let my people go."

The Lord told Moses what to do
Let my people go;
To lead the children of Israel through,
Let my people go.

Go down, Moses,
Way down in Egyptland,
Tell old Pharaoh,
"Let my people go!"

# I Thank God I'm Free at Last

Free at last, free at last.
I thank God I'm free at last,
Free at last, free at last,
I thank God I'm free at last.

Way down yonder in the graveyard walk,
I thank God I'm free at last.
Me and my Jesus goin' to meet and talk,
I thank God I'm free at last.

On my knees when the light passes by,
I thank God I'm free at last.
Thought my soul would arise and fly,
I thank God I'm free at last.

Some of these mornings bright and fair,
I thank God I'm free at last,
Going to meet my Jesus in the middle of the air,
I thank God I'm free at last.

---

### YOU AND THE POEMS

(1) Even in the oldest poems written in English, poets were not telling entirely new stories, but were in part *reminding* their listeners of traditional stories of gods and heroes. When a poet reminds us of a traditional story in a very brief mention or hint, we call the reference an **allusion.** In several of the old Negro spirituals that go back to the times of slavery, a traditional story from the Bible (often the Old Testament) is more than hinted at, but it is still retold in a very simple form. Only what mattered most to the listeners was kept. How much do you remember of the traditional Bible story about the Israelites in Egypt? What in the story mattered most to the people who made "Go Down, Moses" one of the best-known old-time spirituals? What are some of the things that gave this story such a powerful appeal?

(2) Many old spirituals owe their power to a basic promise repeated over and over: release from suffering and oppression—if not in this world, then in the hereafter. Look at some of the words used in many of the spirituals and poems dealing with this basic theme: *oppression, bondage, toil, slavery.* How do these differ in what they bring to mind? (Look at some of the words that are used for the opposite idea—the idea of liberation: *freedom, liberty, emancipation.* How do these words differ from each other in meaning or use?)

(3) In many traditional hymns and ballads, the last line of each stanza is repeated in the same or very similar form as a **refrain.** In these two spirituals, the refrain sums up in especially strong and memorable form the basic message of each poem. How does each refrain sum up the central message? (Why do you think each became a much-quoted and well-remembered line?)

---

### Your Turn

Can you find a recording that includes these and other spirituals? (Or can you arrange for a group to sing some of the spirituals for your class?)

## Langston Hughes

# Uncle Tom

Within—
The beaten pride.
Without—
The grinning face,
The low, obsequious,
Double bow,
The sly and servile grace
Of one the white folks
Long ago
Taught well
To know his
Place.

# Porter

I must say
Yes, sir,
To you all the time.
Yes, sir!
Yes, sir!
All my days
Climbing up a great big mountain
Of yes, sirs!

Rich old white man
Owns the world.
Gimme yo' shoes
To shine.

Yes, sir!

# Graduation

Cinnamon and rayon,
Jet and coconut eyes,
Mary Lulu Jackson
Smooths the skirt
At her thighs.

Mama, portly oven,
Brings remainders from the kitchen
Where the people all are icebergs
Wrapped in checks and wealthy.

DIPLOMA in its new frame:
Mary Lulu Jackson,
Eating chicken,
Tells her mama she's a typist
And the clicking of the keys
Will spell the name
Of a job in a fine office
Far removed from basic oven,
Cookstoves,
And iceberg's kitchen.

Mama says, *Praise Jesus!*
*Until then*
*I'll bring home chicken!*

The DIPLOMA bursts its frame
To scatter star-dust in their eyes.

Mama says, *Praise Jesus!*
*The colored race will rise!*
Mama says,
*Praise Jesus!*

Then,
Because she's tired,
She sighs.

## YOU AND THE POEMS

Langston Hughes (1902–1967) was the most famous of an earlier generation of black American poets. Besides being the most widely admired black poet of his time, Hughes made it his lifework to help collect and preserve the folklore and history of black Americans. He also was a leader in the movement that made black Americans explore the roots of Afro-American culture and tradition in the African past. Some of his best-known poems use the folk speech and the everyday experiences of ordinary people. Answer the following questions about these examples:

(1) Older people often complain how hard it is to make the younger generation understand what they had to go through. They often find it hard to make a young person understand what they think and feel. Pretend you are one of the three older people in these poems: "Uncle Tom," the porter, or Mama. Try to explain to a grandson or a granddaughter what kind of person you are: Explain what kind of experience you had to go through. Say what you really think and feel.

(2) Be the grandson or granddaughter of one of the older people in these poems. Write a poem or short passage in answer to what one of them has said to you.

Arna Bontemps
# A Black Man Talks of Reaping

I have sown beside all waters in my day.
I planted deep, within my heart the fear
That wind or fowl would take the grain away.
I planted safe against this stark, lean year.

I scattered seed enough to plant the land
In rows from Canada to Mexico,
But for my reaping only what the hand
Can hold at once is all that I can show.

Yet what I sowed and what the orchard yields
My brother's sons are gathering stalk and root,
Small wonder then my children glean in fields
They have not sown, and feed on bitter fruit.

## YOU AND THE POEM

(1) A story often carries its message most powerfully when it is stripped to its essentials. This poem is like a biblical **parable** in its use of a simple story to carry a basic point. Do you remember any biblical parable that involves sowing and reaping?

(2) What do the words *stark* and *lean* have in common? How and why do farmers "scatter seed"? How is "gleaning" different from "reaping"?

(3) For centuries, most people lived on farms; they were close to the soil. The rhythms of seed-time and harvest were part of everybody's life. In this poem, the poet carries through a detailed comparison between the cycle of sowing and reaping on the one hand and the history of black Americans on the other. We are not *told* the poet is making a comparison. We are merely *shown* the images of seed-time and reaping. These images "speak for themselves"—we ourselves conclude that these pictures have a meaning other than the ordinary one of real harvests. We call language that speaks to us through pictures such as these metaphorical. A **metaphor** is an image that carries with it not its ordinary everyday meaning but another meaning that is more important to the poet. In this poem, we see a **sustained metaphor** at work: The comparison is carried through into many separate details that all are part of the whole picture. How many different parts of the larger picture can you find in the poem? What meaning does each carry?

(4) In poetry that is traditional in form, a

**rhyme** word often concludes a sentence. This way, it can make us pause; it can help a thought sink in. (Show several examples in this poem.) The last rhyme word in this poem is part of the phrase "bitter fruit." This phrase stays with us as we think about the poem as a whole. Show how this phrase sums up the message of the poem—show how the whole poem leads up to it.

(5) How do you think this poem should be read? When it is read right, how do you think it would affect the listeners? How would they feel? What would they think?

### Your Turn

Arna Bontemps (born 1902) became known both as a poet himself and as a collector and editor of black American poetry from the earliest days to modern times.

Introducing his collection, *American Negro Poetry* (1963), he mentioned the following especially as among the best-known poems by black American writers: Paul Laurence Dunbar, "We Wear the Mask"; Countee Cullen, "Yet Do I Marvel"; Claude McKay, "If We Must Die"; Langston Hughes, "The Negro Speaks of Rivers"; Margaret Walker, "For My People." Other poems among the most often mentioned and quoted poems by black writers include Paul Laurence Dunbar, "Sympathy"; Langston Hughes, "Mother to Son"; Gwendolyn Brooks, "The Chicago *Defender* Sends a Man to Little Rock"; Nikki Giovanni, "Nikki-Rosa." You and your classmates may want to select from among these and other possible choices for a special reading of poetry by black American authors.

Robert Hayden

# Runagate, Runagate

[NARRATOR'S VOICE]    Runs falls rises stumbles on from darkness
          into darkness
and the darkness thicketed with shapes of
          terror
and the hunters pursuing and the hounds
          pursuing
and the night cold and the night long and
          the river
to cross and the jack-muh-lanterns
          beckoning beckoning
and blackness ahead and when shall I
          reach that somewhere
morning and keep on going and never
          turn back and keep on going

[MANY VOICES]    Runagate
          Runagate
               Runagate

[CHORUS]    Many thousands rise and go
many thousands crossing over

[SINGLE VOICE]    O mythic North
O star-shaped yonder Bible city

[NARRATOR'S VOICE]    Some go weeping and some rejoicing
some in coffins and some in carriages
some in silks and some in shackles

[SINGLE VOICE]    Rise and go or fare you well

[CHORUS]    No more auction block for me
no more driver's lash for me

[OWNER'S VOICE]    "If you see my Pompey, 30 yrs of age,
new breeches, plain stockings, negro
          shoes;
if you see my Anna, likely young
          mulatto

branded E on the right cheek, R on the
  left,
catch them if you can and notify subscriber.''
[NARRATOR'S VOICE]  Catch them if you can, but it won't be
  easy.

They'll dart underground when you try
   to catch them,
plunge into quicksand, whirlpools,
mazes,
turn into scorpions when you try to
catch them.

[CHORUS]    And before I'll be a slave
I'll be buried in my grave

[NARRATOR'S VOICE]    North star and bonanza gold
I'm bound for the freedom, freedombound
and oh Susyanna don't you cry for me

[MANY VOICES]    Runagate
Runagate

---

## YOU AND THE POEM

(1) This poem vividly recreates a key page in American history. During much of the nineteenth century, American political life was dominated by the issue of slavery vs. abolition. Even in states where slavery was illegal, the issue of slavery was kept before people's consciences by the arrival of runaway slaves—the "runagates" of Robert Hayden's poem. Could you give a quick capsule report to fill in the *historical background* for this poem? What was the "underground railroad"? What was the Fugitive Slave Law? Who were Harriet Tubman, William Lloyd Garrison, and Harriet Beecher Stowe?

(2) Robert Hayden (born 1913) often uses some of the techniques of experimental modern poetry. His poems often make us follow impressions, memories, and quotations as they might pass through someone's mind. We follow a flow or stream of associations that have a common thread or a common theme. Look at some of the passages that sound like quoted talk or songs in this poem. Why would they be passing through the fugitive's mind? Where do some of them seem to come from? Are any of them familiar?

(3) What is the overall mood of this poem? Is it a poem of hope or despair? What is the overall pattern?

---

### Your Turn

Prepare this poem for a choral reading by members of your class. (You may want to change or adapt the distribution of voices as necessary.) How do you think the different voices should sound? How do you think the different parts should be read?

## Robert Hayden
# Frederick Douglass

When it is finally ours, this freedom, this liberty, this
    beautiful
and terrible thing, needful to man as air,
usable as earth; when it belongs at last to all,
when it is truly instinct, brain matter, diastole, systole,
reflex action; when it is finally won; when it is more
than the gaudy mumbo jumbo of politicians:
this man, this Douglass, this former slave, this Negro
beaten to his knees, exiled, visioning a world
where none is lonely, none hunted, alien,
this man, superb in love and logic, this man
shall be remembered. Oh, not with statues' rhetoric,
not with legends and poems and wreaths of bronze alone,
but with the lives grown out of his life, the lives
fleshing his dream of the beautiful, needful thing.

---

### YOU AND THE POEM

Frederick Douglass (1817–1895), in his famous *Autobiography*, told the story of his own rebellion against and escape from slavery. As a journalist and as a public speaker, he became a leader of the anti-slavery movement in the United States. Answer the following questions about this poem written in his honor:

(1) Freedom is often described as beautiful. What other adjectives are used to describe it in the first three lines of this poem? Are any unexpected? Why?

(2) The "diastole" and the "systole" are two phases of the heartbeat—expansion and contraction. The poet is looking forward to a time when freedom is as naturally a part of life as the heartbeat. What other comparisons, implied or spelled out, help him express this idea?

(3) *Rhetoric* was traditionally the art of public speech. What kind of "speaking" would statues do—and what does the poet think of it? How are "wreaths" and "bronze" traditionally used to help commemorate someone—to make people remember and honor the person?

(4) How does the poet want the man he writes about to be remembered?

---

### Your Turn

Among the leaders who have spoken and written most eloquently about the aspirations of black Americans are Frederick Douglass, W. E. B. DuBois, and Martin Luther King. From the writings or published speeches of one of these, select a passage that you feel still speaks powerfully to people today. Prepare the passage for oral presentation to the class.

• In his book *God's Trombones,* James Weldon Johnson re-created in verse the kind of sermons that he had heard black ministers preach in his youth. Johnson remembered vividly the personal magnetism of the preachers, their gestures and the rhythm of their voices building up the excitement in the room. He remembered the congregation being "moved by the spirit," punctuating the sermon with their "amens" and "hallelujahs." They often provided an accompaniment of soft singing or humming to the sermon in progress. He said about the old-time Negro preacher:

It was through him that the people of diverse languages and customs who were brought here from diverse parts of Africa and thrown into slavery were given their first sense of unity and solidarity. He was the first shepherd of this bewildered flock. His power for good or ill was very great. It was the old-time preacher who for generations was the mainspring of hope and inspiration for the Negro in America.

The old-time preacher was generally a man far above the average in intelligence; he was, not infrequently, a man of positive genius. The earliest of these preachers must have virtually committed many parts of the Bible to memory through hearing the scriptures read or preached from in the white churches which the slaves attended. They were the first of the slaves to learn to read, and their reading was confined to the Bible, and specifically to the more dramatic passages of the Old Testament.

The old-time Negro preacher was above all an orator, and in good measure an actor. . . . He often possessed a voice that was a marvelous instrument, a voice he could modulate from a sepulchral whisper to a crashing thunder clap. . . . He had the power to sweep his hearers before him; and so himself was often swept away.

> Listen!—Listen!
> All you sons of Pharaoh.
> Who do you think can hold God's people
> When the Lord God himself has said,
> Let my people go?

---

James Weldon Johnson

# Noah Built the Ark

[NARRATOR'S VOICE]  Man, as he multiplied on the earth,
Increased in wickedness and sin.
He went on down from sin to sin,
From wickedness to wickedness,
Murder and lust and violence,
Till the earth was corrupt and rotten with flesh,
An abomination in God's sight.
And God was angry at the sins of men.
And God got sorry that he ever made man.

[GOD'S VOICE] And he said: "I will destroy him.
I'll bring down judgment on him with a flood.
I'll destroy ev'rything on the face of the earth,
Man, beasts and birds, and creeping things."
[NARRATOR'S VOICE] And he did—
Ev'rything but the fishes.

But Noah was a just and righteous man.
Noah walked and talked with God.

*Noah Built the Ark*   **539**

|                      | And, one day, God said to Noah, |
| [GOD'S VOICE]        | He said: "Noah, build thee an ark. |

And, one day, God said to Noah,
[GOD'S VOICE] He said: "Noah, build thee an ark.
Build it out of gopher wood.
Build it good and strong.
Pitch it within and pitch it without.
And build it according to the measurements
That I will give to thee.
Build it for you and all your house,
And to save the seeds of life on earth;
For I'm going to send down a mighty flood
To destroy this wicked world."

[NARRATOR'S VOICE] And Noah commenced to work on the ark.
And he worked for about one hundred years.
And ev'ry day the crowd came round
To make fun of Old Man Noah.
[CROWD VOICES] And they laughed and they said: "Tell us, old man,
Where do you expect to sail that boat
Up here amongst the hills?"
[NARRATOR'S VOICE] But Noah kept on a-working.
And ev'ry once in a while Old Noah would stop,
He'd lay down his hammer and lay down his saw,
And take his staff in hand;
And with his long, white beard a-flying in the wind,
And the gospel light a-gleaming from his eye,
Old Noah would preach God's word:

[NOAH'S VOICE] "Sinners, oh, sinners,
Repent, for the judgment is at hand.
Sinners, oh, sinners,
Repent, for the time is drawing nigh.
God's wrath is gathering in the sky.
God's a-going to rain down rain on rain.
God's a-going to loosen up the bottom of the deep,
And drown this wicked world.
Sinners, repent while yet there's time
For God to change his mind."
[YOUNG FELLOW'S VOICE] Some smart young fellow said: "This old man's
Got water on the brain."
[NARRATOR'S VOICE] And the crowd all laughed—Lord, but didn't they
laugh;
And they paid no mind to Noah,
But kept on sinning just the same.

One bright and sunny morning,
Not a cloud nowhere to be seen,

[GOD'S VOICE] God said to Noah: "Get in the ark!"
[NARRATOR'S VOICE] And Noah and his folks all got in the ark,
And all the animals, two by two,
A he and a she marched in.
[GOD'S VOICE] Then God said: "Noah, Bar the door!"
[NARRATOR'S VOICE] And Noah barred the door.

And a little black spot begun to spread,
Like a bottle of ink spilling over the sky;
And the thunder rolled like a rumbling drum;
And the lightning jumped from pole to pole;
And it rained down rain, rain, rain,
Great God, but didn't it rain!
For forty days and forty nights
Waters poured down and waters gushed up;
And the dry land turned to sea.
And the old ark-a she begun to ride;
The old ark-a she begun to rock;
Sinners came a-running down to the ark;
Sinners came a-swimming all round the ark;
Sinners pleaded and sinners prayed—
Sinners wept and sinners wailed—
But Noah'd done barred the door.

And the trees and the hills and the mountain tops
Slipped underneath the waters.
And the old ark sailed that lonely sea—
For twelve long months she sailed that sea,
A sea without a shore.

*Noah Built the Ark* **541**

Then the waters begun to settle down,
And the ark touched bottom on the tallest peak
Of old Mount Ararat.
The dove brought Noah the olive leaf,
And Noah when he saw that the grass was green,
Opened up the ark, and they all climbed down,
The folks, and the animals, two by two,
Down from the mount to the valley.
And Noah wept and fell on his face
And hugged and kissed the dry ground.

And then—

[GOD'S VOICE]  God hung out his rainbow cross the sky,
And he said to Noah: "That's my sign!
No more will I judge the world by flood—
Next time I'll rain down fire."

## YOU AND THE POEM

As you read this "sermon in verse," can you get into the spirit? Can you feel some of the emotions that the congregation felt when it was carried away by the preacher's eloquence? Your class may want to stage a choral reading of this sermon. How would you assign the different speaking parts? How would you help the speakers bring out the strong emotions and the strong rhythms of this poem?

## A Closer Look

(1) In his preface to *God's Trombones*, Johnson explained why he did not write these old-time sermons in the **dialect,** or folk speech, of the old days. The preachers used dialect in their everyday speech, but they went beyond its narrow boundaries when they preached: "They were all saturated with the sublime phraseology of the Hebrew prophets and steeped in the idioms of King James English, so when they preached and warmed to their work they spoke another language, far removed from traditional dialect. It was really a fusion of Negro idioms with Bible English." How familiar is "Bible English" to today's readers? Explain briefly each of the following: *multiply, wicked, corrupt, abomination, righteous, ark, commence, gospel, repent, draw nigh.*

(2) This poem has a strong rhythm brought about by much use of **repetition**. The speaker uses repetition to drive home a point or to build up to a high point in the sermon. He repeats whole phrases, or he echoes words or ideas from a preceding sentence. Often, the same word or expression starts several statements in a row. Find *five* passages of two or more lines that show the preacher's use of repetition. Show how repetition is used in each passage.

- Maya Angelou is a widely traveled actress and writer who has directed stage and television productions. She has written for newspapers and the stage. Her autobiographical *I Know Why the Caged Bird Sings* was published in 1970. The book tells the story of her growing up as a Southern black girl determined to "defy the odds." When she was three, her parents separated. She and her brother Bailey went to live with their grandmother in Stamps, a small town in Arkansas. Their grandmother owned a general merchandise store there that was at the same time a kind of social center for the black people living there. Maya Angelou was raised in the spirit of old-time religion. She went to an all-black school and tried out as a servant girl in a white woman's kitchen. Her book is the story of her strong loyalties to her relatives and her friends, and of her determination to overcome the traditional barriers in a black girl's path. The following chapter from her book tells the story of graduation day at her school.

---

Maya Angelou

# Lift Every Voice and Sing

The children in Stamps trembled visibly with anticipation. Some adults were excited too, but to be certain the whole young population had come down with graduation epidemic. Large classes were graduating from both the grammar school and the high school. Even those who were years removed from their own day of glorious release were anxious to help with preparations as a kind of dry run. The junior students who were moving into the vacating classes' chairs were tradition-bound to show their talents for leadership and management. They strutted through the school and around the campus exerting pressure on the lower grades. Their authority was so new that occasionally if they pressed a little too hard it had to be overlooked. After all, next term was coming, and it never hurt a sixth-grader to have a play sister in the eighth grade, or a tenth-year student to be able to call a twelfth-grader Bubba. So all was endured in a spirit of shared understanding. But the graduating classes themselves were the nobility. Like travelers with exotic destinations on their minds, the graduates were remarkably forgetful. They came to school without their books, or tablets or even pencils. Volunteers fell over themselves to secure replacements for the missing equipment. When accepted, the willing workers might or might not be thanked, and it was of no importance to the pregraduation rites. Even teachers were respectful of the now quiet and aging seniors, and tended to speak to them, if not as equals, as beings only slightly below themselves. After all tests were returned and grades given, the student body, which acted like an extended family, knew who did well, who excelled, and what piteous ones had failed.

Unlike the white high school, Lafayette County Training School distinguished itself by having neither lawn, nor hedges, nor tennis court, nor climbing ivy. Its two buildings (main classrooms, the grade school and home economics) were set on a dirt hill with no fence to limit either its boundaries or those of bordering farms. There was a large expanse to the left of the school which was used alternately as a baseball diamond or a basketball court. Rusty hoops on the swaying poles represented the permanent recreational equipment, although bats and balls could be borrowed from the P. E. teacher if the borrower was qualified and if the diamond wasn't occupied.

Over this rocky area relieved by a few shady tall persimmon trees the graduating class walked. The girls often held hands and no longer bothered to speak to the lower students. There was a sadness about them, as if this old world was not their home and they were bound for higher ground. The boys, on the other hand, had become more friendly, more outgoing—a decided change from the closed attitude they projected while studying for finals. Now they seemed not ready to give up the old school, the familiar paths and classrooms. Only a small percentage would be continuing on to college—one of the South's A & M (agricultural and mechanical) schools, which trained Negro youths to be carpenters, farmers, handymen, masons, maids, cooks, and baby nurses. Their future rode heavily on their shoulders, and blinded them to the collective joy that had pervaded the lives of the boys and girls in the grammar school graduating class.

Parents who could afford it had ordered new shoes and ready-made clothes for themselves from Montgomery Ward or Sears Roebuck. They also engaged the best seamstresses to make the floating graduating dresses and to alter second-hand pants which would be pressed to a military slickness for the important event.

Oh, it was important, all right. White folks would attend the ceremony, and two or three would speak of God and home, and the Southern way of life, and Mrs. Parsons, the principal's wife, would play the graduation march while the lower-grade graduates paraded down the aisles and took their seats below the platform. The high school seniors would wait in empty classrooms to make their dramatic entrance.

In the Store I was the person of the moment: The birthday girl. The center. My class was wearing butter-yellow piqué dresses, and Momma launched out on mine. She smocked the yoke into tiny crisscrossing puckers, then shirred the rest of the bodice. Her dark fingers ducked in and out of the lemony cloth as she embroidered raised daisies around the hem. Before she considered herself finished she had added a crocheted cuff on the puff sleeves, and a crocheted collar.

I was going to be lovely, a walking model of all the various styles of fine hand sewing, and it didn't worry me that I was only twelve years old and merely graduating from the eighth grade. Besides, many teachers in Arkansas Negro schools had only that diploma and were licensed to impart widsom.

The days had become longer and more noticeable. The faded beige of former times had been replaced with strong and sure colors. I began to see my classmates' clothes, their skin tones, and the dust that waved off pussy willows. Clouds that lazed across the sky were objects of great concern to me. Their shiftier shapes might have held a message that in my new

happiness and with a little bit of time I'd soon decipher. During that period I looked at the arch of heaven so religiously my neck kept a steady ache. I had taken to smiling more often, and my jaws hurt from the unaccustomed activity. Between the two physical sore spots, I suppose I could have been uncomfortable, but that was not the case. As a member of the winning team (the graduating class of 1940) I had outdistanced unpleasant sensations by miles. I was headed for the freedom of open fields.

Youth and social approval allied themselves with me and we trammeled memories of slights and insults. The wind of our swift passage remodeled my features. Lost tears were pounded to mud and then to dust. Years of withdrawal were brushed aside and left behind, as hanging ropes of parasitic moss.

My work alone had awarded me a top place and I was going to be one of the first called in the graduating ceremonies. On the classroom blackboard, as well as on the bulletin board in the auditorium, there were blue stars and white stars and red stars. No absences, no tardinesses, and my academic work was among the best of the year. I could say the preamble to the Constitution even faster than my brother Bailey. We had timed ourselves often: "We the people of the United States in order to form a more perfect union . . ." I had memorized the Presidents from Washington to Roosevelt in chronological as well as alphabetical order.

My hair pleased me too. Gradually the black mass had lengthened and thickened, so that it kept at last to its braided pattern, and I didn't have to yank my scalp off when I tried to comb it.

Louise and I had rehearsed the exercises until we tired out ourselves. Henry Reed was class valedictorian. He was a small, very black boy with hooded eyes, a long, broad nose and an oddly shaped head. I had admired him for years because each term he and I vied for the best grades in our class. Most often he bested me, but instead of being disappointed I was pleased that we shared top places between us. Like many Southern black children, he lived with his grandmother, who was as strict as Momma and as kind as she knew how to be. He was courteous, respectful, and soft-spoken to elders, but on the playground he chose to play the roughest games. I admired him. Anyone, I reckoned, sufficiently afraid or sufficiently dull could be polite. But to be able to operate at a top level with both adults and children was admirable.

His valedictory speech was entitled "To Be or Not To Be." The rigid tenth-grade teacher had helped him write it. He'd been working on the dramatic stresses for months.

The weeks until graduation were filled with heady activities. A group of small children were to be presented in a play about buttercups and daisies and bunny rabbits. They could be heard throughout the building practicing their hops and their little songs that sounded like silver bells. The older girls (nongraduates, of course) were assigned the task of making refreshments for the night's festivities. A tangy scent of ginger, cinnamon, nutmeg, and chocolate wafted around the home economics building as the budding cooks made samples for themselves and their teachers.

In every corner of the workshop, axes and saws split fresh timber as the woodshop boys made sets and stage scenery. Only the graduates were left out of the general bustle. We were free to sit in the library at the back of the building or look in quite detachedly, naturally, on the measures being taken for our event.

Even the minister preached on graduation the Sunday before. His subject was, "Let your light so shine that men will see your good works and praise your Father, Who is in Heaven." Although the sermon was addressed to us, he used the occasion to speak to backsliders, gamblers, and general ne'er-do-wells. But since he had called our names at the beginning of the service, we were mollified.

Among Negroes the tradition was to give presents to children going only from one grade to another. How much more important this was when the person was graduating at the top of the class. Uncle Willie and Momma had sent away for a Mickey Mouse watch like Bailey's. Louise gave me four embroidered handkerchiefs. (I gave her three crocheted doilies.) Mrs. Sneed, the minister's wife, made me an underskirt to wear for graduation, and nearly every customer gave me a nickel or maybe even a dime with the instruction "Keep on moving to higher ground," or some such encouragement.

Amazingly the great day finally dawned and I was out of bed before I knew it. I threw open the back door to see it more clearly, but Momma said, "Sister, come away from that door and put your robe on."

I hoped the memory of that morning would never leave me. Sunlight was itself still young, and the day had none of the insistence maturity would bring it in a few hours. In my robe and barefoot in the backyard, under cover of going to see about my new beans, I gave myself up to the gentle warmth and thanked God that no matter what evil I had done in my life He had allowed me to live to see this day. Somewhere in my fatalism I had expected to die, accidentally, and never have the chance to walk up the stairs in the auditorium and gracefully receive my hard-earned diploma. Out of God's merciful bosom I had won reprieve.

Bailey came out in his robe and gave me a box wrapped in Christmas paper. He said he had saved his money for months to pay for it. It felt like a box of chocolates, but I knew Bailey wouldn't save money to buy candy when we had all we could want under our noses.

He was as proud of the gift as I. It was a soft leather-bound copy of a collection of poems by Edgar Allan Poe, or, as Bailey and I called him, "Eap." I turned to "Annabel Lee" and we walked up and down the garden rows, the cool dirt between our toes, reciting the beautifully sad lines.

Momma made a Sunday breakfast although it was only Friday. After we finished the blessing, I opened my eyes to find the watch on my plate. It was a dream of a day. Everything went smoothly and to my credit. I didn't have to be reminded or scolded for anything. Near evening I was too jittery to attend to chores, so Bailey volunteered to do all before his bath.

Days before, we had made a sign for the Store, and as we turned out the lights Momma hung the cardboard over the doorknob. It read clearly: CLOSED. GRADUATION.

My dress fitted perfectly and everyone said that I looked like a sunbeam in it. On the hill, going toward the school, Bailey walked behind with Uncle Willie, who muttered, "Go on, Ju." He wanted him to walk ahead with us because it embarrassed him to have to walk so slowly. Bailey said he'd let the ladies walk together, and the men would bring up the rear. We all laughed, nicely.

Little children dashed by out of the dark like fireflies. Their crepe-paper dresses and butterfly wings were not made for running and we heard more than one rip, dryly, and the regretful "uh uh" that followed.

The school blazed without gaiety. The windows seemed cold and unfriendly from the lower hill. A sense of ill-fated timing crept over me, and if Momma hadn't reached for my hand I would have drifted back to Bailey and Uncle Willie,

and possibly beyond. She made a few slow jokes about my feet getting cold, and tugged me along to the now strange building.

Around the front steps, assurance came back. There were my fellow "greats," the graduating class. Hair brushed back, legs oiled, new dresses and pressed pleats, fresh pocket handkerchiefs and little handbags, all home sewn. Oh, we were up to snuff, all right. I joined my comrades and didn't even see my family go in to find seats in the crowded auditorium.

The school band struck up a march and all classes filed in as had been rehearsed. We stood in front of our seats, as assigned, and on a signal from the choir director, we sat. No sooner had this been accomplished than the band started to play the national anthem. We rose again and sang the song, after which we recited the pledge of allegiance. We remained standing for a brief minute before the choir director and the principal signaled to us, rather desperately I thought, to take our seats. The command was so unusual that our carefully rehearsed, smooth-running machine was thrown off. For a full minute we fumbled for our chairs and bumped into each other awkwardly. Habits change or solidify under pressure, so in our state of nervous tension we had been ready to follow our usual assembly pattern: the American national anthem, then the pledge of allegiance, then the song every black person I knew called the Negro National Anthem. All done in the same key, with the same passion and most often standing on the same foot.

Finding my seat at last, I was overcome with a presentiment of worse things to come. Something unrehearsed, unforeseen was going to happen, and we were going to be made to look bad. I distinctly remember the choice of pronoun. It was "we," the graduating class, the unit, that concerned me then.

The principal welcomed "parents and friends" and asked the Baptist minister to lead us in prayer. His invocation was brief and punchy, and for a second I thought we were getting back on the high road to right action. When the principal came back to the dais, however, his voice had changed. Sounds always affected me profoundly and the principal's voice was one of my favorites. During assembly it melted and lowed weakly into the audience. It had not been in my plan to listen to him, but my curiosity was piqued and I straightened up to give him my attention.

He was talking about Booker T. Washington, our "late great leader," who said we can be as close as the fingers on the hand, etc. . . . Then he said a few vague things about friendship and the friendship of kindly people to those less fortunate than themselves. With that his voice nearly faded, thin, away. Like a river diminished to a stream and then to a trickle. But he cleared his throat and said, "Our speaker tonight, who is also our friend, came from Texarkana to deliver the commencement address, but due to the irregularity of the train schedule, he's going to, as they say, 'speak and run.' " He said that we understood and wanted the man to know that we were most grateful for the time he was able to give us and then something about how we were willing always to adjust to another's program, and without more ado—"I give you Mr. Edward Donleavy."

Not one but two white men came through the door offstage. The shorter one walked to the speaker's platform, and the tall one moved over to the center seat and sat down. But that was our principal's seat, and already occupied. The dislodged gentleman bounced around for a long breath or two before the Baptist minister gave him his chair, then with more dignity than the situation deserved, the minister walked off the stage.

Donleavy looked at the audience once (on reflection, I'm sure that he wanted only to reassure himself that we were really there), adjusted his glasses and began to read from a sheaf of papers.

He was glad "to be here and to see the work going on just as it was in the other schools."

At the first *Amen* from the audience I willed the offender to immediate death by choking on the word. But *Amen*'s and *Yes, sir*'s began to fall around the room like rain through a ragged umbrella.

He told us of the wonderful changes we children in Stamps had in store. The Central School (naturally, the white school was Central) had already been granted improvements that would be in use in the fall. A well-known artist was coming from Little Rock to teach art to them. They were going to have the newest microscopes and chemistry equipment for their laboratory. Mr. Donleavy didn't leave us long in the dark over who made these improvements available to Central High. Nor were we to be ignored in the general betterment scheme he had in mind.

He said that he had pointed out to people at a very high level that one of the first-line football tacklers at Arkansas Agricultural and Mechanical College had graduated from good old Lafayette County Training School. Here fewer *Amen*'s were heard. Those few that did break through lay dully in the air with the heaviness of habit.

He went on to praise us. He went on to say how he had bragged that "one of the best basketball players at Fisk sank his first ball right here at Lafayette County Training School." The white kids were going to have a chance to become Galileos and Madame Curies and Edisons and Gauguins, and our boys (the girls weren't even in on it) would try to be Jesse Owenses and Joe Louises.

Owens and the Brown Bomber were great heroes in our world, but what school official in Little Rock had the right to decide that those two men must be our only heroes? Who decided that for Henry Reed to become a scientist he had to work like George Washington Carver, as a bootblack, to buy a lousy microscope? Bailey was obviously always going to be too small to be an athlete, so which concrete angel glued to what country seat had decided that if my brother wanted to become a lawyer he had to first pay penance for his skin by picking cotton and hoeing corn and studying correspondence books at night for twenty years?

The man's dead words fell like bricks around the auditorium and too many settled in my belly. Constrained by hard-learned manners, I couldn't look behind me, but to my left and right the proud graduating class of 1940 had dropped their heads. Every girl in my row had found something new to do with her handkerchief. Some folded the tiny squares into love knots, and some into triangles, but most were wadding them, then pressing them flat on their yellow laps.

On the dais, the ancient tragedy was being replayed. Professor Parsons sat, a sculptor's reject, rigid. His large, heavy body seemed devoid of will or willingness, and his eyes said he was no longer with us. The other teachers examined the flag (which was draped stage right) or their notes, or the windows which opened on our now-famous playing diamond.

Graduation, the hush-hush magic time of frills and gifts and congratulations and diplomas, was finished for me before my name was called. The accomplishment was nothing. The meticulous maps, drawn in three colors of ink, learning and spelling decasyllabic words, memorizing the whole of *The Rape of Lucrece*—it was for nothing. Donleavy had exposed us.

We were maids and farmers, handymen and washerwomen, and anything higher that we aspired to was quite farcical and presumptuous. . . .

Donleavy was running for election, and assured our parents that if he won we could count on having the only colored paved playing field in that part of Arkansas. Also—he never looked up to acknowledge the grunts of acceptance—also, we were bound to get some new equipment for the home economics building and the workshop.

He finished, and since there was no need to give any more than the most perfunctory *thank-you*'s, he nodded to the men on the stage, and the tall white man who was never introduced joined him at the door. They left with the attitude that now they were off to something really important. (The graduation ceremonies at Lafayette County Training School had been a mere preliminary.)

The ugliness they left was palpable—an uninvited guest who wouldn't leave. The choir was summoned and sang a modern arrangement of "Onward, Christian Soldiers," with new words pertaining to graduates seeking their place in the world. But it didn't work. Elouise, the daughter of the Baptist minister, recited "Invictus," and I could have cried at the impertinence of "I am the master of my fate, I am the captain of my soul."

My name had lost its ring of familiarity and I had to be nudged to go and receive my diploma. All my preparations had fled. I neither marched up to the stage like a conquering Amazon, nor did I look in the audience for Bailey's nod of approval. Marguerite Johnson, I heard the name again, my honors were read, there were noises in the audience of appreciation, and I took my place on the stage as rehearsed.

I thought about colors I hated: ecru, puce, lavender, beige, and black.

There was shuffling and rustling around

Henry had been a good student in elocution. His voice rose on tides of promise and fell on waves of warnings. The English teacher had helped him to create a sermon winging through Hamlet's soliloquy. To be a man, a doer, a builder, a leader, or to be a tool, an unfunny joke, a crusher of funky toadstools. I marveled that Henry could go through with the speech as if we had a choice.

I had been listening and silently rebutting each sentence with my eyes closed; then there was a hush, which in an audience warns that something unplanned is happening. I look up and saw Henry Reed, the conservative, the proper, the A student, turn his back to the audience and turn to us (the proud graduating class of 1940) and sing, nearly speaking,

"Lift ev'ry voice and sing
Till earth and heaven ring
Ring with the harmonies of liberty . . ."

It was the poem written by James Weldon Johnson. It was the music composed by J. Rosamond Johnson. It was the Negro National Anthem. Out of habit we were singing it.

Our mothers and fathers stood in the dark hall and joined the hymn of encouragement. A kindergarten teacher led the small children onto the stage and the buttercups and daisies and bunny rabbits marked time and tried to follow:

Stony the road we trod
Bitter the chastening rod
Felt in the days when hope, unborn, had died.
Yet with a steady beat
Have not our weary feet
Come to the place for which our fathers sighed?

Every child I knew had learned that song with his ABC's and along with "Jesus Loves Me, This I Know." But I personally had never heard it before. Never heard the words, despite the thousands of

me, then Henry Reed was giving his valedictory address, "To Be or Not To Be." Hadn't he heard the whitefolks? We couldn't *be,* so the question was a waste of time. Henry's voice came out clear and strong. I feared to look at him. Hadn't he got the message? There was no "nobler in the mind" for Negroes because the world didn't think we had minds, and they let us know it. "Outrageous fortune"? Now, that was a joke. When the ceremony was over I had to tell Henry Reed some things. That is, if I still cared. Not "rub," Henry, "erase." "Ah, there's the erase." Us.

times I had sung them. Never thought they had anything to do with me.

On the other hand, the words of Patrick Henry had made such an impression on me that I had been able to stretch myself tall and trembling and say, "I know not what course others may take, but as for me, give me liberty or give me death." Now I heard, really for the first time:

We have come over a way that with tears
  has been watered,
We have come, treading our path through the
  blood of the slaughtered.

While echoes of the song shivered in the air, Henry Reed bowed his head, said "Thank you," and returned to his place in the line. The tears that slipped down many faces were not wiped away in shame.

We were on top again. As always, again. We survived. The depths had been icy and dark, but now a bright sun spoke to our souls. I was no longer simply a member of the proud graduating class of 1940; I was a proud member of the wonderful, beautiful Negro race.

---

## YOU AND THE STORY

In some things we read, there is much external action: quarrels, accidents, escapes. But in some of our reading the action is internal: the important developments take place in the thoughts and feelings of the people we read about. What is happening is happening in the minds and hearts of the people. In this chapter from Maya Angelou's book, the important changes are changes in **mood**. Much of what we see and hear mirrors the mood of the people involved. Can you trace the three major stages as the mood changes in this selection? Your teacher may ask you to do one or more of the following:

—Describe as fully as you can the *holiday mood* at the beginning of the chapter. Choose details or examples that would help a reader get into the spirit of the occasion. (What are some of the details that mirror this holiday mood best?)

—Describe as fully as you can the mood of *disappointment* at the actual ceremony. What caused it? How did people feel, and how did they show it? (Where do we get first hints of the change that is going to take place? What details would help the reader share in the general sense of being let down?)

—How would you describe the mood of the author and the audience *at the end*? How would you help an outsider share in the emotions felt by these people?

---

## A Closer Look

(1) This selection shows something about the nature of *segregation* as a traditional feature of the lives of the people involved. What have you previously learned or read about segregation? Drawing on this selection and your previous background, provide a brief account of segregation as part of our history to a visitor from a different planet.

(2) Members of America's minorities look for worthy *models* for their young people to follow or to imitate. What kind of models do you think this author would set up for young people? What does she admire in her classmates and in her teachers? What are some of the major qualities that you think she would try to teach young people?

A valedictory address given by a member of the graduating class is literally a "farewell speech." Assume your school practiced the custom of having a member of *each* class give a send-off speech to his or her classmates at the conclusion of the school year. Prepare the talk you would give. (What *kind* of talk would it be? Discuss your plans, and theirs, with your classmates.)

---

Language/Composition Activity C3

WORKING WITH ETYMOLOGY

# Going to the Roots

Often a combination of two things helps us understand a new or difficult word: (1) *context*—the way a word fits into a sentence or a paragraph: (2) *etymology*—our knowledge of word roots, of the building blocks that helped make up the word. Sometimes a word grew from its root in a roundabout way. For instance, Maya Angelou talks about the "meticulous" maps she and her classmates prepared. The root *met-* means "fear." When we do something meticulously, we do it very carefully, very accurately—as if we are *fearful* we might do a poor job. But in many other words, the root or roots show more directly. For instance, a "valedictorian" gives his speech at graduation. *Vale* is the Latin word for "farewell." *Dict-* is a Latin root that means "spoken." The valedictorian is literally giving a "farewell speech." For each of the italicized words in the following sentences, can you show how *both* the context and our knowledge of word roots help us "make sense" of the word?

1. The children trembled with *anticipation*. (*ante*, "ahead of time"; *cip-*, "take")
2. The student body knew who *excelled* and who failed. (*ex*, "out"; *cel-*, "rise")
3. A large *expanse* to the left of the school was used as a baseball diamond. (*ex*, "out"; *pans-*, "stretch")
4. The clouds held a message that I'd soon *decipher*. (*de*, "out of"; *cipher*, "code")
5. In my *fatalism*, I had expected to die accidentally. (*fate*, "what the oracle has spoken")
6. Out of God's merciful bosom, I had won *reprieve*. (*re*, "again"; *prieve*, *prove* "test")
7. What we aspired to was farcical and *presumptuous*. (*pre*, "before"; *sum*, "take, reach")
8. Now they were to do something really important—the ceremonies at Lafayette had been a mere *preliminary*. (*pre* "before"; *limin-* "threshold")
9. Henry had been a good student in *elocution;* his voice rose on tides of promise and fell on waves of warning. (*e* "out"; *locut-*, "speak")
10. The English teacher had helped him create a sermon winging through Hamlet's *soliloquy*. (*sol-*, "alone"; *loqui*, "speak")

● Ralph Ellison was born in Oklahoma City in 1914. He became famous as the author of the novel *Invisible Man*, which was published in 1952. Its hero traveled a familiar route in his search for who he was: He experienced segregated schools in the South and life in the ghetto of the big city. He became politically involved with groups trying to use him for their purposes. He watched a grass-roots leader trying to make his people proud of their roots in Africa. Wherever he went, he felt no one ever saw him as a person in his own right: He was typed as a member of his racial group. His own identity as a human being was invisible to the world. In the following short story, Ralph Ellison writes about two young boys who are learning pride in their history and in who they are.

## Ralph Ellison

# Mister Toussan

*Once upon a time*
*The goose drink wine*
*Monkey chew tobacco*
*And he spit white lime.*

—Rhyme used as a prologue
to Negro slave stories

"I hope they all gits rotten and the worms git in 'em," the first boy said.

"I hopes a big windstorm comes and blows down all the trees," said the second boy.

"Me too," the first boy said. "And when old Rogan comes out to see what happened I hope a tree falls on his head and kills him."

"Now jus' look a-yonder at them birds," the second boy said, "they eating all they want and when we asked him to let us git some off the ground he had to come calling us names and chasing us home!"

"Doggonit," said the second boy, "I hope them birds got poison in they feet!"

The two small boys, Riley and Buster, sat on the floor of the porch, their bare feet resting upon the cool earth as they stared past the line on the paving where the sun consumed the shade, to a yard directly across the street. The grass in the yard was very green and a house stood against it, neat and white in the morning sun. A double row of trees stood alongside the house, heavy with cherries that showed deep red against the dark green of the leaves and dull dark brown of the branches. They were watching an old man who rocked himself in a chair as he stared back at them across the street.

"Just look at him," said Buster. "Ole Rogan's so scared we gonna git some of his ole cherries he ain't even got sense enough to go in outa the sun!"

"Well, them birds is gitting theirs," said Riley.

"They mockingbirds."

"I don't care what kinda birds they is, they sho in them trees."

"Yeah, old Rogan don't see *them*. Man, white folks ain't got no sense."

They were silent now, watching the

darting flight of the birds into the trees. Behind them they could hear the clatter of a sewing machine: Riley's mother was sewing for the white folks. It was quiet and, as the woman worked, her voice rose above the whirring machine in song.

"Your mamma sho can sing, man," said Buster.

"She sings in the choir," said Riley, "and she sings all the leads in church."

"Shucks, I know it," said Buster. "You tryin' to brag?"

As they listened they heard the voice rise clear and liquid to float upon the morning air:

I got wings, you got wings,
All God's chillun got a-wings
When I git to heaven gonna put on my wings
Gonna shout all ovah God's heaven.
Heab'n, heab'n
Everybody talkin' bout heab'n ain't going
   there
Heab'n, heab'n, Ah'm gonna fly all ovah God's
   heab'n. . . .

She sang as though the words possessed a deep and throbbing meaning for her, and the boys stared blankly at the earth, feeling the somber, mysterious calm of church. The street was quiet and even old Rogan had stopped rocking to listen. Finally the voice trailed off to a hum and became lost in the clatter of the busy machine.

"Sure wish I could sing like that," said Buster.

Riley was silent, looking down to the end of the porch where the sun had eaten a bright square into the shade, fixing a flitting butterfly in its brilliance.

"What would you do if you had wings?" he said.

"Shucks, I'd outfly an eagle, I wouldn't stop flying till I was a million, billion, trillion, zillion miles away from this ole town."

"Where'd you go, man?"

"Up north, maybe to Chicago."

"Man, if I had wings I wouldn't never settle down."

"Me, neither. With wings you could go anywhere, even up to the sun if it wasn't too hot. . . ."

". . . I'd go to New York. . . ."

"Even around the stars. . ."

"Or Dee-troit, Michigan. . ."

"You could git some cheese off the moon and some milk from the Milky Way. . . ."

"Or anywhere else colored is free. . . ."

"I bet I'd loop-the-loop. . . ."

"And parachute. . . ."

"I'd land in Africa and git me some diamonds. . . ."

"Yeah, and them cannibals would eat you too," said Riley.

"The heck they would, not fast as I'd fly away. . . ."

"Man, they'd catch you and stick soma them long spears in you!" said Riley.

Buster laughed as Riley shook his head gravely: "Boy, you'd look like a black pincushion when they got through with you," said Riley.

"Shucks, man, they couldn't catch me, them suckers is too lazy. The geography book says they 'bout the most lazy folks in the whole world," said Buster with disgust, "just black and lazy!"

"Aw naw, they ain't neither," exploded Riley.

"They is too! The geography book says they is!"

"Well, my ole man says they ain't!"

"How come they ain't then?"

" 'Cause my ole man says that over there they got kings and diamonds and gold and ivory, and if they got all them things, all of 'em cain't be lazy," said Riley. "Ain't many colored folks over here got them things."

"Sho ain't, man. The white folks won't let 'em," said Buster.

It was good to think that all the Africans were not lazy. He tried to remember all he had heard of Africa as he watched a purple pigeon sail down into the street and scratch where a horse had passed. Then, as he remembered a story his teacher had told him, he saw a car rolling swiftly up the street and the pigeon stretching its wings and lifting easily into the air, skimming the top of the car in its slow, rocking flight. He watched it rise and disappear where the taut telephone wires cut the sky above the curb. Buster felt good. Riley scratched his initials in the soft earth with his big toe.

"Riley, you know all them African guys ain't really that lazy," he said.

"I know they ain't," said Riley, "I just tole you so."

"Yeah, but my teacher tole me, too. She tole us 'bout one of them African guys named Toussan what she said whipped Napoleon!"

Riley stopped scratching the earth and looked up, his eyes rolling in disgust:

"Now how come you have to start lying?"

"Thass what she said."

"Boy, you oughta quit telling them things."

"I hope God may kill me."

"She said he was a *African*?"

"Cross my heart, man. . . ."

"Really?"

"Really, man. She said he come from a place named Hayti."

Riley looked hard at Buster and seeing the seriousness of the face felt the excitement of a story rise up within him.

"Buster, I'll bet a fat man you lyin'. What'd that teacher say?"

"Really, man, she said that Toussan and his men got up on one of them African mountains and shot down them pecker-wood soldiers fass as they'd try to come up. . . ."

"Why good-a-mighty!" yelled Riley.

"Oh boy, they shot'em down!" chanted Buster.

"Tell me about it, man!"

"And they throwed 'em all off the mountain. . . ."

". . . Goool-leee! . . ."

". . . And Toussan drove 'em cross the sand. . . ."

". . . Yeah! And what was they wearing, Buster? . . ."

"Man, they had on red uniforms and blue hats all trimmed with gold, and they had some swords, all shining what they called sweet blades of Damascus. . . ."

"Sweet blades of Damascus! . . ."

" . . . They really had 'em," chanted Buster.

"And what kinda guns?"

"Big, black cannon!"

"And where did ole what-you-call-'im run them guys? . . .

"His name was Toussan."

"Toussan! Just like Tarzan. . ."

"Not *Taar*-zan, dummy, *Toou*-zan!"

"Toussan! And where'd ole Toussan run 'em?"

"Down to the water, man. . ."

". . . To the river water . . ."

". . . Where some great big ole boats was waiting for 'em. . ."

". . . Go on, Buster!"

"An' Toussan shot into them boats. . . ."

". . . He shot into 'em. . . ."

"With his great big cannons. . ."

". . . Yeah!. . ."

". . . Made a-brass. . ."

". . . Brass. . ."

". . . An' his big black cannonballs started killin' them peckerwoods. . . ."

". . . Lawd, Lawd. . ."

". . . Boy, till them peckerwoods hollowed *'Please, please, Mister Toussan, we'll be good!'*"

"An' what'd Toussan tell em, Buster?"

" 'Boy,' he said in his big deep voice, *'I oughta drown all a-you.' *"

"An' what'd the peckerwoods say?"

"They said, 'Please, Please, *Please, Mister Toussan* . . .' "

". . . 'We'll be good,' " broke in Riley.

"Thass right, man," said Buster excitedly. He clapped his hands and kicked his heels against the earth, his black face glowing in a burst of rhythmic joy.

"Boy!"

"And what'd ole Toussan say then?"

"He said in his big deep voice: 'You all peckerwoods better be good, 'cause this is sweet Papa Toussan talking and my men is crazy 'bout white meat!' "

"Ho, ho, ho!" Riley bent double with laughter. The rhythm still throbbed within him and he wanted the story to go on and on. . . .

"Buster, you know didn't no teacher tell you that lie," he said.

"Yes she did, man."

"That teacher said there was really a guy like that what called hisself Sweet Papa Toussan?"

Riley's voice was unbelieving and there was a wistful expression in his eyes which Buster could not understand. Finally he dropped his head and grinned.

"Well," he said, "I bet thass what ole

Toussan said. You know how grown folks is, they cain't tell a story right, 'cepting real old folks like grandma."

"They sho cain't," said Riley. "They don't know how to put the right stuff to it."

Riley stood, his legs spread wide, and stuck his thumbs in the top of his trousers, swaggering sinisterly.

"Come on, watch me do it now, Buster. Now I bet ole Toussan looked down at them white folks standing just about like this and said in a soft easy voice: 'Ain't I done begged you white folks to quit messin' with me? . . .'"

"Thass right, quit messing with 'im," chanted Buster.

"'But naw, you-all had to come on anyway. . . .'"

". . . Jus' 'cause they was black . . ."

"Thass right," said Riley. "Then ole Toussan felt so bad and mad the tears come a-trickling down. . . ."

". . . He was really mad."

"And then, man, he said in his big bass voice: 'white folks, how come you-all cain't let us colored alone?'"

". . . An' he was crying. . . ."

". . . An' Toussan tole them peckerwoods: 'I been beggin' you-all to quit bothering us. . . .'"

". . . Beggin' on his bended knees! . . ."

"Then, man, Toussan got real mad and snatched off his hat and started stompin' up and down on it and the tears was tricklin' down and he said: 'You-all come tellin' me about Napoleon. . . .'"

"They was tryin' to make him scared, man. . . ."

"Toussan said: 'I don't care about no Napoleon. . . .'"

". . . Wasn't studyin' 'bout him. . . ."

". . . Toussan said: 'Napoleon ain't nothing but a man!' Then Toussan pulled back his shining sword like this, and twirled it at them peckerwoods' throats so hard it z-z-z-zinged in the air!"

"Now keep on, finish it, man," said Buster. "What'd Toussan do then?"

"Then you know what he did, he said: 'I oughta beat you peckerwoods!'"

"Thass right, and he did it too," said Buster. He jumped to his feet and fenced violently with five desperate imaginary soldiers, running each through with his imaginary sword. Buster watched from the porch, grinning.

"Toussan musta scared them white folks almost to death!"

"Yeah, thass 'bout the way it was," said Buster. The rhythm was dying now and he sat back upon the porch, breathing tiredly.

"It sho is a good story," said Riley.

"Hecks, man, all the stories my teacher tells us is good. She's a good ole teacher— but you know one thing?"

"Naw; what?"

"Ain't none of them stories in the books! Wonder why?"

"You know why, ole Toussan was too hard on them white folks, thass why."

"Oh, he was a hard man!"

"He was mean. . . ."

"But a good mean!"

"Toussan was clean. . . ."

". . . He was a good, clean mean," said Riley.

"Aw, man, he was sooo-preme" said Buster.

"Riiiley!!"

The boys stopped short in their word play, their mouths wide.

"Riley I say!" It was Riley's mother's voice.

"Ma'am?"

"She musta heard us cussin'," whispered Buster.

"Shut up, man. . . . What you want, Ma?"

"I says I wants you-all to go around in the backyard and play, you keeping up too much fuss out there. White folks says we tear up a neighborhood when we move in it and you-all out there jus' provin' them out true. Now git on round in the back."

"Aw, ma, we was jus' playing, ma. . . ."

"Boy, I said for you-all to go on."

"But, ma . . ."

"You hear me, boy!"

"Yessum, we going," said Riley. "Come on, Buster."

Buster followed slowly behind, feeling the dew upon his feet as he walked upon the shaded grass.

"What else did he do, man?" Buster said.

"Huh? Rogan?"

"Heck, naw! I mean Toussan."

"Doggone if I know, man—but I'm gonna ask that teacher."

"He was a fightin' son-of-a-gun, wasn't he, man?"

"He didn't stand for no foolishness," said Riley reservedly. He thought of other things now, and as he moved along he slid his feet easily over the short-cut grass, dancing as he chanted

Iron is iron,
And tin is tin,
And that's the way
The story . . .

"Aw come on man," interrupted Buster. "Let's go play in the alley. . . ."

And that's the way . . .

"Maybe we can slip around and git some cherries," Buster went on.

". . . the story ends," chanted Riley.

---

### YOU AND THE STORY

The "Mister Toussan" of this story is Toussaint L'Ouverture (1743–1803), who was the military and political leader of the people of Haiti in their fight against French colonial rule. Napoleon was rising to power as emperor of France at the time. How much can you find out about the historical events behind this story?

### A Closer Look

(1) Members of a group often object to unflattering stereotypes. Things are said about their group that do not apply to all members—and that may apply only to very few (or none). What stereotypes about black people did the author of this story want to help his readers overcome? Where and how? Are you aware of any stereotypes about a group to which you yourself belong? What are they? How do you react to them?

(2) In explaining words, a dictionary often gives *synonyms*, words that have nearly the same meaning. In each of the following sets, three of the words are synonyms of the italicized word. Find the one that is *not* a synonym. Explain what the other three have in common.

a. the *somber*, mysterious calm of church
   gloomy          serious
   melancholy      strange
b. the *taut* telephone lines
   tense           flabby
   stretched       tight
c. a *wistful* expression in his eyes
   cheerful        thoughtful
   longing         yearning
d. swaggering *sinisterly*
   threateningly   frighteningly
   noisily         evilly
e. he was *supreme*
   outstanding     highest
   ruling          attractive

(3) The boys in this story truly delight in *wordplay,* in playing games with words. For instance, they like to exaggerate, going all out to drive home a point or call a striking picture to our minds. Give several examples. What other kinds of wordplay can you find in this story?

## Your Turn

Find material for the life story of one of the following famous people. Prepare a short biographical report. Choose one:

Paul Laurence Dunbar
Harriet Tubman
Frederick Douglass
William E. B. Du Bois
Marian Anderson
Paul Robeson
Leontyne Price
Martin Luther King
Mahalia Jackson
Alexander Haley
Thurgood Marshall
Cicely Tyson

Language/Composition Activity C4

FOR SENTENCE PRACTICE

# The Added Touch

Ralph Ellison knows how to provide the kind of added detail that makes a scene real for the reader. In each of the following sentences, the main part of the statement gives us the main point or the essential information. But after the comma, the author provides the added touch that makes the scene come to life. Use each of these as a model sentence. Write a sentence of your own in which you follow the structure of the original sentence as closely as you can.

1. The two small boys sat on the floor of the porch, *their bare feet resting upon the cool earth.*

(Write your own sentence about someone you observed or noticed.)

2. A double row of trees stood alongside the house, *heavy with cherries that showed deep red against the dark green of the leaves.*

(Write your own sentence about a flower, tree, or other plant life.)

3. They were silent now, *watching the darting flight of the birds into the trees.*

(Write your own sentence about people watching something happen or being done.)

4. He fenced violently with five desperate imaginary soldiers, *running each through with his imaginary sword.*

(Write your own sentence about playacting or make-believe.)

• In the late fifties, a young gifted black woman named Lorraine Hansberry wrote a play that won the award given by the New York drama critics for the best play of the season. Her play, *A Raisin in the Sun,* was later made into a motion picture starring Sidney Poitier, Claudia MacNeil, and Ruby Dee. Lorraine Hansberry was born in Chicago in 1930 and grew up and went to school there. She moved to New York in 1950. In her play, the members of a black family in Chicago live out their daily struggles, their disappointments, and their hopes for the future. At the time the author wrote her play, black writers were beginning to tell white people some bitter truths about how America treated its black citizens. But part of the power of the play was that many spectators and readers for a few short hours forgot they were black or white. As one of the drama critics said when the play was first put on, "It is honest drama, catching up real people . . . It will make you proud of human beings."

## Lorraine Hansberry

# A Raisin in the Sun

To Mama: *in gratitude for the dream*

> What happens to a dream deferred?
> Does it dry up
> Like a raisin in the sun?
> Or fester like a sore—
> And then run?
> Does it stink like rotten meat?
> Or crust and sugar over—
> Like a syrupy sweet?
>
> Maybe it just sags
> Like a heavy load.
>
> *Or does it explode?*
>
> —Langston Hughes

## Cast of Characters

| | |
|---|---|
| RUTH YOUNGER | JOSEPH ASAGAI |
| TRAVIS YOUNGER | GEORGE MURCHISON |
| WALTER LEE YOUNGER (BROTHER) | KARL LINDNER |
| BENEATHA YOUNGER | BOBO |
| LENA YOUNGER (MAMA) | MOVING MEN |

# Act One

## Scene One

*The Younger living room would be a comfortable and well-ordered room if it were not for a number of contradictions to this state of being. Its furnishings are typical and undistinguished and their primary feature now is that they have clearly had to accommodate the living of too many people for too many years—and they are tired. Still, we can see that at some time, a time probably no longer remembered by the family (except perhaps for Mama) the furnishings of this room were actually selected with care and love and even hope—and brought to this apartment and arranged with taste and pride.*

*That was a long time ago. Now the once-loved pattern of the couch upholstery has to fight to show itself from under acres of crocheted doilies and couch covers which have themselves finally come to be more important than the upholstery. And here a table or a chair has been moved to disguise the worn places in the carpet; but the carpet has fought back by showing its weariness, with depressing uniformity, elsewhere on its surface.*

*Weariness has, in fact, won in this room. Everything has been polished, washed, sat on, used, scrubbed too often. All pretenses but living itself have long since vanished from the very atmosphere of this room.*

*Moreover, a section of this room, for it is not really a room unto itself, though the landlord's lease would make it seem so, slopes backward to provide a small kitchen area, where the family makes the meals that are eaten in the living room proper, which must also serve as dining room. The single window that has been provided for these "two" rooms is located in this kitchen area. The sole natural light the family may enjoy in the course of a day is only that which fights its way through this little window.*

*At left, a door leads to a bedroom which is shared by Mama and her daughter, Beneatha. At right, opposite, is a second room (which in the beginning of the life of this apartment was probably a breakfast room) which serves as a bedroom for Walter and his wife, Ruth.*

*Time: Sometime between World War II and the present.*

*Place: Chicago's South Side.*

*At Rise: It is morning dark in the living room. Travis is asleep on the make-down bed at center. An alarm clock sounds from within the bedroom at right, and presently Ruth enters from that room and closes the door behind her. She crosses sleepily toward the window. As she passes her sleeping son she reaches down and shakes him a little. At the window she raises the shade and a dusky South Side morning light comes in feebly. She fills a pot with water and puts it on to boil. She calls to the boy, between yawns, in a slightly muffled voice.*

*Ruth is about thirty. We can see that she was a pretty girl, even exceptionally so, but now it is apparent that life has been little that she expected, and disappointment has already begun to hang in her face. In a few years, before thirty-five even, she will be known among her people as a "settled woman."*

*She crosses to her son and gives him a good, final, rousing shake.*

RUTH: Come on now, boy, it's seven-thirty! [*Her son sits up at last, in a stupor of sleepiness.*] I say hurry up, Travis! You ain't the only person in the world got to use a bathroom! [*The child, a sturdy, handsome little boy of ten or eleven, drags himself out of the bed and almost blindly takes his towels and "today's clothes" from drawers and a closet and goes out to the bathroom, which is in an outside hall and which is shared by another family or families on the same floor. Ruth crosses to the bedroom door at right and opens it and calls in to her husband.]* Walter Lee! . . . It's after seven-thirty! Lemme see you do some waking up in there now! *[She waits.]* You better get up from there, man! It's after seven-thirty, I tell you. *[She waits again.]* All right, you just go ahead and lay there and next thing you know Travis be finished and Mr. Johnson'll be in there and you'll be fussing and cussing round here like a mad man! And be late too! *[She waits, at the end of patience.]* Walter Lee—it's time for you to get up! *[She waits another second and then starts to go into the bedroom, but is apparently satisfied that her husband has begun to get up. She stops, pulls the door to, and returns to the kitchen area. She wipes her face with a moist cloth and then runs her fingers through her sleep-disheveled hair in a vain effort and ties an apron around her housecoat. The bedroom door at right opens and her husband stands in the doorway in his pajamas, which are rumpled and mismated. He is a lean, intense young man in his middle thirties, inclined to quick nervous movements and erratic speech habits—and always in his voice there is an undertone of indictment.]*

WALTER: Is he out yet?

RUTH: What do you mean *out*? He ain't hardly got in there good yet.

WALTER: *[slowly wandering in, still more oriented to sleep than to a new day]* Well, what was you doing all that loud yelling for if I can't even get in there yet? *[stopping and thinking]* Check coming today?

RUTH: They *said* Saturday and this is just Friday and I hopes to God you ain't going to get up here first thing this morning and start talking to me 'bout no money—'cause I 'bout don't want to hear it.

WALTER: Something the matter with you this morning?

RUTH: No—I'm just sleepy as the devil. What kind of eggs you want?

WALTER: Not scrambled. *[Ruth starts to scramble eggs.]* Paper come? *[Ruth points impatiently to the rolled-up* Tribune *on the table, and he gets it and spreads it out and vaguely reads the front page.]* Set off another bomb yesterday.

RUTH: *[with maximum indifference]* Did they?

WALTER: *[looking up]* What's the matter with you?

RUTH: Ain't nothing the matter with me. And don't keep asking me that this morning.

WALTER: Ain't nobody bothering you. *[reading the news of the day absently again]* Say Colonel McCormick is sick.

RUTH: *[affecting tea-party interest]* Is he now? Poor thing.

WALTER: *[sighing and looking at his watch]* Oh, me. *[He waits.]* Now what is that boy doing in that bathroom all this time? He just going to have to start getting up earlier. I can't be being late to work on account of him fooling around in there.

RUTH: *[turning on him]* Oh, no he ain't going to be getting up no earlier no such thing! It ain't his fault that he can't get to bed no earlier nights 'cause he got a bunch of crazy good-for-nothing clowns sitting up running their mouths in what is supposed to be his bedroom after ten o'clock at night.

WALTER: That's what you mad about, ain't it? The things I want to talk about with my friends just couldn't be important in your mind, could they?

[*He rises and finds a cigarette in her handbag on the table and crosses to the little window and looks out, smoking and deeply enjoying this first one.*]

RUTH: [*almost matter-of-factly, a complaint too automatic to deserve emphasis*] Why you always got to smoke before you eat in the morning?

WALTER: [*at the window*] Just look at 'em down there . . . running and racing to work. . . . [*He turns and faces his wife and watches her a moment at the stove, and then, suddenly*] You look young this morning, baby.

RUTH: [*indifferently*] Yeah?

WALTER: Just for a second—stirring them eggs. It's gone now—just for a second it was—you looked real young again. [*then, drily*] It's gone now—you look like yourself again.

RUTH: Man, if you don't shut up and leave me alone.

WALTER: [*looking out to the street again*] The first thing a man ought to learn in life is not to make love to no colored woman the first thing in the morning. You all some evil people at eight o'clock in the morning.

[*Travis appears in the hall doorway, almost fully dressed and quite wide awake now, his towels and pajamas across his shoulders. He opens the door and signals for his father to make the bathroom in a hurry.*]

TRAVIS: [*watching the bathroom*] Daddy, come on! [*Walter gets his bathroom utensils and runs to the bathroom.*]

RUTH: Sit down and have your breakfast, Travis.

TRAVIS: Mama, this is Friday. [*gleefully*] Check coming tomorrow, huh?

RUTH: You get your mind off money and eat your breakfast.

TRAVIS: [*eating*] This is the morning we supposed to bring the fifty cents to school.

RUTH: Well, I ain't got no fifty cents this morning.

TRAVIS: Teacher say we have to.

RUTH: I don't care what your teacher say. I ain't got it. Eat your breakfast, Travis.

TRAVIS: I *am* eating.

RUTH: Hush up now and just eat! [*The boy gives her an exasperated look for her lack of understanding, and eats grudgingly.*]

TRAVIS: You think Grandmamma would have it?

RUTH: No! And I want you to stop asking your grandmother for money, you hear me?

TRAVIS: [*outraged*] Gaaaleee! I don't ask her, she just gimme it sometimes!

RUTH: Travis Willard Younger—I got too much on me this morning to be—

TRAVIS: Maybe Daddy—

RUTH: *Travis!* [*The boy hushes abruptly. They are both quiet and tense for several seconds.*]

TRAVIS: [*presently*] Could I maybe go carry some groceries in front of the supermarket for a little while after school then?

RUTH: Just hush, I said. [*Travis jabs his spoon into his cereal bowl viciously, and rests his head in anger upon his fists.*] If you through eating, you can get over there and make up your bed.

[*The boy obeys stiffly and crosses the room, almost mechanically, to the bed and more or less carefully folds the covering. He carries the folded bedding into his mother's room and returns with his books and cap.*]

TRAVIS: [*sulking and standing apart from

*her unnaturally*] I'm gone.

RUTH: [*looking up from the stove to inspect him automatically*] Come here. [*He crosses to her and she studies his head.*] If you don't take this comb and fix this here head, you better! [*Travis puts down his books with a great sigh of oppression, and crosses to the mirror. His mother mutters under her breath about his "slubbornness."*] 'Bout to march out of here with that head looking just like chickens slept in it! I just don't know where you get your slubborn ways. . . . And get your jacket, too. Looks chilly out this morning.

TRAVIS: [*with conspicuously brushed hair and jacket*] I'm gone.

RUTH: Get carfare and milk money— [*waving one finger*]—and not a single penny for no caps, you hear me?

TRAVIS: [*with sullen politeness*] Yes'm.

[*He turns in outrage to leave. His mother watches after him as in his frustration he approaches the door almost comically. When she speaks to him, her voice has become a very gentle tease.*]

RUTH: [*mocking; as she thinks he would say it*] Oh, Mama makes me so mad sometimes, I don't know what to do! [*She waits and continues to his back as he stands stock-still in front of the door.*] I wouldn't kiss that woman good-bye for nothing in this world this morning! [*The boy finally turns around and rolls his eyes at her, knowing the mood has changed and he is vindicated; he does not, however, move toward her yet.*] Not for nothing in this world! [*She finally laughs aloud at him and holds out her arms to him and we see that it is a way between them, very old and practiced. He crosses to her and allows her to embrace him warmly but keeps his face fixed with masculine rigidity. She holds him back from her presently and looks at him and runs her fingers over the features of his face. With utter gentleness—*] Now—whose little old angry man are you?

TRAVIS: [*The masculinity and gruffness start to fade at last.*] Aw gaalee— Mama . . .

RUTH: [*mimicking*] Aw—gaaaaalleeeee, Mama! [*She pushes him, with rough playfulness and finality, toward the door.*] Get on out of here or you going to be late.

TRAVIS: [*in the face of love, new aggressiveness*] Mama, could I *please* go carry groceries?

RUTH: Honey, it's starting to get so cold evenings.

WALTER: [*coming in from the bathroom and drawing a make-believe gun from a make-believe holster and shooting at his son*] What is it he wants to do?

RUTH: Go carry groceries after school at the supermarket.

WALTER: Well, let him go. . . .

TRAVIS: [*quickly, to the ally*] I have to— she won't gimme the fifty cents. . . .

WALTER: [*to his wife only*] Why not?

RUTH: [*simply, and with flavor*] 'Cause we don't have it.

WALTER: [*to Ruth only*] What you tell the boy things like that for? [*reaching down into his pants with a rather important gesture*] Here, son—

[*He hands the boy the coin, but his eyes are directed to his wife's. Travis takes the money happily.*]

TRAVIS: Thanks, Daddy.

[*He starts out. Ruth watches both of them with murder in her eyes. Walter stands and stares back at her with defiance, and suddenly reaches into his pocket again on an afterthought.*]

WALTER: [*without even looking at his son, still staring hard at his wife*] In fact, here's another fifty cents. . . . Buy yourself some fruit today—or take a taxicab to school or something!

TRAVIS: Whoopee—

[*He leaps up and clasps his father around the middle with his legs, and they face each other in mutual appreciation; slowly Walter Lee peeks around the boy to catch the violent rays from his wife's eyes and draws his head back as if shot.*]

WALTER: You better get down now—and get to school, man.

TRAVIS: [*at the door*] OK. Good-bye.

[*He exits.*]

WALTER: [*after him, pointing with pride*] That's *my* boy. [*She looks at him in disgust and turns back to her work.*] You know what I was thinking 'bout in the bathroom this morning?

RUTH: No.

WALTER: How come you always try to be so pleasant!

RUTH: What is there to be pleasant 'bout!

WALTER: You want to know what I was thinking 'bout in the bathroom or not!

RUTH: I know what you thinking 'bout.

WALTER: [*ignoring her*] 'Bout what me and Willy Harris was talking about last night.

RUTH: [*responding immediately—like a refrain*] Willy Harris is a good-for-nothing loudmouth.

WALTER: Anybody who talks to me has got to be a good-for-nothing loud-mouth, ain't he? And what you know about who is just a good-for-nothing loudmouth? Charlie Atkins was just a "good-for-nothing loudmouth" too, wasn't he! When he wanted me to go in the dry-cleaning business with him. And now—he's grossing a hundred thousand a year. A hundred thousand dollars a year! You still call *him* a loud mouth!

RUTH: [*bitterly*] Oh, Walter Lee . . .

[*She folds her head on her arms over the table.*]

WALTER: [*rising and coming to her and standing over her*] You tired, ain't you? Tired of everything. Me, the boy, the way we live—this beat-up hole—everything. Ain't you? [*Ruth doesn't look up, doesn't answer.*] So tired—moaning and groaning all the time, but you wouldn't do nothing to help, would you? You couldn't be on my side that long for nothing, could you?

RUTH: Walter, please leave me alone.

WALTER: A man needs for a woman to back him up. . . .

RUTH: Walter—

WALTER: Mama would listen to you. You know she listen to you more than she do me and Bennie. She think more of you. All you have to do is just sit down with her when you drinking your coffee one morning and talking 'bout things like you do and—[*He sits down beside her and demonstrates graphically what he thinks her methods and tone should be.*]—you just sip your coffee, see, and say easy-like that you been thinking 'bout that deal Walter Lee is so interested in, 'bout the store and all, and sip some more coffee, like what you saying ain't really that important to you—And the next thing you know, she be listening good and asking you questions and when I come home—I can tell her the details. This ain't no fly-by-night proposition, baby. I mean we figured it out, me and Willy and Bobo.

RUTH: [*with a frown*] Bobo?

WALTER: Yeah. You see, this little liquor store we got in mind cost seventy-five thousand and we figured the initial investment on the place be 'bout thirty thousand, see. That be ten thousand each. Of course, there's a couple of hundred you got to pay so's you don't spend your life just waiting for them clowns to let your license get approved—

RUTH: You mean graft?

WALTER: [frowning impatiently] Don't call it that. See there, that just goes to show you what women understand about the world. Baby, don't *nothing* happen for you in this world 'less you pay *somebody* off!

RUTH: Walter, leave me alone! [She raises her head and stares at him vigorously—then says, more quietly] Eat your eggs, they gonna be cold.

WALTER: [straightening up from her and looking off] That's it. There you are. Man say to his woman: I got me a dream. His woman say: Eat your eggs. [sadly, but gaining in power] Man say: I got to take hold of this here world, baby! And a woman will say: Eat your eggs and go to work. [passionately now] Man say: I got to change my life, I'm choking to death, baby! And his woman say—[in utter anguish as he brings his fists down on his thighs]— Your eggs is getting cold!

RUTH: [softly] Walter, that ain't none of our money.

WALTER: [not listening at all or even looking at her] This morning, I was lookin' in the mirror and thinking about it. . . . I'm thirty-five years old; I been married eleven years and I got a boy who sleeps in the living room—[very, very quietly]—and all I got to give him is stories about how rich white people live. . . .

RUTH: Eat your eggs, Walter.

WALTER: *Damn my eggs . . . damn all the eggs that ever was!*

RUTH: Then go to work.

WALTER: [looking up at her] See—I'm trying to talk to you 'bout myself—[He shakes his head with the repetition] and all you can say is eat them eggs and go to work.

RUTH: [wearily] Honey, you never say nothing new. I listen to you every day, every night and every morning, and you never say nothing new. [shrugging her shoulders] So you would rather *be* Mr. Arnold than be his chauffeur. So— I would *rather* be living in Buckingham Palace.

WALTER: That is just what is wrong with the colored woman in this world . . . they don't understand about building their men up and making 'em feel like they's somebody. Like they can do something.

RUTH: [drily, but intended to hurt] There *are* colored men who do things.

WALTER: Yeah, no thanks to the colored woman.

RUTH: Well, being a colored woman, I guess I can't help myself none.

[She rises and gets the ironing board and sets it up and attacks a huge pile of rough-dried clothes, sprinkling them in preparation for the ironing and then rolling them into tight fat balls.]

WALTER: [mumbling] We one group of men tied to a race of women with small minds.

[His sister Beneatha enters. She is about twenty, as slim and intense as her brother. She is not as pretty as her sister-in-law, but her lean, almost intellectual face has a handsomeness of its own. She wears a bright-red flannel nightie, and her thick hair stands wildly about her head. Her speech is a mixture of many things; it is different from the rest of the family's insofar as education has permeated her sense of English—and perhaps the Midwest rather than the South has finally—at last—won out in her inflection; but not altogether, because over all *of it is a soft slurring and transformed use of vowels which is the decided influence of the South Side. She passes through the room without looking at either Ruth or Walter and goes to the outside door and looks, a little blindly, out to the bathroom. She sees that it has been lost to the Johnsons. She closes the door with a sleepy vengeance and crosses to the table and sits down a little defeated.]*

BENEATHA: I am going to start timing those people.

WALTER: You should get up earlier.

BENEATHA: [*Her face in her hands. She is still fighting the urge to go back to bed.*] Really—would you suggest dawn? Where's the paper?

WALTER: [*pushing the paper across the table to her as he studies her almost clinically, as though he has never seen her before*] You a horrible-looking chick at this hour.

BENEATHA: [*drily*] Good morning, everybody.

WALTER: [*senselessly*] How is school coming along?

BENEATHA: [*in the same spirit*] Lovely. Lovely. And you know, biology is the greatest. [*looking up at him*] I dissected something that looked just like you yesterday.

WALTER: I just wondered if you've made up your mind and everything.

BENEATHA: [*gaining in sharpness and impatience*] And what did I answer yesterday morning—and the day before that?

RUTH: [*from the ironing board, like someone disinterested and old*] Don't be so nasty, Bennie.

BENEATHA: [*still to her brother*] And the day before that and the day before that!

WALTER: [*defensively*] I'm interested in you. Something wrong with that? Ain't many girls who decide—

WALTER and BENEATHA: [*in unison*] —"to be a doctor."

[*silence*]

WALTER: Have we figured out yet just exactly how much medical school is going to cost?

RUTH: Walter Lee, why don't you leave that girl alone and get out of here to work?

BENEATHA: [*Exits to the bathroom and bangs on the door.*] Come on out of there, please!

[*She comes back into the room.*]

WALTER: [*looking at his sister intently*] You know that the check is coming tomorrow.

BENEATHA: [*turning on him with a sharpness all her own*] That money belongs to Mama, Walter, and it's for her to decide how she wants to use it. I don't care if she wants to buy a house or a rocket ship or just nail it up somewhere and look at it. It's hers. Not ours—*hers*.

WALTER: [*bitterly*] Now ain't that fine! You just got your mother's interest at heart, ain't you, girl? You such a nice girl—but if Mama got that money she can always take a few thousand and help you through school—can't she?

BENEATHA: I have never asked anyone around here to do anything for me!

WALTER: No! And the line between asking and just accepting when the time comes is big and wide—ain't it!

BENEATHA: [*with fury*] What do you want from me, Brother—that I quit school or just drop dead, which!

WALTER: I don't want nothing but for you to stop acting holy 'round here. Me and Ruth done made some sacrifices for you—why can't you do something for the family?

RUTH: Walter, don't be dragging me in it.

WALTER: You are in it—don't you get up and go work in somebody's kitchen for the last three years to help put clothes on her back?

RUTH: Oh, Walter—that's not fair. . . .

WALTER: It ain't that nobody expects you to get on your knees and say thank you, Brother; thank you, Ruth; thank you, Mama—and thank you, Travis, for wearing the same pair of shoes for two semesters—

BENEATHA: [*as she drops to her knees*] Well—I *do*—all right?—thank everybody . . . and forgive me for ever wanting to be anything at all . . . forgive me, forgive me!

RUTH: Please stop it! Your mama'll hear you.

WALTER: Who told you you had to be a doctor? If you so crazy 'bout messing 'round with sick people—then go be a nurse like other women—or just get married and be quiet. . . .

BENEATHA: Well—you finally got it said. It took you three years but you finally got it said. Walter, give up; leave me alone—it's Mama's money.

WALTER: *He was my father, too!*

BENEATHA: So what? He was mine, too— and Travis's grandfather—but the insurance money belongs to Mama. Picking on me is not going to make her give it to you to invest in any liquor stores—[*under breath, dropping into a chair*]—and I for one say, God bless Mama for that!

WALTER: [*to Ruth*] See—did you hear? Did you hear!

RUTH: Honey, please go to work.

WALTER: Nobody in this house is ever going to understand me.

BENEATHA: Because you're a nut.

WALTER: Who's a nut?

BENEATHA: You—you are a nut. Thee is mad, boy.

WALTER: [*looking at his wife and sister*

*from the door, very sadly*] The world's most backward race of people, and that's a fact.

BENEATHA: [*turning slowly in her chair*] And then there are all those prophets who would lead us out of the wilderness—[*Walter slams out of the house.*]—into the swamps!

RUTH: Bennie, why you always gotta be pickin' on your brother? Can't you be a little sweeter sometimes? [*Door opens. Walter walks in.*]

WALTER: [*to Ruth*] I need some money for carfare.

RUTH: [*Looks at him, then warms; teasing, but tenderly*] Fifty cents? [*She goes to her bag and gets money.*] Here, take a taxi.

[*Walter exits. Mama enters. Mama is a woman in her early sixties, full-bodied and strong. She is one of those women of a certain grace and beauty who wear it so unobtrusively that it takes a while to notice. Her dark-brown face is surrounded by the total whiteness of her hair, and, being a woman who has adjusted to many things in life and overcome many more, her face is full of strength. She has, we can see, wit and faith of a kind that keep her eyes lit and full of interest and expectancy. She is, in a word, a beautiful woman. Her bearing is perhaps most like the noble bearing of the women of the Hereros of Southwest Africa—rather as if she imagines that as she walks she still bears a basket or a vessel upon her head. Her speech, on the other hand, is as careless as her carriage is precise—she is inclined to slur everything—but her voice is perhaps not so much quiet as simply soft.*]

MAMA: Who that 'round here slamming doors at this hour?

[*She crosses through the room, goes to the window, opens it, and brings in a feeble little plant growing doggedly in a small pot on the window sill. She feels the dirt and puts it back out.*]

RUTH: That was Walter Lee. He and Bennie was at it again.

MAMA: My children and they tempers. Lord, if this little old plant don't get more sun than it's been getting, it ain't never going to see spring again. [*She turns from the window.*] What's the matter with you this morning, Ruth? You looks right peaked. You aiming to iron all them things? Leave some for me. I'll get to 'em this afternoon. Bennie honey, it's too drafty for you to be sitting 'round half dressed. Where's your robe?

BENEATHA: In the cleaner's.

MAMA: Well, go get mine and put it on.

BENEATHA: I'm not cold, Mama, honest.

MAMA: I know—but you so thin. . . .

BENEATHA: [*irritably*] Mama, I'm not cold.

MAMA: [*seeing the make-down bed as Travis has left it*] Lord have mercy, look at that poor bed. Bless his heart—he tries, don't he?

[*She moves to the bed Travis has sloppily made up.*]

RUTH: No—he don't half try at all 'cause he knows you going to come along behind him and fix everything. That's just how come he don't know how to do nothing right now—you done spoiled that boy so.

MAMA: Well—he's a little boy. Ain't supposed to know 'bout housekeeping. My baby, that's what he is. What you fix for his breakfast this morning?

RUTH: [*angrily*] I feed my son, Lena!

MAMA: I ain't meddling—[*under breath; busybodyish*] I just noticed all last week he had cold cereal, and when it starts getting this chilly in the fall a child ought to have some hot grits or something when he goes out in the cold—

RUTH: [furious] I gave him hot oats—is that all right!

MAMA: I ain't meddling. [pause] Put a lot of nice butter on it? [Ruth shoots her an angry look and does not reply.] He likes lots of butter.

RUTH: [exasperated] Lena—

MAMA: [To Beneatha, Mama is inclined to wander conversationally sometimes.] What was you and your brother fussing 'bout this morning?

BENEATHA: It's not important, Mama.

[She gets up and goes to look out at the bathroom, which is apparently free, and she picks up her towels and rushes out.]

MAMA: What was they fighting about?

RUTH: Now you know as well as I do.

MAMA: [slowly shaking her head] Brother still worrying hisself sick about that money?

RUTH: You know he is.

MAMA: You had breakfast?

RUTH: Some coffee.

MAMA: Girl, you better start eating and looking after yourself better. You almost thin as Travis.

RUTH: Lena—

MAMA: Un-hunh?

RUTH: What are you going to do with it?

MAMA: Now don't you start, child. It's too early in the morning to be talking about money. It ain't Christian.

RUTH: It's just that he got his heart set on that store—

MAMA: You mean that liquor store that Willy Harris want him to invest in?

RUTH: Yes—

MAMA: We ain't no business people, Ruth. We just plain working folks.

RUTH: Ain't nobody business people till they go into business. Walter Lee say colored people ain't never going to start getting ahead till they start gambling on some different kinds of things

in the world—make investments and things.

MAMA: What done got into you, girl? Walter Lee done finally sold you on investing.

RUTH: No. Mama, something is happening between Walter and me. I don't know what it is—but he needs something—something I can't give him any more. He needs this chance, Lena.

MAMA: [frowning deeply] But liquor, honey—

RUTH: Well—just like Walter say—I spec people going to always be drinking themselves some liquor.

MAMA: Well—whether they drinks it or not ain't none of my business. But whether I go into business selling it to 'em is, and I don't want that on my ledger this late in life. [stopping suddenly and studying her daughter-in-law] Ruth Younger, what's the matter with you today? You look like you could fall over right there.

RUTH: I'm tired.

MAMA: Then you better stay home from work today.

RUTH: I can't stay home. She'd be calling up the agency and screaming at them, "My girl didn't come in today—send me somebody! My girl didn't come in!" Oh, she just have a fit. . . .

MAMA: Well, let her have it. I'll just call her up and say you got the flu—

RUTH: [laughing] Why the flu?

MAMA: 'Cause it sounds respectable to 'em. Something white people get, too. They know 'bout the flu. Otherwise they think you been cut up or something when you tell 'em you sick.

RUTH: I got to go in today. We need the money.

MAMA: Somebody would of thought my children done all but starved to death the way they talk about money here late. Child, we got a great big old check coming tomorrow.

RUTH: [sincerely, and self-righteously] Now that's your money. It ain't got nothing to do with me. We all feel like that—Walter and Bennie and me—even Travis.

MAMA: [thoughtfully, and suddenly very far away] Ten thousand dollars—

RUTH: Sure is wonderful.

MAMA: Ten thousand dollars.

RUTH: You know what you should do, Miss Lena? You should take yourself a trip somewhere. To Europe or South America or someplace—

MAMA: [throwing up her hands at the thought] Oh, child!

RUTH: I'm serious. Just pack up and leave! Go on away and enjoy yourself some. Forget about the family and have yourself a ball for once in your life—

MAMA: [drily] You sound like I'm just about ready to die. Who'd go with me? What I look like wandering 'round Europe by myself?

RUTH: Shoot, Mama—these here rich white women do it all the time. They don't think nothing of packing up they suitcases and piling on one of them big steamships and—swoosh!—they gone, child.

MAMA: Something always told me I wasn't no rich white woman.

RUTH: Well—what are you going to do with it then?

MAMA: I ain't rightly decided. [Thinking. She speaks now with emphasis.] Some of it got to be put away for Beneatha and her schoolin'—and ain't nothing going to touch that part of it. Nothing. [She waits several seconds, trying to make up her mind about something, and looks at Ruth a little tentatively before going on.] Been thinking that we maybe could meet the notes on a little old two-story somewhere, with a yard where Travis could play in the summertime, if we use part of the insurance for a down payment and everybody kind of pitch in. I could maybe take on a little day work again, few days a week—

RUTH: [studying her mother-in-law furtively and concentrating on her ironing, anxious to encourage without seeming to] Well, Lord knows, we've put enough rent into this here rattrap to pay for four houses by now. . . .

MAMA: [looking up at the words "rattrap" and then looking around and leaning back and sighing—in a suddenly reflective mood—] "Rattrap"—yes, that's all it is. [smiling] I remember just as well the day me and Big Walter moved in here. Hadn't been married but two weeks and wasn't planning on living here no more than a year. [She shakes her head at the dissolved dream.] We was going to set away, little by little, don't you know, and buy a little place out in Morgan Park. We had even picked out the house. [chuckling a little] Looks right dumpy today. But Lord, child, you should know all the dreams I had 'bout buying that house and fixing it up and making me a little garden in the back—[She waits and stops smiling.] And didn't none of it happen. [dropping her hands in a futile gesture]

RUTH: [Keeps her head down, ironing.] Yes, life can be a barrel of disappointments, sometimes.

MAMA: Honey, Big Walter would come in here some nights back then and slump down on that couch there and just look at the rug, and look at me and look at the rug and then back at me—and I'd know he was down then . . . really down. [After a second very long and thoughtful pause; she is seeing back to times that only she can see.] And then, Lord, when I lost that baby—little Claude—I almost thought I was going to lose Big Walter too. Oh, that man grieved hisself! He was one man to love his children.

RUTH: Ain't nothin' can tear at you like losin' your baby.

MAMA: I guess that's how come that man finally worked hisself to death like he done. Like he was fighting his own war with this here world that took his baby from him.

RUTH: He sure was a fine man, all right. I always liked Mr. Younger.

MAMA: Crazy 'bout his children! God knows there was plenty wrong with Walter Younger—hardheaded, mean, kind of wild with women—plenty wrong with him. But he sure loved his children. Always wanted them to have something—to be something. That's where Brother gets all these notions, I reckon. Big Walter used to say, he'd get right wet in the eyes sometimes, lean his head back with the water standing in his eyes and say, "Seem like God didn't see fit to give the black man nothing but dreams—but He did give us children to make them dreams seem worthwhile." [*She smiles.*] He could talk like that, don't you know.

RUTH: Yes, he sure could. He was a good man, Mr. Younger.

MAMA: Yes, a fine man—just couldn't never catch up with his dreams, that's all.

[*Beneatha comes in, brushing her hair and looking up to the ceiling, where the sound of a vacuum cleaner is heard.*]

BENEATHA: What could be so dirty on that woman's rugs that she has to vacuum them every single day?

RUTH: I wish certain young women 'round here who I could name would take inspiration about certain rugs in a certain apartment I could also mention.

BENEATHA: [*shrugging*] How much cleaning can a house need, for _____ sakes.

MAMA: [*not liking the Lord's name used thus*] Bennie!

RUTH: Just listen to her—just listen!

MAMA: If you use the Lord's name just one more time—

BENEATHA: [*somewhat like a whine*] Oh, Mama—

RUTH: Fresh—just fresh as salt, this girl!

BENEATHA: [*drily*] Well—if the salt loses its savor—

MAMA: Now that will do. I just ain't going to have you 'round here reciting the scriptures in vain—you hear me?

BENEATHA: How did I manage to get on everybody's wrong side by just walking into a room?

RUTH: If you weren't so fresh—

BENEATHA: Ruth, I'm twenty years old.

MAMA: What time you be home from school today?

BENEATHA: Kind of late. [*with sudden enthusiasm*] Madeline is going to start my guitar lessons today.

[*Mama and Ruth look up with the same expression.*]

MAMA: Your *what* kind of lessons?

BENEATHA: Guitar.

RUTH: Oh, Father!

MAMA: How come you done taken it in your mind to learn how to play the guitar?

BENEATHA: I just want to, that's all.

MAMA: [*smiling*] Lord, child, don't you know what to do with yourself? How long it going to be before you get tired of this now—like you got tired of that little play-acting group you joined last year? [*looking at Ruth*] And what was it the year before that?

RUTH: The horseback-riding club for which she bought that fifty-five-dollar riding habit that's been hanging in the closet ever since!

MAMA: [*to Beneatha*] Why you got to flit so from one thing to another, baby?

BENEATHA: [*sharply*] I just want to learn

to play the guitar. Is there anything wrong with that?

MAMA: Ain't nobody trying to stop you. I just wonders sometimes why you has to flit so from one thing to another all the time. You ain't never done nothing with all that camera equipment you brought home—

BENEATHA: I don't flit! I—I experiment with different forms of expression—

RUTH: Like riding a horse?

BENEATHA: —People have to express themselves one way or another.

MAMA: What is it you want to express?

BENEATHA: [angrily] Me! [Mama and Ruth look at each other and burst into raucous laughter.] Don't worry—I don't expect you to understand.

MAMA: [to change the subject] Who you going out with tomorrow night?

BENEATHA: [with displeasure] George Murchison again.

MAMA: [pleased] Oh—you getting a little sweet on him?

RUTH: You ask me, this child ain't sweet on nobody but herself—[under her breath] Express herself!

[They laugh.]

BENEATHA: Oh—I like George all right, Mama. I mean I like him enough to go out with him and stuff, but—

RUTH: [for devilment] What does and stuff mean?

BENEATHA: Mind your own business.

MAMA: Stop picking at her now, Ruth. [a thoughtful pause, and then a suspicious sudden look at her daughter as she turns in her chair for emphasis] What does it mean?

BENEATHA: [wearily] Oh, I just mean I couldn't ever really be serious about George. He's—he's so shallow.

RUTH: Shallow—what do you mean he's shallow? He's Rich!

MAMA: Hush, Ruth.

BENEATHA: I know he's rich. He knows he's rich, too.

RUTH: Well—what other qualities a man got to have to satisfy you, little girl?

BENEATHA: You wouldn't even begin to understand. Anybody who married a man like Walter could not possibly understand.

MAMA: [outraged] What kind of way is that to talk about your brother?

BENEATHA: Brother is a flip—let's face it.

MAMA: [to Ruth, helplessly] What's a flip?

RUTH: [glad to add kindling] She's saying he's crazy.

BENEATHA: Not crazy. Brother isn't really crazy yet—he—he's just an elaborate neurotic.

MAMA: Hush your mouth!

BENEATHA: As for George. Well. George looks good—he's got a beautiful car and he takes me to nice places and, as my sister-in-law says, he is probably the richest boy I will ever get to know and I even like him sometimes—but if the Youngers are sitting around waiting to see if their little Bennie is going to tie up the family with the Murchisons, they are wasting their time.

RUTH: You mean you wouldn't marry George Murchison if he asked you someday? That pretty, rich thing? Honey, I knew you was odd—

BENEATHA: No, I would not marry him if all I felt for him was what I feel now. Besides, George's family wouldn't really like it.

MAMA: Why not?

BENEATHA: Oh, Mama—the Murchisons are real-*live*-rich colored people, and the only people in the world who are more snobbish than rich white people are rich colored people. I thought everybody knew that. I've met Mrs. Murchison. She's a scene!

MAMA: You must not dislike people 'cause they well off, honey.

BENEATHA: Why not? It makes just as much sense as disliking people 'cause they are poor, and lots of people do that.

RUTH: [*a wisdom-of-the-ages manner; to Mama*] Well, she'll get over some of this—

BENEATHA: Get over it? What are you talking about, Ruth? Listen, I'm going to be a doctor. I'm not worried about who I'm going to marry yet—if I ever get married.

MAMA *and* RUTH: *If!*

MAMA: Now, Bennie—

BENEATHA: Oh, I probably will . . . but first I'm going to be a doctor, and George, for one, still thinks that's pretty funny. I couldn't be bothered with that. I am going to be a doctor and everybody around here better understand that!

MAMA: [*kindly*] 'Course you going to be a doctor, honey, God willing.

BENEATHA: [*drily*] God hasn't got a thing to do with it.

MAMA: You 'bout to get your fresh little jaw slapped!

RUTH: That's just what she needs, all right!

BENEATHA: Why? Why can't I say what I want to around here, like everybody else?

MAMA: It don't sound nice for a young girl to say things like that—you wasn't brought up that way. Me and your father went to trouble to get you and Brother to church every Sunday.

BENEATHA: Mama, you don't understand. It's all a matter of ideas, and God is just one idea I don't accept. It's not important. I am not going out and be immoral or commit crimes. It's just that I get tired of Him getting credit for all the things the human race achieves through its own stubborn effort. There is only man and it is he who makes miracles!

[*Mama absorbs this speech, studies her daughter and rises slowly and crosses to Beneatha and slaps her powerfully across the face. After, there is only silence and the daughter drops her eyes from her mother's face, and Mama is very tall before her.*]

MAMA: Now—you say after me, in my mother's house there is still God. [*There is a long pause and Beneatha stares at the floor wordlessly. Mama repeats the phrase with precision and cool emotion.*] In my mother's house there is still God.

BENEATHA: In my mother's house there is still God.

[*a long pause*]

MAMA: [*walking away from Beneatha, too disturbed for triumphant posture; then stopping and turning back to her daughter*] There are some ideas we ain't going to have in this house. Not long as I am at the head of this family.

BENEATHA: Yes, ma'am.

[*Mama walks out of the room.*]

RUTH: [*almost gently, with profound understanding*] You think you a woman, Bennie—but you still a little girl. What you did was childish—so you got treated like a child.

BENEATHA: I see. [*quietly*] I also see that everybody thinks it's all right for Mama to be a tyrant. But all the tyranny in the world will never put a God in the heavens!

[*She picks up her books and goes out.*]

RUTH: [*goes to Mama's door*] She said she was sorry.

MAMA: [*coming out of her room, going to her plant*] They frightens me, Ruth. My children.

RUTH: You got good children, Lena. They

just a little off sometimes—but they're good.

MAMA: No—there's something come down between me and them that don't let us understand each other and I don't know what it is. One done almost lost his mind thinking 'bout money all the time and the other done commence to talk about things I can't seem to understand in no form or fashion. What is it that's changing, Ruth?

RUTH: [*soothingly, older than her years*] Now . . . you taking it all too seriously. You just got strong-willed children and it takes a strong woman like you to keep 'em in hand.

MAMA: [*looking at her plant and sprinkling a little water on it*] They spirited all right, my children. Got to admit they got spirit—Bennie and Walter. Like this little plant that ain't never had enough sunshine or nothing—and look at it. . . .

[*She has her back to Ruth, who has had to stop ironing and lean against something and put the back of her hand against her forehead.*]

RUTH: [*trying to keep Mama from noticing*] You . . . sure . . . loves that little old thing, don't you? . . .

MAMA: Well, I always wanted me a garden like I used to see sometimes at the back of the houses down home. This plant is close as I ever got to having one. [*She looks out of the window as she replaces the plant.*] Lord, ain't nothing as dreary as the view from this window on a dreary day, is there? Why ain't you singing this morning, Ruth? Sing that "No Ways Tired." That song always lifts me up so—[*She turns at last to see that Ruth has slipped silently into a chair, in a state of semiconsciousness.*] Ruth! Ruth honey—what's the matter with you . . . Ruth!

## Scene Two

*It is the following morning; a Saturday morning, and housecleaning is in progress at the Youngers. Furniture has been shoved hither and yon and Mama is giving the kitchen-area walls a washing down. Beneatha, in dungarees, with a handkerchief tied around her face, is spraying insecticide into the cracks in the walls. As they work, the radio is on and a South Side disk-jockey program is inappropriately filling the house with a rather exotic saxophone blues. Travis, the sole idle one, is leaning on his arms, looking out of the window.*

TRAVIS: Grandmama, that stuff Bennie is using smells awful. Can I go downstairs, please?

MAMA: Did you get all them chores done already? I ain't seen you doing much.

TRAVIS: Yes'm—finished early. Where did Mama go this morning?

MAMA: [*looking at Beneatha*] She had to go on a little errand.

TRAVIS: Where?

MAMA: To tend to her business.

TRAVIS: Can I go outside then?

MAMA: Oh, I guess so. You better stay right in front of the house, though . . . and keep a good clear lookout for the postman.

TRAVIS: Yes'm. [*He starts out and decides to give his Aunt Beneatha a good swat on the legs as he passes her.*] Leave them poor little old cockroaches alone, they ain't bothering you none.

[*He runs as she swings the spray gun at him both viciously and playfully. Walter enters from the bedroom and goes to the phone.*]

MAMA: Look out there, girl, before you be spilling some of that stuff on that child!

TRAVIS: [*teasing*] That's right—look out now!

[*He exits.*]

BENEATHA: [*drily*] I can't imagine that it would hurt him—it has never hurt the roaches.

MAMA: Well, little boys' hides ain't as tough as South Side roaches.

WALTER: [*into phone*] Hello—Let me talk to Willy Harris.

MAMA: You better get over there behind the bureau. I seen one marching out of there like Napoleon yesterday.

WALTER: Hello, Willy? It ain't come yet. It'll be here in a few minutes. Did the lawyer give you the papers?

BENEATHA: There's really only one way to get rid of them, Mama—

MAMA: How?

BENEATHA: Set fire to this building.

WALTER: Good. Good. I'll be right over.

BENEATHA: Where did Ruth go, Walter?

WALTER: I don't know.

[*He exits abruptly.*]

BENEATHA: Mama, where did Ruth go?

MAMA: [*looking at her with meaning*] To the doctor, I think.

BENEATHA: The doctor? What's the matter? [*They exchange glances.*] You don't think—

MAMA: [*with her sense of drama*] Now I ain't saying what it is I think. But I ain't never been wrong 'bout a woman neither.

[*The phone rings.*]

BENEATHA: [*at the phone*] Hay-lo. . . . [*pause, and a moment of recognition*] Well—when did you get back! . . . And how was it? . . . Of course I've missed you—in my way. . . . This morning? No. . . house cleaning and all that and Mama hates it if I let people come over when the house is like this. . . . You *have*? Well, that's different. . . . What is it—Oh, what the hell, come on over. . . . Right, see you then.

[*She hangs up.*]

MAMA: [*who has listened vigorously, as is her habit*] Who is that you inviting over here with this house looking like this? You ain't got the pride you was born with!

BENEATHA: Asagai doesn't care how houses look, Mama—he's an intellectual.

MAMA: *Who?*

BENEATHA: Asagai—Joseph Asagai. He's an African boy I met on campus. He's been studying in Canada all summer.

MAMA: What's his name?

BENEATHA: Asagai, Joseph. Ah-sah-guy. He's from Nigeria.

MAMA: Oh, that's the little country that was founded by slaves a long ways back. . . .

BENEATHA: No, Mama—that's Liberia.

MAMA: I don't think I never met no African before.

BENEATHA: Well, do me a favor and don't ask him a whole lot of ignorant questions about Africans. I mean, do they wear clothes and all that—

MAMA: Well, now, I guess if you think we so ignorant 'round here, maybe you shouldn't bring your friends here—

BENEATHA: It's just that people ask such crazy things. All anyone seems to know about when it comes to Africa is Tarzan—

MAMA: [*indignantly*] Why should I know anything about Africa?

BENEATHA: Why do you give money at church for the missionary work?

MAMA: Well, that's to help save people.

BENEATHA: You mean save them from *heathenism*—

MAMA: [*innocently*] Yes.

BENEATHA: I'm afraid they need more salvation from the British and the French.

[*Ruth comes in forlornly and pulls off her coat with dejection. They both turn and* look at her expectantly.]

RUTH: [*dispiritedly*] Well, I guess from all the happy faces—everybody knows.

BENEATHA: You pregnant?

MAMA: Lord have mercy, I sure hope it's a little old girl. Travis ought to have a sister.

[*Beneatha and Ruth give her a hopeless look in response to this grandmotherly enthusiasm.*]

BENEATHA: How far along are you?

RUTH: Two months.

BENEATHA: Did you mean to? I mean did you plan it or was it an accident?

MAMA: What do you know about planning or not planning?

BENEATHA: Oh, Mama.

RUTH: [*wearily*] She's twenty years old, Lena.

BENEATHA: Did you plan it, Ruth?

RUTH: Mind your own business.

BENEATHA: It is my business—where is he going to live, on the *roof*? [*There is silence following the remark as the three women react to the sense of it.*] Gee—I didn't mean that, Ruth, honest. Gee, I don't feel like that at all. I— I think it is wonderful.

RUTH: [*dully*] Wonderful.

BENEATHA: Yes—really.

MAMA: [*looking at Ruth, worried*] Doctor say everything going to be all right?

RUTH: [*far away*] Yes—she says everything is going to be fine. . . .

MAMA: [*immediately suspicious*] "She" —What doctor you went to?

[*Ruth folds over, near hysteria.*]

MAMA: [*worriedly hovering over Ruth*] Ruth honey—what's the matter with you—you sick?

[*Ruth has her fists clenched on her thighs and is fighting hard to suppress a scream that seems to be rising in her.*]

BENEATHA: What's the matter with her, Mama?

MAMA: [*working her fingers in Ruth's shoulder to relax her*] She be all right. Women gets right depressed sometimes when they get her way. [*speaking softly, expertly, rapidly*] Now you just relax. That's right . . . just lean back, don't think 'bout nothing at all . . . nothing at all—

RUTH: I'm all right. . . .

[*The glassy-eyed look melts and then she collapses into a fit of heavy sobbing. The bell rings.*]

BENEATHA: Oh, my God—that must be Asagai.

MAMA: [*to Ruth*] Come on now, honey. You need to lie down and rest . . . then have some nice hot food.

[*They exit, Ruth's weight on her mother-in-law. Beneatha, herself profoundly disturbed, opens the door to admit a rather dramatic-looking young man with a large package.*]

ASAGAI: Hello, Alaiyo—

BENEATHA: [*holding the door open and regarding him with pleasure*] Hello. . . . [*long pause*] Well—come in. And please excuse everything. My mother was very upset about my letting anyone come here with the place like this.

ASAGAI: [*coming into the room*] You look disturbed too. . . . Is something wrong?

BENEATHA: [*still at the door, absently*] Yes . . . we've all got acute ghetto-itis. [*She smiles and comes toward him, finding a cigarette and sitting.*] So—sit down! How was Canada?

ASAGAI: [*a sophisticate*] Canadian.

BENEATHA: [*looking at him*] I'm very glad you are back.

ASAGAI: [*looking back at her in turn*] Are you really?

BENEATHA: Yes—very.

ASAGAI: Why—you were quite glad when I went away. What happened?

BENEATHA: You went away.

ASAGAI: Ahhhhhhhh.

BENEATHA: Before—you wanted to be so serious before there was time.

ASAGAI: How much time must there be before one knows what one feels?

BENEATHA: [*stalling this particular conversation; her hands pressed together, in a deliberately childish gesture*] What did you bring me?

ASAGAI: [*handing her the package*] Open it and see.

BENEATHA: [*eagerly opening the package and drawing out some records and the colorful robes of a Nigerian woman*] Oh, Asagai! . . . You got them for me! How beautiful . . . and the records too! [*She lifts out the robes and runs to the mirror with them and holds the drapery up in front of herself.*]

ASAGAI: [*coming to her at the mirror*] I shall have to teach you how to drape it properly. [*He flings the material about her for the moment and stands back to look at her.*] Ah—Oh-pay-gay-day, oh-gbah-mu-shay. [*a Yoruba exclamation for admiration*] You wear it well, Beneatha . . . very well . . . mutilated hair and all.

BENEATHA: [*turning suddenly*] My hair—what's wrong with my hair?

ASAGAI: [*shrugging*] Were you born with it like that?

BENEATHA: [*reaching up to touch it*] No, no . . . of course not.

[*She turns and looks into the mirror again, disturbed.*]

ASAGAI: [*smiling*] How then?

BENEATHA: You know perfectly well how. It's as crinkly as yours . . . that's how.

ASAGAI: And it is ugly to you that way?

BENEATHA: [*quickly*] Oh, no—not ugly. [*more slowly and apologetically*] But it's so hard to manage when it's, well—raw.

ASAGAI: And so you accommodate that—you mutilate it every week?

BENEATHA: It's not mutilation!

ASAGAI: [*laughing aloud at her seriousness*] Oh . . . please! I am only teasing you because you are so very serious about these things. [*He stands back from her and folds his arms across his chest as he watches her pulling at her hair and frowning in the mirror.*] Do you remember the first time you met me at school? . . . [*He laughs.*] You came up to me and you said—and I thought you were the most serious little thing I had ever seen—you said: [*He imitates her.*] "Mr. Asagai—I want very much to talk with you. About Africa. You see, Mr. Asagai, I am looking for my *identity*!"

[*He laughs.*]

BENEATHA: [*turning to him, not laughing*] Yes—

[*Her face is quizzical and profoundly disturbed.*]

ASAGAI: [*still teasing and reaching out and taking her face in his hands and turning her profile to him*] Well . . . it is true that this is not so much a profile of a Hollywood queen as perhaps a queen of the Nile—[*a mock dismissal of the importance of the question*] But what does it matter? Assimilationism is so popular in your country.

BENEATHA: [*wheeling, sharply, passionately*] I am not an assimilationist!

ASAGAI: [*The protest hangs in the room for a moment and Asagai studies her, his laughter fading.*] Such a serious one. [*There is a pause.*] So—you like the robes? You must take excellent care of them—they are from my sister's personal wardrobe.

BENEATHA: [*with incredulity*] You—you sent all the way home—for me?

ASAGAI: [*with charm*] For you—I would do much more. . . . Well, that is what I came for. I must go.

BENEATHA: Will you call me Monday?

ASAGAI: Yes. . . . We have a great deal to talk about. I mean about identity and time and all that.

BENEATHA: Time?

ASAGAI: Yes. About how much time one needs to know what one feels.

BENEATHA: You never understood that there is more than one kind of feeling which can exist between a man and a woman—or, at least, there should be.

ASAGAI: [*shaking his head negatively but gently*] No. Between a man and a woman there need be only one kind of feeling. I have that for you . . . now even . . . right this moment. . . .

BENEATHA: I know—and by itself—it won't do. I can find that anywhere.

ASAGAI: For a woman it should be enough.

BENEATHA: I know—because that's what it says in all the novels that men write. But it isn't. Go ahead and laugh—but I'm not interested in being someone's little episode in America or—[*with feminine vengeance*]—one of them! [*Asagai has burst into laughter again.*] That's funny, huh!

ASAGAI: It's just that every American girl I have known has said that to me. White—black—in this you are all the same. And the same speech, too!

BENEATHA: [*angrily*] Yuk, yuk, yuk!

ASAGAI: It's how you can be sure that the world's most liberated women are not liberated at all. You all talk about it too much!

[*Mama enters and is immediately all social charm because of the presence of a guest.*]

BENEATHA: Oh, Mama, this is Mr. Asagai.

MAMA: How do you do?

ASAGAI: [*total politeness to an elder*] How do you do, Mrs. Younger. Please forgive me for coming at such an outrageous hour on a Saturday.

MAMA: Well, you are quite welcome. I just hope you understand that our house don't always look like this. [*chatterish*] You must come again. I would love to hear all about—[*not sure of the name*]—your country. I think it's so sad the way our American Negroes don't know nothing about Africa 'cept Tarzan and all that. And all that money they pour into these churches when they ought to be helping your people over there drive out them French and Englishmen done taken away your land.

[*The mother flashes a slightly superior look at her daughter upon completion of the recitation.*]

ASAGAI: [*taken aback by this sudden and acutely unrelated expression of sympathy*] Yes . . . yes. . . .

MAMA: [*smiling at him suddenly and relaxing and looking him over*] How many miles is it from here to where you come from?

ASAGAI: Many thousands.

MAMA: [*looking at him as she would look at Walter*] I bet you don't half look after yourself, being away from your mama either. I spec you better come 'round here from time to time and get yourself some decent home-cooked meals. . . .

ASAGAI: [*moved*] Thank you. Thank you very much. [*They are all quiet, then—*] Well . . . I must go. I will call you Monday, Alaiyo.

MAMA: What's that he call you?

ASAGAI: Oh—"Alaiyo." I hope you don't mind. It is what you would call a nickname, I think. It is a Yoruba word. I am a Yoruba.

MAMA: [looking at Beneatha] I thought he was from—

ASAGAI: [understanding] Nigeria is my country. Yoruba is my tribal origin—

BENEATHA: You didn't tell us what Alaiyo means . . . for all I know, you might be calling me Little Idiot or something.

ASAGAI: Well . . . let me see . . . I do not know how just to explain it. . . . The sense of a thing can be so different when it changes languages.

BENEATHA: You're evading.

ASAGAI: No—really it is difficult. . . . [thinking] It means . . . it means One for Whom Bread—Food—Is Not Enough. [He looks at her.] Is that all right?

BENEATHA: [understanding, softly] Thank you.

MAMA: [looking from one to the other and not understanding any of it] Well, that's nice. . . . You must come see us again—Mr.—

ASAGAI: Ah-sah-guy. . . .

MAMA: Yes. . . . Do come again.

ASAGAI: Good-bye.

[He exits.]

MAMA: [after him] Lord, that's a pretty thing just went out here! [insinuatingly, to her daughter] Yes, I guess I see why we done commence to get so interested in Africa 'round here. Missionaries my aunt Jenny!

[She exits.]

BENEATHA: Oh, Mama! . . .

[She picks up the Nigerian dress and holds it up to her in front of the mirror again. She sets the headdress on haphazardly and then notices her hair again and clutches at it and then replaces the headdress and frowns at herself. Then she starts to wriggle in front of the mirror as she thinks a Nigerian woman might. Travis enters and regards her.]

TRAVIS: You cracking up?

BENEATHA: Shut up.

[She pulls the headdress off and looks at herself in the mirror and clutches at her hair again and squinches her eyes as if trying to imagine something. Then, suddenly, she gets her raincoat and kerchief and hurriedly prepares for going out.]

MAMA: [coming back into the room] She's resting now. Travis, baby, run next door and ask Miss Johnson to please let me have a little kitchen cleanser. This here can is empty as Jacob's kettle.

TRAVIS: I just came in.

MAMA: Do as you told. [He exits and she looks at her daughter.] Where you going?

BENEATHA: [halting at the door] To become a queen of the Nile!

[She exits in a breathless blaze of glory. Ruth appears in the bedroom doorway.]

MAMA: Who told you to get up?

RUTH: Ain't nothing wrong with me to be lying in no bed for. Where did Bennie go?

MAMA: [drumming her fingers] Far as I could make out—to Egypt. [Ruth just looks at her.] What time is it getting to?

RUTH: Ten-twenty. And the mailman going to ring that bell this morning just like he done every morning for the last umpteen years.

[Travis comes in with the cleanser can.]

TRAVIS: She say to tell you that she don't have much.

MAMA: [angrily] Lord, some people I could name sure is tight fisted! [directing her grandson] Mark two cans of cleanser down on the list there. If she that hard up for kitchen cleanser, I sure don't want to forget to get her none!

*A Raisin in the Sun* **583**

RUTH: Lena—maybe the woman is just short on cleanser—

MAMA: [*not listening*] —Much baking powder as she done borrowed from me all these years, she could of done gone into the baking business!

[*The bell sounds suddenly and sharply and all three are stunned—serious and silent—in mid-speech. In spite of all the other conversations and distractions that have taken place that morning, this is what they have been waiting for, even Travis, who looks helplessly from his mother to his grandmother. Ruth is the first to come to life again.*]

RUTH: [*to Travis*] Get down them steps, boy!

[*Travis snaps to life and flies out to get the mail.*]

MAMA: [*her eyes wide, her hand to her breast*] You mean it done really come?

RUTH: [*excited*] Oh, Miss Lena!

MAMA: [*collecting herself*] Well . . . I don't know what we all so excited about 'round here for. We known it was coming for months.

RUTH: That's a whole lot different from having it come and being able to hold it in your hands . . . a piece of paper worth ten thousand dollars. . . . [*Travis bursts back into the room. He holds the envelope high above his head, like a little dancer, his face is radiant and he is breathless. He moves to his grandmother with sudden slow ceremony and puts the envelope into her hands. She accepts it, and then merely holds it and looks at it.*] Come on! Open it. . . . Lord have mercy, I wish Walter Lee was here!

TRAVIS: Open it, Grandmama!

MAMA: [*staring at it*] Now you all be quiet. It's just a check.

RUTH: Open it. . . .

MAMA: [*still staring at it*] Now don't act silly. . . . We ain't never been no people to act silly 'bout no money—

RUTH: [*swiftly*] We ain't never had none before—open it!

[*Mama finally makes a good strong tear and pulls out the thin blue slice of paper and inspects it closely. The boy and his mother study it raptly over Mama's shoulders.*]

MAMA: Travis! [*She is counting off with doubt.*] Is that the right number of zeros?

TRAVIS: Yes'm . . . ten thousand dollars. Gaalee, Grandmama, you rich.

MAMA: [*She holds the check away from her, still looking at it. Slowly her face sobers into a mask of unhappiness.*] Ten thousand dollars. [*She hands it to Ruth*] Put it away somewhere, Ruth. [*She does not look at Ruth; her eyes seem to be seeing something somewhere very far off.*] Ten thousand dollars they give you. Ten thousand dollars.

TRAVIS: [*to his mother, sincerely*] What's the matter with Grandmama—don't she want to be rich?

RUTH: [*distractedly*] You go on out and play now, baby. [*Travis exits. Mama starts wiping dishes absently, humming intently to herself. Ruth turns to her, with kind exasperation.*] You've gone and got yourself upset.

MAMA: [*not looking at her*] I spec if it wasn't for you all . . . I would just put that money away or give it to the church or something.

RUTH: Now what kind of talk is that. Mr. Younger would just be plain mad if he could hear you talking foolish like that.

MAMA: [*stopping and staring off*] Yes . . . he sure would. [*sighing*] We got enough to do with that money, all right. [*She halts then, and turns and looks at her*

*daughter-in-law hard; Ruth avoids her eyes and Mama wipes her hands with finality. Mama starts to speak firmly to Ruth.*] Where did you go today, girl?

RUTH: To the doctor.

MAMA: [*impatiently*] Now, Ruth . . . you know better than that. Old Doctor Jones is strange enough in his way but there ain't nothing 'bout him make somebody slip and call him "she"— like you done this morning.

RUTH: Well, that's what happened—my tongue slipped.

MAMA: You went to see that woman, didn't you?

RUTH: [*defensively, giving herself away*] What woman you talking about?

MAMA: [*angrily*] That woman who—

[*Walter enters in great excitement.*]

WALTER: Did it come?

MAMA: [*quietly*] Can't you give people a Christian greeting before you start asking about money?

WALTER: [*to Ruth*] Did it come? [*Ruth unfolds the check and lays it quietly before him, watching him intently with thoughts of her own. Walter sits down and grasps it close and counts off the zeros.*] Ten thousand dollars— [*He turns suddenly, frantically to his mother and draws some papers out of his breast pocket.*] Mama—look. Old Willy Harris put everything on paper—

MAMA: Son—I think you ought to talk to your wife. . . . I'll go on out and leave you alone if you want—

WALTER: I can talk to her later— Mama, look—

MAMA: Son—

WALTER: WILL SOMEBODY PLEASE LISTEN TO ME TODAY!

MAMA: [*quietly*] I don't 'low no yellin' in

this house, Walter Lee, and you know it—[*Walter stares at them in frustration and starts to speak several times.*] And there ain't going to be no investing in no liquor stores. I don't aim to have to speak on that again. [*a long pause*]

WALTER: Oh—so you don't aim to have to speak on that again? So *you* have decided. . . . [*crumpling his papers*] Well, *you* tell that to my boy tonight when you put him to sleep on the living room couch. . . . [*turning to Mama and speaking directly to her*] Yeah—and tell it to my wife, Mama, tell her tomorrow when she has to go out of here to look after somebody else's kids. And tell it to *me*, Mama, every time we need a new pair of curtains and I have to watch *you* go out and work in somebody's kitchen. Yeah, you tell me then!

[*Walter starts out.*]

RUTH: Where you going?

WALTER: I'm going out!

RUTH: Where?

WALTER: Just somewhere out of this house—

RUTH: [*getting her coat*] I'll come too.

WALTER: I don't want you to come!

RUTH: I got something to talk to you about, Walter.

WALTER: That's too bad.

MAMA: [*still quietly*] Walter Lee—[*She waits and he finally turns and looks at her.*] Sit down.

WALTER: I'm a grown man, Mama.

MAMA: Ain't nobody said you wasn't grown. But you still in my house and my presence. And as long as you are—you'll talk to your wife civil. Now sit down.

RUTH: [*suddenly*] Oh, let him go on out and drink himself to death! He makes me sick to my stomach! [*She flings her coat against him.*]

WALTER: [*violently*] And you turn mine too, baby! [*Ruth goes into their bedroom and slams the door behind her.*] That was my greatest mistake—

MAMA: [*still quietly*] Walter, what is the matter with you?

WALTER: Matter with me? Ain't nothing the matter with *me*!

MAMA: Yes, there is. Something eating you up like a crazy man. Something more than me not giving you this money. The past few years I been watching it happen to you. You get all nervous acting and kind of wild in the eyes—[*Walter jumps up impatiently at her words.*] I said sit there now, I'm talking to you!

WALTER: Mama—I don't need no nagging at me today.

MAMA: Seem like you getting to a place where you always tied up in some kind of knot about something. But if anybody ask you 'bout it you just yell at 'em and bust out the house and go out and drink somewheres. Walter Lee, people can't live with that. Ruth's a good, patient girl in her way—but you getting to be too much. Boy, don't make the mistake of driving that girl away from you.

WALTER: Why—what she do for me?

MAMA: She loves you.

WALTER: Mama—I'm going out. I want to go off somewhere and be by myself for a while.

MAMA: I'm sorry 'bout your liquor store, son. It just wasn't the thing for us to do. That's what I want to tell you about—

WALTER: I got to go out, Mama—

[*He rises.*]

MAMA: It's dangerous, son.

WALTER: What's dangerous?

MAMA: When a man goes outside his home to look for peace.

WALTER: [*beseechingly*] Then why can't

there never be no peace in this house then?

MAMA: You done found it in some other house?

WALTER: No—there ain't no woman! Why do women always think there's a woman somewhere when a man gets restless. [*coming to her*] Mama—Mama—I want so many things. . . .

MAMA: Yes, son—

WALTER: I want so many things that they are driving me kind of crazy. . . . Mama—look at me.

MAMA: I'm looking at you. You a good-looking boy. You got a job, a nice wife, a fine boy and—

WALTER: A job. [*looks at her*] Mama, a job? I open and close car doors all day long. I drive a man around in his limousine and I say, "Yes, sir; no, sir; very good, sir; shall I take the Drive, sir?" Mama, that ain't no kind of job . . . that ain't nothing at all. [*very quietly*] Mama, I don't know if I can make you understand.

MAMA: Understand what, baby?

WALTER: [*quietly*] Sometimes it's like I can see the future stretched out in front of me—just plain as day. The future, Mama. Hanging over there at the edge of my days. Just waiting for me—a big, looming blank space—full of *nothing*. Just waiting for *me*. [*pause*] Mama—sometimes when I'm downtown and I pass them cool and quiet-looking restaurants where them white boys are sitting back and talking 'bout things . . . sitting there turning deals worth millions of dollars . . . sometimes I see guys don't look much older than me—

MAMA: Son—how come you talk so much 'bout money?

WALTER: [*with immense passion*] Because it is life, Mama!

MAMA: [*quietly*] Oh—[*very quietly*] So

now it's life. Money is life. Once upon a time freedom used to be life—now it's money. I guess the world really do change. . . .

WALTER: No—it was always money, Mama. We just didn't know about it.

MAMA: No . . . something has changed. [*She looks at him.*] You something new, boy. In my time we was worried about not being lynched and getting to the North if we could and how to stay alive and still have a pinch of dignity too. . . . Now here come you and Beneatha—talking 'bout things we ain't never even thought about hardly, me and your daddy. You ain't satisfied or proud of nothing we done. I mean that you had a home; that we kept you out of trouble till you was grown; that you don't have to ride to work on the back of nobody's streetcar— You my children—but how different we done become.

WALTER: You don't understand, Mama, you just don't understand.

MAMA: Son—do you know your wife is expecting another baby? [*Walter stands, stunned, and absorbs what his mother has said.*] That's what she wanted to talk to you about. [*Walter sinks down into a chair.*] This ain't for me to be telling—but you ought to know. [*She waits.*] I think Ruth is thinking 'bout getting rid of that child.

WALTER: [*slowly understanding*] No— no—Ruth wouldn't do that.

MAMA: Son, when the world gets ugly enough—a woman will do anything for her family. *The part that's already living.*

WALTER: You don't know Ruth, Mama, if you think she would do that.

[*Ruth opens the bedroom door and stands there a little limp.*]

RUTH: [*beaten*] Yes I would too, Walter. [*pause*] I gave her a five-dollar down payment.

[*There is total silence as the man stares at his wife and the mother stares at her son.*]

MAMA: [*presently*] Well—[*tightly*] Well— son, I'm waiting to hear you say something. . . . I'm waiting to hear how you be your father's son. Be the man he was. . . . [*pause*] Your wife say she going to destroy your child. And I'm waiting to hear you talk like him and say we a people who give children life, not who destroys them—[*She rises.*] I'm waiting to see you stand up and look like your daddy and say we done give up one baby to poverty and that we ain't going to give up nary another one . . . I'm waiting.

WALTER: Ruth—

MAMA: If you a son of mine, tell her! [*Walter turns, looks at her and can say nothing. She continues, bitterly.*] You . . . you are a disgrace to your father's memory. Somebody get me my hat.

---

## YOU AND ACT ONE

Drama is the Greek word for action, for "doings." When the events are dramatic, things are "happening." In a truly dramatic play, the action we see on the stage is often *inter*action. There is interaction among several strong **characters**. Lorraine Hansberry's *A Raisin in the Sun* is a play built around several strong characters who interact with each other. They have much in common: their common past, the poverty and narrow limits of their present environment. But each major character is also *different*—he or she is a different, unique human being. They each have their own view of the world, their own plans for the future. They try to explain, to defend, and to act out these beliefs and plans. As they try to "have their way," their goals and values come into conflict. We are kept in suspense as we wonder how the conflict will work itself out. Our attention is kept focused on the stage by the most basic question in much effective drama: "How is it all going to come out?"

As you read this play, how well do you get to know the major characters? How well do you come to understand what they think and feel? The following exercise in *role-playing* may help you and your class remember what you have learned about each different major character in Act One:

(1) In the play, Ruth keeps things going from day to day. Have someone in the class play Ruth's role. Let her tell the story of her *family:* Who are the members of the family? What kind of place do they live in? What is their daily routine? What kind of people are they? The questions should be answered as Ruth would answer them.

(2) In this family, Mama is the link with the *past.* She reminds the younger generation of things they may be ready to forget. Have someone in the class play Mama's role. Have her tell her story—how she looks at the past, how she looks at the history of her people and the history of her family.

(3) Several of the major characters in this family "have a dream." They have their own vision of the *future.* In this first act, Walter and Mama especially have a chance to tell us what they want, what they hope for. Have someone in the class volunteer for one of these two roles. Let each of these characters tell the audience about his or her dream.

(4) Though there is some expression of love and respect in these first few scenes, there is also much *resentment* or anger.

What makes the different characters angry? As you listen to them, can you say: "I understand how you feel"? Have people in the class choose the role of a character with whom they especially sympathize: Mama, Walter, Ruth, Beneatha. Have them answer the question: "What bothers you? What makes you angry?"

(5) What is it like to *grow up* in the Younger household? Have someone in the class tell Travis's story. Have him describe the members of the family—how they act toward him, how he feels toward them.

---

## A Closer Look

Like many other playwrights, Lorraine Hansberry gives detailed **stage directions** explaining how she expects the actors to look and act. If you were acting in the play, how well would you understand her directions? How would you answer questions like the following?

(1) The author calls Walter an "intense" young man with "erratic" speech habits. What does she mean by "intense" and "erratic"?

(2) The author says about Walter, "Always in his voice, there is a quality of indictment." What would be a simpler or more familiar word for *indictment*?

(3) When Walter reads items from the morning newspaper, Ruth responds with "maximum indifference." What is meant by "maximum indifference"?

(4) A little later in the same scene, Ruth is "affecting tea-party interest." What do we do when we "affect" interest? What is an "affected" manner or an "affected" way of talking?

(5) At breakfast, Walter studies his wife "almost *clinically,* as though he has never seen her before." What does *clinically* mean here?

(6) When Travis leaves home, his hair and jacket are "conspicuously" brushed. What does *conspicuous* mean?

(7) While seeming to concentrate on her ironing, Ruth studies her mother-in-law "furtively." What does *furtively* mean?

(8) Mama tells Ruth about the place she never got to buy in Morgan Park. Then she drops her hand in "a futile gesture." What does *futile* mean?

(9) Beneatha says her brother "isn't really crazy" but "an elaborate neurotic"? What is a "neurotic"?

(10) When Travis brings in the long-expected envelope, he holds the envelope high over his head and his face is "radiant." What does *radiant* mean?

---

WORKING WITH USAGE

# Down-Home Talk

In *I Know Why the Caged Bird Sings*, Maya Angelou talks about the difference between the language of the classroom and the language she and her black classmates spoke in the streets and in their homes. She says:

We learned to slide out of one language and into another without being conscious of the effort. At school, in a given situation, we might respond with "That's not unusual." But in the street, meeting the same situation, we easily said, "It be's like that sometimes."

We call a kind of language that is different from mainstream or standard language a **dialect**. In Lorraine Hansberry's play, Mama, the old-timer, comes closest to speaking a real "down-home" dialect. The younger people in the play seem to be able to "slide out of one language and into another"—as Walter would do on the job, or as Beneatha would have to do in school. Look at the following examples of black dialect. For each of these, how would you say the same thing in school language?

1. You wasn't brought up that way.
2. You think you a woman, but you still a little girl.
3. Ain't nobody said you wasn't grown.
4. Whether they drinks it or not ain't none of my business.
5. You'll talk to your wife civil.
6. Something eating you up like a crazy man.
7. That man finally worked hisself to death.
8. You still in my house.
9. You getting to be too much.
10. Death done come in this here house.
11. You ain't old enough to marry nobody.
12. You know how these young folks is nowadays.
13. Somebody would of thought my children done all but starved to death.
14. What's the matter with them stockings?
15. There's something come down between me and them that don't let us understand each other.

# Act Two

## Scene One

*Time: Later the same day.*

*At rise: Ruth is ironing again. She has the radio going. Presently Beneatha's bedroom door opens. Ruth's mouth falls when she sees Beneatha, and she puts down the iron in fascination.*

RUTH: What have we got on tonight!

BENEATHA: [*emerging grandly from the doorway so that we can see her thoroughly robed in the costume Asagai brought*] You are looking at what a well-dressed Nigerian woman wears— [*She parades for Ruth, her hair completely hidden by the headdress; she is coquettishly fanning herself with an ornate oriental fan, mistakenly more like Butterfly than any Nigerian that ever was.*] Isn't it beautiful? [*She promenades to the radio and, with an arrogant flourish, turns off the good loud blues that is playing.*] Enough of this assimilationist junk! [*Ruth follows her with her eyes as she goes to the phonograph and puts on a record and turns and waits ceremoniously for the music to come up. Then, with a shout—*] OCOMOGOSIAY!

[*Ruth jumps. The music comes up, a lovely Nigerian melody. Beneatha listens, enraptured, her eyes far away— "back to the past." She begins to dance. Ruth is dumfounded.*]

RUTH: What kind of dance is that?

BENEATHA: A folk dance.

RUTH: [*Pearl Bailey*] What kind of folks do that, honey?

BENEATHA: It's from Nigeria. It's a dance of welcome.

RUTH: Who you welcoming?

BENEATHA: The men back to the village.

RUTH: Where they been?

BENEATHA: How should I know—out hunting or something. Anyway, they are coming back now. . . .

RUTH: Well, that's good.

BENEATHA: [*with the record*]
Alundi, alundi
Alundi alunya
Jop pu a jeepua
Ang gu soooooooooo
Ai yai yae . . .
Ayehaye—alundi . . .

[*Walter comes in during this performance; he has obviously been drinking. He leans against the door heavily and watches his sister, at first with distaste. Then his eyes look off—"back to the past"—as he lifts both his fists to the roof, screaming.*]

WALTER: YEAH . . . AND ETHIOPIA STRETCH FORTH HER HANDS AGAIN! . . .

RUTH: [*drily, looking at him*] Yes—and Africa sure is claiming her own tonight. [*She gives them both up and starts ironing again.*]

WALTER: [*all in a drunken, dramatic shout*] Shut up! . . . I'm digging them drums . . . them drums move me! . . . [*He makes his weaving way to his wife's face and leans in close to her.*] In my *heart of hearts*—[*He thumps his chest.*]—I am much warrior!

RUTH: [*without even looking up from her ironing*] In your heart of hearts you are much drunkard.

WALTER: [*coming away from her and starting to wander around the room, shouting*] Me and Jomo . . . [*Intently, in his sister's face. She has stopped dancing to watch him in this unknown mood.*] That's my man, Kenyatta. [*shouting and thumping his chest*] FLAMING SPEAR! [*He is suddenly in possession of an imaginary spear and actively spearing enemies all over the room.*] OCOMOGOSIAY . . . THE LION IS WAKING. . . . OWIMOWEH! [*He pulls his shirt open and leaps up on a table and gestures with his spear. The bell rings. Ruth goes to answer.*]

BENEATHA: [*to encourage Walter, thoroughly caught up with this side of him*] OCOMOGOSIAY, FLAMING SPEAR!

WALTER: [*On the table, very far gone, his eyes pure glass sheets. He sees what we cannot, that he is a leader of his people, a great chief, a descendant of Chaka, and that the hour to march has come at last.*] Listen, my black brothers—

BENEATHA: OCOMOGOSIAY!

WALTER: —Do you hear the cold waters rushing against the shores of the coastlands—

BENEATHA: OCOMOGOSIAY!

WALTER: —Do you hear the screeching of the cocks in yonder hills beyond where the chiefs meet in council for the coming of the mighty war—

BENEATHA: OCOMOGOSIAY!

WALTER: —Do you hear the beating of the wings of the birds flying low over the mountains and the low places of our land—

[*Ruth opens the door. George Murchison enters.*]

BENEATHA: OCOMOGOSIAY!

WALTER: —Do you hear the singing of the women, singing the war songs of our fathers to the babies in the great houses . . . singing the sweet war songs? OH, DO YOU HEAR, MY BLACK BROTHERS!

BENEATHA: [*completely gone*] We hear you, Flaming Spear—

WALTER: Telling us to prepare for the greatness of the time—[*to George*] Black Brother!

[*He extends his hand for the fraternal clasp.*]

GEORGE: Black Brother, h——!

RUTH: [*having had enough, and being embarrassed for the family*] Beneatha, you got company—what's the matter with you? Walter Lee Younger, you get down off that table and stop acting like a fool. . . .

[*Walter suddenly comes down off the table and makes a quick exit to the bathroom.*]

RUTH: He's had a little to drink. . . . I don't know what her excuse is.

GEORGE: [*to Beneatha*] Look, honey, we're going *to* the theater—we're not going to be *in* it. . . so go change, huh?

RUTH: You expect this boy to go with you looking like that?

BENEATHA: [*looking at George*] That's up to George. If he's ashamed of his own heritage—

GEORGE: Oh, don't be so proud of yourself, Bennie—just because you look eccentric.

BENEATHA: How can something that's natural be eccentric?

GEORGE: That's what being eccentric means—being natural. Get dressed.

BENEATHA: I don't like that, George.

RUTH: Why must you and your brother make an argument out of everything people say?

BENEATHA: Because I hate assimilationist Negroes!

RUTH: Will somebody please tell me what assimila-whoever means!

GEORGE: Oh, it's just a college girl's way of calling people Uncle Toms—but that isn't what it means at all.

RUTH: Well, what does it mean?

BENEATHA: [*cutting George off and staring at him as she replies to Ruth*] It means someone who is willing to give

up his own culture and submerge himself completely in the dominant, and in this case, *oppressive* culture!

GEORGE: Oh, dear, dear, dear! Here we go! A lecture on the African past! On our Great West African Heritage! In one second we will hear all about the great Ashanti empires; the great Songhay civilizations; and the great sculpture of Bénin—and then some poetry in the Bantu—and the whole monologue will end with the word *heritage*! [*nastily*] Let's face it, baby, your heritage is nothing but a bunch of spirituals and some grass huts!

BENEATHA: *Grass huts!* [*Ruth crosses to her and forcibly pushes her toward the bedroom.*] See there . . . you are standing there in your splendid ignorance talking about people who were the first to smelt iron on the face of the earth! [*Ruth is pushing her through the door.*] The Ashanti were performing surgical operations when the English—[*Ruth pulls the door to, with Beneatha on the other side, and smiles graciously at George. Beneatha opens the door and shouts the end of the sentence defiantly at George.*]—were still tattooing themselves with blue dragons. . . . [*She goes back inside.*]

RUTH: Have a seat, George. [*They both sit. Ruth folds her hands rather primly on her lap, determined to demonstrate the civilization of the family.*] Warm, ain't it? I mean for September. [*pause*] Just like they always say about Chicago weather: If it's too hot or cold for you, just wait a minute and it'll change. [*She smiles happily at this cliché of clichés.*] Everybody say it's got to do with them bombs and things they keep setting off. [*pause*] Would you like a nice cold beer?

GEORGE: No, thank you. I don't care for beer. [*He looks at his watch.*] I hope she hurries up.

RUTH: What time is the show?

GEORGE: It's an eight-thirty curtain. That is just Chicago, though. In New York standard curtain time is eight forty.

[*He is rather proud of this knowledge.*]

RUTH: [*properly appreciating it*] You get to New York a lot?

GEORGE: [*offhand*] Few times a year.

RUTH: Oh—that's nice. I've never been to New York.

[*Walter enters. We feel he has relieved himself, but the edge of unreality is still with him.*]

WALTER: New York ain't got nothing Chicago ain't. Just a bunch of hustling people all squeezed up together—being "Eastern."

[*Walter turns his face into a screw of displeasure.*]

GEORGE: Oh—you've been?

WALTER: *Plenty* of times.

RUTH: [*shocked at the lie*] Walter Lee Younger!

WALTER: [*staring her down*] Plenty! [*pause*] What we got to drink in this house? Why don't you offer this man some refreshment. [*to George*] They don't know how to entertain people in this house, man.

GEORGE: Thank you—I don't really care for anything.

WALTER: [*feeling his head; sobriety coming*] Where's Mama?

RUTH: She ain't come back yet.

WALTER: [*looking Murchison over from head to toe, scrutinizing his carefully casual tweed sports jacket over cashmere V-neck sweater over soft eyelet shirt and tie, and soft slacks, finished off with white buckskin shoes*] Why all you college boys wear them white shoes?

RUTH: Walter Lee!

[*George Murchison ignores the remark.*]

WALTER: [*to Ruth*] Well, they look so crazy—white shoes, cold as it is.

RUTH: [*crushed*] You have to excuse him—

WALTER: No he don't! Excuse me for what? What you always excusing me for! I'll excuse myself if I needs to be excused! [*a pause*] They look as funny as them black knee socks Beneatha wears out of here all the time.

RUTH: It's the college *style*, Walter.

WALTER: She looks like she got burnt legs or something!

RUTH: Oh, Walter—

WALTER: [*an irritable mimic*] Oh, Walter! Oh, Walter! [*to Murchison*] How's your old man making out? I understand you all going to buy that big hotel on the Drive? [*He finds a beer in the refrigerator, wanders over to Murchison, sipping and wiping his lips with the back of his hand, and straddling a chair backwards to talk to the other man.*] Shrewd move. Your old man is all right, man. [*tapping his head and half winking for emphasis*] I mean he knows how to operate. I mean he thinks *big*, you know what I mean, I mean for a *home*, you know? But I think he's kind of running out of ideas now. I'd like to talk to him. Listen, man, I got some plans that could turn this city upside down. I mean I think like he does. *Big.* Invest big, gamble big, lose *big* if you have to, you know what I mean. It's hard to find a man on this whole South Side who understands my kind of thinking—you dig? [*He scrutinizes Murchison again, drinks his beer, squints his eyes and leans in close, confidential, man to man.*] Me and you ought to sit down and talk sometimes, man. Man, I got me some ideas. . . .

MURCHISON: [*with boredom*] Yeah—

sometime we'll have to sit down and talk, Walter.

WALTER: [*understanding the indifference, and offended*] Yeah—well, when you get the time, man. I know you a busy little boy.

RUTH: Walter, please—

WALTER: [*bitterly, hurt*] I know ain't nothing in this world as busy as you colored college boys with your fraternity pins and white shoes. . . .

RUTH: [*covering her face with humiliation*] Oh, Walter Lee—

WALTER: I see you all the time, with the books tucked under your arms, going to your [*British A—a mimic*] "clahsses." And for what! What you learning over there? Filling up your heads—[*counting off on his fingers*]—with the sociology and the psychology—but they teaching you how to be a man? How to take over and run the world? They teaching you how to run a rubber plantation or a steel mill? Naw—just to talk proper and read books and wear white shoes . . .

GEORGE: [*looking at him with distaste, a little above it all*] You're all wacked up with bitterness, man.

WALTER: [*intently, almost quietly, between the teeth, glaring at the boy*] And you—ain't you bitter, man? Ain't you just about had it yet? Don't you see no stars gleaming that you can't reach out and grab? You happy? You got it made? Bitter? Man, I'm a volcano. Bitter? Here I am—a giant—surrounded by ants! Ants who can't even understand what it is the giant is talking about.

RUTH: [*passionately and suddenly*] Oh, Walter—ain't you with nobody!

WALTER: [*violently*] No! 'Cause ain't nobody with me! Not even my own mother!

RUTH: Walter, that's a terrible thing to say!

[Beneatha enters, dressed for the evening in a cocktail dress and earrings.]

GEORGE: Well—hey, you look great.

BENEATHA: Let's go, George. See you all later.

RUTH: Have a nice time.

GEORGE: Thank you. Good night. [to Walter, sarcastically] Good night, Prometheus.*

[Beneatha and George exit.]

WALTER: [to Ruth] Who is Prometheus?

RUTH: I don't know. Don't worry about it.

WALTER: [in fury, pointing after George] See there—they get to a point where they can't insult you man to man—they got to talk about something ain't nobody never heard of!

RUTH: How do you know it was an insult? [to humor him] Maybe Prometheus is a nice fellow.

WALTER: Prometheus! I bet there ain't even no such thing! I bet that simple-minded clown—

RUTH: Walter—

[She stops what she is doing and looks at him.]

WALTER: [yelling] Don't start!

RUTH: Start what?

WALTER: Your nagging! Where was I? Who was I with? How much money did I spend?

RUTH: [plaintively] Walter Lee—why don't we just try to talk about it . . .

WALTER: [not listening] I been out talking with people who understand me. People who care about the things I got on my mind.

RUTH: [wearily] I guess that means people like Willy Harris.

WALTER: Yes, people like Willis Harris.

*Prometheus: the Greek god who stole fire from heaven to give it to man. In punishment, Zeus put him to great torture.

RUTH: [with a sudden flash of impatience] Why don't you all just hurry up and go into the banking business and stop talking about it!

WALTER: Why? You want to know why? 'Cause we all tied up in a race of people that don't know how to do nothing but moan, pray, and have babies!

[The line is too bitter even for him and he looks at her and sits down.]

RUTH: Oh, Walter . . . [softly] Honey, why can't you stop fighting me?

WALTER: [without thinking] Who's fighting you? Who even cares about you?

[This line begins the retardation of his mood.]

RUTH: Well—[She waits a long time, and then with resignation starts to put away her things.] I guess I might as well go on to bed. . . . [more or less to herself] I don't know where we lost it . . . but we have . . . [then, to him] I—I'm sorry about this new baby, Walter. I guess maybe I better go on and do what I started. . . . I guess I just didn't realize how bad things was with us. . . . I guess I just didn't really realize—[She starts out of the bedroom and stops.] You want some hot milk?

WALTER: Hot milk?

RUTH: Yes—hot milk.

WALTER: Why hot milk?

RUTH: 'Cause after all that liquor you come home with you ought to have something hot in your stomach.

WALTER: I don't want no milk.

RUTH: You want some coffee then?

WALTER: No, I don't want no coffee. I don't want nothing hot to drink. [almost plaintively] Why you always trying to give me something to eat?

RUTH: [standing and looking at him helplessly] What else can I give you, Walter Lee Younger?

[*She stands and looks at him. Presently she turns to leave again. He lifts his head and watches her going away from him in a new mood which began to emerge when he asked her "Who cares about you?"*]

WALTER: It's been rough, ain't it, baby? [*She hears and stops but does not turn around and he continues to her back.*] I guess between two people there ain't never as much understood as folks generally thinks there is. I mean like between me and you—[*She turns to face him.*] How we gets to the place where we scared to talk softness to each other. [*He waits, thinking hard himself.*] Why you think it got to be like that? [*He is thoughtful, almost as a child would be.*] Ruth, what is it gets into people ought to be close?

RUTH: I don't know, honey. I think about it a lot.

WALTER: On account of you and me, you mean? The way things are with us. The way something done come down between us.

RUTH: There ain't so much between us, Walter. . . . Not when you come to me and try to talk to me. Try to be with me . . . a little even.

WALTER: [*total honesty*] Sometimes . . . sometimes . . . I don't even know how to try.

RUTH: Walter—

WALTER: Yes?

RUTH: [*coming to him, gently and with misgiving, but coming to him*] Honey, life don't have to be like this. Sometimes people can do things so that things are better. You remember how we used to talk when Travis was born . . . about the way we were going to live . . . the kind of house . . . [*She is stroking his head.*] Well, it's all starting to slip away from us.

[*Mama enters, and Walter jumps up and shouts at her.*]

WALTER: Mama, where have you been?

MAMA: My— them steps is longer than they used to be. Whew! [*She sits down and ignores him.*] How you feeling this evening, Ruth?

[*Ruth shrugs, disturbed some at having been prematurely interrupted and watching her husband knowingly*]

WALTER: Mama, where have you been all day?

MAMA: [*still ignoring him and leaning on the table and changing to more comfortable shoes*] Where's Travis?

RUTH: I let him go out earlier and he ain't come back yet. Boy is he going to get it!

WALTER: Mama!

MAMA: [*as if she has heard him for the first time*] Yes, son?

WALTER: Where did you go?

MAMA: I went downtown to tend to some business that I had to tend to.

WALTER: What kind of business?

MAMA: You know better than to question me like a child, Brother.

WALTER: [*rising, bending over the table*] Where were you, Mama? [*bringing his fists down and shouting*] Mama, you didn't go do something with that insurance money, something crazy?

[*The front door opens slowly, interrupting him, and Travis peeks his head in, less than hopefully.*]

TRAVIS: [*to his mother*] Mama, I—

RUTH: "Mama I" nothing! You're going to get it, boy! Get on in that bedroom and get yourself ready!

TRAVIS: But I—

MAMA: Why don't you all never let the child explain hisself.

RUTH: Keep out of it now, Lena.

[*Mama clamps her lips together, and Ruth menacingly advances toward her son.*]

RUTH: A thousand times I have told you not to go off like that—

MAMA: [holding out her arms to her grandson] Well—at least let me tell him something. I want him to be the first one to hear. . . . Come over here, Travis. [Travis obeys, gladly.] Travis— [She takes him by the shoulder and looks into his face.]—you remember that money we got in the mail this morning?

TRAVIS: Yes'm—

MAMA: Well—what you think your grandmama gone and done with that money?

TRAVIS: I don't know, Grandmama.

MAMA: [putting her finger on his nose for emphasis] She went out and she bought you a house! [The explosion comes from Walter at the end of the revelation and he jumps up and turns away from all of them in a fury. Mama continues, to Travis.] You glad about the house? It's going to be yours when you get to be a man.

TRAVIS: Yeah—I always wanted to live in a house.

MAMA: All right, gimme some sugar then—[Travis puts his arms around her neck as she watches her son over the boy's shoulder. Then, to Travis, after the embrace] Now when you say your prayers tonight, you thank God and your grandfather—'cause it was him who give you the house—in his way.

RUTH: [taking the boy from Mama and pushing him toward the bedroom] Now you get out of here and get ready for your beating.

TRAVIS: Aw, Mama—

RUTH: Get on in there—[closing the door behind him and turning radiantly to her mother-in-law] So you went and did it!

MAMA: [quietly, looking at her son with pain] Yes, I did.

RUTH: [raising both arms classically] Praise God! [Ruth looks at Walter a moment, who says nothing. She crosses rapidly to her husband.] Please, honey—let me be glad . . . you be glad too. [She has laid her hands on his shoulders, but he shakes himself free of her roughly, without turning to face her.] Oh, Walter . . . a home . . . a home. [She comes back to Mama.] Well—where is it? How big is it? How much it going to cost?

MAMA: Well—

RUTH: When we moving?

MAMA: [smiling at her] First of the month.

RUTH: [throwing back her head with jubilance] Praise God!

MAMA: [tentatively, still looking at her son's back turned against her and Ruth] It's—it's a nice house too. . . . [She cannot help speaking directly to him. An imploring quality in her voice, her manner, makes her almost like a girl now.] Three bedrooms— nice big one for you and Ruth. . . . Me and Beneatha still have to share our room, but Travis have one of his own—and [with difficulty] I figure if the—new baby—is a boy, we could get one of the double-decker outfits. . . . And there's a yard with a little patch of dirt where I could maybe get to grow me a few flowers. . . . And there's a nice big basement. . . .

RUTH: Walter honey, be glad—

MAMA: [still to his back, fingering things on the table] 'Course I don't want to make it sound fancier than it is. . . . It's just a plain little old house—but it's made good and solid—and it will be ours. Walter Lee—it makes a difference in a man when he can walk on floors that belong to him. . . .

RUTH: Where is it?

MAMA: [She hesitates, frightened at this telling.] Well—well—it's out there in

Clybourne Park—

[*Ruth's radiance fades abruptly, and Walter finally turns slowly to face his mother with incredulity and hostility.*]

RUTH: Where?

MAMA: [*matter-of-factly*] Four-o-six Clybourne Street, Clybourne Park.

RUTH: Clybourne Park? Mama, there ain't no colored people living in Clybourne Park.

MAMA: [*almost idiotically*] Well, I guess there's going to be some now.

WALTER: [*bitterly*] So that's the peace and comfort you went out and bought for us today!

MAMA: [*finally raising her eyes to meet his*] Son—I just tried to find the nicest place for the least amount of money for my family.

RUTH: [*trying to recover from the shock*] Well—well—'course I ain't one never been 'fraid of no crackers, mind you—but—well, wasn't there no other houses nowhere?

MAMA: Them houses they put up for colored in them areas way out all seem to cost twice as much as other houses. I did the best I could.

RUTH: [*Struck senseless with the news, in its various degrees of goodness and trouble, she sits a moment, her fists propping her chin in thought, and then she starts to rise, bringing her fists down with vigor, the radiance spreading from cheek to cheek again.*] Well—well!—All I can say is—if this is my time in life—my time—to say good-bye—[*And she builds with momentum as she starts to circle the room with an exuberant, almost tearfully happy release.*]—to these cracking walls!—[*She pounds the walls.*]—and these marching roaches!—[*She wipes at an imaginary army of marching roaches.*]—and this cramped little closet which ain't now or never was no

kitchen! . . . then I say it loud and good. *Hallelujah! and good-bye, misery . . . I don't never want to see your ugly face again!* [*She laughs joyously, having practically destroyed the apartment, and flings her arms up and lets them come down happily, slowly, reflectively, over her abdomen, aware for the first time perhaps that the life therein pulses with happiness and not despair.*] Lena?

MAMA: [*moved, watching her happiness*] Yes, honey?

RUTH: [*looking off*] Is there—is there a whole lot of sunlight?

MAMA: [*understanding her*] Yes, child, there's a whole lot of sunlight. [*long pause*]

RUTH: [*collecting herself and going to the door of the room Travis is in*] Well—I guess I better see 'bout Travis. [*to Mama*] Lord, I sure don't feel like whipping nobody today!

[*She exits.*]

MAMA: [*The mother and son are left alone now and the mother waits a long time, considering deeply, before she speaks.*] Son—you—you understand what I done, don't you? [*Walter is silent and sullen.*] I—I just seen my family falling apart today . . . just falling to pieces in front of my eyes. . . . We couldn't of gone on like we was today. We was going backwards 'stead of forwards—talking 'bout killing babies and wishing each other dead. . . . When it gets like that in life—you just got to do something different, push on out and do something bigger. . . . [*She waits.*] I wish you say something, son. I wish you'd say how deep inside you think I done the right thing—

WALTER: [*crossing slowly to his bedroom door and finally turning there and speaking measuredly*] What you need me to say you done right for? *You the* head of this family. You run our lives like you want to. It was your money and you did what you wanted with it. So what you need for me to say it was all right for? [*bitterly, to hurt her as deeply as he knows is possible*] So you butchered up a dream of mine—you—who always talking 'bout your children's dreams. . . .

MAMA: Walter Lee—

[*He just closes the door behind him. Mama sits alone, thinking heavily.*]

## Scene Two

*Time: Friday night. A few weeks later. At rise: Packing crates mark the intention of the family to move. Beneatha and George come in, presumably from an evening out again.*

GEORGE: OK . . . OK, whatever you say. [*They both sit on the couch. He tries to kiss her. She moves away.*] Look, we've had a nice evening; let's not spoil it, huh? . . .

[*He again turns her head and tries to nuzzle in and she turns away from him, not with distaste but with momentary lack of interest; in a mood to pursue what they were talking about.*]

BENEATHA: I'm *trying* to talk to you.

GEORGE: We always talk.

BENEATHA: Yes—and I love to talk.

GEORGE: [*exasperated; rising*] I know it and I don't mind it sometimes. . . . I want you to cut it out, see—The moody stuff, I mean. I don't like it. You're a nice-looking girl . . . all over. That's all you need, honey, forget the atmosphere. Guys aren't going to go for the atmosphere—they're going to go for what they see. Be glad for that. Drop the Garbo routine. It doesn't

go with you. As for myself, I want a nice—[*groping*]—simple [*thoughtfully*] —sophisticated girl . . . not a poet—OK?

[*She rebuffs him again and he starts to leave.*]

BENEATHA: Why are you angry?

GEORGE: Because this is stupid! I don't go out with you to discuss the nature of "quiet desperation" or to hear all about your thoughts—because the world will go on thinking what it thinks regardless—

BENEATHA: Then why read books? Why go to school?

GEORGE: [*with artificial patience, counting on his fingers*] It's simple. You read books—to learn facts—to get grades— to pass the course—to get a degree. That's all—it has nothing to do with thoughts.

[*a long pause*]

BENEATHA: I see. [*a longer pause as she looks at him*] Good night, George.

[*George looks at her a little oddly, and starts to exit. He meets Mama coming in.*]

GEORGE: Oh—hello, Mrs. Younger.

MAMA: Hello, George, how you feeling?

GEORGE: Fine—fine, how are you?

MAMA: Oh, a little tired. You know them steps can get you after a day's work. You all have a nice time tonight?

GEORGE: Yes—a fine time. Well, good night.

MAMA: Good night. [*He exits. Mama closes the door behind her.*] Hello, honey. What you sitting like that for?

BENEATHA: I'm just sitting.

MAMA: Didn't you have a nice time?

BENEATHA: No.

MAMA: No? What's the matter?

BENEATHA: Mama, George is a fool—honest. [She rises.]

MAMA: [Hustling around unloading the packages she has entered with. She stops.] Is he, baby?

BENEATHA: Yes.

[Beneatha makes up Travis's bed as she talks.]

MAMA: You sure?

BENEATHA: Yes.

MAMA: Well—I guess you better not waste your time with no fools.

[Beneatha looks up at her mother, watching her put groceries in the refrigerator. Finally she gathers up her things and starts into the bedroom. At the door she stops and looks back at her mother.]

BENEATHA: Mama—

MAMA: Yes, baby—

BENEATHA: Thank you.

MAMA: For what?

BENEATHA: For understanding me this time.

[Beneatha exits quickly and the mother stands, smiling a little, looking at the place where Beneatha just stood. Ruth enters.]

RUTH: Now don't you fool with any of this stuff, Lena—

MAMA: Oh, I just thought I'd sort a few things out.

[The phone rings. Ruth answers.]

RUTH: [at the phone] Hello—Just a minute. [goes to door] Walter, it's Mrs. Arnold. [waits, goes back to the phone, tense] Hello. Yes, this is his wife speaking . . . He's lying down now . . . Yes . . . well, he'll be in tomorrow. He's been very sick. Yes, I know we should have called, but we were so sure he'd be able to come in today. Yes—yes, I'm very sorry. Yes. . . . Thank you very much. [She hangs up. Walter is standing in the doorway of the bedroom behind her.] That was Mrs. Arnold.

WALTER: [indifferently] Was it?

RUTH: She said if you don't come in tomorrow that they are getting a new man. . . .

WALTER: Ain't that sad—ain't that crying sad.

RUTH: She said Mr. Arnold has had to take a cab for three days. . . . Walter, you ain't been to work for three days! [This is a revelation to her.] Where you been, Walter Lee Younger? [Walter looks at her and starts to laugh.] You're going to lose your job.

WALTER: That's right. . . .

RUTH: Oh, Walter, and with your mother working like a dog every day—

WALTER: That's sad too—Everything is sad.

MAMA: What you been doing for these three days, son?

WALTER: Mama—you don't know all the things a man what got leisure can find to do in this city. . . . What's this—Friday night? Well—Wednesday I borrowed Willy Harris' car and I went for a drive . . . just me and myself and I drove and drove. . . . Way out . . . way past South Chicago, and I parked the car and I sat and looked at the steel mills all day long. I just sat in the car and looked at them big black chimneys for hours. Then I drove back and I went to the Green Hat. [pause] And Thursday—Thursday I borrowed the car again and I got in it and I pointed it the other way and I drove the other way—for hours—way, way up to Wisconsin, and I looked at the farms. I just drove and looked at the farms. Then I drove back and I went to the Green Hat. [pause] And today—today I didn't get the car. Today I just walked. All over the South Side. And I looked at the Negroes and they looked at me and finally I just sat down on the curb at Thirty-ninth and South Parkway and I just sat there and watched the Negroes go by. And then I went to the Green Hat. You all sad? You all depressed? And you know where I am going right now—

[*Ruth goes out quietly.*]

MAMA: Oh, Big Walter, is this the harvest of our days?

WALTER: You know what I like about the Green Hat? [*He turns the radio on and a steamy, deep blues pours into the room.*] I like this little cat they got there who blows a sax. . . . He blows. He talks to me. He ain't but 'bout five feet tall and he's got a conked head and his eyes is always closed and he's all music—

MAMA: [*rising and getting some papers out of her handbag*] Walter—

WALTER: And there's this other guy who plays the piano . . . and they got a sound. I mean they can work on some music. . . . They got the best combo in the world in the Green Hat. . . . You can just sit there and drink and listen to them three men play and you realize that don't nothing matter in this world, but just being there—

MAMA: I've helped do it to you, haven't I, son? Walter, I been wrong.

WALTER: Naw—you ain't never been wrong about nothing, Mama.

MAMA: Listen to me, now. I say I been wrong, son. That I been doing to you what the rest of the world been doing to you. [*She stops and he looks up slowly at her and she meets his eyes pleadingly.*] Walter—what you ain't never understood is that I ain't got nothing, don't own nothing, ain't never really wanted nothing that wasn't for you. There ain't nothing as precious to me. . . . There ain't nothing worth holding on to, money, dreams,

nothing else—if it means—if it means it's going to destroy my boy. [*She puts her papers in front of him and he watches her without speaking or moving.*] I paid the man thirty-five hundred dollars down on the house. That leaves sixty-five hundred dollars. Monday morning I want you to take this money and take three thousand dollars and put it in a savings account for Beneatha's medical schooling. The rest you put in a checking account—with your name on it. And from now on any penny that come out of it or that go in it is for you to look after. For you to decide. [*She drops her hands a little helplessly.*] It ain't much, but it's all I got in the world and I'm putting it in your hands. I'm telling you to be the head of this family from now on like you supposed to be.

WALTER: [*Stares at the money.*] You trust me like that, Mama?

MAMA: I ain't never stop trusting you. Like I ain't never stop loving you.

[*She goes out, and Walter sits looking at the money on the table as the music continues in its idiom, pulsing in the room. Finally, in a decisive gesture, he gets up, and, in mingled joy and desperation, picks up the money. At the same moment, Travis enters for bed.*]

TRAVIS: What's the matter, Daddy? You drunk?

WALTER: [*sweetly, more sweetly than we have ever known him*] No, Daddy ain't drunk. Daddy ain't going to never be drunk again. . . .

TRAVIS: Well, good night, Daddy.

[*The Father has come from behind the couch and leans over, embracing his son.*]

WALTER: Son, I feel like talking to you tonight.

TRAVIS: About what?

WALTER: Oh, about a lot of things. About you and what kind of man you going to be when you grow up. . . . Son—son, what do you want to be when you grow up?

TRAVIS: A bus driver.

WALTER: [laughing a little] A what? Man, that ain't nothing to want to be!

TRAVIS: Why not?

WALTER: 'Cause, man—it ain't big enough—you know what I mean.

TRAVIS: I don't know then. I can't make up my mind. Sometimes Mama asks me that too. And sometimes when I tell you I just want to be like you—she says she don't want me to be like that and sometimes she says she does. . . .

WALTER: [gathering him up in his arms] You know what, Travis? In seven years you going to be seventeen years old. And things is going to be very different with us in seven years, Travis. . . . One day when you are seventeen I'll come home—home from my office downtown somewhere—

TRAVIS: But you don't work in no office, Daddy.

WALTER: No—but after tonight. After what your daddy gonna do tonight, there's going to be offices—a whole lot of offices. . . .

TRAVIS: What are you gonna do tonight, Daddy?

WALTER: You wouldn't understand yet, son, but your daddy's gonna make a transaction . . . a business transaction that's going to change our lives. . . . That's how come one day when you 'bout seventeen years old I'll come home and I'll be pretty tired, you know what I mean, after a day of conferences and secretaries getting things wrong the way they do . . . 'cause an executive's life is hell, man—[The more he talks the farther away he gets.] And I'll pull the car up on the driveway . . . just a plain black Chrysler, I think, with white walls—no—black tires. More elegant. Rich people don't have to be flashy . . . though I'll have to get something a little sportier for Ruth—maybe a Cadillac convertible to do her shopping in. . . . And I'll come up the steps to the house and the gardener will be clipping away at the hedges and he'll say, "Good evening, Mr. Younger." And I'll say, "Hello, Jefferson, how are you this evening?" And I'll go inside and Ruth will come downstairs and meet me at the door and we'll kiss each other and she'll take my arm and we'll go up to your room to see you sitting on the floor with the catalogues of all the great schools in America around you. . . . All the great schools in the world! And—and I'll say, all right son—it's your seventeenth birthday, what is it you've decided? . . . Just tell me where you want to go to school and you'll go. Just tell me, what it is you want to be—and you'll be it. . . . Whatever you want to be—Yessir! [He holds his arms open for Travis.] You just name it, son. . . . [Travis leaps into them.] and I hand you the world!

[Walter's voice has risen in pitch and hysterical promise and on the last line he lifts Travis high.]

## Scene Three

*Time: Saturday, moving day, one week later.*

*Before the curtain rises, Ruth's voice, a strident, dramatic church alto, cuts through the silence.*

*It is, in the darkness, a triumphant surge, a penetrating statement of expectation: "Oh, Lord, I don't feel no ways tired! Children, oh, glory hallelujah!"*

*As the curtain rises we see that Ruth is*

*alone in the living room, finishing up the family's packing. It is moving day. She is nailing crates and tying cartons. Beneatha enters, carrying a guitar case, and watches her exuberant sister-in-law.*

RUTH: Hey!

BENEATHA: [*putting away the case*] Hi.

RUTH: [*pointing at a package*] Honey— look in that package there and see what I found on sale this morning at the South Center. [*Ruth gets up and moves to the package and draws out some curtains.*] Lookahere—hand-turned hems!

BENEATHA: How do you know the window size out there?

RUTH: [*who hadn't thought of that*] Oh— Well, they bound to fit something in the whole house. Anyhow, they was too good a bargain to pass up. [*Ruth slaps her head, suddenly remembering something.*] Oh, Bennie—I meant to put a special note on that carton over there. That's your mama's good china and she wants 'em to be very careful with it.

BENEATHA: I'll do it.

[*Beneatha finds a piece of paper and starts to draw large letters on it.*]

RUTH: You know what I'm going to do soon as I get in that new house?

BENEATHA: What?

RUTH: Honey—I'm going to run me a tub of water up to here. . . . [*with her fingers practically up to her nostrils*] And I'm going to get in it—and I am going to sit . . . and sit . . . and sit in that hot water and the first person who knocks to tell *me* to hurry up and come out—

BENEATHA: Gets shot at sunrise.

RUTH: [*laughing happily*] You said it, sister! [*noticing how large Beneatha is absent mindedly making the note*] Honey, they ain't going to read that from no airplane.

BENEATHA: [*laughing herself*] I guess I always think things have more emphasis if they are big, somehow.

RUTH: [*looking up at her and smiling*] You and your brother seem to have that as a philosophy of life. Lord, that man—done changed so 'round here. You know—you know what we did last night? Me and Walter Lee?

BENEATHA: What?

RUTH: [*smiling to herself*] We went to the movies. [*looking at Beneatha to see if she understands*] We went to the movies. You know the last time me and Walter went to the movies together?

BENEATHA: No.

RUTH: Me neither. That's how long it been. [*smiling again*] But we went last night. The picture wasn't much good, but that didn't seem to matter. We went—and we held hands.

BENEATHA: Oh, Lord!

RUTH: We held hands—and you know what?

BENEATHA: What?

RUTH: When we come out of the show it was late and dark and all the stores and things was closed up . . . and it was kind of chilly and there wasn't many people on the streets . . . and we was still holding hands, me and Walter.

BENEATHA: You're killing me.

[*Walter enters with a large package. His happiness is deep in him; he cannot keep still with his new-found exuberance. He is singing and wiggling and snapping his fingers. He puts his package in a corner and puts a phonograph record, which he has brought in with him, on the record player. As the music comes up he dances over to Ruth and tries to get her to dance with him. She gives in at last to his raunchiness and in a fit of giggling allows herself to be drawn into his mood and together they deliberately burlesque an old social dance of their youth.*]

BENEATHA: [*regarding them a long time as they dance, then drawing in her breath for a deeply exaggerated comment which she does not particularly mean*] Talk about—oldddddddddddfashionedddddddddd—Negroes!

WALTER: [*stopping momentarily*] What kind of Negroes? [*He says this in fun. He is not angry with her today, nor with anyone. He starts to dance with his wife again.*]

BENEATHA: Old-fashioned.

WALTER: [*as he dances with Ruth*] You know, when these *New Negroes* have their convention—[*pointing at his sister*]—that is going to be the chairman of the Committee on Unending Agitation. [*He goes on dancing, then stops.*] Race, race, race! . . . Girl, I do believe you are the first person in the history of the entire human race to successfully brainwash yourself. [*Beneatha breaks up and he goes on dancing. He stops again, enjoying his tease.*] Even the N double A C P takes a holiday sometimes! [*Beneatha and Ruth laugh. He dances with Ruth some more and starts to laugh and stops and pantomimes someone over an operating table.*] I can just see that chick someday looking down at some poor cat on an operating table before she starts to slice him, saying . . . [*pulling his sleeves back maliciously*] "By the way, what are your views on civil rights down there? . . ."

[*He laughs at her again and starts to dance happily. The bell sounds.*]

BENEATHA: Sticks and stones may break my bones but . . . words will never hurt me!

[*Beneatha goes to the door and opens it as Walter and Ruth go on with the clowning. Beneatha is somewhat surprised to see a quiet-looking middle-aged white man in a business suit holding his hat and a briefcase in his hand and consulting a small piece of paper.*]

MAN: Uh—how do you do, miss. I am looking for a Mrs.—[*He looks at the slip of paper.*] Mrs. Lena Younger?

BENEATHA: [*smoothing her hair in slight embarrassment*] Oh—yes, that's my mother. Excuse me. [*She closes the door and turns to quiet the other two.*] Ruth! Brother! Somebody's here. [*Then she opens the door. The man casts a curious quick glance at all of them.*] Uh—come in please.

MAN: [*coming in*] Thank you.

BENEATHA: My mother isn't here just now. Is it business?

MAN: Yes . . . well, of a sort.

WALTER: [*freely, assuming the role of Man of the House*] Have a seat. I'm Mrs. Younger's son. I look after most of her business matters.

[*Ruth and Beneatha exchange amused glances.*]

MAN: [*regarding Walter, and sitting*] Well —My name is Karl Lindner. . . .

WALTER: [*stretching out his hand*] Walter Younger. This is my wife—[*Ruth nods politely.*]—and my sister.

LINDNER: How do you do.

WALTER: [*amiably, as he positions himself easily on a chair, leaning with interest forward on his knees and looking into the newcomer's face expectantly*] What is it we can do for you, Mr. Lindner!

LINDNER: [*some minor shuffling of the hat and briefcase on his knees*] Well— I am a representative of the Clybourne Park Improvement Association—

WALTER: [*pointing*] Why don't you sit your things on the floor?

LINDNER: Oh—yes. Thank you. [*He slides the briefcase and hat under the chair.*] And as I was saying—I am from the Clybourne Park Improvement Association and we have had it brought to our attention at the last meeting that you people—or at least your mother—has bought a piece of residential property at—[*He digs for the slip of paper again.*]—four o six Clybourne Street. . . .

WALTER: That's right. Care for something to drink? Ruth, get Mr. Lindner a beer.

LINDNER: [*upset for some reason*] Oh—no, really. I mean thank you very much, but no thank you.

RUTH: [*innocently*] Some coffee?

LINDNER: Thank you, nothing at all.

[*Beneatha, suspicious, is watching the man carefully.*]

LINDNER: Well, I don't know how much you folks know about our organization. [*He is a gentle man; thoughtful and somewhat labored in his manner.*] It is one of these community organizations set up to look after—oh, you know, things like block upkeep and special projects and we also have what we call our New Neighbors Orientation Committee. . . .

BENEATHA: [*drily*] Yes—and what do they do?

LINDNER: [*turning a little to her and then returning the main force to Walter*] Well—it's what you might call a sort of welcoming committee, I guess. I mean they, we, I'm the chairman of the committee—go around and see the new people who move into the neighborhood and sort of give them the lowdown on the way we do things out in Clybourne Park.

BENEATHA: [*with appreciation of the two meanings, which escape Ruth and Walter*] Un-huh.

LINDNER: And we also have the category of what the association calls—[*He looks elsewhere.*]—uh—special community problems. . . .

BENEATHA: Yes—and what are some of those?

WALTER: Girl, let the man talk.

LINDNER: [*with understated relief*] Thank you. I would sort of like to explain this thing in my own way. I mean I want to explain to you in a certain way.

WALTER: Go ahead.

LINDNER: Yes. Well. I'm going to try to get right to the point. I'm sure we'll all appreciate that in the long run.

BENEATHA: Yes.

WALTER: Be still now!

LINDNER: Well—

RUTH: [*still innocently*] Would you like another chair—you don't look like you're comfortable.

LINDNER: [*more frustrated than annoyed*] No, thank you very much. Please. Well—to get right to the point I—[*a great breath, and he is off at last*] I am sure you people must be aware of some of the incidents which have happened in various parts of the city when colored people have moved into certain areas—[*Beneatha exhales heavily and starts tossing a piece of fruit up and down in the air.*] Well—because we have what I think is going to be a unique type of organization in American community life—not only do we deplore that kind of thing—but we are trying to do something about it. [*Beneatha stops tossing and turns with a new and quizzical interest to the man.*] We feel—[*gaining confidence in his mission because of the interest in the faces of the people he is talking to*]—we feel that most of the trouble in this world, when you come right down to it—[*He hits his knee for emphasis.*]—most of the trouble exists because people just don't sit down and talk to each other.

RUTH: [*nodding as she might in church,*

*pleased with the remark*] You can say that again, mister.

LINDNER: [*more encouraged by such affirmation*] That we don't try hard enough in this world to understand the other fellow's problem. The other guy's point of view.

RUTH: Now that's right.

[*Beneatha and Walter merely watch and listen with genuine interest.*]

LINDNER: Yes—that's the way we feel out in Clybourne Park. And that's why I was elected to come here this afternoon and talk to you people. Friendly like, you know, the way people should talk to each other and see if we couldn't find some way to work this thing out. As I say, the whole business is a matter of *caring* about the other fellow. Anybody can see that you are a nice family of folks, hardworking and honest I'm sure. [*Beneatha frowns slightly, quizzically, her head tilted regarding him.*] Today everybody knows what it means to be on the outside of *something*. And of course, there is always somebody who is out to take advantage of people who don't always understand.

WALTER: What do you mean?

LINDNER: Well—you see our community is made up of people who've worked hard as the dickens for years to build up that little community. They're not rich and fancy people; just ordinary, hardworking, honest people who don't really have much but those little homes and a dream of the kind of community they want to raise their children in. Now, I don't say we are perfect and there is a lot of wrong in some of the things they want. But you've got to admit that a man, right or wrong, has the right to want to have the neighborhood he lives in a certain kind of way.

And at the moment the overwhelming majority of our people out there feel that people get along better, take more of a common interest in the life of the community, when they share a common background. I want you to believe me when I tell you that race prejudice simply doesn't enter into it. It is just a matter of the people of Clybourne Park believing, rightly or wrongly, as I say, that for the happiness of all people concerned that our Negro families are happier when they live in their *own* communities.

BENEATHA: [*with a grand and bitter gesture*] This, friends, is the Welcoming Committee!

WALTER: [*dumfounded, looking at Lindner*] Is this what you came marching all the way over here to tell us?

LINDNER: Well, now, we've been having a fine conversation. I hope you'll hear me all the way through.

WALTER: [*tightly*] Go ahead, man.

LINDNER: You see—in the face of all things I have said, we are prepared to make your family a very generous offer. . . .

BENEATHA: Thirty pieces and not a coin less!

WALTER: Yeah?

LINDNER: [*putting on his glasses and drawing a form out of the briefcase*] Our association is prepared, through the collective effort of our people, to buy the house from you at a financial gain to your family.

RUTH: Lord have mercy, ain't this the living gall!

WALTER: All right, you through?

LINDNER: Well, I would like to explain to you the exact terms of the financial arrangement—

WALTER: We don't want to hear no exact terms of no arrangements. I want to know if you got any more to tell us 'bout getting together?

LINDNER: [taking off his glasses] Well—I don't suppose that you feel . . .

WALTER: Never mind how I feel—you got any more to say 'bout how people ought to sit down and talk to each other? . . . Get out of my house, man.

[He turns his back and walks to the door.]

LINDNER: [looking around at the hostile faces and reaching and assembling his hat and briefcase] Well—I don't understand why you people are reacting this way. What do you think you are going to gain by moving into a neighborhood where you just aren't wanted and where some elements—well—people can get awful worked up when they feel that their whole way of life and everything they've ever worked for is threatened.

WALTER: Get out.

LINDNER: [at the door, holding a small card] Well—I'm sorry it went like this.

WALTER: Get out.

LINDNER: [almost sadly regarding Walter] You just can't force people to change their hearts, son.

[He turns and puts his card on a table and exits. Walter pushes the door to with stinging hatred, and stands looking at it. Ruth just sits and Beneatha just stands. They say nothing. Mama enters with Travis.]

MAMA: Well—this all the packing got done since I left out of here this morning? I testify before God that my children got all the energy of the dead. What time the moving men due?

BENEATHA: Four o'clock. You had a caller, Mama.

[She is smiling, teasingly.]

MAMA: Sure enough—who?

BENEATHA: [her arms folded saucily] The Welcoming Committee.

[Walter and Ruth giggle.]

MAMA: [innocently] Who?

BENEATHA: The Welcoming Committee. They said they're sure going to be glad to see you when you get there.

WALTER: [devilishly] Yeah, they said they can't hardly wait to see your face.

[laughter]

MAMA: [recognizing their facetiousness] What's the matter with you all?

WALTER: Ain't nothing the matter with us. We just telling you 'bout the gentleman who came to see you this afternoon. From the Clybourne Park Improvement Association.

MAMA: What he want?

RUTH: [in the same mood as Beneatha and Walter] To welcome you, honey.

WALTER: He said they can't hardly wait. He said the one thing they don't have, that they just *dying* to have out there is a fine family of colored people! [to Ruth and Beneatha] Ain't that right!

RUTH and BENEATHA: [mockingly] Yeah! He left his card in case—

[They indicate the card, and Mama picks it up and throws it on the floor—understanding and looking off as she draws her chair up to the table on which she has put her plant and some sticks and some cord.]

MAMA: Father, give us strength. [then knowingly—and without fun] Did he threaten us?

BENEATHA: Oh—Mama—they don't do it like that any more. He talked Brotherhood. He said everybody ought to learn how to sit down and hate each other with good Christian fellowship.

[She and Walter shake hands to ridicule the remark.]

MAMA: [sadly] Lord, protect us. . . .

RUTH: You should hear the money those folks raised to buy the house from us. All we paid and then some.

BENEATHA: What they think we going to do—eat 'em?

RUTH: No, honey, marry 'em.

MAMA: [shaking her head] Lord, Lord, Lord . . .

RUTH: Well—that's the way the crackers crumble. Joke.

BENEATHA: [laughingly noticing what her mother is doing] Mama, what are you doing?

MAMA: Fixing my plant so it won't get hurt none on the way. . . .

BENEATHA: Mama, you going to take that to the new house?

MAMA: Un-huh—

BENEATHA: —That raggedy-looking old thing?

MAMA: [stopping and looking at her] It expresses me.

RUTH: [with delight, to Beneatha] So there, Miss Thing!

[Walter comes to Mama suddenly and bends down behind her and squeezes her in his arms with all his strength. She is overwhelmed by the suddenness of it and, though delighted, her manner is like that of Ruth with Travis.]

MAMA: Look out now, boy! You make me mess up my thing here!

WALTER: [His face lit, he slips down on his knees beside her, his arms still about her.] Mama . . . you know what it means to climb up in the chariot?

MAMA: [gruffly, very happy] Get on away from me now. . . .

RUTH: [near the gift-wrapped package, trying to catch Walter's eye] Psst—

WALTER: What does the old song say, Mama. . . .

RUTH: Walter—Now?

[She is pointing at the package.]

WALTER: [speaking the lines, sweetly, playfully, in his mother's face]

I got wings . . . you got wings . . .
All God's Children got wings . . .

MAMA: Boy—get out of my face and do some work. . . .

WALTER: When I get to heaven gonna put on my wings,
Gonna fly all over God's heaven . . .

BENEATHA: [teasingly, from across the room] Everybody talking 'bout heaven ain't going there!

WALTER: [to Ruth, who is carrying the box across to them] I don't know, you think we ought to give her that. . . . Seems to me she ain't been very appreciative around here.

MAMA: [eying the box, which is obviously a gift] What is that?

WALTER: [taking it from Ruth and putting it on the table in front of Mama] Well—what you all think? Should we give it to her?

RUTH: Oh—she was pretty good today.

MAMA: I'll good you—

[She turns her eyes to the box again.]

BENEATHA: Open it, Mama.

[She stands up, looks at it, turns and looks at all of them, and then presses her hands together and does not open the package.]

WALTER: [sweetly] Open it, Mama. It's for you. [Mama looks in his eyes. It is the first present in her life without its being Christmas. Slowly she opens her package and lifts out, one by one, a brand-new sparkling set of gardening tools. Walter continues, prodding.] Ruth made up the note—read it. . . .

MAMA: [picking up the card and adjusting her glasses] "To our own Mrs. Miniver—Love from Brother, Ruth and Beneatha." Ain't that lovely. . . .

TRAVIS: [tugging at his father's sleeve] Daddy, can I give her mine now?

WALTER: All right, son. [Travis flies to get his gift.] Travis didn't want to go in with the rest of us, Mama. He got his own. [somewhat amused] We don't know what it is. . . .

TRAVIS: [racing back in the room with a large hatbox and putting it in front of his grandmother] Here!

MAMA: Lord have mercy, baby. You done gone and bought your grandmother a hat?

TRAVIS: [very proud] Open it!

[She does and lifts out an elaborate, but very elaborate, wide gardening hat, and all the adults break up at the sight of it.]

RUTH: Travis, honey, what is that?

TRAVIS: [who thinks it is beautiful and appropriate] It's a gardening hat! Just like the ladies always have on in the magazines when they work in their gardens.

BENEATHA: [giggling fiercely] Travis—we were trying to make Mama Mrs. Miniver—not Scarlett O'Hara!

MAMA: [indignantly] What's the matter with you all! This here is a beautiful hat! [absurdly] I always wanted me one just like it!

[She pops it on her head to prove it to her grandson, and the hat is ludicrous and considerably oversized.]

RUTH: Hot dog! Go, Mama!

WALTER: [doubled over with laughter] I'm sorry, Mama—but you look like you ready to go out and chop you some cotton sure enough!

[They all laugh except Mama, out of deference to Travis' feelings.]

MAMA: [gathering the boy up to her] Bless your heart—this is the prettiest hat I ever owned—[Walter, Ruth and Beneatha chime in—noisily, festively and insincerely congratulating Travis on his gift.] What are we all standing around here for? We ain't finished packin' yet. Bennie, you ain't packed one book.

[The bell rings.]

BENEATHA: That couldn't be the movers. It's not hardly two good yet—

[Beneatha goes into her room. Mama starts for door.]

WALTER: [turning and stiffening] Wait—wait—I'll get it.

[He stands and looks at the door.]

MAMA: You expecting company, son?

WALTER: [just looking at the door] Yeah—yeah. . . .

[Mama looks at Ruth, and they exchange innocent and unfrightened glances.]

MAMA: [not understanding] Well, let them in, son.

BENEATHA: [from her room] We need some more string.

MAMA: Travis—you run to the hardware and get me some string cord.

[Mama goes out and Walter turns and looks at Ruth. Travis goes to a dish for money.]

RUTH: Why don't you answer the door, man?

WALTER: [suddenly bounding across the floor to her] 'Cause sometimes it hard to let the future begin! [stooping down in her face]
    I got wings! You got wings!
    All God's children got wings!
[He crosses to the door and throws it open. Standing there is a very slight little man in a not too prosperous business suit and with haunted frightened eyes and a hat pulled down

tightly, brim up, around his forehead. Travis passes between the men and exits. Walter leans deep in the man's face, still in his jubilance.]

When I get to heaven gonna put on my wings,
Gonna fly all over God's heaven . . .

[The little man just stares at him.]

Heaven—

[Suddenly he stops and looks past the little man into the empty hallway.] Where's Willy, man?

BOBO: He ain't with me.

WALTER: [not disturbed] Oh—come on in. You know my wife.

BOBO: [dumbly, taking off his hat] Yes—h-you, Miss Ruth.

RUTH: [quietly, a mood apart from her husband already] Hello, Bobo.

WALTER: You right on time today . . . right on time. That's the way! [He slaps Bobo on his back.] Sit down . . . lemme hear.

[Ruth stands stiffly and quietly in back of them, as though somehow she senses death, her eyes fixed on her husband.]

BOBO: [his frightened eyes on the floor, his hat in his hands] Could I please get a drink of water, before I tell you about it, Walter Lee?

[Walter does not take his eyes off the man. Ruth goes blindly to the tap and gets a glass of water and brings it to Bobo.]

WALTER: There ain't nothing wrong, is there?

BOBO: Lemme tell you—

WALTER: Man, didn't nothing go wrong?

BOBO: Lemme tell you—Walter Lee. [looking at Ruth and talking to her more than to Walter] You know how it was. I got to tell you how it was. I mean first I got to tell you how it was

all the way . . . I mean about the money I put in, Walter Lee. . . .

WALTER: [with taut agitation now] What about the money you put in?

BOBO: Well—it wasn't much as we told you—me and Willy—[He stops.] I'm sorry, Walter. I got a bad feeling about it. I got a real bad feeling about it. . . .

WALTER: Man, what you telling me about all this for? . . . Tell me what happened in Springfield. . . .

BOBO: Springfield.

RUTH: [like a dead woman] What was supposed to happen in Springfield?

BOBO: [to her] This deal that me and Walter went into with Willy— Me and Willy was going to go down to Springfield and spread some money 'round so's we wouldn't have to wait so long for the liquor license. . . . That's what we were going to do. Everybody said that was the way you had to do, you understand, Miss Ruth?

WALTER: Man—what happened down there?

BOBO: [a pitiful man, near tears] I'm trying to tell you, Walter.

WALTER: [screaming at him suddenly] THEN TELL ME! . . . WHAT'S THE MATTER WITH YOU?

BOBO: Man . . . I didn't go to no Springfield, yesterday.

WALTER: [halted, life hanging in the moment] Why not?

BOBO: [the long way, the hard way to tell] 'Cause I didn't have no reasons to. . . .

WALTER: Man, what are you talking about!

BOBO: I'm talking about the fact that when I got to the train station yesterday morning—eight o'clock like we planned. . . . Man—Willy didn't never show up.

WALTER: Why . . . where was he . . . where is he?

BOBO: That's what I'm trying to tell you.

I don't know . . . I waited six hours . . . I called his house . . . and I waited . . . six hours . . . I waited in that train station six hours. . . . [*breaking into tears*] That was all the extra money I had in the world. . . . [*looking up at Walter with the tears running down his face*] Man, Willy is gone.

WALTER: Gone, what do you mean Willy is gone? Gone where? You mean he went by himself. You mean he went off to Springfield by himself—to take care of getting the license—[*Turns and looks anxiously at Ruth.*] You mean maybe he didn't want too many people in on the business down there? [*Looks to Ruth again, as before.*] You know Willy got his own ways. [*Looks back to Bobo.*] Maybe you was late yesterday and he just went on down there without you. Maybe—maybe—he's been callin' you at home all this time tryin' to tell you what happened or something. Maybe—maybe—he just got sick. He's somewhere—he's got to be somewhere. We just got to find him—me and you got to find him. [*Grabs Bobo senselessly by the collar and starts to shake him.*] We got to!

BOBO: [*in sudden angry and frightened agony*] What's the matter with you, Walter! *When a cat take off with your money he don't leave you no maps!*

WALTER: [*turning madly, as though he is looking for Willy in the very room*] Willy! . . . Willy . . . don't do it . . . Please don't do it . . . Man, not with that money . . . Man, please, not with that money . . . Oh, God . . . Don't let it be true . . . [*He is wandering around, crying out for Willy and looking for him or perhaps for help from God.*] Man . . . I trusted you . . . Man, I put my life in your hands . . . [*He starts to crumple down on the floor as Ruth just covers her face in horror. Mama opens the door and comes into the room, with Beneatha behind her.*] Man . . . [*He starts to pound on the floor with his fists, sobbing wildly.*] That money is made out of my father's flesh. . . .

BOBO: [*Standing over him helplessly*] I'm sorry, Walter. . . . [*Only Walter's sobs reply. Bobo puts on his hat.*] I had my life staked on this deal, too. . . .

[*He exits.*]

MAMA: [*to Walter*] Son—[*She goes to him, bends down to him, talks to his bent head.*] Son . . . Is it gone? Son, I gave you sixty-five hundred dollars. Is it gone? All of it? Beneatha's money too?

WALTER: [*lifting his head slowly*] Mama, I . . . I never . . . went to the bank at all. . . .

MAMA: [*not wanting to believe him*] You mean . . . your sister's school money . . . you used that too . . . Walter? . . .

WALTER: Yessss! . . . All of it . . . It's all gone. . . .

[*There is total silence. Ruth stands with her face covered with her hands and Beneatha leans forlornly against a wall, fingering a piece of red ribbon from the mother's gift. Mama stops, looks at her son without recognition and then, quite without thinking about it, starts to beat Walter senselessly in the face. Beneatha goes to them and stops it.*]

BENEATHA: Mama!

[*Mama stops, looks at her children and rises slowly. She wanders vaguely, aimlessly away from them.*]

MAMA: I seen him . . . night after night . . . come in . . . and look at that rug . . . and then look at me . . . the red showing in his eyes, the veins moving in his head . . . I seen him grow thin and old before he was forty . . . working

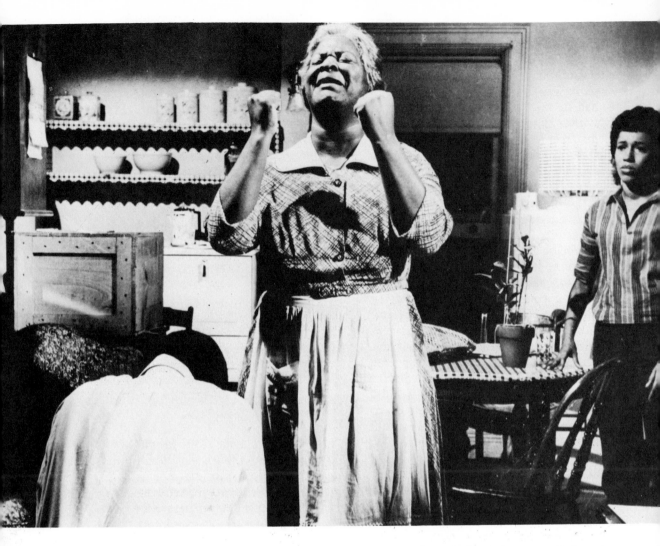

and working and working . . . like somebody's old horse . . . killing himself . . . and you—you give it all away in a day. . . .

BENEATHA: Mama—

MAMA: Oh, God . . . [*She looks up to Him.*] Look down here—and show me the strength.

BENEATHA: Mama—

MAMA: [*folding over*] strength . . .

BENEATHA: [*plaintively*] Mama . . .

MAMA: Strength!

---

## YOU AND ACT TWO

Even people who are strong individuals do not live alone, on a desert island. When we talk about people, much of the time we talk about where they live and where they work. We talk about the family and larger groups of which they are a part. A place, a job, family, friends—this is the **setting** that provides people with the stage on which they act out their feelings and desires, their hopes and fears. *A Raisin in the Sun* is a play in which the setting plays a very strong role. What the characters in the play can do is in large part determined by where and how they live. What they can do is limited in drastic ways by the larger society of which they are a part.

In the second act, especially, we are made to think about the setting that surrounds and hems in the characters in the play:

(1) George Murchison knows the Youngers, but his *status* in society is different. How? Have someone in the class play George's role. Let him tell the class about himself—his background, his goals, his philosophy. Have him talk about the Youngers and what he thinks of them. (What label would you use to describe George? What kind or type of person is he? How would you "classify" him?)

(2) Like other members of minority groups in recent decades, the characters in this play are taking a second look at themselves and their *country*. They are asking themselves: "How do I fit in?" In Acts One and Two, we see some of the characters rebel against "assimilation." America to them no longer is the "melting pot" with everyone trying desperately to become assimilated—to become like everyone else. The play was written when young blacks were beginning to decide they *wanted* to be different. Many of them were beginning to discover their African heritage. Have two people in the class choose the roles of Asagai and Beneatha. Have them tell the audience about Africa.

(3) Though the characters in this play are strong individuals, their lives are shaped by the *environment* in which they live. In the play, the forces that shape their environment remain off the stage. But we get a glimpse of these forces when Mr. Lindner comes as a messenger from the world of "the Man." Pretend you live in Clybourne Park. You are attending a meeting of the Clybourne Park Improvement Association. Have someone be Mr. Lindner and give the group a report on the new neighbors expected in the neighborhood. Have him explain his proposal for handling the situation. When your time comes to join the discussion, what are you going to say?

(4) Of the characters in this play, Walter is most nearly in open *rebellion* against his environment. In this second act, his bitterness comes to the surface in many ways. Have someone be Walter. Have him select and assemble some of what Walter says in this act. Have him present it to the class as a **monologue**—a speech in which a character has a chance to speak for himself and to tell the audience what he thinks and feels. (You may want to assign a group to help select and adapt the material for the monologue.)

## A Closer Look

On the stage, as in real life, we interpret what we hear in the light of what we know about the speaker. We understand better what is being said when we remember *who is talking*. What is the meaning of the italicized word in each of the following statements? (As you explain the meaning of the word, does it help you to remember who is talking?)

1. George called Beneatha's African costume *eccentric*.

2. Beneatha says George is ashamed of his *heritage*.

3. According to Beneatha, *assimilation* means giving up your own culture.

4. Beneatha calls the *dominant* white culture "oppressive."

5. George wants a nice *sophisticated* girl.

# Act Three

*An hour later.*

*At curtain, there is a sullen light of gloom in the living room, gray light not unlike that which began the first scene of Act One. At left we can see Walter within his room, alone with himself. He is stretched out on the bed, his shirt out and open, his arms under his head. He does not smoke, he does not cry out, he merely lies there, looking up at the ceiling, much as if he were alone in the world.*

*In the living room Beneatha sits at the table, still surrounded by the now almost ominous packing crates. She sits looking off. We feel that this is a mood struck perhaps an hour before, and it lingers now, full of the empty sound of profound disappointment. We see on a line from her brother's bedroom the sameness of their attitudes. Presently the bell rings and Beneatha rises without ambition or interest in answering. It is Asagai, smiling broadly at her, striding into the room with energy and happy expectation and conversation.*

ASAGAI: I came over . . . I had some free time. I thought I might help with the packing. Ah, I like the look of packing crates! A household in preparation for a journey! It depresses some people . . . but for me . . . it is another feeling. Something full of the flow of life, do you understand? Movement, progress. It makes me think of Africa.

BENEATHA: Africa!

ASAGAI: What kind of a mood is this? Have I told you how deeply you move me?

BENEATHA: He gave away the money, Asagai. . . .

ASAGAI: Who gave away what money?

BENEATHA: The insurance money. My brother gave it away.

ASAGAI: Gave it away?

BENEATHA: He made an investment! With a man even Travis wouldn't have trusted.

ASAGAI: And it's gone?

BENEATHA: Gone!

ASAGAI: I'm very sorry. . . . And you, now?

BENEATHA: Me? . . . Me? . . . Me I'm nothing . . . me. When I was very small . . . we used to take our sleds out in the wintertime and the only hills we had were the ice-covered stone steps of some houses down the street. And we used to fill them in with snow and make them smooth and slide down them all day . . . and it was very dangerous you know . . . far too steep . . . and sure enough one day a kid named Rufus came down too fast and hit the sidewalk . . . and we saw his face just split open right there in front of us. . . . And I remember standing there looking at his bloody open face thinking that was the end of Rufus. But the ambulance came and they took him to the hospital and they fixed the broken bones and they sewed it all up . . . and the next time I saw Rufus he just had a little line down the middle of his face . . . I never got over that. . . .

[*Walter sits up, listening on the bed. Throughout this scene it is important that we feel his reaction at all times, that he visibly respond to the words of his sister and Asagai.*]

ASAGAI: What?

BENEATHA: That that was what one person could do for another, fix him up— sew up the problem, make him all right again. That was the most marvelous thing in the world. . . . I wanted to do that. I always thought it was the one concrete thing in the world that a human being could do. Fix up the sick, you know—and make them whole again. This was truly being God. . . .

ASAGAI: You wanted to be God?

BENEATHA: No—I wanted to cure. It used to be so important to me. I wanted to cure. It used to matter. I used to care. I mean about people and how their bodies hurt. . . .

ASAGAI: And you've stopped caring?

BENEATHA: Yes—I think so.

ASAGAI: Why?

[Walter rises, goes to the door of his room and is about to open it, then stops and stands listening, leaning on the door jamb.]

BENEATHA: Because it doesn't seem deep enough, close enough to what ails mankind—I mean this thing of sewing up bodies or administering drugs Don't you understand? It was a child's reaction to the world. I thought that doctors had the secret to curing all the hurts. . . . That's the way a child sees things—or an idealist.

ASAGAI: Children see things very well sometimes—and idealists see them even better.

BENEATHA: I know that's what you think. Because you are still where I left off— you still care. This is what you see for the world, for Africa. You with your glorious dreams of the future will patch up all Africa—you are going to cure the Great Sore of colonialism with Independence—

ASAGAI: Yes!

BENEATHA: Yes—and you think that a single word is the penicillin of the human spirit: "Independence!" But then what?

ASAGAI: That will be the problem for another time. First we must get there.

BENEATHA: And where does it end?

ASAGAI: End? Who even spoke of an end? To life? To living?

BENEATHA: An end to misery!

ASAGAI: [smiling] You sound like a French intellectual.

BENEATHA: No! I sound like a human being who just had her future taken right out of her hands! While I was sleeping in my bed in there, things were happening in this world that directly concerned me—and nobody asked me, consulted me—they just went out and did things—and changed my life. Don't you see there isn't any real progress, Asagai, there is only one large circle that we march in, around and around, each of us with our own little picture—in front of us—our own little mirage that we think is the future.

ASAGAI: That is the mistake.

BENEATHA: What?

ASAGAI: What you just said—about the circle. It isn't a circle—it is simply a long line—as in geometry, you know, one that reaches into infinity. And because we cannot see the end—we also cannot see how it changes. And it is very odd but those who see the changes are called "idealists"—and those who cannot, or refuse to think, they are the "realists." It is very strange, and amusing too, I think.

BENEATHA: Asagai, you—you are almost religious.

ASAGAI: Yes . . . I think I have the religion of doing what is necessary in the world—and of worshipping man—because he is so marvelous, you see.

BENEATHA: Man is foul! And the human race deserves its misery!

ASAGAI: You see: *you* have become the religious one in the old sense. Already, and after such a small defeat, you are worshipping despair.

BENEATHA: From now on, I worship the

truth—and the truth is that people are puny, small, and selfish. . . .

ASAGAI: Truth? Why is it that you despairing ones always think that only you have the truth? I never thought to see *you* like that. You! Your brother made a stupid, childish mistake—and you are grateful to him. So that now you can give up the ailing human race on account of it. You talk about what good is struggle; what good is anything? Where are we all going? And why are we bothering?

BENEATHA: *And you cannot answer it!* All your talk and dreams about Africa and Independence. Independence and then what? What about all the crooks and petty thieves and just plain idiots who will come into power to steal and plunder the same as before—only now they will be black and do it in the name of the new Independence— You cannot answer that.

ASAGAI: [*shouting over her*] *I live the answer!* [*pause*] In my village at home it is the exceptional man who can even read a newspaper . . . or who ever *sees* a book at all. I will go home and much of what I will have to say will seem strange to the people of my village. . . . But I will teach and work and things will happen, slowly and swiftly. At times it will seem that nothing changes at all . . . and then again . . . the sudden dramatic events which make history leap into the future. And then quiet again. Retrogression even. Guns, murder, revolution. And I even will have moments when I wonder if the quiet was not better than all that death and hatred. But I will look about my village at the illiteracy and disease and ignorance and I will not wonder long. And perhaps . . . perhaps I will be a great man . . . I mean perhaps I will hold on to the substance of truth and find my way always with the right course . . . and perhaps for it I will be butchered in my bed some night by the servants of empire . . .

BENEATHA: *The martyr!*

ASAGAI: . . . or perhaps I shall live to be a very old man, respected and esteemed in my new nation. . . . And perhaps I shall hold office and this is what I'm trying to tell you, Alaiyo; perhaps the things I believe now for my country will be wrong and outmoded, and I will not understand and do terrible things to have things my way or merely to keep my power. Don't you see that there will be young men and women, not British soldiers then, but my own black countrymen . . . to step out of the shadows some evening and slit my then useless throat? Don't you see they have always been there . . . that they always will be. And that such a thing as my own death will be an advance? They who might kill me even . . . actually replenish me!

BENEATHA: Oh, Asagai, I know all that.

ASAGAI: Good! Then stop moaning and groaning and tell me what you plan to do.

BENEATHA: Do?

ASAGAI: I have a bit of a suggestion.

BENEATHA: What?

ASAGAI: [*rather quietly for him*] That when it is all over—that you come home with me—

BENEATHA: [*slapping herself on the forehead with exasperation born of misunderstanding*] Oh—Asagai—at this moment you decide to be romantic!

ASAGAI: [*quickly understanding the misunderstanding*] My dear, young creature of the New World—I do not mean across the city—I mean across the ocean; home—to Africa.

BENEATHA: [*slowly understanding and turning to him with murmured amazement*] To—to Nigeria?

ASAGAI: Yes! . . . [*smiling and lifting his*

*arms playfully*] Three hundred years later the African Prince rose up out of the seas and swept the maiden back across the middle passage over which her ancestors had come—

BENEATHA: [*unable to play*] Nigeria?

ASAGAI: Nigeria. Home. [*coming to her with genuine romantic flippancy*] I will show you our mountains and our stars; and give you cool drinks from gourds and teach you the old songs and the ways or our people—and, in time, we will pretend that—[*very softly*]—you have only been away for a day—

[*She turns her back to him, thinking. He swings her around and takes her full in his arms in a long embrace which proceeds to passion.*]

BENEATHA: [*pulling away*] You're getting me all mixed up—

ASAGAI: Why?

BENEATHA: Too many things—too many things have happened today. Right now I must sit down and think. I don't know what I feel about anything right this minute.

[*She promptly sits down and props her chin on her fist.*]

ASAGAI: [*charmed*] All right, I shall leave you. No—don't get up. [*touching her, gently, sweetly*] Just sit awhile and think. . . . Never be afraid to sit awhile and think. [*He goes to door and looks at her.*] How often I have looked at you, Beneatha, and said, "Ah—so this is what the New World hath finally wrought. . . ."

[*He exits. Beneatha sits on alone. Presently Walter enters from his room and starts to rummage through things, feverishly looking for something. She looks up and turns in her seat.*]

BENEATHA: [*hissingly*] Yes—just look at what the New World hath wrought!

Just look! [*She gestures with bitter disgust.*] There he is! *Monsieur le petit bourgeois noir*—himself!* There he is—Symbol of a Rising Class! Entrepreneur! Titan of the system! [*Walter ignores her completely and continues frantically and destructively looking for something and hurling things to floor and tearing things out of their place in his search. Beneatha ignores the eccentricity of his actions and goes on with the monologue of insult.*] Did you dream of yachts on Lake Michigan, Brother? Did you see yourself on that Great Day sitting down at the Conference Table, surrounded by all the mighty bald-headed men in America? All halted, waiting, breathless, waiting for your pronouncements on industry? Waiting for you—Chairman of the Board? [*Walter finds what he is looking for—a small piece of white paper—and pushes it in his pocket and puts on his coat and rushes out without ever having looked at her. She shouts after him.*] I look at you and I see the final triumph of stupidity in the world!

[*The door slams and she returns to just sitting again. Ruth comes quickly out of Mama's room.*]

RUTH: Who was that?

BENEATHA: Your husband.

RUTH: Where did he go?

BENEATHA: Who knows—maybe he has an appointment at U.S. Steel.

RUTH: [*anxiously, with frightened eyes*] You didn't say nothing bad to him, did you?

BENEATHA: Bad? Say anything bad to him? No—I told him he was a sweet boy and full of dreams and everything is strictly peachy keen, as the ofay kids say!

*****Monsieur . . . himself:** Mr. Black Middle-Class himself.

[*Mama enters from her bedroom. She is lost, vague, trying to catch hold, to make some sense of her former command of the world, but it still eludes her. A sense of waste overwhelms her gait; a measure of apology rides on her shoulders. She goes to her plant, which has remained on the table, looks at it, picks it up and takes it to the windowsill and sets it outside, and she stands and looks at it a long moment. Then she closes the window, straightens her body with effort and turns around to her children.*]

MAMA: Well—ain't it a mess in here, though? [*a false cheerfulness, a beginning of something*] I guess we all better stop moping around and get some work done. All this unpacking and everything we got to do. [*Ruth raises her head slowly in response to the sense of the line; and Beneatha in similar manner turns very slowly to look at her mother.*] One of you all better call the moving people and tell 'em not to come.

RUTH: Tell 'em not to come?

MAMA: Of course, baby. Ain't no need in 'em coming all the way here and having to go back. They charges for that too. [*She sits down, fingers to her brow, thinking.*] Lord, ever since I was a little girl, I always remembers people saying, "Lena—Lena Eggleston, you aims too high all the time. You needs to slow down and see life a little more like it is. Just slow down some." That's what they always used to say down home—"Lord, that Lena Eggleston is a high-minded thing. She'll get her due one day!"

RUTH: No, Lena. . . .

MAMA: Me and Big Walter just didn't never learn right.

RUTH: Lena, no! We gotta go. Bennie—tell her. . . . [*She rises and crosses to Beneatha with her arms outstretched.*

*Beneatha doesn't respond.*] Tell her we can still move . . . the notes ain't but a hundred and twenty-five a month. We got four grown people in this house—we can work. . . .

MAMA: [*to herself*] Just aimed too high all the time—

RUTH: [*turning and going to Mama fast—the words pouring out with urgency and desperation*] Lena—I'll work . . . I'll work twenty hours a day in all the kitchens in Chicago . . . I'll strap my baby on my back if I have to and scrub all the floors in America and wash all the sheets in America if I have to—but we got to move . . . We got to get out of here. . . .

[*Mama reaches out absently and pats Ruth's hand.*]

MAMA: No—I sees things differently now. Been thinking 'bout some of the things we could do to fix this place up some. I seen a second-hand bureau over on Maxwell Street just the other day that could fit right there. [*She points to where the new furniture might go. Ruth wanders away from her*] Would need some new handles on it and then a little varnish and then it look like something brand-new. And—we can put up them new curtains in the kitchen. . . . Why this place be looking fine. Cheer us all up so that we forget trouble ever came. . . . [*to Ruth*] And you could get some nice screens to put up in your room round the baby's bassinet. . . . [*She looks at both of them, pleadingly.*] Sometimes you just got to know when to give up some things . . . and hold on to what you got.

[*Walter enters from the outside, looking spent and leaning against the door, his coat hanging from him.*]

MAMA: Where you been, son?

WALTER: [breathing hard] Made a call.

MAMA: To who, son?

WALTER: To The Man.

MAMA: What man, baby?

WALTER: The Man, Mama. Don't you know who The Man is?

RUTH: Walter Lee?

WALTER: *The Man.* Like the guys in the streets say—The Man. Captain Boss—Mistuh Charley . . . Old Captain Please Mr. Bossman. . . .

BENEATHA: [suddenly] Lindner!

WALTER: That's right! That's good. I told him to come right over.

BENEATHA: [fiercely, understanding] For what? What do you want to see him for!

WALTER: [looking at his sister] We going to do business with him.

MAMA: What you talking 'bout, son?

WALTER: Talking 'bout life, Mama. You all always telling me to see life like it is. Well—I laid in there on my back today . . . and I figured it out. Life just like it is. Who gets and who don't get. [He sits down with his coat on and laughs.] Mama, you know it's all divided up. Life is. Sure enough. Between the takers and the "tooken." [He laughs.] I've figured it out finally. [He looks around at them.] Yeah. Some of us always getting "tooken." [He laughs.] People like Willy Harris, they don't never get "tooken." And you know why the rest of us do? 'Cause we all mixed up. Mixed up bad. We get to looking 'round for the right and the wrong; and we worry about it and cry about it and stay up nights trying to figure out 'bout the wrong and the right of things all the time. . . . And all the time, man, them takers is out there operating, just taking and taking. Willy Harris? Shoot—Willy Harris don't even count. He don't even count in the big scheme of things. But I'll say one thing for old Willy Harris . . . he's taught me something. He's taught me to keep my eye on what counts in this world. Yeah—[shouting out a little] Thanks, Willy!

RUTH: What did you call that man for, Walter Lee?

WALTER: Called him to tell him to come on over to the show. Gonna put on a show for the man. Just what he wants to see. You see, Mama, the man came here today and he told us that them people out there where you want us to move—well they so upset they willing to pay us not to move out there. [He laughs again.] And—and oh, Mama—you would of been proud of the way me and Ruth and Bennie acted. We told him to get out. . . . Lord have mercy! We told the man to get out. Oh, we was some proud folks this afternoon, yeah. [He lights a cigarette.] We were still full of that old-time stuff. . . .

RUTH: [coming toward him slowly] You talking 'bout taking them people's money to keep us from moving in that house?

WALTER: I ain't just talking 'bout it, baby—I'm telling you that's what's going to happen.

BENEATHA: Oh, God! Where is the bottom! Where is the real honest-to-God bottom so he can't go any farther!

WALTER: See—that's the old stuff. You and that boy that was here today. You all want everybody to carry a flag and a spear and sing some marching songs, huh? You wanna spend your life looking into things and trying to find the right and the wrong part, huh? Yeah. You know what's going to happen to that boy someday—he'll find himself sitting in a dungeon, locked in forever, and the takers will have the key! Forget it, baby! There ain't no causes—there ain't nothing but taking in this world, and he who takes most is smartest—and it don't make a damn bit of difference *how.*

MAMA: You making something inside me cry, son. Some awful pain inside me.

WALTER: Don't cry, Mama. Understand. That white man is going to walk in that door able to write checks for more money than we ever had. It's important to him and I'm going to help him out. I'm going to put on the show, Mama.

MAMA: Son—I come from five generations of people who was slaves and sharecroppers—but ain't nobody in my family never let nobody pay 'em no money that was a way of telling us we wasn't fit to walk the earth. We ain't never been that poor. [*raising her eyes and looking at him*] We ain't never been that dead inside.

BENEATHA: Well—we are dead now. All the talk about dreams and sunlight that goes on in this house. All dead.

WALTER: What's the matter with you all! I didn't make this world! It was give to me this way! Hell, yes, I want me some yachts someday! Yes, I want to hang some real pearls 'round my wife's neck. Ain't she supposed to wear no pearls? Somebody tell me—tell me, who decides which women is suppose to wear pearls in this world. I tell you I am a *man*—and I think my wife should wear some pearls in this world!

[*This last line hangs a good while and Walter begins to move about the room. The word "Man" has penetrated his consciousness; he mumbles it to himself repeatedly between strange agitated pauses as he moves about.*]

MAMA: Baby, how you going to feel on the inside?

WALTER: Fine! . . . Going to feel fine . . . a man . . .

MAMA: You won't have nothing left then, Walter Lee.

WALTER: [*coming to her*] I'm going to feel fine, Mama. I'm going to look that dirty louse in the eyes and say—[*He falters.*]—and say, "All right, Mr. Lindner—[*He falters even more.*]—that's your neighborhood out there. You got the right to keep it like you want. You got the right to have it like you want. Just write the check and—the house is yours." And, and I am going to say—[*His voice almost breaks.*] And you—you people just put the money in my hand and you won't have to live next to this bunch! . . . [*He straightens up and moves away from his mother, walking around the room.*] Maybe—maybe I'll just get down on my black knees. . . . [*He does so; Ruth and Bennie and Mama watch him in frozen horror.*] Captain, Mistuh, Bossman. [*He starts crying.*] A-hee-hee-hee! [*wringing his hands in profoundly anguished imitation*] Yasssssuh! Great White Father, just gi' ussen de money, and we's ain't gwine come out deh and dirty up yo' white folks' neighborhood . . .

[*He breaks down completely, then gets up and goes into the bedroom.*]

BENEATHA: That is not a man. That is nothing but a toothless rat.

MAMA: Yes—death done come in this here house. [*She is nodding, slowly, reflectively.*] Done come walking in my house. On the lips of my children. You what supposed to be my beginning again. You—what supposed to be my harvest. [*to Beneatha*] You—you mourning your brother?

BENEATHA: He's no brother of mine.

MAMA: What you say?

BENEATHA: I said that that individual in that room is no brother of mine.

MAMA: That's what I thought you said. You feeling like you better than he is today? [*Beneatha does not answer.*]

Yes? What you tell him a minute ago? That he wasn't a man? Yes? You give him up for me? You done wrote his epitaph too—like the rest of the world? Well, who done give you the privilege?

BENEATHA: Be on my side for once! You saw what he just did, Mama! You saw him—down on his knees. Wasn't it you who taught me—to despise any man who would do that. Do what he's going to do.

MAMA: Yes—I taught you that. Me and your daddy. But I thought I taught you something else too . . . I thought I taught you to love him.

BENEATHA: Love him? There is nothing left to love.

MAMA: There is always something left to love. And if you ain't learned that, you ain't learned nothing. [looking at her] Have you cried for that boy today? I don't mean for yourself and for the family 'cause we lost the money. I mean for him; what he been through and what it done to him. Child, when do you think is the time to love somebody the most; when they done good and made things easy for everybody? Well then, you ain't through learning—because that ain't the time at all. It's when he's at his lowest and can't believe in hisself 'cause the world done whipped him so. When you starts measuring somebody, measure him right, child, measure him right. Make sure you done taken into account what hills and valleys he come through before he got to wherever he is.

[Travis bursts into the room at the end of the speech, leaving the door open.]

TRAVIS: Grandmama—the moving men are downstairs! The truck just pulled up.

MAMA: [turning and looking at him] Are they, baby? They downstairs?

[She sighs and sits. Lindner appears in the doorway. He peers in and knocks lightly, to gain attention, and comes in. All turn to look at him.]

LINDNER: [hat and briefcase in hand] Uh—hello. . . .

[Ruth crosses mechanically to the bedroom door and opens it and lets it swing open freely and slowly as the lights come up on Walter within, still in his coat, sitting at the far corner of the room. He looks up and out through the room to Lindner.]

RUTH: He's here.

[A long minute passes and Walter slowly gets up.]

LINDNER: [coming to the table with efficiency, putting his briefcase on the table and starting to unfold papers and unscrew fountain pens] Well, I certainly was glad to hear from you people. [Walter has begun the trek out of the room, slowly and awkwardly, rather like a small boy, passing the back of his sleeve across his mouth from time to time.] Life can really be so much simpler than people let it be most of the time. Well—with whom do I negotiate? You, Mrs. Younger, or your son here? [Mama sits with her hands folded on her lap and her eyes closed as Walter advances. Travis goes close to Lindner and looks at the papers curiously.] Just some official papers, sonny.

RUTH: Travis, you go downstairs.

MAMA: [opening her eyes and looking into Walter's] No. Travis, you stay right here. And you make him understand what you doing, Walter Lee. You teach him good. Like Willy Harris taught you. You show where our five generations done come to. Go ahead, son—

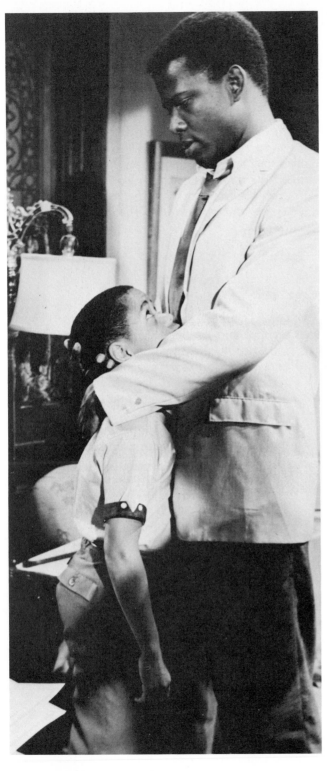

WALTER: [Looks down into his boy's eyes. Travis grins at him merrily and Walter draws him beside him with his arm lightly around his shoulders.] Well, Mr. Lindner. [Beneatha turns away.] We called you—[There is a profound, simple groping quality in his speech.]—because, well, me and my family [He looks around and shifts from one foot to the other.] Well—we are very plain people. . . .

LINDNER: Yes—

WALTER: I mean—I have worked as a chauffeur most of my life—and my wife here, she does domestic work in people's kitchens. So does my mother. I mean—we are plain people. . . .

LINDNER: Yes, Mr. Younger—

WALTER: [really like a small boy, looking down at his shoes and then up at the man] And—uh—well, my father, well, he was a laborer most of his life.

LINDNER: [now absolutely confused] Uh, yes—

WALTER: [looking down at his toes once again] My father almost beat a man to death once because this man called him a bad name or something, you know what I mean?

LINDNER: No, I'm afraid I don't.

WALTER: [finally straightening up] Well, what I mean is that we come from people who had a lot of pride. I mean—we are very proud people. And that's my sister over there and she's going to be a doctor—and we are very proud—

LINDNER: Well—I am sure that is very nice, but—

WALTER: [starting to cry and facing the man eye to eye] What I am telling you is that we called you over here to tell you that we are very proud and that this is—this is my son, who makes the sixth generation of our family in this country, and that we have all thought about your offer and we have decided to move into our house because my father—my father—he earned it. [*Mama has her eyes closed and is rocking back and forth as though she were in church, with her head nodding the amen yes.*] We don't want to make no trouble for nobody or fight no causes—but we will try to be good neighbors. That's all we got to say. [*He looks the man absolutely in the eyes.*] We don't want your money.

[*He turns and walks away from the man.*]

LINDNER: [*looking around at all of them*] I take it then that you have decided to occupy.

BENEATHA: That's what the man said.

LINDNER: [*turning to Mama in her reverie*] Then I would like to appeal to you, Mrs. Younger. You are older and wiser and understand things better, I am sure. . . .

MAMA: [*Rising*] I am afraid you don't understand. My son said we was going to move and there ain't nothing left for me to say. [*shaking her head with double meaning*] You know how these young folks is nowadays, mister. Can't do a thing with 'em. Good-bye.

LINDNER: [*putting away his materials*] Well—if you are that final about it. . . . There is nothing left for me to say. [*He finishes. He is almost ignored by the family, who are concentrating on Walter Lee. At the door Lindner halts and looks around.*] I sure hope you people know what you're doing.

[*He shakes his head and exits.*]

RUTH: [*looking around and coming to life*] Well, for God's sake—if the moving men are here—LET'S GET OUT OF HERE!

MAMA: [*into action*] Ain't it the truth! Look at all this here mess. Ruth, put Travis's good jacket on him. . . . Walter Lee, fix your tie and tuck your shirt in, you look just like somebody's hoodlum. Lord have mercy, where is my plant? [*She flies to get it amid the general bustling of the family, who are deliberately trying to ignore the nobility of the past moment.*] You all start on down . . . Travis child, don't go empty-handed . . . Ruth, where did I put that box with my skillets in it? I want to be in charge of it myself . . . I'm going to make us the biggest dinner we ever ate tonight . . . Beneatha, what's the matter with them stockings? Pull them things up, girl. . . .

[*The family starts to file out as two moving men appear and begin to carry out the heavier pieces of furniture, bumping into the family as they move about.*]

BENEATHA: Mama, Asagai—asked me to marry him today and go to Africa—

MAMA: [*in the middle of her getting-ready activity*] He did? You ain't old enough to marry nobody—[*seeing the moving men lifting one of her chairs precariously*] Darling, that ain't no bale of cotton, please handle it so we can sit in it again. I had that chair twenty-five years. . . .

[*The movers sigh with exasperation and go on with their work.*]

BENEATHA: [*girlishly and unreasonably trying to pursue the conversation*] To go to Africa, Mama—be a doctor in Africa. . . .

MAMA: [*distracted*] Yes, baby—

WALTER: Africa! What he want you to go to Africa for?

BENEATHA: To practice there . . .

WALTER: Girl, if you don't get them silly ideas out your head! You better marry yourself a man with some loot. . . .

BENEATHA: [*angrily, precisely as in the first scene of the play*] What have you got to do with who I marry!

WALTER: Plenty. Now I think George Murchison—

[*He and Beneatha go out yelling at each other vigorously; Beneatha is heard saying that she would not marry George Murchison if he were Adam and she were Eve, etc. The anger is loud and real till their voices diminish. Ruth stands at the door and turns to Mama and smiles knowingly.*]

MAMA: [*fixing her hat at last*] Yeah—they something all right, my children. . . .

RUTH: Yeah—they're something. Let's go, Lena.

MAMA: [*stalling, starting to look around at the house*] Yes—I'm coming. Ruth—

RUTH: Yes?

MAMA: [*quietly, woman to woman*] He finally come into his manhood today, didn't he? Kind of like a rainbow after the rain . . .

RUTH: [*biting her lip lest her own pride explode in front of Mama*] Yes, Lena.

[*Walter's voice is heard calling for them raucously.*]

MAMA: [*waving Ruth out vaguely*] All right, honey—go on down. I be down directly.

[*Ruth hesitates, then exits. Mama stands, at last alone in the living room, her plant on the table before her as the lights start to come down. She looks around at all the walls and ceilings and suddenly, despite herself, while the children call below, a great heaving thing rises in her and she puts her fist to her mouth, takes a final desperate look, pulls her coat about her, pats her hat and goes out. The lights dim down. The door opens and she comes back in, grabs her plant, and goes out for the last time.*]

---

## YOU AND ACT THREE

A good play is not like a race in which a contestant heads for the goal in a straight line. It is more like a game in which the ball moves back and forth as the players use their best energies to make it move the way they want it to move. A truly dramatic play charts the moves and countermoves of major characters. The moves and countermoves of opposed forces produce the end result. When we outline the way the main story of a play develops, we are tracing the **plot** of the play. The plot is the major story line that shapes up as different characters make their moves to influence the course of events.

Assume you could ask one of the major characters at the end of the last act: "What happened in this play?" What kind of *plot summary* or *plot outline* do you think you would get? Assume you are *one* of the four: Mama, Ruth, Walter, or Beneatha. Tell us what happened in the play.

---

### A Closer Look

(1) Misfortunes put people to the test. In Acts Two and Three, we watch the reactions of the different major characters to the loss of the money. Choose two of the major characters. *Compare and contrast* their reactions.

(2) Pretend you are Asagai. Give a brief speech about how you see your personal future and the future of Africa.

---

## YOU AND THE PLAY

(1) To judge from the play as a whole, *what future* does the author think is ahead

for black Americans like those in her play? What kind of future does the play point to? Would you call the author an "optimist"? Would you call her a "pessimist"? Would you call her a "realist"?

(2) When we watch a play like *A Raisin in the Sun,* we are not just spectators. We are not just watching as a neutral observer who says "What's it to me?" The playwright wants us to think. She wants us to care. The play has a message for us as fellow human beings. We call the human message of a play its **theme**. In some plays, a major theme reaches us as clearly and as strongly as a message from a billboard. In other plays, we know we are being told something important—but we may not be able to put it into simple words. We have to sort out what we think and feel.

Look at the following statements from the play. Choose one that you think sums up an important message from the author. Show us why you selected the statement you did. Show us how it sums up something important that is acted out in the play. (The class may want to decide on the statement that comes closest to summing up the major theme of the play.)

a. "We are a proud people."
b. "There is always something left to love."
c. "Sometimes it's hard to let the future begin."
d. "Seems like God didn't see fit to give the black man nothing but dreams."
e. "When it gets like that in life—you just got to do something different, push on out and do something bigger."
f. "There is only man, and it is he who makes miracles."

(3) When Mama first appears in the play in the first scene, the author describes her as follows:

She is a woman in her early sixties, full-bodied and strong. She is one of those women of a certain grace and beauty who wear it so unobtrusively that it takes a while to notice. Her dark-brown face is surrounded by the total whiteness of her hair, and, being a woman who has adjusted to many things in life and overcome many more, her face is full of strength. She has, we can see, wit and faith of a kind that keep her eyes lit and full of interest and expectancy. She is, in a word, a beautiful woman.

Suppose you could write to the author asking her to spell out what she meant: What kind of "strength" does Mama have? What kind of "wit"? What kind of "beauty"? What kind of "faith"? Pretend you are the author. Write a letter that answers these questions.

---

## Your Turn

---

(1) What kind of future do *you* think is ahead for the people in this play? Pretend you are the playwright. You are writing an **epilogue** to the play twenty years after it was first performed in 1959. An epilogue gives an author a chance to have a "last word" with the audience after the play is over. Tell your audience what has happened to the people in the play in the years that have passed. What has become of them?

(2) Is this play dated? Have things changed to the point where the play seems out-of-date? How would the play have to be changed to make it "true to life" as it exists *today*? Look at the four major characters in the play as kinds or types of people. Choose *one:* What has happened to this kind of character in the intervening years? How would you change the description of this kind of person to help bring the play up to date? Choose one of the following types:

—(Mama) the black matriarch: the strong older woman as head of the family
—(Walter) the frustrated, angry young male
—(Ruth) the wife and young mother
—(Beneatha) the politically aware black student

# Between Two Worlds

Eloquence is the ability to speak with telling effect and power about things that deeply concern people. One of the most basic concerns of people throughout history has been the ability of different groups to live together in peace. Basic in the American creed has long been respect for the rights and human dignity of others —others who are different from the way we happen to be. Some of the most eloquent voices in American history and American literature have been those raised on behalf of minorities, asking that their birthright not be denied.

In the American melting pot, people from many nationalities found a new identity. Within a generation or two, the sons and daughters of Scandinavians, Poles, and Italians became fully Americanized. Their families often kept some of their Old Country ways. However, the children grew up in a world in which pizza and Polish sausage were rapidly becoming as American as apple pie.

For millions of other young Americans, however, the road from Old Country ways to a new American identity was less straight. It turned out to be rocky, full of detours and dead ends. Some nationality groups held on to their own language and their own customs. They kept their own religious and social traditions. In the Mexican barrios, in Chinatown, or in Spanish Harlem, young Americans grew up for whom English was truly a second language. For many of them, the familiar world of baseball, Coca-Cola, and the red-white-and-blue was a second culture. Many of them were torn between pride in their own culture and the desire to be accepted in the larger society. Many bilingual young Americans at some point in their lives ask

themselves: "Who am I? Where do I come from? Where am I headed?" In talking about young Mexican-Americans, for instance, Ramón E. Ruiz says that at one time many of them "rebelled against traditional values in their urge to join the American mainstream." But more recently, "a new generation of Mexican-Americans has come of age." They "call themselves Chicanos and demand their share of the good life in the United States." Their search for identity is an "all-powerful drive that encourages youthful Chicanos to study Mexican history and to probe their southwestern heritage in the hope of discovering themselves."

Much powerful literature of the past and the present records the quest of young people for their own true identity. It records their attempt to find out who they really are and who they want to be. We see them listen to the conflicting voices telling them what to do with their lives. The following selections allow us to share in that search for identity.

## POEMS: **If Sun Comes**

In the earliest days of poetry, poets had two important functions. First, they kept alive the memory of the past. They recorded the deeds of heroes; they handed on knowledge of the ancient ways. But, second, they also looked into the future. They were prophets and seers. What pictures of the past and the future do you see in the following poems?

Stephen Berg

# Five Aztec Poems

### 1

now my friends
listen
the dream I am singing
is
each spring life
in the corn
put on a collar of rare stones

### 2

my soul fills to the brim with what I say
Oh friends
I am going to let my heart roam the earth
looking for peace
looking for good luck
no one is born twice

### 3

Oh nothing will cut down the flower of war
there it is on the edges of the river
here it is opening its petals
flower of the tiger flower of the shield
dust rises over the bells

### 4

until today my heart was happy
I hear this song I see a flower
if only they would never wither

### 5

we disappear
eagles tigers
nothing in the gold
nothing in the emeralds
nothing in the feathers
nothing in the word

*Symbolic picture, drawn by an Aztec Indian, of Quetzalcoatl (keht SAL kwahtl), the Toltec god of the morning star adopted by the Aztecs.*

## YOU AND THE POEMS

These poems were adapted from poems that the Aztec Indians knew before the Spaniards first came to the New World. What common human experiences play a role in these poems? Look at the objects, plants, and animals in these poems. What did they mean to the poets? Which of them are used with symbolic or figurative meanings? Would we still use them the same way today?

## Nikki Giovanni
# **Legacies**

her grandmother called her from the playground
    "yes, ma'am"
    "i want chu to learn how to make rolls" said the old
woman proudly
but the little girl didn't want
to learn how because she knew
even if she couldn't say it that
that would mean when the old one died she would be less
dependent on her spirit so
she said
    "i don't want to know how to make no rolls"
with her lips poked out
and the old woman wiped her hands on
her apron saying "lord
    these children"
and neither of them ever
said what they meant
and i guess nobody ever does

(1) How much do we learn about the grandmother? What kind of person is she? (Are there things about her that you recognize or that seem familiar to you?) Making rolls meant something more than a routine household task to both of the people in the poem. What does it symbolize for the grandmother?

(2) What is going on in the little girl's mind? Is she disrespectful? What does the making of rolls symbolize for the girl? (Why or how would knowing how to make rolls make a person "less dependent on her spirit"?

(3) Does the little girl represent the "younger generation"? Why or why not? Does she just speak for herself, or for many other younger people?

(4) What is a "legacy"? Where do we usually hear the word used? Why did the poet call this poem "Legacies"?

## A Closer Look

Like some other modern poetry, this poem departs from the usual *conventions* of the written page. For instance, there is almost no use of punctuation. (Can you find the one or two exceptions?) There is no use of capital letters. (Point out several places in the poem where a capital letter would be conventionally used.) Is it surprising or is it fitting that this poem is unconventional in its outward form? Explain your answer.

## Your Turn

Study the following set of *synonyms* and related words. What do they all have in common? How are they different—how do they differ in what they mean and in how or where they are used?

legacy        heritage
convention        tradition
heirloom        bequest        birthright

## YOU AND THE POEM

The poet says about the grandmother and the little girl, "neither of them ever said what they meant." What *did* they mean? Answer the following questions about this poem:

Gwendolyn Brooks

# Truth

And if sun comes
How shall we greet him?
Shall we not dread him,
Shall we not fear him
After so lengthy a
Session with shade?

Though we have wept for him,
Though we have prayed
All through the night-years—
What if we wake one shimmering morning to
Hear the fierce hammering
Of his firm knuckles
Hard on the door?

Shall we not shudder?—
Shall we not flee
Into the shelter, the dear thick shelter
Of the familiar
Propitious haze?

Sweet is it, sweet is it
To sleep in the coolness
Of snug unawareness.

The dark hangs heavily
Over the eyes.

## YOU AND THE POEM

The poet is one of those who have prayed for the arrival of "truth" and the passing of "unawareness." However, as she imagines the actual arrival of truth, her feelings are **paradoxical**—they are in some way the opposite of what we would expect. What are these feelings, and how does she make us share in them? Answer the following questions about the poem:

(1) What makes the sun a good **symbol** for truth? What makes morning a good symbol for truth? Find three or four things in this poem that the poet uses to symbolize the *opposite* of truth.

(2) Usually, we would expect people to welcome truth with open arms, and to reject the opposite. But in much of this poem, these feelings seem to be paradoxically reversed. Indicate the first hint of these contradictory feelings about truth in the first stanza. Then show how we are asked to imagine truth in the second stanza. A **paradox** is something that at first seems contradictory or strange, but that makes

634 Between Two Worlds

sense as we think about it. Does the description of truth in the second stanza make sense? How?

(3) What do all of the following words have in common: *dear, familiar, propitious, sweet, snug*? What are they applied to in the poem? Why is their use unexpected? How does it make sense?

### A Closer Look

Through the centuries, poets and orators have used **repetition** to build up a solemn feeling. By using similar words and similar phrases, they can channel our attention in one desired direction. They can build up a feeling until it becomes a strong, dominant **mood**.

(1) For each of the following words from this poem, find one or more related or similar words that the poet uses to drive home the same point: *fear, wept, fierce*.

(2) Point out several examples of how the poet repeats the same or very similar phrases—groups of words with very similar *rhythm* or *structure*.

## Imamu Amiri Baraka
### (LeRoi Jones)
# Preface to a Twenty-Volume Suicide Note

Jacob Lawrence, *Tombstones*, (detail). 1942. Gouache. 28³/4 × 20¹/2 inches. Collection of the Whitney Museum of American Art. Purchase.

Lately, I've become accustomed to the way
The ground opens up and envelops me
Each time I go out to walk the dog.
Or the broad edged silly music the wind
Makes when I run for a bus—

Things have come to that.

And now, each night I count the stars,
And each night I get the same number.
And when they will not come to be counted
I count the holes they leave.

Nobody sings anymore.

And then last night, I tiptoed up
To my daughter's room and heard her
Talking to someone, and when I opened
The door, there was no one there . . .
Only she on her knees,
Peeking into her own clasped hands.

## YOU AND THE POEM

(1) What are the poet's feelings at the beginning of the poem? Describe or try to explain the state of mind he finds himself in. Is there some explanation for the way he feels about the ground or the wind? Can you think of any reason why anyone would start counting the stars?

(2) In much ordinary prose, we expect one thing to follow logically from another. In a poem, we are more likely to be prepared for an imaginative leap—something comes into the poem that may at first seem strange or out of place. Look at the phrase, "Nobody sings anymore." How does it fit in with what comes before? Is it in any way related to or connected with the earlier part of the poem? What is the poet trying to tell us?

(3) What is happening in the daughter's room? How are the poet's feelings changed by looking at his daughter?

### Your Turn

Write an imaginary news item of the future under the headline, "NOBODY SINGS ANYMORE." Explain what has happened, or is happening, to produce this result.

James A. Emanuel
# Get Up, Blues

Blues
Never climb a hill
Or sit on a roof
In starlight.

Blues
Just bend low
And moan in the street
And shake a borrowed cup.

Blues
Just sit around
Sipping,
Hatching yesterdays.

Get up, Blues.
Fly.
Learn what it means
To be up high.

## YOU AND THE POEM

(1) What is it like to have the blues? Why does the poet claim that the blues wouldn't go with climbing a hill or "sitting on a roof in starlight"? Why and where is the cup being shaken in the second stanza? What do people do when they "hatch yesterdays"?

(2) Suppose you were talking to someone who felt low, and you were trying to make the person feel "up high." What would you ask the person to think of?

● Amado Muro was born in Mexico. He came to Texas to live and work in El Paso, the town "by the ford" across the Rio Grande. He has published stories about the Mexican-Americans of the Southwest in publications like the *Arizona Quarterly* and the *New Mexico Quarterly.* In the story that follows, he takes us back to his high school days. He tells of his struggles with two tasks that teenagers have had on their minds since times immemorial: to assert their independence from the influence of their parents, and to impress the other sex.

## Amado Muro

# Cecilia Rosas

When I was in the ninth grade at Bowie High School in El Paso, I got a job hanging up women's coats at La Feria Department Store on Saturdays. It wasn't the kind of a job that had much appeal for a Mexican boy or for boys of any other nationality either. But the work wasn't hard, only boring. Wearing a smock, I stood around the Ladies' Wear Department all day long waiting for women customers to finish trying on coats so I could hang them up.

Having to wear a smock was worse than the work itself. It was an agonizing ordeal. To me it was a loathsome stigma of unmanly toil that made an already degrading job even more so. The work itself I looked on as onerous and effeminate for a boy from a family of miners, shepherds, and ditchdiggers. But working in Ladies' Wear had two compensations: earning three dollars every Saturday was one; being close to the Señorita Cecilia Rosas was the other.

This alluring young woman, the most beautiful I had ever seen, more than made up for my mollycoddle labor and the smock that symbolized it. My chances of looking at her were almost limitless. And like a good Mexican, I made the most of

them. But I was only too painfully aware that I wasn't the only one who thought this saleslady gorgeous.

La Feria had water fountains on every one of its eight floors. But men liked best the one on the floor where Miss Rosas worked. So they made special trips to Ladies' Wear all day long to drink water and look at her.

Since I was only fourteen and in love for the first time, I looked at her more chastely than most. The way her romantic lashes fringed her eyes was especially enthralling to me. Then, too, I never tired of admiring her shining raven hair, her Cupid's-bow lips, the warmth of her gleaming white smile. Her rich olive skin was almost as dark as mine. Sometimes she wore a San Juan rose in her hair. When she did, she looked so very lovely I forgot all about what La Feria was paying me to do and stood gaping at her instead. My admiration was decorous but complete. I admired her hourglass figure as well as her wonderfully radiant face.

Other men admired her too. They inspected her from the water fountain. Some stared at her boldly. Others, less frank and open, gazed furtively. Their

effrontery made me indignant. I, too, looked at Miss Rosas. But I prided myself on doing so more romantically, far more poetically than they did, with much more love than desire.

Then, too, Miss Rosas was the friendliest as well as the most beautiful saleslady in Ladies' Wear. But the other salesladies, Mexican girls all, didn't like her. She was so nice to them that they were hard put to justify their dislike. They couldn't very well admit they disliked her because she was pretty. So they all said she was haughty and imperious. Their claim was partly true. Her beauty was Miss Rosas' only obvious vanity. But she had still another. She prided herself on being more American than Mexican because she was born in El Paso. And she did her best to act, dress, and talk the way Americans do. She hated to speak Spanish, disliked

her Mexican name. She called herself Cecile Roses instead of Cecilia Rosas. This made the other salesladies smile derisively. They called her La Americana or the Gringa from Xochimilco every time they mentioned her name.

Looking at this beautiful girl was more important than money to me. It was my greatest compensation for doing work that I hated. She was so lovely that a glance at her sweetly expressive face was enough to make me forget my shame at wearing a smock and my dislike for the daily routine of my job with its eternal waiting around.

Miss Rosas was an exemplary saleslady. She could be frivolous, serious, or demure, primly efficient too, molding herself to each customer's personality. Her voice matched her exotically mysterious eyes. It was the richest, the softest I had ever heard. Her husky whisper, gentle as a rain breeze, was like a tender caress. Hearing it made me want to dream and I did. Romantic thoughts burgeoned up in my mind like rosy billows of hope scented with Miss Rosas' perfume. These thoughts made me so languid at my work that the floor manager, Joe Apple, warned me to show some enthusiasm for it or else suffer the consequences.

But my dreams sapped my will to struggle, making me oblivious to admonitions. I had neither the desire nor the energy to respond to Joe Apple's warnings. Looking at Miss Rosas used up so much of my energy that I had little left for my work. Miss Rosas was twenty, much too old for me, everyone said. But what everyone said didn't matter. So I soldiered on the job and watched her, entranced by her beauty, her grace. While I watched I dreamed of being a hero. It hurt me to have her see me doing such menial work. But there was no escape from it. I needed the job to stay in school. So more and more I took refuge in dreams.

When I had watched her as much, if not more, than I could safely do without attracting the attention of other alert Mexican salesladies, I slipped out of Ladies' Wear and walked up the stairs to the top floor. There I sat on a window ledge smoking Faro cigarettes, looking down at the city's canyons, and best of all, thinking about Miss Rosas and myself.

They say Chihuahua Mexicans are good at dreaming because the mountains are so gigantic and the horizons so vast in Mexico's biggest state that men don't think pygmy thoughts there. I was no exception. Lolling on the ledge, I became what I wanted to be. And what I wanted to be was a handsome American Miss Rosas could love and marry. The dreams I dreamed were imaginative masterpieces, or so I thought. They transcended the insipid realities of a casual relationship,

making it vibrantly thrilling and infinitely more romantic. They transformed me from a colorless Mexican boy who put women's coats away into the debonair American, worldly and dashing, that I longed to be for her sake. For the first time in my life I reveled in the magic of fantasy. It brought happiness. Reality didn't.

But my window ledge reveries left me bewildered and shaken. They had a narcotic quality. The more thrillingly romantic fantasies I created, the more I needed to create. It got so I couldn't get enough dreaming time in Ladies' Wear. My kind of dreaming demanded disciplined concentration. And there was just too much hubbub, too much gossiping, too many coats to be put away there.

So I spent less time in Ladies' Wear. My flights to the window ledge became more recklessly frequent. Sometimes I got tired sitting there. When I did, I took the freight elevator down to the street floor and brazenly walked out of the store without so much as punching a time clock. Walking the streets quickened my imagination, gave form and color to my thoughts. It made my brain glow with impossible hopes that seemed incredibly easy to realize. So absorbed was I in thoughts of Miss Rosas and myself that I bumped into Americans, apologizing mechanically in Spanish instead of English, and wandered down South El Paso Street like a somnambulist, without really seeing its street vendors, cafés and arcades, tattoo shops, and shooting galleries at all.

But if there was confusion in these walks there was some serenity too. Something good did come from the dreams that prompted them. I found I could tramp the streets with a newly won tranquillity, no longer troubled by, or even aware of, girls in tight skirts and drop-stitch stockings. My love for Miss Rosas was my shield against the furtive thoughts and indiscriminate desires that had made me so uneasy for a year or more before I met her.

Then, too, because of her, I no longer looked at the pictures of women in the *Vea* and *Vodevil* magazines at Zamora's newsstand. The thoughts Mexicans call *malos deseos* were gone from my mind. I no longer thought about women as I did before I fell in love with Miss Rosas. Instead, I thought about a woman, only one. This clear-cut objective and the serenity that went with it made me understand something of one of the nicest things about love.

I treasured the walks, the window-ledge sittings, and the dreams that I had then. I clung to them just as long as I could. Drab realities closed in on me chokingly just as soon as I gave them up. My future was a time clock with an American Mister telling me what to do and this I knew only too well. A career as an ice-dock laborer stretched ahead of me. Better said, it dangled over me like a Veracruz machete. My uncle, Rodolfo Avitia, a straw boss on the ice docks, was already training me for it. Every night he took me to the mile-long docks overhanging the Southern Pacific freight yards. There he handed me tongs and made me practice tripping three-hundred-pound ice blocks so I could learn how to unload an entire boxcar of ice blocks myself.

Thinking of this bleak future drove me back into my fantasies, made me want to prolong them forever. My imagination was taxed to the breaking point by the heavy strain I put on it.

I thought about every word Miss Rosas had ever said to me, making myself believe she looked at me with unmistakable tenderness when she said them. When she said: "Amado, please hang up this fur coat," I found special meaning in her tone. It was as though she had said: "Amadito, I love you."

When she gave these orders, I pushed into action like a man blazing with a desire to perform heroic feats. At such times I felt capable of putting away not one but a thousand fur coats, and would have done so joyously.

Sometimes on the street I caught myself murmuring: "Cecilia, *linda amorcita*,[1] I love you." When these surges swept over me, I walked down empty streets so I could whisper: "Cecilia, *te quiero con toda mi alma*"[2] as much as I wanted to and mumble everything else that I felt. And so I emptied my heart on the streets and window ledge while women's coats piled up in Ladies' Wear.

But my absences didn't go unnoticed. Once an executive-looking man, portly, gray, and efficiently brusque, confronted me while I sat on the window ledge with a Faro cigarette pasted to my lips, a cloud of tobacco smoke hanging over my head, and many perfumed dreams inside it. He had a no-nonsense approach that jibed with his austere mien. He asked me what my name was, jotted down my work number, and went off to make a report on what he called "sordid malingering."

Other reports followed his. Gruff warnings, stern admonitions, and blustery tirades developed from them. They came from both major and minor executives. These I was already inured to. They didn't matter anyway. My condition was far too advanced, already much too complex to be cleared up by mere lectures, fatherly or otherwise. All the threats and rebukes in the world couldn't have made me give up my window-ledge reveries or kept me from roaming city streets with Cecilia Rosas' name on my lips like a prayer.

The reports merely made me more cunning, more doggedly determined to city-slick La Feria out of work hours I owed it. The net result was that I timed

[1] *linda amorcita:* Spanish, pretty little love.

[2] *te . . . alma:* I love you with all my soul.

my absences more precisely and contrived better lies to explain them. Sometimes I went to the men's room and looked at myself in the mirror for as long as ten minutes at a time. Such self-studies filled me with gloom. The mirror reflected an ordinary Mexican face, more homely than comely. Only my hair gave me hope. It was thick and wavy, deserving a better face to go with it. So I did the best I could with what I had, and combed it over my temples in ringlets just like the poets back in my hometown of Parral, Chihuahua, used to do.

My inefficiency, my dreams, my general lassitude could have gone on indefinitely, it seemed. My life at the store wavered between bright hope and leaden despair, unrelieved by Miss Rosas' acceptance or rejection of me. Then one day something happened that almost made my overstrained heart stop beating.

It happened on the day Miss Rosas stood behind me while I put a fur coat away. Her heady perfume, the fragrance of her warm healthy body, made me feel faint. She was so close to me I thought about putting my hands around her lissome waist and hugging her as hard as I could. But thoughts of subsequent disgrace deterred me, so instead of hugging her I smiled wanly and asked her in Spanish how she was feeling.

"Amado, speak English," she told me. "And pronounce the words slowly and carefully so you won't sound like a country Mexican."

Then she looked at me in a way that made me the happiest employee who ever punched La Feria's time clock.

"Amadito," she whispered the way I had always dreamed she would.

"Yes, Señorita Cecilia," I responded expectantly.

Her smile was warmly intimate. "Amadito, when are you going to take me to the movies?" she asked.

Other salesladies watched us, all smiling. They made me so nervous I couldn't answer.

"Amadito, you haven't answered me," Miss Rosas said teasingly. "Either you're bashful as a village sweetheart or else you don't like me at all."

In Spanish, I quickly assured her the latter wasn't the case. I was just getting ready to say "Señorita Cecilia, I more than like you, I love you" when she frowned and told me to speak English. So I slowed down and tried to smooth out my ruffled thoughts.

"Señorita Cecilia," I said. "I'd love to take you to the movies any time."

Miss Rosas smiled and patted my cheek. "Will you buy me candy and popcorn?" she said.

I nodded, putting my hand against the imprint her warm palm had left on my face.

"And hold my hand?"

I said "yes" so enthusiastically it made her laugh. Other salesladies laughed too. Dazed and numb with happiness, I watched Miss Rosas walk away. How proud and confident she was, how wholesomely clean and feminine. Other salesladies were looking at me and laughing.

Miss Sandoval came over to me. *"Ay papacito,"* she said. "With women you're the divine tortilla."

Miss de la Rosa came over too. "When you take the Americana to the movies, remember not to speak Christian," she said. "And be sure you wear the pants that don't have any patches on them."

What they said made me blush and wonder how they knew what we had been talking about. Miss Arroyo came over to join them. So did Miss Torres.

"Amado, remember women are weak and men aren't made of sweet bread," Miss Arroyo said.

This embarrassed me but it wasn't altogether unpleasant. Miss Sandoval winked at Miss de la Rosa, then looked back at me.

"Don't go too fast with the Americana, Amado," she said. "Remember the procession is long and the candles are small."

Then they all laughed and slapped me on the back. They all wanted to know when I was going to take Miss Rosas to the movies. "She didn't say," I blurted out without thinking.

This brought another burst of laughter. It drove me back up to the window ledge where I got out my package of Faros and thought about the wonderful thing that had happened. But I was too nervous to stay there. So I went to the men's room and looked at myself in the mirror again, wondering why Miss Rosas liked me so well. The mirror made it brutally clear that my looks hadn't influenced her. So it must have been something else, perhaps character. But that didn't seem likely either. Joe Apple had told me I didn't have much of that. And other store officials had bulwarked his opinion. Still, I had seen homely men walking the streets of El Paso's Little Chihuahua quarter with beautiful Mexican women and no one could explain that either. Anyway it was time for another walk. So I took one.

This time I trudged through Little Chihuahua, where both Miss Rosas and I lived. Little Chihuahua looked different to me that day. It was a broken-down Mexican quarter honeycombed with tenements, Mom and Pop groceries, herb shops, cafés, and spindly salt-cedar trees; with howling children running its streets and old Mexican revolutionaries sunning themselves on its curbs like iguanas. But on that clear frosty day it was the world's most romantic place because Cecilia Rosas lived there.

While walking, I reasoned that Miss Rosas might want to go dancing after the movies. So I went to Professor Toribio

Ortega's dance studio and made arrangements to take my first lesson. Some neighborhood boys saw me when I came out. They bawled "Mariquita" and made flutteringly effeminate motions, all vulgar. It didn't matter. On my lunch hour I went back and took my first lesson anyway. Professor Ortega danced with me. Softened by weeks of dreaming, I went limp in his arms imagining he was Miss Rosas.

The rest of the day was the same as many others before it. As usual I spent most of it stealing glances at Miss Rosas and slipping up to the window ledge. She looked busy, efficient, not like a woman in love. Her many other admirers trooped to the water fountain to look at the way her black silk dress fitted her. Their profane admiration made me scowl even more than I usually did at such times.

When the day's work was done, I plodded home from the store just as dreamily as I had gone to it. Since I had no one else to confide in, I invited my oldest sister, Dulce Nombre de María, to go to the movies with me. They were showing Jorge Negrete and María Felix in *El Rapto* at the Colon Theater. It was a romantic movie, just the kind I wanted to see.

After it was over, I bought Dulce Nombre *churros* and hot *champurrado*[3] at the Golden Taco Cafe. And I told my sister all about what had happened to me. She looked at me thoughtfully, then combed my hair back with her fingertips as though trying to soothe me. "Manito," she said, softly. "I wouldn't . . ." Then she looked away and shrugged her shoulders.

On Monday I borrowed three dollars from my Uncle Rodolfo without telling him what it was for. Miss Rosas hadn't told me what night she wanted me to take her to the movies. But the way she had

---

[3] *churros:* fritters; *champurrado:* a drink of corn gruel and chocolate.

looked at me made me think that almost any night would do. So I decided on Friday. Waiting for it to come was hard. But I had to keep my mind occupied. So I went to Zamora's newsstand to get the Alma Norteña songbook. Poring through it for the most romantic song I could find, I decided on *La Cecilia.*

All week long I practiced singing it on my way to school and in the shower after basketball practice with the Little Chihuahua Tigers at the Sagrado Corazón gym. But, except for singing this song, I tried not to speak Spanish at all. At home I made my mother mad by saying in English, "Please pass the sugar."

My mother looked at me as though she couldn't believe what she had heard. Since my Uncle Rodolfo couldn't say anything more than "hello" and "good-bye" in English, he couldn't tell what I had said. So my sister Consuelo did.

"May the Dark Virgin with the benign look make this boy well enough to speak Christian again," my mother whispered.

This I refused to do. I went on speaking English even though my mother and uncle didn't understand it. This shocked my sisters as well. When they asked me to explain my behavior, I parroted Miss Rosas, saying "We're living in the United States now."

My rebellion against being a Mexican created an uproar. Such conduct was unorthodox, if not scandalous, in a neighborhood where names like Burciaga, Rodríguez, and Castillo predominated. But it wasn't only the Spanish language that I lashed out against.

"Mother, why do we always have to eat *sopa, frijoles refritos, mondongo,* and *pozole?*"[4] I complained once. "Can't we ever eat roast beef or ham and eggs like Americans do?"

My mother didn't speak to me for two days after that. My Uncle Rodolfo grimaced and mumbled something about renegade Mexicans who want to eat ham and eggs even though the Montes Packing Company turned out the best *chorizo*[5] this side of Toluca. My sister Consuelo giggled and called me a Rio Grande Irishman, an American Mister, a gringo, and a *bolillo.*[6] Dulce Nombre looked at me worriedly.

Life at home was almost intolerable. Cruel jokes and mocking laughter made it so. I moped around looking sad as a day without bread. My sister Consuelo suggested I go to the courthouse and change my name to Beloved Wall which is English for Amado Muro. My mother didn't agree. "If *Nuestro Señor*[7] had meant for Amadito to be an American he would have given him a name like Smeeth or Jonesy," she said. My family was unsympathetic. With a family like mine, how could I ever hope to become an American and win Miss Rosas?

Friday came at last. I put on my only suit, slicked my hair down with liquid vaseline, and doused myself with Dulce Nombre's perfume.

"Amado's going to serenade that pretty girl everyone calls La Americana," my sister Consuelo told my mother and uncle when I sat down to eat. "Then he's going to take her to the movies."

This made my uncle laugh and my mother scowl.

"Quépantalones tiene (what nerve that boy's got)," my uncle said, "to serenade a twenty-year-old woman."

"La Americana," my mother said derisively. "That one's Mexican as pulque cured with celery."

---

[4] *sopa, frijoles refritos, mondongo, pozole:* soup, refried beans, tripe, pork-and-corn stew.

[5] *chorizo:* highly spiced pork sausage.

[6] *bolillo:* Mexican slang for an English-speaking person.

[7] *Neustro Señor:* Our Lord (Christ).

They made me so nervous I forgot to take off my cap when I sat down to eat.

"Amado, take off your cap," said my mother. "You're not in La Lagunilla Market."

My uncle frowned. "All this boy thinks about is kissing girls," he said gruffly.

"But my boy's never kissed one," my mother said proudly.

My sister Consuelo laughed. "That's because they won't let him," she said.

This wasn't true. But I couldn't say so in front of my mother. I had already kissed Emalina Uribe from Porfirio Díaz Street not once but twice. Both times I'd kissed her in a darkened doorway less than a block from her home. But the kisses were over so soon we hardly had time to enjoy them. This was because Ema was afraid her big brother, the husky one nicknamed Toro, would see us. But if we'd had more time it would have been better, I knew.

Along about six o'clock the three musicians who called themselves the Mariachis of Tecalitlán came by and whistled for me, just as they had said they would do. They never looked better than they did on that night. They had on black and silver charro uniforms and big black, Zapata sombreros.

My mother shook her head when she saw them. "Son, who ever heard of serenading a girl at six o'clock in the evening," she said. "When your father had the mariachis sing for me it was always at two o'clock in the morning—the only proper time for a six-song gallo."

But I got out my Ramírez guitar anyway. I put on my cap and rushed out to give the mariachis the money without even kissing my mother's hand or waiting for her to bless me. Then we headed for Miss Rosas' home. Some boys and girls I knew were out in the street. This made me uncomfortable. They looked at me wonderingly as I led the mariachi band to Miss Rosas' home.

A block away from Miss Rosas' home I could see her father, a grizzled veteran who had fought for Pancho Villa,[8] sitting on the curb reading the Juárez newspaper, *El Fronterizo*.

The sight of him made me slow down for a moment. But I got back in stride when I saw Miss Rosas herself.

She smiled and waved at me. "Hello, Amadito," she said.

"Hello, Señorita Cecilia," I said.

She looked at the mariachis, then back at me.

"Ay, Amado, you're going to serenade your girl," she said. I didn't reply right away. Then when I was getting ready to say "Señorita Cecilia, I came to serenade you," I saw the American man sitting in the sports roadster at the curb.

Miss Rosas turned to him. "I'll be right there, Johnny," she said.

She patted my cheek. "I've got to run now, Amado," she said. "Have a real nice time, darling."

I looked at her silken legs as she got into the car. Everything had happened so fast I was dazed. Broken dreams made my head spin. The contrast between myself and the poised American in the sports roadster was so cruel it made me wince.

She was happy with him. That was obvious. She was smiling and laughing, looking forward to a good time. Why had she asked me to take her to the movies if she already had a boyfriend? Then I remembered how the other salesladies had laughed, how I had wondered why they were laughing when they couldn't even hear what we were saying. And I realized it had all been a joke, everyone had known it but me. Neither Miss Rosas nor the other salesladies had ever dreamed I would think she was serious about wanting me to take her to the movies.

[8] *Pancho Villa:* Mexican bandit chief and revolutionary leader and hero; born 1877, died 1923.

The American and Miss Rosas drove off. Gloomy thoughts oppressed me. They made me want to cry. To get rid of them I thought of going to one of the "bad death" cantinas in Juárez where tequila starts fights and knives finish them. There I could forget her in style with mariachis, tequila, and night-life women. Then I remembered I was so young that night-life women would shun me and *cantineros* wouldn't serve me tequila.

So I thought some more. Emalina Uribe was the only other alternative. If we went over to Porfirio Díaz Street and serenaded her I could go back to being a Mexican again. She was just as Mexican as I was, Mexican as *chicharrones*.[9] I thought about smiling, freckle-faced Ema.

Ema wasn't like the Americana at all. She wore wash dresses that fitted loosely and even ate the *melcocha*[10] candies Mexicans like so well on the street. On Sundays she wore a Zamora shawl to church

⁹ *chicharrones:* pork cracklings.

¹⁰ *melcocha:* molasses.

and her mother wouldn't let her use lipstick or let her put on high heels.

But with a brother like Toro who didn't like me anyway, such a serenade might be more dangerous than romantic. Besides that, my faith in my looks, my character, or whatever it was that made women fall in love with men, was so undermined I could already picture her getting into a car with a handsome American just like Miss Rosas had done.

The Mariachis of Tecalitlán were getting impatient. They had been paid to sing six songs and they wanted to sing them. But they were all sympathetic. None of them laughed at me.

"Amado, don't look sad as I did the day I learned I'd never be a millionaire," the captain said, putting his arm around me. "If not that girl, then another."

But without Miss Rosas there was no one we could sing *La Cecilia* to. The street seemed bleak and empty now that she was gone. And I didn't want to serenade Ema Uribe even though she hadn't been faithless as Miss Rosas had been. It was true she hadn't been faithless, but only lack of opportunity would keep her from getting into a car with an American, I reasoned cynically.

Just about then Miss Rosas' father looked up from his newspaper. He asked the mariachis if they knew how to sing *Cananea Jail*. They told him they did. Then they looked at me. I thought it over for a moment. Then I nodded and started strumming the bass strings of my guitar. What had happened made it only too plain I could never trust Miss Rosas again. So we serenaded her father instead.

---

## YOU AND THE STORY

(1) Many autobiographical stories tell us about the first time the author was in love. Could you explain to someone what it felt like for this author to be in love? Do any of his feelings and attitudes seem familiar or expected to you? (Have you read or watched stories about other people experiencing similar feelings?)

(2) In this story, as in many similar stories, some of the outsiders *make fun* of someone who is in love. What makes people act that way? Do you think you would have been one of those who made fun of Amado? Why or why not? What would you tell the scoffers if you had a chance to give them your opinion?

### A Closer Look

(1) Though the story deals mostly with Amado's feelings and dreams, we do get glimpses of the **setting**. Give a thumbnail sketch of one of the following as you imagine it, based on what you read in the story: the Mexican neighborhood; the store; the mariachis and other features of the folkways and traditions of Amado's people.

(2) People often show a strong interest in other people. But we all know it is not *good manners* to stare at other people—or to seem to ignore them, either. Explain some of the words the author uses in talking about this question of etiquette: What does "decorous" mean? What are "furtive" looks? What is "effrontery"? Could you give a country boy like Amado some instructions on the approved etiquette for looking at other people—some of the things to do and not to do? (Is this type of etiquette *changing* today?)

### Your Turn

(1) The boy in the story considers himself homely and the girl beautiful. Much autobiographical writing deals with how we look

at ourselves, how others look at us, and how we look at others. Do one of the following:

—Do a *self-portrait* in words, describing yourself as you think you really are.
—Do two *contrasting* descriptions of yourself: one as you think you really are, one as you would like to be.
—Do an *imaginary portrait* of what you would consider an attractive or admirable person of the other sex.

(2) Have you ever rebelled against part of your own background or your own upbringing? Tell the story of your rebellion. What happened? Why? What did you learn from the experience?

(3) Much education takes place not in school but *on the job.* Have you had a job that taught you a few things you had not learned in school? Tell your listeners or readers about the experience.

Language/Composition Activity C6

STUDYING COHERENCE

# Charting Related Terms

When we try to communicate effectively, we do not just state an idea and then drop it. We try to make it sink in. We follow up; we "follow through." In a well-developed piece of writing, we often find that several different words strike the same note. A number of closely related words or expressions develop the idea or build up the impression that the writer aims at. We can often chart a *network* of words that work together to help the same basic idea sink in. Amado Muro is the kind of writer who is rarely at a loss for words when he becomes enthusiastic about an idea. Look at the following sets of related words that he uses to help drive home some of the ideas in his story. Do you see how all the words in each set work together? Explain briefly the meaning of each term in a set:

1. The author uses many words to make it clear that his job did not have much appeal:
agonizing—ordeal—loathsome—stigma—unmanly—toil—degrading—onerous—menial—drab.

2. The author often describes the girl in the most glowing terms:
alluring—gorgeous—romantic—enthralling—lovely—radiant—exotic.

3. The other girls in the story think of Cecilia in less infatuated terms:
haughty—imperious—vanity.

4. The boy's daydreams are often interrupted by nagging superiors:
admonitions—brusque—austere—gruff—stern—blustery—tirades—rebukes.

5. Amado often hints at the kind of young man he would like to be or to imitate:
debonair—dashing—worldly—heroic—poised.

6. When the boy "rebels against being a Mexican," the parents think of his attitude in very unfavorable terms:
unorthodox—scandalous—renegade.

Edna Ferber

# An Iowa Childhood

My father had decided that Chicago was not, after all, the ideal spot on which to lay the foundations of our future fortunes. A year had gone by during which we had stayed on in the house on Calumet Avenue. During that year my father was off for days at a time looking for a business location. He realized that he might much better have stayed on in Kalamazoo, but it was too late to think of that now. Perhaps he had discovered that the steps toward becoming a second Marshall Field or Carson Pirie Scott & Company were not so simple. He had, after all, been a small-town man always. Some miracle of mischance led him to a small Iowa coal-mining town distinguished by the Indian name of Ottumwa. The word is said to mean Place of Perseverance. Whatever Ottumwa means in the Indian language, it meant only bad luck for the Ferbers. My father had been told that there was absolutely no general store in the town. Ottumwa clamored, apparently, for Ferber's Bazaar. He inspected the place (he must have been blindfolded) and returned with glowing stories of this Iowa town in a farming and coal-mining district. The fact that it boasted more than sixteen thousand population without a decent shop for china, toys, notions, and all sorts of household goods should have been significant enough to serve as a warning.

My mother was anguished. She had left Kalamazoo happy at the thought of again becoming a Chicagoan. Now she was to live in an Iowa coal-mining town apparently for the rest of her days. Heavy-hearted with misgivings, she gathered up her household goods and her two children, left Chicago and her people behind her, and came to Ottumwa. As soon as she had a good look at the sordid, clay-and-gully Iowa town, she knew. There it lay flanked by the muddy Des Moines River; unpaved, bigoted, anti-Semitic, undernourished. Julia Ferber's days of youth and peace and happiness were over.

Those next seven years—from 1890 to 1897—must be held accountable for anything in me that is hostile toward the world in which I live. Child though I was, the brutality and ignorance of that little town penetrated to my consciousness, perhaps through casual talk as I heard it between my young parents; certainly as it was visited upon me.

I have since visited the town once, some ten years ago, and I found it a tree-shaded, sightly, modern American town of its size; clean, progressive. I had planned to stay overnight in the new and comfortable hotel. Memory was too strong. At eight that evening I drove through the starlit night back to Des Moines, past the rich black-loam farmlands of Iowa, past the substantial square-built fine farm homes, certainly the most modern and even luxurious farmhouses in the world. It was a purple velvet spring night; the air was rich with the smells of freshly turned earth and the first flowers; the highway ran its flawless length, mile on mile; the sky was lavish with brilliants.

For the first time in my life, out of the deep well of repression where they had so long festered, I dragged those seven years of my bitter little-girlhood and looked at them. And the cool clean Iowa air cleansed them, and I saw them then, not as bitter corroding years, but as strengthening years; years whose adversity had given me and mine a solid foundation of stamina and determination and a profound love of justice.

We moved into a new eight-room house on Wapello Street at the foot of a steep hill. The town ran from almost perpendicular hill streets to the flats near the Des Moines River. In the wintertime it was thrilling to be able to coast, gaining rocketlike velocity, down the length of Wapello or Marian Street hill. It was before the day of automobiles, there was little danger of being run down as you whizzed past street intersections. An occasional team, plop-plopping along in the snow, pulled up at the hill street crossings. In the summer Wapello hill was almost as exciting because you could count on the runaways. There were runaway horses every few days and, as we lived at the foot of the hill, they usually wound up with a grand flourish and splintering of wood and screaming of occupants practically in our laps. Faulty brakes, steep hill, and frightened horse combined to bring about this state of affairs. The best runaway I remember was a heavily laden hay wagon whose driver, helpless, sat perched atop his precarious load. I still can see the unwieldy mass careening wildly down the hill like a vast drunken fat woman. The usually phlegmatic farm horses, teased by the overladen wagon nipping at their heels, had taken fright, had galloped frantically down the steep slope, the mass had overturned, and the farmer lay unconscious, his head bleeding, his arm dislocated at the shoulder and broken. It was midmorning. There were no men about. I remember the doctor, hastily summoned, looking about him in his shirt-sleeves for likely help in this emergency.

"Which one of you ladies will pull this man's arm with all your strength while I set it?"

Julia Ferber came forward. "I will." And she pulled with all her strength while the sweat poured down the doctor's face and that of the groaning farmer.

My sister Fannie and I were left increasingly alone as my mother realized that there was more to my father's business than opening a store, stocking it, and waiting for customers. With instinctive common sense, though she knew nothing of business, she felt that something was amiss, and she set about finding out what this might be. She was still too young, too newly married, and too life-loving to admit that the whole structure was wrong. She got into the way of going to the store early after midday and staying there through the afternoon. There was the hired girl to look after my sister and myself, and we lived the normal outdoor life of small-town children.

The American maid-of-all-work, then known as the hired girl, was an institution in the middle-class life of that day and until the emigration restrictions largely stopped her. She should have a rich, colorful, and important book all to herself. The American hired girl was, in that day, a farm girl, daughter of foreign-born parents; or she was an immigrant newly landed; perhaps at most of five years' standing in this country. She was any one of a half-dozen nationalities: Irish, German, Swedish, Bohemian, Hungarian, Polish. Poverty, famine, persecution, ambition, a spirit of adventure—any one of these may have been the force which catapulted her across the ocean and into the melting pot. She brought into the Eastern and Midwestern middle-class American household a wealth of European ways, manners, customs in speech, cooking, religion, festivals, morals, clothing. If Hungarian, she brought the household such dishes as goulash and strudel; if Irish, stew and shortbread; if Bohemian, noodle-kraut; if Swedish, meatballs and flaky pastry; if Austrian, wiener schnitzel and the best of coffee. She brought her native peasant costume overseas in her funny corded trunk and could be coaxed to don it for the entertainment of the children of the household. To them, too, she brought old-world folktales, dances, myths, songs. She was warmhearted, simple, honest, and had to be taught to brush her teeth. Her hair, tightly braided, was wound around her head or skewered into an eye-straining knot. She rose at five-thirty to start the kitchen fire; she rose at four on Mondays to do the family wash. She loved to dance, she loved to sing, she loved to work.

Of the Ottumwa hired girls the first I remembered is Sophy. Sophy was swarthy, rather heavily mustached, a superb cook and definitely "touched." Her mental maladjustment was, however, confined to one narrow theme. She thought all men were in love with her. I don't know whether she was Polish or Hungarian. She was somewhere in her forties, very plain. She spoke with an accent, and she was always rushing in, after her days off, with an account of the passionate advances of some strange male.

After Sophy there was Sarah, a dear Welsh girl. Sometimes I used to go to early Mass with her. During my childhood I often went to early Mass when the household maid happened to be Catholic. I liked the drama of it; the color, the rich robes, the procession, the choir boys' fresh young voices; the sweetish prick of incense. Once or twice I went with Sarah to the little cottage where her parents lived, near the mines, and my first trip down into the deep black shaft of a coal mine was made with Sarah and her father. We stumbled through the eerie galleries where the men were at work, their tiny cap lamps casting weird shadows. I remember being shocked to learn that people worked in the earth like grubs. I felt sorry for them, and when we came up into the open air again I was relieved. I had felt somehow doomed never to see daylight again.

More and more of my mother's time was spent at the store, though she did little but watch and learn. It was as though scales and scales were falling from her eyes and she were seeing the hard world as it was for the first time. On Saturdays she was there until nine or ten o'clock waiting for her husband, for Saturdays and Saturday nights were the busy times. The farmers and their wives would come in to sell their produce and put in supplies; and the miners would spend their pay. The coal mines lay very near the town. The miners were, for the most part, Welshmen, brought over from the black pits of Cardiff. I would see them coming home from work in the evening, their eyes grotesquely rimmed with black, their trade caps, with the little miner's lamp, on their heads, their tin lunch pails in their tired hands. A lean gaunt lot with few enough quarters and half-dollars to exchange for goods at Ferber's Bazaar.

The town swirled down Main Street on Saturday night. On Saturday afternoon my sister and I went to a matinee if there happened to be a stock company in temporary residence. On Saturday night I was allowed to sit in a tiny chair in a corner and survey the crowds shuffling by. This I insisted on doing. I don't know why a child of five or thereabouts should have enjoyed this diversion, but I did, and I do to this day. My notion of bliss would be to sit in an armchair at the corner of Broadway and 42nd, or State and Madison, or any other busy intersection in America, and watch the town go by. The passer-by does not notice you or care about you; they, the people, are intent on getting somewhere, their faces are open to the reader; they betray themselves by their walk, their voices, their hands, clenched or inert; their feet, their clothes, their eyes.

Ottumwa of that day was a tough town. There were seven murders in it one year, and no convictions. This annoyed certain of the citizenry. They decided to take steps. Consequently, one day as I was rounding the corner on Main Street I saw people running and I was aware of a strange and bloodcurdling sound, not human. It was like the sound made by animals as I remembered them in Chicago's Lincoln Park Zoo at their mealtime. I quickened my steps and cleared the corner just in time to see an odd bundle jerking its way in midair up the electric light pole. It had legs and arms that waved like those of an insect, then they ceased to wave, the thing straightened itself and became decorous and limp, its head dropping as though in contrition. The animal sounds from the crowd below swelled, then ceased. Suddenly they melted away, seeming to flow up and down the streets in all directions. I heard the clang of the police patrol wagon.

Whatever there was to see I saw. Yearly there were held Methodist camp meetings in a great tent. People "got religion," they came down the aisle clapping their hands and shouting, rolling their eyes, shrieking and sobbing in an hysteria of induced emotion. They would drop to the floor at the foot of the platform. I was astonished to learn that these frenzies were occasioned by religious fervor. I had thought of religion as something dignified, solemn, and a little sad.

Somehow or other I attended Chautauquas, revival meetings, political rallies, political parades, ten-twenty-and-thirties, the circus. We always went to the circus at night because my parents could not very well get away in the daytime. I pitied my small friends who were obliged to be content with the afternoon performance. I thought it must be very dull to see this strange world by daylight, exposed beneath a blazing sun. Under the gas flares it was mysterious, romantic. Spangles glittered, color blazed, there was more menace in the snarls and growls of the wild animals. Then, too, there was the added thrill of being up so late. When we stumbled out after the performance, drunk with sound and color and dazzling sights, the smaller tents already had been whisked away like an Arabian Nights dream; hoarse men were shouting to one another and charging about with poles and weird canvas bundles. One heard the thick rich sound of heavy circus wheels on the roadway, like no other sound in the world. It stirred something in me, vague and terrible—something that went back, back, perhaps, to Egyptian days and the heavy wheels of chariots.

Going to school, playing with Ora Burney and Maude Hayward and the Trost boys, I had plenty of normal childish pleasure. But there in Ottumwa it was smirched with constant and cruel persecution. Through the seven years during which we lived in Ottumwa I know that I never went out on the street without being subjected to some form of devilment. It was a fine school for a certain sort of fortitude, but it gave me a strong dash of bitterness at an early age, together with

a bewildered puzzlement at what was known as the Christian world. Certainly I wasn't wise enough or old enough at five, six, seven, eight, nine, ten, to philosophize about this. But these people seemed to me to be barbarians.

On Saturdays, and on unusually busy days when my father could not take the time to come home to the noon dinner, it became my duty to take his midday meal down to him, very carefully packed in a large basket; soup, meat, vegetables, dessert. This must be carried with the utmost care so as not to spill or slop. No one thought of having a sandwich and a cup of coffee in the middle of the day, with a hot dinner to be eaten at leisure in the peace of the evening.

This little trip from the house on Wapello Street to the store on Main Street amounted to running the gauntlet. I didn't so much mind the Morey girl. She sat in front of her house perched on the white gatepost, waiting, a child about my age, with long red curls, a freckled face, very light green eyes. She swung her long legs, idly. At sight of me her listlessness fled.

"Hello, sheeny!" Then variations on this. This, one learned to receive equably. Besides, the natural retort to her baiting was to shout, airily, "Red Head! Wets the bed!"

But as I approached the Main Street corner there sat a row of vultures perched on the iron railing at the side of Sargent's drugstore. These were not children, they were men. Perhaps to me, a small child, they seemed older than they were, but their ages must have ranged from eighteen to thirty. There they sat, perched on the black iron rail, their heels hooked behind the lower rung. They talked almost not at all. The semicircle of spit rings grew richer and richer on the sidewalk in front of them. Vacant-eyed, they stared and spat and sat humped and round-shouldered, doing nothing, thinking nothing, being nothing. Suddenly their lackluster eyes brightened, they shifted, they licked their lips a little and spat with more relish. From afar they had glimpsed their victim, a plump little girl in a clean starched gingham frock, her black curls confined by a ribbon bow.

Every fiber of me shrieked to run the other way. My eyes felt hot and wide. My face became scarlet. I must walk carefully so as not to spill the good hot dinner. Now then. Now.

"Sheeny! Has du gesak de Isaac! De Moses! De Levi! Hoh, sheeny, what you got!" Good Old Testament names. They doubtless heard them in their Sunday worship, but did not make the connection, quite. Then they brought their hands, palms up, above the level of their shoulders and wagged them back and forth, "Oy-yoy, sheeny! Run! Go on, run!"

I didn't run. I glared. I walked by with as much elegance and aloofness as was compatible with a necessity to balance a basket of noodle soup, pot roast, potatoes, vegetable, and pudding.

Of course it was nothing more than a couple of thousand years of bigotry raising its hideous head again to spit on a defenseless and shrinking morsel of humanity. Yet it all must have left a deep scar on a sensitive child. It was unreasoning and widespread in the town. My parents were subject to it. The four or five respectable Jewish families of the town knew it well. They were intelligent men and women, American born and bred, for the most part. It probably gave me a ghastly inferiority, and out of that inferiority doubtless was born inside me a fierce resolution, absurd and childish, such as, "You wait! I'll show you! I'll be rich and famous and you'll wish you could speak to me." I have lived to see entire nations behaving precisely like the idle frustrated bums perched on the drugstore railing.

(1) The "bums" and "vultures" that baited the girl are seen here from the perspective of a frightened child. What do you think they were really like? What do you think made them act the way they did? What was going on in their minds?

(2) The author says that her years in Iowa gave her a "solid foundation of stamina and determination, and a profound love of justice." Can you explain why or how the experiences she describes would help produce these qualities?

(3) Pretend you are a teacher, preacher, police officer, or just plain ordinary citizen happening upon the scene the author describes at the end of this selection. What would you tell the people involved?

---

**Your Turn**

---

Is the kind of prejudice Edna Ferber describes in this selection a thing of the past? Whatever your answer, be prepared to explain it to someone who asks: "What makes you think so?" Discuss in detail several personal observations or experiences that help determine your answer to the original question.

---

Language/Composition Activity C7

IMAGINATIVE DESCRIPTION
# A Scene I Would Like to See

Edna Ferber gives us brief glimpses of childhood scenes from long ago. Which of these scenes becomes most vivid in your own mind? Could you *reconstruct* one of these scenes, using your own imagination to fill in some of the details the author has left out? Write a passage in which you make us see a scene like the following:

—a prosperous Iowa farm of yesteryear
—an old-fashioned country store
—work in an old-style coal mine
—an old-fashioned circus coming to town
—an old-style carriage accident
—an old-style religious camp meeting
—working in the kitchen as the "hired girl"

● Simon J. Ortiz, a Pueblo Indian, has been called a "distinguished representative of an Indian Renaissance which has forced white writers to reevaluate the Indian and his part in the American experience." Ortiz writes about American Indians as the "forgotten people" in our society. In the following story, he makes us think about what happens when two ways of life, two ways of looking at things, come into conflict. When people from different backgrounds meet, problems of communication often result. Within our own group, we know the rules, the signals, the penalties, the laws. But when we talk to people from a different background, we often discover they have different standards of what is right and what is wrong. What seems reasonable to us may seem silly to them. What seems tried and true to them may seem like mere foolishness to us. What is the communication gap in the following story?

## Simon J. Ortiz

# Kaiser and the War

Kaiser got out of the state pen when I was in the fourth grade. I don't know why people called him Kaiser. Some called him Hitler, too, since he was Kaiser, but I don't think he cared at all what they called him. He was probably just glad to get out of the state pen anyway.

Kaiser got into the state pen because he didn't go into the army. That's what my father said anyway, and because he was a crazy nut according to some people, which was probably why he didn't want to go into the army in the first place, which was what my father said also.

The army wanted him anyway, or maybe they didn't know he was crazy or supposed to be. They came for him out at home on the reservation, and he said he wasn't going to go because he didn't speak good English. Kaiser didn't go to school more than just the first or second grade. He said what he said in Indian and his sister said it in English for him. The army men, somebody from the county draft

board, said they'd teach him English, don't worry about it, and how to read and write and give him clothes and money when he got out of the army so that he could start regular as any American. Just like anybody else, and they threw in stuff about how it would be good for our tribe and the people of the U.S.A.

Well, Kaiser, who didn't understand that much English anyway, listened quietly to his sister telling him what the army draft-board men were saying. He didn't ask any questions, just once in a while said, "Yes," like he'd been taught to say in the first grade. Maybe some of the interpretation was lost the way his sister was doing it, or maybe he went nuts like some people said he did once in a while because the next thing he did was to burst out the door and start running for Black Mesa.

The draft-board men didn't say anything at first and then they got pretty mad. Kaiser's sister cried because she didn't want Kaiser to go into the army but she didn't want him running out just like that either. She had gone to the Indian school in Albuquerque, and she learned that stuff about patriotism, duty, honor—even if you were said to be crazy.

At about that time, their grandfather, Faustin, cussed in Indian at the draft-board men. Nobody had noticed when he came into the house, but there he was, fierce-looking as usual, although he wasn't fierce at all. Then he got mad at his granddaughter and the men, asked what they were doing in his house, making the women cry and not even sitting down like friendly people did. Old Faustin and the army confronted each other. The army men were confused and getting more and more nervous. The old man told the girl to go out of the room and he'd talk to the army himself, although he didn't speak a word of English.

Those army men tried to get the girl to come back, but the old man wouldn't let her. He told her to get to grinding corn or something useful. They tried sign language and when Faustin figured out what they were waving their hands around for, he laughed out loud. He wouldn't even take the cigarettes offered him, so the army men didn't say anything more. The last thing they did though was give the old man a paper which they didn't try to explain what it was for. They probably hoped it would get read somehow.

Well, after they left, the paper did get read by the girl, and she told Faustin what it was about. The law was going to come and take Kaiser to jail because he wouldn't go into the army by himself. Grandfather Faustin sat down and talked quietly to himself for a while and then he got up to look for Kaiser.

Kaiser was on his way home by then, and his grandfather told him what was going to happen. They sat down by the side of the road and started to make plans.

Kaiser would go hide up on Black Mesa and maybe go up all the way to Brushy Mountain if the law really came to poking around seriously. Faustin would take him food and tell him the news once in a while.

Everybody in the village knew what was going on pretty soon. Some approved, and some didn't. Some thought it was pretty funny. My father, who couldn't go in the army even if he wanted to because there were too many of us kids, laughed about it for days. The people who approved of it and thought it funny were the ones who knew Kaiser was crazy and that the army must be even crazier. The ones who disapproved were mostly those who were scared of him. A lot of them were parents or brothers of girls who they must have suspected of liking Kaiser. Kaiser was pretty good-looking and funny in the way he talked for a crazy guy. And he was a hard worker. He worked every day out in the fields or up at the sheep camp for his parents while they were alive and for his sister and nephew and grandfather. These people, who were scared of him and said he should have gone into the army perhaps it'll do him good, didn't want him around their daughters or sisters. Mostly these people were scared he would do something, and there was one too many nuts around in the village anyway, they said.

My old man didn't care though. He was buddies with Kaiser. When there was a corn dance up at the community hall, they would have a whole lot of fun singing and laughing and joking, and once in a while when someone brought around a bottle or two they would really get going and the officers of the tribe would have to warn them to behave themselves.

Kaiser was okay, though. He came around home quite a lot. His own kinfolks didn't care for him too much because he was crazy, and they didn't go out of their way to invite him to eat or spend the night when he dropped by their homes and it happened to get dark before he left. My mother didn't mind him around. When she served him something to eat, she didn't act like he was nuts, or supposed to be; she just served him and fussed over him like he was a kid, which Kaiser acted like a lot of the time. I guess she didn't feel a guy who acted like a kid was crazy.

Right after we finished eating, if it happened to be supper, my own grandfather, who was a medicine man, would talk to him and to all of us kids who were usually paying only half attention. He would tell us advice, about how the world was, how each person, everything, was important. And then he would tell us stories about the olden times. Legends mostly, about the katzina, Spider Woman, where our hano, people, came from. Some of the stories were funny, some sad, and some pretty boring. Kaiser would sit there, not saying anything except "Eheh," which is what you're supposed to say once in a while to show that you're listening to the olden times.

After half of us kids were asleep, grandfather would quit talking, only Kaiser wouldn't want him to quit and he'd ask for more, but grandfather wouldn't tell any more. What Kaiser would do was start telling himself about the olden times. He'd lie on the floor in the dark, or sometimes up on the roof which was where he'd sleep in the summer, talking. And sometimes he'd sing, which is also part of the old times. I would drift off to sleep just listening to him.

Well, he didn't come around home after he went up on Black Mesa. He just went up there and stayed there. The law, which was the county sheriff, an officer, and the Indian agent from the Indian Affairs office in Albuquerque, came out to get him, but nobody would tell them where he was. The law had a general idea where he was, but that didn't get them very far because they didn't know the country around Black Mesa. It's rough up here, just a couple of sheep camps in a lot of country.

The Indian agent had written a letter to the officers of the tribe that they would come up for Kaiser on a certain day. There were a lot of people waiting for them when they drove up to the community meeting hall. The county sheriff had a bulging belly and he had a six-shooter strapped to his hip. When the men standing outside the community hall saw him step out of the government car, they made jokes. Just like the Lone Ranger, someone said. The law didn't know what they were laughing about, and they said, Hello, and paid no attention to what they couldn't understand.

Faustin was among them. But he was silent and he smoked a roll-your-own. The agent stopped before him, and Faustin took a slow drag on his roll-your-own but he didn't look at the man.

"Faustin, my old friend," the agent said. "How are you?"

The old man didn't say anything. He let the tobacco smoke out slowly and looked straight ahead. Someone in the crowd told Faustin what the agent had said, but the old man didn't say anything at all.

The law thought he was praying or that he was a wise man contemplating his answer, the way he was so solemn-like, so they didn't press him. What Faustin was doing was ignoring the law. He didn't want them to talk with him. He turned to a man at his side.

"Tell this man I do not want to talk. I can't understand what they are saying in American anyway. And I don't want anyone to tell me what they say. I'm not interested." He looked at the government then, and he dismissed their presence with his indignation.

"The old man isn't gonna talk to you," someone said.

The agent and sheriff big belly glared at the man. "Who's in charge around here?" the sheriff said.

The Indians laughed. They joked by calling each other big belly. The governor of the tribe and two chiefs soon came. They greeted the law, and then they went into the meeting hall to confer about Kaiser.

"Well, have you brought Kaiser?" the Indian agent asked, although he saw that they hadn't and knew that they wouldn't.

"No," the governor said. And someone interpreted for him. "He will not come."

"Well, why don't you bring him? If he doesn't want to come, why don't you bring him? A bunch of you can bring him," the agent said. He was becoming irritated.

The governor, chiefs, and men talked to each other. One old man held the floor a while, until others got tired of him telling about the old times and how it was and how the Americans had said a certain thing and did another and so forth. Someone said, "We can bring him. Kaiser should come by himself anyway. Let's go get him." He was a man who didn't like Kaiser. He looked around carefully when he got through speaking and sat down.

"Tell the Americans that is not the way," one of the chiefs said. "If our son wants to meet these men he will come." And the law was answered with the translation.

"I'll be switched," the sheriff said, and the Indians laughed quietly. He glared at them and they stopped. "Let's go get him ourselves," he continued.

The man who had been interpreting said, "He is crazy."

"Who's crazy?" the sheriff yelled, like he was refuting an accusation. "I think you're all crazy."

"Kaiser, I think he is crazy," the interpreter said like he was ashamed of saying so. He stepped back, embarrassed.

Faustin then came to the front. Although he said he didn't want to talk with the law, he shouted, "Go get Kaiser your-self. If he's crazy, I hope he kills you. Go get him."

"Okay," the agent replied when the interpreter finished. "We'll go get him ourselves. Where is he?" The agent knew no one would tell him, but he asked it anyway.

Upon that, the Indians assumed the business that the law came to do was over, and that the law had resolved what it came to do in the first place. The Indians began to leave.

"Wait," the agent said. "We need some-one to go with us. He's up on Black Mesa, but we need someone to show us where."

The men kept on leaving. "We'll pay you. The government will pay you to go with us. You're deputized," the agent said. "Stop them, Sheriff," he said to the county sheriff, and the sheriff yelled, "Stop, come back here," and put a hand to his six-shooter. When he yelled, some of the Indians looked at him to laugh. He sure looked funny and talked funny. But some of them came back. "All right, you're deputies, you'll get paid," the sher-iff said. Some of them knew what that meant, others weren't too sure. Some of them decided they'd come along for the fun of it.

The law and the Indians piled into the government car and a pickup truck which belonged to one of the deputies who was assured that he would get paid more than the others.

Black Mesa is fifteen miles back on the reservation. There are dirt roads up to it, but they aren't very good, nobody uses them except sheep herders and hunters in the fall. Kaiser knew what he was doing when he went up there, and he probably saw them when they were coming. But it wouldn't have made any difference be-cause when the law and the deputies come up to the foot of the mesa, they still weren't getting anywhere. The deputies, who were still Indians too, wouldn't tell or didn't really know where Kaiser was at the moment. So they sat for a couple of hours at the foot of the mesa, debating what should be done. The law tried to get the deputies to talk. The sheriff was boiling mad by this time, getting madder too, and he was for persuading one of the deputies into telling where Kaiser was exactly. But he reasoned the deputy wouldn't talk being that he was Indian too, and so he shut up for a while. He had figured out why the Indians laughed so frequently even though it was not as loud as before they were deputized.

Finally, they decided to walk up Black Mesa. It's rough going and when they didn't know which was the best way to go up they found it was even rougher. The real law dropped back one by one to rest on a rock or under a piñon tree until only the deputies were left. They watched the officer from the Indian Affairs office sit-ting on a fallen log some yards back. He was the last one to keep up so far, and he was unlacing his shoes. The deputies waited patiently for him to start again and for the others to catch up.

"It's sure hot," one of the deputies said.

"Yes, maybe it'll rain soon," another said.

"No, it rained for the last time last month, maybe next year."

"Snow then," another said.

They watched the sheriff and the Indian agent walking toward them half a mile back. One of them limped.

"Maybe the Americans need a rest," someone said. "We walked a long ways."

"Yes, they might be tired," another said. "I'll go tell that one that we're going to stop to rest," he said and walked back to the law sitting on the log. "We gonna stop to rest," he told the law. The law didn't say anything as he massaged his feet. And the deputy walked away to join the others.

They didn't find Kaiser that day or the next day. The deputies said they could walk all over the mesa without finding him for all eternity, but they wouldn't find him. They didn't mind walking, they said. As long as they got paid for their time, their crops were already in, and they'll just hire someone to haul winter wood for them now that they had the money. But they refused to talk. The ones who wanted to tell where Kaiser was, if they knew, didn't say so out loud, but they didn't tell anyway so it didn't make any difference. They were too persuaded by the newly found prosperity of being employed.

The sheriff, exhausted by the middle of the second day of walking the mesa, began to sound like he was for going back to Albuquerque. Maybe Kaiser'd come in by himself, he didn't see any sense in looking for some Indian anyway just to get him into the army. Besides, he'd heard the Indian was crazy. When the sheriff had first learned the Indian's name was Kaiser he couldn't believe it, but he was assured that wasn't his real name, just something he was called because he was crazy. But the sheriff didn't feel any better or less tired, and he was getting jumpy about the crazy part.

At the end of the second day, the law decided to leave. Maybe we'll come back, they said; we'll have to talk this over with the Indian Affairs officials, maybe it'll be all right if that Indian didn't have to be in the army after all. And they left. The sheriff, his six-shooter off his hip now, was pretty tired out, and he didn't say anything.

The officials for the Indian Affairs didn't give up though. They sent back some more men. The county sheriff had decided it wasn't worth it, besides he had a whole county to take care of. And the Indians were deputized again. More of them volunteered this time, some had to be turned away. They had figured out how to work it: they wouldn't have to tell, if they knew, where Kaiser was. All they would have to do was walk and say from time to time, "Maybe he's over there by that canyon. Used to be there was some good hiding places back when the Apache and Navaho were raising Cain." And some would go over there and some in the other direction, investigating good hiding places. But after camping around Black Mesa for a week this time, the Indian Affairs gave up. They went by Faustin's house the day they left for Albuquerque and left a message: the government would wait and when Kaiser least expected it, they would get him and he would have to go to jail.

Kaiser decided to volunteer for the army. He had decided to after he had watched the law and the deputies walk all over the mesa. Grandfather Faustin had come to visit him up at one of the sheep camps, and the old man gave him all the news at home and then he told Kaiser the message the government had left.

"Okay," Kaiser said. And he was silent for a while and nodded his head slowly like his grandfather did. "I'll join the army."

"No," his grandfather said. "I don't want you to. I will not allow you."

"Grandfather, I do not have to mind you. If you were my grandfather or uncle on my mother's side, I would listen to you and probably obey you, but you are not, and so I will not obey you."

"You are really crazy then," Grandfather Faustin said. "If that's what you want to do, go ahead." He was angry and he was sad, and he got up and put his hand on his grandson's shoulder and blessed him in the people's way. After that the old man left. It was evening when he left the sheep camp, and he walked for a long time away from Black Mesa before he started to sing.

The next day, Kaiser showed up at home. He ate with us, and after we ate we sat in the living room with my grandfather.

"So you've decided to go into the Americans' army," my grandfather said. None of us kids, nor even my parents, had known he was going but my grandfather had known all along. He probably knew as soon as Kaiser had walked into the house. Maybe even before that.

My grandfather blessed him then, just like Faustin had done, and he talked to him of how a man should behave and what he should expect. Just general things, and grandfather turned sternly toward us kids who are playing around as usual. My father and mother talked with him also, and when they were through, my grandfather put cornmeal in Kaiser's hand for him to pray with. Our parents told us kids to tell Kaiser good-bye and good luck and after we did, he left.

The next thing we heard was that Kaiser was in the state pen.

Later on, some people went to visit him up at the state pen. He was okay and getting fat, they said, and he was getting on okay with everybody and the warden told them. And when someone had asked Kaiser if he was okay, he said he was fine and he guessed he would be American pretty soon being that he was around them so much. The people left Kaiser some home-baked bread and dried meat and came home after being assured by the warden that he'd get out pretty soon, maybe right after the war. Kaiser was a model inmate. When the visitors got home to the reservation, they went and told Faustin his grandson was okay, getting fat and happy as any American. Old Faustin didn't have anything to say about that.

Well, the war was over after a while.

Faustin died sometime near the end of it. Nobody had heard him mention Kaiser at all. Kaiser's sister and nephew were the only ones left at their home. Sometimes someone would ask about Kaiser, and his sister and nephew would say, "Oh, he's fine. He'll be home pretty soon, right after the war." But after the war was over, they just said he was fine.

My father and a couple of other guys went down to the Indian Affairs office to see what they could find out about Kaiser. They were told that Kaiser was going to stay in the pen longer now because he had tried to kill somebody. Well, he just went crazy one day, and he made a mistake so he'll just have to stay in for a couple more years or so, the Indian Affairs said. That was the first anybody heard of Kaiser trying to kill somebody, and some people said why didn't they put him in the army for that like they wanted to in the first place. So Kaiser remained in the pen long after the war was over and most of the guys who had gone into the army from the tribe had come home. When he was due to get out, the Indian Affairs sent a letter to the governor and several men from the village went to get him.

My father said Kaiser was quiet all the way home on the bus. Some of the guys tried to joke with him, but he just wouldn't laugh or say anything. When they got off the bus at the highway and began to walk home, the guys broke into song, but that didn't bring Kaiser around. He kept walking quiet and reserved in his gray suit. Someone joked that Kaiser probably owned the only suit in the whole tribe.

"You lucky so and so. You look like a rich man," the joker said. The others looked at him sharply and he quit joking, but Kaiser didn't say anything.

When they reached home, his sister and nephew were very happy to see him. They cried and laughed at the same time, but

Kaiser didn't do anything except sit at the kitchen table and look around. My father and the other guys gave him advice and welcomed him home again and left.

After that, Kaiser always wore his gray suit. Every time you saw him, he was wearing it. Out in the fields or at the plaza watching the katzina, he wore the suit. He didn't talk much any more, my father said, and he didn't come around home any more either. The suit was getting all beat-up looking, but he just kept on wearing it so that some people began to say that he was showing off.

"That Kaiser," they said, "he's always wearing this suit, just like he was an American or something. Who does he think he is anyway?" And they'd snicker, looking at Kaiser with a sort of envy. Even when the suit was torn and soiled so that it hardly looked anything like a suit, Kaiser wore it. And some people said, "When he dies, Kaiser is going to be wearing his suit." And they said that like they wished they had gotten a suit like Kaiser's.

Well, Kaiser died, but without his gray suit. He died up at one of his distant relatives' sheep camps one winter. When someone asked about the suit, they were told by Kaiser's sister that it was rolled up in some newspaper at their home. She said that Kaiser had told her, before he went up to the sheep camp, that she was to send it to the government. But, she said, she couldn't figure out what he meant, whether Kaiser had meant the law or somebody, maybe the state pen or the Indian Affairs.

The person who asked about the suit wondered about this Kaiser's instructions. He couldn't figure out why Kaiser wanted to send a beat-up suit back. And then he figured, well, maybe that's the way it was when you either went into the state pen or the army and became an American.

---

## YOU AND THE STORY

Do you think Kaiser was treated unjustly by the law? Why or why not?

---

## A Closer Look

(1) There seem to be some contradictory opinions about Kaiser even before the "army men" came for him. Do you think Kaiser was "crazy"? What kind of person was he?

(2) The "law people" come to the reservation from a different world, and they don't always understand what is going on. Could you help people like them in a similar situation? What is the attitude of the Indians toward the representatives of the law?

(3) Apparently, Kaiser misunderstood the way the law worked or was going to work in his case. Why or how? If you had a chance to explain to him how things worked in his case, what would you say?

(4) Why do you think Kaiser kept wearing the suit that he brought home with him? Why did he want it sent back to the government after he died?

(5) When people misunderstand each other, the results are often funny, and often sad. Which parts of the story do you think were funny? Are there parts that are funny and sad at the same time?

---

## Your Turn

Many people believe in justice. But in individual cases they often find it hard to agree on whether an injustice has occurred, or whether "justice" was done. Can you describe in detail a clear-cut case of "injustice"? Discuss a case that you know well from your own observation, experience, or reading.

● Some writers are fascinated with the rich and famous. They describe the glamorous or adventurous lives of people that we may envy or that may give us something to daydream about. But other writers write about the poor and unknown. They write about the underdog, the outcast, the loner. John Steinbeck wrote many of his stories about people who do not appear in the society pages or in the history books. In his early years, he had worked as a sailor, fruit picker, surveyor, and caretaker. One of his first successful books was *Tortilla Flat* (1935), a story about the Spanish-Indian *paisanos* of the Monterey area in central California, where Steinbeck grew up. *Of Mice and Men* (1937), like some of his other books, was a story about migratory workers. His *Grapes of Wrath* (1939), read by millions, told the story of Oklahoma farmers driven from their homes during the Dust Bowl years of the Great Depression. It followed them on their journey through the hobo jungles and workers' camps of the West in search of a new life. In the story that follows Steinbeck takes us to the Monterey coast, his favorite setting. The characters of the story speak Spanish and have Spanish names. They are poor, and they are proud.

John Steinbeck

# Flight

About fifteen miles below Monterey, on the wild coast, the Torres family had their farm, a few sloping acres above a cliff that dropped to the brown reefs and to the hissing white waters of the ocean. Behind the farm the stone mountains stood up against the sky. The farm buildings huddled like little clinging aphids on the mountain skirts, crouched low to the ground as though the wind might blow them into the sea. The little shack, the rattling, rotting barn were gray-bitten with sea salt, beaten by the damp wind until they had taken on the color of the granite hills. Two horses, a red cow and a red calf, half a dozen pigs and a flock of lean, multicolored chickens stocked the place. A little corn was raised on the sterile slope, and it grew short and thick under the wind, and all the cobs formed on the landward sides of the stalks.

Mama Torres, a lean, dry woman with ancient eyes, had ruled the farm for ten years, ever since her husband tripped over a stone in the field one day and fell full length on a rattlesnake. When one is bitten on the chest there is not much that can be done.

Mama Torres had three children, two undersized black ones of twelve and fourteen, Emilio and Rosy, whom Mama kept fishing on the rocks below the farm when the sea was kind and when the truant officer was in some distant part of Monterey County. And there was Pepé, the tall smiling son of nineteen, a gentle, affectionate boy, but very lazy. Pepé had a tall head, pointed at the top, and from its

peak, coarse black hair grew down like a thatch all around. Over his smiling little eyes Mama cut a straight bang so he could see. Pepé had sharp Indian cheekbones and an eagle nose, but his mouth was as sweet and shapely as a girl's mouth, and his chin was fragile and chiseled. He was loose and gangling, all legs and feet and wrists, and he was very lazy. Mama thought him fine and brave, but she never told him so. She said, "Some lazy cow must have got into thy father's family, else how could I have a son like thee." And she said, "When I carried thee, a sneaking lazy coyote came out of the brush and looked at me one day. That must have made thee so."

Pepé smiled sheepishly and stabbed at the ground with his knife to keep the blade sharp and free from rust. It was his inheritance, that knife, his father's knife. The long heavy blade folded back into the black handle. There was a button on the handle. When Pepé pressed the button, the blade leaped out ready for use. The knife was with Pepé always, for it had been his father's knife.

One sunny morning when the sea below the cliff was glinting and blue and the white surf creamed on the reef, when even the stone mountains looked kindly, Mama Torres called out the door of the shack, "Pepé, I have a labor for thee."

There was no answer. Mama listened. From behind the barn she heard a burst of laughter. She lifted her full long skirt and walked in the direction of the noise.

Pepé was sitting on the ground with his back against a box. His white teeth glistened. On either side of him stood the two black ones, tense and expectant. Fifteen feet away a redwood post was set in the ground. Pepé's right hand lay limply in his lap, and in the palm the big black knife rested. The blade was closed back into the handle. Pepé looked smiling at the sky.

Suddenly Emilio cried, "Ya!"

Pepé's wrist flicked like the head of a snake. The blade seemed to fly open in mid-air, and with a thump the point dug into the redwood post, and the black handle quivered. The three burst into excited laughter. Rosy ran to the post and pulled out the knife and brought it back to Pepé. He closed the blade and settled the knife carefully in his listless palm again. He grinned self-consciously at the sky.

"Ya!"

The heavy knife lanced out and sunk into the post again. Mama moved forward like a ship and scattered the play.

"All day you do foolish things with the knife, like a toy-baby," she stormed. "Get up on thy huge feet that eat up shoes. Get up!" She took him by one loose shoulder and hoisted at him. Pepé grinned sheepishly and came halfheartedly to his feet. "Look!" Mama cried. "Big lazy, you must catch the horse and put on him thy father's saddle. You must ride to Monterey. The medicine bottle is empty. There is no salt. Go thou now, Peanut! Catch the horse."

A revolution took place in the relaxed figure of Pepé. "To Monterey, me? Alone? Sí, Mama."

She scowled at him. "Do not think, big sheep, that you will buy candy. No, I will give you only enough for the medicine and the salt."

Pepé smiled, "Mama, you will put the hatband on the hat?"

She relented then. "Yes, Pepé. You may wear the hatband."

His voice grew insinuating, "And the green handkerchief, Mama?"

"Yes, if you go quickly and return with no trouble, the silk green handkerchief will go. If you make sure to take off the handkerchief when you eat so no spot may fall on it. . . ."

'Sí, Mama. I will be careful. I am a man."

"Thou? A man? Thou art a peanut."

He went into the rickety barn and brought out a rope, and he walked agilely enough up the hill to catch the horse.

When he was ready and mounted before the door, mounted on his father's saddle that was so old that the oaken frame showed through torn leather in many places, then Mama brought out the round black hat with the tooled leather band, and she reached up and knotted the green silk handkerchief about his neck. Pepé's blue denim coat was much darker than his jeans, for it had been washed much less often.

Mama handed up the big medicine bottle and the silver coins. "That for the medicine," she said, "and that for the salt. That for a candle to burn for the papa. That for *dulces*[1] for the little ones. Our friend Mrs. Rodriguez will give you dinner and maybe a bed for the night. When you go to the church say only ten Paternosters and only twenty-five Ave Marias.[2] Oh! I know, big coyote. You would sit there flapping your mouth over Aves all day while you looked at the candles and the holy pictures. That is not good devotion to stare at the pretty things."

The black hat, covering the high pointed head and black thatched hair of Pepé, gave him dignity and age. He sat the rangy horse well. Mama thought how handsome he was, dark and lean and tall. "I would not send thee now alone, thou little one, except for the medicine," she said softly. "It is not good to have no medicine, for who knows when the toothache will come, or the sadness of the stomach. These things are."

"Adios, Mama," Pepé cried. "I will come back soon. You may send me often alone. I am a man."

"Thou art a foolish chicken."

He straightened his shoulders, flipped the reins against the horse's shoulder and rode away. He turned once and saw that they still watched him, Emilio and Rosy and Mama. Pepé grinned with pride and gladness and lifted the tough buckskin horse to a trot.

When he had dropped out of sight over a little dip in the road, Mama turned to the black ones, but she spoke to herself. "He is nearly a man now," she said. "It will be a nice thing to have a man in the house again." Her eyes sharpened on the children. "Go to the rocks now. The tide is going out. There will be abalones to be found." She put the iron hooks into their hands and saw them down the steep trail to the reefs. She brought the smooth stone *metate*[3] to the doorway and sat grinding her corn to flour and looking occasionally at the road over which Pepé had gone. The noonday came and then the afternoon, when the little ones beat the abalones on a rock to make them tender and Mama patted the tortillas to make them thin. They ate their dinner as the red sun was plunging down toward the ocean. They sat on the doorsteps and watched the big white moon come over the mountaintops.

Mama said, "He is now at the house of our friend Mrs. Rodriguez. She will give him nice things to eat and maybe a present."

Emilio said, "Some day I too will ride to Monterey for medicine. Did Pepé come to be a man today?"

Mama said wisely, "A boy gets to be a man when a man is needed. Remember this thing. I have known boys forty years old because there was no need for a man."

Soon afterwards they retired, Mama in her big oak bed on one side of the room, Emilio and Rosy in their boxes full of

---

[1]*dulces*: Spanish, sweets.

[2]**Paternosters . . . Ave Marias:** prayers that begin "Our Father" and "Hail, Mary."

[3]*metate*: a stone used for grinding meal.

straw and sheepskins on the other side of the room.

The moon went over the sky and the surf roared on the rocks. The roosters crowed the first call. The surf subsided to a whispering surge against the reef. The moon dropped toward the sea. Again the roosters crowed.

The moon was near down to the water when Pepé rode on a winded horse to his home flat. His dog bounced out and circled the horse yelping with pleasure. Pepé slid off the saddle to the ground. The weathered little shack was silver in the moonlight and the square shadow of it was black to the north and east. Against the east the piling mountains were misty with light; their tops melted into the sky.

Pepé walked wearily up the three steps and into the house. It was dark inside. There was a rustle in the corner.

Mama cried out from her bed. "Who comes? Pepé is it thou?"

"*Sí*, Mama."

"Did you get the medicine?"

"*Sí*, Mama."

"Well, go to sleep, then. I thought you would be sleeping at the house of Mrs. Rodriguez." Pepé stood silently in the dark room. "Why do you stand there, Pepé? Did you drink wine?"

"*Sí*, Mama."

"Well, go to bed and sleep out the wine."

His voice was tired and patient, but very firm. "Light the candle, Mama. I must go away into the mountains."

"What is this, Pepé? You are crazy." Mama struck a sulphur match and held the little blue burr until the flame spread up the stick. She set light to the candle on the floor beside her bed. "Now, Pepé, what is this you say?" She looked anxiously into his face.

He was changed. The fragile quality seemed to have gone from his chin. His mouth was less full than it had been, the lines of the lips were straighter, but in his eyes the greatest change had taken place. There was no laughter in them any more, nor any bashfulness. They were sharp and bright and purposeful.

He told her in a tired monotone, told her everything just as it had happened. A few people came into the kitchen of Mrs. Rodriguez. There was wine to drink. Pepé drank wine. The little quarrel—the man started toward Pepé and then the knife—it went almost by itself. It flew, it darted before Pepé knew it. As he talked, Mama's face grew stern, and it seemed to grow more lean. Pepé finished. "I am a man now, Mama. The man said names to me I could not allow."

Mama nodded. "Yes, thou art a man, my poor little Pepé. Thou art a man. I have seen it coming on thee. I have watched you throwing the knife into the post, and I have been afraid." For a moment her face had softened, but now it grew stern again. "Come! We must get you ready. Go. Awaken Emilio and Rosy. Go quickly."

Pepé stepped over to the corner where his brother and sister slept among the sheepskins. He leaned down and shook them gently. "Come, Rosy! Come, Emilio! The mama says you must arise."

The little black ones sat up and rubbed their eyes in the candlelight. Mama was out of bed now, her long black skirt over her nightgown. "Emilio," she cried. "Go up and catch the other horse for Pepé. Quickly, now! Quickly." Emilio put his legs in his overalls and stumbled sleepily out the door.

"You heard no one behind you on the road?" Mama demanded.

"No, Mama. I listened carefully. No one was on the road."

Mama darted like a bird about the room. From a nail on the wall she took a canvas water bag and threw it on the floor. She stripped a blanket from her bed and rolled it into a tight tube and tied the ends with string. From a box beside the stove she lifted a flour sack half full of black stringy jerky. "Your father's black coat, Pepé. Here, put it on."

Pepé stood in the middle of the floor watching her activity. She reached behind the door and brought out the rifle, a long 38-56, worn shiny the whole length of the barrel. Pepé took it from her and held it in the crook of his elbow. Mama brought a little leather bag and counted the cartridges into his hand. "Only ten left," she warned. "You must not waste them."

Emilio put his head in the door. " *'Qui 'st 'l caballo,*[4] Mama."

"Put on the saddle from the other horse. Tie on the blanket. Here, tie the jerky to the saddle horn."

Still Pepé stood silently watching his mother's frantic activity. His chin looked hard, and his sweet mouth was drawn and thin. His little eyes followed Mama about the room almost suspiciously.

Rosy asked softly, "Where goes Pepé?"

Mama's eyes were fierce. "Pepé goes on a journey. Pepé is a man now. He has a man's thing to do."

Pepé straightened his shoulders. His mouth changed until he looked very much like Mama.

At last the preparation was finished. The loaded horse stood outside the door. The water bag dripped a line of moisture down the bay shoulder.

The moonlight was being thinned by the dawn and the big white moon was near down to the sea. The family stood by the shack. Mama confronted Pepé. "Look, my son! Do not stop until it is dark again. Do not sleep even though you are tired. Take care of the horse in order that he may not stop of weariness. Remember to be careful with the bullets—there are only ten. Do not fill thy stomach with jerky or it will make thee sick. Eat a little jerky and fill thy stomach with grass. When thou comest to the high mountains, if thou seest any of the dark watching men, go not near to them nor try to speak to them. And forget not thy prayers." She put her lean hands on Pepé's shoulders, stood on her toes and kissed him formally on both cheeks, and Pepé kissed her on both cheeks. Then he went to Emilio and Rosy and kissed both of their cheeks.

Pepé turned back to Mama. He seemed to look for a little softness, a little weakness in her. His eyes were searching, but Mama's face remained fierce. "Go now," she said. "Do not wait to be caught like a chicken."

Pepé pulled himself into the saddle. "I am a man," he said.

It was the first dawn when he rode up the hill toward the little canyon which let a trail into the mountains. Moonlight and daylight fought each other, and the two warring qualities made it difficult to see. Before Pepé had gone a hundred yards, the outlines of his figure were misty; and long before he entered the canyon, he had become a gray, indefinite shadow.

Mama stood stiffly in front of her doorstep, and on either side of her stood Emilio and Rosy. They cast furtive glances at Mama now and then.

When the grey shape of Pepé melted into the hillside and disappeared, Mama relaxed. She began the high, whining keen of the death wail. "Our beautiful—our brave," she cried. "Our protector, our son is gone." Emilio and Rosy moaned beside her. "Our beautiful—our brave, he is gone." It was the formal wail. It rose to a high piercing whine and subsided to a moan. Mama raised it three times and then she turned and went into the house and shut the door.

[4] **Qui . . . caballo:** Spanish, Here is the horse.

Emilio and Rosy stood wondering in the dawn. They heard Mama whimpering in the house. They went out to sit on the cliff above the ocean. They touched shoulders. "When did Pepé come to be a man?" Emilio asked.

"Last night," said Rosy. "Last night in Monterey." The ocean clouds turned red with the sun that was now behind the mountains.

"We will have no breakfast," said Emilio. "Mama will not want to cook." Rosy did not answer him. "Where is Pepé gone?" he asked.

Rosy looked around at him. She drew her knowledge from the quiet air. "He has gone on a journey. He will never come back."

"Is he dead? Do you think he is dead?"

Rosy looked back at the ocean again. A little steamer, drawing a line of smoke sat on the edge of the horizon. "He is not dead," Rosy explained. "Not yet."

Pepé rested the big rifle across the saddle in front of him. He let the horse walk up the hill and he didn't look back. The stony slope took on a coat of short brush so that Pepé found the entrance to a trail and entered it.

When he came to the canyon opening, he swung once in his saddle and looked back, but the houses were swallowed in the misty light. Pepé jerked forward again. The high shoulder of the canyon closed in on him. His horse stretched out its neck and sighed and settled to the trail.

It was a well-worn path, dark soft leaf-mold earth strewn with broken pieces of sandstone. The trail rounded the shoulder of the canyon and dropped steeply into the bed of the stream. In the shallows the water ran smoothly, glinting in the first morning sun. Small round stones on the bottom were as brown as rust with sun moss. In the sand along the edges of the stream the tall, rich wild mint grew, while in the water itself the cress, old and tough, had gone to heavy seed.

The path went into the stream and emerged on the other side. The horse sloshed into the water and stopped. Pepé dropped his bridle and let the beast drink of the running water.

Soon the canyon sides became steep and the first giant sentinel redwoods guarded the trail, great round red trunks bearing foliage as green and lacy as ferns. Once Pepé was among the trees, the sun was lost. A perfumed and purple light lay in the pale green of the underbrush. Gooseberry bushes and blackberries and tall ferns lined the stream, and overhead the branches of the redwoods met and cut off the sky.

Pepé drank from the water bag, and he reached into the flour sack and brought out a black string of jerky. His white teeth gnawed at the string until the tough meat parted. He chewed slowly and drank occasionally from the water bag. His little eyes were slumberous and tired, but the muscles of his face were hard set. The earth of the trail was black now. It gave up a hollow sound under the walking hoofbeats.

The stream fell more sharply. Little waterfalls splashed on the stones. Five-fingered ferns hung over the water and dripped spray from their fingertips. Pepé rode half over in his saddle, dangling one leg loosely. He picked a bay leaf from a tree beside the way and put it into his mouth for a moment to flavor the dry jerky. He held the gun loosely across the pommel.

Suddenly he squared in his saddle, swung the horse from the trail and kicked it hurriedly up behind a big redwood tree. He pulled up the reins tight against the bit to keep the horse from whinnying. His face was intent and his nostrils quivered a little.

A hollow pounding came down the trail, and a horseman rode by, a fat man with red cheeks and a white stubble beard. His horse put down its head and blubbered at the trail when it came to the place where Pepé had turned off. "Hold up!" said the man and he pulled up his horse's head.

When the last sound of the hoofs died away, Pepé came back into the trail again. He did not relax in the saddle any more. He lifted the big rifle and swung the lever to throw a shell into the chamber, and then he let down the hammer to half cock.

The trail grew very steep. Now the redwood trees were smaller and their tops were dead, bitten dead where the wind reached them. The horse plodded on; the sun went slowly overhead and started down toward the afternoon.

Where the stream came out of a side canyon, the trail left it. Pepé dismounted and watered his horse and filled up his water bag. As soon as the trail had parted from the stream, the trees were gone and only the thick brittle sage and manzanita and chaparral edged the trail. And the soft black earth was gone, too, leaving only the light tan broken rock for the trail bed. Lizards scampered away into the brush as the horse rattled over the little stones.

Pepé turned in his saddle and looked back. He was in the open now: he could be seen from a distance. As he ascended the trail the country grew more rough and terrible and dry. The way wound about the bases of great square rocks. Little gray rabbits skittered in the brush. A bird made a monotonous high creaking. Eastward the bare rock mountaintops were pale and powder-dry under the dropping sun. The horse plodded up and up the trail toward a little V ridge which was the pass.

Pepé looked suspiciously back every minute or so, and his eyes sought the tops of the ridges ahead. Once, on a white barren spur, he saw a black figure for a moment, but he looked quickly away, for it was one of the dark watchers. No one knew who the watchers were, nor where they lived, but it was better to ignore them and never to show interest in them. They did not bother one who stayed on the trail and minded his own business.

The air was parched and full of light dust blown by the breeze from the eroding mountains. Pepé drank sparingly from his bag and corked it tightly and hung it on the horn again. The trail moved up the dry shale hillside, avoiding rocks, dropping under clefts, climbing in and out of old water scars. When he arrived at the little pass he stopped and looked back for a long time. No dark watchers were to be seen now. The trail behind was empty. Only the high tops of the redwoods indicated where the stream flowed.

Pepé rode on through the pass. His little eyes were nearly closed with weariness, but his face was stern, relentless and manly. The high mountain wind coasted sighing through the pass and whistled on the edges of the big blocks of broken granite. In the air, a red-tailed hawk sailed over close to the ridge and screamed angrily. Pepé went slowly through the broken jagged pass and looked down on the other side.

The trail dropped quickly, staggering among broken rock. At the bottom of the slope there was a dark crease, thick with brush, and on the other side of the crease a little flat, in which a grove of oak trees grew. A scar of green grass cut across the flat. And behind the flat another mountain rose, desolate with dead rocks and starving little black bushes. Pepé drank from the bag again for the air was so dry that it encrusted his nostrils and burned his lips. He put the horse down the trail. The hooves slipped and struggled on the steep way, starting little stones that rolled off into the brush. The sun was gone behind the westward mountain now, but still it glowed brilliantly on the oaks and on the grassy flat. The rocks and the hill-sides still sent up waves of the heat they had gathered from the day's sun.

Pepé looked up to the top of the next dry withered ridge. He saw a dark form against the sky, a man's figure standing on top of a rock, and he glanced away quickly not to appear curious. When a moment later he looked up again, the figure was gone.

Downward the trail was quickly covered. Sometimes the horse floundered for footing, sometimes set his feet and slid a little way. They came at last to the bottom where the dark chaparral was higher than Pepé's head. He held up his rifle on one side and his arm on the other to shield his face from the sharp brittle fingers of the brush.

Up and out of the crease he rode, and up a little cliff. The grassy flat was before him, and the round comfortable oaks. For a moment he studied the trail down which he had come, but there was no movement and no sound from it. Finally he rode out over the flat, to the green streak, and at the upper end of the damp he found a little spring welling out of the earth and dropping into a dug basin before it seeped out over the flat.

Pepé filled his bag first, and then he let the thirsty horse drink out of the pool. He led the horse to the clump of oaks, and in the middle of the grove, fairly protected from sight on all sides, he took off the saddle and the bridle and laid them on the ground. The horse stretched his jaws sideways and yawned. Pepé knotted the lead rope about the horse's neck and tied him to a sapling among the oaks, where he could graze in a fairly large circle.

When the horse was gnawing hungrily at the dry grass, Pepé went to the saddle and took a black string of jerky from the sack and strolled to an oak tree on the edge of the grove, from under which he could watch the trail. He sat down in the crisp oak leaves and automatically felt for his big black knife to cut the jerky, but he had no knife. He leaned back on his elbow and gnawed at the tough strong meat. His face was blank, but it was a man's face.

The bright evening light washed the eastern ridge, but the valley was darkening. Doves flew down from the hills to the spring, and the quail came running out of the brush and joined them, calling clearly to one another.

Out of the corner of his eye Pepé saw a shadow grow out of the brushy crease. He turned his head slowly. A big spotted wildcat was creeping toward the spring, his belly to the ground, moving like thought.

Pepé cocked his rifle and edged the muzzle slowly around. Then he looked apprehensively up the trail and dropped the hammer again. From the ground beside him he picked an oak twig and threw it toward the spring. The quail flew up with a roar and the doves whistled away. The big cat stood up: for a long moment he looked at Pepé with cold yellow eyes, and then fearlessly walked back into the gulch.

The dusk gathered quickly in the deep valley. Pepé muttered his prayers, put his head down on his arm and went instantly to sleep.

The moon came up and filled the valley with cold blue light, and the wind swept rustling down from the peaks. The owls worked up and down the slopes looking for rabbits. Down in the brush of the gulch a coyote gabbled. The oak trees whispered softly in the night breeze.

Pepé started up, listening. His horse had whinnied. The moon was just skipping behind the western ridge, leaving the valley in darkness behind it. Pepé sat tensely gripping his rifle. From far up the trail he heard an answering whinny and the crash of shod hooves on the broken rock. He jumped to his feet, ran to his horse and led it under the trees. He threw on the saddle and cinched it tight for the steep trail, caught the unwilling head and forced the bit into the mouth. He felt the saddle to make sure the water bag and the sack of jerky were there. Then he mounted and turned up the hill.

It was velvet dark. The horse found the entrance to the trail where it left the flat, and started up, stumbling and slipping on the rocks. Pepé's hand rose up to his head. His hat was gone. He had left it under the oak tree.

The horse had struggled far up the trail when the first change of dawn came into the air, a steel grayness as light mixed thoroughly with dark. Gradually the sharp snaggled edge of the ridge stood out above him, rotten granite tortured and eaten by the winds of time. Pepé had dropped his reins on the horn, leaving direction to the horse. The brush grabbed at his legs in the dark until one knee of his jeans was ripped.

Gradually the light flowed down over the ridge. The starved brush and rocks stood out in the half light, strange and lonely in high perspective. Then there came warmth into the light. Pepé drew up and looked back, but he could see nothing in the darker valley below. The sky turned blue over the coming sun. In the waste of the mountainside, the poor dry brush grew only three feet high. Here and there, big outcroppings of unrotted granite stood up like mouldering houses. Pepé relaxed a little. He drank from his water bag and bit off a piece of jerky. A single eagle flew over, high in the light.

Without any warning, Pepé's horse screamed and fell on its side. He was almost down before the rifle crash echoed up from the valley. From a hole behind the struggling shoulder, a stream of crimson blood pumped and stopped and pumped and stopped. The hooves threshed on the

ground. Pepé lay half stunned beside the horse. He looked slowly down the hill. A piece of sage slipped off beside his head and another crash echoed up from side to side of the canyon. Pepé flung himself frantically behind a bush.

He crawled up the hill on his knees and one hand. His right hand held the rifle up off the ground and pushed it ahead of him. He moved with the instinctive care of an animal. Rapidly he wormed his way toward one of the big outcroppings of granite on the hill above him. Where the brush was high he doubled up and ran but where the cover was slight he wriggled forward on his stomach, pushing the rifle ahead of him. In the last little distance there was no cover at all. Pepé poised and then he darted across the space and flashed around the corner of the rock.

He leaned panting against the stone. When his breath came easier he moved along behind the big rock until he came to a narrow split that offered a thin section of vision down the hill. Pepé lay on his stomach and pushed the rifle barrel through the slit and waited.

The sun reddened the western ridges now. Already the buzzards were settling down toward the place where the horse lay. A small brown bird scratched in the dead sage leaves directly in front of the rifle muzzle. The coasting eagle flew back toward the rising sun.

Pepé saw a little movement in the brush far below. His grip tightened on the gun. A little brown doe stepped daintily out on the trail and crossed it and disappeared into the brush again. For a long time Pepé waited. Far below he could see the little flat and the oak trees and the slash of green. Suddenly his eyes flashed back at the trail again. A quarter of a mile down there had been a quick movement in the chaparral. The rifle swung over. The front sight nestled in the v of the rear sight. Pepé studied for a moment and then raised the rear sight a notch. The little movement in the brush came again. The sight settled on it. Pepé squeezed the trigger. The explosion crashed down the mountain and up the other side, and came rattling back. The whole side of the slope grew still. No more movement. And then a white streak cut into the granite of the slit and a bullet whined away and a crash sounded from below. Pepé felt a sharp pain in his right hand. A sliver of granite was sticking out from between his first and second knuckles and the point protruded from his palm. Carefully he pulled out the sliver of stone. The wound bled evenly and gently. No vein was cut.

Pepé looked into a little dusty cave in the rock and gathered a handful of spider web, and he pressed the mass into the cut, plastering the soft web into the blood. The flow stopped almost at once.

The rifle was on the ground. Pepé picked it up, levered a new shell into the chamber. And then he slid into the brush on his stomach. Far to the right he crawled, and then up the hill, moving slowly and carefully, crawling to cover and resting and then crawling again.

In the mountains the sun is high in its arc before it penetrates the gorges. The hot face looked over the hill and brought instant heat with it. The white light beat on the rocks and reflected from them and rose up quivering from the earth again, and the rocks and brushes seemed to quiver behind the air.

Pepé crawled in the general direction of the ridge peak, zigzagging for cover. The deep cut between his knuckles began to throb. He crawled close to a rattlesnake before he saw it, and when it raised its dry head and made a soft beginning whirr, he backed up and took another way. The quick gray lizards flashed in front of him, raising a tiny line of dust. He found another mass of spider web and pressed it against his throbbing hand.

Pepé was pushing the rifle with his left hand now. Little drops of sweat ran to the ends of his coarse black hair and rolled down his cheeks. His lips and tongue were growing thick and heavy. His lips writhed to draw saliva into his mouth. His little dark eyes were uneasy and suspicious. Once when a gray lizard paused in front of him on the parched ground and turned its head sideways he crushed it flat with a stone.

When the sun slid past noon he had not gone a mile. He crawled exhaustedly a last hundred yards to a patch of high sharp manzanita, crawled desperately, and when the patch was reached he wriggled in among the tough gnarly trunks and dropped his head on his left arm. There was little shade in the meager brush, but there was cover and safety. Pepé went to sleep as he lay and the sun beat on his back. A few little birds hopped close to him and peered and hopped away. Pepé squirmed in his sleep and he raised and dropped his wounded hand again and again.

The sun went down behind the peaks and the cool evening came, and then the dark. A coyote yelled from the hillside. Pepé started awake and looked about with misty eyes. His hand was swollen and heavy; a little thread of pain ran up the inside of his arm and settled in a pocket in his armpit. He peered about and then stood up, for the mountains were black and the moon had not yet risen. Pepé stood up in the dark. The coat of his father pressed on his arm. His tongue was swollen until it nearly filled his mouth. He wriggled out of the coat and dropped it in the brush, and then he struggled up the hill, falling over rocks and tearing his way through the brush. The rifle knocked against stones as he went. Little dry avalanches of gravel and shattered stone went whispering down the hill behind him.

After a while the old moon came up and showed the jagged ridge top ahead of him. By moonlight Pepé traveled more easily. He bent forward so that his throbbing arm hung away from his body. The journey uphill was made in dashes and rests, a frantic rush up a few yards and then a rest.

The wind coasted down the slope rattling the dry stems of the bushes.

The moon was at meridian when Pepé came at last to the sharp backbone of the ridge top. On the last hundred yards of the rise no soil had clung under the wearing winds. The way was on solid rock. He clambered to the top and looked down on the other side. There was a draw like the last below him, misty with moonlight, brushed with dry struggling sage and chaparral. On the other side the hill rose up sharply and at the top the jagged rotten teeth of the mountain showed against the sky. At the bottom of the cut the brush was thick and dark.

Pepé stumbled down the hill. His throat was almost closed with thirst. At first he tried to run, but immediately he fell and rolled. After that he went more carefully. The moon was just disappearing behind the mountains when he came to the bottom. He crawled into the heavy brush feeling with his fingers for water. There was no water in the bed of the stream, only damp earth. Pepé laid his gun down and scooped up a handful of mud and put it in his mouth, and then he spluttered and scraped the earth from his tongue with his finger, for the mud drew at his mouth like a poultice. He dug a hole in the streambed with his fingers, dug a little basin to catch water; but before it was very deep his head fell forward on the damp ground and he slept.

The dawn came and the heat of the day fell on the earth, and still Pepé slept. Late in the afternoon his head jerked up. He looked slowly around. His eyes were slits of wariness. Twenty feet away in the heavy brush a big tawny mountain lion stood looking at him. Its long thick tail waved gracefully, its ears were erect with interest, not laid back dangerously. The lion squatted down on its stomach and watched him.

Pepé looked at the hole he had dug in

the earth. A half inch of muddy water had collected in the bottom. He tore the sleeve from his hurt arm, with his teeth ripped out a little square, soaked it in the water and put it in his mouth. Over and over he filled the cloth and sucked it.

Still the lion sat and watched him. The evening came down but there was no movement on the hills. No birds visited the dry bottom of the cut. Pepé looked occasionally at the lion. The eyes of the yellow beast drooped as though he were about to sleep. He yawned and his long thin red tongue curled out. Suddenly his head jerked around and his nostrils quivered. His big tail lashed. He stood up and slunk like a tawny shadow into the thick brush.

A moment later Pepé heard the sound, the faint far crash of horses' hooves on gravel. And he heard something else, a high whining yelp of a dog.

Pepé took his rifle in his left hand and he glided into the brush almost as quietly as the lion had. In the darkening evening he crouched up the hill toward the next ridge. Only when the dark came did he stand up. His energy was short. Once it was dark he fell over the rocks and slipped to his knees on the steep slope, but he moved on and on up the hill, climbing and scrabbling over the broken hillside.

When he was far up toward the top, he lay down and slept for a little while. The withered moon, shining on his face, awakened him. He stood up and moved up the hill. Fifty yards away he stopped and turned back, for he had forgotten his rifle. He walked heavily down and poked about in the brush, but he could not find his gun. At last he lay down to rest. The pocket of pain in his armpit had grown more sharp. His arm seemed to swell out and fall with every heartbeat. There was no position lying down where the heavy arm did not press against his armpit.

With the effort of a hurt beast, Pepé got up and moved again toward the top of the ridge. He held his swollen arm away from his body with his left hand. Up the steep hill he dragged himself, a few steps and a rest, and a few more steps. At last he was nearing the top. The moon showed the uneven sharp back of it against the sky.

Pepé's brain spun in a big spiral up and away from him. He slumped to the ground and lay still. The rock ridge top was only a hundred feet above him.

The moon moved over the sky. Pepé half turned on his back. His tongue tried to make words, but only a thick hissing came from between his lips.

When the dawn came, Pepé pulled himself up. His eyes were sane again. He drew his great puffed arm in front of him and looked at the angry wound. The black line ran up from his wrist to his armpit. Automatically he reached in his pocket for the big black knife, but it was not there. His eyes searched the ground. He picked up a sharp blade of stone and scraped the wound, sawed at the proud flesh and then squeezed the green juice out in big drops. Instantly he threw back his head and whined like a dog. His whole right side shuddered at the pain, but the pain cleared his head.

In the gray light he struggled up the last slope to the ridge and crawled over and lay down behind a line of rocks. Below him lay a deep canyon exactly like the last, waterless and desolate. There was no flat, no oak trees, not even heavy brush in the bottom of it. And on the other side a sharp ridge stood up, thinly brushed with starving sage, littered with broken granite. Strewn over the hill there were giant outcroppings, and on the top the granite teeth stood out against the sky.

The new day was light now. The flame of the sun came over the ridge and fell on Pepé where he lay on the ground. His coarse black hair was littered with twigs and bits of spider web. His eyes had retreated back into his head. Between his lips the tip of his black tongue showed.

He sat up and dragged his great arm into his lap and nursed it, rocking his body and moaning in his throat. He threw back his head and looked up into the pale sky. A big black bird circled nearly out of sight; far to the left another was sailing near.

He lifted his head to listen, for a familiar sound had come to him from the valley he had climbed out of; it was the crying yelp of hounds, excited and feverish, on a trail.

Pepé bowed his head quickly. He tried to speak rapid words but only a thick hiss came from his lips. He drew a shaky cross on his breast with his left hand. It was a long struggle to get to his feet. He crawled slowly and mechanically to the top of a big rock on the ridge peak. Once there, he arose slowly, swaying to his feet, and stood erect. Far below he could see the dark brush where he had slept. He braced his feet and stood there, black against the morning sky.

There came a ripping sound at his feet. A piece of stone flew up and a bullet droned off into the next gorge. The hollow crash echoed up from below. Pepé looked down for a moment and then pulled himself straight again.

His body jarred back. His left hand fluttered helplessly toward his breast. The second crash sounded from below. Pepé swung forward and toppled from the rock. His body struck and rolled over and over, starting a little avalanche. And when at last he stopped against a bush, the avalanche slid slowly down and covered up his head.

## YOU AND THE STORY

Look at the role the boy's knife plays in this story. It is a weapon, but it means more than that. It helps us understand what kind of people we are watching. It helps show what their ideas and feelings and values are. The knife becomes a central **symbol** in the story: It sums up much of what the story is all about. Look at the different parts of the story where the knife plays a role. Where did it come from? What does it mean to the children? What does the mother think about it? What does the knife mean to Pepé? What role does it play in the story as a whole? Tell the story of the knife as completely as you can.

## A Closer Look

(1) John Steinbeck skillfully creates an authentic **setting** for his story by carefully filling in detail after detail. There are many things for us to look at, to take in. How successful is the author in making the countryside come to life before your eyes? Use some vivid details from the story to describe one of the following:

—the farm by the sea
—the trail up into the mountains
—the wildlife in the countryside along the trail

(2) John Steinbeck was a born storyteller. If you were asked for a *plot summary*, how would you retell in brief what happens in this story? Why do you think some of the key events of the story are not told directly—they happen "offstage," so to speak? How would it change the story if we could watch what actually happened during Pepé's fateful trip to town?

(3) To understand a character, we have to know what the character says and

does—but also what the character *thinks and feels*. Mama Torrez is the kind of person who does not say everything she thinks. Tell her story—who she is, what she thinks about her children and especially the oldest boy, what she thinks about the events in the story.

(4) Pepé has his own strong ideas about what is right, about what "a man" is and should do. He does not talk much about these ideas, but he acts the way he thinks he should. It is as if his ideas were part of an unwritten *code*. Many young people take over such an unwritten set of standards from the group or society around them. Suppose a young person had asked you to help initiate him or her into the code that Pepé lives by. What would you say?

---

### Your Turn

---

How do you react to Pepé's actions in this story? Do you approve? Do you disapprove? Are your own reactions the same as those of your classmates, or are they different? The story deals with questions on which people strongly *disagree*, depending on their own personal values. People disagree on how strongly we should value our personal pride, how and when we should take offense. They disagree on whether and when we should "take the law into our own hands."

When we find ourselves in disagreement with other people on an important matter, we can clarify our own thinking by lining up the pro's and con's. On which of the following questions do you think something could be said for either side? Line up what you would say in support of the one side, and then of the other.

(1) Pepé's mother considers him brave, but the story is mostly about his running away. Is he brave, or could he be called "cowardly"?

(2) Pepé is called gentle and affectionate early in the story. Does this mean that the "manlike" code he lives by does not really fit him as a person?

(3) Many people today feel that quarrels like the one in the story should be settled according to the laws, not by personal violence. Is Pepé's kind of code out of date in our modern civilized world?

(Your teacher may ask you to prepare a "pro and con" paper based on one of these topics.)

---

Language/Composition Activity C8

---

FOR SENTENCE PRACTICE

# Writing the Close-Up Sentence

John Steinbeck was a writer who took a close look at scenes and people and described in loving detail what he saw. He told his readers what they needed to know to visualize what he described. Look at how the following sentences from his story answer questions that might arise in the reader's mind:

BARE FACT: A horseman rode by. (What did he look like? What kind of person was he?)

CLOSE-UP VIEW: A horseman rode by, *a fat man with red cheeks and a white stubble beard.*

---

<dl>
<dt>BARE FACT:</dt>
<dd>He moved on and on up the hill. (How did he manage? How did it go?)</dd>
<dt>CLOSE-UP VIEW:</dt>
<dd>He moved on and on up the hill, climbing and scrabbling over the broken hillside.</dd>
</dl>

A. In the first example, the close-up view adds a detailed description that we could paste like a label or caption beneath a picture of what is being described. Here are additional examples from the story:

Mama Torres, *a lean dry woman with ancient eyes,* had ruled the farm for ten years.

The first giant sentinel redwoods guarded the trail, *great round red trunks bearing foliage as green and lacy as ferns.*

It was a well-worn path, *dark soft leaf-mold earth strewn with broken pieces of sandstone.*

On a separate sheet of paper, complete the following sentence frames by filling in a close-up description similar to those used in the model sentences above.

The President spoke on TV, a _____.

My favorite actor (actress), a _____, usually plays _____ roles.

The plants I know best are _____, _____.

Some day you should visit our street, _____.

B. The second type of sentence illustrated in the original two pairs above follows a slightly different pattern: For the close-up view, we add material following a word that ends in *-ing*. The added material tells us how something is done or what happens as a result. Here are additional examples from the story:

In the shallows the water ran smoothly, *glinting in the first morning sun.*

The hooves slipped and struggled on the steep way, *starting little stones that rolled off into the brush.*

The trail moved up the dry shale hillside, *avoiding rocks, dropping under clefts, climbing in and out of old water scars.*

On a separate sheet of paper, complete the following sentence frames by filling in "what is happening" details similar to those used in the model sentences above:

The plane was taking off, _____.

In our rivers today the water runs _____, _____.

Teenage drivers were driving around the neighborhood, _____.

Our group moved on, _____, _____, _____.

# Handbook of Literary Terms

# Alphabetical Index of Literary Terms

**abstract** *422, 683*

**alliteration** *687*

**allusion** *255, 529, 685*

**ambiguity** A deliberate choice of words intended to make the meaning uncertain and to stimulate several interpretations and streams of thought in the reader's mind. *348*

**anapest** *688*

**antithesis** *19*

**apostrophe** A figure of speech that addresses a person who is absent or an object that is personified. *424*

**aside** *699*

**assonance** A resemblance in sound in two or more words, such as *stony* and *holy*, often called partial, near, or half rhyme. *17, 379*

**ballad** A poem that tells a story. It is divided into stanzas and often has a refrain. (See **stanza** and **refrain**.) Usually the poem is about a dramatic event in the life of a heroic or very colorful character. *62, 417*

**blank verse** *263, 688*

**caricature** A description that distorts or exaggerates the characteristics of a person, an object, or an idea. *349*

**character** *40, 98, 99, 373, 588, 691*

**chorus** In Greek plays, a group of singers and dancers who commented on the action and pointed out the significance of events. *425*

**chronological order** *693*

**climax** *98, 285, 327, 693, 699*

**closed couplet** *689*

**comedy** *700*

**concrete** *422, 683*

**confidant(e)** *699*

**conflict** *98, 362, 374, 699*

**couplet** *420, 689*

**dactyl** *688*

**denouement** *693*

**dialect** A form of speech characteristic of a group in a particular geographical area or social class. Authors use this technique of characterization to bring a character to life and to reveal the character's education, geographical background, and social status. *542, 590*

**dialogue** *692, 698*

**didactic** *695*

**elegy** A mournful, melancholy poem, often expressing sorrow at a death. *198*

**epilogue** A speech delivered at the end of a play, or a concluding section of a novel or poem, that sums up or interprets the literary work. *627*

**episode** *693*

**epitaph** *145*

**exposition** *698*

**figurative language** *381, 683*

**first-person observer** *694*

**first-person participant** *694*

**flashback** *362, 525, 693*

**flat character** A character who is not fully developed and who changes little over the course of the story. This type of character often has a single trait or motive; the reader is seldom in doubt about what the character will do or think in a given situation. *40*

**foot** *688*

**foreshadowing** *693*

**form** In a poem, the organization of metrical units, feet, lines and stanzas and the devices of rhyme and repetition that work together to create a unified whole. (See **meter, foot, stanza, rhyme,** and **repetition**.) *65*

**free verse** *188, 689*

**gestures** *698*

**grotesque** *235*

**hexameter** *688*

**hubris** *700*

**iamb** *688*

**iambic pentameter** *689*

**image** *683*

**irony** *305, 318, 320, 415, 685*

**literal language** *683*

**lyric** A short songlike poem expressing personal emotion. *414*

**macabre** *235*

**melodrama** *245*

**metaphor** *149, 416, 532, 684*

**meter** *254, 688*

**minor character** *698*

**monologue** *69, 471, 615, 699*

**mood** *335, 552, 635, 695*

**motivation** The reasons behind a character's behavior. To make the events believable, an author must provide a clear and convincing explanation for what the character does in a given situation. A character's actions, or lack of action, may be accounted for by circumstance, temperament, attitude, or a combination of these. Whether a character's motives are implied or stated, they must

account realistically for his or her behavior. *373*

**narrator** *275, 694, 698*

**objective third-person narrator** *694*

**octameter** *688*

**omniscient narrator** *361, 694*

**onomatopoeia** *685*

**oral literature** *485*

**parable** A brief story that teaches some truth or moral lesson. *415, 532*

**paradox** *280, 421, 634, 685*

**pentameter** *688*

**personification** *258, 376, 416, 684*

**plot** *458, 626, 693*

**point of view** *99, 181, 361, 693*

**prologue** An introduction to a long poem, novel, or play. In ancient Greek tragedy, it introduced the subject of the play. *426*

**prop** *698*

**realism** The portrayal of life as it actually is. Realism is achieved in a fictional work when events are ordinary, when characters are true to life and their actions are convincing, and when the details of the setting—whether real or imaginary—are consistent with an actual time and place. Because it mirrors life, the work as a whole seems believable. *206*

**refrain** *417, 529, 689*

**repetition** The repeating of a word or phrase within a poem that creates a unity of sound and meaning. *65, 327, 542, 635*

**resolution** *699*

**rhyme** *17, 65, 418, 533, 687*

**rhyme scheme** A sequence of rhyme in a poem. (See **rhyme**.) A regular rhyme scheme, in which lines that rhyme fall into a consistent pattern, contributes to the unity of the poem. *254, 260*

**rounded character** A character that is fully developed throughout the course of a story. The reader comes to know the character well as many facets of his or her personality are revealed. A rounded character has depth and complexity and is often changed in some fundamental way by the end of the story. *40, 99*

**saga** A legend, myth, or tale that gives a detailed account of the marvelous deeds and experiences of a heroic character. *Saga* often refers to a Scandinavian story of this kind from medieval times. *75*

**satire** *147, 235, 700*
**scansion** *688*
**scenery** *698*
**setting** *25, 86, 443, 614, 647, 677, 691*
**simile** *416, 684*
**soliloquy** *699*
**sonnet** *417, 420, 422, 689*
**stage directions** *472, 589, 698*

**stanza** *17, 65, 418, 689*
**stock character** *700*
**stream of consciousness** *361, 694*
**surprise ending** *693*
**suspense** *693*
**sustained metaphor** *155, 532, 684*
**symbol** *17, 26, 260, 280, 380, 381, 399, 419, 423, 634, 677, 684*
**symbolic incident** *695*
**tall tale**   A story in which the events and abilities of the hero are exagger-

ated and hard to believe. *235*
**tetrameter** *688*
**theme** *305, 362, 373, 471, 525, 627, 694*
**tone** *19, 695*
**tragedy** *699*
**tragic dilemma** *700*
**tragic flaw** *699*
**tragic hero** *699*
**trimeter** *688*
**trochee** *688*

# The Language of Poetry   1

The language of poetry tells us *more* than ordinary language does. It has more to offer to our ears—we can be pleased or charmed or excited by listening to its sounds. It has more to offer to our senses—it gives us things that we can imagine as if we were there to see them, hear them, or touch them. It has more to offer to our minds—it makes us think and feel.

The following are important elements in the language of poetry:

| | |
|---|---|
| image | symbol |
| literal and figurative language | allusion |
| | irony |
| simile | paradox |
| metaphor | onomatopoeia |
| personification | |

**image**   Much of poetry is made up of experiences we can grasp and understand through our senses. These appeals to our senses make poetry **concrete**—they give us things that we can see, hear, or feel. The concreteness is created by the poet's use of images. We look in the mirror and see an "image" of ourselves, something we can identify because we see it. The poet uses similar images. Most are *visual* images—things we can see. Others are *sound* images—things we can hear. Still others are *touch* images—textures, surfaces, and the like. Finally there are *taste* images—the sourness of a lemon, for example, that makes the mouth pucker.

In "Those Winter Sundays" (page 146), Robert Hayden conveys a feeling of bitter cold by appealing to our sense of sight and touch. We can visualize the "blue-black cold" and almost feel "cracked hands that ached." Our sense of sound is called upon in the image of the blazing fire dispelling the icy cold when the speaker says "I wake and hear the cold splintering, breaking." Images which appeal to our senses create vivid pictures of the cold house in our minds.

• Poets often use imagery to make **abstract** ideas more concrete for the reader. Emily Dickinson defines the abstract idea "presentiment" (page 376) as "that long shadow on the lawn/Indicative that suns go down." In "I Stepped From Plank to Plank," (page 379), Dickinson uses concrete images to help us visualize the process of learning from experience:

> I stepped from plank to plank,
> A slow and cautious way.
> The stars about my head I felt,
> About my feet the sea.
>
> I knew not but the next
> Would be my final inch—
> This gave me that precarious gait
> Some call experience.

**literal and figurative language**   Figurative language uses imaginative comparisons to present concrete pictures for our senses. When writers describe things exactly as they see them, they are being literal. In "The Tuft of Flowers" (page 256), Robert Frost describes flowers beside a brook in literal language:

> But he turned first, and led my eye to look
> At a tall tuft of flowers beside a brook

However, when he goes on to describe the flowers in the next two lines, he uses figurative language:

A leaping tongue of bloom the scythe had spared
Beside a reedy brook the scythe had bared.

The flowers are not really "leaping," nor are they truly a "tongue." But this figurative use of language brings the scene to life and calls to mind colors and feelings that might be hard to sum up in ordinary literal words.

**simile**  The easiest kind of figurative language to understand is the simile. A simile is a comparison using the word *like* or *as*. It says outright that something is *like* something else. We use similes all the time in our conversation. When we say that the fog is like pea soup, we are using a simile. We mean that the fog is *like* pea soup because we can't see through it, just as we can't see through pea soup.

Similes are often used to convey an idea or mood that literal language cannot achieve. Henry Wadsworth Longfellow used the following similes in "Afternoon in February" (page 254) to lend a feeling of sorrow and gloom to his description of a February afternoon.

> Through clouds *like ashes*
> The red sun flashes
> . . . . . . . . . . . . . . . . . . . . . . . . .
> While through the meadows,
> *Like fearful shadows,*
> Slowly passes
> A funeral train.
> . . . . . . . . . . . . . . . . . . . . . . . . .
> Shadows are trailing,
> My heart is bewailing
> And tolling within
> *Like a funeral bell.*

Clouds "like ashes," a funeral train passing "like fearful shadows," and a beating heart tolling "like a funeral bell" are all carefully chosen comparisons designed to create the desired effect—a somber mood.

**metaphor**  The kind of comparison that calls something by a different name is a metaphor. A metaphor does not say something is *like* something else; a metaphor says something *is* something else. Because metaphors do not make use of *like* or *as,* the comparisons they express are stronger than similes.

When we say of a hockey or football player, "He's a tiger," we mean that he is fearless, aggressive, and unbeatable. We are using a metaphor. "Song of

Defeat" (page 485) contains a similar metaphor, which compares the speaker to a wolf:

> A wolf
> I considered myself,
> But the owls are hooting
> And the night
> I fear.

This simple comparison creates an image of a strong, fearless hunter while also revealing much about the speaker's attitudes, pride, and self-image.

• "Because I Could Not Stop for Death" (page 380) by Emily Dickinson uses a **sustained metaphor.** The journey in the carriage is a metaphor for the journey of life toward death. The images throughout the poem all represent aspects of life and death, and so sustain the comparison.

**personification**  Writers often talk about an object, animal, or idea as if it were human. This is called *personification*—making it a person. When you give human traits to a feeling or thing, you are *personifying* it. Gwendolyn Brooks personifies the sun in her poem "Truth" (page 634). The sun is a man—"And if sun comes/How shall we greet him?" The sun has hands—"What if we wake one shimmering morning to/Hear the fierce hammering/Of his knuckles/Hard on the door?" Because the sun acts and looks like a human, it is personified.

**symbol**  When an object or living thing comes to stand in our minds for an idea or feeling, we call it a symbol. For instance, a rose has often been used as a symbol of love. A symbol has a larger meaning beyond itself. When we look at the world around us, we often find there a mirror of our thoughts and feelings. A storm makes us think of anger or rage. We see the wind lash out in anger at houses and trees. A century-old oak makes us think of lasting strength. When we make a natural object stand for an idea like rage or strength, we are using it as a symbol. Nations choose animals like the lion or eagle as symbols of courage. The dove has come to be a symbol of peace.

In "Four Poems" (page 414), Stephen Crane used symbols to represent abstract ideas. In Poem 1, the speaker says, "I saw a man pursuing the horizon." The horizon symbolizes goals that can never be reached. In Poem 2, the "ball of gold" is a symbol for our illusions:

A man saw a ball of gold in the sky;
He climbed for it,
And eventually he achieved it—
It was clay.

The poem makes the point that people sometimes choose to hold on to pleasant illusions rather than accept unpleasant realities.

**allusion**   An allusion is a brief mention that makes us remember an event, a person, or a historical place. It makes us remember a story. That story may be similar to something in the poem. When you have just taken a tough test or exam, you may walk out of class saying "That was my Waterloo." If your friends remember European history, they will know that Napoleon met his downfall at the battle of Waterloo. They will know that the exam was not only a hard one, but that it felt like a final defeat. An allusion jogs our memories. It is a shorthand way of bringing into a poem something that we have heard about or read about before.

"Runagate, Runagate" (page 534) by Robert Hayden is about the escape of slaves into the North prior to the Civil War. The lines "Many thousands rise and go/many thousands crossing over" refer to crossing the line to freedom in the North. They are also a biblical allusion to the crossing of the Red Sea by the Israelite slaves in their exodus from Egypt. The parallel drawn between these two struggles for freedom adds another dimension to the poem and heightens its emotional impact.

**irony**   Sometimes a writer will make a point by saying the opposite of what he or she really means. We can tell that the writer is not serious, and we understand exactly what point is being made. This is called *irony*. People use irony in everyday conversations as well as in literature. For instance, suppose you have kept a friend waiting in the rain for half an hour. When you finally arrive, your friend says, "Oh, don't apologize . . . I just love standing in the rain!" By the words and tone, you have no doubt that your friend is being ironic.

Edna St. Vincent Millay used irony in "Apostrophe to Man" (page 424), a poem focusing on the absurdity of war. Following a scathing denunciation of the stupidity of mankind, Millay concluded the poem with "Breed, crowd, encroach, expand, expunge yourself, die out,/ *Homo* called *sapiens.*" *Homo sapiens,* or mankind, is derived from Latin—*Homo* means "man" and *sapiens* means "wise or intelligent." Millay created irony by calling mankind "intelligent." She did not think this at all—a fact made clear in the preceding lines of the poem. Since "intelligent and wise" is the opposite of what she really meant, the final line of the poem is ironic.

**paradox**   A paradox is a statement that at first does not make sense. It strikes us as puzzling or contradictory. But as we think about it (or as the poet tells us more), we begin to see the point. In many traditional love poems, the poet calls a loved person a "sweet foe" or a "beautiful tyrant." Though love is sweet, it also causes people much disappointment and suffering. In many of the most beautiful love poems through the ages, love is paradoxically "bittersweet." Freedom is called both beautiful and terrible in "Frederick Douglass" (page 537) by Robert Hayden. This description at first seems contradictory, but on further reflection we can see that freedom brings joy to those who possess it and suffering to those struggling to attain it. The poem goes on to say that freedom is "needful to man as air." As such, the threat of a loss of freedom would be alarming.

In "The Tuft of Flowers" (page 256), Robert Frost deals with a different paradox:

But he had gone his way, the grass all mown,
And I must be, as he had been,—alone.

"As all must be," I said within my heart,
"Whether they work together or apart."

The apparent contradiction that one can work with others and yet be alone reflects the speaker's belief that people, though together, do not share common thoughts and experiences. However, the paradox is reversed at the end of the poem:

"Men work together," I told him from the heart,
"Whether they work together or apart."

The apparent contradiction here is that people, though apart, still work together. Because of the event described in the poem, the speaker no longer feels isolated from others. He now recognizes a common bond of feelings between himself and the man who had mowed the grass earlier in the day.

**onomatopoeia**   When we listen to a poem, we expect the sound to mirror and reinforce the meaning. We expect a poem about tenderness to be read tenderly, softly, gently. We expect an angry poem to sound harsh or threatening. Often the poet chooses words and rhythms that help us read it in such a way that sound and sense go together. The ancient Greek name for sound mirroring sense is *onomatopoeia.*

Edna St. Vincent Millay makes effective use of onomatopoeia in "Dirge Without Music" (page 423).

> I am not resigned to the shutting away of loving hearts in the hard ground.

Words like *resigned, shutting,* and *hard ground,* with their hard sound, *sound* harsh and bitter and reflect the speaker's bitterness toward death.

In contrast to these sounds is this line from the same poem:

The answers quick and keen, the honest look, the laughter, the love,—

The words *quick* and *keen* and the numerous breaks between short phrases give this line a more lively sound that echoes the exuberance and activity of life. Sound again mirrors sense in the following line:

> Down, down, down into the darkness of the grave.

Because of the drawn-out vowel sounds and the heavy consonant sounds, this line *sounds* dark, dull, and mournful.

# Review

## Exercise 1

Read the poem and answer the questions that follow.

> I have studied many times
> The marble which was chiseled for me—
> A boat with a furled sail at rest in a harbor.
> In truth it pictures not my destination
> But my life.
> For love was offered me and I shrank from its
>     disillusionment;
> Sorrow knocked at my door, but I was afraid;
> Ambition called to me, but I dreaded the chances.
> Yet all the while I hungered for meaning in my life.
> And now I know that we must lift the sail
> And catch the winds of destiny
> Wherever they drive the boat.
> To put meaning in one's life may end in madness,
> But life without meaning is the torture
> Of restlessness and vague desire—
> It is a boat longing for the sea and yet afraid.
>
> Edgar Lee Masters, "George Gray"

1. Find two examples of **personification**—ideas which are given human form. What human abilities do they have?

2. George Gray says that life without meaning is "a boat longing for the sea and yet afraid." What do we call this kind of **figurative language**? Write a **literal** interpretation of this statement showing the ideas and emotions expressed in these few words.

3. The boat with a furled sail chiseled on Gray's gravestone represents a ship at rest in the harbor after an exciting voyage. Why is this **ironic**?

## Exercise 2

Read the poem and answer the questions that follow.

> Nothing would sleep in that cellar, dank as a ditch,
> Bulbs broke out of boxes hunting for chinks in the
>     dark,
> Shoots dangled and drooped,
> Lolling obscenely from mildewed crates,
> Hung down long yellow evil necks, like tropical
>     snakes.
> And what a congress of stinks!—
> Roots ripe as old bait,
> Pulpy stems, rank, silo-rich,
> Leaf-mold, manure, lime, piled against slippery
>     planks.
> Nothing would give up life:
> Even the dirt kept breathing a small breath.
>
> Theodore Roethke, "Root Cellar"

1. The poem is rich in **concrete images** that appeal to the senses of sight, sound, smell, and touch. Using each of these senses as a column heading, list as many words from the poem as you can that form concrete images in your mind by appealing to your senses.

2. Find two examples of **personification** and explain what human abilities the objects are given.

3. Find three examples of **similes**—comparisons using *like* or *as.* Replace these similes with comparisons that lend a different feeling to the poem. You may want to replace other words in the lines containing similes to create the impression you want.

Read each poem and answer the question that follows it.

> Had I not seen the Sun
> I could have borne the shade
> But Light a newer Wilderness
> My Wilderness has made—
>
> Emily Dickinson

1. What do the sun and shade **symbolize**? What do the first two lines mean?

> Hear the sledges with the bells,
> Silver bells!
> What a world of merriment their melody foretells!
> How they tinkle, tinkle, tinkle,
> In the icy air of night!
>
> Edgar Allan Poe, "The Bells"

2. This description of sleigh bells contains a word whose meaning can be heard in its sound. Find this example of **onomatopoeia**. Think of other onomatopoetic words that might be used in a poem about sleigh bells.

> Stone walls do not a prison make,
> Nor iron bars a cage;
> Minds innocent and quiet take
> That for an hermitage;
> If I have freedom in my love
> And in my soul am free,
> Angels alone, that soar above,
> Enjoy such liberty.
>
> Richard Lovelace, "To Althea, from Prison"

3. The first two lines seem to be contradictions or **paradoxes**. On further reading, however, the poet's meaning becomes clear. Explain the meaning of the first two lines.

# The Form of Poetry   2

Poetry has a *pattern* that gives us pleasure as we listen to it. Poets repeat and echo sounds to please our ears. They also use these effects to hold our attention and to mirror or reinforce the meaning. Words have rhythm, or beat, as well as sound, and the rhythm of poetry is usually more regular than we hear in ordinary language. Often a poem is divided into sections of lines that follow the same pattern of sound and rhythm, so that we quickly learn the pattern as we read or listen, and enjoy knowing what to expect.

The following are important terms for the different forms of poetry and the ways poets create these forms.

| rhyme | blank verse | refrain |
|---|---|---|
| alliteration | couplet | free verse |
| meter | stanza | sonnet |

**rhyme**   Poets use rhyme to make the endings of two or more lines sound alike:

> Great-grandmother talks by the hour to me
> Of a little cottage in Ballybree
> Of whitewashed walls and a roof of thatch
> And a gay green ribbon that raised the latch.
>
> Katherine Edelman, "Irish Grandmother" (page 109)

The words in the following pairs rhyme: love/dove, moon/June, sad/glad, season/reason, nation/celebration. Words rhyme when the strongest vowel sound and what follows are the same in both words. Rhyme is one of the ways poets repeat or echo sounds. They often use rhyme to mark off lines, and sometimes to mark off half-lines.

**alliteration**   Alliteration is a way of connecting words by repeating the same sound or sounds at the beginning of two or more words: *s*afe and *s*ound, *sp*ick and *sp*an, *k*it and *c*aboodle. Many centuries ago, English poets used alliteration instead of rhyme:

> A *f*air *f*ield *f*ull of *f*olk *f*ound I there. . .
>
> *P*reach to the *p*eople, but *p*ractice it yourself.

**meter** The rhythm of poetry is more regular than that of prose. In much traditional poetry, each line is roughly the same length—the number of syllables is similar or the same. Stressed or accented syllables appear at roughly the same points. The meter of a poem is the pattern set by the length of the line and the number of stressed syllables. By far the most common meter used in English poetry is a five-beat line of ten or more syllables:

A thíng of beaúty ís a jóy foréver.

John Keats, "Endymion"

To bé or nót to bé, thát is the quéstion.

William Shakespeare, Hamlet

• Like music, poetry may have a free-floating rhythm that we hardly notice. Or it may have a very definite beat. Meter is the kind of rhythm a poem has when its lines are regular enough to be measured. Measuring the meter of a poem is called **scansion**. To determine the meter of a line, we scan, or measure, its rhythm by breaking it up into groups of syllables. Usually each group contains just one stressed syllable and one or more unstressed syllables. Each group is called a **foot**. In the following example from Alexander Pope, there are five feet to the line, and each foot contains one unstressed and one stressed syllable:

To érr/is hú/man, tó/forgíve/divíne.

• Because there are five feet to the line, it is called **pentameter**. There are, however, many types of meter, all determined by the number of feet in a line. A three-foot line is called **trimeter**; a four-foot line, **tetrameter**; a six-foot line, **hexameter**; and an eight-foot line, **octameter**. The following line is an example of octameter:

Ónce up/ón a/mídnight/dréary,/whíle I/póndered,/wéak and/wéary,

Edgar Allan Poe, "The Raven"

The terms *trimeter, tetrameter, pentameter, hexameter,* and *octameter* all indicate the number of feet in a line of poetry. The number and arrangement of syllables within each foot is indicated by the terms *iamb, anapest, trochee,* and *dactyl.*

• In much English poetry, a typical foot is a pair of syllables, with the stressed one *last.* Such a pair of syllables is called an **iamb**. Each foot in the following example contains an unstressed syllable followed by a stressed one, and so is iambic:

For Í/was bórn/on Sát/urdáy—

Countee Cullen, "Saturday's Child" (page 19)

(Detroít/Detroít/Detroít/Detroít)

Because there are four iambic feet in this line, it is called *iambic tetrameter.* Usually not every iambic line follows exactly this pattern. For instance, for variety, two unstressed syllables may take the place of one:

His lús/trous brícks/are bríght/er than blóod,
His smók/ing mór/tar whít/er than bóne.

Elinor Wylie, "Sanctuary" (page 418)

• We call a foot in which a stressed syllable comes after two unstressed ones an **anapest**:

(New Rochélle/New Rochélle/New Rochélle)

Anapestic lines often have a speeded-up feeling:

Ah, flý!—/let us flý!—/for we múst.

Edgar Allan Poe, "Ulalume" (page 326)

• When a line falls mainly into pairs of syllables and the stressed syllable comes *first* in each pair, we call the rhythm or meter *trochaic.* The word **trochee** comes from an ancient Greek word that means "runner." The people who named this kind of meter were thinking of the CLIP-clop CLIP-clop sound of someone running. These lines contain four trochees:

Dáy by/ dáy did / Hía/wátha
Gó to / wáit and / wátch be/síde it;

Henry Wadsworth Longfellow, "Hiawatha"

(Bóston/Bóston/Bóston/Bóston)

• When unstressed syllables double up after the beat, the foot is called **dactyl**. This meter is rare in English poetry. Here is a dactylic line:

Táke her up/ténderly;/Líft her with/cáre

(Báltimore/Báltimore/Báltimore)

**blank verse** Blank verse is the basic line in much traditional English poetry and in the plays of Shakespeare. It is made up of unrhymed iambic lines with five feet. A line with five feet, or beats, is a pentameter line (from the Greek word *penta* meaning "five"). Blank verse, thus, is unrhymed **iambic pentameter**.

The following lines from "Mending Wall" (page 142) by Robert Frost are blank verse:

I let my neighbor know beyond the hill;
And on a day we meet to walk the line
And set the wall between us once again.

**couplet** A pair of lines that rhyme and have the same meter and length is a couplet. We call the two lines a **closed couplet** when they end with a period and sum up an image or thought. "Once by the Pacific" (page 258) by Robert Frost is made up of seven couplets. The final couplet of the poem is a closed couplet:

There would be more than ocean-water broken
Before God's last *Put out the Light* was spoken.

**stanza** Many poems are divided into stanzas. Stanzas are groups of lines that follow the same or a very similar pattern. In the following two stanzas, the length and rhythm of each set of four lines are very similar. They use the same rhyme scheme: The first and third lines rhyme (Saturday/say, life/wife) and the second and fourth lines rhyme (seed/feed, Sorrow/borrow).

For I was born on Saturday—
"Bad time for planting a seed,"
Was all my father had to say,
And, "One mouth more to feed."

Death cut the strings that gave me life,
And handed me to Sorrow,
The only kind of middle wife
My folks could beg or borrow.

Countee Cullen, "Saturday's Child" (page 19)

Some traditional stanza forms are not as simple as this one. They may weave as many as eight or twelve lines into a complicated pattern. Part of the pleasure of reading or listening to poetry comes from recognizing the stanza form and being able to follow it.

**refrain** A refrain is a line or part of a line that comes back in the same or very similar form several times in a poem. In many songs and songlike poems, the refrain is the last line of each stanza. Through the refrain, a basic idea or feeling seems to echo throughout the poem. In this way, the refrain helps set the mood or tone of the poem. In the following example, the refrain is continued throughout the poem:

The Lord told Moses what to do
Let my people go;
To lead the children of Israel through,
Let my people go.

"Go Down, Moses" (page 528)

**free verse** Free verse is a freely moving, varied kind of modern poetry. It does not follow the strict requirements of traditional meter and rhyme. Lines may vary much in length, and they are often longer than in traditional poems. Though the lines may have a free-moving rhythm, they seldom fall into a strict metrical pattern. There may be some repetition and echoing of words and phrases but no regular or predictable rhyme.

The poets who first experimented with free verse often used it to produce a chantlike effect. Here are some lines by the American nineteenth-century poet Walt Whitman, who wrote most of his poetry in free verse:

Sing on, sing on you gray-brown bird,
Sing from the swamps, the recesses, pour your chant
from the bushes,
Limitless out of the dusk, out of the cedars and pines.

"When Lilacs Last in the Dooryard Bloomed" (page 195)

**sonnet** The sonnet is a traditional poem of 14 lines that follows an intricate rhyme scheme. Generally, each line is iambic pentameter, that is, it has five iambic feet. The sonnet was already popular with poets and their readers and listeners in the fourteenth century. Shakespeare and many poets of his time wrote many, many sonnets that are still admired and memorized by people who love poetry. Here is a famous sonnet from the nineteenth century by the English poet Elizabeth Barrett Browning. Notice that the same rhyme is repeated over and over in the first eight lines. Then a second rhyme (or near rhyme) is repeated several times in the last six lines:

How do I love thee? Let me count the ways.    a
I love thee to the depth and breadth and height    b
My soul can reach, when feeling out of sight    b
For the ends of Being and ideal Grace.    a
I love thee to the level of everyday's    a
Most quiet need, by sun and candle light.    b
I love thee freely, as men strive for Right;    b
I love thee purely, as they turn from Praise.    a
I love thee with the passion put to use    c
In my old griefs, and with my childhood's faith.    d

I love thee with a love I seemed to lose    c
With my lost saints—I love thee with the breath,    d
Smiles, tears, of all my life!—and, if God choose,    c
I shall but love thee better after death.    d

Like this example, most of the sonnets written through the ages have been poems about love. Often they are about the sorrows and despair of a lover to whom love matters more than anything else in life.

# Review

## Exercise 1

Copy each of the following lines of poetry and mark the stressed syllables ( ˊ ). Separate the feet with a slanted line (/). Tell whether the foot is **iambic** (Detróit), **anapestic** (New Rochélle), **trochaic** (Bóston), or **dactylic** (Báltimore). Tell whether the line is **trimeter** (3 feet), **tetrameter** (4 feet), or **pentameter** (5 feet).

1. Double, double, toil and trouble,

   William Shakespeare, *Macbeth*

2. But, soft! What light through yonder window breaks?

   William Shakespeare, *Romeo and Juliet*

3. 'Twas the night before Christmas, when all through the house,

   Clement Moore, *A Visit from St. Nicholas*

4. I could not love thee, Dear, so much
   Loved I not Honor more.

   Richard Lovelace "To Lucasta, on Going to the Wars"

cate the **rhyme** scheme by writing *a* after each word that rhymes with *day*, *b* after rhymes of *temperate*, *c* after rhymes of *shines*, *d* after rhymes of *dimmed*, *e* after rhymes of *fade*, *f* after rhymes of *ow'st*, and *g* after rhymes of *see*.

3. Find and copy the **closed couplet**—a pair of lines that rhyme, have the same meter, and sum up an image.

Shall I compare thee to a summer's day?
Thou art more lovely and more temperate:
Rough winds do shake the darling buds of May,
And summer's lease hath all too short a date;
Sometimes too hot the eye of heaven shines,
And often is his gold complexion dimmed;
And every fair from fair sometime declines,
By chance or nature's changing course untrimmed:
But thy eternal summer shall not fade
Nor lose possession of that fair thou ow'st;
Nor shall Death brag thou wander'st in his shade,
When in eternal lines to time thou grow'st:
So long as men can breathe, or eyes can see,
So long lives this, and this gives life to thee.

"Shall I Compare Thee to a Summer's Day?"
William Shakespeare

## Exercise 2

Read the **sonnet** and demonstrate your understanding of this poetry form by doing the following:

1. Copy the ninth line. Show that it is **iambic pentameter** by separating the feet (/) and marking the stressed ( ˊ ) syllables.
2. Copy the last word in each line in column form. Indi-

## Exercise 3

"Beat! Beat! Drums" is an example of free verse. Read the first stanza of this poem and do the following:

1. Find examples of **alliteration**—words with the same initial sound—and copy them down.
2. Practice reading the **stanza** aloud in such a way that its strong *irregular rhythm* comes through.

Beat! beat! drums!—blow! bugles! blow!
Through the windows—through doors—burst like a
 ruthless force,
Into the solemn church, and scatter the congregation,
Into the school where the scholar is studying;
Leave not the bridegroom quiet—no happiness must he

have now with his bride,
Nor the peaceful farmer any peace, ploughing his field
 or gathering his grain,
So fierce you whirr and pound you drums—so shrill you
 bugles blow.

Walt Whitman, "Beat! Beat! Drums!"

# Elements of the Short Story    3

A short story makes us share in a series of events. The writer of a short story creates a place for things to happen. He or she makes us share in the experiences of other people (or sometimes other creatures). In a good story, we are caught up in the action: we begin to wonder about the outcome. Some things turn out as we expect, and we are surprised by others. We often come to understand the characters and their motives—why they act the way they do. Often a good story makes us share in others' feelings—of sadness, happiness, bitterness, or disappointment. A good story gives us something to watch, to care about, and to think about.

The following are important elements of the short story:

| | |
|---|---|
| setting | point of view |
| character | theme |
| plot | tone |

**setting** Setting is the time and place of the events of a story. Often the setting helps shape the characters and events. Village or city, north or south, poor or wealthy neighborhood, mountain country or coast—all these help decide how people live. They help decide what the people will be like and what is most important in their lives.

In "The Leader of the People" (page 87) by John Steinbeck, the worlds which shaped the values of the boy's father and grandfather are so different that these men fail to understand each other. If we are to understand their different outlooks on life, we must know the time and place in which these characters lived. The grandfather lived during the westward movement—a time when heroic deeds were accomplished and the West was tamed. The achievements of the old pioneering days, of the *past,* are most important to the grandfather. The present offers different challenges to the boy's father. In his world, the westward trek is over, and survival depends on remaining in one place, settling the land and making his living from it. These goals are most important to him; he has no patience with storytelling that glorifies deeds no longer relevant. Steinbeck draws us into the lives of the characters. We wonder why the father fails to understand the grandfather; we want to understand him ourselves. To do so, we must recognize the time and place that shaped his life.

**character** Often the focus of a short story, as in a play, is on the characters created by the writer. We come to know them as people. We come to understand or share their thoughts and feelings. We imagine what it would be like to be in their places or what it would be like to meet them. In a good story, the writer does not simply *tell* us what a character is like and what we are supposed to think of the person. We have a chance to observe the characters for ourselves; we judge them by what they say and do. A writer may help us understand a character in a variety of ways:

• *Outward appearance* often tells us something about a person. Sometimes it gives us a wrong impression. But just as often it gives us insight into what a person is like. This visual description of the matchmaker in Bernard Malamud's "The Magic Barrel" (page 111) tells us more than what he looks like:

The matchmaker appeared one night out of the dark fourth-floor hallway of the graystone rooming house, grasping a black, strapped portfolio that had been worn thin with use. Salzman, who had been long in the business, was of slight but dignified build, wearing an old hat and an overcoat too short and tight for him. He smelled frankly of fish, which he loved to eat, and although he was missing a few teeth, his presence was not displeasing, because of an amiable manner curiously contrasted by mournful eyes. His voice, his lips, his wisp of beard, his bony fingers were animated, but give him a moment of repose, and his mild blue eyes soon revealed a depth of sadness, a characteristic that put Leo a little at ease although the situation, for him, was inherently tense.

• The **dialogue** in a short story is often our main clue to what people think and feel. We learn much about people by listening to what they say.

The following dialogue between Lawrence and his fellow classmates in "A Turn With the Sun" (page 27) by John Knowles dramatizes the urgency of Lawrence's plea for acceptance, and at the same time reveals the reason for his rejection by the group. As we listen, we begin to understand him better and see what it is that makes him different from his classmates:

"I have some cousins, two cousins, you know, Ging—George and Carter—they're in clubs at Harvard, I mean a club at Harvard, one club, both of 'em are in the same club. It's the . . . the . . ." Lawrence was suddenly stricken with the thought that George and Carter might very easily not be in the best Harvard club, or even the second best; but everyone, even Marvel, was listening with interest, "It's called," he felt his color rising at the inelegance of the name, "The Gas—or something."

"Oh yes," said Vinnie crisply, "that's a very good club, for New Yorkers mostly, they have some very good men."

"Oh," Lawrence breathed with fake innocence and real relief. . . .

"Devon is like some kind of country-club penitentiary, where the inmates don't take walks around the courtyard, they go to the private penitentiary golf course for eighteen holes. And the dean, is that who he is? that queer, stuttery old bird, you know, the one in chapel the first day, the one who looks like Hoover with an Oxford accent. . . ."

"Yes, that's the dean," said Vinnie, fingering his water glass, "Dean Eleazer Markham Bings-Smith."

"No!" exploded Lawrence, "is that his name! His honest name?" He regretted the *honest,* it should have been *actual.*

"Why does he talk that way, and *look* that way! Like my beagle, that's the way he looks, like the beagle I've got at home, my beagle looks just like that right after he's had a bath."

There was something like consternation passing around the table. Lawrence felt it and looked wonderingly from one to the other. Ging was watching an elderly couple making their way toward the door. The others examined their desserts.

"Was that the dean?" Lawrence asked in a shocked whisper. "Did he hear me?"

No one really answered. . . .

• *Actions* often speak louder than words. To understand or judge people, we often have to see what they will do. We want to see especially what they will do when a challenge or important decision puts them to the test. In Eudora Welty's "A Visit of Charity" (page 21), Marian is confronted for the first time by the realities of being old. How does she respond?

"Well, it was a real visit," said the old woman, following Marian through the doorway and all the way out into the hall. Then from behind she suddenly clutched the child with her sharp little fingers. In an affected, high-pitched whine she cried, "Oh, little girl, have you a penny to spare for a poor old woman that's not got anything of her own? We don't have a thing in the world—not a penny for candy—not a thing! Little girl, just a nickel—a penny—"

Marian pulled violently against the old hands for a moment before she was free. Then she ran down the hall, without looking behind her and without looking at the nurse, who was reading *Field & Stream* at her desk. The nurse, after another triple motion to consult her wrist watch, asked automatically the question put to visitors in all institutions: "Won't you stay and have dinner with *us?*"

Marian never replied. She pushed the heavy door open into the cold air and ran down the steps.

Under the prickly shrub she stooped and quickly, without being seen, retrieved a red apple she had hidden there.

Her yellow hair under the white cap, her scarlet coat, her bare knees all flashed in the sunlight as she ran to meet the big bus rocketing through the street.

"Wait for me!" she shouted. As though at an imperial command, the bus ground to a stop.

She jumped on and took a big bite out of the apple.

• A writer often makes us share in the *thoughts* and *feelings* of the characters. What people think to themselves is as important as what they say out loud. Many modern writers aim at being faithful to what really goes on in people's minds. In "I Stand Here Ironing" (page 175), Tillie Olsen allows us to share in a mother's thoughts as she tries to analyze where she went wrong in raising her daughter:

> "Who needs help." Even if I came, what good would it do? You think because I am her mother I have a key, or that in some way you could use me as a key? She has lived for nineteen years. There is all that life that has happened outside of me, beyond me.
> And when is there time to remember, to sift, to weigh, to estimate, to total? I will start and there will be an interruption and I will have to gather it all together again. Or I will become engulfed with all I did or did not do, with what should have been and what cannot be helped.

**plot**    The most basic kind of question that makes us go on reading is: "What is going to happen next? How will it all come out?" We call the series of events that keep a story moving the plot of the story. We expect the characters of a story to do something. We expect things to happen to them. We expect them to interact with each other, to establish some kind of relationship among themselves. The events that make up the plot of a story may be loosely strung together, or they may be very tightly related. There may be much physical or external action or very little. Here are some kinds of plot that are familiar to readers:

• Different events may follow each other as they happen in time—in simple **chronological order.** Some stories are written almost as if they were part of a diary or a journal. They note things as they happen during a period in someone's life.

• Some of the oldest kinds of storytelling tell us different things that happened during a trip—a journey by land or by sea, often in search of something. Mark Twain's *The Adventures of Huckleberry Finn* (page 208) tells the story of the different things that happened to Huck after he ran away and traveled down the Mississippi on a raft with the runaway slave Jim. We call the plot of such a story **episodic.** It is made up of different **episodes:** different stages of the journey, encounters with different people, different adventures, different problems to solve.

• In many modern short stories, we find a more tightly structured plot. We find ourselves in some kind of situation in which a challenge or a problem creates **suspense.** Events have led us to expect something very good or very bad will happen, but we don't know what it will be. In a well-written story, things may come to a head at a point where an important decision has to be made or when everything hangs in the balance. We call this high point the **climax** of the story. Toward the end of the story, things are settled one way or the other. A true effort may end in success or failure, or a problem may be solved. We call this winding up the resolution, or **denouement,** of the story. In Bret Harte's story "The Outcasts of Poker Flat" (page 237), the conflict is between the characters and the forces of nature. They are "snowed in," trapped in the Sierra Mountains. The suspense builds as the snow piles higher and higher and food and firewood become scarcer with each passing day. The climax is reached when both time and food have nearly run out. The characters' only hope of survival rests with Tom, who must walk through the snow to Poker Flat and bring back help before time runs out. The conflict is resolved when the forces of nature triumph and the rescue party returns too late.

• Many writers make the plots of their stories more complicated or more interesting by special effects. **Foreshadowing,** for instance, provides us with hints or clues about what is going to happen later in the story. **Flashbacks** take us backward in time from the current action to act out for us something important from the character's past that helps explain the present. In "A Turn With the Sun" (page 27), John Knowles makes effective use of flashbacks throughout the story to help us understand Lawrence's thoughts and feelings. Many writers of popular stories like to end them with a clever twist or **surprise ending.** In "The Black Cat" (page 328), just when we are beginning to feel as confident as the narrator that the police do not suspect him of murder, the "one long, loud, and continuous scream, utterly anomalous and inhuman" is heard.

**point of view**    When authors write stories, they make us look at the events of the story as seen through someone's eyes. The eyes, or point of view, of the story may be that of a character in the story who is different from the author. In "A Separate Road" (page 401), Richard Wright tells the story from the main character's point of view:

> I went to school, feeling that my life depended not so much upon my learning as upon getting into another world of people.
> Until I entered Jim Hill public school, I had had but one year of unbroken study. With the exception of one year at the church school, each time I had begun a school term something happened to disrupt it. Already my personality was lopsided. My knowledge of feeling was far greater than my knowledge of fact.

The following are examples of different points of view:

• In many traditional novels and short stories, the storyteller, or **narrator,** tells us everything important that goes on. We simply assume that the narrator knows the past history of the characters as well as what they are doing at a given point in the story. When the narrator is all-knowing, or **omniscient,** we are told not only what is happening but also what the characters feel and think. Sometimes the storyteller turns directly to us as readers, commenting on the action or giving us a personal opinion.

• Many modern writers have felt that a *limited point of view* would make fiction more realistic or lifelike. In real life, we never know everything that goes on in other people's minds or in places where we are not present. Some writers tell us only what a person who is present might have seen and heard. They use an **objective third-person narrator.** We as readers then often have to draw our own conclusions and make our own judgments. In "The Open Boat" (page 287), Stephen Crane describes the plight of the four men as if he were observing the scene:

> In the meantime the oiler and the correspondent rowed. And also they rowed. They sat together in the same seat, and each rowed an oar. Then the oiler took both oars; then the correspondent took both oars; then the oiler; then the correspondent. They rowed and they rowed. The very ticklish part of the business was when the time came for the reclining one in the stern to take his turn at the oars. By the very last star of truth, it is easier to steal eggs from under a hen than it was to change seats in the dinghy. First the man in the stern slid his hand along the thwart and moved with care. Then the man in the rowingseat slid his hand along the other thwart. It was all done with the most extraordinary care. As the two sidled past each other, the whole party kept watchful eyes on the coming wave, and the captain cried: "Look out, now! Steady, there!"

• Sometimes we see the story through the eyes of a **first-person observer**, a character who plays a minor role in the actions or events. This person lets us share in whatever scenes or events an eyewitness to the story would be able to see.

• When the narrator is a **first-person participant,** again someone is talking to us directly, telling us "I did this" or "I observed such and such." But the person telling the story is at the same time a major character or even the central character in the story. He or she participates in the story. We then come to know the central character especially well—sharing the person's experiences, thoughts, and feelings. An all-time favorite told from this point of view is Mark Twain's novel *The Adventures of Huckleberry Finn* (page 208), in which Huck tells his own story. We see everything through the eyes of this unspoiled country boy:

> Three or four months run along, and it was well into the winter now. I had been to school most all the time, and could spell, read, and write just a little, and could say the multiplication table up to six times seven is thirty-five, and I don't reckon I could ever get any further than that if I was to live forever. I don't take no stock in mathematics anyway.

• Some modern writers have experimented with letting us share in the thoughts and feelings of one major character—exactly as they pass through that character's mind. The writers set down on paper that person's **stream of consciousness.** For instance, we might share in the thoughts of a sick person alone in a room. The story would be a stream of memories, half-finished thoughts, wishes, guesses about what is going on outside, and the like. Here is an example of stream-of-consciousness writing from "I Stand Here Ironing" (page 175) by Tillie Olsen. We are allowed to share in Momma's thoughts and feelings as she stands ironing, trying to sort out her feelings of failure in bringing up her daughter Emily:

> She always had a reason why we should stay home. Momma, you look sick, Momma. I feel sick. Momma, the teachers aren't there today, they're sick. Momma, we can't go, there was a fire there last night. Momma, it's a holiday today, no school, they told me.
>
> But never a direct protest, never rebellion. I think of our others in their three-, four-year-oldness—the explosions, the tempers, the denunciations, the demands—and I feel suddenly ill. I put the iron down. What in me demanded that goodness in her? And what was the cost, the cost to her of such goodness?

**theme**  The theme of a short story, play, or novel is the idea or thought that stays in our minds when we think about the meaning of a story as a whole. A good story often gets us involved in its action. It makes us share in emotions—in feelings of hope or anger, of love or disappointment. But a good story also makes us think. It raises some question in our minds that the story as a whole answers.

In practice, we use the term *theme* in two slightly different ways. Sometimes we use the word to label the *question* that the story raises in our minds. The theme then is a challenge or a problem that plays a major role in a story. For instance, in many stories about growing up, young people face a conflict between the old or traditional ways of their parents and the different or new ways of their own friends. Children of immigrant parents have often had to steer their way between the old-country ways of their family and Americanized ways. This is a theme in "Fifth Chinese Daughter" (page 125) by Jade Snow Wong. The conflict between the old and the new is made clear in the following **symbolic incident:**

My clothes were limited but I changed to look more graceful in silk stockings and found a bright ribbon for my long black hair. Daddy watched, catching my mood, observing the dashing preparations. He asked me where I was going without his permission and with whom.

I refused to answer him. I thought of my rights! I thought he surely would not try to understand. Thereupon Daddy thundered his displeasure and forbade my departure.

I found a new courage as I heard my voice announce calmly that I was no longer a child, and if I could work my way through college, I would choose my own friends. It was my right as a person.

My mother heard the commotion and joined my father to face me; both appeared shocked and incredulous. Daddy at once demanded the source of this unfilial, non-Chinese theory. And when I quoted my college professor, reminding him that he had always felt teachers should be revered, my father denounced that professor as a foreigner who was disregarding the superiority of our Chinese culture, with its sound family strength. My father did not spare me; I was condemned as an ingrate for echoing dishonorable opinions which should only be temporary whims, yet nonetheless inexcusable.

At other times, we use the word *theme* to stand for the *answer* to the basic question the story raises. In "Lift Every Voice and Sing" (page 543) by Maya Angelou, the basic question is, "Can one overcome barriers along the road to success placed in one's way by society, and is there any point in trying?" The story ends by answering this question. The theme is that success is possible, and the struggle worthwhile. Success lies in never allowing yourself to be defeated, in never giving up. Sometimes both the question and answer are stated in a *thematic passage,* as in this selection from "Lift Every Voice and Sing":

There was shuffling and rustling around me, then Henry Reed was giving his valedictory address, "To Be or Not To Be." Hadn't he heard the whitefolks? We couldn't *be,* so the question was a waste of time. Henry's voice came out clear and strong. I feared to look at him. Hadn't he got the message? There was no "nobler in the mind" for Negroes because the world didn't think we had minds, and they let us know it. "Outrageous fortune"? Now, that was a joke. When the ceremony was over I had to tell Henry Reed some things. That is, if I still cared. Not "rub," Henry, "erase." "Ah, there's the erase." Us.

Henry had been a good student in elocution. His voice rose on tides of promise and fell on waves of warnings. The English teacher had helped him to create a sermon winging through Hamlet's soliloquy. To be a man, a doer, a builder, a leader, or to be a tool, an unfunny joke, a crusher of funky toadstools. I marveled that Henry could go through with the speech as if we had a choice.

The thematic question here is, "Who is right, Henry or the narrator?" The answer is summed up in these concluding paragraphs:

While echoes of the song shivered in the air, Henry Reed bowed his head, said "Thank you," and returned to his place in the line. The tears that slipped down many faces were not wiped away in shame.

We were on top again. As always, again. We survived. The depths had been icy and dark, but now a bright sun spoke to our souls. I was no longer simply a member of the proud graduating class of 1940; I was a proud member of the wonderful, beautiful Negro race.

Most modern readers like to think about a story and reach their own conclusions about its meaning. When the author uses the story too directly to teach a lesson, we call the story **didactic**. A didactic story makes us feel that the author is teaching us something we already know.

**tone**    As in a poem, the way a story affects us depends not only on *what* we are told, but also on *how* we are told. Should we take the events seriously—should we worry about the characters and share their sorrow or even despair? Or are we expected to smile at what happens or even laugh out loud? The author's tone suggests what our reaction should be. It sets the **mood**—light-hearted or solemn, affectionate or bitter.

The opening paragraphs of Ralph Ellison's "Mister Toussan" (page 554) creates a playful, humorous mood:

"I hope they all gits rotten and the worms git 'em," the first boy said.

"I hopes a big windstorm comes and blows down all the trees," said the second boy.

"Me too," the first boy said. "And when old Rogan comes out to see what happened I hope a tree falls on his head and kills him."

"Now jus' look a-yonder at them birds," the second boy said, "they eating all they want and when we asked him to let us git some off the ground he had to come calling us names and chasing us home!"

"Doggonit," said the second boy, "I hope them birds got poison in they feet!"

The harmless, childlike dialogue of the two young boys causes us to laugh affectionately at them. They delight us; we immediately like them and are ready to listen to what they have to teach us.

The mood of Joe Vergara's "A Letter From Home" (page 137), on the other hand, is sorrow. The author prepares us for the seriousness of the events to come with these opening paragraphs:

One evening, shortly after Pop came home, Mom told him that a letter had come from Calabria.

"Why you don't tell me before? Read-a to me right away."

We knew how important these letters were to Pop, so while Mom went to get the letter and Pop stretched out on the couch, Al, Wheezer, and I left the piano and other preoccupations and sat around on the floor.

The opening paragraphs of "Deerslayer Escapes" (page 199) by James Fenimore Cooper immediately create tension, suspicion, concern. We worry about the hero. There is a feeling of impending danger:

It was an imposing scene into which Deerslayer now found himself advancing. All the older warriors were seated on the trunk of the fallen tree, waiting his approach with grave decorum. On the right stood the young men, armed, while the left was occupied by the women and children. In the center was an open space of considerable extent, always canopied by leaves, but from which the underbrush, dead wood, and other obstacles had been carefully removed.

# Review

## Exercise 1

Read the story and answer the questions that follow it.

Two strangers entered a village just as night was falling. They sought out the chief to greet him, according to custom, and to ask him for a place to spend the night. The chief replied, "Welcome, O strangers. We welcome you. There is a guesthouse in which you may sleep and there is food for you to eat. But know that in this village there is a custom of long standing. Strangers may sleep here, but on pain of death they may not snore. Remember this well, for if you snore you will be killed as you sleep." The chief then took the strangers to the guesthouse and they composed themselves for the night's rest.

The visitors had not been asleep for long when one of them began to snore: "Vo, vo, vo." His companion awoke. He heard also, "Ts, ts, ts." This was the sound the villagers made sharpening their knives. The stranger then knew that they were getting ready to kill the snorer. He thought quickly of a way that he might save his companion. As one stranger snored, "Vo, vo, vo," the other stranger composed a song:

> Vo, vo, lio, vo. Vo, vo, lio, vo.
> We walked on the road.
> We came to this town.
> We were welcomed.
> Vo, vo, lio, vo.
> Vo, vo, lio, vo.

He sang this song with a stronger voice and the people could not hear the snoring above the song. They let their knives fall and began to dance. The drums were brought out and played. The people took up the song and sang. All the people, women, children, the chief, and all the men, came to join the dance.

All that night one stranger snored, one stranger sang, and the townspeople danced and played.

In the morning the strangers went to bid farewell to the chief before they took to the road again. The chief wished them a good journey and presented them with a good-sized purse. "I give you this present of money for your fine song. Because of you, strangers, we spent the night in dance and play. We are most grateful."

The strangers went out of the village. Once again on the road, they began to argue. How should the money be shared? The snorer said, "It is to me that the larger portion should fall. If I had not snored, you would not have been moved to compose the song, and we should have received no present at all."

The singer said, "True. If you had not snored, I would not have composed the song, but if I had not, you would have been killed. The people were already sharpening their knives. So I certainly get the larger portion of the money." Thus they argued and could not decide. Can you?

1. Where are we in this story? Does the **setting** make any difference to the tale? How?
2. What do we learn about the **characters** in this story?
3. How would you sum up what happens in the story? Give a brief **plot** summary.
4. What is the **theme** of this story? Does the theme raise a question or answer one?

## Exercise 2

As you read these passages from short stories in this volume, find examples of the following elements of a short story. Explain each element in terms of the appropriate passage.

| | |
|---|---|
| tone | first-person observer |
| suspense | first-person participant |
| climax | narrator |
| denouement | symbolic incident |
| foreshadowing | flashback |

One might write a book concerning our flight from the chicken farm into town. Mother and I walked the entire eight miles—she to be sure that nothing fell from the wagon and I to see the wonders of the world. On the seat of the wagon beside father was his greatest treasure. I will tell you of that.

On a chicken farm where hundreds and even thousands of chickens come out of eggs, surprising things sometimes happen. Grotesques are born out of eggs as out of people. The accident does not often occur—perhaps once in a thousand births. A chicken is, you see, born that has four legs, two pairs of wings, two heads, or

what not. The things do not live. They go quickly back to the hand of their maker that has for a moment trembled. The fact that the poor little things could not live was one of the tragedies of life to father. He had some sort of notion that if he could but bring into henhood or roosterhood a five-legged hen or a two-headed rooster his fortune would be made. He dreamed of taking the wonder about the county fairs and of growing rich by exhibiting it to other farmhands.

Sherwood Anderson, "The Egg" (page 166)

"Give way, men," whispered Starbuck, drawing still further aft the sheet of his sail. "There is time to kill a fish yet before the squall comes. There's white water again!—close to! Spring!"

Soon after, two cries in quick succession on each side of us denoted that the other boats had got fast. Hardly were they overheard when with a lightninglike hurtling whisper Starbuck said "Stand up!" and Queequeg, harpoon in hand, sprang to his feet.

Though not one of the oarsmen was then facing the life and death peril so close to them ahead, yet with their eyes on the intense countenance of the mate in the stern of the boat, they knew that the instant had come. They heard, too, an enormous wallowing sound as of fifty elephants stirring in their litter. Meanwhile the boat was still booming through the mist, the waves curling and hissing around us like enraged serpents.

"That's his hump. *There, there*, give it to him!" whispered Starbuck.

A short rushing sound leaped out of the boat. It was the darted iron of Queequeg. Then all in one welded commotion came an invisible push from astern, while forward the boat seemed striking on a ledge. The sail collapsed and exploded; a gush of scalding vapor shot up nearby; something rolled and tumbled like an earthquake beneath us. The whole crew were half suffocated as they were tossed helter-skelter into the white curdling cream of the squall. Squall, whale, and harpoon had all blended together; and the whale, merely grazed by the iron, escaped.

Herman Melville, *Moby Dick* (page 268)

## Exercise 3

Read or re-read "My Sister's Marriage" (page 364) by Cynthia Rich, paying particular attention to what the narrator says about her sister, Olive, and to what Olive herself says and does. Then write a **character** sketch of Olive using excerpts from the text that provide a clue to Olive's appearance, personality, thoughts, and feelings. Include excerpts of **dialogue** and action, as well as descriptions from the narrator.

# Elements of Drama    4

Drama is an age-old form of shared experience. Through the centuries, audiences have watched live actors act out events on a stage. The theater can create for us a powerful illusion of watching things as they happen. As good actors weave their spells, we seem to share directly in the thoughts and emotions of others. In a good performance, there is a strong bond between the performers and the audience. Through their rapt attention, their laughter, and their applause, the spectators show that the play has come to life for them and that the magic of the stage is doing its work.

In talking about drama, we use many terms, such as *character* and *plot*, that we also use in talking about other kinds of literature. The following terms are especially important for an understanding of the playwright's craft:

| stage directions | dialogue | tragedy |
| narrator | conflict | comedy |

**stage directions**    The author's stage directions describe what the spectators are supposed to see happening on the stage. An author may give very detailed instructions about **scenery**—the setting where the action takes place. Sometimes the scenery re-creates a place with realistic detail, to make it look like an actual room, a street, a forest setting, or the like. Sometimes the stage is almost bare, with many details of the setting left vague. The stage directions describe the appearance and use of important objects, or **props,** that may play a role in the events: a painting, a vase, a pistol, a bunch of flowers, or the like. Often the stage directions give detailed instructions for the *entrances* and *exits* of the actors. There may be much guidance to the actors for the language of **gestures,** which is an important part of the language of the theater. A look on the actor's face, an outstretched hand, a sudden turning away—all these can tell us as much as the spoken word, and sometimes more. In addition, the directions may call for sound effects—thunder, a shot, hoofbeats, or whatever else is needed.

**narrator**    In some modern plays (and in many short plays originally written for radio), a narrator tells part of the story. The narrator may look back into the past or summarize the events between major scenes. The narrator can make us feel that we are looking *behind* the scenes of the main events. In *Our Town* (page 426) by Thornton Wilder, the stage manager functions as a narrator.

**dialogue**    When we watch a play, our attention focuses on the words being spoken. To appreciate the play, we must be good listeners. *Dialogue* is our term for the give-and-take of the spoken word among characters on the stage. Playwrights use dialogue to let us know indirectly what a short story writer or a novelist may tell us directly, through the narrator. When a play does not have a narrator, the characters on stage may have to tell us *where* they are, *who* the other people are, and *what* is happening. But as we listen to them, we not only learn "the facts," we also find out what goes on in their minds and why they do what they do. These are some of the important ways dialogue is used in a play:

• We call the important facts and background that we are told early in the play the **exposition.** Much of what the characters say at the beginning will introduce us to a situation or location. We may learn about the past history of a person, a family, or a community. Gradually, a major problem or challenge may come into focus. Then the main action of the play is ready to start. During the exposition of Lorraine Hansberry's *A Raisin in the Sun* (page 562), we see not only *where* the characters live, but *how* they live. We see their day-to-day struggle with poverty in their small apartment, the arguments over a bathroom shared by other tenants, the conflict between mother and son, husband and wife over insignificant sums of money. We learn something of the characters' thoughts and feelings—their dreams, frustrations, disillusionments. During the exposition we learn enough about the characters and their situation to prepare us for the main action of the play: the dispute over how the insurance money should be spent to free them all from a life of poverty.

• The **minor characters** of a play often help bring out the important character traits of the major characters. In *A Raisin in the Sun*, Momma, Ruth, Walter, and Beneatha all reveal basic values and attitudes toward life in their interactions with George Murchison.

- In a **soliloquy,** a major character talks to himself or herself at some length. If other characters are present on stage, either they are not listening or they are listening secretly. (In a **monologue,** only one character speaks, but he or she may be speaking *to* other characters.) A soliloquy lets us hear the speaker's private thoughts. Sometimes this is our best chance to learn the character's real feelings.
- A **confidant** or confidante (female) is someone whom a major character trusts with his or her secrets. The confidant(e) provides the audience with another way of learning about feelings or problems that the major character hides from the rest of the world.
- In an **aside,** a character makes a brief comment that is not for the ears of the other characters on the stage. In many comedies, we laugh at funny or disrespectful things people mutter in asides while they pretend to be listening seriously to others.

**conflict** In a play, as in a short story or novel, the main character has a problem. The heart of this problem is the conflict of the play. These are some of the different kinds of conflicts often found in plays:
- Sometimes the conflict is created by *two people or groups* with opposite wants or needs. The major characters in *A Raisin in the Sun* (page 562) are all in conflict over how the money should be spent. Walter wants the money to start a business; Beneatha, to further her education; Ruth, to buy a house. There is also a conflict between the family and society, represented by Mr. Lindner, who calls on the family to deter them from moving into a white neighborhood.
- Sometimes the conflict is created by opposite wants or needs *within one person*. In *A Raisin in the Sun*, Momma is faced with a difficult choice. With her limited amount of money, should she satisfy her daughter's desire to further her education and become a doctor, her son's dream of starting his own business, or her own desire to have a house and provide her grandson Travis with a better environment? As the events in the play make her decision more and more crucial to their happiness, her struggle to resolve the problem becomes increasingly difficult until, witnessing Walter's desperation, the conflict rages within her.
- The conflict may also be a struggle *between a person or group and an impersonal force*, such as a natural disaster or illness. A central conflict in *A Raisin in the Sun* is the family's struggle with poverty.
- In many plays, conflict is the essential element that makes the play come to life. The truly dramatic scenes

in a play are often the scenes where opposites meet face to face, where opposing forces confront each other. Often the exposition of a play sketches in the background or history of the people or groups that are in conflict. We learn something about the reasons for a quarrel or the causes of a disagreement. Often the play reaches its high point, or **climax,** in a scene where a smoldering conflict comes out into the open. During the climax, two characters may finally explain or justify their conflicting goals. A hidden resentment may turn into open rebellion. The **resolution,** or denouement, may lead to triumph for one side and defeat for the other. It may lead to some kind of agreement or understanding. It may make us see another way out of the clash of opposing forces.

**tragedy** A tragedy is a play in which the central character, or protagonist, is a great or admirable person who goes down to defeat. To be a true **tragic hero** or heroine, he or she needs the right personal qualities: the person (or persons) should have the kind of dignity or stature that calls for our admiration or even awe. But at the same time, the tragic hero and heroine should still be human, in some ways like other people—so that we can feel pity, or compassion, for them in their sufferings. A tragedy brings great sorrow and loss to someone we admire or respect. Much discussion of tragedy deals with *how* the downfall of the tragic hero comes about. In a great tragedy, we look for one or more of the following:
- A **tragic flaw** is a shortcoming, or weakness, in the tragic hero; it helps bring on his or her downfall. Though the character may have admirable goals and great strength, some shortsightedness or personal weakness helps explain the final defeat. In several of Shakespeare's plays, a tragic flaw of the main character is the inability to control a rash, passionate, or impulsive nature. In *Romeo and Juliet*, one major cause of death and suffering is the old feud between the two noble families of the Montagues and the Capulets. But we also hear many warnings in the play about the hotheaded, hot-blooded young people. Juliet has misgivings about her first lovers' meeting with Romeo; it is "too rash, too unadvised, too sudden." Friar Lawrence warns the lovers, "These violent delights have violent ends!" We see several situations in the play where people lose control when their passions become too strong and sweep them along.
- The tragic hero may be struggling against fate, a power that has the final word in all human effort. In the

ancient Greek tragedies, human beings who struggle against fate gain nothing but greater suffering. Their tragic flaw is pride—they think they can change fate, but they are destroyed in the attempt. The pride that made people rebel against fate was called **hubris** by the ancient Greeks.

• A **tragic dilemma** puts the hero in a situation where either way out is equally, or almost equally, bad. The character has two choices that are both in some way evil, or that may each lead to disaster. In Shakespeare's *Julius Caesar,* Brutus is an admirable man faced with a tragic dilemma. Should he support his friend Caesar, who seems tempted by his ambition to be emperor, and who with such power might become a tyrant? Or, for the sake of the people, should he join the plot to kill Caesar and in that way save Roman democracy? Brutus is an admirable man, torn between love and loyalty to Caesar and to his country Rome. He is a patriot, willing to do a terrible thing for the sake of Rome.

**comedy**   Comedy is the kind of drama that entertains us and makes us laugh. Its main characters are often ordinary people—people who do not frighten us or fill us with awe. We can smile at their weaknesses, and we can easily share in their joys and sorrows. Writers who have a gift for comedy know how to appeal to our sense of humor. Different kinds of comedy make us laugh for different reasons.

• We respond with laughter when something surprising happens that makes us happy. Even when the characters in a comedy meet with problems or barriers, the play often shows that wishes can come true.

We expect a *happy ending.* The happy ending is often brought about by good luck—a fortunate coincidence, an unexpected inheritance, or a sudden change of heart by some important person. Favorite comedy plots through the ages have been built around events like the following:

—Young lovers are separated by events or misunderstandings, but they are finally reunited.
—Domineering older people try to deny younger people their place in the sun, but they finally have to give in.
—A sneaky crook or hypocrite threatens to get the better of an innocent victim, but he or she is foiled in the end.

• Favorite comedy characters are often well-meaning, lovable people who get into every kind of trouble. We smile at their innocence or their mistakes. We sympathize with them and wish them no ill, but we cannot help laughing at their weaknesses. We laugh with *affection* because we know they mean no harm.

• **Satire** is a way of criticizing human nature by making people with bad character traits look foolish. We are meant to laugh at them with scorn rather than affection. A satire often uses a **stock character**—someone with one very *exaggerated* flaw, like greed or conceit—to show us how *not* to behave. Satire can be a powerful teacher, because no one in the audience wants to resemble this ridiculous character.

• Many writers of comedy delight in quick, clever remarks and nimble word play. We laugh at conversations full of quick-witted answers, called *repartee.* We laugh at *puns,* which use the same (or very similar) words in several surprising and different ways.

# Review

## Exercise 1

Select any *five* of the following **characters.** For each, find and copy two or three lines spoken by the character that tell us a great deal about the person. Explain what the lines disclose about the character.

*Our Town* (page 426)
Dr. Gibbs
Mrs. Gibbs
Mr. Webb
Mrs. Webb
Emily Webb
Wally Webb
George Gibbs
Rebecca Gibbs

*A Raisin in the Sun*
 (page 562)
Lena Younger (Mama)
Ruth Younger
Walter Younger
Beneatha Younger

## Exercise 2

Read *Our Town* (page 426) by Thornton Wilder. In Act Three, Emily struggles with a **conflict** between leaving the world of the living and joining the world of the dead. Rewrite the scene in which Emily chooses to go back to the world of the living and relive the days of her childhood. Create a different **resolution** to the conflict.

## Exercise 3

Re-read the scene in Act One of *Our Town* in which Professor Willard gives "a kind of scientific account" of the history of Grover's Corners. Explain how this character introduces humor into the play. How do we react to the professor himself and to the way he relates what he knows about the town? Which of the following elements of humor is displayed in this scene? Explain your answer.

happy ending
satire
affectionate laughter

puns
repartee
surprise

## Exercise 4

The **stage directions** in *Our Town* specify what type of **scenery** should be used and what expressions and **gestures** should accompany the lines.

1. What kind of **props** are used in *Our Town?* Is the **setting** *realistic,* or does it rely on the audience's *imagination?* Choose a scene in the play and explain how the props work to create the desired setting. If you were writing the same scene, what props would you use to achieve a similar effect?

2. As you re-read the **stage directions,** notice how they guide the actors and actresses toward the interpretation of the lines that the author intended. Choose *five* stage directions. Based on what they say, explain how you as an actor or actress would interpret the lines in a performance of the play that is faithful to the author's intentions.

# Author Biographies

*Sherwood Anderson*

*Maya Angelou*

SHERWOOD ANDERSON (1876–1941), short story writer and novelist, was born in Camden, Ohio. Because his family moved aimlessly around Ohio, each of the seven children was born in a different place and Anderson's schooling was very spotty. He served in Cuba during the Spanish-American War and became manager of a factory. He later lived in Chicago, where he worked as an advertising copywriter. His first collection of stories, *Winesburg, Ohio*, was published in 1919 through the assistance of one of his admirers, Carl Sandburg. He published another successful collection of short stories, *The Triumph of the Egg*, in 1921.

Sherwood Anderson was among the first American writers to develop characters in his stories that could be evaluated and judged in terms of modern psychology. His stories did not rely very heavily upon plot and external action. Instead, he was more interested in disclosing the interior thought processes of his characters.

MAYA ANGELOU (born 1928) was born in St. Louis, Missouri, and spent her early years in Arkansas and California. She studied music and dance and was a member of the cast of *Porgy and Bess* in 1954–1955, when the musical was sponsored by the United States Department of State on a 22-nation tour. She subsequently appeared in a number of Off Broadway productions. She worked for Dr. Martin Luther King and wrote columns for newspapers in Ghana and Egypt. Her autobiography, *I Know Why the Caged Bird Sings*, was published in 1970. Its sequel, *Gather Together in My Name*, appeared in 1974. She has also published poetry collections, has written plays and screenplays, and is a songwriter and composer. She is fluent in Spanish, French, Italian, and Arabic.

IMAMU AMIRI BARAKA (LEROI JONES) (born 1934), American poet, dramatist, novelist, and essayist, was born in Newark, New Jersey. He attended Rutgers University for a year and later transferred to Howard University, from which he graduated at the age of nineteen. After two years of service in the Strategic Air Command, he settled in New York City where he continued his studies and developed a reputation as a very knowledgeable jazz critic. He published his first collection of poetry, *Preface to a Twenty-Volume Suicide Note*, in 1961. Dedicated to the development of the black community and its culture, he established a black theatre and community center in his native city of Newark in 1966. He has also written on music in *Blues People* (1963) and *Black Music* (1967). The former book has been universally praised and is considered to be the foremost work in the field.

STEPHEN VINCENT BENÉT (1898–1943), was born in Bethlehem, Pennsylvania. His father, like his grandfather and great-grandfather before him, was an army officer, so Benét's boyhood was spent in many places. He went to school in California and Georgia and later graduated from Yale University. He published his first volume of poetry when he was 17. His long narrative poem *John Brown's Body* won the Pulitzer Prize for poetry in 1929. His short stories and novels were always popular, and *The Devil and Daniel Webster* became a minor classic in a very short period of time.

As a poet, Stephen Vincent Benét was a master of the ballad form in particular and of narrative poetry in general. Many of his short stories are haunting and suspenseful. Those that use folklore for their story base are genuinely American and wholly delightful.

STEPHEN BERG (born 1934), American poet, was born in Philadelphia, Pennsylvania. He graduated from the State University of Iowa in 1959. He has taught English for a number of years at the college level. *Bearing Weapons*, his first collection of poetry, was published in 1963. He has translated a number of Spanish authors into English and has edited a number of anthologies. His poetry has appeared frequently in a number of magazines and literary journals.

ARNA BONTEMPS (1902–1973), American poet, novelist, and biographer, was born in Alexandria, Louisiana. He was raised in California and graduated from Pacific Union College in 1923. His poetry first appeared in *Crisis* magazine in 1924 and continued to appear in that magazine for the next three years. He turned to the novel, publishing *God Sends Sunday* in 1931, *Black Thunder* in 1936, and *Drums at Dusk* in 1939.

Bontemps' interest in his own black heritage accounts for the many books he has written about black Americans. His *Story of the Negro* received the Jane Adams Children's Book Award in 1956. In *Anyplace But Here* he gathered together brief biographies of courageous black Americans. He published a much-read biography of Frederick Douglass in 1959 and an anthology of poetry written by blacks in 1963.

KAY BOYLE (born 1903), poet, short story writer, and novelist, was born in St. Paul, Minnesota. From 1922 until 1941 she lived in Europe, mostly in France. She published her first collection of short stories in 1929 and her first novel in the following year. From the early thirties until the early forties she published a number of novels, short story collections, and poems. Her presence in Europe at the beginning of World War II led directly to three books that described the unfolding war— *Primer for Combat, Avalanche,* and

*1939.* Her novel *Generation Without Farewell* dealt with conditions in postwar Germany. She was appointed Professor of English at San Francisco State University in 1963.

ANNE BRADSTREET (1612–1672), was born in England, the daughter of Thomas Dudley, who eventually became a governor of the Massachusetts Bay Colony. At the age of 16, she married Simon Bradstreet and sailed for America with her father, her husband, and other colonists two years later. She had eight children but still found the time to write. In 1650 the first edition of her poems was published in England under the title *The Tenth Muse Lately Sprung Up in America*. A second edition was published in Boston in 1678. This was the first volume of original poetry published in the British Colonies of North America. She also wrote several other poems and a short autobiography entitled *Religious Experiences*.

GWENDOLYN BROOKS (born 1917), American poet, was born in Topeka, Kansas, but has spent all except the first month of her life in Chicago. She loved poetry as a child and her first published poem appeared in a children's magazine when she was ten. While she was in high school, several of her poems were published in the *Defender*, a black newspaper in Chicago. In the early 1940's she won many prizes for her poetry and published her first poetry collection in 1945. *Annie Allen*, her second book of poetry, received a Pulitzer Prize in 1950.

Gwendolyn Brooks' poetry draws upon her own personal and racial experiences. But she deals with universal human concerns. Her poems are sometimes bold and experimental, but they are also natural and down-to-earth.

WILLIAM CULLEN BRYANT (1794–1878), journalist and poet, was born in Cummington, Massachusetts. He

*Gwendolyn Brooks*

*William Cullen Bryant*

*Willa Cather*

*James Fenimore Cooper*

published his first poem when he was 13 years old. His most famous poem "Thanatopsis," a meditation upon death, was written when he was 17. He was recognized as America's greatest poet by the time he was thirty. In 1825 he moved from Massachusetts to New York City to become the co-editor of a magazine. The following year he became editor of the *Evening Post*, one of New York's daily newspapers, and held that position until his death. He had little time for poetry after 1840, devoting all his energy to the newspaper and to national and city affairs. He was instrumental in the founding of New York's Central Park and the Metropolitan Museum of Art.

William Cullen Bryant was mainly a poet of nature. To him, nature was the outward sign of God's beauty and goodness and was therefore beneficial to human beings. His poetry describes nature and finds moral and spiritual significance in it.

WILLA CATHER (1873–1947), novelist, was born in Gore, Virginia, a small town near the larger city of Winchester. She grew up in Nebraska, where her father had moved to pursue a career in ranching. She graduated from the University of Nebraska. After teaching high school in Pittsburgh for five years, she joined the staff of *McClure's Magazine* and later became its managing editor. She left the magazine in 1912 when *Alexander's Bridge*, her first novel, was published. *My Antonia*, the story of a young girl who grows up on a farm, perhaps her best-known novel, followed in 1918. She won the Pulitzer Prize in 1923 for *One of Ours*, the story of a Nebraska farm boy who is killed during World War I. *Death Comes for the Archbishop*, 1927, is considered by most of the critics to be her finest novel.

In all of her fiction Willa Cather portrayed the beauty of the land and the uncomplicated but harsh nature of pioneer life. Her books communicate her own love for the American prairies and for the southwest section of the country and her admiration for the people who settled and survived on those lands.

JAMES FENIMORE COOPER (1789–1851) was born in Burlington, New Jersey, and grew up in Cooperstown, New York, a town named for his father and at the time located on the American frontier. He joined the U.S. Navy when he was 17 and served for five years. He returned to Cooperstown, intending to become a gentleman farmer, but turned to writing instead. He published his first novel in 1820, but its appearance went largely unnoticed. *The Spy*, his second novel, appeared in the following year. A story about the Revolutionary War, it was warmly praised and widely read. Cooper's most famous books are those that make up the Leatherstocking Tales, a series of five novels about Natty Bumppo, a brave Indian who struggles to maintain a life of freedom as the American settlers advance westward. These novels, in their order of publication, are *The Pioneers* (1823), *The Last of the Mohicans* (1826), *The Prairie* (1827), *The Pathfinder* (1840), and *The Deerslayer* (1841).

James Fennimore Cooper was a great admirer of a life of freedom lived close to nature. His memorable character Natty Bumppo is such a person, a brave and noble Indian who grieves as the settlers thoughtlessly and selfishly misuse the wilderness. Cooper was a great champion of individual freedom, but he feared that majority rule would bring disaster. He felt the United States should be governed by a small group of cultured and public-spirited landowners.

STEPHEN CRANE (1871–1900), poet, short story writer, and novelist, was born in Newark, New Jersey, and spent most of his youth in upstate New York. After attending college for two years, he moved to New York City to become a free-lance journalist. He published his first novel in 1893. In 1895 his second and greatest novel appeared, *The Red Badge of Courage*. This realistic novel about the Civil War became an immediate success. His fame as a writer grew with the publication in the same year of *The Black Riders*, a collection of free verse. "The Open Boat," one of his two most famous short stories, appeared in 1897. The other, "The Blue Hotel," was published the year before his early death.

Stephen Crane was one of the earliest realistic writers in America. So convincingly and authentically did he describe the horrors of war in *The Red Badge of Courage* that veterans of the conflict were sure he had served. He was born six years after the war's end.

COUNTEE CULLEN (1903–1946), poet, was born and raised in New York City. He graduated from New York University in 1925 and received a master's degree from Harvard the following year. He published his first collection of poetry, *Color*, the year he graduated from college. Two additional collections, *Copper Sun* and *The Ballad of a Brown Girl*, appeared two years later. *Caroling Dusk*, a collection of black poetry that he edited, appeared in the same year. His only novel, *One Way to Heaven*, a description of life in Harlem, appeared in 1932. His selection of his own favorite poems, entitled *On These I Stand*, appeared a year after his death.

Countee Cullen's poetry is known for its musical, lyrical quality. He deals memorably with the joys and sorrows of the black American in his verses. He was a moving force in what has come to be called the Harlem renaissance, a period in the 1930's and 1940's of artistic production in Harlem by writers such as Cullen, Claude McKay, Langston Hughes, J. W. Johnson, and James Baldwin.

EDWARD ESTLIN CUMMINGS (1894–1962) or, as he preferred it, e. e. cummings,

was born in Cambridge, Massachusetts. He was educated at Harvard University; his father had been an English professor at Harvard and later a famous Congregational minister. Before America entered the First World War, Cummings went to France and served as a volunteer ambulance driver. After the war he spent several years in Paris, where he studied art. He was a very talented painter and exhibited his work several times throughout his life.

Cummings published his first volume of poetry in 1923. From the very beginning he was both criticized and praised for his unusual use of language and punctuation. He was among the first of the modern twentieth-century American poets. He has been called "the most truly delightful lyric poet in America" and "one of the major lyric poets of our time." The freshness and directness of his poetry has always appealed to young people.

EMILY DICKINSON (1830–1886), poet, was born in Amherst, Massachusetts, and spent her entire life there. She wrote over 1700 poems, but only seven were published, without her consent, during her lifetime. Because she wrote in secret, most of her poetry was discovered by her sister after her death. She lived a life of almost total seclusion and welcomed only a few close friends to her home. Her first volume of poetry did not appear until 1890, four years after her death.

Emily Dickinson's poetry suggests that she felt that she had to withdraw from the world before she could react to it. Many of her poems contain dramatic statements of the relationship between her inner being and the world outside. Her poems are short and have no titles. Most were written in four-line stanzas. Many deal with loneliness and anxiety, but they are not depressing. The emotions they communicate apply to all people, although the poet chose to avoid people throughout her 56 years.

*Countee Cullen*

*E. E. Cummings*

*Jonathan Edwards*

*Ralph Waldo Emerson*

JONATHAN EDWARDS (1703–1758) was born in East Windsor, Connecticut. He entered Yale University at the age of 13 and graduated when he was 17 years old. Many of his relatives had been Congregationalist clergymen, and he himself entered that church's ministry, becoming assistant pastor of the church at Northampton, Massachusetts, in 1726. He became the chief pastor three years later. He was a forceful and compelling speaker, and his sermons were instrumental in beginning a religious revival throughout New England that came to be called the "Great Awakening." In addition to his numerous sermons, he also wrote several works on religion during this period. Because of a doctrinal argument with his congregation, he was dismissed as its minister in 1750. For the next six years he served as a missionary minister to the Indian settlement in Stockbridge, Massachusetts. In the midst of that ministry he wrote *Freedom of Will*, his major philosophical work.

RALPH ELLISON (born 1914), American novelist, was born in Oklahoma City, Oklahoma. He attended Tuskegee Institute in Alabama but left before graduation to join the Federal Writers' Project, which was created to provide employment during the Great Depression. He has lectured and taught at numerous American colleges and universities and was a member of the National Council for the Arts from 1965 to 1967. His novel *Invisible Man* was published in 1952, was immediately hailed as a masterpiece, and won the National Book Award. It is considered by many critics to be the most significant work of fiction written in the 20 year period between 1945 and 1965. In 1964 he published a collection of largely autobiographical essays entitled *Shadow and Act* that traces his spiritual and intellectual growth. It too was acclaimed by American critics. For more than a decade he has been working on a second novel that he refuses to release until he is sure it will be the greatest American novel ever written.

Ralph Ellison's *Invisible Man* tells how it is to be a black writer in America. Its author has never been a political activist, preferring instead to remain a black American, working through his art to create the kind of society that will readily embrace what both allegiances suggest.

JAMES A. EMANUEL (born 1921), American poet, biographer, and critic, was born in Alliance, Nebraska. He graduated from Howard University in 1950, received his master's degree from Northwestern University three years later, and his doctorate from Columbia University in 1962. He is currently Professor of English at New York City's City University of New York. His first book, a biography of the American poet Langston Hughes, appeared in 1967. He has edited a number of poetry collections and has contributed his own poetry to a number of periodicals. His book reviews have appeared in a number of journals, and he has written numerous scholarly articles.

RALPH WALDO EMERSON (1803–1882), poet and essayist, was born in Boston, Massachusetts. His father, a Unitarian minister, died when Emerson was 11 years old, and his mother had to raise, in poverty, five sons, two of whom were very sickly. Emerson himself was in ill health through most of his youth and suffered from temporary blindness and a lung disease. He entered Harvard University in 1817, briefly taught school after graduation, and then returned to the Harvard Divinity School to study theology. He was ordained in 1829, but for personal and religious reasons resigned his ministry three years later. He traveled in Europe for a year and then returned to begin his career as a lecturer and writer. In 1836 his first book, *Nature*, appeared and was very well received. In it he sketched out the main principles of his philosophy of transcendentalism. A year later he gave an address at Harvard entitled "The American Scholar," which announced America's intellectual independence of Europe. His next two books, both called *Essays*, appeared four years later and contain some of his most memorable prose. Only two volumes of poetry appeared during his lifetime: *Poems* (1846) and *May-Day* (1867).

Ralph Waldo Emerson wrote some of the classical pieces of American literature. His essays, collections of loosely connected maxims, proverbs, and impressions, are memorable examples of understandable wisdom. His poetry is traditional and noteworthy in its simplicity and economy. His influence is apparent in the later works of some of America's most famous writers.

WILLIAM FAULKNER (1897–1962), novelist and short story writer, was born in New Albany, Mississippi, and grew up in Oxford, Mississippi, an area that bears close resemblance to the mythical "Yoknapatawpha County" that is featured in his novels. Because he could not meet the U.S. requirements for size, he went to Canada and joined the British Royal Air Force in World War I. He worked for a while on a New Orleans newspaper. His first publication was *A Marble Fawn*, a collection of poems in a rural setting. Among his most famous novels are *The Sound and the Fury* (1929), *As I Lay Dying* (1930), and *Requiem for a Nun* (1951). He also published many collections of short stories in the 1930's and 1940's. He won Pulitzer Prizes in 1955 for *A Fable* and in 1963 for *The Reivers*. He was awarded the Nobel Prize for literature in 1949.

William Faulkner ranks among the leading American authors of the twentieth century. His novels are known for the varied stylistic techniques that he employed in writing them. In many of his books he chooses the history and

traditions of the South for his theme and handles it sympathetically and knowledgeably. But above all else his books deal with the universal values of honor, pity, pride, sympathy, and love. In his acceptance speech for the Nobel Prize, he said that it was "the writer's duty to write about these things."

EDNA FERBER (1887–1968), American novelist, was born in Kalamazoo, Michigan. She grew up in Appleton, Wisconsin. She became a reporter for the local newspaper when her father's blindness forced her to abandon her ambition to become an actress. She later wrote for the Milwaukee *Journal* and the Chicago *Tribune*. She published her first novel in 1911, but her first significant success did not come until 1924, when *So Big* was published. Two years later *Show Boat* appeared. It eventually became a popular Broadway musical and Hollywood film. *Cimarron*, published in 1929, was also made into a very successful movie. Two of her later novels, *Giant* (1952) and *Ice Palace* (1958), also became extremely successsful box office attractions.

EDWARD FIELD (born 1924), American poet, was born in Brooklyn, New York, and attended New York University. He served in the United States Army Air Force during World War II. After the war he wrote narrations for film documentaries. *Stand Up, Friend, With Me*, his first collection of poems, appeared in 1962. He published a collection of Eskimo songs and stories in 1973.

BENJAMIN FRANKLIN (1706–1790) was born in Boston, Massachusetts, the fifteenth child and youngest son of a soap and candle maker. His formal schooling ended after two years, and the young Franklin worked in his father's shop until the age of 10. He was an avid reader and devoured every book he could get his hands on. At the same time he

*William Faulkner*

*Edna Ferber*

*Robert Frost*

*Nikki Giovanni*

worked on his writing style, eventually producing prose that was clear and sharp. At the age of 12 he became an apprentice to one of his older brothers, a printer. He soon became expert at the trade. After a dispute with his brother, he moved to Philadelphia in 1723. Seven years later he owned his own print shop and began publishing *The Pennsylvania Gazette*, writing much of the material for this newspaper himself. In 1733 he published the first of 25 annual editions of *Poor Richard's Almanac*, a publication in which his own wise and witty sayings were scattered throughout. He excelled in everything he did. He became Philadelphia's postmaster in 1737 and made an efficient operation out of the poorly run British Colonial Posts in both America and Canada. His inquisitive mind led him into scientific discovery, and he invented the lightning rod, bifocal lenses, and the Franklin stove. His lifelong concern for human betterment led him to the establishment of the first public library and the first fire department. He was instrumental in the founding of the new nation and laid the groundwork for the Articles of Confederation and was a signer of the Declaration of Independence. He served as American emissary to Paris during the Revolutionary War and secured vital French aid, both military and financial. He also served as the first Postmaster General of the United States.

ROBERT FROST (1874–1963), poet, was born in San Francisco, but at the age of 10 he returned to his native New England upon the death of his father. After briefly attending Dartmouth and Harvard, he worked as a shoemaker, schoolteacher, editor, and farmer during the last decade of the nineteenth century. His first collection of poetry, *A Boy's Will*, appeared in 1913 during a three-year period spent in England. His reputation became firmly established in 1914 through the publication of *North of Boston*, a collection that contained what

were to become some of Frost's most popular poems. These included "Mending Wall" and "The Death of the Hired Man." Returning to the United States in 1915, Frost settled on a New Hampshire farm. He won his first Pulitzer Prize for poetry in 1924 with the publication of *New Hampshire*. Many of the poems in this collection dealt with informal subjects. His next Pulitzer Prize came in 1931 for *Collected Poems*. Frost was subsequently awarded two other Pulitzer Prizes, one for *A Further Range* in 1937 and one for *A Witness Tree* in 1943. In 1961 he read one of his poems, "The Gift Outright," at the inauguration of President John F. Kennedy. He was the first poet ever to be involved in the inauguration of a president of the United States.

Robert Frost's poetry is closely linked with rural New England, specifically the north-of-Boston areas of Vermont and New Hampshire. The speech, the land, and the people of those areas live in all his poetry. The style he uses is graceful and the language plain. Much of his poetry proclaims that true peacefulness comes to those who labor amidst the external forces of nature.

DANIELA GIOSEFFI (born 1941) was born in Orange, New Jersey. She graduated from New Jersey's Montclair State College in 1963 and received a master's degree from the Catholic University of America two years later. She was a professional actress for five years. She has given poetry readings at colleges and universities. She has written poetry-plays that have been produced in Off Broadway theaters and her poetry has appeared in several anthologies. She has also contributed many poems to journals in this country, England, Canada, and Australia.

NIKKI GIOVANNI (born 1943), American poet, was born in Knoxville, Tennessee. She graduated from Fisk University in

Nashville in 1967 and later did graduate work at both the University of Pennsylvania and Columbia University. She has taught on the college level and established her own publishing firm in 1970. *Black Feeling, Black Talk*, her first volume of poetry, appeared in 1968. She has published several poetry collections since then, many of which were intended for young readers. Much of her poetry has been recorded. She has contributed her works to a number of nationally circulated magazines.

ELLEN GLASGOW (1874–1945), novelist, was born in Richmond, Virginia, and lived there all her life. Because she was in ill health as a child, she mostly educated herself through her father's large library. Although she never enrolled in a college or university, she was granted honorary degrees by several, including the University of North Carolina and the College of William and Mary. Her early writing was produced in secret. Her first novel, *The Descendant*, appeared in 1897 without her family's realizing she was doing any serious writing. Her finest novels include *Barren Ground* (1925), *The Romantic Comedians* (1926), *They Stooped to Folly* (1929), and *Vein of Iron* (1935). *In This Our Life* received the Pulitzer Prize for the novel in 1942.

Ellen Glasgow's works demonstrate her deep understanding of human nature. Her novels reveal her as a social historian who described, in a Southern setting, the eternal conflict between human beings and human nature.

LORRAINE HANSBERRY (1930–1965), American playwright, was born in Chicago, Illinois, the daughter of a prosperous real estate broker. She was interested in the theater during her high school years but was even more fascinated by painting. She studied art first at the Art Institute of Chicago and later at the University of Wisconsin and in Guadalajara, Mexico. She decided eventually that she wasn't a very good painter and turned her attention to the theater exclusively. After writing several unpublished stories and a few unfinished plays, she began working on *A Raisin in the Sun*. The play opened in New York in 1959 and was universally praised. It was awarded the New York Drama Critics Circle Award as the best American play of that year. It was adapted for film in 1961. Her second play, *The Sign in Sidney Brustein's Window*, opened in 1964.

Lorraine Hansberry was the first black woman to have a play produced on a Broadway stage. *A Raisin in the Sun* ran for nineteen consecutive months. But she never considered herself to be a black playwright, preferring instead to be thought of as a playwright who happened to be black. She died prematurely of cancer three months after the opening of her second play.

*Lorraine Hansberry*

*Bret Harte*

BRET HARTE (1836–1902), short story writer, was born in Albany, New York. He moved to California in 1854 and remained there during the height of the gold rush. He settled in San Francisco in 1860, where he became a printer and journalist. He contributed tales about Spanish California and the gold rush to two magazines and immediately became a famous literary personality. In 1868 he became editor of a new magazine, *The Overland Monthly*. His story "The Luck of Roaring Camp" appeared in an early issue of that magazine and won for Harte a nationwide reputation. Some of his best-known stories were published in subsequent issues of the magazine in 1869: "The Outcasts of Poker Flat" and "Tennessee's Partner." He returned to the East in 1871, settled in Boston, and began an unsuccessful relationship with the *Atlantic Monthly* magazine. From 1878 to 1885 he served as U.S. counsel, first in Prussia and then in Glasgow, Scotland.

Bret Harte is famous for the vivid descriptions that are found in his stories.

*Nathaniel Hawthorne*

*Ernest Hemingway*

They helped to establish a movement in American literature called "local color" writing. Like Harte, those who practiced local color writing had the ability to capture the feeling of a particular place and the people who inhabited it.

NATHANIEL HAWTHORNE (1804–1864), novelist and short story writer, was born in Salem, Massachusetts. He graduated from Bowdoin College in Maine in 1825. He returned to Salem and began his writing career but worked at many other jobs at the same time. In 1839 and 1840 he worked in the Boston Custom House, moved to Concord, Massachusetts, in 1842, and was Surveyor of Customs for the Port of Salem from 1846 to 1849. He was appointed to the four-year post of U.S. Consul in Liverpool, England, in 1853 by President Franklin Pierce, who had been a college classmate of his. In a 25 year period beginning in 1825, Hawthorne wrote more than 100 short stories that were eventually published in collections like *Twice-Told Tales*. *The Scarlet Letter*, his first novel, appeared in 1850 and gained him international fame. *The House of the Seven Gables* was published in 1851, *The Blithdale Romance* in 1852, and *The Marble Faun* in 1860.

Nathaniel Hawthorne's works frequently focus upon the darker side of human nature. Many of his stories are set against the rather grim background of Puritan New England. His ancestors had helped shape that society, and one of his forefathers, Colonel John Hawthorne, had been a judge during the infamous Salem witchcraft trials. Hawthorne characterized his writing as "romantic," but to him the term means confronting reality rather than escaping from it. Morality and redemption are themes that run through virtually everything he wrote.

ROBERT HAYDEN (1913–1980), American poet, was born in Detroit, Michigan. He graduated from Wayne State University in Detroit and did graduate work at the University of Michigan. He later joined the faculty of Fisk University. *Heart-shape in the Dust*, his first poetry collection, was published in 1940. His poetry has appeared in several nationally distributed journals and magazines. Another collection, *A Ballad of Remembrance*, was published in 1963 and received the grand prize at the *World Festival of Negro Arts*.

ERNEST HEMINGWAY (1898–1961) was born in Oak Park, Illinois, and was raised in northern Michigan. He volunteered as an ambulance driver in World War I and was seriously wounded in Italy at the age of 18. *In Our Time*, a collection of his early short stories, was published in 1925. *The Sun Also Rises* and *A Farewell to Arms*, the two novels that made him unquestionably famous, appeared in 1926 and 1929 respectively. The first captures the aimlessness of Americans living in post–World War I Europe. The second is a moving commentary on the pointlessness of war. *For Whom the Bell Tolls* appeared in 1940 and received great critical acclaim. The publication of *The Old Man and the Sea* in 1952 led directly to his being awarded the Nobel Prize for literature in 1954.

Ernest Hemingway influenced modern writers in many ways. His economical style and his ideas of courage and honor were widely admired and duplicated. He was a vital man who was a soldier, a war correspondent, a big game hunter, and a realistic, forceful writer.

RUTH HERSCHEBERGER (born 1917) was born in Philipse Manor, New York, a suburb of New York City. She grew up in Chicago and attended the University of Chicago and the University of Michigan. She published her first book of poems, *A Way of Happening*, in 1948. It was warmly welcomed by the critics. *Adam's Rib*, a prose work that examined the position of women in modern society, appeared that same year. She won the Harriet Monroe Memorial Prize for poetry in 1953. She has also written short stories.

M. Carl Holman (born 1919), American poet, was born in Minter City, Mississippi, and grew up in St. Louis, Missouri. He graduated from Lincoln University in Jefferson City, Missouri, and earned a master's degree at the University of Chicago. He won a Fiske Poetry Prize while he was in Chicago, as well as a fellowship for further study and creative writing. He has taught English on the college level in Georgia and Virginia. He has served as an information officer and as deputy staff director with the United States Commission on Civil Rights and as a vice president of the National Urban Coalition.

Langston Hughes (1902–1967), was born in Joplin, Missouri. He went to high school in Cleveland, Ohio, and his first published poems appeared in the school's literary magazine. He attended New York's Columbia University for a year and then worked at various jobs, including trans-Atlantic seaman and hotel busboy. His first poetry collection, *The Weary Blues*, appeared in 1926. In 1929 he graduated from Lincoln University in Pennsylvania. In addition to numerous collections of poetry, Hughes also wrote novels, short stories, plays, radio and motion picture scripts, juvenile stories, and nonfiction.

Hughes concerned himself mainly with demonstrating what it was like to be black in the United States. This thread runs through all his writings. He did everything in his power to stimulate other members of his race to write and urged young people to become writers in his frequent lecture appearances at black colleges throughout the South. He also translated into English the poetry of many black writers from other parts of the world. His own poetry was translated into many of the world's languages.

David Ignatow (born 1914) was born in Brooklyn, the son of a Russian-born father and a Hungarian-born mother. He graduated from high school in the depth of the Great Depression. His father wanted him to join his bindery business, but Ignatow felt compelled to become a writer. In 1933 he managed to sell his first story, and it was listed among the best written in that year. On the strength of that story he was accepted into the newly formed and federally funded Writers' Project. His own private writing turned more and more to poetry, but his first collection of poems did not appear until 1948.

The great majority of David Ignatow's poems deal with the ordinary labors of life. Many deal with the dangers—and sometimes the benefits—of living in the city. All of the topics he chooses to write about are described and considered in great depth.

Robinson Jeffers (1887–1962) was born in Pittsburgh, Pennsylvania, but he spent most of his productive life as a writer on the rugged coast of California. He found in the physical characteristics of that area the inspiration he needed to express his observations about mankind. He published his first collection of poetry in 1912, and many other collections followed. His adaptation of the ancient Greek tragedy *Medea* was widely performed after its appearance in 1946 and was warmly praised by the critics. He produced other adaptations of classic Greek drama in the 1950's.

Robinson Jeffers had a less than positive view of human beings. He believed that the human race was largely responsible for its own misery. At the same time, however, he appreciated the human ability to appreciate nature's beauty and majesty. In much of his more interesting poetry he chooses nature as his subject.

*Langston Hughes*

*Robinson Jeffers*

James Weldon Johnson

Denise Levertov

Henry Wadsworth
Longfellow

JAMES WELDON JOHNSON (1871–1938), American poet and songwriter, was born in Jacksonville, Florida. After attending Atlanta University, he began a varied career. He served as a school principal, a lawyer, and a diplomat, eventually becoming a professor of literature at Fisk University. *Fifty Years and Other Poems*, his first collection of verse, appeared in 1917, followed by *God's Trombones* in 1927 and *St. Peter Relates an Incident of the Resurrection Day* in 1930. He edited and compiled the *Book of American Negro Poetry* that was first published in 1922. With his brother he wrote in 1900 "Lift Every Voice and Sing," a song that is well known among America's black population.

JOHN KNOWLES (born 1926), travel writer and novelist, was born in Fairmont, West Virginia. He was educated at Phillips Exeter Academy and at Yale University. He graduated from Yale in 1949 and spent two years as a reporter for a Connecticut newspaper. He was an associate editor for *Holiday* magazine for three years. *A Separate Peace*, his first and much-praised novel, appeared in 1959. Its popularity was postponed until a number of years after its publication when it was widely read by young people.

DENISE LEVERTOV (born 1923) was born in Ilford, a London suburb, and became an American citizen in 1955. She had no formal education and was taught by her mother up to the age of 13. From that point on, she used her father's vast library to continue her education. He was a biblical scholar and ordained Anglican priest. She took naturally to the writing of poetry from a very early age and published her first collection in 1946. Her second collection, *Here and Now*, did not appear until 1957, but she has published many since then.

Many of Denise Levertov's poems are clear and simple statements that effectively communicate her impressions. Others celebrate what it means to be a woman, a wife, and a mother. Many critics have praised her work, some calling her the most profound and moving of modern poets.

HENRY WADSWORTH LONGFELLOW (1807–1882) was born in Portland, Maine, and was educated at Bowdoin College, where he was a classmate of Nathaniel Hawthorne. His first poem appeared in a Portland newspaper when he was 13 years old. After three years of study in Europe, he joined the Bowdoin faculty, moving to Harvard University in 1836, where he taught French and Spanish for 18 years. Beginning in 1833 and ending in 1882, Longfellow published a lengthy series of books, most of which were collections of verse. Many of America's most beloved poems appeared in these volumes: "The Village Blacksmith," "The Children's Hour," "The Arsenal at Springfield," and "Paul Revere's Ride." "Evangeline," his narrative poem of the Acadians that is numbered among the world's epics by many critics, appeared in 1847.

Henry Wadsworth Longfellow is the only American poet to be honored with a statue in "Poets' Corner" of London's Westminster Abbey. The musical nature and simplicity of his verse appealed to his fellow citizens in mid-nineteenth-century America and retain their appeal today.

ARCHIBALD MACLEISH (born 1892), poet, dramatist, and politician, was born in Glencoe, Illinois. He served at the front in World War I. After the war ended, he went to Yale University, graduating in 1915. He received a law degree from Harvard Law School in 1919. He grew tired of the practice of law and turned to the study of literature, reading the works of the most famous poets of the times, T. S. Eliot and Ezra Pound. In 1932 he published *Conquistador*, a lengthy poem that described in epic terms the Spanish exploration of the New World. President Franklin Roosevelt appointed him Librarian of Congress in 1939. He served as Assistant Secretary of State during the final two years of World War II. His *Collected Poems 1917–1952* won him a second Pulitzer Prize in 1953. His successful and widely praised verse-drama, *J.B.*, won him a third Pulitzer Prize for drama in 1959. He taught at Harvard University from 1949 to 1962 and at Amherst College from 1963 to 1967.

BERNARD MALAMUD (born 1914), short story writer and novelist, was born in Brooklyn, New York, the son of Russian immigrants. He worked in his father's grocery store in his youth. He graduated from City College of New York and held a number of odd jobs. He studied for a master's degree at Columbia University. To support himself, he found a job teaching in an evening high school. He wrote during the day for almost ten years in a furnished room. He published his first novel, *The Natural*, in 1952. *The Magic Barrel*, his first collection of short stories, appeared in 1959 and won for him a National Book Award. Malamud has taught at Oregon State University and at Bennington College in Vermont.

All of Bernard Malamud's writing contains a conversational directness. Both a sense of compassion and a sense of humor run through everything he has written.

He masterfully captures the Jewish character, which he knows so well. "I write," he has said, "to explain life to myself and to keep me related to men."

EDGAR LEE MASTERS (1868–1950), biographer, poet, and novelist, was born in Garnett, Kansas, the son of a lawyer and politician. He grew up in Petersburg and Lewistown, Illinois. He went to college for a year and then studied law in his father's office and passed his law exams in 1891. He went to Chicago, opened a law office there, and soon had a large and successful practice. In 1915 he published a single volume of poems upon which his literary reputation largely rests. He was to publish more than 15 other collections of poetry, seven novels, and numerous works during his long career, but his fame rests upon *Spoon River Anthology*. The entire work consists of more than 200 short poems in free verse.

Masters captured the country in *Spoon River Anthology*. The technique of having each of the people in the imaginary Spoon River cemetery interpret life from the grave was called "one of the most original pieces of imaginative literature."

*Bernard Malamud*

*Herman Melville*

HERMAN MELVILLE (1819–1891), novelist and short story writer, was born in New York City of a prominent family that had undergone financial difficulties. He left school at an early age, worked briefly in a bank and in his brother's fur store, and then went to sea as a cabin boy. He made many other voyages and developed a respect and love for the sea, which is found in most of his books. *Typee*, his first book (1846), is based upon his adventure in the South Seas. *Omoo* (1847) describes Tahiti, an island he lived on between voyages on a whaler. The adventures described in his first books made him a very popular writer. But his popularity had begun to vanish before the 1851 publication of his greatest work, *Moby Dick*. In 1866, after his popularity had disappeared completely, he received a position as a customs inspector and worked on the New York piers for the next 19 years. In his last few years, he slipped from public view completely and died virtually unknown. *Billy Budd*, one of the first novellas, was written shortly before his death but published after his death. Melville's position of importance in American literature was not recognized until the 1920's.

*Edna St. Vincent Millay*

*Amado Muro*

Herman Melville was a master of realistic and poetic description. His books contain a mixture of fact, fiction, and symbolism. Throughout much of what he wrote runs the theme of human beings grasping to find true value and faith in a skeptical world that is attracted to material things.

EVE MERRIAM (born 1916) was born in Philadelphia, Pennsylvania, and grew up in a suburb of that city. She graduated from the University of Pennsylvania in 1937 and did further study at the University of Wisconsin and Columbia University. She published her first collection of poetry, *Family Circle,* in 1946. It received the Yale Younger Poets Prize. She wanted to share her lifelong love of words with children, so she began writing poetry designed for young people. The first of these collections appeared in 1962 under the title *There Is No Rhyme for Silver.* Other titles followed: *It Doesn't Always Have to Rhyme, Catch a Little Rhyme,* and *Independent Voices.*

EDNA ST. VINCENT MILLAY (1892–1950) was born in Rockland, Maine. She wrote poetry in her childhood and was encouraged by her mother, who recognized her talent. A major poem of hers appeared in a poetry collection in 1912, when she was still a student. She graduated from Vassar College in 1917 and published her first volume of poetry in that same year. In 1923 Millay won a Pulitzer Prize for a collection of her poems entitled *The Harp-Weaver.* She was one of the most famous and successful poets of the 1920's, 30's, and 40's and published more than twenty volumes of verse.

Edna St. Vincent Millay's poetry is known for its down-to-earth language and simple meter. In much of her poetry she deals with common events and feelings, but her treatment of them is memorable and dramatic. She has the ability to give meaning to the apparently simple and unimportant.

N. SCOTT MOMADAY (born 1934) was born in Lawton, Oklahoma, the son of a father who was an art teacher and painter and of a mother who was a painter and writer. He graduated from the University of New Mexico in 1958 and received both a master's degree and a doctorate from Stanford University. He began his academic career teaching English at the University of California, Santa Barbara, in 1963 and became Professor of English and comparative literature at the University of California, Berkley, in 1973. A Kiowa Indian, his first non-academic book was a collection of retold folktales of his people entitled *The Journey of Tai-me,* published in 1968 and republished the following year under the title *The Way to Rainy Mountain.* His novel *The House Made of Dawn* won the Pulitzer Prize for literature in 1969. A collection of poetry, *Angle of Geese and Other Poems,* appeared in 1974.

N. Scott Momaday's writings reflect his vital interest in the history, art, and culture of the American Indian. When he writes about this interest, his prose closely resembles poetry. In much of what he has written, he deals movingly with a time that is gone forever, a landscape that is incomparable, and a human spirit which endures.

AMADO MURO (born 1931), Mexican-American writer, was born in Parral, Chihuahua, Republic of Mexico, the son of a singer and composer. He moved to El Paso, Texas at an early age. He has worked as a construction worker and as a farm laborer. He has traveled widely in South America and Europe as a seaman.

Muro very clearly describes life in the Mexican-American community in his short stories. It is a very active and exciting life because the musicians, singers, poets, philosophers, and shrewd observers of life in the Mexican-American *barrio* are anything but dull.

MARY OLIVER (born 1935), American poet, was born in Cleveland, Ohio, and attended both Ohio State University and Vassar College. She worked as secretary to the sister of the famous poet Edna St. Vincent Millay. She has also served as chairman of the writing department at the Five Arts Work Center at Provincetown, Massachusetts. Her first collection of poetry, *No Voyage, and Other Poems*, appeared in 1963, then again in 1965 with 19 additional poems. Her second collection, *The River Styx, Ohio, and Other Poems*, was published in 1972. She has contributed numerous poems to journals in both England and the United States.

TILLIE OLSEN (born 1931) was born in Omaha, Nebraska. She worked in industry, as a clerk typist, and raised her four children. *Tell Me a Riddle*, a collection of her short stories, was published in 1961. Her stories have consistently appeared in major American short story collections, including *The Fifty Best American Stories 1915–1965*. She won the O. Henry Award for the best short story of 1961. She has recorded several of her stories for radio presentation.

SIMON J. ORTIZ was born at the Acoma Pueblo in New Mexico. He spent his first 20 years at the pueblo, his mother's ancestral home. He has been a teacher, a journalist, a public relations director, a laborer, and a baker's helper. He writes about the people of his native New Mexico and about their legends and traditions. Among his recent works are *Going for the Rain* (1976) and *A Good Journey* (1977).

THOMAS PAINE (1737–1809) was born in England and became a corset-maker's apprentice at an early age. The first 37 years of his life were quite unsettled as he pursued a variety of occupations including teacher, tobacconist, grocer, and tax collector. He was dismissed twice from his tax collector's job because of his efforts to obtain higher pay for the people who did that work. While fighting for that cause, he met Benjamin Franklin, who was impressed by Paine's intelligence and helped him begin a new life in America. In 1774 he arrived in Philadelphia and began to contribute to many magazines and journals of the times. He became well known in 1776 with the publication of *Common Sense*, a collection of essays that urged immediate independence from Great Britain. He served in the Continental Army and continued to write in support of the Revolutionary War. He later became actively involved in defending the French Revolution.

*Thomas Paine*

*Sylvia Plath*

LINDA PASTAN (born 1932), American poet, was born in New York City. She graduated from Radcliffe College in 1954, earned a master's degree from Simmons College, and another graduate degree from Brandeis University. Her first poetry collection, *A Perfect Circle of Sun*, was published in 1971, followed by two other collections, both of which appeared in 1975.

MARGE PIERCY (born 1936), American poet and novelist, was born in Detroit, Michigan. She completed her undergraduate education at the University of Michigan and earned a graduate degree at Northwestern University. She has been a full-time writer all her life. Her first collection of poems, *Breaking Camp*, appeared in 1968. *Going Down Fast*, her first novel, was published the following year. She has contributed poetry, book reviews, essays, and short stories to numerous national magazines.

SYLVIA PLATH (1932–1963), poet and novelist, was born in Boston, Massachusetts. Her father, who had been

*Edgar Allan Poe*

*Katherine Anne Porter*

born in Austria, taught at Boston University and was a recognized expert on bees. While she was in high school, she sold several stories and poems to *Seventeen* magazine. She entered Smith College and graduated with the highest praise in 1955. She studied at Cambridge University in England. In 1956 she married the English poet Ted Hughes. *The Colossus*, her first collection of poetry, appeared in 1960. *The Bell Jar*, her only novel, was published under the name of Victoria Lucas in 1963 and under her own name in 1966.

Sylvia Plath's poetry contains a burning intensity that is almost unmatched. But her verse is very disciplined and written deliberately in a set rhythm.

EDGAR ALLAN POE (1809–1849), poet and short story writer, was born in Boston, Massachusetts, the son of actors. Orphaned at the age of two, he was taken into the home of a wealthy Richmond, Virginia, family by the name of Allan. His youth was troubled constantly by conflicts with his foster father. He was a student for a time at the University of Virginia but had to leave because Allan would not provide him with enough money to live. He joined the U.S. Army and rose to the rank of sergeant major. He entered the United States Military Academy at West Point but got himself deliberately dismissed after it became clear that he would never be reconciled with Allan. He became a magazine editor and was a success at it. In 1840 he published *Tales of the Grotesque and Arabesque*, a collection of his first 25 stories. The collection brought him neither success nor money. But in 1843 his tale "The Gold Bug" sold 300,000 copies. In 1845 he published 12 additional stories in *Tales* and 30 poems in *The Raven and Other Poems*. His ability as a writer was praised in print by James Russell Lowell. After a tragic four-year period, Poe died

under mysterious circumstances in Baltimore.

Edgar Allan Poe's most well-known tales are filled with the strange, the unusual, and the terrible. Generations of readers have thrilled to his suspenseful, eerie stories. His poetry is known for the haunting quality that is produced through its obvious and repetitious rhythm.

KATHERINE ANNE PORTER (born 1890), an American short story writer and novelist, was born in Indian Creek, Texas, a small town near San Antonio. She grew up in Texas and Louisiana. She began writing at about the same time as she could hold a pencil but did not attempt to publish anything until she was 30 years old. *Flowering Judas*, her first collection of short stories, appeared in 1930, followed in 1939 by *Pale Horse, Pale Rider*, a collection of three short novels. *Ship of Fools*, her only full-length novel, was published in 1962.

Katherine Anne Porter has always been an extremely slow writer, and her solid reputation is built upon a very small published output. Her prose is compact like poetry and extremely clear. Her aim, as she herself said, is always "to tell a straight story and to give true testimony."

DUNCAN CAMPBELL SCOTT (1862–1947) was born in Ottawa, Ontario, Canada, the son of a Methodist minister who traveled from assignment to assignment throughout Canada. Scott entered the Canadian Civil Service in the Department of Indian Affairs, retiring as Deputy Superintendent General in 1932. While associated with the Department of Indian Affairs, he instituted numerous improvements in the fields of health care and education. He published his first collection of poetry in 1893. His *Complete Poems* appeared in 1926. He also was an accomplished writer of short stories. *The Village of Viger*, an anthology of his short stories, appeared in 1896 and again in 1945.

Most of Scott's writing was about the Indians to whom he had devoted most of his professional life. The conflict between man and nature and the heroic endurance of man were his major themes.

W. D. SNODGRASS (born 1926), American poet, was born in Wilkinson, Pennsylvania. He graduated in 1949 from the State University of Iowa and eventually received two graduate degrees from that same institution. He has taught English and creative writing at American colleges and universities and has lectured and given poetry readings at several writers' conferences. *Heart's Needle*, his first collection of poetry, was published in 1959 and received the 1960 Pulitzer Prize for poetry. He has contributed poetry to many journals, has assembled a number of poetry collections, and has translated several German poets into English.

WILLIAM STAFFORD (born 1914), American poet, was born in Hutchinson, Kansas. He grew up in various small towns of central Kansas and hunted, camped, and fished in the pleasant countryside. He received two degrees from the University of Kansas and received his doctorate in English from the State University of Iowa. He was a professor of English at Lewis and Clark College in Portland, Oregon, where he started to teach in 1948. A year earlier his first collection of poems appeared. His third collection, *Traveling Through the Dark*, received the National Book Award for poetry in 1963.

Almost all of William Stafford's poems are short and to the point. He uses simple images and everyday language. He believes that poetry should capture the most commonplace daily events.

JOHN STEINBECK (1902–1968) was born in Salinas, California, an area that provides

the setting for his novels about California's poor laborers and farmers. The area figures in his first novel, *Cup of Gold* (1929), and his next book, a collection of short stories, *Pastures of Heaven* (1932), both of which were unsuccessful. *Tortilla Flat* (1935) was his first novel to receive critical praise. His most famous novel, *The Grapes of Wrath* (1939), a story about victims of the Great Depression, received the 1940 Pulitzer Prize. *East of Eden*, a symbolic tale about the need for tolerance and brotherhood, appeared in 1952. In *Travels with Charley* (1962) Steinbeck describes modern America by relating a transcontinental journey that he made with his pet dog. In 1962 John Steinbeck was awarded the Nobel Prize for literature.

In most of what he wrote, John Steinbeck described the simple people who worked hard, loved the land, and were sometimes exploited by events beyond their direct control. His Nobel Prize for literature cited him for "realistic and imaginative writings, distinguished as they are by a sympathetic humor and a social perception."

IRVING STONE (born 1903) was born in San Francisco. He worked his way through the University of California, graduated with honors, received a master's degree in economics, and taught that subject at the University of Southern California. At the age of 23, he left the teaching profession, moved to New York, and began to write full time. He wrote 18 full-length plays over a 10–year period, but only two were produced without success. While in Europe in 1930, he became aware of the works and life of the painter Vincent van Gogh. In 1934 he published a biography of van Gogh, *Lust for Life*. This was but the first of many biographical works about famous people: *Sailor on Horseback* (Jack London), *Clarence Darrow for the Defense*, *Love Is Eternal* (Mary Todd and

*William Stafford*

*John Steinbeck*

*Irving Stone*

*Henry David Thoreau*

Abraham Lincoln), *The President's Lady* (Rachel and Andrew Jackson), and *The Agony and the Ecstasy* (Michelangelo).

Irving Stone set out to reshape and enliven the literary biography. He sought to make biography as dramatic and moving as any novel or play. He has become a master of what can best be called the biographical novel.

EDWARD TAYLOR (1645–1729) was born in England and emigrated to Boston in 1668. After graduating from Harvard College in 1671, he became pastor of the Puritan Church in the Massachusetts frontier town of Westfield and physician to the settlement. He remained in this community until his death. He has been called the greatest New England poet before the year 1800. Before his death, he asked that his works not be published. His grandson carried out his request, and his poetry remained in manuscripts until they were discovered in 1937 and published in 1939. A more complete edition of his poems did not appear until 1960.

Edward Taylor joins simple, ordinary language with strong religious feeling in his poetry. He also made use of striking imagery, apparent contradictions, and fantastic comparisons in his poems. These characteristics were associated with the so-called "metaphysical" poetry of the English poets John Donne (1572–1631) and Richard Crashaw (1612–1649).

HENRY DAVID THOREAU (1817–1862) was born in Concord, Massachusetts. His father was a pencil maker, and his mother took in boarders to make ends meet. He graduated from Harvard College in 1837. He received encouragement to write and criticism of what he wrote from Ralph Waldo Emerson, also a resident of Concord. He worked for a time as Emerson's gardener and general handyman. He published only two books during his lifetime: *A Week on the Concord and Merrimac Rivers* in 1849 and *Walden* in 1854. In gathering raw material for the latter book, his most famous work, he lived for two years on the shores of Concord's Walden Pond, observing nature, reading, and thinking about the connection between human beings and nature.

Henry David Thoreau was a great believer in the rights of the individual. In his observations of nature recorded in *Walden* and in his recounting of how he built his house by Walden Pond and managed his affairs there, he expresses the importance of self-reliance. The book expresses the belief that human beings live best when they live in harmony and peace with nature.

MARK TWAIN (SAMUEL LANGHORNE CLEMENS) (1835–1910) was born in Florida, Missouri. He grew up in the Mississippi River town of Hannibal, the main setting for his famous novels *The Adventures of Huckleberry Finn* and *The Adventures of Tom Sawyer*. He left school to become a printer, but his first job was as a reporter for his brother's newspaper. He abandoned his plans to seek his fortune in South America in favor of a career as a steamboat pilot. He served as an apprentice pilot for three years and as a licensed pilot for two more. He left the river in 1861 when the outbreak of the Civil War closed the waterway to commercial traffic. He recounts his experiences on the river in *Life on the Mississippi*, published in 1883. Twain wrote about the frontier in *The Celebrated Jumping Frog of Calaveras County and Other Sketches* (1867) and in *Roughing It* (1872), about his often humorous travel experiences in *The Innocents Abroad* (1869) and *A Tramp Abroad* (1880), and about the comic shortcomings of human nature in *A Connecticut Yankee in King Arthur's Court* (1889).

Mark Twain is without question one of America's most important writers. Humor runs through most of what he wrote, and it both amuses and teaches. His writing is both graceful and to the point. He can make episodes come alive, and his characters become very real. In many of his works Twain deals with the important theme of the difference between human ideals and human actions.

JOHN UPDIKE (born 1932), novelist, poet, and short story writer, was born in Shillington, Pennsylvania, in the midst of the "Pennsylvania Dutch" region. He was president of his local high school class, editor of its newspaper, and an excellent student. He earned a scholarship to Harvard University, where he majored in English. After graduation, he joined the staff of the *New Yorker* magazine and began contributing stories, verse, and essays to the magazine. His first book, *The Carpentered Hen*, a collection of many of his early poems, appeared in 1958. *The Same Door*, a collection of stories from the *New Yorker*, appeared the following year.

John Updike is a storyteller of modern America. His characters deal with and help explain contemporary life. In all of Updike's works, he expresses an insight into human relationships and uses his painter's eye to describe the colors, shapes, and movements of modern living.

JOE VERGARA (born 1915) was born in New York City. He graduated from New York's City College in 1937. For eight years he was a professional piano player. But after serving in the U.S. Army during World War II, he joined the editorial staff of a New York publisher. He published his first novel in 1968 and has been a frequent contributor of both fiction and nonfiction to national magazines.

EUDORA WELTY (born 1909) was born in Jackson, Mississippi. Except for a few years when she attended the University of Wisconsin and Columbia University, she has spent her entire life in the area in which she was born. *A Curtain of Green*, her first collection of short stories, appeared in 1941, followed in 1943 and 1955 by two other collections. Her novels include *Delta Wedding* (1946), *Losing Battles* (1970), and *The Optimist's Daughter* (1972). She received the 1973 Pulitzer Prize for the latter work.

Eudora Welty combines realism and fantasy in most of her writing. Her love for the South comes through clearly in all of her work. However, while her stories tell about the small region in which she lives, her major themes of the need for people to understand their neighbors and themselves, the pain of growing up, and the agony of loneliness are universal.

WALT WHITMAN (1819–1892) was born on Long Island, New York. He grew up and was educated in Brooklyn. His first job as a printer's apprentice led naturally to newspaper work. He became at one point editor of the Brooklyn *Eagle*. He went to New Orleans with his brother and edited a newspaper there for a short time. He returned to newspaper work in Brooklyn and became very involved in politics. At the same time he became interested in the lives of the ordinary working people who lived around the New York City area. These people, who to Whitman represented America's dynamic character, are featured in *Leaves of Grass*, his greatest poem. It appeared first as a collection of twelve poems in 1855, and was further enlarged and republished in 1856, 1860, 1867, 1871, and at intervals thereafter. He served as a volunteer nurse during the Civil War, ministering to the wounded from both the North and South. In 1865 and 1866 he published *Drum Taps* and *Sequel to Drum Taps*, collections that contained his famous poems about Abraham Lincoln. He spent the last 19 years of his life at Camden, New Jersey. During his final years his contribution to American literature began to be more widely recognized.

*John Updike*

*Eudora Welty*

*Richard Wilbur*

*Thornton Wilder*

*Jade Snow Wong*

Walt Whitman's poetry shocked his readers because it contained features previously unseen. He used repetition and parallelism frequently and used the phrase rather than the poetic foot as his basic rhythm. His "free verse" later became more common in modern poetry. He attempted in his "different" type of poetry to capture America, a nation "different" from all others.

RICHARD WILBUR (born 1921), was born in New York City and grew up in rural New Jersey. His father was Lawrence Wilbur, an artist who had come east from Omaha. His mother's father and grandfather were newspaper editors. He attended Amherst College and served in the Army in Europe during World War II. After the war he attended the Harvard University graduate school and joined the faculty in 1950. His first poetry collection, *The Beautiful Changes*, appeared in 1947. In 1957 he won the Pulitzer Prize for poetry for his volume *Things of This World*.

Richard Wilbur's poems are always written in a formal style. They have a musical quality and are both witty and serious at the same time. In his poems he tries to demonstrate that the senses and the mind in combination can deepen our understanding of the world.

THORNTON WILDER (1897–1975), playwright and novelist, was born in Madison, Wisconsin, but grew up in China, where his father served as American Consul-General at Hong Kong and Shanghai. He returned to the United States for his college education and graduated from Yale University in 1920. His first novel, *The Cabala*, dealt with the decaying Italian nobility and was published in 1926. His second, *The Bridge of San Luis Rey*, appeared the following year and won the Nobel Prize for literature in 1928. *Our Town* won the Pulitzer Prize for drama in 1938. *The Merchant Yonkers* (1938), another of his plays, was revised in 1954 as *The Matchmaker*. It was redone by others in 1963 as *Hello, Dolly!*

Thornton Wilder has greatly influenced modern American literature. *The Bridge of San Luis Rey* gave birth to a new type of story in which characters are brought together by chance and geography at a critical moment in their lives. In *Our Town* the histories of many generations in a community are told at roughly the same time, thus departing from the general notions of time in the theater.

C. K. WILLIAMS (born 1936) was born in Newark, New Jersey. He graduated from the University of Pennsylvania in 1959. He published his first collection of poems in 1969 and has published three additional collections since then. He has taught poetry at several colleges and is a contributing editor to the *American Poetry Review*. He has also translated works of classical Greek authors.

JADE SNOW WONG (born 1922) was born in San Francisco, California, to first-generation Chinese parents. Her early years growing up in Chinatown amidst the influences of two cultures is the subject of her moving autobiography, *Fifth Chinese Daughter*. Written when she was 27 years old, her book has been translated into many foreign languages.

In 1942, Jade Snow Wong graduated from Mills College and worked for the navy during the remainder of World War II. Soon after, she began making and selling ceramics in San Francisco. A distinguished pictoral and ceramic artist, her works are part of permanent museum collections. She again showed herself to be a gifted author with the publication of *No Chinese Stranger* in 1975.

RICHARD WRIGHT (1908–1960) was born on a plantation near Natchez, Mississippi. His father was a farm worker, and his mother was a country schoolteacher. Because his parents' poverty made his support impossible, he was passed from relative to relative and even spent some time in an orphanage. He struck out on his own at 15 and made his way to Memphis, where he worked at several unskilled jobs before becoming a postal clerk. A devoted reader since his early teen years, he finally decided to become a writer. He went to Chicago, published a few free-verse poems, and qualified for a position on the Federal Writers' Project, a government program designed to employ writers during the Depression. He moved to New York, where he ultimately wrote *Native Son* after eight months of intense work. The story of a young black who grows up in the slums of Chicago, it appeared in 1940 and became a best seller. His other novels include *The Outsiders* (1953), *The Long Dream* (1958), and *Black Boy* (1945).

ELINOR WYLIE (1885–1928) novelist and poet, was born in Somerville, New Jersey, the daughter of wealthy parents. She grew up in a suburb of Philadelphia. She moved to Washington at the age of 12 when her father was named Solicitor General of the United States. Her first poetry appeared in 1912, and her first novel, *Jennifer Lorn*, was published in 1923. An accidental fall suffered in England in 1927 led to a severe injury and her accidental death.

Elinor Wylie's poetry is noted for its rich vocabulary and for its crystal-clear images. She explores a wide range of subjects in her poems but prefers the starkness of a landscape and the graceful movements of animals. She uses a wide variety of poetic forms to develop her subjects.

*Richard Wright*

# Glossary

## Full Pronunciation Key

The pronunciation of each word is shown just after the word, in this way: **ab bre vi ate** (ə brē′vē āt). The letters and signs used are pronounced as in the words below. The mark ′ is placed after a syllable with primary or heavy accent, as in the example above. The mark ′ after a syllable shows a secondary or lighter accent, as in **ab bre vi a tion** (ə brē′vē ā′shən).

Some words, taken from foreign languages, are spoken with sounds that do not otherwise occur in English. Symbols for these sounds are given in the key as "foreign sounds."

| | | | | | | |
|---|---|---|---|---|---|---|
| a | hat, cap | j | jam, enjoy | u | cup, butter | |
| ā | age, face | k | kind, seek | u̇ | full, put | |
| ä | father, far | l | land, coal | ü | rule, move | |
| | | m | me, am | | | |
| b | bad, rob | n | no, in | v | very, save | |
| ch | child, much | ng | long, bring | w | will, woman | |
| d | did, red | | | y | young, yet | |
| | | o | hot, rock | z | zero, breeze | |
| e | let, best | ō | open, go | zh | measure, seizure | |
| ē | equal, be | ô | order, all | | | |
| ėr | term, learn | oi | oil, voice | ə | represents: | |
| | | ou | house, out | | a in about | |
| f | fat, if | | | | e in taken | |
| g | go, bag | p | paper, cup | | i in pencil | |
| h | he, how | r | run, try | | o in lemon | |
| | | s | say, yes | | u in circus | |
| i | it, pin | sh | she, rush | | | |
| ī | ice, five | t | tell, it | | | |
| | | th | thin, both | | | |
| | | ᵺ | then, smooth | | | |

FOREIGN SOUNDS

Y as in French *du*.
Pronounce (ē) with the lips rounded as for (ü).

à as in French *ami*.
Pronounce (ä) with the lips spread and held tense.

œ as in French *peu*.
Pronounce (ā) with the lips rounded as for (ō).

N as in French *bon*.
The N is not pronounced, but shows that the vowel before it is nasal.

H as in German *ach*.
Pronounce (k) without closing the breath passage.

## Grammatical Key

| | | | | | | | |
|---|---|---|---|---|---|---|---|
| *adj.* | adjective | *interj.* | interjection | *pron.* | pronoun | *v.t.* | transitive verb |
| *adv.* | adverb | *n.* | noun | *v.* | verb | *sing.* | singular |
| *conj.* | conjunction | *prep.* | preposition | *v.i.* | intransitive verb | *pl.* | plural |

From Thorndike-Barnhart Advanced Dictionary *by E. L. Thorndike and Clarence L. Barnhart. Copyright © 1974 by Scott, Foresman and Company. Reprinted by permission.*

**ab a lo ne** (ab′ə lō′nē), *n.* an edible salt-water fish with a large, rather flat shell lined with mother-of-pearl.

**a bash** (ə bash′), *v.t.* embarrass and confuse; make uneasy and somewhat ashamed.

**a bate** (ə bāt′), *v.t.* 1 lessen in force or intensity; reduce or decrease. 2 put an end to; stop. — *v.i.* become less in force or intensity; diminish.

**ab er ra tion** (ab′ə rā′shən), *n.* 1 a deviating from the right path or usual course of action. 2 an abnormal structure or development. 3 a temporary mental disorder.

**ab ject** (ab′jekt, ab jekt′), *adj.* 1 so low or degraded as to be hopeless; wretched; miserable. 2 deserving contempt; despicable. 3 slavish. — **ab ject′ly,** *adv.*

**a bode** (ə bōd′), *n.* place of residence; dwelling; house or home.

**a bom i na ble** (ə bom′ə nə bəl), *adj.* 1 arousing disgust and hatred; detestable. 2 very unpleasant; disagreeable.

**a bom i na tion** (ə bom′ə nā′shən), *n.* 1 something that arouses strong disgust. 2 a feeling of disgust.

**a breast** (ə brest′), *adv., adj.* 1 side by side. 2 up with; alongside of.

**ab solve** (ab solv′, ab zolv′), *v.t.* 1 pronounce or set (a person) free from sin, guilt, blame, or their penalties or consequences. 2 set free (*from* a promise, obligation, or duty); release.

**a byss** (ə bis′), *n.* 1 a bottomless or very great depth. 2 anything too deep or great to be measured; lowest depth.

**ac cord ing ly** (ə kôr′ding lē), *adv.* 1 in agreement with what is expected or stated; correspondingly. 2 for this reason; therefore; consequently.

**ac cost** (ə kôst′, ə kost′), *v.t.* approach and speak to first; address.

**ac count** (ə kount′), *n.* 1 statement telling in detail about an event or thing. 2 statement explaining one's conduct, especially to a superior. 3 statement of reasons, causes, etc., explaining some event. — *v.t.* hold to be; consider.

**ac qui es cence** (ak′wē es′ns), *n.* consent given without making objections; assent. — *v.i.* to assent.

**ad a mant** (ad′ə mənt, ad′ə mant), *adj.* 1 not giving in readily; firm and unyielding; immovable. 2 too hard to be cut or broken. — **ad′a mant ly,** *adv.*

**ad dle** (ad′l), *v.t., v.i.* 1 make or become muddled. 2 make or become rotten. — *adj.* muddled; confused.

**ad mon ish** (ad mon′ish), *v.t.* 1 advise against something; warn. 2 scold gently. 3 urge strongly; advise earnestly. 4 recall to a duty overlooked or forgotten; remind.

**ad mo ni tion** (ad′mə nish′ən), *n.* act of admonishing; gentle reproof or warning.

**ad vent** (ad′vent), *n.* a coming; arrival.

**ad ver si ty** (ad vėr′sə tē), *n.* condition of being in unfavorable circumstances, especially unfavorable financial circumstances; misfortune; distress.

**af fect** (ə fekt′), *v.t.* 1 pretend to have or

feel; feign; simulate. 2 choose to use, wear, own, etc.; fancy. 3 make a show of liking; adopt falsely or ostentatiously.

**af fright** (ə frīt′), ARCHAIC. — *v.t.* excite with sudden fear; frighten. — *n.* sudden fear; fright; terror.

**af front** (ə frunt′), *n.* 1 word or act that openly and purposely expresses disrespect; open insult. 2 a slight or injury to one's dignity. — *v.t.* 1 insult openly. 2 face courageously and defiantly.

**aft** (aft), *adv.* at or toward the stern. — *adj.* in or near the stern.

**ag ate** (ag′it), *n.* a variety of rock with variously colored stripes, clouded colors, or mosslike formations.

**air** (er, ar), *n.* 1 atmosphere. 2 space overhead; sky. 3 a simple melody or tune. 4 **airs,** *pl.* unnatural or affected manners.

**a lac ri ty** (ə lak′rə tē), *n.* 1 liveliness. 2 cheerful willingness.

**al che my** (al′kə mē), *n.* 1 the chemistry of the Middle Ages, which combined science, magic, and philosophy. 2 any miraculous power of transformation.

**al ien ate** (ā′lyə nāt, ā′lē ə nāt), *v.t.* turn away the normal feelings, fondness, or devotion of anyone; make unfriendly.

**al ien a tion** (ā′lyə nā′shən, ā′lē ə nā′-shən), *n.* 1 an alienating. 2 a being alienated.

**a light** (ə līt′), *v.i.* 1 get out of, off, or down from. 2 descend and lightly settle, as a bird, a snowflake, etc.

**al lay** (ə lā′), *v.t.* 1 put at rest; quiet. 2 relieve (pain, trouble, thirst, etc.); alleviate.

**al le go ri cal** (al′ə gôr′ə kəl, al′ə gor′ə-kəl), *adj.* explaining or teaching something by a story.

**al le vi ate** (ə lē′vē āt), *v.t.* 1 make easier to endure (suffering of the body or mind); relieve. 2 lessen or lighten; diminish.

**al lot** (ə lot′), *v.t.* 1 divide and distribute in parts or shares. 2 give as a share, task, duty, etc; assign. 3 appropriate (anything) to a special purpose; allocate.

**al lure** (ə lür′), *v.t.* tempt or attract very strongly; fascinate; charm.

**al lur ing** (ə lür′ing), *adj.* 1 strongly attracting; tempting. 2 charming; fascinating.

**al lu sion** (ə lü′zhən), *n.* act of alluding; slight or incidental mention of something.

**al ly** (ə lī′), *v.t.* 1 combine for some special purpose. 2 associate; connect.

**al oe** (al′ō), *n.* 1 plant of the lily family having a long spike of flowers and thick, narrow leaves. 2 **aloes,** a bitter drug made from the dried juice of this plant's leaves.

**al right** (ôl rīt′), *adv., adj.* INFORMAL. all right.

**a mi a bil i ty** (ā′mē ə bil′ə tē), *n.* a being amiable; good nature.

**a mi a ble** (ā′mē ə bəl), *adj.* having a good-natured and friendly disposition; pleasant and agreeable. — **a′mi a bly,** *adv.*

**am i ca ble** (am′ə kə bəl), *adj.* having or

showing a friendly attitude; peaceable.

**am phi the a ter** (am′fə thē′ə tər), *n.* a circular or oval building with tiers of seats around a central open space.

**an ar chist** (an′ər kist), *n.* 1 person who seeks to bring about the destruction of government and law. 2 person who promotes disorder and stirs up revolt.

**a nath e ma** (ə nath′ə mə), *n.* 1 a solemn curse by church authorities excommunicating some person from the church. 2 denunciation of some person or thing as evil; curse. 3 person or thing that has been cursed or is utterly detested.

**an guish** (ang′gwish), *n.* 1 severe physical pain; great suffering. 2 extreme mental pain or suffering.

**an guished** (ang′gwisht), *adj.* full of anguish; distressed with severe pain; tormented.

**an i mat ed** (an′ə mā′tid), *adj.* 1 lively; vigorous. 2 gay; joyful. 3 seeming to be alive. 4 living; alive; animate.

**a nom a lous** (ə nom′ə ləs), *adj.* irregular; abnormal.

**an o nym i ty** (an′ə nim′ə tē), *n.* condition or quality of being anonymous.

**an ti-Sem ite** (an′ti sem′īt), *n.* person who shows dislike or hatred of Jews.

**a peak** (ə pēk′), *adj., adv.* being in a vertical position.

**a phid** (ā′fid, af′id), *n.* any of various very small insects that live by sucking juices from plants; plant louse.

**ap pa ri tion** (ap′ə rish′ən), *n.* a supernatural sight or thing; ghost or phantom.

**ap pease** (ə pēz′), *v.t.* 1 put an end to by satisfying (an appetite or desire). 2 make calm or quiet; pacify.

**ap pel la tion** (ap′ə lā′shən), *n.* 1 name or title describing or identifying someone. 2 act of calling by a name.

**ap pre hen sion** (ap′ri hen′shən), *n.* expectation of misfortune; dread of impending danger; fear.

**ap pre hen sive** (ap′ri hen′siv), *adj.* afraid that some misfortune is about to occur; anxious about the future; fearful. — **ap′pre hen′sive ly,** *adv.*

**ap pro ba tion** (ap′rə bā′shən), *n.* 1 favorable opinion; approval. 2 act of formally and authoritatively approving.

**ap ro pos** (ap′rə pō′), *adv.* 1 fittingly. 2 **apropos of,** with regard to. — *adj.* to the point; fitting; suitable.

**apt** (apt), *adj.* 1 fitted by nature; likely. 2 fit for the occasion; suitable; fitting. — **apt′ly,** *adv.*

**ar bi trar y** (är′bə trer′ē), *adj.* 1 based on one's own wishes, notions, or will; not going by rule or law. 2 fixed or determined by chance. 3 using or abusing unlimited power.

**ar bi tra tor** (är′bə trā′tər), *n.* person chosen to decide or settle a dispute.

**ar cade** (är kād′), *n.* passageway with an

arched roof, often lined with small stores.

**ar che type** (är′kə tīp), *n.* an original model or pattern from which copies are made, or out of which later forms develop.

**ar dent** (ärd′nt), *adj.* 1 glowing with passion; passionate. 2 eager; keen. 3 burning; fiery; hot.

**ar dor** (är′dər), *n.* 1 warmth of emotion; passion. 2 great enthusiasm; eagerness.

**a right** (ə rīt′), *adv.* correctly; rightly.

**ar tic u late** (*adj.* är tik′yə lit; *v.* är tik′yə lāt), *adj.* 1 uttered in distinct syllables of words. 2 able to put one's thoughts into words easily and clearly. — *v.t.* speak distinctly. — *v.i.* express oneself in words.

**as cet ic** (ə set′ik), *n.* 1 person who practices unusual self-denial or severe discipline over himself, especially for religious reasons. 2 person who refrains from pleasures and comforts. — *adj.* refraining from pleasures and comforts; practicing unusual self-denial.

**as cribe** (ə skrīb′), *v.t.* 1 think of as caused by or coming from; assign; attribute (*to*). 2 consider as belonging (*to*).

**ash en** (ash′ən), *adj.* like ashes; pale as ashes.

**as sail** (ə sāl′), *v.t.* 1 attack repeatedly with violent blows. 2 attack with hostile words, arguments, or abuse. 3 trouble.

**as sail ant** (ə sā′lənt), *n.* person who attacks.

**as sent** (ə sent′), *v.i.* express agreement; consent. — *n.* acceptance of a proposal, statement, etc.; agreement.

**as sert** (ə sèrt′), *v.t.* 1 state positively; declare firmly. 2 maintain (a right, a claim, etc.); insist upon.

**as sim i late** (ə sim′ə lāt), *v.t.* 1 take in and make part of oneself; absorb; digest. 2 cause to be like the people of a nation in customs, viewpoint, character, etc. — *v.i.* 1 become absorbed; be digested. 2 become like the people of a nation in customs, viewpoint, character, etc. 3 become like. — **as sim′i la′tor,** *n.*

**a stride** (ə strīd′), *prep.* with one leg on each side of.

**a sun der** (ə sun′dər), *adv.* in pieces; into separate parts. — *adj.* apart or separate from each other.

**a thwart** (ə thwôrt′), *adv.* across from side to side; crosswise. — *prep.* 1 across. 2 across the line or course of.

**at tain** (ə tān′), *v.t.* 1 reach (a state or condition) by living, growing, or developing. 2 win, gain, or acquire by effort. 3 reach (a place).

**au di tor** (ô′də tər), *n.* 1 person who audits business accounts. 2 hearer; listener.

**aught** (ôt), *n.* zero; cipher; nothing.

**au gur** (ô′gər), *n.* soothsayer; fortune-teller. — *v.t.* guess from signs or omens; predict; foretell.

**aus tere** (ô stir′), *adj.* 1 stern in manner or appearance; harsh. 2 severe in self-discipline; strict in morals. 3 severely simple. 4 serious.

**au thor i ta tive** (ə thôr′ə tā′tiv, ə thor′ə tā′tiv), *adj.* 1 proceeding from a recognized authority; official. 2 of or characterized by authority; commanding. 3 entitled to obedience and respect.

**a ver sion** (ə vėr′zhən, ə vėr′shən), *n.* 1 a strong or fixed dislike. 2 thing or person disliked.

**av id** (av′id), *adj.* extremely eager; greatly desirous. — **av′id ly,** *adv.*

**awe** (ô), *n.* 1 a feeling of wonder and deep respect inspired by anything of great beauty, majesty, or power. 2 dread mingled with respect.

**a wry** (ə rī′), *adv.* 1 with a twist or turn to one side. 2 wrong; out of order.

**back slide** (bak′slīd′), *v.i.* slide back into wrongdoing, especially to practices forbidden by the church. — **back′slid′er,** *n.*

**ban dy** (ban′dē), *v.t.* 1 hit or throw back and forth. 2 give and take; exchange. — *adj.* having a bend or curve outward.

**bane** (bān), *n.* 1 cause of death, ruin, or harm. 2 destruction of any kind.

**ban shee** (ban′shē, ban shē′), *n.* a female spirit whose wail means that there will soon be a death in the family.

**ban zai** (bän′zī′), *interj.* a Japanese greeting, patriotic cheer, or battle cry. It means "May you live ten thousand years!"

**bar** (bär), *v.t.* 1 put bars across. 2 block. 3 exclude or forbid. — *prep.* except; excluding.

**bard** (bärd), *n.* a Celtic minstrel and poet who from earliest times to the Middle Ages sang his own poems, usually to harp accompaniment, celebrating daring deeds, etc.

**bark** (bärk), *n.* the tough outside covering of trees. — *v.t.* scrape the skin from (shins, knuckles, etc.).

**bar ri o** (bär′ē ō), *n.* U.S. section of a city inhabited chiefly by Spanish-speaking people.

**bar ter** (bär′tər), *v.i.* trade by exchanging one kind of goods or services for other goods or services without using money.

**ba salt** (bə sôlt′, bā′sôlt), *n.* a hard, dark-colored rock of volcanic origin.

**base** (bās), *adj.* 1 morally low or mean; selfish and cowardly. 2 fit for an inferior person or thing; menial; unworthy. — **base′ness,** *n.*

**batch** (bach), *n.* 1 quantity of bread, cookies, etc., made at one baking. 2 quantity of anything made as one lot or set. 3 number of persons or things put or treated together.

**bay** (bā), *n.* 1 a deep, prolonged barking of a dog when pursuing or attacking. 2 position of a hunted animal that turns to face its pursuers when further flight is impossible.

**bear grass** (ber′gras′, bar′gras′), *n.* any of several plants of the lily family with foliage resembling coarse blades of grass.

**be daz zle** (bi daz′əl), *v.t.* dazzle completely; confuse by dazzling.

**beet ling** (bēt′ling), *adj.* projecting or overhanging.

**be fall** (bi fôl′), *v.t.* happen to. — *v.i.* happen.

**be get** (bi get′), *v.t.* 1 become the father of. 2 cause to be; produce.

**be guile** (bi gīl′), *v.t.* 1 trick or mislead (a person); deceive. 2 entertain. 3 while away (time) pleasantly.

**be held** (bi held′), *v.t.* looked at; saw.

**be hoove** (bi hüv′), *v.t.* 1 be necessary for. 2 be proper for.

**be jug gle** (bi jug′əl), *v.t.* delude; cheat.

**be lie** (bi lī′), *v.t.* 1 give a false idea of; misrepresent. 2 show to be false; prove to be mistaken.

**bel li cose** (bel′ə kōs), *adj.* fond of fighting and quarreling; inclined to war, warlike.

**be nef i cent** (bə nef′ə sənt), *adj.* doing good; kind.

**be night ed** (bi nī′tid), *adj.* 1 not knowing right from wrong; ignorant. 2 ARCHAIC. overtaken by darkness.

**be nign** (bi nīn′), *adj.* 1 kindly in feeling; gracious. 2 gentle.

**be nig nant** (bi nig′nənt), *adj.* having or showing a kindly feeling toward inferiors and dependents. — **be nig′nant ly,** *adv.*

**be queath** (bi kwēᴛʜ′, bi kwēth′), *v.t.* 1 give or leave (especially money or other personal property) by a will. 2 pass along.

**be quest** (bi kwest′), *n.* money or other property left to a person by the will of someone who has died; legacy.

**be reave** (bi rēv′), *v.t.* leave desolate and alone.

**be reft** (bi reft′), *adj.* bereaved.

**be seech** (bi sēch′), *v.t.* ask earnestly; beg. — **be seech′ing ly,** *adv.*

**be set** (bi set′), *v.t.* 1 attack from all sides; set upon in attack. 2 surround; hem in.

**be stow** (bi stō′), *v.t.* 1 give (something) as a gift; give. 2 ARCHAIC. find quarters for; lodge.

**be take** (bi tāk′), *v.t.* **betake oneself, a** make one's way; go. **b** apply oneself.

**bi as** (bī′əs), *adj.* slanting across the threads of cloth; diagonal.

**bid** (bid), *v.t.* 1 tell (someone) what to do, where to go, etc.; command; order. 2 ARCHAIC. invite.

**big ot ed** (big′ə tid), *adj.* obstinately and unreasonably attached to a particular opinion, belief, party, etc., and intolerant of all who have different views.

**big ot ry** (big′ə trē), *n.* bigoted conduct or attitude; intolerance.

**bil low** (bil′ō), *n.* a great, swelling wave or surge of the sea.

**blaze** (blāz), *n.* 1 a bright flame or fire. 2 a glow of brightness. 3 a bright display. — *v.i.* show bright colors or lights.

**bleak** (blēk), *adj.* 1 exposed to cold and winds; bare. 2 chilly; cold; raw. 3 cheerless and depressing; dismal.

**blight** (blīt), *n.* 1 disease of plants that causes leaves, stems, fruits, and tissues to wither and die. 2 anything that withers hope or causes destruction or ruin.

**blood root** (blud′rüt′, blud′rùt′), *n.* a wild plant of the same family as the poppy, that has a red root, orange-red sap, and a single white flower that blooms in early spring.

**blub ber** (blub′ər), *n.* 1 fat of whales and some other sea animals from which oil is obtained. 2 noisy weeping. — *v.i.* weep noisily; sob.

**boc cie** (boch′ē), *n.* Italian lawn bowling played in a long narrow court.

**bog gy** (bog′ē, bôg′ē), *adj.* soft and wet like a bog; marshy; swampy.

**bond** (bond), *n.* 1 anything that binds or fastens, as a rope, cord, or other band. 2 ARCHAIC. imprisonment. 3 any agreement or binding engagement.

**boon** (bün), *n.* great benefit; blessing.

**bo reen** (bō′rēn), *n.* IRISH. a narrow country road.

**bor ough** (bėr′ō), *n.* 1 an incorporated town with certain privileges, smaller than a city. 2 one of the five administrative divisions of New York City.

**bow sprit** (bou′sprit′, bō′sprit′), *n.* pole or spar projecting forward from the bow of a ship.

**brach y ce phal ic** (brak′ē sə fal′ik), *adj.* having a short, broad skull.

**bran dish** (bran′dish), *v.t.* wave or shake threateningly.

**brant** (brant), *n.* either of two kinds of small, dark, wild geese that breed in arctic regions.

**brash** (brash), *adj.* 1 showing lack of respect. 2 hasty; rash.

**bra va do** (brə vä′dō), *n.* a show of courage or boldness without much real courage.

**breach** (brēch), *n.* an opening made by breaking down something solid, as a gap made in a wall or fortification.

**brick bat** (brik′bat′), *n.* piece of broken brick, especially one used as a missile.

**brim stone** (brim′stōn′), *n.* sulfur.

**broach** (brōch), *v.t.* begin conversation or discussion about; introduce.

**brow** (brou), *n.* 1 part of the face above the eyes; forehead. 2 eyebrow. 3 edge of a steep place; top of a slope.

**brusque** (brusk), *adj.* abrupt in manner or speech; blunt.

**buck ler** (buk′lər), *n.* 1 a small, round shield used to ward off blows or thrusts. 2 means of protection; defense.

**bul ly rag** (bùl′ē rag′), *v.t.* INFORMAL. 1 attack with abusive language; bully. 2 tease.

**bul wark** (bùl′wərk), *n.* person, thing, or idea that is a defense or protection. — *v.t.* defend; protect.

**bur dock** (bėr′dok′), *n.* a coarse weed

with burs and broad leaves.

**bur geon** (bėr′jən), *v.i.* 1 grow or shoot forth; bud; sprout. 2 grow or develop rapidly; flourish.

**bur lesque** (bər lesk′), *n.* kind of vaudeville characterized by coarse, vulgar comedy and dancing. — *v.t.* imitate so as to make fun of. — *adj.* making people laugh; comically imitative.

**bur ly** (bėr′lē), *adj.* great in bodily size; big and strong; sturdy.

**bur nish** (bėr′nish), *v.t.* make (metal) smooth and bright; polish (a surface) by rubbing until shiny.

**bur sar** (bėr′sər, bėr′sär), *n.* treasurer, especially of a college or university.

**Bu shi do** (bü′shē dō), *n.* the moral code of the knights and warriors of feudal Japan.

**butt** (but), *n.* object of ridicule or scorn.

**butte** (byüt), *n.* a steep, flat-topped hill standing alone.

**but tress** (but′ris), *n.* 1 a support built against a wall or building to strengthen it. 2 a support like this.

**cache** (kash), *n.* a hiding place, especially of goods, treasure, food, etc. — *v.t.* hide.

**ca dence** (kād′ns), *n.* the measure or beat of music, dancing, marching, or any movement regularly repeating itself.

**cal lig ra phy** (kə lig′rə fē), *n.* 1 handwriting. 2 beautiful handwriting.

**cal lous** (kal′əs), *adj.* unfeeling; insensitive. — **cal′lous ness,** *n.*

**cal low** (kal′ō), *adj.* 1 young and inexperienced. 2 not fully developed.

**can did** (kan′did), *adj.* saying openly what one really thinks; frank and sincere.

**can ti na** (kan tē′nə), *n.* a saloon.

**cap sule** (kap′səl, kap′syül), *n.* 1 a small case or covering. 2 the enclosed front section of a rocket. 3 a concise summary. — *adj.* very short; condensed or abridged.

**ca reen** (kə rēn′), *v.i.* lean to one side or sway sharply; tilt; tip.

**ca reer** (kə rir′), *n.* 1 a general course of action or progress through life. 2 occupation. 3 a run at full speed. — *v.i.* rush along wildly; dash.

**car mine** (kär′mən, kär′mīn), *n., adj.* deep-red with a tinge of purple.

**ca rouse** (kə rouz′), *v.i.* drink heavily. — *n.* a noisy drinking party.

**caste** (kast), *n.* 1 an exclusive social group; distinct class. 2 a social system having distinct classes separated by differences of birth, rank, wealth, or position.

**cas u al** (kazh′ü əl), *adj.* 1 happening by chance. 2 without plan or method. 3 informal in manner; offhand. — **cas′u al ly,** *adv.*

**ca tal pa** (kə tal′pə), *n.* tree with large, heart-shaped leaves, clusters of bell-shaped flowers, and long pods.

**cat a ract** (kat′ə rakt′), *n.* 1 a large, steep waterfall. 2 a violent rush or downpour of water; flood.

**cav al cade** (kav′əl kād′, kav′əl kād), *n.* procession of persons riding on horses, in carriages, or in automobiles.

**cede** (sēd), *v.t.* give up; surrender; hand over to another.

**ce les tial** (sə les′chəl), *adj.* 1 of the sky; having to do with the heavens. 2 heavenly.

**cen sure** (sen′shər), *n.* 1 expression of disapproval. 2 penalty, as a public rebuke or suspension from office. — *v.t.* express disapproval of.

**ces sa tion** (se sā′shən), *n.* a ceasing; a stopping.

**chafe** (chāf), *v.t.* rub so as to wear away, scrape, or make sore. — *n.* a chafing; irritation.

**chand ler** (chand′lər), *n.* 1 maker or seller of candles. 2 dealer in groceries and supplies.

**chan nel** (chan′l), *n.* 1 the bed of a stream, river, etc. 2 body of water joining two larger bodies of water. 3 course of action; field of activity. — *v.t.* direct into a particular course.

**chap ar ral** (chap′ə ral′, shap′ə ral′), *n.* a dense, often thorny thicket of low brushy vegetation.

**chap man** (chap′mən), *n.* BRITISH. peddler.

**char ro** (chä′rō), *n.* a Mexican horseman or cowboy dressed in close-fitting pants, jacket or serape, and sombrero.

**chase** (chās), *v.t.* decorate (metal, etc.) with embossed or engraved work.

**chaste** (chāst), *adj.* 1 pure; virtuous. 2 decent; modest.

**chas ten** (chā′sn), *v.t.* punish to improve; discipline.

**check rein** (chek′rān′), *n.* a short rein attached to the saddle or harness to keep a horse from lowering its head.

**chi a** (chē′ə), *n.* any of several plants of Mexico and the southwestern United States from the seeds of which a beverage is made.

**chide** (chīd), *v.t.* find fault with; blame; scold.

**chi mer a** (kə mir′ə, kī mir′ə), *n.* 1 a horrible creature of the imagination. 2 an absurd or impossible idea; wild fancy.

**chink** (chingk), *n.* a narrow opening; crack.

**chron ic** (kron′ik), *adj.* 1 lasting a long time. 2 never stopping; constant.

**ci ca da** (sə kā′də, sə kä′də), *n.* a large insect, commonly called a locust, with two

hat, āge, fär; let, ēqual, tėrm; it, īce; hot, ōpen, ôrder; oil, out; cup, pùt, rüle; ch, child; ng, long; sh, she; th, thin; ᵺ, then; zh, measure.

ə represents *a* in about, *e* in taken, *i* in pencil, *o* in lemon, *u* in circus.

pairs of thin, transparent wings.

**cinque foil** (singk′foil′), *n.* plant belonging to the rose family, having small, five-petaled yellow, white, or red flowers and leaves divided into five parts.

**cite** (sīt), *v.t.* **1** quote (a passage, book, or author), especially as an authority. **2** summon officially to appear before a court of law.

**ci vil i ty** (sə vil′ə tē), *n.* polite behavior; courtesy.

**clasp knife** (clasp′nīf′), *n.* knife with a blade or blades folding into the handle, which, when open, may be secured in place by a catch.

**cleave** (klēv), *v.i.* hold fast; cling.

**cleft** (kleft), *adj.* split; divided. — *n.* space or opening made by splitting; crack.

**cli en tele** (klī′ən tel′), *n.* **1** clients as a group. **2** customers.

**clime** (klīm), *n.* **1** country or region, especially one having pleasant conditions for living. **2** climate.

**clo ven-hoofed** (klō′vən hüft′, klō′vən-hüft′), *adj.* **1** having cloven hoofs. **2** devilish.

**co erce** (kō ėrs′), *v.t.* **1** compel; force. **2** control or restrain by force or authority.

**cog ni zance** (kog′nə zəns, kon′ə zəns), *n.* **1** knowledge; perception; awareness. **2 take cognizance of,** take notice of; give attention to.

**co her ent** (kō hir′ənt), *adj.* logically connected; consistent.

**coin** (koin), *n.* piece of metal stamped and issued by a government for use as money. — *v.t.* **1** make (money) by stamping metal. **2** make up; invent.

**col leen** (kol′ēn′, kə lēn′), *n.* IRISH. girl.

**comb** (kōm), *n.* **1** piece of metal, plastic, rubber, bone, etc., with teeth, used to arrange or straighten the hair or to hold it in place. **2** top of a wave rolling over or breaking. — *v.t.* search through; look everywhere in. — *v.i.* (of waves) roll over or break at the top.

**comb er** (kō′mər), *n.* breaker.

**come ly** (kum′lē), *adj.* **1** pleasant to look at; attractive. **2** fitting; suitable; proper.

**com men tar y** (kom′ən ter′ē), *n.* **1** series of notes explaining parts of a book. **2** series of comments.

**com mer cial ize** (kə mėr′shə līz), *v.t.* apply the methods and spirit of commerce to; make a matter of business or trade.

**com mit** (kə mit′), *v.t.* **1** do or perform (usually something wrong). **2** hand over for safekeeping. **3** give over; carry over; transfer.

**com mu ni ca ble** (kə myü′nə kə bəl), *adj.* that can be communicated.

**com mu ni ca tive** (kə myü′nə kā′tiv, kə myü′nə kə tiv), *adj.* ready to give information; talkative.

**com par a tive** (kəm par′ə tiv), *adj.* measured by comparison with something else;

relative. — **com par′a tive ly,** *adv.*

**com pe tent** (kom′pə tənt), *adj.* properly qualified; able; fit.

**com pla cent** (kəm plā′snt), *adj.* pleased with oneself or what one has; self-satisfied. — **com pla′cent ly,** *adv.*

**com posed** (kəm pōzd′), *adj.* calm; quiet; self-controlled. — **com pos′ed ly,** *adv.*

**com post** (kom′pōst), *n.* mixture of decaying leaves, manure, etc., for improving and fertilizing soil.

**com po sure** (kəm pō′zhər), *n.* calmness; quietness; self-control.

**com pre hend** (kom′pri hend′), *v.t.* **1** understand the meaning of. **2** include; contain.

**con cede** (kən sēd′), *v.t.* **1** admit as true; acknowledge. **2** allow to have; grant; yield.

**con ceiv a ble** (kən sē′və bəl), *adj.* that can be conceived or thought of; imaginable.

**con ceive** (kən sēv′), *v.t.* form in the mind; think up. — *v.i.* have an idea or feeling; think; imagine.

**con cen tric** (kən sen′trik), *adj.* having the same center.

**con cert ed** (kən sėr′tid), *adj.* arranged by agreement; planned or made together.

**con fla gra tion** (kon′flə grā′shən), *n.* a great and destructive fire.

**con form** (kən fôrm′), *v.i.* **1** act according to law or rule; be in agreement with generally accepted standards of business, conduct, or worship. **2** become the same in form; correspond in form or character.

**con front** (kən frunt′), *v.t.* **1** meet face to face; stand facing. **2** face boldly; oppose.

**con fute** (kən fyüt′), *v.t.* **1** prove (an argument, testimony, etc.) to be false or incorrect. **2** prove (a person) to be wrong; overcome by argument.

**con gen ial** (kən jē′nyəl), *adj.* **1** having similar tastes and interests; getting on well together. **2** agreeable; suitable.

**con gre ga tion al** (kong′grə gā′shə-nəl), *adj.* **1** of or done by a congregation. **2 Congregational,** of Congregationalism or Congregationalists.

**con jec ture** (kən jek′chər), *n.* formation of an opinion admittedly without sufficient evidence for proof; guessing. — *v.t., v.i.* guess.

**con jure** (kon′jər, kun′jər), *v.t.* **1** compel (a spirit, devil, etc.) to appear or disappear by a set form of words. **2** cause to appear or happen as if by magic. **3** cause to appear in the mind.

**conk** (kongk), *n.* hair which is straightened out and flattened down or waved.

**con science-strick en** (kon′shəns-strik′ ən), *adj.* suffering from a feeling of having done wrong.

**con scrip tion** (kən skrip′shən), *n.* compulsory service of men in the armed forces; draft.

**con sid er a tion** (kən sid′ə rā′shən), *n.* **1** act of thinking about in order to decide. **2** something thought of as a reason. **3** thoughtfulness. **4** money or other payment.

**con sign** (kən sīn′), *v.t.* **1** hand over; deliver. **2** send; transmit. **3** set apart; assign.

**con so la tion** (kon′sə lā′shən), *n.* a comforting person, thing, or event.

**con stan cy** (kon′stən sē), *n.* **1** firmness in belief or feeling; determination. **2** loyalty.

**con ster na tion** (kon′stər nā′shən), *n.* great dismay; paralyzing terror.

**con sti tute** (kon′stə tüt, kon′stə tyüt), *v.t.* make up; form; comprise.

**con sti tu tion** (kon′stə tü′shən, kon′-stə tyü′shən), *n.* way in which a person or thing is organized; nature; make-up.

**con sul** (kon′səl), *n.* official appointed by a government to live in a foreign city to look after the business interests of his or her own country and to protect citizens who are traveling or living there.

**con sume** (kən süm′), *v.t.* **1** use up; spend. **2** eat or drink up. **3** destroy; burn up. — *v.i.* waste away; be destroyed.

**con sum mate** (kon′sə māt), *v.t.* bring to completion; realize; fulfill.

**con ta gion** (kən tā′jən), *n.* **1** the spreading of disease by direct or indirect contact. **2** the spreading of any influence from one to another.

**con tem pla tive** (kon′təm plā′tiv, kən-tem′plə tiv), *adj.* deeply thoughtful.

**con tempt** (kən tempt′), *n.* the feeling that a person, act, or thing is mean, low, or worthless.

**con temp tu ous** (kən temp′chü əs), *adj.* showing contempt; scornful. — **con-temp′tu ous ly,** *adv.*

**con tend** (kən tend′), *v.i.* **1** work hard against difficulties; struggle. **2** take part in a contest. **3** argue. — *v.t.* declare to be a fact; maintain as true.

**con tor tion** (kən tôr′shən), *n.* a twisting or bending out of shape; distorting.

**con tract** (kən trakt′), *v.t.* draw together; make shorter, narrower, or smaller.

**con trite** (kən trīt′, kon′trīt), *adj.* **1** broken in spirit by a sense of guilt. **2** showing deep regret and sorrow. — **con trite′ly,** *adv.*

**con trive** (kən trīv′), *v.t.* **1** plan with cleverness or skill; invent; design. **2** plan; scheme; plot.

**con va les cent** (kon′və les′nt), *adj.* recovering health and strength after illness.

**con vene** (kən vēn′), *v.i.* meet for some purpose; gather together; assemble.

**con ven tion al** (kən ven′shə nəl), *adj.* **1** customary. **2** acting or behaving according to commonly accepted and approved ways. **3** (in the arts) following custom and traditional models; formal.

**con vex** (kon veks′, kon′veks), *adj.* curved out like the outside of a circle or sphere.

**con vulse** (kən vuls′), *v.t.* **1** shake violently. **2** cause violent disturbance in. **3** throw into fits of laughter.

**coop er** (kü′pər, kúp′ər), *n.* man who makes or repairs barrels, casks, etc.

**cop ing** (kō'ping), *n.* the top layer of a brick or stone wall, usually with a slope to shed water.

**co pi ous** (kō'pē əs), *adj.* **1** more than enough; plentiful; abundant. **2** containing many words. — **co'pi ous ly,** *adv.* — **co'pi ous ness,** *n.*

**co quette** (kō ket'), *n.* woman who tries to attract men merely to please her vanity; flirt.

**co quet tish** (kō ket'ish), *adj.* **1** of a coquette. **2** like a coquette. — **co quet'- tish ly,** *adv.*

**cord** (kôrd), *n.* measure of cut wood equal to 128 cubic feet.

**cord wood** (kôrd'wüd'), *n.* **1** wood sold by the cord. **2** firewood piled in cords.

**cor ner stone** (kôr'nər stōn'), *n.* **1** stone at the corner of two walls that holds them together. **2** such a stone built into the corner of a building as its formal beginning. **3** something of fundamental importance; foundation; basis.

**cor nice** (kôr'nis), *n.* a molding around the walls of a room just below the ceiling or over the top of a window.

**cor rode** (kə rōd'), *v.t.* eat away gradually, especially by or as if by chemical action. — *v.i.* become corroded.

**cor rup tion** (kə rup'shən), *n.* **1** a making evil or wicked. **2** a being made evil or wicked. **3** evil conduct; wickedness. **4** bribery; dishonesty.

**Cos sack** (kos'ak), *n.* one of a people living on the steppes in the southwestern Soviet Union, noted as horsemen.

**coun te nance** (koun'tə nəns), *n.* **1** expression of the face. **2** face; features. **3** approval. **4** calmness.

**coun ter bal ance** (*n.* koun'tər bal'əns; *v.* koun'tər bal'əns), *n.* weight balancing another weight. — *v.t., v.i.* offset.

**coun ter pane** (koun'tər pān'), *n.* an outer covering for a bed; bedspread.

**cov e nant** (kuv'ə nənt), *n.* **1** a solemn agreement between two or more persons or groups to do or not to do a certain thing. **2** (in the Bible) the solemn promises of God to man; compact between God and man.

**cov ert** (kuv'ərt, kō'vərt), *adj.* kept from sight; concealed; secret; hidden. — *n.* a hiding place; shelter.

**cov et** (kuv'it), *v.t.* desire eagerly (something that belongs to another).

**cov et ous** (kuv'ə təs), *adj.* desiring things that belong to others. — **cov'et ous ness,** *n.*

**cov ey** (kuv'ē), *n.* **1** brood of partridge, quail, etc. **2** a small group.

**cow hide** (kou'hīd'), *n.* **1** the hide of a cow. **2** a strong, heavy whip made of rawhide or braided leather. — *v.t.* whip with a cowhide.

**crack er** (krak'ər), *n.* **1** a thin, crisp biscuit or wafer. **2** firecracker. **3** U.S. DIALECT. a poor white person living in the hills and backwoods regions of Georgia, Florida, etc.

**crape** (krāp), *n.* **1** crepe; a thin, light cloth with a finely crinkled surface. **2** piece of black crepe used as a sign of mourning.

**craw** (krô), *n.* **1** crop of a bird or insect. **2** stomach of any animal.

**cre do** (krē'dō, krā'dō), *n.* belief; creed.

**crest fall en** (krest'fô'lən), *adj.* discouraged.

**cringe** (krinj), *v.i.* shrink from danger or pain; crouch in fear.

**crock** (krok), *n.* pot or jar made of earthenware.

**crone** (krōn), *n.* a withered old woman.

**cro ny** (krō'nē), *n.* a very close friend; chum.

**cru cial** (krü'shəl), *adj.* **1** very important or decisive; critical. **2** very trying; severe.

**crypt** (kript), *n.* an underground room or vault.

**crys tal line** (kris'tl ən, kris'tl īn), *adj.* **1** made of crystals. **2** clear and transparent like crystal.

**cul tur al** (kul'chər əl), *adj.* of or having to do with culture.

**cul ture** (kul'chər), *n.* fineness of feelings, thoughts, tastes, manners, etc.

**cur** (kėr), *n.* **1** a dog of mixed breed; mongrel. **2** a surly, contemptible person.

**curt** (kėrt), *adj.* rudely brief; short; abrupt. — **curt'ly,** *adv.*

**cut ler** (kut'lər), *n.* person who makes, sells, or repairs knives, scissors, and other cutting instruments.

**cut wa ter** (kut'wô'tər, kut'wot'ər), *n.* the front part of a ship's prow.

**cyn i cal** (sin'ə kəl), *adj.* **1** doubting the sincerity and goodness of others. **2** sneering; sarcastic.

**cyn i cism** (sin'ə siz'əm), *n.* **1** cynical quality or disposition. **2** a cynical remark.

**da is** (dā'is), *n.* a raised platform at one end of a hall or large room for a throne, seats of honor, a lectern, etc.

**dal ly** (dal'ē), *v.i.* **1** act in a playful manner. **2** toy or trifle (with a thing or subject).

**dan dy** (dan'dē), *n.* **1** man who is too careful about his dress and appearance. **2** INFORMAL. an excellent or first-rate thing.

**dank** (dangk), *adj.* unpleasantly damp or moist.

**dap ple** (dap'əl), *adj.* marked with spots; spotted. — *n.* a spotted appearance or condition.

**dark** (därk), *adj.* **1** without light; with very

little light. **2** gloomy; dull. **3** evil; wicked.

**dead pan** (ded'pan'), SLANG. *n.* an expressionless face, person, or manner. — *adj.* showing no expression or feeling.

**dearth** (dėrth), *n.* too small a supply; great scarcity or lack.

**de bauch** (di bôch'), *v.t.* lead away from duty, virtue, or morality; corrupt or seduce. — *n.* period or bout of excessive indulgence in eating, drinking, etc.

**de camp** (di kamp'), *v.i.* leave quickly and secretly; run away; flee.

**dec a syl lab ic** (dek'ə sə lab'ik), *adj.* having ten syllables.

**dec or ous** (dek'ər əs, di kôr'əs, di kōr'əs), *adj.* acting properly; in good taste; well-behaved; dignified.

**de co rum** (di kôr'əm, di kōr'əm), *n.* **1** proper behavior; good taste in conduct, speech, dress, etc. **2** observance or requirement of polite society.

**deem** (dēm), *v.t., v.i.* form or have an opinion; think, believe, or consider.

**de fer** (di fėr'), *v.t., v.i.* put off to some later time; delay; postpone.

**def er ence** (def'ər əns), *n.* **1** a yielding to the judgment, opinion, wishes, etc., of another. **2** great respect.

**def e ren tial** (def'ə ren'shəl), *adj.* showing deference; respectful.

**de gen e rate** (di jen'ər it), *adj.* showing a decline in physical, mental, or moral qualities. — *n.* person having a degenerate or unwholesome character.

**de jec tion** (di jek'shən), *n.* lowness of spirits; sadness; discouragement.

**de lir i um** (di lir'ē əm), *n.* a temporary disorder of the mind that occurs during fevers, insanity, drunkenness, etc., characterized by restlessness, excitement, irrational talk, and hallucinations.

**de lude** (di lüd'), *v.t.* mislead the mind or judgment of; trick or deceive.

**de mean** (di mēn'), *v.t.* lower in dignity or standing; humble; degrade.

**dem i john** (dem'ē jon), *n.* a large bottle of glass or earthenware enclosed in wicker.

**de mo ni ac** (di mō'nē ak), *adj.* **1** of or like demons. **2** devilish; fiendish. — *n.* person supposed to be possessed by an evil spirit.

**de mo ni a cal** (dē'mə nī'ə kəl), *adj.* demoniac.

**de nun ci a tion** (di nun'sē ā'shən), *n.* **1** expression of strong disapproval. **2** accusation.

**de pict** (di pikt'), *v.t.* **1** represent by drawing, painting, or carving; picture. **2** describe in words, music, etc.; portray.

**de plore** (di plôr', di plōr'), *v.t.* be very

---

hat, āge, fär; let, ēqual, tėrm; it, īce; hot, ōpen, ôrder; oil, out; cup, pút, rüle; ch, child; ng, long; sh, she; th, thin; ᴛH, then; zh, measure.

ə represents *a* in about, *e* in taken, *i* in pencil, *o* in lemon, *u* in circus.

sorry about; regret deeply.

**de ploy** (di ploi′), *v.t.*, *v.i.* **1** spread out (troops, military units, etc.) from a column into a long battle line. **2** spread out or extend (anything).

**de pot** (dē′pō *for 1;* dep′ō *for 2),* *n.* **1** a railroad or bus station. **2** place where recruits are brought together and trained.

**de ri sive** (di rī′siv), *adj.* that ridicules; mocking. **— de ri′sive ly,** *adv.* **— de ri′sive ness,** *n.*

**de rive** (di rīv′), *v.t.* **1** obtain from a source. **2** trace (a word, custom, etc.) from or to a source or origin.

**de scry** (di skrī′), *v.t.* **1** catch sight of; be able to see. **2** discover by observation.

**de sist** (di zist′), *v.i.* stop doing something.

**des o late** (des′ə lit), *adj.* **1** laid waste; devastated; barren. **2** not lived in; deserted. **3** unhappy. **4** lonely. **5** dreary.

**de spond** (di spond′), *v.i.* lose heart, courage, or hope.

**des tine** (des′tən), *v.t.* **1** set apart for a particular purpose or use; intend. **2** cause by fate.

**dev as tate** (dev′ə stāt), *v.t.* make desolate; lay waste; destroy. **— dev′as ta′tion,** *n.*

**de vi a tion** (dē′vē ā′shən), *n.* **1** act of turning aside; swerving. **2** straying from a policy or course of action.

**de void** (di void′), *adj.* entirely without; empty; lacking.

**de volve** (di volv′), *v.i.* be handed down to someone else; be transferred.

**de vo tion al** (di vō′shə nəl), *adj.* having to do with religious devotion; used in worship.

**dex ter i ty** (dek ster′ə tē) *n.* **1** skill in using the hands or body. **2** skill in using the mind; cleverness.

**dex ter ous** (dek′stər əs), *adj.* **1** skillful in using the hands or body. **2** having or showing skill in using the mind; clever.

**di a bol ic** (dī′ə bol′ik), *adj.* very cruel or wicked; devilish; fiendish.

**di a bol i cal** (dī′ə bol′ə kəl), *adj.* diabolic.

**Di as po ra** (dī as′pər ə), *n.* **1** the scattering of the Jews after their captivity in Babylon. **2 diaspora,** the scattering of any group.

**di as to le** (dī as′tl ē) *n.* the normal, rhythmical enlargement of the heart.

**dif fuse** (di fyüs′), *adj.* not concentrated together at a single point; spread out.

**di gress** (də gres′, dī gres′), *v.i.* turn aside from the main subject in talking or writing.

**din** (din), *n.* a continuing loud, confused noise. **—** *v.t.* say over and over again; repeat in a tiresome way.

**dire ful** (dīr′fəl), *adj.* dreadful; terrible.

**dirge** (dėrj), *n.* a funeral song or tune.

**dis af fect ed** (dis′ə fek′tid), *adj.* unfriendly, disloyal, or discontented.

**dis cern** (də zėrn′, də sėrn′), *v.t.* see

clearly; distinguish or recognize.

**dis charge** (dis chärj′), *v.t.* fire off; shoot.

**dis close** (dis klōz′), *v.t.* **1** open to view; uncover. **2** make known; reveal.

**dis com fi ture** (dis kum′fi chúr, dis-kum′fi chər), *n.* **1** a complete defeat. **2** defeat of plans or hopes; frustration.

**dis con cert** (dis′kən sért′), *v.t.* **1** disturb the self-possession of; embarrass greatly; confuse. **2** upset or frustrate (plans, etc.).

**dis con so late** (dis kon′sə lit), *adj.* **1** without hope; unhappy. **2** causing discomfort; cheerless.

**dis course** (n. dis′kôrs, dis′kōrs; v. dis-kôrs′, dis kōrs′), *n.* **1** a formal or extensive speech or writing. **2** talk; conversation. **—** *v.i.* talk; converse.

**dis creet** (dis krēt′), *adj.* very careful and sensible in speech and action; having or showing good judgment.

**dis cre tion** (dis kresh′ən), *n.* **1** great carefulness in speech or action; good judgment. **2** freedom to decide or choose.

**dis crim i nate** (dis krim′ə nāt), *v.i.* **1** make or see a difference; make a distinction. **2** accord a particular person, class, etc., distinctive (and usually unfair) treatment.

**dis il lu sion** (dis′i lü′zhən), *v.t.* set free from illusion; disenchant.

**dis joint ed** (dis join′tid), *adj.* without proper connection; incoherent.

**dis pas sion ate** (dis pash′ə nit), *adj.* free from emotion or prejudice; calm and impartial. **— dis pas′sion ate ly,** *adv.*

**dis perse** (dis pėrs′), *v.t.* send or drive off in different directions; scatter.

**dis pu ta tious** (dis′pyə tā′shəs), *adj.* fond of disputing; inclined to argue.

**dis sev er** (di sev′ər), *v.t.* cut into parts; sever; separate.

**dis si pate** (dis′ə pāt), *v.t.* **1** scatter. **2** cause to disappear. **3** spend foolishly; waste on things of little value.

**dis so lute** (dis′ə lüt), *adj.* living an immoral life; loose in morals.

**dis tinc tive** (dis tingk′tiv), *adj.* distinguishing from others; special; characteristic.

**di verge** (də vėrj′, dī vėrj′), *v.i.* move or lie in different directions from the same point; branch off.

**di vers** (dī′vərz), *adj.* more than one; several different; various.

**di verse** (də vėrs′, dī vėrs′), *adj.* **1** not alike; different. **2** varied.

**di ver sion** (də vėr′zhən, dī vėr′zhən), *n.* **1** a turning aside. **2** distraction from work, care, etc.; amusement.

**di vine** (də vīn′), *adj.* **1** of God or a god. **2** sacred; holy. **—** *n.* clergyman; minister; priest. **—** *v.t.* foresee or foretell by inspiration, by magic, or by signs and omens; predict.

**di vin i ty** (də vin′ə tē), *n.* **1** a divine being; god or goddess. **2** divine nature or quality.

**doc ile** (dos′əl), *adj.* **1** easily managed or dealt with; obedient. **2** easily taught; will-

ing to learn.

**do cil i ty** (do sil′ə tē), *n.* docile quality.

**dod der** (dod′ər), *v.i.* be unsteady; tremble or shake from frailty.

**dog ged** (dô′gid, dog′id), *adj.* not giving up; stubborn; persistent.

**dole ful** (dōl′fəl), *adj.* very sad or dreary; mournful; dismal.

**do mes tic** (də mes′tik), *adj.* of the home, household, or family affairs.

**do min ion** (də min′yən), *n.* power or right of governing and controlling; rule.

**dost** (dust), *v.* ARCHAIC. do. "Thou dost" means "you do."

**dou ble-banked,** (dub′əl bangkt′), *adj.* having two lines of rowers sitting side by side.

**dove tail** (duv′tāl′), *v.i.* fit together exactly.

**drag gle** (drag′əl), *v.t.* make wet or dirty (a garment, etc.) by dragging it through mud, water, dust, etc.

**draw nigh** (drô′ nī′), *v.i.* come; approach.

**dread ful ly** (dred′fə lē), *adv.* **1** in a dreadful manner. **2** very; exceedingly.

**drear** (drir), *adj.* ARCHAIC. dreary.

**drear y** (drir′ē), *adj.* **1** without cheer; gloomy. **2** ARCHAIC. sad.

**dredge** (drej), *v.t.* dig up; collect.

**droll** (drōl), *adj.* odd and amusing.

**dung** (dung), *n.* waste matter from the intestines of animals, much used as a fertilizer.

**du plic i ty** (dü plis′ə tē, dyü plis′ə tē), *n.* a secretly acting in one way and openly acting in another in order to deceive.

**dys en ter y** (dis′n ter′ē), *n.* disease of the intestines, producing diarrhea.

**ec cle si as ti cal** (i klē′zē as′tə kəl), *adj.* of or having to do with the church or the clergy.

**ec ru** (ek′rü, ā′krü), *adj.* pale-brown; light-tan.

**ed dy** (ed′ē), *n.* water, air, smoke, etc., moving against the main current, especially when having a whirling motion. **—** *v.i., v.t.* move against the main current in a whirling motion; whirl.

**e dict** (ē′dikt), *n.* **1** decree or law proclaimed by a king or other ruler on his sole authority. **2** any similar order or command.

**eer ie** (ir′ē), *adj.* **1** causing fear because of strangeness or weirdness. **2** timid because of superstition; fearful.

**ef face** (ə fās′), *v.t.* rub out; blot out; wipe out.

**ef fec tu al** (ə fek′chü əl), *adj.* producing or capable of producing the desired effect. **— ef fec′tu al ly,** *adv.*

**ef fem i nate** (ə fem′ə nit), *adj.* (of a man or boy) lacking in forceful qualities; showing weakness or softness.

**ef fer ves cent** (ef′ər ves′nt), *adj.* **1** giving off bubbles of gas. **2** lively and gay.

**ef fron ter y** (ə frun′tər ē), *n.* shameless boldness; rudeness.

**e jac u late** (i jak′yə lāt), *v.t., v.i.* say suddenly and briefly.

**e la tion** (i lā′shən), *n.* high spirits.

**el o cu tion** (el′ə kyü′shən), *n.* art of speaking or reading clearly and expressively in public.

**el o quence** (el′ə kwəns), *n.* 1 flow of speech that has grace and force. 2 power to win by speaking.

**e ma ci ate** (i mā′shē āt), *v.t.* make unnaturally thin; cause to lose flesh or waste away.

**em bark** (em bärk′), *v.i.* 1 go on board a ship or an aircraft. 2 begin an undertaking; set out; start.

**em bold en** (em bōl′dən), *v.t.* make bold; encourage.

**ém i gré** (em′ə grā; *French* ā mē grā′), *n.* 1 person who leaves his own country to settle in another; emigrant. 2 refugee.

**em met** (em′it), *n.* ARCHAIC. ant.

**e nam or** (e nam′ər), *v.t.* 1 inflame or arouse to love. 2 charm; fascinate.

**en camp** (en kamp′), *v.i.* 1 make a camp. 2 live in a camp for a time.

**en croach** (en krōch′), *v.i.* 1 go beyond proper or usual limits. 2 intrude.

**en cum ber** (en kum′bər), *v.t.* 1 hold back (from running, doing, etc.); hinder. 2 block up; fill. 3 burden with weight, difficulties, cares, debt, etc.

**en cum brance** (en kum′brəns), *n.* 1 something useless or in the way; hindrance; burden. 2 claim, mortgage, etc., on property.

**en gen der** (en jen′dər), *v.t.* bring into existence; produce; cause.

**en mi ty** (en′mə tē), *n.* the feeling that enemies have for each other; hostility or hatred.

**en snare** (en sner′, en snar′), *v.t.* catch in a snare; trap; snare.

**en tice** (en tīs′), *v.t.* attract by arousing hopes or desires; tempt.

**en trails** (en′trālz, en′trəlz), *n.pl.* 1 the inner parts of the body of a man or animal. 2 the intestines; bowels.

**en trance** (en trans′), *v.t.* 1 fill with joy or wonder; delight; charm. 2 put into a trance.

**en trap** (en trap′), *v.t.* 1 catch in a trap. 2 bring into difficulty or danger; trick.

**en treat** (en trēt′), *v.t.* ask or keep asking earnestly; beg. — **en treat′ing ly,** *adv.*

**en treat y** (en trē′tē), *n.* an earnest request; prayer or appeal.

**ep i sode** (ep′ə sōd), *n.* an outstanding incident or experience in a person's life, in the history of a country, the world, an institution, etc.

**ep i taph** (ep′ə taf), *n.* a short statement in memory of a dead person, usually put on a gravestone or tombstone.

**ep i thet** (ep′ə thet), *n.* 1 a descriptive expression; word or phrase expressing some quality or attribute. 2 an insulting or contemptuous word or phrase used in place of a person's name.

**ep och** (ep′ək, ē′pok), *n.* 1 period of time; era; age. 2 period of time in which striking things happened.

**eq ua ble** (ek′wə bəl, ē′kwə bəl), *adj.* changing little; uniform; even. — **eq′ua bly,** *adv.*

**e qui nox** (ē′kwə noks), *n.* either of the two times in the year when the center of the sun crosses the celestial equator, and day and night are of equal length in all parts of the earth.

**eq ui ty** (ek′wə tē), *n.* a being equal or fair; fairness; justice.

**e quiv o cal** (i kwiv′ə kəl), *adj.* 1 having two or more meanings; intentionally vague. 2 undecided; uncertain. 3 questionable; suspicious.

**ere** (er, ar), ARCHAIC. *prep.* before. — *conj.* 1 before. 2 sooner than; rather than.

**er ra ta** (ə rā′tə, ə rä′tə), *n., pl.* of **erratum.** 1 errors in writing or printing. 2 errors and corrections in printing listed and inserted in a book.

**es pres so** (e spres′ō), *n.* a very strong black coffee made of coffee beans roasted black, and brewed under steam pressure, usually in a special machine.

**etch** (ech), *v.t.* 1 engrave (a drawing or design) on a metal plate, glass, etc., by means of acid that eats away the lines. 2 impress deeply; fix firmly.

**e vade** (i vād′), *v.t.* get away from by trickery; avoid by cleverness. — **e vad′er,** *n.*

**e va sion** (i vā′zhən), *n.* 1 a getting away from something by trickery; avoiding by cleverness. 2 an attempt to escape an argument, a charge, a question, etc.

**e ven tide** (ē′vən tīd′), *n.* ARCHAIC. evening.

**e vince** (i vins′), *v.t.* 1 show clearly. 2 show that one has (a certain quality, trait, etc.).

**e volve** (i volv′), *v.t.* 1 develop gradually. 2 develop by a process of growth and change to a more highly organized condition.

**ex alt** (eg zôlt′), *v.t.* 1 make high in rank, honor, power, character, or quality. 2 fill with pride. 3 honor; glorify.

**ex as pe rate** (eg zas′pə rāt′), *v.t.* irritate very much; annoy extremely; make angry.

**ex clu sive** (ek sklü′siv, ek sklü′ziv), *adj.* 1 shutting out all or most others. 2 very selective in choosing friends, members, patrons, etc.

**ex em plar y** (eg zem′plər ē, eg′zəm pler′ē), *adj.* worth imitating; serving as a model or pattern.

**ex hil a rate** (eg zil′ə rāt′), *v.t.* make merry or lively; put into high spirits; cheer.

**ex hil a ra tion** (eg zil′ə rā′shən), *n.* a being or feeling exhilarated; high spirits.

**ex hort** (eg zôrt′), *v.t.* urge strongly; advise or warn earnestly.

**ex hor ta tion** (eg′zôr tā′shən, ek′sôr tā′shən), *n.* 1 strong urging; earnest advice or warning. 2 speech, sermon, etc., that exhorts.

**ex o dus** (ek′sə dəs), *n.* a going out; departure, usually of a large number of people.

**ex pa tri ate** (*v.* ek spā′trē āt; *n.,* ek spā′trē it, ek spā′trē āt), *v.t.* 1 force to leave one's country; banish; exile. 2 withdraw (oneself) from one's country; give up one's citizenship. — *n.* an expatriated person; exile.

**ex pe di ent** (ek spē′dē ənt), *adj.* 1 helping to bring about a desired result; desirable or suitable under the circumstances; useful; advantageous. 2 giving or seeking personal advantage. — *n.* means of bringing about a desired result.

**ex pi a tion** (ek′spē ā′shən), *n.* 1 a making amends for a wrong, sin, etc.; atonement. 2 means of atonement; amends.

**ex ple tive** (ek′splə tiv), *n.* 1 syllable, word, or phrase used for filling out a sentence or a line of verse, without adding to the sense. 2 oath or exclamation.

**ex ploit** (ek sploit′), *v.t.* 1 make use of; turn to practical account. 2 make unfair or selfish use of.

**ex pound** (ek spound′), *v.t.* make clear; explain, interpret, etc.

**ex punge** (ek spunj), *v.t.* remove completely; erase.

**ex tem po rize** (ek stem′pə rīz′), *v.i., v.t.* prepare offhand; make for the occasion.

**ex tol** (ek stōl′, ek stol′), *v.t.* praise highly; commend.

**ex trem i ty** (ek strem′ə tē), *n.* 1 the very end; farthest possible place. 2 very great danger or need. 3 an extreme degree. 4 an extreme action or measure.

**ex ult** (eg zult′), *v.i.* be very glad; rejoice greatly.

**fa cade** (fə säd′), *n.* outward appearance.

**fa ce tious** (fə sē′shəs), *adj.* 1 having the habit of joking; being slyly humorous. 2 said in fun. — **fa ce′tious ly,** *adv.*

---

hat, āge, fär; let, ēqual, tèrm; it, īce; hot, ōpen, ôrder; oil, out; cup, pùt, rüle; ch, child; ng, long; sh, she; th, thin; ŦH, then; zh, measure.

ə represents *a* in about, *e* in taken, *i* in pencil, *o* in lemon, *u* in circus.

— **fa ce′tious ness,** *n.*

**fac ul ty** (fak′əl tē), *n.* power of the mind or body; capability.

**fain** (fān), ARCHAIC. *adv.* gladly; willingly. — *adj.* **1** willing, but not eager. **2** obliged. **3** glad. **4** eager.

**fal si fy** (fôl′sə fī), *v.t.* make false; change to deceive.

**fan ci ful** (fan′sə fəl), *adj.* **1** showing fancy in design. **2** led by fancy; imaginative. **3** suggested by fancy; unreal.

**fan cy** (fan′sē), *v.t.* **1** picture to oneself; imagine; conceive. **2** have an idea or belief; suppose.

**farce** (färs), *n.* a ridiculous mockery.

**far ci cal** (fär′sə kəl), *adj.* of or like a farce; ridiculous; absurd.

**fa tal ism** (fā′tl iz′əm), *n.* **1** belief that fate controls everything that happens. **2** acceptance of everything that happens because of this belief.

**fath om a ble** (faᴛʜ′ə mə bəl), *adj.* **1** that can be fathomed. **2** understandable.

**fe al ty** (fē′əl tē), *n.* loyalty; faithfulness; allegiance.

**fe do ra** (fi dôr′ə, fi dōr′ə), *n.* a man's low, soft felt hat with a curved brim, having the crown creased lengthwise.

**fe lic i ty** (fə lis′ə tē), *n.* **1** great happiness; bliss. **2** good fortune; blessing.

**fel on** (fel′ən), *n.* person who has committed a felony; criminal.

**fen** (fen), *n.* low, marshy land covered wholly or partially with shallow, often stagnant water.

**fer ment** (fər ment′), *v.i.* undergo or produce a gradual chemical change in which bacteria, yeast, etc., change sugar into alcohol and produce carbon dioxide.

**fe roc i ty** (fə ros′ə tē), *n.* savage cruelty; fierceness.

**fer vid** (fėr′vid), *adj.* full of strong feeling; intensely emotional; spirited.

**fer vor** (fėr′vər), *n.* great warmth of feeling; intense emotion; enthusiasm.

**fes ter** (fes′tər), *v.i.* **1** form pus. **2** cause soreness or pain; irritate. **3** decay; rot.

**fes toon** (fe stün′), *n.* a string or chain of flowers, leaves, ribbons, etc., hanging in a curve between two points. — *v.t.* decorate with festoons.

**fetch** (fech), *v.t.* **1** go to another place and bring back; go and get; bring. **2** cause to come; succeed in bringing.

**fet lock** (fet′lok), *n.* tuft of hair above a horse's hoof on the back part of its leg.

**fe ver ish** (fē′vər ish), *adj.* excited; restless.

**fi del i ty** (fī del′ə tē, fə del′ə tē), *n.* steadfast faithfulness; loyalty.

**fig ment** (fig′mənt), *n.* something imagined; made-up story.

**fig ure** (fig′yər), *n.* person or character noticed or remembered.

**fil i al** (fil′ē əl), *adj.* of a son or daughter; due from a son or daughter toward a mother or father.

**fi nite** (fī′nīt), *adj.* having limits or bounds; not infinite. — **fi′nite ness,** *n.*

**fir ma ment** (fėr′mə mənt), *n.* arch of the heavens; sky.

**fit ful** (fit′fəl), *adj.* going on and then stopping for a while; irregular.

**flail** (flāl), *n.* instrument for threshing grain. — *v.t.* beat; thrash.

**flam beau** (flam′bō), *n.,* *pl.* **-beaux** or **-beaus** (-bōz). a flaming torch.

**flay** (flā), *v.t.* **1** strip off the skin or outer covering of; skin. **2** scold severely; criticize without pity or mercy.

**fleet ing** (flē′ting), *adj.* passing swiftly; soon gone.

**flick** (flik), *n.* SLANG. movie.

**flot sam** (flot′səm), *n.* **1** wreckage of a ship or its cargo found floating on the sea. **2** odds and ends; useless things.

**fluke** (flük), *n.* either of the two halves of a whale's tail.

**flume** (flüm), *n.* a deep and very narrow valley with a stream running through it.

**flut ed** (flü′tid), *adj.* having long, round grooves.

**fo li age** (fō′lē ij), *n.* leaves of a plant.

**folk sy** (fōk′sē), *adj.* INFORMAL. **1** friendly. **2** simple; common.

**folk way** (fōk′wā′), *n.* custom or habit that has grown up within a social group and is very common among the members of this group.

**for bear ance** (fôr ber′əns), *n.* patience.

**fore bear** (fôr′ber, fôr′bar), *n.* ancestor.

**fore bod ing** (fôr bō′ding, fōr bō′ding), *n.* **1** prediction; warning. **2** a feeling that something bad is going to happen.

**fore stall** (fôr stôl′, fōr stôl′), *v.t.* **1** prevent by acting first. **2** act sooner than.

**for mi da ble** (fôr′mə də bəl), *adj.* hard to overcome; hard to deal with; to be dreaded.

**for sake** (fôr sāk′), *v.t.* give up; leave alone; leave; abandon.

**for sooth** (fôr süth′), *adv.* ARCHAIC. in truth; indeed.

**forth with** (fôrth′with′), *adv.* at once; immediately.

**for ti tude** (fôr′tə tüd, fôr′tə tyüd), *n.* courage in facing pain, danger, or trouble; firmness of spirit.

**foun der** (foun′dər), *v.i.* fill with water and sink. — *v.t.* cause to fill with water and sink.

**fren zy** (fren′zē), *n.* **1** state of near madness. **2** condition of very great excitement.

**fro** (frō), *adv.* **1** from; back. **2 to and fro,** first one way and then back again.

**frus trate** (frus′trāt), *v.t.* **1** make useless or worthless; bring to nothing; defeat. **2** prevent from accomplishing; oppose.

**fum ble** (fum′bəl), *v.t.* handle (something) awkwardly and with nervous clumsiness. — *n.* an awkward attempt to find or handle something.

**furze** (fėrz), *n.* a low, prickly, evergreen shrub of the pea family, having yellow flowers, common on wastelands in Europe.

**fuse** (fyüz), *v.t.* **1** join together by melting. **2** blend; unite. — *v.i.* **1** become melted. **2** become blended; unite.

**gab ble** (gab′əl), *v.i.* talk rapidly with little or no meaning; jabber.

**gai ter** (gā′tər), *n.* **1** an outer covering for the lower leg or ankle, made of cloth, leather, etc., for outdoor wear. **2** shoe with an elastic strip in each side.

**gal lo** (gal′ō), *n.* rooster.

**gar ish** (ger′ish, gar′ish), *adj.* **1** obtrusively bright in color; showy. **2** adorned to excess.

**gar ret** (gar′it), *n.* **1** space in a house just below a sloping roof; attic. **2** room or apartment in such a place.

**gaud y** (gô′dē), *adj.* too bright and gay to be in good taste. — **gaud′i ly,** *adv.*

**gaunt let** (gônt′lit, gänt′lit), *n.* **1** a former punishment or torture in which the offender had to run between two rows of men who struck him with clubs or other weapons as he passed. **2 run the gauntlet, a** pass between two rows of men each of whom strikes the runner as he passes. **b** be exposed to unfriendly attacks or severe criticism.

**gen e ra tion** (jen′ə rā′shən), *n.* **1** all the people born about the same period. Parents belong to one generation and their children to the next. **2** the time from the birth of one generation to the birth of the next generation; about thirty years.

**gen ius** (jē′nyəs, jē′nē əs), *n.* **1** great natural ability of some special kind. **2** the special character or spirit of a person, nation, age, language, etc.

**gen tile** (jen′tīl), *n.* person who is not a Jew. — *adj.* not Jewish.

**gen til i ty** (jen til′ə tē), *n.* **1** gentle birth; being of good family and social position. **2** good manners. **3** refinement.

**ges tic u la tion** (je stik′yə la′shən), *n.* a lively or excited gesture.

**ghast ly** (gast′lē), *adj.* **1** causing terror; horrible; shocking. **2** like a dead person or ghost; deathly pale.

**ghet to** (get′ō), *n.* **1** (formerly) a section of a city where Jews were required to live. **2** section of a city where any racial or other minority group lives.

**ghoul** (gül), *n.* a horrible demon that robs graves and feeds on corpses.

**gild** (gild), *v.t.* cover with a thin layer of gold or similar material.

**gilt** (gilt), *n.* a thin layer of gold or similar material with which a surface is gilded.

**gin ger ly** (jin′jər lē), *adv.* with extreme care or caution.

**gist** (jist), *n.* the essential part; real point; main idea; substance of a longer statement.

**glean** (glēn), *v.i.* gather grain left on a field by reapers.

**glib** (glib), *adj.* speaking or spoken too smoothly and easily to be believed.

**goad** (gōd), *n.* **1** a sharp-pointed stick for driving cattle. **2** anything which drives or urges one on. — *v.t.* drive or urge on.

**gore** (gôr, gōr), *n.* blood that is shed; thick blood; clotted blood.

**gos sa mer** (gos′ə mər), *n.* **1** film or thread of cobweb spun by small spiders, which is seen floating in the air in calm weather. **2** anything very light and thin. — *adj.* like gossamer; very light and thin; filmy.

**grap ple** (grap′əl), *v.t.* seize and hold fast. — *v.i.* **1** struggle by seizing one another. **2** try to overcome, solve, or deal (with a problem, question, etc.).

**grat i fi ca tion** (grat′ə fə kā′shən), *n.* something that satisfies or pleases.

**grat i fy** (grat′ə fī), *v.t.* **1** give pleasure to; please. **2** give satisfaction to; satisfy.

**grave**[1] (grāv), *adj.* **1** earnest; thoughtful; serious. **2** not gay; dignified; solemn.

**grave**[2] (grāv), *v.t.* **1** engrave; carve. **2** impress deeply; fix firmly.

**grav i ty** (grav′ə tē), *n.* seriousness; earnestness.

**great coat** (grāt′kōt′), *n.* a heavy overcoat.

**green ing** (grē′ning), *n.* apple with a yellowish-green skin when ripe.

**grille** (gril), *n.* an openwork, metal structure or screen, used as a gate, door, or window.

**gris tle** (gris′əl), *n.* cartilage, especially when found in meat.

**gris tly** (gris′lē), *adj.* of, containing, or like gristle.

**griz zled** (griz′əld), *adj.* **1** grayish; gray. **2** gray-haired.

**gro tesque** (grō tesk′), *adj.* **1** odd or unnatural in shape, appearance, manner, etc.; fantastic; queer. **2** ridiculous; absurd.

**guf faw** (gu fô′), *n.* burst of loud, coarse laughter. — *v.i.* laugh loudly and coarsely.

**guile less** (gīl′lis), *adj.* without guile; honest; frank; straightforward.

**gun wale** (gun′l), *n.* the upper edge of the side of a ship or boat.

**hag gard** (hag′ərd), *adj.* looking worn from pain, fatigue, worry, hunger, etc.; careworn; gaunt.

**hag gle** (hag′əl), *v.i.* dispute, especially about a price or the terms of a bargain. — *v.t.* mangle in cutting; hack.

**hair breadth**   or   **hairs breadth** (herz′bredth′, herz′bretth′; harz′bredth, harz′bretth′), *adj.* very narrow; extremely close.

**hank** (hangk), *n.* **1** coil or loop. **2** roll of yarn.

**hap less** (hap′lis), *adj.* unlucky; unfortu-

nate.

**hap ly** (hap′lē), *adv.* ARCHAIC. by chance; perhaps.

**har le quin** (här′lə kwən, här′lə kən), *n.* a mischievous person; clown.

**hash** (hash), *n.* **1** mixture of cooked meat, potatoes, and other vegetables, chopped into small pieces and fried or baked. **2** mixture; jumble. — *v.t.* chop into small pieces.

**haunt** (hônt, hänt), *v.t.* **1** go often to; visit frequently. **2** be often with; come often to. — *n.* place often gone to or visited.

**haw**[1] (hô), *interj., n.* a stammering sound between words.

**haw**[2] (hô), *n.* the red berry of the hawthorn.

**head y** (hed′ē), *adj.* **1** hasty; rash; headlong. **2** apt to affect the head and make one dizzy; intoxicating.

**heath er** (heᴛʜ′ər), *n.* a low, evergreen shrub with stalks of small, purple or pink, bell-shaped flowers.

**heath er y** (heᴛʜ′ər ē), *adj.* **1** of or like heather. **2** covered with heather.

**he li o trope** (hē′lē ə trōp, hē′lyə trōp), *n.* a plant that has clusters of small, fragrant purple or white flowers.

**hem** (hem), *interj., n.* sound like clearing the throat, used to attract attention or show doubt or hesitation. — *v.i.* **hem and haw,** hesitate in speaking.

**herb age** (ėr′bij, hėr′bij), *n.* **1** grass and other low-growing plants covering a large extent of ground, especially as used for pasture; herbs collectively. **2** the green leaves and soft stems of plants.

**hew** (hyü), *v.t.* cut with an ax, sword, etc.; chop. — *v.i.* hold firmly *(to);* stick fast or cling *(to).*

**hid e ous** (hid′ē əs), *adj.* very ugly; frightful; horrible. — **hid′e ous ness,** *n.*

**hid ing** (hī′ding), *n.* INFORMAL. a beating; thrashing.

**hill ock** (hil′ək), *n.* a little hill.

**hin der** (hin′dər), *v.t.* keep back; get in the way of; make difficult.

**hith er to** (hiᴛʜ′ər tü′), *adv.* until now.

**hoar y** (hôr′ē, hōr′ē), *adj.* white or gray with age.

**ho cus** (hō′kəs), *v.t.* play a trick on; hoax; cheat.

**hogs head** (hogz′hed, hôgz′hed), *n.* a large barrel or cask. In the United States, a hogshead contains from 63 to 140 gallons.

**home stead** (hōm′sted′), *n.* **1** house with its buildings and grounds; farm with its buildings. **2** U.S. parcel of 160 acres of public land granted to a settler under certain conditions by the United States government. **3** the place of one's dwelling or home.

***Ho mo sa pi ens*** (hō′mō sā′pē enz; hō′-mō sap′ē enz), *n.* human beings.

**horn y** (hôr′nē), *adj.* hard like a horn; calloused.

**how be it** (hou bē′it), *adv.* ARCHAIC. nevertheless.

**hu mil i ty** (hyü mil′ə tē), *n.* humbleness of mind; lack of pride; meekness.

**hum mock** (hum′ək), *n.* **1** a very small, rounded hill; knoll; hillock. **2** a bump or ridge in a field of ice.

**hu mor** (hyü′mər, yü′mər), *v.t.* give in to the fancies or whims of (a person); indulge.

**hump** (hump), *n.* a rounded lump that sticks out. — *v.i.* **1** rise in a hump. **2** SLANG. exert oneself; make an effort.

**hunch** (hunch), *v.t.* draw, bend, or form into a hump. — *v.i.* draw, bend, or form oneself into a hump.

**hus band man** (huz′bənd mən), *n.* person who farms.

**hy poth e sis** (hī poth′ə sis), *n.* something assumed because it seems likely to be a true explanation.

**id i om** (id′ē əm), *n.* **1** phrase or expression whose meaning cannot be understood from the ordinary meanings of the words in it. **2** the language or dialect of a particular area or group.

**id i o syn cra sy** (id′ē ō sing′krə sē), *n.* a personal peculiarity of taste, behavior, opinion, etc.

**i dyl lic** (ī dil′ik), *adj.* suitable for an idyll; simple and charming.

**ig no ble** (ig nō′bəl), *adj.* **1** without honor; disgraceful; base. **2** not of noble birth or position; humble.

**im age** (im′ij), *n.* a comparison, description, or figure of speech that helps the mind to form forceful or beautiful pictures. Poetry often contains images.

**im me mo ri al** (im′ə môr′ē əl, im′ə-mōr′ē əl), *adj.* extending back beyond the bounds of memory; extremely old.

**im mi nent** (im′ə nənt), *adj.* likely to happen soon; about to occur.

**im pair** (im per′, im par′), *v.t.* make worse; damage; harm; weaken.

**im pale** (im pāl′), *v.t.* pierce through with something pointed; fasten upon something pointed.

**im part** (im pärt′), *v.t.* **1** give a part or share of; give. **2** communicate; tell.

**im pel** (im pel′), *v.t.* **1** drive or force; cause. **2** cause to move; push along.

**im pend ing** (im pen′ding), *adj.* likely to happen soon; threatening; about to occur.

**im per cep ti ble** (im′pər sep′tə bəl), *adj.* very slight, gradual, or indistinct.

---

hat, āge, fär; let, ēqual, tėrm; it, īce; hot, ōpen, ôrder; oil, out; cup, pùt, rüle; ch, child; ng, long; sh, she; th, thin; ᴛʜ, then; zh, measure.

ə represents *a* in about, *e* in taken, *i* in pencil, *o* in lemon, *u* in circus.

**im per i ous** (im pir′ē əs), *adj.* haughty or arrogant; domineering.

**im per vi ous** (im pėr′vē əs), *adj.* allowing no passage or entrance. — **im per′vi ous ness,** *n.*

**im pi ous** (im′pē əs, im pī′əs), *adj.* not religious; not having or not showing reverence for God; wicked; profane.

**im pla ca ble** (im plā′kə bəl, im plak′ə bəl), *adj.* unable to be satisfied or calmed; unyielding.

**im plore** (im plôr′, im plōr′), *v.t.* **1** beg or pray earnestly for. **2** beg (a person) to do something.

**im pose** (im pōz′), *v.t.* **1** put (a burden, tax, or punishment) on. **2** force or thrust (oneself or one's company) on another or others.

**im pos ing** (im pō′zing), *adj.* impressive because of size, appearance, dignity, etc.

**im pov er ished** (im pov′ər isht), *adj.* very poor.

**im promp tu** (im promp′tü, im promp′tyü), *adj.* made or done without previous thought or preparation.

**in ac ces si ble** (in′ək ses′ə bəl), *adj.* **1** hard to get at; hard to reach or enter. **2** that cannot be reached or entered at all.

**in ar tic u late** (in′är tik′yə lit), *adj.* **1** not uttered in distinct syllables or words. **2** unable to speak in words.

**in can ta tion** (in′kan tā′shən), *n.* set of words spoken as a magic charm or to cast a magic spell.

**in car nate** (in kär′nit, in kär′nāt), *adj.* embodied in flesh, especially in human form; lifelike.

**in cense** (in sens′), *v.t.* make very angry; fill with rage.

**in com pe tence** (in kom′pə təns), *n.* lack of ability, power, or fitness.

**in com pe ten cy** (in kom′pə tən sē), *n.* incompetence.

**in con se quent** (in kon′sə kwent, in-kon′sə kwənt), *adj.* **1** not logical; not logically connected. **2** not to the point; irrelevant.

**in cor ri gi ble** (in kôr′ə jə bəl, in kor′ə jə bəl), *adj.* **1** too firmly fixed in bad ways, an annoying habit, etc., to be reformed or changed. **2** so fixed that it cannot be changed or cured.

**in cre du li ty** (in′krə dü′lə tē, in′krə dyü′lə tē), *n.* lack of belief; doubt.

**in cred u lous** (in krej′ə ləs), *adj.* **1** not ready to believe; doubting; skeptical. **2** showing a lack of belief.

**in cur** (in kėr′), *v.t.* run or fall into (something unpleasant or inconvenient); bring on oneself.

**in den ture** (in den′chər), *n.* **1** a written agreement, such as a contract or deed. **2** Also, **indentures,** *pl.* contract by which a servant or apprentice is bound to serve or work for someone else.

**in dic a tive** (in dik′ə tiv), *adj.* pointing out; showing; being a sign; suggestive.

**in dif fer ent** (in dif′ər ənt), *adj.* **1** having or showing no interest or attention. **2** not inclined to prefer one person or thing to another; neutral; fair. **3** not mattering much; unimportant.

**in dig na tion** (in′dig nā′shən), *n.* anger at something unworthy, unjust, unfair, or mean; anger mixed with scorn; righteous anger.

**in dis crim i nate** (in′dis krim′ə nit), *adj.* **1** mixed up; confused. **2** not distinguishing carefully between persons, things, etc.

**in di vid u al ism** (in′də vij′ü ə liz′əm), *n.* **1** theory that individual freedom is as important as the welfare of the community or group as a whole. **2** any moral, economic, or political theory that emphasizes the importance of individuals. **3** the pursuit of one's own ends or ideas as a mode or principle of life.

**in do lent** (in′dl ənt), *adj.* disliking work; lazy; idle.

**in duce** (in düs′, in dyüs′), *v.t.* **1** lead on; influence; persuade. **2** bring about; cause.

**in dulge** (in dulj′), *v.i.* give in to one's pleasure; let oneself have, use, or do what one wants. — *v.t.* **1** give in to; let oneself have, use, or do. **2** give in to the wishes or whims of; humor.

**in dul gent** (in dul′jənt), *adj.* giving in to another's wishes or whims; too kind or agreeable.

**in ept** (in ept′), *adj.* **1** not suitable; out of place; inappropriate. **2** awkward; clumsy.

**in fa my** (in′fə mē), *n.* **1** a very bad reputation; public disgrace. **2** shameful badness; extreme wickedness.

**in fat u at ed** (in fach′ü ā′tid), *adj.* having an exaggerated fondness or passion; foolishly in love.

**in fat u a tion** (in fach′ü ā′shən), *n.* exaggerated fondness or passion; foolish love.

**in fer no** (in fėr′nō), *n.* **1** hell. **2** place of torment like hell.

**in fest** (in fest′), *v.t.* trouble or disturb frequently or in large numbers.

**in fi del** (in′fə dəl), *n.* person who does not believe in religion. — *adj.* not believing in religion.

**in firm** (in fėrm′), *adj.* lacking strength or health; physically weak or feeble, especially through age.

**in flec tion** (in flek′shən), *n.* a change in the tone or pitch of the voice.

**in gen u ous** (in jen′yü əs), *adj.* **1** free from restraint or reserve; frank and open; sincere. **2** simple and natural; innocent. — **in gen′u ous ly,** *adv.*

**in grate** (in′grāt), *n.* an ungrateful person.

**in her ent** (in hir′ənt, in her′ənt), *adj.* belonging to a person or thing as a permanent and essential quality. — **in her′ent ly,** *adv.*

**in hib it** (in hib′it), *v.t.* **1** hold back; hinder or restrain; check. **2** prohibit; forbid.

**in junc tion** (in jungk′shən), *n.* an authoritative or emphatic order; command.

**in nu en do** (in′yü en′dō), *n.* **1** an indirect hint or reference; insinuation. **2** an indirect suggestion meant to discredit a person.

**in scru ta bil i ty** (in skrü′tə bil′ə tē), *n.* **1** a being inscrutable. **2** something inscrutable.

**in scru ta ble** (in skrü′tə bəl), *adj.* that cannot be understood; so mysterious or obscure that one cannot make out its meaning; incomprehensible.

**in stru men tal i ty** (in′strə men tal′ə-tē), *n.* helpfulness; agency; means.

**in teg ri ty** (in teg′rə tē), *n.* **1** honesty or sincerity; uprightness. **2** wholeness; completeness.

**in tem per ance** (in tem′pər əns), *n.* **1** lack of moderation or self-control; excess. **2** excessive drinking of intoxicating liquor.

**in tent** (in tent′), *n.* **1** purpose; intention. **2** meaning; significance. **3 to all intents and purposes,** in almost every way; practically speaking.

**in ter** (in tėr′), *v.t.* put (a dead body) into a grave or tomb; bury.

**in ter ac tion** (in′tər ak′shən), *n.* action on each other.

**in ter mi na ble** (in tėr′mə nə bəl), *adj.* **1** never stopping; unceasing; endless. **2** so long as to seem endless; very long and tiring.

**in ter tinge** (in′tər tinj′), *v.t.* alter slightly by a blend of colors.

**in ti mate** (in′tə māt), *v.t.* **1** suggest indirectly; hint. **2** make known; announce; notify.

**in tox i cate** (in tok′sə kāt), *v.t.* **1** make drunk. **2** excite greatly; exhilarate.

**in tu i tion** (in′tü ish′ən, in′tyü ish′ən), *n.* **1** immediate perception or understanding of truths, facts, etc., without reasoning. **2** truth, fact, etc., so perceived or understood.

**in un date** (in′un dāt, in un′dāt), *v.t.* **1** overspread with a flow of water; flood. **2** overspread as if with a flood.

**in ure** (in yùr′), *v.t.* toughen or harden; accustom.

**in var i a ble** (in ver′ē ə bəl, in var′ē ə-bəl), *adj.* always the same; unchanging. — **in var′i a bly,** *adv.*

**in vest** (in vest′), *v.t.* clothe; cover; surround.

**in vo ca tion** (in′və kā′shən), *n.* **1** a calling upon in prayer; appeal for help or protection. **2** a calling forth of spirits with magic words or charms.

**in voke** (in vōk′), *v.t.* **1** call on in prayer; appeal to for help or protection. **2** appeal to for confirmation or judgment. **3** ask earnestly for; beg for.

**ir i des cent** (ir′ə des′nt), *adj.* displaying changing colors; changing color when moved or turned.

**i ron i cal** (ī ron′ə kəl), *adj.* contrary to what would naturally be expected. — **i ron′i cal ly,** *adv.*

**ir re cov er a ble** (ir′i kuv′ər ə bəl),

*adj.* **1** that cannot be regained or got back. **2** that cannot be remedied.

**ir re press i ble** (ir′i pres′ə bəl), *adj.* that cannot be restrained; uncontrollable.

**ir rev er ent** (i rev′ər ənt), *adj.* disrespectful. — **ir rev′er ent ly,** *adv.*

**ir rev o ca ble** (i rev′ə kə bəl), *adj.* **1** not able to be taken back; final. **2** impossible to call or bring back.

**jack pine** (jak′pīn′), *n.* a slender pine tree growing in barren or rocky soil in the northeastern and midwestern United States and in Canada.

**jamb** (jam), *n.* an upright piece forming the side of a doorway, window, or fireplace.

**jibe** (jīb), *v.i.* INFORMAL. be in harmony; agree.

**joc u lar** (jok′yə lər), *adj.* speaking or acting in jest; said or done in jest; funny; joking.

**jour ney man** (jėr′nē mən), *n.* **1** workman who knows his trade. **2** workman who has served his apprenticeship and is qualified to practice his trade, but has not become an employer or master workman.

**keel** (kēl), *n.* the main timber or steel piece that extends the whole length of the bottom of a ship or boat. The whole ship is built up on the keel.

**keen** (kēn), *adj.* **1** so shaped as to cut well. **2** sharp; piercing; cutting. **3** highly sensitive.

**kid** (kid), *n.* **1** a young goat. **2** leather made from its skin, used for gloves and shoes.

**kiln** (kil, kiln), *n.* furnace or oven for burning, baking, or drying something.

**kin dred** (kin′drid), *adj.* **1** related in character or properties; like; similar. **2** related by birth or descent.

**kirk** (kėrk), *n.* **1** SCOTTISH. church. **2 the Kirk,** the national church of Scotland; the Scottish Presbyterian Church as distinguished from the Church of England or the Scottish Episcopal Church.

**knell** (nel), *n.* **1** sound of a bell rung slowly after a death or at a funeral. **2** a warning sign of death, failure, etc. **3** a mournful sound.

**lace** (lās), *v.t.* INFORMAL. lash; beat; thrash.

**lac e ra tion** (las′ə rā′shən), *n.* a rough tear; mangled place.

**lack lus ter** (lak′lus′tər), *adj.* lacking

brightness; dull and drab.

**la con ic** (lə kon′ik), *adj.* using few words; brief in speech or expression; concise.

**la crosse** (lə krôs′, lə kros′), *n.* game played on a field with a ball and long-handled, loosely-strung rackets by two teams, usually of 10 players each. The players carry the ball in the rackets, trying to send it into the other team's goal.

**lag** (lag), *n.* **1** a barrel stave. **2** a stave, slat, or strip.

**la ment** (lə ment′), *v.t.* **1** express grief for. **2** regret. — *v.i.* express grief; mourn; weep.

**lam en ta ble** (lam′ən tə bəl), *adj.* **1** to be regretted or pitied. **2** inferior. **3** ARCHAIC. sorrowful. — **lam′en ta bly,** *adv.*

**lam en ta tion** (lam′ən tā′shən), *n.* loud grief; cries of sorrow; mourning; wailing.

**lan guid** (lang′gwid), *adj.* **1** without energy; drooping; weak; weary. **2** without interest or enthusiasm; indifferent; listless. **3** not brisk or lively; sluggish; dull.

**lar board** (lär′bərd, lär′bôrd, lär′bōrd), *n.* side of a ship to the left of a person looking from the stern toward the bow.

**lash** (lash), *v.t.* **1** beat or drive with a whip, etc.; flog. **2** attack severely in words.

**las si tude** (las′ə tüd, las′ə tyüd), *n.* lack of energy; weariness.

**lath** (lath), *n.* one of the thin, narrow strips of wood used to form a support for plaster or to make a lattice.

**lathe** (lāTH), *n.* machine for holding pieces of wood, metal, etc., and turning them rapidly against a cutting tool which shapes them.

**lau rel** (lôr′əl, lor′əl), *n.* a small evergreen tree with smooth, shiny leaves.

**ledg er** (lej′ər), *n.* book of accounts in which a business keeps a final record of all transactions.

**lee** (lē), *n.* **1** shelter; protection. **2** side or part sheltered or away from the wind.

**lee beam** (lē′ bēm′), *n.* a beam on the side of a ship that is farthest from the point from which the wind blows.

**leg a cy** (leg′ə sē), *n.* money or other property left to a person by the will of someone who has died.

**lest** (lest), *conj.* **1** for fear that. **2** that (after words meaning fear, danger, etc.).

**lin e age** (lin′ē ij), *n.* **1** descent in a direct line from a common ancestor. **2** the descendants of a common ancestor. **3** family or race.

**lin sey-wool sey** (lin′zē wul′zē), *n.* a strong, coarse fabric made of linen and wool or of cotton and wool.

**lis some** (lis′əm), *adj.* bending easily; limber.

**loathe** (lōTH), *v.t.* feel strong dislike and disgust for; hate.

**loath ing** (lō′THing), *n.* strong dislike and disgust.

**loath some** (lōTH′səm), *adj.* making one feel sick; disgusting.

**lob by** (lob′ē), *n.* **1** an entrance hall. **2** room or hall outside a legislative chamber. **3** person or group that tries to influence legislators.

**loft y** (lôf′tē, lof′tē), *adj.* **1** very high; towering. **2** exalted or dignified; grand. **3** proud; haughty. — **loft′i ly,** *adv.*

**loll** (lol), *v.i.* **1** recline or lean in a lazy manner. **2** hang loosely or droop.

**loom** (lüm), *v.i.* appear dimly or vaguely as a large, threatening shape.

**low-key** (lō′kē′), *adj.* understated; played down.

**lu cid** (lü′sid), *adj.* **1** marked by clearness of reasoning, expression, or arrangement; easy to follow or understand. **2** shining; bright; luminous.

**lu di crous** (lü′də krəs), *adj.* causing scornful laughter; amusingly absurd; ridiculous.

**lu gu bri ous** (lü gü′brē əs, lü gyü′brē-əs), *adj.* too sad; overly mournful. — **lu gu′bri ous ness,** *n.*

**lull** (lul), *v.i.* become calm or more nearly calm. — *n.* period of less noise or violence; brief calm.

**lu pin** (lü′pən), *n.* any of a large genus of plants of the pea family, having long spikes of flowers, radiating clusters of grayish, hairy leaflets, and flat pods with bean-shaped seeds.

**lur id** (lur′id), *adj.* **1** lighted up with a red or fiery glare. **2** glaring in brightness or color. **3** shockingly terrible, repulsive, etc.; sensational; startling.

**lu te fisk** (lüd′ ə fisk), *n.* NORWEGIAN. stockfish that have been soaked in lye water, skinned, boned, and boiled.

**lux ur i ant** (lug zhur′ē ənt, luk shur′ē-ənt), *adj.* growing thick and green; lush.

**ma ca bre** (mə kä′brə, mə kä′bər), *adj.* causing horror; gruesome; horrible; ghastly.

**mach i na tion** (mak′ə nā′shən, mash′ə-nā′shən), *n.* **1** evil or artful plotting; scheming against authority. **2** Usually, **machinations,** *pl.* an evil plot; secret or cunning scheme.

**Ma don na** (mə don′ə), *n.* **1** Mary, the mother of Jesus. **2** picture or statue of her.

**mag nan i mous** (mag nan′ə məs), *adj.* **1** noble in soul or mind; generous in forgiving; free from mean or petty feelings or

hat, āge, fär; let, ēqual, tėrm; it, īce; hot, ōpen, ôrder; oil, out; cup, put, rüle; ch, child; ng, long; sh, she; th, thin; ŦH, then; zh, measure.

ə represents *a* in about, *e* in taken, *i* in pencil, *o* in lemon, *u* in circus.

acts; unselfish. **2** showing or arising from a generous spirit.

**mag net ism** (mag′nə tiz′əm), *n.* power to attract or influence; personal charm.

**maim** (mām), *v.t.* cut off or make useless an arm, leg, ear, etc., of; cripple; disable.

**main spring** (mān′spring′), *n.* the main cause, motive, or influence.

**main tain** (mān tān′), *v.t.* **1** keep in existence or continuance. **2** support, uphold, or defend. **3** declare to be true.

**mal e dic tion** (mal′ə dik′shən), *n.* a calling forth of evil upon someone; curse.

**ma lev o lence** (mə lev′ə ləns), *n.* the wish that evil may happen to others; ill will; spite.

**ma lin ger** (mə ling′ger), *v.i.* pretend to be sick, injured, etc., in order to escape work or duty; shirk.

**mal treat** (mal trēt′), *v.t.* treat roughly or cruelly; abuse.

**man i fes ta tion** (man′ə fə stā′shən), *n.* a showing; making easy to see.

**man i fes to** (man′ə fes′tō), *n.* a public declaration of intentions, purposes, or motives by an important person or group.

**man-of-war** (man′əv wôr′), *n.* warship of a type used in former times.

**manse** (mans), *n.* parsonage, especially in Scotland.

**man tle** (man′tl), *n.* a loose cloak without sleeves.

**man za ni ta** (man′zə nē′tə), *n.* any of various evergreen shrubs or small trees that grow in western North America.

**ma ri a chi** (mär′ē ä′chē), *n.* member of a Mexican band of strolling singers and musicians.

**mar tyr** (mär′tər), *n.* person who chooses to die or suffer rather than renounce his religious faith.

**ma tri arch** (mā′trē ärk), *n.* **1** mother who is the ruler of a family or tribe. **2** an important, respected old woman, especially one who dominates the group of which she is a member.

**maud lin** (môd′lən), *adj.* sentimental in a weak, silly way.

**mav er ick** (mav′ər ik), *n.* U.S. **1** calf or other animal not marked with an owner's brand. **2** INFORMAL. person who refuses to affiliate with a regular political party.

**mea ger** (mē′gər), *adj.* **1** lacking fullness or richness; poor or scanty. **2** thin; lean.

**me di o cre** (mē′dē ō′kər, mē′dē ō′kər), *adj.* neither good nor bad; of average quality; ordinary.

**me di oc ri ty** (mē′dē ok′rə tē), *n.* mediocre quality.

**med i ta tive** (med′ə tā′tiv), *adj.* **1** fond of or given to meditating; thoughtful. **2** expressing meditation. — **med′i ta‑ tive ly**, *adv.*

**mel an chol y** (mel′ən kol′ē), *n.* condition of sadness and low spirits. — *adj.* **1** depressed in spirits; sad; gloomy.

**2** causing sadness; depressing.

**mel o dra mat ic** (mel′ə drə mat′ik), *adj.* of, like, or suitable for melodrama; sensational and exaggerated.

**me ni al** (mē′nē əl, mē′nyəl), *adj.* suited to or belonging to a servant; low; servile.

**me no rah** (mə nôr′ə, mə nōr′ə), *n.* candlestick with eight branches used during the Jewish festival of Hanukkah.

**mer can tile** (mėr′kən til, mėr′kən tīl), *adj.* of or having to do with merchants or trade; commercial.

**mer ce nar y** (mėr′sə ner′ē), *n.* soldier serving for pay in a foreign army.

**me squite** (me skēt′), *n.* a deep-rooted tree that often grows in dense clumps or thickets and bears pods that are used as livestock fodder.

**mess** (mes), *n.* group of people who take meals together regularly, especially such a group in the armed forces.

**met al lur gy** (met′l ėr′jē), *n.* science or art of working with metals.

**me thinks** (mi thingks′), *v.* ARCHAIC. it seems to me.

**me thod i cal** (mə thod′ə kəl), *adj.* done according to a method; systematic; orderly. — **me thod′i cal ly**, *adv.*

**me tic u lous** (mə tik′yə ləs), *adj.* extremely or excessively careful about small details.

**mien** (mēn), *n.* manner of holding the head and body; way of acting and looking; bearing.

**mill** (mil), *n.* machine for grinding grain into flour or meal. — *v.i.* move (around) in confusion.

**mirth** (mėrth), *n.* merry fun; being joyous or gay; merriment.

**mis giv ing** (mis giv′ing), *n.* a feeling of doubt, suspicion, or anxiety.

**mish mash** (mish′mash′), *n.* a confused mixture; hodgepodge; jumble.

**miz zen** (miz′n), *n.* a fore-and-aft sail, or mast nearest the stern.

**mode** (mōd), *n.* manner or way in which a thing is done; method.

**mod e ra tion** (mod′ə rā′shən), *n.* freedom from excess; proper restraint; control.

**mold er** (mōl′dər), *v.i.* turn into dust by natural decay; waste away; crumble.

**mol li fy** (mol′ə fī), *v.t.* soften in temper; calm, pacify; make less severe.

**mol ly cod dle** (mol′ē kod′l), *n.* person, especially a boy or man, accustomed to being fussed over and pampered.

**mo ral ize** (môr′ə līz, mor′ə līz), *v.i.* think, talk, or write about questions of right and wrong. — **mo′ral iz′er**, *n.*

**mo rass** (mə ras′), *n.* **1** piece of low, soft, wet ground; swamp; marsh. **2** a difficult situation; puzzling mess.

**mor row** (môr′ō, mor′ō), *n.* **1** the following day or time. **2** ARCHAIC. morning.

**mor ti fy** (môr′tə fī), *v.t.* wound the feelings of; make feel humbled and ashamed; humiliate.

**mor tise** (môr′tis), *n.* hole cut in or through one piece of wood to receive the

tenon on another piece so as to form a joint. — *v.t.* fasten or join by a mortise and tenon.

**mo ti vate** (mō′tə vāt), *v.t.* provide with a motive or incentive; cause to act.

**mot ley** (mot′lē), *adj.* made up of parts or kinds that are different or varied.

**mould er** (mōl′dər), *v.i.* molder.

**mus ing** (myü′zing), *adj.* meditative. *n.* meditation.

**mus ke toon** (mus′kə tün′), *n.* a short musket.

**mus ter** (mus′tər), *n.* **1** assembly; collection. **2** a bringing together of men or troops for review, service, roll call, etc.

**myr i ad** (mir′ē əd), *n.* **1** ten thousand. **2** a very great number.

**mys tic** (mis′tik), *adj.* **1** mystical. **2** of hidden meaning or nature; mysterious.

**mys ti cal** (mis′tə kəl), *adj.* **1** having some secret meaning; beyond human understanding; mysterious. **2** spiritually symbolic.

**na ïve** (nä ēv′), *adj.* simple in nature; like a child; not sophisticated.

**nar ra tive** (nar′ə tiv), *n.* story or account; tale.

**nat ur al ism** (nach′ər ə liz′əm), *n.* **1** (in art and literature) close adherence to nature and reality. **2** principles and methods of a group of writers of the late 1800's and early 1900's whose realism includes all the details however repulsive.

**nat ur al is tic** (nach′ər ə lis′tik), *adj.* of naturalism, especially in art or literature.

**nat ur al ize** (nach′ər ə līz), *v.t.* admit (a foreigner) to citizenship.

**neb u lous** (neb′yə ləs), *adj.* **1** hazy; vague; confused. **2** cloudlike.

**neg li gi ble** (neg′lə jə bəl), *adj.* that can be disregarded; unimportant; insignificant.

**nep o tism** (nep′ə tiz′əm), *n.* the showing of too much favor by one in power to his relatives, especially by giving them desirable positions.

**net tle** (net′l), *v.t.* sting the mind of; irritate.

**niche** (nich), *n.* **1** recess or hollow in a wall for a statue, vase, etc.; nook. **2** a suitable place or position; place for which a person is suited.

**nigh** (nī), *adv.* **1** near (in position, time, relationship, etc.) **2** nearly; almost. — *adj.* near; close. — *prep.* near. — *v.t., v.i.* draw near.

**noc tur nal** (nok tėr′nl), *adj.* of the night.

**noc turne** (nok′tėrn′), *n.* **1** a dreamy or pensive musical piece. **2** a painting of a night scene.

**nom i nal** (nom′ə nəl), *adj.* **1** existing in name only; not real. **2** too small to be considered.

**non cha lant** (non′shə lənt, non′shə‑ länt′), *adj.* without enthusiasm; indifferent. — **non′cha lant ly**, *adv.*

**non con form i ty** (non′kən fôr′mə tē), *n.* **1** lack of conformity; failure or refusal to act like others. **2** failure or refusal to conform to an established church.

**nos tal gia** (no stal′jə), *n.* a painful yearning for one's home, country, city, or for anything far removed in space or time.

**nos tal gic** (no stal′jik), *adj.* feeling or showing nostalgia.

**no to ri ous** (nō tôr′ē əs, nō tōr′ē əs), *adj.* well-known, especially because of something bad; having a bad reputation.

**not with stand ing** (not′wiŦH stan′ding, not′with stan′ding), *prep.* in spite of. — *adv.* in spite of it; nevertheless.

**nov ice** (nov′is), *n.* one who is new to what he is doing; beginner.

**nu ance** (nü äns′, nü′äns; nyü äns′, nyü′-äns), *n.* shade of expression, meaning, feeling, etc.

**nup tial** (nup′shəl), *adj.* of marriage or weddings.

**nur ture** (nėr′chər), *v.t.* bring up; care for; rear; train. — *n.* a bringing up; rearing; training; education.

**nuz zle** (nuz′əl), *v.i.* nestle; snuggle; cuddle.

**ob jec tive** (əb jek′tiv), *adj.* **1** existing outside the mind as something actual and not merely in the mind as an idea; real. **2** giving facts as they are without bias; impersonal.

**o blige** (ə blīj′), *v.t.* bind by a promise, contract, duty, etc.; force.

**o blique** (ə blēk′; *military* ə blīk′), *adj.* neither perpendicular to nor parallel with a given line or surface; slanting. — **o blique′ly,** *adv.*

**o bliv i ous** (ə bliv′ē əs), *adj.* not mindful; forgetful.

**ob nox ious** (əb nok′shəs), *adj.* very disagreeable; offensive; hateful.

**ob scure** (əb skyúr′), *adj.* **1** not clearly expressed; hard to understand. **2** not well known. **3** not easily discovered. **4** not distinct; not clear. — **ob scure′ly,** *adv.*

**ob scu ri ty** (əb skyúr′ə tē), *n.* **1** lack of clearness. **2** a little-known person or place.

**ob se qui ous** (əb sē′kwē əs), *adj.* polite or obedient from hope of gain or from fear.

**ob sess** (əb ses′), *v.t.* fill the mind of; keep the attention of to an unreasonable or unhealthy extent; haunt.

**ob strep er ous** (əb strep′ər əs), *adj.* **1** loud or noisy; boisterous. **2** unruly; disorderly.

**oc cult** (ə kult′, ok′ult), *adj.* **1** beyond the bounds of ordinary knowledge; mysterious. **2** outside the laws of the natural world; magical.

**o di ous** (ō′dē əs), *adj.* very displeasing; hateful; offensive.

**o fay** (ō′fā), *n.* a white person, usually used in an uncomplimentary way.

**off ing** (ô′fing, of′ing), *n.* **1** the more distant part of the sea as seen from the shore. **2 in the offing, a** just visible from the shore. **b** in the making.

**O lym pi ad** (ō lim′pē ad), *n.* **1** period of four years reckoned from one celebration of the Olympic games to the next, by which Greeks computed time from 776 B.C. **2** celebration of the modern Olympic games.

**om i nous** (om′ə nəs), *adj.* of bad omen; unfavorable; threatening.

**om ni bus** (om′nə bus), *n.* bus.

**om nip o tent** (om nip′ə tənt), *adj.* **1** having all power; almighty. **2** having very great power or influence.

**om nis cient** (om nish′ənt), *adj.* knowing everything; having complete or infinite knowledge.

**on er ous** (on′ər əs), *adj.* hard to take or carry; burdensome.

**on set** (ôn′set′, on′set′), *n.* **1** the beginning or start. **2** attack.

**op press** (ə pres′), *v.t.* **1** govern harshly; keep down unjustly or by cruelty. **2** weigh down; lie heavily on; burden.

**op pres sive** (ə pres′iv), *adj.* **1** hard to bear; burdensome. **2** harsh; unjust; tyrannical.

**op pro bri ous** (ə prō′brē əs), *adj.* **1** expressing scorn, reproach, or abuse. **2** disgraceful; shameful; infamous.

**op u lent** (op′yə lənt), *adj.* **1** having wealth; rich. **2** showing wealth; costly and luxurious. **3** abundant; plentiful.

**o ra cle** (ôr′ə kəl, or′ə kəl), *n.* **1** (in ancient Greece and Rome) an answer believed to be given by a god through a priest or priestess to some question. **2** the priest, priestess, or other means by which the god's answer was believed to be given. **3** a very wise person.

**or di na tion** (ôrd′n ā′shən), *n.* **1** act or ceremony of officially welcoming a clergyman into the ministry. **2** condition of being ordained as a clergyman.

**os ten ta tious** (os′ten tā′shəs), *adj.* **1** done for display. **2** showing off. — **os′-ten ta′tious ly,** *adv.*

**os tra cism** (os′trə siz′əm), *n.* **1** banishment from one's native country. **2** a being shut out from society, favor, privileges, or association with one's fellows.

**out crop** (out′krop), *n.* a coming (of a rock, stratum, etc.) to the surface of the earth.

**out land ish** (out lan′dish), *adj.* not familiar; strange or ridiculous; odd.

**out rage** (out′rāj), *n.* act showing no regard for the rights or feelings of others; an overturning of the rights of others by force.

**out rid er** (out′rī′dər), *n.* servant or attendant riding on a horse before or beside a carriage, wagon, etc.

**o ver bear ing** (ō′vər ber′ing, ō′vər-bar′ing), *adj.* inclined to dictate; forcing others to one's own will; domineering.

**o ver ture** (ō′vər chúr, ō′vər chər), *n.* proposal or offer.

**Ox ford** (ok′sfərd), *n.* **1** city in S England. **2** the very old and famous English university located there.

**pa cif ic** (pə sif′ik), *adj.* **1** tending to make peace. **2** loving peace; not warlike. **3** peaceful; calm; quiet.

**pa dro ne** (pä drō′nä *for 1;* pə drō′nē *for 2*), *n.* **1** ITALIAN. **a** master; boss. **b** innkeeper. **2** person who provides Italian laborers on contract with an employer, as in America.

**pa gan** (pā′gən), *n.* person who is not a Christian, Jew, or Moslem; one who worships many gods, or no gods. — *adj.* of or having to do with pagans.

**paint er** (pān′tər), *n.* a rope, usually fastened to the bow of a boat, for tying it to a ship, pier, etc.

**pai sa no** (pī sä′nō), *n.* **1** person of mixed Spanish and Indian ancestry living in California. **2** peasant.

**pa lav er** (pə lav′ər), *v.i.* **1** talk, especially talk profusely or unnecessarily. **2** talk fluently and flatteringly.

**pale** (pāl), *n.* a long, narrow board, pointed on top, used for fences; picket.

**pal ing** (pā′ling), *n.* fence of pales.

**pall** (pôl), *n.* **1** a heavy, dark cloth spread over a coffin, a hearse, or a tomb. **2** a dark, gloomy covering.

**pal lor** (pal′ər), *n.* lack of normal color from fear, illness, death, etc.; paleness.

**pal pa ble** (pal′pə bəl), *adj.* **1** readily seen or heard and recognized; obvious. **2** that can be touched or felt; tangible.

**pal try** (pôl′trē), *adj.* **1** almost worthless; trifling; petty. **2** of no worth; despicable; mean.

**pa lus tral** (pə lus′trəl), *adj.* marshy.

**par a dox i cal** (par′ə dok′sə kəl), *adj.* of paradoxes; involving a paradox.

**par al lel** (par′ə lel), *adj.* similar; corresponding; like.

**par al lel ism** (par′ə lel′iz′əm), *n.* **1** a being parallel. **2** likeness or similarity; correspondence. **3** parallel statements in writing, expressed in the same grammatical form.

**pa ri ah** (pə rī′ə, pär′ē ə), *n.* any person or

---

hat, āge, fär; let, ēqual, tėrm; it, īce; hot, ōpen, ôrder; oil, out; cup, pút, rüle; ch, child; ng, long; sh, she; th, thin; ŦH, then; zh, measure.

ə represents *a* in about, *e* in taken, *i* in pencil, *o* in lemon, *u* in circus.

animal generally despised; outcast.

**par ti al i ty** (pär/shē al/ə tē, pär shal/ə-
tē), *n.* 1 the favoring of one more than
another or others. 2 a particular liking;
fondness.

**par ti san** (pär/tə zən), *n.* a strong sup-
porter of a person, party, or cause; one
whose support is based on feeling rather
than on reasoning. — *adj.* of or like a
partisan.

**pas ta** (pä/stə), *n.* any of various foods, as
macaroni, spaghetti, etc., made of flour,
water, salt, and sometimes milk or eggs,
shaped in tubular or other forms and dried.

**pas tor al** (pas/tər əl), *adj.* 1 of shepherds
or country life. 2 simple or naturally beautiful like the country.

**pat ent** (pat/nt), *adj.* 1 given or protected
by a patent. 2 evident; plain.

**path o log i cal** (path/ə loj/ə kəl), *adj.*
1 of pathology; dealing or concerned with
diseases. 2 due to or accompanying disease. — **path/o log/i cal ly**, *adv.*

**pa thos** (pā/thos), *n.* quality in speech,
writing, music, events, or a scene that
arouses a feeling of pity or sadness; power
of evoking tender or melancholy emotion.

**pa tri arch** (pā/trē ärk), *n.* 1 father and
ruler of a family or tribe, especially one of
the ancestral figures in the Bible. 2 person
thought of as the father or founder of
something. 3 a venerable old man, especially the elder of a village, community, etc.

**pa tron ize** (pā/trə nīz, pat/rə nīz), *v.t.*
treat in a haughty, condescending way.

**paunch** (pônch, pänch), *n.* 1 belly; stomach. 2 a large, protruding belly; pot-
belly.

**paunch y** (pôn/chē, pän/chē), *adj.* having
a big paunch.

**peak ed** (pē/kid), *adj.* sickly in appearance; wan; thin.

**peal** (pēl), *n.* 1 a loud, long sound. 2 the
loud ringing of bells.

**pe cul iar** (pi kyü/lyər), *adj.* 1 out of the
ordinary; strange; odd; unusual. 2 belonging to one person or thing and not to
another.

**pee vish** (pē/vish), *adj.* 1 feeling cross;
fretful; complaining. 2 showing annoyance
or irritation.

**pel let** (pel/it), *n.* a little ball of mud,
paper, food, medicine, etc.; pill. — *v.t.* hit
with pellets.

**pen sive** (pen/siv), *adj.* thoughtful in a
serious or sad way.

**pent-up** (pent/up/), *adj.* shut up; closely
confined.

**per ceive** (pər sēv/), *v.t.* 1 be aware of
through the senses; see, hear, taste, smell,
or feel. 2 take in with the mind; observe;
understand.

**per func to ry** (pər fungk/tər ē), *adj.*
done merely for the sake of getting rid of
the duty; done from force of habit; mechanical; indifferent.

**pe riph er y** (pə rif/ər ē), *n.* an outside
boundary.

**per me ate** (pèr/mē āt), *v.t.* spread
through the whole of; pass through.

**per se ver ance** (pèr/sə vir/əns), *n.* a
sticking to a purpose or an aim.

**per se vere** (pèr/sə vir/), *v.i.* continue
steadily in doing something hard; persist.

**per son a ble** (pèr/sə nə bəl), *adj.* having
a pleasing appearance; good-looking; attractive.

**per spi cu i ty** (pèr/spə kyü/ə tē), *n.* ease
in being understood; clearness in expression.

**per ti nac i ty** (pèrt/n as/ə tē), *n.* great
persistence; holding firmly to a purpose,
action, or opinion.

**per vade** (pər vād/), *v.t.* go or spread
throughout.

**per verse** (pər vèrs/), *adj.* 1 contrary and
willful; obstinately opposing what is wanted, reasonable, or required. 2 persistent in
wrong. 3 morally bad.

**pes ti lence** (pes/tl əns), *n.* any infectious
or contagious epidemic disease that spreads
rapidly, often causing many deaths.

**pe tite** (pə tēt/), *adj.* of small stature or
size; little, especially with reference to a
woman or girl.

**pet ri fy** (pet/rə fī), *v.t.* paralyze with fear,
horror, or surprise.

**pet tish** (pet/ish), *adj.* peevish; cross.

**pe wee** (pē/wē), *n.* any (bird) of several
small American flycatchers with an olive-
colored or gray back.

**pew ter** (pyü/tər), *n.* alloy of tin with lead,
copper, or other metals. — *adj.* made of
pewter.

**phan tasm** (fan/taz/əm), *n.* 1 thing seen
only in one's imagination; unreal fancy. 2 a
supposed appearance of an absent person,
living or dead. 3 a deceiving likeness (of
something).

**phe nom e non** (fə nom/ə non), *n.* fact,
event, or circumstance that can be observed.

**phi los o pher** (fə los/ə fər), *n.* student,
teacher, or lover of philosophy.

**phi los o phy** (fə los/ə fē), *n.* study of the
truth or principles underlying all real
knowledge; study of the most general causes and principles of the universe.

**phleg mat ic** (fleg mat/ik), *adj.* 1 not
easily aroused to feeling or action; sluggish;
indifferent. 2 cool; calm.

**phos pho res cence** (fos/fə res/ns), *n.*
1 act or process of giving out light without burning or by very slow burning without
noticeable heat. 2 light given out in this
way.

**pic tur esque** (pik/chə resk/), *adj.* quaint
or interesting enough to be used as the
subject of a picture.

**piece work** (pēs/wèrk/), *n.* work paid for
by the amount done, not by the time it
takes.

**pil lage** (pil/ij), *v.t.* rob with violence;
plunder.

**pil lor y** (pil/ər ē), *n.* frame of wood with

holes through which a person's head and
hands were put formerly in a public place as
punishment for an offense. — *v.t.* 1 put in
the pillory. 2 expose to public ridicule,
contempt, or abuse.

**pince-nez** (pans/nā/, pins/nā/), *n.* eyeglasses kept in place by a spring that clips on
to the bridge of the nose.

**pine** (pīn), *v.i.* 1 long eagerly; yearn.
2 waste away with pain, hunger, grief, or
desire.

**pin ion** (pin/yən), *v.t.* bind; bind the arms
of; bind (to something.)

**pip** (pip), *n.* a contagious disease of poultry
and other birds, characterized by the secre-
tion of thick mucus in the mouth and throat
and sometimes by white scale on the
tongue.

**pip ing** (pī/ping), *adj.* sounding shrilly;
shrill.

**pique** (pēk), *v.t.* arouse; stir up.

**pi qué** (pi kā/), *n.* fabric of cotton, rayon,
or silk, with narrow ribs or raised stripes.

**pit** (pit), *v.t.* set to fight or compete; match.

**pitch y** (pich/ē), *adj.* 1 full of pitch. 2 like
pitch; sticky. 3 black.

**pith** (pith), *n.* the central column of spongy
tissue in the stems of most herbaceous
plants and of some trees.

**plain tive** (plān/tiv), *adj.* expressive of
sorrow; mournful; sad. — **plain/tive ly**,
*adv.*

**plait** (plāt, plat), *n.* braid.

**plash** (plash), *n.* splash.

**plau si ble** (plô/zə bəl), *adj.* 1 appearing
true, reasonable, or fair. 2 apparently worthy of confidence but often not really so.

**plen i tude** (plen/ə tüd, plen/ə tyüd), *n.*
fullness; completeness; abundance.

**plumb** (plum), *n.* a small weight used on
the end of a line to find the depth of water
or to see if a wall is vertical.

**plumb line**, *n.* line with a plumb at the
end, used to find the depth of water or to
test the straightness of a wall.

**plun der** (plun/dər), *v.t.* rob by force; rob.

**ply** (plī), *v.t.* keep up work on; work away at
or on.

**pock mark** (pok/märk/), *n.* mark or pit
on the skin; pock.

**po grom** (pō grom/, pō/grəm), *n.* an organized massacre, especially of Jews.

**po lar i ty** (pō lar/ə tē), *n.* possession or
exhibition of two opposite or contrasted
principles or tendencies.

**po lar ize** (pō/lə rīz/), *v.t.* give polarity to;
cause polarization in.

**pol i tic** (pol/ə tik), *adj.* 1 wise in looking
out for one's own interests; prudent;
shrewd. 2 showing wisdom or shrewdness.
3 scheming; crafty. 4 political.

**Pol ly an na** (pol/ē an/ə), *n.* person who
is untiringly cheerful and optimistic about
everything and everyone.

**pom mel** (pum/əl, pom/əl), *n.* part of a
saddle that sticks up at the front.

**pom pos i ty** (pom pos/ə tē), *n.* pompous
quality.

**pom pous** (pom/pəs), *adj.* trying to seem

magnificent or very important; self-important.

**pone** (pōn), *n.* U.S. bread made of corn meal, popular in the southern United States.

**pore** (pôr, pōr), *v.i.* 1 gaze earnestly or steadily. 2 study long and steadily.

**pose** (pōz), *n.* 1 position of the body. 2 attitude assumed for effect. — *v.i.* put forward for discussion; state.

**pos sess** (pə zes′), *v.t.* 1 own. 2 hold as property. 3 control; influence strongly. 4 control by an evil spirit.

**prec e dence** (pres′ə dəns, pri sēd′ns), *n.* 1 higher position or rank; greater importance. 2 right to precede others in ceremonies or social affairs; social superiority.

**prec i pice** (pres′ə pis), *n.* a very steep or almost vertical face of a rock, etc.; cliff, crag, or steep mountainside.

**pre cip i tate** (pri sip′ə tit, pri sip′ə tāt), *adj.* 1 very hurried; sudden. 2 with great haste and force; plunging or rushing headlong; hasty; rash.

**pre em i nent** (prē em′ə nənt), *adj.* standing out above all others; superior to others. — **pre em′i nent ly,** *adv.*

**preen** (prēn), *v.t.* dress (oneself) carefully; primp.

**pre oc cu pa tion** (prē ok′yə pā′shən), *n.* condition of being preoccupied; absorption.

**pre oc cu pied** (prē ok′yə pīd), *adj.* absorbed; engrossed.

**prep** (prep), INFORMAL. *adj.* preparatory. — *n.* preparatory school.

**pre pos ter ous** (pri pos′tər əs), *adj.* contrary to nature, reason, or common sense; absurd; senseless.

**Pres by ter i an** (prez′bə tir′ē ən, pres′-bə tir′ē ən), *adj.* of or belonging to a Protestant denomination or church governed by elected presbyters or elders all of equal rank and having beliefs based on Calvinism. — *n.* member of a Presbyterian church.

**pre sen ti ment** (pri zen′tə mənt), *n.* a feeling or impression that something, especially something evil, is about to happen; vague sense of approaching misfortune; foreboding.

**pres tige** (pre stēzh′, pre stēj′), *n.* reputation, influence, or distinction based on what is known of one's abilities, achievements, opportunities, associations, etc.

**pre tense** (prē′tens, pri tens′), *n.* 1 make-believe; pretending. 2 a false appearance. Also, **pretence.**

**pre vail** (pri vāl′), *v.i.* 1 be the most usual or strongest. 2 be the stronger; win the victory; succeed.

**prim** (prim), *adj.* stiffly precise, neat, proper, or formal. — **prim′ly,** *adv.*

**pri ma don na** (prē′mə don′ə), *n.* 1 the principal woman singer in an opera. 2 a temperamental person.

**prith ee** (priᴛʜ′ē), *interj.* ARCHAIC. I pray thee; I ask you.

**pro ceed ing** (prə sē′ding), *n.* 1 what is done; action; conduct. 2 **proceedings,** *pl.* a action in a case in a court of law. b record of what was done at the meetings of a society, club, etc.

**proc tor** (prok′tər), *n.* official in a university or school designated to supervise students, especially during an examination.

**pro cure** (prə kyùr′), *v.t.* 1 obtain by care or effort; secure. 2 bring about; cause.

**prod** (prod), *v.t.* 1 poke or jab with something pointed. 2 stir up; urge on.

**prod i gal** (prod′ə gəl), *adj.* given to extravagant or reckless spending; wasteful.

**prod i gy** (prod′ə jē), *n.* 1 person endowed with amazing brilliance, talent, etc., especially a remarkably talented child. 2 a marvelous example.

**pro fane** (prə fān′), *adj.* 1 characterized by contempt or disregard for God or holy things. 2 not sacred; worldly.

**pro fess** (prə fes′), *v.t.* 1 lay claim to; pretend; claim. 2 declare one's belief in.

**pro fi cien cy** (prə fish′ən sē), *n.* a being proficient; knowledge; skill; advanced state of expertness.

**pro fu sion** (prə fyü′zhən), *n.* great abundance.

**pro jec tile** (prə jek′təl), *n.* any object that is thrown, hurled, or shot, such as a stone or bullet.

**pro lif ic** (prə lif′ik), *adj.* 1 producing offspring or fruit abundantly. 2 highly productive; fertile.

**prompt** (prompt), *v.t.* 1 cause (someone) to do something. 2 give rise to; suggest; inspire.

**pro nounce ment** (prə nouns′mənt), *n.* 1 a formal or authoritative statement; declaration. 2 opinion or decision.

**pro pi tious** (prə pish′əs), *adj.* holding well; favorable.

**pro pri e ty** (prə prī′ə tē), *n.* 1 quality or condition of being proper; fitness. 2 proper behavior.

**pro sa ic** (prō zā′ik), *adj.* like prose; matter-of-fact; ordinary; not exciting.

**pro sce ni um** (prō sē′nē əm), *n.* the part of the stage in front of the curtain.

**pro scrip tion** (prō skrip′shən), *n.* a proscribing or a being proscribed; banishment.

**pros e lyte** (pros′ə līt), *n.* person who has been converted from one opinion, religious belief, etc., to another.

**pros pect** (pros′pekt), *n.* 1 thing expected or looked forward to. 2 act of looking forward; expectation. — *v.i.* explore a region for oil, gold, or other minerals.

**pro spec tive** (prə spek′tiv), *adj.* that is looked forward to as likely or promised; probable; expected.

**pro té gé** (prō′tə zhā), *n.* person who has been taken under the protection or kindly care of a friend or patron.

**prot es ta tion** (prot′ə stā′shən), *n.* 1 a solemn declaration; protesting. 2 a protest.

**pro to type** (prō′tə tīp), *n.* the first or primary type of anything; the original or model.

**prov i dence** (prov′ə dəns), *n.* 1 God's care and help. 2 **Providence,** God. 3 instance of God's care and help.

**prov ince** (prov′əns), *n.* 1 one of the main divisions of a country. 2 **the provinces,** part of a country outside the capital or the largest cities.

**pro vin cial** (prə vin′shəl), *adj.* 1 having the manners, speech, dress, point of view, etc., of people living in a province. 2 lacking refinement or polish; narrow. — **pro vin′cial ly,** *adv.*

**pro vi sion** (prə vizh′ən), *n.* 1 statement making a condition. 2 care taken for the future. 3 supply; food. — *v.t.* supply with provisions.

**prov o ca tion** (prov′ə kā′shən), *n.* 1 act of provoking. 2 something that stirs up or provokes.

**pro voke** (prə vōk′), *v.t.* 1 make angry. 2 stir up; excite.

**prow** (prou), *n.* the front part of a ship or boat; bow.

**pru dence** (prüd′ns), *n.* 1 wise thought before acting; good judgment. 2 good management; economy.

**pru dent** (prüd′nt), *adj.* 1 planning carefully ahead of time; sensible. 2 characterized by good judgment or good management. — **pru′dent ly,** *adv.*

**pru den tial** (prü den′shəl), *adj.* of, marked by, or showing prudence.

**psy che** (sī′kē), *n.* 1 the human soul or spirit. 2 the mind.

**puce** (pyüs), *n.* purplish brown.

**pul let** (pùl′it), *n.* a young hen, usually less than a year old.

**pul que** (pùl′kē), *n.* an alcoholic beverage made from the fermented juice of certain maguey plants, much used in Mexico and Central America.

**pul sate** (pul′sāt), *v.i.* 1 expand and contract rhythmically, as the heart or an artery; beat; throb. 2 vibrate; quiver.

**pul sa tion** (pul sā′shən), *n.* 1 a beating; throbbing. 2 vibration; quiver.

**pun cheon** (pun′chən), *n.* a large cask for liquor, varying in size from 70 to 120 gallons.

---

hat, āge, fär; let, ēqual, tėrm; it, īce; hot, ōpen, ôrder; oil, out; cup, pùt, rüle; ch, child; ng, long; sh, she; th, thin; ᴛʜ, then; zh, measure.

ə represents *a* in about, *e* in taken, *i* in pencil, *o* in lemon, *u* in circus.

**punch y** (pun′chē), *adj.* INFORMAL. forceful.

**purl** (pėrl), *v.i.* flow with rippling motions and a murmuring sound.

**pu tres cent** (pyü tres′nt), *adj.* rotting.

**qua dran gu lar** (kwo drang′gyə lər), *adj.* having four corners or angles.

**quag mire** (kwag′mīr′, kwog′mīr′), *n.* 1 soft, muddy ground. 2 a difficult situation.

**quail** (kwāl), *v.i.* be afraid; lose courage; shrink back in fear.

**Quak er** (kwā′kər), *n.* member of a Christian group called the Society of Friends, founded by George Fox about 1650, whose principles and practices include the observance of simplicity in religious worship, manners, etc., and opposition to war and to taking oaths; Friend.

**qual i fy** (kwol′ə fī), *v.t.* 1 make fit or competent. 2 change somewhat.

**quea sy** (kwē′zē), *adj.* inclined to nausea; easily upset.

**quer u lous** (kwer′ə ləs, kwer′yə ləs), *adj.* complaining; fretful; cross. — **quer′u lous ly,** *adv.*

**ques tion** (kwes′chən), *v.t.* 1 ask a question or questions of; seek information from. 2 ask or inquire about. 3 doubt; dispute. — **ques′tion ing ly,** *adv.*

**rab id** (rab′id), *adj.* 1 unreasonably extreme; fanatical; violent. 2 furious; raging.

**rag a muf fin** (rag′ə muf′ən), *n.* a ragged, disreputable fellow.

**ram pant** (ram′pənt), *adj.* angry; violent.

**ran cor** (rang′kər), *n.* bitter resentment or ill will; extreme hatred or spite.

**rang y** (rān′jē), *adj.* 1 fitted for ranging or moving about. 2 slender and long-limbed.

**rap scal lion** (rap skal′yən), *n.* rascal; rogue; scamp.

**rapt** (rapt), *adj.* lost in delight.

**rasp** (rasp), *v.i.* make a harsh, grating sound. — *v.t.* 1 utter with a grating sound. 2 have a harsh or irritating effect on.

**rasp y** (ras′pē), *adj.* 1 grating; harsh; rough. 2 irritable.

**ra tion al** (rash′ə nəl), *adj.* 1 reasoned out; sensible; reasonable. 2 able to think and reason clearly. — **ra′tion al ly,** *adv.*

**raunch y** (rôn′chē), *adj.* 1 SLANG. sloppy; shabby. 2 noisy.

**rav age** (rav′ij), *v.t.* damage greatly; lay waste; destroy. — *n.* violence; destruction.

**rav en ous** (rav′ə nəs), *adj.* 1 very hungry. 2 greedy.

**realm** (relm), *n.* region or sphere in which something rules or prevails.

**re buff** (ri buf′), *n.* a blunt or sudden check to a person who makes advances, offers help, makes a request, etc. — *v.t.* give a rebuff to.

**re cep tiv i ty** (rē′sep tiv′ə tē), *n.* ability or readiness to receive.

**re cess** (rē′ses, ri ses′), *n.* 1 part in a wall set back from the rest; alcove. 2 quiet, secluded place.

**re cip ro cate** (ri sip′rə kāt), *v.t.* give, do, feel, or show in return.

**reck on ing** (rek′ə ning), *n.* 1 method of computing; count; calculation. 2 settlement of an account.

**rec og nize** (rek′əg nīz), *v.t.* acknowledge; accept; admit.

**re dound** (ri dound′), *v.i.* come back as a result; contribute.

**re flec tion** (ri flek′shən), *n.* 1 thinking, especially careful thinking. 2 idea or remark resulting from careful thinking; idea; remark.

**re flec tive** (ri flek′tiv), *adj.* thoughtful. — **re flec′tive ly,** *adv.*

**re frain** (ri frān′), *v.i.* hold oneself back, especially from satisfying a momentary impulse.

**re gard** (ri gärd′), *v.t.* 1 think of; consider or look on. 2 show thought or consideration for. — *n.* 1 consideration; thought; care. 2 a steady look; gaze.

**reg is trar** (rej′ə strär, rej′ə strär′), *n.* official who keeps a register; official recorder.

**re im burse** (rē′im bėrs′), *v.t.* pay back; repay (a person or a sum expended).

**re join der** (ri join′dər), *n.* an answer to a reply; response.

**re lent** (ri lent′), *v.i.* become less harsh or cruel; be more tender and merciful.

**rel e vant** (rel′ə vənt), *adj.* bearing upon or connected with the matter in hand; to the point.

**re lief** (ri lēf′), *n.* 1 projection of figures or designs from a surface in sculpture, drawing, or painting. 2 figure or design standing out from the surface from which it is cut, shaped, or stamped.

**re li gious** (ri lij′əs), *adj.* very careful; strict; scrupulous. — **re li′gious ly,** *adv.*

**re lin quish** (ri ling′kwish), *v.t.* 1 give up; let go; release. 2 abandon.

**re mote** (ri mōt′), *adj.* far away; far off.

**rend** (rend), *v.t.* 1 pull apart violently; tear. 2 split.

**ren dez vous** (rän′də vü), *n.* an appointment or engagement to meet at a fixed place or time; meeting by agreement.

**re nounce** (ri nouns′), *v.t.* declare that one gives up; give up entirely; give up.

**ren o vate** (ren′ə vāt), *v.t.* make new again; restore to good condition.

**re plete** (ri plēt′), *adj.* abundantly supplied; filled.

**re pose** (ri pōz′), *n.* 1 rest or sleep. 2 quietness; ease. 3 peace; calmness.

**re press** (ri pres′), *v.t.* 1 prevent from acting; check; curb. 2 keep down; put down; suppress.

**re pres sion** (ri presh′ən), *n.* act of repressing.

**rep ri mand** (rep′rə mand), *v.t.* fault severely or formally; express disapproval of.

**re pulse** (ri puls′), *v.t.* 1 drive back; repel. 2 refuse to accept; reject.

**re pul sive** (ri pul′siv), *adj.* 1 causing strong dislike. 2 tending to drive back or repel.

**rep u ta ble** (rep′yə tə bəl), *adj.* having a good reputation; well thought of; in good repute. — **rep′u ta bly,** *adv.*

**re pute** (ri pyüt′), *n.* 1 reputation. 2 good reputation.

**re serve** (ri zėrv′), *n.* 1 act of keeping back or holding back. 2 act or condition of being kept, set apart, or saved for use later. 3 a keeping one's thoughts, feelings, and affairs to oneself; self-restraint in action or speech.

**res i due** (rez′ə dü, rez′ə dyü), *n.* what remains after a part is taken; remainder.

**res ig na tion** (rez′ig nā′shən), *n.* patient acceptance; quiet submission.

**re source ful** (ri sôrs′fəl, ri sōrs′fəl), *adj.* good at thinking of ways to do things; quick-witted.

**re spec tive ly** (ri spek′tiv lē), *adv.* as regards each of several persons or things in turn or in the order mentioned.

**res pite** (res′pit), *n.* time of relief and rest; lull.

**res to ra tion** (res′tə rā′shən), *n.* 1 a restoring; establishing again. 2 a bringing back to a former condition.

**re straint** (ri strānt′), *n.* 1 a restraining; holding back or hindering from action or motion. 2 tendency to restrain natural feeling; reserve.

**re sult** (ri zult′), *n.* that which happens because of something.

**re sult ant** (ri zult′nt), *adj.* that results; resulting.

**re tal i ate** (ri tal′ē āt), *v.i.* pay back wrong, injury, etc.; return like for like, usually to return evil for evil.

**re tar da tion** (re′tär dā′shən), *n.* 1 act of retarding or slowing. 2 that which retards; hindrance.

**ret i cule** (ret′ə kyül), *n.* a woman's small handbag, especially one with a drawstring.

**ret ri bu tion** (ret′rə byü′shən), *n.* a deserved punishment; return for evil done.

**ret ro gress** (ret′rə gres, ret′rə gres′), *v.i.* 1 move backward, especially to an earlier or less advanced condition. 2 become worse. — **ret′ro gres′sion,** *n.*

**rev el** (rev′əl), *v.i.* take pleasure *(in)*.

**re ver ber ate** (ri vėr′bə rāt′), *v.i.* echo back. — *v.t.* reecho (a sound or noise). — **re ver′be ra′tion,** *n.*

**re vere** (ri vir′), *v.t.* love and respect deeply; honor greatly.

**rev er ie** (rev′ər ē), *n.* 1 dreamy thoughts; dreamy thinking of pleasant things. 2 condition of being lost in dreamy thoughts.

**re vi tal ize** (rē vī′tə līz), *v.t.* restore to vitality; put new life into.

**rib** (rib), *n.* one of the curved timbers in a ship's frame.

**ridge pole** (rij′pōl′), *n.* the horizontal timber along the top of a roof or tent.

**rift** (rift), *n.* an opening or break in clouds or mist. — *v.t., v.i.* split.

**right eous** (rī′chəs), *adj.* **1** doing right; behaving justly. **2** proper; just; right. — **right′eous ness,** *n.*

**rig or ous** (rig′ər əs), *adj.* **1** severe; strict. **2** thoroughly logical and scientific; exact.

**riv en** (riv′ən), *adj.* torn apart; split.

**riv u let** (riv′yə lit), *n.* a very small stream.

**rock-ribbed** (rok′ribd′), *adj.* **1** having ridges of rock. **2** unyielding; rigid; inflexible.

**roust** (roust), *v.t.* INFORMAL. force out; move; stir.

**row lock** (rō′lok′), *n.* oarlock.

**rud dy** (rud′ē), *adj.* red or reddish.

**rue** (rü), *n.* a strong-smelling, woody herb of the same family as the citrus, with yellow flowers, and bitter leaves that were formerly much used in medicine.

**run a gate** (run′ə gāt′), *n.* ARCHAIC. **1** runaway. **2** vagabond; wanderer.

**sa ble** (sā′bəl), *adj.* ARCHAIC. black; dark.

**saf fron** (saf′rən), *n.* an orange yellow.

**sa ga cious** (sə gā′shəs), *adj.* **1** wise in a keen, practical way; shrewd. **2** intelligent.

**sage** (sāj), *n.* a very wise man.

**sa ke** (sä′kē), *n.* an alcoholic beverage made from a fermented mash of rice, popular in Japan.

**sal ly** (sal′ē), *v.i.* **1** go suddenly from a defensive position to attack an enemy. **2** rush forth suddenly; go out.

**salt y** (sôl′tē), *adj.* **1** containing salt; tasting of salt. **2** brief, witty, and a bit improper.

**sam o var** (sam′ə vär, sam′ə vär′), *n.* a metal urn used for heating water for tea.

**sam u rai** (sam′u̇ rī′), *n.* **1** the military class in feudal Japan, consisting of the retainers of the great nobles. **2** member of this class.

**sanc ti ty** (sangk′tə tē), *n.* **1** holiness of life; saintliness; godliness. **2** holy character; sacredness.

**sap** (sap), *v.t.* **1** dig under or wear away the foundation of. **2** weaken; use up.

**sau cy** (sô′sē), *adj.* **1** showing lack of respect; impudent; rude. **2** pert; smart. — **sau′ci ly,** *adv.*

**sa van na** (sə van′ə), *n.* **1** a treeless plain in the southeastern United States or tropical America. **2** grassland with scattered trees between the equatorial forests and the hot deserts in either hemisphere.

**sa vant** (sə vänt′, sav′ənt), *n.* scholar.

**save** (sāv), *prep.* except; but. — *conj.* excepting.

**scal a ble** (skā′lə bəl), *adj.* that can be scaled or climbed.

**scant** (skant), *adj.* **1** not enough in size or quantity; poor. **2** barely enough.

**scathe less** (skāᴛʜ′lis), *adj.* without harm; unhurt.

**scowl** (skoul), *v.i.* look angry or sullen by lowering the eyebrows; frown. — *n.* an angry, sullen look; frown.

**scrape** (skrāp), *n.* situation hard to get out of; difficulty.

**scru ple** (skrü′pəl), *n.* **1** a feeling of doubt about what one ought to do. **2** a feeling of uneasiness that keeps a person from doing something.

**scru pu lous** (skrü′pyə ləs), *adj.* **1** very careful to do what is right; conscientious. **2** attending thoroughly to details; very careful. — **scru′pu lous ly,** *adv.*

**scru ti ny** (skrüt′n ē), *n.* **1** close examination; careful inspection. **2** a looking searchingly at something; searching gaze.

**scud** (skud), *v.i.* run or move swiftly. — *n.* clouds or spray driven by the wind.

**scull** (skul), *n.* oar worked with a side twist over the stern of a boat to propel it. — *v.t.* propel (a boat) by a scull or by sculls.

**scut tle** (skut′l), *v.i.* run with quick, hurried steps; scamper; scurry.

**sec re tar i at** (sek′rə ter′ē it, sek′rə ter′ē at), *n.* **1** group of secretaries. **2** place where a secretary transacts business.

**se duce** (si düs′, si dyüs′), *v.t.* **1** tempt to wrongdoing; persuade to do wrong. **2** lead away from virtue.

**seer** (sir), *n.* person who foresees or foretells future events; prophet.

**seethe** (sēᴛʜ), *v.i.* be excited; be disturbed.

**sem i nar** (sem′ə när), *n.* **1** group of students engaged in discussion and research under the guidance of a professor. **2** course of study or work for such a group.

**sen ti nel** (sen′tə nəl), *n.* **1** person stationed to keep watch and guard against surprise attacks. **2 stand sentinel,** keep watch.

**sep ul cher** (sep′əl kər), *n.* place of burial; tomb; grave. Also, **sepulchre.**

**se pul chral** (sə pul′krəl), *adj.* **1** of sepulchers or tombs. **2** deep and gloomy; dismal; suggesting a tomb.

**sep ul chre** (sep′əl kər), *n., v.t.* sepulcher.

**ser aph** (ser′əf), *n.* one of the highest order of angels.

**sere** (sir), *adj.* ARCHAIC. dried; withered.

**se rene** (sə rēn′), *adj.* peaceful; calm.

**se ren i ty** (sə ren′ə tē), *n.* **1** peace and quiet; calmness. **2** clearness; brightness.

**ser vile** (sėr′vəl), *adj.* **1** like that of slaves; mean; base. **2** of or having to do with slaves. **3** yielding through fear, lack of spirit, etc.

**ser vi tude** (sėr′və tüd, sėr′və tyüd), *n.* **1** condition of being a slave; slavery; bondage. **2** forced labor as punishment.

**shack le** (shak′əl), *n.* **1** a metal band fastened around the ankle or wrist of a prisoner, slave, etc. Shackles are usually fastened to each other, the wall, floor, etc., by chains. **2 shackles,** *pl.* anything that prevents freedom of action, thought, etc.

**sheath ing** (shē′ᴛʜing, shē′thing), *n.* casing; covering.

**sheen** (shēn), *n.* brightness; luster.

**sheen y** (shē′nē), *adj.* bright; lustrous.

**sheer** (shir), *adj.* **1** very thin; almost transparent. **2** unmixed with anything else; complete.

**shin** (shin), *v.i., v.t.* climb by clasping or holding fast with the hands or arms and legs and drawing oneself up.

**shirk** (shėrk), *v.t., v.i.* avoid or get out of doing (work, a duty, etc.).

**shirr** (shėr), *v.t.* draw up or gather (cloth) on parallel threads.

**short com ing** (shôrt′kum′ing), *n.* fault; defect.

**shroud** (shroud), *n.* **1** cloth or garment in which a dead person is wrapped or dressed for burial. **2** something that covers, conceals, or veils. — *v.t.* cover; conceal.

**si dle** (sī′dl), *v.i.* **1** move sideways. **2** move sideways slowly so as not to attract attention.

**sig ni fy** (sig′nə fī), *v.t.* be a sign of; mean.

**sil i cate** (sil′ə kit, sil′ə kāt), *n.* compound containing silicon with oxygen and metal.

**silt** (silt), *n.* very fine particles of earth, sand, etc., carried by moving water and deposited as sediment.

**sim plic i ty** (sim plis′ə tē), *n.* **1** a being simple. **2** freedom from difficulty; clearness. **3** plainness. **4** absence of show or pretense; sincerity.

**si mul ta ne ous** (sī′məl tā′nē əs, sim′əl-tā′nē əs), *adj.* existing, done, or happening at the same time. — **si′mul ta′ne ous ly,** *adv.*

**sin ew** (sin′yü), *n.* **1** tendon. **2** strength; energy; force. **3** means of strength.

**sing song** (sing′sông′, sing′song′), *n.* a monotonous, up-and-down rhythm.

**sin gu lar** (sing′gyə lər), *adj.* extraordinary; unusual.

**sin gu lar i ty** (sing′gyə lar′ə tē), *n.* **1** condition or quality of being singular. **2** something singular; peculiarity; oddity.

**sin is ter** (sin′ə stər), *adj.* **1** showing ill will; threatening. **2** bad; evil; dishonest.

**skiff** (skif), *n.* **1** a small, light rowboat. **2** a

hat, āge, fär; let, ēqual, tėrm; it, īce; hot, ōpen, ôrder; oil, out; cup, pu̇t, rüle; ch, child; ng, long; sh, she; th, thin; ᴛʜ, then; zh, measure.

ə represents *a* in about, *e* in taken, *i* in pencil, *o* in lemon, *u* in circus.

small, light boat with a mast for a single triangular sail.

**ski jor ing** (skē′jôr′ing), *n.* a winter sport in which a person wearing skis is drawn over snow or ice by a horse or vehicle.

**skirl** (skėrl), *n.* sound of a bagpipe.

**skoal** (skōl), *n., interj.* a Scandinavian word used in drinking a toast to health. It means "May you prosper."

**skulk** (skulk), *v.i.* move in a stealthy, sneaking way.

**skull cap** (skul′kap′), *n.* a close-fitting cap without a brim.

**slake** (slāk), *v.t.* satisfy (thirst, revenge, wrath, etc.).

**sla lom** (slä′ləm, slal′əm), *n.* (in skiing) a zigzag race downhill.

**slav ish** (slā′vish), *adj.* 1 like a slave; mean. 2 weakly submitting.

**sloop** (slüp), *n.* a sailboat.

**sloth** (slôth, slōth), *n.* unwillingness to work or exert oneself; laziness; idleness.

**slough** (slü), *n.* a swampy place; marshy inlet.

**small age** (smôl′ij), *n.* a strongly scented herb.

**smart weed** (smärt′wēd′), *n.* any of various weeds of the same family as the buckwheat, that grow in wet places and cause an irritation when brought into contact with the skin.

**smelt** (smelt), *v.t.* fuse or melt (ore) in order to separate the metal contained.

**smite** (smīt), *v.t.* 1 give a hard blow to (a person, etc.) with the hand, a stick, or the like; strike. 2 impress suddenly with a strong feeling, sentiment, etc.

**smor gas bord** (smôr′gəs bôrd, smôr′-gəs bōrd), *n.* a buffet luncheon or supper consisting of a large variety of meats, salads, hors d'oeuvres, etc.

**snarl** (snärl), *n.* 1 a tangled or knotted mass. 2 confusion. — *v.t., v.i.* 1 tangle. 2 confuse.

**snuff** (snuf), *n.* **up to snuff,** INFORMAL. in perfect order or condition; as good as expected.

**sol ace** (sol′is), *v.t.* comfort or relieve; cheer.

**sol dier** (sōl′jər), *v.i.* INFORMAL. pretend to work but do very little.

**so lic it** (sə lis′it), *v.t.* 1 ask earnestly; try to get. 2 influence to do wrong; tempt.

**so lic i tude** (sə lis′ə tüd, sə lis′ə tyüd), *n.* anxious care; anxiety; concern.

**sol i dar i ty** (sol′ə dar′ə tē), *n.* unity or fellowship arising from common responsibilities and interests.

**so lil o quize** (sə lil′ə kwīz), *v.i.* 1 talk to oneself. 2 speak a soliloquy.

**so lil o quy** (sə lil′ə kwē), *n.* speech made by an actor to himself when alone on the stage. It reveals his thoughts and feelings to the audience, but not to the other characters in the play.

**sol stice** (sol′stis), *n.* either of the two

times in the year when the sun is at its greatest distance from the celestial equator.

**som nam bu list** (som nam′byə list), *n.* sleepwalker.

**som no lence** (som′nə ləns), *n.* sleepiness; drowsiness.

**sor did** (sôr′did), *adj.* 1 dirty; filthy. 2 mean; low; base; contemptible.

**sor ghum** (sôr′gəm), *n.* 1 any of a genus of tall, tropical cereal grasses which resemble corn. 2 molasses or syrup made from a sweet sorghum plant.

**sound ing** (soun′ding), *n.* 1 act of measuring the depth of water. 2 take **soundings,** try to find out quietly how matters stand.

**spar** (spär), *n.* a stout pole used to support or extend the sails of a ship; mast, yard, gaff, boom, etc., of a ship.

**Spar tan** (spärt′n), *adj.* of or having to do with Sparta or its people. — *n.* native of Sparta. The Spartans were noted for simplicity of life, severity, and courage.

**spec ter** (spek′tər), *n.* 1 phantom or ghost, especially one of a terrifying nature or appearance. 2 thing causing terror or dread.

**spec u la tive** (spek′yə lā′tiv, spek′yə lə-tiv), *adj.* carefully thoughtful; reflective.

**spell** (spel), *n.* 1 period of work or duty 2 relief of one person by another in doing something. — *v.t.* INFORMAL. work in place of (another) for a while; relieve.

**sperm whale,** *n.* a large, square-headed, toothed whale that has a large cavity in its head filled with sperm oil.

**spike horn** (spīk′hôrn′), *n.* a deer having spikes, or antlers.

**spile** (spīl), *n.* a heavy stake or beam driven into the ground as a support; pile.

**splice** (splīs), *v.t.* join together (ropes, etc.) by weaving together ends which have been untwisted. — *n.* a joining of ropes, timbers, film, etc., by splicing.

**spon ta ne ous** (spon tā′nē əs), *adj.* caused by natural impulse or desire; not planned beforehand. — **spon ta′ne ous-ly,** *adv.*

**squal id** (skwol′id), *adj.* 1 foul through neglect or want of cleanliness; dirty; filthy. 2 morally repulsive or wretched; degraded.

**squall** (skwôl), *n.* a sudden, violent gust of wind, often with rain, snow, or sleet.

**squash** (skwosh), *n.* either of two games somewhat like handball and tennis, played in a walled court with rackets and a rubber ball.

**stanch** (stänch, stanch), *v.t.* stop the flow of blood from (a wound).

**stan chion** (stan′shən), *n.* an upright bar, post, or support, as for a window, a roof, or the deck of a ship.

**stan dard-bear er** (stan′dərd ber′ər, stan′dərd bar′ər), *n.* 1 officer or soldier who carries a flag or standard. 2 a conspicuous leader of a movement.

**stark** (stärk), *adj.* 1 downright; complete. 2 stiff; rigid. 3 harsh; stern. — *adv.* entirely; completely. — **stark′ly,** *adv.*

**state ly** (stāt′lē), *adj.* having dignity; majestic.

**stat ure** (stach′ər), *n.* 1 height. 2 physical, mental, or moral growth; development.

**staunch** (stônch, stänch), *adj.* 1 strong or firm. 2 loyal; steadfast.

**stave** (stāv), *v.t.* 1 break up (a barrel, cask, etc.) into staves. 2 break a hole in (a boat, etc.). 3 smash (a hole) in a boat, door, etc.

**stead fast** (sted′fast′), *adj.* 1 firm of purpose; loyal and unwavering. 2 firmly fixed; not moving or changing. — **stead′fast′-ly,** *adv.*

**steer age** (stir′ij), *n.* the part of a passenger ship occupied by passengers traveling at the cheapest rate.

**ster e o type** (ster′ē ə tīp′, stir′ē ə tīp′), *n.* a fixed form, character, image, etc.; conventional type.

**stick ler** (stik′lər), *n.* person who contends or insists stubbornly, sometimes over trifles.

**stiff** (stif), *adj.* 1 not easily bent; fixed; rigid. 2 not easy or natural in manner; formal.

**stile** (stīl), *n.* step or steps for getting over a fence or wall.

**stilt ed** (stil′tid), *adj.* stiffly dignified or formal.

**stock** (stok), *n.* supply of goods for sale. — *v.t.* **take stock in,** INFORMAL. take an interest in; consider important; trust.

**stol id** (stol′id), *adj.* hard to arouse; not easily excited; seeming dull.

**sto ried** (stôr′ēd, stōr′ēd), *adj.* celebrated in story or history.

**stout** (stout), *adj.* 1 fat and large. 2 strongly built. 3 brave; bold.

**strag gle** (strag′əl), *v.i.* 1 wander in a scattered fashion. 2 stray from the rest.

**strait** (strāt), *n., pl.* **straits.** difficulty; need; distress. — *adj.* ARCHAIC. narrow; limited; confining. — **strait′ness,** *n.*

**strat a gem** (strat′ə jəm), *n.* scheme or trick for deceiving an enemy; trickery.

**strat i fy** (strat′ə fī), *v.t.* arrange in layers or strata; form into layers or strata.

**stri dent** (strīd′nt), *adj.* making or having a harsh sound; creaking; grating; shrill.

**strife** (strīf), *n.* a quarreling; fighting.

**stu por** (stü′pər, styü′pər), *n.* a dazed condition; loss of the power to feel.

**sub due** (səb dü′, səb dyü′), *v.t.* 1 conquer. 2 keep down; hold back.

**sub ject** (sub′jikt, sub′jekt), *n.* something thought about, discussed, investigated, etc. — *adj.* liable (to suffer from); likely to have.

**sub jec tion** (səb jek′shən), *n.* a bringing under some power or influence; conquering.

**sub jec tive** (səb jek′tiv), *adj.* 1 existing in the mind; belonging to the person thinking rather than to the object thought of. 2 dealing with the thoughts and feelings of the speaker, writer, painter, etc.; personal.

**sub ju gate** (sub′jə gāt), *v.t.* 1 subdue; conquer. 2 bring under complete control.

**sub lime** (sə blīm′), *adj.* lofty or elevated in thought, feeling, language, etc.; noble;

grand; exalted.

**sub mis sion** (səb mish′ən), *n.* a yielding to the power, control, or authority of another; submitting.

**sub side** (səb sīd′), *v.i.* grow less; die down; become less active.

**sub sist** (səb sist′), *v.i.* 1 keep alive; live. 2 continue to be; exist.

**sub stan ti ate** (səb stan′shē āt), *v.t.* establish by evidence; prove.

**sub ter fuge** (sub′tər fyüj), *n.* trick, excuse, or expedient used to escape something unpleasant.

**sub ter ra ne an** (sub′tə rā′nē ən), *adj.* 1 underground. 2 carried on secretly.

**sub tle** (sut′l), *adj.* 1 so fine or delicate as to elude observation or analysis. 2 faint; mysterious.

**suc cint** (sək singkt′), *adj.* expressed briefly and clearly; expressing much in few words; concise. — **suc cinct′ly,** *adv.*

**suc cor** (suk′ər), *v.t.* help, assist, or aid (a person, etc.).

**suc cumb** (sə kum′), *v.i.* 1 give way; yield. 2 die.

**suck le** (suk′əl), *v.t.* bring up; nourish.

**suf fer** (suf′ər), *v.t.* 1 have or feel (pain, grief, etc.). 2 be subjected to; experience; undergo. 3 bear with patiently; endure.

**suf frage** (suf′rij), *n.* 1 the right to vote. 2 a vote, usually in support of a proposal, candidate, etc. 3 a humble prayer.

**su mach** (sü′mak, shü′mak), *n.* any of a genus of shrubs or small trees having divided leaves that turn scarlet in the autumn and cone-shaped clusters of small, red or white, one-seeded fruit.

**su per nat ur al** (sü′pər nach′ər əl), *adj.* above or beyond what is natural. — *n.* **the supernatural,** supernatural agencies, influences, or phenomena.

**su per struc ture** (sü′pər struk′chər), *n.* 1 structure built on something else. 2 all of a building above the foundation.

**sup pli ant** (sup′lē ənt), *adj.* asking humbly and earnestly.

**sup pli cant** (sup′lə kənt), *adj., n.* suppliant.

**sup po si tion** (sup′ə zish′ən), *n.* thing supposed; belief; opinion.

**sup press** (sə pres′), *v.t.* 1 put an end to; stop by force; put down. 2 keep in; hold back.

**sur mise** (sər mīz′), *v.t., v.i.* infer or guess.

**sur mount** (sər mount′), *v.t.* overcome.

**sus tain** (sə stān′), *v.t.* 1 hold up; support. 2 bear; endure. 3 suffer; experience.

**swag ger** (swag′ər), *v.i.* walk with a bold, rude, or superior air; strut about or show off in a vain or insolent way.

**swart** (swôrt), *adj.* dark; swarthy.

**swarth** (swôrth,), *adj.* ARCHAIC. swarthy.

**swarth y** (swôr′ᴛʜē, swôr′ᴛʜē), *adj.* having a dark skin.

**swathe** (swāᴛʜ), *v.t.* 1 wrap up closely or fully. 2 bind, wrap, or bandage. 3 envelop or surround like a wrapping.

**swoon** (swün), *v.i.* faint.

**syn o nym** (sin′ə nim), *n.* word having a meaning that is the same or nearly the same as that of another word.

**sys to le** (sis′tl ē), *n.* the normal rhythmical contraction of the heart, especially that of the ventricles, when blood is pumped from the heart into the arteries.

**tab leau** (tab′lō), *n.* a striking scene.

**tack** (tak), *v.i.* 1 in nautical use: **a** sail zigzag into the wind. **b** turn and sail at the same angle to the wind on the other side. 2 move along any zigzag route.

**tack le** (tak′əl), *n.* 1 equipment; apparatus; gear. Fishing tackle means the rod, line, hooks, etc. 2 set of ropes and pulleys for lifting, lowering, or moving heavy things. The sails of a ship are raised and moved by tackle.

**tal low** (tal′ō), *n.* the hard fat from sheep, cows, etc., used for making candles, soap, etc.

**tal ly** (tal′ē), *v.i.* correspond; agree.

**tan gi ble** (tan′jə bəl), *adj.* 1 that can be touched or felt by touch. 2 real; actual; definite.

**tan ner y** (tan′ər ē), *n.* place where hides are tanned.

**tan ta lize** (tan′tl īz), *v.t.* torment or tease by keeping something desired in sight but out of reach, or by holding out hopes that are repeatedly disappointed.

**tan yard** (tan′yärd′), *n.* the part of a tannery housing tanning vats.

**tarn** (tärn), *n.* a small lake or pool in the mountains.

**tar ry** (tar′ē), *v.i.* delay leaving; remain; stay.

**taunt** (tônt, tänt), *v.t.* 1 jeer at; mock. 2 provoke. — **taunt′ing ly,** *adv.*

**taw ny** (tô′nē), *adj.* brownish-yellow.

**te di ous** (tē′dē əs, tē′jəs), *adj.* long and tiring; boring; wearisome.

**te di um** (tē′dē əm), *n.* 1 condition of being wearisome; tiresomeness. 2 boredom.

**tem per ance** (tem′pər əns), *n.* a being moderate in action, speech, habits, etc.; self-control.

**tem pest** (tem′pist), *n.* 1 a violent windstorm, usually accompanied by rain, hail, or snow. 2 a violent disturbance.

**tem por al** (tem′pər əl), *adj.* lasting for a time only; temporary.

**tend** (tend), *v.i.* 1 be apt; be likely; incline *(to).* 2 move; be directed.

**ten der** (ten′dər), *v.t.* offer formally.

**ten on** (ten′ən), *n.* projection on the end of a piece of wood cut so as to fit into the mortise in another piece and so form a joint. — *v.t., v.i.* cut so as to form a tenon.

**ten u ous** ten′yü əs), *adj.* having slight importance; not substantial.

**ter mi nate** (tėr′mə nāt), *v.t.* bring to an end; put an end to; conclude.

**thence** (ᴛʜens, thens), *adv.* 1 from that place. 2 for that reason.

**thence forth** (ᴛʜens′fôrth′, ᴛʜens′-fôrth′; thens′fôrth′, thens′fôrth′), *adv.* from then on; from that time forward.

**thence for ward** (ᴛʜens′fôr′wərd, thens fôr′wərd), *adv.* thenceforth.

**the oc ra cy** (thē ok′rə sē), *n.* 1 government in which God is recognized as the supreme civil ruler and in which religious authorities rule the state as God's representatives. 2 any government headed by religious authorities.

**the ol o gy** (thē ol′ə jē), *n.* 1 doctrines concerning God and His relations to man and the universe. 2 study of religion and religious beliefs.

**thith er** (thiᴛʜ′ər, ᴛʜiᴛʜ′ər), *adv.* to that place; toward that place; there.

**thrib let** (thrib′let), *n.* triplet.

**throat y** (thrō′tē), *adj.* 1 produced in the throat. 2 low-pitched.

**throe** (thrō), *n.* 1 a violent pang; great pain. 2 **throes,** *pl.* **a** anguish; agony. **b** a desperate struggle; violent disturbance.

**throng** (thrông, throng), *n.* 1 a crowd. 2 crowded condition. — *v.t.* crowd. — *v.i.* come together in a crowd.

**thumb nail** (thum′nāl′), *adj.* very small or short.

**thwart** (thwôrt), *n.* 1 seat across a boat, on which a rower sits. 2 brace between the gunwales of a canoe.

**tim or ous** (tim′ər əs), *adj.* easily frightened; timid.

**tim o thy** (tim′ə thē), *n.* a coarse grass with long, cylindrical spikes, often grown for hay.

**tinc ture** (tingk′chər), *n.* solution of medicine in alcohol. — *v.t.* give a trace or tinge to.

**tin ny** (tin′ē), *adj.* like tin in looks, sound, or taste.

**tit ter** (tit′ər), *v.i.* laugh in a half-restrained manner, because of nervousness or silliness; giggle.

**ton al** (tō′nl), *adj.* of or having to do with tone or quality of sound.

**tor pid** (tôr′pid), *adj.* 1 dull, inactive, or sluggish. 2 not moving or feeling; dormant.

hat, āge, fär; let, ēqual, tėrm; it, īce; hot, ōpen, ôrder; oil, out; cup, pùt, rüle; ch, child; ng, long; sh, she; th, thin; ᴛʜ, then; zh, measure.

ə represents *a* in about, *e* in taken, *i* in pencil, *o* in lemon, *u* in circus.

**tor por** (tôr′pər), *n.* torpid condition or quality; apathy; lethargy.

**tor toise-shell** (tôr′təs shel′), *adj.* 1 made of tortoise shell. 2 mottled or colored like tortoise shell.

**touch stone** (tuch′stōn′), *n.* 1 a black stone used to test the purity of gold or silver by the color of the streak made on the stone by rubbing it with the metal. 2 any means of testing; a test.

**tram mel** (tram′əl), *v.t.* 1 hinder; restrain. 2 catch in or as if in a trammel; entangle.

**trans fig u ra tion** (tran sfig′yə rā′shən), *n.* a change in form or appearance; transformation.

**tran spire** (tran spīr′), *v.i.* take place; happen; occur.

**trans port** (*v.* tran spôrt′, tran spōrt′; *n.* tran′spôrt, tran′spōrt), *v.t.* 1 carry from one place to another. 2 send away to another country as a punishment, especially to a penal colony. — *n.* a strong feeling.

**tra vail** (trə vāl′, trav′āl), *n.* 1 toil; labor. 2 trouble, hardship; suffering.

**tread** (tred), *v.i.* set the foot down; walk; step. — *v.t.* set the feet on; walk on or through.

**trem or** (trem′ər), *n.* an involuntary shaking or trembling.

**trem u lous** (trem′yə ləs), *adj.* 1 trembling; quivering. 2 timid; fearful. 3 that wavers; shaky.

**trep i da tion** (trep′ə dā′shən), *n.* nervous dread; fear; fright.

**trip ham mer** (trip′ham′ər), *n.* a heavy iron or steel block raised by machinery and then tripped by a mechanism and allowed to drop.

**triv et** (triv′it), *n.* a three-legged stand for supporting a pot or kettle over an open fire.

**triv i al** (triv′ē əl), *adj.* not important; insignificant.

**truck** (truk), *n.* 1 vegetables raised for market. 2 small articles of little value; odds and ends.

**trun dle** (trun′dl), *v.t.* roll along; push along. — *v.i.* 1 move or be moved by trundling. 2 whirl; revolve.

**tump line** (tump′līn′), *n.* strap across the forehead and over the shoulders, used to help to carry loads on the back, especially by American Indians.

**tu mul tu ous** (tü mul′chü əs, tyü mul′chü əs), *adj.* rough; stormy.

**turf** (tėrf), *n.* the upper surface of the soil covered with grass and other small plants.

**tur ret** (tėr′it), *n.* a small tower, often on the corner of a building.

**twin kle** (twing′kəl), *n.* 1 sparkle; gleam. 2 time required for a wink.

**ul ti mate** (ul′tə mit), *adj.* coming at the end; final. — **ul′ti mate ly,** *adv.*

---

**un ap peas a ble** (un′ə pē′zə bəl), *adj.* not to be calmed or quieted.

**un as ser tive** (un′ə sėr′tiv), *adj.* not insistent or forward; reserved in speech or actions.

**un can ny** (un kan′ē), *adj.* strange and mysterious; weird.

**un con ven tion al** (un′kən ven′shə nəl), *adj.* not bound by or conforming to convention, rule, or precedent; free from conventionality. — **un′con ven′tion al ly,** *adv.*

**un der cur rent** (un′dər kėr′ənt), *n.* an underlying quality or tendency.

**un der lie** (un′dər lī′), *v.t.* 1 lie under; be beneath. 2 be at the basis of; form the foundation of.

**un der mine** (un′dər mīn′, un′dər mīn′), *v.t.* weaken by secret or unfair means.

**un de sir a ble** (un′di zī′rə bəl), *adj.* objectionable; disagreeable. — *n.* an undesirable person or thing.

**un earth ly** (un ėrth′lē), *adj.* 1 not of this world; supernatural. 2 strange; weird; ghostly.

**un hal lowed** (un hal′ōd), *adj.* 1 not made holy; not sacred. 2 wicked; sinful; evil.

**u ni form i ty** (yü′nə fôr′mə tē), *n.* uniform condition or character; sameness throughout.

**un ion** (yü′nyən), *n.* marriage.

**u ni son** (yü′nə sən, yü′nə zən), *n.* 1 harmonious combination or union. 2 identity in pitch of two or more sounds, tones, etc.

**un leav ened** (un lev′ənd), *adj.* not leavened. Unleavened bread is made without yeast, so is not raised or made lighter.

**un ob tru sive** (un′əb trü′siv), *adj.* not obtrusive; modest; inconspicuous. — **un′ob tru′sive ly,** *adv.*

**un pre ten tious** (un′pri ten′shəs), *adj.* not pretentious; unassuming; modest.

**un seem ly** (un sēm′lē), *adj.* not seemly; not suitable; improper.

**un sheathe** (un shēᴛʜ′), *v.t.* 1 draw (a sword, knife, etc.) from a sheath. 2 bring or put forth from a covering.

**un sta ble** (un stā′bəl), *adj.* 1 not firmly fixed; easily moved, shaken, or overthrown. 2 not constant; variable.

**un ut ter a ble** (un ut′ər ə bəl), *adj.* that cannot be expressed in words; unspeakable.

**un whole some** (un hōl′səm), *adj.* bad for the body or the mind; unhealthy.

**un wield y** (un wēl′dē), *adj.* not easily handled or managed, because of size, shape, or weight; bulky and clumsy.

**up braid** (up brād′), *v.t.* find fault with; blame; reprove.

**up shot** (up′shot′), *n.* 1 conclusion; result. 2 the essential facts.

**ut ter** (ut′ər), *adj.* complete; total.

---

**vale** (vāl), *n.* valley.

---

**var mint** (vär′mənt), *n.* DIALECT. 1 vermin. 2 an objectionable animal or person.

**veer** (vir), *v.i.* change in direction; shift; turn.

**ven er a ble** (ven′ər ə bəl), *adj.* worthy of reverence; deserving respect because of age, character, or importance.

**vent** (vent), *n.* free expression.

**ver ein** (və rīn′, fə rīn′), *n.* social or political organization or association.

**verge** (vėrj), *n.* 1 the point at which something begins or happens. 2 a limiting edge, margin, or bound of something; border.

**ver i ly** (ver′ə lē), *adv.* ARCHAIC. in truth; truly; really.

**ver min** (vėr′mən), *n. pl. or sing.* 1 small animals that are troublesome or destructive. 2 very unpleasant or vile person or persons.

**versed** (vėrst), *adj.* experienced; practiced; skilled.

**ves tige** (ves′tij), *n.* trace mark.

**ves ture** (ves′chər), *n.* covering.

**vex** (veks), *v.t.* 1 anger by trifles; annoy; provoke. 2 worry; trouble; harass.

**vex a tion** (vek sā′shən), *n.* 1 a vexing. 2 a being vexed. 3 thing that vexes.

**vi al** (vī′əl), *n.* a small glass or plastic bottle for holding medicines or the like; phial.

**vi brant** (vī′brənt), *adj.* throbbing with vitality, enthusiasm, etc. — **vi′brant ly,** *adv.*

**vice** (vīs), *n.* an evil, immoral, or wicked habit or tendency.

**vict ual** (vit′l), *n.* **victuals,** *pl.* food or provisions.

**vie** (vī), *v.i.* strive for superiority; contend in rivalry; compete.

**vig i lance** (vij′ə ləns), *n.* watchfulness; alertness; caution.

**vile** (vīl), *adj.* evil; low; immoral.

**vin di cate** (vin′də kāt), *v.t.* clear from suspicion, dishonor, a hint or charge of wrongdoing, etc.

**vir tu al** (vėr′chü əl), *adj.* being something in effect, though not so in name; for all practical purposes; actual; real. — **vir′tu al ly,** *adv.*

**vis age** (viz′ij), *n.* 1 face. 2 appearance or aspect.

**vis ta** (vis′tə), *n.* 1 view seen through a narrow opening or passage. 2 a mental view.

**vi tal** (vī′tl), *adj.* of or having to do with life. — *n.* **vitals,** *pl.* parts or organs necessary to life.

**vi tu pe ra tive** (vī tü′pə rā′tiv, vī tyü′pə rā′tiv), *adj.* abusive; reviling.

**void** (void), *n.* 1 an empty space; vacuum. 2 a feeling of emptiness or great loss.

**vol ley** (vol′ē), *n.* a rapid outpouring or burst of words, oaths, shouts, cheers, etc.

**vor tex** (vôr′teks), *n.* a whirling mass of water, etc., that sucks everything near it toward its center; whirlpool.

**vul ner a ble** (vul′nər ə bəl), *adj.* 1 that can be wounded or injured; open to attack. 2 sensitive to criticism, temptations, influences, etc.

**wad** (wod), *n.* a tight roll; compact bundle or mass. — *v.t.* make into a wad; press into a wad.

**waft** (waft), *v.i.* float.

**waif** (wāf), *n.* person without home or friends, especially a homeless or neglected child.

**wake** (wāk), *n.* track left behind a moving ship.

**wan** (won), *adj.* looking worn or tired; faint; weak. — **wan'ly,** *adv.*

**wane** (wān), *v.i.* **1** lose size; become smaller gradually. **2** decline in power, influence, or importance. **3** decline in strength or intensity. **4** draw to a close. — *n.* act or process of waning.

**wan ton** (won'tən), *adj.* **1** reckless, heartless, or malicious. **2** without reason or excuse. **3** not moral; not chaste.

**war i ness** (wer'ē nis, war'ē nis), *n.* caution; care.

**wax** (waks), *v.i.* grow bigger or greater; increase.

**way far er** (wā'fer'ər, wā'far'ər), *n.* traveler, especially one who travels on foot.

**way lay** (wā'lā', wā'lā'), *v.t.* **1** lie in wait for; attack on the way. **2** stop (a person) on his way.

**way ward** (wā'wərd), *adj.* turning from the right way; disobedient; willful.

**weft** (weft), *n.* **1** the threads running from side to side across a fabric; woof. **2** something woven or spun, as a web.

**weight y** (wā'tē), *adj.* **1** having much weight; heavy; ponderous. **2** convincing.

**wel ter** (wel'tər), *v.i.* (of waves, the water, or sea) surge.

**whence** (hwens), *adv.* **1** from what place; from where. **2** from what place, source, or cause. **3** from which. — *conj.* from what place, source, or cause.

**whet** (hwet), *v.t.* sharpen by rubbing.

**whet stone** (hwet'stōn'), *n.* stone for sharpening knives or tools.

**whip cord** (hwip'kôrd'), *n.* **1** a thin, tough, tightly twisted cord, sometimes used for the lashes of whips. **2** a strong, closely woven worsted cloth with diagonal ridges on it.

**whip staff** (hwip'staf'), *n.* a lever used to help steer a boat.

**white fish** (hwīt'fish'), *n.* any of a family of freshwater food fishes with white or silvery sides.

**whith er** (hwiŦH'ər), *adv., conj.* to what place; to which place; where.

**whorl** (hwėrl, hwôrl), *n.* **1** circle of leaves or flowers round a single node or point on the stem of a plant. **2** anything that circles or turns on or around something else.

**who so** (hü'sō), *pron.* whoever.

**wick er** (wik'ər), *n.* twigs or branches woven together. — *adj.* covered with wicker.

**wick i up** (wik'ē up'), *n.* an Indian hut made of brushwood or covered with mats, formerly used by nomadic tribes in the western and southwestern United States.

**wield** (wēld), *v.t.* hold and use; manage; control.

**wile** (wīl), *n.* **1** a trick to deceive. **2** subtle trickery; slyness.

**wil ly-nil ly** (wil'ē nil'ē), *adv.* willingly or not; with or against one's wishes.

**wil y** (wī'lē), *adj.* using wiles or subtle tricks to deceive; sly. — **will'i ly,** *adv.*

**wince** (wins), *v.i.* draw back suddenly; flinch slightly.

**wind flow er** (wind'flou'ər), *n.* anemone.

**wind lass** (wind'ləs), *n.* machine for pulling or lifting things. It is used to hoist water from a well or an anchor out of the water.

**wisp** (wisp), *n.* **1** a small bundle; small bunch. **2** a little thing.

**wist ful** (wist'fəl), *adj.* longing; yearning. — **wist'ful ly,** *adv.*

**with al** (wi ŦHôl', wi thôl'), *adv.* **1** with it all; as well; besides; also. **2** ARCHAIC. in spite of all.

**wont** (wont, wōnt, wunt), *adj.* accustomed.

**word play** (wėrd'plā'), *n.* play of or upon words.

**wrack** (rak), *v.t., v.i.* wreck or be wrecked.

**wran gle** (rang'gəl), *v.i.* dispute noisily; quarrel angrily.

**wrath** (rath), *n.* **1** very great anger; rage. **2** vengeance or punishment caused by anger.

**wrench** (rench), *n.* distortion of the original or proper meaning, interpretation, etc.

**wrest** (rest), *v.t.* twist, pull, or tear away with force; wrench away.

**wretch ed** (rech'id), *adj.* **1** very unfortunate or unhappy. **2** very unsatisfactory; miserable. **3** very bad. — **wretch'ed ness,** *n.*

**writhe** (rīŦH), *v.i.* **1** twist and turn; twist about. **2** suffer mentally; be very uncomfortable.

**wrought** (rôt), *adj.* made.

**wry** (rī), *adj.* **1** turned to one side; twisted. **2** ironic.

**yes ter year** (yes'tər yir'), *n., adv.* **1** ARCHAIC. last year; the year before this. **2** of yesteryear, of yore.

**Yid dish** (yid'ish), *n.* language which developed from a dialect of Middle High German, containing many Hebrew and Slavic words, and written in Hebrew characters.

**ze nith** (zē'nith), *n.* **1** the point in the heavens directly overhead. **2** the highest point.

---

hat, āge, fär; let, ēqual, tėrm; it, īce; hot, ōpen, ôrder; oil, out; cup, pùt, rüle; ch, child; ng, long; sh, she; th, thin; ŦH, then; zh, measure.

ə represents *a* in about, *e* in taken, *i* in pencil, *o* in lemon, *u* in circus.

# Acknowledgments

Sherwood Anderson. "The Egg" is reprinted by permission of Harold Ober Associates, Inc. Copyright 1921 by B. W. Heubsch, Inc., renewed 1948 by Eleanor C. Anderson.

Maya Angelou. "Lift Every Voice and Sing," from *I Know Why the Caged Bird Sings,* is reprinted by permission of Random House, copyright © 1969 by Maya Angelou.

W. H. Auden. Lines from "In Memory of W. B. Yeats" are used by permission of Random House.

Mary Austin. "The Grass on the Mountain" is from *The American Rhythm,* revised edition by Mary Austin. Reprinted by permission of Houghton Mifflin Company. Copyright renewed 1958 by Kenneth M. Chapman and Mary C. Wheelwright.

Imamu Amiri Baraka. "Preface to a Twenty-Volume Suicide Note" is reprinted by permission of Corinth Books. Copyright © 1961 by LeRoi Jones.

Stephen Vincent Benét. "Western Star," plus a two-line epigram, is reprinted from *Western Star,* copyright renewed © 1971 by Rachel Benét Lewis, Thomas C. Benét, and Stephanie Benét Mahin. Reprinted by permission of Brandt & Brandt. First published by Holt, Rinehart and Winston, Inc.

Stephen Berg. "Five Aztec Poems" is from *Nothing in the World* by Stephen Berg. Reprinted by permission of Viking Penguin, Inc. All rights reserved.

Black Elk. "The Earth Is All That Lasts" is from *Black Elk Speaks* by John G. Neihardt, Simon & Schuster Publishers, copyright © 1959-1961. Reprinted by permission of the John G. Neihardt Trust.

Arna Bontemps. "A Black Man Talks of Reaping" is reprinted by permission of Harold Ober Associates, Inc. Copyright © 1963 by Arna Bontemps.

Kay Boyle. "October 1954," copyright © 1954 by Kay Boyle, is reprinted by permission of A. Watkins, Inc.

Gwendolyn Brooks. "The Sonnet Ballad," copyright © 1949, and "Truth," copyright © 1945 by Gwendolyn Brooks Blakely, from *The World of Gwendolyn Brooks,* are reprinted by permission of Harper and Row, Publishers, Inc.

Olga Cabral. Lines from the poem "Occupation: Spinster," copyright © 1975 by Olga Cabral, are used by permission of the author. First published in *We Became New: Poems of Contemporary American Women,* Bantam Books, Inc.

Willa Cather. "The New Country," from *My Antonia* by Willa Cather is reprinted by permission of Houghton Mifflin Company. Copyright © 1954.

Countee Cullen. "Any Human to Another," copyright © 1953 by Harper & Row, Publishers, Inc., renewed 1963 by Ida M. Cullen and "Saturday's Child," copyright 1925 by Harper & Row, Publishers, Inc., renewed 1953 by Ida M. Cullen, are reprinted by permission of Harper & Row, Publishers, Inc., from *On These I Stand* by Countee Cullen.

E. E. Cummings. "in Just spring," copyright 1923, 1951 by E. E. Cummings, is reprinted from his volume *Complete Poems 1913-1962,* by permission of Harcourt Brace Jovanovich, Inc.

Daniel de Poala. "The Returning" is reprinted by permission from *Prairie Schooner,* copyright © 1964 by the University of Nebraska Press.

Emily Dickinson. "A Bird Came Down the Walk," "A Narrow Fellow in the Grass," "Because I Could Not Stop for Death," "Had I Not Seen the Sun," "Hope Is the Thing With Feathers," "I Stepped From Plank to Plank," "Presentiment," "The Bustle in a House" Reprinted by permission of the publishers and the Trustees of Amherst College from THE POEMS OF EMILY DICKINSON, edited by Thomas H. Johnson, Cambridge, Massachusetts: Harvard University Press, Copyright © 1951, 1955 by the President and Fellows of Harvard College."

Thomas A. Dorsey. "Take My Hand, Precious Lord" is reprinted by permission of Chappell Music Company. Copyright © 1938 by Hill and Range Songs, Inc. Copyright renewed, assigned to Unichappell Music, Inc. All rights reserved.

Paul Lawrence Dunbar. "Compensation," from *The Complete Poems of Paul Lawrence Dunbar,* is reprinted by permission of Dodd, Mead & Company.

Katherine Edelman. "Irish Grandmother" is reprinted by special permission by Mrs. Ardis Glenn and Glenn Books, Kansas City, Missouri.

T. S. Eliot. Lines from "The Waste Land," from *Collected Poems* 1909-1962 by T. S. Eliot, are reprinted by permission of Harcourt Brace Jovanovich, Inc.

Ralph Ellison. "Mister Toussan" is reprinted by permission of William Morris Agency, Inc. on behalf of author. Copyright © 1941 (renewed) by Ralph Ellison.

James A. Emanuel. "Get Up, Blues" is reprinted by permission of the author.

William Faulkner. "The Tall Men," from *The Collected Stories of William Faulkner,* is reprinted by permission of Random House. Copyright 1941 and renewed 1969 by Estelle Faulkner and Jill Faulkner Summer.

Edna Ferber. "An Iowa Childhood," from *A Peculiar Treasure,* is reprinted by permission of Doubleday & Company, Inc. Copyright 1938, 1939 by Edna Ferber; copyright © 1960 by Morris L. Ernst et al., trustees.

Edward Field. "My Polish Grandma" is reprinted by permission of the author.

Robert Frost. "Mending Wall" is copyright 1930, © 1969 by Holt, Rinehart and Winston, copyright © 1958 by Robert Frost, copyright © 1967 by Leslie Frost Ballantine. "Once by the Pacific" and "The Tuft of Flowers," copyright 1928, 1934, © 1969 by Holt, Rinehart and Winston, copyright © 1956, 1962 by Robert Frost. All are taken from *The Poetry of Robert Frost* edited by Edward Connery Lathem and are reprinted by permission of Holt, Rinehart and Winston, Publishers.

Daniela Gioseffi. "Some Slippery Afternoon" is reprinted by permission of Daniela Gioseffi, copyright © 1979 in her book of poems, *Eggs in the Lake,* Boa Editions, 92 Park Ave., Brockport, N.Y. with acknowledgment to *Choice #9, We Became New, The Poetry of Contemporary American Women* (Bantam Books, 1975), and *The Ardis Anthology & New American Poetry* (The Ardis Press, Ann Arbor, Michigan, 1977).

Nikki Giovanni. "Legacies," from *My House* by Nikki Giovanni, is reprinted by permission of William Morrow & Company, Inc. Copyright © 1972 by Nikki Giovanni.

Ellen Glasgow. "Only Yesterday," from *Vein of Iron,* copyright 1935 by Ellen Glasgow; copyright © 1963 by First and Merchants Bank of Richmond is reprinted by permission of Harcourt Brace Jovanovich, Inc.

Pete Hamill. "Notes On the Irish," from *New York Magazine,* is reprinted by permission of International Creative Management.

Lorraine Hansberry. *A Raisin in the Sun,* copyright © 1958, 1959, 1966 by Robert Nemiroff as Executor of the Estate of Lorraine Hansberry, is reprinted by permission of Random House, Inc.

CAUTION: Professionals and amateurs are hereby warned that *A Raisin in the Sun,* being fully protected under the Copyright Laws of the United States of America, the British Empire, including the Dominion of Canada, and all other countries of the Universal Copyright and Berne Conventions, is subject to royalty. All rights, including professional, amateur, motion picture, recitation, lecturing, public reading, radio and television broadcasting, and the rights of translation into foreign languages, are strictly reserved. Particular emphasis is laid on the question of readings, permission for which must be secured in writing. All inquiries should be addressed to the publisher.

Robert Hayden. "Frederick Douglass," "Runagate, Runagate" (Part I), and "Those Winter Sundays" are reprinted from *Angle of Ascent,* New and Selected Poems, by Robert Hayden, by permission of Liveright Publishing Corporation. Copyright © 1966, 1970, 1972, 1975 by Robert Hayden.

Ernest Hemingway. Part I "Big Two-Hearted River" is reprinted by permission of Charles Scribner's Sons from *In Our Time* by Ernest Hemingway. Copyright 1925 Charles Scribner's Sons.

Ruth Herschberger. "Displays of Skill: The Bat" is reprinted from *Nature and Love Poems* (Eakins Press) by permission of the author. Copyright © 1969 by Ruth Herschberger.

M. Carl Holman. "The Afternoon of a Young Poet" is from *Anger, and Beyond: The Negro Writer in the United States,* edited by Herbert Hill, copyright © 1966 by Herbert Hill. Is reprinted by permission of Harper & Row, Publishers, Inc.

Langston Hughes. "Graduation," copyright 1948 by Alfred A. Knopf, "Harlem," copyright 1951, "Porter," copyright renewed 1955, "Uncle Tom," copyright © 1959 by Langston Hughes from *Selected Poems of Langston Hughes,* are reprinted by permission of Alfred A. Knopf, Inc.

Evelyn Tooley Hunt. "Taught Me Purple," from *Negro Digest,* February 1964, is reprinted by permission of the author.

David Ignatow. "Europe and America" is reprinted from *Figures of the Human,* by permission of Wesleyan University Press. Copyright © 1948 by David Ignatow.

Alta Jablow. "The Two Strangers," from *Yes and No: The Intimate Folklore of Africa* by Alta Jablow. Copyright © 1967, is reprinted by permission of the publisher, Horizon Press.

Robinson Jeffers. "Vulture," from *The Beginning and the End and Other Poems,* by Robinson Jeffers, is reprinted by permission of Random House. Copyright © 1954, 1963 by Garth Jeffers and Donnan Jeffers.

James Weldon Johnson. "Noah Built the Ark," from *God's Trombone* by James Weldon Johnson, is reprinted by permission of Viking Penguin Inc. Copyright 1927 by The Viking Press, Inc., copyright © renewed 1955 by Grace Nail Johnson.

John Knowles. "A Turn With the Sun," from *Phineas* by John Knowles, is reprinted by permission of Random House, Inc. Copyright © 1953.

Denise Levertov. "The Sharks" is from *Overland to the Islands,* copyright © 1958 by Denise Levertov. Reprinted by permission of New Directions Publishing Corporation, Agents.

*Life* Special Report on Remarkable American Women 1776-1976 © 1976 Time Inc. Reprinted by permission.

Vachel Lindsay. "The Flower-Fed Buffaloes," from *Going to the Stars* by Vachel Lindsay, copyright 1926 by D. Appleton & Co., copyright renewed © 1954 by Elizabeth C. Lindsay, is reprinted by permission.

Archibald MacLeish. "To Thomas Jefferson, Esquire," from "Empire Builders" by Archibald MacLeish from his volume *Collected Poems 1917-1952,* is reprinted by permission of Houghton Mifflin Company.

Bernard Malamud. "The Magic Barrel" is reprinted by permission of Farrar, Straus & Giroux, Inc. from *The Magic Barrel* by Bernard Malamud. Copyright © 1954, 1958 by Bernard Malamud.

Edgar Lee Masters. "George Gray," and "Lucinda Matlock," from *Spoon River Anthology,* by Edgar Lee Masters, are reprinted by permission of Ellen C. Masters, Macmillan, Inc., Publishers, copyright © 1963, 1944.

Eve Merriam. "Landscape," from *Finding a Poem,* copyright © 1970 by Eve Merriam, is reprinted by permission of Atheneum Publishers. "Robin Hood," copyright © 1970 by Eve Merriam, is reprinted by permission of Eve Merriam, c/o International Creative Management.

Edna St. Vincent Millay. "Apostrophe to Man," "Dirge Without Music," "I Shall Go Back Again to the Bleak Shore," "Love Is Not All," "Pity Me Not Because the Light of Day" are reprinted by permission of Norma Millay Ellis from *Collected Poems,* Harper & Row, Publishers, Inc. Copyright 1923, 1928, 1931, 1934, 1951, 1955, 1958, 1962 by Edna St. Vincent Millay and Norma Millay Ellis.

N. Scott Momaday. "Earth and I Gave You Turquoise," from *The Gourd Dancer* by N. Scott Momaday, is reprinted by permission of Harper & Row, Publishers, Inc. Copyright © 1957 by N. Scott Momaday. "The Way to Rainy Mountain," adapted from *The Way To Rainy Mountain,* copyright © 1969 by the University of New Mexico Press, is reprinted by permission. First published in *The Reporter,* January 26, 1967.

Amado, Muro. "Cecilia Rosas" is reprinted by permission of Mrs. Chester Seltzer.

*Newsweek* "Mark Twain," reprinted by permission. Copyright © 1976 by Newsweek, Inc. All rights reserved.

Terrence O'Flaherty. "Through the Golden Door" is reprinted by permission of the San Francisco Chronicle, copyright © 1976 by Chronicle Publishing Company.

Mary Oliver. "Stark Boughs on the Family Tree," copyright © 1968 by The New York Times Company, is reprinted by permission.

Tillie Olsen. "I Stand Here Ironing," excerpted from *Tell Me a Riddle* by Tillie Olsen, is reprinted by permission of Delacorte Press/Seymour Lawrence. Copyright © 1956 by Tillie Olsen.

Simon J. Ortiz. "Kaiser and the War" is reprinted by permission of the author.

Linda Pastan. "My Grandmother" is reprinted from *The First Stages of Grief,* poems by Linda Pastan, by permission of W. W. Norton & Company, Inc. Copyright © 1978 by Linda Pastan.

Elisabeth Peck. "Walthena," from *American Frontier* by Elisabeth Peck is reprinted by permission of Doubleday & Company, Inc. Copyright 1937 by Elisabeth Peck.

Marge Piercy. "Simple Song" is reprinted from *Hard Loving* by permission of Wesleyan University Press. Copyright © 1969 by Marge Piercy.

Sylvia Plath. "Frog Autumn," and "The Water Rat," from "Watercolor of Grantchester Meadows," from *The Colossus and Other Poems* by Sylvia Plath, are reprinted by permission of Alfred A. Knopf, Inc. Copyright © 1959, 1960, by Sylvia Plath. First appeared in *The New Yorker.*

Katherine Anne Porter. "The Grave," from *The Leaning Tower and Other Stories,* copyright 1944, 1972 by Katherine Anne Porter. Reprinted by permission of Harcourt Brace Jovanovich, Inc.

Cynthia Rich. "My Sister's Marriage," reprinted from *Mademoiselle,* by permission of the author. Copyright © 1955 by Street & Smith Publications, Inc.

Theodore Roethke. "Root Cellar," from *The Collected Poems of Theodore Roethke,* copyright 1943 by Modern Poetry Association, Inc., is reprinted by permission of Doubleday & Company, Inc.

Vern Rutsala. Lines from "Looking in the Album" are reprinted from *The Window* by permission of Wesleyan University Press.

Duncan Campbell Scott. "On the Way to the Mission," is reprinted by permission of John G. Aylen, Ottawa, Canada.

Louis Simpson. "American Poetry," from *The End of the Road* by Louis Simpson, Wesleyan University Press, 1963, is reprinted by permission.

W. D. Snodgrass. "Powwow" from *After Experience* by W. D. Snodgrass, is reprinted by permission of Harper & Row, Publishers, Inc. Copyright © 1962 by W. D. Snodgrass. Originally appeared in *The New Yorker.*

William Stafford. "One Home" is reprinted from *The Rescued Year* by William Stafford by permission of Harper & Row, Publishers, Inc. Copyright © 1960 by William E. Stafford.

John Steinbeck. "Flight" and "The Leader of the People" are reprinted from *The Long Valley* by John Steinbeck by permission of The Viking Press. Copyright 1938, copyright © renewed 1966 by John Steinbeck.

Irving Stone. "Death Valley Earns Its Name," from *Men to Match My Mountain,* by Irving Stone, is reprinted by permission of Doubleday & Company, Inc. Copyright © 1956 by Irving Stone.

John Updike. "Home Movies," from "Midpoint and Other Poems" by John Updike, is reprinted by permission of Alfred A. Knopf, Inc. Copyright © 1965 by John Updike.

Joe Vergara. "A Letter From Home," from *Love and Pasta,* reprinted by permission of Harper & Row, Publishers, Inc. Copyright © 1969 by Joseph R. Vergara.

Eudora Welty. "A Visit of Charity," copyright 1941, 1969 by Eudora Welty, is reprinted from her volume *A Curtain of Green and Other Stories* by permission of Harcourt Brace Jovanovich, Inc.

Richard Wilbur. "Running" is reprinted from *Walking to Sleep* by Richard Wilbur by permission of Harcourt Brace Jovanovich, Inc. Copyright © 1968 by Richard Wilbur.

Thornton Wilder. *Our Town,* copyright © 1938, 1957 by Thornton Wilder, is reprinted by permission of Harper & Row, Publishers, Inc.

Caution! *Our Town* is the sole property of the author and is fully protected by copyright. It may not be acted by professionals or amateurs without formal

# Art Credits

## Illustrations

Jan Naimo Jones   23
Elissa della Piana   29, 37
Jan Naimo Jones   45, 51
Robert Masheris   81
Susan Spellman   90, 95
Karen Watson   115, 120
Ted Rand   127, 130, 133
Gail Burroughs   139
Lydia Dabcovich   144, 145
Al Lorenz   169, 173
Judy Love   178
Howard Post   209, 222, 230
John Whalley   239
Susan Spellman   247
Ron Rudat   289, 292, 297, 303
Austin Stevens   309, 313

Leslie Morrill   318, 319, 320, 321
Karen Watson   323
Charles Shaw   326, 327, 330, 333
Irene Roman   338, 344
George Ulrich   353, 357
Winona Taylor   377, 378, 379, 380, 381
Troy Howell   402, 405, 409
Judy Oliver   421, 422, 423
Michael Cobb   519
Floyd Sowell   528, 529, 530, 531
Sandy Rabinowitz   545, 548, 551
Jerry Pinkney   632, 633
Michael Compton   639, 646
Lane Yerkes   653
Yoshi Miyaki   659
Charles Shaw   665, 673

## Photography

The Bettmann Archive, Inc.   2
The Bettmann Archive, Inc.   *top, middle, bottom, 3*
The Bettmann Archive, Inc.   *top, 4*
Merrimack Valley Textile Museum   *middle, 4*
The Bettmann Archive, Inc.   *bottom, 4*
Library of Congress   *top, 5*
Culver Pictures   *middle, 5*
NASA   *bottom, 5*
The Bettmann Archive, Inc.   *top, 6*
By permission of the Trustees of Amherst College, Amherst, Mass.   *bottom, 6*
Yale University   *top, 7*
The Stow-Day Foundation, Hartford, Connecticut   *bottom, 7*
The Bettmann Archive, Inc.   *top, 8*
Photograph © 1980 by Jill Krementz   *bottom, 8 and top, 9*
Courtesy of Harper & Row Publishers   *bottom, 9*
"Sea Wind" by Robert Vickrey. Photo courtesy of Hirschl & Adler Galleries, Inc.   *10–13*
Michael P. Gadomski/Photo Researchers   *14*
"Her World" by Philip Evergood. The

Metropolitan Museum of Art, Arthur H. Hearn Fund, 1950   *17*
John E. Fogle   *18*
Eugene Richards/The Picture Cube   *20*
"Emigrants and Indians" by E. L. Spybuck. The Carl S. Dentzel Collection, photo by J. R. Eyerman   *55*
Pilgrim Hall Museum, Plymouth, Mass.   *56, 58*
"Lewis and Clark at Black Eagle Falls" by O. C. Seltzer. The Thomas Gilcrease Institute of American History and Art, Tulsa, Oklahoma   *59*
"Hudson Bay Trading Post on Flathead Indian Reservation" by Peter Petersen Tofft. Museum of Fine Arts, Boston, The Karolik Collection   *61*
Peter Vandermark   *63*
Jack Gill   *65*
Rare Book Division, the New York Public Library, Astor, Lenox & Tilden Foundations   *66*
Woolaroc Museum, Bartlesville, Oklahoma   *71*
David Muench   *73*
"Hester Street" by George Luks. The Brooklyn

Museum, Dick S. Ramsay Fund  *101*
Library of Congress  *102*
Susan McCartney/Photo Researchers  *105*
"The Last of England" by Ford Madox Brown.
   Birmingham Museum and Art Gallery  *107*
American Jewish Historical Society  *108*
Susan McCartney/Photo Researchers  *109*
Museum of the City of New York  *110*
"The Artist and His Mother" by Arshile Gorky.
   Collection of Whitney Museum of American
   Art  *136*
Eric Anderson/Stock Boston  *143*
Hella Hammid/Rapho/Photo Researchers  *146*
Cary Wolinsky/Stock Boston  *147*
S. J. Krasemann/Photo Researchers  *149*
The Metropolitan Museum of Art, Rogers Fund,
   1946  *150*
Library of Congress  *153*
Copyright © The White House Historical
   Association. Photograph by National
   Geographic Society  *157*
Free Library of Philadelphia, photos by Joseph
   J. Kelly  *160*
From the Collection of Vivian & Ira Brichta,
   photo by Arthur Shay  *165*
"Bauerhaus and Carousel at Rockaway
   Beach," artist unknown. Museum of the City
   of New York  *182–186*
"Corn Husking" by Eastman Johnson. Everson
   Museum of Art  *188*
"Young Soldier" by Winslow Homer. Courtesy
   of the Cooper-Hewitt Museum, Smithsonian
   Institution's National Museum of
   Design  *193*
"Abraham Lincoln's Funeral in New York City,"
   Anne S. K. Brown Military Collection, Brown
   University Library  *196*
"The Last of the Mohicans," by Thomas Cole
   (detail). New York State Historical
   Association, Cooperstown  *201*
The Bettmann Archive, Inc.  *204*
W. B. Finch/Stock Boston  *252*
Rich Friedman/The Picture Cube  *255*
Grant Heilman  *top and bottom, 256*
John Serrano/Photo Researchers  *257*
W. B. Finch/Stock Boston  *258*
Bob Llewellyn/The Picture Cube  *259*
G. Engman/The Picture Cube  *260*
"The Oxbow" by Thomas Cole (detail). The
   Metropolitan Museum of Art. Gift of Mrs.

Russell Sage, 1908  *262*
Jeff Albertson/Stock Boston  *264*
Index of American Design, National Gallery of
   Art, Washington, D. C.  *267*
The Peabody Museum of Salem, Mass. Photos
   by Mark Sexton  *266, 271, 272, 274, 278*
"Sperm Whaling No. 2—The Conflict."
   Courtesy of the Shelburne Museum,
   Shelburne, Vermont  *283*
John Marmaras/Woodfin Camp &
   Associates  *317*
Valentine Museum  *325*
"Girl Combing Her Hair" by William M. Paxton.
   Courtesy of the Vose Galleries of Boston,
   Inc.  *365*
"Raising of the Liberty Pole" by John McRae.
   The Kennedy Galleries, Inc.  *383*
"Man with a Knapsack" by Winslow Homer.
   Courtesy of the Cooper-Hewitt Museum,
   Smithsonian Institution's National Museum of
   Design  *390*
Ivan Massar/Black Star  *394*
Courtesy Thoreau Lyceum  *397*
Roland Wells Robbins  *398*
John E. Fogle  *415*
John Cole/The Picture Cube  *417*
Peter Vandermark  *418*
"To Fight Again." The Metropolitan Museum of
   Art, Rogers Fund, 1942  *419*
Museum of the City of New York  *426*
Billy Rose Theatre Collection, Performing Arts
   Research Center, New York Public Library of
   Lincoln Center, Astor, Lenox and Tilden
   Foundations  *429, 432, 439, 441, 457*
Museum of the City of New York  *453*
Library of Congress  *top left, 461*
The Halbe Collection, Kansas State Historical
   Society, Topeka, Kansas  *top right, 461*
Pennell Collection, Kansas Collection, Kenneth
   Spencer Research Library, University of
   Kansas  *middle left, 461*
Culver Pictures  *bottom left, 461*
Charles Van Schaik Collection, State Historical
   Society of Wisconsin  *bottom right, 461*
The Bettmann Archive, Inc.  *465*
Murals by Aaron Douglas. Courtesy of Fisk
   University, Nashville, Tennessee. Photos by
   J. Clark Thomas  *474–477*
Library of Congress  *479*
New York Public Library, Rare Book Division,

# Index of Authors and Titles

Afternoon in February   254
Afternoon of a Young Poet, The   42
American Crisis, The   382
Anderson, Sherwood   166, 702
Angelou, Maya   543, 702
Annabel Lee   324
Any Human to Another   416
Apostrophe to Man   424
Austin, Mary   487
Autobiography   157

Baraka, Imamu Amiri   636, 702
Because I Could Not Stop for Death   380
Benét, Stephen Vincent   56, 702
Berg, Stephen   630, 703
Big Two-Hearted River   307
Bird Came Down the Walk, A   377
Black Cat, The   328
Black Elk   497
Black Man Talks of Reaping, A   532
Bontemps, Arna   532, 703
Boyle, Kay   260, 703
Bradstreet, Anne   150, 703
Brooks, Gwendolyn   417, 634, 703
Browning, Elizabeth Barrett   689, 690
Bryant, William Cullen   261, 264, 703
Bustle in a House, The   381

Calling for Rain   480
Cather, Willa   77, 704
Cecilia Rosas   638
Cooper, James Fenimore   199, 704
Crane, Stephen   287, 414, 704
Creation, The   149
Cullen, Countee   19, 416, 705
Cummings, E. E.   255, 705

Death Valley Earns Its Name   70
Deerslayer Escapes   199
dePaola, Daniel   517
Dickinson, Emily   6, 376–381, 687, 705
Dirge Without Music   423
Displays of Skill: The Bat   321

Earth and I Gave You Turquoise   490
Earth Is All That Lasts, The   497
Edelman, Katherine   109
Edwards, Jonathan   152, 706

Egg, The   166
Ellison, Ralph   8, 554, 706
Emanuel, James A.   637, 706
Emerson, Ralph Waldo   388, 706
Europe and America   107
Experiment in Simple Living, An   392

Faulkner, William   351, 707
Ferber, Edna   649, 707
Field, Edward   104, 707
Fifth Chinese Daughter   125
Five Aztec Poems   630
Flight   664
Flower-Fed Buffaloes, The   486
Four Poems   414
Franklin, Benjamin   157, 707
Frederick Douglass   537
Frog Autumn   259
Frost, Robert   142, 256, 258, 708

George Gray   686
Get Up, Blues   637
Gioseffi, Daniela   322, 708
Giovanni, Nikki   632, 708
Glasgow, Ellen   66, 709
Go Down, Moses   528
Golden Key, The   148
Graduation   531
Grass on the Mountain, The   487
Grave, The   246
Groves Were God's First Temples, The   264

Had I Not Seen the Sun   687
Hansberry, Lorraine   562, 709
Harte, Bret   237, 709
Hawthorne, Nathaniel   338, 710
Hayden, Robert   146, 534, 537, 710
Hemingway, Ernest   307, 710
Herschberger, Ruth   321, 710
Holman, M. Carl   42, 711
Home Movies   16
Hood   20
Hope Is the Thing With Feathers   381
Huck Runs Away   207
Hughes, Langston   530, 531, 711
Human Vanity   150
Hunt, Evelyn Tooley   17

*I Am One of the Nation*  189
*I Shall Go Back Again to the Bleak Shore*  421
*I Stand Here Ironing*  175
*I Stepped From Plank to Plank*  379
*I Thank God I'm Free at Last*  529
Ignatow, David  107, 711
*in Just-spring*  255
*Iowa Childhood, An*  649
*Irish Grandmother*  109

Jablow, Alta  696
Jeffers, Robinson  319, 711
*Jewish Cemetery, The*  103
Johnson, James Weldon  538, 712

*Kaiser and the War*  656
Knowles, John  27, 712

*Landscape*  147
*Leader of the People, The*  87
*Legacies*  632
*Letter From Home, A*  137
Levertov, Denise  320, 712
*Lift Every Voice and Sing*  543
Lindsay, Vachel  486
Longfellow, Henry Wadsworth  103, 254, 712
*Love Is Not All*  422
*Love of Nature, The*  261
*Lucinda Matlock*  145

MacLeish, Archibald  59, 712
*Magic Barrel, The*  111
Malamud, Bernard  111, 713
*March in the Ranks Hard-Pressed, A*  193
Masters, Edgar Lee  145, 686, 713
Melville, Herman  266, 713
*Mending Wall*  142
Merriam, Eve  147, 714
Millay, Edna St. Vincent  420–424, 714
*Mister Toussan*  554
*Moby Dick*  266
Momaday, N. Scott  9, 490, 491, 714
Muro, Amado  638, 714
*My Grandmother*  108
*My Polish Grandma*  104
*My Sister's Marriage*  364

*Narrow Fellow in the Grass, A*  378
*New Country, The*  77
*Noah Built the Ark*  538

Oates, Joyce Carol  9
*October 1954*  260
Oliver, Mary  63, 715
Olsen, Tillie  175, 715
*On Self-Reliance*  388
*On the Way to the Mission*  61
*Once by the Pacific*  258
*One Home*  144
*Only Yesterday*  66
*Open Boat, The*  287
Ortiz, Simon J.  656, 715
*Our Town*  425
*Outcasts of Poker Flat, The*  237

Paine, Thomas  382, 715
Pastan, Linda  108, 715
Peck, Elisabeth  64
Piercy, Marge  419, 715
*Pity Me Not Because the Light of Day*  420
Plath, Sylvia  259, 318, 715
Poe, Edgar Allan  324, 326, 328, 716
*Poet's Art, The*  150
*Porter*  530
Porter, Katherine Anne  246, 716
*Powwow*  488
*Prayer to the Dead, A*  483
*Preface to a Twenty-Volume Suicide Note*  636
*Presentiment*  376

*Raisin in the Sun, A*  562
*Returning, The*  517
Rich, Cynthia  364
*Robin Hood*  147
Roethke, Theodore  686
*Root Cellar*  686
*Runagate, Runagate*  534
*Running*  18

*Sanctuary*  418
Saroyan, William  8
*Saturday's Child*  19
Scott, Duncan Campbell  61, 716
*Separate Road, A*  401
Shakespeare, William  690
*Shall I Compare Thee to a Summer's Day?*  690
*Sharks, The*  320
*Simple Song*  419
Simpson, Louis  184
*Sinners in the Hands of an Angry God*  152
Snodgrass, W. D.  488, 717

Some Slippery Afternoon   322
Song of Defeat   485
Song of the Sky Loom   484
Sonnet 43   690
Sonnet-Ballad, The   417
Spiderweb, The   149
Stafford, William   144, 717
Stark Boughs on the Family Tree   63
Steinbeck, John   87, 664, 717
Stone, Irving   70, 717
Stowe, Harriet Beecher   7

Tall Men, The   351
Taught Me Purple   17
Taylor, Edward   148, 149, 718
Thoreau, Henry David   392, 718
Those Winter Sundays   146
To Thomas Jefferson, Esquire   59
Truth   634
Tuft of Flowers, The   256
Turn With the Sun, A   27
Twain, Mark   7, 207, 718
Two Strangers, The   696

Ulalume   326
Uncle Tom   530
Updike, John   16, 719

Vergara, Joe   137, 719
Visit of Charity, A   21
Vulture   319

Walthena   64
War God's Horse Song, The   482
Water Rat, The   318
Way to Rainy Mountain, The   491
Welty, Eudora   21, 719
Western Star   56
When Lilacs Last in the Dooryard
   Bloomed   195
Whitman, Walt   6, 188–195, 719
Wilbur, Richard   18, 720
Wilder, Thornton   425, 720
Williams, C. K.   20, 720
Wong, Jade Snow   125, 720
Wright, Richard   401, 720
Wylie, Elinor   418, 721

Young Goodman Brown   338